Easy to use

Whether you know exactly in which town you want to stay or have only an idea of the area you wish to visit, it couldn't be easier to find accommodation to suit you in *Where to Stay*.

For this reason, we've included a comprehensive town index and full colour location maps to help you locate your accommodation easily. We've also listed establishment entries in alphabetical order by location, region by region. In fact, you'll find all the information you need is listed in an easy-to-follow format.

Turn to the Information section beginning on page 567 for lots of useful information and advice on making a booking, as well as events and location maps. It's all there to make finding your accommodation easy and put your mind at rest - and make sure you've nothing to think about but planning what to visit when you arrive!

A SIGN OF QUALITY

Knowing what to expect is vital when choosing a place to stay whether you're taking a short break, are away on business, or visiting family or friends. Whatever type of accommodation you are looking for, you'll find that establishments in *Where to Stay* offer reassurance provided by the English Tourist Board's official National Quality Grading and Classification Scheme.

Classification of facilities

An establishment's assessment under the Scheme will usually consist of two parts: the first, using the Crown symbol, classifies the range of services and facilities provided for guests; the second, from De Luxe to Approved, indicates the overall quality standard of these services and facilities.

The range of services and facilities provided is classified under one of six bands: from **Listed** (clean and comfortable accommodation, but limited range of services and facilities) to **Five Crown** (providing a full range of services and facilities). Quite simply, the more Crowns, the wider the range.

Please note that a higher number of Crowns does not necessarily imply that the quality on offer is superior to that available at an establishment with fewer Crowns.

Quality grading

A separate quality grading indicates the overall standard of services and facilities. Graded establishments are awarded one of the following quality gradings:

DE LUXE
(excellent overall standard)

HIGHLY COMMENDED
(very good overall standard)

COMMENDED
(good overall standard)

APPROVED
(acceptable overall standard)

Before awarding a quality grading, Tourist Board inspectors check in as a guest, only identifying themselves after paying the bill. They assess the warmth of the welcome and level of care and service they receive, as well as the standard and state of the decor, furnishings and fittings. Their overall assessment takes the nature and size of the establishments into account; you will therefore find that all types of accommodation have been able to achieve a Highly Commended or De Luxe quality grading.

If no quality grade appears alongside the Crown classification, it means that the proprietor has applied for but was still awaiting inspection at the time of going to press.

Range of facilities

Listed and then **One to Five Crown** tell you the range of facilities provided. The more Crowns, the wider the range. Below is an indication of some of the facilities you can expect under each classification.

Listed Clean and comfortable accommodation, but limited range of facilities and services.

👑 There will be additional facilities, including washbasin and chair in your bedroom, and you will have the use of a telephone.

👑👑 There will be a colour TV in your bedroom or in a lounge and you can enjoy morning tea/coffee in your room. At least some of the bedrooms will have private bath (or shower) and WC.

👑👑👑 At least half of the bedrooms will have private bath (or shower) en-suite. You will also be able to order a hot evening meal.

👑👑👑👑 Your bedroom will have a colour TV, radio and telephone; 90% of bedrooms will have private bath and/or shower and WC en-suite. There will be lounge service until midnight and evening meals can be ordered up to 2030 hours.

👑👑👑👑👑 Every bedroom will have private bath, fixed shower and WC en-suite. The restaurant will be open for breakfast, lunch and dinner (or you can take meals into your room from breakfast until midnight) and you will benefit from an all-night lounge service. A night porter will also be on duty.

Lodge accommodation

The Lodge classification covers purpose-built bedroom accommodation that you will find along major roads and motorways. The range of facilities is indicated by **One** to **Three Moon** symbols. A separate quality grading indicates the overall standard of these facilities.

☾ Your bedroom will have at least a washbasin and radio or colour TV. Tea/coffee may be from a vending machine in a public area.

☾☾ Your room will have colour TV, tea/coffee-making facilities and en-suite bath or shower with WC.

☾☾☾ You will find colour TV and radio, tea/coffee-making facilities and comfortable seating in your bedroom and there will be a bath, shower and WC en-suite. The reception will be manned throughout the night.

Accessible Scheme

If you have difficulty walking or are a wheelchair user, it is important to be able to identify those establishments that will be able to cater for your requirements. If you book accommodation displaying an Accessible symbol, there's no longer any guesswork involved. Establishments can be awarded one of these categories of accessibility:

Category 1 accessible to all wheelchair users including those travelling independently

Category 2 accessible to a wheelchair user with assistance

Category 3 accessible to a wheelchair user able to walk short distances and up at least three steps.

See page 10 for a full list of establishments in this guide who have an Accessible symbol.

FINDING YOUR IDEAL ACCOMMODATION

Whatever your requirements, your preferences or your price range, *Where to Stay* will lead you straight to a selection of fine accommodation in England. From prices, quality and facilities on offer, you can see what's available at a glance.

Regional sections

The guide is divided into eleven regional sections. See the map on page 12. Each section contains an alphabetical listing of the region's cities, towns and villages with their accommodation establishments.

At the beginning of each section is a brief description of the area and a selection of interesting places to visit which may persuade you to stay a little longer - an illustrative map shows where they can be found.

Town index and location maps

The town index on page 591 and the colour location maps at the back of the guide show all the places featuring accommodation in this guide.

WHERE TO STAY ENGLAND 1997
CONTENTS

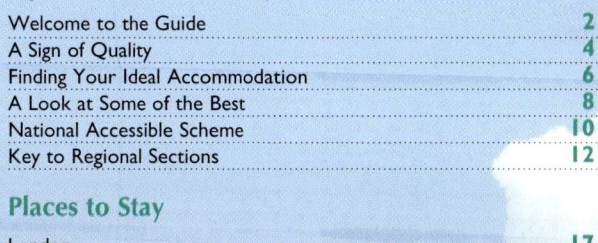

Upfront

Welcome to the Guide	2
A Sign of Quality	4
Finding Your Ideal Accommodation	6
A Look at Some of the Best	8
National Accessible Scheme	10
Key to Regional Sections	12

Places to Stay

London	17
Cumbria	51
Northumbria	99
North West	125
Yorkshire	157
Heart of England	217
Middle England	287
East Anglia	321
West Country	369
South of England	473
South East England	523

Information Pages

National Grading and Classification Scheme	568
General Advice and Information	569
About the Guide Entries	572
Hotel Group Central Reservations Offices	574
Events for 1997	576
Tourist Information Centres	582
Enquiry Coupons	583

Town Index and Location Maps

Town Index	591
Index to Advertisers	597
Mileage Chart	598
Location Maps	601
Your Quick Guide	616

Key to Symbols

Inside back cover

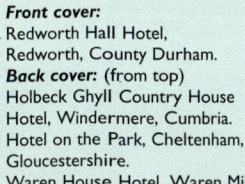

Front cover:
Redworth Hall Hotel, Redworth, County Durham.
Back cover: (from top)
Holbeck Ghyll Country House Hotel, Windermere, Cumbria.
Hotel on the Park, Cheltenham, Gloucestershire.
Waren House Hotel, Waren Mill, Northumberland.

WELCOME TO THE GUIDE

You may be in England for business or pleasure. Rushing around or enjoying a well-earned holiday. Wherever you're heading, at the end of the day if you're looking for accommodation, you can depend on *Where to Stay.*

Sure signs of where to stay

Many different types of accommodation are described in this guide, though they all have one thing in common. Each entry has been inspected (or applied for inspection) under the ETB's official National Quality Grading and Classification Scheme. The Scheme is your assurance of facilities and service: Crowns show you the range of facilities provided to guests; Quality Gradings indicate the overall standard of welcome, service and accommodation. To find out more, turn to page 4.

If the place you plan to visit is included in the town index, turn to the page number given for accommodation.

If, however, it is not included in the town index - or you just have a general idea of the area in which you wish to stay - use the colour location maps. You will find accommodation in all the places printed in black. Then simply refer back to the town index for the relevant page.

Service and facilities

Each accommodation listing contains detailed information to help you decide if it is right for you. This information has been provided by the proprietors themselves, and our aim has been to ensure that it is as objective and factual as possible.

Below the establishment name you will find the Crown classification, Listed or One to Five Crown, which indicates the range of services and facilities provided. The quality grading, De Luxe, Highly Commended, Commended or Approved tells you the overall standard of services and facilities. Detailed information on classification and gradings can be found on page 568.

At-a-glance symbols at the end of each entry give you additional information on services and facilities - a key to symbols can be found on the back cover flap. Keep this open to refer to as you read.

Accessibility

If you are a wheelchair user or have difficulty walking, look for the Accessible symbol. You will find a full list of entries participating in the National Accessible Scheme on page 10.

Check for changes

Please remember that changes may occur after the guide is printed. When you have found a suitable place to stay we advise you to contact the establishment to check availability, and also to confirm prices and any specific facilities which may be important to you. The coupons at the back of the guide will help you with your enquiries.

Then make your booking and, if you have time, confirm it in writing.

Further information

You may find it useful to read the information pages at the back of this guide (see page 567), particularly the section on cancellations.

Town Name ▶	**TAUNTON**
Map reference ▶	Somerset Map Ref 1D1
Town description ▶	County town, well-known for its public schools, sheltered by gentle hill-ranges on the River Tone
Establishment name ▶	**Tower Hotel**
National Crown classification and quality grading ▶	👑👑👑 COMMENDED
Address, telephone and fax numbers ▶	River Street, Taunton TA9 2PW ☎ (01823) 000111 Fax (01823) 000111
Establishment description ▶	Charming family-run hotel with walled garden and conservatory restaurant. Ideal base for exploring.
National wheelchair access category ▶	Wheelchair access category 2 Bedrooms: 10 single, 20 twin, 13 double Bathrooms: 43 private
Accommodation, price guide and facilities ▶	**Bed & breakfast** **per night:** £min £max Double 53.00 104.00 Lunch available Evening meal 1930 (last orders 2130) Parking for 40 Cards accepted: Access, Visa, Amex
At-a-glance symbols - see flap on back cover ▶	❦ 🏛 ✆ 📺 🍴 S 🚻 ♿ 🎱 🎬 🛏 🍷 10-70 ⛳ ► ✺ ❀ SP 🏪 T

7

A LOOK AT SOME OF THE BEST

The award of a DE LUXE quality grade recognises an establishment's excellent overall standard of such things as warmth of welcome, general atmosphere and ambience, efficiency of service, as well as the quality of facilities and standard of fittings.

The inspector's overall assessment takes the nature and size of an establishment into account; you will therefore find all types of accommodation can achieve a DE LUXE quality grading.

These pages feature those establishments in *Where to Stay* that have achieved the highest quality grade of DE LUXE. Use the Town Index at the back of the guide to find page numbers for their fully detailed entries.

Gilpin Lodge Country House Hotel and Restaurant, Windermere, Cumbria.

Ashdown Park Hotel, Wych Cross, East Sussex
The Bath Spa Hotel, Bath, Bath and North East Somerset
Brereton House, Holmes Chapel, Cheshire
Broadview, Crewkerne, Somerset
Chewton Glen Hotel, Health & Country Club, New Milton, Hampshire
Crit Hall, Benenden, Kent
De Vere Grand Harbour, Southampton, Hampshire
Devonshire Arms Country House Hotel, Bolton Abbey, North Yorkshire
The Dorchester, London, Greater London
Gidleigh Park, Chagford, Devon
Gilpin Lodge Country House Hotel and Restaurant, Windermere, Cumbria
Hall House, Hertford, Hertfordshire
Holbeck Ghyll Country House Hotel and Restaurant, Windermere, Cumbria
Holly Lodge, Bath, Bath and North East Somerset
Hope House, Tynemouth, Tyne & Wear
Hotel On The Park, Cheltenham, Gloucestershire

The Swan Hotel, Bibury, Gloucestershire.

Linthwaite House Hotel, Windermere, Cumbria.

Hotel Riviera, Sidmouth, Devon
Linthwaite House Hotel, Windermere, Cumbria
Malt House, Diss, Norfolk
Marriott Hanbury Manor Hotel and Country Club, Ware, Hertfordshire
Number Thirty One, Carlisle, Cumbria
The Old Parsonage, Royal Tunbridge Wells, Kent
The Old Plough, Retford, Nottinghamshire
The Old Rectory, Broadway, Hereford & Worcester
Old Vicarage Hotel, Bridgnorth, Shropshire
Pickett Howe, Buttermere, Cumbria
Severn Lodge, Ironbridge, Shropshire
Swallow Hotel, Birmingham
The Swan Hotel, Bibury, Gloucestershire
Swinside Lodge, Keswick, Cumbria
Tavern House, Tetbury, Gloucestershire
Wyck Hill House, Stow-on-the-Wold, Gloucestershire

Holly Lodge, Bath, Bath and North East Somerset.

NATIONAL ACCESSIBLE SCHEME

Throughout Britain, the Tourist Boards are inspecting all types of places to stay, on holiday or business, that provide accessible accommodation for wheelchair users and others who may have difficulty walking.

The Tourist Boards recognise three categories of accessibility:

Category 1
Accessible to all wheelchair users including those travelling independently.

Category 2
Accessible to a wheelchair user with assistance.

Category 3
Accessible to a wheelchair user able to walk short distances and up at least three steps.

If you have additional needs or special requirements of any kind, we strongly recommend that you make sure these can be met by your chosen establishment before you confirm your booking.

The criteria the Tourist Boards have adopted do not, necessarily, conform to British Standards or to Building Regulations. They reflect what the Boards understand to be acceptable to meet the practical needs of wheelchair users.

The following establishments listed in this *Where to Stay* guide had been inspected and given an access category at the time of going to press. Use the Town Index at the back of the guide to find page numbers for their full entries.

Category 1

BOLTON, GREATER MANCHESTER
 - Bolton Moat House
BRACKNELL, BERKSHIRE
 - Coppid Beech Hotel
CHESHUNT, HERTFORDSHIRE
 - Cheshunt Marriott Hotel
CROOKHAM, NORTHUMBERLAND
 - The Coach House
DURHAM,
 - Royal County Hotel
HULL,
 KINGSTON UPON HULL
 - Kingstown Hotel
OXFORD, OXFORDSHIRE
 - Westwood Country Hotel
SELSEY, WEST SUSSEX
 - St Andrews Lodge
SOUTHAMPTON, HAMPSHIRE
 - Botley Park Hotel, Golf & Country Club
WILMSLOW, CHESHIRE
 - Dean Bank Hotel
WIMBORNE MINSTER, DORSET
 - Northill House
YORK
 - Swallow Hotel

Category 2

BRIDGNORTH, SHROPSHIRE
 - Old Vicarage Hotel
BRIDGWATER, SOMERSET
 - Friarn Court Hotel
CASTLE DONINGTON, LEICESTERSHIRE
 - Park Farmhouse Hotel
CHESTER, CHESHIRE
 - Chester Moat House
EVESHAM, HEREFORD & WORCESTER
 - Northwick Arms Hotel
GARBOLDISHAM, NORFOLK
 - Ingleneuk Lodge
GREAT YARMOUTH, NORFOLK
 - Horse & Groom Motel
LANCASTER, LANCASHIRE
 - Lancaster House Hotel
LEICESTER, LEICESTERSHIRE
 - The Red Cow
LONDON, GREATER LONDON
 - The Bonnington in Bloomsbury
NEWHAVEN, EAST SUSSEX
 - The Brighton Motel
NEWTON AYCLIFFE, DURHAM
 - Redworth Hall
NORWICH, NORFOLK
 - Beeches Hotel & Victorian Gardens
 - Hotel Norwich
PETERBOROUGH, CAMBRIDGESHIRE
 - Swallow Hotel
SHAP, CUMBRIA
 - Shap Wells Hotel

Category 3

ALDERLEY EDGE, CHESHIRE
 - The Alderley Edge Hotel
AMBLESIDE, CUMBRIA
 - Borrans Park Hotel
 - Kirkstone Foot Country House
 - Rowanfield Country Guesthouse
BAKEWELL, DERBYSHIRE
 - The Croft Country House Hotel
BASSENTHWAITE LAKE, CUMBRIA
 - Pheasant Inn
BEESTON, CHESHIRE
 - Wild Boar Hotel
BOLTON ABBEY, NORTH YORKSHIRE
 - Devonshire Arms Country House

BOURNEMOUTH, DORSET
- Norfolk Royale Hotel
BRADFORD, WEST YORKSHIRE
- Novotel Bradford
BRATTON FLEMING, DEVON
- Bracken House Country Hotel
BRIGHTON & HOVE, EAST SUSSEX
- Brighton Oak Hotel
CHELTENHAM, GLOUCESTERSHIRE
- The Prestbury House Hotel
CHESTER, CHESHIRE
- Dene Hotel
- Green Bough Hotel
- Plantation Inn Hotel
CHESTERFIELD, DERBYSHIRE
- Abbeydale Hotel
CHIPPING, LANCASHIRE
- Gibbon Bridge Hotel
CRESSBROOK, DERBYSHIRE
- Cressbrook Hall
CREWE, CHESHIRE
- Hunters Lodge Hotel
CROMER, NORFOLK
- Cliftonville Hotel
DEVIZES, WILTSHIRE
- Pinecroft
EARLS COLNE, ESSEX
- Riverside Inn Motel
EASTBOURNE, EAST SUSSEX
- Congress Hotel
- Heatherdene Hotel
ELLERBY, NORTH YORKSHIRE
- Ellerby Hotel
EXETER, DEVON
- St Andrews Hotel
FALMOUTH, CORNWALL
- Broadmead Hotel
FAREHAM, HAMPSHIRE
- Avenue House Hotel
FROME, SOMERSET
- Fourwinds Guest House
GRANGE-OVER-SANDS, CUMBRIA
- Netherwood Hotel
GRANTHAM, LINCOLNSHIRE
- Kings Hotel
GRIMSBY, NORTH EAST LINCOLNSHIRE
- Millfields
HASTINGS, EAST SUSSEX
- Grand Hotel
HELMSLEY, NORTH YORKSHIRE
- Pheasant Hotel
HEMEL HEMPSTEAD, HERTFORDSHIRE
- The Bobsleigh Inn
ILFRACOMBE, DEVON
- Sunnymeade Country House

INGATESTONE, ESSEX
- The Heybridge Hotel
IPSWICH, SUFFOLK
- Courtyard Ipswich
- Novotel Ipswich
KESWICK, CUMBRIA
- Derwentwater Hotel
KIDDERMINSTER, HEREFORD & WORCESTER
- The Granary Hotel
KINGSBURY, WARWICKSHIRE
- Lea Marston Hotel & Leisure Complex
LANGHO, LANCASHIRE
- Mytton Fold Hotel & Golf Complex
LINCOLN, LINCOLNSHIRE
- Damon's Motel
LONDON, GREATER LONDON
- Westland Hotel
LUDLOW, SHROPSHIRE
- The Feathers at Ludlow
LYTHAM ST ANNES, LANCASHIRE
- Chadwick Hotel
MILDENHALL, SUFFOLK
- Smoke House
NEWCASTLE UPON TYNE,
- Newcastle Marriott (Gateshead)
NEWMARKET, SUFFOLK
- Heath Court Hotel
NORTHALLERTON, NORTH YORKSHIRE
- Sundial Hotel
NORTHAMPTON, NORTHAMPTONSHIRE
- Courtyard Daventry
NORWICH, NORFOLK
- Elm Farm Chalet Hotel
- Old Rectory
NOTTINGHAM, NOTTINGHAMSHIRE
- The Nottingham Gateway Hotel
RAVENSTONEDALE, CUMBRIA
- The Black Swan Hotel
REDCAR, TEES VALLEY
- Falcon Hotel
ROTHERHAM, SOUTH YORKSHIRE
- Best Western Elton Hotel
ROYAL TUNBRIDGE WELLS, KENT
- The Spa Hotel
SKEGNESS, LINCOLNSHIRE
- Saxby Hotel
SKIPTON, NORTH YORKSHIRE
- Randells Hotel, Conference & Leisure Centre

SOUTH CAVE, EAST RIDING OF YORKSHIRE
- Rudstone Walk Farmhouse & Country Cottages
SOUTH NORMANTON, DERBYSHIRE
- Swallow Hotel
SOUTHPORT, MERSEYSIDE
- Scarisbrick Hotel
STAMFORD, LINCOLNSHIRE
- Garden House Hotel
STRATFORD-UPON-AVON, WARWICKSHIRE
- Grosvenor House Hotel
SWANAGE, DORSET
- The Pines Hotel
TARPORLEY, CHESHIRE
- The Swan Hotel
TENTERDEN, KENT
- Little Silver Country Hotel
WANSFORD, CAMBRIDGESHIRE
- Haycock Hotel
WARRINGTON, CHESHIRE
- The Park Royal International
WESTON-SUPER-MARE, NORTH SOMERSET
- Moorlands
WHITLEY BAY, TYNE & WEAR
- York House Hotel
WINDERMERE, CUMBRIA
- The Burn How Garden House
- Linthwaite House Hotel
WISBECH, CAMBRIDGESHIRE
- Crown Lodge Hotel
WOODHALL SPA, LINCOLNSHIRE
- Petwood House Hotel
YORK
- Clifton Bridge Hotel
- Hotel Fairmount
- Heworth Court Hotel
- Savages Hotel

The National Accessible Scheme forms part of the Tourism for All Campaign that is being promoted by all three National Tourist Boards. Additional help and guidance on finding suitable holiday accommodation for those with special needs can be obtained from:
Holiday Care Service
2 Old Bank Chambers,
Station Road,
Horley, Surrey RH6 9HW.
Tel: (01293) 774535.
Fax: (01293) 784647.
Minicom: (01293) 776943.

KEY TO REGIONAL SECTIONS

This *Where to Stay* guide is divided into 11 regional sections as shown on the map below. To identify each regional section and its page number, please refer to the key opposite. The index lists the counties of England and indicates under which regional section you will find them.

Colour location maps showing all the cities, towns and villages with accommodation listed in this guide, and an index to the place names, can be found at the back of the guide.

As you are probably aware, during 1996 the boundaries and names of a number of counties in England were changed as the result of local government reorganisation. The main county changes that had been announced at the time of compiling the 1997 guide have been reflected in *Where to Stay*, particularly in the county index opposite, the regional section maps, in the colour location maps at the back and in the town descriptions.**

If you want to find out more about what there is to see and do in a particular area, contact the appropriate Regional Tourist Board. Details are given both at the beginning and end of each regional section.

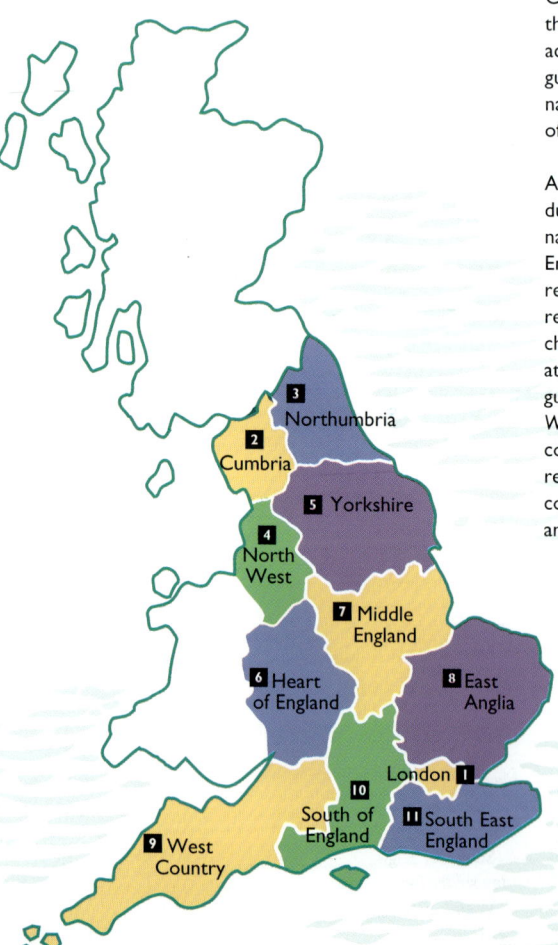

KEY TO MAP

1	London	17
2	Cumbria	51
3	Northumbria	99
4	North West	125
5	Yorkshire	157
6	Heart of England	217
7	Middle England	287
8	East Anglia	321
9	West Country	369
10	South of England	473
11	South East England	523

** This is how you will find the following county changes have been reflected in *Where to Stay*:
Avon is replaced by Bath & North East Somerset, City of Bristol, North Somerset and South Gloucestershire
Cleveland is replaced by Tees Valley
Humberside is replaced by East Riding of Yorkshire, North Lincolnshire and North East Lincolnshire.

Although there have been changes to the unitary authority boundaries in the following areas, you will see that the familiar regional names have been retained for: Greater Manchester, Merseyside, South Yorkshire, Tyne & Wear, West Midlands and West Yorkshire

Please note that further changes are planned for 1997 which have yet to be confirmed.

COUNTY INDEX

Bath & North East Somerset:
West Country
Bedfordshire:
East Anglia
Berkshire:
South of England
Buckinghamshire:
South of England
Cambridgeshire:
East Anglia
Cheshire:
North West
City of Bristol:
West Country
Cornwall:
West Country
Cumbria:
Cumbria
Derbyshire:
Middle England
Derbyshire High Peak District:
North West
Devon:
West Country
Dorset (Eastern):
West Country
Dorset (Western):
South of England
Durham:
Northumbria
East Riding of Yorkshire:
Yorkshire
Essex:
East Anglia
Gloucestershire:
Heart of England
Greater London:
London
Greater Manchester:
North West
Hampshire:
South of England
Hereford & Worcester:
Heart of England
Hertfordshire:
East Anglia
Isle of Wight:
South of England
Isles of Scilly:
West Country
Kent:
South East England

Lancashire:
North West
Leicestershire:
Middle England
Lincolnshire:
Middle England
Merseyside:
North West
Norfolk:
East Anglia
North East Lincolnshire:
Yorkshire
North Lincolnshire:
Yorkshire
North Somerset:
West Country
North Yorkshire:
Yorkshire
Northamptonshire:
Middle England
Northumberland:
Northumbria
Nottinghamshire:
Middle England
Oxfordshire:
South of England
Shropshire:
Heart of England
Somerset:
West Country
South Gloucestershire:
West Country
South Yorkshire:
Yorkshire
Staffordshire:
Heart of England
Suffolk:
East Anglia
Surrey:
South East England
Tees Valley:
Northumbria
Tyne & Wear:
Northumbria
Warwickshire:
Heart of England
West Midlands:
Heart of England
West Sussex:
South East England
Wiltshire:
West Country

Telephone:
0181 943 1862

Facsimile:
0181 943 9363

10 minutes from
Hampton Court
Palace

20 minutes from
the centre of
London

HOTEL

AN AWARD WINNING HOTEL

with style and elegance set in tranquil surroundings at affordable prices

- Quality en suite bedrooms
- Full English Breakfast
- À la carte menu
- Licensed bar
- Wedding receptions

- Honeymoon Suite
- Natural health therapies
- Easy access to Kingston town centre and all major transport links
- 20 minutes Heathrow Airport

Weekend breaks available on request

FOR BUSINESS OR PLEASURE - **Reservations: 0181 943 1862** Fax: 0181 943 9363
10 Park Road, Hampton Wick, Kingston upon Thames KT1 4AS

ALL MAJOR CREDIT CARDS ACCEPTED.

RASOOL COURT HOTEL

19-21 Penywern Road, Earl's Court, London, SW5 9TT
Tel: (0171) 373 8900 & 4893   Fax: (0171) 244 6835

57-bedroom hotel located just near the Earl's Court Tube Station.

Very convenient for the West End and Heathrow Airport.
All rooms with colour TV and direct-dial telephone.

Prices:
Singles from £26
Doubles from £37
Triple from £49
(including taxes and continental breakfast).

BRANSTON HALL HOTEL

AA approved Country House Hotel

Branston Hall Hotel is a magnificent country manor house which enjoys a fine reputation for its warm welcome and hospitality. Steeped in history, the Hall is situated in 88 acres of private wooded parkland, private lakes and with commanding views and gardens famous for their interest and splendour. Branston Hall Hotel provides the ultimate oasis of tranquillity and true country living, yet only 5 miles from Lincoln City centre. Within the hotel, all the rooms have en suite bathrooms, tea/coffee making facilities, direct dial telephone, TV text and radio. Amongst the traditional oak paneled splendour of yesteryear, is the famed Lakeside Restaurant which is internationally acclaimed independently of the hotel.

Bedrooms 29 (29 en suite) Prices £38.75 bed and breakfast, based on double occupancy.
Mini breaks available (minimum 2 persons, 2 nights) on dinner, bed and breakfast £45

TEL (01522) 793305   Branston Hall Hotel, Lincoln Road, Branston, Lincoln, LN4 1PD   FAX (01522) 790549

THE ENGLAND FOR EXCELLENCE AWARDS
WINNERS 1995

The England for Excellence Awards were created by the English Tourist Board to recognise and reward the highest standards of excellence and quality in all major sectors of tourism in England. The coveted Leo statuette, presented each year to winners, has become firmly established as the ultimate accolade in the English tourism industry.

Over the past eight years the Leo has been won by all types and sizes of business with one common attribute - excellence in the facilities and services they offer.

Hotel of the Year
Sponsored by Yellow Pages
The Four Seasons Hotel, London
(Five Crown, De Luxe)
London

Bed and Breakfast of the Year
Sponsored by Blackpool Pleasure Beach
Tree Tops
(Two Crown, De Luxe)
Berwick-upon-Tweed,
Northumberland

Holiday Centre of the Year
Sponsored by Senior King
Potters Leisure
Hopton on Sea, Norfolk

Self-Catering Holiday of the Year
Sponsored by Country Holidays Group
The Corbyn Holidays Suites & Villas - Brights of Nettlebed
(Five Key, De Luxe)
Torquay, Devon

Visitor Attraction of the Year
Sponsored by Hilton National
Hampton Court Palace
Surrey

Tourism Town of the Year
Sponsored by Marks & Spencer
Manchester - The City Visitor Destination

Tourism for All Award
Sponsored by Gould & Portmans
Cheshire County Council 'Tourism for All' Programme

Tourist Information Centre of the Year
Sponsored by Ordnance Survey
Sunderland Tourist Information Centre
Tyne and Wear

Outstanding Contribution to English Tourism Award
Sponsored by Hilton International
BBC TV / Pride and Prejudice

WHERE TO STAY IN ENGLAND

Published by: English Tourist Board, Thames Tower, Black's Road, Hammersmith, London W6 9EL.
ISBN 0 86143 198 7
Managing Editor: Jane Collinson
Technical Manager: Marita Sen
Compilation & Production: Guide Associates, Croydon
Design and illustrations: Jackson Lowe Marketing, Lewes, East Sussex
Colour Photography: Mike Williams (front cover)
Cartography: Colin Earl
Typesetting: Reed Technologies and Information Services, London and Jackson Lowe Marketing, Lewes
Printing and Binding: Bemrose Security Printing, Derby
Advertisement Sales: Madison Bell Ltd, 3 St. Peter's Street, Islington Green, London N1 8JD. (0171) 359 7737.
© English Tourist Board (except where stated)

Important:
The information contained in this guide has been published in good faith on the basis of information submitted to the English Tourist Board by the proprietors of the premises listed, who have paid for their entries to appear. The English Tourist Board cannot guarantee the accuracy of the information in this guide and accepts no responsibility for any error or misrepresentation. All liability for loss, disappointment, negligence or other damage caused by reliance on the information contained in this guide, or in the event of bankruptcy, or liquidation, or cessation of trade of any company, individual or firm mentioned, is hereby excluded. Please check carefully all prices and other details before confirming a reservation.

The English Tourist Board
The Board is a statutory body created by the Development of Tourism Act 1969 to develop and market England's tourism. Its main objectives are to provide a welcome for people visiting England; to encourage people living in England to take their holidays there; and to encourage the provision and improvement of tourist amenities and facilities in England. The Board has a statutory duty to advise the Government on tourism matters relating to England and, with Government approval and support, administers the national classification and grading schemes for tourist accommodation in England.

LONDON

No one can capture the atmosphere of London in words alone. One of the eternally great cities, it remains true that 'if you're tired of London, you're tired of life'.

Buckingham Palace, the Tower and Madame Tussaud's are just the beginning... London has more than 100 museums and galleries, the finest theatres in the world and some of the most exciting shops, restaurants and markets.

Stroll through the many gracious parks, discover Jack the Ripper's East End, explore 'the City', follow in the footsteps of Dickens. Or if you prefer, hop on a red bus or catch a black cab. Whichever way you go, seeing the sights of London is an unforgettable experience.

FOR MORE INFORMATION CONTACT:
London Tourist Board
26 Grosvenor Gardens, London SW1W 0DU

Where to Go in London - see pages 18-20
Where to Stay in London - see pages 25-49

LONDON

Where to Go and What to See

You will find hundreds of interesting places to visit during your stay in London, just some of which are listed in these pages. Contact any Tourist Information Centre in the region for more ideas on days out in London.

■ **Bankside Gallery**
48 Hopton Street,
London SE1 9JH
Tel: (0171) 928 7521
Home of The Royal Watercolour Society and The Royal Society of Painter-Printmakers. Changing exhibitions of watercolours and prints.

■ **British Museum**
Great Russell Street,
London WC1B 3DG
Tel: (0171) 636 1555
One of the great museums of the world, showing the works of man from all over the world from prehistoric times to the present day.

■ **Cabinet War Rooms**
Clive Steps,
King Charles Street,
London SW1A 2AQ
Tel: (0171) 930 6961
The underground headquarters used by Winston Churchill and the British Government during World War II. Includes Cabinet Room, transatlantic telephone room and Map Room.

■ **Design Museum**
Shad Thames,
London SE1 2YD
Tel: (0171) 403 6933
A study collection showing the development of design in mass production. Review of new products, graphics gallery, and changing programme of exhibitions.

■ **Dickens House**
48 Doughty Street,
London WC1N 2LF
Tel: (0171) 405 2127
Charles Dickens' home from 1837-1839. Collection of letters, pictures, first editions, furniture, memorabilia, restored rooms.

■ **Fan Museum**
12 Crooms Hill,
London SE10 8ER
Tel: (0181) 305 1441
The only venue in the world devoted entirely to the art and craft of the fan. Changing exhibitions. Beautifully restored 18thC houses. Gift shop.

■ **Guards Museum**
Wellington Barracks,
Birdcage Walk,
London SW1E 6HQ
Tel: (0171) 414 3428
Collection of uniforms, colours and artefacts spanning over 300 years of history of the Foot Guards.

■ **Hampton Court Palace**
Hampton Court,
Surrey KT8 9AU
Tel: (0181) 781 9500
Oldest Tudor palace in England. Tudor kitchens, tennis courts, maze, state apartments and King's apartments.

■ **HMS Belfast**
Morgan's Lane, Tooley Street,
London SE1 2JH
Tel: (0171) 407 6434
11,500 tonne World War II cruiser moored on the Thames. Now a

floating naval museum, with seven decks to explore. Many naval exhibits on show.

■ Imperial War Museum
Lambeth Road,
London SE1 6HZ
Tel: (0171) 416 5000
The story of 20thC war from Flanders to Bosnia. Features include the Blitz Experience, Operation Jericho and the Trench Experience.

■ London Dungeon
28-34 Tooley Street,
London SE1 2SZ
Tel: (0171) 403 0606
World's first medieval horror museum. Now featuring two major shows: "The Jack the Ripper Experience" and "The Theatre of the Guillotine".

■ Madame Tussaud's
Marylebone Road,
London NW1 5LR
Tel: (0171) 935 6861
Wax figures in themed settings, including The Garden Party, 200 Years, Superstars, The Grand Hall, The Chamber of Horrors and The Spirit of London.

■ Museum of London
150 London Wall,
London EC2Y 5HN
Tel: (0171) 600 3699
Galleries illustrate over 2000 years of the capital's social history, from prehistoric times to the 20thC. Regular temporary exhibitions, lunchtime lecture programmes.

■ Museum of the Moving Image
South Bank, Waterloo,
London SE1 8XT
Tel: (0171) 928 3535
A celebration of cinema and television. 44 exhibit areas offer plenty of hands-on participation, and a cast of actors to tell visitors more.

■ National Gallery
Trafalgar Square,
London WC2N 5DN
Tel: (0171) 839 3321
Western painting from 1260-1920, including work by Van Gogh, Rembrandt, Cezanne, Turner, Gainsborough, Leonardo da Vinci, Renoir and Botticelli.

■ National Maritime Museum
Romney Road, Greenwich,
London SE10 9NF
Tel: (0181) 858 4522
Britain's maritime heritage illustrated through actual and model ships, paintings, uniforms, navigation and astronomy instruments, archives and photographs. Queen's House.

■ National Portrait Gallery
St Martin's Place,
London WC2H 0HE
Tel: (0171) 306 0055
Permanent collection of portraits of famous men and women from the Middle Ages to the present day.

■ National Postal Museum
King Edward Building,
King Edward Street,
London EC1A 1LP
Tel: (0171) 239 5420
One of the most important and extensive collections of postage stamps in the world, including the Phillips and Berne Collections. Temporary exhibitions.

■ Natural History Museum
Cromwell Road,
London SW7 5BD
Tel: (0171) 938 9123
Home of the wonders of the natural world, one of the most popular museums in the world, and one of London's finest landmarks.

■ Old Royal Observatory
(Flamsteed House),
Greenwich Park,
London SE10 9NF
Tel: (0181) 858 4422

Museum of time and space. Greenwich Meridian, working telescopes, planetarium and timeball. Wren's Octagon Room. Intricate clocks and computer simulations. Restored in 1993.

■ **Rock Circus**
London Pavilion, Piccadilly Circus,
London W1V 9LA
Tel: (0171) 734 7203
The exhibition is an amazing combination of stereo sound through personal headsets, audio animatronic (moving) and Madame Tussauds (wax) figures of over 50 rock stars.

■ **Royal Air Force Museum**
Grahame Park Way,
London NW9 5LL
Tel: (0181) 205 2266
Britain's National Museum of aviation features over 70 full size aircraft, Flight Simulator, "Touch & Try" Jet Provost Trainer and Eurofighter 2000 Theatre.

■ **Science Museum**
Exhibition Road,
London SW7 2DD
Tel: (0171) 938 8000
National Museum of Science and Industry. Full size replica of Apollo 11 Lunar Lander, launch pad, Wellcome Museum of History of Medicine, flight lab, food for thought, optics.

■ **Sherlock Holmes Museum**
221B Baker Street,
London NW1 6XE
Tel: (0171) 935 8866
Grade 2 listed lodging house. 1st floor Holmes' apartment. Second floor Mrs Hudson's room and Doctor Watson's room. Third floor souvenir shop. Reading room and exhibition room.

■ **Thames Barrier Visitors' Centre**
Unity Way, London SE18 5NJ
Tel: (0181) 854 1373
Exhibition with 10-min video, a working scale model and a multi-media show. Also riverside walkways, children's play area and Thames Barrier Buffet.

■ **Tower Bridge**
London SE1 2UP
Tel: (0171) 403 3761
Exhibition explains the history of the bridge and how it operates. Original steam powered engines on view. Panoramic views from fully-glazed walkways. Gift shop.

■ **Tower of London**
Tower Hill,
London EC3N 4AB
Tel: (0171) 709 0765
Building spans 900 years of British history. The nation's Crown Jewels, regalia and armoury robes on display. Home of the "Beefeaters" and ravens.

■ **Victoria and Albert Museum**
Cromwell Road,
London SW7 2RL
Tel: (0171) 938 8500
The V & A is the world's finest museum of the decorative arts. Its collection, housed in magnificent Victorian buildings, span 2000 years including sculpture and furniture.

FIND OUT MORE

A free information pack about holidays and attractions in London is available on written request from:
London Tourist Board and Convention Bureau,
26 Grosvenor Gardens,
London SW1W 0DU.

TOURIST INFORMATION

Tourist and leisure information can be obtained from Tourist Information Centres throughout England. Details of centres and other information services in Greater London are given below. The symbol ⌘ means that an accommodation booking service is provided.

Tourist Information Centres

Points of arrival
Victoria Station, Forecourt, SW1 ⌘
Easter-October, daily 0800-1900.
November-Easter, reduced opening hours.
Liverpool Street Underground Station, EC2 ⌘
Monday-Friday 0800-1800.
Saturday-Sunday 0845-17.30.
Heathrow Terminals 1, 2, 3 Underground Station Concourse (Heathrow Airport) ⌘
Daily 0800-1800.
Heathrow Terminal 3 Arrivals Concourse ⌘
0600-2300.
Waterloo International Arrivals Hall ⌘
0830-2100
The above information centres provide a London and Britain tourist information service, offer a hotel accommodation booking service, stock free and saleable publications on Britain and London and sell theatre tickets, tourist tickets for bus and underground and tickets for sightseeing tours.

Inner London
British Travel Centre ⌘
12 Regent Street, Piccadilly Circus, SW1Y 4PQ
Monday-Friday 0900-1830.
Saturday-Sunday 1000-1600
(0900-1700 Saturdays May-September).

Tower Hamlets Tourist Information Centre
107a Commercial Street, E1 6BG
Tel: (0181) 375 2549
Monday-Friday 0930-1630.
Greenwich Tourist Information Centre ⌘
46 Greenwich Church Street, SE10 9BL
Tel: (0181) 858 6376
April-September, daily 1015-1645. October-March, reduced opening hours.
Hackney Museum and Tourist Information Centre
Central Hall, Mare Street, E8
Tel: (0181) 985 9055
Tuesday-Friday 1000-1700.
Saturday 1330-1700.
Islington Tourist Information Centre ⌘
44 Duncan Street, N1 8BW
Tel: (0171) 278 8787
Monday 1400-1600.
Tuesday-Saturday 1000-1700.
Lewisham Tourist Information Centre
Lewisham Library, Lewisham High Street, SE13 6LG
Tel: (0181) 297 8317
Monday 1000-1700.
Tuesday-Friday 0900-1700
Selfridges ⌘
Oxford Street, W1. Basement Services Arcade
Open during normal store hours.
Southwark Tourist Information Centre ⌘
Hay's Galleria,
Tooley Street, SE1 2HD
Tel: (0171) 403 8299

Monday-Friday 1030-1700.
Saturday-Sunday 1100-1700.
(Reduced winter opening).

Outer London
Bexley Tourist Information Centre
Central Library, Townley Road, Bexleyheath DA6 7HJ
Tel: (0181) 303 9052
Monday, Tuesday, Thursday 0930-2000.
Wednesday & Friday 0930-1730.
Saturday 0930-1700.
Also at Hall Place Visitor Centre
Bourne Road, Bexley
Tel: (01322) 558676
June-September, daily 1130-1630.
Croydon Tourist Information Centre ⌘
Katharine Street,
Croydon CR9 1ET
Tel: (0181) 253 1009
Monday-Wednesday & Friday 0900-1800. Thursday 0930-1800.
Saturday 0900-1700.
Sunday 1200-1700.
Foots Cray Tourist Information Centre ⌘
Tesco Store Car Park,
Edgington Way, Sidcup DA14 5AH
Summer only, Monday-Saturday 1000-1800.
Sunday 1000-1600.
Harrow Tourist Information Centre
Civic Centre, Station Road,
Harrow HA1 2XF
Tel: (0181) 424 1103
Monday-Friday 0900-1700.

Hillingdon Tourist Information Centre
Central Library,
14 High Street,
Uxbridge UB8 1HD
Tel: Uxbridge (01895) 250706
Monday, Tuesday
& Thursday 0930-2000.
Friday & Wednesday 0930-1730.
Saturday 0930-1600.

Hounslow Tourist Information Centre
24 The Treaty Centre,
Hounslow High Street,
Hounslow TW3 1ES
Tel: (0181) 572 8279
Monday, Wednesday, Friday
& Saturday 0930-1730.
Tuesday, Thursday 0930-2000.

Kingston Tourist Information Centre
The Market House,
The Market Place,
Kingston upon Thames
KT1 1JS
Tel: (0181) 547 5592
Monday-Friday 1000-1700.
Saturday 0900-1600.

Redbridge Tourist Information Centre
Town Hall, High Road, Ilford,
Essex IG1 1DD
Tel: (0181) 478 3020
Monday-Friday 0830-1700.

Richmond Tourist Information Centre 🛏
Old Town Hall,
Whittaker Avenue,
Richmond upon Thames
TW9 1TP
Tel: (0181) 940 9125
Monday-Friday 1000-1800.
Saturday 1000-1700.
May-October,
also Sunday 1015-1615.

Twickenham Tourist Information Centre
The Altrium, Civic Centre,
York Street,
Twickenham TW1 3BZ
Tel: (0181) 891 7272
Monday-Friday 0900-1700.

Visitorcall

The London Tourist Board and Convention Bureau's 'Phone Guide to London' operates 24 hours a day. To access a full range of information call 0839 123456. To access specific lines dial 0839 123 followed by:

What's on this week - 400
What's on next 3 months - 401
Sunday in London - 407
Rock and pop concerts - 422
Popular attractions - 480
Where to take children - 424
Museums - 429
Palaces (including Buckingham Palace) - 481
Current exhibitions - 403
Changing the Guard - 411
Popular West End shows - 416
London dining - 485
Calls cost 45p per minute cheap rate, 50p per minute at all other times (as at October '96).
To order a Visitorcall card please call (0171) 971 0026.
Information for callers using push-button telephones:
(0171) 971 0027.

Artsline

London's information and advice service for disabled people on arts and entertainment.
Call (0171) 388 2227.

Hotel Accommodation Service

The London Tourist Board and Convention Bureau helps visitors to find and book accommodation at a wide range of prices in hotels and guesthouses, including budget accommodation, throughout the Greater London area.

Reservations are made with hotels which are members of LTB, denoted in this guide with the symbol 🛏 by their name. Reservations can be made by credit card holders via the telephone accommodation reservations service on (0171) 824 8844 by simply giving the reservation clerk your card details (Access or Visa) and room requirements. LTB takes an administrative booking fee. The service operates Monday-Friday 0930-1730.

Reservations on arrival are handled at the Tourist Information Centres operated by LTB at Victoria Station, Liverpool Street Station, Waterloo International, Selfridges and Heathrow. Go to any of them on the day when you need accommodation. A communication charge and a refundable deposit are payable when making a reservation.

Which part of London?

The majority of tourist accommodation is situated in the central parts of London and is therefore very convenient for most of the city's attractions and night life.

However, there are many hotels in outer London which provide other advantages, such as easier parking. In the *'Where to Stay'* pages which follow, you will find accommodation listed under INNER LONDON (covering the E1 to W14 London Postal Area) and OUTER LONDON (covering the remainder of Greater London). Colour maps 6 and 7 at the back of the guide show place names and London Postal Area codes and will help you to locate accommodation in your chosen area of London.

LONDON INDEX

If you are looking for accommodation in a particular establishment in London and you know its name, this index will give you the page number of the full entry in the guide.

A — page no

Aaron (Wembley Park) Hotel Wembley	48
Abbey Court Hotel W2	37
Abbey Lodge Hotel W5	41
Abcone Hotel SW7	35
Acton Park Hotel W3	41
Adelphi Hotel Wembley	48
Airways Hotel, NationLodge Ltd SW1	29
Albany Hotel WC1	42
Albro House Hotel W2	39
Alfa Hotel SW1	29
Allandale Hotel W2	39
Alpha Guest House Croydon	44
Anchor Hotels (Golders Green) Ltd NW11	28
Hotel Antoinette of Kingston Kingston upon Thames	47
Arena Hotel Wembley	48
Arlington (Heathrow) Hotel Hayes	46
Ashdowne Guest House Hounslow	46
Ashley Hotel W2	39
Ashling Tara Hotel Sutton	48
Hotel Atlas W8	42

B — page no

Balfour Hotel Ilford	46
Bardon Lodge Hotel SE3	28
The Basil Street Hotel SW3	32
Beaver Hotel SW5	32
Bedknobs SE22	28
Bentinck House Hotel W1	36
Beverley House Hotel W2	39
The Bingham Hotel on Thames Richmond	47

C — page no

Blair House Hotel SW3	32
Blooms Hotel WC1	42
The Bonnington in Bloomsbury WC1	42
The Brewers Inn SW18	35
Briarley Hotel Croydon	44
The Brookside Hotel Wembley	48
Buxted Lodge Bexley	43

Carnarvon Hotel W5	41
Caswell Hotel SW1	29
Cavendish Guest House NW6	27
Central House Hotel SW1	29
Charles Bernard Hotel NW3	27
Charlotte Guest House & Restaurant NW6	27
Chester House SW1	29
Chumleigh Lodge Hotel N3	26
Clarendon Hotel SE3	28
Colliers Hotel SW1	30
Compton Guest House SW19	36
Corona Hotel SW1	30
Crescent Hotel Harrow	45
Crescent Hotel WC1	42
Croydon Hotel Croydon	44
Cumberland Hotel Harrow	45

D — page no

Dalmacia Hotel W6	41
Dereen Croydon	44
Diana Hotel SE21	28
Dillons Hotel NW3	27
Dolphin Square Hotel SW1	30
The Dorchester W1	36
Dover Hotel SW1	30

Durley Dene Country House Bromley	44

E — page no

The Edward Lear Hotel W1	36
Elizabeth Hotel SW1	30
Elm Hotel Wembley	48

F — page no

Five Kings Guest House N7	26
Five Sumner Place Hotel SW7	35
Forest View Hotel E7	25

G — page no

Garden Court Hotel W2	39
Garth Hotel WC1	42
George Hotel WC1	43
Glendevon House Hotel Bromley	44
Gower House Hotel WC1	43
Grange Lodge Hotel W5	41
Grangewood Lodge Hotel E7	25

H — page no

Hamilton House Hotel SW1	30
Harrow Hotel Harrow	45
Hendon Hall Hotel NW4	27
Henry VIII Hotel W2	39
Hindes Hotel Harrow	46
Hobart Hall Richmond	47
Huttons Hotel SW1	30
Hyde Park Rooms Hotel W2	39

ENQUIRY COUPONS

To help you obtain further information about advertisers and accommodation featured in this guide you will find enquiry coupons at the back. Send these directly to the establishments in which you are interested.

Remember to complete both sides of the coupon.

LONDON INDEX

J — page no
J and T Guest House NW10 — 28

K — page no
Kandara Guest House N1 — 25
Kensington Court Hotel SW5 — 32
Kent Hall Hotel N4 — 26
Kenwood House Hotel W1 — 36
Kings Arms W2 — 39
Kings Lodge Hotel SW19 — 36
Kirkdale Hotel Croydon — 44
Knightsbridge Green Hotel SW1 — 31

L — page no
The Langorf Hotel NW3 — 27
The Leonard W1 — 36
Lincoln House Hotel W1 — 37
Lindal Hotel Harrow — 46
London Continental Hotel W1 — 37
London Tourist Hotel SW5 — 32
Lord Jim Hotel SW5 — 33
Luna-Simone Hotel SW1 — 31

M — page no
Magnolia Hotel, Chelsea SW3 — 32
Mandeville Hotel W1 — 37
Marble Arch Inn W1 — 37
Markington Hotel Croydon — 45
The Mary Rose Hotel Orpington — 47
Mayflower House SW5 — 33
Meadow Croft Lodge SE9 — 28
Melbourne House SW1 — 31
Melita House Hotel SW1 — 31
Merlyn Court Hotel SW5 — 33
Montana Hotel SW7 — 35

N — page no
Nayland Hotel W2 — 40
New Aquarius Hotel SW5 — 33
Hotel Number Sixteen SW7 — 35

O — page no
Hotel Oliver SW5 — 34
Oliver Plaza Hotel SW5 — 34

P — page no
Packfords Hotel Woodford Green — 49
Park Hotel Ilford — 47
Parkland Walk Guest House N19 — 26
Parkwood Hotel W2 — 40
The Pavilion Hotel W2 — 40
Pearl Hotel SW5 — 34
Hotel La Place W1 — 37
The Plough Inn SW14 — 35
Prince Regent Hotel W1 — 37

Q — page no
Quinns Hotel Richmond — 47

R — page no
Raglan Hall Hotel N10 — 26
Rasool Court Hotel SW5 — 34
Rilux House NW4 — 27
Riverside Hotel Richmond — 48
Rose Court Hotel W2 — 40
Royal Adelphi Hotel WC2 — 43
Royal Chace Hotel Enfield — 45
Royal Park Hotel W2 — 40
Ruddimans Hotel W2 — 40
Rushmore Hotel SW5 — 34

S — page no
St. Athan's Hotel WC1 — 43
St. David's and Norfolk Court Hotel W2 — 40
Selsdon Park Croydon — 45
Shalimar Hotel Hounslow — 46
Shepiston Lodge Hayes — 46
Sidney Hotel SW1 — 31
Sleeping Beauty Motel E10 — 25
Stanley House Hotel SW1 — 31
Swallow Hotel Bexleyheath — 43
Swallow International Hotel SW5 — 34
Swiss House Hotel SW5 — 34

T — page no
Thanet Hotel WC1 — 43

V — page no
Vegas Hotel SW1 — 31
Vicarage Private Hotel W8 — 42

W — page no
West Lodge Park Barnet — 43
Westland Hotel W2 — 41
Weston House SE9 — 28
Westpoint Hotel W2 — 41
The White House NW1 — 26
The White House SE27 — 29
White Lodge Hotel N8 — 26
Windermere Hotel SW1 — 31
Windmill on the Common SW4 — 32
Windsor House W5 — 35
Wyndham Hotel W1 — 37

AT-A-GLANCE SYMBOLS

Symbols at the end of each accommodation entry give useful information about services and facilities. A key to symbols can be found inside the back cover flap.

Keep this open for easy reference.

LONDON

WHERE TO STAY (LONDON)

Accommodation entries in this section are listed under **Inner London** (covering the postcode areas E1 to W14) and **Outer London** (covering the remainder of Greater London) - please refer to the colour location maps 6 and 7 at the back of this guide.

If you want to look up a particular establishment, use the index on the previous pages which will give you the page number.

At-a-glance symbols at the end of each accommodation entry give useful information about services and facilities. A key to symbols can be found inside the back cover flap. Keep this open for easy reference.

INNER LONDON

Colour maps 6 & 7 at the back of the guide show place names and London Postal Area Codes and will help you locate accommodation in your chosen area of London

LONDON E7

Forest View Hotel

APPROVED

227 Romford Road, Forest Gate, London E7 9HL
☎ (0181) 534 4844
Fax (0181) 534 8959

Catering for business and tourist clientele, this hotel has en-suite rooms with tea/coffee making, direct-dial telephone and TV. Full English breakfast. Warm and friendly atmosphere, competitive rates.
Bedrooms: 8 single, 5 double, 2 twin, 2 triple, 3 family rooms
Bathrooms: 3 en-suite, 4 private, 3 public

Bed & breakfast
per night:	£min	£max
Single	32.90	32.90
Double	47.00	56.40

Half board per
person:	£min	£max
Daily	39.40	45.50
Weekly	275.80	318.50

Evening meal 1830 (last orders 2100)
Parking for 15
Cards accepted: Access, Visa

Grangewood Lodge Hotel

Listed

104 Clova Road, Forest Gate, London E7 9AF
☎ (0181) 534 0637 & 503 0941
Fax (0181) 257 0392

Comfortable budget accommodation in a quiet road. Pleasant garden. Easy access to central London, Docklands and M11. 12 minutes to Liverpool Street station.
Bedrooms: 10 single, 1 double, 5 twin, 2 triple
Bathrooms: 3 public, 1 private shower

Bed & breakfast
per night:	£min	£max
Single	17.50	19.00
Double	28.00	34.00

Parking for 2
Cards accepted: Access, Visa

LONDON E10

Sleeping Beauty Motel

APPROVED

543 Lea Bridge Road, Leyton, London E10 7EB
☎ (0181) 556 8080
Fax (0181) 556 8080

All rooms en-suite with bath and shower, satellite TV, direct-dial telephone, hairdryer, hospitality tray,

trouser press, mini fridge, safe. Ironing facilities, 24-hour reception, lift, free car park, bar.
Bedrooms: 15 double, 21 twin, 4 triple
Bathrooms: 40 en-suite

Bed & breakfast
per night:	£min	£max
Single	40.00	45.00
Double	45.00	50.00

Parking for 34
Cards accepted: Access, Visa, Diners, Amex, Switch/Delta

LONDON N1

Kandara Guest House

Listed

68 Ockendon Road, London N1 3NW
☎ (0171) 226 5721 & 226 3379

Small family-run guesthouse near the Angel, Islington. Free street parking and good public transport to West End and City.
Bedrooms: 4 single, 2 double, 3 twin, 1 triple
Bathrooms: 3 public

Bed & breakfast
per night:	£min	£max
Single	26.00	29.00
Double	36.00	39.00

Cards accepted: Access, Visa

A key to symbols can be found inside the back cover flap.

LONDON

LONDON N3

Chumleigh Lodge Hotel

226-228 Nether Street, Finchley, London N3 1HU
☎ (0181) 346 1614 & 346 0059
Fax (0181) 346 1614
Easy access to M1/A1, North Circular, Alexandra Palace, Wembley and West End. Restaurant, residents' bar, full English breakfast. Parking.
Bedrooms: 7 single, 4 double, 3 twin, 4 triple, 2 family rooms
Bathrooms: 16 en-suite, 2 public

Bed & breakfast per night:

	£min	£max
Single	25.00	35.00
Double	43.00	49.00

Evening meal 1900 (last orders 2130)
Parking for 11
Cards accepted: Access, Visa

LONDON N4

Kent Hall Hotel

Listed
414 Seven Sisters Road, London N4 2LX
☎ (0181) 802 0800 & 802 5100
Fax (0181) 802 9070
Close to Manor House underground, 10 minutes from central London. Ideal for groups and school parties.
Bedrooms: 4 single, 6 double, 7 twin, 8 triple
Bathrooms: 10 en-suite, 15 private showers

Bed & breakfast per night:

	£min	£max
Single	25.00	35.00
Double	35.00	50.00

Parking for 4

LONDON N7

Five Kings Guest House

59 Anson Road, Tufnell Park, London N7 0AR
☎ (0171) 607 3996 & 607 6466
Privately-run guesthouse in a quiet residential area. 15 minutes to central London. Unrestricted parking in road.
Bedrooms: 6 single, 3 double, 3 twin, 2 triple, 2 family rooms
Bathrooms: 9 en-suite, 3 public, 2 private showers

Bed & breakfast per night:

	£min	£max
Single	18.00	27.00
Double	30.00	38.00

Cards accepted: Access, Visa

LONDON N8

White Lodge Hotel

1 Church Lane, Hornsey, London N8 7BU
☎ (0181) 348 9765
Fax (0181) 340 7851
Small, friendly, family hotel offering personal service. Easy access to all transport, for sightseeing and business trips.
Bedrooms: 7 single, 3 double, 3 twin, 3 family rooms
Bathrooms: 8 en-suite, 3 public

Bed & breakfast per night:

	£min	£max
Single	26.00	28.00
Double	36.00	44.00

Evening meal 1800 (last orders 1900)
Cards accepted: Access, Visa

LONDON N10

Raglan Hall Hotel

COMMENDED
8-12 Queens Avenue, Muswell Hill, London N10 3NR
☎ (0181) 883 5700 & 883 9836
Fax (0181) 883 5002
Best Western
Located in a quiet tree-lined avenue of north London. Lovely secluded garden and patio. Modern English food. Friendly relaxed atmosphere.
Bedrooms: 13 single, 16 double, 9 twin, 8 triple
Bathrooms: 46 en-suite

Bed & breakfast per night:

	£min	£max
Single	85.00	90.00
Double	95.00	100.00

Half board per person:

	£min	£max
Daily	101.00	106.00
Weekly	707.00	742.00

Lunch available
Evening meal 1900 (last orders 2145)
Parking for 8
Cards accepted: Access, Visa, Diners, Amex, Switch/Delta

For ideas on places to visit refer to the introduction at the beginning of this section.

LONDON N19

Parkland Walk Guest House

Listed COMMENDED
12 Hornsey Rise Gardens, London N19 3PR
☎ (0171) 263 3228 & 0973 382982
Fax (0171) 831 9489
Friendly Victorian family house in residential area, Highgate/Crouch End. Near many restaurants and convenient for central London. Non-smokers only. Recent British Tourist Authority award winner - Best Small Hotel in London competition.
Bedrooms: 3 single, 1 double, 1 twin, 1 family room
Bathrooms: 3 en-suite, 1 private, 1 public

Bed & breakfast per night:

	£min	£max
Single	25.00	35.00
Double	42.00	56.00

Cards accepted: Amex

LONDON NW1

The White House

COMMENDED
Albany Street, Regent's Park, London NW1 3UP
☎ (0171) 387 1200
Fax (0171) 388 0091
Utell International
Near Regent's Park, the zoo and Madame Tussaud's. A few minutes from Euston Station and about 10 minutes' walk from Oxford Circus. There are 3 underground stations within walking distance.
Bedrooms: 53 single, 216 double, 239 twin, 53 triple
Suites available
Bathrooms: 561 en-suite

Bed & breakfast per night:

	£min	£max
Single	150.00	175.00
Double	168.00	197.00

Half board per person:

	£min	£max
Daily	174.00	200.00

Lunch available
Evening meal 1830 (last orders 2230)
Parking for 7
Cards accepted: Access, Visa, Diners, Amex, Switch/Delta

Establishments should be open throughout the year, unless otherwise stated.

LONDON

LONDON NW3

Charles Bernard Hotel
COMMENDED

5 Frognal, Hampstead, London
NW3 6AL
☎ (0171) 794 0101
Fax (0171) 794 0100
Purpose-built hotel approximately 4 miles from Oxford Circus, offering a happy, friendly atmosphere. Ideal for business, shopping or leisure visits to the capital.
Bedrooms: 9 double, 48 twin
Bathrooms: 57 en-suite

Bed & breakfast per night:	£min	£max
Single	60.00	64.00
Double	70.00	74.00

Half board per person:	£min	£max
Daily	48.00	52.00
Weekly	302.00	327.00

Lunch available
Evening meal 1830 (last orders 2130)
Parking for 18
Cards accepted: Access, Visa, Diners, Amex, Switch/Delta

Dillons Hotel
Listed

21 Belsize Park, Hampstead, London NW3 4DU
☎ (0171) 794 3360
Fax (0171) 586 1104
Small private guesthouse, close to central London, with excellent transport facilities nearby.
Bedrooms: 4 single, 1 double, 5 twin, 1 triple, 2 family rooms
Bathrooms: 7 private, 3 public

Bed & breakfast per night:	£min	£max
Single	26.00	32.00
Double	36.00	42.00

The Langorf Hotel
COMMENDED

20 Frognal, Hampstead, London NW3 6AG
☎ (0171) 794 4483
Fax (0171) 435 9055
Three minutes' walk from Finchley Road underground, this elegant Edwardian residence in Hampstead boasts attractive bedrooms with full facilities. BTA Spencer Trophy runner-up.
Bedrooms: 1 single, 18 double, 8 twin, 4 triple
Bathrooms: 31 en-suite

Bed & breakfast per night:	£min	£max
Single	62.00	75.00
Double	80.00	95.00

Lunch available
Evening meal 1800 (last orders 2300)
Cards accepted: Access, Visa, Diners, Amex

LONDON NW4

Hendon Hall Hotel

Ashley Lane, off Parson Street, Hendon, London NW4 1HF
☎ (0181) 203 3341
Fax (0181) 203 9709
Utell International
Elegant 18th C Georgian mansion set in its own grounds.
Bedrooms: 22 single, 10 double, 18 twin, 2 triple
Bathrooms: 52 en-suite

Bed & breakfast per night:	£min	£max
Single	89.95	108.95
Double	114.90	129.90

Half board per person:	£min	£max
Daily	106.70	125.70
Weekly	746.90	879.90

Lunch available
Evening meal 1900 (last orders 2200)
Parking for 70
Cards accepted: Access, Visa, Diners, Amex

Rilux House

1 Lodge Road, London NW4 4DD
☎ (0181) 203 0933
Fax (0181) 203 6446
High standard, all private facilities, kitchenette and garden. Quiet. Close to underground, buses, M1, 20 minutes West End. Convenient for Wembley, easy route to Heathrow, direct trains to Gatwick and Luton airports. Close to Middlesex University.
Bedrooms: 1 double
Bathrooms: 1 en-suite

Bed & breakfast per night:	£min	£max
Single	27.50	30.00
Double	45.00	50.00

Parking for 1

LONDON NW6

Cavendish Guest House

24 Cavendish Road, London NW6 7XP
☎ (0181) 451 3249
In a quiet residential street, 5 minutes' walk from Kilburn underground station, 15 minutes' travelling time to the West End.
Bedrooms: 4 single, 3 double, 1 twin
Bathrooms: 1 en-suite, 3 public

Bed & breakfast per night:	£min	£max
Single	25.00	27.00
Double	38.00	44.00

Parking for 4

Charlotte Guest House & Restaurant
Listed

221 West End Lane, West Hampstead, London NW6 1XJ
☎ (0171) 794 6476
Fax (0171) 431 3584

Rooms with private facilities. Restaurant and coffee lounge. French and German spoken. Bus, underground and BR adjacent. 15 minutes from West End and city. Free London Travel Card for a week's stay or longer.
Bedrooms: 12 single, 12 double, 12 twin
Bathrooms: 18 en-suite, 6 public

Bed & breakfast per night:	£min	£max
Single	20.00	35.00
Double	30.00	45.00

Half board per person:	£min	£max
Daily	25.00	45.00
Weekly	175.00	315.00

Lunch available
Evening meal 1800 (last orders 2200)
Cards accepted: Amex

The symbol after an establishment name indicates that it is a Regional Tourist Board member.

LONDON

LONDON NW10

J and T Guest House
Listed

98 Park Avenue North, Willesden Green, London NW10 1JY
☎ (0181) 452 4085
Fax (0181) 450 2503

Small guesthouse in north west London close to underground. Easy access to Wembley Stadium complex. 5 minutes from M1.

Bedrooms: 1 single, 1 double, 3 twin, 1 triple
Bathrooms: 2 en-suite, 4 private

Bed & breakfast per night:	£min	£max
Single	29.00	35.00
Double	42.00	52.00

Parking for 2
Cards accepted: Access, Visa, Switch/Delta

LONDON NW11

Anchor Hotels (Golders Green) Ltd
Listed APPROVED

10 West Heath Drive, Golders Green, London NW11 7QH
☎ (0181) 458 8764
Fax (0181) 455 3204

Small well-furnished hotel, 150 yards from underground/High Street. En-suite rooms with remote control satellite TV, coffee tray. Huge buffet breakfast. Warm, welcoming atmosphere.

Bedrooms: 3 single, 5 double, 3 twin
Bathrooms: 8 en-suite, 1 public

Bed & breakfast per night:	£min	£max
Single	29.00	33.00
Double	45.00	49.00

Parking for 4
Cards accepted: Access, Visa, Switch/Delta

LONDON SE3

Bardon Lodge Hotel
COMMENDED

15-17 Stratheden Road, Blackheath, London SE3 7TH
☎ (0181) 853 4051
Fax (0181) 858 7357

Victorian residence close to Greenwich Park and the A2. Reception rooms retain their original grandeur, whilst the bedrooms have been completely modernised.

Bedrooms: 13 single, 11 double, 3 twin, 1 triple, 3 family rooms
Bathrooms: 27 en-suite, 2 public, 4 private showers

Bed & breakfast per night:	£min	£max
Single	45.00	60.00
Double	65.00	85.00

Evening meal 1900 (last orders 2130)
Parking for 32
Cards accepted: Access, Visa, Diners, Amex, Switch/Delta

Clarendon Hotel
APPROVED

8-16 Montpelier Row, Blackheath, London SE3 0RW
☎ (0181) 318 4321
Fax (0181) 318 4378

Facing the heath and 22 minutes by train from central London. 10 minutes' walk from Greenwich, 5 minutes' walk from Greenwich Royal Park.

Bedrooms: 44 single, 54 double, 69 twin, 24 triple, 2 family rooms Suites available
Bathrooms: 158 en-suite, 6 private, 14 public

Bed & breakfast per night:	£min	£max
Single	39.50	49.50
Double	72.50	84.00

Half board per person:	£min	£max
Daily	61.50	
Weekly	400.50	

Lunch available
Evening meal 1830 (last orders 2145)
Parking for 80
Cards accepted: Access, Visa, Diners, Amex, Switch/Delta

LONDON SE9

Meadow Croft Lodge
COMMENDED

96-98 Southwood Road, New Eltham, London SE9 3QS
☎ (0181) 859 1488
Fax (0181) 850 8054

Between A2 and A20, near New Eltham station with easy access to London. Warm and friendly atmosphere. TV in rooms. British Tourist Authority London B&B award 1990.

Bedrooms: 4 single, 3 double, 9 twin, 1 family room
Bathrooms: 1 private, 4 public, 9 private showers

Bed & breakfast per night:	£min	£max
Single	21.00	26.00
Double	39.00	42.00

Parking for 9
Cards accepted: Access, Visa, Amex

Weston House
APPROVED

8 Eltham Green, Eltham, London SE9 5LB
☎ (0181) 850 5191
Fax (0181) 850 0030

Recently refurbished, friendly, comfortable hotel in Greenwich conservation area close to National Maritime Museum. 20 minutes from central London, convenient for A2, M20 and A205.

Bedrooms: 3 single, 2 double, 3 twin, 1 triple
Bathrooms: 3 en-suite, 1 public, 6 private showers

Bed & breakfast per night:	£min	£max
Single	30.00	30.00
Double	40.00	45.00

Parking for 6
Cards accepted: Access, Visa, Switch/Delta

LONDON SE21

Diana Hotel

88 Thurlow Park Road, London SE21 8HY
☎ (0181) 670 3250
Fax (0181) 761 9152

Comfortable and friendly family-run hotel near Dulwich Village, a pleasant suburb 10 minutes by train from central London.

Bedrooms: 1 single, 4 double, 3 twin, 2 triple, 1 family room
Bathrooms: 4 en-suite, 2 public, 2 private showers

Bed & breakfast per night:	£min	£max
Single	28.00	38.00
Double	38.00	48.00

Evening meal 1800 (last orders 1930)
Parking for 3
Cards accepted: Access, Visa

LONDON SE22

Bedknobs
Listed COMMENDED

58 Glengarry Road, East Dulwich, London SE22 8QD
☎ (0181) 299 2004
Fax (0181) 693 5611

Carefully restored Victorian family-run house offering many home comforts, excellent service and a warm welcome. BTA London B&B Award 1992.

LONDON

Bedrooms: 1 double, 2 twin
Bathrooms: 2 public
Bed & breakfast
per night: £min   £max
Single   20.00   32.00
Double   40.00   60.00

LONDON SE27

The White House
Listed

242 Norwood Road, West
Norwood, London SE27 9AW
☎ (0181) 670 3607 & 761 8892
Fax (0181) 670 6440
Listed Georgian house with forecourt parking, on main road. Buses and trains to the city. Close to Crystal Palace National Sports Centre.
Bedrooms: 2 single, 1 triple
Bathrooms: 3 en-suite, 2 public
Bed & breakfast
per night: £min   £max
Single   15.00   17.00
Double   25.00   27.00
Parking for 3

LONDON SW1

Airways Hotel, NationLodge Ltd
Listed APPROVED

29-31 St. George's Drive, Victoria,
London SW1V 4DG
☎ (0171) 834 0205
Fax (0171) 932 0007
Within walking distance of Buckingham Palace and Westminster Abbey. Convenient for Harrods and theatreland. Friendly personal service.
Bedrooms: 6 single, 8 double, 12 twin, 4 triple, 5 family rooms
Bathrooms: 35 en-suite, 1 public
Bed & breakfast
per night: £min   £max
Single   35.00   49.00
Double   45.00   59.00

Cards accepted: Access, Visa, Diners, Amex, Switch/Delta

Alfa Hotel
Listed

78-82 Warwick Way, London
SW1V 1RZ
☎ (0171) 828 8603
Fax (0171) 976 6536
Close to Victoria station, behind a period facade, the Alfa offers comfort, service and interior-decorated accommodation.
Bedrooms: 9 single, 10 double, 9 twin, 4 triple, 1 family room
Bathrooms: 33 private
Bed & breakfast
per night: £min   £max
Single   35.00   49.00
Double   55.00   63.00

Cards accepted: Access, Visa, Diners, Amex

Caswell Hotel
Listed

25 Gloucester Street, London
SW1V 2DB
☎ (0171) 834 6345
Pleasant, family-run hotel, near Victoria coach and rail stations, yet in a quiet location.
Bedrooms: 1 single, 6 double, 6 twin, 3 triple, 2 family rooms
Bathrooms: 7 en-suite, 5 public
Bed & breakfast
per night: £min   £max
Single   28.00   52.00
Double   39.00   65.00

> A key to symbols can be found inside the back cover flap.

Central House Hotel
Listed APPROVED

39 Belgrave Road, London
SW1V 2BB
☎ (0171) 834 8036 & 828 0644
Fax (0171) 834 1854
Situated within minutes of Victoria coach, rail and underground stations. All rooms have en-suite facilities, telephones, etc. Newly refurbished with lift serving all floors.
Bedrooms: 4 single, 18 double, 19 twin, 6 triple, 3 family rooms
Bathrooms: 50 en-suite, 1 public
Bed & breakfast
per night: £min   £max
Single   35.00   49.00
Double   55.00   69.00

Cards accepted: Access, Visa

Chester House
Listed

134 Ebury Street, London
SW1W 9QQ
☎ (0171) 730 3632
Fax (0171) 824 8446
Small, friendly bed and breakfast close to Sloane Square and 10 minutes' walk from Harrods. Convenient for public transport.
Bedrooms: 3 single, 2 double, 5 twin, 2 triple
Bathrooms: 6 private, 2 public
Bed & breakfast
per night: £min   £max
Single   32.00   45.00
Double   50.00   60.00

Cards accepted: Access, Visa, Diners, Amex

> Please check prices and other details at the time of booking.

ELIZABETH HOTEL
CENTRAL LONDON SW1

Friendly, private Hotel ideally located for all parts of the Capital
37 Eccleston Square, VICTORIA,
London SW1V 1PB.
Telephone (0171) 828 6812

HIGHLY COMMENDED
in the Considerate Hoteliers of Westminster 1994 Awards.

Situated in stately garden square (c. 1835), close to Belgravia and a few doors from one of the residences of the late Sir Winston Churchill. Within two minutes' walk of Victoria Station/Coach Station/Air Terminals. Parking nearby.
Comfortable single, twin, double and family rooms.
Attractive lounge and pleasant Breakfast Room. Lift.
Good ENGLISH BREAKFAST, or Continental breakfast at any time for EARLY DEPARTURES.
MODERATE PRICES include accommodation, breakfast and Tax.
FREE COLOUR BROCHURE AVAILABLE

LONDON

LONDON SW1
Continued

Colliers Hotel
Listed
97 Warwick Way, London
SW1V 1QL
☎ (0171) 834 6931 & 828 0210
Fax (0171) 834 8439
Modern-style family hotel with spacious rooms. Very clean, budget priced, centrally located. Ideal for easy connections to London's major tourist spots.
Bedrooms: 4 single, 7 double, 5 twin, 1 triple, 1 family room
Bathrooms: 2 en-suite, 3 public, 3 private showers

Bed & breakfast per night:	£min	£max
Single	22.00	28.00
Double	32.00	42.00

Cards accepted: Access, Visa, Diners, Amex

Corona Hotel
87-89 Belgrave Road, Victoria,
London SW1V 2BQ
☎ (0171) 828 9279
Fax (0171) 931 8576
Utell International

Small in stature, but big on hospitality, Corona offers a uniquely friendly atmosphere which has endeared it to hundreds who regularly stay here.
Bedrooms: 9 single, 13 double, 9 twin, 2 triple, 2 family rooms
Bathrooms: 29 en-suite, 2 public, 2 private showers

Bed & breakfast per night:	£min	£max
Single	34.00	52.00
Double	45.00	66.00

Cards accepted: Access, Visa, Diners, Amex, Switch/Delta

Dolphin Square Hotel
COMMENDED
Dolphin Square, London SW1V 3LX
☎ (0171) 834 3800
Fax (0171) 798 8735
Grand Heritage

An all-suite hotel and apartment complex, set amongst private gardens in central London. Extensive leisure facilities include own sports and health club with swimming pool.
Bedrooms: 19 single, 95 double, 35 twin, 2 triple
Bathrooms: 151 en-suite

Bed & breakfast per night:	£min	£max
Single	91.95	111.50
Double	121.90	180.00

Half board per person:	£min	£max
Daily	102.90	112.95
Weekly	635.30	779.15

Lunch available
Evening meal 1800 (last orders 2230)
Parking for 200
Cards accepted: Access, Visa, Diners, Amex, Switch/Delta

Dover Hotel
Listed APPROVED
44 Belgrave Road, London
SW1V 1RG
☎ (0171) 821 9085
Fax (0171) 834 6425
Small friendly bed and breakfast hotel with easy access to all major attractions and 3 minutes from Victoria rail/coach station.
Bedrooms: 1 single, 4 double, 6 twin, 4 triple, 1 family room
Bathrooms: 13 en-suite, 1 private, 1 public, 2 private showers

Bed & breakfast per night:	£min	£max
Single	40.00	45.00
Double	50.00	60.00

Cards accepted: Access, Visa, Diners, Amex, Switch/Delta

Elizabeth Hotel
37 Eccleston Square, Victoria,
London SW1V 1PB
☎ (0171) 828 6812

Friendly, quiet hotel overlooking magnificent gardens of stately residential square (circa 1835), close to Belgravia yet within 5 minutes' walk of Victoria. Free colour brochure.
Bedrooms: 6 single, 5 double, 4 twin, 16 triple, 7 family rooms
Bathrooms: 26 en-suite, 8 private, 1 public, 1 private shower

Bed & breakfast per night:	£min	£max
Single	36.00	55.00
Double	62.00	84.00

Ad See display advertisement on page 29

Hamilton House Hotel
APPROVED
60 Warwick Way, London
SW1V 1SA
☎ (0171) 821 7113
Fax (0171) 630 0806

Hotel close to Victoria station and the West End. Warm and friendly atmosphere. Modern decor. Satellite TV.
Bedrooms: 5 single, 10 double, 23 twin, 2 triple
Bathrooms: 18 en-suite, 7 private, 5 public

Bed & breakfast per night:	£min	£max
Single	38.00	48.00
Double	48.00	58.00

Cards accepted: Access, Visa

Huttons Hotel
Listed APPROVED
55 Belgrave Road, London
SW1V 2BB
☎ (0171) 834 3726
Fax (0171) 834 3389

Please check prices and other details at the time of booking.

LONDON

5 minutes' walk from Victoria and central London.
Bedrooms: 5 single, 11 double, 27 twin, 8 triple, 2 family rooms
Bathrooms: 26 en-suite, 10 public
Bed & breakfast

per night:	£min	£max
Single	31.00	31.00
Double	41.00	41.00

Cards accepted: Access, Visa, Diners, Amex

Knightsbridge Green Hotel ⋀
HIGHLY COMMENDED
159 Knightsbridge, London
SW1X 7PD
☎ (0171) 584 6274
Fax (0171) 225 1635
Small family-owned and run hotel close to Harrods, offering spacious accommodation at competitive rates.
Bedrooms: 5 single, 3 double, 5 twin, 12 triple
Suites available
Bathrooms: 25 en-suite
Bed & breakfast

per night:	£min	£max
Single	91.50	91.50
Double	133.00	133.00

Cards accepted: Access, Visa, Diners, Amex

Luna-Simone Hotel ⋀
Listed
47 Belgrave Road, London
SW1V 2BB
☎ (0171) 834 5897
Fax (0171) 828 2474
Friendly, good value, bed and breakfast hotel. Within easy walking distance of Victoria rail, underground and coach stations. Opposite bus stop.
Bedrooms: 3 single, 11 double, 11 twin, 10 triple
Bathrooms: 19 private, 4 public, 5 private showers
Bed & breakfast

per night:	£min	£max
Single	22.00	28.00
Double	38.00	56.00

Cards accepted: Access, Visa

Melbourne House ⋀
Listed COMMENDED
79 Belgrave Road, London
SW1V 2BG
☎ (0171) 828 3516
Fax (0171) 828 7120
Family-run bed and breakfast. All rooms en-suite with tea and coffee facilities, colour TV. Good value.
Bedrooms: 2 single, 5 double, 5 twin, 1 triple, 1 family room
Suites available
Bathrooms: 14 en-suite
Bed & breakfast

per night:	£min	£max
Single	25.00	45.00
Double	50.00	65.00

Cards accepted: Access, Visa

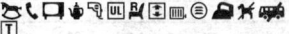

Melita House Hotel ⋀
Listed
35 Charlwood Street, London
SW1V 2DU
☎ (0171) 828 0471 & 834 1387
Fax (0171) 932 0988
Family-run, budget B & B (full English breakfast), close to Victoria station. Warm, friendly and with extensive facilities.
Bedrooms: 5 single, 6 double, 5 twin, 1 triple, 2 family rooms
Bathrooms: 11 en-suite, 2 private, 2 public, 4 private showers
Bed & breakfast

per night:	£min	£max
Single	28.00	38.00
Double	40.00	52.00

Cards accepted: Access, Visa, Amex, Switch/Delta

Sidney Hotel ⋀
76 Belgrave Road, London
SW1V 2BP
☎ (0171) 834 2738
Fax (0171) 630 0973
Utell International

Friendly establishment, a few minutes' walk from Victoria rail and coach stations.
Bedrooms: 14 single, 11 double, 7 twin, 4 triple, 3 family rooms
Bathrooms: 26 en-suite, 3 public, 6 private showers
Bed & breakfast

per night:	£min	£max
Single	34.00	52.00
Double	48.00	66.00

Cards accepted: Access, Visa, Diners, Amex, Switch/Delta

Stanley House Hotel ⋀
19-21 Belgrave Road, London
SW1V 1RB
☎ (0171) 834 5042 & 834 7292
Fax (0171) 834 8439
In elegant Belgravia, only a few minutes' walk from Victoria station and with easy access to West End. All rooms en-suite, with colour TV, direct-dial telephone, hairdryer. Friendly, relaxing atmosphere at affordable rates.
Bedrooms: 3 single, 5 double, 12 twin, 8 triple, 13 family rooms
Bathrooms: 30 en-suite, 5 public
Bed & breakfast

per night:	£min	£max
Single	26.00	35.00
Double	40.00	49.00

Cards accepted: Access, Visa, Diners, Amex, Switch/Delta

Vegas Hotel ⋀
Listed APPROVED
104 Warwick Way, London
SW1V 1SD
☎ (0171) 834 0082
Fax (0171) 834 5623
Close to Victoria coach and underground station and 15 minutes from Buckingham Palace. Satellite colour TV, telephone, radio, alarm clock in all rooms.
Bedrooms: 1 single, 3 double, 9 twin
Bathrooms: 11 en-suite, 1 public, 2 private showers
Bed & breakfast

per night:	£min	£max
Single	35.00	50.00
Double	40.00	65.00

Cards accepted: Access, Visa, Diners, Amex, Switch/Delta

Windermere Hotel ⋀
COMMENDED
142-144 Warwick Way, Victoria, London SW1V 4JE
☎ (0171) 834 5163 & 834 5480
Fax (0171) 630 8831
Previous winner of BTA Trophy and Certificate of Distinction for small hotels. A friendly, charming hotel with well-appointed rooms and a licensed restaurant.
Bedrooms: 3 single, 11 double, 5 twin, 1 triple, 3 family rooms
Bathrooms: 19 en-suite, 2 public
Bed & breakfast

per night:	£min	£max
Single	34.00	57.00
Double	59.00	86.00

Continued ▶

LONDON

LONDON SW1
Continued

Half board per person:
	£min	£max
Daily	40.00	52.50

Evening meal 1800 (last orders 2130)
Cards accepted: Access, Visa, Amex, Switch/Delta

LONDON SW3

The Basil Street Hotel
HIGHLY COMMENDED

Basil Street, Knightsbridge, London SW3 1AH
☎ (0171) 581 3311
Fax (0171) 581 3693
Ⓖ Utell International
An English country house in the centre of London, a short distance from Harrods.
Bedrooms: 42 single, 20 double, 25 twin, 4 triple
Bathrooms: 89 en-suite, 6 public
Bed & breakfast per night:
	£min	£max
Single	138.50	147.50
Double	202.00	215.00

Half board per person:
	£min	£max
Daily	155.50	129.50

Lunch available
Evening meal 1830 (last orders 2200)
Cards accepted: Access, Visa, Diners, Amex, Switch/Delta

Blair House Hotel
APPROVED

34 Draycott Place, London SW3 2SA
☎ (0171) 581 2323 & 225 0771
Fax (0171) 823 7752
Homely hotel in a quiet, elegant street, close to Harrods and museums.
Bedrooms: 1 single, 4 double, 6 twin
Bathrooms: 11 en-suite, 1 public
Bed & breakfast per night:
	£min	£max
Single	70.00	
Double	90.00	98.00

Cards accepted: Access, Visa, Diners, Amex, Switch/Delta

Magnolia Hotel, Chelsea
Listed APPROVED

104-105 Oakley Street, London SW3 5NT
☎ (0171) 352 0187 & 352 3610
Small hotel in Chelsea with a country atmosphere, close to King's Road and all main amenities. Out of season discount. All rooms have colour TV.
Bedrooms: 6 single, 6 double, 7 twin, 1 triple
Bathrooms: 3 en-suite, 1 private, 4 public, 6 private showers
Bed & breakfast per night:
	£min	£max
Single	30.00	48.00
Double	45.00	65.00

Cards accepted: Access, Visa, Amex

LONDON SW4

Windmill on the Common
HIGHLY COMMENDED

Southside, Clapham Common, London SW4 9DE
☎ (0181) 673 4578
Fax (0181) 675 1486
Well-appointed bedrooms overlooking Clapham Common. A la carte/table d'hote restaurant and traditional busy Youngs pub serving good bar food. Easy access into central London (underground station 5 minutes' walk from hotel).
Bedrooms: 20 double, 9 twin
Bathrooms: 29 en-suite
Bed & breakfast per night:
	£min	£max
Single	80.00	
Double	90.00	115.00

Lunch available
Evening meal 1900 (last orders 2200)
Parking for 30
Cards accepted: Access, Visa, Diners, Amex, Switch/Delta

LONDON SW5

Beaver Hotel

57-59 Philbeach Gardens, London SW5 9ED
☎ (0171) 373 4553
Fax (0171) 373 4555
In a quiet, tree-lined crescent of late Victorian terraced houses, close to Earl's Court Exhibition Centre and 10 minutes from the West End.
Bedrooms: 17 single, 6 double, 10 twin, 4 triple
Bathrooms: 24 en-suite, 5 public

Bed & breakfast per night:
	£min	£max
Single	29.00	49.00
Double	42.00	66.00

Parking for 23
Cards accepted: Access, Visa, Diners, Amex

Kensington Court Hotel
APPROVED

33 Nevern Place, Earl's Court, London SW5 9NP
☎ (0171) 370 5151
Fax (0171) 370 3499
Ⓖ Utell International
Purpose-built hotel with private car park. Centrally situated for both the underground and exhibition centres. All rooms with en-suite facilities.
Bedrooms: 10 single, 5 double, 5 twin, 10 triple, 5 family rooms
Bathrooms: 35 en-suite
Bed & breakfast per night:
	£min	£max
Single	59.00	
Double	75.00	

Evening meal 1900 (last orders 2100)
Parking for 10
Cards accepted: Access, Visa, Amex, Switch/Delta

London Tourist Hotel
COMMENDED

15 Penywern Road, Earl's Court, London SW5 9TT
☎ (0171) 370 4356
Fax (0171) 370 7923

Situated within 2 minutes' walk of Earl's Court underground, with direct connections to Heathrow, Victoria and Piccadilly Circus. Recently refurbished, all rooms with en-suite facilities, colour TV, telephone and hairdryer. Children under 3 free of charge.
Bedrooms: 9 single, 4 double, 13 twin, 6 triple
Bathrooms: 32 en-suite
Bed & breakfast per night:
	£min	£max
Single	42.00	49.00
Double	62.00	72.00

Parking for 4
Cards accepted: Access, Visa, Diners, Amex

LONDON

Lord Jim Hotel
Listed
23-25 Penywern Road, London SW5 9TT
☎ (0171) 370 6071 & 0860 691644
Fax (0171) 373 8919

Budget-priced, well-serviced bed and breakfast, ideally situated for Earl's Court and Olympia exhibition halls. Convenient for museums, city, and Heathrow and Gatwick airports (via Victoria).
Bedrooms: 8 single, 6 double, 5 twin, 9 triple, 7 family rooms
Bathrooms: 11 en-suite, 6 public, 3 private showers

Bed & breakfast per night:	£min	£max
Single	25.00	40.00
Double	30.00	48.00

Cards accepted: Access, Visa, Diners, Amex

Mayflower House
Listed
26-28 Trebovir Road, Earls Court, London SW5 9NJ
☎ (0171) 370 0991
Fax (0171) 370 0994
Family-run centrally located hotel. Easy access to shops and theatres. Friendly and attentive service. Well-appointed en-suite bedrooms with all facilities.
Bedrooms: 8 single, 17 double, 14 twin, 7 triple, 2 family rooms
Bathrooms: 46 en-suite, 1 public

Bed & breakfast per night:	£min	£max
Single	49.00	55.00
Double	59.00	65.00

Cards accepted: Access, Visa, Diners, Amex, Switch/Delta

Merlyn Court Hotel
2 Barkston Gardens, London SW5 0EN
☎ (0171) 370 1640
Fax (0171) 370 4986

Well-established, family-run, good value hotel in quiet Edwardian square, close to Earl's Court and Olympia. Direct underground link to Heathrow, the West End and rail stations. Car park nearby.

Bedrooms: 4 single, 4 double, 4 twin, 2 triple, 3 family rooms
Bathrooms: 8 en-suite, 3 private, 6 public, 1 private shower

Bed & breakfast per night:	£min	£max
Single	25.00	50.00
Double	35.00	60.00

Cards accepted: Access, Visa

New Aquarius Hotel
Listed
20-22 Hogarth Road, London SW5 0PT
☎ (0171) 373 6155 & 370 6582
Fax (0171) 373 5182
Medium size budget hotel, 1 minute from Earl's Court underground station.
Bedrooms: 13 single, 7 double, 7 twin, 9 triple, 2 family rooms
Bathrooms: 26 en-suite, 10 private, 2 public, 2 private showers

Bed & breakfast per night:	£min	£max
Single	25.00	35.00
Double	35.00	45.00

Cards accepted: Access, Visa, Diners, Amex

ENQUIRY COUPONS

To help you obtain further information about advertisers featured in this guide you will find enquiry coupons at the back. Send these directly to the establishments in which you are interested. Remember to complete both sides of the coupon.

LONDON HOTEL

BEST RATES

SINGLES FROM £22 - £38
DOUBLES FROM £16 pp to £28 pp
FAMILIES 3/4/5 FROM £13-£20 pp
GROUP RATES FROM £13 pp

WINDSOR HOUSE HOTEL,
12 PENYWERN ROAD,
LONDON SW5 9ST
Tel: 0171 373 9087 Fax: 0171 385 2417

5 Mins to Piccadilly

Call, fax or write now!
WELCOME TO LONDON

LONDON

LONDON SW5
Continued

Hotel Oliver
APPROVED
198 Cromwell Road, London SW5 0SN
☎ (0171) 370 6881
Fax (0171) 370 6556

All rooms en-suite with colour TV and telephone. Full central heating, lift service to all floors. 2 minutes' walk to Earl's Court underground station. Heathrow Airbus stops outside hotel.
Bedrooms: 20 single, 11 double, 11 twin, 2 triple, 4 family rooms
Bathrooms: 48 en-suite

Bed & breakfast

per night:	£min	£max
Single	35.00	45.00
Double	50.00	60.00

Cards accepted: Access, Visa, Diners, Amex

Oliver Plaza Hotel
Listed
33 Trebovir Road, Earl's Court, London SW5 0LR
☎ (0171) 373 7183
Fax (0171) 244 6021
A small hotel with emphasis on efficiency of service and comfort for guests.
Bedrooms: 3 single, 13 double, 8 twin, 3 triple, 5 family rooms
Bathrooms: 32 en-suite, 1 public

Bed & breakfast

per night:	£min	£max
Single	40.00	45.00
Double	50.00	55.00

Parking for 7
Cards accepted: Access, Visa, Diners, Amex, Switch/Delta

Pearl Hotel
Listed APPROVED
40 West Cromwell Road, Earl's Court, London SW5 9QL
☎ (0171) 373 9610 & 835 2007
Fax (0171) 244 6835
Located near Earl's Court underground station, 15 minutes from West End. Direct train from Heathrow Airport.
Bedrooms: 13 single, 2 double, 4 twin, 1 triple

Bathrooms: 1 en-suite, 1 private, 5 public, 12 private showers

Bed & breakfast

per night:	£min	£max
Single	20.00	26.00
Double	33.00	36.00

Cards accepted: Access, Visa, Amex

Rasool Court Hotel
Listed APPROVED
19-21 Penywern Road, Earl's Court, London SW5 9TT
☎ (0171) 373 8900 & 373 4893
Fax (0171) 244 6835
Located near Earl's Court underground station. Few minutes' tube journey to the West End and direct route to Heathrow Airport. All rooms have colour TV and direct-dial telephone.
Bedrooms: 27 single, 15 double, 7 twin, 8 triple
Bathrooms: 20 en-suite, 4 public, 25 private showers

Bed & breakfast

per night:	£min	£max
Single	25.00	31.00
Double	36.00	42.00

Cards accepted: Access, Visa, Diners, Amex, Switch/Delta

See display advertisement on page 15

Rushmore Hotel
Listed
11 Trebovir Road, London SW5 9LS
☎ (0171) 370 3839 & 370 6505
Fax (0171) 370 0274
Minotel/Logis of Great Britain
Each room stylishly and individually themed, making the hotel unique in its category. All rooms have cable TV and direct-dial telephone. Within a minute's walk of both Earl's Court underground station and exhibition centre.
Bedrooms: 4 single, 7 double, 6 twin, 2 triple, 3 family rooms
Bathrooms: 22 en-suite

Bed & breakfast

per night:	£min	£max
Single	55.00	69.00
Double	65.00	79.00

Evening meal 1800 (last orders 1930)
Parking for 6
Cards accepted: Access, Visa, Diners, Amex

For ideas on places to visit refer to the introduction at the beginning of this section.

Swallow International Hotel
COMMENDED
Cromwell Road, London SW5 0TH
☎ (0171) 973 1000
Fax (0171) 244 8194
Swallow
Bright modern hotel offering an exclusive leisure club. Near Earl's Court and Olympia Exhibition Halls, fashionable Knightsbridge and Kensington's parks and museums. Short break packages available.
Bedrooms: 28 single, 132 double, 220 twin, 36 triple
Suites available
Bathrooms: 416 en-suite

Bed & breakfast

per night:	£min	£max
Single	110.00	135.00
Double	120.00	147.50

Lunch available
Evening meal 1800 (last orders 2345)
Parking for 70
Cards accepted: Access, Visa, Diners, Amex

Swiss House Hotel
Listed COMMENDED
171 Old Brompton Road, London SW5 0AN
☎ (0171) 373 2769 & 373 9383
Fax (0171) 373 4983

High quality budget priced hotel, conveniently situated near London museums, shopping/exhibition centres. Gloucester Road underground station is within easy walking distance. Winner of BTA award for best value B&B in London.
Bedrooms: 5 single, 5 double, 2 twin, 4 triple
Bathrooms: 15 en-suite, 1 public, 1 private shower

Bed & breakfast

per night:	£min	£max
Single	39.00	56.00
Double	72.00	72.00

Cards accepted: Access, Visa, Diners, Amex, Switch/Delta

LONDON

Windsor House

Listed

12 Penywern Road, London
SW5 9ST
☎ (0171) 373 9087
Fax (0171) 385 2417

Budget-priced bed and breakfast establishment in Earl's Court. Easily reached from airports and motorway. The West End is minutes away by underground. NCP parking.
Bedrooms: 2 single, 4 double, 4 twin, 1 triple, 7 family rooms
Bathrooms: 10 en-suite, 6 public, 6 private showers

Bed & breakfast per night:	£min	£max
Single	24.00	38.00
Double	32.00	48.00

See display advertisement on page 33

LONDON SW7

Abcone Hotel

APPROVED

10 Ashburn Gardens, London
SW7 4DG
☎ (0171) 370 3383
Fax (0171) 373 3082

Close to Gloucester Road underground and convenient for High Street Kensington, Knightsbridge, Olympia, Earl's Court, museums and Hyde Park.
Bedrooms: 17 single, 15 double, 3 twin
Bathrooms: 28 en-suite, 4 public

Bed & breakfast per night:	£min	£max
Single	40.00	74.00
Double	50.00	89.00

Evening meal 1900 (last orders 2130)
Cards accepted: Access, Visa, Diners, Amex, Switch/Delta

Five Sumner Place Hotel

Listed HIGHLY COMMENDED

5 Sumner Place, South Kensington, London SW7 3EE
☎ (0171) 584 7586
Fax (0171) 823 9962
Recent winner of the Best Small Hotel in London Award. Situated in South Kensington, the most fashionable area.

This family owned and run hotel offers first-class service and personal attention.
Bedrooms: 3 single, 10 double
Bathrooms: 13 en-suite, 1 public

Bed & breakfast per night:	£min	£max
Single	72.00	82.00
Double	96.00	116.00

Cards accepted: Access, Visa, Amex

Montana Hotel

APPROVED

67 Gloucester Road, London
SW7 4PG
☎ (0171) 584 7654
Fax (0171) 581 3109

Centrally located hotel. Convenient for Knightsbridge, Kensington, Earl's Court and Olympia exhibitions. Gloucester Road underground opposite gives direct link to Heathrow Airport and West End.
Bedrooms: 14 single, 5 double, 21 twin, 15 triple
Bathrooms: 51 en-suite, 6 public, 4 private showers

Bed & breakfast per night:	£min	£max
Single	25.00	45.00
Double	35.00	60.00

Lunch available
Evening meal 1800 (last orders 2330)
Cards accepted: Access, Visa, Diners, Amex

Hotel Number Sixteen

HIGHLY COMMENDED

16 Sumner Place, London SW7 3EG
☎ (0171) 589 5232
Fax (0171) 584 8615
With atmosphere of a comfortable town house in very attractive street. Secluded award-winning gardens. Winner of the Spencer Trophy.
Bedrooms: 9 single, 24 double, 3 triple
Bathrooms: 32 en-suite, 2 private, 1 private shower

Bed & breakfast per night:	£min	£max
Single	80.00	105.00
Double	140.00	170.00

Cards accepted: Access, Visa, Diners, Amex

LONDON SW14

The Plough Inn

APPROVED

42 Christchurch Road, East Sheen, London SW14 7AF
☎ (0181) 876 7833 & 876 4533
Fax (0181) 392 8801
Delightful old pub, part 16th C, next to Richmond Park. En-suite accommodation, traditional ales, home-cooked food.
Bedrooms: 3 double, 3 twin, 1 triple
Bathrooms: 6 en-suite, 1 private

Bed & breakfast per night:	£min	£max
Single	50.00	55.00
Double	65.00	70.00

Half board per person:	£min	£max
Daily	55.00	65.00

Lunch available
Evening meal 1930 (last orders 2130)
Parking for 4
Cards accepted: Access, Visa, Amex

LONDON SW18

The Brewers Inn

COMMENDED

147 East Hill, Wandsworth, London SW18 2QB
☎ (0181) 874 4128
Fax (0181) 877 1953
En-suite bedrooms, large bar, restaurant and car park.
Bedrooms: 4 single, 9 double, 3 twin
Bathrooms: 16 en-suite

Bed & breakfast per night:	£min	£max
Single	50.00	70.00
Double	60.00	80.00

Half board per person:	£min	£max
Daily	75.00	95.00
Weekly	560.00	700.00

Lunch available
Evening meal 1800 (last orders 2200)
Parking for 10
Cards accepted: Access, Visa, Diners, Amex, Switch/Delta

Please mention this guide when making your booking.

LONDON

LONDON SW19

Compton Guest House
Listed

65 Compton Road, Wimbledon, London SW19 7QA
☎ (0181) 947 4488 & 879 3245
Fax (0181) 947 4488

Family-run guesthouse in pleasant, peaceful area, 5 minutes from Wimbledon station (British Rail and District Line). Easy access to the West End, central London, M1, M2, M3, M4 and M25. Quality rooms, with excellent service. About 12 minutes' walk to Wimbledon tennis courts.

Bedrooms: 2 single, 1 double, 2 twin, 1 triple, 2 family rooms
Bathrooms: 2 public

Bed & breakfast per night:

	£min	£max
Single	33.00	38.00
Double	45.00	64.00

Parking for 2

Kings Lodge Hotel
COMMENDED

5 Kings Road, Wimbledon, London SW19 8PL
☎ (0181) 545 0191
Fax (0181) 545 0381

For an overnight stop or a longer stay, your comfort is assured in our family-run town centre hotel. Join our list of guests who return time and time again. We have a sister hotel in Shanklin, Isle of Wight.

Bedrooms: 1 single, 2 double, 1 twin, 3 triple
Bathrooms: 7 en-suite

Bed & breakfast per night:

	£min	£max
Single	45.00	69.00
Double	59.00	85.00

Lunch available
Evening meal 1800 (last orders 2000)
Parking for 6
Cards accepted: Access, Visa, Diners, Amex, Switch/Delta

LONDON W1

Bentinck House Hotel
Listed

20 Bentinck Street, London W1M 5RL
☎ (0171) 935 9141
Fax (0171) 224 5903

Family-run bed and breakfast hotel in the heart of London's fashionable West End, close to Bond Street underground and Oxford Street.

Bedrooms: 8 single, 1 double, 3 twin, 5 triple
Bathrooms: 12 en-suite, 4 public

Bed & breakfast per night:

	£min	£max
Single	45.00	55.00
Double	69.00	79.00

Half board per person:

	£min	£max
Daily	45.00	65.00
Weekly	300.00	450.00

Evening meal 1800 (last orders 2200)
Cards accepted: Access, Visa, Diners, Amex, Switch/Delta

The Dorchester
DE LUXE

Park Lane, London W1A 2HJ
☎ (0171) 629 8888
Fax (0171) 409 0114
Utell International

De luxe hotel in traditional English country house style. All modern facilities, including a spa and 3 restaurants. Prices shown are room only, plus VAT and are valid until 31 March 1997.

Bedrooms: 32 single, 120 double, 92 twin
Suites available
Bathrooms: 244 en-suite

Bed & breakfast per night:

	£min	£max
Single	225.00	250.00
Double	250.00	280.00

Half board per person:

	£min	£max
Daily	332.50	357.50

Lunch available
Evening meal 1800 (last orders 2330)
Parking for 24
Cards accepted: Access, Visa, Diners, Amex

The Edward Lear Hotel

30 Seymour Street, Marble Arch, London W1H 5WD
☎ (0171) 402 5401
Fax (0171) 706 3766

Family-run Georgian town residence, once the home of Edward Lear, famous poet and painter, with informal but efficient atmosphere. In a central location, 1 minute from Oxford Street and Marble Arch.

Bedrooms: 13 single, 4 double, 10 twin, 2 triple, 2 family rooms
Bathrooms: 3 en-suite, 1 private, 6 public, 9 private showers

Bed & breakfast per night:

	£min	£max
Single	39.50	49.50
Double	55.00	79.50

Cards accepted: Access, Visa, Diners, Switch/Delta

Kenwood House Hotel

114 Gloucester Place, London W1H 3DB
☎ (0171) 935 3473 & 935 9455
Fax (0171) 224 0582

Friendly, family-run hotel in a central location, with budget prices.

Bedrooms: 4 single, 6 double, 4 twin, 2 family rooms
Bathrooms: 9 en-suite, 4 public

Bed & breakfast per night:

	£min	£max
Single	27.00	48.00
Double	44.00	58.00

Cards accepted: Access, Visa, Amex, Switch/Delta

The Leonard
HIGHLY COMMENDED

15 Seymour Street, London W1H 5AA
☎ (0171) 935 2010
Fax (0171) 935 6700
Grand Heritage

Four 18th C town houses, elegantly restored. Accommodation is mainly suites, all with air conditioning and hifi systems. 24-hour room service and friendly staff.

Bedrooms: 22 double, 1 triple, 3 family rooms
Suites available
Bathrooms: 26 en-suite

Bed & breakfast per night:

	£min	£max
Single	195.00	400.00
Double	195.00	400.00

Lunch available
Cards accepted: Access, Visa, Diners, Amex, Switch/Delta

LONDON

Lincoln House Hotel
COMMENDED

33 Gloucester Place, London
W1H 3PD
☎ (0171) 486 7630
Fax (0171) 486 0166
Georgian hotel of distinctive character. En-suite rooms with all modern comforts. Superb location, competitively priced, in the heart of London's West End.
Bedrooms: 6 single, 8 double, 4 twin, 3 triple, 1 family room
Bathrooms: 20 en-suite, 2 private, 1 public

Bed & breakfast per night:	£min	£max
Single	39.00	59.00
Double	59.00	79.00

Cards accepted: Access, Visa, Diners, Amex, Switch/Delta

London Continental Hotel
Listed COMMENDED

88 Gloucester Place, Marble Arch, London W1H 3HN
☎ (0171) 486 8670 & 0860 642345
Fax (0171) 486 8671
Centrally located hotel, off Oxford Street, ideal for businessmen and tourists. En-suite rooms with hairdryer, direct-dial telephone, satellite TV, fridge/freezer, tea/coffee making. Nearest underground station Baker Street.
Bedrooms: 8 single, 8 double, 5 twin, 1 triple, 3 family rooms
Bathrooms: 23 en-suite, 1 public, 2 private showers

Bed & breakfast per night:	£min	£max
Single	57.00	59.00
Double	67.00	69.00

Cards accepted: Access, Visa, Diners, Amex, Switch/Delta

Mandeville Hotel
COMMENDED

Mandeville Place, London W1M 6BE
☎ (0171) 935 5599
Fax (0171) 935 9588
Utell International
In the heart of London's West End, within 3 minutes' walking distance of Oxford Street, Bond Street and Regent Street. Convenient for theatreland. Recently refurbished bedrooms.
Bedrooms: 74 single, 91 twin
Bathrooms: 165 en-suite

Bed & breakfast per night:	£min	£max
Single	60.00	100.00
Double	80.00	130.00

Half board per person:	£min	£max
Daily	83.30	115.00

Lunch available
Evening meal 1700 (last orders 2230)
Cards accepted: Access, Visa, Diners, Amex, Switch/Delta

Marble Arch Inn
Listed APPROVED

49-50 Upper Berkeley Street, Marble Arch, London W1H 7PN
☎ (0171) 723 7888
Fax (0171) 723 6060
Friendly hotel at Marble Arch, within minutes of Hyde Park and Oxford Street and within easy reach of other major attractions.
Bedrooms: 2 single, 8 double, 9 twin, 6 triple, 4 family rooms
Bathrooms: 25 en-suite, 2 public, 4 private showers

Bed & breakfast per night:	£min	£max
Single	38.00	45.00
Double	50.00	60.00

Cards accepted: Access, Visa, Diners, Amex, Switch/Delta

Hotel La Place
COMMENDED

17 Nottingham Place, London W1M 3FF
☎ (0171) 486 2323
Fax (0171) 486 4335
Small, friendly, centrally located hotel with bar and restaurant, offering good value for money.
Bedrooms: 7 single, 6 double, 3 twin, 2 triple, 3 family rooms
Bathrooms: 21 en-suite

Bed & breakfast per night:	£min	£max
Single	75.00	130.00
Double	87.00	140.00

Lunch available
Evening meal 1800 (last orders 2030)
Cards accepted: Access, Visa, Diners, Amex, Switch/Delta

Prince Regent Hotel

37 Nottingham Place, London W1M 3FE
☎ (0171) 935 4276 & 487 5153
Fax (0171) 224 1582
In the heart of the West End yet in a dignified, quiet position. Ideal for people coming to Harley Street hospitals and clinics. Near Regent's Park and Baker Street underground stations.
Bedrooms: 7 single, 4 double, 5 twin, 4 triple
Bathrooms: 20 en-suite

Bed & breakfast per night:	£min	£max
Single	45.00	50.00
Double	55.00	70.00

Cards accepted: Access, Visa, Diners, Amex

Wyndham Hotel
Listed

30 Wyndham Street, London W1H 1DD
☎ (0171) 723 7204 & 723 9400
Fax (0171) 723 7204
Small family-run B&B in a Georgian terrace, around the corner from Baker Street and a short walk from Oxford Street.
Bedrooms: 5 single, 4 double, 2 twin
Bathrooms: 1 public, 9 private showers

Bed & breakfast per night:	£min	£max
Single	32.00	34.00
Double	42.00	44.00

LONDON W2

Abbey Court Hotel
Listed

174 Sussex Gardens, London W2 1TP
☎ (0171) 402 0704
Fax (0171) 262 2055
Central London hotel, reasonable prices. Within walking distance of Lancaster Gate, Paddington station and Hyde Park. Easy access to tourist attractions and shopping. Car parking at modest charge.
Bedrooms: 14 single, 24 double, 7 twin, 10 triple, 2 family rooms
Bathrooms: 57 en-suite

Bed & breakfast per night:	£min	£max
Single	30.00	39.00
Double	38.00	58.00

Parking for 20
Cards accepted: Access, Visa, Amex

See display advertisement on page 38

Establishments should be open throughout the year, unless otherwise stated.

ACCOMMODATION

Central London — *Budget Prices*

WESTPOINT HOTEL
170 Sussex Gardens, Hyde Park, London W2 1PT.
Tel: (0171) 402 0281 (Reservations) Fax: (0171) 224 9114.

Most rooms with private shower & toilet, radio/intercom & colour TV. Children welcome. TV lounge.

This hotel has long been a popular choice amongst tourists because of its central location, being near to Hyde Park and only 2 minutes from Paddington and Lancaster Gate tube stations. The West End's tourist attractions, including theatres, museums and Oxford Street stores, are within easy reach. Individuals, families and groups are all welcome.

• PRIVATE CAR PARK • DIRECT A2 BUS FROM HEATHROW •

RATES:

Low Season
Singles from £24 per person.
Doubles from £15 per person.
Family rooms from £13 per person.

High Season
Singles from £28 per person.
Doubles from £20 per person.
Family rooms from £18 per person.

ABBEY COURT HOTEL
174 Sussex Gardens, Hyde Park, London W2 1TP.
Tel: (0171) 402 0704 Fax: (0171) 262 2055.

Open all year. Radio Intercom in every room. Children welcome.
Most rooms with private shower, toilet and colour TV.

• CAR PARKING AVAILABLE • A2 BUS FROM HEATHROW •

Central London hotel in a pleasant avenue near Hyde Park and within 2 minutes' walking distance of Paddington main line and tube station and Lancaster Gate tube station. The tourist attractions of the West End including theatres, museums and Oxford Street are within easy reach. Individuals, families, school parties and groups are all welcome and group tours can be arranged.

TERMS per person:
Low Season: Single from £26, double from £16 p.p., family rooms from £14 p.p.
High Season: Single from £28, double from £23 p.p., family rooms from £18 p.p.

SASS HOUSE HOTEL
11 Craven Terrace, Hyde Park, London W2 3QD.
Tel: (0171) 262 2325 Fax: (0171) 262 0889

★ Centrally located – within easy reach of London's most famous tourist attractions.
★ Nearest underground Paddington and Lancaster Gate. ★ Served by a network of bus routes.
★ Colour television lounge. ★ Centrally heated. ★ Radio and intercom in all rooms.
★ Most rooms with showers/toilets. ★ Parking facilities available.
★ A2 bus from Heathrow.

TERMS per person:
Low season: Singles from £22, doubles from £16 p.p., family rooms from £15 p.p.
High season: Singles from £34, doubles from £19 p.p., family rooms from £18 p.p.

LONDON

Albro House Hotel
APPROVED
155 Sussex Gardens, London W2 2RY
☎ (0171) 724 2931 & 706 8153
Fax (0171) 262 2278
Ideally located in pleasant area near public transport. Nice rooms, all en-suite. English breakfast. Languages spoken. Friendly and safe. Some parking available.
Bedrooms: 2 single, 6 double, 5 twin, 4 triple, 1 family room
Suites available
Bathrooms: 17 en-suite, 1 public, 1 private shower
Bed & breakfast

per night:	£min	£max
Single	34.00	48.00
Double	44.00	78.00

Parking for 1
Cards accepted: Access, Visa, Diners, Amex

Allandale Hotel
Listed APPROVED
3 Devonshire Terrace, Lancaster Gate, London W2 3DN
☎ (0171) 723 8311 & 723 7807
Fax (0181) 905 4891

Small, select family hotel will impress you with its careful service. Full English breakfast. All bedrooms have private shower and toilet, colour TV and central heating. Close to Hyde Park, West End, Lancaster Gate/Paddington stations.
Bedrooms: 2 single, 8 double, 5 twin, 2 triple, 3 family rooms
Bathrooms: 18 en-suite, 1 public
Bed & breakfast

per night:	£min	£max
Single	37.00	39.95
Double	44.00	49.95

Cards accepted: Access, Visa, Diners, Amex, Switch/Delta

Ashley Hotel
Listed APPROVED
15 Norfolk Square, London W2 1RU
☎ (0171) 723 3375
Fax (0171) 723 0173
Very popular town house hotel in quiet garden square. Quality rooms with private showers and toilets, TV,

tea-making facilities. Owned and managed by the same Welsh family for 27 years.
Bedrooms: 17 single, 16 double, 6 twin, 8 triple, 5 family rooms
Bathrooms: 36 en-suite, 8 public
Bed & breakfast

per night:	£min	£max
Single	30.00	41.00
Double	60.00	63.00

Cards accepted: Access, Visa, Switch/Delta

Beverley House Hotel
142 Sussex Gardens, London W2 1UB
☎ (0171) 723 3380
Fax (0171) 262 0324
Refurbished bed and breakfast hotel, serving traditional English breakfast and offering high standards at low prices. Close to Paddington station, Hyde Park and museums.
Bedrooms: 6 single, 5 double, 6 twin, 6 triple
Bathrooms: 23 en-suite
Bed & breakfast

per night:	£min	£max
Single	39.00	48.00
Double	44.00	66.00

Evening meal 1800 (last orders 2200)
Parking for 2
Cards accepted: Access, Visa, Diners, Amex

Garden Court Hotel
30-31 Kensington Gardens Square, London W2 4BG
☎ (0171) 229 2553
Fax (0171) 727 2749
Friendly, family-run town house hotel established in 1954, in a quiet Victorian garden square in central London. Convenient for all transport. All rooms have TV, telephone and hairdryers.
Bedrooms: 13 single, 7 double, 6 twin, 6 triple, 2 family rooms
Bathrooms: 16 en-suite, 5 public, 1 private shower
Bed & breakfast

per night:	£min	£max
Single	32.00	45.00
Double	48.00	65.00

Cards accepted: Access, Visa

Henry VIII Hotel
APPROVED
19 Leinster Gardens, London W2 3AN
☎ (0171) 262 0117
Fax (0171) 706 0472
Convenient for Queensway and Bayswater underground stations, with Hyde Park nearby. Banqueting accommodation for up to 100 persons.
Bedrooms: 30 single, 13 double, 57 twin, 7 triple
Bathrooms: 107 en-suite
Bed & breakfast

per night:	£min	£max
Single		95.00
Double		115.00

Evening meal 1800 (last orders 2200)
Cards accepted: Access, Visa, Diners, Amex, Switch/Delta

Hyde Park Rooms Hotel
Listed
137 Sussex Gardens, Hyde Park, London W2 2RX
☎ (0171) 723 0225 & 723 0965
Small centrally located private hotel with personal service. Clean, comfortable and friendly. Within walking distance of Hyde Park and Kensington Gardens. Car parking available.
Bedrooms: 5 single, 6 double, 2 twin, 1 triple
Bathrooms: 7 en-suite, 2 private, 2 public
Bed & breakfast

per night:	£min	£max
Single	24.00	38.00
Double	36.00	48.00

Parking for 3
Cards accepted: Access, Visa, Diners, Amex, Switch/Delta

Kings Arms
APPROVED
254 Edgware Road, Paddington, London W2 1DS
☎ (0171) 262 8441
Fax (0171) 258 0556
Conveniently located for public transport and West End shopping. Recently decorated and furnished to a comfortable standard.
Bedrooms: 2 single, 3 double, 5 twin, 1 triple, 1 family room
Bathrooms: 7 en-suite, 1 private, 2 public, 1 private shower

Continued ▶

LONDON

LONDON W2
Continued

(previous hotel)

Bed & breakfast per night:
	£min	£max
Single	28.50	38.50
Double	47.00	57.00

Half board per person:
	£min	£max
Daily	33.00	43.00
Weekly	198.00	258.00

Lunch available
Evening meal 1700 (last orders 2200)
Cards accepted: Access, Visa, Amex, Switch/Delta

Nayland Hotel
COMMENDED

132-134 Sussex Gardens, London W2 1UB
☎ (0171) 723 4615
Fax (0171) 402 3292
Centrally located, close to many amenities and within walking distance of Hyde Park and Oxford Street. Quality you can afford.
Bedrooms: 11 single, 8 double, 17 twin, 5 triple
Bathrooms: 41 en-suite

Bed & breakfast per night:
	£min	£max
Single	40.00	55.00
Double	48.00	74.00

Evening meal 1800 (last orders 2100)
Parking for 5
Cards accepted: Access, Visa, Diners, Amex

Parkwood Hotel
APPROVED

4 Stanhope Place, London W2 2HB
☎ (0171) 402 2241
Fax (0171) 402 1574

Smart town house only 1 minute's walk away from Oxford Street and Speakers' Corner, Hyde Park.
Bedrooms: 5 single, 2 double, 7 twin, 4 triple
Bathrooms: 12 en-suite, 2 public

Bed & breakfast per night:
	£min	£max
Single	44.50	64.50
Double	59.50	79.50

Evening meal 1830 (last orders 2130)
Cards accepted: Access, Visa

The Pavilion Hotel
Listed COMMENDED

37 Leinster Gardens, London W2 3AR
☎ (0171) 258 0269
Fax (0171) 723 7295
Friendly hotel within easy walking distance of Hyde Park and the West End. Six conference rooms.
Bedrooms: 36 single, 18 double, 34 twin, 8 triple
Bathrooms: 96 en-suite

Bed & breakfast per night:
	£min	£max
Single	95.00	105.00
Double	115.00	130.00

Evening meal 1800 (last orders 2130)
Cards accepted: Access, Visa, Diners, Amex, Switch/Delta

Rose Court Hotel

1-3 Talbot Square, London W2 1TR
☎ (0171) 723 5128 & 723 8671
Fax (0171) 723 1855
Privately-run Victorian town house in a quiet garden square. Close to Paddington and the West End.
Bedrooms: 6 single, 11 double, 13 twin, 5 triple, 3 family rooms
Bathrooms: 38 en-suite, 1 public

Bed & breakfast per night:
	£min	£max
Single	38.00	54.00
Double	46.00	68.00

Half board per person:
	£min	£max
Daily	48.00	62.00
Weekly	310.00	370.00

Lunch available
Evening meal 1800 (last orders 2100)
Cards accepted: Access, Visa, Diners, Amex, Switch/Delta

Royal Park Hotel
APPROVED

2-5 Westbourne Terrace, London W2 3UL
☎ (0171) 402 6187
Fax (0171) 224 9426
Modernised hotel built in 1854.

Comfortable and well-placed for bus and underground to the West End. Free car parking available.
Bedrooms: 8 single, 10 double, 35 twin, 8 triple, 2 family rooms
Bathrooms: 63 en-suite

Bed & breakfast per night:
	£min	£max
Single	59.00	61.00
Double	76.00	80.00

Evening meal 1800 (last orders 2200)
Parking for 15
Cards accepted: Access, Visa, Amex, Switch/Delta

Ruddimans Hotel
Listed APPROVED

160-162 Sussex Gardens, London W2 1UD
☎ (0171) 723 1026 & 723 6715
Fax (0171) 262 2983
Comfortable hotel close to West End and London's attractions, offering generous English breakfast and good service at reasonable prices. Car park.
Bedrooms: 9 single, 12 double, 13 twin, 6 triple, 1 family room
Bathrooms: 33 en-suite, 3 public

Bed & breakfast per night:
	£min	£max
Single	25.00	35.00
Double	38.00	48.00

Parking for 6
Cards accepted: Access, Visa

St. David's and Norfolk Court Hotel
Listed APPROVED

16 Norfolk Square, Hyde Park, London W2 1RS
☎ (0171) 723 3856 & 723 4963
Fax (0171) 402 9061
Small, friendly hotel in front of a quiet garden square. Central location, economical prices. Reckons to serve the "best English breakfast" in London.
Bedrooms: 14 single, 8 double, 14 twin, 12 triple
Bathrooms: 2 private, 16 public, 4 private showers

Bed & breakfast per night:
	£min	£max
Single	28.00	38.00
Double	44.00	54.00

Cards accepted: Access, Visa, Diners, Amex

LONDON

Westland Hotel

154 Bayswater Road, London
W2 4HP
☎ (0171) 229 9191
Fax (0171) 727 1054
CR The Independents
Small, friendly hotel. Well located for West End shopping, touring or relaxing in a beautiful park. Your home-from-home.
Wheelchair access category 3
Bedrooms: 2 single, 5 double, 19 twin, 3 triple, 1 family room
Bathrooms: 30 en-suite

Bed & breakfast per night:	£min	£max
Single	75.00	80.00
Double	95.00	100.00
Half board per person:	£min	£max
Daily	85.00	90.00
Weekly	535.00	600.00

Lunch available
Evening meal 1830 (last orders 2230)
Parking for 9
Cards accepted: Access, Visa, Diners, Amex, Switch/Delta

Westpoint Hotel

Listed
170-172 Sussex Gardens, London
W2 1TP
☎ (0171) 402 0281
Fax (0171) 224 9114
Inexpensive accommodation in central London. Close to Paddington and Lancaster Gate underground stations. Easy access to tourist attractions, shopping and Hyde Park.
Bedrooms: 12 single, 15 double, 16 twin, 14 triple, 6 family rooms
Bathrooms: 31 en-suite, 10 public, 9 private showers

Bed & breakfast per night:	£min	£max
Single	24.00	38.00
Double	29.00	48.00

Parking for 15
Cards accepted: Access, Visa, Diners, Amex

Ad See display advertisement on page 38

LONDON W3

Acton Park Hotel

116 The Vale, Acton, London
W3 7JT
☎ (0181) 743 9417
Fax (0181) 743 9417
Small, friendly, family-run hotel, just off
the North Circular Road. Between Heathrow and the West End, overlooking parkland. Ample parking.
Bedrooms: 7 single, 4 double, 8 twin, 2 triple
Bathrooms: 21 en-suite

Bed & breakfast per night:	£min	£max
Single	40.00	40.00
Double	52.00	52.00

Lunch available
Evening meal 1800 (last orders 2200)
Parking for 15
Cards accepted: Access, Visa, Diners, Amex, Switch/Delta

LONDON W5

Abbey Lodge Hotel

51 Grange Park, Ealing, London
W5 3PR
☎ (0181) 567 7914
Fax (0181) 579 5350
Recently refurbished. All rooms en-suite and with remote-control colour TV. Complimentary hot drinks 24 hours a day. Very close to 3 underground lines.
Bedrooms: 11 single, 1 double, 1 twin, 3 triple
Bathrooms: 16 en-suite

Bed & breakfast per night:	£min	£max
Single	35.00	39.00
Double	46.00	52.00

Cards accepted: Access, Visa, Diners, Switch/Delta

Carnarvon Hotel

COMMENDED
Ealing Common, London W5 3HN
☎ (0181) 992 5399
Fax (0181) 992 7082
CR Consort

Modern purpose-built 5-storey building close to Ealing town centre and within easy reach of central London.
Bedrooms: 45 double, 100 twin
Bathrooms: 145 en-suite

Bed & breakfast per night:	£min	£max
Single	92.00	102.00
Double	110.00	120.00
Half board per person:	£min	£max
Daily	108.00	118.00

Lunch available
Evening meal 1830 (last orders 2130)
Parking for 150
Cards accepted: Access, Visa, Diners, Amex

Grange Lodge Hotel

APPROVED
48-50 Grange Road, Ealing, London
W5 5BX
☎ (0181) 567 1049
Fax (0181) 579 5350
Quiet, comfortable hotel within a few hundred yards of the underground station. Midway between central London and Heathrow.
Bedrooms: 7 single, 2 double, 2 twin, 2 triple
Bathrooms: 9 en-suite, 2 public

Bed & breakfast per night:	£min	£max
Single	27.00	39.00
Double	38.00	51.00

Parking for 10
Cards accepted: Access, Visa, Diners, Switch/Delta

LONDON W6

Dalmacia Hotel

Listed APPROVED
71 Shepherds Bush Road, Hammersmith, London W6 7LS
☎ (0171) 603 2887 & 602 5701
Fax (0171) 602 9226

Family-run bed and breakfast within easy reach of the West End. All rooms en-suite with 16 satellite TV channels, hairdryer, tea and coffee facilities and direct-dial telephone.
Bedrooms: 3 single, 6 double, 4 twin, 3 triple
Bathrooms: 16 en-suite

Bed & breakfast per night:	£min	£max
Single	28.00	34.00
Double	48.00	58.00
Half board per person:	£min	£max
Daily	36.00	42.00

Continued ▶

41

LONDON

LONDON W6
Continued

Evening meal 1830 (last orders 2100)
Cards accepted: Access, Visa, Diners, Amex, Switch/Delta

LONDON W8

Hotel Atlas

24-30 Lexham Gardens, London W8 5JE
☎ (0171) 835 1155
Fax (0171) 370 4853
The Independents/Utell International

Friendly, long established hotel, situated close to Earl's Court and Olympia exhibition centres and the shopping areas of Knightsbridge and Kensington High Street.
Bedrooms: 12 single, 6 double, 18 twin, 8 triple, 1 family room
Bathrooms: 45 en-suite, 4 public
Bed & breakfast

per night:	£min	£max
Single	58.00	65.00
Double	68.00	75.00

Cards accepted: Access, Visa, Diners, Amex, Switch/Delta

Vicarage Private Hotel

10 Vicarage Gate, Kensington, London W8 4AG
☎ (0171) 229 4030

Delightful, family-run Victorian townhouse hotel, situated in a quiet garden square, offering a generous freshly-cooked English breakfast and a "home-from-home" atmosphere. Ideally located for tourist attractions and transport facilities.
Bedrooms: 7 single, 2 double, 5 twin, 4 triple
Bathrooms: 5 public
Bed & breakfast

per night:	£min	£max
Single	38.00	40.00
Double	58.00	60.00

LONDON WC1

Albany Hotel
Listed APPROVED
34 Tavistock Place, London WC1H 9RE
☎ (0171) 837 9139 & 833 0459
Fax (0171) 833 0459
Small, friendly hotel in central London.

Bedrooms: 3 single, 3 double, 4 twin, 1 triple
Bathrooms: 4 public
Bed & breakfast

per night:	£min	£max
Single	32.00	35.00
Double	42.00	47.00

Lunch available
Evening meal 1830 (last orders 2130)
Cards accepted: Access, Visa, Diners, Amex

Blooms Hotel
HIGHLY COMMENDED
7 Montague Street, London WC1B 5BP
☎ (0171) 323 1717
Fax (0171) 636 6498
Utell International

Town-house style hotel located in Bloomsbury.
Bedrooms: 5 single, 15 double, 7 twin
Bathrooms: 27 en-suite
Bed & breakfast

per night:	£min	£max
Single	100.00	130.00
Double	150.00	180.00

Lunch available
Cards accepted: Access, Visa, Diners, Amex, Switch/Delta

The Bonnington in Bloomsbury
COMMENDED
92 Southampton Row, London WC1B 4BH
☎ (0171) 242 2828
Fax (0171) 831 9170
The Independents/Logis of Great Britain

Between the City and West End. Close to mainline stations and on the underground to Heathrow Airport.
Wheelchair access category 2
Bedrooms: 109 single, 44 double, 45 twin, 17 triple
Bathrooms: 215 en-suite
Bed & breakfast

per night:	£min	£max
Single	63.00	90.00
Double	95.00	114.00

Lunch available
Evening meal 1730 (last orders 2230)

Cards accepted: Access, Visa, Diners, Amex, Switch/Delta

Crescent Hotel
Listed
49-50 Cartwright Gardens, London WC1H 9EL
☎ (0171) 387 1515
Fax (0171) 383 2054

Recently refurbished, comfortable, family-run hotel in a quiet Georgian crescent, with private gardens and tennis courts. All rooms have colour TV and tea/coffee tray, most are en-suite.
Bedrooms: 9 single, 2 double, 2 twin, 9 triple, 2 family rooms
Bathrooms: 15 en-suite, 4 public, 3 private showers
Bed & breakfast

per night:	£min	£max
Single	38.00	54.00
Double	65.00	70.00

Cards accepted: Access, Visa

Garth Hotel
Listed
69 Gower Street, London WC1E 6HJ
☎ (0171) 636 5761
Fax (0171) 637 4854
Centrally situated family-run bed and breakfast accommodation, convenient for shops, theatres and travel. TV in rooms. Tea/coffee-making facilities. Some rooms en-suite.
Bedrooms: 3 single, 4 double, 5 twin, 3 triple, 2 family rooms
Bathrooms: 1 en-suite, 3 public, 10 private showers
Bed & breakfast

per night:	£min	£max
Single	32.00	42.00
Double	45.00	60.00

Cards accepted: Access, Visa, Amex, Switch/Delta

All accommodation in this guide has been graded, or is awaiting a grading, by a trained Tourist Board inspector.

LONDON

George Hotel

58-60 Cartwright Gardens, London
WC1H 9EL
☎ (0171) 387 8777
Fax (0171) 387 8666
Central London hotel in a quiet square. Comfortable, bright rooms with satellite TV, direct-dial telephone, tea/coffee. Gardens and tennis courts available for guest use.
Bedrooms: 16 single, 5 double,
4 twin, 8 triple, 8 family rooms
Bathrooms: 4 en-suite, 14 public,
4 private showers

Bed & breakfast per night:	£min	£max
Single	35.50	39.50
Double	49.50	59.50

Cards accepted: Access, Visa, Amex, Switch/Delta

Gower House Hotel
Listed   APPROVED

57 Gower Street, London
WC1E 6HJ
☎ (0171) 636 4685
Fax (0171) 636 4685
Friendly bed and breakfast hotel, close to Goodge Street underground station and within easy walking distance of British Museum, shops, theatres and restaurants.
Bedrooms: 4 single, 2 double, 6 twin,
3 triple, 1 family room
Bathrooms: 3 private, 3 public

Bed & breakfast per night:	£min	£max
Single	34.00	37.00
Double	43.00	48.00

Cards accepted: Access, Visa

St. Athan's Hotel

20 Tavistock Place, Russell Square,
London WC1H 9RE
☎ (0171) 837 9140 & 837 9627
Fax (0171) 833 8352
Simple, small but clean family-run hotel offering bed and breakfast.
Bedrooms: 16 single, 15 double,
15 twin, 4 triple, 5 family rooms
Bathrooms: 15 en-suite, 12 public

Bed & breakfast per night:	£min	£max
Single	36.00	
Double	46.00	

Lunch available
Cards accepted: Access, Visa, Diners, Amex

Thanet Hotel
Listed   COMMENDED

8 Bedford Place, London WC1B 5JA
☎ (0171) 580 3377 & 636 2869
Fax (0171) 323 6676
Comfortable, family-run hotel, with colour TV, tea and coffee and direct-dial telephones. All en-suite rooms. Next to British Museum, close to London's famous Theatreland. Full English breakfast.
Bedrooms: 4 single, 4 double, 4 twin,
1 triple, 1 family room
Bathrooms: 14 en-suite

Bed & breakfast per night:	£min	£max
Single	54.00	54.00
Double	69.00	69.00

Cards accepted: Access, Visa, Diners, Amex, Switch/Delta

LONDON WC2

Royal Adelphi Hotel

21 Villiers Street, London
WC2N 6ND
☎ (0171) 930 8764
Fax (0171) 930 8735
Centrally located and ideal for theatreland, near Embankment and Charing Cross underground. All rooms with colour TV, hairdryer, tea/coffee facilities. Most rooms have private bathrooms.
Bedrooms: 20 single, 12 double,
13 twin, 2 triple
Bathrooms: 34 en-suite, 4 public

Bed & breakfast per night:	£min	£max
Single	38.00	55.00
Double	55.00	72.00

Lunch available
Evening meal 1800 (last orders 2300)
Cards accepted: Access, Visa, Diners, Amex, Switch/Delta

OUTER LONDON

Colour maps 6 & 7 at the back of the guide show place names and London Postal Area Codes and will help you locate accommodation in your chosen area of London

BARNET

West Lodge Park
HIGHLY COMMENDED

Cockfosters Road, Hadley Wood,
Barnet, Hertfordshire EN4 0PY
☎ (0181) 440 8511
Fax (0181) 449 3698
White-painted William IV country house set in 35 acres of grounds in rolling countryside. Fine restaurant, leisure club nearby.
Bedrooms: 15 single, 22 double,
7 twin
Bathrooms: 44 en-suite

Bed & breakfast per night:	£min	£max
Single	75.00	115.00
Double	110.00	155.00

Lunch available
Evening meal 1915 (last orders 2145)
Parking for 200
Cards accepted: Access, Visa, Amex, Switch/Delta

BEXLEY

Tourist Information Centre
☎ (0181) 303 9052

Buxted Lodge
APPROVED

40 Parkhurst Road, Bexley, Kent
DA5 1AS
☎ Crayford (01322) 554010 & 0831 794031
Victorian lodge retaining many original features, with beautiful grounds. 30 minutes to central London by British Rail.
Bedrooms: 2 single, 3 double, 2 twin,
2 triple
Bathrooms: 3 en-suite, 4 public,
5 private showers

Bed & breakfast per night:	£min	£max
Single	20.00	30.00
Double	40.00	50.00

Half board per person:	£min	£max
Daily	26.00	36.00
Weekly	140.00	200.00

Evening meal 1830 (last orders 2000)
Parking for 14

BEXLEYHEATH

Swallow Hotel
HIGHLY COMMENDED

1 Broadway, Bexleyheath, Kent
DA6 7JZ
☎ (0181) 298 1000
Fax (0181) 298 1234
Swallow
Easy access to London and just minutes from junction 2 of the M25. Spacious, double-size bedrooms with marble-finish bathrooms, leisure club
Continued ▶

LONDON

BEXLEYHEATH
Continued

with extensive facilities including fitness room with the latest computerised equipment. Short break packages available.
Bedrooms: 49 single, 37 double, 38 twin, 10 triple, 8 family rooms
Bathrooms: 142 en-suite

Bed & breakfast per night:

	£min	£max
Single	70.00	100.00
Double	80.00	115.00

Half board per person:

	£min	£max
Daily	89.75	126.00

Lunch available
Evening meal 1830 (last orders 2245)
Parking for 86
Cards accepted: Access, Visa, Diners, Amex, Switch/Delta

BROMLEY

Durley Dene Country House

COMMENDED

82 Shortlands Road, Bromley, Kent BR2 0JP
☎ (0181) 290 0032
Fax (0181) 460 0215
Attractive 19th C country house with oak-beamed hallway, situated in beautiful secluded gardens. Ideal for visiting London (20 minutes) and Kent countryside. All bedrooms have full facilities.
Bedrooms: 3 single, 5 double
Bathrooms: 8 en-suite

Bed & breakfast per night:

	£min	£max
Single	50.00	55.00
Double	78.00	100.00

Evening meal 1600 (last orders 1950)
Parking for 8
Cards accepted: Access, Visa, Amex, Switch/Delta

Glendevon House Hotel

80 Southborough Road, Bickley, Bromley BR1 2EN
☎ (0181) 467 2183
Small hotel with private car park. Convenient for central London. Caters for tourists and businessmen.
Bedrooms: 4 single, 3 double, 1 twin, 1 triple
Bathrooms: 3 en-suite, 1 private, 1 public, 1 private shower

Bed & breakfast per night:

	£min	£max
Single	24.00	32.00
Double	42.00	42.00

Parking for 6
Cards accepted: Access, Visa

CROYDON

Tourist Information Centre
☎ (0181) 253 1009

Alpha Guest House

99 Brigstock Road, Thornton Heath, Surrey CR7 7JL
☎ (0181) 684 4811 & 665 0032
Modern, family-run residence in ideal location near Croydon (20 minutes from Victoria Station). Tea and coffee-making facilities, satellite TV, free parking and varied breakfasts.
Bedrooms: 4 single, 1 double, 5 twin, 1 triple
Bathrooms: 3 en-suite, 3 public

Bed & breakfast per night:

	£min	£max
Single	20.00	22.00
Double	33.00	38.00

Parking for 5

Briarley Hotel

APPROVED

8 Outram Road, Croydon CR0 6XE
☎ (0181) 654 1000
Fax (0181) 656 6084
The Independents
Gracious Victorian exterior but 1990s hotel standards and all rooms en-suite. Restaurant, attractive garden, parking, launderette. Good public transport. Minimum B&B prices shown are for weekend stays.
Bedrooms: 19 single, 9 double, 10 twin
Bathrooms: 38 en-suite

Bed & breakfast per night:

	£min	£max
Single	35.00	55.00
Double	45.00	65.00

Evening meal 1830 (last orders 2200)
Parking for 25
Cards accepted: Access, Visa, Diners, Amex, Switch/Delta

Croydon Hotel

112 Lower Addiscombe Road, Croydon CR0 6AD
☎ (0181) 656 7233
Fax (0181) 655 0211
Close to central Croydon (route A222) and 10 minutes' walk from East Croydon station. Opposite shops and restaurants. Frequent direct trains to Victoria and Gatwick Airport.
Bedrooms: 1 single, 2 double, 3 twin, 2 triple
Bathrooms: 6 en-suite, 1 public

Bed & breakfast per night:

	£min	£max
Single	24.00	34.00
Double	40.00	46.00

Parking for 4
Cards accepted: Access, Visa

Dereen

Listed APPROVED

14 St. Augustines Avenue, South Croydon, Surrey CR2 6BS
☎ (0181) 686 2075
Small, family guesthouse. Tea/coffee-making facilities. Colour TV in all rooms. Breakfast by arrangement. Weekly rates available.
Bedrooms: 1 single, 2 double
Bathrooms: 2 public

Bed & breakfast per night:

	£min	£max
Single	16.00	17.00
Double	32.00	34.00

Kirkdale Hotel

22 St. Peter's Road, Croydon CR0 1HD
☎ (0181) 688 5898
Fax (0181) 680 6001
Large detached corner house close to Croydon's shopping, restaurant and business centre, on bus route and with easy commuting to London. Five minutes from Fairfield Halls.
Bedrooms: 8 single, 9 double, 2 twin
Bathrooms: 19 en-suite

Bed & breakfast per night:

	£min	£max
Single	25.00	40.00
Double	40.00	50.00

Parking for 12
Cards accepted: Access, Visa, Amex

A key to symbols can be found inside the back cover flap.

Please check prices and other details at the time of booking.

LONDON

Markington Hotel

9 Haling Park Road, South Croydon, Surrey CR2 6NG
☎ (0181) 681 6494
Fax (0181) 688 6530

Friendly, comfortable private hotel with fully equipped rooms, all en-suite. Free car parking. Bar, restaurant. Close to public transport.

Bedrooms: 10 single, 6 double, 2 twin, 2 triple
Bathrooms: 20 en-suite, 2 public

Bed & breakfast per night:	£min	£max
Single	35.00	49.50
Double	45.00	55.00

Evening meal 1830 (last orders 2030)
Parking for 17
Cards accepted: Access, Visa, Amex, Switch/Delta

Selsdon Park HIGHLY COMMENDED

Sanderstead, South Croydon, Surrey CR2 8YA
☎ (0181) 657 8811
Fax (0181) 651 6171

Country house hotel, 10 minutes from the M25, 30 minutes from London and Gatwick, set in 200 acres of parkland. Special weekend rates.

Bedrooms: 40 single, 50 double, 80 twin
Suite available
Bathrooms: 170 en-suite

Bed & breakfast per night:	£min	£max
Single	69.00	99.00
Double	138.00	198.00

Half board per person:	£min	£max
Daily	79.00	109.00

Lunch available
Evening meal 1930 (last orders 2200)
Parking for 265
Cards accepted: Access, Visa, Diners, Amex, Switch/Delta

ENFIELD

Royal Chace Hotel

162 The Ridgeway, Enfield, Middlesex EN2 3AR
☎ (0181) 366 6500
Fax (0181) 367 7191
Ⓡ The Independents

Pleasant hotel of character, set in Green Belt, with access to London and M25. Ideal for businessmen and tourists. Special weekend rates available.

Bedrooms: 49 double, 40 twin, 3 family rooms
Bathrooms: 92 en-suite

Bed & breakfast per night:	£min	£max
Single	55.00	76.50
Double	70.00	100.00

Half board per person:	£min	£max
Daily	75.00	95.00
Weekly	525.00	665.00

Lunch available
Evening meal 1900 (last orders 2145)
Parking for 300
Cards accepted: Access, Visa, Diners, Amex, Switch/Delta

HARROW

Tourist Information Centre
☎ (0181) 424 1103 or 424 1100

Crescent Hotel COMMENDED

58-62 Welldon Crescent, Harrow, Middlesex HA1 1QR
☎ (0181) 863 5491 & 863 5163
Fax (0181) 427 5965
Ⓡ The Independents

Modern, friendly hotel with full facilities in the heart of Harrow. Five minutes to underground, easy access to Wembley, West End, Heathrow and major motorways. Email: JIVRAJ@crsnthtl.demon.co.uk

Bedrooms: 10 single, 3 double, 6 twin, 1 triple, 2 family rooms
Bathrooms: 14 en-suite, 3 public

Bed & breakfast per night:	£min	£max
Single	35.00	45.00
Double	50.00	60.00

Half board per person:	£min	£max
Daily	50.00	60.00
Weekly	350.00	420.00

Lunch available
Evening meal 1900 (last orders 2030)
Parking for 7
Cards accepted: Access, Visa, Diners, Amex, Switch/Delta

Cumberland Hotel COMMENDED

St. John's Road, Harrow, Middlesex HA1 2EF
☎ (0181) 863 4111
Fax (0181) 861 5668
Ⓡ Best Western

Close to Wembley, 25 minutes to West End and Heathrow. Bar, restaurant and meeting/conference suites. All rooms with full modern facilities.

Bedrooms: 33 single, 31 double, 14 twin, 3 triple, 3 family rooms
Bathrooms: 84 en-suite

Bed & breakfast per night:	£min	£max
Single	45.00	48.00
Double	60.00	65.00

Lunch available
Evening meal 1900 (last orders 2130)
Parking for 65
Cards accepted: Access, Visa, Diners, Amex, Switch/Delta

Harrow Hotel COMMENDED

12-22 Pinner Road, Harrow, Middlesex HA1 4HZ
☎ (0181) 427 3435
Fax (0181) 861 1370
Ⓡ The Independents/Logis of Great Britain

Friendly, family-run hotel near Wembley and convenient for central London. Restaurant and bar meals, free parking. Easy access to motorways and airports. Family rooms available. Each 7th night free.

Bedrooms: 30 single, 21 double, 19 twin, 4 triple, 2 family rooms

Continued ▶

LONDON

HARROW
Continued

Suites available
Bathrooms: 76 en-suite
Bed & breakfast
per night:	£min	£max
Single	65.00	79.00
Double	79.00	90.00

Half board per
person:	£min	£max
Daily	80.00	94.00

Lunch available
Evening meal 1800 (last orders 2130)
Parking for 58
Cards accepted: Access, Visa, Diners, Amex, Switch/Delta

Hindes Hotel

8 Hindes Road, Harrow, Middlesex HA1 1SJ
☎ (0181) 427 7468
Fax (0181) 424 0673
Homely owner-run bed and breakfast hotel near the M1. West End 15 minutes by underground. Convenient for Wembley Stadium complex.
Bedrooms: 4 single, 4 double, 6 twin
Bathrooms: 7 en-suite, 2 public
Bed & breakfast
per night:	£min	£max
Single	29.00	39.00
Double	39.00	49.00

Parking for 20
Cards accepted: Access, Visa, Amex

Lindal Hotel
COMMENDED

2 Hindes Road, Harrow, Middlesex HA1 1SJ
☎ (0181) 863 3164
Fax (0181) 427 5435
In busy town centre. Easy reach motorways, central London, Wembley complex and Heathrow. 8 minutes' walk to tube stations.
Bedrooms: 8 single, 4 double, 6 twin, 1 triple, 1 family room
Bathrooms: 17 en-suite, 1 public
Bed & breakfast
per night:	£min	£max
Single	37.00	40.00
Double	46.50	50.00

Half board per
person:	£min	£max
Daily		47.00

Lunch available
Evening meal 1900 (last orders 2045)

Parking for 17
Cards accepted: Access, Visa

HAYES

Arlington (Heathrow) Hotel

Shepiston Lane, Hayes, Middlesex UB3 1LP
☎ (0181) 573 6162
Fax (0181) 848 1057
Utell International
Modern hotel on the quieter side of Heathrow, with friendly and helpful staff. Courtesy bus service to and from all terminals at Heathrow at regular intervals throughout the day.
Bedrooms: 17 single, 12 double, 47 twin, 3 triple, 1 family room
Bathrooms: 80 en-suite
Bed & breakfast
per night:	£min	£max
Single	45.00	59.50
Double	55.00	69.50

Half board per
person:	£min	£max
Daily	66.50	81.45

Lunch available
Evening meal 1830 (last orders 2200)
Parking for 80
Cards accepted: Access, Visa, Amex, Switch/Delta

Shepiston Lodge
Listed APPROVED

31 Shepiston Lane, Hayes, Middlesex UB3 1LJ
☎ (0181) 573 0266 & 569 2536
Fax (0181) 569 2536
Homely guesthouse, 10 minutes from Heathrow Airport. Close M4, M25 and convenient for London. Rooms with colour TV, tea/coffee facilities. Parking facility for holiday periods. Bar and evening meals.
Bedrooms: 3 single, 1 double, 6 twin, 3 triple
Bathrooms: 3 public, 7 private showers
Bed & breakfast
per night:	£min	£max
Single	28.50	33.00
Double	41.50	45.00

Evening meal 1800 (last orders 2100)
Parking for 13
Cards accepted: Access, Visa, Diners, Amex, Switch/Delta

HEATHROW AIRPORT
See under Hayes, Hounslow

HOUNSLOW
Tourist Information Centre
☎ (0181) 572 8279

Ashdowne Guest House

9 Pownall Gardens, Hounslow, Middlesex TW3 1YW
☎ (0181) 572 0008
Fax (0181) 570 1939
Very comfortable Victorian house with elegant rooms, all en-suite and non smoking. Conveniently situated for travel to Heathrow and central London.
Bedrooms: 2 single, 2 double, 2 twin
Bathrooms: 6 en-suite
Bed & breakfast
per night:	£min	£max
Single		41.00
Double		57.00

Parking for 4
Cards accepted: Access, Visa

Shalimar Hotel

215-221 Staines Road, Hounslow, Middlesex TW3 3JJ
☎ (0181) 572 2816 & 577 7070
Fax (0181) 569 6789
Family-run hotel, close to Heathrow, M4, M25, underground and shopping centre. Residents' bar, dining room and lounge.
Bedrooms: 12 single, 5 double, 10 twin, 4 triple
Bathrooms: 20 en-suite, 11 private showers
Bed & breakfast
per night:	£min	£max
Single	35.00	39.00
Double	45.00	49.00

Evening meal 1800 (last orders 2000)
Parking for 7
Cards accepted: Access, Visa, Diners, Amex

ILFORD

Balfour Hotel

31 Balfour Road, Ilford, Essex IG1 4HP
☎ (0181) 514 3238
Small friendly hotel close to Ilford station, M11 and M25. All rooms with colour TV, clock radio/alarm and tea facilities.

LONDON

Bedrooms: 2 single, 2 double, 1 twin
Bathrooms: 3 en-suite, 1 public

Bed & breakfast per night:	£min	£max
Single	22.00	34.00
Double	36.00	44.00

Parking for 3

Park Hotel
APPROVED
327 Cranbrook Road, Ilford, Essex
IG1 4UE
☎ (0181) 554 9616 & 554 7187
Fax (0181) 518 2700

Homely, comfortable establishment opposite Valentines Park. Within walking distance of underground and BR stations. M11, A406, A12 and A13 are minutes away. All rooms have Sky TV and tea/coffee-making facilities.
Bedrooms: 9 single, 7 double, 2 twin, 2 triple
Bathrooms: 17 en-suite, 1 private, 1 public, 2 private showers

Bed & breakfast per night:	£min	£max
Single	28.50	40.50
Double	40.00	54.00

Evening meal 1830 (last orders 2000)
Parking for 23
Cards accepted: Access, Visa, Switch/Delta

KINGSTON UPON THAMES

Hotel Antoinette of Kingston
APPROVED
Beaufort Road, Kingston upon Thames, Surrey KT1 2TQ
☎ (0181) 546 1044
Fax (0181) 547 2595
Minotel
Tourist hotel located 20 minutes by train from London. Ideal base for visiting Hampton Court, Kew, Windsor, Chessington World of Adventures and Thorpe Park.
Bedrooms: 24 single, 8 double, 34 twin, 24 triple, 9 family rooms
Bathrooms: 99 en-suite

Bed & breakfast per night:	£min	£max
Single	42.00	52.00
Double	55.00	62.00

Evening meal 1830 (last orders 2115)
Parking for 100
Cards accepted: Access, Visa, Amex, Switch/Delta

ORPINGTON

The Mary Rose Hotel
APPROVED
40-50 High Street, St Mary Cray, Orpington, Kent BR5 3NJ
☎ (01689) 871917 & 875369
Fax (01689) 839445
16th C listed inn. Land traversed by River Cray. 30 minutes from Hever and Leeds Castle, Chartwell, Greenwich. 25 minutes from central London, convenient for M25 and British Rail.
Bedrooms: 3 single, 9 double, 5 twin, 3 triple, 12 family rooms
Bathrooms: 24 en-suite, 3 private, 2 public

Bed & breakfast per night:	£min	£max
Single	22.50	34.50
Double	37.50	49.50

Half board per person:	£min	£max
Daily	32.50	44.50
Weekly	227.50	311.50

Lunch available
Evening meal 1900 (last orders 2145)
Parking for 50
Cards accepted: Access, Visa, Diners, Amex, Switch/Delta

RICHMOND

Tourist Information Centre
☎ (0181) 940 9125

The Bingham Hotel on Thames
COMMENDED
61-63 Petersham Road, Richmond, Surrey TW10 6UT
☎ (0181) 940 0902
Fax (0181) 948 8737
Country house style hotel, ideally situated midway between Heathrow and central London, overlooking the River Thames.
Bedrooms: 9 single, 11 double, 3 twin
Bathrooms: 23 en-suite

Bed & breakfast per night:	£min	£max
Single	75.00	85.00
Double	95.00	115.00

Half board per person:	£min	£max
Daily	87.00	106.00
Weekly	609.00	742.00

Evening meal 1900 (last orders 2130)
Parking for 8
Cards accepted: Access, Visa, Diners, Amex

Hobart Hall
APPROVED
43-47 Petersham Road, Richmond, Surrey TW10 6UL
☎ (0181) 940 0435 & 940 1702
Fax (0181) 332 2996
Family-run, 17th C former home of the Duke of Clarence, set on the banks of the River Thames. Spacious and comfortable rooms. Convenient for Heathrow, London, Kew Gardens and Hampton Court.
Bedrooms: 7 single, 5 double, 3 twin, 4 triple
Bathrooms: 15 en-suite, 3 private, 3 public

Bed & breakfast per night:	£min	£max
Single	45.00	50.00
Double	68.00	72.00

Lunch available
Parking for 15
Cards accepted: Access, Visa, Amex

Quinns Hotel
APPROVED
48 Sheen Road, Richmond, Surrey TW9 1AW
☎ (0181) 940 5444
Fax (0181) 940 1828
Ideally located for business or pleasure, within easy reach of central London, airports and local places of interest.
Bedrooms: 4 single, 22 double, 5 twin, 4 triple, 1 family room
Bathrooms: 20 en-suite, 5 public

Bed & breakfast per night:	£min	£max
Single	30.00	60.00
Double	45.00	70.00

Parking for 14
Cards accepted: Access, Visa, Diners, Amex, Switch/Delta

A key to symbols can be found inside the back cover flap.

LONDON

RICHMOND
Continued

Riverside Hotel
23 Petersham Road, Richmond, Surrey TW10 6UH
☎ (0181) 940 1339
Elegant Victorian house overlooking the Thames, close to Richmond Bridge. Colour TVs, tea and coffee facilities.
Bedrooms: 4 single, 5 double, 3 twin, 1 triple
Bathrooms: 12 en-suite, 1 private shower

Bed & breakfast per night:	£min	£max
Single	38.00	48.00
Double	63.00	68.00

Parking for 5
Cards accepted: Access, Visa, Amex

SUTTON

Ashling Tara Hotel
COMMENDED
50 Rosehill, Sutton, Surrey SM1 3EU
☎ (0181) 641 6142
Fax (0181) 644 7872
House hotel opposite open parkland. Short walk to Sutton town centre. All rooms en-suite, lounge/bar and restaurant. On-site parking. Convenient M25, Heathrow/Gatwick Airports. Underground station 1 mile from hotel.
Bedrooms: 5 single, 4 double, 4 twin, 2 family rooms
Bathrooms: 14 en-suite, 1 private shower

Bed & breakfast per night:	£min	£max
Single	40.00	60.00
Double	52.50	70.00

Half board per person:	£min	£max
Daily	52.00	72.00
Weekly	370.00	450.00

Evening meal 1900 (last orders 2100)
Parking for 32
Cards accepted: Access, Visa, Amex, Switch/Delta

WEMBLEY

Aaron (Wembley Park) Hotel
APPROVED
8 Forty Lane, Wembley, Middlesex HA9 9EB
☎ (0181) 904 6329
Fax (0181) 385 0472

Guesthouse close to Wembley Park station, stadium, arena and conference centre. Easy access to major routes and city. Parking available.
Bedrooms: 4 single, 3 triple
Bathrooms: 3 en-suite, 1 public

Bed & breakfast per night:	£min	£max
Single	25.00	35.00
Double	35.00	50.00

Half board per person:	£min	£max
Daily	30.00	40.00
Weekly	200.00	280.00

Lunch available
Evening meal 1800 (last orders 2000)
Parking for 10
Cards accepted: Access, Visa, Diners, Amex

Adelphi Hotel
APPROVED
4 Forty Lane, Wembley, Middlesex HA9 9EB
☎ (0181) 904 5629
Fax (0181) 908 5314
Close to Wembley Stadium and Wembley Park underground, 15 minutes from West End. Attractive decor. TV lounge, tea/coffee in rooms.
Bedrooms: 4 single, 4 double, 3 twin
Bathrooms: 7 en-suite, 2 public

Bed & breakfast per night:	£min	£max
Single	28.00	35.00
Double	38.00	45.00

Half board per person:	£min	£max
Daily	38.00	65.00

Evening meal 2000 (last orders 2100)
Parking for 12
Cards accepted: Access, Visa, Amex

Arena Hotel
6 Forty Lane, Wembley, Middlesex HA9 9EB
☎ (0181) 908 0670 & 908 2850
Fax (0181) 908 2007
Spacious en-suite accommodation with TV and satellite link in every room. Recent refurbishment, only 1800 yards from Wembley Stadium complex. Easy access by all transport routes. Parking.

Bedrooms: 1 single, 3 double, 3 twin, 3 triple, 3 family rooms
Bathrooms: 13 en-suite, 1 public

Bed & breakfast per night:	£min	£max
Single	35.00	39.00
Double	45.00	49.00

Half board per person:	£min	£max
Daily	45.00	49.00
Weekly	210.00	280.00

Evening meal 2000 (last orders 2100)
Parking for 15
Cards accepted: Access, Visa, Diners, Amex, Switch/Delta

The Brookside Hotel
APPROVED
32 Brook Avenue, Wembley, Middlesex HA9 8PH
☎ (0181) 904 0252 & 908 5725
Fax (0181) 385 0800
20 minutes from central London, a stone's throw from Wembley Stadium and Conference Centre. Overlooks Wembley Park station.
Bedrooms: 5 single, 1 double, 1 twin, 2 triple, 2 family rooms
Suites available
Bathrooms: 8 en-suite, 2 public

Bed & breakfast per night:	£min	£max
Single	20.00	38.00
Double	35.00	48.00

Parking for 8
Cards accepted: Access, Visa, Amex, Switch/Delta

Elm Hotel
APPROVED
1-7 Elm Road, Wembley, Middlesex HA9 7JA
☎ (0181) 902 1764
Fax (0181) 903 8365
The Independents
Ten minutes' walk (1200 yards) from Wembley Stadium and Conference Centre. 150 yards from Wembley Central underground and mainline station.
Bedrooms: 6 single, 8 double, 8 twin, 4 triple, 1 family room
Suites available
Bathrooms: 24 en-suite, 2 public

Bed & breakfast per night:	£min	£max
Single	35.00	45.00
Double	45.00	55.00

Evening meal 1800 (last orders 2000)

LONDON

Parking for 7
Cards accepted: Access, Visa, Switch/Delta
🛏🍴📞📺♿📶Ⓢ🔊📻🍽🛎🍽30

WOODFORD GREEN

Packfords Hotel

👑👑👑 COMMENDED

16 Snakes Lane (West), Woodford Green, Essex IG8 0BS
☎ (0181) 504 2642
Fax (0181) 505 5778
Small hotel with individually designed rooms. Banqueting and conference facilities available.
Bedrooms: 1 single, 8 double, 1 twin, 1 triple
Bathrooms: 11 en-suite

Bed & breakfast per night:	£min	£max
Single	45.00	50.00
Double	60.00	65.00

Evening meal 1830 (last orders 2000)
Parking for 15
Cards accepted: Access, Visa, Diners, Amex, Switch/Delta
🛏🍴📞📺♿📶Ⓢ🔊📺🍽🛎
🍽60▶✱🚌 SP

USE YOUR *i*'s

There are more than 550 Tourist Information Centres throughout England offering friendly help with accommodation and holiday ideas as well as suggestions of places to visit and things to do. You'll find the address of your nearest Tourist Information Centre in your local Phone Book.

AT-A-GLANCE SYMBOLS

Symbols at the end of each accommodation entry give useful information about services and facilities. A key to symbols can be found inside the back cover flap.

Keep this open for easy reference.

USE YOUR *i*'s

There are more than 550 Tourist Information Centres throughout England offering friendly help with accommodation and holiday ideas as well as suggestions of places to visit and things to do. There may well be a centre in your home town which can help you before you set out. You'll find the address of your nearest Tourist Information Centre in your local Phone Book.

ENQUIRY COUPONS

To help you obtain further information about advertisers and accommodation featured in this guide you will find enquiry coupons at the back. Send these directly to the establishments in which you are interested. Remember to complete both sides of the coupon.

AT-A-GLANCE SYMBOLS

Symbols at the end of each accommodation entry give useful information about services and facilities. A key to symbols can be found inside the back cover flap.

Keep this open for easy reference.

CUMBRIA

Cumbria is simply one of the most extraordinarily beautiful places on earth. Wordsworth lived here among its shimmering lakes and towering crags, and called it 'the loveliest spot that man hath ever found'; a 'spot' which attracts walkers, climbers and watersports enthusiasts, all year round.

But you don't have to be energetic! There are pretty villages, working farms, museums, visitors centres - plus the whole of the Lake District National Park to explore.

To the west of the Lakes lies Cumbria's unspoilt coastline. To the north you'll find the wild North Pennines and Borderlands. To the southeast, the peaceful Eden Valley. And between... paradise.

FOR MORE INFORMATION CONTACT:
Cumbria Tourist Board
Ashleigh, Holly Road, Windermere,
Cumbria LA23 2AQ
Tel: (015394) 44444 **Fax:** (015394) 44041

Where to Go in Cumbria – see pages 52-55
Where to Stay in Cumbria – see pages 56-98

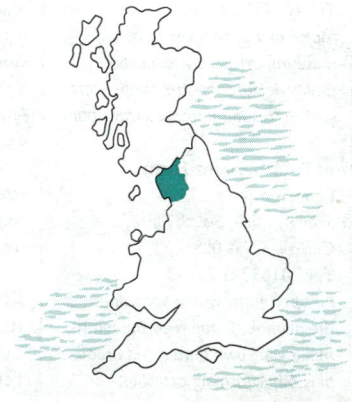

CUMBRIA

Where to Go and What to See

You will find hundreds of interesting places to visit during your stay in Cumbria, just some of which are listed in these pages. The number against each name will help you locate it on the map (page 55). Contact any Tourist Information Centre in the region for more ideas on days out in Cumbria.

1 Linton Tweeds
Shaddon Mills, Shaddon Gate,
Carlisle, Cumbria CA2 5TZ
Tel: (01228) 27569
Shows history of weaving in Carlisle up to Lintons today. Available for visitors to have hands on weaving and other activities.

2 Tullie House Museum and Art Gallery
Castle Street, Carlisle,
Cumbria CA3 8TP
Tel: (01228) 34781
Major tourist complex housing: museum, art gallery, education facility, lecture theatre, shops, herb garden, restaurant and terrace bars.

3 Four Seasons Farm Experience
Sceugh Mire, Southwaite,
Carlisle CA4 0LS
Tel: (016974) 73753
An open farm where you can meet the animals, bottle feed the lambs, make your own butter and bread, plus other farming activities.

4 Senhouse Roman Museum
The Battery, Sea Brows,
Maryport, Cumbria CA15 6JD
Tel: (01900) 816168
Once the headquarters of Hadrian's Coastal Defence system. UK's largest group of Roman altars, stones and inscriptions from a single site. Roman military equipment, stunning sculpture.

5 Lakeland Sheep and Wool Centre
Egremont Road, Cockermouth,
Cumbria CA13 0QX
Tel: (01900) 822673
An all weather attraction with live sheep shows and working dog demonstrations. Includes large screen and other tourism exhibitions on the area, a wool shop and seafood restaurant.

6 The Printing House Museum
102 Main Street, Cockermouth,
Cumbria CA13 9LX
Tel: (01900) 824984
Printing machinery and equipment. Tour of the museum follows the development of printing from the 15thC to the present day.

7 Dalemain Historic House and Gardens
Dalemain Estate Office
Penrith,
Cumbria CA11 0HB
Tel: (017684) 86450
Historic house with Georgian furniture. Westmorland and Cumberland Yeomanry Museum, agricultural bygones, adventure playground, licensed restaurant, famous gardens.

8 Mirehouse
Underskiddaw,
Cumbria CA12 4QE
Tel: (017687) 72287
17thC house with wide ranging literary and artistic connections. Grounds to Bassenthwaite Lake include playgrounds, garden, tearoom.

9 Dove Cottage & Wordsworth Museum
Town End, Grasmere,
Ambleside, Cumbria LA22 9SH
Tel: (015394) 35544
Wordsworth's home 1799-1808. Poet's possessions, museum with manuscripts, farmhouse reconstruction, paintings and drawings. Special events throughout the year.

10 Rydal Mount
Ambleside, Cumbria LA22 9LU
Tel: (015394) 33002
William Wordsworth's home for 37 years. Family portraits, furniture, first editions and personal possessions. Garden landscaped by the poet. 9thC Norse Mound, magnificent views.

11 Sellafield Visitors Centre
Sellafield, Seascale,
Cumbria CA20 1PG
Tel: (019467) 27027
Exhibition of nuclear power and the nuclear industry.

12 Eskdale Corn Mill
Boot, Holmrook,
Cumbria CA19 1TG
Tel: (019467) 23235
A historic water-powered corn mill near Dalegarth Station, approached via packhorse bridge. Early wooden machinery, milling and farming. Exhibition and waterfalls.

13 Brockhole - Lake District National Park Visitor Centre
Windermere,
Cumbria LA23 1LJ
Tel: (015394) 46601
Exhibitions include National Park Story, slide shows, films, shop, gardens, grounds, adventure playground, drystone walling area, trails, events. Gaddums restaurant, tearoom, putting.

14 Muncaster Castle, Gardens and Owl Centre
Ravenglass,
Cumbria CA18 1RQ
Tel: (01229) 717614
14thC pele tower with 15th and 19thC additions. Gardens contain an exceptional collection of rhododendrons and azaleas. Extensive collection of owls.

15 Ravenglass and Eskdale Railway
Ravenglass, Cumbria CA18 1SW
Tel: (01229) 717171
England's oldest narrow-guage railway runs for 7 miles through glorious scenery to the foot of England's highest hills. Most trains steam hauled.

16 Steam Yacht Gondola
Pier Cottage, Coniston,
Cumbria LA21 8AJ
Tel: (015394) 41288
Victorian steam powered vessel now National Trust owned and completely renovated with opulently upholstered saloon.

17 Amazonia
Glebe Road, Bowness-on-Windermere, Windermere,
Cumbria LA23 3HE
Tel: (015394) 48002
Large display of exotic reptiles and insects from around the world including pythons, crocodiles and tarantula spiders! Visitors are able to handle certain animals.

18 The World of Beatrix Potter
The Old Laundry, Crag Brow, Bowness-on-Windermere, Windermere, Cumbria LA23 3BX
Tel: (015394) 88444
The life and works of Beatrix Potter presented on a 9 screen video wall, film on her life, and three-dimensional recreations of some of the scenes from her popular tales.

19 Levens Hall
Levens, Kendal, Cumbria LA8 0PD
Tel: (015395) 60321
Elizabethan mansion, incorporating a pele tower. Famous topiary

garden laid out in 1694, steam collection, plant centre, shop, play and picnic areas.

20 Sizergh Castle
Kendal, Cumbria LA8 8AE
Tel: (015395) 60070
Strickland family home for 750 years, now National Trust owned. With 14thC pele tower, 15thC great hall, 16thC wings. Stuart connections. Rock garden, rose garden, daffodils.

23 Lakeside & Haverthwaite Railway
Haverthwaite Station,
Ulverston,
Cumbria LA12 8AL
Tel: (015395) 31594
Standard gauge steam railway operating a daily seasonal service through the beautiful Leven Valley. Steam and diesel locomotives on display.

26 South Lakes Wild Animal Park
Crossgates,
Dalton-in-Furness,
Cumbria LA15 8JR
Tel: (01229) 466086
Wild animal park in over 14 acres with over 120 species of animals from all over the world. Large water-fowl ponds. Miniature railway.

21 Heron Corn Mill and Museum of Papermaking
Waterhouse Mills,
Beetham, Milnthorpe,
Cumbria LA7 7AR
Tel: (015395) 63363
Restored working corn mill featuring 14ft high waterwheel. The museum shows paper-making both historic and modern with artefacts, displays and diagrams.

22 Heron Glass
54 The Gill, Ulverston,
Cumbria LA12 7BL
Tel: (01229) 581121
A combined visitor centre and workshop. Traditional glassmaking demonstrations daily. Factory shop.

24 Phil Cotton's Classic Bikes Working Museum
Victoria Road,
Ulverston,
Cumbria LA12 0BY
Tel: (01229) 586099
Classic motorcycle display, with video, restoration areas and small shop.

25 Holker Hall and Gardens
Cark in Cartmel,
Cumbria LA11 7PL
Tel: (015395) 58328
Victorian wing, formal and woodland garden, deer park, motor museum, adventure playground and gift shop. Exhibitions including Timeless Toys and Teddies.

27 The Dock Museum
North Road,
Barrow-in-Furness,
Cumbria LA14 2PW
Tel: (01229) 870871
Presents the story of steel shipbuilding for which Barrow is famous. Interactive displays, nautical adventure playground.

28 Furness Abbey
Barrow-in-Furness,
Cumbria LA13 0TJ
Tel: (01229) 823420
Ruins of a 12C Cistercian abbey. Extensive remains include transepts, choir, west tower of church, canopied seats and arches.

FIND OUT MORE

Further information about holidays and attractions in Cumbria is available from:
Cumbria Tourist Board,
Ashleigh,
Holly Road,
Windermere,
Cumbria LA23 2AQ.
Tel: (015394) 44444

These publications are available from the Cumbria Tourist Board:

■ **Cumbria The Lake District Touring Map** - including tourist information and touring caravan and camping parks £3.45. Laminated poster £2.95.

■ **Days Out in Cumbria** - Over 200 ideas for a great day out £1.25.

■ **Short Walks** - Good for Families - route descriptions, maps and information for 14 walks in lesser known areas of Cumbria 95p.

■ **Wordsworth's Lake District** - folded map showing major Wordsworthian sites plus biographical details 60p. Japanese language version £1. Laminated poster £1.

WHERE TO STAY (CUMBRIA)

Accommodation entries in this region are listed in alphabetical order of place name, and then in alphabetical order of establishment.

Map references refer to the colour location maps at the back of this guide. The first number indicates the map to use; the letter and number which follow refer to the grid reference on the map.

At-a-glance symbols at the end of each accommodation entry give useful information about services and facilities. A key to symbols can be found inside the back cover flap. Keep this open for easy reference.

ALSTON

Cumbria
Map ref 5B2

Alston is the highest market town in England, set amongst the highest fells of the Pennines and close to the Pennine Way in an Area of Outstanding Natural Beauty. Mainly 17th C buildings and steep, cobbled streets.

Lovelady Shield Country House Hotel

HIGHLY COMMENDED

Nenthead Road, Alston CA9 3LF
☎ (01434) 381203
Fax (01434) 381515
Attractive Georgian-style country house standing in its own grounds. Idyllic and peaceful location in beautiful Pennine countryside. Noted for cuisine and service.
Bedrooms: 1 single, 7 double, 3 twin
Bathrooms: 11 en-suite

Bed & breakfast per night:	£min	£max
Single	49.00	49.00
Double	98.00	114.00

Half board per person:	£min	£max
Daily	71.50	81.50
Weekly	400.00	456.00

Lunch available
Evening meal 1930 (last orders 2030)
Parking for 25
Open February–December
Cards accepted: Access, Visa, Diners, Amex

AMBLESIDE

Cumbria
Map ref 5A3

Market town situated at the head of Lake Windermere and surrounded by fells. The historic town centre is now a conservation area and the country around Ambleside is rich in historic and literary associations. Good centre for touring, walking and climbing.
Tourist Information Centre
☎ (015394) 32582

Barnes Fell Guest House

Listed COMMENDED

Low Gale, Ambleside LA22 0BB
☎ Windermere (015394) 33311
Convenient yet peaceful non-smoking Victorian guesthouse, furnished with antiques. Delicious food, fine views and a warm welcome.
Bedrooms: 3 double
Bathrooms: 1 en-suite, 1 public

Bed & breakfast per night:	£min	£max
Single	16.00	37.00
Double	30.00	54.00

Half board per person:	£min	£max
Daily	24.00	39.00
Weekly	149.00	245.00

Evening meal 1930 (last orders 2030)

Borrans Park Hotel

HIGHLY COMMENDED

Borrans Road, Ambleside LA22 0EN
☎ (015394) 33454
Fax (015394) 33003

Peacefully situated between the village and lake. Enjoy candlelit dinners, 120 fine wines, and four-poster bedrooms with private spa baths.
Wheelchair access category 3
Bedrooms: 9 double, 1 twin, 2 triple
Bathrooms: 12 en-suite

Bed & breakfast per night:	£min	£max
Single	29.00	49.00
Double	58.00	78.00

Half board per person:	£min	£max
Daily	45.00	55.00
Weekly	255.00	329.00

Evening meal 1900 (last orders 1800)
Parking for 20
Cards accepted: Access, Visa, Switch/Delta

Claremont House

APPROVED

Compston Road, Ambleside LA22 9DJ
☎ (015394) 33448
Fax (015394) 33448
All rooms have colour TV and tea/coffee makers, most are en-suite. Family-run, friendly atmosphere.
Bedrooms: 2 single, 3 double, 1 triple
Bathrooms: 4 en-suite, 1 public

Bed & breakfast per night:	£min	£max
Single	12.50	25.00
Double	30.00	45.00

Cards accepted: Access, Visa, Switch/Delta

CUMBRIA

Crow How Hotel
COMMENDED
Rydal Road, Ambleside LA22 9PN
☎ (015394) 32193
Lovely old Lakeland hotel, set in 2-acre seclusion on rural outskirts. Private car park, spacious en-suite rooms, dogs welcome.
Bedrooms: 6 double, 1 twin, 2 triple
Bathrooms: 8 en-suite, 1 private

Bed & breakfast
per night:	£min	£max
Single	18.00	33.00
Double	36.00	66.00

Half board per
person:	£min	£max
Daily	31.50	47.00
Weekly	255.00	300.00

Evening meal 1930 (last orders 1730)
Parking for 12
Open February–November
Cards accepted: Access, Visa

Easedale Guest House
Compston Road, Ambleside LA22 9DJ
☎ (015394) 32112
Victorian house with private car park. Overlooking Lochrigg Fell and tennis court. Friendly and comfortable, serving generous breakfasts. Advice given for walking and sightseeing. No smoking, please.
Bedrooms: 6 double, 1 twin
Bathrooms: 3 en-suite, 1 private, 1 public

Bed & breakfast
per night:	£min	£max
Single	16.00	22.50
Double	32.00	45.00

Parking for 6

Elder Grove Hotel
COMMENDED
Lake Road, Ambleside LA22 0DB
☎ (015394) 32504
Delightful small hotel, owned and managed by the Haywood family, offering comfortable en-suite bedrooms; delicious food and wines. Heating. Parking.
Bedrooms: 2 single, 7 double, 2 twin, 1 triple
Bathrooms: 12 en-suite

Bed & breakfast
per night:	£min	£max
Single	27.00	
Double	54.00	58.00

Half board per
person:	£min	£max
Daily	43.00	45.00
Weekly	266.00	283.00

Evening meal 1915 (last orders 2015)
Parking for 14
Open February–November
Cards accepted: Access, Visa, Amex, Switch/Delta

Fisherbeck Hotel
COMMENDED
Lake Road, Ambleside LA22 0DH
☎ (015394) 33215
Fax (015394) 33600

Noted for hospitality, service and comfort. Fine food, sheltered garden, car parking, fell views. Ideally situated for touring and all Lakeland activities. Special breaks available. Leisure club facilities. Fishing.

Continued ▶

ENQUIRY COUPONS

To help you obtain further information about advertisers featured in this guide you will find enquiry coupons at the back. Send these directly to the establishments in which you are interested. Remember to complete both sides of the coupon.

WHERE THE SPIRIT SOARS

LANGDALE

This naturally beautiful Estate is a haven of peace and tranquillity; an ideal touring base to discover and enjoy all that the Lake District has to offer. Founded on the site of a 19th century gunpowder works, it is dotted with massive millstones and other carefully preserved reminders of its history. The Hotel has two restaurants, a traditional Lakeland pub and leisure facilities. So much to do and so much to remember... the scenery, the comfort, the good food and the warm and friendly service.

Langdale Hotel & Country Club,
Great Langdale, Nr. Ambleside, Cumbria LA22 9JD
Telephone 015394 37302 Facsimile 015394 37694
ETB ★★★★★ RAC ★★★★ AA ★★★ BTA Award of Distinction
Egon Ronay Recommended Civic Trust Award

CUMBRIA

AMBLESIDE
Continued

Bedrooms: 1 single, 14 double, 2 twin, 3 triple
Bathrooms: 17 en-suite, 2 public

Bed & breakfast per night:	£min	£max
Single	25.00	45.00
Double	50.00	74.00

Half board per person:	£min	£max
Daily	32.00	53.00
Weekly	224.00	353.00

Lunch available
Evening meal 1900 (last orders 2030)
Parking for 20
Cards accepted: Access, Visa

The Gables Hotel
COMMENDED

Compston Road, Ambleside LA22 9DJ
☎ (015394) 33272
In a quiet residential area overlooking the park, tennis courts, bowling green and Loughrigg Fell. Convenient for shops, walking and water sports.
Bedrooms: 3 single, 5 double, 1 twin, 4 triple
Bathrooms: 13 en-suite

Bed & breakfast per night:	£min	£max
Single	28.00	
Double	46.00	

Evening meal 1845 (last orders 1915)
Parking for 7
Open January–November
Cards accepted: Access, Visa

Ghyll Head Hotel
APPROVED

Waterhead, Ambleside LA22 0HD
☎ (015394) 32360
Family hotel in a good position overlooking Lake Windermere and ideal for touring the Lake District.
Bedrooms: 1 single, 6 double, 1 twin, 3 triple, 1 family room
Bathrooms: 10 en-suite, 1 private, 1 private shower

Bed & breakfast per night:	£min	£max
Single	21.50	27.50
Double	43.00	55.00

Half board per person:	£min	£max
Daily	31.50	37.50
Weekly	215.00	255.00

Evening meal 1830 (last orders 1930)
Parking for 12

Hillsdale

Church Street, Ambleside LA22 0BT
☎ (015394) 33174
Family-run hotel in centre of village. 10 minutes' walk from lake. Central for touring all lakes and near bowling green, tennis courts and putting green.
Bedrooms: 1 single, 6 double, 1 twin
Bathrooms: 1 en-suite, 1 public, 4 private showers

Bed & breakfast per night:	£min	£max
Single	15.00	20.00
Double	30.00	40.00

The Horseshoe Hotel

Rothay Road, Ambleside LA22 0EE
☎ (015394) 32000
Fax (015394) 31007

Georgian house hotel with magnificent mountain views. Super bar meals and candlelit dinners. Individually designed bedrooms, honeymoon suites. Warm, friendly and informal.
Bedrooms: 1 single, 12 double, 3 twin, 2 triple, 2 family rooms
Bathrooms: 18 en-suite, 1 public

Bed & breakfast per night:	£min	£max
Single	29.00	38.00
Double	50.00	68.00

Half board per person:	£min	£max
Daily	29.50	44.50
Weekly	210.00	270.00

Lunch available
Evening meal 1900 (last orders 2030)
Parking for 20
Cards accepted: Access, Visa, Amex, Switch/Delta

Kingswood

Old Lake Road, Ambleside LA22 0AE
☎ (015394) 34081
Comfortable and well-equipped bedrooms. Tea/coffee making facilities. Short distance to shops and lake. Pleasant lounge/dining area. Parking. Non-smoking.
Bedrooms: 1 double, 1 twin, 1 triple
Bathrooms: 1 public

Bed & breakfast per night:	£min	£max
Single	14.50	18.50
Double	31.00	

Evening meal from 1900
Parking for 5

Kirkstone Foot Country House Hotel
HIGHLY COMMENDED

Kirkstone Pass Road, Ambleside LA22 9EH
☎ (015394) 32232
Fax (015394) 32232

Secluded 17th C manor house and renowned restaurant, set in its own grounds, with adjoining self-contained apartments and cottages.
Wheelchair access category 3
Bedrooms: 12 double, 1 twin, 1 triple
Bathrooms: 14 en-suite

Bed & breakfast per night:	£min	£max
Single	35.00	45.00
Double	70.00	92.00

Half board per person:	£min	£max
Daily	48.00	70.00
Weekly	231.00	372.00

Evening meal 1930 (last orders 2030)
Parking for 30
Open February–December
Cards accepted: Access, Visa, Diners, Amex, Switch/Delta

Langdale Hotel & Country Club
HIGHLY COMMENDED

Great Langdale, Ambleside LA22 9JD
☎ (015394) 37302
Fax (015394) 37694

Please check prices and other details at the time of booking.

CUMBRIA

En-suite hotel, winner of 1986 Civic Trust environmental award, in 35 acres of wooded grounds. Indoor country club, large pool, spa-bath, sports facilities, restaurants and bars. Minimum stay 2 nights.
Bedrooms: 41 double, 24 twin
Bathrooms: 65 en-suite

Bed & breakfast per night:	£min	£max
Single	90.00	105.00
Double	140.00	170.00
Half board per person:	£min	£max
Daily	105.00	120.00
Weekly	427.00	504.00

Lunch available
Evening meal 1900 (last orders 2200)
Parking for 120
Cards accepted: Access, Visa, Diners, Amex, Switch/Delta

See display advertisement on page 57

Lattendales
COMMENDED

Compston Road, Ambleside LA22 9DJ
☎ (015394) 32368
Traditional Lakeland home in the heart of Ambleside. A central base for walking or touring, offering comfortable accommodation and local produce.
Bedrooms: 2 single, 2 double, 2 twin
Bathrooms: 4 en-suite, 1 public

Bed & breakfast per night:	£min	£max
Single	15.00	17.50
Double	32.00	40.00
Half board per person:	£min	£max
Daily	28.00	32.00
Weekly	189.00	215.00

Evening meal 1830 (last orders 1700)

Laurel Villa
HIGHLY COMMENDED

Lake Road, Ambleside LA22 0DB
☎ (015394) 33240
Detached Victorian house, visited by Beatrix Potter. En-suite bedrooms overlooking the fells. Within easy reach of Lake Windermere and the village. Private car park.
Bedrooms: 7 double, 1 twin
Bathrooms: 8 en-suite

Bed & breakfast per night:	£min	£max
Single	50.00	50.00
Double	60.00	80.00

Half board per person:	£min	£max
Daily	50.00	60.00

Evening meal 1900 (last orders 1700)
Parking for 10
Cards accepted: Access, Visa, Amex

Lyndhurst Hotel
COMMENDED

Wansfell Road, Ambleside LA22 0EG
☎ (015394) 32421
Lovely rooms and delicious food make a stay at this small Lakeland hotel a delightful experience - everything you could wish for.
Bedrooms: 5 double, 1 twin
Bathrooms: 6 en-suite

Bed & breakfast per night:	£min	£max
Double	35.00	50.00
Half board per person:	£min	£max
Daily	31.50	38.50
Weekly	215.00	250.00

Evening meal 1830 (last orders 1830)
Parking for 9

The Old Vicarage
COMMENDED

Vicarage Road, Ambleside LA22 9DH
☎ (015394) 33364
Fax (015394) 34734

Quietly situated in own grounds in heart of village. Car park, quality en-suite accommodation, friendly service. Family-run. Pets welcome.
Bedrooms: 7 double, 1 twin, 1 triple, 1 family room
Bathrooms: 10 en-suite

Bed & breakfast per night:	£min	£max
Single	28.00	
Double	46.00	

Parking for 12
Cards accepted: Access, Visa, Switch/Delta

Queens Hotel
COMMENDED

Market Place, Ambleside LA22 9BU
☎ (015394) 32206
Fax (015394) 32721
In the heart of the Lakes and convenient for walking, climbing and other leisure activities. 2 fully licensed bars, choice of restaurant or bar meals.
Bedrooms: 4 single, 14 double, 3 twin, 2 triple, 3 family rooms
Bathrooms: 26 en-suite

Bed & breakfast per night:	£min	£max
Single	23.50	34.00
Double	47.00	68.00
Half board per person:	£min	£max
Daily	36.50	47.00

Lunch available
Evening meal 1900 (last orders 2130)
Parking for 12
Cards accepted: Access, Visa, Diners, Amex, Switch/Delta

Riverside Lodge Country House
COMMENDED

Nr. Rothay Bridge, Ambleside LA22 0EH
☎ (015394) 34208
Georgian country house of character with 2 acres of grounds through which the River Rothay flows. 500 yards from the centre of Ambleside.
Bedrooms: 1 single, 2 double, 1 twin
Bathrooms: 2 en-suite, 2 private

Bed & breakfast per night:	£min	£max
Double	42.00	59.00

Parking for 20
Cards accepted: Access, Visa

Rothay Garth Hotel
COMMENDED

Rothay Road, Ambleside LA22 0EE
☎ (015394) 32217
Fax (015394) 34400
Distinctive Victorian country house with elegant Loughrigg restaurant overlooking lovely gardens and nearby mountains. Close to village centre and Lake Windermere. All-season breaks.
Bedrooms: 2 single, 9 double, 2 twin, 2 triple, 1 family room
Suite available
Bathrooms: 15 en-suite, 1 public

Bed & breakfast per night:	£min	£max
Single	34.00	49.00
Double	68.00	98.00

Continued ▶

CUMBRIA

AMBLESIDE
Continued

Half board per person:	£min	£max
Daily	54.00	69.00
Weekly	338.00	395.00

Lunch available
Evening meal 1900 (last orders 2100)
Parking for 17
Cards accepted: Access, Visa, Diners, Amex, Switch/Delta

Rothay Manor Hotel
HIGHLY COMMENDED
Rothay Bridge, Ambleside LA22 0EH
☎ (015394) 33605
Fax (015394) 33607

Elegant Regency country house hotel with a well-known restaurant. Balcony rooms overlook the garden. Suites for families and disabled guests. Free use of nearby leisure club.
Bedrooms: 2 single, 5 double, 3 twin, 5 triple, 3 family rooms
Suites available
Bathrooms: 18 en-suite

Bed & breakfast per night:	£min	£max
Single	78.00	
Double	118.00	132.00

Half board per person:	£min	£max
Daily	75.00	105.00

Lunch available
Evening meal 1945 (last orders 2100)
Parking for 50
Open February–December
Cards accepted: Access, Visa, Diners, Amex

Rowanfield Country Guesthouse
HIGHLY COMMENDED
Kirkstone Road, Ambleside
LA22 9ET
☎ (015394) 33686
Fax (015394) 31569

Idyllic setting, panoramic lake and mountain views. Laura Ashley style decor. Scrumptious food created by proprietor/chef. Superior room available at supplement.
Wheelchair access category 3
Bedrooms: 5 double, 1 twin, 1 triple
Bathrooms: 7 en-suite

Bed & breakfast per night:	£min	£max
Double	52.00	56.00

Half board per person:	£min	£max
Daily	42.00	45.00
Weekly	255.00	271.00

Evening meal 1900 (last orders 1900)
Parking for 8
Open March–December
Cards accepted: Access, Visa, Switch/Delta

The Rysdale Hotel
COMMENDED
Rothay Road, Ambleside LA22 0EE
☎ (015394) 32140
Fax (015394) 31111
Family-run hotel with magnificent views over park and fells. Good food, licensed bar. Friendly, personal service. Ideal walking base. No smoking.
Bedrooms: 4 single, 4 double, 1 triple
Bathrooms: 6 en-suite, 2 public

Bed & breakfast per night:	£min	£max
Single	16.00	24.00
Double	32.00	48.00

Parking for 2
Cards accepted: Access, Visa

The Salutation Hotel
COMMENDED
Lake Road, Ambleside LA22 9BX
☎ (015394) 32244
Fax (015394) 34157
Ⓒ Consort
Traditional hotel overlooking central Ambleside, with comfortable rooms and leisure facilities available. Warm and friendly welcome assured.
Bedrooms: 17 double, 8 twin, 4 triple
Bathrooms: 29 en-suite

Bed & breakfast per night:	£min	£max
Single	30.50	42.50
Double	61.00	85.00

Half board per person:	£min	£max
Daily	45.50	57.50
Weekly	281.00	345.00

Lunch available
Evening meal 1900 (last orders 2100)
Parking for 40
Cards accepted: Access, Visa, Amex, Switch/Delta

Smallwood House Hotel
COMMENDED
Compston Road, Ambleside
LA22 9DJ
☎ (015394) 32330
Family-run hotel in central position, offering warm and friendly service, good home cooking and value-for-money quality and standards.
Bedrooms: 7 double, 3 twin, 1 triple, 2 family rooms
Bathrooms: 11 en-suite, 2 private

Bed & breakfast per night:	£min	£max
Single	25.00	29.50
Double	34.00	43.00

Half board per person:	£min	£max
Daily	30.00	33.50
Weekly	205.00	225.00

Lunch available
Evening meal 1800 (last orders 2000)
Parking for 11
Cards accepted: Access, Visa

Thorneyfield Guest House
COMMENDED
Compston Road, Ambleside
LA22 9DJ
☎ (015394) 32464
Fax (015394) 32464
Cosy family-run guesthouse in the town centre with friendly and helpful service. Close to the park, miniature golf, tennis and lake. Large family rooms available.
Bedrooms: 1 single, 2 double, 1 triple, 2 family rooms
Bathrooms: 4 en-suite, 1 public

Bed & breakfast per night:	£min	£max
Single	14.00	16.00
Double	28.00	38.00

Please mention this guide when making your booking.

CUMBRIA

Cards accepted: Access, Visa, Switch/Delta

Wateredge Hotel
HIGHLY COMMENDED
Waterhead Bay, Ambleside
LA22 0EP
☎ (015394) 32332
Fax (015394) 31878

Delightfully situated on shores of Windermere, the family- run Wateredge offers quiet relaxation, elegant comfort, excellent cuisine, beautiful lake views and, above all, personal unobtrusive service.
Bedrooms: 3 single, 12 double, 8 twin
Bathrooms: 23 en-suite

Half board per person:

	£min	£max
Daily	53.00	87.00
Weekly	365.00	580.00

Lunch available
Evening meal 1900 (last orders 2030)
Parking for 25
Open February–December
Cards accepted: Access, Visa, Amex, Switch/Delta

Waterhead Hotel
COMMENDED
Lake Road, Ambleside LA22 0ER
☎ (015394) 32566
Fax (015394) 31255
Best Western
On the edge of Lake Windermere, an ideal central base for touring the lovely English Lakes.
Bedrooms: 4 single, 10 double, 11 twin, 1 triple
Bathrooms: 26 en-suite

Bed & breakfast per night:

	£min	£max
Single	38.00	40.00
Double	76.00	106.00

Half board per person:

	£min	£max
Daily	50.00	66.00
Weekly	300.00	396.00

Lunch available
Evening meal 1900 (last orders 2100)

Parking for 50
Cards accepted: Access, Visa, Diners, Amex, Switch/Delta

APPLEBY-IN-WESTMORLAND
Cumbria
Map ref 5B3

Former county town of Westmorland, at the foot of the Pennines in the Eden Valley. The castle was rebuilt in the 17th C, except for its Norman keep, ditches and ramparts. It now houses a Rare Breeds Survival Trust Centre. Good centre for exploring the Eden Valley.
Tourist Information Centre
☎ (017683) 51177

Appleby Manor Country House Hotel
HIGHLY COMMENDED
Roman Road,
Appleby-in-Westmorland CA16 6JB
☎ Appleby (017683) 51571
Fax (017683) 52888
Best Western
Award-winning country house hotel with fine timber features, in wooded grounds overlooking Appleby Castle. Panoramic views of the Pennines and the Lakeland fells. Indoor leisure club.
Bedrooms: 14 double, 8 twin, 1 triple, 7 family rooms
Suite available
Bathrooms: 30 en-suite

Bed & breakfast per night:

	£min	£max
Single	61.50	69.50
Double	88.00	118.00

Half board per person:

	£min	£max
Daily	49.50	69.50
Weekly	297.00	417.00

Lunch available
Evening meal 1900 (last orders 2100)
Parking for 51
Cards accepted: Access, Visa, Diners, Amex, Switch/Delta

Information on accommodation listed in this guide has been supplied by the proprietors. As changes may occur you are advised to check details at the time of booking.

Bongate House
COMMENDED
Appleby-in-Westmorland
CA16 6UE
☎ Appleby (017683) 51245
Family-run Georgian guesthouse on the outskirts of a small market town. Large garden. Relaxed friendly atmosphere, good home cooking.
Bedrooms: 1 single, 3 double, 2 twin, 1 triple, 1 family room
Bathrooms: 5 en-suite, 1 public

Bed & breakfast per night:

	£min	£max
Single	17.00	19.50
Double	34.00	39.00

Half board per person:

	£min	£max
Daily	25.00	27.50
Weekly	160.00	180.00

Evening meal 1900 (last orders 1800)
Parking for 10

ARNSIDE
Cumbria
Map ref 5A3

Small coastal village in an Area of Outstanding Natural Beauty, with spectacular views across the Kent Estuary of the Lakeland hills. Excellent base for bird-watching. The incoming tide creates an impressive tidal bore.

Willowfield Hotel
COMMENDED
The Promenade, Arnside, Carnforth, Lancashire LA5 0AD
☎ (01524) 761354
Non-smoking, relaxed, family-run hotel with panoramic outlook over estuary to Lakeland hills. Good home cooking and quiet situation.
Bedrooms: 2 single, 3 double, 3 twin, 2 triple
Bathrooms: 6 en-suite, 2 public

Bed & breakfast per night:

	£min	£max
Single	19.00	23.00
Double	38.00	46.00

Half board per person:

	£min	£max
Daily	30.00	34.00
Weekly	196.00	224.00

Evening meal from 1830
Parking for 8
Cards accepted: Access, Visa

CUMBRIA

BARROW-IN-FURNESS
Cumbria
Map ref 5A3

On the Furness Peninsula in Morecambe Bay, an industrial and commercial centre with sandy beaches and nature reserves on Walney Island. Ruins of 12th C Cistercian Furness Abbey. The Dock Museum tells the story of the area and Forum 28 houses a modern theatre and arts centre.
Tourist Information Centre ☎ (01229) 870156

Abbey House Hotel
Abbey Road, Barrow-in-Furness LA13 0PA
☎ Barrow (01229) 838282
Fax (01229) 820403
Friendly country house hotel, in idyllic location for that romantic weekend and an excellent base for touring the Lake District. Half board prices are for weekends only.
Bedrooms: 3 single, 14 double, 5 twin, 6 triple
Bathrooms: 28 en-suite, 1 public

Bed & breakfast
per night:	£min	£max
Single	59.95	59.95
Double	74.95	74.95

Half board per
person:	£min	£max
Daily	37.25	52.50

Lunch available
Evening meal 1900 (last orders 2130)
Parking for 60
Cards accepted: Access, Visa, Diners, Amex, Switch/Delta

Arlington House Hotel and Restaurant
HIGHLY COMMENDED
200/202 Abbey Road, Barrow-in-Furness LA14 5LD
☎ (01229) 831976
Relaxed hotel with an elegant restaurant. In the town, yet not far away from the Lakes and sea.
Bedrooms: 2 double, 6 twin
Bathrooms: 8 en-suite

Bed & breakfast
per night:	£min	£max
Single	52.00	57.00
Double	70.00	77.00

Evening meal 1930 (last orders 2045)
Parking for 20
Cards accepted: Access, Visa

Clarence House Country Hotel and Restaurant
HIGHLY COMMENDED
Skelgate, Dalton-in-Furness LA15 8BQ
☎ Dalton-in-Furness (01229) 462508
Fax (01229) 467177
Elegant, family-run, late Victorian country hotel and restaurant, set in 3 acres of beautiful grounds.
Bedrooms: 14 double, 3 twin
Bathrooms: 17 en-suite

Bed & breakfast
per night	£min	£max
Single	45.00	60.00
Double	50.00	75.00

Half board per
person:	£min	£max
Daily	57.50	78.95
Weekly	458.95	541.60

Lunch available
Evening meal 1830 (last orders 2130)
Parking for 40
Cards accepted: Access, Visa, Amex, Switch/Delta

Hotel Majestic
COMMENDED
Duke Street, Barrow-in-Furness LA14 1HP
☎ (01229) 870448
Fax (01229) 870448
Recently modernised Victorian building with restaurant, conference facilities, cafe bar, games room. All rooms en suite and include all modern amenities. Centrally located.
Bedrooms: 10 single, 13 double, 10 twin, 2 family rooms
Bathrooms: 35 en-suite

Bed & breakfast
per night:	£min	£max
Single	34.00	45.00
Double	46.50	58.00

Lunch available
Evening meal 1830 (last orders 2130)
Parking for 25
Cards accepted: Access, Visa, Amex

White House Hotel
Abbey Road, Barrow-in-Furness LA13 9AE
☎ (01229) 827303
Fax (01229) 835534

Map references apply to the colour maps at the back of this guide.

Always a warm welcome at this long established hotel catering for tourists and travellers. Large car/coach park, security patrolled.
Bedrooms: 25 single, 2 double, 8 twin
Bathrooms: 5 en-suite, 3 private, 4 public

Bed & breakfast
per night:	£min	£max
Single	23.50	36.00
Double	33.00	46.00

Lunch available
Evening meal 1730 (last orders 2100)
Parking for 67
Cards accepted: Access, Visa, Switch/Delta

BASSENTHWAITE
Cumbria
Map ref 5A2

Standing in an idyllic setting, nestled at the foot of Skiddaw and Ullock Pike, this village is just a mile from Bassenthwaite Lake, the one true "lake" in the Lake District. The area is visited by many varieties of migrating birds.

Kiln Hill Barn
COMMENDED
Bassenthwaite, Keswick CA12 4RG
☎ Bassenthwaite Lake (017687) 76454
Family rooms with en-suite facilities, log fires and central heating. Meals served in the Barn dining room, adjacent to the farmhouse.
Bedrooms: 2 single, 4 double, 1 twin
Bathrooms: 5 en-suite, 1 public

Bed & breakfast
per night:	£min	£max
Single	19.00	19.00
Double	38.00	38.00

Half board per
person:	£min	£max
Daily	26.00	26.00
Weekly	172.00	172.00

Evening meal 1830 (last orders 1900)
Parking for 15
Open January–November

CUMBRIA

Ravenstone Hotel
HIGHLY COMMENDED

Bassenthwaite, Keswick CA12 4QG
☎ (017687) 76240
Fax (017687) 76240

Charming dower house offering comfort and relaxation in beautiful surroundings. Elegant lounge and bar with log fires. Games room with full-size snooker table.
Bedrooms: 2 single, 10 double, 7 twin, 1 triple
Bathrooms: 20 en-suite

Bed & breakfast per night:
	£min	£max
Single	30.00	32.00
Double	60.00	64.00

Half board per person:
	£min	£max
Daily	40.00	45.00
Weekly	262.50	304.50

Evening meal 1900 (last orders 1930)
Parking for 20
Open January–October

BASSENTHWAITE LAKE
Cumbria
Map ref 5A2

The northernmost and only true "lake" in the Lake District. Visited annually by many species of migratory birds.

Link House Hotel
COMMENDED

Bassenthwaite Lake, Cockermouth CA13 9YD
☎ Bassenthwaite (017687) 76291
Fax (017687) 76670

Licensed country house at Bassenthwaite Lake. Superb views. Traditional home cooking, log fire, conservatory bar, nearby leisure club facilities.
Bedrooms: 2 single, 3 double, 2 twin, 1 triple
Bathrooms: 8 en-suite, 1 public

Bed & breakfast per night:
	£min	£max
Single	15.00	26.00
Double	50.00	52.00

Half board per person:
	£min	£max
Daily	38.00	39.00
Weekly	240.00	240.00

Evening meal 1900 (last orders 1900)
Parking for 8

Open February–November and Christmas
Cards accepted: Access, Visa, Switch/Delta

Pheasant Inn
HIGHLY COMMENDED

Bassenthwaite Lake, Cockermouth CA13 9YE
☎ (017687) 76234
Fax (017687) 76002
Logis of Great Britain

Peacefully situated just off the A66 at the northern end of Bassenthwaite Lake. A 16th C farmhouse with all the charm and character of that age.
Wheelchair access category 3
Bedrooms: 5 single, 8 double, 7 twin
Bathrooms: 20 en-suite

Bed & breakfast per night:
	£min	£max
Single	58.00	60.00
Double	72.00	100.00

Half board per person:
	£min	£max
Daily	78.00	88.00
Weekly	350.00	460.00

Lunch available
Evening meal 1900 (last orders 2030)
Parking for 80
Cards accepted: Access, Visa

BORROWDALE
Cumbria
Map ref 5A3

Stretching south of Derwentwater to Seathwaite in the heart of the Lake District, the valley is walled by high fellsides. It can justly claim to be the most scenically impressive valley in the Lake District. Excellent centre for walking and climbing.

Derwent House
COMMENDED

Grange-in-Borrowdale, Borrowdale, Keswick CA12 5UY
☎ (017687) 77658
Fax (017687) 77217

Victorian, family-run guesthouse in lovely Borrowdale. Comfortable rooms enjoy beautiful views of surrounding fells. No smoking in bedrooms and dining rooms, please.
Bedrooms: 1 single, 5 double, 3 twin, 1 triple
Bathrooms: 6 en-suite, 1 public

Bed & breakfast per night:
	£min	£max
Single	25.00	30.00
Double	40.00	50.00

Half board per person:
	£min	£max
Daily	34.00	39.00
Weekly	238.00	252.00

Evening meal 1900 (last orders 1900)
Parking for 15
Open February–December

Hazel Bank
HIGHLY COMMENDED

Rosthwaite, Borrowdale, Keswick CA12 5XB
☎ (017687) 77248 & 77373

Comfortable and well-appointed country house in the beautiful, peaceful Borrowdale Valley. Ideal base for walking or touring. Non-smokers only, please.
Bedrooms: 1 single, 2 double, 3 twin
Bathrooms: 6 en-suite

Half board per person:
	£min	£max
Daily	40.00	45.00
Weekly	280.00	280.00

Evening meal 1900 (last orders 1900)
Parking for 12
Open April–October
Cards accepted: Access, Visa, Switch/Delta

Leathes Head Hotel and Restaurant
HIGHLY COMMENDED

Borrowdale, Keswick CA12 5UY
☎ (017687) 77247
Fax (017687) 77363

Beautiful country house with a warm welcome and magnificent views in the heart of Borrowdale. Menus change daily, with emphasis on fresh local produce.
Bedrooms: 2 single, 3 double, 2 twin, 2 triple, 1 family room

Continued ▶

CUMBRIA

BORROWDALE
Continued

Bathrooms: 10 en-suite

Bed & breakfast per night:

	£min	£max
Single	29.50	40.00
Double	59.00	80.00

Half board per person:

	£min	£max
Daily	44.50	54.50
Weekly	298.00	330.00

Evening meal 1900 (last orders 2030)
Parking for 25
Open February–December
Cards accepted: Access, Visa, Switch/Delta

Mary Mount

Borrowdale, Keswick CA12 5UU
☎ (017687) 77223
Set in 4.5 acres of gardens and woodlands on the shores of Derwentwater, 2.5 miles from Keswick. Views across lake to Catbells and Maiden Moor. Families and pets welcome.
Bedrooms: 1 single, 5 double, 5 twin, 2 triple, 1 family room
Bathrooms: 14 en-suite

Bed & breakfast per night:

	£min	£max
Single	21.00	27.50
Double	42.00	55.00

Lunch available
Evening meal 1830 (last orders 2045)
Parking for 40
Open February–December
Cards accepted: Access, Visa

Royal Oak Hotel
COMMENDED

Rosthwaite, Borrowdale, Keswick CA12 5XB
☎ (017687) 77214
Fax (017687) 77214
Small, family-run, traditional Lakeland hotel 6 miles south of Keswick. Cosy atmosphere, home cooking and friendly service.
Bedrooms: 2 single, 4 double, 2 twin, 3 triple, 1 family room
Bathrooms: 8 en-suite, 3 public

Bed & breakfast per night:

	£min	£max
Single	20.00	28.00
Double	40.00	56.00

Half board per person:

	£min	£max
Daily	24.00	38.00
Weekly	180.00	238.00

Evening meal 1900 (last orders 1900)
Parking for 12
Cards accepted: Access, Visa

Seatoller House
Listed COMMENDED

Seatoller, Borrowdale, Keswick CA12 5XN
☎ (017687) 77218
This 300-year-old house has accommodated visitors to Borrowdale for well over a century. It continues to be known for its homely, friendly and informal atmosphere, good food and fine location.
Bedrooms: 1 double, 3 twin, 5 triple
Bathrooms: 3 en-suite, 6 private

Bed & breakfast per night:

	£min	£max
Single	28.00	
Double	54.00	

Half board per person:

	£min	£max
Daily	36.00	
Weekly	210.00	

Evening meal 1900 (last orders 1800)
Parking for 15
Open March–November

Stakis Keswick Lodore Hotel
HIGHLY COMMENDED

Borrowdale, Keswick CA12 5UX
☎ (017687) 77285
Fax (017687) 77343
Utell International
Largely refurbished hotel with excellent sports and family facilities. Fantastic views of lake and fells beyond. Beautiful grounds and gardens for a relaxing holiday. Half board overnight price based on minimum 2-night stay.
Bedrooms: 10 single, 20 double, 44 twin, 1 triple
Suite available
Bathrooms: 75 en-suite, 1 public

Bed & breakfast per night:

	£min	£max
Single	35.00	60.00
Double	70.00	120.00

Half board per person:

	£min	£max
Daily	38.00	72.00
Weekly	266.00	454.00

Lunch available
Evening meal 1930 (last orders 2130)
Parking for 123
Cards accepted: Access, Visa, Diners, Amex, Switch/Delta

BRAITHWAITE

Cumbria
Map ref 5A3

Braithwaite nestles at the foot of the Whinlatter Pass and has a magnificent backdrop of the mountains forming the Coledale Horseshoe.

Coledale Inn

Braithwaite, Keswick CA12 5TN
☎ (017687) 78272
Victorian country house hotel and Georgian inn, in a peaceful hillside position away from traffic, with superb mountain views. Families and pets welcome.
Bedrooms: 1 single, 6 double, 1 twin, 3 triple, 1 family room
Bathrooms: 12 en-suite

Bed & breakfast per night:

	£min	£max
Single	17.00	20.00
Double	42.00	55.00

Lunch available
Evening meal 1830 (last orders 2100)
Parking for 15
Cards accepted: Access, Visa

BRAMPTON

Cumbria
Map ref 5B3

Excellent centre for exploring Hadrian's Wall. Wednesday is market day around the Moot Hall in this delightful sandstone-built town. Wall plaque marks the site of Bonnie Prince Charlie and his Jacobite army headquarters whilst they laid siege to Carlisle Castle in 1745.

Sands House Hotel
COMMENDED

The Sands, Brampton CA8 1UG
☎ (016977) 3085
Fax (016977) 3297

17th C coaching inn. Fully licensed, famous restaurant. En-suite rooms with colour TV, tea-maker and telephone. On A69, close to Hadrian's Wall and Lanercost Priory.
Bedrooms: 4 double, 4 twin, 2 triple
Bathrooms: 10 en-suite, 1 public

Bed & breakfast per night:	£min	£max
Single	32.00	36.00
Double	46.00	50.00

Lunch available
Evening meal 1800 (last orders 2200)
Parking for 50
Cards accepted: Access, Visa, Diners

BROUGHTON-IN-FURNESS

Cumbria
Map ref 5A3

Old market village whose historic charter to hold fairs is still proclaimed every year on the first day of August in the market square. Good centre for touring the pretty Duddon Valley.

The Garner Guest House
APPROVED
Church Street,
Broughton-in-Furness LA20 6HJ
☎ (01229) 716462
Comfortable Victorian family house of character, with a sunny walled garden. On the outskirts of this old market town.
Bedrooms: 1 double, 1 twin
Bathrooms: 2 en-suite, 1 public

Bed & breakfast per night:	£min	£max
Single	23.00	
Double	40.00	

Evening meal from 1900

Manor Arms
The Square, Broughton-in-Furness LA20 6HY
☎ Barrow (01229) 716286
18th C family-run freehouse with a welcoming atmosphere, in a picturesque market town. Awards for range of excellent traditional ales, well-appointed bedrooms.
Bedrooms: 2 double, 1 triple
Bathrooms: 3 en-suite

Bed & breakfast per night:	£min	£max
Single	19.00	23.00
Double	28.00	42.00

Cards accepted: Access, Visa, Switch/Delta

BUTTERMERE

Cumbria
Map ref 5A3

Small village surrounded by high mountains, between Buttermere Lake and Crummock Water. An ideal centre for walking and climbing the nearby peaks and for touring.

Bridge Hotel
HIGHLY COMMENDED
Buttermere, Cockermouth
CA13 9UZ
☎ Keswick (017687) 70252
Fax (017687) 70252

Historic Lakeland hotel with modern comforts and facilities, in an Area of Outstanding Natural Beauty. Superb walking country.
Bedrooms: 2 single, 8 double, 12 twin
Bathrooms: 21 en-suite, 1 private

Bed & breakfast per night:	£min	£max
Single	35.00	40.00
Double	70.00	80.00

Half board per person:	£min	£max
Daily	45.00	59.00
Weekly	310.00	335.00

Lunch available
Evening meal 1900 (last orders 2030)
Parking for 60
Cards accepted: Access, Visa, Switch/Delta

The symbol (CR) and a group name following an hotel address indicates that bookings can be made through a central reservations office. These offices are listed in the information pages at the back of this guide.

The Fish Hotel
COMMENDED
Buttermere, Cockermouth
CA13 9XA
☎ (017687) 70253
Below Honister Pass and Newlands Hause between the twin lakes of Buttermere and Crummock Water. 2 comfortable lounges, one with a cocktail bar. Pleasant rooms, all en-suite.
Bedrooms: 6 double, 1 twin, 3 triple
Bathrooms: 10 en-suite, 2 public

Bed & breakfast per night:	£min	£max
Single	37.00	39.00
Double	60.00	

Half board per person:	£min	£max
Daily	34.00	36.00
Weekly	210.00	215.00

Lunch available
Evening meal from 1900
Parking for 35
Open March–November
Cards accepted: Access, Visa, Switch/Delta

Pickett Howe
DE LUXE
Buttermere Valley, Cockermouth
CA13 9UY
☎ Lorton (01900) 85444
Fax (01900) 85209

Recent National winner of English Tourist Board's England for Excellence award. Luxuriously appointed and peacefully situated 17th C farmhouse, renowned for creative cooking, relaxing atmosphere and jacuzzis!
Bedrooms: 3 double, 1 twin
Bathrooms: 4 en-suite

Bed & breakfast per night:	£min	£max
Double	72.00	72.00

Half board per person:	£min	£max
Daily	57.00	57.00
Weekly	371.00	371.00

Evening meal from 1915
Parking for 6
Open April–November
Cards accepted: Access, Visa

CUMBRIA

CALDBECK
Cumbria
Map ref 5A2

Quaint limestone village lying on the northern fringe of the Lake District National Park. John Peel, the famous huntsman who is immortalised in song, is buried in the churchyard. The fells surrounding Caldbeck were once heavily mined, being rich in lead, copper and barytes.

Parkend Restaurant and Country Hotel
COMMENDED

Parkend, Caldbeck, Wigton
CA7 8HH
☎ (016974) 78494
17th C farmhouse restaurant with en-suite rooms. Situated in Caldbeck in the wonderful walking country of the northern lakes. Fine food in tranquil surroundings.
Bedrooms: 3 double
Bathrooms: 3 en-suite

Bed & breakfast per night:	£min	£max
Single	24.00	32.00
Double		48.00

Evening meal 1730 (last orders 2200)
Parking for 16
Cards accepted: Access, Visa, Diners, Amex

CARLISLE
Cumbria
Map ref 5A2

Cumbria's only city is rich in history. Attractions include the small red sandstone cathedral and 900-year-old castle with magnificent view from the keep. Award-winning Tullie House Museum and Art Gallery brings 2,000 years of Border history dramatically to life. Excellent centre for shopping.
Tourist Information Centre ☎ *(01228) 512444*

Avondale
HIGHLY COMMENDED

3 St. Aidan's Road, Carlisle CA1 1LT
☎ (01228) 23012
Michael and Angela Hayes welcome you to their attractive Edwardian house. Comfortable, spacious rooms. Quiet situation. Private parking. Close to centre.
Bedrooms: 1 double, 2 twin
Bathrooms: 1 en-suite, 2 private, 1 public

Bed & breakfast per night:	£min	£max
Double	36.00	40.00

Evening meal 1830 (last orders 1200)
Parking for 3

Calreena Guest House
APPROVED

123 Warwick Road, Carlisle
CA1 1JZ
☎ (01228) 25020

Comfortable, friendly guesthouse. Central heating, home cooking. Colour TV and tea-making facilities in all rooms. 2 minutes from city centre, railway and bus stations and from M6, junction 43.
Bedrooms: 1 single, 1 double, 1 twin, 1 triple
Bathrooms: 2 public

Bed & breakfast per night:	£min	£max
Single	14.00	14.00
Double	25.00	25.00

Half board per person:	£min	£max
Daily	17.50	17.50
Weekly	119.00	119.00

Evening meal 1700 (last orders 1500)
Cards accepted: Access, Visa

Central Plaza Hotel

Victoria Viaduct, Carlisle CA3 8AL
☎ (01228) 20256
Fax (01228) 514457
Elegant hotel with modern comforts in traditional surroundings. Conference facilities. Group theme/entertainment breaks a speciality. Close to many attractions.
Bedrooms: 17 single, 29 double, 35 twin, 3 triple
Bathrooms: 84 en-suite

Bed & breakfast per night:	£min	£max
Single	60.00	70.00
Double	80.00	95.00

Half board per person:	£min	£max
Daily	70.00	85.00

Lunch available
Evening meal 1900 (last orders 2115)

Parking for 15
Cards accepted: Access, Visa, Amex

Chatsworth Guesthouse
COMMENDED

22 Chatsworth Square, Carlisle
CA1 1HF
☎ (01228) 24023
Ornate city centre listed Victorian town house in quiet conservation area overlooking Chatsworth Gardens. 5 minutes from bus and rail stations, convenient for Sands Centre (sports and leisure). Street parking.
Bedrooms: 1 single, 1 double, 3 twin, 1 family room
Bathrooms: 3 en-suite, 1 public

Bed & breakfast per night:	£min	£max
Single	15.00	17.00
Double	26.00	38.00

Half board per person:	£min	£max
Daily	21.00	23.00
Weekly	140.00	150.00

Evening meal 1700 (last orders 1830)
Cards accepted: Access, Visa, Amex

Corner House Hotel and Bar
APPROVED

4 Grey Street, Off London Road, Carlisle CA1 2JP
☎ (01228) 33239
Fax (01228) 46628
Warm welcome for short or long stay guests. Good food, bar, games room, Sky TV in lounge. All rooms en-suite, four- poster beds. Easy access bus/train and M6 junctions 42/43.
Bedrooms: 4 single, 3 double, 2 twin, 1 triple
Bathrooms: 10 en-suite, 1 public

Bed & breakfast per night:	£min	£max
Single	20.00	25.00
Double	35.00	40.00

Half board per person:	£min	£max
Daily	23.50	33.50
Weekly	160.00	210.00

Lunch available
Evening meal 1730 (last orders 2030)

You are advised to confirm your booking in writing.

CUMBRIA

Cornerways Guest House
107 Warwick Road, Carlisle
CA1 1EA
☎ (01228) 21733
Five minutes to rail and bus stations and city centre. M6 exit 43. Colour TV, central heating in all bedrooms. Tea and coffee facilities. Lounge, pool table, payphone.
Bedrooms: 3 single, 1 double, 4 twin, 1 triple, 1 family room
Bathrooms: 1 en-suite, 2 public
Bed & breakfast

per night:	£min	£max
Single	14.00	16.00
Double	26.00	32.00

Half board per

person:	£min	£max
Daily	19.00	21.00
Weekly	125.00	140.00

Evening meal 1600 (last orders 1900)
Parking for 6

County Hotel
COMMENDED
9 Botchergate, Carlisle CA1 1QP
☎ (01228) 31316
Fax (01228) 515456
Built in 1853 and extensively refurbished with every modern convenience. City centre location, adjacent to railway station. Parking on premises.
Bedrooms: 27 single, 16 double, 27 twin, 10 triple, 4 family rooms
Bathrooms: 84 en-suite
Bed & breakfast

per night:	£min	£max
Single	42.94	71.94
Double	55.93	78.93

Half board per

person:	£min	£max
Daily	55.89	84.89

Lunch available
Evening meal 1900 (last orders 2145)
Parking for 100
Cards accepted: Access, Visa, Diners, Amex

Crosby Lodge Country House Hotel
HIGHLY COMMENDED
High Crosby, Crosby-on-Eden, Carlisle CA6 4QZ
☎ Crosby-on-Eden (01228) 573618
Fax (01228) 573428

18th C country mansion overlooking parkland and the river. Chef/proprietor provides a varied English and continental menu. Full afternoon teas available on request.
Bedrooms: 1 single, 4 double, 3 twin, 3 triple
Bathrooms: 11 en-suite
Bed & breakfast

per night:	£min	£max
Single	68.00	70.00
Double	95.00	115.00

Half board per

person:	£min	£max
Daily	75.00	85.00
Weekly	490.00	525.00

Lunch available
Evening meal 1930 (last orders 2100)
Parking for 40
Open February–December
Cards accepted: Access, Visa, Amex, Switch/Delta

Kates Guest House
6 Lazonby Terrace, London Road, Carlisle CA1 2PZ
☎ (01228) 39577
Tastefully decorated refurbished town house, offering a warm Cumbrian welcome, comfortable accommodation, delicious home cooking and a relaxing atmosphere. All rooms have satellite TV and welcome tray.
Bedrooms: 1 single, 2 twin
Bathrooms: 1 public
Bed & breakfast

per night:	£min	£max
Single	15.00	17.50
Double	25.00	30.00

Half board per

person:	£min	£max
Daily	17.50	22.50
Weekly	122.50	140.00

Lunch available
Evening meal 1800 (last orders 2100)

Number Thirty One
DE LUXE
31 Howard Place, Carlisle CA1 1HR
☎ (01228) 597080
Fax (01228) 597080
Number Thirty One Howard Place has recently been restored by Philip and Judith into a gracious, comfortable home, furnished in period with pictures, ornaments and china. All rooms provide private bath, shower and toilet.
Bedrooms: 1 single, 2 double
Bathrooms: 3 en-suite
Bed & breakfast

per night:	£min	£max
Single	35.00	40.00
Double	40.00	50.00

Half board per

person:	£min	£max
Daily	32.50	40.00
Weekly	227.50	280.00

Evening meal 1800 (last orders 1930)
Open February–December

Royal Hotel
APPROVED
9 Lowther Street, Carlisle CA3 8ES
☎ (01228) 22103
Fax (01228) 23904
Family-run hotel. All bedrooms have colour TV. Breakfast, bar lunches and evening meals served.
Bedrooms: 8 single, 4 double, 8 twin, 3 triple
Bathrooms: 16 en-suite, 3 public
Bed & breakfast

per night:	£min	£max
Single	21.00	30.00
Double	35.00	46.00

Half board per

person:	£min	£max
Daily	26.00	38.00

Lunch available
Evening meal 1830 (last orders 2030)
Cards accepted: Access, Visa

Swallow Hilltop Hotel
COMMENDED
London Road, Carlisle CA1 2PQ
☎ (01228) 29255
Fax (01228) 25238
Swallow
Modern comfortable hotel with leisure facilities. Ideal touring base for the Border, Lakes, Roman Wall and the Solway Coast. Special cabaret weekends. Short break packages available.
Bedrooms: 2 single, 38 double, 52 twin
Bathrooms: 92 en-suite
Bed & breakfast

per night:	£min	£max
Single	65.00	85.00
Double	79.00	95.00

Continued ▶

CUMBRIA

CARLISLE
Continued

Half board per person: £min £max
Daily 82.95 102.95

Lunch available
Evening meal 1900 (last orders 2200)
Parking for 350
Cards accepted: Access, Visa, Diners, Amex

CARTMEL

Cumbria
Map ref 5A3

Picturesque conserved village based on a 12th C priory with a well-preserved church and gatehouse. Just half a mile outside the Lake District National Park, this is a peaceful base for walking and touring, with historic houses and beautiful scenery.

Aynsome Manor Hotel
HIGHLY COMMENDED

Cartmel, Grange-over-Sands
LA11 6HH
☎ (015395) 36653
Fax (015395) 36016

Lovely old manor house, nestling in the vale of Cartmel. Good food, attentive service and log fire comfort. Lunches served on Sundays. No smoking in restaurant.
Bedrooms: 6 double, 4 twin, 2 triple
Bathrooms: 12 en-suite, 1 public

Half board per person: £min £max
Daily 43.00 60.00
Weekly 285.00 285.00

Evening meal 1900 (last orders 2030)
Parking for 20
Open February–December
Cards accepted: Access, Visa, Amex, Switch/Delta

The Cavendish at Cartmel
Listed COMMENDED

Cavendish Street, Cartmel,
Grange-over-Sands LA11 6QA
☎ (015395) 36240 & 0860 700334
Fax (015395) 36620
Cartmel's oldest hostelry, voted best pub 1996 by Good Pub Guide for its award-winning beers. Very popular with locals and visitors.
Bedrooms: 5 double, 2 twin
Bathrooms: 7 en-suite

Bed & breakfast per night: £min £max
Single 25.00 30.00
Double 46.00 60.00

Half board per person: £min £max
Daily 37.50 45.00
Weekly 210.00 250.00

Lunch available
Evening meal 1800 (last orders 2130)
Parking for 20
Cards accepted: Access, Visa

The Grammar Hotel
COMMENDED

Cartmel, Grange-over-Sands
LA11 7SG
☎ (015395) 36367
Fax (015395) 36026
Minotel

17th C country hotel in beautiful Vale of Cartmel. All rooms en-suite, with colour TV and tea-making facilities. Peace, tranquillity and good food guaranteed. Non-smoking restaurant.
Bedrooms: 5 double, 3 twin, 1 triple, 1 family room
Bathrooms: 10 en-suite

Bed & breakfast per night: £min £max
Single 36.00 42.00
Double 58.00 72.00

Half board per person: £min £max
Daily 44.00 50.00
Weekly 280.00 320.00

Lunch available
Evening meal 1830 (last orders 2030)
Parking for 50
Open March–December
Cards accepted: Access, Visa, Amex

A key to symbols can be found inside the back cover flap.

CLEATOR

Cumbria
Map ref 5A3

6 miles from the Georgian port of Whitehaven and with easy access to the western fells. Features a grotto similar to that in Lourdes, France.

Grove Court
COMMENDED

Cleator Gate, Cleator CA23 3DT
☎ Cleator Moor (01946) 810503
Fax (01946) 815412
Family-run hotel with reputation for food. Convenient for Lake District and Solway coast. Popular meeting place for meals.
Bedrooms: 2 single, 5 double, 4 twin
Suite available
Bathrooms: 11 en-suite

Bed & breakfast per night: £min £max
Single 47.50 55.00
Double 65.00 75.00

Lunch available
Evening meal 1900 (last orders 2200)
Parking for 100
Cards accepted: Access, Visa, Diners, Amex

COCKERMOUTH

Cumbria
Map ref 5A2

Ancient market town at confluence of Rivers Cocker and Derwent. Birthplace of William Wordsworth in 1770. The house where he was born is at the end of the town's broad, tree-lined main street and is now owned by the National Trust. Good touring base for the Lakes. *Tourist Information Centre* ☎ *(01900) 822634*

Rose Cottage
COMMENDED

Lorton Road, Cockermouth
CA13 9DX
☎ (01900) 822189

In a pleasant position, this guesthouse is within easy reach of the Lakes and the coast.
Bedrooms: 3 double, 1 twin, 2 triple
Bathrooms: 3 en-suite, 2 public

CUMBRIA

Bed & breakfast

per night:	£min	£max
Single	20.00	25.00
Double	30.00	42.00

Half board per

person:	£min	£max
Daily	25.00	30.00
Weekly	175.00	210.00

Evening meal 1900 (last orders 2030)
Parking for 12
Cards accepted: Access, Visa, Amex

The Shepherds Hotel

COMMENDED

Egremont Road, Cockermouth CA13 0QX
☎ (01900) 822673
Fax (01900) 822673

All rooms have modern decor and facilities to suit both tourist and business clientele. Sky TV in all rooms.
Bedrooms: 4 double, 9 twin
Bathrooms: 13 en-suite

Bed & breakfast

per night:	£min	£max
Single	35.00	40.00
Double	35.00	40.00

Half board per

person:	£min	£max
Daily	31.00	50.00
Weekly	217.00	350.00

Lunch available
Evening meal 1800 (last orders 2130)
Parking for 100
Cards accepted: Access, Visa, Switch/Delta

Trout Hotel

HIGHLY COMMENDED

Crown Street, Cockermouth CA13 0EJ
☎ (01900) 823591
Fax (01900) 827514

Attractive black and white listed building, dating from c 1670, on banks of River Derwent adjacent to own award-winning gardens. 12 miles west of Keswick off A66.
Bedrooms: 6 single, 12 double, 2 twin, 1 triple, 1 family room
Suites available
Bathrooms: 22 en-suite

Bed & breakfast

per night:	£min	£max
Single	59.95	95.00
Double	76.95	120.00

Half board per

person:	£min	£max
Daily	45.00	95.00
Weekly	315.00	390.00

Lunch available
Evening meal 1900 (last orders 2130)
Parking for 50
Cards accepted: Access, Visa, Amex, Switch/Delta

CONISTON

Cumbria
Map ref 5A3

The 803m fell Coniston Old Man dominates the skyline to the east of this village at the northern end of Coniston Water. Arthur Ransome set his "Swallows and Amazons" stories here. Coniston's most famous resident was John Ruskin, whose home, Brantwood, is open to the public. Good centre for walking.

Black Bull Hotel

COMMENDED

Yewdale Road, Coniston LA21 8DU
☎ Windermere (015394) 41335
Fax (015394) 41168

16th C old world inn, Known for fine food and comfort. Real ales from on-site "micro" brewery are served in the bar. Special offers on room rates during the year - ask for details.
Bedrooms: 2 single, 10 double, 3 twin
Bathrooms: 15 en-suite, 1 public

Bed & breakfast

per night:	£min	£max
Single	35.00	
Double	59.00	

Lunch available
Evening meal 1730 (last orders 2130)
Parking for 20
Cards accepted: Access, Visa, Switch/Delta

Coniston Lodge

HIGHLY COMMENDED

Sunny Brow, Coniston LA21 8HH
☎ (015394) 41201

Small family-run hotel in beautiful surroundings, offering superior accommodation and good home cooking. Non-smoking.
Bedrooms: 3 double, 3 twin
Bathrooms: 6 en-suite

Bed & breakfast

per night:	£min	£max
Single	27.00	40.00
Double	54.00	80.00

Half board per

person:	£min	£max
Daily	43.00	56.00
Weekly	301.00	332.50

Evening meal 1900 (last orders 1930)
Parking for 9
Cards accepted: Access, Visa, Amex

Crown Hotel

APPROVED

Coniston LA21 8EA
☎ (015394) 41243
Fax (015394) 41804

At the foot of Coniston Old Man, 10 minutes' walk to the lake where Donald Campbell attempted to break the world water speed record.
Bedrooms: 4 double, 1 twin, 3 triple
Bathrooms: 1 private, 2 public

Bed & breakfast

per night:	£min	£max
Single	20.00	25.00
Double	36.00	40.00

Half board per

person:	£min	£max
Daily	25.00	45.00
Weekly	160.00	350.00

Lunch available
Evening meal 1900 (last orders 2100)
Parking for 30
Cards accepted: Access, Visa, Diners, Amex, Switch/Delta

Old Rectory Hotel

HIGHLY COMMENDED

Torver, Coniston LA21 8AY
☎ (015394) 41353
Fax (015394) 41156

Tastefully converted rectory offering delightful accommodation, set in 3 acres with pastoral views. Imaginative cooking in conservatory dining room. Superb local walks.
Bedrooms: 4 double, 2 twin, 1 triple
Bathrooms: 7 en-suite

Bed & breakfast

per night:	£min	£max
Single	17.50	29.50
Double	35.00	73.00

Continued ▶

For ideas on places to visit refer to the introduction at the beginning of this section.

CUMBRIA

CONISTON
Continued

Half board per person:
	£min	£max
Daily	29.50	48.50
Weekly	189.00	318.00

Evening meal 1930 (last orders 1930)
Parking for 10
Cards accepted: Access, Visa

Sun Hotel Coniston
COMMENDED
Coniston LA21 8HQ
☎ (015394) 41248

Country house hotel and 16th C inn, in spectacular mountain setting on the fringe of the village and at the foot of the Coniston Old Man.
Bedrooms: 1 single, 7 double, 3 twin
Bathrooms: 9 en-suite, 2 private

Bed & breakfast per night:
	£min	£max
Single	25.00	45.00
Double	50.00	70.00

Half board per person:
	£min	£max
Daily	40.00	60.00
Weekly	280.00	420.00

Lunch available
Evening meal 1900 (last orders 2045)
Parking for 20
Cards accepted: Access, Visa, Diners

Wheelgate Country House Hotel
HIGHLY COMMENDED
Little Arrow, Torver, Coniston LA21 8AU
☎ (015394) 41418
Delightful 17th C country house with attractive bedrooms, oak-beamed lounge and dining room. Excellent restaurant. Complimentary leisure facilities. Perfect Lakeland retreat.
Bedrooms: 2 single, 6 double
Bathrooms: 8 en-suite

Bed & breakfast per night:
	£min	£max
Single	27.00	34.00
Double	48.00	68.00

Half board per person:
	£min	£max
Daily	41.00	51.00
Weekly	245.00	308.00

Evening meal 1930 (last orders 1930)
Parking for 8
Open March–November
Cards accepted: Access, Visa, Amex

Yewdale Hotel
COMMENDED
Yewdale Road, Coniston LA21 8LU
☎ (015394) 41280
Fax (015394) 41662
Built of local materials in 1896 as a bank, now a modern hotel skilfully refurbished throughout. Reduced rate breaks available.
Bedrooms: 5 double, 1 twin, 2 triple, 2 family rooms
Bathrooms: 9 en-suite, 1 private

Bed & breakfast per night:
	£min	£max
Single	21.95	31.50
Double	43.90	63.00

Half board per person:
	£min	£max
Daily	32.90	42.45
Weekly	148.89	189.00

Lunch available
Evening meal (last orders 2100)
Parking for 6
Cards accepted: Access, Visa, Switch/Delta

CROSTHWAITE
Cumbria
Map ref 5A3

Small village in the picturesque Lyth Valley off the A5074. St Kentigern's church is home to a memorial of the poet Robert Southey. The valley itself is famous for its Damson plums.

Crosthwaite House
HIGHLY COMMENDED
Crosthwaite, Kendal LA8 8BP
☎ (015395) 68264
Mid-18th C building with unspoilt views of the Lyth and Winster valleys, 5 miles from Bowness and Kendal. Family atmosphere and home cooking. Self-catering cottages also available.
Bedrooms: 1 single, 3 double, 2 twin
Bathrooms: 6 en-suite

Bed & breakfast per night:
	£min	£max
Single	20.00	22.00
Double	40.00	44.00

Half board per person:
	£min	£max
Daily	32.00	34.00
Weekly	210.00	225.00

Evening meal 1900 (last orders 1900)
Parking for 10
Open March–November
Cards accepted: Amex

DENT
Cumbria
Map ref 5B3

Very picturesque village with narrow cobbled streets, lying within the boundaries of the Yorkshire Dales National Park.

George & Dragon Hotel
COMMENDED
Main Street, Dent, Sedbergh LA10 5QL
☎ (01539) 625256
Excellent centre for exploring the Yorkshire Dales National Park. Owned by, and serves beer from, Dent's own small brewery.
Bedrooms: 4 double, 3 twin, 2 triple
Bathrooms: 3 private, 2 public

Bed & breakfast per night:
	£min	£max
Single	25.00	33.00
Double	40.00	50.00

Half board per person:
	£min	£max
Daily	30.00	35.00
Weekly	190.00	220.00

Lunch available
Evening meal 1900 (last orders 2200)
Parking for 14
Cards accepted: Access, Visa

EGREMONT
Cumbria
Map ref 5A3

Old market town with a wide tree-lined street. One of its attractions is the 12th C Norman castle built of red sandstone.
Tourist Information Centre ☎ (01946) 820693

Old Vicarage Guest House
Listed COMMENDED
Thornhill, Egremont CA22 2NX
☎ Beckermet (01946) 841577
Imposing 19th C vicarage of character in attractive grounds. Within easy reach of sea and mountains.

CUMBRIA

Bedrooms: 3 triple
Bathrooms: 2 public

Bed & breakfast per night:	£min	£max
Single	13.50	15.50
Double	27.00	31.00

Parking for 6

ENDMOOR

Cumbria
Map ref 5B3

Village situated between Kendal and Kirkby Lonsdale on the A65, convenient for touring South Lakes and for the M6.

Summerlands Tower

HIGHLY COMMENDED

Endmoor, Kendal LA8 0ED
☎ Sedgwick (015395) 61081
Fine Victorian country guesthouse offering spacious and tastefully decorated accommodation, surrounded by 3 acres of mature gardens and woodlands. 3 miles from M6 junction 36.
Bedrooms: 1 double, 1 twin
Bathrooms: 1 en-suite, 1 private

Bed & breakfast per night:	£min	£max
Single	24.50	29.50
Double	39.00	49.00

Parking for 6

ESKDALE

Cumbria
Map ref 5A3

Several minor roads lead to the west end of this beautiful valley, or it can be approached via the east over the Hardknott Pass, the Lake District's steepest pass. Scafell Pike and Bow Fell lie to the north and a miniature railway links the Eskdale Valley with Ravenglass on the coast.

Bower House Inn

COMMENDED

Eskdale CA19 1TD
☎ (019467) 23244
Fax (019467) 23308
A 17th C inn, full of charm and character, in one of Lakeland's loveliest valleys. All rooms en-suite. Good food, real ales, conference facilities. Ideal for walking, touring or business.
Bedrooms: 3 single, 11 double, 7 twin, 3 triple
Bathrooms: 24 en-suite

Bed & breakfast per night:	£min	£max
Single	40.00	48.00
Double	60.00	64.00

Half board per person:	£min	£max
Daily	49.50	67.50
Weekly	294.00	378.00

Lunch available
Evening meal 1900 (last orders 2030)
Parking for 60
Cards accepted: Access, Visa, Amex, Switch/Delta

Woolpack Inn

APPROVED

Boot, Eskdale CA19 1TH
☎ (01946) 723230
Fax (01946) 723230
Comfortable hotel serving real ale and home-cooked food, set in beautiful scenery at the head of the Eskdale Valley.
Bedrooms: 3 double, 4 twin, 1 family room
Bathrooms: 1 public, 4 private showers

Bed & breakfast per night:	£min	£max
Single	19.50	24.50
Double	39.00	49.00

Half board per person:	£min	£max
Daily	24.45	38.45
Weekly	175.00	270.00

Lunch available
Evening meal 1830 (last orders 2100)
Parking for 40
Cards accepted: Access, Visa

GOSFORTH

Cumbria
Map ref 5A3

This large village lies on the western boundary of the Lake District National Park. Noted for its famous 14 ft high 10th C cross which stands in the churchyard and bears Christian, pagan and Norse symbols.

Westlakes Hotel and Restaurant

Gosforth, Seascale CA20 1HP
☎ (019467) 25221
Fax (019467) 25099
Traditional Georgian country house hotel set in 2.5 acres of well

maintained grounds with views of Scafell and Wasdale. Prices per room.
Bedrooms: 2 single, 5 double, 1 twin, 1 triple
Bathrooms: 9 en-suite

Bed & breakfast per night:	£min	£max
Single	44.50	46.00
Double	46.50	53.50

Lunch available
Evening meal 1900 (last orders 2100)
Parking for 20
Cards accepted: Access, Visa, Amex

GRANGE-OVER-SANDS

Cumbria
Map ref 5A3

Set on the beautiful Cartmel Peninsula, this tranquil resort, known as Lakeland's Riviera, overlooks Morecambe Bay. Pleasant seafront walks and beautiful gardens. The bay attracts many species of wading birds.

Clare House

COMMENDED

Park Road, Grange-over-Sands LA11 7HQ
☎ (015395) 33026 & 34253

Charming hotel with well-appointed bedrooms and pleasant lounges, set in grounds with magnificent bay views. Delightful meals prepared from the best ingredients.
Bedrooms: 3 single, 2 double, 11 twin, 1 triple
Bathrooms: 16 en-suite, 1 public

Bed & breakfast per night:	£min	£max
Single	29.50	30.00
Double	59.00	60.00

Half board per person:	£min	£max
Daily	41.00	44.00
Weekly	255.00	270.00

Lunch available
Evening meal 1845 (last orders 1915)
Parking for 16
Open April–October

CUMBRIA

GRANGE-OVER-SANDS
Continued

The Cumbria Grand Hotel
COMMENDED

Lindale Road, Grange-over-Sands
LA11 6EN
☎ (015395) 32331
Fax (015395) 34534

In 25 acres of grounds overlooking Morecambe Bay, with easy access to the M6 and the Lake District. Tennis court, trim trail, snooker room.
Bedrooms: 12 single, 23 double, 82 twin, 6 triple
Bathrooms: 123 en-suite

Bed & breakfast per night:	£min	£max
Single	39.00	48.00
Double	58.00	76.00

Half board per person:	£min	£max
Daily	44.00	53.00
Weekly	190.00	217.00

Lunch available
Evening meal 1830 (last orders 2030)
Parking for 120
Cards accepted: Access, Visa, Diners, Amex, Switch/Delta

Elton Hotel
COMMENDED

Windermere Road,
Grange-over-Sands LA11 6EQ
☎ (015395) 32838
A warm, generous welcome, good food and superior accommodation. An ideal base for exploring the impressive Lakeland scenery.
Bedrooms: 4 double, 2 twin, 1 family room
Bathrooms: 5 en-suite, 2 private showers

Bed & breakfast per night:	£min	£max
Single	27.00	31.00
Double	44.00	52.00

Evening meal 2100 (last orders 2200)
Open March–December

Hampsfell House Hotel
COMMENDED

Hampsfell Road, Grange-over-Sands
LA11 6BG
☎ (015395) 32567
Peaceful country setting in own grounds. Fresh and imaginatively prepared food. Extensive wine list. Ample safe parking.
Bedrooms: 4 double, 4 twin, 1 triple
Bathrooms: 9 en-suite, 1 public

Bed & breakfast per night:	£min	£max
Single	25.00	30.00
Double	50.00	58.00

Half board per person:	£min	£max
Daily	35.00	45.00
Weekly	230.00	250.00

Lunch available
Evening meal 1830 (last orders 2030)
Parking for 20
Cards accepted: Access, Visa

Mayfields
COMMENDED

3 Mayfield Terrace, Kents Bank Road, Grange-over-Sands
LA11 7DW
☎ (015395) 34730
Victorian terraced town house, tastefully furnished and equipped to a high standard. In a pleasant position on fringe of town close to promenade and open countryside.
Bedrooms: 1 single, 1 double, 1 twin
Bathrooms: 2 en-suite, 1 private shower

Bed & breakfast per night:	£min	£max
Single	17.00	18.00
Double	37.00	39.00

Half board per person:	£min	£max
Daily	26.00	28.50
Weekly	173.00	189.00

Lunch available
Evening meal from 1830
Parking for 3

Netherwood Hotel
COMMENDED

Grange-over-Sands LA11 6ET
☎ (015395) 32552
Fax (015395) 34121
Built in 1893 and a building of high architectural and historic interest.
Wheelchair access category 3
Bedrooms: 4 single, 10 double, 8 twin, 3 triple, 4 family rooms
Bathrooms: 29 en-suite, 2 public

Bed & breakfast per night:	£min	£max
Single	45.00	55.00
Double	90.00	110.00

Half board per person:	£min	£max
Daily	61.00	71.00
Weekly	420.00	483.00

Lunch available
Evening meal 1900 (last orders 2030)
Parking for 160
Cards accepted: Access, Visa, Switch/Delta

GRASMERE
Cumbria
Map ref 5A3

Described by William Wordsworth as "the loveliest spot that man hath ever found", this village, famous for its gingerbread, is in a beautiful setting overlooked by Helm Grag. Wordsworth lived at Dove Cottage. The cottage and museum are open to the public.

Bridge House Hotel
COMMENDED

Stock Lane, Grasmere, Ambleside
LA22 9SN
☎ (015394) 35425
Fax (015394) 35523
Comfortable hotel, close to the village centre, in 2 acres of garden. Relaxing atmosphere, home cooking and ample parking. Room with four-poster available for special occasions, such as honeymoon and anniversary.
Bedrooms: 2 single, 6 double, 4 twin
Bathrooms: 12 en-suite

Bed & breakfast per night:	£min	£max
Single	25.00	37.00
Double	50.00	74.00

Half board per person:	£min	£max
Daily	35.00	47.50
Weekly	235.00	287.50

Evening meal 1900 (last orders 1930)
Parking for 20
Open February–November and Christmas
Cards accepted: Access, Visa, Switch/Delta

Please mention this guide when making your booking.

CUMBRIA

The Grasmere Hotel
HIGHLY COMMENDED
Grasmere, Ambleside LA22 9TA
☎ (015394) 35277
Fax (015394) 35277
In the midst of beautiful mountain scenery with the restaurant overlooking a large garden, the river and surrounding hills.
Bedrooms: 1 single, 9 double, 2 twin
Bathrooms: 11 en-suite, 1 private shower

Bed & breakfast per night:
	£min	£max
Single	20.00	30.00
Double	40.00	60.00

Half board per person:
	£min	£max
Daily	30.00	50.00
Weekly	175.00	350.00

Evening meal 1930 (last orders 2030)
Parking for 16
Open February–December
Cards accepted: Access, Visa

Lake View Country House
COMMENDED
Lake View Drive, Grasmere, Ambleside LA22 9TD
☎ (015394) 35384
In private grounds overlooking the lake and with private access. Located in the village but off the main road.
Bedrooms: 1 single, 4 double, 1 twin
Bathrooms: 3 en-suite, 1 public

Bed & breakfast per night:
	£min	£max
Single	24.00	28.00
Double	48.00	56.00

Half board per person:
	£min	£max
Daily	33.50	37.50
Weekly	225.00	253.00

Evening meal 1830 (last orders 1500)
Parking for 10
Open February–November

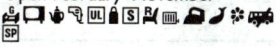

Moss Grove Hotel
COMMENDED
Grasmere, Ambleside LA22 9SW
☎ (015394) 35251
Fax (015394) 35691
Minotel

Elegant Lakeland hotel. Some four-poster bedrooms with south-facing balconies. Cosy bar, conservatory, sauna and use of adjacent indoor swimming pool.
Bedrooms: 2 single, 7 double, 3 twin, 1 triple, 1 family room
Bathrooms: 13 en-suite, 2 public

Bed & breakfast per night:
	£min	£max
Single	25.00	38.50
Double	50.00	77.00

Half board per person:
	£min	£max
Daily	33.00	56.00
Weekly	237.00	338.00

Lunch available
Evening meal 1930 (last orders 2030)
Parking for 16
Open February–November
Cards accepted: Access, Visa, Switch/Delta

Oak Bank Hotel
Broadgate, Grasmere, LA22 9TA
☎ (015394) 35217
Fax (015395) 35685

Built 100 years ago in Lakeland stone and now modernised throughout. Cordon bleu cuisine, good cellar - pamper yourself with people who care.
Bedrooms: 1 single, 9 double, 4 twin, 1 family room
Bathrooms: 15 en-suite

Bed & breakfast per night:
	£min	£max
Single	25.00	45.00
Double	50.00	90.00

Half board per person:
	£min	£max
Daily	30.00	59.00
Weekly	250.00	350.00

Evening meal 1900 (last orders 2300)
Parking for 15
Open February–December
Cards accepted: Access, Visa, Switch/Delta

Redmayne
HIGHLY COMMENDED
Keswick Road, Grasmere, Ambleside LA22 9QY
☎ (015394) 35635
Superb private situation overlooking the Vale of Grasmere. Comfortable, beautifully appointed en-suite bedrooms. Non-smoking. Private parking.
Bedrooms: 1 double, 1 twin
Bathrooms: 2 en-suite

Bed & breakfast per night:
	£min	£max
Double	36.00	48.00

Parking for 2
Open February–November

The Swan
HIGHLY COMMENDED
Grasmere, Ambleside LA22 9RF
☎ (015394) 35551
Fax (015394) 35741
Forte
A homely hotel at the foot of Dunmail Raise on the Windermere to Keswick road.
Bedrooms: 2 single, 20 double, 14 twin
Bathrooms: 36 en-suite

Bed & breakfast per night:
	£min	£max
Single	40.00	70.00
Double	70.00	130.00

Half board per person:
	£min	£max
Daily	50.00	80.00
Weekly	300.00	450.00

Lunch available
Evening meal 1900 (last orders 2100)
Parking for 40
Cards accepted: Access, Visa, Diners, Amex

Please check prices and other details at the time of booking.

Establishments should be open throughout the year, unless otherwise stated.

A key to symbols can be found inside the back cover flap.

CUMBRIA

GREAT LANGDALE

Cumbria
Map ref 5A3

Picturesque valley at the foot of the Langdale Pikes, popular with walkers and climbers of every ability, with some of the Lake District's loveliest waterfalls.

New Dungeon Ghyll Hotel

Great Langdale, Ambleside LA22 9JY
☎ Langdale (015394) 37213
Fax (015394) 37666
An early Victorian hotel set in its own lawned gardens, at the head of the famed Langdale Valley.
Bedrooms: 11 double, 5 twin
Bathrooms: 16 en-suite

Bed & breakfast per night:

	£min	£max
Single	45.00	45.00
Double	70.00	70.00

Half board per person:

	£min	£max
Daily	47.50	47.50
Weekly	300.00	300.00

Lunch available
Evening meal 1900 (last orders 2100)
Parking for 18
Cards accepted: Access, Visa, Amex, Switch/Delta

HAWKSHEAD

Cumbria
Map ref 5A3

Lying near Esthwaite Water, this village has great charm and character. Its small squares are linked by flagged or cobbled alleys and the main square is dominated by the market house, or Shambles, where the butchers had their stalls in days gone by.

Greenbank House Hotel

Hawkshead, Ambleside LA22 0NS
☎ (015394) 36497
Well-appointed family-run country house hotel in this picturesque village. Central for all activities. Good home cooking.
Bedrooms: 3 single, 7 double, 2 twin
Bathrooms: 5 en-suite, 3 public

Bed & breakfast per night:

	£min	£max
Single	21.00	23.00
Double	42.00	50.00

Half board per person:

	£min	£max
Daily	32.50	36.00
Weekly	206.50	217.00

Evening meal 1830 (last orders 1600)
Parking for 12

Grizedale Lodge Hotel & Restaurant in the Forest

COMMENDED

Grizedale, Hawkshead, Ambleside LA22 0QL
☎ (015394) 36532
Fax (015394) 36572
Comfortable former shooting lodge with sun-terrace and log fires. In magnificent Grizedale Forest, midway between Coniston and Windermere. Close to forest walks and sculpture trails.
Bedrooms: 6 double, 2 twin, 1 triple
Bathrooms: 9 en-suite

Bed & breakfast per night:

	£min	£max
Single	37.50	46.50
Double	65.00	75.00

Half board per person:

	£min	£max
Daily	40.00	52.50
Weekly	250.00	315.00

Lunch available
Evening meal 1900 (last orders 2030)
Parking for 25
Open February–December
Cards accepted: Access, Visa, Amex, Switch/Delta

Queens Head Hotel

COMMENDED

Main Street, Hawkshead, Ambleside LA22 0NS
☎ Ambleside (015394) 36271
Fax (015394) 36722
Located between Lakes Windermere and Coniston. The home of Beatrix Potter, Wordsworth's grammar school and Ann Tyson's cottage. Fishing and bowling green facilities available.
Bedrooms: 10 double, 1 twin, 2 triple
Bathrooms: 11 en-suite, 2 private, 2 public

Bed & breakfast per night:

	£min	£max
Single	35.00	45.00
Double	53.00	70.00

Half board per person:

	£min	£max
Daily		
Weekly	233.00	260.00

Lunch available
Evening meal 1815 (last orders 2130)
Cards accepted: Access, Visa, Switch/Delta

Silverholme

COMMENDED

Graythwaite LA12 8AZ
☎ Newby Bridge (015395) 31332

Set in its own grounds, overlooking Lake Windermere and with lake access, this small mansion house provides a quiet, comfortable, relaxed atmosphere. Home cooking.
Bedrooms: 1 double, 1 triple, 1 family room
Bathrooms: 2 en-suite, 1 private

Bed & breakfast per night:

	£min	£max
Single	29.50	32.00
Double	43.00	46.00

Half board per person:

	£min	£max
Daily	34.00	36.00
Weekly	210.00	226.00

Lunch available
Evening meal 1800 (last orders 1800)
Parking for 7

HELTON

Cumbria
Map ref 5B3

"A place on the side of a hill", Helton nestles in a quiet, undisturbed corner of the Lakes yet has easy access to Penrith and junction 40 of the M6.

Beckfoot Country House

COMMENDED

Helton, Penrith CA10 2QB
☎ Bampton (01931) 713241
Fax (01931) 713391
Logis of Great Britain
Nestling in the Lakeland Fells of the Lowther Valley near Haweswater. Ideal walking base. M6 exit 39 (south) and 40 (north).
Bedrooms: 1 single, 2 double, 2 twin, 1 triple
Bathrooms: 6 en-suite

CUMBRIA

Bed & breakfast per night:	£min	£max
Single	26.00	30.00
Double	52.00	60.00

Half board per person:	£min	£max
Daily	40.00	44.00

Evening meal 1900 (last orders 1930)
Parking for 12
Open March–November
Cards accepted: Amex

HEVERSHAM

Cumbria
Map ref 5B3

This attractive village is set on a hill, and has a grammar school founded in 1613.

The Blue Bell at Heversham
HIGHLY COMMENDED

Princes Way, Heversham, Milnthorpe LA7 7EE
☎ Milnthorpe (015395) 62018
Fax (015395) 62455

Country hotel in a rural haven, an ideal touring centre. Adjacent to A6 south of Kendal.
Bedrooms: 1 single, 14 double, 6 twin, 1 triple
Bathrooms: 22 en-suite

Bed & breakfast per night:	£min	£max
Single	37.50	49.50
Double	64.00	95.00

Half board per person:	£min	£max
Daily	55.50	67.50

Lunch available
Evening meal 1900 (last orders 2130)
Parking for 100
Cards accepted: Access, Visa, Amex, Switch/Delta

For ideas on places to visit refer to the introduction at the beginning of this section.

KENDAL

Cumbria
Map ref 5B3

The "Auld Grey Town" lies in the valley of the River Kent with a backcloth of limestone fells. Situated just outside the Lake District National Park, it is a good centre for touring the Lakes and surrounding country. Ruined castle, reputed birthplace of Catherine Parr.
Tourist Information Centre ☎ (01539) 725758

Brantholme
Listed COMMENDED

7 Sedbergh Road, Kendal LA9 6AD
☎ (01539) 722340
Family-run guesthouse in own grounds. All rooms with private facilities. Good meals from fresh local produce.
Bedrooms: 3 twin
Bathrooms: 2 en-suite, 1 private

Bed & breakfast per night:	£min	£max
Single	25.00	28.00
Double	38.00	40.00

Half board per person:	£min	£max
Daily	25.00	31.00
Weekly	161.00	217.00

Evening meal 1830 (last orders 1730)
Parking for 6
Open March–November

Burrow Hall Country Guesthouse
HIGHLY COMMENDED

Plantation Bridge, Kendal LA8 9JR
☎ Staveley (01539) 821711
Tastefully furnished, 17th C Lakeland house enjoying modern day comforts. Sits peacefully in idyllic south Lakeland countryside between Kendal and Windermere, on A591.
Bedrooms: 2 double, 1 twin
Bathrooms: 3 en-suite

Bed & breakfast per night:	£min	£max
Single	25.00	
Double	40.00	

Parking for 8
Cards accepted: Access, Visa, Switch/Delta

The County Hotel

Station Road, Kendal LA9 6BT
☎ (01539) 722461
Fax (01539) 732644
In the centre of Kendal and ideal for touring the Lakes, coast of Cumbria and the Yorkshire Dales. Market day Saturday.
Bedrooms: 4 single, 6 double, 10 twin, 7 triple, 2 family rooms
Bathrooms: 27 en-suite, 2 public

Bed & breakfast per night:	£min	£max
Single	39.00	45.00
Double	59.00	78.00

Evening meal 1900 (last orders 2130)
Parking for 11
Cards accepted: Access, Visa, Switch/Delta

Garden House
HIGHLY COMMENDED

Fowling Lane, Kendal LA9 6PH
☎ (01539) 731131
Fax (01539) 740064
Elegant country house offering personal service. Ideal touring base for Lakes and dales. Ample parking. 2-day breaks available.
Bedrooms: 2 single, 3 double, 3 twin, 2 triple
Bathrooms: 10 en-suite

Bed & breakfast per night:	£min	£max
Single	45.00	55.00
Double	60.00	80.00

Half board per person:	£min	£max
Daily	50.00	65.00
Weekly	300.00	405.00

Lunch available
Evening meal 1900 (last orders 2130)
Parking for 15
Cards accepted: Access, Visa, Diners, Amex, Switch/Delta

Heaves Hotel

Kendal LA8 8EF
☎ Sedgwick (015395) 60269 & 60396
Fax (015395) 60269

Georgian mansion in 10 acres, 4 miles from M6, junction 36, and Kendal. Billiard room, library. Family owned and run.

Continued ▶

CUMBRIA

KENDAL
Continued

Bedrooms: 4 single, 4 double, 5 twin, 1 triple, 1 family room
Bathrooms: 10 en-suite, 1 private, 2 public

Bed & breakfast
per night:	£min	£max
Single	20.00	28.00
Double	40.00	60.00

Half board per person:
	£min	£max
Daily	31.00	41.00
Weekly	203.00	266.00

Lunch available
Evening meal 1900 (last orders 2000)
Parking for 24
Cards accepted: Access, Visa, Diners, Amex, Switch/Delta

Hillside Guest House
COMMENDED

4 Beast Banks, Kendal LA9 4JW
☎ (01539) 722836
Small guesthouse near the shops and town facilities, convenient for the Lakes, Yorkshire Dales and Morecambe Bay.
Bedrooms: 2 single, 3 double, 1 twin
Bathrooms: 4 en-suite, 2 public

Bed & breakfast
per night:	£min	£max
Single	15.00	18.00
Double	30.00	36.00

Parking for 2
Open March–November

Newlands
APPROVED

37 Milnthorpe Road, Kendal
LA9 5QG
☎ (01539) 725340
Open door to a friendly Victorian guesthouse. Town centre, shops, museums within walking distance. Ideally situated for the Lakes and Yorkshire Dales.
Bedrooms: 1 single, 2 double, 2 triple
Suite available
Bathrooms: 2 en-suite, 1 public

Bed & breakfast
per night:	£min	£max
Single	15.00	20.00
Double	30.00	40.00

Half board per person:
	£min	£max
Daily	22.50	27.50
Weekly	135.00	170.00

Evening meal from 1830
Parking for 5

Roadchef Lodge
COMMENDED

Killington Lake Motorway Service Area, M6 Southbound, Kendal
LA8 0NW
☎ Killington (015396) 21666 & 20739
Fax (015396) 21660
RoadChef
RoadChef Lodges offer high specification rooms at affordable prices, in popular locations suited to both the business and private traveller. Prices are per room and do not include breakfast.
Bedrooms: 14 double, 20 twin, 2 family rooms
Bathrooms: 36 en-suite

Bed & breakfast
per night:	£min	£max
Single	37.95	39.95

Lunch available
Parking for 100
Cards accepted: Access, Visa, Diners, Amex, Switch/Delta

KESWICK
Cumbria
Map ref 5A3

Beautifully positioned town beside Derwentwater and below the mountains of Skiddaw and Blencathra. Excellent base for walking, climbing, watersports and touring. Motor-launches operate on Derwentwater and motor boats, rowing boats and canoes can be hired.
Tourist Information Centre
☎ *(017687) 72645*

Acorn House Hotel
HIGHLY COMMENDED

Ambleside Road, Keswick
CA12 4DL
☎ (017687) 72553
Fax (017687) 75332
Elegant Georgian house set in colourful garden. All bedrooms tastefully furnished, some four-poster beds. Cleanliness guaranteed. Close to town centre.
Bedrooms: 6 double, 1 twin, 3 triple
Bathrooms: 9 en-suite, 1 private

Bed & breakfast
per night:	£min	£max
Single	25.00	35.00
Double	48.00	60.00

Parking for 10
Open February–November
Cards accepted: Access, Visa

The Anchorage
COMMENDED

14 Ambleside Road, Keswick
CA12 4DL
☎ (017687) 72813
Comfortable house, serving good home cooking, with owners who make every effort to please.
Bedrooms: 1 single, 3 double, 2 triple
Bathrooms: 6 en-suite, 1 public

Derwentwater
PORTINSCALE, KESWICK, CA12 5RE
ON THE LAKE SHORE - IN THE HEART OF THE LAKE DISTRICT
Set in 16 acres of conservation grounds on the shores of Lake Derwentwater, yet only 1 mile from the centre of Keswick. Two country style houses offer:-
Traditional Hotel Accommodation
or
Self - Catering Apartments with Style.
Many facilities available - Children and Pets Welcome.
FULL COLOUR BROCHURE TEL. 017687-72538.
'A WARM WELCOME AWAITS'
DAILY TELEGRAPH HIGHLY RECOMMENDED

AA ★★★ RAC ★★★

CUMBRIA

Bed & breakfast per night:	£min	£max
Single	18.00	21.00
Double	36.00	42.00

Half board per person:	£min	£max
Daily	28.00	31.00
Weekly	190.00	210.00

Evening meal 1830 (last orders 1500)
Parking for 7
☎5🖂□🚿🍴🛏️🚭S🛌🏡📺🚻🚗✱
✈️🚲SP

Applethwaite Country House Hotel ♨

👑👑👑 COMMENDED

Applethwaite, Underskiddaw, Keswick CA12 4PL
☎ (017687) 72413

Characterful Victorian Lakeland-stone residence in idyllic, peaceful setting 1.5 miles from Keswick. Superb elevated position, stunning panoramic views. Relaxed informal atmosphere. Delicious home cooking, vegetarians welcomed.
Bedrooms: 1 single, 5 double, 2 twin, 4 triple
Bathrooms: 12 en-suite, 1 public

Bed & breakfast per night:	£min	£max
Single	29.00	32.00
Double	58.00	64.00

Half board per person:	£min	£max
Daily	42.00	46.50
Weekly	265.00	295.00

Evening meal 1900 (last orders 1850)
Parking for 10
Cards accepted: Access, Visa
☎🖂🚿🍴🛏️S🛌🏡📺🚻🚗✱
🍴✈️🚲SP🏠T

Avondale Guest House ♨

👑👑 COMMENDED

20 Southey Street, Keswick CA12 4EF
☎ (017687) 72735

High quality, comfortable guesthouse with well-appointed en-suite rooms. Close to town centre, lake and parks. Non-smokers only, please.
Bedrooms: 1 single, 4 double, 1 twin,
Bathrooms: 4 en-suite, 1 public

Bed & breakfast per night:	£min	£max
Single	18.50	19.50
Double	37.00	39.00

Cards accepted: Access, Visa, Switch/Delta
☎12🖂□🚿🍴🛏️🚭S🛌🏡🚗✱
🐕SP T

Berkeley Guest House ♨

👑👑

The Heads, Keswick CA12 5ER
☎ (017687) 74222
On a quiet road overlooking Borrowdale Valley, with splendid views from each comfortable room. Close to the town centre and lake.
Bedrooms: 4 double, 1 triple
Bathrooms: 3 en-suite, 1 public

Bed & breakfast per night:	£min	£max
Double	29.00	42.00

Open February–November
☎1🚿🖂□🍴🛏️🚭S🛌🏡🚗
🐕🚲

Bonshaw Guest House ♨

Listed COMMENDED

20 Eskin Street, Keswick CA12 4DG
☎ (017687) 73084
Small, friendly, comfortable guesthouse, providing good home cooking. Convenient for town centre and all amenities. En-suite rooms available.
Non-smokers only, please.
Bedrooms: 3 single, 2 double, 1 twin, 1 triple
Bathrooms: 2 en-suite, 1 public

Bed & breakfast per night:	£min	£max
Single	15.00	20.00
Double	28.00	37.00

Half board per person:	£min	£max
Daily	24.00	28.50
Weekly	168.00	199.50

Evening meal 1830 (last orders 1600)
Parking for 6
Cards accepted: Access, Visa, Amex
☎5□🚿🍴🛏️🛌🏡🚲

Borrowdale Hotel ♨

👑👑👑👑 COMMENDED

Borrowdale, Keswick CA12 5UY
☎ Borrowdale (017687) 77224
Fax (017687) 77338
Traditional, friendly, licensed Lakeland hotel renowned for service and cuisine. All rooms en-suite. Family and four-poster rooms available.
Bedrooms: 5 single, 15 double, 12 twin, 2 triple
Bathrooms: 34 en-suite

Bed & breakfast per night:	£min	£max
Single	34.50	
Double	63.00	89.00

Half board per person:	£min	£max
Daily	50.00	63.00

Lunch available
Evening meal 1900 (last orders 2115)
Parking for 100
Cards accepted: Access, Visa, Switch/Delta
☎🖂🕿🖂□🚿🍴🛏️S🛌🏡🚗✱
U🍴✱🐕🚲SP

Brierholme Guest House ♨

👑👑👑

21 Bank Street, Keswick CA12 5JZ
☎ (017687) 72938
Select guesthouse in town centre. High quality accommodation, all rooms having mountain views, tea-making facilities and colour TV. Private parking.
Bedrooms: 6 double
Bathrooms: 4 en-suite, 1 private, 1 private shower

Bed & breakfast per night:	£min	£max
Double	35.00	43.00

Evening meal (last orders 1500)
Parking for 6
☎□🚿🛌🏡🚗🐕SP T

Castle Inn Hotel ♨

👑👑👑👑 COMMENDED

Bassenthwaite, Keswick CA12 4RG
☎ Bassenthwaite (017687) 76401
Fax (017687) 76604
🅶🆁 Best Western

Hotel with extensive leisure facilities, including a large indoor swimming pool. Good restaurant. Free children's accommodation. Friendliest welcome. Superb views.
Bedrooms: 2 single, 21 double, 18 twin, 2 triple, 6 family rooms
Bathrooms: 49 en-suite

Bed & breakfast per night:	£min	£max
Single	59.00	59.00
Double	98.00	98.00

Half board per person:	£min	£max
Daily	59.00	59.00
Weekly	354.00	354.00

Continued ▶

77

CUMBRIA

KESWICK
Continued

Lunch available
Evening meal 1830 (last orders 2130)
Parking for 100
Cards accepted: Access, Visa, Diners, Amex, Switch/Delta

Chaucer House Hotel
COMMENDED
Derwentwater Place, Keswick CA12 4DR
☎ (017687) 72318 & 73223
Fax (017687) 75551
Minotel
Beautiful Victorian house. Quiet family-run hotel overlooked by Skiddaw, Grisedale and Derwentwater. Delicious, home-cooked meals including bread, jams and chutney.
Bedrooms: 9 single, 22 double, 12 twin, 3 triple, 1 family room
Bathrooms: 42 en-suite, 4 public

Bed & breakfast per night:	£min	£max
Single	29.00	37.00
Double	56.00	41.00

Half board per person:	£min	£max
Daily	39.00	54.00
Weekly	243.00	334.00

Lunch available
Evening meal 1830 (last orders 2100)
Parking for 26
Open February–November
Cards accepted: Access, Visa, Amex

Clarence House
COMMENDED
14 Eskin Street, Keswick CA12 4DQ
☎ (017687) 73186
High quality accommodation, all en-suite. Four-poster and ground floor rooms. 5 minutes' walk from lake, parks and shops. Non-smoking.
Bedrooms: 1 single, 4 double, 3 twin, 1 triple
Bathrooms: 8 en-suite, 1 private

Bed & breakfast per night:	£min	£max
Single	18.00	20.00
Double	38.00	46.00

Half board per person:	£min	£max
Daily	28.00	32.00
Weekly	190.00	200.00

Evening meal from 1830

Craglands
HIGHLY COMMENDED
Penrith Rd, Keswick CA12 4LJ
☎ (017687) 74406
Well-appointed Victorian house in a quiet position on the outskirts of Keswick. Superb views, friendly atmosphere and good food using fresh local produce.
Bedrooms: 3 double, 1 twin
Bathrooms: 4 en-suite

Bed & breakfast per night:	£min	£max
Single	25.00	27.00
Double	40.00	50.00

Half board per person:	£min	£max
Daily	37.00	42.00
Weekly	220.00	250.00

Evening meal 1900 (last orders 2000)
Parking for 5

Crow Park Hotel
COMMENDED
The Heads, Keswick CA12 5ER
☎ (017687) 72208
Fax (017687) 74776
Quiet but central, between the lake and the town centre. Magnificent views all round of the Lakeland fells.
Bedrooms: 4 single, 16 double, 6 twin, 1 triple
Bathrooms: 27 en-suite

Bed & breakfast per night:	£min	£max
Single	21.50	29.50
Double	43.00	59.00

Half board per person:	£min	£max
Daily	32.50	42.50
Weekly	195.00	279.00

Evening meal 1845 (last orders 2000)
Parking for 26
Cards accepted: Access, Visa

Dalegarth House Country Hotel
COMMENDED
Portinscale, Keswick CA12 5RQ
☎ (017687) 72817
Edwardian house 1 mile from Keswick, with views of Skiddaw and Derwentwater. Licensed bar, 2 lounges and 6-course evening meal. Non-smokers only, please.

Bedrooms: 2 single, 4 double, 3 twin, 1 triple
Bathrooms: 10 en-suite

Bed & breakfast per night:	£min	£max
Single	26.00	28.00
Double	52.00	56.00

Half board per person:	£min	£max
Daily	39.00	41.00
Weekly	250.00	260.00

Evening meal 1900 (last orders 1730)
Parking for 12
Cards accepted: Access, Visa

Dalkeith House
1 Leonards Street, Keswick CA12 4EJ
☎ (017687) 72696
Fax (017687) 72696
Family-run Victorian guesthouse. En-suite and standard rooms. Home cooking, evening meal optional. Close to Derwentwater, shops and parks.
Bedrooms: 1 single, 3 double, 1 twin, 1 triple
Bathrooms: 3 en-suite, 1 public

Bed & breakfast per night:	£min	£max
Single	15.00	20.00
Double	30.00	46.00

Half board per person:	£min	£max
Daily	24.00	29.00
Weekly	160.00	195.00

Evening meal 1830 (last orders 1830)

Derwentwater Hotel
HIGHLY COMMENDED
Portinscale, Keswick CA12 5RE
☎ (017687) 72538
Fax (017687) 71002

Well-positioned on the shore of Lake Derwentwater in 16 acres of grounds, offering comfortable accommodation. Half board price is based on a minimum 2-night stay. Premier rooms, suites and four-poster rooms, all with lake views, available.
Wheelchair access category 3
Bedrooms: 5 single, 23 double, 20 twin, 2 triple

CUMBRIA

Suites available
Bathrooms: 50 en-suite

Bed & breakfast

per night:	£min	£max
Single	69.00	79.00
Double	99.00	148.00

Half board per

person:	£min	£max
Daily	68.00	89.00
Weekly	340.00	445.00

Evening meal 1900 (last orders 2130)
Parking for 140
Cards accepted: Access, Visa, Diners, Amex, Switch/Delta

Ad See display advertisement on page 76

The Grange Country House Hotel ♙
HIGHLY COMMENDED

Manor Brow, Ambleside Road, Keswick CA12 4BA
☎ (017687) 72500
A building of charm, fully restored and refurbished, with many antiques. Quiet, overlooking Keswick with panoramic mountain views. Log fires, freshly prepared food and attractive bedrooms.
Bedrooms: 7 double, 3 twin
Bathrooms: 10 en-suite, 1 public

Bed & breakfast

per night:	£min	£max
Double	62.00	75.00

Half board per

person:	£min	£max
Daily	46.00	52.00
Weekly	315.00	329.00

Evening meal 1900 (last orders 2030)
Parking for 13
Open March–November
Cards accepted: Access, Visa

Greystones ♙
HIGHLY COMMENDED

Ambleside Road, Keswick CA12 4DP
☎ (017687) 73108
Established family-run hotel, tastefully furnished and with all the comforts you would expect. Ideally situated for town, lake and fells.
Bedrooms: 1 single, 5 double, 2 twin
Bathrooms: 7 en-suite, 1 private shower

Bed & breakfast

per night:	£min	£max
Single	22.50	22.50
Double	46.00	46.00

Half board per

person:	£min	£max
Daily	36.00	36.00

Evening meal 1900 (last orders 1400)
Parking for 9
Open February–November
Cards accepted: Access, Visa

Hazeldene Hotel ♙
APPROVED

The Heads, Keswick CA12 5ER
☎ (017687) 72106
Fax (017687) 75435
Beautiful and central with open views of Skiddaw and Borrowdale and Newlands Valleys. Midway between town centre and Lake Derwentwater.
Bedrooms: 5 single, 9 double, 4 twin, 4 triple
Bathrooms: 17 en-suite, 3 private, 2 public

Bed & breakfast

per night:	£min	£max
Single	23.00	29.00
Double	46.00	58.00

Half board per

person:	£min	£max
Daily	37.00	43.00
Weekly	249.00	288.00

Evening meal 1830 (last orders 1600)
Parking for 18
Open February–November

Hunters Way Guest House ♙
COMMENDED

4 Eskin Street, Keswick CA12 4DH
☎ (017687) 72324 & 0374 818366
Spacious, attractive guesthouse, 5 minutes' walk from town centre and beautiful countryside. Imaginative menu with home cooking - vegetarians welcome. Non-smoking.
Bedrooms: 2 single, 3 double, 1 twin
Bathrooms: 4 en-suite, 1 public

Bed & breakfast

per night:	£min	£max
Single	14.00	16.00
Double	36.00	40.00

Half board per

person:	£min	£max
Daily	23.50	29.50
Weekly	164.50	192.50

Evening meal from 1830

You are advised to confirm your booking in writing.

King's Arms Hotel ♙
COMMENDED

Main Street, Keswick CA12 5BL
☎ (017687) 72083

Charming 18th C coaching inn with oak-beamed bar/lounge and refurbished air-conditioned restaurant. Traditional English home cooking. Bedrooms of high quality, all en-suite. Free use of nearby leisure club.
Bedrooms: 9 double, 4 twin
Bathrooms: 13 en-suite

Bed & breakfast

per night:	£min	£max
Single	37.00	44.00
Double	50.00	60.00

Half board per

person:	£min	£max
Daily	32.50	37.50
Weekly	227.50	262.50

Lunch available
Evening meal 1800 (last orders 2200)
Cards accepted: Access, Visa, Switch/Delta

Ladstock Country House Hotel ♙
COMMENDED

Thornthwaite, Keswick CA12 5RZ
☎ (017687) 78210
Fax (017687) 78088
CR Consort
18th C country house hotel 3 miles from Keswick, set in own grounds. Panoramic views. Rooms with four-poster beds. 3 day breaks. Weddings and conferences.
Bedrooms: 11 double, 5 twin, 1 triple, 2 family rooms
Bathrooms: 18 en-suite, 1 private, 2 public

Bed & breakfast

per night:	£min	£max
Single	45.00	
Double	70.00	80.00

Half board per

person:	£min	£max
Daily	45.00	55.00

Lunch available
Evening meal 1900 (last orders 2030)
Parking for 100
Cards accepted: Access, Visa

CUMBRIA

KESWICK
Continued

Linnett Hill Hotel ♠
COMMENDED
4 Penrith Road, Keswick CA12 4HF
☎ (017687) 73109
Charming 1812 hotel overlooking Skiddaw and Latrigg Hills. Opposite parks, gardens and river. Fresh home-cooked food, including a la carte menus with quality wines. Secure car park. Non-smoking establishment.
Bedrooms: 1 single, 7 double, 2 twin
Bathrooms: 10 en-suite

Bed & breakfast per night:	£min	£max
Single	24.50	30.00
Double	45.00	47.00

Half board per person:	£min	£max
Daily	35.50	39.50
Weekly	238.00	273.00

Evening meal 1900 (last orders 1830)
Parking for 12
Cards accepted: Access, Visa

Littletown Farm ♠
COMMENDED
Newlands, Keswick CA12 5TU
☎ Braithwaite (017687) 78353
150-acre mixed farm. In the beautiful, unspoilt Newlands Valley. En-suite bedrooms. Comfortable residents' lounge, dining room and cosy bar. Traditional 4-course dinner 6 nights a week.
Bedrooms: 4 double, 2 twin, 2 triple, 2 family rooms
Bathrooms: 6 en-suite, 1 public

Bed & breakfast per night:	£min	£max
Single	24.00	28.00
Double	48.00	56.00

Half board per person:	£min	£max
Daily	35.00	39.00
Weekly	215.00	240.00

Evening meal from 1900
Parking for 10
Open March–December
Cards accepted: Access, Visa

Lyzzick Hall Hotel ♠
HIGHLY COMMENDED
Underskiddaw, Keswick CA12 4PY
☎ (017687) 72277
Fax (017687) 72278
Peaceful country house hotel in its own grounds, with panoramic views, good food and a friendly, relaxed atmosphere. Heated indoor swimming pool.
Bedrooms: 3 single, 12 double, 7 twin, 3 family rooms
Bathrooms: 25 en-suite, 1 public

Bed & breakfast per night:	£min	£max
Single	37.00	39.00
Double	74.00	78.00

Half board per person:	£min	£max
Daily	47.00	49.00
Weekly	310.00	340.00

Lunch available
Evening meal 1900 (last orders 2130)
Parking for 30
Open January, March–December
Cards accepted: Access, Visa, Diners, Amex, Switch/Delta

Maple Bank ♠
COMMENDED
Braithwaite, Keswick CA12 5RY
☎ Braithwaite (017687) 78229
Friendly country guesthouse with magnificent views of Skiddaw and surrounding countryside. Delicious home cooking. Open four seasons, including Christmas and New Year.
Bedrooms: 6 double, 1 twin
Bathrooms: 7 en-suite

Bed & breakfast per night:	£min	£max
Single	22.00	24.00
Double	44.00	48.00

Half board per person:	£min	£max
Daily	32.00	34.00
Weekly	209.00	215.00

Evening meal 1830 (last orders 1600)
Parking for 10
Cards accepted: Access, Visa

Priorholme Hotel ♠
COMMENDED
Borrowdale Road, Keswick CA12 5DD
☎ (017687) 72745
This Georgian hotel with charm and character has a 200-year-old bar and is on a quiet road 3 minutes' walk from the town, the lake and the theatre.
Bedrooms: 2 single, 3 double, 1 twin
Bathrooms: 6 en-suite, 1 public

Bed & breakfast per night:	£min	£max
Single	22.00	26.00
Double		52.00

Half board per person:	£min	£max
Daily	38.00	42.00
Weekly	252.00	280.00

Evening meal 1900 (last orders 1930)
Parking for 7
Open February–December
Cards accepted: Access, Visa, Switch/Delta

Queen's Hotel
Main Street, Keswick CA12 5JF
☎ (017687) 73333
Fax (017687) 71144
GR The Independents
In the centre of Keswick, well placed for both the shops and countryside.
Bedrooms: 9 single, 20 double, 8 triple
Bathrooms: 37 en-suite

Bed & breakfast per night:	£min	£max
Single	24.50	30.00
Double	49.00	60.00

Lunch available
Evening meal 1830 (last orders 2030)
Parking for 8
Cards accepted: Access, Visa, Diners, Amex, Switch/Delta

Ravensworth Hotel ♠
HIGHLY COMMENDED
29 Station Street, Keswick CA12 5HH
☎ (017687) 72476
Small, family-run licensed hotel, decorated to a high standard of comfort, situated close to Keswick's amenities. An ideal Lake District base.
Bedrooms: 7 double, 1 twin
Bathrooms: 7 en-suite, 1 private

Bed & breakfast per night:	£min	£max
Single	21.00	35.00
Double	30.00	50.00

Parking for 5
Open March–November
Cards accepted: Access, Visa

The ♠ symbol after an establishment name indicates that it is a Regional Tourist Board member.

CUMBRIA

Rickerby Grange
COMMENDED
Portinscale, Keswick CA12 5RH
☎ (017687) 72344

Detached country hotel in its own gardens, in a quiet village on the outskirts of Keswick. Provides imaginative cooking, a cosy bar and quiet lounge. Ground floor bedrooms available.
Bedrooms: 1 single, 7 double, 1 twin, 3 triple
Bathrooms: 11 en-suite, 1 private

Bed & breakfast per night:	£min	£max
Single	27.00	27.00
Double	54.00	54.00

Half board per person:	£min	£max
Daily	38.00	39.00
Weekly	255.50	255.50

Evening meal 1900 (last orders 1800)
Parking for 14
Open February–November

Skiddaw Hotel
HIGHLY COMMENDED
Market Square, Keswick CA12 5BN
☎ (017687) 72071
Fax (017687) 74850
Logis of Great Britain

Family-owned town centre hotel, offering true hospitality and excellent cuisine. In-house saunas, free midweek golf, free use of nearby exclusive leisure club.
Bedrooms: 10 single, 11 double, 11 twin, 8 triple
Bathrooms: 40 en-suite

Bed & breakfast per night:	£min	£max
Single	34.00	38.00
Double	62.00	70.00

Half board per person:	£min	£max
Daily	45.00	53.00

Lunch available
Evening meal 1830 (last orders 2130)
Parking for 8
Cards accepted: Access, Visa, Amex

Skiddaw Grove Hotel
COMMENDED
Vicarage Hill, Keswick CA12 5QB
☎ (017687) 73324

Family-run Georgian hotel in peaceful situation on fringe of town. Magnificent views. Gardens, heated outdoor pool, parking.
Bedrooms: 1 single, 6 double, 2 twin, 1 triple
Bathrooms: 9 en-suite, 1 private, 1 public

Bed & breakfast per night:	£min	£max
Single	22.00	24.50

Half board per person:	£min	£max
Daily	34.00	36.00

Evening meal 1900 (last orders 1700)
Parking for 12

Swinside Lodge
DE LUXE
Newlands, Keswick CA12 5UE
☎ (017687) 72948
Fax (017687) 72948
Quietly situated informal country hotel offering the highest standards of comfort, service and hospitality. Noted for enjoyable food which demonstrates a serious and dedicated approach to the cooking.
Bedrooms: 5 double, 2 twin
Bathrooms: 7 en-suite

Bed & breakfast per night:	£min	£max
Single	40.00	53.00
Double	66.00	102.00

Half board per person:	£min	£max
Daily	58.00	78.00

Evening meal 1930 (last orders 2000)
Parking for 12
Open February–November and Christmas

Winchester House
COMMENDED
58 Blencathra Street, Keswick CA12 4HT
☎ (017687) 73664
Comfortable, well-appointed and quietly situated spacious guesthouse with good views from most rooms and friendly atmosphere. Substantial full English breakfast. Non-smokers only, please. Evening meals available winter months only.
Bedrooms: 1 single, 2 double, 1 twin, 1 triple, 1 family room
Bathrooms: 2 public

Bed & breakfast per night:	£min	£max
Single	15.50	16.00
Double	31.00	32.00

Half board per person:	£min	£max
Daily	22.50	24.00
Weekly	157.50	168.00

Evening meal 1830 (last orders 1600)

KIRKBY LONSDALE

Cumbria
Map ref 5B3

Charming old town of narrow streets and Georgian buildings, set in the superb scenery of the Lune Valley. The Devil's Bridge over the River Lune is probably 13th C.
Tourist Information Centre
☎ (015242) 71437

The Copper Kettle
Listed APPROVED
3 & 5 Market Street, Kirkby Lonsdale, Carnforth, Lancashire LA6 2AU
☎ (015242) 71714
Part of an old manor house, built in 1610, on the border between the Yorkshire Dales and the Lakes.
Bedrooms: 2 double, 1 twin, 1 triple
Bathrooms: 1 en-suite, 3 public

Bed & breakfast per night:	£min	£max
Single	21.00	21.00
Double	30.00	36.00

Half board per person:	£min	£max
Daily	21.00	27.00
Weekly	145.00	170.00

Lunch available
Evening meal 1800 (last orders 2100)
Cards accepted: Access, Visa, Diners, Amex, Switch/Delta

CUMBRIA

KIRKBY LONSDALE
Continued

Pheasant Inn
COMMENDED

Casterton, Kirkby Lonsdale,
Carnforth, Lancashire LA6 2RX
☎ (015242) 71230
Fax (015242) 71230

Old world country inn specialising in food and service, ideal for touring the Lakes, dales and coast. Situated amidst the peaceful Lunesdale Fells.
Bedrooms: 2 single, 6 double, 2 twin
Bathrooms: 10 en-suite

Bed & breakfast per night:	£min	£max
Single	35.00	37.50
Double	60.00	64.00

Lunch available
Evening meal 1830 (last orders 2100)
Parking for 40
Cards accepted: Access, Visa, Diners, Switch/Delta

Whoop Hall Inn
COMMENDED

Burrow with Burrow, Kirkby Lonsdale (A65), Carnforth, Lancashire LA6 2HP
☎ (01524) 271284
Fax (01524) 272154
Minotel

17th C coaching inn offering super food and local specialities. Between Lakes and dales, 6 miles from M6, junction 36. Ideal for business or pleasure.
Bedrooms: 4 single, 12 double, 3 twin, 2 triple, 1 family room
Suites available
Bathrooms: 22 en-suite

Bed & breakfast per night:	£min	£max
Single	47.50	55.00
Double	60.00	80.00

Half board per person:	£min	£max
Weekly	280.00	

Lunch available
Evening meal 1800 (last orders 2200)
Parking for 120
Cards accepted: Access, Visa, Diners, Amex, Switch/Delta

Map references apply to the colour maps at the back of this guide.

KIRKBY STEPHEN
Cumbria
Map ref 5B3

Old market town close to the River Eden, with many fine Georgian buildings and an attractive market square. St Stephen's Church is known as the "Cathedral of the Dales". Good base for exploring the Eden Valley and the Dales.

Ing Hill Lodge
COMMENDED

Mallerstang Dale, Mallerstang, Kirkby Stephen CA17 4JT
☎ (017683) 71153
Fax (017683) 71153

Delightful Georgian country home in Mallerstang Valley with glorious views. Peace, quiet, open fires, home cooking and a warm welcome.
Bedrooms: 2 double, 1 triple
Bathrooms: 3 en-suite, 1 public

Bed & breakfast per night:	£min	£max
Double	40.00	50.00

Half board per person:	£min	£max
Daily	32.50	37.50

Evening meal from 1930
Parking for 5

LANGDALE
Cumbria
Map ref 5A3

The two Langdale valleys (Great Langdale and Little Langdale) lie in the heart of beautiful mountain scenery. The craggy Langdale Pikes are almost 2500 ft high. An ideal walking and climbing area and base for touring.

Britannia Inn
COMMENDED

Elterwater, Ambleside LA22 9HP
☎ (015394) 37210
Fax (015394) 37311
Wayfarer

A 400-year-old traditional Lake District inn on a village green in the beautiful Langdale Valley. Cosy bars with log fires, home-cooked food and real ales. Very well-appointed accommodation.

Bedrooms: 1 single, 9 double, 3 twin
Bathrooms: 9 en-suite, 1 public

Bed & breakfast per night:	£min	£max
Single	20.00	23.50
Double	38.00	60.00

Lunch available
Evening meal 1830 (last orders 2130)
Parking for 7
Cards accepted: Access, Visa, Switch/Delta

Eltermere Country House Hotel
COMMENDED

Elterwater, Ambleside LA22 9HY
☎ Ambleside (015394) 37207

Friendly country house hotel in a quiet rural setting in the heart of the Langdale Valley. Personally run by the owners.
Bedrooms: 3 single, 9 double, 6 twin
Bathrooms: 15 en-suite, 3 public

Bed & breakfast per night:	£min	£max
Single	27.00	35.00
Double	54.00	77.00

Half board per person:	£min	£max
Daily	35.00	51.50
Weekly	221.00	323.50

Evening meal 1900 (last orders 2000)
Parking for 20

Three Shires Inn
COMMENDED

Little Langdale, Ambleside LA22 9NZ
☎ (015394) 37215

Traditional Lakeland inn near foot of Wrynose Pass in beautiful Little Langdale Valley. An ideal area for walkers and touring.
Bedrooms: 4 double, 5 twin, 1 triple
Bathrooms: 10 en-suite

Bed & breakfast per night:	£min	£max
Single	25.00	40.00
Double	50.00	80.00

Lunch available
Evening meal 1900 (last orders 2000)
Parking for 22
Open February–December

LORTON

Cumbria
Map ref 5A3

High and Low Lorton are set in a beautiful vale north of Crummock Water and at the foot of the Whinlatter Pass. Church of St Cuthbert is well worth a visit.

New House Farm

HIGHLY COMMENDED

Lorton, Cockermouth CA13 9UU
☎ (01900) 85404
Fax (01900) 85404

The very best of small country guest houses in quiet Lakeland valley. Old fashioned hospitality and traditional cuisine. Major tourism award winners 1994 and 1995.
Bedrooms: 3 double
Bathrooms: 3 en-suite

Bed & breakfast per night:	£min	£max
Single	30.00	40.00
Double	50.00	60.00

Half board per person:	£min	£max
Daily	45.00	50.00

Lunch available
Evening meal 1930 (last orders 1930)
Parking for 20

Establishments should be open throughout the year, unless otherwise stated.

All accommodation in this guide has been graded, or is awaiting a grading, by a trained Tourist Board inspector.

LUPTON

Cumbria
Map ref 5B3

Village divided by A65 between Kirkby Lonsdale and Kendal. Appears in the Domesday Book. Boasts many fine farmhouses dating back to the 17th C and a disused mill that has stood on Lupton Beck for 700 years.

The Plough Hotel

COMMENDED

Cow Brow, Lupton LA6 1PJ
☎ Crooklands (015395) 67227
Fax (015395) 67848
Tastefully refurbished country inn renowned for the warmth of its welcome. Superb food, real ales and well-appointed rooms.
Bedrooms: 8 double, 2 twin, 1 triple, 2 family rooms
Suite available
Bathrooms: 13 en-suite

Bed & breakfast per night:	£min	£max
Single	32.50	35.00
Double	49.50	69.50

Lunch available
Evening meal 1800 (last orders 2115)
Parking for 80
Cards accepted: Access, Visa, Switch/Delta

MUNGRISDALE

Cumbria
Map ref 5A2

Set in an unspoilt valley, this hamlet has a simple, white church with a 3-decker pulpit and box pews.

Near Howe Farm Hotel

COMMENDED

Mungrisdale, Penrith CA11 0SH
☎ Penrith (017687) 79678
Farmhouse in quiet surroundings 1 mile from Mungrisdale, half a mile from the A66 and within easy reach of all the lakes.
Bedrooms: 3 double, 1 twin, 2 triple, 1 family room
Bathrooms: 4 en-suite, 1 public

Bed & breakfast per night:	£min	£max
Single	20.00	20.00
Double	34.00	40.00

Half board per person:	£min	£max
Daily	27.00	30.00
Weekly	189.00	210.00

Evening meal 1700 (last orders 1700)
Parking for 10

NEWBY BRIDGE

Cumbria
Map ref 5A3

At the southern end of Windermere on the River Leven, this village has an unusual stone bridge with arches of unequal size. The Lakeside and Haverthwaite Railway has a stop here, and steamer cruises on Lake Windermere leave from nearby Lakeside.

Swan Hotel

HIGHLY COMMENDED

Newby Bridge, Ulverston LA12 8NB
☎ (015395) 31681
Fax (015395) 31917
Logis of Great Britain
Privately-owned hotel enjoying a beautiful site at the foot of Lake Windermere. We offer facilities appreciated by both holiday and business visitors.
Bedrooms: 7 single, 13 double, 10 twin, 6 triple
Suite available
Bathrooms: 36 en-suite

Bed & breakfast per night:	£min	£max
Single	50.00	87.50
Double	80.00	135.00

Half board per person:	£min	£max
Daily	62.00	100.00

Lunch available
Evening meal 1900 (last orders 2130)
Parking for 106
Cards accepted: Access, Visa, Diners, Amex, Switch/Delta

Whitewater Hotel

The Lakeland Village, Backbarrow, Newby Bridge, Ulverston LA12 8PX
☎ (015395) 31133
Fax (015395) 31881
Minotel
Old mill built of Lakeland stone, converted into a hotel with all facilities, including a leisure centre in the grounds.
Bedrooms: 4 single, 14 double, 7 twin, 10 triple
Bathrooms: 35 en-suite

Continued ▶

CUMBRIA

NEWBY BRIDGE
Continued

Bed & breakfast per night: £min £max
Single 65.00 75.00
Double 95.00 110.00

Lunch available
Evening meal 1915 (last orders 2100)
Parking for 50
Cards accepted: Access, Visa, Diners, Amex, Switch/Delta

ORTON
Cumbria
Map ref 5B3

Small, attractive village with the background of Orton Scar, it has some old buildings and a spacious green. George Whitehead, the itinerant Quaker preacher, was born here in 1636.

Tebay Mountain Lodge Hotel

Orton, Penrith CA10 3SB
☎ (015396) 24351
Fax (015396) 24354
Friendly country hotel overlooking Howgill Mountains. Ideal for touring Lakes, dales or en route north-south stopover, with easy M6 access.
Bedrooms: 4 single, 18 double, 26 twin, 2 triple, 4 family rooms
Bathrooms: 54 en-suite

Bed & breakfast per night: £min £max
Single 45.00
Double 50.00

Evening meal 1900 (last orders 2100)
Parking for 30
Cards accepted: Access, Visa, Diners, Amex, Switch/Delta

Please check prices and other details at the time of booking.

A key to symbols can be found inside the back cover flap.

PENRITH
Cumbria
Map ref 5B2

Ancient and historic market town, the northern gateway to the Lake District. Penrith Castle was built as a defence against the Scots. Its ruins, open to the public, stand in the public park. High above the town is the Penrith Beacon, made famous by William Wordsworth.
Tourist Information Centre ☎ (01768) 867466

Beacon Bank Hotel
HIGHLY COMMENDED

Beacon Edge, Penrith CA11 7BD
☎ (01768) 862633
Victorian house of character, set in peaceful landscaped gardens. Residential licence, good food and service, spacious, comfortable, high standard accommodation. Five minutes from M6 junction 40. A no smoking hotel.
Bedrooms: 2 single, 5 double, 1 twin
Bathrooms: 8 en-suite

Bed & breakfast per night: £min £max
Single 29.00 50.00
Double 40.00 60.00

Half board per person: £min £max
Daily 41.50

Evening meal 1900 (last orders 1900)
Parking for 10

Brantwood Country Hotel
COMMENDED

Stainton, Penrith CA11 0EP
☎ (01768) 862748
Fax (01768) 890164

Family-owned and run. Standing in secluded gardens in rural location, 1.5 miles from M6 junction 40 and 3 miles from Ullswater.
Bedrooms: 2 single, 9 double, 2 triple
Bathrooms: 13 en-suite, 1 public

Bed & breakfast per night: £min £max
Single 36.00 45.00
Double 54.00 68.00

Half board per person: £min £max
Daily 43.00 61.00

Lunch available
Evening meal 1830 (last orders 2100)
Parking for 40
Cards accepted: Access, Visa, Switch/Delta

George Hotel
COMMENDED

Penrith CA11 7SU
☎ (01768) 862696
Fax (01768) 868223
Logis of Great Britain
300-year-old, famous coaching inn providing modern facilities, in the centre of Penrith. Privately owned and managed.
Bedrooms: 11 single, 10 double, 9 twin
Bathrooms: 30 en-suite, 1 public

Bed & breakfast per night: £min £max
Single 40.75
Double 54.00

Lunch available
Evening meal 1900 (last orders 2100)
Parking for 30
Cards accepted: Access, Visa, Switch/Delta

Norcroft Guesthouse
COMMENDED

Graham Street, Penrith CA11 9LQ
☎ (01768) 862365
Fax (01768) 862365
Spacious Victorian house with large comfortable rooms. In a quiet residential area near the town centre.
Bedrooms: 1 single, 2 double, 2 twin, 1 triple, 2 family rooms
Bathrooms: 6 en-suite, 1 public

Bed & breakfast per night: £min £max
Single 17.00 28.00
Double 32.00 42.00

Half board per person: £min £max
Daily 27.00 36.50
Weekly 174.00 195.00

Evening meal 1900 (last orders 1630)
Parking for 8

CUMBRIA

Old Victoria Hotel

APPROVED

46 Castlegate, Penrith CA11 7HY
☎ (01768) 862467
Fax (01768) 890438
Family-run hotel with public bar. Bar lunches and evening meals with home-cooked specialities. Your hosts are Roy and Christine Bacon.
Bedrooms: 1 single, 4 double, 2 twin
Bathrooms: 3 en-suite, 1 public, 4 private showers

Bed & breakfast per night:

	£min	£max
Single	25.00	25.00
Double	44.00	48.00

Half board per person:

	£min	£max
Daily	30.00	32.00

Lunch available
Evening meal 1900 (last orders 2030)
Parking for 12

The White House

COMMENDED

Clifton, Penrith CA10 2EL
☎ (01768) 865115

Situated in a rural area, an 18th C converted farmhouse where guests' comfort and enjoyment take priority. Ullswater, Haweswater, Eden Valley nearby. Fully licensed. For non-smokers only.
Bedrooms: 2 single, 1 twin, 2 triple
Bathrooms: 3 en-suite, 2 private

Bed & breakfast per night:

	£min	£max
Single	19.00	28.00
Double	42.00	42.00

Half board per person:

	£min	£max
Daily	31.50	33.50
Weekly	199.50	213.50

Evening meal 1900 (last orders 1200)
Parking for 8
Open January–October and Christmas

Map references apply to the colour maps at the back of this guide.

Woodland House Hotel

COMMENDED

Wordsworth Street, Penrith CA11 7QY
☎ (01768) 864177
Fax (01768) 890152
Elegant and spacious red sandstone house with library of books and maps for walkers, nature lovers and sightseers. Ideal base for exploring Eden Valley, Lakes, Pennines. A no-smoking hotel. email: idaviesa@cix.compulink.co.uk.
Bedrooms: 3 single, 2 double, 2 twin, 1 triple
Bathrooms: 7 en-suite, 1 private

Bed & breakfast per night:

	£min	£max
Single	26.00	26.00
Double	42.00	42.00

Half board per person:

	£min	£max
Daily	35.50	35.50
Weekly	239.00	239.00

Evening meal 1845 (last orders 1430)
Parking for 10

RAVENSTONEDALE

Cumbria
Map ref 5B3

Surrounded by fells, the Howgills to the south-west and Wild Boar Fell to the south-east, this village has a fine church with an unusual interior where sections of the congregation sit facing one another.

The Black Swan Hotel

COMMENDED

Ravenstonedale, Kirkby Stephen CA17 4NG
☎ Newbiggin-on-Lune (015396) 23204
Fax (015396) 23604
Delightful family-run hotel, set amidst beautiful countryside in a picturesque village. Renowned for food, comfort and hospitality. Private fishing. 5 minutes from M6 junction 38.
Wheelchair access category 3
Bedrooms: 1 single, 9 double, 5 twin
Bathrooms: 8 en-suite, 6 private, 1 public

Bed & breakfast per night:

	£min	£max
Single	25.00	45.00
Double	30.00	75.00

Half board per person:

	£min	£max
Daily	32.00	68.00
Weekly	242.00	395.00

Lunch available
Evening meal 1800 (last orders 2100)
Parking for 30
Cards accepted: Access, Visa, Diners, Amex

RYDAL

Cumbria
Map ref 5A3

Small hamlet next to Rydal Water, a small, beautiful lake sheltered by Rydal Fell. Once the home of William Wordsworth, Rydal Mount is open to the public. It is a good centre for walking and touring.

The Glen Rothay Hotel

Rydal, Ambleside LA22 9LR
☎ Ambleside (015394) 32524
Fax (015394) 31079

17th C historic inn with Wordsworth associations, in a beautiful setting facing Rydal Water. Suite available.
Bedrooms: 2 single, 7 double, 1 twin, 1 triple
Bathrooms: 11 en-suite, 1 public

Bed & breakfast per night:

	£min	£max
Single	27.50	32.50
Double	55.00	115.00

Half board per person:

	£min	£max
Daily	45.00	70.00
Weekly	287.00	462.00

Lunch available
Evening meal 1930 (last orders 2030)
Parking for 40
Cards accepted: Access, Visa, Diners, Amex, Switch/Delta

The symbols in each entry give information about services and facilities. A 'key' to these symbols appears at the back of this guide.

CUMBRIA

SANDSIDE

Cumbria
Map ref 5A3

On the extensive sands of the Kent Estuary between Milnthorpe and Arnside. Magnificent views across the bay. Immediately behind the village lie the remains of the dismantled railway and station and behind this the old quarry face dominates the landscape.

Kingfisher House & Restaurant
COMMENDED

Sandside, Milnthorpe LA7 7HW
☎ Milnthorpe (015395) 63909
Overlooking Kent Estuary and Lakeland hills, perfect for bird-watching, golf, rambling. All food home-cooked using fresh produce.
Bedrooms: 1 single, 2 double, 1 twin, 1 family room
Bathrooms: 5 private
Bed & breakfast

per night:	£min	£max
Single	25.00	
Double	40.00	

Half board per

person:	£min	£max
Daily	33.75	

Lunch available
Evening meal 1630 (last orders 2030)
Parking for 22
Cards accepted: Access, Visa

SAWREY

Cumbria
Map ref 5A3

Far Sawrey and Near Sawrey lie near Esthwaite Water. Both villages are small but Near Sawrey is famous for Hill Top Farm, home of Beatrix Potter, now owned by the National Trust and open to the public.

Buckle Yeat Guest House
COMMENDED

Sawrey, Ambleside LA22 0LF
☎ Hawkshead (015394) 36446 & 36538
Fax (015394) 36446
Old cottage guesthouse with log fires. Centrally situated for touring Lakeland, walking, bird-watching. Central heating throughout.
Bedrooms: 1 single, 4 double, 2 twin
Bathrooms: 6 en-suite, 1 private
Bed & breakfast

per night:	£min	£max
Single	20.00	22.50
Double	40.00	45.00

Parking for 9
Cards accepted: Access, Visa, Amex

Sawrey Hotel
COMMENDED

Far Sawrey, Ambleside LA22 0LQ
☎ Windermere (015394) 43425

Country inn on the quieter side of Windermere, 1 mile from the car ferry on B5285 to Hawkshead. The bar is in the old stables and has log fires.
Bedrooms: 3 single, 6 double, 6 twin, 3 triple
Bathrooms: 16 en-suite, 1 public
Bed & breakfast

per night:	£min	£max
Single	23.00	27.00
Double	46.00	54.00

Half board per

person:	£min	£max
Daily	31.00	36.00
Weekly	199.00	225.00

Lunch available
Evening meal 1900 (last orders 2045)
Parking for 30
Cards accepted: Access, Visa, Switch/Delta

Sawrey House Country Hotel
HIGHLY COMMENDED

Near Sawrey, Ambleside LA22 0LF
☎ Hawkshead (015394) 36387
Fax (015394) 36010
Near Sawrey (home of Beatrix Potter). Warm friendly atmosphere, comfortable accommodation, good food, magnificent views, 3 acres and large car park.
Bedrooms: 1 single, 5 double, 2 twin, 2 triple
Bathrooms: 10 en-suite
Bed & breakfast

per night:	£min	£max
Single	37.50	39.00
Double	75.00	95.00

Half board per

person:	£min	£max
Daily	53.00	65.00
Weekly	340.00	370.00

Evening meal 1930 (last orders 1830)
Parking for 20

Open February–December
Cards accepted: Access, Visa

West Vale Country Guest House
HIGHLY COMMENDED

Far Sawrey, Hawkshead, Ambleside LA22 0LQ
☎ Windermere (015394) 42817
A warm welcome awaits you at this peaceful family-run guesthouse, with home cooking, log fire and fine views.
Bedrooms: 5 double, 1 twin, 2 triple
Bathrooms: 6 en-suite, 2 private, 1 public
Bed & breakfast

per night:	£min	£max
Single	22.50	22.50
Double	45.00	45.00

Half board per

person:	£min	£max
Daily	33.00	33.00
Weekly	217.00	217.00

Lunch available
Evening meal 1900 (last orders 1600)
Parking for 8
Open March–October

SEDBERGH

Cumbria
Map ref 5B3

This busy market town set below the Howgill Fells is an excellent centre for walkers and touring the Dales and Howgills. The noted boys' school was founded in 1525.

Dalesman Country Inn
COMMENDED

Main Street, Sedbergh LA10 5BN
☎ (015396) 21183
On entering Sedbergh from the M6 the Dalesman is the first inn on the left. 17th C but recently refurbished by local craftsmen. 10% discount on weekly bookings. Winter breaks available.
Bedrooms: 1 single, 1 twin, 3 triple, 1 family room
Bathrooms: 5 en-suite, 1 private shower
Bed & breakfast

per night:	£min	£max
Single	25.00	37.50
Double	50.00	50.00

Lunch available
Evening meal 1800 (last orders 2130)
Parking for 12
Cards accepted: Access, Visa

CUMBRIA

SHAP
Cumbria
Map ref 5B3

Village lying nearly 1000 ft above sea-level, amongst impressive moorland scenery. Shap Abbey, open to the public, is hidden in a valley nearby. Most of the ruins date from the early 13th C, but the tower is 16th C. The famous Shap granite and limestone quarries are nearby.

Shap Wells Hotel

Shap, Penrith CA10 3QU
☎ (01931) 716628
Fax (01931) 716377
The Independents

In a secluded valley in the Shap Fells. Ideal for exploring the Lakes, dales and Border country. Half board price is based on minimum 2 night stay.
Wheelchair access category 2
Bedrooms: 13 single, 33 double, 39 twin, 4 triple, 4 family rooms
Bathrooms: 93 en-suite, 2 public

Bed & breakfast per night:	£min	£max
Single	45.00	50.00
Double	70.00	80.00

Half board per person:	£min	£max
Daily	35.00	60.00

Lunch available
Evening meal 1900 (last orders 2030)
Parking for 200
Open February–December
Cards accepted: Access, Visa, Diners, Amex, Switch/Delta

STAVELEY
Cumbria
Map ref 5A3

Large village built in slate, set between Kendal and Windermere at the entrance to the lovely Kentmere Valley.

Tarn House

18 Danes Road, Staveley, Kendal LA8 9PW
☎ Kendal (01539) 821656

Comfortable accommodation with a homely atmosphere, ideal for touring the Lakes.
Bedrooms: 1 double, 1 family room
Bathrooms: 1 public

Bed & breakfast per night:	£min	£max
Double	28.00	28.00

Parking for 3
Open February–October

THORNTHWAITE
Cumbria
Map ref 5A3

Small village, west of Keswick, at the southern tip of Bassenthwaite Lake. Forest trails in Thornthwaite Forest.

Thwaite Howe Hotel
HIGHLY COMMENDED

Thornthwaite, Keswick CA12 5SA
☎ Braithwaite (017687) 78281
Fax (017687) 78529

Stone-built country hotel in a tranquil position with magnificent panoramic views. Noted for good home-cooked food and fine wines.
Bedrooms: 5 double, 3 twin
Bathrooms: 8 en-suite

Half board per person:	£min	£max
Daily	41.00	45.00

Evening meal 1900 (last orders 1900)
Parking for 12
Open March–October
Cards accepted: Access, Visa, Switch/Delta

TROUTBECK
Cumbria
Map ref 5A2

On the Penrith to Keswick road, Troutbeck was the site of a series of Roman camps. The village now hosts a busy weekly sheep market.

Lane Head Farm Guest House

Troutbeck, Penrith CA11 0SY
☎ Threlkeld (017687) 79220

Charming 17th C former farmhouse in quiet location, 4 miles from Ullswater lake. Good home cooking, table licence. Log fire, some en-suite and four-poster rooms.
Bedrooms: 1 single, 5 double, 2 twin, 1 family room
Bathrooms: 5 en-suite, 1 public

Bed & breakfast per night:	£min	£max
Single	16.00	25.00
Double	32.00	44.00

Half board per person:	£min	£max
Daily	23.95	32.95
Weekly	150.00	207.00

Evening meal 1900 (last orders 2000)
Parking for 10

TROUTBECK
Cumbria
Map ref 5A3

Most of the houses in this picturesque village are 17th C, some retain their spinning galleries and oak-mullioned windows. At the south end of the village is Townend, owned by the National Trust and open to the public, an excellently preserved example of a yeoman farmer's or statesman's house.

Broadoaks Country House
Listed

Bridge Lane, Troutbeck, Windermere LA23 1LA
☎ Windermere (015394) 45566
Fax (015394) 88766

Country house in 7 acres of gardens, splendid views. All en-suite. Four-poster and Victorian beds. Jacuzzi, spa, free use of leisure centre. Licensed for civil marriage ceremonies.
Bedrooms: 8 double, 1 twin, 1 family room
Bathrooms: 10 en-suite

Bed & breakfast per night:	£min	£max
Single	45.00	60.00
Double	60.00	140.00

Half board per person:	£min	£max
Daily	70.00	85.00

Lunch available
Evening meal 1900 (last orders 2000)
Parking for 40
Cards accepted: Access, Visa

High Green Lodge

High Green, Troutbeck, Windermere LA23 1PN
☎ Ambleside (015394) 33005

Here all mornings are magical - sun, swans, Swallows and Amazons. Cosy en-suite/king-size rooms in peaceful
Continued ▶

CUMBRIA

TROUTBECK
Continued

lodge with fantastic views down valley/Lake Garbon Pass. Walkers'/motorists' paradise. Fabulous breakfast, gourmet food at pubs nearby.
Bedrooms: 2 double, 1 twin
Bathrooms: 3 en-suite

Bed & breakfast per night:	£min	£max
Single		35.00
Double	40.00	55.00

Parking for 6

Mortal Man Hotel
COMMENDED

Troutbeck, Windermere LA23 1PL
☎ Windermere (015394) 33193
Fax (015394) 31261
Ideal centre for walking, touring or for a very quiet and restful holiday. Beautiful location with homely charm.
Bedrooms: 2 single, 4 double, 6 twin
Bathrooms: 12 en-suite

Half board per person:	£min	£max
Daily	50.00	60.00
Weekly	330.00	350.00

Lunch available
Evening meal 1930 (last orders 2000)
Parking for 30
Open February–November

ULLSWATER
Cumbria
Map ref 5A3

This beautiful lake, which is over 7 miles long, runs from Glenridding to Pooley Bridge. Lofty peaks ranging around the lake make an impressive background. A steamer service operates along the lake between Pooley Bridge, Howtown and Glenridding in the summer.

Glenridding Hotel
HIGHLY COMMENDED

Glenridding, Penrith CA11 0PB
☎ Glenridding (017684) 82228
Fax (017684) 82555
Best Western
Old established family hotel, adjacent to the lake and surrounded by mountains. We offer value breaks, log fires, real ales and good food. 2 restaurants, pub. Children and pets welcome.
Bedrooms: 5 single, 23 double, 12 twin

Bathrooms: 40 en-suite

Bed & breakfast per night:	£min	£max
Single	64.00	66.00
Double	88.00	90.00

Half board per person:	£min	£max
Daily	65.00	70.00
Weekly	342.00	357.00

Lunch available
Evening meal 1900 (last orders 2030)
Parking for 30
Cards accepted: Access, Visa, Diners, Amex, Switch/Delta

Patterdale Hotel

Patterdale, Lake Ullswater, Penrith CA11 0NN
☎ Glenridding (017684) 82231
Fax (017684) 82440
Family-run hotel, within the same family for 65 years. All rooms with private facilities, colour TV and telephone.
Bedrooms: 14 single, 16 double, 23 twin, 2 triple, 2 family rooms
Bathrooms: 57 en-suite, 5 public

Bed & breakfast per night:	£min	£max
Single	20.00	27.50
Double	40.00	55.00

Half board per person:	£min	£max
Daily	35.00	45.00
Weekly	220.00	280.00

Lunch available
Evening meal 1900 (last orders 2000)
Parking for 100
Open March–December
Cards accepted: Access, Visa, Switch/Delta

Ullswater House
COMMENDED

Pooley Bridge, Penrith CA10 2NN
☎ Pooley Bridge (017684) 86259
Centrally situated in Pooley Bridge. The well appointed rooms are quiet, each having a fridge containing alcoholic and soft drinks.
Bedrooms: 2 double, 1 twin
Bathrooms: 3 en-suite

Bed & breakfast per night:	£min	£max
Single	19.50	29.00
Double	39.00	39.00

Half board per person:	£min	£max
Daily	29.50	29.50
Weekly	200.00	200.00

Evening meal 1900 (last orders 1900)
Parking for 4

ULVERSTON
Cumbria
Map ref 5A3

Market town lying between green fells and the sea. There is a replica of the Eddystone lighthouse on the Hoad which is a monument to Sir John Barrow, founder of the Royal Geographical Society. Birthplace of Stan Laurel, of Laurel and Hardy.
Tourist Information Centre ☎ (01229) 587120

Lonsdale House Hotel

Daltongate, Ulverston LA12 7BD
☎ (01229) 582598
Fax (01229) 581260
Located in beautiful walled garden. All rooms with bathroom, TV, video, tea/coffee facilities, trouser press and telephone.
Bedrooms: 8 single, 6 double, 5 twin, 1 triple
Bathrooms: 20 en-suite

Bed & breakfast per night:	£min	£max
Single	30.00	60.00
Double	55.00	75.00

Half board per person:	£min	£max
Daily	40.00	60.00

Lunch available
Evening meal 1900 (last orders 2100)
Parking for 2
Cards accepted: Access, Visa, Diners, Amex, Switch/Delta

Trinity House Hotel
COMMENDED

Prince's Street, Ulverston LA12 7NB
☎ (01229) 587639
Fax (01229) 587639
Georgian former rectory, elegant licensed restaurant with local food. En-suite bedrooms are spacious and stylishly decorated.
Bedrooms: 1 single, 4 double, 1 twin
Bathrooms: 6 en-suite

Bed & breakfast per night:	£min	£max
Single	38.00	41.00
Double	50.00	60.00

Half board per person:	£min	£max
Daily	39.00	44.00
Weekly	240.00	270.00

CUMBRIA

Lunch available
Evening meal 1900 (last orders 2100)
Parking for 7
Cards accepted: Access, Visa, Amex, Switch/Delta

WASDALE
Cumbria
Map ref 5A3

A very dramatic valley with England's deepest lake, Wastwater, highest mountain, Scafell Pike, and smallest church. The eastern shore of Wastwater is dominated by the 1,500 ft screes dropping steeply into the lake. A good centre for walking and climbing.

Low Wood Hall Hotel
COMMENDED
Wasdale CA20 1ET
☎ (019467) 26289
Fax (019467) 26289

Gracious Victorian country house with fine views across Wasdale. Close to Scafell, Wastwater and sea. Bar, billiard room. Extensive dinner menu.
Bedrooms: 1 single, 6 double, 7 twin
Bathrooms: 13 en-suite, 1 private

Bed & breakfast per night: £min £max
Single   35.00
Double   57.00

Half board per person: £min £max
Daily   33.00   44.00
Weekly   199.00 276.00

Evening meal 1830 (last orders 2045)
Parking for 24
Cards accepted: Access, Visa, Amex

WHITEHAVEN
Cumbria
Map ref 5A3

Historic Georgian port on the west coast. The town was developed in the 17th C and many fine buildings have been preserved. The Beacon Heritage Centre includes a Meteorological Office Weather Gallery. Start or finishing point of Coast to Coast, Whitehaven to Sunderland, cycleway.
Tourist Information Centre ☎ (01946) 695678

Corkickle Guest House
COMMENDED
1 Corkickle, Whitehaven CA28 8AA
☎ (01946) 692073 & 0850 172828
Fax (01946) 692073
Small Georgian guesthouse offering high standards of comfort. Conveniently situated for business or leisure visitors. Residential licence.
Bedrooms: 2 single, 2 double, 2 twin
Bathrooms: 4 en-suite, 1 private, 1 public, 1 private shower

Bed & breakfast per night: £min £max
Single   25.00   32.00
Double   45.00

Half board per person: £min £max
Daily   38.00   45.00

Evening meal from 1900
Parking for 2

WINDERMERE
Cumbria
Map ref 5A3

Once a tiny hamlet before the introduction of the railway in 1847, now adjoins Bowness which is on the lakeside. Centre for sailing and boating. A good way to see the lake is a trip on a passenger steamer. Steamboat Museum has a fine collection of old boats.
Tourist Information Centre
☎ (015394) 46499

Adam Place Guest House
COMMENDED
1 Park Avenue, Windermere
LA23 2AR
☎ (015394) 44600
Small, friendly guesthouse, close to lake and all amenities.
Bedrooms: 1 single, 2 double, 1 triple, 1 family room
Bathrooms: 2 en-suite, 1 public

Bed & breakfast per night: £min £max
Single   13.00   15.00
Double   26.00   36.00

Parking for 2

Applegarth Hotel
COMMENDED
College Road, Windermere
LA23 1BU
☎ (015394) 43206
Elegant Victorian mansion house with individually designed bedrooms and four-poster suites. Lovely fell views from most rooms. Cosy restaurant and bar. Please pre-book dinner to avoid disappointment. Complimentary use of local country club.
Bedrooms: 4 single, 9 double, 2 triple, 1 family room
Bathrooms: 16 en-suite

Bed & breakfast per night: £min £max
Single   22.00   40.00
Double   39.00   80.00

Half board per person: £min £max
Daily   33.00   55.00
Weekly   231.00 266.00

Evening meal 1900 (last orders 1930)
Parking for 25
Open February–December
Cards accepted: Access, Visa, Amex

Ashleigh Guest House
COMMENDED
11 College Road, Windermere
LA23 1BU
☎ (015394) 42292
Beautiful, comfortable Victorian home in quiet, central location with mountain views. All rooms en-suite, old pine furniture, brass and pine beds. Breakfast choice. Non-smoking.
Bedrooms: 3 double, 1 twin
Bathrooms: 4 en-suite

Bed & breakfast per night: £min £max
Double   30.00   44.00

Parking for 1

Autumn Leaves
COMMENDED
29 Broad Street, Windermere
LA23 2AB
☎ (015394) 48410
A comfortable Victorian guesthouse located in the heart of Windermere,
Continued ▶

National gradings and classifications were correct at the time of going to press but are subject to change. Please check at the time of booking.

CUMBRIA

WINDERMERE
Continued

providing an excellent quality of service and friendly atmosphere.
Bedrooms: 1 single, 3 double, 1 twin, 1 triple
Bathrooms: 3 en-suite, 1 public

Bed & breakfast
per night:	£min	£max
Single	20.50	24.50
Double	31.00	39.00

Half board per
person:	£min	£max
Daily	24.00	33.00
Weekly	146.00	209.00

Evening meal 1800 (last orders 1930)
Cards accepted: Access, Visa, Switch/Delta

Bay House Lake View Guesthouse
Listed
Bay House, Fallbarrow Road, Bowness-on-Windermere, Windermere LA23 3DJ
☎ (015394) 43383
Informal guesthouse with lake view, in the heart of old Bowness. Vegetarians catered for. Dogs welcome. Lots of fun.
Bedrooms: 3 double, 1 twin, 1 triple, 1 family room
Bathrooms: 2 public

Bed & breakfast
per night:	£min	£max
Double	25.00	40.00

Half board per
person:	£min	£max
Daily	20.00	28.00

Evening meal 1700 (last orders 2100)
Parking for 6

The Beaumont Hotel
HIGHLY COMMENDED
Holly Road, Windermere LA23 2AF
☎ (015394) 47175
Fax (015394) 47175

Elegant Victorian house hotel with beautiful lounge. All rooms are en-suite, with colour TV, hairdryer, tea/coffee making facilities. Some four-posters. Warm, personal service.

Bedrooms: 1 single, 7 double, 1 twin, 1 family room
Suites available
Bathrooms: 10 en-suite

Bed & breakfast
per night:	£min	£max
Single	25.00	36.00
Double	46.00	56.00

Parking for 10
Open March–October
Cards accepted: Access, Visa, Amex

Beech Hill Hotel
COMMENDED
Newby Bridge Road, Bowness-on-Windermere, Windermere LA23 3LR
☎ (015394) 42137 & Freephone 0800 592294
Fax (015394) 43745
Consort
Perfectly situated on the shore of Lake Windermere, north of Newby Bridge. Majestic views over the lake, the Langdale Pikes and surrounding fells. On A592.
Bedrooms: 2 single, 38 double, 11 twin, 4 triple
Bathrooms: 55 en-suite

Bed & breakfast
per night:	£min	£max
Single	50.00	56.00
Double	100.00	110.00

Half board per
person:	£min	£max
Daily	58.00	70.00

Lunch available
Evening meal 1900 (last orders 2130)
Parking for 40
Cards accepted: Access, Visa, Amex, Switch/Delta

Belsfield House
COMMENDED
4 Belsfield Terrace, Kendal Road, Bowness-on-Windermere, Windermere LA23 3EQ
☎ (015394) 45823
Family-run guesthouse in the heart of Bowness, 2 minutes' walk from the lake front.
Bedrooms: 2 single, 3 double, 4 triple
Bathrooms: 9 en-suite

Bed & breakfast
per night:	£min	£max
Single	21.00	26.00
Double	38.00	50.00

Parking for 9

Biskey Howe Villa Hotel
APPROVED
Craig Walk, Bowness-on-Windermere, Windermere LA23 3AX
☎ (015394) 43988
Fax (015394) 88379
In a peaceful spot close to Bowness Bay. Detached Victorian villa with some bedrooms having spectacular views of lake and mountains. Friendly, family-run establishment.
Bedrooms: 1 single, 5 double, 1 twin, 2 triple, 1 family room
Suite available
Bathrooms: 10 en-suite, 1 public

Bed & breakfast
per night:	£min	£max
Single	30.00	38.00
Double	44.00	56.00

Half board per
person:	£min	£max
Daily	35.00	42.00

Evening meal 1830 (last orders 2000)
Parking for 10
Open March–October
Cards accepted: Access, Visa, Amex

Bowfell Cottage
APPROVED
Middle Entrance Drive, Storrs Park, Bowness-on-Windermere, Windermere LA23 3JY
☎ (015394) 44835
Cottage in a delightful setting, about 1 mile south of Bowness just off the A5074, offering traditional Lakeland hospitality.
Bedrooms: 1 double, 1 twin, 1 triple
Bathrooms: 1 public

Bed & breakfast
per night:	£min	£max
Single	18.00	18.00
Double	34.00	36.00

Half board per
person:	£min	£max
Daily	27.00	28.00
Weekly	170.00	175.00

Evening meal 1800 (last orders 2000)
Parking for 6

Braemount House Hotel
HIGHLY COMMENDED
Sunny Bank Road, Windermere LA23 2EN
☎ (015394) 45967
Fax (015394) 45967
Small, comfortable family-run hotel with a relaxed, friendly atmosphere.

CUMBRIA

Offering fine cuisine (chef-patron) along with a genuine, cheerful welcome.
Bedrooms: 3 double, 1 twin, 1 family room
Bathrooms: 5 en-suite

Bed & breakfast per night:	£min	£max
Single	32.50	50.00
Double	45.00	80.00

Half board per person:	£min	£max
Daily	38.00	55.50
Weekly	245.00	280.00

Evening meal 1900 (last orders 2030)
Parking for 6
Cards accepted: Access, Visa

The Burn How Garden House Hotel & Motel

HIGHLY COMMENDED

Back Belsfield Road, Windermere LA23 3HH
☎ (015394) 46226
Fax (015394) 47000
Best Western

Unique combination of Victorian houses and private chalets in secluded gardens in the heart of a picturesque village. Full facilities. Four-poster beds available.
Wheelchair access category 3
Bedrooms: 2 single, 8 double, 8 twin, 8 triple
Bathrooms: 25 en-suite, 1 private

Bed & breakfast per night:	£min	£max
Single	48.00	62.00
Double	76.00	99.00

Half board per person:	£min	£max
Daily	44.00	62.00
Weekly	230.00	370.00

Lunch available
Evening meal 1900 (last orders 2030)
Parking for 30
Cards accepted: Access, Visa, Diners, Amex, Switch/Delta

Cedar Manor Hotel

HIGHLY COMMENDED

Ambleside Road, Windermere LA23 1AX
☎ (015394) 43192
Fax (015394) 45970

Traditional Lakeland house with interesting architectural features. Elegantly furnished and in a country garden setting. Some rooms have lake views.
Bedrooms: 9 double, 3 twin
Bathrooms: 12 en-suite

Bed & breakfast per night:	£min	£max
Single	28.00	37.50
Double	56.00	75.00

Half board per person:	£min	£max
Daily	40.00	52.00
Weekly	203.00	294.00

Lunch available
Evening meal 1930 (last orders 2030)
Parking for 20
Cards accepted: Access, Visa

College House

COMMENDED

15 College Road, Windermere LA23 1BU
☎ (015394) 45767
Warm, comfortable, Victorian family house. En-suite rooms with gorgeous mountain views. Nice garden. Quiet location. Close to village centre. Non-smoking.
Bedrooms: 2 double, 1 twin
Bathrooms: 2 en-suite, 1 private

Bed & breakfast per night:	£min	£max
Double	32.00	48.00

Parking for 3

Cranleigh Hotel

COMMENDED

Kendal Road,
Bowness-on-Windermere,
Windermere LA23 3EW
☎ (015394) 43293
Comfortable, quiet hotel, 2 minutes' walk from lake and village centre. Free use of private leisure club. Garden, private parking, bar.

Bedrooms: 9 double, 2 twin, 2 triple, 2 family rooms
Bathrooms: 14 en-suite, 1 private

Bed & breakfast per night:	£min	£max
Single	18.00	32.00
Double	36.00	64.00

Half board per person:	£min	£max
Daily	27.00	41.00

Lunch available
Evening meal 1900 (last orders 2100)
Parking for 15
Cards accepted: Access, Visa

Damson Dene Hotel

COMMENDED

Crosthwaite, Kendal LA8 8JE
☎ Crosthwaite (015395) 68676
Fax (015395) 68227
Experience the unique atmosphere of this hotel, set in the tranquil Lyth Valley near Windermere. Leisure centre open all year, roaring log fires in winter.
Bedrooms: 5 single, 17 double, 10 twin, 2 family rooms
Bathrooms: 34 en-suite

Bed & breakfast per night:	£min	£max
Single	25.00	42.00
Double	50.00	84.00

Half board per person:	£min	£max
Daily	37.00	54.00
Weekly	222.00	324.00

Lunch available
Evening meal 1900 (last orders 2100)
Parking for 102
Cards accepted: Access, Visa, Switch/Delta

Eastbourne Hotel

COMMENDED

Biskey Howe Road,
Bowness-on-Windermere,
Windermere LA23 2JR
☎ (015394) 43525
Family-run hotel situated below the Biskey Howe viewpoint and within easy walking distance of the lake and all amenities.
Bedrooms: 2 single, 4 double, 1 triple, 1 family room
Bathrooms: 5 en-suite, 1 private, 1 public

Bed & breakfast per night:	£min	£max
Single	17.00	27.00
Double	34.00	54.00

Continued ▶

CUMBRIA

WINDERMERE
Continued

Parking for 6
Cards accepted: Access, Visa

Fairfield Country House Hotel
COMMENDED
Brantfell Road,
Bowness-on-Windermere,
Windermere LA23 3AE
☎ (015394) 46565
Fax (015394) 46565
Small, friendly 200-year-old country house with half an acre of peaceful secluded gardens. 2 minutes' walk from Lake Windermere and village. Private car park, leisure facilities.
Bedrooms: 1 single, 5 double, 1 twin, 1 triple, 1 family room
Bathrooms: 8 en-suite, 1 private, 1 public

Bed & breakfast
per night:	£min	£max
Single	24.00	28.00
Double	48.00	56.00

Half board per
person:	£min	£max
Daily	39.00	43.00
Weekly	255.00	285.00

Evening meal 1900 (last orders 1900)
Parking for 14
Cards accepted: Access, Visa

Fayrer Garden House Hotel
HIGHLY COMMENDED
Lyth Valley Road,
Bowness-on-Windermere,
Windermere LA23 3JP
☎ (015394) 88195
Logis of Great Britain
Beautiful, well-appointed country house in splendid grounds overlooking Lake Windermere. Noted for food. Four-posters, jacuzzis, free leisure facilities. Special breaks.
Bedrooms: 1 single, 10 double, 3 triple
Bathrooms: 13 en-suite, 1 private

Bed & breakfast
per night:	£min	£max
Double	50.00	110.00

Half board per
person:	£min	£max
Daily	39.50	75.00

Evening meal 1930 (last orders 2030)

Parking for 20
Cards accepted: Access, Visa, Amex

Fir Trees
HIGHLY COMMENDED
Lake Road, Windermere LA23 2EQ
☎ (015394) 42272
Fax (015394) 42272
Well-situated and handsome Victorian gentleman's residence offering elegant accommodation. Lovely bedrooms, scrumptious breakfasts and warm hospitality, all at exceptional value for money.
Bedrooms: 6 double, 1 twin, 1 triple
Bathrooms: 8 en-suite

Bed & breakfast
per night:	£min	£max
Single	25.00	31.00
Double	40.00	52.00

Parking for 8
Cards accepted: Access, Visa, Amex

Gilpin Lodge Country House Hotel & Restaurant
DE LUXE
Crook Road, Windermere LA23 3NE
☎ (015394) 88818
Fax (015394) 88058

Elegant and friendly hotel in rural setting, 2 miles from Windermere. Sumptuous bedrooms, renowned cuisine, gardens. Country club nearby. Telephone 0800 269460 (toll free in UK).
Bedrooms: 9 double, 1 twin, 1 triple
Bathrooms: 11 en-suite

Bed & breakfast
per night:	£min	£max
Single	65.00	85.00
Double	80.00	140.00

Half board per
person:	£min	£max
Daily	55.00	85.00
Weekly	365.00	555.00

Lunch available
Evening meal 1900 (last orders 2045)
Parking for 40
Cards accepted: Access, Visa, Diners, Amex, Switch/Delta

Glenville Hotel
COMMENDED
Lake Road, Windermere LA23 2EQ
☎ (015394) 43371

Standing in its own grounds, midway between Windermere and Bowness and perfectly positioned for access to all amenities. The lake is an easy 10-minute walk. Car park.
Bedrooms: 5 double, 3 triple
Bathrooms: 7 en-suite, 1 private, 1 public

Bed & breakfast
per night:	£min	£max
Single	20.00	30.00
Double	35.00	48.00

Parking for 12
Open February–December
Cards accepted: Access, Visa

Grey Walls Hotel
COMMENDED
Elleray Road, Windermere LA23 1AG
☎ (015394) 43741
Fax (015394) 47546
Comfortable hotel with the leisurely atmosphere found in family-run businesses of this size.
Bedrooms: 2 single, 7 double, 2 twin, 2 triple, 1 family room
Bathrooms: 14 en-suite, 1 public

Bed & breakfast
per night:	£min	£max
Single	20.00	25.00
Double	35.00	60.00

Half board per
person:	£min	£max
Daily	32.50	37.50
Weekly	195.00	255.00

Lunch available
Evening meal 1730 (last orders 2130)
Parking for 20
Cards accepted: Access, Visa, Diners, Amex, Switch/Delta

Hideaway Hotel
COMMENDED
Phoenix Way, Windermere LA23 1DB
☎ (015394) 43070

CUMBRIA

Friendly, small hotel away from the main road, with a pleasant garden, well-trained chefs, open fires and well-equipped, comfortable bedrooms.
Bedrooms: 2 single, 7 double, 3 twin, 3 triple
Bathrooms: 15 en-suite

Bed & breakfast per night:	£min	£max
Single	28.00	39.00
Double	50.00	94.00

Half board per person:	£min	£max
Daily	38.00	55.00
Weekly	210.00	320.00

Evening meal 1930 (last orders 2000)
Parking for 16
Open February–December
Cards accepted: Access, Visa, Amex

Holbeck Ghyll Country House Hotel and Restaurant ⚜

DE LUXE

Holbeck Lane, Windermere LA23 1LU
☎ Ambleside (015394) 32275
Fax (015394) 34743

Magnificent 19th C country house overlooking Lake Windermere. Set in peaceful grounds. Spacious lounges, log fires, numerous leisure facilities on site.
Bedrooms: 10 double, 3 twin, 1 triple
Suites available
Bathrooms: 14 en-suite

Half board per person:	£min	£max
Daily	65.00	120.00
Weekly	409.50	756.00

Lunch available
Evening meal 1900 (last orders 2045)
Parking for 22
Cards accepted: Access, Visa, Diners, Amex

Holly Lodge ⚜

COMMENDED

6 College Road, Windermere LA23 1BX
☎ (015394) 43183
Fax (015394) 43183

Traditional Lakeland stone guesthouse, built in 1854. In a quiet area off the main road, close to the village centre, buses, railway station and all amenities.
Bedrooms: 1 single, 5 double, 2 twin, 3 triple
Bathrooms: 6 en-suite, 2 public

Bed & breakfast per night:	£min	£max
Single	17.00	20.00
Double	34.00	40.00

Half board per person:	£min	£max
Daily	28.00	31.00

Evening meal from 1830
Parking for 7

Holly Park House ⚜

COMMENDED

1 Park Road, Windermere LA23 2AW
☎ (015394) 42107

Elegant stone-built Victorian guesthouse with nicely furnished spacious rooms. Quiet area, convenient for village shops and coach/rail services.
Bedrooms: 2 double, 4 triple
Bathrooms: 6 en-suite

Bed & breakfast per night:	£min	£max
Single	24.00	28.00
Double	34.00	42.00

Evening meal 1830 (last orders 1930)
Parking for 4
Cards accepted: Access, Visa, Amex, Switch/Delta

Knoll Hotel ⚜

Lake Road, Windermere LA23 2JF
☎ (015394) 43756

In quiet grounds, with magnificent views overlooking Lake Windermere and the mountains. Free use of Parklands leisure club.
Bedrooms: 4 single, 4 double, 1 twin, 3 triple
Bathrooms: 9 en-suite, 1 public

Bed & breakfast per night:	£min	£max
Single	26.00	32.00
Double	60.00	64.00

Half board per person:	£min	£max
Daily	39.00	44.00
Weekly	246.00	278.00

Evening meal 1900 (last orders 1930)
Parking for 15
Cards accepted: Access, Visa

Langdale Chase Hotel ⚜

HIGHLY COMMENDED

Windermere LA23 1LW
☎ Ambleside (015394) 32201
Fax (015394) 32604

Country house hotel in landscaped gardens on the edge of Lake Windermere. Excellent views of mountains and lake. Great dining experience.
Bedrooms: 2 single, 11 double, 17 twin, 1 triple, 1 family room
Bathrooms: 32 en-suite

Bed & breakfast per night:	£min	£max
Single	45.00	55.00
Double	95.50	147.00

Half board per person:	£min	£max
Daily	68.25	94.50
Weekly	477.75	661.50

Lunch available
Evening meal 1900 (last orders 2045)
Parking for 50
Cards accepted: Access, Visa, Diners, Amex, Switch/Delta

Lindeth Fell Country House Hotel ⚜

HIGHLY COMMENDED

Windermere LA23 3JP
☎ (015394) 43286 & 44287
Fax (015394) 47455

Beautifully situated in magnificent private grounds on the hills above Lake Windermere, Lindeth Fell offers brilliant views, modern English cooking and elegant surroundings. All bedrooms have full facilities, many have lake views.
Bedrooms: 2 single, 5 double, 5 twin, 2 triple
Bathrooms: 14 en-suite

Continued ▶

Please mention this guide when making your booking.

CUMBRIA

WINDERMERE
Continued

Half board per
person: £min   £max
Daily   57.50   65.00
Weekly   385.00   430.00

Lunch available
Evening meal 1930 (last orders 2030)
Parking for 20
Open March–November
Cards accepted: Access, Visa

Lindeth Howe Country House Hotel
HIGHLY COMMENDED

Longtail Hill,
Bowness-on-Windermere,
Windermere LA23 3JF
☎ (015394) 45759
Fax (015394) 46368

19th C country house hidden in 6 acres of beautiful, secluded gardens overlooking Lake Windermere. Cosy bar and log fires on chilly evenings. All rooms have satellite colour TV, direct-dial telephone and baby listening, some have spa bath. Sauna, sunbeds. Free membership of local leisure club.
Bedrooms: 9 double, 2 twin, 3 triple
Bathrooms: 14 en-suite
Bed & breakfast
per night: £min   £max
Single   48.50   48.50
Double   64.00   104.00

Half board per
person: £min   £max
Daily   49.50   69.50
Weekly   312.00

Evening meal 1900 (last orders 2030)
Parking for 30
Cards accepted: Access, Visa, Switch/Delta

Half board prices are given per person, but in some cases these may be based on double/twin occupancy.

Lindisfarne
Listed

Sunny Bank Road, Windermere LA23 2EN
☎ (015394) 46295
Traditional detached Lakeland stone house. Ideally situated in quiet area, close to lake, shops and scenic walks. Friendly and flexible hosts.
Bedrooms: 2 double, 1 twin, 1 family room
Bathrooms: 2 en-suite, 1 private, 1 public
Bed & breakfast
per night: £min   £max
Single   15.00   20.00
Double   26.00   35.00

Half board per
person: £min   £max
Daily   23.00   28.00
Weekly   138.00   168.00

Evening meal 1800 (last orders 2000)
Parking for 4

Linthwaite House Hotel
DE LUXE

Crook Road,
Bowness-on-Windermere,
Windermere LA23 3JA
☎ (015394) 88600
Fax (015394) 88601
Grand Heritage
Peaceful location in 14 acres of gardens, 1 mile south of village and with panoramic views over the lake. English Tourist Board's Hotel of the Year, 1994.
Wheelchair access category 3
Bedrooms: 1 single, 13 double, 4 twin
Suite available
Bathrooms: 18 en-suite
Bed & breakfast
per night: £min   £max
Single   85.00   100.00
Double   120.00   190.00

Half board per
person: £min   £max
Daily   79.00   110.00
Weekly   498.00   693.00

Lunch available
Evening meal 1915 (last orders 2045)
Parking for 30
Cards accepted: Access, Visa, Amex, Switch/Delta

You are advised to confirm your booking in writing.

Low Wood Hotel
COMMENDED

Windermere LA23 1LP
☎ Ambleside (015394) 33338
Fax (015394) 34072
Best Western

Almost a mile of lake frontage. Boat launching, water ski tuition and superb lake and mountain views. Also leisure centre, indoor heated swimming pool, bubble beds, sauna room, health and beauty centre, gymnasium, conference centre.
Bedrooms: 16 single, 31 double, 52 twin
Bathrooms: 99 en-suite
Bed & breakfast
per night: £min   £max
Single   49.50   67.00
Double   99.00   134.00

Half board per
person: £min   £max
Daily   59.50   77.00

Lunch available
Evening meal 1900 (last orders 2130)
Parking for 200
Cards accepted: Access, Visa, Diners, Amex, Switch/Delta

Mountain Ash Hotel
COMMENDED

Ambleside Road, Windermere LA23 1AT
☎ (015394) 43715
Fax (015394) 88480
Lakeland stone hotel refurbished to provide comfortable accommodation, including four-poster beds and spa baths. Cocktail bar, conservatory and locally renowned traditional cuisine.
Bedrooms: 1 single, 19 double
Bathrooms: 20 en-suite
Bed & breakfast
per night: £min   £max
Single   24.50   39.00

Half board per
person: £min   £max
Daily   39.50   63.50

Lunch available
Evening meal 1900 (last orders 2100)
Parking for 30
Cards accepted: Access, Visa, Switch/Delta

CUMBRIA

Oakbank House ⚜

👑👑 COMMENDED

Helm Road,
Bowness-on-Windermere,
Windermere LA23 3BU
☎ (015394) 43386

Panoramic views of Lake Windermere,
1 minute from shops and restaurants.
Spacious, comfortable, tastefully
furnished rooms, all en-suite. Friendly
family-run hotel.
Bedrooms: 3 double, 2 twin, 6 triple
Bathrooms: 10 en-suite, 1 private
Bed & breakfast

per night:	£min	£max
Single	22.00	30.00
Double	42.00	60.00

Parking for 10
Cards accepted: Access, Visa,
Switch/Delta

Oldfield House ⚜

👑👑 COMMENDED

Oldfield Road, Windermere
LA23 2BY
☎ (015394) 88445
Fax (015394) 43250

Friendly, informal atmosphere within a
traditionally-built Lakeland residence.
Quiet central location, free use of
swimming and leisure club.
Bedrooms: 2 single, 4 double,
1 triple, 1 family room
Bathrooms: 8 en-suite, 1 public
Bed & breakfast

per night:	£min	£max
Single	21.50	32.50
Double	38.00	60.00

Parking for 7
Open February–December
Cards accepted: Access, Visa, Amex,
Switch/Delta

Map references apply to
the colour maps at the
back of this guide.

Orrest Close Guest House ⚜

👑👑👑 COMMENDED

3 The Terrace, Windermere
LA23 1AJ
☎ (015394) 43325
Fax (015394) 43325

Charming Victorian listed residence,
delightfully furnished and centrally
situated in a quiet position within easy
reach of both village and lake.
Bedrooms: 3 double, 2 twin, 1 family
room
Bathrooms: 4 en-suite, 2 private
Bed & breakfast

per night:	£min	£max
Single	20.00	25.00
Double	37.00	45.00

Half board per

person:	£min	£max
Daily		32.00
Weekly		190.00

Evening meal from 1900
Parking for 7
Cards accepted: Access, Visa,
Switch/Delta

Osborne Guest House

👑👑

3 High Street, Windermere
LA23 1AF
☎ (015394) 46452
Traditional Lakeland house, central for
all transport, tours and walks. Clean,
comfortable accommodation. Full
breakfast. Developed by present
owners since 1982.
Bedrooms: 1 double, 2 triple
Bathrooms: 3 en-suite
Bed & breakfast

per night:	£min	£max
Single	14.00	18.50
Double	28.00	37.00

Cards accepted: Access, Visa

The Poplars ⚜

👑👑👑 COMMENDED

Lake Road, Windermere LA23 2EQ
☎ (015394) 42325 & 46590
Small family-run guesthouse on the
main lake road, offering en-suite
accommodation coupled with fine
cuisine and homely atmosphere. Golf
and fishing can be arranged.
Bedrooms: 1 single, 3 double, 2 twin,
1 triple

Bathrooms: 6 en-suite, 1 private,
1 public
Bed & breakfast

per night:	£min	£max
Single	17.50	20.50
Double	35.00	41.00

Half board per

person:	£min	£max
Daily	29.50	32.50
Weekly	189.00	210.50

Evening meal 1800 (last orders
1800)
Parking for 7
Open February–December

Quarry Garth Country House Hotel and Restaurant ⚜

👑👑👑👑 HIGHLY COMMENDED

Troutbeck Bridge, Windermere
LA23 1LF
☎ (015394) 88282 & 43761
Fax (015394) 46584
Ⓖ Logis of Great Britain
This gracious and mellow Edwardian
country house is set in 8 acres of
lakeland gardens near Lake
Windermere. Residents are captivated
by excellent cuisine, antique furniture,
original paintings, collectors' items,
open fires, four-poster beds, candlelight
and a relaxed family-style welcome.
Bedrooms: 1 single, 8 double, 2 twin,
1 triple
Bathrooms: 12 en-suite
Bed & breakfast

per night:	£min	£max
Single	40.00	55.00
Double	70.00	80.00

Half board per

person:	£min	£max
Daily	48.00	65.00

Lunch available
Evening meal 1900 (last orders
2100)
Parking for 50
Cards accepted: Access, Visa, Diners,
Amex, Switch/Delta

Ravensworth Hotel ⚜

👑👑👑

Ambleside Road, Windermere
LA23 1BA
☎ (015394) 43747
Fax (015394) 43903
Close to the village centre, lake and
fells. English and continental cooking.
Variety of accommodation including
four poster beds.
Bedrooms: 2 single, 9 double, 2 twin,
1 triple
Bathrooms: 14 en-suite

Continued ▶

CUMBRIA

WINDERMERE
Continued

Bed & breakfast
per night:	£min	£max
Single	27.50	29.50
Double	55.00	73.00

Half board per
person:	£min	£max
Daily	40.50	49.50
Weekly	255.00	275.00

Evening meal 1900 (last orders 2030)
Parking for 16
Cards accepted: Access, Visa

Rocklea ♠
COMMENDED
Brookside, Lake Road, Windermere LA23 2BX
☎ (015394) 45326
Charming, family-run, traditional Lakeland-stone guesthouse in a quiet central location. Very comfortable with a warm, friendly atmosphere. Parking.
Bedrooms: 1 single, 5 double, 2 twin
Bathrooms: 6 en-suite, 1 public

Bed & breakfast
per night:	£min	£max
Single	17.00	21.00
Double	30.00	42.00

Parking for 6
Cards accepted: Access, Visa

Rockside
Ambleside Road, Windermere LA23 1AQ
☎ (015394) 45343
Fax (015394) 45533
100 yards from Windermere village and its amenities. Tours and walks arranged if required. Railway and bus station 250 yards. Large car park.
Bedrooms: 2 single, 6 double, 5 twin, 1 triple, 1 family room
Bathrooms: 10 en-suite, 2 public

Bed & breakfast
per night:	£min	£max
Single	16.50	22.50
Double	33.00	48.00

Parking for 12
Cards accepted: Access, Visa, Diners, Amex, Switch/Delta

Rosemount Private Hotel ♠
COMMENDED
Lake Road, Windermere LA23 2EQ
☎ (015394) 43739
Fax (015394) 43739

Well situated guesthouse, tastefully decorated and furnished. Warm hospitality, scrumptious breakfast, all at unbeatable prices. Golf can be arranged. Non-smokers only, please.
Bedrooms: 2 single, 5 double, 1 twin
Bathrooms: 5 en-suite, 3 private

Bed & breakfast
per night:	£min	£max
Single	18.50	25.00
Double	37.00	48.00

Parking for 8
Open February–November
Cards accepted: Access, Visa

St. John's Lodge ♠
COMMENDED
Lake Road, Windermere LA23 2EQ
☎ (015394) 43078
Small private hotel midway between Windermere and the lake, managed by the chef/proprietor and convenient for all amenities and services. Facilities of local sports and leisure club available to guests.
Bedrooms: 1 single, 9 double, 2 twin, 2 triple
Bathrooms: 12 en-suite, 2 private

Bed & breakfast
per night:	£min	£max
Single	20.00	25.00
Double	37.00	50.00

Half board per
person:	£min	£max
Daily	30.00	35.00
Weekly	198.00	215.00

Evening meal 1900 (last orders 1800)
Parking for 11
Open February–November
Cards accepted: Access, Visa

Sandown ♠
COMMENDED
Lake Road, Bowness-on-Windermere, Windermere LA23 2JF
☎ (015394) 45275
Large modern detached house, set in landscaped area with trees and shrubs, 10 minutes' walk from Lake Windermere. Golf, riding, sailing nearby. Safe parking in grounds. SAE or telephone for details.
Bedrooms: 6 double, 1 twin
Bathrooms: 7 en-suite

Bed & breakfast
per night:	£min	£max
Double	38.00	54.00

Parking for 8

South View ♠
Cross Street, Windermere LA23 1AE
☎ (015394) 42951
Unique in Windermere village - the only guesthouse with own heated indoor swimming pool open all year. Excellent breakfast. Quiet yet central.
Bedrooms: 3 double, 1 twin, 1 family room
Bathrooms: 5 en-suite, 2 public

Bed & breakfast
per night:	£min	£max
Single	18.00	27.00
Double	36.00	54.00

Evening meal 1830 (last orders 1600)
Parking for 6
Cards accepted: Access, Visa, Amex

Villa Lodge ♠
COMMENDED
Cross Street, Windermere LA23 1AE
☎ (015394) 43318
Fax (015394) 43318

Friendliness and cleanliness guaranteed. Peacefully situated in quiet cul-de-sac overlooking Windermere village. Splendid views. Safe private parking.
Bedrooms: 1 single, 4 double, 1 twin, 1 family room
Bathrooms: 3 en-suite, 4 private

Bed & breakfast
per night:	£min	£max
Single	16.00	18.00
Double	32.00	50.00

Parking for 9
Open February–December
Cards accepted: Access, Visa

Westbourne Hotel ♠
COMMENDED
Biskey Howe Road, Bowness-on-Windermere, Windermere LA23 2JR
☎ (015394) 43625 & Mobile (04020) 25305
In a peaceful area of Bowness within a short walk of the lake and shops. Highly recommended by our regular guests for comfort, decor and efficient, friendly service.
Bedrooms: 1 single, 5 double, 2 twin, 1 triple

CUMBRIA

Bathrooms: 9 en-suite

Bed & breakfast per night:	£min	£max
Single	21.00	28.50
Double	36.00	52.00
Half board per person:	£min	£max
Daily	33.50	41.00
Weekly	234.50	287.00

Evening meal 1830 (last orders 1900)
Parking for 10
Cards accepted: Access, Visa, Amex

White Lodge Hotel

COMMENDED

Lake Road, Windermere LA23 2JS
☎ (015394) 43624
Fax (015394) 47000

Victorian family-owned hotel with good home cooking, only a short walk from Bowness Bay. All bedrooms have private bathroom, colour TV and tea making facilities, some with lake views and four-posters.

Bedrooms: 3 single, 6 double, 2 twin, 1 triple
Bathrooms: 12 en-suite

Bed & breakfast per night:	£min	£max
Single	22.00	29.00
Double	44.00	58.00
Half board per person:	£min	£max
Daily	35.00	41.00
Weekly	220.00	260.00

Lunch available
Evening meal 1900 (last orders 2000)
Parking for 20
Open March–November
Cards accepted: Access, Visa

Wild Boar Hotel

COMMENDED

Crook, Kendal LA23 3NF
☎ (015394) 45225
Fax (015394) 42198
Best Western

17th C former inn, renowned for its food. In Gilpin Valley, on B5284, 3 miles from the lake and half-a-mile from golf-course.

Bedrooms: 1 single, 16 double, 17 twin, 2 triple
Bathrooms: 36 en-suite

Bed & breakfast per night:	£min	£max
Single	67.50	72.00
Double	95.00	104.00

Half board per person:	£min	£max
Daily	59.50	74.50
Weekly	357.00	447.00

Lunch available
Evening meal 1900 (last orders 2100)
Parking for 80
Cards accepted: Access, Visa, Diners, Amex

The Willowsmere Hotel

Ambleside Road, Windermere LA23 1ES
☎ (015394) 43575

Offers a comfortable and friendly atmosphere. Run by the fifth generation of local hoteliers. Varied food using fresh local produce.

Bedrooms: 2 single, 3 double, 1 twin, 7 triple
Bathrooms: 13 en-suite

Bed & breakfast per night:	£min	£max
Single	25.00	26.00
Double	50.00	52.00
Half board per person:	£min	£max
Daily	34.50	39.00
Weekly	175.00	241.00

Lunch available
Evening meal 1900 (last orders 1900)
Parking for 40
Open February–November
Cards accepted: Access, Visa, Diners, Amex, Switch/Delta

Woodlands

HIGHLY COMMENDED

New Road, Windermere LA23 2EE
☎ (015394) 43915 & (0468) 596142
Fax (015394) 48558

Family-run hotel in a convenient location. Renowned for its high standard of cleanliness and comfort. Ample car parking.

Bedrooms: 2 single, 11 double, 1 twin
Suites available
Bathrooms: 14 en-suite

Bed & breakfast per night:	£min	£max
Single	22.00	29.00
Double	40.00	58.00

Evening meal from 1900
Parking for 14
Cards accepted: Access, Visa, Switch/Delta

WITHERSLACK

Cumbria
Map ref 5A3

Tranquil village on the east bank of the River Winster, at the south end of the Lyth Valley, famed for its damsons. Good base for touring.

The Old Vicarage Country House Hotel

HIGHLY COMMENDED

Church Road, Witherslack, Grange-over-Sands LA11 6RS
☎ (015395) 52381
Fax (015395) 52373

Near to the Lakes, far from the crowds, in historic country vicarage in a beautiful setting. Comfortable and family-owned with a relaxed atmosphere. Award-winning restaurant.

Bedrooms: 1 single, 9 double, 4 twin, 1 triple
Bathrooms: 15 en-suite

Bed & breakfast per night:	£min	£max
Single	59.00	79.00
Double	98.00	138.00
Half board per person:	£min	£max
Daily	55.00	77.50
Weekly	385.00	542.50

Evening meal 2000 (last orders 2030)
Parking for 25
Cards accepted: Access, Visa, Amex, Switch/Delta

WORKINGTON

Cumbria
Map ref 5A2

A deep-water port on the west Cumbrian coast. There are the ruins of the 14th C Workington Hall, where Mary Queen of Scots stayed in 1568.

Morven Guest House

APPROVED

Siddick Road, Siddick, Workington CA14 1LE
☎ (01900) 602118

Continued ▶

CUMBRIA

WORKINGTON
Continued

Detached house north-west of town. Ideal base for western lakes and coast. Start of coast to coast cycleway. Car park, cycle storage.
Bedrooms: 3 single, 1 double, 3 twin, 1 triple
Bathrooms: 8 en-suite

Bed & breakfast per night:

	£min	£max
Single	24.00	32.00
Double	38.00	46.00

Half board per person:

	£min	£max
Daily	36.00	42.00

Lunch available
Evening meal 1800 (last orders 1600)
Parking for 20

Osborne House
Listed
31 Brow Top, Workington
CA14 2DP
☎ (01900) 603400
Town centre location. Homely accommodation and full English breakfast. Parking available.
Bedrooms: 5 twin, 1 family room
Bathrooms: 2 public

Bed & breakfast per night:

	£min	£max
Single	11.00	11.00
Double	22.00	22.00

Half board per person:

	£min	£max
Daily	15.00	15.00
Weekly	105.00	105.00

Evening meal 1700 (last orders 1900)
Parking for 3

COUNTRY CODE

Always follow the Country Code ⚜ Enjoy the countryside and respect its life and work ⚜ Guard against all risk of fire ⚜ Fasten all gates ⚜ Keep your dogs under close control ⚜ Keep to public paths across farmland ⚜ Use gates and stiles to cross fences, hedges and walls ⚜ Leave livestock, crops and machinery alone ⚜ Take your litter home ⚜ Help to keep all water clean ⚜ Protect wildlife, plants and trees ⚜ Take special care on country roads ⚜ Make no unnecessary noise

CHECK THE MAPS

The colour maps at the back of this guide show all the cities, towns and villages for which you will find accommodation entries.

Refer to the town index to find the page on which it is listed.

NORTHUMBRIA

Spectacular countryside awaits the visitor to Northumbria. The high Cheviots and the rugged Pennines leave an indelible impression while the majestic coastline offers sandy beaches, quaint fishing villages and surprisingly lively seaside resorts!

In contrast, Northumbria is also a region with vibrant industrial heritage, cosmopolitan cities and a long tradition of excellence in both the sporting and cultural arenas.

Soak up the history - don't miss Durham Cathedral - explore Catherine Cookson country and visit a traditional Northern pub. Or why not the Metro Centre, Europe's largest shopping city! Wherever you go, you'll be sure of a warm, northern welcome.

FOR MORE INFORMATION CONTACT:
Northumbria Tourist Board
Aykley Heads, Durham DH1 5UX
Tel: (0191) 375 3000 **Fax:** (0191) 386 0899

Where to Go in Northumbria - see pages 100-103
Where to Stay in Northumbria - see pages 104-124

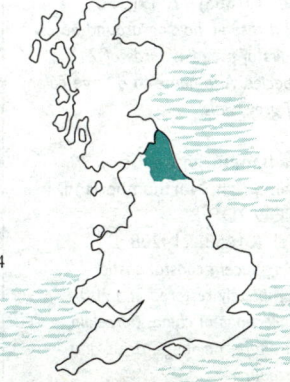

NORTHUMBRIA

Where to Go and What to See

You will find hundreds of interesting places to visit during your stay in Northumbria, just some of which are listed in these pages. The number against each name will help you locate it on the map (page 103). Contact any Tourist Information Centre in the region for more ideas on days out in Northumbria.

1 Lindisfarne Castle
Holy Island,
Berwick-upon-Tweed
Northumberland TD15 2SH
Tel: (01289) 89244
Fort converted into a private home in 1903 for Edward Hudson by the architect Edwin Lutyens.

2 Farne Islands
Seahouses off Northumberland coast,
Northumberland
Tel: (01665) 720651
Bird reserve holding around 55,000 pairs of breeding birds of 21 species. Also home to a large colony of grey seals.

3 Bamburgh Castle
Bamburgh, Northumberland,
NE69 7DF
Tel: (01668) 214208
Magnificent coastal castle completely restored in 1900. Collections of china, porcelain, furniture, paintings, arms and armour.

4 Alnwick Castle
Alnwick,
Northumberland NE66 1NQ
Tel: (01665) 510777
Largest inhabited castle in England after Windsor Castle. Home of the Percys, Dukes of Northumberland since 1309.

5 Cragside House, Gardens and Grounds
Cragside, Rothbury,
Northumberland NE65 7PX
Tel: (01669) 620333
House built 1864-84 for the first Lord Armstrong, Tyneside Industrialist. The first house to be lit by electricity generated by water power.

6 Kielder Water Leaplish Waterside Park
Kielder,
Northumberland NE48 1BX
Tel: (01434) 240395
Largest man made lake in Western Europe. Water sports, fishing, log cabins and caravan site. Cycle hire, crazy golf and restaurant.

7 Wallington House Walled Garden and Grounds
Wallington, Cambo,
Northumberland NE61 4AR
Tel: (01670) 74283
Built 1688 on site of earlier medieval castle. Altered in 1740s. Interior has plasterwork, porcelain, furniture, pictures and needlework.

8 Morpeth Chantry Bagpipe Museum
The Chantry, Bridge Street,
Morpeth,
Northumberland NE61 1PJ
Tel: (01670) 519466
Set in a 13thC church building, this unusual museum specialises in the history and development of Northumbrian small pipes and their music.

9 Sea Life Centre
Grand Parade, Long Sands,
Tynemouth,
Tyne & Wear NE30 4JF
Tel: (0191) 257 6100
Journey beneath the North Sea and

discover thousands of amazing creatures. Over 30 hi-tech displays.

10 Wet 'N Wild
Rotary Way,
North Shields,
Tyne & Wear NE29 6DA
Tel: (0191) 296 1233
Tropical indoor waterpark. A fun water playground providing the UK's wildest and wettest indoor rapid experience.

11 Castle Keep
Saint Nicholas Street,
Castle Garth,
Newcastle upon Tyne NE1 1RQ
Tel: (0191) 232 7938
Built 1168-1178. One of the finest surviving examples of a Norman keep in the country. Panoramic views of the city from the roof. Small museum within keep.

12 Bede's World
Church Bank,
Jarrow,
Tyne & Wear NE32 3DY
Tel: (0191) 489 2106
New museum opened May 1995. Late 18thC hall, excavated finds from Anglo-Saxon and medieval monastery of St Pauls Jarrow nearby. Anglo-Saxon farm with rare breeds.

13 Metroland
Gateshead,
Tyne & Wear NE11 9YZ
Tel: (0191) 493 2048
Europe's only indooor theme park within a large shopping complex. Rollercoaster, dodgems, swinging chairs, pirate ship plus live entertainment.

14 Housesteads Roman Fort
Hadrian's Wall,
Northumberland NE47 6NN
Tel: (01434) 344363
Best preserved and most impressive of the Roman forts. Vercovicium was a 5-acre fort for extensive civil settlement. Only example of a Roman hospital.

15 Wildfowl & Wetlands Trust
Washington,
Tyne & Wear NE38 8LE
Tel: (0191) 416 5454
Collection of 1,250 wildfowl of 108 varieties. Viewing gallery, picnic areas, hides and winter wild bird feeding station. Flamingos, wild grey heron. Food available.

16 Beamish – The North of England Open Air Museum
Beamish, Co Durham DH9 0RG
Tel: (01207) 231811
Visit a town, colliery village, farm and railway station recreated to show life in the North of England early this century. Pockerley Manor illustrates life in the early 1800s.

17 Durham Castle
Palace Green,
Durham DH1 3RW
Tel: (0191) 374 3863
Fine Bailey castle founded in 1072, Norman chapel dating from 1080. Kitchens and great hall dated 1499 and 1284 respectively.

18 Durham Cathedral
Durham DH1 3EH
Tel: (0191) 386 4266
Widely considered to be the finest example of Norman church architecture in England. Has the tombs of St Cuthbert and The Venerable Bede.

19 Killhope Leadmining Centre
Cowshill,
St John's Chapel,
Co Durham DL13 1AR
Tel: (01388) 537505
Most complete lead mining site in Great Britain. Includes crushing mill with 34ft water wheel, reconstruction of Victorian machinery and miners accommodation.

20 High Force Waterfall
Forest-in-Teesdale,
Middleton-in-Teesdale,
Co Durham DL12
Tel: (01833) 640209
High Force is the most majestic of the waterfalls on the River Tees. The falls are only a short walk from a bus stop, car park and picnic area.

21 Raby Castle
Staindrop,
Co Durham DL2 3AH
Tel: (01833) 660202
Medieval castle in 200-acre park. 600-year-old kitchen and carriage collection. Walled gardens and deer park. Home of Lord Barnard's family for over 350 years.

22 Butterfly World
Preston Park, Yarm Road,
Stockton-on-Tees,
Tees Valley TS18 3RH
Tel: (01642) 791414
An indoor tropical garden populated by exotic free-flying butterflies and complemented by a display of fascinating insects and reptiles.

23 Preston Hall Museum
Yarm Road, Stockton-on-Tees,
Tees Valley TS18 3RH
Tel: (01642) 781184
A Georgian country house set in a park which is a museum of Victoriana. Return to a bygone age, stroll along a high street, explore 100 acres of parkland overlooking the Tees.

24 Captain Cook Birthplace Museum
Stewart Park,
Marton,
Middlesbrough,
Tees Valley TS7 6AS
Tel: (01642) 311211
Early life and voyages of Captain Cook and the countries he visited. Temporary exhibitions.

25 Ormesby Hall
Church Lane,
Ormesby,
Middlesbrough,
Tees Valley TS7 9AB
Tel: (01642) 324188
18thC Palladian mansion with impressive contemporary plasterwork. Magnificent stableblock attributed to Carr of York. Model railway exhibition and children's play area.

26 Hartlepool Historic Quay
Maritime Avenue,
Hartlepool,
Tees Valley TS24 0XZ
Tel: (01429) 860006
An exciting reconstruction of a seaport of the 1800s with buildings and lively quayside.

27 Saltburn Smugglers Heritage Centre
Ship Inn, Saltburn-by-the-Sea,
Tees Valley TS12 1HF
Tel: (01287) 625252
Experience the authentic sights, sounds and smells of Saltburn's smuggling heritage. Listen to tales of John Andrew, "King of the Smugglers".

FIND OUT MORE
Further information about holidays and attractions in Northumbria is available from: **Northumbria Tourist Board**, Aykley Heads, Durham DH1 5UX. Tel: (0191) 375 3000

These publications are available free from the Northumbria Tourist Board:
- **Northumbria Breaks 1997**
- **Bed & Breakfast Map - Northumbria and Cumbria**
- **Great Days Out - regional attraction guide**
- **Freedom Caravan and Camping Guide - Northumbria, Yorkshire, East Riding, Cumbria and North West**
- **Schools Out - educational brochure**

Also available are (prices include postage and packaging):
- **Northumbria Touring Map and Guide** £4.75
- **Leisure Guide to Northumbria** £10.99
- **Walk Northumbria** £6.

NORTHUMBRIA

WHERE TO STAY (NORTHUMBRIA)

Accommodation entries in this region are listed in alphabetical order of place name, and then in alphabetical order of establishment.

Map references refer to the colour location maps at the back of this guide. The first number indicates the map to use; the letter and number which follow refer to the grid reference on the map.

At-a-glance symbols at the end of each accommodation entry give useful information about services and facilities. A key to symbols can be found inside the back cover flap. Keep this open for easy reference.

ALNMOUTH

Northumberland
Map ref 5C1

Quiet village with pleasant old buildings, at the mouth of the River Aln where extensive dunes and sands stretch along Alnmouth Bay. 18th C granaries, some converted to dwellings, still stand.

Famous Schooner Hotel
APPROVED
Northumberland Street, Alnmouth, Alnwick NE66 2RS
☎ Alnwick (01665) 830216
Fax (01665) 830216
17th C coaching inn, only 100 yards from beach, river and golf course and only 1 mile from railway station. This freehouse is renowned for good food and its extensive selection of real ales.
Bedrooms: 3 single, 3 double, 5 twin, 13 triple, 2 family rooms
Bathrooms: 26 en-suite
Bed & breakfast

per night:	£min	£max
Single	29.50	37.50
Double	59.00	75.00

Half board per person:	£min	£max
Daily	37.50	49.50
Weekly	199.00	346.50

Lunch available
Evening meal 1900 (last orders 2200)
Parking for 50
Cards accepted: Access, Visa, Diners, Amex, Switch/Delta

Saddle Hotel
APPROVED
24-25 Northumberland Street, Alnmouth, Alnwick NE66 2RA
☎ Alnwick (01665) 830476
Personally supervised by owners and offering a high standard of accommodation. Fourteen awards for food in seven years.
Bedrooms: 4 double, 4 twin, 1 triple
Bathrooms: 9 en-suite
Bed & breakfast

per night	£min	£max
Single	25.00	35.00
Double	36.00	56.00

Half board per person:	£min	£max
Daily	35.00	38.00

Lunch available
Evening meal 1830 (last orders 2100)
Cards accepted: Access, Visa, Switch/Delta

WELCOME HOST

This is a nationally recognised customer care programme which aims to promote the highest standards of service and a warm welcome. Establishments who are taking part in this initiative are indicated by the symbol.

ALNWICK

Northumberland
Map ref 5C1

Ancient and historic market town, entered through the Hotspur Tower, an original gate in the town walls. The medieval castle, the second biggest in England and still the seat of the Dukes of Northumberland, was restored from ruin in the 18th C.
Tourist Information Centre ☎ (01665) 510665

1 Beaconsfield Terrace
Alnwick NE66 1XB
☎ (01665) 602617
Imposing Victorian house in quiet residential area, yet only 4 minutes' walk to centre of town, 10 minutes' walk to castle.
Bedrooms: 2 double, 1 twin
Bathrooms: 2 public
Bed & breakfast

per night:	£min	£max
Single	16.00	17.00
Double	32.00	34.00

Parking for 6

Bondgate House Hotel
COMMENDED
20 Bondgate Without, Alnwick NE66 1PN
☎ (01665) 602025
Fax (01665) 602554
Small family-run hotel near the medieval town gateway and interesting local shops. Well-placed for touring. Most rooms are en-suite.

NORTHUMBRIA

Bedrooms: 1 single, 2 double, 2 twin, 2 triple, 1 family room
Bathrooms: 5 en-suite, 2 private, 1 public, 1 private shower

Bed & breakfast per night:	£min	£max
Single	23.00	25.00
Double	40.00	42.00
Half board per person:	£min	£max
Daily	35.00	37.00
Weekly	230.00	244.00

Evening meal 1830 (last orders 1630)
Parking for 8
Cards accepted: Access, Visa, Switch/Delta

The Georgian Guest House
APPROVED
3 Hotspur Street, Alnwick
NE66 1QE
☎ (01665) 602 398
Fax (01665) 602 398
Georgian house situated 200 yards from town centre, next to famous Hotspur Tower.
Bedrooms: 1 single, 3 double, 4 twin, 1 triple
Bathrooms: 4 private, 2 public

Bed & breakfast per night:	£min	£max
Single	15.00	18.00
Double	30.00	35.00

Parking for 8
Cards accepted: Access, Visa

Hotspur Hotel
APPROVED
Bondgate Without, Alnwick
NE66 1PR
☎ (01665) 510101
Fax (01665) 605033
Originally a coaching inn, centrally located, offering a warm welcome and friendly hospitality. Traditional and continental dishes, fine real ales.
Bedrooms: 5 single, 9 double, 12 twin, 1 family room
Bathrooms: 20 en-suite, 3 public

Bed & breakfast per night:	£min	£max
Single	30.00	35.00
Double	50.00	60.00
Half board per person:	£min	£max
Daily	42.50	47.50

Lunch available
Evening meal 1900 (last orders 2100)

Parking for 20
Cards accepted: Access, Visa, Diners, Amex

Masons Arms
COMMENDED
Stamford Cott, Rennington, Alnwick
NE66 3RX
☎ (01665) 577275
Fax (01665) 577894

Country inn offering real ale and good food. En-suite bedrooms. 3.5 miles from A1 towards coast and beaches, on B1340.
Bedrooms: 3 double, 1 twin, 1 triple
Suites available
Bathrooms: 5 en-suite

Bed & breakfast per night:	£min	£max
Single	38.00	38.00
Double	48.00	52.00

Lunch available
Evening meal 1900 (last orders 2100)
Parking for 20
Cards accepted: Access, Visa, Switch/Delta

BAMBURGH
Northumberland
Map ref 5C1

Village with a spectacular red sandstone castle standing 150 ft above the sea. On the village green the magnificent Norman church stands opposite a museum containing mementoes of the heroine Grace Darling.

Mizen Head Hotel
APPROVED
Lucker Road, Bamburgh NE69 7BS
☎ (01668) 214254
Privately-owned, fully licensed hotel in own grounds, with accent on good food and service. Convenient for beaches, castle and golf. 2 minutes' walk from village centre.
Bedrooms: 2 single, 5 double, 4 twin, 4 family rooms
Bathrooms: 11 en-suite, 2 public

Bed & breakfast per night:	£min	£max
Single	21.50	42.50
Double	43.00	74.00
Half board per person:	£min	£max
Daily	33.50	50.00
Weekly	224.00	300.00

Lunch available
Evening meal 1830 (last orders 2000)
Parking for 30
Cards accepted: Access, Visa

Waren House Hotel
HIGHLY COMMENDED
Waren Mill, Belford NE70 7EE
☎ (01668) 214581
Fax (01668) 214484
Logis of Great Britain
Traditional, beautifully restored, award-winning country house in 6 acres overlooking Holy Island. Quality accommodation and food, 250+ bin wine list. Adults only.
Bedrooms: 8 double, 2 twin
Suites available
Bathrooms: 10 en-suite

Bed & breakfast per night:	£min	£max
Single	55.00	80.00
Double	110.00	130.00
Half board per person:	£min	£max
Daily	55.00	77.50
Weekly	328.00	448.00

Evening meal 1900 (last orders 2030)
Parking for 26
Cards accepted: Access, Visa, Diners, Amex, Switch/Delta

BARDON MILL
Northumberland
Map ref 5B2

Small hamlet midway between Haydon Bridge and Haltwhistle, within walking distance of Vindolanda, an excavated Roman settlement, and near the best stretches of Hadrian's Wall.

Vallum Lodge Hotel
COMMENDED
Military Road, Twice Brewed, Bardon Mill, Hexham NE47 7AN
☎ Hexham (01434) 344248
Fax (01434) 344488
Small, quiet, comfortable hotel on the
Continued ▶

NORTHUMBRIA

BARDON MILL
Continued

B6318, in the Northumberland National Park. Close to the most spectacular part of Hadrian's Wall and the Pennine Way. Good choice of freshly cooked food.
Bedrooms: 1 single, 3 double, 2 twin, 1 triple
Bathrooms: 2 en-suite, 2 private, 2 public

Bed & breakfast per night:	£min	£max
Single	21.00	25.00
Double	40.00	51.00

Half board per person:	£min	£max
Daily	32.50	36.00
Weekly	224.00	252.00

Lunch available
Evening meal 1930 (last orders 2030)
Parking for 25
Open March–November
Cards accepted: Access, Visa, Amex

BARRASFORD
Northumberland
Map ref 5B2

Lovely village on the North Tyne River, overlooked by the restored 14th C Haughton Castle on the opposite bank.

Barrasford Arms
APPROVED
Barrasford, Hexham NE48 4AA
☎ Hexham (01434) 681237
Small country hotel in this lovely hamlet, only 8 miles from Hexham and 4 miles to the Roman Wall. An ideal centre for touring Northumberland.
Bedrooms: 1 double, 3 twin, 1 triple
Bathrooms: 4 en-suite, 1 public

Bed & breakfast per night:	£min	£max
Single	20.00	26.00
Double	26.00	36.00

Half board per person:	£min	£max
Daily	57.50	57.50
Weekly		350.00

Evening meal 1930 (last orders 2115)
Parking for 46
Cards accepted: Access, Visa

BEADNELL
Northumberland
Map ref 5C1

Charming fishing village on Beadnell Bay. Seashore lime kilns (National Trust), dating from the 18th C, recall busier days as a coal and lime port and a pub is built on to a medieval pele tower which survives from days of the border wars.

Beadnell Towers Hotel
COMMENDED
Beadnell, Chathill NE67 5AU
☎ Seahouses (01665) 721211
Fax (01665) 720424
An old hotel, full of character, in this beautiful coastal village near the Farne Islands.
Bedrooms: 1 single, 4 double, 4 twin, 3 triple
Bathrooms: 11 en-suite, 1 public

Bed & breakfast per night:	£min	£max
Single	27.50	27.50
Double	55.00	55.00

Half board per person:	£min	£max
Daily	35.00	38.50
Weekly	200.00	269.50

Lunch available
Evening meal 1900 (last orders 2100)
Parking for 25
Cards accepted: Access, Visa, Diners, Amex, Switch/Delta

BELFORD
Northumberland
Map ref 5B1

Small market town on the old coaching road, close to the coast, the Scottish border and the north-east flank of the Cheviots. Built mostly in stone and very peaceful now that the A1 has by-passed the town, Belford makes an ideal centre for excursions to the moors and coast.

Purdy Lodge
COMMENDED
Adderstone Services, Belford NE70 7JU
☎ (01668) 213000
Fax (01668) 213111

Please check prices and other details at the time of booking.

Situated 40 miles north of Newcastle, 75 miles south of Edinburgh on the A1. Comfortable accommodation. 5.5 miles away from breathtaking Bamburgh coast. Prices shown below are per room per night for single, double or family, excluding breakfast.
Bedrooms: 3 double, 10 twin, 6 triple, 1 family room
Bathrooms: 20 en-suite

Bed & breakfast per night:	£min	£max
Single	37.50	37.50
Double	37.50	37.50

Lunch available
Evening meal 1830 (last orders 2130)
Parking for 60
Cards accepted: Access, Visa, Diners, Amex, Switch/Delta

BELLINGHAM
Northumberland
Map ref 5B2

Set in the beautiful valley of the North Tyne close to the Kielder Forest, Kielder Water and lonely moorland below the Cheviots. The church has an ancient stone wagon roof fortified in the 18th C with buttresses.
Tourist Information Centre ☎ (01434) 220616

Riverdale Hall Hotel
COMMENDED
Bellingham, Hexham NE48 2JT
☎ (01434) 220254
Fax (01434) 220457
The Independents
Spacious country hall in large grounds. Indoor swimming pool, sauna, fishing, cricket field and golf opposite. Award-winning restaurant in hospitable family-run hotel.
Bedrooms: 3 single, 4 double, 9 twin, 4 triple
Bathrooms: 20 en-suite, 2 public

Bed & breakfast per night:	£min	£max
Single	40.00	45.00
Double	69.00	78.00

Half board per person:	£min	£max
Daily	52.00	63.00
Weekly	289.00	315.00

NORTHUMBRIA

Lunch available
Evening meal 1900 (last orders 2130)
Parking for 60
Cards accepted: Access, Visa, Diners, Amex, Switch/Delta

BERWICK-UPON-TWEED

Northumberland
Map ref 5B1

Guarding the mouth of the Tweed, England's northernmost town with the best 16th C city walls in Europe. The handsome Guildhall and barracks date from the 18th C. Three bridges cross to Tweedmouth, the oldest built in 1634.
Tourist Information Centre ☎ (01289) 330733

Kings Arms Hotel
COMMENDED
Hide Hill, Berwick-upon-Tweed TD15 1EJ
☎ (01289) 307454
Fax (01289) 308867

Well-known Georgian coaching inn with a walled garden, an ideal centre for touring the Borders and the coast.
Bedrooms: 9 single, 10 double, 14 twin, 3 triple
Bathrooms: 36 en-suite

Bed & breakfast per night:

	£min	£max
Single	39.50	53.50
Double	59.50	79.50

Half board per person:

	£min	£max
Daily	39.75	49.50
Weekly	244.30	320.60

Lunch available
Evening meal 1800 (last orders 2200)
Cards accepted: Access, Visa, Diners, Amex

Miranda's Guest House
43 Church Street, Berwick-upon-Tweed TD15 1EE
☎ (01289) 306483
Small, friendly guesthouse in the town centre of old Berwick yet away from traffic.

Bedrooms: 1 single, 2 double, 1 twin, 2 triple
Bathrooms: 2 public
Evening meal 1800 (last orders 1900)
Parking for 4

Queens Head Hotel
Sandgate, Berwick-upon-Tweed TD15 1EP
☎ (01289) 307852
Fax (01289) 307852
Near the town centre, opposite the swimming baths and adjacent to the historic town walls.
Bedrooms: 1 single, 1 double, 2 twin, 2 triple
Bathrooms: 6 en-suite, 1 public

Bed & breakfast per night:

	£min	£max
Single	30.00	35.00
Double	50.00	55.00

Half board per person:

	£min	£max
Daily	40.00	50.00
Weekly	250.00	

Lunch available
Evening meal 1830 (last orders 2100)
Cards accepted: Access, Visa, Amex

BLANCHLAND

Northumberland
Map ref 5B2

Beautiful medieval village rebuilt in the 18th C with stone from its ruined abbey, for lead miners working on the surrounding wild moors. The village is approached over a stone bridge across the Derwent or, from the north, through the ancient gatehouse.

Lord Crewe Arms Hotel
HIGHLY COMMENDED
Blanchland, Consett, County Durham DH8 9SP
☎ Hexham (01434) 675251
Fax (01434) 675 337
Originally Blanchland Abbey (built in 13th C), now a hotel, reputedly with a delightful ghost. Set in the Derwent Valley and surrounded by Northumberland moors.
Bedrooms: 10 double, 6 twin, 2 triple
Bathrooms: 18 en-suite

Bed & breakfast per night:

	£min	£max
Single	75.00	75.00
Double	105.00	105.00

Evening meal 1900 (last orders 2115)
Cards accepted: Access, Visa, Diners, Amex, Switch/Delta

CHOLLERFORD

Northumberland
Map ref 5B2

At the crossing of the military road and Hadrian's Wall over the North Tyne River and close to an important fort. Chesters Roman fort with the remains of its bridge, its living quarters and its bath houses stands in the park of an 18th C mansion.

The George Hotel
HIGHLY COMMENDED
Chollerford, Hexham NE46 4EW
☎ Hexham (01434) 681611
Fax (01434) 681727
CR Swallow
Lovely riverside setting close to Hadrian's Wall and Chesters Fort, 5 miles from Hexham. Many bedrooms and the restaurant overlook the attractive gardens and river. Leisure centre. Short break packages available.
Bedrooms: 3 single, 31 double, 14 twin
Bathrooms: 48 en-suite

Bed & breakfast per night:

	£min	£max
Single	90.00	110.00
Double	110.00	125.00

Half board per person:

	£min	£max
Daily	109.50	129.50

Lunch available
Evening meal 1900 (last orders 2130)
Parking for 100
Cards accepted: Access, Visa, Diners, Amex

The symbol CR and a group name following an hotel address indicates that bookings can be made through a central reservations office. These offices are listed in the information pages at the back of this guide.

NORTHUMBRIA

CONSETT

Durham
Map ref 5B2

Former steel town on the edge of rolling moors. Modern development includes the shopping centre and a handsome Roman Catholic church, designed by a local architect. To the west, the Derwent Reservoir provides water sports and pleasant walks.

Bee Cottage Farm ⚐

⚜⚜⚜ HIGHLY COMMENDED

Castleside, Consett, County Durham DH8 9HW
☎ (01207) 508224

46-acre livestock farm. 1.5 miles west of the A68, between Castleside and Tow Law. Unspoilt views. Ideally located for Beamish Museum and Durham. No smoking. Tea-room open 1-6 pm.
Bedrooms: 1 single, 3 double, 2 twin, 1 triple, 2 family rooms
Bathrooms: 1 en-suite, 2 private, 5 public
Bed & breakfast

per night:	£min	£max
Single	24.00	
Double	40.00	

Half board per person:	£min	£max
Daily	32.00	
Weekly	224.00	

Lunch available
Evening meal 1930 (last orders 2100)
Parking for 20

WELCOME HOST

This is a nationally recognised customer care programme which aims to promote the highest standards of service and a warm welcome. Establishments who are taking part in this initiative are indicated by the ✿ symbol.

CORBRIDGE

Northumberland
Map ref 5B2

Small town on the River Tyne. Close by are extensive remains of the Roman military town Corstopitum, with a museum housing important discoveries from excavations. The town itself is attractive with shady trees, a 17th C bridge and interesting old buildings, notably a 14th C vicarage.

Angel Inn ⚐

⚜⚜⚜ COMMENDED

Main Street, Corbridge NE45 5LA
☎ Hexham (01434) 632119
Old coaching inn in the centre of Corbridge providing an excellent base for touring the Roman Wall area and Northumberland.
Bedrooms: 3 double, 2 twin
Bathrooms: 5 en-suite
Bed & breakfast

per night:	£min	£max
Single		42.00
Double		64.00

Lunch available
Evening meal 1900 (last orders 2115)
Parking for 20
Cards accepted: Access, Visa, Diners, Amex

Fox & Hounds Hotel ⚐

⚜⚜⚜ COMMENDED

Stagshaw Bank, Corbridge NE45 5QW
☎ Hexham (01434) 633024
Fax (01434) 633024

400-year-old coaching inn with a 70-seat conservatory restaurant. Owners operate and live on premises.
Bedrooms: 4 double, 4 twin
Bathrooms: 8 en-suite
Bed & breakfast

per night:	£min	£max
Single	25.00	30.00
Double	40.00	40.00

Lunch available
Evening meal 1700 (last orders 2130)
Parking for 40

Lion of Corbridge Hotel

⚜⚜⚜ COMMENDED

Bridge End, Corbridge NE45 5AX
☎ Hexham (01434) 632504
Fax (01434) 632571
Ⓡ The Independents
Family-run hotel on a bank of the River Tyne with emphasis on comfort and good food. Room on ground floor especially equipped for disabled.
Special 2-3 day breaks available (room, breakfast and dinner £150.00 to £190.00 respectively).
Bedrooms: 8 double, 6 twin
Bathrooms: 14 en-suite
Bed & breakfast

per night:	£min	£max
Single		46.00
Double		56.00

Lunch available
Evening meal 1830 (last orders 2130)
Parking for 60
Cards accepted: Access, Visa, Diners, Amex, Switch/Delta

CROOK

Durham
Map ref 5C2

Pleasant market town sometimes referred to as "the gateway to Weardale". The town's shopping centre surrounds a large, open green, attractively laid out with lawns and flowerbeds around the Devil's Stone, a relic from the Ice Age.

Kensington Hall Hotel ⚐

⚜⚜⚜ COMMENDED

Kensington Terrace, Willington, Crook, County Durham DL15 0PJ
☎ Bishop Auckland (01388) 745071
Fax (01388) 745800
Comfortable family-run hotel with lounge bar, restaurant and function suite. Good meals daily. 8 miles from Durham on A690 to Crook.
Bedrooms: 2 double, 5 twin, 3 family rooms
Bathrooms: 10 en-suite
Bed & breakfast

per night:	£min	£max
Single	32.50	35.00
Double	45.00	48.00

Half board per person:	£min	£max
Daily	42.50	45.00

Lunch available
Evening meal 1900 (last orders 2145)
Parking for 40

NORTHUMBRIA

Cards accepted: Access, Visa, Diners, Amex, Switch/Delta

CROOKHAM

Northumberland
Map ref 5B1

Pretty hamlet taking its name from the winding course of the River Till which flows in the shape of a shepherd's crook. Three castles - Etal, Duddo and Ford - can be seen, and nearby the restored Heatherslaw Mill is of great interest.

The Coach House
HIGHLY COMMENDED

Crookham, Cornhill-on-Tweed TD12 4TD
☎ (01890) 820293 & 820284
Fax (01890) 820284

Spacious rooms, arranged around a courtyard, in rolling country near the Scottish border. Home-cooked, quality fresh food. Rooms specially equipped for disabled guests.
Wheelchair access category 1
Bedrooms: 2 single, 2 double, 5 twin
Bathrooms: 7 en-suite, 2 public

Bed & breakfast
per night: £min £max
Single 23.00 34.00
Double 46.00 68.00

Half board per
person: £min £max
Daily 38.50 49.50

Evening meal 1930 (last orders 1930)
Parking for 12
Open March–November
Cards accepted: Access, Visa

DARLINGTON

Durham
Map ref 5C3

Largest town in County Durham, standing on the River Skerne and home of the earliest passenger railway which first ran to Stockton in 1825. Now the home of a railway museum. Originally a prosperous market town occupying the site of an Anglo-Saxon settlement, it still holds an open market.
Tourist Information Centre ☎ (01325) 382698

Aberlady Guest House
APPROVED

51 Corporation Road, Darlington, County Durham DL3 6AD
☎ (01325) 461449
Large Victorian house near town centre.

Short walking distance to Railway Museum. Within easy reach of 4 golf courses and leisure centre.
Bedrooms: 2 single, 3 twin, 2 triple
Bathrooms: 2 public

Bed & breakfast
per night: £min £max
Single 13.50 16.00
Double 25.00 27.00

Parking for 2

Grange Hotel

South End, Coniscliffe Road, Darlington, County Durham DL3 7HZ
☎ (01325) 464555
Fax (01325) 464555

Imposing stately mansion built 1804, once the home of Joseph Pease, first Quaker MP and promoter of early railways. Was also a convent from 1905 to 1975. Here we offer you the comfort and contentment of gracious living.
Bedrooms: 2 single, 2 double, 5 twin, 1 triple
Bathrooms: 10 private

Bed & breakfast
per night: £min £max
Single 25.00 38.00
Double 40.00 52.00

Evening meal 1700 (last orders 1800)
Parking for 50

Greenbank Guest House
APPROVED

90 Greenbank Road, Darlington, County Durham DL3 6EL
☎ (01325) 462624
Large Victorian town property, 5 minutes from town centre and all amenities. Just off A68.
Bedrooms: 5 single, 3 double, 6 twin, 6 triple
Bathrooms: 4 en-suite, 5 public

Bed & breakfast
per night: £min £max
Single 16.00 19.00
Double 32.00 38.00

Half board per
person: £min £max
Daily 20.00 25.00
Weekly 140.00 150.00

Evening meal 1800 (last orders 1900)
Parking for 3

Swallow King's Head Hotel
COMMENDED

Priestgate, Darlington, County Durham DL1 1NW
☎ (01325) 380222
Fax (01325) 382006
Swallow

Comfortable hotel with restaurant, coffee shop and bar, in the town centre close to shops and entertainments. Short break packages available.
Bedrooms: 46 single, 14 double, 22 twin, 3 family rooms
Suite available
Bathrooms: 85 en-suite

Bed & breakfast
per night: £min £max
Single 55.00 89.00
Double 80.00 99.00

Half board per
person: £min £max
Daily 71.95 105.95

Lunch available
Evening meal 1900 (last orders 2130)
Parking for 28
Cards accepted: Access, Visa, Diners, Amex, Switch/Delta

Walworth Castle Hotel

Walworth, Darlington, County Durham DL2 2LY
☎ (01325) 485470
Fax (01325) 462257

A 12th C castle in 18 acres of lawns and woods, privately owned, offering comfort and food at modest prices. 3 miles west of Darlington off the A68.
Bedrooms: 4 single, 23 double, 5 twin, 4 triple
Bathrooms: 36 en-suite, 2 public

Bed & breakfast
per night: £min £max
Single 35.00 50.50
Double 56.50 76.50

Half board per
person: £min £max
Daily 45.00 65.00

Lunch available
Evening meal 1900 (last orders 2200)
Parking for 250

Continued ▶

109

NORTHUMBRIA

DARLINGTON
Continued

Cards accepted: Access, Visa, Diners, Amex, Switch/Delta

Woodland House
COMMENDED

63 Woodland Road, Darlington, County Durham DL3 7BQ
☎ (01325) 461908
Victorian town house built in 1876. Tastefully decorated bedrooms with all amenities.
Bedrooms: 2 single, 1 double, 2 twin, 3 triple
Bathrooms: 3 en-suite, 2 public

Bed & breakfast per night:	£min	£max
Single	21.00	28.00
Double	36.00	42.00

DURHAM
Durham
Map ref 5C2

Ancient city with its Norman castle and cathedral, now a World Heritage site, set on a bluff high over the Wear. A market and university town and regional centre, spreading beyond the market-place on both banks of the river.
Tourist Information Centre ☎ (0191) 384 3720

Bay Horse Inn
COMMENDED

Brandon Village, Durham, County Durham DH7 8ST
☎ (0191) 378 0498
Ten stone-built chalets 3 miles from Durham city centre. All have shower, toilet, TV, tea and coffee facilities and telephone. Ample car parking.
Bedrooms: 3 double, 6 twin, 1 family room
Bathrooms: 10 en-suite

Bed & breakfast per night:	£min	£max
Single	30.00	30.00
Double	39.00	39.00

Lunch available
Evening meal 1900 (last orders 2200)
Parking for 25
Cards accepted: Access, Visa

Bees Cottage Guest House
COMMENDED

Bridge Street, Durham, County Durham DH1 4RT
☎ (0191) 384 5775
Durham's oldest cottage, in city centre and convenient for shops, rail and bus. Hospitality tray, English or vegetarian breakfast, early morning call. All rooms en-suite with TV. No smoking, please. Private parking.
Bedrooms: 1 double, 2 twin, 1 triple
Bathrooms: 4 en-suite

Bed & breakfast per night:	£min	£max
Single	33.00	33.00
Double	45.00	45.00

Parking for 4

Castle View Guest House
COMMENDED

4 Crossgate, Durham, County Durham DH1 4PS
☎ (0191) 386 8852
Fax (0191) 386 8852
250-year-old, listed building in the heart of the old city, with woodland and riverside walks and a magnificent view of the cathedral and castle.
Bedrooms: 1 single, 2 double, 2 twin, 1 triple
Bathrooms: 3 en-suite, 2 private, 1 public

Bed & breakfast per night:	£min	£max
Single	25.00	38.00
Double	38.00	48.00

Crossways Hotel
COMMENDED

Dunelm Road, Thornley, Durham, County Durham DH6 3HT
☎ Wellfield (01429) 821248
Fax (01429) 820034
The Independents
Well-appointed private hotel, all rooms en-suite, satellite TV. Solarium, 3 bars, ballroom and a la carte restaurant. Entertainment certain nights. Durham Cathedral 6 miles.
Bedrooms: 5 single, 5 double, 8 twin, 1 triple
Bathrooms: 19 en-suite

Bed & breakfast per night:	£min	£max
Single	39.00	48.00
Double	48.00	65.00

Half board per person:	£min	£max
Daily	49.00	65.00
Weekly	238.00	280.00

Lunch available
Evening meal 1900 (last orders 2145)
Parking for 100
Cards accepted: Access, Visa, Diners, Amex

Drumforke
COMMENDED

25 Crossgate Peth, Durham, County Durham DH1 4PZ
☎ (0191) 384 2966
Near the city centre and providing a useful base for touring the beautiful dales of Weardale and Teesdale.
Bedrooms: 2 twin, 1 triple
Bathrooms: 1 public

Bed & breakfast per night:	£min	£max
Single	20.00	
Double	35.00	

Parking for 4

Hill Rise Guest House
HIGHLY COMMENDED

13 Durham Road West, Bowburn, Durham DH6 5AU
☎ (0191) 377 0302
Fax (0191) 3770302
Conveniently placed 200 yards from A1(M). Family, twin and double rooms with en-suite facilities. Quality home-cooked evening meals available.
Bedrooms: 2 single, 1 twin, 2 triple, 1 family room
Suites available
Bathrooms: 4 en-suite, 1 public

Bed & breakfast per night:	£min	£max
Single	18.00	25.00
Double	40.00	40.00

Half board per person:	£min	£max
Daily	28.00	35.00
Weekly	196.00	245.00

Evening meal 1850 (last orders 1900)
Parking for 4

Queens Head Hotel
APPROVED

Gilesgate, Durham DH1 2JR
☎ (0191) 386 5649
Under a mile from the city centre in a main road position. Bar with pool and darts.
Bedrooms: 1 single, 3 double, 3 twin, 1 triple, 1 family room
Bathrooms: 2 private, 2 public

Bed & breakfast per night:	£min	£max
Single	18.00	26.00
Double	36.00	40.00

NORTHUMBRIA

Lunch available
Parking for 12

Ramside Hall Hotel
HIGHLY COMMENDED
Carrville, Durham, County Durham
DH1 1TD
☎ (0191) 386 5282
Fax (0191) 386 0399
Consort
Attractive en-suite bedrooms, 3 eating areas, entertainment nightly. Surrounded by 27-hole golf course, just 3 miles from Durham.
Bedrooms: 2 single, 48 double, 32 twin
Suites available
Bathrooms: 82 en-suite
Bed & breakfast
per night:	£min	£max
Single	60.00	95.00
Double	80.00	120.00

Half board per
person:	£min	£max
Daily	75.00	110.00

Lunch available
Evening meal 1900 (last orders 2230)
Parking for 500
Cards accepted: Access, Visa, Diners, Amex, Switch/Delta

Redhills Hotel
APPROVED
Redhills Lane, Crossgate Moor, Durham, County Durham
DH1 4AW
☎ (0191) 386 4331
Small, friendly hotel with well-appointed bedrooms and personal service, only 2 minutes from Durham city centre.
Bedrooms: 5 single, 1 double
Bathrooms: 2 public
Bed & breakfast
per night:	£min	£max
Single	25.00	30.00
Double	30.00	36.00

Half board per
person:	£min	£max
Daily	37.00	42.00
Weekly	200.00	280.00

Lunch available
Evening meal 1900 (last orders 2200)
Parking for 80
Cards accepted: Access, Visa, Diners, Amex

Roadchef Lodge
COMMENDED
Durham Motorway Service Area, A1(M), Tursdale Road, Bowburn, Durham DH6 5NP
☎ (0191) 3773666 & Freephone 0800 834719
Fax (0191) 377 1448
RoadChef
RoadChef Lodges offer high specification rooms at affordable prices, in popular locations suited to both the business and private traveller. Prices are per room and do not include breakfast.
Bedrooms: 21 double, 16 twin, 1 family room
Bathrooms: 38 en-suite
Bed & breakfast
per night:	£min	£max
Single	37.95	39.95

Parking for 158
Cards accepted: Access, Visa, Diners, Amex, Switch/Delta

Royal County Hotel
HIGHLY COMMENDED
Old Elvet, Durham, County Durham
DH1 3JN
☎ (0191) 386 6821
Fax (0191) 386 0704
Swallow
In the heart of a historic cathedral city, this well-appointed hotel with a superb leisure club has a fascinating history. Choice of restaurants. Short break packages available.
Wheelchair access category 1
Bedrooms: 53 single, 46 double, 47 twin, 4 family rooms
Bathrooms: 150 en-suite
Bed & breakfast
per night:	£min	£max
Single	75.00	110.00
Double	85.00	130.00

Half board per
person:	£min	£max
Daily	90.00	131.00

Lunch available
Evening meal 1900 (last orders 2215)
Parking for 85
Cards accepted: Access, Visa, Diners, Amex, Switch/Delta

For further information on accommodation establishments use the coupons at the back of this guide.

St. Aidan's College
University of Durham, Windmill Hill, Durham, County Durham DH1 3LJ
☎ (0191) 374 3269
Comfortable, modern college in beautiful landscaped gardens overlooking the cathedral. Adjacent to golf-course. Standard and en-suite single and twin-bedded rooms.
Bedrooms: 293 single, 66 twin
Bathrooms: 92 en-suite, 48 public
Bed & breakfast
per night:	£min	£max
Single	16.50	27.00
Double	30.00	49.00

Half board per
person:	£min	£max
Daily	24.50	35.00
Weekly	155.00	220.00

Lunch available
Evening meal 1830 (last orders 1930)
Parking for 80
Open January, March–April, July–September, December
Cards accepted: Visa

Three Tuns Hotel
COMMENDED
New Elvet, Durham, County Durham DH1 3AQ
☎ (0191) 386 4326
Fax (0191) 386 1406
Swallow
Originally a coaching inn, the hotel has been tastefully modernised to provide first-class facilities. Within easy walking distance of the magnificent Norman cathedral. Short break packages available.
Bedrooms: 15 single, 12 double, 18 twin, 1 triple, 1 family room
Suite available
Bathrooms: 47 en-suite
Bed & breakfast
per night:	£min	£max
Single	80.00	95.00
Double	90.00	110.00

Half board per
person:	£min	£max
Daily	95.50	110.50

Lunch available
Evening meal 1900 (last orders 2130)
Parking for 60
Cards accepted: Access, Visa, Diners, Amex, Switch/Delta

Please mention this guide when making your booking.

NORTHUMBRIA

DURHAM
Continued

Trevelyan College
Elvet Hill Road, Durham, County Durham DH1 3LN
☎ (0191) 374 3765 & 374 3768
Fax (0191) 374 3789
Set in parkland within easy walking distance of Durham City. Comfortable Cloister Bar, TV lounges, ample parking. Standard and en-suite rooms available.
Bedrooms: 253 single, 8 double, 27 twin
Bathrooms: 58 en-suite, 47 public

Bed & breakfast per night:	£min	£max
Single	16.95	27.50

Half board per person:	£min	£max
Daily	29.90	49.50

Lunch available
Evening meal 1800 (last orders 1930)
Parking for 100
Open January, March–April, June–September, December

Van Mildert College (Tunstall Stairs)
Mill Hill Lane, Durham, County Durham DH1 3LH
☎ (0191) 3743900
Fax (0191) 3743974
College and conference centre in beautiful lakeside surroundings. Adjacent to golf course, half a mile from Durham Cathedral and Castle World Heritage Site.
Bedrooms: 30 single
Bathrooms: 30 en-suite

Bed & breakfast per night:	£min	£max
Single	27.50	27.50
Double	41.25	41.25

Half board per person:	£min	£max
Daily	35.00	35.00
Weekly	209.60	209.60

Lunch available
Parking for 100
Open March–April, July–September, December

Map references apply to the colour maps at the back of this guide.

EAGLESCLIFFE
Tees Valley
Map ref 5C3

Railway suburb of Stockton-on-Tees on the road to Yarm. Preston Hall Park has a museum, zoo, Butterfly World, riverside walks, fishing and picnic areas.

Sunnyside Hotel
COMMENDED
580-582 Yarm Road, Eaglescliffe, Stockton-on-Tees, Cleveland TS16 0DF
☎ (01642) 780075
Fax (01642) 783789
Friendly family hotel, ideal for touring Cleveland and North Yorkshire, with easy access to main roads, the station and Teesside Airport.
Bedrooms: 9 single, 9 double, 3 twin, 2 triple
Bathrooms: 23 en-suite, 2 public

Bed & breakfast per night:	£min	£max
Single	20.00	36.00
Double	40.00	55.00

Lunch available
Evening meal 1845 (last orders 2000)
Parking for 20
Cards accepted: Access, Visa, Amex, Switch/Delta

EBCHESTER
Durham
Map ref 5B2

Old village standing on the 4-acre Roman fort Vindomara close to the place where the Roman road Dere Street crossed the River Derwent.

The Raven Country Hotel
HIGHLY COMMENDED
Broomhill, Ebchester, Consett, County Durham DH8 6RY
☎ (01207) 560367 & 562562
Fax (01207) 560262
Stone-built, traditionally decorated hotel with fine views over Derwent Valley. Conservatory Restaurant serving quality food. Lounge bar with excellent range of beers and bar meals. Twenty minutes from both Durham and Gateshead MetroCentre.
Bedrooms: 11 double, 14 twin, 3 triple
Bathrooms: 28 en-suite

Bed & breakfast per night:	£min	£max
Single	41.00	52.00
Double	57.00	69.00

Half board per person:	£min	£max
Daily	54.00	65.00

Lunch available
Evening meal 1900 (last orders 2200)
Parking for 100
Cards accepted: Access, Visa, Diners, Amex, Switch/Delta

EMBLETON
Northumberland
Map ref 5C1

Coastal village beside a golf-course spread along the edge of Embleton Bay. The old church was extensively restored in the 19th C. The vicarage incorporates a medieval pele tower.

Dunstanburgh Castle Hotel
COMMENDED
Embleton, Alnwick NE66 3UN
☎ Alnwick (01665) 576111

Coaching hotel in coastal village, minutes by foot from golden sandy beaches and National Trust coastline. 2 bars, restaurant and lounge.
Bedrooms: 2 single, 3 double, 9 twin, 2 triple, 1 family room
Bathrooms: 15 en-suite, 2 private

Bed & breakfast per night:	£min	£max
Single	18.50	29.50
Double	37.00	59.00

Half board per person:	£min	£max
Daily	33.95	42.25
Weekly	218.75	276.50

Lunch available
Evening meal 1900 (last orders 2000)
Parking for 25
Open March–November
Cards accepted: Access, Visa, Switch/Delta

A key to symbols can be found inside the back cover flap.

NORTHUMBRIA

The Sportsman ⚐
Listed COMMENDED
Embleton, Alnwick NE66 3XF
☎ Alnwick (01665) 576588
Fax (01665) 576524
Family-run hotel, recently refurbished. Includes dormitory facilities for golfing parties, etc. Bar meals available.
Bedrooms: 2 single, 2 double, 2 twin, 3 family rooms
Bathrooms: 6 en-suite, 3 private

Bed & breakfast
per night:	£min	£max
Single	20.00	25.00
Double	40.00	50.00

Half board per person:	£min	£max
Daily	30.00	35.00
Weekly	210.00	245.00

Lunch available
Evening meal 1830 (last orders 2100)
Cards accepted: Access, Visa, Amex, Switch/Delta

FIR TREE
Durham
Map ref 5C2

Attractive Pennine village on the scenic route to Scotland (A68), midway between Edinburgh and York and at the entrance to Weardale. Beautiful dales scenery. Convenient rural stopover for Durham City and cathedral.

Duke of York Inn ⚐
HIGHLY COMMENDED
Fir Tree, Crook, County Durham
DL15 8DG
☎ Bishop Auckland (01388) 762848

Please check prices and other details at the time of booking.

Early 18th C coaching inn with log fires. Furnished by "Mouseman" Thompson. Restaurant, en-suite bedrooms. Midway Edinburgh/York and convenient for Durham City and dales.
Bedrooms: 3 double, 1 twin
Bathrooms: 4 en-suite

Bed & breakfast
per night:	£min	£max
Single	48.00	
Double	65.00	

Lunch available
Evening meal 1830 (last orders 2200)
Parking for 60
Cards accepted: Access, Visa, Switch/Delta

Greenhead Country House Hotel ⚐

HIGHLY COMMENDED
Fir Tree, Crook, County Durham
DL15 8BL
☎ Bishop Auckland (01388) 763143

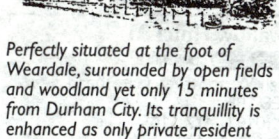

Perfectly situated at the foot of Weardale, surrounded by open fields and woodland yet only 15 minutes from Durham City. Its tranquillity is enhanced as only private resident guests are catered for - no public bars or discos.
Bedrooms: 4 double, 2 twin
Bathrooms: 6 private

Bed & breakfast
per night:	£min	£max
Single	35.00	38.00
Double	45.00	50.00

Evening meal 1800 (last orders 1700)
Parking for 15
Cards accepted: Access, Visa

Helme Park Hall Hotel ⚐
HIGHLY COMMENDED
Fir Tree, Crook, County Durham
DL13 4NW
☎ Bishop Auckland (01388) 730970
Fax (01388) 730970

Comfortable, fully refurbished hotel with open fires and warm welcoming atmosphere, in 5 acres of grounds and with spectacular views over the dales. A haven of peace and tranquillity.
Bedrooms: 2 single, 7 double, 2 twin, 2 triple
Bathrooms: 13 en-suite

Bed & breakfast
per night:	£min	£max
Single	38.00	38.00
Double	60.00	91.50

Lunch available
Evening meal 1900 (last orders 2100)
Parking for 70
Cards accepted: Access, Visa, Amex, Switch/Delta

Ad See display advertisement on this page

HELME PARK HALL COUNTRY HOUSE HOTEL
Near Fir Tree, Bishop Auckland,
Co. Durham. DL13 4NW
Tel: 01388 730970

A68 midway between Darlington and Corbridge,
14th century hunting lodge now a unique family run hotel. 25 miles of glorious views, immense character, log fires, extensive gardens.
Convenient touring centre for Lake District, Scottish Borders, Yorkshire Dales, and spectacular coast line.

Famous for food - A La Carte and Table d' Hote menus in the restaurant.
Bar meals approximately 125 main courses + starters and puds, approximately 100 Scotch Malt Whiskys, extensive wine list .

The Warmest Welcome in Northern England

R.A.C. Award of merit for Comfort, Hospitality & Service
R.A.C. ☆☆☆ A.A.
Northumbria Tourist Board 4 Crowns - Highly Commended

NORTHUMBRIA

FOREST-IN-TEESDALE

Durham
Map ref 5B2

An area in Upper Teesdale of widely-dispersed farmsteads set in wild but beautiful scenery with High Force Waterfall and Cauldron Snout. Once the hunting park of the Earls of Darlington.

High Force Hotel

Forest-in-Teesdale, Barnard Castle, County Durham DL12 0XH
☎ Teesdale (01833) 622222
Fax (01833) 622264
Hotel with own brewery in beautiful Upper Teesdale. Adjacent to the famous waterfall and the Pennine Way.
Bedrooms: 2 single, 2 twin, 2 triple
Bathrooms: 6 en-suite, 1 public

Bed & breakfast per night:	£min	£max
Single	15.00	22.00
Double	30.00	42.00

Lunch available
Evening meal 1900 (last orders 2130)
Parking for 20
Cards accepted: Access, Visa

GATESHEAD

Tyne and Wear
Map ref 5C2

Facing Newcastle across the Tyne, a busy industrial centre which grew rapidly early this century. Now it is a town of glass, steel and concrete buildings. Home of Europe's largest indoor shopping and leisure complex, the MetroCentre.
Tourist Information Centre ☎ (0191) 477 3478

Bewick Lodge

APPROVED

93-95 Bewick Road, Gateshead NE8 1RR
☎ Tyneside (0191) 477 3401
Fax (0191) 477 6146
Situated in a mixed commercial/residential area. Close to all amenities. Secure parking behind the lodge.
Bedrooms: 3 single, 3 double, 4 twin, 2 triple
Bathrooms: 10 en-suite, 2 public

Bed & breakfast per night:	£min	£max
Single	17.00	20.00
Double	30.00	34.00

Half board per person:	£min	£max
Daily	21.50	24.50
Weekly	140.00	154.00

Evening meal 1700 (last orders 1830)
Parking for 7

Shaftesbury House Hotel

APPROVED

245 Prince Consort Road, Gateshead NE8 4DT
☎ (0191) 478 2544
Fax (0191) 478 2544
Charming, Victorian, small family hotel. Central for MetroCentre, trains, buses, stadium, Team Valley, Newcastle, beaches and Beamish. Opposite Gateshead leisure centre. A1 to Gateshead South, then A167.
Bedrooms: 2 single, 2 double, 4 twin, 2 triple
Bathrooms: 2 en-suite, 3 public

Bed & breakfast per night:	£min	£max
Single	17.00	32.00
Double	28.00	40.00

Half board per person:	£min	£max
Daily	28.00	38.00
Weekly	175.00	260.00

Lunch available
Evening meal 1700 (last orders 1830)
Parking for 12

Swallow Hotel

COMMENDED

High West Street, Gateshead NE8 1PE
☎ (0191) 477 1105
Fax (0191) 478 7214
Swallow
Modern hotel 1 mile from Newcastle city centre just south of the River Tyne. Leisure complex incorporating pool, sauna, solarium and mini-gym. Well placed for visiting the MetroCentre. Short breaks packages available.
Bedrooms: 40 single, 46 double, 13 twin, 4 family rooms
Bathrooms: 103 en-suite

Bed & breakfast per night:	£min	£max
Single	70.00	85.00
Double	75.00	95.00

Half board per person:	£min	£max
Daily	87.50	102.50

Lunch available
Evening meal 1900 (last orders 2200)
Parking for 210

Cards accepted: Access, Visa, Diners, Amex, Switch/Delta

HAMSTERLEY FOREST

Durham

See under Crook, Fir Tree

HARTLEPOOL

Tees Valley
Map ref 5C2

Major industrial port north of Tees Bay. Occupying an ancient site, the town's buildings are predominantly modern. Local history can be followed in the Museum of Hartlepool and adjacent historic quay and there is a marina with restored ships.
Tourist Information Centre ☎ (01429) 266522 ext 2407

Grand Hotel

COMMENDED

Swainson Street, Hartlepool, Cleveland TS24 8AA
☎ (01429) 266345
Fax (01429) 265217
Traditional 19th C city centre hotel close to modern enclosed shopping centre. Extensively refurbished and an excellent base for visiting MetroCentre, Beamish and Durham.
Bedrooms: 15 single, 17 double, 12 twin, 3 family rooms
Suites available
Bathrooms: 47 en-suite

Bed & breakfast per night:	£min	£max
Single	47.50	65.00
Double	60.00	80.00

Lunch available
Evening meal 1930 (last orders 2200)
Parking for 10
Cards accepted: Access, Visa, Diners, Amex, Switch/Delta

Ryedale Moor Hotel

COMMENDED

3 Beaconsfield Street, Hartlepool, Cleveland TS24 ONX
☎ (01429) 231436
Fax (01429) 863787
The Independents/Logis of Great Britain
Family-run hotel with sea views. Licensed bar, all rooms en-suite. Close to new marina and quay developement.
Bedrooms: 5 single, 1 double, 6 twin
Bathrooms: 11 en-suite, 1 public, 1 private shower

NORTHUMBRIA

Bed & breakfast per night:	£min	£max
Single	35.00	43.00
Double	48.00	60.00

Half board per person:	£min	£max
Daily	40.00	60.00
Weekly	210.00	350.00

Lunch available
Evening meal 1900 (last orders 2100)
Parking for 6
Cards accepted: Access, Visa, Diners, Amex

HEXHAM

Northumberland
Map ref 5B2

Old coaching and market town near Hadrian's Wall. Since pre-Norman times a weekly market has been held in the centre with its market-place and abbey park, and the richly-furnished 12th C abbey church has a superb Anglo-Saxon crypt.
Tourist Information Centre ☎ *(01434) 605225*

County Hotel ♠
APPROVED

Priestpopple, Hexham NE46 1PS
☎ (01434) 602030
Fax (01434) 603202
Warm and comfortable hotel in the town centre. Ideal for touring the Roman Wall and border country, Kielder Water and Forest.
Bedrooms: 2 single, 4 double, 3 twin
Bathrooms: 8 en-suite, 1 private, 1 public

Bed & breakfast per night:	£min	£max
Single	35.00	42.00
Double	55.00	65.00

Half board per person:	£min	£max
Daily	45.00	50.00

Lunch available
Evening meal 1900 (last orders 2130)
Parking for 2
Cards accepted: Access, Visa, Diners, Amex, Switch/Delta

Stotsfold Hall ♠

Steel, Hexham NE47 0HP
☎ (01434) 673270
Beautiful house surrounded by 15 acres of gardens and woodland with streams and flowers. 6 miles south of Hexham.
Bedrooms: 2 single, 1 double, 1 twin
Bathrooms: 3 public

Bed & breakfast per night:	£min	£max
Single	20.00	20.00
Double	40.00	40.00

Parking for 6

HOLY ISLAND

Northumberland
Map ref 5B1

Still an idyllic retreat, tiny island and fishing village and cradle of northern Christianity. It is approached from the mainland at low water by a causeway. The clifftop castle (National Trust) was restored by Sir Edwin Lutyens.

Lindisfarne Hotel ♠

Holy Island, Berwick-upon-Tweed TD15 2SQ
☎ Berwick-upon-Tweed (01289) 389273
Fax (01289) 389284
Small, comfortable, family-run hotel providing coffees, lunches and evening meals. An ideal place for ornithologists and within walking distance of Lindisfarne Castle and Priory.
Bedrooms: 2 single, 1 double, 1 twin, 3 triple
Bathrooms: 5 en-suite, 1 public

Bed & breakfast per night:	£min	£max
Single	16.50	30.00
Double	33.00	52.00

Lunch available
Evening meal 1800 (last orders 2030)
Parking for 12
Cards accepted: Access, Visa, Diners, Amex, Switch/Delta

North View ♠
HIGHLY COMMENDED

Marygate, Holy Island, Berwick-upon-Tweed TD15 2SD
☎ Berwick-upon-Tweed (01289) 389222
400-year-old listed building on historic and beautiful island. Ideally situated for visiting many of Northumberland's tourist attractions.
Bedrooms: 2 double, 1 twin
Bathrooms: 3 en-suite

Bed & breakfast per night:	£min	£max
Single	22.50	30.00
Double	45.00	49.00

Half board per person:	£min	£max
Daily	34.50	42.00

Lunch available
Evening meal 1900 (last orders 2100)
Parking for 6
Cards accepted: Access, Visa

KIELDER FOREST

Northumberland

See under Bellingham, Kielder Water

KIELDER WATER

Northumberland
Map ref 5B2

A magnificent man-made lake, the largest in Northern Europe, with over 27 miles of shoreline. On the edge of the Northumberland National Park and near the Scottish border, Kielder can be explored by car, on foot or by ferry.

The Pheasant Inn (by Kielder Water) ♠
COMMENDED

Stannersburn, Falstone, Hexham NE48 1DD
☎ Hexham (01434) 240382
Logis of Great Britain

Historic inn with beamed ceilings and open fires. Home cooking. Fishing, riding and all water sports nearby. Close to Kielder Water, Hadrian's Wall and the Scottish border.
Bedrooms: 4 double, 3 twin, 1 family room
Bathrooms: 8 en-suite

Bed & breakfast per night:	£min	£max
Single	30.00	35.00
Double	52.00	56.00

Half board per person:	£min	£max
Daily	45.00	48.00

Continued ▶

> For ideas on places to visit refer to the introduction at the beginning of this section.

NORTHUMBRIA

KIELDER WATER
Continued

Lunch available
Evening meal 1900 (last orders 2100)
Parking for 30
Cards accepted: Access, Visa, Switch/Delta

LANGLEY-ON-TYNE

Northumberland
Map ref 5B2

Small hamlet by a tiny lake, set in beautiful countryside south of Haydon Bridge and the River South Tyne. The road from Haydon Bridge to Langley winds through woodland and past the Derwentwater Memorial and Langley Castle.

Langley Castle
COMMENDED

Langley-on-Tyne, Hexham NE47 5LU
☎ Haydon Bridge (01434) 688888
Fax (01434) 684019
14th C castle restored to a magnificent and comfortable hotel. 2 miles south west of Haydon Bridge, 30 minutes from Newcastle Airport. A69-A686 junction.
Bedrooms: 14 double, 2 twin
Bathrooms: 16 en-suite

Bed & breakfast per night:	£min	£max
Single	65.00	95.00
Double	90.00	135.00

Half board per person:	£min	£max
Daily	57.50	69.50

Lunch available
Evening meal 1900 (last orders 2100)
Parking for 100
Cards accepted: Access, Visa, Diners, Amex

MIDDLESBROUGH

Tees Valley
Map ref 5C3

Boom-town of the mid 19th C, today's Teesside industrial and conference town has a modern shopping complex and predominantly modern buildings. An engineering miracle of the early 20th C is the Transporter Bridge which replaced an old ferry.
Tourist Information Centre ☎ (01642) 243425 or 264330

Hospitality Inn
COMMENDED

Fry Street, Middlesbrough, Cleveland TS1 1JH
☎ (01642) 232000
Fax (01642) 232655
Utell International
City centre hotel with all modern amenities.
Bedrooms: 100 single, 78 twin, 2 triple
Suites available
Bathrooms: 180 en-suite

Bed & breakfast per night:	£min	£max
Single	39.00	91.50
Double	78.00	99.00

Half board per person:	£min	£max
Daily	47.00	105.00

Lunch available
Evening meal 1900 (last orders 2200)
Parking for 40
Cards accepted: Access, Visa, Diners, Amex

MIDDLETON-IN-TEESDALE

Durham
Map ref 5B3

Small stone town of hillside terraces overlooking the river, developed by the London Lead Company in the 18th C. Five miles up-river is the spectacular 70-ft waterfall, High Force.

Teesdale Hotel
COMMENDED

Middleton-in-Teesdale, Barnard Castle, County Durham DL12 0QG
☎ Teesdale (01833) 640264 & 640537
Fax (01833) 640651
Tastefully modernised, family-run 18th C coaching inn serving home cooking and fine wines. All rooms have telephone, radio and TV. Also 4 comfortable holiday cottages in hotel courtyard. Dogs welcome free of charge.
Bedrooms: 2 single, 5 double, 3 twin
Bathrooms: 10 en-suite

Bed & breakfast per night:	£min	£max
Single	38.50	42.50
Double	50.00	60.00

Half board per person:	£min	£max
Daily	57.45	
Weekly	300.85	

Lunch available
Evening meal 1930 (last orders 2030)
Parking for 24
Cards accepted: Access, Visa, Amex

NEWCASTLE UPON TYNE

Tyne and Wear
Map ref 5C2

Commercial and cultural centre of the North East, with a large indoor shopping centre, Quayside market, museums and theatres which offer an annual 6 week season by the Royal Shakespeare Company. Norman castle keep, medieval alleys, old Guildhall.
Tourist Information Centre ☎ (0191) 261 0610 or 230 0030

Brighton Guest House
APPROVED

47-49 Brighton Grove, Fenham, Newcastle upon Tyne NE4 5NS
☎ (0191) 273 3600
Fax (0191) 226 0563

Family-run guesthouse where you will receive a warm welcome. Rooms to suit all budgets.
Bedrooms: 4 single, 2 double, 8 twin, 3 triple, 1 family room
Suites available
Bathrooms: 8 en-suite, 3 public

Bed & breakfast per night:	£min	£max
Single	15.00	25.00
Double	30.00	45.00

Half board per person:	£min	£max
Daily	21.00	31.00

The map references refer to the colour maps towards the end of the guide. The first figure is the map number; the letter and figure which follow indicate the grid reference on the map.

NORTHUMBRIA

Evening meal 1700 (last orders 1900)
Parking for 10

Cairn Hotel
COMMENDED

97-103 Osborne Road, Jesmond, Newcastle upon Tyne NE2 2TJ
☎ (0191) 281 1358
Fax (0191) 281 9031
CR The Independents
The Cairn is situated in Jesmond, close to the Metro and bus route and near the city centre.
Bedrooms: 8 single, 24 double, 18 twin
Bathrooms: 50 en-suite

Bed & breakfast
per night:	£min	£max
Single	38.00	55.00
Double	40.00	70.00

Lunch available
Evening meal 1800 (last orders 2115)
Parking for 17
Cards accepted: Access, Visa, Diners, Amex, Switch/Delta

Comfort Inn Carlton
COMMENDED

82-86 Osborne Road, Jesmond, Newcastle upon Tyne NE2 2AP
☎ (0191) 281 3361
Fax (0191) 281 7722
CR The Independents
Recently refurbished hotel in a quiet residential area, on a direct bus route to the city centre.
Bedrooms: 17 single, 8 double, 7 twin, 2 triple
Bathrooms: 34 en-suite

Bed & breakfast
per night:	£min	£max
Single	40.00	60.00
Double	48.00	75.00

Lunch available
Evening meal 1830 (last orders 2100)
Parking for 12
Cards accepted: Access, Visa, Diners, Amex, Switch/Delta

The Copthorne Newcastle
HIGHLY COMMENDED

The Close, Quayside, Newcastle upon Tyne, Tyne & Wear NE1 3RT
☎ (0191) 222 0333
Fax (0191) 230 1111
CR Millennium & Copthorne/Utell International
Set amidst the historic quayside, all bedrooms, restaurants, bars and leisure club pool overlook the river. Free on-site car parking.
Bedrooms: 132 double, 24 twin
Bathrooms: 156 en-suite

Bed & breakfast
per night:	£min	£max
Single	79.00	160.00
Double	89.00	170.00

Lunch available
Evening meal 1830 (last orders 2215)
Parking for 180
Cards accepted: Access, Visa, Diners, Amex, Switch/Delta

Dene Hotel
COMMENDED

38-42 Grosvenor Road, Jesmond, Newcastle upon Tyne NE2 2RP
☎ (0191) 281 1502
Fax (0191) 281 8110
In a quiet residential area close to beautiful Jesmond Dene with its small children's zoo. Within easy reach of the city centre. Passenger lift.
Bedrooms: 13 single, 5 double, 5 twin
Bathrooms: 15 en-suite, 2 public, 8 private showers

Bed & breakfast
per night:	£min	£max
Single	27.50	37.50
Double	47.50	57.50

Half board per
person:	£min	£max
Daily	31.25	39.25

Lunch available
Evening meal 1730 (last orders 2000)
Parking for 17
Cards accepted: Access, Visa, Diners, Amex, Switch/Delta

Grosvenor Hotel
APPROVED

Grosvenor Road, Jesmond, Newcastle upon Tyne NE2 2RR
☎ (0191) 281 0543
Fax (0191) 281 9217
Friendly hotel in quiet residential suburb, offering a wide range of facilities. Close to city centre.
Bedrooms: 17 single, 8 double, 9 twin, 6 triple
Bathrooms: 32 en-suite, 5 public

Bed & breakfast
per night:	£min	£max
Single	20.00	40.00
Double	30.00	60.00

Half board per
person:	£min	£max
Daily	25.00	50.00
Weekly	175.00	350.00

Lunch available
Evening meal 1830 (last orders 2100)
Parking for 30
Cards accepted: Access, Visa, Diners, Amex, Switch/Delta

Hospitality Inn

Osborne Road, Jesmond, Newcastle upon Tyne NE2 2AT
☎ (0191) 281 7881
Fax (0191) 281 6241
CR Utell International
In a quiet residential area of Newcastle, just 1 mile from the centre and close to the city's Exhibition Park and Jesmond Dene.
Bedrooms: 10 single, 17 double, 52 twin, 6 triple
Suite available
Bathrooms: 85 en-suite

Bed & breakfast
per night:	£min	£max
Single	45.00	85.00
Double	70.00	160.00

Half board per
person:	£min	£max
Daily	59.00	100.00

Lunch available
Evening meal 1830 (last orders 2230)
Parking for 45
Cards accepted: Access, Visa, Diners, Amex

Imperial Swallow Hotel
COMMENDED

Jesmond Road, Newcastle upon Tyne NE2 1PR
☎ (0191) 281 5511
Fax (0191) 281 8472
CR Swallow
Newly refurbished hotel 10 minutes' walk from the city centre, near Jesmond Metro station, with leisure facilities and popular bar with a friendly atmosphere. Car park free to residents. Short break packages available.
Bedrooms: 53 single, 45 double, 18 twin, 3 triple, 3 family rooms
Bathrooms: 122 en-suite

Bed & breakfast
per night:	£min	£max
Single	68.00	85.00
Double	78.00	95.00

Continued ▶

NORTHUMBRIA

NEWCASTLE UPON TYNE
Continued

Half board per person:	£min	£max
Daily	84.00	101.00

Lunch available
Evening meal 1900 (last orders 2145)
Parking for 130
Cards accepted: Access, Visa, Diners, Amex, Switch/Delta

Jesmond Park Hotel

74-76 Queens Road, Jesmond, Newcastle upon Tyne NE2 2PR
☎ (0191) 281 2821 & 281 1913
Fax (0191) 281 0515
Clean and friendly hotel offering good English breakfast, in a quiet area close to city centre.
Bedrooms: 8 single, 2 double, 3 twin, 1 triple, 2 family rooms
Bathrooms: 7 en-suite, 3 public, 1 private shower

Bed & breakfast per night:	£min	£max
Single	24.00	34.00
Double	39.00	44.00

Parking for 14
Cards accepted: Access, Visa

Newcastle Marriott (Gateshead)
HIGHLY COMMENDED

Metro Centre, Gateshead, Newcastle upon Tyne NE11 9XF
☎ Tyneside (0191) 493 2233
Fax (0191) 493 2030
Utell International/Whitbread
Beautifully appointed hotel, ideally located off A1. 5 minutes' walk from MetroCentre, shopping and leisure development. Health club, restaurant and bars. Conference facilities and free parking.
Wheelchair access category 3
Bedrooms: 148 double
Suites available
Bathrooms: 148 en-suite, 2 public

Bed & breakfast per night:	£min	£max
Single	108.00	125.00
Double	118.00	147.00

Evening meal 1900 (last orders 2230)
Parking for 250
Cards accepted: Access, Visa, Diners, Amex, Switch/Delta

Royal Station Hotel
COMMENDED

Neville Street, Newcastle upon Tyne NE1 5DH
☎ (0191) 232 0781
Fax (0191) 222 0786
The Independents
Opened by Queen Victoria in 1858, the hotel combines elegant Victorian architecture with up-to-date facilities. Fully refurbished, family-run. We take pride in offering a friendly and courteous service to all our clients.
Bedrooms: 40 single, 40 double, 40 twin, 2 triple, 4 family rooms
Bathrooms: 126 en-suite

Bed & breakfast per night:	£min	£max
Single	45.00	65.00
Double	60.00	75.00

Lunch available
Evening meal 1900 (last orders 2130)
Parking for 100
Cards accepted: Access, Visa, Diners, Amex, Switch/Delta

Surtees Hotel
COMMENDED

12-16 Dean Street, Newcastle upon Tyne NE1 1PG
☎ (0191) 261 7771
Fax (0191) 230 1322
Minotel
City-centre hotel within walking distance of Eldon Square, the Quayside and station, with a 24-hour multi-storey car park adjacent. Cocktail and public bar, restaurant and nightclub. All bedrooms are en-suite with satellite TV and tea making facilities.
Bedrooms: 12 single, 7 double, 8 twin
Bathrooms: 27 en-suite

Bed & breakfast per night:	£min	£max
Single	45.00	61.50
Double	55.00	81.50

Lunch available
Evening meal 1700 (last orders 2230)
Cards accepted: Access, Visa, Diners, Amex, Switch/Delta

Swallow Hotel
COMMENDED

Newgate Arcade, Newcastle upon Tyne NE1 5SX
☎ (0191) 232 5025
Fax (0191) 232 8428
Swallow
Comfortable, modern hotel with a roof-top restaurant, in the heart of Newcastle city centre. An ideal base for a shopping weekend. Short break packages available.
Bedrooms: 1 single, 17 double, 72 twin, 3 triple
Bathrooms: 93 en-suite

Bed & breakfast per night:	£min	£max
Single	60.00	85.00
Double	70.00	95.00

Half board per person:	£min	£max
Daily	75.50	100.50

Lunch available
Evening meal 1830 (last orders 2130)
Parking for 100
Cards accepted: Access, Visa, Diners, Amex

Swallow Gosforth Park Hotel
HIGHLY COMMENDED

High Gosforth Park, Newcastle upon Tyne NE3 5HN
☎ (0191) 236 4111
Fax (0191) 236 8192
Swallow
Beautifully appointed hotel set in 12 acres of woodland, 5 miles north of city centre. Facilities include restaurants, bars, leisure complex and conference facilities. Short break packages available.
Bedrooms: 110 double, 63 twin, 5 triple
Suites available
Bathrooms: 178 en-suite

Bed & breakfast per night:	£min	£max
Single	70.00	110.00
Double	80.00	125.00

Half board per person:	£min	£max
Daily	85.75	132.00

Lunch available
Evening meal 1800 (last orders 2230)
Parking for 300
Cards accepted: Access, Visa, Diners, Amex, Switch/Delta

Information on accommodation listed in this guide has been supplied by the proprietors. As changes may occur you are advised to check details at the time of booking.

NORTHUMBRIA

NEWTON AYCLIFFE

Durham
Map ref 5C3

Northern England's first New Town growing from 60 persons in 1947 to over 27,000 today. Leisure centres in the town centre and at Spennymoor offer a wide range of facilities.

Redworth Hall
HIGHLY COMMENDED

Redworth, Newton Aycliffe, County Durham DL5 6NL
☎ Bishop Auckland (01388) 772442
Fax (01388) 775112
Grand Heritage

Beautiful 17th C country house hotel, providing excellent leisure and conference facilities. An ideal venue for business or pleasure.
Wheelchair access category 2
Bedrooms: 3 single, 35 double, 42 twin, 7 triple, 13 family rooms
Bathrooms: 100 en-suite

Bed & breakfast per night:	£min	£max
Single	105.00	115.00
Double	125.00	160.00

Half board per person:	£min	£max
Daily	74.50	79.50
Weekly	521.50	556.50

Lunch available
Evening meal 1900 (last orders 2200)
Parking for 200
Cards accepted: Access, Visa, Diners, Amex, Switch/Delta

OTTERBURN

Northumberland
Map ref 5B1

Small village set at the meeting of the River Rede with Otter Burn, the site of the Battle of Otterburn in 1388. A peaceful tradition continues in the sale of Otterburn tweeds in this beautiful region, which is ideal for exploring the Border country and the Cheviots.

The Butterchurn Guest House
COMMENDED

Main Street, Otterburn NE19 1NP
☎ (01830) 520585

In village centre, on the River Rede. Central for Roman Wall and Kielder Water. Within easy reach of Northumberland coast. Fishing permits available.
Bedrooms: 2 double, 2 twin, 3 triple
Bathrooms: 7 en-suite

Bed & breakfast per night:	£min	£max
Single	22.00	22.00
Double	34.00	36.00

Half board per person:	£min	£max
Daily	27.00	31.00
Weekly	189.00	217.00

Evening meal 1900 (last orders 1900)
Parking for 10
Cards accepted: Access, Visa

Redesdale Arms Hotel
COMMENDED

Rochester, Otterburn, Newcastle upon Tyne NE19 1TA
☎ (01830) 520668
Fax (01830) 520063

Family-run old coaching inn with log fires. Central for Hadrian's Wall and Kielder Forest. All rooms en-suite.
Bedrooms: 3 double, 5 twin, 2 triple
Bathrooms: 10 en-suite

Bed & breakfast per night:	£min	£max
Single	33.00	38.00
Double	50.00	60.00

Lunch available
Evening meal 1900 (last orders 2200)
Parking for 30
Cards accepted: Access, Visa, Diners, Switch/Delta

REDCAR

Tees Valley
Map ref 5C3

Lively holiday resort near Teesside with broad sandy beaches, a fine racecourse, a large indoor funfair at Coatham and other seaside amusements. Britain's oldest existing lifeboat can be seen at the Zetland Museum.

Claxton Hotel

196 High Street, Redcar, Cleveland TS10 3AW
☎ (01642) 486745
Fax (01642) 486522

Hotel facing the sea with traditionally-styled dining room and bar featuring huge inglenook fireplace.
Bedrooms: 3 single, 3 double, 17 twin, 1 triple, 1 family room
Bathrooms: 23 en-suite, 2 public, 2 private showers

Bed & breakfast per night:	£min	£max
Single	20.00	25.00
Double	38.00	40.00

Evening meal 1730 (last orders 2100)
Parking for 10

Falcon Hotel
APPROVED

13 Station Road, Redcar, Cleveland TS10 1AH
☎ (01642) 484300

Small licensed hotel in centre of town, providing home cooking and a warm welcome. Within easy reach of the Cleveland Hills and surrounding countryside.
Wheelchair access category 3
Bedrooms: 4 single, 3 twin, 1 triple, 4 family rooms
Bathrooms: 4 en-suite, 3 public

Bed & breakfast per night:	£min	£max
Single	16.00	18.00
Double	27.00	34.00

Half board per person:	£min	£max
Daily	21.50	24.50
Weekly	150.50	171.50

Evening meal 1700 (last orders 1900)

ROTHBURY

Northumberland
Map ref 5B1

Old market town on the River Coquet near the Simonside Hills. It makes an ideal centre for walking and fishing or for exploring this beautiful area from the coast to the Cheviots. Cragside House and Gardens (National Trust) are open to the public.

Orchard Guest House
HIGHLY COMMENDED

High Street, Rothbury, Morpeth NE65 7TL
☎ (01669) 620684

Charming guesthouse in the middle of a lovely village, an ideal centre for visiting all Northumbria's attractions. Comfortable surroundings.
Bedrooms: 2 double, 4 twin
Bathrooms: 4 en-suite, 1 private, 3 public

Continued ▶

NORTHUMBRIA

ROTHBURY
Continued

Bed & breakfast per night: £min / £max
Single 20.00 / 23.50
Double 40.00 / 47.00

Half board per person: £min / £max
Daily 33.50 / 37.00
Weekly 227.00 / 252.00

Evening meal 1900 (last orders 1900)
Open March–October

ROWLANDS GILL
Tyne and Wear
Map ref 5C2

Adjacent to the Derwent Walk Country Park on the side of the River Derwent, opposite the National Trust Gibside Chapel.

Towneley Arms Hotel
Listed APPROVED
Station Road, Rowlands Gill, Gateshead NE39 1QF
☎ (01207) 542274
Fax (01207) 542523
On Station Road, with excellent views over the Derwent Valley. Only minutes away from Gateshead MetroCentre.
Bedrooms: 4 single, 13 double
Bathrooms: 17 en-suite

Bed & breakfast per night: £min / £max
Single 30.00 / 40.00
Double 50.00 / 70.00

Half board per person: £min / £max
Daily 35.00 / 45.00
Weekly 245.00 / 315.00

Lunch available
Evening meal 1800 (last orders 2130)
Parking for 200
Cards accepted: Access, Visa, Amex, Switch/Delta

Map references apply to the colour maps at the back of this guide.

Establishments should be open throughout the year, unless otherwise stated.

RUSHYFORD
Durham
Map ref 5C2

Small village on the old Great North Road.

Eden Arms Swallow Hotel
COMMENDED
Rushyford, Durham DL17 0LL
☎ Bishop Auckland (01388) 720541
Fax (01388) 721871
Swallow
17th C coaching inn with leisure club, 10 miles south of Durham City. Ideal base for visiting Durham and the Tees Valley. Short break packages available.
Bedrooms: 13 single, 14 double, 15 twin, 4 triple
Bathrooms: 46 en-suite

Bed & breakfast per night: £min / £max
Single 60.00 / 90.00
Double 85.00 / 105.00

Half board per person: £min / £max
Daily 76.95 / 106.95

Lunch available
Evening meal 1900 (last orders 2200)
Parking for 150
Cards accepted: Access, Visa, Diners, Amex, Switch/Delta

SEAHOUSES
Northumberland
Map ref 5C1

Small modern resort developed around a 19th C herring port. Just offshore, and reached by boat from here, are the rocky Farne Islands (National Trust) where there is an important bird reserve. The bird observatory occupies a medieval pele tower.

Beach House Hotel
COMMENDED
Sea Front, Seahouses NE68 7SR
☎ (01665) 720337
Fax (01665) 720921
Logis of Great Britain

Quiet, comfortable and friendly, family-run hotel overlooking the Farne Islands. Specialising in imaginative home cooking and baking.
Bedrooms: 2 single, 4 double, 6 twin, 2 triple
Bathrooms: 14 en-suite, 2 public

Bed & breakfast per night: £min / £max
Single 29.50 / 37.00
Double 59.00 / 74.00

Half board per person: £min / £max
Daily 39.50 / 48.00

Evening meal 1900 (last orders 2030)
Parking for 16
Open April–October
Cards accepted: Access, Visa, Amex, Switch/Delta

Links Hotel
COMMENDED
8 King Street, Seahouses NE68 7XP
☎ Alnwick (01665) 720062
Fax (01665) 721305
All rooms with colour TV and tea-making facilities. Lounge, bar and dining room. 2 minutes from harbour.
Bedrooms: 5 double, 3 twin, 1 family room
Bathrooms: 4 en-suite, 2 public

Bed & breakfast per night: £min / £max
Single 20.00 / 35.00
Double 36.00 / 50.00

Half board per person: £min / £max
Daily 30.00 / 47.00
Weekly 180.00 / 220.00

Lunch available
Evening meal 1900 (last orders 2030)
Parking for 16
Cards accepted: Access, Visa

Olde Ship Hotel
COMMENDED
Seahouses NE68 7RD
☎ (01665) 720200
Fax (01665) 721383
Hotel with a long-established reputation for food and drink in comfortably relaxing old-fashioned surroundings.
Bedrooms: 1 single, 9 double, 5 twin, 1 triple
Suites available
Bathrooms: 16 en-suite, 2 public

Bed & breakfast per night: £min / £max
Single 29.50 / 35.00
Double 59.00 / 70.00

NORTHUMBRIA

Half board per person:	£min	£max
Daily	42.50	48.50
Weekly	280.00	295.00

Lunch available
Evening meal 1900 (last orders 2030)
Parking for 12
Open February–November
Cards accepted: Access, Visa, Switch/Delta

St Aidan Hotel

COMMENDED

On the Seafront, Seahouses NE68 7SR
☎ (01665) 720355
Fax (01665) 830333
Unrivalled seafront location, overlooking the Farne Islands. All food is prepared and presented by the internationally trained chef/proprietor.
Bedrooms: 1 single, 5 double, 3 twin
Bathrooms: 9 en-suite

Bed & breakfast per night:	£min	£max
Single	25.00	35.00
Double	50.00	65.00

Half board per person:	£min	£max
Daily	35.00	45.00
Weekly	220.00	280.00

Lunch available
Evening meal 1830 (last orders 1930)
Parking for 12
Open February–November
Cards accepted: Access, Visa, Diners, Amex

White Swan Hotel

Main Street, Seahouses NE68 7UB
☎ (01665) 720211
Next to a riding school and only a short walk to the beach and harbour. Close to numerous castles and golf-courses. Its famous restaurant specialises in seafood and its bars in real ales. Home of the "Cow Pie".
Bedrooms: 1 single, 7 double, 3 twin, 3 triple, 3 family rooms
Bathrooms: 16 en-suite, 1 private, 1 public

Bed & breakfast per night:	£min	£max
Single	19.50	29.50
Double	39.00	59.00

Half board per person:	£min	£max
Daily	27.50	39.50
Weekly	175.00	276.50

Lunch available
Evening meal 1900 (last orders 2130)
Parking for 40
Open March–October, December
Cards accepted: Access, Visa, Diners, Amex

SLALEY

Northumberland
Map ref 5B2

Small hamlet, now a major golfing venue, south of Corbridge near the Derwent Reservoir.

Slaley Hall

HIGHLY COMMENDED

Slaley, Hexham NE47 0BY
☎ Hexham (01434) 673350
Fax (01434) 673962
Edwardian former mansion, set in 1000 acres. International 18-hole championship standard golf course. 23m swimming pool, health and beauty spa.
Bedrooms: 75 double, 50 twin, 17 family rooms
Suites available
Bathrooms: 142 en-suite

Bed & breakfast per night:	£min	£max
Single	107.00	132.00
Double	125.00	150.00

Half board per person:	£min	£max
Daily	79.50	

Lunch available
Evening meal 1900 (last orders 2200)
Parking for 500
Cards accepted: Access, Visa, Diners, Amex, Switch/Delta

A key to symbols can be found inside the back cover flap.

The symbols in each entry give information about services and facilities. A 'key' to these symbols appears at the back of this guide.

SOUTH SHIELDS

Tyne and Wear
Map ref 5C2

At the mouth of the Tyne, shipbuilding and industrial centre developed around a 19th C coalport and occupying the site of an important Roman fort and granary port. The town's museum has mementoes of the earliest self-righting lifeboat, built here in 1789.
Tourist Information Centre ☎ *(0191) 454 6612*

Sea Hotel

Sea Road, South Shields NE33 2LD
☎ (0191) 427 0999
Fax (0191) 454 0500
Consort
On the seafront in the heart of Catherine Cookson country. Popular restaurant offering French and English cooking. Secure car park.
Bedrooms: 20 single, 6 double, 5 twin, 2 triple
Bathrooms: 33 en-suite

Bed & breakfast per night:	£min	£max
Single	58.00	60.00
Double	63.00	75.00

Lunch available
Evening meal 1900 (last orders 2130)
Parking for 70
Cards accepted: Access, Visa, Diners, Amex, Switch/Delta

STANLEY

Durham
Map ref 5C2

Small town on the site of a Roman cattle camp. At the Beamish North of England Open Air Museum numerous set-pieces and displays recreate industrial and social conditions prevalent during the area's past.

Harperley Hotel

Harperley, Stanley, County Durham DH9 9TY
☎ (01207) 234011
Converted granary on the outskirts of Stanley, in the country park area close to the old water mill. Fishing and shooting can be arranged.
Bedrooms: 2 single, 3 double
Bathrooms: 5 en-suite

Continued ▶

NORTHUMBRIA

STANLEY
Continued

Bed & breakfast per night:	£min	£max
Single	26.00	31.00
Double	39.50	43.00

Half board per person:	£min	£max
Daily	36.00	40.00

Lunch available
Evening meal 1930 (last orders 2130)
Parking for 200
Cards accepted: Access, Visa, Switch/Delta

STOCKTON-ON-TEES
Tees Valley
Map ref 5C3

Teesside town first developed in the 19th C around the ancient market town with its broad main street which has been the site of a regular market since 1310. Green Dragon Yard has a Georgian theatre and there is a railway heritage trail around the town.
Tourist Information Centre ☎ *(01642) 615080*

Parkmore Hotel and Leisure Club
HIGHLY COMMENDED

636 Yarm Road, Eaglescliffe, Stockton-on-Tees, Cleveland TS16 0DH
☎ Eaglescliffe (01642) 786815
Fax (01642) 790485
Best Western
Warm, friendly hotel with leisure club, opposite golf-course near Yarm. Ideal for visiting North York Moors, the dales, Durham and York.
Bedrooms: 18 single, 18 double, 16 twin, 3 triple
Bathrooms: 55 en-suite

Bed & breakfast per night:	£min	£max
Single	45.00	70.00
Double	54.00	84.00

Lunch available
Evening meal 1845 (last orders 2130)
Parking for 100
Cards accepted: Access, Visa, Diners, Amex

Swallow Hotel
COMMENDED

John Walker Square, High Street, Stockton-on-Tees, Cleveland TS18 1AQ
☎ Middlesbrough (01642) 679721
Fax (01642) 601714
Swallow
Smart, modern hotel in Stockton town centre, with Swallow Leisure Club, bar, restaurant and brasserie. An ideal base for visiting the north east for business or pleasure. Short break packages available.
Bedrooms: 3 single, 73 double, 49 twin
Suites available
Bathrooms: 125 en-suite

Bed & breakfast per night:	£min	£max
Single	88.00	103.00
Double	100.00	115.00

Half board per person:	£min	£max
Daily	104.50	119.50

Lunch available
Evening meal 1900 (last orders 2200)
Parking for 400
Cards accepted: Access, Visa, Diners, Amex, Switch/Delta

SUNDERLAND
Tyne and Wear
Map ref 5C2

Ancient coal and shipbuilding port on Wearside, with important glassworks since the 17th C, although glassmaking here dates back more than 1,000 years.
Tourist Information Centre ☎ *(0191) 565 0990 or 565 0960*

Bed & Breakfast Stop
COMMENDED

183 Newcastle Road, Fulwell, Sunderland SR5 1NR
☎ (0191) 548 2291
Tudor-style semi-detached house on the A1018 Newcastle to Sunderland road. 5 minutes to the railway station and 10 minutes to the seafront and city centre.
Bedrooms: 1 single, 1 twin, 1 triple
Bathrooms: 1 public

Bed & breakfast per night:	£min	£max
Single	15.00	17.00
Double	28.00	30.00

Half board per person:	£min	£max
Daily	21.00	23.00
Weekly	133.00	140.00

Evening meal 1800 (last orders 1200)
Parking for 3

The Shipwrights Hotel
COMMENDED

Ferry Boat Lane, North Hylton, Sunderland SR5 3HW
☎ (0191) 549 5139
Fax (0191) 549 7464

A warm welcome awaits you at this small riverside hotel, 4 miles from Sunderland, 6 miles from Newcastle. En-suite rooms, with TV and tea/coffee-making facilities, tastefully decorated in keeping with this beautiful listed building.
Bedrooms: 2 single, 1 double, 1 twin, 1 triple
Bathrooms: 5 en-suite

Bed & breakfast per night:	£min	£max
Single	35.00	35.00
Double	42.00	42.00

Lunch available
Evening meal 1900 (last orders 2130)
Parking for 18
Cards accepted: Access, Visa, Switch/Delta

Swallow Hotel
HIGHLY COMMENDED

Queens Parade, Seaburn, Sunderland SR6 8DB
☎ (0191) 529 2041
Fax (0191) 529 4227
Swallow
Highly commended hotel with leisure facilities and spectacular seaside location. Good base for seeing Northumbria's coastline and castles.
Bedrooms: 3 single, 36 double, 23 twin, 3 family rooms
Bathrooms: 65 en-suite

Bed & breakfast per night:	£min	£max
Single	75.00	95.00
Double	95.00	125.00

Half board per person:	£min	£max
Daily	94.50	114.50

Lunch available
Evening meal 1900 (last orders 2145)
Parking for 100

NORTHUMBRIA

TYNEMOUTH
Tyne and Wear
Map ref 5C2

At the mouth of the Tyne, old Tyneside resort adjoining North Shields with its fish quay and market. The pier is overlooked by the gaunt ruins of a Benedictine priory and a castle. Splendid sands, amusement centre and park.

Grand Hotel
COMMENDED

Grand Parade, Tynemouth, North Shields NE30 4ER
☎ (0191) 293 6666
Fax (0191) 293 6665

High on the cliffs overlooking beautiful Long Sands beach, this imposing Victorian building was the seaside home of the Duchess of Northumberland. Building is now completely modernised to offer every comfort.
Bedrooms: 22 double, 7 twin, 8 triple, 2 family rooms
Bathrooms: 39 en-suite

Bed & breakfast per night:	£min	£max
Single	44.00	55.00
Double	49.00	60.00

Lunch available
Evening meal 1800 (last orders 2130)
Parking for 30
Cards accepted: Access, Visa, Diners, Amex

Hope House
DE LUXE

47 Percy Gardens, Tynemouth, North Shields NE30 4HH
☎ (0191) 257 1989
Fax (0191) 257 1989
Logis of Great Britain
Double-fronted Victorian house with superb coastal views from most rooms. Tastefully furnished, with large bedrooms. Fine cuisine and quality wines.

Bedrooms: 2 double, 1 twin
Bathrooms: 2 en-suite, 1 private, 1 public

Bed & breakfast per night:	£min	£max
Single	37.50	45.00
Double	42.50	57.50

Lunch available
Evening meal 1800 (last orders 2100)
Parking for 5
Cards accepted: Access, Visa, Diners, Amex

Park Hotel
APPROVED

Grand Parade, Tynemouth, North Shields NE30 4JQ
☎ (0191) 257 1406
Fax (0191) 257 1716
Large, recently modernised hotel in an elevated position with bedrooms and attractive bars overlooking the sea. The beach is only 1 minute's walk away.
Bedrooms: 11 single, 16 double, 17 twin, 5 triple
Bathrooms: 44 en-suite, 2 public

Bed & breakfast per night:	£min	£max
Single	37.00	49.50
Double	49.50	58.00

Half board per person:	£min	£max
Daily	49.00	62.00

Lunch available
Evening meal 1900 (last orders 2130)
Parking for 400
Cards accepted: Access, Visa, Diners, Amex, Switch/Delta

WHITLEY BAY
Tyne and Wear
Map ref 5C2

Traditional seaside resort with long beaches of sand and rock and many pools to explore. St Mary's lighthouse is open to the public.
Tourist Information Centre ☎ (0191) 200 8535

Marlborough Hotel
COMMENDED

20-21 East Parade, The Promenade, Whitley Bay NE26 1AP
☎ (0191) 251 3628
Fax (0191) 251 3628
Traditional seaside hotel with fine sea views. Comfortable, modern accommodation with friendly service.
Bedrooms: 5 single, 5 double, 4 twin, 1 triple, 1 family room
Bathrooms: 13 en-suite, 2 public

Bed & breakfast per night:	£min	£max
Single	20.00	32.00
Double	45.00	48.00

Half board per person:	£min	£max
Daily	29.00	41.00

Evening meal 1800 (last orders 1830)
Parking for 7
Cards accepted: Access, Visa, Amex, Switch/Delta

Shan-Gri-La
29 Esplanade, Whitley Bay NE26 2AL
☎ (0191) 253 0230
Small family-run guesthouse. Close to all amenities, near seafront and shopping area.
Bedrooms: 4 single, 3 twin, 3 triple
Bathrooms: 2 public

Bed & breakfast per night:	£min	£max
Single	15.00	17.00
Double	28.00	31.00

Half board per person:	£min	£max
Daily	20.00	22.00

Evening meal 1800 (last orders 1900)

Windsor Hotel
COMMENDED

South Parade, Whitley Bay NE26 2RF
☎ (0191) 251 8888 & 297 0272

Private hotel close to the seafront and town centre. An excellent base in the north east for business or pleasure.
Bedrooms: 5 single, 16 double, 43 twin
Bathrooms: 64 en-suite

Bed & breakfast per night:	£min	£max
Single	44.00	55.00
Double	50.00	65.00

Continued ▶

NORTHUMBRIA

WHITLEY BAY
Continued

Lunch available
Evening meal 1800 (last orders 2130)
Parking for 26
Cards accepted: Access, Visa, Diners, Amex, Switch/Delta

York House Hotel

COMMENDED

30 Park Parade, Whitley Bay
NE26 1DX
☎ (0191) 252 8313 & 251 3953
Fax (0191) 251 3953

Ideally located for exploring historic Northumbria or visiting the excellent shopping facilities at Newcastle and MetroCentre. High standard en-suite accommodation and imaginative menu choice. No charge for children when sharing. Ground floor bedrooms suitable for disabled. Secure car parking.
Wheelchair access category 3
Bedrooms: 1 single, 6 double, 6 twin, 2 triple
Bathrooms: 13 en-suite, 1 private, 1 private shower

Bed & breakfast per night:	£min	£max
Single	20.00	30.00
Double	40.00	50.00

Half board per person:	£min	£max
Daily	30.00	70.00
Weekly	200.00	320.00

Lunch available
Evening meal 1800 (last orders 2030)
Parking for 3
Cards accepted: Access, Visa, Amex, Switch/Delta

WOOLER
Northumberland
Map ref 5B1

Old grey-stone town, market-place for foresters and hill farmers, set at the edge of the north-east Cheviots. This makes a good base for excursions to Northumberland's loveliest coastline, or for angling and walking in the Borderlands.

Loreto Guest House

APPROVED

1 Ryecroft Way, Wooler NE71 6BW
☎ (01668) 281 350

Family-run early Georgian house in spacious grounds, in lovely Cheviot village. Central for touring and walking and close to coastline. All home cooking, all rooms en-suite.
Bedrooms: 1 single, 3 double, 2 twin
Bathrooms: 6 en-suite

Bed & breakfast per night:	£min	£max
Single	19.00	21.00
Double	35.00	40.00

Half board per person:	£min	£max
Daily	25.00	25.00
Weekly	150.00	160.00

Evening meal 1800 (last orders 1830)
Parking for 12

Tankerville Arms Hotel

HIGHLY COMMENDED

22 Cottage Road, Wooler
NE71 6AD
☎ (01668) 281581
Fax (01668) 281387

Charming 17th C family-owned coaching inn. All facilities, fine cuisine. Central for beautiful coast, National Trust properties and Scottish borders.
Bedrooms: 2 single, 6 double, 6 twin, 1 triple, 1 family room
Bathrooms: 16 en-suite

Bed & breakfast per night:	£min	£max
Single	43.50	43.50
Double	72.00	72.00

Half board per person:	£min	£max
Daily	46.50	46.50
Weekly	309.50	309.50

Lunch available
Evening meal 1900 (last orders 2130)
Parking for 104
Cards accepted: Access, Visa

WELCOME HOST

This is a nationally recognised customer care programme which aims to promote the highest standards of service and a warm welcome. Establishments who are taking part in this initiative are indicated by the symbol.

NORTH WEST

The legacy of the Industrial Revolution can be seen in the North West's fine Victorian architecture, magnificent mill buildings and miles of canals - once used for transportation but today, navigated for pleasure.

Manchester and Liverpool are vibrant centres of popular and 'high' culture while stylish Lytham St Anne's, Southport or glittering Blackpool are among Britain's most famous coastal resorts.

Explore elegant Chester, the historic city of Lancaster or, in total contrast, the pretty villages of the Wirral and the unspoilt border country of Cheshire. From birdlife to nightlife, markets to music festivals, the North West has it all.

FOR MORE INFORMATION CONTACT:
North West Tourist Board
Swan House, Swan Meadow Road,
Wigan Pier, Wigan WN3 5BB
Tel: (01942) 821222 **Fax:** (01942) 820002

Where to Go in the North West -
see pages 126-129
Where to Stay in the North West -
see pages 130-156

NORTH WEST

Where to Go and What to See

You will find hundreds of interesting places to visit during your stay in the North West, just some of which are listed in these pages. The number against each name will help you locate it on the map (page 129). Contact any Tourist Information Centre in the region for more ideas on days out in the North West.

1 Frontierland Western Theme Park
Marine Road, Morecambe,
Lancashire LA4 4DG
Tel: (01524) 410024
Over 40 thrill rides and attractions including the Texas Tornado, the Polo Tower Perculator and Stampede Roller Coaster.

2 Lancaster Castle
Shire Hall, Castle Parade,
Lancaster, Lancashire
Tel: (01524) 64998
Collection of coats of arms, dungeons, crown court, Jane Scott's chair. Grand Jury Room. External tour of castle walls.

3 Blackpool Pleasure Beach
Ocean Boulevard,
Blackpool, Lancashire FY4 1EZ
Tel: (01253) 341033
Amusement park with rides including Space Invader, Big Dipper and Revolution. Funshineland for children. Summer season ice show, Mystique illusion show in Horseshoe Bar.

4 Blackpool Sea Life Centre
The Promenade,
Blackpool,
Lancashire FY1 5AA
Tel: (01253) 22445
Tropical sharks up to 8 feet in length housed in a 100,000 gallon display with underwater walk-through.

5 Blackpool Tower
Promenade,
Blackpool,
Lancashire FY1 4BJ
Tel: (01253) 22242
Tower Ballroom, Bug World, Jungle Jim's playground. Out of this World. Children's entertainment in Hornpipe Galley, Undersea World. Tower Circus, Laser fantasy and Lift Ride.

6 Ribchester Museum of Childhood
Church Street,
Ribchester,
Lancashire PR3 3YE
Tel: (01254) 878520
Large 10-room building contaning childhood toys, dolls and dolls' houses, 20-piece model fairground, Tom Thumb replica, collectors' toy shop.

7 Pleasureland Amusement Park
Marine Drive,
The Fun Coast,
Southport,
Merseyside PR8 1RX
Tel: (01704) 532717
Traditional amusement park with wide variety of thrilling and family rides.

8 Astley Hall
Astley Park,
Chorley,
Lancashire PR7 1NP
Tel: (01257) 262166
Hall dates from 1580 with subsequent additions. Unique collection of furniture including a fine Elizabethan bed and the famous shovel board table in the Long Gallery.

9 Camelot Theme Park and Rare Breeds Farm
Park Hall Road, Charnock Richard,
Lancashire PR7 5LP
Tel: (01257) 453044
Magical kingdom offering over 100 thrilling rides, attractions and medieval entertainment.

10 Wildfowl and Wetland Centre
Martin Mere, Burscough,
Lancashire L40 0TA
Tel: (01704) 895181
45 acres of gardens with over 1600 ducks geese and swans of 120 different kinds. Two flocks of flamingos. 300-acre wild area with 20-acre lake.

11 East Lancashire Railway
Bolton Street Station,
Bury, Lancashire BL9 0EY
Tel: (0161) 764 7790
Eight-mile-long preserved railway operated principally by steam traction, transport museum nearby.

12 Rufford Old Hall
Rufford, Ormskirk,
Lancashire L40 1SG
Tel: (01704) 821254
Fine 15thC building with a magnificent Great Hall, particularly noted for its immense moveable screen.

13 Wigan Pier
Wallgate, Wigan,
Lancashire WN3 4EU
Tel: (01942) 323666
The Way We Were – life in Wigan in 1900. World's largest steam mill engine, cotton machinery hall, shops, picnic gardens, cafeteria, waterbuses and Victorian classroom.

14 Granada Studios Tour
Water Street, Manchester,
Greater Manchester M60 9EA
Tel: (0161) 832 9090
Major television theme park providing an insight into the fascinating world behind the TV screen. Visit three of the most famous streets in Britain.

15 Museum of Science and Industry in Manchester
Liverpool Road, Castlefield,
Manchester,
Greater Manchester M3 4JP
Tel: (0161) 832 2244
The Museum of Science and Industry in Manchester based in the world's oldest passenger railway station, with 15 galleries that amaze, amuse and entertain.

16 Knowsley Safari Park
Prescot,
Merseyside L34 4AN
Tel: (0151) 430 9009
Five-mile drive through game reserves, set in 400 acres of parkland containing lions, tigers, elephants, rhinos, etc. Large picnic areas and children's amusement park.

17 Albert Dock
The Colonnades,
Albert Dock,
Liverpool, L3 4AA
Tel: (0151) 708 8854
Britain's largest Grade 1 listed historic building. Restored 4-sided dock, including shops, bars, restaurants, entertainment, marina and maritime museum.

18 Croxteth Hall and Country Park
Off Muirhead Avenue East,
Liverpool,
Merseyside L12 0HB
Tel: (0151) 228 5311
500 acre country park and hall with displays, furnished rooms and walled garden. Farm with rare breeds, miniature railway, gift shop, picnic area, riding centre, adventure playground.

19 Tate Gallery Liverpool
Albert Dock, Liverpool L3 4BB
Tel: (0151) 709 3223
The national collection of modern art in the North of England.

20 Dunham Massey Hall and Park
Altrincham, Cheshire WA14 4SJ
Tel: (0161) 941 1025
Historic house, garden and park with restaurant and shop.

21 Lyme Park
Disley, Cheshire SK12 2NX
Tel: (01663) 762023
Country estate within 1377 acres of moorland, woodland and park. Magnificent house with 17 acres of historic gardens.

22 Quarry Bank Mill
Styal, Cheshire SK9 4LA
Tel: (01625) 527468
Georgian water-powerd cotton-spinning mill. Four floors of displays and demonstrations, 284 acres of parkland.

23 Norton Priory Museum and Gardens
Tudor Road, Runcorn, Cheshire WA7 1SX
Tel: (01928) 569895
Excavated Augustinian priory, remains of church, cloister and chapter house. Later site of Tudor mansion and Georgian house. Walled garden and woodland.

24 Boat Museum
Dock Yard Road, Ellesmere Port, Cheshire L65 4FW
Tel: (0151) 355 5017
Over 50 historic craft, largest floating collection in the world with restored buildings, traditional cottages, workshops, steam engines, boat trips, shop and cafe.

25 Arley Hall and Gardens
Arley, Northwich, Cheshire CW9 6NA
Tel: (01565) 777353
Early Victorian building set in 12 acres of magnificent gardens. 15thC Tythe barn. Unique collection of water colours of the area.

26 Macclesfield Silk Museum
The Heritage Centre, Roe Street, Macclesfield, Cheshire SK11 6UT
Tel: (01625) 613210
Information centre, town history exhibition, silk museum, Sunday school, history exhibition, guided trails.

27 Jodrell Bank Science Centre and Arboretum
Lower Withington, Macclesfield, Cheshire SK11 9DL
Tel: (01477) 571339
Exhibition and interactive exhibits on astronomy, space, satellites, energy and the environment. Planetarium and the world-famous Lovell telescope and 35 acre arboretum.

28 Cheshire Oaks Designer Outlet Village
Ellesmere Port, The Wirral L65 9JJ
Over 60 individual stores selling famous branded goods.

29 Chester Zoo
Upton-by-Chester, Chester, Cheshire CH2 1LH
Tel: (01244) 380280
Penguin pool with underwater views, tropical house, spectacular displays of spring and summer bedding plants. Chimpanzee house and new monorail.

FIND OUT MORE

Further information about holidays and attractions in the North West is available from:
North West Tourist Board,
Swan House,
Swan Meadow Road,
Wigan Pier,
Wigan WN3 5BB.
Tel: (01942) 821222

These publications are available free from the North West Tourist Board:
- **North West Welcome Guide**
- **Discover England's North West**
- **Attraction Map**
- **Group Travel Guide**
- **Bed & Breakfast Map**
- **Caravan and Camping Parks Guide**

WHERE TO STAY (NORTH WEST)

Accommodation entries in this region are listed in alphabetical order of place name, and then in alphabetical order of establishment.

Map references refer to the colour location maps at the back of this guide. The first number indicates the map to use; the letter and number which follow refer to the grid reference on the map.

At-a-glance symbols at the end of each accommodation entry give useful information about services and facilities. A key to symbols can be found inside the back cover flap. Keep this open for easy reference.

ALDERLEY EDGE

Cheshire
Map ref 4B2

Picturesque town taking its name from the wooded escarpment towering above the Cheshire plain, with fine views and walks. A romantic local legend tells of the Wizard and sleeping warriors who will save the country in crisis. Excellent shops. Chorley Hall, nearby, boasts a moat.

The Alderley Edge Hotel M
HIGHLY COMMENDED

Macclesfield Road, Alderley Edge SK9 7BJ
☎ (01625) 583033
Fax (01625) 586343
Converted country mansion built originally for one of the Manchester cotton barons. Close to the Edge beauty spot and near the village of Alderley, Jodrell Bank and Gawsworth Hall. Restaurant featuring fish and produce from the hotel bakery. Award-winning head chef.
Wheelchair access category 3
Bedrooms: 21 single, 11 double
Bathrooms: 32 en-suite
Bed & breakfast
per night: £min   £max
Single   36.00   95.50
Double   67.00 116.50
Lunch available
Evening meal 1900 (last orders 2200)
Parking for 90
Cards accepted: Access, Visa, Diners, Amex

Milverton House Hotel M

Wilmslow Road, Alderley Edge SK9 7QL
☎ (01625) 583615 & 585555
Well-appointed Victorian villa on main road with open country views. Home cooking.
Bedrooms: 1 single, 7 double, 4 twin
Bathrooms: 7 en-suite, 1 private, 4 public
Bed & breakfast
per night: £min   £max
Single   25.00   35.00
Double   45.00   55.00
Half board per
person: £min   £max
Daily   35.00   55.00
Weekly   200.00 250.00
Evening meal from 1830
Parking for 16
Cards accepted: Access, Visa

The M symbol after an establishment name indicates that it is a Regional Tourist Board member.

Information on accommodation listed in this guide has been supplied by the proprietors. As changes may occur you are advised to check details at the time of booking.

ALTRINCHAM

Greater Manchester
Map ref 4A2

Historic market town developed as a residential area in the 19th C. Preserves the best of the old at its fascinating Old Market Place, with the best of the new on pedestrianised George Street. International fashion and high style interior design rub shoulders with boutiques and speciality shops.
Tourist Information Centre ☎ (0161) 912 5931

Beech Mount Hotel M

46 Barrington Road, Altrincham, Cheshire WA14 1HN
☎ (0161) 928 4523
Fax (0161) 928 1055
Family-run hotel within easy reach of Manchester Airport and city centre. Convenient for public transport and shopping centre.
Bedrooms: 12 single, 7 double, 10 twin, 3 triple
Bathrooms: 32 en-suite, 2 public
Bed & breakfast
per night: £min   £max
Single   22.00   28.00
Double   38.00   45.00
Evening meal 1830 (last orders 2030)
Parking for 36
Cards accepted: Access, Visa

NORTH WEST

Cresta Court Hotel
♛♛♛♛ COMMENDED
Church Street, Altrincham, Cheshire
WA14 4DP
☎ (0161) 927 7272
Fax (0161) 926 9194
Ⓒ Best Western
Privately owned town centre hotel, opened in 1973 and designed to provide all modern facilities. Easy access to M56, M6, M62, M63. 10 minutes to Manchester International Airport.
Bedrooms: 111 single, 13 double, 8 twin, 3 triple
Bathrooms: 135 en-suite

Bed & breakfast per night:	£min	£max
Single	36.00	65.00
Double	70.00	85.00

Half board per person:	£min	£max
Daily	46.00	75.00

Lunch available
Evening meal 1830 (last orders 2200)
Parking for 200
Cards accepted: Access, Visa, Diners, Amex, Switch/Delta

ASHTON-UNDER-LYNE
Greater Manchester
Map ref 4B1

The largest town in the borough of Tameside, with excellent access to central Manchester and to the foothills of Pennines. Famous for its 700-year-old market and the confluence of 3 canals at Portland Basin. The Church of St Michael and All Angels has a spectacular window.
Tourist Information Centre ☎ (0161) 343 4343

Lynwood Hotel
♛♛ COMMENDED
3 Richmond Street,
Ashton-under-Lyne, Lancashire
OL6 7TX
☎ (0161) 330 5358
Small, comfortable, family-run hotel in quiet position. Convenient for motorways, G-Mex, The Arena and National Cycling Centre. 20 minutes to Manchester Airport.
Bedrooms: 2 single, 2 twin
Bathrooms: 2 en-suite, 1 public

Bed & breakfast per night:	£min	£max
Single	23.00	23.00
Double	44.00	44.00

Parking for 4

York House Hotel
♛♛♛♛ HIGHLY COMMENDED
York Place, Off Richmond Street,
Ashton-under-Lyne, Lancashire
OL6 7TT
☎ (0161) 330 5899
Fax (0161) 343 1613
Ⓒ The Independents
Refurbished hotel with restaurant and function room. Emphasis on good food and fine wines. Garden ("Britain in Bloom" winner). Ideal base for touring north of England.
Bedrooms: 8 single, 19 double, 5 twin, 2 triple
Bathrooms: 34 en-suite

Bed & breakfast per night:	£min	£max
Single	49.00	58.00
Double	72.00	75.00

Half board per person:	£min	£max
Daily	66.00	75.00

Lunch available
Evening meal 1900 (last orders 2130)
Parking for 36
Cards accepted: Access, Visa, Diners, Amex, Switch/Delta

BEESTON
Cheshire
Map ref 4A2

Hamlet below the Peckforton Hills which rise from the Cheshire Plain to 740 ft. Medieval Beeston Castle (English Heritage) was originally occupied by the Romans.

Wild Boar Hotel
♛♛♛♛ HIGHLY COMMENDED
Whitchurch Road, Beeston,
Tarporley CW6 9NW
☎ Bunbury (01829) 260309
Fax (01829) 261081

17th C black and white building of character, in typical style of Cheshire. 13 miles from Chester and ideally located for exploring the Cheshire countryside.
Wheelchair access category 3
Bedrooms: 15 double, 3 twin, 19 triple
Bathrooms: 37 private

Bed & breakfast per night:	£min	£max
Single	55.00	200.00
Double	75.00	200.00

Half board per person:	£min	£max
Daily	55.00	70.00

Lunch available
Evening meal 1900 (last orders 2200)
Parking for 100
Cards accepted: Access, Visa, Diners, Amex, Switch/Delta

BIRKENHEAD
Merseyside
Map ref 4A2

Founded in the 12th C by monks who operated the first Mersey ferry service, Birkenhead has some fine Victorian architecture and one of the best markets in the north west. Attractions include the famous Mersey Ferry and Birkenhead Park, opened in 1847, the first public park in the country.
Tourist Information Centre ☎ (0151) 647 6780

Central Hotel
♛♛♛
Clifton Crescent, Birkenhead
L41 2QH
☎ (0151) 647 6347
Fax (0151) 647 5476
Town centre hotel opposite railway station with direct service to Liverpool and Chester. Near Liverpool tunnel entrance.
Bedrooms: 13 single, 8 double, 9 twin, 1 triple
Bathrooms: 27 en-suite, 2 public

Bed & breakfast per night:	£min	£max
Single	29.00	40.00
Double	39.00	49.00

Half board per person:	£min	£max
Daily	39.00	50.00
Weekly	317.00	

Lunch available
Evening meal 1830 (last orders 2045)
Parking for 12
Cards accepted: Access, Visa, Diners, Amex, Switch/Delta

NORTH WEST

BIRKENHEAD
Continued

Shrewsbury Lodge Hotel
APPROVED

31 Shrewsbury Road, Oxton, Birkenhead L43 2JB
☎ (0151) 652 4029 & Mobile 0973 776694
Fax (0151) 653 4179
Family-run hotel with en-suite facilities, restaurant and fully licensed bar. Satellite TV. Convenient for M23, Liverpool Tunnel and train station.
Bedrooms: 7 single, 4 double, 3 twin, 1 triple, 1 family room
Bathrooms: 10 en-suite, 4 public
Bed & breakfast

per night:	£min	£max
Single	22.00	28.00
Double	36.00	38.00

Half board per

person:	£min	£max
Daily	31.00	37.00
Weekly	200.00	245.00

Evening meal 1700 (last orders 2100)
Parking for 12
Cards accepted: Access, Visa, Diners, Switch/Delta

BLACKBURN
Lancashire
Map ref 4A1

North east Lancashire town. Architecture reflects Victorian prosperity from the cotton industry. Daniel Thwaites, founder of Thwaites Brewery, is buried in St John's churchyard. Lewis Textile Museum is dedicated to the history of the textile industry.
Tourist Information Centre ☎ *(01254) 53277*

Northcote Manor Hotel
HIGHLY COMMENDED

Northcote Road, Old Langho, Blackburn BB6 8BE
☎ (01254) 240555
Fax (01254) 246568

Privately-owned refurbished manor house with an outstanding restaurant, offering the best in hospitality. Ideal location 9 miles from M6 junction 31, off A59.

Bedrooms: 10 double, 4 twin
Bathrooms: 14 en-suite
Bed & breakfast

per night:	£min	£max
Single	75.00	95.00
Double	95.00	115.00

Half board per

person:	£min	£max
Daily	100.00	130.00

Lunch available
Evening meal 1900 (last orders 2130)
Parking for 50
Cards accepted: Access, Visa, Diners, Amex, Switch/Delta

BLACKPOOL
Lancashire
Map ref 4A1

Britain's largest fun resort, with Blackpool Pleasure Beach, 3 piers and the famous Tower. Host to the spectacular autumn illuminations - "the greatest free show on earth".
Tourist Information Centre ☎ *(01253) 21623*

Alderley Hotel
COMMENDED

581 South Promenade, Blackpool FY4 1NG
☎ (01253) 342173
Quiet seafront licensed hotel, with en-suite and ground-floor bedrooms. Main course choice of 10 dishes.
Bedrooms: 1 single, 6 double, 3 twin, 1 triple, 2 family rooms
Bathrooms: 13 en-suite
Bed & breakfast

per night:	£min	£max
Single	17.00	21.00
Double	34.00	42.00

Half board per

person:	£min	£max
Daily	23.00	27.00
Weekly	145.00	179.00

Lunch available
Evening meal 1800 (last orders 1800)
Parking for 8
Cards accepted: Access, Visa, Diners, Amex

Ash Lodge
Listed

131 Hornby Road, Blackpool FY1 4JG
☎ (01253) 27637
Small, private licensed hotel with a warm friendly welcome and home cooking. Centrally located with ample car parking.
Bedrooms: 7 double, 2 twin, 2 triple, 1 family room
Bathrooms: 7 en-suite, 2 public
Bed & breakfast

per night:	£min	£max
Single	15.00	19.50
Double	30.00	39.00

Half board per

person:	£min	£max
Daily	20.50	25.00
Weekly	136.00	168.00

Evening meal 1700 (last orders 1830)
Parking for 15

Ashbeian Hotel
COMMENDED

49 High Street, Blackpool FY1 2BN
☎ (01253) 26301
All en-suite bedrooms, good public parking. Privately owned. Splendid menus. Terrific value. Just off seafront, an easy walk to everything.
Bedrooms: 1 single, 2 double, 2 triple
Bathrooms: 5 en-suite
Bed & breakfast

per night:	£min	£max
Single	11.00	22.00
Double	22.00	44.00

Half board per

person:	£min	£max
Daily	18.00	30.00
Weekly	112.00	150.00

Evening meal 1700 (last orders 1930)
Cards accepted: Access, Visa

Ashcroft Hotel
COMMENDED

42 King Edward Avenue, Blackpool FY2 9TA
☎ (01253) 351538
Small friendly hotel off Queens Promenade, 2 minutes from sea and Gynn Gardens. Offering personal service. Cleanliness assured.
Bedrooms: 3 single, 3 double, 1 twin, 2 triple, 1 family room
Bathrooms: 7 en-suite, 1 public
Bed & breakfast

per night:	£min	£max
Single	16.00	21.00
Double	32.00	42.00

Half board per

person:	£min	£max
Daily	21.00	26.00
Weekly	154.00	161.00

NORTH WEST

Evening meal from 1700
Parking for 3
Cards accepted: Access, Visa

The Hotel Bambi
HIGHLY COMMENDED
27 Bright Street, Blackpool FY4 1BS
☎ (01253) 343756
Friendly, family-run guesthouse with good facilities. Ideally situated for Pleasure Beach, Promenade and South Shore shopping area.
Bedrooms: 2 double, 1 twin, 1 triple, 1 family room
Bathrooms: 5 en-suite

Bed & breakfast per night:	£min	£max
Single	17.00	
Double	32.00	

Evening meal from 1700
Parking for 2
Open February–November
Cards accepted: Access, Visa, Diners, Amex

Beachcomber Hotel
Listed
78 Reads Avenue, Blackpool FY1 4DE
☎ (01253) 21622
Comfortable hotel having en-suite rooms with TV, tea/coffee facilities and central heating. Choice of menu, table licence - no noisy bar. Car park.
Bedrooms: 1 single, 5 double, 1 twin, 2 triple, 2 family rooms
Bathrooms: 11 en-suite

Bed & breakfast per night:	£min	£max
Single	15.00	20.00
Double	30.00	40.00

Half board per person:	£min	£max
Daily	19.00	24.00
Weekly	105.00	140.00

Evening meal 1700 (last orders 1730)
Parking for 10
Cards accepted: Access, Visa

Bedford Hotel
COMMENDED
298-300 North Promenade, Blackpool FY1 2EY
☎ (01253) 23475 & 290263
Fax (01253) 21878
Well-managed family-run hotel on the seafront, with indoor swimming pool, sauna, spa and large comfortable bedrooms. Choice of menu at all meals. Large, free car park.

Bedrooms: 20 double, 5 twin, 12 triple, 5 family rooms
Suites available
Bathrooms: 42 en-suite, 1 public

Bed & breakfast per night:	£min	£max
Single	20.00	80.00
Double	40.00	80.00

Half board per person:	£min	£max
Daily	25.00	85.00
Weekly	140.00	280.00

Lunch available
Evening meal 1800 (last orders 1900)
Parking for 24
Cards accepted: Access, Visa, Amex

Carlton Hotel
282-286 North Promenade, Blackpool FY1 2EZ
☎ (01253) 28966 & 21494
Fax (01253) 752587
On the quieter North Promenade and conveniently situated within walking distance of the town centre and all conference venues.
Bedrooms: 18 single, 23 double, 8 twin, 8 triple, 1 family room
Bathrooms: 58 en-suite

Bed & breakfast per night:	£min	£max
Single	20.00	35.00
Double	40.00	80.00

Half board per person:	£min	£max
Daily	25.00	40.00
Weekly	170.00	280.00

Evening meal 1800 (last orders 1900)
Parking for 62
Cards accepted: Access, Visa, Diners, Amex

Claremont House Hotel
COMMENDED
14 Gynn Avenue, Blackpool FY1 2LD
☎ (01253) 351783
Fax (01253) 596618
Licensed private hotel with home cooking. Close to town centre and theatres, on quiet North Shore. Family owned and managed. All en-suite.
Bedrooms: 5 double, 2 twin, 2 triple, 1 family room
Bathrooms: 10 en-suite

Bed & breakfast per night:	£min	£max
Single	15.00	50.00
Double	30.00	75.00

Half board per person:	£min	£max
Daily	21.00	56.00

Lunch available
Evening meal 1700 (last orders 1730)
Parking for 6
Cards accepted: Access, Visa, Diners, Amex

Collingwood Hotel
8-10 Holmfield Road, Blackpool FY2 9SL
☎ (01253) 352929
Fax (01253) 352929

In a select area just off Queens Promenade and Gynn Gardens. Good reputation for service, home cooking, cleanliness and value for money. All rooms en-suite. Excellence is our standard.
Bedrooms: 2 single, 9 double, 2 twin, 2 triple, 2 family rooms
Bathrooms: 17 en-suite

Bed & breakfast per night:	£min	£max
Single	18.00	23.00
Double	36.00	46.00

Half board per person:	£min	£max
Daily	25.00	28.00
Weekly	130.00	150.00

Lunch available
Evening meal from 1700
Parking for 13
Cards accepted: Access, Visa, Diners, Amex

Glenshee Hotel
6-8 Harrow Place, New South Promenade, Blackpool FY4 1RP
☎ (01253) 402259 & 341446
Fax (01253) 346308
Family-run hotel, offering special package weeks with entertainment in hotel. Something for everyone. Friendly, homely atmosphere where the guest comes first.
Bedrooms: 5 single, 20 double, 10 twin, 5 triple, 2 family rooms
Bathrooms: 37 en-suite, 2 public

Continued ▶

NORTH WEST

BLACKPOOL
Continued

Bed & breakfast

per night:	£min	£max
Single	20.00	30.00
Double	40.00	60.00

Half board per

person:	£min	£max
Daily	22.00	35.00
Weekly	99.50	165.00

Lunch available
Evening meal 1730 (last orders 1830)
Parking for 12
Cards accepted: Access, Visa, Diners, Amex, Switch/Delta

The Headlands ⋔
Listed COMMENDED

611-613 South Promenade, Blackpool FY4 1NJ
☎ (01253) 341179
Fax (01253) 342047
Superior seafront hotel, all rooms en-suite. Lift, parking, entertainment. Weekend breaks, midweek specials. Excellent service, cuisine, quality. Open Christmas and New Year.
Bedrooms: 10 single, 8 double, 14 twin, 10 triple, 1 family room
Bathrooms: 43 en-suite

Bed & breakfast

per night:	£min	£max
Single	26.85	46.50
Double	53.70	93.00

Half board per

person:	£min	£max
Daily	34.30	50.90
Weekly	248.40	303.95

Lunch available
Evening meal 1800 (last orders 2030)
Parking for 40
Cards accepted: Access, Visa, Diners, Amex, Switch/Delta

The Knowlsley Private Hotel
Listed APPROVED

68 Dean Street, Blackpool FY4 1BP
☎ (01253) 343414
Friendly family-run hotel in quiet area of South Shore. Close to beach, shops, Pleasure Beach. Easy access to M55 and airport.
Bedrooms: 2 single, 5 double, 2 twin, 2 triple, 2 family rooms
Bathrooms: 3 en-suite, 4 private, 1 public

Bed & breakfast

per night	£min	£max
Single	17.00	20.00
Double	30.00	40.00

Half board per

person:	£min	£max
Daily	20.00	25.00
Weekly	140.00	175.00

Evening meal from 1700
Parking for 12
Cards accepted: Access, Visa

May-Dene Licensed Hotel
Listed APPROVED

10 Dean Street, Blackpool FY4 1AU
☎ (01253) 343464
In a sun-trap area close to South Promenade, Sandcastle, Pleasure Beach, markets and pier. Clean, friendly and good food.
Bedrooms: 1 single, 6 double, 1 twin, 4 family rooms
Bathrooms: 5 en-suite, 2 public

Bed & breakfast

per night:	£min	£max
Single	14.00	25.00
Double	28.00	50.00

Half board per

person:	£min	£max
Daily	18.00	29.00
Weekly	98.00	150.00

Evening meal from 1700
Parking for 5
Cards accepted: Access, Visa, Diners, Amex

Motel Mimosa ⋔
Listed APPROVED

24a Lonsdale Road, Blackpool FY1 6EE
☎ (01253) 341906
Purpose built apartotel, personally supervised by resident owners. Central yet in quiet location. Evening meal by arrangement. Car parking.
Bedrooms: 9 double, 3 twin, 3 family rooms
Bathrooms: 15 en-suite

Bed & breakfast

per night:	£min	£max
Single	16.00	25.00
Double	32.00	45.00

Half board per

person:	£min	£max
Daily	19.00	28.50

Lunch available
Evening meal 1700 (last orders 2130)
Parking for 16
Cards accepted: Access, Visa

The Old Coach House ⋔
👑👑👑 COMMENDED

50 Dean Street, Blackpool FY4 1BP
☎ (01253) 344330
Fax (01253) 344330
Large detached house set in beautiful gardens, near the promenade and South Pier.
Bedrooms: 3 double, 2 twin, 1 triple, 1 family room
Bathrooms: 7 en-suite

Bed & breakfast

per night:	£min	£max
Single	23.50	32.50
Double	47.00	65.00

Half board per

person:	£min	£max
Daily	31.45	40.85
Weekly	220.15	285.95

Evening meal 1700 (last orders 2100)
Parking for 8
Cards accepted: Access, Visa, Amex, Switch/Delta

Park House Hotel ⋔
👑👑👑

308 North Promenade, Blackpool FY1 2HA
☎ (01253) 20081
Fax (01253) 290181
Beautifully situated on promenade within easy reach of Winter Gardens, piers, golf-courses, town centre and Stanley Park.
Bedrooms: 13 single, 34 double, 35 twin, 14 triple, 8 family rooms
Bathrooms: 104 en-suite, 3 public

Bed & breakfast

per night:	£min	£max
Single	25.10	36.45
Double	44.00	75.60

Half board per

person:	£min	£max
Daily	28.10	40.90
Weekly	154.00	245.00

Lunch available
Evening meal 1800 (last orders 2030)
Parking for 52
Cards accepted: Access, Visa, Amex

Pembroke Private Hotel ⋔
👑👑👑 COMMENDED

11 King Edward Avenue, Blackpool FY2 9TD
☎ (01253) 351306
Warm welcome assured to all at this small beautifully decorated hotel, which offers a quiet relaxed atmosphere.
Bedrooms: 4 single, 4 double, 2 twin, 1 triple
Bathrooms: 9 en-suite, 1 public

NORTH WEST

Bed & breakfast per night:	£min	£max
Single	16.00	22.00
Double	32.00	44.00
Half board per person:	£min	£max
Daily	20.00	26.00
Weekly	115.00	147.00

Evening meal 1730 (last orders 1830)
Parking for 8
Open March–October and Christmas

Ruskin Hotel ⋀
 COMMENDED
Albert Road, Blackpool FY1 4PW
☎ (01253) 24063
Fax (01253) 23571

One of the town's premier hotels, totally refurbished and providing a central haven of excellence. The Tower, Winter Gardens and theatres all within 400 yards.
Bedrooms: 7 single, 27 double, 25 twin, 10 triple, 3 family rooms
Bathrooms: 72 en-suite

Bed & breakfast per night:	£min	£max
Single	31.00	45.00
Double	62.00	80.00
Half board per person:	£min	£max
Daily	35.00	50.00
Weekly	173.25	276.00

Lunch available
Evening meal 1800 (last orders 2030)
Parking for 8
Cards accepted: Access, Visa, Switch/Delta

St Chads Hotel ⋀
317-321 Promenade, Blackpool FY1 6BN
☎ (01253) 346148
Fax (01253) 348240
Splendid promenade location offering live entertainment in season. Choice of menu. Home-from-home.
Bedrooms: 7 single, 21 double, 22 twin, 2 triple, 6 family rooms
Bathrooms: 58 en-suite

Bed & breakfast per night:	£min	£max
Single	20.00	40.00
Double	40.00	80.00
Half board per person:	£min	£max
Daily	25.00	40.00
Weekly	175.00	230.00

Lunch available
Evening meal 1700 (last orders 2030)
Parking for 25
Cards accepted: Access, Visa

Seabank Hotel
219-221 Central Promenade, Blackpool FY1 5DL
☎ (01253) 22717 & 22173
Fax (01253) 295148

This newly refurbished hotel enjoys one of the finest positions on the Central Promenade, with unobstructed views of the Irish Sea. Only 700 yards from the Tower.
Bedrooms: 6 single, 17 double, 15 twin, 16 triple, 3 family rooms
Bathrooms: 57 en-suite

Bed & breakfast per night:	£min	£max
Single	17.50	31.50
Double	31.00	59.00
Half board per person:	£min	£max
Daily	20.50	34.50
Weekly	143.50	221.50

Evening meal 1700 (last orders 1720)
Cards accepted: Access, Visa

Sunray ⋀
COMMENDED
42 Knowle Avenue, Blackpool FY2 9TQ
☎ (01253) 351937
Fax (01253) 593307
Ⓡ Logis of Great Britain
Modern semi in quiet residential part of north Blackpool. Friendly personal service and care. 1.75 miles north of tower along promenade. Turn right at Uncle Tom's Cabin. Sunray is about 300 yards on left.
Bedrooms: 3 single, 2 double, 2 twin, 2 triple
Bathrooms: 9 en-suite, 1 public

Bed & breakfast per night:	£min	£max
Single	25.00	28.00
Double	50.00	56.00
Half board per person:	£min	£max
Daily	37.00	40.00
Weekly	220.00	240.00

Evening meal 1750 (last orders 1500)
Parking for 6
Cards accepted: Access, Visa, Amex

Surrey House Hotel
9 Northumberland Avenue, Blackpool FY2 9SB
☎ (01253) 351743
Friendly, family-run hotel close to promenade, Gynn Gardens and with easy access to town's entertainments. Central heating and en-suite facilities.
Bedrooms: 2 single, 3 double, 4 triple, 2 family rooms
Bathrooms: 10 en-suite, 1 private, 2 public

Bed & breakfast per night:	£min	£max
Single	19.00	24.00
Double	38.00	48.00
Half board per person:	£min	£max
Daily	25.50	30.50
Weekly	171.50	213.50

Evening meal 1700 (last orders 1600)
Parking for 7

Waverley Hotel
COMMENDED
95 Reads Avenue, Blackpool FY1 4DG
☎ (01253) 21633
Small, licensed hotel close to Tower, Winter Gardens, shopping precinct and promenade. For those special occasions, book our four-poster or canopied rooms. Comfort and quality assured, at prices you can afford.
Bedrooms: 1 single, 9 double, 2 triple, 1 family room
Bathrooms: 11 en-suite, 1 public

Bed & breakfast per night:	£min	£max
Single	15.00	30.00
Double	30.00	50.00
Half board per person:	£min	£max
Daily	21.00	36.00
Weekly	105.00	140.00

Continued ▶

BLACKPOOL
Continued

Evening meal 1700 (last orders 1800)
Parking for 8
Cards accepted: Access, Visa

The Windsor Hotel
COMMENDED

21 King Edward Avenue, North Shore, Blackpool FY2 9TA
☎ (01253) 353735
Quality furnishings in all bedrooms. Fine rooms displaying antiques and watercolours. Exquisite dining room serving traditional English cuisine.
Bedrooms: 3 single, 4 double, 1 twin, 1 triple
Bathrooms: 9 en-suite

Bed & breakfast per night:	£min	£max
Single	19.50	24.50
Double	39.00	49.00

Half board per person:	£min	£max
Daily	24.50	29.50
Weekly	119.00	159.00

Evening meal 1700 (last orders 1900)
Parking for 4
Open April–October and Christmas

Windsor Hotel
APPROVED

53 Dean Street, Blackpool FY4 1BP
☎ (01253) 400232 & 346886
Fax (01253) 400232
Clean, comfortable en-suite rooms. Four-posters available. Good home cooking. Guests' individual needs catered for. Close to promenade and entertainments.
Bedrooms: 2 single, 5 double, 3 twin, 2 triple
Bathrooms: 12 en-suite

Bed & breakfast per night:	£min	£max
Single	16.00	23.00
Double	32.00	46.00

Half board per person:	£min	£max
Daily	21.00	28.00
Weekly	126.00	144.00

Evening meal 1700 (last orders 1900)
Parking for 8
Cards accepted: Access, Visa, Switch/Delta

BOLTON
Greater Manchester
Map ref 4A1

On the edge of the West Pennine Moors and renowned for its outstanding town centre architecture and fine shopping facilities. The Octagon Theatre has national recognition for its "theatre in the round". Samuel Crompton, inventor of the "spinning mule", is buried here.
Tourist Information Centre ☎ *(01204) 364333*

Bolton Moat House
HIGHLY COMMENDED

1 Higher Bridge Street, Bolton BL1 2EW
☎ (01204) 879988
Fax (01204) 380777
Queens Moat/Utell International
Town centre hotel, 20 minutes to Manchester city centre and Manchester Airport. Accessible to M61 and M6. Leisure, conference and restaurant facilities. Disabled guests catered for.
Wheelchair access category 1
Bedrooms: 72 double, 52 twin, 4 triple
Bathrooms: 128 en-suite

Bed & breakfast per night:	£min	£max
Single	64.75	98.75
Double	74.50	124.50

Half board per person:	£min	£max
Daily	80.25	114.25

Lunch available
Evening meal 1900 (last orders 2200)
Parking for 70
Cards accepted: Access, Visa, Diners, Amex, Switch/Delta

BOLTON-BY-BOWLAND
Lancashire
Map ref 4B1

Unspoilt village near the Ribble Valley with 2 greens, one with stump of 13th C market cross and stocks. Whitewashed and greystone cottages.

Copy Nook Hotel
COMMENDED

Bolton-by-Bowland, Clitheroe BB7 4NL
☎ Clitheroe (01200) 447205
Fax (01200) 447004
Traditional country inn, set in rural countryside. All the charm and atmosphere of yesteryear combined with the modern comforts of today. Only 3 minutes from A59.
Bedrooms: 4 double, 2 twin
Bathrooms: 6 en-suite

Bed & breakfast per night:	£min	£max
Single	30.00	
Double	50.00	

Lunch available
Evening meal 1900 (last orders 2130)
Cards accepted: Access, Visa, Diners, Amex, Switch/Delta

BURNLEY
Lancashire
Map ref 4B1

"A town amidst the Pennines". Towneley Hall has fine period rooms and is home to Burnley's art gallery and museum. The Kay-Shuttleworth collection of lace and embroidery can be seen at Gawthorpe Hall (National Trust). Burnley Mechanics Arts Centre is a well-known jazz and blues venue.
Tourist Information Centre ☎ *(01282) 455485*

Alexander Hotel
HIGHLY COMMENDED

2 Tarleton Avenue, Todmorden Road, Burnley BB11 3ET
☎ (01282) 422684
Fax (01282) 424094
The Independents
Family-run hotel with accent on personal service. Near the town centre, in quiet residential area close to Towneley Hall.
Bedrooms: 8 single, 5 double, 2 twin, 1 family room
Bathrooms: 13 en-suite, 1 public

Bed & breakfast per night:	£min	£max
Single	25.00	38.00
Double	38.00	49.00

Half board per person:	£min	£max
Daily	29.00	52.00
Weekly	189.00	300.00

Lunch available
Evening meal 1815 (last orders 2045)
Parking for 22
Cards accepted: Access, Visa

NORTH WEST

Ormerod Hotel
HIGHLY COMMENDED
121-123 Ormerod Road, Burnley
BB11 3QW
☎ (01282) 423255
Small bed and breakfast hotel in quiet, pleasant surroundings facing local parks. Recently refurbished, all en-suite facilities. 5 minutes from town centre.
Bedrooms: 4 single, 2 double, 2 twin, 2 triple
Bathrooms: 10 en-suite

Bed & breakfast per night:	£min	£max
Single	20.00	24.00
Double	34.00	37.00

Parking for 7

BURWARDSLEY
Cheshire
Map ref 4A2

The Pheasant Inn
COMMENDED
Higher Burwardsley, Tattenhall, Chester CH3 9PF
☎ Tattenhall (01829) 770434
Fax (01829) 771097
Ⓒ Wayfarer/Logis of Great Britain

300-year-old inn, half-timber and sandstone construction, nestling on the top of the Peckforton Hills. Accommodation in delightfully converted barn affording pleasant views towards Chester.
Bedrooms: 7 double, 2 twin, 1 triple
Bathrooms: 10 en-suite

Bed & breakfast per night:	£min	£max
Single	45.00	45.00
Double	70.00	80.00

Half board per person:	£min	£max
Daily	85.00	90.00

Lunch available
Evening meal 1930 (last orders 2130)
Parking for 60
Cards accepted: Access, Visa, Diners, Amex

Please mention this guide when making your booking.

BURY
Greater Manchester
Map ref 4B1

Famous for its black puddings, huge open market and East Lancashire Steam Railway. Birthplace of Sir Robert Peel, founder of the police force and Prime Minister. Bury Art Gallery has an important collection of Turner and Constable paintings.
Tourist Information Centre ☎ (0161) 705 5111

The Bolholt Country Park Hotel
COMMENDED
Walshaw Road, Bury BL8 1PU
☎ (0161) 764 5239 & 763 7007
Fax (0161) 763 1789
Ⓒ The Independents

Family-run hotel and conference centre in 50 acres of beautiful parkland, lakes and gardens. Large swimming pool and full leisure facilities.
Bedrooms: 12 single, 26 double, 5 twin, 4 family rooms
Bathrooms: 45 en-suite, 2 private

Bed & breakfast per night:	£min	£max
Single	44.00	50.00
Double	55.00	61.00

Half board per person:	£min	£max
Daily	57.50	63.50
Weekly	402.50	444.50

Lunch available
Evening meal 1900 (last orders 2130)
Parking for 150
Cards accepted: Access, Visa, Diners, Amex

Normandie Hotel
HIGHLY COMMENDED
Elbut Lane, Birtle, Bury, Lancashire BL9 6UT
☎ (0161) 764 3869 & 764 1170
Fax (0161) 764 4866
Modern comfortable hotel, noted nationally for the preparation and presentation of modern French/British cooking.
Bedrooms: 7 single, 10 double, 6 twin
Bathrooms: 23 en-suite

Bed & breakfast per night:	£min	£max
Single	49.00	69.00
Double	59.00	79.00

Half board per person:	£min	£max
Daily	64.00	84.00

Lunch available
Evening meal 1900 (last orders 2130)
Parking for 60
Cards accepted: Access, Visa, Diners, Amex, Switch/Delta

Rostrevor Hotel and Bistro
COMMENDED
148 Manchester Road, Bury, Lancashire BL9 0TL
☎ (0161) 764 3944
Fax (0161) 764 8266
Small, family-run hotel and bistro opposite open parkland, close to town centre, markets and steam railway. Warm welcome and friendly atmosphere.
Bedrooms: 5 single, 4 double, 4 twin, 1 triple
Bathrooms: 10 en-suite, 2 public

Bed & breakfast per night:	£min	£max
Single	29.00	34.00
Double	42.00	48.00

Half board per person:	£min	£max
Daily	39.00	44.00
Weekly	245.00	294.00

Lunch available
Evening meal 1800 (last orders 2000)
Parking for 14
Cards accepted: Access, Visa, Amex, Switch/Delta

CHEADLE HULME
Greater Manchester
Map ref 4B2

Residential area near Manchester with some older buildings dating from 19th C once occupied by merchants and industrialists from surrounding towns. Several fine timber-framed houses, shopping centre and easy access to Manchester Airport.

Spring Cottage Guest House
Listed HIGHLY COMMENDED
60 Hulme Hall Road, Cheadle Hulme, Stockport, Cheshire SK8 6JZ
☎ (0161) 485 1037

Continued ▶

NORTH WEST

CHEADLE HULME
Continued

Beautifully furnished Victorian house in historic part of Cheadle Hulme. Convenient for airport, rail station and variety of local restaurants.
Bedrooms: 1 single, 1 double, 4 twin
Bathrooms: 3 en-suite, 1 public

Bed & breakfast
per night:	£min	£max
Single	18.50	27.00
Double	32.50	39.00

Parking for 6
Cards accepted: Access, Visa

CHESTER
Cheshire
Map ref 4A2

Roman and medieval walled city rich in treasures. Black and white buildings are a hallmark, including "The Rows" - two-tier shopping galleries. The racecourse is the only one in the country where horses race anti-clockwise. 900-year-old cathedral, zoo.
Tourist Information Centre ☎ *(01244) 317962 or 351609 or 322220*

Brookside Hotel
COMMENDED
Brook Lane, Chester CH2 2AN
☎ (01244) 381943
Fax (01244) 379701
Character, charm and friendly atmosphere, where our reputation is based on your recommendation. Off Liverpool Road near Northgate Arena and city centre. Weekly half board less 10 per cent.
Bedrooms: 8 single, 5 double, 6 twin, 6 triple
Bathrooms: 25 en-suite

Bed & breakfast
per night:	£min	£max
Single	30.00	34.00
Double	44.00	48.00

Half board per
person:	£min	£max
Daily	32.00	44.00

Evening meal 1900 (last orders 2130)
Parking for 13
Cards accepted: Access, Visa, Switch/Delta

Please check prices and other details at the time of booking.

Chester Moat House
HIGHLY COMMENDED
Trinity Street, Chester CH1 2BD
☎ (01244) 899988
Fax (01244) 316118
Queens Moat/Utell International
Modern city centre hotel, within ancient city walls. Close to racecourse and with views over North Wales. Rates shown below apply at weekends only.
Wheelchair access category 2
Bedrooms: 29 single, 40 double, 83 twin
Suites available
Bathrooms: 152 en-suite

Bed & breakfast
per night:	£min	£max
Single	50.00	55.00
Double	100.00	110.00

Half board per
person:	£min	£max
Daily	60.00	70.00

Lunch available
Evening meal 1800 (last orders 2230)
Parking for 80
Cards accepted: Access, Visa, Diners, Amex

Cheyney Lodge Hotel
COMMENDED
77-79 Cheyney Road, Chester CH1 4BS
☎ (01244) 381925
Small, friendly hotel of unusual design, featuring indoor garden and fish pond. 10 minutes' walk from city centre and on main bus route. Personally supervised with emphasis on good food.
Bedrooms: 1 single, 4 double, 2 twin, 1 triple
Bathrooms: 8 en-suite

Bed & breakfast
per night:	£min	£max
Single	24.00	24.00
Double	39.00	44.00

Half board per
person:	£min	£max
Daily	28.95	31.95
Weekly	202.65	223.65

Lunch available
Evening meal 1800 (last orders 2000)
Parking for 12
Cards accepted: Access, Visa

A key to symbols can be found inside the back cover flap.

City Walls Hotel & Restaurant
City Walls Road, 14 Stanley Place, Chester CH1 2LU
☎ (01244) 313416
Fax (01244) 313416
The Independents
Charming Georgian hotel situated on the old city walls, overlooking Chester racecourse. Noted for accommodation, food and service.
Bedrooms: 4 single, 6 double, 2 twin, 4 triple
Bathrooms: 16 en-suite

Bed & breakfast
per night:	£min	£max
Single	36.00	42.50
Double	46.40	55.00

Half board per
person:	£min	£max
Daily	34.45	49.45
Weekly	210.00	258.65

Lunch available
Evening meal 1900 (last orders 2130)
Parking for 3
Cards accepted: Access, Visa, Amex, Switch/Delta

Curzon Hotel
COMMENDED
52-54 Hough Green, Chester CH4 8JQ
☎ (01244) 678581
Fax (01244) 680866

A warm welcome awaits in this privately owned large Victorian house with beautiful gardens. Close to racecourse, River Dee and golf. Fine cuisine prepared by chef-proprietor Markus Imfeld.
Bedrooms: 4 single, 4 double, 1 twin, 4 triple, 3 family rooms
Bathrooms: 16 en-suite

Bed & breakfast
per night:	£min	£max
Single	35.00	40.00
Double	45.00	65.00

Half board per
person:	£min	£max
Daily	40.00	50.00
Weekly	245.00	385.00

Evening meal 1900 (last orders 2100)
Parking for 24

NORTH WEST

Cards accepted: Access, Visa, Diners, Amex

Dene Hotel
COMMENDED
Hoole Road, Chester CH2 3ND
☎ (01244) 321165
Fax (01244) 350177
Logis of Great Britain
Hotel in own grounds, adjacent to Alexandra Park and 1 mile from city centre. A la carte restaurant, rooms for non-smokers, ample parking.
Wheelchair access category 3
Bedrooms: 9 single, 23 double, 12 twin, 3 triple, 2 family rooms
Bathrooms: 49 en-suite

Bed & breakfast per night:
	£min	£max
Single	37.00	39.00
Double	47.00	49.00

Half board per person:
	£min	£max
Daily	36.00	38.00
Weekly	216.00	228.00

Lunch available
Evening meal 1900 (last orders 2100)
Parking for 51
Cards accepted: Access, Visa, Amex, Switch/Delta

Eaton Hotel
APPROVED
29-31 City Road, Chester CH1 4AE
☎ (01244) 320840
Fax (01244) 320850
Minotel
Welcoming and relaxing hotel, convenient for station and 5 minutes' walk from the famous shopping centre, Roman walls and river. Bargain breaks available all year.
Bedrooms: 3 single, 5 double, 5 twin, 2 triple, 3 family rooms
Bathrooms: 11 en-suite, 7 private showers

Bed & breakfast per night:
	£min	£max
Single	28.50	39.50
Double	37.50	49.50

Half board per person:
	£min	£max
Daily	27.50	47.50
Weekly	175.00	227.50

Lunch available
Evening meal 1830 (last orders 2000)
Parking for 10
Cards accepted: Access, Visa, Diners, Amex, Switch/Delta

Edwards House Hotel
HIGHLY COMMENDED
61-63 Hoole Road, Chester CH2 3NJ
☎ (01244) 318055 & 319888
Victorian property with well proportioned bedrooms, all en-suite. Convenient for city centre, Chester Zoo, M53/M56 motorways and A55 North Wales trunk road.
Bedrooms: 2 single, 5 double, 3 triple
Bathrooms: 10 en-suite

Bed & breakfast per night:
	£min	£max
Single	21.00	29.00
Double	35.00	49.00

Half board per person:
	£min	£max
Daily	27.50	37.00
Weekly	192.50	259.00

Evening meal 1830 (last orders 1930)
Parking for 10
Cards accepted: Access, Visa

Green Bough Hotel and Restaurant
HIGHLY COMMENDED
60 Hoole Road, Chester CH2 3NL
☎ (01244) 326241
Fax (01244) 326265
Comfortable, family-run Victorian hotel with friendly, relaxed atmosphere. Tastefully decorated with many antique furnishings. Restaurant renowned for traditional English cooking.
Wheelchair access category 3
Bedrooms: 2 single, 14 double, 1 twin, 3 triple
Bathrooms: 20 en-suite

Bed & breakfast per night:
	£min	£max
Single	36.00	44.00
Double	52.00	60.00

Lunch available
Evening meal 1900 (last orders 2030)
Parking for 21
Cards accepted: Access, Visa, Amex, Switch/Delta

Malvern Guest House
21 Victoria Road, Chester CH2 2AX
☎ (01244) 380865
Victorian terraced town house comprising 2-storeys, within 8 minutes' walk of the cathedral and the city centre.
Bedrooms: 2 single, 1 double, 2 twin, 2 triple

Bathrooms: 2 public

Bed & breakfast per night:
	£min	£max
Single		13.00
Double		25.00

Half board per person:
	£min	£max
Daily		17.50
Weekly		91.50

Evening meal 1800 (last orders 1700)

Mollington Banastre Hotel
Parkgate Road, Mollington, Chester CH1 6NN
☎ (01244) 851471
Fax (01244) 851242
Best Western
Country house hotel in its own grounds, only 1.5 miles from historic Chester. Leisure complex.
Bedrooms: 4 single, 37 double, 14 twin, 8 triple
Bathrooms: 63 en-suite

Bed & breakfast per night:
	£min	£max
Single	65.00	85.00
Double	76.00	115.00

Half board per person:
	£min	£max
Daily	50.00	65.00

Lunch available
Evening meal 1900 (last orders 2200)
Parking for 200
Cards accepted: Access, Visa, Diners, Amex

Plantation Inn Hotel
Liverpool Road, Chester CH2 1AG
☎ (01244) 374100
Fax (01244) 379240
Utell International

Ideally situated 500 metres from the medieval city centre, the hotel offers dinner and dancing Thursday to Saturday, good food and friendly staff.
Wheelchair access category 3
Bedrooms: 21 single, 15 double, 34 twin, 3 triple
Bathrooms: 73 en-suite

Continued ▶

139

NORTH WEST

CHESTER
Continued

Bed & breakfast per night:

	£min	£max
Single	72.00	82.00
Double	92.00	102.00

Half board per person:

	£min	£max
Daily	56.00	66.00
Weekly	392.00	462.00

Lunch available
Evening meal 1900 (last orders 2200)
Parking for 90
Cards accepted: Access, Visa, Diners, Amex

Stafford Hotel
COMMENDED
City Road, Chester CH1 3AE
☎ (01244) 326052
Fax (01244) 311403
Comfortable, family-run hotel, close to city centre and railway station. Restaurant and licensed bar. Parking available. Short breaks available all year. Brochure on request.
Bedrooms: 7 single, 10 double, 3 twin, 1 triple, 1 family room
Bathrooms: 22 en-suite, 1 public

Bed & breakfast per night:

	£min	£max
Single	38.00	40.00
Double	50.00	50.00

Evening meal 1830 (last orders 2045)
Parking for 2
Cards accepted: Access, Visa, Diners, Amex, Switch/Delta

CHIPPING
Lancashire
Map ref 4A2

Delightful small village with 3 pubs, teashop, ancient church and ghost.

Gibbon Bridge Hotel
HIGHLY COMMENDED
Forest of Bowland, Chipping, Preston PR3 2TQ
☎ (01995) 61456
Fax (01995) 61277
Privately-owned country house hotel in the heart of some of Lancashire's finest countryside, yet only 20 minutes from M6, exit 32. Award-winning gardens. Excellent dining facilities and executive accommodation, leisure facilities and beauty salon.

Wheelchair access category 3
Bedrooms: 3 single, 8 double, 15 twin, 4 triple
Bathrooms: 30 en-suite

Bed & breakfast per night:

	£min	£max
Single	60.00	110.00
Double	80.00	175.00

Half board per person:

	£min	£max
Daily	50.00	75.00

Lunch available
Evening meal 1900 (last orders 2030)
Parking for 151
Cards accepted: Access, Visa, Diners, Amex, Switch/Delta

CHORLEY
Lancashire
Map ref 4A1

Set between the Pennine moors and the Lancashire Plain, Chorley has been an important town since medieval times, with its "Flat-Iron" and covered markets. The rich heritage includes Astley Hall and Park, Hoghton Tower, Rivington Country Park and the Leeds-Liverpool Canal.

Park Hall Hotel, Leisure & Conference Centre
HIGHLY COMMENDED
Park Hall Road, Charnock Richard, Chorley, Preston PR7 5LP
☎ Eccleston (01257) 452090
Fax (01257) 451838
Hotel, village and conference centre set in 130 acres of beautiful grounds, close to both the M6 and M61 motorways. Conference and leisure facilities.
Bedrooms: 43 double, 64 twin, 33 family rooms
Suites available
Bathrooms: 140 en-suite

Bed & breakfast per night:

	£min	£max
Single	49.99	77.45
Double	69.98	84.95

Half board per person:

	£min	£max
Daily	44.99	90.95

Lunch available
Evening meal 1830 (last orders 2145)
Parking for 2500
Cards accepted: Access, Visa, Diners, Amex, Switch/Delta

CLITHEROE
Lancashire
Map ref 4A1

Ancient market town with an 800-year-old castle keep and a wide range of award-winning shops. Good base for touring Ribble Valley, Trough of Bowland and Pennine moorland. Country market on Tuesdays and Saturdays.
Tourist Information Centre ☎ (01200) 25566

Brooklyn
HIGHLY COMMENDED
32 Pimlico Road, Clitheroe BB7 2AH
☎ (01200) 28268
Small, family-run licensed guesthouse, close to town centre, where the proprietors assure you of a warm and friendly welcome.
Bedrooms: 1 single, 1 double, 2 twin
Bathrooms: 4 en-suite

Bed & breakfast per night:

	£min	£max
Single	23.00	25.00
Double	38.00	40.00

Half board per person:

	£min	£max
Daily	33.00	35.00

Evening meal 1830 (last orders 1930)
Cards accepted: Access, Visa, Amex

Mitton Hall Lodgings
APPROVED
Mitton Road, Mitton, Blackburn BB7 9PQ
☎ Stonyhurst (01254) 826544
Fax (01254) 826386
16th C listed hall in Ribble Valley. Restaurant, pizzeria, tavern, lodgings. Two miles Whalley Abbey, 3 miles Clitheroe Castle, close Trough of Bowland. Eleven miles junction 31 of M6, 7 miles M65.
Bedrooms: 2 single, 6 double, 5 twin, 1 triple
Bathrooms: 14 en-suite

Bed & breakfast per night:

	£min	£max
Single	35.75	37.50
Double	38.50	42.00

Half board per person:

	£min	£max
Daily	48.00	

Lunch available
Evening meal 1830 (last orders 2230)

NORTH WEST

Parking for 150
Cards accepted: Access, Visa, Amex, Switch/Delta

Shireburn Arms Hotel
COMMENDED

Whalley Road, Hurst Green,
Clitheroe BB7 9QJ
☎ Stonyhurst (01254) 826518
Fax (01254) 826208
The Independents
16th C family-run hotel, with unrivalled views, renowned for food and comfort, log fires, real ale, bar food. Within easy reach of the motorway network.
Bedrooms: 6 double, 4 twin, 2 family rooms
Bathrooms: 12 en-suite

Bed & breakfast
per night:	£min	£max
Single	30.00	39.00
Double		54.00

Half board per
person:	£min	£max
Daily		42.50

Lunch available
Evening meal 1900 (last orders 2130)
Parking for 80
Cards accepted: Access, Visa, Amex, Switch/Delta

CREWE
Cheshire
Map ref 4A2

Famous for its railway junction, this small market town is at the heart of the beautiful south Cheshire countryside and well located for visiting local attractions. Original home of the Rolls Royce motor car.

Hunters Lodge Hotel

Sydney Road, Crewe CW1 5LU
☎ (01270) 583440 & 588216
Fax (01270) 500553
Family-run country-style hotel with conference and leisure facilities, set in 14 acres, 1 mile from Crewe and 6 miles from M6.
Wheelchair access category 3
Bedrooms: 10 single, 28 double, 4 twin
Bathrooms: 42 en-suite

Bed & breakfast
per night:	£min	£max
Single	25.00	50.00
Double	42.00	64.00

Half board per
person:	£min	£max
Daily	34.50	91.00

Lunch available
Evening meal 1900 (last orders 2130)
Parking for 250
Cards accepted: Access, Visa, Amex

DARWEN
Lancashire
Map ref 4A1

Small town on the edge of the West Pennine moors, close to Blackburn.

Old Rosins Inn
COMMENDED

Treacle Row, Pickup Bank, Darwen BB3 3QD
☎ (01254) 771264
Fax (01254) 873894
Country hotel with panoramic views, yet close to all main towns and main road systems in Lancashire.
Bedrooms: 7 double, 5 twin, 3 triple
Bathrooms: 15 en-suite

Bed & breakfast
per night:	£min	£max
Single	45.00	55.00
Double	55.00	65.00

Half board per
person:	£min	£max
Daily	59.00	69.00
Weekly	350.00	350.00

Lunch available
Evening meal 1900 (last orders 2200)
Parking for 200
Cards accepted: Access, Visa, Diners, Amex, Switch/Delta

All accommodation in this guide has been graded, or is awaiting a grading, by a trained Tourist Board inspector.

The symbols in each entry give information about services and facilities. A 'key' to these symbols appears at the back of this guide.

GARSTANG
Lancashire
Map ref 4A1

Picturesque country market town. The gateway to the fells, it stands on the Lancaster Canal and is a popular cruising centre. Close by are the remains of Greenhalgh Castle (no public access) and the Bleasdale Circle. Discovery Centre shows history of Over Wyre and Bowland fringe areas.
Tourist Information Centre ☎ (01995) 602125

Crofters Hotel
HIGHLY COMMENDED

A6, Cabus, Garstang, Preston PR3 1PH
☎ (01995) 604128
Fax (01995) 601646
Family owned and managed hotel with all modern facilities, situated midway between Preston and Lancaster.
Bedrooms: 1 single, 5 double, 10 twin, 3 triple
Bathrooms: 19 en-suite

Bed & breakfast
per night:	£min	£max
Single	45.00	55.00
Double	55.00	80.00

Lunch available
Evening meal 1900 (last orders 2200)
Parking for 200
Cards accepted: Access, Visa, Diners, Amex, Switch/Delta

Guy's Thatched Hamlet
COMMENDED

Canalside, St. Michael's Road, Bilsborrow, Garstang, Preston PR3 0RS
☎ Brock (01995) 640849 & 640010
Fax (01995) 640141
Logis of Great Britain

Friendly, family-run thatched canalside tavern, restaurant, pizzeria, lodgings, craft shops, cricket ground with thatched pavilion and crown green bowling. Conference centre. Off junction 32 of M6, then 3 miles north on A6 to Garstang.
Bedrooms: 28 double, 20 twin, 5 family rooms

Continued ▶

NORTH WEST

GARSTANG
Continued

Bathrooms: 53 en-suite
Bed & breakfast
per night:

	£min	£max
Double	44.00	59.50

Half board per
person:

	£min	£max
Daily	35.00	42.00

Lunch available
Evening meal 1800 (last orders 2330)
Parking for 300
Cards accepted: Access, Visa, Amex, Switch/Delta

HOLMES CHAPEL
Cheshire
Map ref 4A2

Large village with some interesting 18th C buildings and St Luke's Church encased in brick hiding the 15th C original.

Brereton House
DE LUXE

Mill Lane, Brereton, Holmes Chapel CW4 8AU
☎ (01477) 534511
Fax (01477) 544149

Award-winning country house with oak beams, antiques and four-poster beds. Delicious food. Amidst open farmland yet only 5 minutes M6. Convenient for many National Trust attractions. No smoking.
Bedrooms: 1 single, 4 double, 1 twin
Bathrooms: 6 en-suite
Bed & breakfast
per night:

	£min	£max
Single	35.00	59.50
Double	55.00	65.00

Half board per
person:

	£min	£max
Daily	50.00	74.50

Evening meal 1930 (last orders 2030)
Parking for 6
Cards accepted: Access, Visa, Diners, Amex

Holly Lodge Hotel
COMMENDED

70 London Road, Holmes Chapel CW4 7AS
☎ (01477) 537033
Fax (01477) 535823
Charming Victorian country hotel, professionally managed and family-owned. Friendly and efficient service. Close to junction 18 of M6. A la carte restaurant, conference and meeting rooms. Four-poster, jacuzzi and water bed.
Bedrooms: 6 single, 21 double, 9 twin, 2 triple
Bathrooms: 38 en-suite
Bed & breakfast
per night:

	£min	£max
Single	34.50	69.50
Double	56.50	82.50

Half board per
person:

	£min	£max
Daily	48.90	83.90

Lunch available
Evening meal 1930 (last orders 2145)
Parking for 80
Cards accepted: Access, Visa, Diners, Amex, Switch/Delta

HOYLAKE
Merseyside
Map ref 4A2

Overlooking the North Wales coastline across the River Dee, this residential resort has good beaches, a 4-mile promenade and, nearby, the Royal Liverpool Golf Club. Variety of bird life on Hilbre Islands accessible on foot at low tide.

Kings Gap Court Hotel
APPROVED

Valentia Road, Hoylake, Wirral L47 2AN
☎ (0151) 632 2073
Fax (0151) 632 0247
Old established family hotel close to seafront and many championship golf-courses. Ideal centre for Wales, Chester and Liverpool.
Bedrooms: 3 single, 2 double, 21 twin, 1 triple
Bathrooms: 23 en-suite, 5 public
Bed & breakfast
per night:

	£min	£max
Single	32.00	32.00
Double	42.00	57.00

Half board per
person:

	£min	£max
Daily	28.00	36.00
Weekly	172.00	240.00

Lunch available
Evening meal 1830 (last orders 2000)
Parking for 89
Cards accepted: Access, Visa

KNUTSFORD
Cheshire
Map ref 4A2

Delightful town with many buildings of architectural and historic interest. The setting of Elizabeth Gaskell's "Cranford". Annual May Day celebration and decorative "sanding" of the pavements are unique to the town. Popular Heritage Centre. *Tourist Information Centre* ☎ (01565) 632611 or 632210

Longview Hotel and Restaurant
HIGHLY COMMENDED

Manchester Road, Knutsford WA16 0LX
☎ (01565) 632119
Fax (01565) 652402
Logis of Great Britain
Period Victorian hotel with many antiques and a relaxed, comfortable atmosphere, overlooking town common. High quality varied food. Close to exit 19 of M6 and airport.
Bedrooms: 6 single, 9 double, 7 twin, 1 triple
Bathrooms: 23 en-suite
Bed & breakfast
per night:

	£min	£max
Single	38.00	75.00
Double	58.00	80.00

Lunch available
Evening meal 1900 (last orders 2100)
Parking for 17
Cards accepted: Access, Visa, Diners, Amex

WELCOME HOST

This is a nationally recognised customer care programme which aims to promote the highest standards of service and a warm welcome. Establishments who are taking part in this initiative are indicated by the symbol.

NORTH WEST

LANCASTER

Lancashire
Map ref 5A3

Interesting old county town on the River Lune with history dating back to Roman times. Norman castle, St Mary's Church, Customs House, City and Maritime Museums, Ashton Memorial and Butterfly House are among places of note. Good centre for touring the Lake District.
Tourist Information Centre ☎ (01524) 32878

Lancaster House Hotel

HIGHLY COMMENDED

Green Lane, Lancaster LA1 4GJ
☎ (01524) 844822
Fax (01524) 844766
Best Western
Elegant country house with extensive leisure facilities, perfectly located for exploring the nearby Lake District, Yorkshire Dales and historic Lancaster.
Wheelchair access category 2
Bedrooms: 36 double, 42 twin, 2 triple
Bathrooms: 80 en-suite

Bed & breakfast per night:	£min	£max
Single	59.50	82.00
Double	77.00	92.00

Half board per person:	£min	£max
Daily	57.00	62.00
Weekly	342.00	372.00

Lunch available
Evening meal 1900 (last orders 2130)
Parking for 100
Cards accepted: Access, Visa, Diners, Amex, Switch/Delta

LANGHO

Lancashire
Map ref 4A1

This parish can trace its history back to Saxon times when in 798 AD a battle was fought at Billangohoh from which the names of Billington and Langho were derived. A flourishing community of mainly cattle farms, near both the River Ribble and the River Calder.

Mytton Fold Hotel and Golf Complex

HIGHLY COMMENDED

Whalley Road, Langho, Blackburn BB6 8AB
☎ Blackburn (01254) 240662
Fax (01254) 248119

10 miles from exit 31 of M6. Peacefully secluded, yet only 300 yards from the A59. Own private 18-hole golf-course.
Wheelchair access category 3
Bedrooms: 13 double, 14 twin
Bathrooms: 27 en-suite

Bed & breakfast per night:	£min	£max
Single	36.00	46.00
Double	58.00	67.00

Half board per person:	£min	£max
Daily	43.00	51.00

Lunch available
Evening meal 1830 (last orders 2130)
Parking for 200
Cards accepted: Access, Visa, Amex, Switch/Delta

Petre Lodge

HIGHLY COMMENDED

Northcote Road, Langho, Blackburn BB6 8BG
☎ Blackburn (01254) 245506
Fax (01254) 245506

Charming village school conversion in semi-rural location. Combines the comfort of a hotel with the privacy of a finely furnished home.
Bedrooms: 1 single, 6 double, 2 twin
Bathrooms: 9 en-suite

Bed & breakfast per night:	£min	£max
Single	35.00	40.00
Double	45.00	50.00

Evening meal 1900 (last orders 2100)
Parking for 10
Cards accepted: Access, Visa, Switch/Delta

Map references apply to the colour maps at the back of this guide.

For ideas on places to visit refer to the introduction at the beginning of this section.

LIVERPOOL

Merseyside
Map ref 4A2

Vibrant city which became prominent in the 18th C as a result of its sugar, spice and tobacco trade with the Americas. Today the historic waterfront is a major attraction. Home to the Beatles, the Grand National and 2 20th C cathedrals, as well as many museums and galleries.
Tourist Information Centre ☎ (0151) 709 3631 or 708 8854

Aachen Hotel

COMMENDED

89-91 Mount Pleasant, Liverpool L3 5TB
☎ (0151) 709 3477 & 709 1126
Fax (0151) 709 1126
In city centre close to theatres, shops, cinemas, boat/rail/coach stations. Albert Dock and Maritime Museum close by. Winner of regional and local awards for best small hotel.
Bedrooms: 6 single, 1 double, 5 twin, 5 triple
Bathrooms: 9 en-suite, 2 public

Bed & breakfast per night:	£min	£max
Single	22.00	30.00
Double	36.00	44.00

Half board per person:	£min	£max
Daily	30.00	35.00
Weekly	210.00	245.00

Lunch available
Evening meal 1830 (last orders 2030)
Parking for 2
Cards accepted: Access, Visa, Diners, Amex

Antrim Hotel

APPROVED

73 Mount Pleasant, Liverpool L3 5TB
☎ (0151) 709 5239 & 709 9212
Fax (0151) 709 7169
Friendly, family-run city centre hotel, convenient for shops, railway and bus stations, Albert Dock and all major tourist attractions. Twenty minutes from the airport.
Bedrooms: 8 single, 2 double, 8 twin, 2 family rooms
Bathrooms: 7 en-suite, 1 public, 8 private showers

Bed & breakfast per night:	£min	£max
Single	25.00	40.00
Double	38.00	50.00

Continued ▶

143

LIVERPOOL
Continued

Half board per person:

	£min	£max
Daily	37.00	52.00
Weekly	259.00	364.00

Evening meal 1800 (last orders 2000)
Parking for 2
Cards accepted: Access, Visa, Diners, Amex

Atlantic Tower Hotel
COMMENDED

Chapel Street, Liverpool L3 9RE
☎ (0151) 227 4444
Fax (0151) 236 3973
Utell International

A well known landmark, this modern hotel overlooks Liverpool's business quarter and has a magnificent view of the River Mersey from its rooms and celebrated restaurant.
Bedrooms: 58 single, 59 double, 109 twin
Suites available
Bathrooms: 226 en-suite

Bed & breakfast per night:

	£min	£max
Single	40.00	94.50
Double	80.00	128.50

Lunch available
Evening meal 1900 (last orders 2200)
Parking for 80
Cards accepted: Access, Visa, Diners, Amex

Blundellsands Hotel
COMMENDED

The Serpentine, Blundellsands, Crosby, Liverpool L23 6YB
☎ (0151) 924 6515
Fax (0151) 931 5364
Stagecoach

Majestic Victorian character hotel in a quiet suburb of Crosby. Easy access to Liverpool centre and Southport.
Bedrooms: 21 single, 13 double, 5 twin, 2 triple
Suite available
Bathrooms: 41 en-suite

Bed & breakfast per night:

	£min	£max
Single	35.00	60.50
Double	65.00	75.00

Half board per person:

	£min	£max
Daily	46.25	74.35

Lunch available
Evening meal 1900 (last orders 2130)
Parking for 250
Cards accepted: Access, Visa, Diners, Amex, Switch/Delta

Green Park Hotel
APPROVED

4-6 Green Bank Drive, Liverpool L17 1AN
☎ (0151) 733 3382
Fax (0151) 734 1161

Two miles from city centre and 3 miles from Liverpool Airport.
Bedrooms: 2 single, 6 double, 10 twin, 2 triple, 1 family room
Bathrooms: 21 en-suite, 1 public

Bed & breakfast per night:

	£min	£max
Single	24.00	28.00
Double	36.00	42.00

Half board per person:

	£min	£max
Daily	30.00	36.00

Lunch available
Evening meal 1830 (last orders 2100)
Parking for 25
Cards accepted: Access, Visa, Diners, Amex

Holme Leigh Guest House

93 Woodcroft Road, Wavertree, Liverpool L15 2HG
☎ (0151) 734 2216 & 427 9806

Victorian red brick 3-storey corner dwelling and fashion shop, facing on to Lawrence Road. Just 2.5 miles from city centre.
Bedrooms: 4 single, 2 double, 4 twin
Bathrooms: 3 en-suite, 1 public

Bed & breakfast per night:

	£min	£max
Single	15.00	17.00
Double	25.00	29.00

Cards accepted: Access, Visa, Amex

Rockland Hotel
APPROVED

View Road, Rainhill, Prescot L35 0LG
☎ (0151) 426 4603
Fax (0151) 426 0107

Georgian hotel set in own grounds in quiet suburban location. Easy access to motorway (1 mile) and 10 miles from Liverpool city centre.
Bedrooms: 4 single, 2 double, 3 twin, 2 triple
Bathrooms: 10 en-suite, 1 public

Bed & breakfast per night:

	£min	£max
Single	25.00	33.50
Double	35.00	44.00

Lunch available
Evening meal 1830 (last orders 2030)
Parking for 30
Cards accepted: Access, Visa, Diners, Amex

Woodlands Guest House
COMMENDED

10 Haigh Road, Waterloo, Liverpool L22 3XP
☎ (0151) 920 5373

Situated in conservation area within short walking distance of all major amenities. Superb road and rail links to Liverpool and Southport.
Bedrooms: 3 single, 6 twin
Bathrooms: 9 en-suite, 1 public

Bed & breakfast per night:

	£min	£max
Single	25.00	25.00
Double	36.00	38.00

Parking for 10

LONGRIDGE
Lancashire
Map ref 4A1

Situated at the foot of Longridge Fell. Several civic buildings in Preston are built of Longridge stone.

Ferraris Country House
COMMENDED

Chipping Road, Thornley, Longridge, Preston PR3 2TB
☎ (01772) 783148
Fax (01772) 786174

Country house hotel, set in mature gardens and offering value, quality and service.
Bedrooms: 1 single, 6 double, 1 twin, 2 triple, 1 family room
Bathrooms: 11 en-suite

Bed & breakfast per night:

	£min	£max
Single	30.00	
Double	45.00	

Half board per person:

	£min	£max
Daily	42.95	
Weekly	275.00	

Lunch available
Evening meal 1830 (last orders 2215)
Parking for 50
Cards accepted: Access, Visa, Switch/Delta

NORTH WEST

LYTHAM ST ANNES

Lancashire
Map ref 4A1

Pleasant resort famous for its championship golf-courses, notably the Royal Lytham and St Annes. Fine sands and attractive gardens. Some half-timbered buildings and an old windmill recently restored.
Tourist Information Centre ☎ (01253) 725610

Blue Sands Hotel

COMMENDED

45 South Promenade, Lytham St Annes FY8 1LZ
☎ St Annes (01253) 713535
Recently built, family-run hotel on seafront, close to St Anne's Square. Enjoy excellent food and hospitality.
Bedrooms: 4 double, 10 twin
Bathrooms: 14 en-suite

Bed & breakfast

per night:	£min	£max
Single	35.00	45.00
Double	50.00	70.00

Half board per

person:	£min	£max
Daily	35.00	55.00
Weekly	180.00	

Evening meal 1900 (last orders 2030)
Parking for 13
Cards accepted: Access, Visa, Switch/Delta

Chadwick Hotel

COMMENDED

South Promenade, Lytham St Annes FY8 1NP
☎ St. Annes (01253) 720061
Fax (01253) 714455
Ⓒ Logis of Great Britain

Modern family-run hotel and leisure complex with reputation for food, comfort, personal service and value for money.
Wheelchair access category 3
Bedrooms: 10 single, 11 double, 29 twin, 14 triple, 8 family rooms
Bathrooms: 72 en-suite

Bed & breakfast

per night:	£min	£max
Single	36.00	39.00
Double	50.00	54.00

Half board per

person:	£min	£max
Daily	36.50	43.00
Weekly	262.40	299.50

Lunch available
Evening meal 1900 (last orders 2030)
Parking for 40
Cards accepted: Access, Visa, Diners, Amex, Switch/Delta

See display advertisement on this page

Dalmeny Hotel

19-33 South Promenade, Lytham St Annes FY8 1LX
☎ St Annes (01253) 712236
Fax (01253) 724447
The Dalmeny is a rare find these days. Well-appointed promenade hotel, managed by the Webb family since 1945.
Bedrooms: 1 single, 25 double, 69 triple
Bathrooms: 95 private

Bed & breakfast

per night:	£min	£max
Single	57.50	57.50
Double	62.00	102.00

Lunch available
Evening meal 1700 (last orders 2230)
Parking for 95
Cards accepted: Access, Visa, Amex, Switch/Delta

The Grand Hotel

South Promenade, Lytham St Annes FY8 1NB
☎ St. Annes (01253) 721288
Fax (01253) 714459
On the South Promenade overlooking the bay. Splendid Victorian building offering excellent food and accommodation. Close to championship golf-course.
Bedrooms: 4 single, 17 double, 14 twin, 5 triple
Suites available
Bathrooms: 40 en-suite

Bed & breakfast

per night:	£min	£max
Single	49.50	67.50
Double	60.00	90.00

Half board per

person:	£min	£max
Daily	51.50	61.50

Lunch available
Evening meal 1800 (last orders 2130)
Parking for 152
Cards accepted: Access, Visa, Amex, Switch/Delta

Lindum Hotel

COMMENDED

63-67 South Promenade, Lytham St Annes FY8 1LZ
☎ St. Annes (01253) 721534 & 722516
Fax (01253) 721364
Ⓒ Logis of Great Britain
Family-run, seafront hotel with good reputation for food and comfortable
Continued ▶

The Chadwick Hotel

South Promenade, Lytham St. Annes, FY8 1NP Tel:(01253) 720061

Enjoy the luxury of this modern, family-run seventy bedroom hotel. The hotel is renowned for good food and comfortable en-suite bedrooms with in-house movies and satellite television.

Other facilities include an indoor pool, spa bath, sauna, Turkish room, solarium, games room, soft play adventure area.

Vegetarian dishes and a 24-hour menu. Dinner room and breakfast terms from £36.70 Daily per person.

145

NORTH WEST

LYTHAM ST ANNES
Continued

accommodation. Close to fine shops and championship golf-courses.
Bedrooms: 8 single, 30 double, 18 twin, 22 triple
Bathrooms: 78 en-suite, 2 public

Bed & breakfast per night:

	£min	£max
Single	30.00	35.00
Double	50.00	55.00

Half board per person:

	£min	£max
Daily	35.00	40.00

Lunch available
Evening meal 1800 (last orders 1900)
Parking for 25
Cards accepted: Access, Visa, Amex, Switch/Delta

MACCLESFIELD
Cheshire
Map ref 4B2

Cobbled streets and quaint old buildings stand side by side with modern shops and three markets. Centuries of association with the silk industry; museums feature working exhibits and social history. Stunning views of the Peak District National Park.
Tourist Information Centre ☎ (01625) 504114

Chadwick House
COMMENDED
55 Beech Lane, Macclesfield SK10 2DS
☎ (01625) 615558 & Mobile (0858) 154816
Fax (01625) 615558
Tastefully refurbished large town house, close to town centre and stations. Licensed bar, restaurant, sauna, solarium and gym available. Sky TV in all rooms.
Bedrooms: 6 single, 6 double, 1 twin
Bathrooms: 13 en-suite, 2 public

Bed & breakfast per night:

	£min	£max
Single	30.00	45.00
Double		60.00

Half board per person:

	£min	£max
Daily	39.00	54.00

Evening meal from 1930
Parking for 10
Cards accepted: Access, Visa, Diners, Amex

Moorhayes House Hotel
COMMENDED
27 Manchester Road, Tytherington, Macclesfield SK10 2JJ
☎ (01625) 433228

Modern, comfortable house in attractive garden, half a mile from town centre. 5 minutes from Peak District National Park, 20 minutes from Manchester Airport.
Bedrooms: 2 single, 6 double, 1 twin
Bathrooms: 7 en-suite, 2 public

Bed & breakfast per night:

	£min	£max
Single	25.00	35.00
Double	38.00	44.00

Evening meal 1800 (last orders 1900)
Parking for 14

MANCHESTER
Greater Manchester
Map ref 4B1

The Gateway to the North, offering one of Britain's largest selections of arts venues and theatre productions, a wide range of chain stores and specialist shops, a legendary, lively nightlife, spectacular architecture and a plethora of eating and drinking places.
Tourist Information Centre ☎ (0161) 234 3157 or 234 3158 or 436 3344

Albany Hotel
21 Albany Road, Chorlton-cum-Hardy, Manchester M21 1AY
☎ (0161) 881 6774
Fax (0161) 862 9405
Renovated and refurbished to the highest standards. All bedrooms fully fitted for your needs and comfort, majority with private bathroom. 10 minutes city and airport, 1 mile M56/M63. Here, the customer is king.
Bedrooms: 2 single, 7 double, 9 twin, 1 family room
Bathrooms: 15 private, 2 public, 4 private showers

Bed & breakfast per night:

	£min	£max
Single	29.00	37.00
Double	45.00	49.00

Half board per person:

	£min	£max
Daily	40.00	47.00
Weekly	250.00	335.00

Lunch available
Evening meal 1900 (last orders 2200)
Parking for 8
Cards accepted: Access, Visa

Baron Hotel
116 Palatine Road, West Didsbury, Manchester M20 9ZA
☎ (0161) 445 3877 & 434 3688
Fax (01203) 520680
Comfortable, friendly, family-run hotel, all rooms with en-suite facilities. Ten minutes from Manchester Airport and city centre. Half a mile from the motorway network.
Bedrooms: 10 single, 5 twin, 1 triple
Bathrooms: 16 en-suite

Bed & breakfast per night:

	£min	£max
Single	28.50	35.00
Double	42.00	49.00

Evening meal 1900 (last orders 2030)
Parking for 25
Cards accepted: Access, Visa

The Beechwood Hotel
193 Withington Road, Whalley Range, Manchester M16 8HT
☎ (0161) 226 9015
Fax (0161) 226 9015
Recently opened hotel in Victorian building with period furnishings. Home cooking and friendly bar with traditional beer. Ideal base, 5 minutes from city centre and motorways, 15 minutes from airport.
Bedrooms: 2 single, 3 double, 5 twin
Bathrooms: 10 en-suite, 1 public

Bed & breakfast per night:

	£min	£max
Single	35.00	45.00
Double	45.00	55.00

Evening meal 1800 (last orders 2030)
Parking for 10
Cards accepted: Access, Visa, Diners, Amex

Establishments should be open throughout the year, unless otherwise stated.

NORTH WEST

Bentley Guest House
COMMENDED

64 Hill Lane, Blackley, Manchester
M9 6PF
☎ (0161) 795 1115
Comfortable, friendly house, 10 minutes from M62 and close to shops and bus for city centre. Private parking, garden, patio. Personal attention, freshly-cooked meals, dinner optional.
Bedrooms: 1 single, 2 double
Bathrooms: 1 en-suite, 1 public

Bed & breakfast per night:	£min	£max
Single	16.00	20.00
Double	30.00	40.00

Half board per person:	£min	£max
Daily	26.00	30.00
Weekly	182.00	130.00

Evening meal 1800 (last orders 2000)
Parking for 3
Open February–December

The Copthorne Manchester
HIGHLY COMMENDED

Clippers Quay, Salford Quays,
Manchester M5 2XP
☎ (0161) 873 7321
Fax (0161) 873 7318
Millennium & Copthorne/Utell International
Waterfront location, close to city centre. Local attractions include Old Trafford, Granada TV studio tours, G-Mex Centre and China Town.
Bedrooms: 111 double, 55 twin Suites available
Bathrooms: 166 en-suite

Bed & breakfast per night:	£min	£max
Single	115.00	
Double	130.00	

Lunch available
Evening meal 1830 (last orders 2215)
Parking for 120
Cards accepted: Access, Visa, Diners, Amex, Switch/Delta

Crescent Gate Hotel
COMMENDED

Park Crescent, Victoria Park,
Manchester M14 5RE
☎ (0161) 224 0672
Fax (0161) 257 2822
Logis of Great Britain
Two miles from city centre, in quiet residential crescent, convenient for airport. One of Manchester's most popular independent hotels.

Bedrooms: 20 single, 2 double,
2 twin, 1 triple
Bathrooms: 20 en-suite, 2 public

Bed & breakfast per night:	£min	£max
Single	28.00	35.00
Double	40.00	48.00

Half board per person:	£min	£max
Daily	30.00	45.00

Lunch available
Evening meal 1900 (last orders 2000)
Parking for 18
Cards accepted: Access, Visa, Diners, Amex, Switch/Delta

Elm Grange Hotel

559-561 Wilmslow Road,
Withington, Manchester M20 4GJ
☎ (0161) 445 3336
Fax (0161) 445 3336
The Independents
On main bus routes to city centre and airport. Cleanliness, service, value for money. Convenient for theatres, shops, restaurants, hospitals and university. Special weekend discounts. Restaurant open evenings.
Bedrooms: 16 single, 5 double,
10 twin
Bathrooms: 17 en-suite, 3 public

Bed & breakfast per night:	£min	£max
Single	24.50	39.50
Double	36.00	56.00

Half board per person:	£min	£max
Daily	34.50	76.00

Lunch available
Evening meal 1800 (last orders 2000)
Parking for 41
Cards accepted: Access, Visa, Amex

Forte Posthouse Manchester
COMMENDED

Palatine Road, Northenden,
Manchester M22 4FH
☎ (0161) 998 7090
Fax (0161) 946 0139
Forte
This modern hotel is in a pleasant suburb just off the M56 and M62/63 motorways. The city centre is within easy reach.
Bedrooms: 49 single, 89 double,
52 twin
Bathrooms: 190 en-suite

Bed & breakfast per night:	£min	£max
Single	29.00	
Double	58.00	

Half board per person:	£min	£max
Daily	43.00	

Lunch available
Evening meal 1700 (last orders 2230)
Parking for 243
Cards accepted: Access, Visa, Diners, Amex, Switch/Delta

Gardens Hotel
COMMENDED

55 Piccadilly, Manchester M1 2AP
☎ (0161) 236 5155
Fax (0161) 228 7287
This modern hotel, only 7 years old, is situated in the heart of the city, overlooking Piccadilly Gardens.
Bedrooms: 11 single, 47 double,
42 twin
Bathrooms: 100 en-suite

Bed & breakfast per night:	£min	£max
Single	55.00	80.00
Double	65.00	95.00

Half board per person:	£min	£max
Daily	67.50	100.00

Lunch available
Evening meal 1830 (last orders 2200)
Cards accepted: Access, Visa, Diners, Amex, Switch/Delta

Granada Hotel
APPROVED

404 Wilmslow Road, Withington,
Manchester M20 9BM
☎ (0161) 286 9551 & 434 3480
Fax (0161) 286 9553
Comfortable hotel close to Manchester city centre and airport. En-suite rooms, colour TV, telephone, hairdryer. Lounge, bar and restaurant.
Bedrooms: 3 single, 2 double, 3 twin,
2 triple
Bathrooms: 10 en-suite

Bed & breakfast per night:	£min	£max
Single	25.00	35.00
Double	35.00	45.00

Half board per person:	£min	£max
Daily	35.00	45.00
Weekly	180.00	250.00

Evening meal 1800 (last orders 2330)

Continued ▶

NORTH WEST

MANCHESTER
Continued

Parking for 20
Cards accepted: Access, Visa, Diners, Amex

Imperial Hotel

157 Hathersage Road, Manchester
M13 0HY
☎ (0161) 225 6500
Fax (0161) 225 6500
Privately owned hotel offering personal and friendly service. Close to the university and teaching hospital, 1.25 miles from city centre.
Bedrooms: 13 single, 5 double, 9 twin
Bathrooms: 21 en-suite, 3 public

Bed & breakfast
per night:	£min	£max
Single	30.00	36.00
Double	35.00	44.00

Half board per person:
	£min	£max
Daily		35.00

Evening meal 1830 (last orders 2030)
Parking for 30
Cards accepted: Access, Visa, Diners, Amex

Mitre Hotel

Cathedral Gates, Manchester
M3 1SW
☎ (0161) 834 4128
Fax (0161) 839 1646
Located in the heart of the city. Comfortable and friendly, with bars, restaurants and 3 conference rooms.
Bedrooms: 11 single, 7 double, 10 twin
Bathrooms: 22 en-suite, 6 public

Bed & breakfast
per night:	£min	£max
Single	30.00	49.00
Double	39.00	57.00

Half board per person:
	£min	£max
Daily	35.00	65.00
Weekly	240.00	420.00

Lunch available
Evening meal 1900 (last orders 2100)
Cards accepted: Access, Visa, Diners, Amex, Switch/Delta

Hotel Montana

59 Palatine Road, West Didsbury, Manchester M20 9LJ
☎ (0161) 445 6427 & 445 0062
Fax (0161) 448 9458

Family-run hotel with pleasant atmosphere. Spanish a la carte restaurant and tapas bar. Sky TV. Large secure car park. 3 miles city centre and airport.
Bedrooms: 7 single, 5 double, 9 twin, 1 triple
Bathrooms: 18 en-suite, 3 public

Bed & breakfast
per night:	£min	£max
Single	25.00	30.00
Double	40.00	50.00

Half board per person:
	£min	£max
Daily	35.00	42.00
Weekly	238.00	280.00

Evening meal 1800 (last orders 2200)
Parking for 40
Cards accepted: Access, Diners

Princess Hotel
APPROVED

101 Portland Street, Manchester
M1 6DF
☎ (0161) 236 5122
Fax (0161) 236 4468

City centre hotel catering for business and holiday clients. Professional service with personal approach. Easily accessed by major motorway, road and rail networks, Manchester Airport and metro link. Close to shops and entertainment.
Bedrooms: 5 single, 48 double, 26 twin, 6 triple
Bathrooms: 85 en-suite

Bed & breakfast
per night:	£min	£max
Single	45.00	75.00
Double	55.00	95.00

Half board per person:
	£min	£max
Daily	55.00	85.00
Weekly	365.00	420.00

Lunch available
Evening meal 1800 (last orders 2200)
Cards accepted: Access, Visa, Diners, Amex, Switch/Delta

The Royals Hotel
COMMENDED

Altrincham Road, Wythenshawe, Manchester M22 4BJ
☎ (0161) 998 9011
Fax (0161) 948 4641
CR Consort
At the heart of Manchester's motorway network, 2 miles from Manchester Airport. Recently renovated mock-Tudor building in own grounds with beautiful Conservatory Restaurant. Ample car parking.
Bedrooms: 11 single, 9 double, 10 twin, 3 triple
Bathrooms: 33 en-suite

Bed & breakfast
per night:	£min	£max
Single	56.00	60.00
Double	70.00	75.00

Half board per person:
	£min	£max
Daily	71.00	75.00

Lunch available
Evening meal 1900 (last orders 2145)
Parking for 100
Cards accepted: Access, Visa, Diners, Amex

Wilmslow Hotel

356 Wilmslow Road, Fallowfield, Manchester M14 6AB
☎ (0161) 225 3030 & 224 5815
Fax (0161) 257 2854
Comfortable, family-run hotel with Sky TV in all rooms. Special group and long term rates available. Convenient for Manchester University, city centre, airport, railway stations and M56, M63.
Bedrooms: 14 single, 4 double, 6 twin, 1 triple, 3 family rooms
Bathrooms: 14 en-suite, 3 public, 2 private showers

Bed & breakfast
per night:	£min	£max
Single	16.65	30.65
Double	28.30	35.50

NORTH WEST

Half board per person:	£min	£max
Daily	26.65	40.65
Weekly	256.55	284.55

Evening meal 1830 (last orders 2100)
Parking for 35
Cards accepted: Access, Visa

MANCHESTER AIRPORT

See under Alderley Edge, Altrincham, Cheadle Hulme, Knutsford, Manchester, Salford, Stockport, Urmston, Wilmslow.

MAWDESLEY

Lancashire
Map ref 4A1

Mawdsleys Eating House and Hotel
COMMENDED

Hall Lane, Mawdsley, Ormskirk L40 2QZ
☎ Rufford (01704) 822552 & 821874
Fax (01704) 822096
In the picturesque village of Mawdsley, voted "best kept village". Its peaceful setting will be appreciated by business people and pleasure travellers alike.
Bedrooms: 34 double, 6 twin
Bathrooms: 40 en-suite

Bed & breakfast per night:	£min	£max
Single	41.00	46.00
Double	51.00	56.00

Half board per person:	£min	£max
Daily	50.00	60.00
Weekly	350.00	450.00

Lunch available
Evening meal 1900 (last orders 2200)
Parking for 100
Cards accepted: Access, Visa, Diners, Amex, Switch/Delta

MOBBERLEY

Cheshire
Map ref 4A2

The Hinton
HIGHLY COMMENDED

Town Lane, Mobberley, Knutsford WA16 7HH
☎ (01565) 873484
Fax (01565) 873484
Bed and breakfast for both business and private guests. Within easy reach of M6, M56, Manchester Airport and

InterCity rail network. Ideal touring base, on the B5085 between Knutsford and Wilmslow.
Bedrooms: 3 single, 2 double, 1 twin
Bathrooms: 4 en-suite, 1 public

Bed & breakfast per night:	£min	£max
Single	29.00	35.00
Double	39.00	48.00

Evening meal 1800 (last orders 1900)
Parking for 10
Cards accepted: Access, Visa, Diners, Amex

MORECAMBE

Lancashire
Map ref 5A3

Famous for its shrimps, Morecambe is a traditional resort on a wide bay with spacious beaches, entertainments and seafront illuminations. Bubbles Leisure Park, Frontierland and various attractions nearby. Stunning views across the bay.
Tourist Information Centre ☎ (01524) 582808 or 582809

Elms Hotel
COMMENDED

Bare Village, Morecambe LA4 6DD
☎ (01524) 411501
Fax (01524) 831979

Set back from promenade and standing in its own grounds. Established hotel ideally located for Lake District, Yorkshire Dales and Trough of Bowland.
Bedrooms: 6 single, 20 double, 14 twin
Bathrooms: 40 en-suite

Bed & breakfast per night:	£min	£max
Single	32.50	
Double	55.00	

Half board per person:	£min	£max
Daily	42.50	
Weekly	245.00	

Lunch available
Evening meal 1900 (last orders 2130)
Parking for 80

Cards accepted: Access, Visa, Diners, Amex, Switch/Delta

NANTWICH

Cheshire
Map ref 4A2

Old market town on the River Weaver made prosperous in Roman times by salt springs. Fire destroyed the town in 1583 and many buildings were rebuilt in Elizabethan style. Churche's Mansion (open to the public) survived the fire.
Tourist Information Centre ☎ (01270) 610983 or 610880

Crown Hotel
APPROVED

24 High Street, Nantwich CW5 5AS
☎ (01270) 625283
Fax (01270) 628047
Best Western
Half-timbered black and white 16th C Grade I listed building, dating from 1583. Oak beams, real fires. Lively interesting bars. Warm and friendly welcome. Italian restaurant.
Bedrooms: 3 single, 4 double, 9 twin, 2 triple
Bathrooms: 18 en-suite

Bed & breakfast per night:	£min	£max
Single	59.50	
Double	69.00	

Half board per person:	£min	£max
Daily	47.50	49.50

Lunch available
Evening meal 1800 (last orders 2200)
Parking for 100
Cards accepted: Access, Visa, Diners, Amex, Switch/Delta

POTT SHRIGLEY

Cheshire
Map ref 4B2

Shrigley Hall Hotel Golf and Country Club

Shrigley Park, Pott Shrigley, Macclesfield SK10 5SB
☎ Macclesfield (01625) 575757
Fax (01625) 573323
Utell International
Country house hotel built in 1825 in the 262-acre estate of Shrigley Park.

Continued ▶

NORTH WEST

POTT SHRIGLEY
Continued

Overlooks the Cheshire plain and Peak District. 18-hole golf-course and full leisure club.
Bedrooms: 25 single, 92 double, 34 twin, 5 triple
Suite available
Bathrooms: 156 en-suite
Bed & breakfast

per night:	£min	£max
Single	95.00	105.00
Double	115.00	130.00

Half board per person:	£min	£max
Daily	115.00	125.00

Lunch available
Evening meal 1900 (last orders 2145)
Parking for 300
Cards accepted: Access, Visa, Diners, Amex, Switch/Delta

PRESTON
Lancashire
Map ref 4A1

Scene of decisive Royalist defeat by Cromwell in the Civil War and later of riots in the Industrial Revolution. Local history exhibited in Harris Museum. Famous for its Guild and the celebration that takes place every 20 years.
Tourist Information Centre ☎ (01772) 253731

Tulketh Hotel
COMMENDED

209 Tulketh Road, Ashton, Preston PR2 1ES
☎ (01772) 728096 & 726250
Fax (01772) 723743
The Independents
Hotel of fine quality and with personal service, in a quiet residential area. A la carte menu. 5 minutes from town centre, 10 minutes from M6 motorway.
Bedrooms: 5 single, 2 double, 5 twin
Bathrooms: 11 en-suite, 1 private
Bed & breakfast

per night:	£min	£max
Single	35.00	38.50
Double	45.00	49.50

Evening meal 1830 (last orders 1930)
Parking for 12
Cards accepted: Access, Visa, Diners, Amex

RADCLIFFE
Greater Manchester
Map ref 4A1

By the River Irwell, originally a coal and cotton town. The ruins of the medieval Radcliffe Tower can still be seen.

Hawthorn Hotel & Restaurant
APPROVED

139-143 Stand Lane, Radcliffe, Manchester M26 1JR
☎ (0161) 723 2706
Fax (0161) 723 2706
Comfortable family hotel convenient for M62 junction 17, motorway network and close to Bury, Bolton and Manchester. Restaurant.
Bedrooms: 4 single, 5 double, 4 twin, 1 triple, 1 family room
Bathrooms: 13 en-suite, 1 public
Bed & breakfast

per night:	£min	£max
Single	27.00	35.00
Double	39.00	47.00

Half board per person:	£min	£max
Daily	36.95	45.45
Weekly	195.00	275.00

Evening meal 1800 (last orders 2100)
Parking for 9
Cards accepted: Access, Visa, Amex, Switch/Delta

RIBBLE VALLEY

See under Chipping, Clitheroe, Langho

ROCHDALE
Greater Manchester
Map ref 4B1

Pennine mill town made prosperous by wool and later cotton-spinning, famous for the Co-operative Movement started in 1844 by a group of Rochdale working men. Birthplace of John Bright (Corn Law opponent) and more recently Gracie Fields. Fine Victorian Gothic town hall.
Tourist Information Centre ☎ (01706) 356592

Broadfield Hotel

Sparrow Hill, Rochdale, Lancashire OL16 1AF
☎ (01706) 44085 & 55180
Fax (01706) 47484
Set in 35 acres of parkland. Ideally situated for Manchester, Blackpool and Lake District. Special rates for weekends.
Bedrooms: 11 single, 5 double, 4 twin, 3 triple
Bathrooms: 23 en-suite
Bed & breakfast

per night:	£min	£max
Single	25.00	45.00
Double	40.00	60.00

Lunch available
Evening meal 1845 (last orders 2130)
Parking for 50
Cards accepted: Access, Visa, Diners, Amex, Switch/Delta

RUNCORN
Cheshire
Map ref 4A2

Now designated as a New Town, Runcorn developed in 18th C with building of barge dock on Manchester-Liverpool Canal. Quarrying became important and sand was used for local buildings.

Forte Posthouse Runcorn
COMMENDED

Wood Lane, Beechwood, Runcorn WA7 3HA
☎ (01928) 714000
Fax (01928) 714611
Forte
From exit 12 on the M56, follow the direction sign Beechwood. 12 miles from Liverpool and 20 miles from Manchester Airport. Business services and leisure club available.
Bedrooms: 105 double, 30 twin
Bathrooms: 135 en-suite
Bed & breakfast

per night:	£min	£max
Single	77.95	
Double	86.90	

Half board per person:	£min	£max
Daily	85.90	

Lunch available
Evening meal 1845 (last orders 2230)
Parking for 250
Cards accepted: Access, Visa, Diners, Amex, Switch/Delta

A key to symbols can be found inside the back cover flap.

NORTH WEST

SADDLEWORTH
Greater Manchester
Map ref 4B1

The stone-built villages of Saddleworth are peppered with old mill buildings and possess a unique Pennine character. The superb scenery of Saddleworth Moor provides an ideal backdrop for canal trips, walking and outdoor pursuits.
Tourist Information Centre ☎ (01457) 870336 or 874093

La Pergola Country House Hotel and Restaurant M
COMMENDED

Rochdale Road, Denshaw, Oldham OL3 5UE
☎ (01457) 871040
Fax (01457) 873804
Country hotel set in Pennine hills, only 5 minutes M62. All bedrooms en-suite with TV, telephone, hairdryer and trouser press (non-smoking available). Lounge bar with log fire, restaurant and pizzeria.
Bedrooms: 1 single, 14 double, 7 twin, 2 triple
Bathrooms: 24 en-suite

Bed & breakfast per night:	£min	£max
Single	35.00	50.00
Double	50.00	70.00

Lunch available
Evening meal 1830 (last orders 2200)
Parking for 65
Cards accepted: Access, Visa, Diners, Amex, Switch/Delta

ST HELENS
Merseyside
Map ref 4A1

St Helens is renowned for its glass industry and exhibits are on show at Pilkington Glass Museum. Town is also famous for Rainhill Trials and for Haydock Park Racecourse. Good shopping and excellent local museum.

Haydock Thistle Hotel M
COMMENDED

Penny Lane, Haydock, St Helens WA11 9SG
☎ Wigan (01942) 272000
Fax (01942) 711092
Utell International
High standard country house hotel set in 11 acres of landscaped gardens, adjacent to the world famous racecourse.

Bedrooms: 2 single, 84 double, 40 twin, 13 triple
Bathrooms: 139 en-suite

Bed & breakfast per night:	£min	£max
Single	83.00	93.00
Double	93.00	103.00

Lunch available
Evening meal 1900 (last orders 2200)
Parking for 180
Cards accepted: Access, Visa, Diners, Amex

SALFORD
Greater Manchester
Map ref 4B1

Industrial city close to Manchester with Roman Catholic cathedral and university. Lowry often painted Salford's industrial architecture and much of his work is in the local art gallery. Salford Quays provide a backdrop to pubs, walkways and a large cinema complex.

Hazeldean Hotel M
APPROVED

467 Bury New Road, Kersal Bar, Salford, Lancashire M7 3NE
☎ (0161) 792 6667 & 792 2079
Fax (0161) 792 6668
Renovated Victorian mansion in residential area of Salford. Two miles exit 17 M62, 2.5 miles city centre on A56. Most rooms en-suite. Fully stocked bar leading on to beautiful garden. Restaurant, TV lounge.
Bedrooms: 10 single, 4 double, 5 twin, 2 triple
Bathrooms: 17 en-suite, 2 public

Bed & breakfast per night:	£min	£max
Single	29.00	40.00
Double	44.00	50.00

Lunch available
Evening meal 1830 (last orders 2030)
Parking for 25
Cards accepted: Access, Visa, Diners, Amex, Switch/Delta

White Lodge Private Hotel

87-89 Great Cheetham Street West, Broughton, Salford M7 9JA
☎ (0161) 792 3047
Small, family-run hotel, close to city centre amenities and sporting facilities.
Bedrooms: 3 single, 3 double, 3 twin
Bathrooms: 2 public

Bed & breakfast per night:	£min	£max
Single	19.00	
Double	32.00	34.00

Parking for 6

SAMLESBURY
Lancashire
Map ref 4A1

Swallow Hotel M
COMMENDED

Preston New Road, Samlesbury, Preston PR5 0UL
☎ (01772) 877351
Fax (01772) 877424
Swallow
Hotel and leisure club, ideal for business and family use, overlooking Ribble Valley countryside, 1 mile from the M6. Short break packages available.
Bedrooms: 24 single, 36 double, 18 twin
Bathrooms: 78 en-suite

Bed & breakfast per night:	£min	£max
Single	60.00	85.00
Double	70.00	110.00

Half board per person:	£min	£max
Daily	76.50	101.50

Lunch available
Evening meal 1900 (last orders 2130)
Parking for 300
Cards accepted: Access, Visa, Diners, Amex

SANDBACH
Cheshire
Map ref 4A2

Small Cheshire town, originally important for salt production. Contains narrow, winding streets, timbered houses and a cobbled market-place. Town square has 2 Anglo-Saxon crosses to commemorate the conversion to Christianity of the King of Mercia's son.

Bears Head Hotel
Listed COMMENDED

Brereton, Sandbach CW11 9RS
☎ Holmes Chapel (01477) 535251
Fax (01477) 535888
17th C half-timbered family-run hotel. Delightful oak-beamed, candlelit a la
Continued ▶

151

NORTH WEST

SANDBACH
Continued

carte restaurant, or cosy bar with inglenook fireplace for a drink and a light home-made meal.
Bedrooms: 9 single, 8 double, 5 twin
Suite available
Bathrooms: 22 en-suite

Bed & breakfast
per night:	£min	£max
Single	47.00	
Double	61.50	70.00

Lunch available
Evening meal 1930 (last orders 2200)
Parking for 100
Cards accepted: Access, Visa, Amex, Switch/Delta

Chimney House Hotel M

Congleton Road, Sandbach
CW11 0ST
☎ Crewe (01270) 764141
Fax (01270) 768916
Whitbread
Set in 7.5 acres, 500 yards from the M6 exit 17. Convenient for breaking your journey north or south, or for your business appointments in the north west.
Bedrooms: 2 single, 39 double, 4 twin, 3 triple
Bathrooms: 48 en-suite

Bed & breakfast
per night:	£min	£max
Single	26.00	68.00
Double	55.00	68.00

Half board per
person:	£min	£max
Daily	46.00	85.00

Lunch available
Evening meal 1900 (last orders 2200)
Parking for 110
Cards accepted: Access, Visa, Diners, Amex, Switch/Delta

Poplar Mount Guest House
COMMENDED

2 Station Road, Elworth, Sandbach
CW11 9JG
☎ Crewe (01270) 761268
Warm and friendly family-run guesthouse, 5 minutes from M6 junction 17. Ideally situated for touring Cheshire.
Bedrooms: 2 single, 2 double, 1 twin, 1 triple, 1 family room
Bathrooms: 4 en-suite, 1 public

Bed & breakfast
per night:	£min	£max
Single	19.00	29.00
Double	28.00	36.00

Lunch available
Evening meal 1830 (last orders 1930)
Parking for 9
Cards accepted: Access, Visa

SOUTHPORT

Merseyside
Map ref 4A1

Delightful Victorian resort noted for gardens, sandy beaches and 6 golf-courses, particularly Royal Birkdale. Attractions include the Atkinson Art Gallery, Southport Railway Centre, Pleasureland and the annual Southport Flower Show. Excellent shopping, particularly in Lord Street's elegant boulevard.
Tourist Information Centre ☎ (01704) 533333

Ambassador Private Hotel
COMMENDED

13 Bath Street, Southport PR9 0DP
☎ (01704) 530459 & 543998
Fax (01704) 536269
Delightful small quality hotel with residential licence, 200 yards from promenade and conference facilities. All bedrooms en-suite. Pets welcome.
Bedrooms: 1 single, 3 double, 4 twin
Bathrooms: 7 en-suite, 2 public

Bed & breakfast
per night:	£min	£max
Single	29.00	29.00
Double	46.00	46.00

Half board per
person:	£min	£max
Daily	39.00	56.00
Weekly	180.00	180.00

Lunch available
Evening meal 1800 (last orders 1900)
Parking for 6
Cards accepted: Access, Visa, Amex

Leicester Hotel
APPROVED

24 Leicester Street, Southport
PR9 0EZ
☎ (01704) 530049
Family-run hotel with personal attention, clean and comfortable, close to all amenities. Car park. Licensed bar. TV in all rooms. En-suite available.
Bedrooms: 2 single, 3 double, 3 twin
Bathrooms: 3 en-suite, 2 public

Bed & breakfast
per night:	£min	£max
Single	16.00	21.00
Double	30.00	40.00

Half board per
person:	£min	£max
Daily	21.00	26.00

Evening meal from 1800
Parking for 8
Cards accepted: Access, Visa, Diners

Metropole Hotel M
COMMENDED

3 Portland Street, Southport
PR8 1LL
☎ (01704) 536836
Fax (01704) 549041
Fully licensed, privately owned family hotel. Centrally located, 50 yards from famous Lord Street shopping boulevard. Close to Royal Birkdale Golf Course.
Bedrooms: 13 single, 3 double, 5 twin, 3 triple
Bathrooms: 21 en-suite, 2 public

Bed & breakfast
per night:	£min	£max
Double	52.00	60.00

Lunch available
Evening meal 1900 (last orders 2030)
Parking for 12
Cards accepted: Access, Visa, Amex, Switch/Delta

Rosedale Hotel M
COMMENDED

11 Talbot Street, Southport
PR8 1HP
☎ (01704) 530604
Fax (01704) 530604
Well-established, centrally situated private hotel with licensed bar and reading room. All bedrooms have colour TV with satellite link. Weekly rates available.
Bedrooms: 4 single, 2 double, 3 twin, 1 triple
Bathrooms: 7 en-suite, 1 public

Bed & breakfast
per night:	£min	£max
Single	20.00	26.00
Double	40.00	52.00

Evening meal 1800 (last orders 1600)
Parking for 8
Cards accepted: Access, Visa, Switch/Delta

NORTH WEST

Scarisbrick Hotel

COMMENDED

239 Lord Street, Southport
PR8 1NZ
☎ (01704) 543000
Fax (01704) 533335
Prominent town-centre traditional hotel. A la carte and table d'hote restaurant, several bars, function rooms and conference suites.
Wheelchair access category 3
Bedrooms: 7 single, 40 double, 24 twin, 6 triple
Bathrooms: 77 en-suite

Bed & breakfast per night:	£min	£max
Single	37.00	70.00
Double	44.00	120.00

Half board per person:	£min	£max
Daily	40.00	82.50
Weekly	252.00	577.50

Lunch available
Evening meal 1830 (last orders 2130)
Parking for 55
Cards accepted: Access, Visa, Diners, Amex, Switch/Delta

Stutelea Hotel and Leisure Club

HIGHLY COMMENDED

Alexandra Road, Southport
PR9 0NB
☎ (01704) 544220
Fax (01704) 500232
Charming, licensed hotel, in pleasant gardens. Heated indoor swimming pool, sauna, jacuzzi, gymnasium, steam room, solarium and games room. Convenient for promenade, marina, golf-courses and shopping centre. Also self-catering apartments. Half-board prices shown are for a minimum 2-night stay.
Bedrooms: 2 single, 8 double, 9 twin, 3 triple
Bathrooms: 22 en-suite, 4 public

Bed & breakfast per night:	£min	£max
Single	50.00	55.00
Double	75.00	80.00

Half board per person:	£min	£max
Daily	45.00	60.00
Weekly	315.00	420.00

Lunch available
Evening meal 1900 (last orders 2100)
Parking for 16
Cards accepted: Access, Visa, Diners, Amex, Switch/Delta

STOCKPORT
Greater Manchester
Map ref 4B2

Once an important cotton-spinning and manufacturing centre, Stockport has an impressive railway viaduct, a shopping precinct built over the River Mersey and a new leisure complex. Lyme Hall and Vernon Park Museum nearby.
Tourist Information Centre ☎ (0161) 474 3320 or 474 3321

Jarvis Alma Lodge Hotel

COMMENDED

149 Buxton Road, Stockport, Cheshire SK2 6EL
☎ (0161) 483 4431
Fax (0161) 483 1983
Jarvis/Utell International
A few miles from the Peak District and a short drive from Manchester city centre. Modern bedrooms, comfortable restaurant.
Bedrooms: 21 single, 13 double, 18 twin
Suite available
Bathrooms: 52 en-suite

Bed & breakfast per night:	£min	£max
Single	37.00	78.00
Double	74.00	95.00

Lunch available
Evening meal 1900 (last orders 2130)
Parking for 250
Cards accepted: Access, Visa, Diners, Amex, Switch/Delta

Pymgate Lodge Hotel

COMMENDED

147 Styal Road, Gatley, Stockport, Cheshire SK8 3TG
☎ (0161) 436 4103
Fax (0161) 499 9171
Within 1 mile of Manchester Airport. Every bedroom overlooks garden or open fields. Decorated and furnished to a high standard. Licensed a la carte restaurant. Courtesy tray in each room. All bedrooms non-smoking.
Bedrooms: 5 twin, 3 triple
Bathrooms: 6 en-suite, 1 public

Bed & breakfast per night:	£min	£max
Single	38.00	44.50
Double	46.00	50.00

Half board per person:	£min	£max
Daily	46.50	49.95
Weekly	325.50	395.15

Lunch available
Evening meal 1800 (last orders 2130)

Parking for 14
Cards accepted: Access, Visa, Amex

West Towers Hotel

Church Lane, Marple SK6 7LB
☎ (0161) 427 7133
Fax (0161) 449 0333
Private hotel, offering a friendly service. Elevated, semi-rural position. Excellent restaurant and wine list. Central for the Greater Manchester, Cheshire and Derbyshire attractions.
Bedrooms: 11 single, 7 double, 3 twin
Bathrooms: 21 en-suite

Bed & breakfast per night:	£min	£max
Single	30.00	40.00
Double	45.00	60.00

Half board per person:	£min	£max
Daily	40.00	50.00
Weekly	250.00	300.00

Lunch available
Evening meal 1900 (last orders 2200)
Parking for 70
Cards accepted: Access, Visa, Diners, Amex, Switch/Delta

TARPORLEY
Cheshire
Map ref 4A2

Old town with gabled houses and medieval church of St Helen containing monuments to the Done family, a historic name in this area. Spectacular ruins of 13th C Beeston Castle nearby.

The Swan Hotel

COMMENDED

50 High Street, Tarporley CW6 0AG
☎ (01829) 733838
Fax (01829) 732932

Historic Georgian coaching inn, attractively and traditionally furnished. High standard of food and warm welcome. Well-appointed en-suite bedrooms. Close to Oulton Park, the Oakland and Portal golf-courses. Also, walking on the Sandstone Trail.

Continued ▶

153

NORTH WEST

TARPORLEY
Continued

Wheelchair access category 3
Bedrooms: 3 single, 7 double, 10 twin
Bathrooms: 20 en-suite

Bed & breakfast per night:

	£min	£max
Single	45.00	50.00
Double	65.00	75.00

Half board per person:

	£min	£max
Daily	60.00	75.00

Lunch available
Evening meal 1800 (last orders 2200)
Parking for 49
Cards accepted: Access, Visa, Amex

URMSTON
Greater Manchester
Map ref 4A2

Manor Hey Hotel

130 Stretford Road, Urmston, Manchester M41 9LT
☎ (0161) 748 3896
Fax (0161) 746 7183
Comfortable and friendly family-run hotel. Five minutes to Trafford Park, 15 minutes to Manchester Airport.
Bedrooms: 1 double, 12 twin
Bathrooms: 13 en-suite

Bed & breakfast per night:

	£min	£max
Single	30.00	45.00
Double	45.00	60.00

Half board per person:

	£min	£max
Daily	38.00	53.00

Lunch available
Evening meal 1830 (last orders 2030)
Parking for 50
Cards accepted: Access, Visa

The symbol CR and a group name following an hotel address indicates that bookings can be made through a central reservations office. These offices are listed in the information pages at the back of this guide.

WADDINGTON
Lancashire
Map ref 4A1

One of the area's best-known villages, with a stream and public gardens gracing the main street.

The Moorcock Inn
COMMENDED

Slaidburn Road, Waddington, Clitheroe BB7 3AA
☎ Clitheroe (01200) 22333
Fax (01200) 29184
Friendly, family-run inn with panoramic views of Ribble Valley. Rooms en-suite. Fresh home-cooked food available in bar and restaurant. Banqueting facilities.
Bedrooms: 2 double, 5 twin
Bathrooms: 7 private

Bed & breakfast per night:

	£min	£max
Single	35.00	35.00
Double	55.00	55.00

Lunch available
Evening meal 1900 (last orders 2130)
Parking for 250
Cards accepted: Access, Visa

WARRINGTON
Cheshire
Map ref 4A2

Has prehistoric and Roman origins. Once the "beer capital of Britain" because so much beer was brewed here. Developed in the 18th and 19th C as a commercial and industrial town. The cast-iron gates in front of the town hall were originally destined for Sandringham.
Tourist Information Centre ☎ (01925) 442180

The Park Royal International Hotel
HIGHLY COMMENDED

Stretton Road, Stretton, Warrington WA4 4NS
☎ Norcott Brook (01925) 730706
Fax (01925) 730740
CR Best Western
Privately owned hotel situated in the heart of the Cheshire countryside, 2 minutes from junction 10 M56 and 5 minutes from junction 20 M6. Special weekend rates available.
Wheelchair access category 3
Bedrooms: 2 single, 61 double, 29 twin, 2 triple, 2 family rooms
Bathrooms: 96 en-suite

WIGAN
Greater Manchester
Map ref 4A1

Bed & breakfast per night:

	£min	£max
Single	73.50	81.50
Double	83.50	91.50

Half board per person:

	£min	£max
Daily	89.95	97.95

Lunch available
Evening meal 1900 (last orders 2200)
Parking for 400
Cards accepted: Access, Visa, Diners, Amex, Switch/Delta

Although a major industrial town, Wigan is an ancient settlement which received a royal charter in 1246. Famous for its pier distinguished in Orwell's "Road to Wigan Pier". The pier has now been developed as a major tourist attraction.
Tourist Information Centre ☎ (01942) 825677

Coaching Inn
COMMENDED

Warrington Road, Lower Ince, Wigan, Lancashire WN3 4NL
☎ (01942) 866330 & 74990
Fax (01942) 517128

Approximately one mile from town centre on good regular bus route. All rooms are en-suite with tea-making facilities and TV.
Bedrooms: 14 single, 3 twin, 1 triple
Bathrooms: 18 en-suite

Bed & breakfast per night:

	£min	£max
Single	18.00	20.00
Double	34.00	36.00

Half board per person:

	£min	£max
Daily	21.00	23.00
Weekly	140.00	154.00

Lunch available
Evening meal 1900 (last orders 2130)
Parking for 24

NORTH WEST

WILLINGTON
Cheshire
Map ref 4A2

Willington Hall Hotel ♠
COMMENDED

Willington, Tarporley CW6 0NB
☎ Kelsall (01829) 752321
Fax (01829) 752596

Country house hotel set in its own park with good views over surrounding countryside.
Bedrooms: 2 single, 3 double, 5 twin
Bathrooms: 10 en-suite, 1 public

Bed & breakfast per night:	£min	£max
Single	42.00	54.00
Double	76.00	80.00

Half board per person:	£min	£max
Daily	59.00	80.00

Lunch available
Evening meal 1930 (last orders 2130)
Parking for 60
Cards accepted: Access, Visa, Diners, Amex, Switch/Delta

WILMSLOW
Cheshire
Map ref 4B2

Nestling in the valleys of the Rivers Bollin and Dane, Wilmslow retains an intimate village atmosphere. Easy-to-reach attractions include Quarry Bank Mill at Styal. Lindow Man was discovered on a nearby common. Romany's Caravan sits in a memorial garden.

Belfry Hotel ♠

Stanley Road, Handforth, Wilmslow SK9 3LD
☎ (0161) 437 0511
Fax (0161) 499 0597
Utell International

Modern hotel on B5358 (old A34), noted for good food and service. Convenient for business in Manchester and Wilmslow area. 10 minutes from Manchester Airport (courtesy transport available with prior notice). Minimum prices shown are weekend rates.
Bedrooms: 25 single, 36 double, 17 twin, 2 triple
Suites available
Bathrooms: 80 en-suite

Bed & breakfast per night:	£min	£max
Single	35.00	90.00
Double	75.00	99.00

Half board per person:	£min	£max
Daily	55.00	115.00

Lunch available
Evening meal 1900 (last orders 2200)
Parking for 150
Cards accepted: Access, Visa, Diners, Amex, Switch/Delta

Dean Bank Hotel ♠
COMMENDED

Adlington Road, Wilmslow SK9 2BT
☎ (01625) 524268
Fax (01625) 549715

Easily accessible from M6, M56, M63 and Manchester Airport (courtesy transport available). Family-run hotel in extensive grounds 2 miles from centre of Wilmslow. Home-cooked evening meals.
Wheelchair access category 1 ♿
Bedrooms: 1 single, 5 double, 6 twin, 5 triple
Bathrooms: 17 en-suite

Bed & breakfast per night:	£min	£max
Single	30.00	35.00
Double	44.00	49.50

Half board per person:	£min	£max
Daily	36.95	43.50

Evening meal 1730 (last orders 1930)
Parking for 24
Cards accepted: Access, Visa, Amex

Lisieux
HIGHLY COMMENDED

199 Wilmslow Road, Handforth, Wilmslow SK9 3JX
☎ (01625) 522113

Deceptively large, homely bungalow with high standard of accommodation. Extensive breakfast menu available early morning. 3 miles from Manchester Airport.
Bedrooms: 1 single, 1 double, 1 twin
Bathrooms: 2 en-suite, 1 private, 1 public

Bed & breakfast per night:	£min	£max
Single	26.00	28.00
Double	36.00	39.00

Half board per person:	£min	£max
Daily	41.00	43.00
Weekly	287.00	301.00

Evening meal 1800 (last orders 1900)
Parking for 5

Stanneylands Hotel ♠
HIGHLY COMMENDED

Stanneylands Road, Wilmslow SK9 4EY
☎ (01625) 525225
Fax (01625) 537282
Utell International

The ideal blend of comfort and facilities makes Stanneylands a perfect setting for business meetings or entertaining in the exclusive restaurant.
Bedrooms: 7 single, 11 double, 14 twin
Suites available
Bathrooms: 32 en-suite

Bed & breakfast per night:	£min	£max
Single	45.00	85.00
Double	70.00	125.00

Lunch available
Evening meal 1900 (last orders 2230)
Parking for 80
Cards accepted: Access, Visa, Diners, Amex, Switch/Delta

WIRRAL
Merseyside

See under Birkenhead, Hoylake

COUNTRY CODE

Always follow the Country Code 🌳Enjoy the countryside and respect its life and work 🌳Guard against all risk of fire 🌳Fasten all gates 🌳Keep your dogs under close control 🌳Keep to public paths across farmland 🌳Use gates and stiles to cross fences, hedges and walls 🌳Leave livestock, crops and machinery alone 🌳Take your litter home 🌳Help to keep all water clean 🌳Protect wildlife, plants and trees 🌳Take special care on country roads 🌳Make no unnecessary noise

ENQUIRY COUPONS

To help you obtain further information about advertisers and accommodation featured in this guide you will find enquiry coupons at the back. Send these directly to the establishments in which you are interested. Remember to complete both sides of the coupon.

CHECK THE MAPS

The colour maps at the back of this guide show all the cities, towns and villages for which you will find accommodation entries.

Refer to the town index to find the page on which it is listed.

YORKSHIRE

Yorkshire encompass an area of vastly differing landscapes and moods. The wildness of the Yorkshire Moors and 'Brontë Country' soften into the mellow valleys of the Yorkshire Dales, contrasted by the coastline of towering cliffs, lively resorts and pleasant fishing ports.

Many of the grandest gardens in Britain are here. It's also where you can taste fish and chips at their best, sample ale straight from the brewery or go down a coalmine!

Don't miss historic York with its world-famous Minster. You'll also find some of the best museums and industrial heritage sites in England.

FOR MORE INFORMATION CONTACT:
Yorkshire Tourist Board
312 Tadcaster Road, York YO2 2HF
Tel: (01904) 707961 or 707070 (24 hour brochure line)
Fax: (01904) 701414

Where to Go in Yorkshire - see pages 158-161
Where to Stay in Yorkshire - see pages 162-216

YORKSHIRE

Where to Go and What to See

You will find hundreds of interesting places to visit during your stay in Yorkshire, just some of which are listed in these pages. The number against each name will help you locate it on the map (page 161). Contact any Tourist Information Centre in the region for more ideas on days out in Yorkshire.

1 Sea Life Centre
Scalby Mills,
Scarborough,
North Yorkshire YO12 6RP
Tel: (01723) 376125
At the Sea Life Centre you have the opportunity to meet creatures that live in and around the oceans of the British Isles, ranging from starfish and crabs to rays and seals.

2 North Yorkshire Moors Railway
Pickering Station,
Pickering,
North Yorkshire YO18 7AJ
Tel: (01751) 472508
Operates the route between Grosmont and Pickering, through some of the most magnificent scenery of the North York Moors National Park.

3 Flamingo Land Theme Park, Zoo and Holiday Village
Kirby Misperton,
North Yorkshire YO17 0UX
Tel: (01653) 668287
One price family funpark with over 100 attractions, nine shows and Europe's largest privately owned zoo. Large lake, children's and thrill rides.

4 Fountains Abbey and Studley Royal
Ripon,
North Yorkshire HG4 3DZ
Tel: (01765) 608888
Largest monastic ruin in Britain, founded by Cistercian monks in 1132. Landscaped garden laid out 1720-40 with lake, formal watergarden, temples and deer park.

5 Lightwater Valley Theme Park
North Stainley, Ripon,
North Yorkshire HG4 3HT
Tel: (01765) 635321
175 acres of country park featuring range of white-knuckle rides (including the world's biggest rollercoaster), skill testing activities, leisurely pursuits, live entertainment.

6 Castle Howard
Malton,
North Yorkshire YO6 7DA
Tel: (01653) 648444
Set in 1,000 acres of magnificent parkland with nature walks, scenic lake and stunning rose gardens. Attractions include important furniture and works of art.

7 Sewerby Hall and Gardens
Sewerby, Bridlington,
East Riding of Yorkshire
YO15 1EA
Tel: (01262) 673769
Children's zoo, aviary, old English walled garden, bowls, putting, golf, children's corner, museum, art gallery, Amy Johnson collection, novel train from park to North Beach.

8 Yorkshire Dales Falconry & Conservation Centre
Crows Nest, Giggleswick,
North Yorkshire LA2 8AS
Tel: (01729) 825164
Falconry centre with many species

of birds of prey from around the world including vultures, eagles, hawks, falcons and owls. Free flying displays, lecture room and aviaries.

9 Ripley Castle
Ripley,
North Yorkshire HG3 3AY
Tel: (01423) 770152
Ingilby family home since 1345, fine armour, furniture, chandeliers, panelling, priests hiding hole. Langley Castle in Barbara Taylor Bradford's book "Voice from the Heart".

10 Beningbrough Hall
Shipton-by-Beningbrough,
York YO6 1DD
Tel: (01904) 470666
Handsome Baroque house built 1716, nearly 100 pictures from the National Portrait Gallery. Victorian laundry, potting shed, garden, adventure playground, National Trust shop.

11 Skipton Castle
Skipton,
North Yorkshire BD23 1AQ
Tel: (01756) 792442
One of the most complete and well-preserved medieval castles in England. Beautiful Conduit Court with famous yew.

12 Archaeological Resource Centre
St Saviourgate, York YO1 2NN
Tel: (01904) 654324
Visitors can "touch the past", handling ancient finds of pottery and bone, stitching Roman sandals and picking a Viking padlock. A/V display and exploration of dig by computer.

13 Jorvik Viking Centre
Coppergate, York YO1 1NT
Tel: (01904) 643211
Visitors travel back in time in a timecar to a recreation of Viking York. They will see excavated remains of Viking houses and a display of objects found.

14 National Railway Museum
Leeman Road, York YO2 4XJ
Tel: (01904) 621261
Experience nearly 200 years of technical and social history on the railways and see the way they shaped the world.

15 York Castle Museum
The Eye of York, York YO1 1RY
Tel: (01904) 653611
England's most popular museum of everyday life including reconstructed streets and period rooms, Edwardian park, costume and jewellery, arms and armour, craft workshops.

16 York Minster
Deangate, York YO1 2JA
Tel: (01904) 624426
The largest Gothic cathedral in England. Museum of Saxon and Norman remains, chapter house and crypt. Unrivalled views from Norman tower.

17 Hornsea Freeport
Hornsea,
East Riding of Yorkshire
HU18 1UT
Tel: (01964) 534211
Brand names such as Laura Ashley and Alexon all at discount prices. Birds of prey, Butterfly World, Neptunes Kingdom and more.

18 Harewood House
Harewood, Leeds LS17 9LQ
Tel: (0113) 288 6225
18thC Carr/Adam house, Capability Brown landscape, fine Sevres and Chinese porcelain, English and Italian paintings, Chippendale furniture. Exotic bird garden.

19 National Museum of Photography, Film and Television
Pictureville, Bradford,
West Yorkshire BD1 1NQ
Tel: (01274) 727488
This free museum houses the largest cinema screen (Imax) in

Britain. Fly on a magic carpet, operate a TV camera, become a newsreader for a day.

20 Transperience
Transperience Way,
Low Moor,
Bradford,
West Yorkshire BD12 7HQ
Tel: (01274) 690909
With historic vehicle rides and state of the art interactive technology. Travel on a unique journey through the past, present and future of public transport.

21 Royal Armouries Museum
Leeds LS10 1LT
Tel: (0113) 220 1999
History in action at Britain's newest museum. The thrill of jousting tournaments and terror of battlefield recaptured. See one of the world's finest collections of arms and armour.

22 Tetley's Brewery Wharf
The Waterfront,
Leeds LS1 1QG
Tel: (0113) 242 0666
A unique new development which brings to life the story through the ages of one of the greatest British traditions – the pub.

23 Museum of Army Transport
Beverley,
East Riding of Yorkshire
HU17 0NG
Tel: (01482) 860445
Army road, rail, sea and air exhibits excitingly displayed in two huge indoor exhibition halls, plus the last remaining Blackburn Beverly aircraft. D-Day exhibition.

24 Eureka! The Museum for Children
Discovery Road, Halifax,
West Yorkshire HX1 2NE
Tel: (01422) 330069
Eureka! is the first museum of its kind designed especially for children up to the age of 12. Wherever you go in Eureka! you can touch, listen, feel and smell, as well as look.

25 Piece Hall
Halifax, West Yorkshire HX1 1RE
Tel: (01422) 358087
Historic, colonnaded cloth hall, surrounding open-air courtyard and comprising 40 speciality shops, art gallery, Tourist Information Centre, three weekly markets and Calderdale Kaleidoscope display.

26 National Coal Mining Museum for England
Caphouse Colliery,
New Road, Overton,
Wakefield,
West Yorkshire WF4 4RH
Tel: (01924) 848806
Exciting, award-winning museum of the Yorkshire coalfield including guided underground tour in authentic old workings, surface displays, working steam winder.

27 Yorkshire Sculpture Park
Bretton, Wakefield,
West Yorkshire WF4 4LG
Tel: (01924) 830302
Beautiful parkland containing regular exhibitions of contemporary sculpture. Permanent collection includes sculpture by Barbara Hepworth and Henry Moore.

28 National Fishing Heritage Centre
Alexandra Dock, Grimsby,
North East Lincolnshire
DN31 1UZ
Tel: (01472) 344867
Spectacular 1950's steam trawler experience. See, hear, smell and touch a series of recreated environments. Museum displays, shop, aquarium and historic fishing vessels.

29 Pleasure Island Theme Park
Kings Road, Cleethorpes,
North East Lincolnshire
DN35 0PL
Tel: (01472) 211511
The East Coast's newest outdoor theme park with great rides, slides and attractions including the Big Splash, Boomerang, Giant Wheel, Mini Mine Train, Terror Rack and Octopus rides.

FIND OUT MORE

Further information about holidays and attractions in Yorkshire, East Riding and Northern Lincolnshire is available from **Yorkshire Tourist Board**, 312 Tadcaster Road, York YO2 2HF.
Tel: (01904) 707961 or 707070 (24 hour brochure line)

These publications are available free from the Yorkshire Tourist Board:
- **Main Holidays and Shortbreaks guide** - information on the region, including hotels, self-catering and caravan and camping parks
- **Days Out in Yorkshire** (available Easter '97) - information on attractions, major events, getting around the region, etc.
- **Bed & Breakfast Touring Map**
- **What's On** - 3 issues per year
- **Overseas Brochure** - French, Dutch, German
- **'Freedom'** - caravan and camping guide
- **Getting Around Yorkshire** - guide to public transport

YORKSHIRE

WHERE TO STAY (YORKSHIRE)

Accommodation entries in this region are listed in alphabetical order of place name, and then in alphabetical order of establishment.

Map references refer to the colour location maps at the back of this guide. The first number indicates the map to use; the letter and number which follow refer to the grid reference on the map.

At-a-glance symbols at the end of each accommodation entry give useful information about services and facilities. A key to symbols can be found inside the back cover flap. Keep this open for easy reference.

APPLETON-LE-MOORS

North Yorkshire
Map ref 5C3

A charming, unspoilt village in the North York Moors National Park. 23 miles inland from Scarborough and 33 miles north of York, it is an excellent centre for the coast, Herriot country, the North Yorkshire Moors Railway and many delightful walks and places of historic interest.

Appleton Hall Country House Hotel

♛♛♛ HIGHLY COMMENDED

Appleton-le-Moors, York YO6 6TF
☎ Lastingham (01751) 417227 & 417452
Fax (01751) 417540

Victorian country house set in 2 acres of mature lawns and gardens. A hideaway place offering elegance, comfort and tranquillity.
Bedrooms: 2 single, 5 double, 2 twin
Suites available
Bathrooms: 9 en-suite
Bed & breakfast
per night: £min   £max
Single   33.00   45.00
Double   66.00   90.00

Half board per
person: £min   £max
Daily   45.00   60.00
Weekly   290.00 330.00

Lunch available
Evening meal 1830 (last orders 2030)
Parking for 20
Cards accepted: Access, Visa, Amex, Switch/Delta

ARDSLEY

South Yorkshire
Map ref 4B1

Ardsley House Hotel

♛♛♛ HIGHLY COMMENDED

Doncaster Road, Ardsley, Barnsley S71 5EH
☎ Barnsley (01226) 309955
Fax (01226) 205374
Best Western

18th C manor house, tastefully converted to a private hotel. Extensive conference and banqueting facilities. French and English cooking.
Bedrooms: 17 single, 22 double, 23 twin, 11 triple
Bathrooms: 73 en-suite
Bed & breakfast
per night: £min   £max
Single   55.00   70.00
Double   65.00   80.00

Half board per
person: £min   £max
Daily   60.00   85.00

Lunch available
Evening meal 1900 (last orders 2230)
Parking for 250

Cards accepted: Access, Visa, Diners, Amex, Switch/Delta

ARKENGARTHDALE

North Yorkshire
Map ref 5B3

Picturesque Yorkshire dale, once an important and prosperous lead-mining valley developed by Charles Bathurst in the 18th C.

The White House

♛♛ COMMENDED

Arkle Town, Arkengarthdale, Richmond DL11 6RB
☎ Richmond (01748) 884203
Family-run guesthouse with panoramic views of this secluded dale. Close to Richmond and Barnard Castle and 3 miles from Reeth in Swaledale. An ideal touring and walking centre. Reduced rates for two or more nights.
Bedrooms: 2 double, 1 twin
Bathrooms: 2 en-suite, 1 public
Bed & breakfast
per night: £min   £max
Single   26.00   29.00
Double   37.00   42.00

Half board per
person: £min   £max
Daily   30.00   32.50
Weekly   375.00 388.00

Evening meal 1830 (last orders 1200)
Parking for 5
Open January–November

YORKSHIRE

ARNCLIFFE

North Yorkshire
Map ref 5B3

On the River Skirfare in Littondale, Arncliffe is an attractive dales village with a green and 17th C stone cottages and houses.

Amerdale House Hotel
HIGHLY COMMENDED

Arncliffe, Skipton BD23 5QE
☎ (01756) 770250
Fax (01756) 770250
Country house hotel with beautiful open views of Littondale. Offering comfortable, elegant accommodation, with emphasis on food and friendly, caring hospitality.
Bedrooms: 7 double, 3 twin, 1 triple
Bathrooms: 11 en-suite, 1 public
Half board per person:

	£min	£max
Daily	54.50	59.50
Weekly	371.50	416.50

Evening meal 1900 (last orders 2030)
Parking for 20
Open March–November
Cards accepted: Access, Visa

ASKRIGG

North Yorkshire
Map ref 5B3

The name of this dales village means "ash tree ridge". It is centred on a steep main street of high, narrow 3-storey houses and thrived on cotton and later wool in 18th C. Once famous for its clock making.

Kings Arms Hotel and Restaurant
COMMENDED

Askrigg, Leyburn DL8 3HQ
☎ Wensleydale (01969) 650258
Fax (01969) 650635
Logis of Great Britain
Old coaching inn of great character, featured as the Drovers Arms in BBC's James Herriot series, in the heart of the Yorkshire Dales National Park.
Bedrooms: 10 double, 1 twin
Bathrooms: 11 en-suite
Bed & breakfast per night:

	£min	£max
Single	50.00	70.00
Double	75.00	108.00

Half board per person:

	£min	£max
Daily	47.50	74.00
Weekly	300.00	465.00

Lunch available
Evening meal 1830 (last orders 2100)
Parking for 15
Cards accepted: Access, Visa, Amex, Switch/Delta

Winville Hotel & Restaurant
APPROVED

Main Street, Askrigg, Leyburn DL8 3HG
☎ Wensleydale (01969) 650515
Fax (01969) 650594
Logis of Great Britain

19th C Georgian residence in the centre of Herriot village. Some rooms have views of the dales. Conservatory, private gardens.
Bedrooms: 4 double, 2 twin, 4 triple
Bathrooms: 10 en-suite
Bed & breakfast per night:

	£min	£max
Single	31.00	35.00
Double	42.00	50.00

Half board per person:

	£min	£max
Daily	37.50	44.50
Weekly	245.00	315.00

Lunch available
Evening meal 1900 (last orders 2130)
Parking for 18
Cards accepted: Access, Visa, Diners

AUSTWICK

North Yorkshire
Map ref 5B3

Picturesque dales village with pleasant cottages, a green, an old cross and an Elizabethan Hall.

The Traddock
COMMENDED

Austwick, Settle LA2 8BY
☎ Clapham (015242) 51224
Fax (015242) 51224

A key to symbols can be found inside the back cover flap.

A well-known Yorkshire gem. This Georgian country house hotel is situated in the walkers' paradise of the Yorkshire Dales. Emphasis on comfort, good food and wines.
Bedrooms: 1 single, 4 double, 3 twin, 2 triple, 1 family room
Bathrooms: 11 en-suite, 1 public
Bed & breakfast per night:

	£min	£max
Single	40.00	55.00
Double	50.00	80.00

Half board per person:

	£min	£max
Daily	42.00	60.00
Weekly	290.00	350.00

Lunch available
Evening meal 1900 (last orders 2030)
Parking for 22
Cards accepted: Access, Visa

BATLEY

West Yorkshire
Map ref 4B1

New industries are replacing heavy woollen goods made at Batley for centuries. All Saints Church, partly 15th C, has fine carved screen. 40-acre Wilton Park has lakes, walks and Bagshaw Museum containing local history and archaeology. Nearby is Oakwell Hall and Country Park.

Alder House Hotel
COMMENDED

Towngate Road, Batley WF17 7HR
☎ (01924) 444777
Fax (01924) 442644
Handsome, tastefully converted Georgian house dating from around 1730. Recently built new wing with 7 bedrooms and function suite. Approached via Healey Lane.
Bedrooms: 5 single, 10 double, 4 twin
Bathrooms: 19 en-suite, 1 public
Bed & breakfast per night:

	£min	£max
Single	47.50	52.50
Double	60.00	72.00

Continued ▶

163

YORKSHIRE

BATLEY
Continued

Lunch available
Evening meal 1900 (last orders 2100)
Parking for 29
Cards accepted: Access, Visa, Amex

BEDALE

North Yorkshire
Map ref 5C3

Ancient church of St Gregory and Georgian Bedale Hall occupy commanding positions over this market town situated in good hunting country. The hall, which contains interesting architectural features including great ballroom and flying-type staircase, now houses a library and museum.

Elmfield House
COMMENDED

Arrathorne, Bedale DL8 1NE
☎ (01677) 450558
Fax (01677) 450557
Country house in own grounds with special emphasis on standards and home cooking. All rooms en-suite. Bar, games room, solarium. Ample secure parking.
Bedrooms: 4 double, 3 twin, 2 triple
Bathrooms: 9 en-suite

Bed & breakfast per night:	£min	£max
Single		29.30
Double	41.00	46.00

Half board per person:	£min	£max
Daily	32.00	41.00
Weekly	217.00	234.50

Evening meal from 1830
Parking for 10
Cards accepted: Access, Visa

For ideas on places to visit refer to the introduction at the beginning of this section.

The 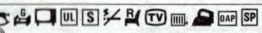 symbol after an establishment name indicates that it is a Regional Tourist Board member.

BEVERLEY

East Riding of Yorkshire
Map ref 4C1

Beverley's most famous landmark is its beautiful medieval Minster with Percy family tomb. Many attractive squares and streets, notably Wednesday and Saturday Market, North Bar Gateway and the Museum of Army Transport, Flemingate. Famous racecourse.
Tourist Information Centre ☎ *(01482) 867430 or 883898*

Eastgate Guest House
COMMENDED

7 Eastgate, Beverley, North Humberside HU17 0DR
☎ Hull (01482) 868464
Fax (01482) 871899
Family-run Victorian guesthouse, established and run by the same proprietor for 28 years. Close to the town centre, Beverley Minster, Museum of Army Transport and railway station.
Bedrooms: 6 single, 3 double, 3 twin, 3 triple, 3 family rooms
Bathrooms: 7 en-suite, 3 public

Bed & breakfast per night:	£min	£max
Single	18.50	32.00
Double	32.00	44.00

Manor House
HIGHLY COMMENDED

Newbald Road, Northlands, Walkington, Beverley, North Humberside HU17 8RT
☎ Hull (01482) 881645
Fax (01482) 866501
Country house hotel, surrounded by trees, in an idyllic setting among meadows and farms. Between Walkington and Bishop Burton, 5 minutes from Beverley.
Bedrooms: 6 double, 1 family room
Bathrooms: 7 en-suite

Bed & breakfast per night:	£min	£max
Single	74.50	84.50
Double	92.00	117.00

Half board per person:	£min	£max
Daily	62.50	75.00

Evening meal 1930 (last orders 2115)
Parking for 50
Cards accepted: Access, Visa, Switch/Delta

Tickton Grange Hotel & Restaurant
COMMENDED

Tickton Grange, Tickton, Beverley, North Humberside HU17 9SH
☎ Hornsea (01964) 543666
Fax (01964) 542556
Logis of Great Britain
Family-run Georgian country house set in rose gardens, 2 miles from historic Beverley. Country house cooking.
Bedrooms: 3 single, 10 double, 3 twin, 2 triple
Bathrooms: 18 en-suite

Bed & breakfast per night:	£min	£max
Single	62.50	
Double	80.00	90.00

Lunch available
Evening meal 1900 (last orders 2130)
Parking for 65
Cards accepted: Access, Visa, Diners, Amex

BINGLEY

West Yorkshire
Map ref 4B1

Bingley Five-Rise is an impressive group of locks on the Leeds and Liverpool Canal. Town claims to have first bred the Airedale terrier originally used for otter hunting. Among fine Georgian houses is Myrtle Grove where John Wesley stayed.

Five Rise Locks Hotel
HIGHLY COMMENDED

Beck Lane, Bingley BD16 4DD
☎ Bradford (01274) 565296
Fax (01274) 568828
Newly renovated Victorian mill owner's house set in a quiet position in its own grounds. Relaxed atmosphere, varied menu and wine list. Prices are per room.
Bedrooms: 7 double, 2 twin
Bathrooms: 9 en-suite

Bed & breakfast per night:	£min	£max
Single	32.50	45.00
Double	48.00	55.00

Half board per person:	£min	£max
Daily	36.00	57.00

Evening meal 1930 (last orders 2030)
Parking for 15
Cards accepted: Access, Visa, Switch/Delta

YORKSHIRE

Jarvis Bankfield Hotel

COMMENDED

Bradford Road, Bingley BD16 1TU
☎ Bradford (01274) 567123
Fax (01274) 551331
Jarvis/Utell International

In its own large gardens on the banks of the River Aire. The beautifully decorated restaurant offers a comfortable and relaxing atmosphere.
Bedrooms: 28 single, 26 double, 42 twin, 7 triple
Bathrooms: 103 en-suite

Bed & breakfast per night:	£min	£max
Single	48.00	77.50
Double	96.00	155.00

Half board per person:	£min	£max
Daily	39.50	92.50
Weekly	237.00	255.00

Lunch available
Evening meal 1930 (last orders 2145)
Parking for 270
Cards accepted: Access, Visa, Diners, Amex, Switch/Delta

Oakwood Hall Hotel

COMMENDED

Lady Lane, Bingley BD16 4AW
☎ Bradford (01274) 564123 & 563569
Fax (01274) 561477

Impressive listed building in quiet woodland. Individually designed bedrooms, some with four-poster beds. Relaxed place to visit, serving fine food.
Bedrooms: 1 single, 15 double, 4 twin
Bathrooms: 20 en-suite

Bed & breakfast per night:	£min	£max
Single	55.00	65.00
Double	80.00	90.00

Half board per person:	£min	£max
Daily	70.00	80.00
Weekly	350.00	560.00

Lunch available
Evening meal 1930 (last orders 2130)
Parking for 120
Cards accepted: Access, Visa, Diners, Amex, Switch/Delta

Establishments should be open throughout the year, unless otherwise stated.

BOLTON ABBEY

North Yorkshire
Map ref 4B1

This hamlet is best known for its priory situated near a bend in the River Wharfe. It was founded in 1151 by Alicia de Romilly and before that was site of Anglo-Saxon manor. Popular with painters, amongst them Landseer.

Devonshire Arms Country House Hotel

DE LUXE

Bolton Abbey, Skipton BD23 6AJ
☎ Skipton (01756) 710441
Fax (01756) 710564

Traditional country house hotel in Yorkshire Dales. Open fires, lounges furnished with antiques from Chatsworth. Leisure, health and beauty therapy club. Winner of silver award for "Hotel of the Year" in England for Excellence 1993.
Wheelchair access category 3
Bedrooms: 22 double, 19 twin
Suite available
Bathrooms: 41 en-suite

Bed & breakfast per night:	£min	£max
Single	100.00	110.00
Double	140.00	165.00

Half board per person:	£min	£max
Daily	170.00	185.00

Lunch available
Evening meal 1900 (last orders 2145)
Parking for 150
Cards accepted: Access, Visa, Diners, Amex

Please check prices and other details at the time of booking.

BOROUGHBRIDGE

North Yorkshire
Map ref 5C3

On the River Ure, Boroughbridge was once an important coaching centre with 22 inns and in the 18th C a port for Knaresborough's linens. It has fine old houses, many trees and a cobbled square with market cross. Nearby stand 3 megaliths known as the Devil's Arrows.

Crown Hotel

COMMENDED

Horsefair, Boroughbridge, York Y05 9LB
☎ (01423) 322328
Fax (01423) 324512
The Independents/Logis of Great Britain

Fully-modernised 12th C coaching inn, 1 mile from A1. Ideal base for Yorkshire Dales, Herriot country, York and Harrogate. Good restaurant.
Bedrooms: 5 single, 14 double, 22 twin, 1 triple
Bathrooms: 42 en-suite

Bed & breakfast per night:	£min	£max
Single	47.25	
Double	69.95	89.95

Half board per person:	£min	£max
Daily	54.00	64.00

Lunch available
Evening meal 1900 (last orders 2130)
Parking for 45
Cards accepted: Access, Visa, Diners, Amex

Rose Manor Hotel

COMMENDED

Horsefair, Boroughbridge, York Y05 9LL
☎ (01423) 322245
Fax (01423) 324920

Country house hotel. Secluded gardens, private car park. Restaurant and cocktail bar. Within 1 mile of A1/A1 (M) Boroughbridge exit.
Bedrooms: 2 single, 8 double, 7 twin
Bathrooms: 17 en-suite

Continued ▶

A key to symbols can be found inside the back cover flap.

YORKSHIRE

BOROUGHBRIDGE
Continued

Bed & breakfast
per night:	£min	£max
Single	69.75	69.75
Double	90.50	95.50

Half board per person:
	£min	£max
Daily	62.75	65.25

Lunch available
Evening meal 1930 (last orders 2100)
Parking for 100
Cards accepted: Access, Visa, Diners, Amex, Switch/Delta

BRADFORD
West Yorkshire
Map ref 4B1

City founded on wool, with fine Victorian and modern buildings. Attractions include the cathedral, city hall, Cartwright Hall, Lister Park, Moorside Mills Industrial Museum and National Museum of Photography, Film and Television.
Tourist Information Centre ☎ (01274) 753678

Cedar Court Hotel Bradford

Mayo Avenue (top of the M606), Off Rooley Lane, Bradford BD5 8HZ
☎ (01274) 406606
Fax (01274) 406600
First purpose-built hotel in Bradford for 20 years. Situated at the top of the M606. The ideal location.
Bedrooms: 81 double, 34 twin, 12 family rooms
Suites available
Bathrooms: 127 en-suite

Bed & breakfast
per night:	£min	£max
Single	60.00	99.00
Double	70.00	108.00

Half board per person:
	£min	£max
Daily	45.00	119.00
Weekly	305.00	610.00

Lunch available
Evening meal 1800 (last orders 2200)
Parking for 320
Cards accepted: Access, Visa, Diners, Amex, Switch/Delta

Ivy Guest House
Listed

3 Melbourne Place, Bradford BD5 0HZ
☎ (01274) 727060 & (0421) 509207
Fax (01274) 306347
Large, detached, listed house built of Yorkshire stone. Car park and gardens. Close to city centre, National Museum of Photography, Film and Television and Alhambra Theatre.
Bedrooms: 3 single, 2 double, 4 twin, 1 triple
Bathrooms: 3 public

Bed & breakfast
per night:	£min	£max
Single	18.00	18.00
Double	30.00	30.00

Half board per person:
	£min	£max
Daily	21.00	24.00
Weekly	147.00	168.00

Lunch available
Evening meal 1800 (last orders 2000)
Parking for 15
Cards accepted: Access, Visa, Diners, Amex, Switch/Delta

Marriott Leeds/Bradford Hotel
HIGHLY COMMENDED

Hollins Hill, Baildon, Shipley BD17 7QW
☎ (01274) 530053
Fax (01274) 530187
Whitbread
Great base for exploring the Yorkshire Dales, an exceptionally attractive building originally built along Elizabethan lines in the 19th C. Convenient for some of the North of England's most romantic attractions, including Bolton Abbey and Haworth Parsonage, home of the Bronte family.
Bedrooms: 33 double, 23 twin, 2 triple, 1 family room
Bathrooms: 59 en-suite

Bed & breakfast
per night:	£min	£max
Single	54.00	64.00
Double	58.00	78.00

Half board per person:
	£min	£max
Daily	41.00	51.00

Lunch available
Evening meal 1900 (last orders 2200)
Parking for 130
Cards accepted: Access, Visa, Diners, Amex, Switch/Delta

New Beehive Inn

171 Westgate, Bradford BD1 3AA
☎ (01274) 721784
Edwardian gaslit oak-panelled inn, full of character, close to centre of Bradford. Antique furniture and individually furnished bedrooms.
Bedrooms: 1 single, 4 double, 2 twin, 1 triple
Bathrooms: 8 en-suite, 2 public

Bed & breakfast
per night:	£min	£max
Single	20.00	26.00
Double	34.00	40.00

Half board per person:
	£min	£max
Daily	27.00	33.00

Lunch available
Evening meal 1900 (last orders 1900)
Parking for 22
Cards accepted: Visa

Novotel Bradford
APPROVED

Adjacent M606, Merrydale Road, Bradford BD4 6SA
☎ (01274) 683683
Fax (01274) 651342
Novotel
10 minutes' drive from Bradford city and 2 minutes from the M62, with easy access to Leeds/Bradford Airport.
Wheelchair access category 3
Bedrooms: 56 double, 56 twin, 15 triple
Bathrooms: 127 en-suite

Bed & breakfast
per night:	£min	£max
Single	35.00	50.00
Double	40.00	57.50

Half board per person:
	£min	£max
Daily	47.50	62.50

Lunch available
Evening meal 1800 (last orders 2359)
Parking for 200
Cards accepted: Access, Visa, Diners, Amex, Switch/Delta

Park Drive Hotel
COMMENDED

12 Park Drive, Heaton, Bradford BD9 4DR
☎ (01274) 480194
Fax (01274) 484869
Victorian former mill owner's residence set in its own grounds in a peaceful tree-lined conservation area, close to Lister Park.

YORKSHIRE

Bedrooms: 5 single, 3 double, 2 twin, 1 triple
Bathrooms: 11 en-suite

Bed & breakfast
per night:	£min	£max
Single	30.00	46.00
Double	48.00	56.00

Half board per
person:	£min	£max
Daily	36.00	58.00

Evening meal 1900 (last orders 2030)
Parking for 9
Cards accepted: Access, Visa, Amex

Park Grove Hotel and Restaurant
COMMENDED

Park Grove, Frizinghall, Bradford BD9 4JY
☎ (01274) 543444
Fax (01274) 495619
Minotel
Victorian establishment in a secluded preserved area of Bradford, 1.5 miles from the city centre. Gateway to the dales.
Bedrooms: 6 single, 5 double, 1 twin, 2 triple
Bathrooms: 14 en-suite

Bed & breakfast
per night:	£min	£max
Single	35.00	46.00
Double	45.00	58.00

Half board per
person:	£min	£max
Daily	35.00	40.00

Evening meal 1800 (last orders 2330)
Parking for 8
Cards accepted: Access, Visa, Amex, Switch/Delta

Pennington Midland Hotel
COMMENDED

Forster Square, Bradford BD1 4HU
☎ (01274) 735735
Fax (01274) 720003
Fully refurbished Victorian hotel with the ambience of a byegone era. Two of the finest ballrooms in Yorkshire. City centre location adjacent to motorway link and rail station. All-day restaurant, 24-hour room service. Truly unbeatable value!
Bedrooms: 12 single, 38 double, 18 twin
Suites available
Bathrooms: 68 en-suite

Bed & breakfast
per night:	£min	£max
Single	35.00	70.00
Double	49.00	95.00

Half board per
person:	£min	£max
Daily	45.00	80.00

Lunch available
Evening meal 1100 (last orders 2300)
Parking for 24
Cards accepted: Access, Visa, Diners, Amex, Switch/Delta

BRANDESBURTON
East Riding of Yorkshire
Map ref 4D1

The village church retains work from the Norman period through to the 15th C, and the shaft of a medieval cross stands on the village green.

Burton Lodge Hotel
HIGHLY COMMENDED

Brandesburton, Driffield, East Yorkshire YO25 8RU
☎ Hornsea (01964) 542847
Fax (01964) 542847
Logis of Great Britain
Charming country hotel situated in own grounds adjoining 18-hole parkland golf-course. 7 miles from Beverley on the A165.
Bedrooms: 2 single, 2 double, 3 twin, 1 triple, 1 family room
Bathrooms: 9 en-suite

Bed & breakfast
per night:	£min	£max
Single	30.00	35.00
Double	40.00	45.00

Half board per
person:	£min	£max
Daily	33.50	48.00
Weekly	220.00	280.00

Evening meal 1900 (last orders 2100)
Parking for 15
Cards accepted: Access, Visa, Amex, Switch/Delta

Information on accommodation listed in this guide has been supplied by the proprietors. As changes may occur you are advised to check details at the time of booking.

BRIDLINGTON
East Riding of Yorkshire
Map ref 5D3

Lively seaside resort with long sandy beaches, Leisure World and busy harbour with fishing trips in cobles. Priory church of St Mary whose Bayle Gate is now a museum. Mementoes of flying pioneer, Amy Johnson, in Sewerby Hall. Harbour Museum and Aquarium.
Tourist Information Centre ☎ (01262) 673474 or 606383

Bay Ridge Hotel
COMMENDED

11 Summerfield Road, Bridlington, North Humberside YO15 3LF
☎ (01262) 673425
Friendly, comfortable and caring family-run hotel near the South Beach and Spa Complex. Good value for money, all mod cons.
Bedrooms: 2 single, 6 double, 2 twin, 4 triple
Bathrooms: 12 en-suite, 2 private, 1 public

Bed & breakfast
per night:	£min	£max
Single	19.50	20.50
Double	38.00	40.00

Half board per
person:	£min	£max
Daily	23.00	26.00
Weekly	150.00	155.00

Lunch available
Evening meal 1745 (last orders 1815)
Parking for 7
Cards accepted: Access, Visa

Expanse Hotel
COMMENDED

North Marine Drive, Bridlington, North Humberside YO15 2LS
☎ (01262) 675347
Fax (01262) 604928
In a unique position overlooking the beach and sea, with panoramic views of the bay and Heritage Coast. Half board prices are based on a minimum 2-night stay.
Bedrooms: 13 single, 11 double, 20 twin, 4 triple
Bathrooms: 48 en-suite

Bed & breakfast
per night:	£min	£max
Double	50.00	75.00

Half board per
person:	£min	£max
Daily	39.50	52.00
Weekly	210.00	312.00

Continued ▶

YORKSHIRE

BRIDLINGTON
Continued

Lunch available
Evening meal 1830 (last orders 2100)
Parking for 30
Cards accepted: Access, Visa, Diners, Amex, Switch/Delta

Park View Licensed Family Hotel

9-11 Tennyson Avenue, Bridlington, North Humberside YO15 2EU
☎ (01262) 672140 & 0800 374370
Small, family-run hotel 250 yards from the beach and close to all amenities including the Leisure World indoor leisure centre.
Bedrooms: 4 single, 4 double, 4 twin, 2 triple, 2 family rooms
Bathrooms: 4 en-suite, 3 public

Bed & breakfast per night:	£min	£max
Single	15.00	17.50
Double	30.00	35.00

Half board per person:	£min	£max
Daily	20.00	22.50
Weekly	129.50	147.00

Evening meal 1700 (last orders 1800)
Parking for 8
Cards accepted: Access, Visa, Amex

The Tennyson Hotel
HIGHLY COMMENDED

19 Tennyson Avenue, Bridlington, North Humberside YO15 2EU
☎ (01262) 604382
Fax (01262) 604382
Hotel offers fine cuisine in attractive surroundings, close to sea and Leisure World. Complimentary newspaper and toiletries.
Bedrooms: 3 double, 3 twin
Bathrooms: 3 en-suite, 1 private, 2 public

Bed & breakfast per night:	£min	£max
Single	24.95	24.95
Double	40.00	46.00

Lunch available
Evening meal 1800 (last orders 2030)
Parking for 4
Cards accepted: Access, Visa, Diners, Amex, Switch/Delta

BRIGG
North Lincolnshire
Map ref 4C1

Small town at an ancient crossing of the River Ancholme, granted a weekly Thursday market and annual horsefair by Henry III in 1235.
Tourist Information Centre ☎ (01652) 657053

Holcombe Guest House
COMMENDED

34 Victoria Road, Barnetby, South Humberside DN38 6JR
☎ Mobile 0850 764002
Pleasant, homely accommodation in centre of Barnetby village. 5 minutes from M180 and railway station, 3 miles from Humberside Airport, 10 minutes from Brigg, 15-30 minutes from Grimsby, Scunthorpe and Hull.
Bedrooms: 3 single, 4 twin, 1 triple
Bathrooms: 4 en-suite, 2 public

Bed & breakfast per night:	£min	£max
Single	17.50	22.50
Double	30.00	35.00

Half board per person:	£min	£max
Daily	22.50	32.00

Evening meal 1900 (last orders 2000)
Parking for 4
Cards accepted: Access, Visa

CATTERICK
North Yorkshire
Map ref 5C3

A military camp since Roman times, known then as Cataractonium, Catterick used to be a major coaching stop on Great North Road. Crowds once gathered to watch cock-fighting where nowadays they come to Catterick Bridge for horse-racing.

Rose Cottage Guest House
Listed APPROVED

26 High Street, Catterick, Richmond DL10 7LJ
☎ Richmond (01748) 811164
Small, friendly stone-built guesthouse. En-suite facilities, guest lounge, private parking. Convenient for Richmond and Yorkshire Dales. Mid-way London/Edinburgh, A1(M) 1 kilometre. Evening meal on request May-September.
Bedrooms: 1 single, 2 twin, 1 triple
Bathrooms: 2 en-suite, 1 public

Bed & breakfast per night:	£min	£max
Single	20.00	25.00
Double	35.00	39.00

Half board per person:	£min	£max
Daily	28.50	33.50
Weekly	203.00	248.50

Evening meal 1730 (last orders 1830)
Parking for 4

CLAPHAM
North Yorkshire
Map ref 5B3

Neat village of grey-stone houses and whitewashed cottages; a pot-holing centre. Upstream are Ingleborough Cave and Gaping Gill with its huge underground chamber. National Park Centre.

Flying Horseshoe Hotel

Clapham Station, Clapham, Lancaster LA2 8ES
☎ (015242) 51229
Family-run Georgian coaching house with real fires, real ales and real food. In superb surroundings, close to Lakes and West Coast, with sea trout and salmon fishing. Bargain breaks available all year.
Bedrooms: 3 double, 1 twin
Bathrooms: 4 en-suite

Bed & breakfast per night:	£min	£max
Single	20.00	25.00
Double	30.00	40.00

Lunch available
Evening meal 1900 (last orders 2100)
Parking for 50

CLECKHEATON
West Yorkshire
Map ref 4B1

West Yorkshire town 4 miles north-west of Dewsbury.

Prospect Hall Hotel
COMMENDED

Prospect Road, Cleckheaton BD19 3HD
☎ (01274) 873022
Fax (01274) 870376
Hall, converted to provide a well-appointed hotel, close to the M62,

YORKSHIRE

Bronte country, the dales and Peak District. Reduced prices for B&B at weekends.
Bedrooms: 7 single, 30 double, 3 twin
Bathrooms: 40 en-suite

Bed & breakfast per night:	£min	£max
Single	40.00	46.50
Double	56.50	56.50

Half board per person:	£min	£max
Daily	50.00	62.50

Lunch available
Evening meal 1900 (last orders 2130)
Parking for 200
Cards accepted: Access, Visa, Diners, Amex, Switch/Delta

CLEETHORPES

North East Lincolnshire
Map ref 4D1

Once a little fishing village, now a thriving holiday resort attracting many visitors to its 3 miles of sands, boating lake, Tropical Garden, promenade and pier. Pleasure Island Fun Park. Attractive views of Humberside coast with Spurn Head light.
Tourist Information Centre ☎ (01472) 200220

Holmhirst Hotel

3 Alexandra Road, Cleethorpes, South Humberside DN35 8LQ
☎ (01472) 692656
Compact family-run hotel specialising in food, comfort and courtesy. In a prime position overlooking the sea.
Bedrooms: 5 single, 2 double, 1 twin
Bathrooms: 3 en-suite, 2 public, 1 private shower

Bed & breakfast per night:	£min	£max
Single	18.00	30.00
Double	39.00	42.00

Half board per person:	£min	£max
Daily	23.00	40.00

Lunch available
Evening meal 1900 (last orders 2000)
Cards accepted: Access, Visa

Please mention this guide when making your booking.

Tudor Terrace Guest House
Listed COMMENDED

11 Bradford Avenue, Cleethorpes, South Humberside DN35 0BB
☎ (01472) 600800
Set in quiet location at the southern end of Cleethorpes, within a conservation area. Ideal base for boating lake/leisure centre and the delights of the Lincolnshire Wolds.
Bedrooms: 1 single, 3 double, 1 twin
Bathrooms: 1 en-suite, 1 public, 3 private showers

Bed & breakfast per night:	£min	£max
Single	16.00	17.00
Double	28.00	32.00

Half board per person:	£min	£max
Daily	20.00	22.00

Evening meal 1800 (last orders 2000)
Parking for 3

DEWSBURY

West Yorkshire
Map ref 4B1

Although this town is most famous for its woollen products, its history stretches back to Saxon times. Robin Hood is reputed to have died and been buried in the Cistercian convent in Kirklees Park nearby.

Heath Cottage Hotel & Restaurant
COMMENDED

Wakefield Road, Dewsbury WF12 8ET
☎ (01924) 465399
Fax (01924) 459405
Impressive Victorian house in well-kept gardens. On the A638, 2.5 miles from M1 junction 40. Conference/banquet facilities. Large car park.
Bedrooms: 9 single, 14 double, 1 twin, 3 triple
Bathrooms: 27 en-suite

Bed & breakfast per night:	£min	£max
Single	36.00	50.00
Double	55.00	65.00

Lunch available
Evening meal 1830 (last orders 2130)
Parking for 65
Cards accepted: Access, Visa, Switch/Delta

DONCASTER

South Yorkshire
Map ref 4C1

Ancient Roman town famous for its heavy industries, butterscotch and racecourse (St Leger), also centre of agricultural area. Attractions include 18th C Mansion House, Cusworth Hall Museum, Doncaster Museum, St George's Church, The Dome and Doncaster Leisure Park.
Tourist Information Centre ☎ (01302) 734309

Danum Swallow Hotel
COMMENDED

High Street, Doncaster DN1 1DN
☎ (01302) 342261
Fax (01302) 329034
Swallow
Town centre hotel built in 1908, now fully modernised but retaining the majestic atmosphere of the past. Free car parking. Short break packages available.
Bedrooms: 22 single, 16 double, 23 twin, 3 triple, 2 family rooms
Suites available
Bathrooms: 66 en-suite

Bed & breakfast per night:	£min	£max
Single	48.00	90.00
Double	58.00	100.00

Half board per person:	£min	£max
Daily	64.95	106.95

Lunch available
Evening meal 1830 (last orders 2115)
Parking for 78
Cards accepted: Access, Visa, Diners, Amex, Switch/Delta

Regent Hotel
COMMENDED

Regent Square, Doncaster DN1 2DS
☎ (01302) 364180 & 364336
Fax (01302) 322331
Logis of Great Britain
Family-run hotel overlooking Regents Park. Two public bars, cocktail bar and a good restaurant. All rooms en-suite.
Bedrooms: 20 single, 9 double, 15 twin, 5 triple
Bathrooms: 49 en-suite

Bed & breakfast per night:	£min	£max
Single	49.50	68.00
Double	70.00	80.00

Half board per person:	£min	£max
Daily	59.50	

Continued ▶

YORKSHIRE

DONCASTER
Continued

Lunch available
Evening meal 1800 (last orders 2200)
Parking for 26
Cards accepted: Access, Visa, Diners, Amex, Switch/Delta

DRIFFIELD
East Riding of Yorkshire
Map ref 4C1

Lively market town on edge of Wolds with fine Early English church, All Saints. Popular with anglers for its trout streams which flow into the River Hull. Its 18th C canal is lined with barges and houseboats.

The Old Rectory
HIGHLY COMMENDED

Cowlam, Driffield, North Humberside YO25 0AD
☎ (01377) 267617
Fax (01377) 267403

Victorian rectory set in the traditional riding of East Yorkshire. We offer classic good food, log fires and elegant en-suite rooms. In the heart of unspoilt countryside.
Bedrooms: 1 double, 2 twin
Bathrooms: 2 en-suite, 1 private
Bed & breakfast
per night:	£min	£max
Double	51.00	55.00

Half board per
person:	£min	£max
Daily	42.00	44.00

Evening meal 1900 (last orders 2100)
Parking for 12

The White Horse Inn
COMMENDED

Main Street, Hutton Cranswick, Driffield, East Riding of Yorkshire YO25 9QN
☎ (01377) 270383
Fax (01377) 270383
Set beside the village green and pond.

A unique combination of village inn/hotel, restaurant, cabaret and function venue.
Bedrooms: 2 single, 3 double, 1 twin, 2 family rooms
Bathrooms: 8 en-suite
Bed & breakfast
per night:	£min	£max
Single	25.00	29.50
Double	40.00	45.00

Half board per
person:	£min	£max
Daily	30.00	
Weekly	210.00	

Lunch available
Evening meal 1730 (last orders 2100)
Parking for 100
Cards accepted: Access, Visa, Switch/Delta

EASINGWOLD
North Yorkshire
Map ref 5C3

Market town of charm and character with a cobbled square and many fine Georgian buildings.

The George
COMMENDED

Market Place, Easingwold, York YO6 3AD
☎ (01347) 821698
Fax (01347) 823448
18th C coaching inn overlooking cobbled square in delightful Georgian market town. 15 minutes York, dales, moors. Good food. Cask beers.
Bedrooms: 7 double, 4 twin, 1 triple, 1 family room
Bathrooms: 13 en-suite
Bed & breakfast
per night:	£min	£max
Single	35.00	45.00
Double	50.00	60.00

Half board per
person:	£min	£max
Daily	37.50	47.50
Weekly	245.00	

Lunch available
Evening meal 1900 (last orders 2130)
Parking for 8
Cards accepted: Access, Visa, Switch/Delta

Map references apply to the colour maps at the back of this guide.

Old Farmhouse Country Hotel & Restaurant
HIGHLY COMMENDED

Raskelf, York YO6 3LF
☎ (01347) 821971
Fax (01347) 822392
Logis of Great Britain
Former farmhouse converted to a comfortable country hotel, offering home cooking, open fires and a warm welcome. In Herriot country, 3 miles from Easingwold and 15 miles from York.
Bedrooms: 6 double, 2 twin, 2 triple
Bathrooms: 10 en-suite
Bed & breakfast
per night:	£min	£max
Single	27.00	31.00
Double	46.00	54.00

Half board per
person:	£min	£max
Daily	38.00	42.00
Weekly	266.00	280.00

Evening meal 1900 (last orders 2030)
Parking for 12
Open February–December

ELLERBY
North Yorkshire
Map ref 5C3

Hamlet 3 miles south of Staithes.

Ellerby Hotel
COMMENDED

Ellerby, Saltburn-by-the-Sea, Cleveland TS13 5LP
☎ Whitby (01947) 840342
Fax (01947) 841221
Residential country inn within the North York Moors National Park, 9 miles north of Whitby, 1 mile inland from Runswick Bay.
Wheelchair access category 3
Bedrooms: 5 double, 4 triple
Bathrooms: 9 en-suite
Bed & breakfast
per night:	£min	£max
Single	33.00	36.00
Double	50.00	56.00

Lunch available
Evening meal 1900 (last orders 2200)
Parking for 60
Cards accepted: Access, Visa, Switch/Delta

Please check prices and other details at the time of booking.

YORKSHIRE

FILEY

North Yorkshire
Map ref 5D3

Resort with elegant Regency buildings along the front and 6 miles of sandy beaches bounded by natural breakwater, Filey Brigg.

The Downcliffe House Hotel
HIGHLY COMMENDED

The Beach, Filey YO14 9LA
☎ Scarborough (01723) 513310
Fax (01723) 516141
Recently refurbished seafront hotel with magnificent views over Filey Bay. All rooms en-suite with telephone, satellite TV and tea-making facilities.
Bedrooms: 1 single, 6 double, 1 twin, 1 triple, 1 family room
Bathrooms: 10 en-suite
Bed & breakfast

per night:	£min	£max
Single	27.00	35.00
Double	54.00	70.00

Half board per

person:	£min	£max
Daily	37.00	49.00
Weekly	245.00	280.00

Lunch available
Evening meal 1800 (last orders 2100)
Parking for 10
Open February–December
Cards accepted: Access, Visa, Switch/Delta

Sea Brink Hotel
COMMENDED

The Beach, Filey YO14 9LA
☎ Scarborough (01723) 513257
Fax (01723) 514139
Seafront hotel overlooking the beach. Magnificent views, delightful en-suite rooms with all facilities. Licensed restaurant and coffee shop. Jacuzzi. French/German spoken.
Bedrooms: 6 double, 5 family rooms
Bathrooms: 9 en-suite, 2 private, 1 public
Bed & breakfast

per night:	£min	£max
Single	20.00	25.00
Double	36.00	44.00

Lunch available
Evening meal 1800 (last orders 1930)
Open January–May, July–November and Christmas
Cards accepted: Access, Visa, Diners, Amex

Seafield Hotel
COMMENDED

9-11 Rutland Street, Filey YO14 9JA
☎ Scarborough (01723) 513715
Small, friendly and comfortable hotel in the centre of Filey, close to the beach and all amenities. Car park. Family rooms.
Bedrooms: 2 single, 3 double, 3 triple, 5 family rooms
Bathrooms: 10 en-suite, 2 public
Bed & breakfast

per night:	£min	£max
Single	18.50	20.50
Double	37.00	41.00

Half board per

person:	£min	£max
Daily	24.00	26.00
Weekly	160.00	174.00

Evening meal 1800 (last orders 1600)
Parking for 7
Cards accepted: Access, Visa, Amex

White Lodge Hotel
APPROVED

The Crescent, Filey YO14 9JX
☎ Scarborough (01723) 514771
Clifftop hotel overlooking the bay, close to town centre and golf-course. A short distance from Bempton Bird Sanctuary. Special mini-breaks available.
Bedrooms: 3 single, 8 double, 7 twin, 1 triple
Bathrooms: 19 en-suite
Bed & breakfast

per night:	£min	£max
Single	31.72	34.07
Double	63.44	68.14

Half board per

person:	£min	£max
Daily	44.72	47.07
Weekly	280.00	313.04

Lunch available
Evening meal 1900 (last orders 2045)
Parking for 8
Cards accepted: Access, Visa, Switch/Delta

The symbols in each entry give information about services and facilities. A 'key' to these symbols appears at the back of this guide.

FLAMBOROUGH

East Riding of Yorkshire
Map ref 5D3

Village with strong seafaring tradition, high on chalk headland dominated by cliffs of Flamborough Head, a fortress for over 2000 years. St Oswald's Church is in the oldest part of Flamborough.

North Star Hotel
HIGHLY COMMENDED

North Marine Road, Flamborough, Bridlington, North Humberside YO15 1BL
☎ Bridlington (01262) 850379
Family-run hotel offering quality en-suite rooms with spectacular sea views. Superb birdwatching and cliff walks at RSPB Bempton. Renowned for good food.
Bedrooms: 2 double, 5 twin
Bathrooms: 7 en-suite
Bed & breakfast

per night:	£min	£max
Single	33.00	40.00
Double	50.00	70.00

Lunch available
Evening meal 1845 (last orders 2130)
Parking for 30
Cards accepted: Access, Visa

GOATHLAND

North Yorkshire
Map ref 5D3

Spacious village has several large greens grazed by sheep and is an ideal centre for walking the North York Moors. Nearby are several waterfalls, among them Mallyan Spout. Plough Monday celebrations held in January. Location for filming of TV "Heartbeat" series.

Fairhaven Country Hotel

The Common, Goathland, Whitby YO22 5AN
☎ Whitby (01947) 896361
Edwardian country house with superb moorland views in the centre of Goathland village. Warm hospitality and fine food in a relaxed atmosphere.
Bedrooms: 2 single, 2 double, 2 twin, 2 triple, 1 family room
Bathrooms: 4 en-suite, 3 public
Bed & breakfast

per night:	£min	£max
Single	19.00	23.50
Double	38.00	47.00

Continued ▶

YORKSHIRE

GOATHLAND
Continued

Half board per person:	£min	£max
Daily	29.00	33.50
Weekly	195.00	220.00

Evening meal 1900 (last orders 1730)
Parking for 10
Cards accepted: Access, Visa, Switch/Delta

Inn on the Moor
COMMENDED

Goathland, Whitby YO22 5LZ
☎ Whitby (01947) 896296
Fax (01947) 896484

Country house hotel overlooking the Yorkshire Moors. A warm welcome, pleasant service, English food, fresh air and peace. All rooms have colour TV, 6 with four-poster beds, 2 family suites. "Heartbeat" country.

Bedrooms: 11 double, 10 twin, 2 triple, 2 family rooms
Bathrooms: 25 en-suite, 1 public

Bed & breakfast per night:	£min	£max
Single	30.00	46.00
Double	56.00	80.00

Half board per person:	£min	£max
Daily	39.00	54.00
Weekly	234.00	324.00

Lunch available
Evening meal 1900 (last orders 2030)
Parking for 30
Cards accepted: Access, Visa, Amex, Switch/Delta

Mallyan Spout Hotel
COMMENDED

Goathland, Whitby YO22 5AN
☎ Whitby (01947) 896486 & 896206
Fax (01947) 896327

Comfortable hotel with old-fashioned comforts, welcoming log fires and good dining facilities. An ideal centre for walking the North York Moors. "Heartbeat" country.

Bedrooms: 4 single, 12 double, 7 twin
Bathrooms: 21 en-suite, 2 private

Bed & breakfast per night:	£min	£max
Single	45.00	65.00
Double	65.00	130.00

Half board per person:	£min	£max
Daily	50.00	75.00
Weekly	325.00	475.00

Lunch available
Evening meal 1900 (last orders 2100)
Parking for 100
Cards accepted: Access, Visa, Diners, Amex, Switch/Delta

Whitfield House Hotel
COMMENDED

Darnholm, Goathland, Whitby YO22 5LA
☎ Whitby (01947) 896215 & 896214

17th C farmhouse providing modern comforts amidst old world charm. Peaceful location. Cottage-style en-suite bedrooms (non-smoking) with every amenity.

Bedrooms: 1 single, 5 double, 2 triple
Bathrooms: 8 en-suite

Bed & breakfast per night:	£min	£max
Single	26.00	28.00
Double	52.00	56.00

Half board per person:	£min	£max
Daily	37.50	39.50
Weekly	255.00	270.00

Evening meal 1900 (last orders 1730)
Parking for 10
Open February–November
Cards accepted: Access, Visa

GOOLE
North Lincolnshire
Map ref 4C1

This busy port on the River Ouse developed with the opening of the Aire and Calder Canal in 1826 and is reminiscent of the Netherlands with its red brick buildings and flat, watery landscape. Goole Museum houses Garside Local History Collection.

Clifton Hotel
APPROVED

Boothferry Road, Goole, North Humberside DN14 6AL
☎ (01405) 761336
Fax (01405) 762350

Small, comfortable and friendly family-run hotel convenient for Humberside, York, East Yorkshire and Lincolnshire. One mile from M62 motorway.

Bedrooms: 4 single, 3 double, 1 twin, 1 family room
Bathrooms: 8 en-suite, 1 private

Bed & breakfast per night:	£min	£max
Single	26.00	39.50
Double	39.50	48.00

Half board per person:	£min	£max
Daily	27.00	

Lunch available
Evening meal 1900 (last orders 2100)
Parking for 8
Cards accepted: Access, Visa, Diners, Amex

GRASSINGTON
North Yorkshire
Map ref 5B3

Tourists visit this former lead-mining village to see its "smiddy", antique and craft shops and Upper Wharfedale Museum of country trades. Popular with fishermen and walkers. Numerous prehistoric sites. Grassington Feast in October. National Park Centre.

Ashfield House Hotel
HIGHLY COMMENDED

Grassington, Skipton BD23 5AE
☎ (01756) 752584

Quiet and secluded 17th C private hotel near the village square. Open fires and creative home cooking using only fresh produce.

Bedrooms: 4 double, 3 twin
Bathrooms: 6 en-suite, 1 private

National gradings and classifications were correct at the time of going to press but are subject to change. Please check at the time of booking.

YORKSHIRE

Bed & breakfast per night:	£min	£max
Single	24.50	39.00
Double	49.00	56.00

Half board per person:	£min	£max
Daily	37.50	43.00
Weekly	234.00	270.00

Evening meal 1900 (last orders 1900)
Parking for 9
Open February–December
Cards accepted: Access, Visa

Clarendon Hotel
COMMENDED

Hebden, Grassington, Skipton BD23 5DE
☎ Skipton (01756) 752446
Yorkshire Dales village inn serving good food and ales. Personal supervision at all times. Steaks and fish dishes are specialities.
Bedrooms: 2 double, 1 twin
Bathrooms: 3 en-suite

Bed & breakfast per night:	£min	£max
Single	25.00	35.00
Double	40.00	50.00

Lunch available
Evening meal 1900 (last orders 2100)
Parking for 30

Grassington House Hotel
COMMENDED

5 The Square, Grassington, Skipton BD23 5AQ
☎ (01756) 752406
Fax (01756) 752135
Friendly, family-run Georgian hotel in the Yorkshire Dales. Renowned for comfort and food. Pets welcome. Ideal touring and walking base. Special terms for weekly stays.
Bedrooms: 2 single, 5 double, 2 twin, 1 triple
Bathrooms: 10 en-suite

Bed & breakfast per night:	£min	£max
Single	26.00	26.00
Double	52.00	52.00

Half board per person:	£min	£max
Daily	36.50	36.50

Lunch available
Evening meal 1900 (last orders 2130)
Parking for 24
Cards accepted: Access, Visa, Switch/Delta

Lodge Guest House
APPROVED

8 Wood Lane, Grassington, Skipton BD23 5LU
☎ (01756) 752518
In a quiet location yet only 100 yards from the square. Ideal walking or touring base, near Harrogate and York. Children and dogs welcome. Full central heating.
Bedrooms: 3 double, 4 twin
Bathrooms: 2 private, 2 public

Bed & breakfast per night:	£min	£max
Single	22.00	
Double	32.00	40.00

Half board per person:	£min	£max
Daily	26.00	32.00

Evening meal from 1900
Parking for 7
Open March–October

GRIMSBY
North East Lincolnshire
Map ref 4D1

Founded 1,000 years ago by a Danish fisherman named Grim, Grimsby is today a major fishing port and docks. It has modern shopping precincts and National Fishing Heritage Centre, voted England's top tourist attraction in 1992.
Tourist Information Centre ☎ *(01472) 342422*

Millfields
COMMENDED

53 Bargate, Grimsby, South Humberside DN34 5AD
☎ (01472) 356068
Fax (01472) 250286
Ⓒ Minotel/The Independents

Exclusive yet competitively priced hotel with a wide range of leisure facilities, situated close to the commercial and retail centre of Grimsby.
Wheelchair access category 3
Bedrooms: 13 double, 9 twin
Bathrooms: 22 en-suite

Bed & breakfast per night:	£min	£max
Single	40.00	51.00
Double	53.00	70.00

Half board per person:	£min	£max
Daily	52.00	63.00

Lunch available
Evening meal 1900 (last orders 2100)
Parking for 50
Cards accepted: Access, Visa, Diners, Amex, Switch/Delta

HALIFAX
West Yorkshire
Map ref 4B1

Founded on the cloth trade, and famous for its building society, textiles, carpets and toffee. Most notable landmark is Piece Hall where wool merchants traded, now restored to house shops, museums and art gallery. Home also to Eureka! The Museum for Children.
Tourist Information Centre ☎ *(01422) 368725*

The Hobbit
COMMENDED

Hob Lane, Norland, Sowerby Bridge HX6 3QL
☎ (01422) 832202
Fax (01422) 835381
Country hotel with panoramic views. Restaurant and bistro have reputation for good food at affordable prices. Friendly inn-type atmosphere.
Bedrooms: 3 single, 10 double, 7 twin, 2 triple
Bathrooms: 22 en-suite

Bed & breakfast per night:	£min	£max
Single	31.00	59.00
Double	45.00	75.00

Half board per person:	£min	£max
Daily	34.00	74.00
Weekly	209.65	251.65

Lunch available
Evening meal 1700 (last orders 2200)
Parking for 100
Cards accepted: Access, Visa, Diners, Amex, Switch/Delta

COLOUR MAPS

Colour maps at the back of this guide pinpoint all places in which you will find accommodation listed.

YORKSHIRE

HARROGATE

North Yorkshire
Map ref 4B1

A major conference, exhibition and shopping centre, renowned for its spa heritage and award winning floral displays, spacious parks and gardens. Famous for antiques, toffee, fine shopping and excellent tea shops, also its Royal Pump Rooms and Baths.
Tourist Information Centre ☎ *(01423) 525666*

Abbey Lodge

COMMENDED

29-31 Ripon Road, Harrogate HG1 2JL
☎ (01423) 569712
Fax (01423) 530570
Ideal touring base for the dales, moors and abbeys. With award-winning restaurant and sofa-filled lounge, our hospitality awaits you.
Bedrooms: 4 single, 6 double, 3 twin, 3 triple, 1 family room
Bathrooms: 14 en-suite, 1 public

Bed & breakfast per night:

	£min	£max
Single	28.00	49.00
Double	49.00	59.00

Half board per person:

	£min	£max
Daily	35.75	43.00

Evening meal 1900 (last orders 2100)
Parking for 25
Cards accepted: Access, Visa, Amex, Switch/Delta

Acacia Lodge

HIGHLY COMMENDED

21 Ripon Road, Harrogate HG1 2JL
☎ (01423) 560752 & 503725
Warm, lovingly restored Victorian house in select town centre area. Fine furnishings/antiques, beautiful lounge with open fire, all rooms en-suite. Award-winning breakfasts, ample floodlit parking. Entirely non-smoking.
Bedrooms: 1 double, 2 twin, 2 triple
Bathrooms: 5 en-suite

Bed & breakfast per night:

	£min	£max
Single	32.00	48.00
Double	48.00	58.00

Parking for 6

Alamah

COMMENDED

88 Kings Road, Harrogate HG1 5JX
☎ (01423) 502187
Fax (01423) 566175
Comfortable rooms, personal attention, friendly atmosphere and full English breakfast. 300 metres from town centre. Garages/parking.
Bedrooms: 2 single, 2 double, 2 twin, 1 family room
Bathrooms: 5 en-suite, 2 private showers

Bed & breakfast per night:

	£min	£max
Single	23.00	25.00
Double	42.00	48.00

Evening meal 1830 (last orders 1400)
Parking for 8

The Alexander

HIGHLY COMMENDED

88 Franklin Road, Harrogate HG1 5EN
☎ (01423) 503348
Friendly, family-run elegant Victorian guesthouse with some en-suite facilities. Ideal for conference centre and Harrogate town. Good touring centre for dales. Non-smokers only, please.
Bedrooms: 2 single, 1 double, 2 triple
Suites available
Bathrooms: 3 en-suite, 1 public

Bed & breakfast per night:

	£min	£max
Single	19.00	22.00
Double	42.00	42.00

Parking for 2

Alvera Court Hotel

COMMENDED

76 Kings Road, Harrogate HG1 5JX
☎ (01423) 505735
Fax (01423) 507996
Extensively refurbished Victorian residence placing special emphasis on comfort and personal service. Directly opposite the conference centre.
Bedrooms: 5 single, 5 double, 2 twin, 4 triple
Bathrooms: 16 en-suite

Bed & breakfast per night:

	£min	£max
Single	29.00	42.30
Double	58.00	84.00

Half board per person:

	£min	£max
Daily	44.50	51.50
Weekly	311.00	361.00

Evening meal 1930 (last orders 1400)

Parking for 8
Cards accepted: Access, Visa, Switch/Delta

Anro

COMMENDED

90 Kings Road, Harrogate HG1 5JX
☎ (01423) 503087
In a central position, 2 minutes from the conference centre and near Valley Gardens, town, bus and rail stations. Ideal for touring the dales. Home cooking.
Bedrooms: 3 single, 1 double, 2 twin, 1 family room
Bathrooms: 4 en-suite, 1 public

Bed & breakfast per night:

	£min	£max
Single	20.00	
Double	40.00	

Half board per person:

	£min	£max
Daily	32.00	

Evening meal 1815 (last orders 1630)

Ascot House Hotel

COMMENDED

53 Kings Road, Harrogate HG1 5HJ
☎ (01423) 531005
Fax (01423) 503523
Minotel
Delightful, refurbished, family-run hotel near town centre assuring you of a friendly welcome and an enjoyable stay. Quality cuisine. Parking. Ring for colour brochure.
Bedrooms: 4 single, 7 double, 7 twin, 1 triple
Bathrooms: 18 en-suite, 1 private shower

Bed & breakfast per night:

	£min	£max
Single	44.50	52.50
Double	65.00	85.00

Half board per person:

	£min	£max
Daily	44.00	53.50
Weekly	264.00	321.00

Evening meal 1900 (last orders 2045)
Parking for 14
Cards accepted: Access, Visa, Diners, Amex

Map references apply to the colour maps at the back of this guide.

YORKSHIRE

Ashley House Hotel
COMMENDED

36-40 Franklin Road, Harrogate
HG1 5EE
☎ (01423) 507474
Fax (01423) 560858

Ron and Linda welcome you to their comfortable home in a quiet street close to the town centre. Friendly atmosphere, personal service, delicious meals and cosy bar.

Bedrooms: 5 single, 5 double, 7 twin
Bathrooms: 17 en-suite, 2 public

Bed & breakfast per night:	£min	£max
Single	30.00	35.00
Double	50.00	65.00

Half board per person:	£min	£max
Daily	40.00	50.00
Weekly	250.00	280.00

Evening meal 1900 (last orders 2100)
Parking for 6
Cards accepted: Access, Visa, Diners, Amex, Switch/Delta

Barkers Guest House

202-204 King's Road, Harrogate
HG1 5JG
☎ (01423) 568494

Small, family-run guesthouse within 10 minutes' walking distance of town centre. Home-from-home accommodation in one of England's nicest towns.

Bedrooms: 1 single, 1 double, 1 triple
Bathrooms: 1 en-suite, 1 public

Bed & breakfast per night:	£min	£max
Single	18.00	19.00
Double	36.00	38.00

Parking for 2

Bay Horse Inn
COMMENDED

Burnt Yates, Harrogate HG3 3EJ
☎ (01423) 770230
(CR) Wayfarer

Renowned 18th C inn with oak beams, open log fires and restaurant serving traditional English fare. In Nidderdale between Ripley and Pateley Bridge. Ideal base for racing in Yorkshire, golf courses and shooting parties.

Bedrooms: 4 double, 6 twin, 2 triple
Bathrooms: 12 en-suite

Bed & breakfast per night:	£min	£max
Single	42.00	42.00
Double	60.00	60.00

Half board per person:	£min	£max
Daily	41.00	57.95
Weekly	275.00	275.00

Lunch available
Evening meal 1900 (last orders 2200)
Parking for 80
Cards accepted: Access, Visa, Switch/Delta

Britannia Lodge Hotel

16 Swan Road, Harrogate HG1 2SA
☎ (01423) 508482
Fax (01423) 526840

Beautiful 19th C town house, delightful garden, own car park. En-suite bedrooms with all facilities, elegant lounge and bar. 5 minutes' walk to town centre, historic attractions and Valley Gardens.

Bedrooms: 4 single, 4 double, 4 twin
Bathrooms: 12 en-suite

Bed & breakfast per night:	£min	£max
Single	35.00	50.00
Double	51.00	70.00

Half board per person:	£min	£max
Daily	38.00	47.50
Weekly	245.00	332.50

Evening meal 1800 (last orders 2030)
Parking for 7
Cards accepted: Access, Visa, Amex

Cavendish Hotel
COMMENDED

3 Valley Drive, Harrogate HG2 0JJ
☎ (01423) 509637

Overlooking the beautiful Valley Gardens in a quiet location yet close to conference centre and extensive shopping area. Ideal for business or pleasure.

Bedrooms: 3 single, 4 double, 2 twin
Bathrooms: 9 en-suite

Establishments should be open throughout the year, unless otherwise stated.

Bed & breakfast

per night:	£min	£max
Single	28.00	45.00
Double	50.00	65.00

Half board per person:	£min	£max
Daily	37.50	54.50
Weekly	262.50	381.50

Evening meal 1900 (last orders 2030)
Cards accepted: Access, Visa

The Dales Hotel
COMMENDED

101 Valley Drive, Harrogate
HG2 0JP
☎ (01423) 507248 & Mobile (01585) 430782
Fax (01423) 507248

A warm welcome for those who prefer comfort and good food with the "personal" touch. Overlooking Valley Gardens. Sports facilities. 7-10 minutes' walk from conference and town centres. Perfect for York, Herriot, Bronte country, Yorkshire Dales and coast.

Bedrooms: 2 single, 3 double, 2 twin, 1 triple
Bathrooms: 6 en-suite, 2 private

Bed & breakfast per night:	£min	£max
Single	28.00	40.00
Double	48.00	56.00

Half board per person:	£min	£max
Daily	34.00	37.00

Evening meal 1800 (last orders 1200)
Parking for 8
Cards accepted: Access, Visa, Amex

Eton House

3 Eton Terrace, Knaresborough Road, Harrogate HG2 7SU
☎ (01423) 886850

Still here after 18 years, this homely guesthouse with spacious comfortable rooms, all with TV and tea/coffee facilities. Situated on A59 on the edge of the Stray and close to town.

Bedrooms: 1 single, 3 triple, 3 family rooms
Bathrooms: 2 en-suite, 2 public

Bed & breakfast per night:	£min	£max
Single	18.00	20.00
Double	36.00	40.00

Parking for 10

YORKSHIRE

HARROGATE
Continued

Garden House Hotel
COMMENDED
14 Harlow Moor Drive, Harrogate
HG2 0JX
☎ (01423) 503059
Small, family-run, Victorian hotel overlooking Valley Gardens, in a quiet location with unrestricted parking. Home cooking using fresh produce only.
Bedrooms: 3 single, 1 double, 3 twin
Bathrooms: 5 en-suite, 2 private showers

Bed & breakfast per night:	£min	£max
Single	21.00	
Double	45.00	

Half board per person:	£min	£max
Daily	33.50	
Weekly	210.00	

Evening meal 1900 (last orders 1200)
Cards accepted: Access, Visa, Diners, Amex

Imperial Hotel
COMMENDED
Prospect Place, Harrogate HG1 1LA
☎ (01423) 565071
Fax (01423) 500082
Principal/Utell International
Recently refurbished and situated in the heart of this historic spa town, this hotel was once the home of Lord Carnaervon. Half board prices below are based on double/twin occupancy for minimum 2-night stay, with free entry into some local attractions.
Bedrooms: 12 single, 22 double, 51 twin
Suite available
Bathrooms: 85 en-suite

Half board per person:	£min	£max
Daily	50.00	80.00

Lunch available
Evening meal 1900 (last orders 2130)
Parking for 45
Cards accepted: Access, Visa, Diners, Amex, Switch/Delta

Establishments should be open throughout the year, unless otherwise stated.

Low Hall Hotel and Coach House Restaurant
COMMENDED
Ripon Road, Killinghall, Harrogate
HG3 2AY
☎ (01423) 508598
Fax (01423) 560848
Charming, privately-owned country hotel, set in attractive gardens. Excellent restaurant and bar meals. 2 miles north of Harrogate.
Bedrooms: 2 single, 4 double, 1 twin
Bathrooms: 7 en-suite

Bed & breakfast per night:	£min	£max
Single	39.00	75.00
Double	49.50	85.00

Half board per person:	£min	£max
Daily	39.00	89.00

Lunch available
Evening meal 1900 (last orders 2130)
Parking for 50
Cards accepted: Access, Visa, Diners, Amex

Lynton House
COMMENDED
42 Studley Road, Harrogate
HG1 5JU
☎ (01423) 504715
In a central, quiet, tree-lined avenue, 100 yards from exhibition halls close to Valley Gardens. Personal supervision. Non-smokers only, please.
Bedrooms: 2 single, 1 twin, 2 triple
Bathrooms: 1 public

Bed & breakfast per night:	£min	£max
Single	17.50	19.50
Double	35.00	36.00

Open March–November

Ruskin Hotel and Restaurant
HIGHLY COMMENDED
1 Swan Road, Harrogate HG1 2SS
☎ (01423) 502045
Fax (01423) 506131
Small, enchanting Victorian hotel, full of graceful charm and character in lovely mature gardens. Close to conference centre and town. Beautiful antique furnished bedrooms, all en-suite including four-poster, offering every comfort and facility. Delightful licensed restaurant. Private car park.
Bedrooms: 1 single, 3 double, 2 triple
Bathrooms: 6 en-suite

Bed & breakfast per night:	£min	£max
Single	39.00	54.00
Double	55.00	85.00

Half board per person:	£min	£max
Daily	53.00	68.00

Evening meal 1900 (last orders 2130)
Parking for 10
Cards accepted: Access, Visa

St George Swallow Hotel
COMMENDED
Ripon Road, Harrogate HG1 2SY
☎ (01423) 561431
Fax (01423) 530037
Swallow
Traditional hotel, tastefully restored, with leisure complex including pool, sauna, solarium, spa bath and exercise gym. Close to the Valley Gardens and other historic attractions. Short break packages available.
Bedrooms: 35 single, 25 double, 19 twin, 8 triple, 6 family rooms
Suites available
Bathrooms: 93 en-suite

Bed & breakfast per night:	£min	£max
Single	65.00	95.00
Double	80.00	115.00

Half board per person:	£min	£max
Daily	81.95	111.95

Lunch available
Evening meal 1900 (last orders 2130)
Parking for 63
Cards accepted: Access, Visa, Diners, Amex, Switch/Delta

Spring Lodge Guest House
COMMENDED
22 Spring Mount, Harrogate
HG1 2HX
☎ (01423) 506036
In a quiet cul-de-sac, a few minutes' walk from the town centre, bus/railway stations, Royal Hall, conference centre and gardens. Ideal for tourist and business visitors.
Bedrooms: 1 single, 4 double, 1 triple
Bathrooms: 2 en-suite, 1 public, 2 private showers

Bed & breakfast per night:	£min	£max
Single	16.00	25.00
Double	32.00	42.00

YORKSHIRE

Half board per person:	£min	£max
Daily	24.00	33.00
Weekly	152.00	208.00

Evening meal 1900 (last orders 2100)
Parking for 1

Stoney Lea Guest House

Listed COMMENDED

13 Spring Grove, Harrogate HG1 2HS
☎ (01423) 501524
Comfortable and attractive Victorian house in a quiet cul-de-sac. Centrally located within walking distance of all the town's tourist and business facilities.
Bedrooms: 2 single, 1 double, 1 twin, 1 triple
Bathrooms: 5 en-suite

Bed & breakfast per night:	£min	£max
Single	26.00	26.00
Double	40.00	45.00

Parking for 2

Studley Hotel

COMMENDED

Swan Road, Harrogate HG1 2SE
☎ (01423) 560425
Fax (01423) 530967
Small, friendly hotel, ideally situated near Valley Gardens, shops and conference/exhibition centre. Le Breton French Restaurant has genuine charcoal grill. Excellent value table d'hote dinner and a la carte menu with extensive wine list.
Bedrooms: 15 single, 10 double, 11 twin
Bathrooms: 36 en-suite

Bed & breakfast per night:	£min	£max
Single	55.00	80.00
Double	70.00	95.00

Lunch available
Evening meal 1900 (last orders 2200)
Parking for 14
Cards accepted: Access, Visa, Diners, Amex, Switch/Delta

Valley Hotel

COMMENDED

93-95 Valley Drive, Harrogate HG2 0JP
☎ (01423) 504868
Fax (01423) 531940
Hotel overlooking Valley Gardens, offering a warm welcome to both tourists and business people. Licensed restaurant.

Bedrooms: 4 single, 3 double, 5 twin, 1 triple, 2 family rooms
Bathrooms: 15 en-suite

Bed & breakfast per night:	£min	£max
Single	26.00	50.00
Double	46.00	60.00

Half board per person:	£min	£max
Daily	32.00	
Weekly	224.00	

Lunch available
Evening meal 1800 (last orders 2130)
Parking for 3
Cards accepted: Access, Visa, Diners, Amex

White Hart Hotel

Cold Bath Road, Harrogate HG2 ONF
☎ (01423) 505681
Fax (01423) 568354
Grade II listed building in the centre of Harrogate, overlooking West Park Stray. Recently upgraded and refurbished.
Bedrooms: 37 single, 4 double, 13 twin
Bathrooms: 54 en-suite

Bed & breakfast per night:	£min	£max
Single	50.00	60.00
Double	70.00	75.00

Lunch available
Evening meal 1830 (last orders 2030)
Parking for 80
Cards accepted: Access, Visa

HAWES

North Yorkshire
Map ref 5B3

The capital of Upper Wensleydale on the famous Pennine Way, renowned for great cheeses. Popular with walkers. Dales National Park Information Centre and Folk Museum. Nearby is spectacular Hardraw Force waterfall.

Cocketts Hotel

HIGHLY COMMENDED

Market Place, Hawes DL8 3RD
☎ Wensleydale (01969) 667312
Fax (01969) 667162
17th C stone-built hotel in the Market Place. Ideally situated for touring the dales. English and French cuisine. Warm, comfortable old world atmosphere, yet all modern facilities.
Bedrooms: 6 double, 2 twin
Bathrooms: 8 en-suite

Bed & breakfast per night:	£min	£max
Single	30.00	40.00
Double	44.00	64.00

Half board per person:	£min	£max
Daily	45.00	55.00
Weekly	315.00	385.00

Lunch available
Evening meal 1900 (last orders 2030)
Cards accepted: Access, Visa, Amex, Switch/Delta

Simonstone Hall

HIGHLY COMMENDED

Hawes DL8 3LY
☎ Wensleydale (01969) 667255
Fax (01969) 667741

18th C country house hotel, rural setting in the heart of Wensleydale. Panoramic views, tranquillity, excellent cuisine, wines and friendly staff. Ideal for a memorable break. Dogs welcome.
Bedrooms: 7 double, 3 twin
Bathrooms: 10 en-suite

Bed & breakfast per night:	£min	£max
Single	39.00	61.00
Double	70.00	110.00

Half board per person:	£min	£max
Daily	55.00	75.00
Weekly	346.00	472.00

Lunch available
Evening meal 1900 (last orders 2030)
Parking for 22
Cards accepted: Access, Visa, Switch/Delta

Steppe Haugh Licensed Country Guest House

COMMENDED

Town Head, Hawes DL8 3RG
☎ Wensleydale (01969) 667645
The house was built in 1643 and is tastefully decorated with antique furnishings and unusual dark pitch and
Continued ▶

YORKSHIRE

HAWES
Continued

pine ceilings and staircase. Cosy lounge with log fire. Children 8 years and over are accepted.
Bedrooms: 1 single, 4 double, 1 twin
Bathrooms: 2 en-suite, 2 public

Bed & breakfast per night:	£min	£max
Single	16.50	18.50
Double	30.00	46.00

Evening meal 1900 (last orders 2000)
Parking for 6

Stone House Hotel
COMMENDED
Sedbusk, Hawes DL8 3PT
☎ Wensleydale (01969) 667571
Fax (01969) 667720

Fine Edwardian country house hotel in a beautiful old English garden with panoramic views of Upper Wensleydale.
Bedrooms: 1 single, 10 double, 7 twin, 1 triple
Bathrooms: 19 en-suite, 1 public

Bed & breakfast per night:	£min	£max
Single	32.50	47.50
Double	55.00	78.00

Half board per person:	£min	£max
Daily	44.00	55.50
Weekly	277.20	349.65

Evening meal 1900 (last orders 2000)
Parking for 15
Open February–December
Cards accepted: Access, Visa, Switch/Delta

White Hart Inn
APPROVED
Main Street, Hawes DL8 3QL
☎ Wensleydale (01969) 667259
17th C coaching inn with a friendly welcome, offering traditional fare. Open fires, Yorkshire ales. Central for exploring the dales.
Bedrooms: 1 single, 4 double, 2 twin
Bathrooms: 2 public

Bed & breakfast per night:	£min	£max
Single	18.00	18.00
Double	34.00	34.00

Lunch available
Evening meal 1900 (last orders 2100)
Parking for 7
Cards accepted: Access, Visa, Amex

HAWORTH
West Yorkshire
Map ref 4B1

This Pennine town is famous as home of the Bronte family. The Parsonage is now a Bronte Museum where furniture and possessions of the family are displayed. Moors and Bronte waterfalls nearby and steam trains on the Keighley and Worth Valley Railway pass through.
Tourist Information Centre ☎ *(01535) 642329*

The Apothecary Guest House & Tea Rooms
Listed APPROVED
86 Main Street, Haworth, Keighley BD22 8DA
☎ Keighley (01535) 643642
Fax (01535) 643642
At the top of Haworth Main Street opposite the famous Bronte church, 1 minute from the parsonage and moors.
Bedrooms: 1 single, 4 double, 2 twin, 1 triple
Bathrooms: 7 en-suite, 1 private

Bed & breakfast per night:	£min	£max
Single	17.00	19.00
Double	32.00	38.00

Parking for 7
Cards accepted: Access, Visa

Bronte Hotel
Listed
Lees Lane, Haworth, Keighley BD22 8RA
☎ Keighley (01535) 644112
Fax (01535) 646725
On the edge of the moors, 5 minutes' walk from the station and 15 minutes' walk to the parsonage, the former home of the Brontes.
Bedrooms: 3 single, 3 double, 2 twin, 3 triple
Bathrooms: 8 en-suite, 1 public

Bed & breakfast per night:	£min	£max
Single	20.00	30.00
Double	34.00	40.00

Lunch available
Evening meal 1900 (last orders 2130)
Parking for 30
Cards accepted: Access, Visa

Ferncliffe
COMMENDED
Hebden Road, Haworth, Keighley BD22 8RS
☎ Keighley (01535) 643405
Well-appointed, private hotel with panoramic views overlooking Haworth and the Worth Valley Steam Railway. Personal attention and good food.
Bedrooms: 2 single, 2 double, 1 twin, 1 triple
Bathrooms: 6 en-suite

Bed & breakfast per night:	£min	£max
Single	19.50	25.00
Double	39.00	50.00

Half board per person:	£min	£max
Daily	29.25	34.75
Weekly	204.75	243.25

Lunch available
Evening meal 1900 (last orders 2100)
Parking for 12
Cards accepted: Access, Visa

Old White Lion Hotel
COMMENDED
Haworth, Keighley BD22 8DU
☎ Keighley (01535) 642313
Fax (01535) 646222
Family-run, centuries old coaching inn. Candlelit restaurant using local fresh produce, cooked to order and featured in good food guides. Old world bars, popular with locals, serving home-made bar meals and traditional ales.
Bedrooms: 3 single, 8 double, 1 twin, 2 triple
Bathrooms: 14 en-suite

Bed & breakfast per night:	£min	£max
Single	38.50	45.00
Double	50.00	60.00

Half board per person:	£min	£max
Daily	37.00	52.00

Lunch available
Evening meal 1900 (last orders 2150)
Parking for 8
Cards accepted: Access, Visa, Diners, Amex

YORKSHIRE

HEBDEN BRIDGE
West Yorkshire
Map ref 4B1

Originally a small town on packhorse route, Hebden Bridge grew into a booming mill town in 18th C with rows of "up-and-down" houses of several storeys built against hillsides. Ancient "pace-egg play" custom held on Good Friday. Tourist Information Centre ☎ (01422) 843831

Carlton Hotel

HIGHLY COMMENDED

Albert Street, Hebden Bridge HX7 8ES
☎ (01422) 844400
Fax (01422) 843117
Victorian emporium converted and lovingly restored to provide comfort and tranquillity from the town set below. Varied and interesting shops to hand and excellent walking nearby.
Bedrooms: 4 single, 10 double, 4 twin
Bathrooms: 18 en-suite

Bed & breakfast per night:	£min	£max
Single	49.00	59.00
Double	65.00	75.00

Half board per person:	£min	£max
Daily	37.50	42.50

Lunch available
Evening meal 1900 (last orders 2130)
Cards accepted: Access, Visa, Amex, Switch/Delta

Redacre Mill

HIGHLY COMMENDED

Redacre, Mytholmroyd, Hebden Bridge HX7 5DQ
☎ Halifax (01422) 885563
Logis of Great Britain
Small country hotel once featured on "Wish You Were Here". Peaceful canalside location, convenient for Bronte country, South Pennines and the Yorkshire Dales.
Bedrooms: 3 double, 2 twin
Bathrooms: 5 en-suite, 1 public

Bed & breakfast per night:	£min	£max
Single	32.50	37.50
Double	45.00	50.00

Half board per person:	£min	£max
Daily	37.50
Weekly	230.00

Evening meal 1800 (last orders 2000)
Parking for 8
Cards accepted: Access, Visa

White Lion Hotel

COMMENDED

Bridge Gate, Hebden Bridge HX7 8EX
☎ (01422) 842197

Family-run inn, dating back to 1657, well known for a wide range of cask ales and good home-cooked food.
Bedrooms: 5 double, 2 twin, 1 triple, 2 family rooms
Bathrooms: 10 en-suite

Bed & breakfast per night:	£min	£max
Single	37.50	37.50
Double	40.00	50.00

Lunch available
Evening meal 1200 (last orders 2100)
Parking for 10
Cards accepted: Access, Visa

HELMSLEY
North Yorkshire
Map ref 5C3

Pretty town on the River Rye at the entrance to Ryedale and the North York Moors, with large square and remains of 12th C castle, several inns and All Saints' Church.

Black Swan Hotel

HIGHLY COMMENDED

Market Place, Helmsley, York YO6 5BJ
☎ (01439) 770466
Fax (01439) 770174
Forte
Charming old world inn in the market place adjacent to the parish church.
Bedrooms: 4 single, 23 double, 17 twin
Bathrooms: 44 en-suite

Half board per person:	£min	£max
Daily	64.00	89.00
Weekly	385.00	455.00

Lunch available
Evening meal 1930 (last orders 2130)
Parking for 60
Cards accepted: Access, Visa, Diners, Amex, Switch/Delta

The Crown Hotel

COMMENDED

Market Place, Helmsley, York YO6 5BJ
☎ (01439) 770297
16th C inn with a Jacobean dining room offering traditional country cooking. Special breaks available. Dogs welcome. Run by the same family for 36 years.
Bedrooms: 5 single, 4 double, 4 twin, 1 triple
Bathrooms: 12 en-suite, 1 public

Bed & breakfast per night:	£min	£max
Single	27.00	35.00
Double	54.00	70.00

Half board per person:	£min	£max
Daily	40.00	49.00
Weekly	270.00	295.00

Lunch available
Evening meal 1915 (last orders 2000)
Parking for 15
Cards accepted: Access, Visa

Pheasant Hotel

COMMENDED

Harome, Helmsley, York YO6 5JG
☎ (01439) 771241
Logis of Great Britain
In a quiet rural village, with a terrace and gardens overlooking the village pond. Oak-beamed bar in a former blacksmith's shop, English food and log fires. Children over 12 years are welcome. Heated indoor swimming pool.
Wheelchair access category 3
Bedrooms: 1 single, 5 double, 6 twin
Bathrooms: 12 en-suite

Half board per person:	£min	£max
Daily	52.00	62.00
Weekly	364.00	434.00

Lunch available
Evening meal 1930 (last orders 2030)
Parking for 20
Open March–December

YORKSHIRE

HELMSLEY
Continued

Stilworth House
⌂⌂ COMMENDED
1 Church Street, Helmsley, York YO6 5AD
☎ (01439) 771072 & 770507
Comfortable relaxed atmosphere in elegant Georgian town house off the market square of Helmsley. Pretty en-suite rooms with colour TV, hairdryer, tea/coffee facilities. Private car park.
Bedrooms: 3 double, 1 twin, 1 triple
Bathrooms: 5 en-suite

Bed & breakfast per night:

	£min	£max
Single	25.00	35.00
Double	35.00	50.00

Parking for 4

HORNSEA
East Riding of Yorkshire
Map ref 4D1

Small holiday town situated on strip of land bordering beach bordering North Sea and Hornsea Mere, a large natural freshwater lake. Some sailing and fishing permitted on protected nature reserve. Hornsea Pottery and retail "freeport" attract many visitors.

Merlstead Private Hotel M
⌂⌂ COMMENDED
59 Eastgate, Hornsea, North Humberside HU18 1NB
☎ (01964) 533068
Fax (01964) 536975
Large, well-built, family-run property offering comfortable, spacious accommodation with a warm and friendly atmosphere, close to the sea.
Bedrooms: 1 double, 3 twin, 1 triple
Bathrooms: 5 en-suite

Bed & breakfast per night:

	£min	£max
Single	30.00	32.00
Double	45.00	48.00

Half board per person:

	£min	£max
Daily	42.50	44.50
Weekly	255.00	420.00

Lunch available
Evening meal 1700 (last orders 1900)
Parking for 4
Cards accepted: Access, Visa

HOWDEN
East Riding of Yorkshire
Map ref 4C1

Small town near the River Ouse, dominated by partly-ruined medieval church of St Peter's which has ancient origins but has been rebuilt in a range of architectural styles over the centuries.

Wellington Hotel M
⌂⌂ COMMENDED
31 Bridgegate, Howden, East Yorkshire DN14 7JG
☎ (01430) 430258
Fax (01430) 432139
16th C coaching inn with modern facilities in historic market town. Popular restaurant, bars and beer garden. Ideal for business or pleasure.
Bedrooms: 3 single, 3 double, 4 twin
Bathrooms: 8 en-suite, 2 private

Bed & breakfast per night:

	£min	£max
Single	20.00	29.50
Double	30.00	39.50

Lunch available
Evening meal 1830 (last orders 2200)
Parking for 60
Cards accepted: Access, Visa, Amex

HUDDERSFIELD
West Yorkshire
Map ref 4B1

Founded on wool and cloth, has a famous choral society. Town centre redeveloped, but several good Victorian buildings remain, including railway station, St Peter's Church, Tolson Memorial Museum, art gallery and nearby Colne Valley Museum.
Tourist Information Centre ☎ (01484) 430808

Ashfield Hotel M
⌂ COMMENDED
93 New North Road, Huddersfield HD1 5ND
☎ (01484) 425916
Fax (01484) 425916
Family-run licensed hotel with emphasis on home-cooked food and friendly service. Half a mile from the town centre and within 2 miles of the M62.
Bedrooms: 6 single, 3 double, 2 twin, 3 triple
Bathrooms: 4 en-suite, 3 public, 3 private showers

Bed & breakfast per night:

	£min	£max
Single	20.00	27.00
Double	34.00	42.00

Half board per person:

	£min	£max
Daily	25.00	32.00
Weekly	175.00	224.00

Evening meal 1830 (last orders 2000)
Parking for 20
Cards accepted: Access, Visa, Diners, Amex

Elm Crest Hotel M
⌂⌂ COMMENDED
2 Queens Road, Edgerton, Huddersfield HD2 2AG
☎ (01484) 530990 & (0421) 458479
Fax (01484) 516227
Logis of Great Britain
Victorian residence with Victorian charm and quality, 1 mile from the town centre and 2 miles from M62.
Bedrooms: 3 single, 1 double, 3 twin, 1 triple
Bathrooms: 5 en-suite, 1 private, 2 public

Bed & breakfast per night:

	£min	£max
Single	25.00	32.00
Double	45.00	57.00

Half board per person:

	£min	£max
Daily	40.00	47.00
Weekly	200.00	300.00

Lunch available
Evening meal 1800 (last orders 2100)
Parking for 12
Cards accepted: Access, Visa, Diners, Amex, Switch/Delta

Huddersfield Hotel and Rosemary Lane Bistro M
⌂⌂⌂ COMMENDED
33-47 Kirkgate, Huddersfield HD1 1QT
☎ (01484) 512111
Fax (01484) 435262
Past winner of "Yorkshire In Bloom". Free secure car park. Continental-style brasserie, traditional pub and nightclub within the complex. Renowned for friendliness.
Bedrooms: 20 single, 16 double, 6 twin, 3 triple, 1 family room
Bathrooms: 46 en-suite

Bed & breakfast per night:

	£min	£max
Single	30.00	49.00
Double	40.00	69.00

YORKSHIRE

Half board per person:	£min	£max
Daily	45.00	60.00

Lunch available
Evening meal 1800 (last orders 2300)
Parking for 120
Cards accepted: Access, Visa, Diners, Amex, Switch/Delta

Old Golf House Hotel
COMMENDED

New Hey Road, Outlane, Huddersfield HD3 3YP
☎ Elland (01422) 379211
Fax (01422) 372694
Whitbread
Stone-built hotel with conference facilities, set in 3 acres of gardens adjacent to the M62. Full restaurant/bar food available.
Bedrooms: 1 single, 31 double, 13 twin, 4 triple
Suites available
Bathrooms: 49 en-suite

Bed & breakfast per night:	£min	£max
Single	25.00	74.50
Double	50.00	82.00

Half board per person:	£min	£max
Daily	36.00	89.50
Weekly	312.00	630.00

Lunch available
Evening meal 1900 (last orders 2200)
Parking for 108
Cards accepted: Access, Visa, Diners, Amex, Switch/Delta

HULL
Kingston upon Hull
Map ref 4C1

Busy seaport with a modern city centre and excellent shopping facilities. Maritime traditions in the town, docks museum, and the home of William Wilberforce, the slavery abolitionist, whose house is now a museum. The Humber Bridge is 5 miles west.
Tourist Information Centre ☎ (01482) 223559 or 223344 or 702118

Kingstown Hotel
HIGHLY COMMENDED

Hull Road, Hedon, Hull HU12 8DJ
☎ (01482) 890461
Fax (01482) 890713
Family-run hotel, stylish, select and very friendly. Ideally placed for visiting Hull

and historic Holderness with its seaside resorts of Hornsea and Withernsea.
Wheelchair access category 1
Bedrooms: 10 single, 19 double, 5 twin
Bathrooms: 34 en-suite

Bed & breakfast per night:	£min	£max
Single	45.00	72.00
Double	55.00	85.00

Half board per person:	£min	£max
Daily	60.95	
Weekly	383.00	

Lunch available
Evening meal 1900 (last orders 2200)
Parking for 96
Cards accepted: Access, Visa, Amex, Switch/Delta

Pearson Park Hotel
APPROVED

Pearson Park, Hull HU5 2TQ
☎ (01482) 343043
Fax (01482) 447679
The Independents
Tastefully converted Victorian villas just outside central area, in a delightful park with bowling greens and conservatory. Under same ownership since 1967.
Bedrooms: 9 single, 16 double, 6 twin, 1 family room
Bathrooms: 32 en-suite

Bed & breakfast per night:	£min	£max
Single	39.00	45.00
Double	45.00	60.00

Half board per person:	£min	£max
Daily	50.00	56.00

Lunch available
Evening meal 1830 (last orders 2100)
Parking for 30
Cards accepted: Access, Visa, Diners, Amex

The symbol **CR** and a group name following an hotel address indicates that bookings can be made through a central reservations office. These offices are listed in the information pages at the back of this guide.

ILKLEY
West Yorkshire
Map ref 4B1

This moorland town is famous for its ballad. The 16th C manor house, now a museum, displays local prehistoric and Roman relics. Popular walk leads up Heber's Ghyll to Ilkley Moor, with the mysterious Swastika Stone and White Wells, 18th C plunge baths.
Tourist Information Centre ☎ (01943) 602319

Crescent Hotel
COMMENDED

Brook Street, Ilkley LS29 8DG
☎ (01943) 600012 & 600062
Fax (01943) 607186
Fully modernised hotel with family rooms and self-catering suites. In a central position in town. Convenient for the dales. Meals can also be provided for residents at The Box Tree, an award-winning restaurant.
Bedrooms: 1 single, 4 double, 15 twin
Bathrooms: 20 en-suite

Bed & breakfast per night:	£min	£max
Single	46.00	55.00
Double	60.00	72.00

Half board per person:	£min	£max
Daily	56.00	65.00

Lunch available
Evening meal 1830 (last orders 2045)
Parking for 25
Cards accepted: Access, Visa, Amex

Grove Hotel
COMMENDED

66 The Grove, Ilkley LS29 9PA
☎ (01943) 600298
Fax (01943) 600298
Small, friendly, private hotel offering well-appointed accommodation. Convenient for Ilkley town centre, shops and gardens. Short breaks available all year.
Bedrooms: 1 single, 3 double, 2 triple
Bathrooms: 6 en-suite, 1 public

Bed & breakfast per night:	£min	£max
Single	30.00	42.00
Double	40.00	54.00

Half board per person:	£min	£max
Daily	32.00	56.00

Continued ▶

YORKSHIRE

ILKLEY
Continued

Lunch available
Evening meal 1900 (last orders 1930)
Parking for 5
Cards accepted: Access, Visa, Diners, Amex, Switch/Delta

Moorview Hotel
COMMENDED

104 Skipton Road, Ilkley LS29 9HE
☎ (01943) 600156 & 816572

Imposing Victorian villa on bank of River Wharfe, at start of the Dales Way. Ideal touring centre for dales and Bronte country. Ample parking.
Bedrooms: 1 single, 4 double, 2 twin, 2 triple, 4 family rooms
Bathrooms: 7 en-suite, 2 private, 3 public

Bed & breakfast per night:	£min	£max
Single	25.00	38.00
Double	40.00	50.00

Half board per person:	£min	£max
Daily	35.00	45.00
Weekly	150.00	175.00

Evening meal 1900 (last orders 2100)
Parking for 15
Cards accepted: Access, Visa, Switch/Delta

Rombalds Hotel and Restaurant
HIGHLY COMMENDED

West View, Wells Road, Ilkley LS29 9JG
☎ (01943) 603201
Fax (01943) 816586

Elegant Georgian restoration on the edge of Ilkley Moor, 600 yards from the town centre. Restaurant.
Bedrooms: 3 single, 5 double, 2 twin, 5 family
Suites available
Bathrooms: 15 en-suite

Bed & breakfast per night:	£min	£max
Single	50.00	95.00
Double	70.00	110.00

Half board per person:	£min	£max
Daily	62.50	107.50
Weekly	375.00	645.00

Lunch available
Evening meal 1900 (last orders 2130)
Parking for 22
Cards accepted: Access, Visa, Diners, Amex, Switch/Delta

INGLETON
North Yorkshire
Map ref 5B3

Thriving tourist centre for fell-walkers, climbers and pot-holers. Popular walks up beautiful Twiss Valley to Ingleborough Summit, Whernside, White Scar Caves and waterfalls.

Bridge End Guest House
COMMENDED

Mill Lane, Ingleton, Carnforth, Lancashire LA6 3EP
☎ (015242) 41413

Georgian house pleasantly situated adjacent to the entrance to the waterfalls walk. It features a cantilevered patio over the River Doe and retains an elegant staircase. All rooms en-suite. Vegetarians welcome.
Bedrooms: 1 single, 1 double, 1 triple
Bathrooms: 3 en-suite

Bed & breakfast per night:	£min	£max
Single	19.00	20.00
Double	34.00	36.00

Half board per person:	£min	£max
Daily	24.00	29.00
Weekly	159.00	185.00

Lunch available
Evening meal 1830 (last orders 2030)
Parking for 10

Ferncliffe Guest House
COMMENDED

55 Main Street, Ingleton, Carnforth, Lancashire LA6 3HJ
☎ (015242) 42405

Lovely detached Victorian house in quiet location, with a growing reputation for good food and high standard of accommodation. All rooms en-suite.
Bedrooms: 1 double, 4 twin
Bathrooms: 5 en-suite

Bed & breakfast per night:	£min	£max
Single	28.00	28.00
Double	44.00	44.00

Half board per person:	£min	£max
Daily	34.50	40.50
Weekly	218.00	255.00

Evening meal 1830 (last orders 2030)
Parking for 4
Open February–October

Ingleborough View
COMMENDED

Main Street, Ingleton, Carnforth, Lancashire LA6 3HH
☎ (015242) 41523

Small, friendly guesthouse offering very comfortable accommodation. Panoramic views of river and mountain. Ideally situated for local walks, touring dales/Lake District.
Bedrooms: 3 double, 1 twin
Bathrooms: 2 en-suite, 2 private

Bed & breakfast per night:	£min	£max
Single	20.00	25.00
Double	36.00	38.00

Parking for 4

Langber Country Guest House

Tatterthorne Road, Ingleton, Carnforth LA6 3DT
☎ (015242) 41587

Detached country house in hilltop position with panoramic views. Good touring centre for dales, lakes and coast. Comfortable accommodation. Friendly service - everyone welcome.
Bedrooms: 1 single, 2 double, 1 twin, 2 triple, 1 family room
Bathrooms: 4 en-suite, 1 public

Bed & breakfast per night:	£min	£max
Single	15.50	25.00
Double	29.50	43.00

Half board per person:	£min	£max
Daily	22.00	28.00
Weekly	142.00	165.00

YORKSHIRE

Evening meal 1830 (last orders 1700)
Parking for 6

Springfield Private Hotel
APPROVED

Main Street, Ingleton, Carnforth, Lancashire LA6 3HJ
☎ (015242) 41280
Detached Victorian villa in its own grounds with a fountain and conservatory. Private fishing.
Bedrooms: 3 double, 1 twin, 1 family room
Bathrooms: 5 en-suite, 1 public

Bed & breakfast per night:	£min	£max
Single	20.00	22.00
Double	40.00	44.00

Half board per person:	£min	£max
Daily	30.00	32.00
Weekly	182.00	196.00

Evening meal 1830 (last orders 1700)
Parking for 12

KEIGHLEY
West Yorkshire
Map ref 4B1

Pleasant Victorian town where Charlotte Bronte used to shop. Cliffe Castle is an art gallery and museum with large collection of Victorian bygones. 17th C East Riddlesden Hall (National Trust) has fine medieval tithe barn. Trips on Keighley and Worth Valley Railway.

Dalesgate Hotel
COMMENDED

406 Skipton Road, Utley, Keighley BD20 6HP
☎ (01535) 664930
Fax (01535) 611253
Charming, family-run hotel near the town. Ideal tourist area for the dales, Haworth, York and the steam railways.
Bedrooms: 7 single, 9 double, 4 twin
Bathrooms: 20 en-suite

Bed & breakfast per night:	£min	£max
Single	30.00	42.00
Double	50.00	60.00

Half board per person:	£min	£max
Daily	36.00	42.00
Weekly	252.00	294.00

Evening meal 1900 (last orders 2100)

Parking for 22
Cards accepted: Access, Visa, Diners, Amex

KIRKBYMOORSIDE
North Yorkshire
Map ref 5C3

Attractive market town with remains of Norman castle. Good centre for exploring moors. Nearby are wild daffodils of Farndale.

George & Dragon Hotel
COMMENDED

Market Place, Kirkbymoorside, York YO6 6AA
☎ (01751) 433334
Fax (01751) 433334
Inn of character adjacent to the North York Moors. Extensively modernised bedrooms, all with colour TV, en-suite bathrooms. Ideal touring location. Good Pub Guide "Newcomer of the Year Award 1995". Half board prices based on minimum 2-night stay.
Bedrooms: 1 single, 12 double, 3 twin, 2 triple, 1 family room
Bathrooms: 19 en-suite

Bed & breakfast per night:	£min	£max
Single	45.00	49.00
Double	72.00	83.00

Half board per person:	£min	£max
Daily	46.75	52.00

Lunch available
Evening meal 1900 (last orders 2130)
Parking for 20
Cards accepted: Access, Visa, Switch/Delta

KNARESBOROUGH
North Yorkshire
Map ref 4B1

Picturesque market town on the River Nidd, famous for its 11th C castle ruins, overlooking town and river gorge. Attractions include oldest chemist's shop in country, prophetess Mother Shipton's cave, Dropping Well and Court House Museum. Boating on river.

Dower House Hotel
COMMENDED

Bond End, Knaresborough HG5 9AL
☎ Harrogate (01423) 863302
Fax (01423) 867665
Best Western
This gracious Grade II listed country house, only 10 minutes from Harrogate, combines traditional hospitality and modern comfort. Perfect base from which to explore historic York, Castle Howard and Harewood House and to discover Herriot and Bronte countryside. Excellent leisure facilities.
Bedrooms: 5 single, 11 double, 16 twin
Suite available
Bathrooms: 32 en-suite

Bed & breakfast per night:	£min	£max
Single	50.00	65.00
Double	75.00	90.00

Half board per person:	£min	£max
Daily	52.00	55.00

Evening meal 1900 (last orders 2130)
Parking for 80
Cards accepted: Access, Visa, Diners, Amex, Switch/Delta

Ebor Mount
COMMENDED

18 York Place, Knaresborough HG5 0AA
☎ Harrogate (01423) 863315
Fax (01423) 863315
Charming 18th C townhouse with private car park, providing bed and breakfast accommodation in recently refurbished rooms. Ideal touring centre.
Bedrooms: 1 single, 4 double, 1 twin, 2 triple
Bathrooms: 8 en-suite, 1 public

Bed & breakfast per night:	£min	£max
Single	18.00	35.00
Double	36.00	40.00

Parking for 10
Cards accepted: Access, Visa

General Tarleton Inn
COMMENDED

Boroughbridge Road, Ferrensby, Knaresborough HG5 0QB
☎ Harrogate (01423) 340284
Fax (01423) 340288

Continued ▶

103

YORKSHIRE

KNARESBOROUGH
Continued

All rooms elegantly furnished. Freehouse, traditional ales. Warm family welcome.
Bedrooms: 3 double, 12 twin
Bathrooms: 15 en-suite

Bed & breakfast per night:	£min	£max
Single	25.00	27.50
Double	50.00	60.00

Half board per person:	£min	£max
Daily	35.00	40.00
Weekly	227.50	262.50

Lunch available
Evening meal 1800 (last orders 2200)
Parking for 100
Cards accepted: Access, Visa, Switch/Delta

Newton House Hotel
COMMENDED

5-7 York Place, Knaresborough HG5 0AD
☎ Harrogate (01423) 863539
Fax (01423) 869748
Charming, family-run, 17th C former coaching inn, situated 2 minutes' walk from the market square, castle and river. 10 minutes Harrogate, 20 minutes York, 30 minutes the dales.
Bedrooms: 1 single, 6 double, 3 twin, 2 triple
Bathrooms: 11 en-suite, 1 private

Bed & breakfast per night:	£min	£max
Single	32.50	37.50
Double	50.00	60.00

Half board per person:	£min	£max
Daily	35.00	49.50
Weekly	220.00	262.00

Evening meal 1900 (last orders 2030)
Parking for 10
Cards accepted: Access, Visa, Switch/Delta

ACCESSIBILITY
Look for the symbols which indicate accessibility for wheelchair users. These are described in detail at the front of this guide.

LEEDS
West Yorkshire
Map ref 4B1

Large city with excellent modern shopping centre and splendid Victorian architecture. Museums and galleries including Temple Newsam House (the Hampton Court of the North), Tetley's Brewery Wharf and the Royal Armouries Museum; also home of Opera North.
Tourist Information Centre ☎ (0113) 242 5242

Adriatic Hotel
APPROVED

87 Harehills Avenue, Leeds LS8 4ET
☎ (0113) 262 0115
Fax (0113) 262 6071
Hotel with a warm and friendly atmosphere, providing a high standard of accommodation and service. All rooms en-suite. A la carte restaurant and lounge bar.
Bedrooms: 10 single, 1 double, 13 twin, 3 triple
Bathrooms: 27 en-suite

Bed & breakfast per night:	£min	£max
Single	25.00	35.00
Double	35.00	45.00

Lunch available
Evening meal 1830 (last orders 2200)
Parking for 50
Cards accepted: Access, Visa, Diners, Amex, Switch/Delta

Aintree Hotel
COMMENDED

38 Cardigan Road, Headingley, Leeds LS6 3AG
☎ (0113) 275 8290
Small, comfortable licensed family hotel in tree-lined road, overlooking Headingley Cricket Ground. Close to university, public transport and shopping centre, 1.5 miles from city centre.
Bedrooms: 4 single, 4 double, 2 twin
Bathrooms: 6 en-suite, 2 public

Bed & breakfast per night:	£min	£max
Single	23.00	30.00
Double	35.00	40.00

Half board per person:	£min	£max
Daily	28.00	30.50

Evening meal 1800 (last orders 1000)
Parking for 10
Cards accepted: Access, Visa

Aragon Hotel

250 Stainbeck Lane, Leeds LS7 2PS
☎ (0113) 275 9306
Fax (0113) 275 7166
The Independents
Converted, late Victorian house in quiet, wooded surroundings, 2 miles from the city centre. TV, telephone and tea-making facilities in all bedrooms. Weekly half board rates negotiable.
Bedrooms: 3 single, 7 double, 3 twin
Bathrooms: 11 en-suite, 2 public

Bed & breakfast per night:	£min	£max
Single	26.75	39.95
Double	42.00	48.95

Half board per person:	£min	£max
Daily	30.00	44.95

Evening meal 1900 (last orders 2100)
Parking for 27
Cards accepted: Access, Visa, Diners, Amex

Broomhurst Hotel
COMMENDED

12 Chapel Lane, Off Cardigan Road, Headingley, Leeds LS6 3BW
☎ (0113) 278 6836 & 278 5764
Fax (0113) 230 7099
Small, comfortable, owner-run hotel in a quiet, pleasantly wooded conservation area, 1.5 miles from the city centre. Convenient for Yorkshire County Cricket Ground and university.
Bedrooms: 8 single, 4 double, 2 twin, 2 triple, 2 family rooms
Bathrooms: 12 en-suite, 3 public

Bed & breakfast per night:	£min	£max
Single	23.50	33.50
Double	35.00	45.00

Half board per person:	£min	£max
Daily	28.00	33.00
Weekly	110.30	148.10

Lunch available
Evening meal 1800 (last orders 0900)
Parking for 16
Cards accepted: Access, Visa, Diners, Switch/Delta

Cardigan Private Hotel
Listed

36 Cardigan Road, Headingley, Leeds LS6 3AG
☎ (0113) 278 4301
Fax (0113) 230 7792

YORKSHIRE

Family-run hotel, next to Headingley Cricket/Rugby League Ground. Near public transport and shopping facilities, 1.5 miles from city centre. Evening meals available Monday to Thursday only.
Bedrooms: 5 single, 1 double, 2 twin, 1 triple, 1 family room
Bathrooms: 6 en-suite, 2 public

Bed & breakfast per night:	£min	£max
Single	25.00	36.00
Double	35.00	46.00

Half board per person:	£min	£max
Daily	35.00	46.00

Evening meal from 1830
Parking for 11

Harewood Arms Hotel
HIGHLY COMMENDED
Harrogate Road, Harewood, Leeds LS17 9LH
☎ (0113) 288 6566
Fax (0113) 288 6064
Stone-built hotel and restaurant of character with a rural aspect, 8 miles from Harrogate and Leeds. Opposite Harewood House and close to all amenities, including golf and racing.
Bedrooms: 2 single, 10 double, 10 twin, 2 triple
Bathrooms: 24 en-suite

Bed & breakfast per night:	£min	£max
Single	45.00	65.00
Double	60.00	78.00

Half board per person:	£min	£max
Daily	59.95	80.95

Lunch available
Evening meal 1900 (last orders 2200)
Parking for 60
Cards accepted: Access, Visa, Diners, Amex, Switch/Delta

Pinewood Hotel
COMMENDED
78 Potternewton Lane, Leeds LS7 3LW
☎ (0113) 262 2561 & 262 8485

Extremely attractively decorated and very well furnished, with many extra touches enhancing guests' comfort. A most comfortable welcome in a small hotel of distinction.
Bedrooms: 5 single, 3 double, 2 twin
Bathrooms: 10 en-suite

Bed & breakfast per night:	£min	£max
Single	35.00	40.00
Double	42.00	51.00

Half board per person:	£min	£max
Daily	31.00	50.00
Weekly	199.00	270.00

Evening meal 1830 (last orders 1000)
Cards accepted: Access, Visa, Amex

St Michael's Tower Hotel
5 St Michael's Villas, Cardigan Road, Headingley, Leeds LS6 3AF
☎ (0113) 275 5557 & 275 6039
Fax (0113) 230 7491
Comfortable, owner-run licensed hotel, 1.5 miles from city centre and close to Headingley Cricket Ground and university. Easy access to Yorkshire countryside.
Bedrooms: 7 single, 7 double, 7 twin, 2 triple, 1 family room
Bathrooms: 16 en-suite, 4 public

Bed & breakfast per night:	£min	£max
Single	22.00	29.00
Double	34.00	39.00

Half board per person:	£min	£max
Daily	26.00	29.00
Weekly	108.00	122.85

Evening meal 1830 (last orders 2000)
Parking for 26
Cards accepted: Access, Visa

De Vere Oulton Hall
HIGHLY COMMENDED
Rothwell Lane, Oulton, Woodlesford, Leeds LS26 8HN
☎ (0113) 282 1000
Fax (0113) 282 8066

Fully renovated hall in the heart of Yorkshire south-east of Leeds, adjacent to a golf course. Full leisure club.
Bedrooms: 88 double, 64 twin
Suites available
Bathrooms: 152 en-suite

Bed & breakfast per night:	£min	£max
Single	115.00	225.00
Double	125.00	225.00

Half board per person:	£min	£max
Daily	70.00	136.50

Lunch available
Evening meal 1900 (last orders 2200)
Parking for 220
Cards accepted: Access, Visa, Diners, Amex

LEEDS/BRADFORD AIRPORT
See under Bingley, Bradford, Leeds, Pool in Wharfedale

LEEMING BAR
North Yorkshire
Map ref 5C3

Just off the A1 between dales and moors.

White Rose Hotel
COMMENDED
Leeming Bar, Northallerton DL7 9AY
☎ Bedale (01677) 422707 & 424941
Fax (01677) 425123
Family-run private hotel and restaurant ideally situated in village half a mile from A1 motorway. Central for Yorkshire Dales, "Heartbeat" country, coastal resorts. Pets welcome.
Bedrooms: 9 single, 1 double, 6 twin, 2 triple
Bathrooms: 18 en-suite

Bed & breakfast per night:	£min	£max
Single	31.00	32.00
Double	45.00	46.00

Half board per person:	£min	£max
Daily	35.50	44.00
Weekly	248.50	308.00

Lunch available
Evening meal 1930 (last orders 2145)
Parking for 40
Cards accepted: Access, Visa, Diners, Amex, Switch/Delta

> Establishments should be open throughout the year, unless otherwise stated.

YORKSHIRE

LEYBURN
North Yorkshire
Map ref 5B3

Attractive dales market town where Mary Queen of Scots was reputedly captured after her escape from Bolton Castle. Fine views over Wensleydale from nearby.
Tourist Information Centre ☎ (01969) 623069 or 622773

Secret Garden House
COMMENDED

Grove Square, Leyburn DL8 5AE
☎ Wensleydale (01969) 623589
Georgian house with secluded walled garden and conservatory, in market town, the heart of James Herriot country. Free off-street parking.
Bedrooms: 2 double, 2 twin
Bathrooms: 4 en-suite, 1 public
Bed & breakfast
per night: £min £max
Single 18.00 25.00
Double 36.00 50.00
Evening meal 1930 (last orders 2000)
Parking for 10
Cards accepted: Access, Visa

White Swan Hotel
COMMENDED

Market Place, Middleham, Leyburn DL8 4PE
☎ Wensleydale (01969) 622093
Refurbished Georgian coaching inn, near the castle, offering all en-suite bedrooms, excellent cuisine and personal service. In the heart of the Yorkshire Dales - an ideal base for touring.
Bedrooms: 4 double, 1 twin, 2 triple
Bathrooms: 3 en-suite, 1 public
Bed & breakfast
per night: £min £max
Single 26.50 29.50
Double 43.00 49.00
Half board per person: £min £max
Daily 34.50 42.50
Weekly 224.00 245.00
Lunch available
Evening meal 1900 (last orders 2130)
Parking for 6
Cards accepted: Access, Visa

LIVERSEDGE
West Yorkshire
Map ref 4B1

Typical West Yorkshire town 3 miles north-west of Dewsbury.

Geordie Pride Lodge Hotel

112 Roberttown Lane, Roberttown, Liversedge WF15 7LZ
☎ Heckmondwike (01924) 402069
Fax (01924) 410136
Two miles from M62 and perfectly placed for both "Summer Wine" country and Yorkshire Dales. 7 miles from Leeds, Huddersfield and Bradford.
Bedrooms: 8 single, 6 double
Bathrooms: 14 en-suite
Bed & breakfast
per night: £min £max
Single 37.50 42.50
Double 42.50 50.00
Half board per person: £min £max
Daily 50.00
Weekly 300.00
Lunch available
Evening meal 1830 (last orders 2200)
Parking for 51
Cards accepted: Access, Visa, Amex, Switch/Delta

Healds Hall Hotel
COMMENDED

Leeds Road, Liversedge WF15 6JA
☎ Heckmondwike (01924) 409112
Fax (01924) 401895

Family-run hotel with award-winning restaurant. Large gardens. On A62, near M1 and M62. Ideal for dales. Special weekend breaks available.
Bedrooms: 7 single, 10 double, 4 twin, 4 triple
Bathrooms: 25 en-suite
Bed & breakfast
per night: £min £max
Single 30.00 53.00
Double 50.00 75.00
Half board per person: £min £max
Daily 35.00 68.00
Weekly 245.00 525.00

Lunch available
Evening meal 1900 (last orders 2100)
Parking for 60
Cards accepted: Access, Visa, Diners, Amex, Switch/Delta

MALHAM
North Yorkshire
Map ref 5B3

Hamlet of stone cottages amid magnificent rugged limestone scenery in the Yorkshire Dales National Park. Malham Cove is a curving, sheer white cliff 240 ft high. Malham Tarn, one of Yorkshire's few natural lakes, belongs to the National Trust. National Park Centre.

Beck Hall Guest House
APPROVED

Malham, Skipton BD23 4DJ
☎ Settle (01729) 830332
Family-run guesthouse set in a spacious riverside garden. Homely atmosphere, four-poster beds, log fires and home cooking.
Bedrooms: 11 double, 3 twin
Bathrooms: 9 en-suite, 2 private, 1 public
Bed & breakfast
per night: £min £max
Single 20.00 25.00
Double 31.00 39.00
Half board per person: £min £max
Daily 22.45 26.45
Lunch available
Evening meal 1900 (last orders 2000)
Parking for 30

Half board prices are given per person, but in some cases these may be based on double/twin occupancy.

Information on accommodation listed in this guide has been supplied by the proprietors. As changes may occur you are advised to check details at the time of booking.

YORKSHIRE

MALTON

North Yorkshire
Map ref 5D3

Thriving farming town on the River Derwent with large livestock market. Famous for racehorse training. The local museum has Roman remains and the Eden Camp Modern History Theme Museum transports visitors back to wartime Britain. Castle Howard within easy reach.
Tourist Information Centre ☎ (01653) 600048

Newstead Grange
HIGHLY COMMENDED

Norton, Malton YO17 9PJ
☎ (01653) 692502
Fax (01653) 696951
Elegant Georgian country house in 2.5 acres, 1.5 miles from Malton on the Beverley road. Antique furniture. Non-smoking establishment. Children 12 years and over and sometimes younger children by arrangement.
Bedrooms: 4 double, 4 twin
Bathrooms: 8 en-suite

Bed & breakfast per night:

	£min	£max
Single	36.50	41.00
Double	63.00	75.00

Half board per person:

	£min	£max
Daily	41.00	56.00
Weekly	250.00	320.00

Evening meal 1930 (last orders 1945)
Parking for 15
Open February–November
Cards accepted: Access, Visa

Wentworth Arms Hotel
APPROVED

Town Street, Old Malton, Malton YO17 0HD
☎ (01653) 692618
Former coaching inn, built early 1700s and run by the same family for 100 years. 20 miles from York. An excellent base for touring the Yorkshire Dales, North York Moors and the East Coast.
Bedrooms: 3 double, 2 twin
Bathrooms: 4 en-suite, 1 public

Bed & breakfast per night:

	£min	£max
Single	23.00	
Double	46.00	

Please mention this guide when making your booking.

Lunch available
Evening meal 1800 (last orders 2045)
Parking for 30
Cards accepted: Access, Visa

MIDDLEHAM

North Yorkshire
Map ref 5C3

Town famous for racehorse training, with cobbled squares and houses of local stone. Norman castle, once principal residence of Warwick the Kingmaker and later Richard III. Ruins of Jervaulx Abbey nearby.

Black Swan Hotel
COMMENDED

Market Place, Middleham DL8 4NP
☎ Wensleydale (01969) 622221
Unspoilt 17th C inn, with open fires and beamed ceilings, allied to 20th C comforts. Emphasis on food.
Bedrooms: 1 single, 4 double, 1 twin, 1 triple
Bathrooms: 7 en-suite

Bed & breakfast per night:

	£min	£max
Single	26.00	30.00
Double	46.00	62.00

Half board per person:

	£min	£max
Daily	32.50	38.50

Lunch available
Evening meal 1830 (last orders 2100)
Parking for 3
Cards accepted: Access, Visa

Millers House Hotel
HIGHLY COMMENDED

Market Place, Middleham, Leyburn DL8 4NR
☎ Wensleydale (01969) 622630
Fax (01969) 623570
Elegant Georgian country house in peaceful village in the heart of Herriot's Yorkshire Dales. Charming en-suite rooms and four-poster, colour TV, telephone, tea/coffee facilities. 20 minutes from A1. 1994 Runner-up in Yorkshire & Humberside Tourist Board's "Hotel of the Year" competition.
Bedrooms: 1 single, 3 double, 3 twin
Bathrooms: 6 en-suite, 1 private

Bed & breakfast per night:

	£min	£max
Single	36.50	88.00
Double	73.00	90.00

Half board per person:

	£min	£max
Daily	54.00	63.00
Weekly	340.00	400.00

Evening meal 1915 (last orders 2030)
Parking for 8
Open February–December
Cards accepted: Access, Visa, Switch/Delta

MONK FRYSTON

North Yorkshire
Map ref 4C1

Village dating back to Saxon times. The prefix "Monk" denotes its former ownership by monks of Selby Abbey. Interesting church, lodge and several early thatched cottages.

Monk Fryston Hall Hotel

Monk Fryston, Leeds LS25 5DU
☎ South Milford (01977) 682369
Fax (01977) 683544
Old manor house with peaceful, comfortable accommodation on the A63 just off the A1. Friendly atmosphere and English cooking. Weekend half board reduction for minimum 2-night stay.
Bedrooms: 5 single, 15 double, 6 twin, 2 triple
Bathrooms: 28 en-suite

Bed & breakfast per night:

	£min	£max
Single	68.50	72.00
Double	95.00	102.00

Half board per person:

	£min	£max
Daily	75.00	85.00

Lunch available
Evening meal 1900 (last orders 2130)
Parking for 60
Cards accepted: Access, Visa, Amex, Switch/Delta

The symbols in each entry give information about services and facilities. A 'key' to these symbols appears at the back of this guide.

YORKSHIRE

MORLEY
West Yorkshire
Map ref 4B1

On the outskirts of Leeds, just off the M62 and close to the M1. The Town Hall dominates the town.

Old Vicarage Guest House
COMMENDED

Bruntcliffe Road, Morley, Leeds
LS27 OJZ
☎ Leeds (0113) 253 2174
Fax (0113) 253 3549
Within minutes of motorways, providing a Yorkshire welcome with home comforts in an authentic Victorian setting. Weekend rates available.
Bedrooms: 12 single, 3 double, 2 twin
Bathrooms: 17 en-suite

Bed & breakfast per night:	£min	£max
Single	25.00	47.00
Double	40.00	62.00

Half board per person:	£min	£max
Daily	34.95	81.90

Evening meal 1800 (last orders 2030)
Parking for 21
Cards accepted: Access, Visa, Amex, Switch/Delta

NEWBY WISKE
North Yorkshire
Map ref 5C3

Village on the River Wiske in the Vale of Mowbray.

Solberge Hall
HIGHLY COMMENDED

Newby Wiske, Northallerton
DL7 9ER
☎ Northallerton (01609) 779191
Fax (01609) 780472
Best Western
Victorian country house in the heart of Herriot country, convenient for the moors and dales.
Bedrooms: 4 single, 16 double, 5 twin
Bathrooms: 25 en-suite

Bed & breakfast per night:	£min	£max
Single	60.00	70.00
Double	80.00	100.00

Half board per person:	£min	£max
Daily	61.00	71.00

Lunch available
Evening meal 1930 (last orders 2130)

Parking for 60
Cards accepted: Access, Visa, Diners, Amex, Switch/Delta

NORTHALLERTON
North Yorkshire
Map ref 5C3

Formerly a staging post on coaching route to the North and later a railway town. Today a lively market town and administrative capital of North Yorkshire. Parish church of All Saints dates from 1200.
Tourist Information Centre ☎ (01609) 776864

Alverton Guest House

26 South Parade, Northallerton
DL7 8SG
☎ (01609) 776207
Family-run guesthouse convenient for county town facilities and ideal for touring the dales, moors and coastal areas.
Bedrooms: 2 single, 1 double, 1 twin, 1 triple
Bathrooms: 3 en-suite, 1 public

Bed & breakfast per night:	£min	£max
Single	17.00	23.00
Double	35.00	38.00

Half board per person:	£min	£max
Daily	26.95	32.95
Weekly	183.00	230.00

Evening meal 1700 (last orders 1900)
Parking for 5

Porch House
HIGHLY COMMENDED

68 High Street, Northallerton
DL7 8EG
☎ (01609) 779831 & Mobile (0589) 776014

16th/17th C Grade II listed family house, with original beams, fireplaces and walled garden. Guests have included Charles I. Centrally positioned, ideal for discovering the Yorkshire Dales, moors and coast. Runner-up White Rose Award for Best B&B 1996.
Bedrooms: 1 single, 2 double, 1 twin
Bathrooms: 4 en-suite

Bed & breakfast per night:	£min	£max
Single	25.00	28.00
Double	36.00	42.00

Half board per person:	£min	£max
Daily	28.00	35.00
Weekly	200.00	250.00

Evening meal 1800 (last orders 1930)
Parking for 5

Sundial Hotel
APPROVED

Darlington Road, Northallerton
DL6 2XF
☎ (01609) 780525
Fax (01609) 780491
Elegantly appointed hotel for businessmen and tourists alike. Fireside cocktail lounge and restaurant, conference facilities. Facilities for disabled.
Wheelchair access category 3
Bedrooms: 3 double, 25 twin
Bathrooms: 28 en-suite

Bed & breakfast per night:	£min	£max
Single	45.00	50.00
Double	55.00	60.00

Lunch available
Evening meal 1900 (last orders 2200)
Parking for 100
Cards accepted: Access, Visa, Amex, Switch/Delta

PATELEY BRIDGE
North Yorkshire
Map ref 5C3

Small market town at centre of Upper Nidderdale. Flax and linen industries once flourished in this remote and beautiful setting.

Grassfields Country House Hotel
COMMENDED

Low Wath Road, Pateley Bridge, Harrogate HG3 5HL
☎ Harrogate (01423) 711412

The National Grading and Classification Scheme is explained in full at the back of this guide.

YORKSHIRE

Georgian building in 2 acres of lawns and trees, within level walking distance of Pateley Bridge. A fine wine cellar and wholesome Yorkshire food.
Bedrooms: 1 single, 4 double, 3 twin, 1 triple
Bathrooms: 9 en-suite

Bed & breakfast per night:	£min	£max
Double	40.00	55.00
Half board per person:	£min	£max
Daily	32.00	39.50

Evening meal 1900 (last orders 1845)
Parking for 15
Open February–November

Yorke Arms Hotel
HIGHLY COMMENDED

Ramsgill, Harrogate HG3 5RL
☎ Harrogate (01423) 755243
Fax (01423) 755243
Best Western
18th C hostelry on village green. In the heart of unspoilt Nidderdale at the head of Gouthwaite Reservoir Nature Reserve.
Bedrooms: 3 single, 3 double, 5 twin, 2 triple
Bathrooms: 13 en-suite

Bed & breakfast per night:	£min	£max
Single	35.00	45.00
Double	70.00	100.00
Half board per person:	£min	£max
Daily	42.00	65.00

Lunch available
Evening meal 1900 (last orders 2100)
Parking for 30
Cards accepted: Access, Visa, Switch/Delta

National gradings and classifications were correct at the time of going to press but are subject to change. Please check at the time of booking.

PICKERING
North Yorkshire
Map ref 5D3

Market town and tourist centre on edge of North York Moors. Parish church has complete set of 15th C wall paintings depicting lives of saints. Part of 12th C castle still stands. Beck Isle Museum. The North York Moors Railway begins here.
Tourist Information Centre ☎ (01751) 473791

Burgate House Hotel & Restaurant
COMMENDED

17 Burgate, Pickering YO18 7AU
☎ (01751) 473463
Quietly situated, close to town centre, station and castle. Quaint 17th C bar. Local reputation for interesting food. Victorian half tester and other antique bedsteads.
Bedrooms: 5 double, 1 twin
Bathrooms: 6 en-suite, 1 public

Bed & breakfast per night:	£min	£max
Single	20.00	30.00
Double	40.00	60.00
Half board per person:	£min	£max
Daily	31.00	42.00

Lunch available
Evening meal from 1900
Parking for 8
Cards accepted: Access, Visa

Cottage Leas Country Hotel
COMMENDED

Nova, Middleton, Pickering YO18 8PN
☎ (01751) 472129
Fax (01751) 474930
Delightful 18th C country hotel set in 2 acres of gardens surrounded by open countryside, close to moors and coast. Fine restaurant, log fire, warm hospitality.
Bedrooms: 7 double, 2 twin, 1 triple, 1 family room
Suite available
Bathrooms: 11 en-suite

Bed & breakfast per night:	£min	£max
Single	34.00	39.00
Double	68.00	70.00
Half board per person:	£min	£max
Daily	41.00	44.00
Weekly	265.00	279.00

Lunch available
Evening meal 1900 (last orders 2130)
Parking for 35
Cards accepted: Access, Visa

Forest & Vale Hotel
COMMENDED

Malton Road, Pickering YO18 7DL
☎ (01751) 472722
Fax (01751) 472972
Consort
Independently-owned Yorkshire stone manor house, comfortable yet elegant. Specialising in imaginative cuisine. Central for moors, coast and York.
Bedrooms: 2 single, 9 double, 3 twin, 3 triple
Bathrooms: 17 en-suite

Bed & breakfast per night:	£min	£max
Single	51.00	
Double	70.00	
Half board per person:	£min	£max
Daily	55.00	
Weekly	370.00	

Lunch available
Evening meal 1900 (last orders 2100)
Parking for 75
Cards accepted: Access, Visa, Diners, Amex

The Sinnington Country Hotel
HIGHLY COMMENDED

Sinnington, York YO6 6SQ
☎ (01751) 431577
Once an old coaching inn. Open fires and period furniture. In tranquil rural setting west of Pickering. Fishing, riding, golf and riverside walks close by. Antique four-poster suite. No smoking restaurant, bedrooms and residents' lounge. Sorry, no pets.
Bedrooms: 2 single, 6 double, 2 twin, 1 triple, 1 family room
Bathrooms: 11 en-suite, 1 private

Bed & breakfast per night:	£min	£max
Single	34.00	44.00
Double	44.00	62.00
Half board per person:	£min	£max
Daily	38.00	47.00

Lunch available
Evening meal 1830 (last orders 2130)
Parking for 30

Continued ▶

YORKSHIRE

PICKERING
Continued

Cards accepted: Access, Visa, Switch/Delta

POOL IN WHARFEDALE
West Yorkshire
Map ref 4B1

Monkman's Bistro with Bedrooms
HIGHLY COMMENDED

Pool Bank, Pool in Wharfedale, Otley LS21 1EH
☎ Leeds (0113) 284 1105
Fax (0113) 284 3115
Fine Georgian mansion 9 miles from Harrogate, Leeds and Bradford. Exceptionally warm welcome and renowned modern bistro cuisine.
Bedrooms: 1 single, 3 double, 2 twin
Bathrooms: 6 en-suite

Bed & breakfast per night:	£min	£max
Single	63.00	73.00
Double	73.00	83.00

Lunch available
Evening meal 1830 (last orders 2200)
Parking for 65
Cards accepted: Access, Visa, Switch/Delta

RAVENSCAR
North Yorkshire
Map ref 5D3

Splendidly-positioned small coastal resort with magnificent views over Robin Hood's Bay. Its Old Peak is the end of the famous Lyke Wake Walk or "corpse way".

Bide-a-While
Listed APPROVED

3 Loring Road, Ravenscar, Scarborough YO13 OLY
☎ Scarborough (01723) 870643
Small guesthouse offering clean, comfortable accommodation in a homely atmosphere. Home cooking with fresh produce. Sea views from all rooms. On the edge of North York Moors and ideal for exploring the dales.
Bedrooms: 1 double, 2 family rooms
Bathrooms: 1 public

Bed & breakfast per night:	£min	£max
Single	18.50	
Double	33.00	

Half board per person:	£min	£max
Daily	22.50	24.50
Weekly	147.00	161.00

Evening meal 1700 (last orders 1830)
Parking for 6

Crag Hill
APPROVED

Ravenhall Road, Ravenscar, Scarborough YO13 ONA
☎ Scarborough (01723) 870925
Magnificent coastal views. Golf and pony trekking available locally. TV in all rooms. Ideal for walking and touring. Please send for brochure.
Bedrooms: 3 double, 2 twin, 2 family rooms
Bathrooms: 4 en-suite, 1 public

Bed & breakfast per night:	£min	£max
Single	25.00	30.00
Double	32.00	40.00

Half board per person:	£min	£max
Daily	25.00	29.00
Weekly	168.00	195.00

Lunch available
Evening meal from 1830
Parking for 9

REETH
North Yorkshire
Map ref 5B3

Once a market town and lead-mining centre, Reeth today serves holiday-makers in Swaledale with its folk museum and 18th C shops and inns lining the green at High Row.

Buck Hotel
Reeth, Richmond DL11 6SW
☎ Richmond (01748) 884210
Fax (01748) 884802
In the heart of Swaledale and within the Yorkshire Dales National Park. Superb walking area.
Bedrooms: 1 single, 5 double, 2 twin, 1 triple, 1 family room
Bathrooms: 10 en-suite

Bed & breakfast per night:	£min	£max
Single	28.00	
Double	55.00	

Lunch available
Evening meal 1830 (last orders 2100)
Parking for 10
Cards accepted: Access, Visa, Switch/Delta

Kings Arms Hotel
Listed APPROVED

High Row, Reeth, Richmond DL11 6SY
☎ Richmond (01748) 884259
Family-run hotel dating from 1736, in a pleasant setting overlooking the village green and with wonderful views of Swaledale.
Bedrooms: 3 double, 1 twin
Bathrooms: 4 private showers

Bed & breakfast per night:	£min	£max
Single	24.00	30.00
Double	40.00	45.00

Lunch available
Evening meal 1830 (last orders 2130)

RICHMOND
North Yorkshire
Map ref 5C3

Market town on edge of Swaledale with 11th C castle, Georgian and Victorian buildings surrounding cobbled market-place. Green Howards' Museum is in the former Holy Trinity Church. Attractions include the Georgian Theatre, Richmondshire Museum and Easby Abbey.
Tourist Information Centre ☎ (01748) 850252 or 825994

Bridge House Hotel
COMMENDED

Catterick Bridge, Richmond DL10 7PE
☎ (01748) 818331
Fax (01748) 818331
Riverside coaching hotel dating back to the 15th C. Easily accessible from the A1. Situated midway between the dales and the North York Moors.
Bedrooms: 2 single, 6 double, 6 twin, 2 triple
Bathrooms: 13 en-suite, 1 public

Bed & breakfast per night:	£min	£max
Single	26.00	36.00
Double	42.00	52.00

YORKSHIRE

Half board per person:	£min	£max
Daily	38.00	48.00
Weekly	248.00	311.00

Lunch available
Evening meal 1830 (last orders 2130)
Parking for 70
Cards accepted: Access, Visa, Diners, Amex, Switch/Delta

⛱🅿📞📺🍴♿🚭S¥📺🏧
†120 ♪❄ SP 🏨 T

King's Head Hotel ♛
👑👑👑 COMMENDED

Market Place, Richmond DL10 4HS
☎ (01748) 850220
Fax (01748) 850635
Ⓒ Consort

Beautiful Georgian hotel in historic market town. Ideal for touring Herriot country/Yorkshire Dales. High standard of accommodation and service. Freshly prepared cuisine, extensive wine list.
Bedrooms: 7 single, 13 double, 7 twin, 1 triple
Bathrooms: 28 en-suite

Bed & breakfast per night:	£min	£max
Single	45.00	53.00
Double	70.00	97.00

Half board per person:	£min	£max
Daily	45.50	63.50
Weekly	273.00	381.00

Lunch available
Evening meal 1900 (last orders 2115)
Parking for 25
Cards accepted: Access, Visa, Diners, Amex, Switch/Delta

⛱🅿📞📺🍴♿🚭S¥📺🌙🏧
†150♪❄SP🏨T

The Restaurant On The Green ♛
Listed COMMENDED

5-7 Bridge Street, Richmond DL10 4RW
☎ (01748) 826229

Grade II listed William and Mary property with Georgian sundials at foot

of Castle bluff. Near town centre, River Swale and countryside. Family run. Bedrooms with colour TV, beverage tray, en-suite or private bathroom. Good food, fine wines. No smoking.
Bedrooms: 1 double, 1 twin
Bathrooms: 1 en-suite, 1 private

Bed & breakfast per night:	£min	£max
Single	29.00	
Double	36.50	

Evening meal 1900 (last orders 2030)
Cards accepted: Access, Visa

⛱10📞♿🚭S¥🍴🏧🎯🚗♿🏨

St Trinians Hall ♛
👑👑 COMMENDED

Easby, Richmond DL10 7ET
☎ (01748) 826248
Grade II listed family-run country house between Richmond and Brompton-on-Swale. Peaceful situation, ample parking, gardens.
Bedrooms: 2 double, 1 twin
Bathrooms: 1 en-suite, 2 private

Bed & breakfast per night:	£min	£max
Single	25.00	
Double	38.00	

Parking for 12
Open February–November

⛱♿🅿UL🚭📺🍴🏧🎯❄🚗♿🏨

Willance House Guesthouse ♛
APPROVED

24 Frenchgate, Richmond DL10 7AG
☎ (01748) 824467
16th C stone-built house with oak beams and open fires. Personal attention from the family. Close to the market place.
Bedrooms: 2 double
Bathrooms: 2 en-suite, 1 public

Bed & breakfast per night:	£min	£max
Single	20.00	25.00
Double	34.00	38.00

Half board per person:	£min	£max
Daily	24.50	30.00
Weekly	171.50	210.00

Evening meal 1900 (last orders 1800)

⛱📞♿🅿UL🚭S¥📺🏧
🎯❄SP🏨T

The ♛ symbol after an establishment name indicates that it is a Regional Tourist Board member.

ROSEDALE ABBEY

North Yorkshire
Map ref 5C3

Sturdy hamlet built around Cistercian nunnery in the reign of Henry II, in the middle of Rosedale, largest of the moorland valleys.

Milburn Arms Hotel ♛
👑👑👑 COMMENDED

Rosedale Abbey, Pickering YO18 8RA
☎ Lastingham (01751) 417312
Fax (01751) 417312
Ⓒ Logis of Great Britain
Historic inn, in a picturesque conservation area village, central to the national park and 15 miles from the Yorkshire Heritage Coast. Restaurant noted for enjoyable, well-prepared food.
Bedrooms: 9 double, 2 twin
Bathrooms: 11 en-suite

Bed & breakfast per night:	£min	£max
Single	41.50	44.50
Double	68.00	74.00

Lunch available
Evening meal 1900 (last orders 2130)
Parking for 30
Cards accepted: Access, Visa, Diners

⛱♿🍴🏧📞📺♿🚭S¥📺🏧
†14♪❄🚗BAP♿SP🏨T⑤

ROTHERHAM

South Yorkshire
Map ref 4B2

In the Don Valley, Rotherham became an important industrial town in 19th C with discovery of coal and development of iron and steel industry by Joshua Walker who built Clifton House, now the town's museum. Magnificent 15th C All Saints Church is town's showpiece.
Tourist Information Centre ☎ (01709) 823611

Best Western Elton Hotel ♛
👑👑👑👑 HIGHLY COMMENDED

Main Street, Bramley, Rotherham S66 0SF
☎ (01709) 545681
Fax (01709) 549100
Ⓒ Best Western
200-year-old, stone-built, Yorkshire house with a modern extension and a restaurant. Half a mile from junction 1 of M18, 2 miles from M1. Minimum prices below for one-day stays apply at weekends only.

Continued ▶

YORKSHIRE

ROTHERHAM
Continued

Wheelchair access category 3
Bedrooms: 9 single, 12 double, 4 twin, 4 triple
Bathrooms: 29 en-suite

Bed & breakfast per night:

	£min	£max
Single	45.00	66.50
Double	58.00	83.00

Half board per person:

	£min	£max
Daily	55.00	86.50

Lunch available
Evening meal 1900 (last orders 2130)
Parking for 50
Cards accepted: Access, Visa, Diners, Amex, Switch/Delta

Consort Hotel, Banqueting & Conference Suite
COMMENDED

Brampton Road, Thurcroft, Rotherham S66 9JA
☎ (01709) 530022
Fax (01709) 531529
Consort
At the junction of M1 and M18 (access exits 31 and 33 of M1 and exit 1 of M18).
Bedrooms: 10 double, 7 twin, 1 family room
Bathrooms: 18 en-suite

Bed & breakfast per night:

	£min	£max
Single	30.00	60.00
Double	45.00	70.00

Half board per person:

	£min	£max
Daily	42.50	72.50

Lunch available
Evening meal 1800 (last orders 2130)
Parking for 96
Cards accepted: Access, Visa, Diners, Amex

Swallow Hotel
COMMENDED

West Bawtry Road, Rotherham S60 4NA
☎ (01709) 830630
Fax (01709) 830549
Swallow
Modern, 4-storey building with extensive conference and banqueting facilities and leisure complex. Easy access from junction 33 of M1.
Bedrooms: 72 double, 27 twin, 2 family rooms

Suites available
Bathrooms: 101 en-suite

Bed & breakfast per night:

	£min	£max
Single	60.00	84.00
Double	72.00	98.00

Half board per person:

	£min	£max
Daily	77.00	101.00
Weekly	539.00	707.00

Lunch available
Evening meal 1900 (last orders 2145)
Parking for 252
Cards accepted: Access, Visa, Diners, Amex, Switch/Delta

RUNSWICK
North Yorkshire
Map ref 5D3

Holiday and fishing village on the west side of Runswick Bay.

Cliffemount Hotel
COMMENDED

Runswick Bay, Runswick, Saltburn-by-the-Sea, Cleveland TS13 5HU
☎ Whitby (01947) 840103
Fax (01947) 841025
Relaxing hotel on the clifftop with panoramic views of Runswick Bay. 9 miles north of Whitby. Noted for cuisine.
Bedrooms: 1 single, 10 double
Bathrooms: 11 en-suite

Bed & breakfast per night:

	£min	£max
Single	24.00	39.50
Double	47.50	67.00

Half board per person:

	£min	£max
Daily	31.50	55.50
Weekly	220.50	388.50

Lunch available
Evening meal 1900 (last orders 2130)
Parking for 30
Cards accepted: Access, Visa

ACCESSIBILITY

Look for the symbols which indicate accessibility for wheelchair users. These are described in detail at the front of this guide.

SCARBOROUGH
North Yorkshire
Map ref 5D3

Large, popular East Coast seaside resort, formerly a spa town. Beautiful gardens and two splendid sandy beaches. Castle ruins date from 1100; fine Georgian and Victorian houses. Scarborough Millennium depicts 1,000 years of town's history. Sea Life Centre.
Tourist Information Centre ☎ *(01723) 373333*

Ambassador Hotel
COMMENDED

Centre of the Esplanade, Scarborough YO11 2AY
☎ (01723) 362841
Fax (01723) 362841
Victorian hotel with en-suite bedrooms, offering unrivalled sea views, excellent cuisine, dinner/dances, leisure, entertainment, satellite, direct-dial telephone, lift, ample free parking and more.
Bedrooms: 9 single, 17 double, 29 twin, 3 triple, 1 family room
Bathrooms: 59 en-suite

Bed & breakfast per night:

	£min	£max
Single	27.00	42.00
Double	54.00	84.00

Half board per person:

	£min	£max
Daily	31.50	52.00
Weekly	245.00	336.00

Lunch available
Evening meal 1800 (last orders 2030)
Cards accepted: Access, Visa, Amex, Switch/Delta

Avoncroft Hotel
COMMENDED

5-7 Crown Terrace, South Cliff, Scarborough YO11 2BL
☎ (01723) 372737
Fax (01723) 372737

Listed Georgian terrace overlooking Crown Gardens. Close to spa and sports facilities. Convenient for town centre and all entertainments.
Bedrooms: 7 single, 10 double, 5 twin, 12 triple
Bathrooms: 20 en-suite, 5 public

YORKSHIRE

Bed & breakfast per night:	£min	£max
Single	19.50	25.50
Double	39.00	51.00
Half board per person:	£min	£max
Daily	26.00	32.00
Weekly	169.00	210.00

Lunch available
Evening meal 1730 (last orders 1815)

Earlsmere Hotel
COMMENDED
5 Belvedere Road, South Cliff, Scarborough YO11 2UU
☎ (01723) 361340
Elegant Edwardian building of character retaining most of the original features. 2 minutes from the Esplanade. Choice of menus.
Bedrooms: 1 single, 3 double, 3 twin
Bathrooms: 4 en-suite, 1 public

Bed & breakfast per night:	£min	£max
Single	20.00	28.00
Double	40.00	48.00
Half board per person:	£min	£max
Daily	33.00	41.00
Weekly	231.00	287.00

Lunch available
Evening meal 1830 (last orders 1900)
Parking for 2
Cards accepted: Access, Visa, Switch/Delta

Esplanade Hotel
COMMENDED
Belmont Road, Scarborough YO11 2AA
☎ (01723) 360382
Fax (01723) 376137
Welcoming period-style hotel in good position on Scarborough's South Cliff. Close to beach, spa and town centre. Landau restaurant, parlour bar and roof terrace.
Bedrooms: 18 single, 19 double, 26 twin, 8 triple, 2 family rooms
Bathrooms: 73 en-suite, 4 public

Bed & breakfast per night:	£min	£max
Single	43.00	43.00
Double	80.00	88.00
Half board per person:	£min	£max
Daily	56.00	60.00
Weekly	300.00	303.00

Lunch available
Evening meal 1830 (last orders 2100)
Parking for 24
Open March–December
Cards accepted: Access, Visa, Diners, Amex, Switch/Delta

Excelsior Private Hotel
APPROVED
1 Marlborough Street, Scarborough YO12 7HG
☎ (01723) 360716
Situated on corner of North Bay seafront. Magnificent views. Personal service, fresh produce, home-made bread, soups and sweets. Over 60s discounts. 100% non-smoking.
Bedrooms: 2 single, 4 double, 1 triple, 2 family rooms
Bathrooms: 7 en-suite, 1 public

Bed & breakfast per night:	£min	£max
Single	18.00	20.00
Double	36.00	40.00
Half board per person:	£min	£max
Daily	22.50	26.00
Weekly	130.00	145.00

Evening meal from 1730
Open April–October

The Grainary
Keasbeck Hill Farm, Harwood Dale, Scarborough YO13 0DT
☎ (01723) 870026
Fax (01723) 870026
200-acre mixed farm. Close to "Heartbeat" country, coast and moors. Wildlife trails. Disabled guests welcome. Pet bedrooms.
Bedrooms: 2 single, 5 double, 3 twin, 2 triple, 2 family rooms
Bathrooms: 14 en-suite, 1 public

Bed & breakfast per night:	£min	£max
Single	18.00	21.00
Double	35.00	42.00
Half board per person:	£min	£max
Daily	26.00	31.00
Weekly	175.00	210.00

Lunch available
Evening meal 1830 (last orders 2000)
Parking for 16
Cards accepted: Access, Visa

The Gresham Hotel
COMMENDED
18 Lowdale Avenue, Northstead, Scarborough YO12 6JW
☎ (01723) 372117

Beautifully appointed, detached, licensed hotel in imposing position next to Peasholm Park. Ideal for North Cliff golf-course. A warm welcome awaits.
Bedrooms: 6 single, 4 double, 1 twin, 2 triple
Bathrooms: 5 en-suite, 2 public

Bed & breakfast per night:	£min	£max
Single	17.00	19.00
Double	34.00	42.00
Half board per person:	£min	£max
Daily	23.00	27.00
Weekly	161.00	189.00

Evening meal from 1800
Parking for 4
Open March–October

Holmelea Guest House
Listed APPROVED
8 Belle Vue Parade, Scarborough YO11 1SU
☎ Scarborough/Minicom (01723) 360139
Family-run guesthouse. Centrally heated rooms with divans, duvets, tea/coffee making, colour TV with satellite/video link, radio alarm and hairdryer.
Bedrooms: 2 single, 1 double, 2 twin, 1 family room
Bathrooms: 1 public

Bed & breakfast per night:	£min	£max
Single	12.00	14.00
Double	24.00	28.00
Half board per person:	£min	£max
Weekly	80.00	92.00

Cards accepted: Access, Visa, Switch/Delta

Lysander Hotel
COMMENDED
22 Weydale Avenue, Scarborough YO12 6AX
☎ (01723) 373369
In a peaceful setting between Peasholm Park and Northstead

Continued ▶

YORKSHIRE

SCARBOROUGH
Continued

Gardens. Close to the beach, swimming pools, boating lakes, golf and theatres.
Bedrooms: 4 single, 8 double, 4 twin, 2 triple
Bathrooms: 15 en-suite, 1 public

Bed & breakfast per night:	£min	£max
Single	19.00	23.00
Double	38.00	46.00

Half board per person:	£min	£max
Daily	24.00	30.00
Weekly	159.50	199.50

Evening meal 1800 (last orders 1900)
Parking for 12
Open April–October
Cards accepted: Access, Visa

Manor Heath Hotel ⋔
⚜⚜⚜ COMMENDED

67 Northstead Manor Drive, Scarborough YO12 6AF
☎ (01723) 365720
Detached hotel with pleasant gardens and a private car park, overlooking Peasholm Park and the sea. Close to all North Bay attractions.
Bedrooms: 1 single, 6 double, 2 triple, 5 family rooms
Bathrooms: 14 en-suite, 1 public

Bed & breakfast per night:	£min	£max
Single	18.00	22.00
Double	36.00	44.00

Half board per person:	£min	£max
Daily	23.00	27.00
Weekly	155.00	180.00

Evening meal from 1800
Parking for 12

Philamon ⋔
⚜⚜

108 North Marine Road, Scarborough YO12 7JA
☎ (01723) 373107
North side, convenient for all attractions. A pleasant stay and good home cooking await you. Some en-suite rooms. Reductions for senior citizens, early and late season. Our aim is to offer an enjoyable holiday.
Bedrooms: 2 single, 3 double, 1 twin, 2 triple
Bathrooms: 3 en-suite, 1 public

Bed & breakfast per night:	£min	£max
Single	13.00	17.00
Double	26.00	34.00

Half board per person:	£min	£max
Daily	17.00	21.00
Weekly	119.00	147.00

Evening meal 1730 (last orders 1730)

Philmore Hotel
⚜⚜⚜ APPROVED

126 Columbus Ravine, Scarborough YO12 7QZ
☎ (01723) 361516
Family-run hotel near all the North Bay attractions.
Bedrooms: 1 single, 9 double, 1 twin, 4 triple, 2 family rooms
Bathrooms: 17 en-suite

Bed & breakfast per night:	£min	£max
Single	17.00	22.00
Double	34.00	44.00

Half board per person:	£min	£max
Daily	22.00	25.00
Weekly	140.00	175.00

Evening meal from 1800
Parking for 12
Open March–November

Red Lea Hotel ⋔
⚜⚜⚜ COMMENDED

Prince of Wales Terrace, Scarborough YO11 2AJ
☎ (01723) 362431
Fax (01723) 371230
Traditional hotel with sea views, close to the Spa Centre. Restaurant, bar, lounges, lift and colour TVs. Solarium and indoor heated swimming pool.
Bedrooms: 19 single, 11 double, 28 twin, 10 triple
Bathrooms: 68 en-suite

Bed & breakfast per night:	£min	£max
Single	32.00	34.00
Double	64.00	68.00

Half board per person:	£min	£max
Daily	44.00	46.00
Weekly	290.00	300.00

Lunch available
Evening meal 1830 (last orders 2000)
Cards accepted: Access, Visa, Amex, Switch/Delta

Ryndle Court Private Hotel ⋔
⚜⚜⚜

47 Northstead Manor Drive, Scarborough YO12 6AF
☎ (01723) 375188 & Mobile 0860 711517
Fax (01723) 375188
Pleasantly situated overlooking Peasholm Park and near the sea. All rooms en-suite with TV and tea-making facilities. Residents' bar, car park.
Bedrooms: 1 single, 6 double, 2 twin, 3 triple, 2 family rooms
Bathrooms: 14 en-suite

Bed & breakfast per night:	£min	£max
Single	26.00	32.00
Double	52.00	54.00

Half board per person:	£min	£max
Daily	32.00	40.00
Weekly	180.00	210.00

Evening meal 1730 (last orders 1700)
Parking for 10
Cards accepted: Access, Visa, Amex

Scarborough Travel and Holiday Lodge ⋔
⚜⚜ APPROVED

33 Valley Road, Scarborough YO11 2LX
☎ (01723) 363537
Fax (01723) 501239
Scarborough Travel and Holiday Lodge is based upon the lodge principle offering inexpensive, quality room-only accommodation for business and recreational purposes. Scarborough Fayre Bistro open 8.00am-9.00pm. Car park.
Bedrooms: 4 single, 4 double, 4 twin, 3 triple, 1 family room
Bathrooms: 16 en-suite

Bed & breakfast per night:	£min	£max
Single	34.50	34.50
Double	34.50	34.50

Lunch available
Evening meal 1830 (last orders 2030)
Parking for 20
Cards accepted: Access, Visa, Switch/Delta

Wharncliffe Hotel
⚜⚜ COMMENDED

26 Blenheim Terrace, Scarborough YO12 7HD
☎ (01723) 374635
Panoramic sea views - cleanliness assured - friendly atmosphere. All rooms en-suite with colour TV,

YORKSHIRE

radio/alarm and tea/coffee facilities.
Close to town centre and amenities.
Bedrooms: 7 double, 1 twin, 2 triple,
2 family rooms
Bathrooms: 12 en-suite
Bed & breakfast
per night: £min £max
Single 25.00 25.00
Double 42.00 42.00
Half board per
person: £min £max
Daily 28.00 28.00
Weekly 189.00 189.00
Evening meal 1800 (last orders 1200)
Parking for 1
Open March–September

SCUNTHORPE
North Lincolnshire
Map ref 4C1

Consisted of 5 small villages until 1860 when extensive ironstone beds were discovered. Today an industrial "garden town" with some interesting modern buildings. Nearby Normanby Hall contains fine examples of Regency furniture.

Beverley Hotel
APPROVED

55 Old Brumby Street, Scunthorpe, South Humberside DN16 2AJ
☎ (01724) 282212
Fax (01724) 270422
In the pleasant, quiet residential district of Old Brumby off the A18, close to Scunthorpe town centre.
Bedrooms: 5 single, 3 double, 5 twin, 2 triple
Bathrooms: 15 en-suite
Bed & breakfast
per night: £min £max
Single 38.50 42.00
Double 48.50 52.00
Lunch available
Evening meal 1830 (last orders 1930)
Parking for 15
Cards accepted: Access, Visa, Switch/Delta

Briggate Lodge Inn
HIGHLY COMMENDED

Ermine Street, Broughton, Brigg, Scunthorpe, South Humberside DN20 0NQ
☎ Brigg (01652) 650770
Fax (01652) 650495
Close to junction 4 of the M180, within easy reach of Lincoln, Hull and York, a beautifully-appointed hotel set in mature woodland, with 27-hole championship golf complex and floodlit driving range.
Bedrooms: 2 single, 41 double, 7 twin
Bathrooms: 50 en-suite
Bed & breakfast
per night: £min £max
Single 72.00 79.00
Double 81.00 87.00
Half board per
person: £min £max
Daily 89.50 96.50
Lunch available
Evening meal 1900 (last orders 2200)
Parking for 220
Cards accepted: Access, Visa, Diners, Amex, Switch/Delta

The Downs Guest House
Listed

33 Deyne Avenue, Scunthorpe, South Humberside DN15 7PZ
☎ (01724) 850710
Clean, comfortable and friendly guesthouse in a quiet setting near town centre.
Bedrooms: 2 single, 2 double, 2 twin, 1 triple
Bathrooms: 2 public
Bed & breakfast
per night: £min £max
Single 16.00 16.00
Double 28.00 28.00
Parking for 6

SELBY
North Yorkshire
Map ref 4C1

Small market town on the River Ouse, believed to have been birthplace of Henry I, with a magnificent abbey containing much fine Norman and Early English architecture.
Tourist Information Centre ☎ (01757) 703263

Loftsome Bridge Coaching House
HIGHLY COMMENDED

Loftsome Bridge, Wressle, Selby YO8 7EN
☎ (01757) 630070
Fax (01757) 630070
Nestling alongside the tranquil River Derwent, just 5 minutes from the M62 and a leisurely 20-minute drive from York. Dating back to 1782, this family-run country house hotel boasts a hand-carved Chippendale four-poster bed.

Bedrooms: 10 double, 4 twin, 1 family room
Bathrooms: 15 en-suite
Bed & breakfast
per night: £min £max
Single 35.00 40.00
Double 45.00 50.00
Half board per
person: £min £max
Daily 50.95 55.95
Lunch available
Evening meal 1900 (last orders 2200)
Parking for 80
Cards accepted: Access, Visa

SETTLE
North Yorkshire
Map ref 5B3

Town of narrow streets and Georgian houses in an area of great limestone hills and crags. Panoramic view from Castleberg Crag which stands 300 ft above town.
Tourist Information Centre ☎ (01729) 825192

The Country House Hotel
COMMENDED

Long Preston, Skipton BD23 4NJ
☎ Long Preston (01729) 840246
Elegant Victorian country house, graciously furnished. Offering well-appointed accommodation in homely, informal and restful surroundings. Reputation for good food. Non-smoking.
Bedrooms: 4 double, 2 twin, 1 triple
Bathrooms: 6 en-suite, 1 private, 1 public
Bed & breakfast
per night: £min £max
Single 27.00 32.00
Double 54.00 54.00
Half board per
person: £min £max
Daily 40.00 40.00
Weekly 261.00
Evening meal from 1900
Parking for 7
Open February–December

Falcon Manor Hotel
COMMENDED

Skipton Road, Settle BD24 9BD
☎ (01729) 823814
Fax (01729) 822087
Privately-owned country house hotel, Grade II listed, in the dales market
Continued ▶

195

YORKSHIRE

SETTLE
Continued

town of Settle. Ideal for walking, motoring and the Settle to Carlisle Railway.
Bedrooms: 10 double, 6 twin, 3 triple
Bathrooms: 19 en-suite

Bed & breakfast per night	£min	£max
Single	55.00	
Double	90.00	120.00

Half board per person	£min	£max
Daily	60.00	75.00
Weekly	420.00	525.00

Lunch available
Evening meal 1900 (last orders 2130)
Parking for 80
Cards accepted: Access, Visa, Diners

Maypole Inn
COMMENDED

Maypole Green, Main Street, Long Preston, Skipton BD23 4PH
☎ Long Preston (01729) 840219 & 840755

17th C inn, with open fires, on the village green. Easy access to many attractive walks in the surrounding dales. 4 miles from Settle.
Bedrooms: 1 single, 2 double, 1 twin, 1 triple, 1 family room
Bathrooms: 6 en-suite

Bed & breakfast per night	£min	£max
Single	24.00	26.00
Double	35.00	39.00

Lunch available
Evening meal 1830 (last orders 2100)
Parking for 25
Cards accepted: Access, Visa, Diners, Amex

New Inn Hotel
COMMENDED

Clapham, Lancaster LA2 8HH
☎ Clapham (015242) 51203
Fax (015242) 51496
Wayfarer

18th C coaching inn in a picturesque Yorkshire Dales village 6 miles north of Settle, in dramatic river, waterfall and fell country.
Bedrooms: 10 double, 3 twin
Bathrooms: 13 en-suite

Bed & breakfast per night	£min	£max
Single	40.00	40.00
Double	63.00	68.00

Half board per person	£min	£max
Daily	31.50	56.50
Weekly	230.50	367.50

Lunch available
Evening meal 1900 (last orders 2030)
Parking for 50
Cards accepted: Access, Visa, Amex, Switch/Delta

Whitefriars Country Guest House
APPROVED

Church Street, Settle BD24 9JD
☎ (01729) 823753

Historic family-run guesthouse, set in spacious gardens, in heart of Settle. Ideal for exploring the Dales, Settle-Carlisle Railway. Non-smokers only, please.
Bedrooms: 1 single, 3 double, 3 twin, 1 triple, 1 family room
Bathrooms: 3 en-suite, 2 public

Bed & breakfast per night	£min	£max
Single	17.00	17.50
Double	34.00	42.00

Half board per person	£min	£max
Daily	27.00	31.50
Weekly	167.10	195.30

Evening meal 1900 (last orders 2000)
Parking for 9

SHEFFIELD
South Yorkshire
Map ref 4B2

Local iron ore and coal gave Sheffield its prosperous steel and cutlery industries. The modern city centre has many interesting buildings - cathedral, Cutlers' Hall, Crucible Theatre, Graves and Mappin Art Galleries - and Meadowhall Shopping Centre nearby.
Tourist Information Centre ☎ (0114) 273 4671 or 273 4672

Andrews Park Hotel
COMMENDED

48 Kenwood Road, Netheredge, Sheffield S7 1NQ
☎ (0114) 250 0111
Fax (0114) 255 5423

High quality hotel, less than 1 mile from the city centre, with free car parking and beautiful landscaped gardens.
Bedrooms: 6 single, 3 double, 2 twin, 1 triple, 1 family room
Bathrooms: 8 en-suite, 1 public, 1 private shower

Bed & breakfast per night	£min	£max
Single	38.50	42.00
Double	51.00	68.00

Lunch available
Evening meal 1830 (last orders 2100)
Parking for 25
Cards accepted: Access, Visa, Amex

Etruria House Hotel
APPROVED

91 Crookes Road, Broomhill, Sheffield S10 5BD
☎ (0114) 266 2241 & 267 0853
Fax (0114) 267 0853

Family-run hotel in elegant Victorian house, close to all amenities and city centre. Ideal base for Peak District.
Bedrooms: 5 single, 3 double, 2 twin, 1 triple
Bathrooms: 7 en-suite, 2 public

Bed & breakfast per night	£min	£max
Single	22.00	32.00
Double	37.00	47.00

Parking for 13
Cards accepted: Access, Visa

Forte Posthouse Sheffield
COMMENDED

Manchester Road, Broomhill, Sheffield S10 5DX
☎ (0114) 267 0067
Fax (0114) 268 2620
Forte

Modern hotel with leisure club, close to city centre, Meadowhall and university. Located in quiet suburb.
Bedrooms: 52 single, 49 double, 35 twin
Suites available
Bathrooms: 136 en-suite

Bed & breakfast per night	£min	£max
Single	66.75	
Double	74.20	

Lunch available
Evening meal 1700 (last orders 2215)
Parking for 120
Cards accepted: Access, Visa, Diners, Amex

YORKSHIRE

Ivory House Hotel
34 Wostenholm Road, Sheffield
S7 1LJ
☎ (0114) 255 1853
Fax (0114) 255 1578
Within easy reach of both the city centre and countryside. Personal service from the family management. TV and tea/coffee facilities in all rooms.
Bedrooms: 5 single, 1 twin, 1 triple, 1 family room
Bathrooms: 2 en-suite, 3 public
Bed & breakfast
per night: £min   £max
Single   18.00   23.00
Double   30.00   34.00
Parking for 11

Lindrick Hotel
COMMENDED
226-230 Chippinghouse Road, Sheffield S7 1DR
☎ (0114) 258 5041
Fax (0114) 255 4758
Family-run hotel with parking at the front and rear, only minutes from the city centre.
Bedrooms: 17 single, 3 double, 2 twin, 1 triple
Bathrooms: 15 en-suite, 2 public
Bed & breakfast
per night: £min   £max
Single   21.00   36.95
Double   39.00   45.00
Evening meal 1800 (last orders 2100)
Parking for 22
Cards accepted: Access, Visa, Amex, Switch/Delta

Peace Guest House
Listed
92 Brocco Bank, Sheffield S11 8RS
☎ (0114) 268 5110 & 267 0760
Established for 15 years. Close to Endcliffe Park, university, hospitals and Peak District Route.
Bedrooms: 3 single, 1 double, 2 twin, 1 triple
Bathrooms: 2 public, 3 private showers
Bed & breakfast
per night: £min   £max
Single   18.00
Double   32.00
Half board per
person: £min   £max
Daily   28.00
Weekly   175.00
Evening meal 1700 (last orders 1900)
Parking for 6

St Pellegrino
Listed
2 Oak Park, Off Manchester Road, Sheffield S10 5DE
☎ (0114) 268 1953 & 266 0151
Comfortable, family-run hotel near university and city centre, yet you can still enjoy the spacious beauty of peaceful surroundings.
Bedrooms: 3 single, 3 double, 3 twin, 1 triple
Bathrooms: 4 en-suite, 2 public
Bed & breakfast
per night: £min   £max
Single   20.00   27.00
Double   34.00   37.00
Evening meal 1830 (last orders 2000)
Parking for 22

Swallow Hotel
HIGHLY COMMENDED
Kenwood Road, Sheffield S7 1NQ
☎ (0114) 258 3811
Fax (0114) 250 0138
 Swallow
Set in extensive landscaped grounds with its own leisure club, this hotel is ideal for the Peaks, Meadowhall and Chatsworth. Short break packages are available.
Bedrooms: 24 single, 56 double, 37 twin
Suite available
Bathrooms: 117 en-suite
Bed & breakfast
per night: £min   £max
Single   70.00   99.00
Double   85.00   115.00
Half board per
person: £min   £max
Daily   88.00   117.00
Lunch available
Evening meal 1900 (last orders 2145)
Parking for 200
Cards accepted: Access, Visa, Diners, Amex, Switch/Delta

Whitley Hall Hotel
HIGHLY COMMENDED
Elliott Lane, Grenoside, Sheffield S30 3NR
☎ (0114) 245 4444
Fax (0114) 245 5414

Elizabethan mansion with 30 acres of gardens, lakes and woodlands, only a few miles from the centres of Sheffield, Rotherham and Barnsley. Food a speciality with full a la carte and daily menus. Open to non-residents.
Bedrooms: 2 single, 5 double, 10 twin, 1 family room
Suite available
Bathrooms: 18 en-suite
Bed & breakfast
per night: £min   £max
Single   52.00   78.00
Double   62.00   98.00
Half board per
person: £min   £max
Daily   51.00   98.00
Lunch available
Evening meal 1900 (last orders 2130)
Parking for 100
Cards accepted: Access, Visa, Diners, Amex, Switch/Delta

SHELLEY
West Yorkshire
Map ref 4B1

West Yorkshire village south of Huddersfield and close to Kirklees Light Railway.

Three Acres Inn and Restaurant
Listed
Roydhouse, Shelley, Huddersfield HD8 8LR
☎ Huddersfield (01484) 602606
Fax (01484) 608411
Attractive country inn, convenient for all Yorkshire's major conurbations and motorway network. Restaurant, traditional beers.
Bedrooms: 6 single, 9 double, 2 twin, 2 triple
Bathrooms: 19 en-suite
Bed & breakfast
per night: £min   £max
Single   30.00   49.50
Double   45.00   62.50
Half board per
person: £min   £max
Daily   40.00   59.50
Weekly   350.00

Continued ▶

For further information on accommodation establishments use the coupons at the back of this guide.

YORKSHIRE

SHELLEY
Continued

Lunch available
Evening meal 1900 (last orders 2130)
Parking for 100
Cards accepted: Access, Visa, Amex, Switch/Delta

SKIPTON

North Yorkshire
Map ref 4B1

Pleasant market town at gateway to dales, with farming community atmosphere, a Palladian Town Hall, parish church and fully roofed castle at the top of the High Street.
Tourist Information Centre ☎ (01756) 792809

Devonshire Hotel
Listed

Newmarket Street, Skipton
BD23 2HR
☎ (01756) 793078 & 426640
Fax (01756) 793078

Family-run, country market town hotel with an attractive garden and children's play area. All bedrooms have TV. Resident proprietors. Real ale. An ideal base for touring the dales and Yorkshire countryside.
Bedrooms: 1 single, 7 double, 4 twin, 1 triple, 2 family rooms
Bathrooms: 6 en-suite, 4 public

Bed & breakfast
per night:	£min	£max
Single	18.00	27.00
Double	30.00	50.00

Half board per
person:	£min	£max
Daily	22.50	40.00
Weekly	157.50	280.00

Lunch available
Evening meal 1800 (last orders 2000)
Parking for 28

Randells Hotel, Conference & Leisure Centre
COMMENDED

Keighley Road, Snaygill, Skipton
BD23 2TA
☎ (01756) 700100
Fax (01756) 700107

Situated at the gateway to the dales. Individually designed rooms and suites, Waterside Restaurant, conference facilities for up to 400 people. Leisure centre with indoor pool and squash courts. Registered children's nursery.

Wheelchair access category 3
Bedrooms: 26 double, 30 twin, 20 triple
Bathrooms: 76 en-suite

Bed & breakfast
per night:	£min	£max
Single	53.00	80.00
Double	68.00	89.00

Half board per
person:	£min	£max
Daily	68.00	95.00

Lunch available
Evening meal 1900 (last orders 2200)
Parking for 200
Cards accepted: Access, Visa, Diners, Amex, Switch/Delta

Unicorn Hotel
COMMENDED

Devonshire Place, Keighley Road, Skipton BD23 2LP
☎ (01756) 794146 & 793376

Centrally situated, with double-glazing to ensure peace and tranquillity. Ideal base for touring Bronte country and the Yorkshire Dales. Recently refurbished to a high standard. Half board prices based on minimum 2 nights stay.
Bedrooms: 6 double, 2 twin, 1 family room
Bathrooms: 9 en-suite

Bed & breakfast
per night:	£min	£max
Single	42.00	44.00
Double	49.00	51.00

Half board per
person:	£min	£max
Daily	32.00	34.00

Evening meal 1900 (last orders 2100)
Cards accepted: Access, Visa, Amex, Switch/Delta

WELCOME HOST

This is a nationally recognised customer care programme which aims to promote the highest standards of service and a warm welcome. Establishments who are taking part in this initiative are indicated by the ✿ symbol.

SOUTH CAVE

East Riding of Yorkshire
Map ref 4C1

Lying on the famous Ermine Street, the Roman road stretching from Lincoln to York. Located only 3 miles from the River Humber, it is an ideal centre for touring the county of Humberside.

Rudstone Walk Farmhouse & Country Cottages
HIGHLY COMMENDED

South Cave, Brough, East Yorkshire
HU15 2AH
☎ Howden (01430) 422230
Fax (01430) 424552

303-acre arable farm. Historic farmhouse with converted buildings around attractive courtyard provides lovely, relaxing en-suite accommodation, good food and a warm welcome.
Wheelchair access category 3
Bedrooms: 7 double, 7 twin
Bathrooms: 14 en-suite, 1 public

Bed & breakfast
per night:	£min	£max
Single	35.00	65.00
Double	49.00	75.00

Half board per
person:	£min	£max
Daily	50.00	80.00
Weekly	250.00	520.00

Evening meal 1900 (last orders 1600)
Parking for 50
Cards accepted: Access, Visa, Diners, Amex, Switch/Delta

THIRSK

North Yorkshire
Map ref 5C3

Thriving market town with cobbled square surrounded by old shops and inns and also with a local museum. St Mary's Church is probably the best example of Perpendicular work in Yorkshire.

Angel Inn
COMMENDED

Long Street, Topcliffe, Thirsk
YO7 3RW
☎ (01845) 577237
Fax (01845) 578000

Well-appointed, attractive village inn, renowned for good food and traditional ales. Ideal centre for touring York and Herriot country.
Bedrooms: 2 single, 8 double, 4 twin, 1 family room
Bathrooms: 15 en-suite

YORKSHIRE

Bed & breakfast per night:

	£min	£max
Single	35.00	39.50
Double	50.00	55.00

Half board per person:

	£min	£max
Daily	37.50	52.50

Lunch available
Evening meal 1830 (last orders 2130)
Parking for 150
Cards accepted: Access, Visa, Switch/Delta

☼ 2 ♦ 🗋 🖺 ♦ ¾ 🛡 S ♪ 📺 🍴 ♿
🅿150 ♣ ♪ ❄ ✗ 🐾 SP T

Fourways Guest House ♠
APPROVED

Town End, Thirsk YO7 1PY
☎ (01845) 522601
Guesthouse close to the town centre, 2 minutes' walk from the surgery of famous vet and author, the late James Herriot. Centrally located for touring North York Moors and Yorkshire Dales.
Bedrooms: 3 single, 3 double, 3 twin, 1 triple
Bathrooms: 7 en-suite, 1 public

Bed & breakfast per night:

	£min	£max
Single	15.00	17.00
Double	30.00	34.00

Half board per person:

	£min	£max
Daily	22.00	24.00
Weekly	139.00	151.00

Lunch available
Evening meal 1830 (last orders 1930)
Parking for 10
Cards accepted: Access, Visa

☼ 🗋 ♦ ¾ 🛡 ♪ 🍴 🐾 SP

Golden Fleece ♠
COMMENDED

Market Place, Thirsk YO7 1LL
☎ (01845) 523108
Fax (01845) 523996
CR Consort/Utell International
Situated in the market place within easy reach of the Yorkshire Dales and Moors, this old coaching inn has a friendly atmosphere and serves traditional ales and fine fare.
Bedrooms: 1 single, 14 double, 2 twin, 1 triple
Bathrooms: 18 en-suite, 5 public

Bed & breakfast per night:

	£min	£max
Single	55.00	
Double	75.00	

Half board per person:

	£min	£max
Daily	70.00	
Weekly	225.00	

Lunch available
Evening meal 1900 (last orders 2100)
Parking for 30
Cards accepted: Access, Visa, Diners, Amex, Switch/Delta

☼ 🗋 ♦ 📧 🖺 ♦ ¾ 🛡 S ♪ 🍴 ♿
🅿110 ♿ ▶ ¾ SP 🎱 T

Old Red House ♠
APPROVED

Station Road, Carlton Miniott, Thirsk YO7 4LT
☎ (01845) 524383
2-storey Georgian building, with a bar lounge and open fire.
Bedrooms: 1 single, 3 double, 1 twin, 1 triple, 4 family rooms
Bathrooms: 10 en-suite

Bed & breakfast per night:

	£min	£max
Single	20.00	22.00
Double	32.00	36.00

Half board per person:

	£min	£max
Daily		
Weekly	145.00	160.00

Lunch available
Evening meal 1900 (last orders 2130)
Parking for 30
Cards accepted: Access, Visa, Diners, Amex

☼ 🗋 ♦ 🛡 S 🍴 ♣ ❄ DAP
¾ SP

Sheppard's Hotel & Restaurant ♠
COMMENDED

Front Street, Sowerby, Thirsk YO7 1JF
☎ (01845) 523655
Fax (01845) 524720
17th C building on the village green. Carefully developed, giving every comfort whilst maintaining its rural atmosphere. An ideal centre for touring Herriot's Yorkshire.
Bedrooms: 7 double, 1 triple
Bathrooms: 8 en-suite

Bed & breakfast per night:

	£min	£max
Single	56.00	62.00
Double	75.00	85.00

Lunch available
Evening meal 1900 (last orders 2200)
Parking for 35
Cards accepted: Access, Visa, Switch/Delta

☼ 10 🗋 ♦ 📧 🖺 ♦ ¾ 🛡 S ¾ ♪
🅿 🍴60 ✗ 🐾 SP

THORNTON WATLASS
North Yorkshire
Map ref 5C3

Picturesque village in Lower Wensleydale.

The Buck Inn ♠
COMMENDED

Thornton Watlass, Ripon HG4 4AH
☎ Bedale (01677) 422461
Friendly village inn overlooking the delightful cricket green in a small village, 3 miles from Bedale on the Masham road, and close to the A1. Ideal centre for exploring both the dales and North York Moors.
Bedrooms: 1 single, 3 double, 2 twin, 1 triple
Bathrooms: 5 en-suite, 1 public

Bed & breakfast per night:

	£min	£max
Single	32.00	
Double	50.00	

Lunch available
Evening meal 1830 (last orders 2130)
Parking for 40
Cards accepted: Access, Visa, Diners, Amex

☼ 🗋 ♦ 🛡 S ¾ ♪ 📺 🍴 ♿ 🅿70
♣ ♪ ❄ 🐾 DAP SP

THWAITE
North Yorkshire
Map ref 5B3

Quiet village, ideal for walking the fells of Great Shunner, Kisdon, High Seat, Rogan's Seat and Lovely Seat. Magnificent scenery.

Kearton Guest House ♠
Listed

Thwaite, Richmond DL11 6DR
☎ Richmond (01748) 886277
Fax (01748) 886590
In the charming village of Thwaite in Swaledale, within easy reach of York, the Lake District, Herriot country and the Yorkshire Dales.
Bedrooms: 1 single, 4 double, 1 twin, 6 triple, 1 family room
Bathrooms: 4 public, 5 private showers

Bed & breakfast per night:

	£min	£max
Single		20.00
Double		40.00

Half board per person:

	£min	£max
Daily		25.50
Weekly		174.50

Continued ▶

YORKSHIRE

THWAITE
Continued

Lunch available
Evening meal from 1830
Parking for 40
Open March–December
Cards accepted: Access, Visa, Switch/Delta

WAKEFIELD

West Yorkshire
Map ref 4B1

Thriving city with cathedral church of All Saints boasting 247-ft spire. Old Bridge, a 9-arched structure, has fine medieval chantry chapels of St Mary's. Fine Georgian architecture and good shopping centre (The Ridings). National Coal Mining Museum for England nearby.
Tourist Information Centre ☎ (01924) 305000 or 305001

Cedar Court Hotel

Denby Dale Road, Calder Grove, Wakefield WF4 3QZ
☎ (01924) 276310 & 261459
Fax (01924) 280221
International hotel, designed for ultimate customer satisfaction. Close to the M1 and M62 motorways, halfway between London and Scotland. Suitable for business people, conferences, private functions and holidaymakers.
Bedrooms: 126 double, 23 twin, 1 triple
Suites available
Bathrooms: 150 en-suite

Bed & breakfast per night:	£min	£max
Single	48.45	88.95
Double	57.40	97.40

Lunch available
Evening meal 1800 (last orders 2200)
Parking for 350
Cards accepted: Access, Visa, Diners, Amex

Dimple Well Lodge Hotel
HIGHLY COMMENDED

The Green, Ossett WF5 8JX
☎ (01924) 264352
Fax (01924) 274024
Family-run, Georgian house hotel in own picturesque gardens, offering charm and character. Close to M1 (junction 40) and M62.
Bedrooms: 5 single, 5 double, 1 twin
Bathrooms: 11 en-suite

Bed & breakfast per night:	£min	£max
Single	43.00	43.00
Double	55.00	55.00

Half board per person:	£min	£max
Daily	55.00	55.00

Evening meal 1900 (last orders 2030)
Parking for 20
Cards accepted: Access, Visa, Amex

Parklands Hotel

143 Horbury Road, Wakefield WF2 8TY
☎ (01924) 377407
Fax (01924) 290348

Elegant Victorian former vicarage overlooking 680 acres of beautiful parkland. Family-run for over 25 years, providing a high standard of service and cuisine and well-appointed en-suite bedrooms.
Bedrooms: 9 single, 2 double, 2 twin
Bathrooms: 11 en-suite, 2 private showers

Bed & breakfast per night:	£min	£max
Single	30.50	39.85
Double	40.85	44.00

Half board per person:	£min	£max
Daily	40.25	49.40

Lunch available
Evening meal 1845 (last orders 2015)
Parking for 20
Cards accepted: Access, Visa, Diners, Amex, Switch/Delta

Swallow Hotel
COMMENDED

Queen Street, Wakefield WF1 1JU
☎ (01924) 372111
Fax (01924) 383648
Swallow
Modern city centre hotel adjacent to Ridings shopping centre. Easy access from M1 and M62, 400 yards from mainline railway station. Short break packages available.
Bedrooms: 36 single, 12 double, 16 twin
Bathrooms: 64 en-suite

Bed & breakfast per night:	£min	£max
Single	55.00	85.00
Double	65.00	95.00

Half board per person:	£min	£max
Daily	68.50	98.50

Lunch available
Evening meal 1900 (last orders 2115)
Parking for 50
Cards accepted: Access, Visa, Diners, Amex, Switch/Delta

Waterton Park Hotel
HIGHLY COMMENDED

Walton Hall, Walton, Wakefield WF2 6PW
☎ (01924) 257911
Fax (01924) 240082
Best Western

Georgian mansion, situated on an island and surrounded by a 26-acre lake. Well-equipped bedrooms, restaurant, swimming pool, steamroom, sauna, solarium, fly-fishing, fitness-room, coffee shop, 18-hole golf.
Bedrooms: 3 single, 31 double, 8 twin
Bathrooms: 42 en-suite

Bed & breakfast per night:	£min	£max
Single	60.00	85.00
Double	90.00	110.00

Half board per person:	£min	£max
Daily	80.00	100.00

Lunch available
Evening meal 1900 (last orders 2130)
Parking for 130
Cards accepted: Access, Visa, Diners, Amex, Switch/Delta

Information on accommodation listed in this guide has been supplied by the proprietors. As changes may occur you are advised to check details at the time of booking.

YORKSHIRE

WEST WITTON

North Yorkshire
Map ref 5B3

Popular Wensleydale village, where the burning of "Owd Bartle", effigy of an 18th C pig rustler, is held in August.

Wensleydale Heifer
COMMENDED

West Witton, Leyburn DL8 4LS
☎ Wensleydale (01969) 622322
Fax (01969) 624183
Consort/Logis of Great Britain

17th C inn situated in Yorkshire Dales National Park. Seafood restaurant and bistro. Four-poster bedrooms. Special breaks. Dogs welcome. Rustic country cooking.
Bedrooms: 8 double, 5 twin, 1 triple, 1 family room
Suite available
Bathrooms: 15 en-suite
Bed & breakfast per night:

	£min	£max
Single	49.50	49.50
Double	64.00	80.00

Half board per person:

	£min	£max
Daily	49.50	57.30

Lunch available
Evening meal 1900 (last orders 2130)
Parking for 40
Cards accepted: Access, Visa, Diners, Amex, Switch/Delta

WETHERBY

West Yorkshire
Map ref 4B1

Prosperous market town on the River Wharfe, noted for horse-racing.
Tourist Information Centre ☎ (01937) 582706

Jarvis Wetherby Hotel
COMMENDED

Leeds Road, Wetherby LS22 5HE
☎ (01937) 583881
Fax (01937) 580062
Jarvis/Utell International
Rural setting. Ideally located off A1, minutes away from the historic city of York and the spa town of Harrogate. Brilliant base for Leeds and Dales.
Bedrooms: 17 double, 53 twin, 2 triple
Bathrooms: 72 en-suite
Bed & breakfast per night:

	£min	£max
Single	39.00	77.50
Double	78.00	95.00

Half board per person:

	£min	£max
Daily	39.50	90.45

Lunch available
Evening meal 1900 (last orders 2145)
Parking for 125
Cards accepted: Access, Visa, Diners, Amex, Switch/Delta

Prospect House
Listed

8 Caxton Street, Wetherby LS22 6RU
☎ (01937) 582428
Established 35 years. En-suite rooms available. Near York, Harrogate, Dales, Herriot country. Midway London/Edinburgh. Restaurants nearby. Pets welcome.
Bedrooms: 1 single, 3 double, 2 twin
Suites available
Bathrooms: 4 en-suite, 1 public
Bed & breakfast per night:

	£min	£max
Single	18.00	20.00
Double	38.00	45.00

Parking for 6

WHITBY

North Yorkshire
Map ref 5D3

Quaint holiday town with narrow streets and steep alleys at the mouth of the River Esk. Captain James Cook, the famous navigator, lived in Grape Lane. 199 steps lead to St Mary's Church and St Hilda's Abbey overlooking harbour. Dracula connections. Sandy beach.
Tourist Information Centre ☎ (01947) 602674

Dunsley Hall Country House Hotel and Leisure Club
HIGHLY COMMENDED

Dunsley, Whitby YO21 3TL
☎ (01947) 893437
Fax (01947) 893505

Peaceful, elegant country hall in 4 acres of secluded grounds within North York Moors National Park. Relaxing and friendly atmosphere. Oak panelling, carved lounge bar with stained-glass windows. Indoor heated swimming pool, fitness room, tennis, croquet and putting green.
Bedrooms: 8 double, 3 twin
Bathrooms: 11 en-suite
Bed & breakfast per night:

	£min	£max
Single	55.00	65.00
Double	85.00	105.00

Half board per person:

	£min	£max
Daily	65.00	75.00

Lunch available
Evening meal 1900 (last orders 2100)
Parking for 22
Cards accepted: Access, Visa, Switch/Delta

Glendale Guest House

16 Crescent Avenue, Whitby YO21 3ED
☎ (01947) 604242
Family-run Victorian guesthouse. Clean and comfortable with a pleasant atmosphere. Emphasis on food.
Bedrooms: 1 single, 5 double
Bathrooms: 5 en-suite, 2 public
Bed & breakfast per night:

	£min	£max
Single	18.00	18.50
Double	38.00	40.00

Half board per person:

	£min	£max
Daily	28.00	29.00
Weekly	180.00	186.00

Evening meal 1600 (last orders 1730)
Parking for 6
Open March–November

All accommodation in this guide has been graded, or is awaiting a grading, by a trained Tourist Board inspector.

YORKSHIRE

WHITBY
Continued

Larpool Hall Country Hotel and Restaurant
COMMENDED

Larpool Lane, Whitby YO22 4ND
☎ (01947) 602737
Fax (01947) 820204
The Independents/Logis of Great Britain
One of the miniature stately homes of England, built in 1796, set in 10 acres overlooking the Esk Valley. One mile from town centre.
Bedrooms: 2 single, 5 double, 5 twin, 1 triple
Bathrooms: 13 en-suite

Bed & breakfast per night:	£min	£max
Single	39.50	50.00
Double	70.00	100.00

Half board per person:	£min	£max
Daily	45.00	55.00
Weekly	280.00	350.00

Lunch available
Evening meal 1900 (last orders 2100)
Parking for 20
Cards accepted: Access, Visa, Diners, Amex

Morningside Hotel
COMMENDED

10 North Promenade, West Cliff, Whitby YO21 3JX
☎ (01947) 602643 & 604030
Within easy distance of the sports ground, indoor swimming pool, Spa Theatre and Pavilion, and half a mile to 18-hole golf course.
Bedrooms: 1 single, 11 double, 3 twin, 1 triple
Bathrooms: 16 en-suite

Bed & breakfast per night:	£min	£max
Single	27.00	27.00
Double	44.00	54.00

Half board per person:	£min	£max
Daily	34.00	39.00
Weekly	228.00	260.00

Evening meal 1830 (last orders 1900)
Parking for 14
Cards accepted: Access, Visa

Saxonville Hotel
COMMENDED

Ladysmith Avenue, Whitby YO21 3HX
☎ (01947) 602631
Fax (01947) 820523
Family-owned hotel, in operation since 1946, proud of its cuisine and friendly atmosphere.
Bedrooms: 3 single, 10 double, 9 twin, 2 triple
Bathrooms: 24 en-suite

Bed & breakfast per night:	£min	£max
Single	30.00	36.00
Double	60.00	72.00

Half board per person:	£min	£max
Daily	40.00	46.00
Weekly	255.00	300.00

Lunch available
Evening meal 1900 (last orders 2030)
Parking for 20
Open April–October
Cards accepted: Access, Visa, Switch/Delta

Seacliffe Hotel
COMMENDED

12 North Promenade, West Cliff, Whitby YO21 3JX
☎ (01947) 603139 & Freephone 0500 202229
Fax (01947) 603139
Friendly hotel overlooking the sea. Seafood a speciality in the a la carte restaurant. Golf nearby.
Bedrooms: 1 single, 13 double, 2 twin, 3 triple, 1 family room
Bathrooms: 20 en-suite, 1 public

Bed & breakfast per night:	£min	£max
Single	29.50	37.50
Double	55.00	59.00

Half board per person:	£min	£max
Daily	35.00	37.00

Evening meal 1800 (last orders 2100)
Parking for 8
Cards accepted: Access, Visa, Diners, Amex, Switch/Delta

Stakesby Manor
COMMENDED

Manor Close, High Stakesby, Whitby YO21 1HL
☎ (01947) 602773 & 602140
Fax (01947) 602773
Georgian house dating back to 1710, in its own grounds, on the outskirts of Whitby in the North York Moors National Park. Facing south with views of the moors.
Bedrooms: 6 double, 2 twin, 1 triple
Bathrooms: 9 en-suite

Bed & breakfast per night:	£min	£max
Single	44.00	44.00
Double	62.00	66.00

Half board per person:	£min	£max
Daily	36.00	44.00
Weekly	252.00	308.00

Lunch available
Evening meal 1900 (last orders 2030)
Parking for 30
Cards accepted: Access, Visa, Amex, Switch/Delta

White House Hotel
COMMENDED

Upgang Lane, West Cliff, Whitby YO21 3JJ
☎ (01947) 600469
Fax (01947) 821600
Family-run hotel in a unique position with panoramic views, overlooking Sandsend Bay, adjoining a golf-course. Emphasis on food.
Bedrooms: 3 single, 3 double, 2 twin, 3 triple
Bathrooms: 9 en-suite, 1 public

Bed & breakfast per night:	£min	£max
Single	20.00	30.00
Double	40.00	60.00

Half board per person:	£min	£max
Daily	35.00	38.00
Weekly	240.00	270.00

Lunch available
Evening meal 1830 (last orders 2130)
Parking for 50
Cards accepted: Access, Visa, Switch/Delta

> Establishments should be open throughout the year, unless otherwise stated.

> Half board prices are given per person, but in some cases these may be based on double/twin occupancy.

YORKSHIRE

YORK

Map ref 4C1

Ancient walled city nearly 2000 years old containing many well-preserved medieval buildings. Its Minster has over 100 stained glass windows. Attractions include Castle Museum, National Railway Museum, Jorvik Viking Centre and York Dungeon.
Tourist Information Centre ☎ (01904) 621756 or 621756 or 620557

Abbots Mews Hotel
👑👑👑 APPROVED

6 Marygate Lane, Bootham, York YO3 7DE
☎ (01904) 634866 & 622395
Fax (01904) 612848
Consort

Converted Victorian coachmen's cottages, quietly located in a mews, with easy access to the city centre.
Bedrooms: 7 single, 17 double, 15 twin, 9 triple
Bathrooms: 48 en-suite, 1 public

Bed & breakfast per night:	£min	£max
Single		42.00
Double		64.00

Half board per person:	£min	£max
Daily		42.00

Lunch available
Evening meal 1900 (last orders 2130)
Parking for 30
Cards accepted: Access, Visa, Diners, Amex, Switch/Delta

See display advertisement on this page

Acorn Guest House
👑👑 COMMENDED

1 Southlands Road, York YO2 1NP
☎ (01904) 620081 & Mobile 0850 560477
Fax (01904) 613331

Victorian town house with spacious accommodation, 10 minutes' walk to city centre and most main attractions. Varied breakfast menu. Most diets catered for. Half board prices shown apply in winter only.
Bedrooms: 1 single, 2 double, 2 triple, 1 family room
Bathrooms: 3 en-suite, 1 public

Bed & breakfast per night:	£min	£max
Single	14.00	18.50
Double	26.00	35.00

Half board per person:	£min	£max
Daily		19.00	25.00

Lunch available
Evening meal 1800 (last orders 1000)
Cards accepted: Access, Visa, Amex

Aldwark Manor Golf Hotel
👑👑👑👑 HIGHLY COMMENDED

Aldwark, Alne, York YO6 2NF
☎ Tollerton (01347) 838146
Fax (01347) 838867

19th C manor in 180 acres of parkland with its own 18-hole golf-course.
Bedrooms: 3 single, 7 double, 8 twin, 2 triple
Bathrooms: 20 en-suite

Bed & breakfast per night:	£min	£max
Single	42.00	50.00
Double	70.00	90.00

Half board per person:	£min	£max
Daily	60.50	68.50

Lunch available
Evening meal 1900 (last orders 2100)
Parking for 100

Continued ▶

·Y·O·R·K·
CITY CENTRE

- Close to Minster • Luxury hotel in gardens
- Elegant Restaurant • Special Breaks • Conference facilities
- Car Parking

Abbots Mews Hotel

👑👑👑 APPROVED

Marygate Lane, Bootham, York, YO3 7DE
Tel. (01904) 634866/622395 Fax. (01904) 612848

YORKSHIRE

YORK
Continued

Cards accepted: Access, Visa, Diners, Amex

Alfreda Guest House
COMMENDED
61 Heslington Lane, Fulford, York YO1 4HN
☎ (01904) 631698

Double-fronted, Edwardian residence in 1.5 acres, close to Fulford Golf Course and York University. Large parking area with security lighting.
Bedrooms: 3 double, 3 twin, 2 triple, 2 family rooms
Bathrooms: 8 en-suite, 1 public
Bed & breakfast

per night:	£min	£max
Single	20.00	35.00
Double	35.00	50.00

Parking for 21
Cards accepted: Access, Visa, Amex

Alhambra Court Hotel
COMMENDED
31 St Mary's, Bootham, York YO3 7DD
☎ (01904) 628474
Fax (01904) 610690

Early Georgian town house in a quiet cul-de-sac near the city centre. Family-run hotel with bar, restaurant, open to non-residents. Lift and parking.
Bedrooms: 3 single, 7 double, 9 twin, 2 triple, 3 family rooms
Bathrooms: 24 en-suite
Bed & breakfast

per night:	£min	£max
Single	31.50	39.50
Double	45.00	62.00

Half board per

person:	£min	£max
Daily		35.00
Weekly		206.50

Evening meal 1800 (last orders 2100)
Parking for 20
Cards accepted: Access, Visa

Arndale Hotel
HIGHLY COMMENDED
290 Tadcaster Road, York YO2 2ET
☎ (01904) 702424

Delightful Victorian house, directly overlooking racecourse. Beautiful enclosed walled gardens giving a country atmosphere within the city. Antiques, fresh flowers, four-poster beds, whirlpool baths. Enclosed gated car park.
Bedrooms: 7 double, 2 twin, 1 triple
Bathrooms: 10 en-suite
Bed & breakfast

per night:	£min	£max
Single	35.00	45.00
Double	45.00	59.00

Parking for 20

Arnot House
Listed COMMENDED
17 Grosvenor Terrace, Bootham, York YO3 7AG
☎ (01904) 641966
Beautifully preserved Victorian town house with original cornices, fireplaces and staircase. Large en-suite rooms, tastefully decorated with brass beds, antiques and paintings. Just 5 minutes' walk from York Minster. Non-smoking throughout.
Bedrooms: 3 double, 1 twin
Bathrooms: 3 en-suite, 1 private
Bed & breakfast

per night:	£min	£max
Single	20.00	50.00
Double	35.00	50.00

Half board per

person:	£min	£max
Daily	30.00	60.00
Weekly	200.00	300.00

Evening meal 1800 (last orders 1930)
Parking for 3

Ascot House
APPROVED
80 East Parade, Heworth, York YO3 7YH
☎ (01904) 426826
Fax (01904) 431077

A most attractive Victorian villa, 15 minutes' walk from city centre. All double rooms are en-suite. Some have four-poster or canopy beds. Private car park. Licensed.
Bedrooms: 2 single, 7 double, 2 twin, 3 triple, 1 family room
Bathrooms: 12 en-suite, 2 public
Bed & breakfast

per night	£min	£max
Single	17.00	22.00
Double	34.00	44.00

Parking for 12
Cards accepted: Access, Visa

Ashbourne House Hotel
COMMENDED
139 Fulford Road, York YO1 4HG
☎ (01904) 639912
Fax (01904) 631332
Charming, comfortable, family-owned and run licensed private hotel. On main route into York from the south and within walking distance of city centre.
Bedrooms: 3 double, 2 twin, 1 family room
Bathrooms: 5 en-suite, 1 private
Bed & breakfast

per night:	£min	£max
Single	34.00	38.00
Double	40.00	50.00

Half board per

person:	£min	£max
Daily	35.00	45.00
Weekly	245.00	315.00

Evening meal 1900 (last orders 1800)
Parking for 6
Cards accepted: Access, Visa, Diners, Amex

The National Grading and Classification Scheme is explained in full at the back of this guide.

YORKSHIRE

Ashcroft Hotel

🛌🛌🛌 COMMENDED

294 Bishopthorpe Road, York
YO2 1LH
☎ (01904) 659286 & 629543
Fax (01904) 640107
Ⓖ Minotel

Victorian former mansion in 2.5 acres of wooded grounds overlooking the River Ouse, only 1 mile from the city centre. All bedrooms have colour TV, radio, telephone, coffee/tea-making facilities, hairdryer and trouser press.
Bedrooms: 1 single, 7 double, 4 twin, 1 triple, 2 family rooms
Bathrooms: 15 en-suite
Bed & breakfast

per night:	£min	£max
Single	42.00	45.00
Double	55.00	80.00

Half board per

person:	£min	£max
Daily	40.00	53.00
Weekly	260.00	295.00

Lunch available
Evening meal 1900 (last orders 2130)
Parking for 40
Cards accepted: Access, Visa, Diners, Amex, Switch/Delta
🛌♿&📞🍴🅿♿📺🖨🚗
↑70 🎿❄🐕 SP T

Ashwood Place

🛌🛌

19 Nunthorpe Avenue, Off Scarcroft Road, York YO2 1PF
☎ (01904) 623412
Fax (01904) 623412
Comfortable guesthouse, close to the city, racecourse and station. Families welcome. Low season breaks.
Non-smokers. No parking restrictions.
Bedrooms: 1 double, 2 triple, 1 family room
Bathrooms: 4 en-suite, 1 public
Bed & breakfast

per night:	£min	£max
Double	34.00	50.00

Half board per

person:	£min	£max
Daily	24.00	28.00
Weekly	161.00	182.00

Open February–November
🛌♿🅿♿🛏S✂♿🖨🚗❄🚌
DAP SP

Astoria Hotel

Listed

6 Grosvenor Terrace, Bootham, York YO3 7AG
☎ (01904) 659558
Spacious Victorian hotel overlooking park and York Minster. Some en-suite rooms available. Parties and groups catered for. Dogs very welcome.
Bedrooms: 5 single, 2 double, 4 twin, 1 triple, 3 family rooms
Bathrooms: 5 en-suite, 3 public
Bed & breakfast

per night	£min	£max
Single	18.00	25.00
Double	36.00	50.00

Parking for 15
Cards accepted: Visa
🛌♿&🅿🛏S♿📺🖨🚗

Avenue Guest House

🛌

6 The Avenue, Clifton, York
YO3 6AS
☎ (01904) 620575
Victorian house in a quiet location with easy parking. Riverside walk to city centre. Colour TV, tea/coffee in all rooms. Families welcome. No smoking.
Bedrooms: 1 single, 2 double, 2 triple, 2 family rooms
Bathrooms: 2 en-suite, 2 public
Bed & breakfast

per night:	£min	£max
Single	15.00	18.00
Double	26.00	40.00

🛌🅿♿🛏S✂♿📺🖨🚗❄ SP

Barbican Hotel

🛌🛌 COMMENDED

20 Barbican Road, York YO1 5AA
☎ (01904) 627617
Fax (01904) 647140

Small in size, large in character.
Overlooks city walls. No smoking. Full English or vegetarian breakfast. Leave car in our car park and walk to city centre.
Bedrooms: 4 double, 1 twin, 1 family room
Bathrooms: 6 en-suite, 1 public
Bed & breakfast

per night:	£min	£max
Single	23.00	35.00
Double	40.00	52.00

Parking for 7
Cards accepted: Access, Visa, Diners, Amex
🛌♿🖨&📞🅿♿🛏S✂♿📺
🖨🚗❄ SP

Bay Tree Guest House

🛌🛌

92 Bishopthorpe Road, York
YO2 1JS
☎ (01904) 659462
Victorian terraced house, 10 minutes' walk from the city centre and half a mile from the racecourse.
Bedrooms: 2 single, 2 double, 1 twin
Bathrooms: 1 en-suite, 1 public
Bed & breakfast

per night:	£min	£max
Single	15.00	17.00
Double	30.00	40.00

Parking for 1
🛌🅿♿♿🛏S✂♿📺🖨🚗 SP
🏠

Bedford Hotel

🛌🛌 COMMENDED

108-110 Bootham, York YO3 7DG
☎ (01904) 624412
Family-run hotel, a short walk along historic Bootham to the famous York Minster and city centre.
Bedrooms: 4 single, 6 double, 2 twin, 3 triple, 1 family room
Bathrooms: 16 en-suite
Bed & breakfast

per night:	£min	£max
Single	28.00	34.00
Double	44.00	50.00

Parking for 14
Cards accepted: Access, Visa
🛌🅿♿📺🖨🚗❄🚌 SP 🏠 ®

Beech House

🛌🛌🛌

6-7 Longfield Terrace, Bootham, York YO3 7DJ
☎ (01904) 634581
Small, family-run guesthouse with a warm welcome and a relaxing atmosphere, only 5 minutes' walk from York Minster.
Bedrooms: 1 single, 5 double, 2 twin
Bathrooms: 8 en-suite
Bed & breakfast

per night:	£min	£max
Single	21.00	30.00
Double	38.00	46.00

Evening meal from 1800
Parking for 5
🛌10&📞🅿♿🛏♿📺🖨🚗❄
🚌 SP T ®

YORKSHIRE

YORK
Continued

Beechwood Close Hotel
COMMENDED
19 Shipton Road, Clifton, York
YO3 6RE
☎ (01904) 658378
Fax (01904) 647124
Ⓒ Minotel

Spacious, detached, family-run hotel set among trees, located on the A19, 1 mile north of the city centre. Restaurant, bar, lounge, car park and a 9-hole putting green.
Bedrooms: 3 single, 4 double, 2 twin, 5 triple
Bathrooms: 14 en-suite
Bed & breakfast

per night:	£min	£max
Single	43.50	45.00
Double	60.00	72.00

Half board per person:	£min	£max
Daily	42.50	57.30
Weekly	283.50	388.50

Lunch available
Evening meal 1900 (last orders 2100)
Parking for 36
Cards accepted: Access, Visa, Diners, Amex, Switch/Delta

Bloomsbury Hotel
127 Clifton, York YO3 6BL
☎ (01904) 634031

An elegantly appointed large Victorian town house, centrally situated with large private car park. Recently totally refurbished. Completely non-smoking.
Bedrooms: 2 single, 8 double, 4 twin, 4 triple
Bathrooms: 18 en-suite
Bed & breakfast

per night:	£min	£max
Single	36.00	50.00
Double	45.00	65.00

Parking for 8
Cards accepted: Access, Visa, Switch/Delta

Blue Bridge Hotel
Fishergate, York YO1 4AP
☎ (01904) 621193
Fax (01904) 671571
Friendly, private hotel with a relaxed atmosphere and a warm welcome. Short riverside walk to city. Private car park.

Bedrooms: 2 single, 6 double, 3 twin, 5 triple
Bathrooms: 14 en-suite, 1 public
Bed & breakfast

per night:	£min	£max
Single	35.00	48.00
Double	50.00	60.00

Parking for 20
Cards accepted: Access, Visa

Bootham Park Hotel
COMMENDED
9 Grosvenor Terrace, Bootham, York YO3 7AG
☎ (01904) 644262
Fax (01904) 645647

Elegant Victorian house 5 minutes' walk from York Minster and tourist attractions. En-suite rooms with hairdryer, alarm clock, colour TV, drinks tray and telephone.
Bedrooms: 3 double, 1 twin, 1 triple, 1 family room
Bathrooms: 6 en-suite
Bed & breakfast

per night:	£min	£max
Double	38.00	50.00

Parking for 6
Cards accepted: Access, Visa

Bowen House
4 Gladstone Street, Huntington Road, York YO3 7RF
☎ (01904) 636881
Within a short walk of York Minster and city centre, this late Victorian, family-run guesthouse combines high quality facilities with old-style charm. Private car park. Traditional or vegetarian breakfasts. Non-smoking throughout.
Bedrooms: 1 single, 2 double, 1 twin, 1 family room
Bathrooms: 3 en-suite, 1 public, 1 private shower
Bed & breakfast

per night:	£min	£max
Single	20.00	23.00
Double	32.00	45.00

Parking for 4
Cards accepted: Access, Visa

Briar Lea Guest House
APPROVED
8 Longfield Terrace, Bootham, York YO3 7DJ
☎ (01904) 635061 & (0589) 178956
Victorian house with all rooms en-suite, 5 minutes' walk from the city centre and railway station.

Bedrooms: 1 double, 1 twin, 1 triple, 1 family room
Bathrooms: 4 en-suite
Bed & breakfast

per night:	£min	£max
Single	18.00	22.00
Double	32.00	40.00

Parking for 1

Byron House Hotel
COMMENDED
7 Driffield Terrace, The Mount, York YO2 2DD
☎ (01904) 632525
Fax (01904) 638904
Ⓒ The Independents

Elegant Georgian building with spacious rooms. Easy walking distance from city centre. Good English cooking including vegetarian dishes and dietary requirements.
Bedrooms: 3 single, 2 double, 1 twin, 3 triple, 1 family room
Bathrooms: 7 en-suite, 1 public
Bed & breakfast

per night:	£min	£max
Single	25.00	43.00
Double	49.00	76.00

Evening meal from 1900
Parking for 7
Cards accepted: Access, Visa, Diners, Amex

Carlton House Hotel
COMMENDED
134 The Mount, York YO2 2AS
☎ (01904) 622265
Hotel in Georgian terraced home, family-run for 50 years. Just outside city walls, close to all attractions and amenities.
Bedrooms: 1 single, 6 double, 1 twin, 4 triple, 1 family room
Bathrooms: 13 en-suite, 1 public
Bed & breakfast

per night:	£min	£max
Single	27.00	
Double	48.00	

Parking for 7

Carousel Guest House
Listed APPROVED
83 Eldon Street, off Stanley Street, Haxby Road, York YO3 7NH
☎ (01904) 646709
Warm, friendly, licensed guesthouse in

YORKSHIRE

central location. All rooms en-suite with tea/coffee making facilities and colour TV. Parking.
Bedrooms: 2 single, 4 double, 1 twin, 1 triple, 1 family room
Bathrooms: 9 en-suite

Bed & breakfast per night:
	£min	£max
Single	16.50	18.50
Double	30.00	36.00

Half board per person:
	£min	£max
Daily	25.00	28.50
Weekly	170.00	195.00

Evening meal 1730 (last orders 1000)
Parking for 15

Cavalier Private Hotel
COMMENDED
39 Monkgate, York YO3 7PB
☎ (01904) 636615
Small family-run hotel close to the city centre, only yards from the ancient Bar Walls and many of York's famous historic landmarks.
Bedrooms: 2 single, 4 double, 2 triple, 2 family rooms
Bathrooms: 7 en-suite, 3 public

Bed & breakfast per night:
	£min	£max
Single	23.00	25.00
Double	40.00	54.00

Parking for 3
Cards accepted: Access, Visa, Amex

Chantry Hotel
COMMENDED
130 The Mount, York YO2 2AS
☎ (01904) 659150
Elegant Georgian listed residence, built in 1830 and tastefully restored. Near the station and Micklegate Bar, an ancient entrance to the old city.
Bedrooms: 2 single, 3 double, 1 triple
Bathrooms: 3 en-suite, 1 private, 1 public

Bed & breakfast per night:
	£min	£max
Single	27.50	37.50
Double	50.00	65.00

Half board per person:
	£min	£max
Daily	39.00	52.50

Evening meal 1830 (last orders 2030)
Parking for 2
Cards accepted: Access, Visa

Chelmsford Place Guest House
APPROVED
85 Fulford Road, York YO1 4BD
☎ (01904) 624491
Small, friendly guesthouse offering accommodation at a moderate price. Ten minutes' walk from York centre.
Bedrooms: 1 single, 2 double, 2 triple
Bathrooms: 2 en-suite, 2 public

Bed & breakfast per night:
	£min	£max
Single	15.00	20.00
Double	25.00	40.00

Parking for 1
Cards accepted: Access, Visa

Chilton Guest House
Listed COMMENDED
1 Claremont Terrace, Gillygate, York YO3 7EJ
☎ (01904) 612465
Small guesthouse in city centre, close to the city's historic attractions. All rooms en-suite with hairdryer, tea/coffee tray.
Bedrooms: 1 double, 1 twin, 1 triple
Bathrooms: 3 en-suite

Bed & breakfast per night:
	£min	£max
Single	25.00	30.00
Double	36.00	44.00

Parking for 2

City Guest House
68 Monkgate, York YO3 7PF
☎ (01904) 622483
Small, friendly, family-run B & B in attractive Victorian town-house. Ideally situated 5 minutes' walk to York Minster and close to attractions. Private parking. Cosy en-suite rooms. Restaurants nearby. Non-smoking.
Bedrooms: 2 single, 3 double, 1 twin, 1 family room
Bathrooms: 5 en-suite, 2 private showers

Bed & breakfast per night:
	£min	£max
Single	14.00	20.00
Double	28.00	44.00

Parking for 4
Cards accepted: Access, Visa

Establishments should be open throughout the year, unless otherwise stated.

Clarence Gardens Hotel
Haxby Road, York YO3 7JS
☎ (01904) 624252
Fax (01904) 671293
Comfortable accommodation with emphasis on service. Pool table. 10 minutes' walk to the city centre and York Minster.
Bedrooms: 1 single, 4 double, 8 twin, 1 triple, 4 family rooms
Bathrooms: 18 en-suite

Bed & breakfast per night:
	£min	£max
Single	30.00	43.00
Double	40.00	60.00

Half board per person:
	£min	£max
Daily	26.00	55.95
Weekly	182.00	391.65

Evening meal 1900 (last orders 2015)
Parking for 60
Cards accepted: Access, Visa, Amex

Clifton Bridge Hotel
COMMENDED
Water End, Clifton, York YO3 6LL
☎ (01904) 610510
Fax (01904) 640208

Ideally situated in its own grounds beside delightful short riverside walk to city centre. Beautifully appointed, with bar and restaurant. All rooms en-suite with colour TV, beverages, telephone, radio, baby listening, etc.
Wheelchair access category 3
Bedrooms: 2 single, 3 double, 8 twin, 1 triple
Bathrooms: 14 en-suite

Bed & breakfast per night:
	£min	£max
Single	30.00	48.00
Double	45.00	64.00

Half board per person:
	£min	£max
Daily	32.50	42.00

Lunch available
Evening meal 1830 (last orders 2000)
Parking for 14
Cards accepted: Access, Visa, Diners, Amex, Switch/Delta

YORKSHIRE

YORK
Continued

Collingwood Hotel
163 Holgate Road, York YO2 4DF
☎ (01904) 783333
Georgian building with adequate parking within its own grounds. Licensed. All rooms private facilities. Four-poster bedroom available. Close to city centre, racecourse and railway station.
Bedrooms: 6 double, 2 twin, 1 triple, 1 family room
Bathrooms: 9 en-suite, 1 private

Bed & breakfast per night:	£min	£max
Single	25.00	35.00
Double	38.00	48.00

Parking for 10
Cards accepted: Access, Visa, Diners, Amex

Copper's Lodge
Listed
15 Alma Terrace, Fulford Road, York YO1 4DQ
☎ (01904) 639871
Family-run guesthouse offering personal service. In a quiet location with a river walk close by and only 5 minutes' walk to the city centre.
Bedrooms: 1 single, 1 double, 5 triple
Bathrooms: 3 public

Bed & breakfast per night:	£min	£max
Single	16.00	18.00
Double	26.00	36.00

Half board per person:	£min	£max
Daily	20.50	26.50

Evening meal 1800 (last orders 1800)
Parking for 7

Cottage Hotel
COMMENDED
1 Clifton Green, York YO3 6LH
☎ (01904) 643711
Fax (01904) 611230
Enchanting family-run hotel within 10 minutes' walking distance of the city centre, overlooking the beautiful Clifton Green.
Bedrooms: 2 single, 9 double, 5 twin, 3 triple
Bathrooms: 19 en-suite

Bed & breakfast per night:	£min	£max
Single	30.00	45.00
Double	40.00	60.00

Half board per person:	£min	£max
Daily	29.50	37.50

Evening meal 1830 (last orders 2100)
Parking for 10
Cards accepted: Access, Visa, Diners, Amex, Switch/Delta

Craig-Y-Don
APPROVED
3 Grosvenor Terrace, Bootham, York YO3 7AG
☎ (01904) 637186 & Mobile 0850 202795
Fax (01904) 637186
Under the Oliver ownership since 1979, where guests have become friends. Early booking is advisable to prevent disappointment.
Bedrooms: 3 single, 3 double, 2 twin
Bathrooms: 1 en-suite, 3 public

Bed & breakfast per night:	£min	£max
Single	16.00	20.00
Double	32.00	40.00

Parking for 5
Open January–October, December
Cards accepted: Access, Visa

Crook Lodge
COMMENDED
26 St Mary's, Bootham, York YO3 7DD
☎ (01904) 655614
Early Victorian residence 450 yards from city centre. Bedrooms all en-suite with colour TV, radio. Private car park. Special breaks, dinner, bed and breakfast.
Bedrooms: 1 single, 4 double, 2 twin
Bathrooms: 7 en-suite

Bed & breakfast per night:	£min	£max
Single	25.00	28.00
Double	36.00	50.00

Half board per person:	£min	£max
Daily	26.00	35.50

Evening meal 1800 (last orders 1000)
Parking for 8
Open February–December

The ⋀ symbol after an establishment name indicates that it is a Regional Tourist Board member.

Curzon Lodge and Stable Cottages
HIGHLY COMMENDED
23 Tadcaster Road, Dringhouses, York YO2 2QG
☎ (01904) 703157

Delightful 17th C listed house and former stables in pretty conservation area overlooking York racecourse, once a home of the Terry "chocolate" family. All en-suite, some four-posters. Many antiques. Large enclosed car park.
Bedrooms: 1 single, 4 double, 3 twin, 1 triple, 1 family room
Bathrooms: 10 en-suite

Bed & breakfast per night:	£min	£max
Single	30.00	40.00
Double	45.00	60.00

Parking for 16
Cards accepted: Access, Visa

Dean Court Hotel
HIGHLY COMMENDED
Duncombe Place, York YO1 2EF
☎ (01904) 625082
Fax (01904) 620305
Best Western

Elegant Victorian hotel, superbly situated next to York Minster in the centre of the city. Tearooms, restaurant, bar and conference facilities. Secure car park with free valet service.
Bedrooms: 18 single, 8 double, 10 twin, 3 triple, 2 family rooms
Suite available
Bathrooms: 41 en-suite

Bed & breakfast per night:	£min	£max
Single	75.00	95.00
Double	110.00	130.00

Half board per person:	£min	£max
Daily	57.00	67.00

Lunch available
Evening meal 1900 (last orders 2130)
Parking for 30

YORKSHIRE

Cards accepted: Access, Visa, Diners, Amex, Switch/Delta

Hotel Fairmount
230 Tadcaster Road, Mount Vale, York YO2 2ES
☎ (01904) 638298
Fax (01904) 639724
Logis of Great Britain
Large, tastefully furnished, Victorian villa with open views over racecourse, 10 minutes from city centre. Ground floor rooms available for people with special needs.
Wheelchair access category 3
Bedrooms: 2 single, 6 double, 2 twin, 2 triple
Bathrooms: 10 en-suite, 2 private

Bed & breakfast per night:	£min	£max
Single	30.00	35.00
Double	54.00	56.00

Half board per person:	£min	£max
Daily	38.00	42.00

Lunch available
Evening meal 1900 (last orders 2100)
Parking for 12
Cards accepted: Access, Visa, Amex, Switch/Delta

Forte Posthouse York
COMMENDED
Tadcaster Road, York YO2 2QF
☎ (01904) 707921
Fax (01904) 702804
Forte
Modern hotel with a pleasant garden, in the south of the city overlooking the racecourse.
Bedrooms: 81 double, 62 twin
Bathrooms: 143 en-suite

Bed & breakfast per night:	£min	£max
Single	39.00	46.00
Double	78.00	92.00

Half board per person:	£min	£max
Daily	53.00	56.00

Lunch available
Evening meal 1700 (last orders 2200)
Parking for 180
Cards accepted: Access, Visa, Diners, Amex, Switch/Delta

Four Seasons Hotel
COMMENDED
7 St Peter's Grove, Bootham, York YO3 6AQ
☎ (01904) 622621
Fax (01904) 620976

Beautiful, high-quality Victorian hotel, in quiet tree-lined grove. Only 5 minutes' walk from city centre. All rooms en-suite. Private car park.
Bedrooms: 2 double, 1 twin, 1 triple, 1 family room
Bathrooms: 5 en-suite

Bed & breakfast per night:	£min	£max
Double	44.00	56.00

Parking for 8
Cards accepted: Access, Visa

Fourposter Lodge Hotel
COMMENDED
68-70 Heslington Road, Barbican Road, York YO1 5AU
☎ (01904) 651170

Victorian villa, lovingly restored and furnished for your comfort. Just 10 minutes' walk from historic York with all its fascinations.
Bedrooms: 8 double, 1 twin, 1 triple
Bathrooms: 10 en-suite

Bed & breakfast per night:	£min	£max
Single	35.00	38.00
Double	50.00	54.00

Half board per person:	£min	£max
Daily	37.50	39.50

Evening meal 1830 (last orders 2000)
Parking for 8
Cards accepted: Access, Visa, Amex

Establishments should be open throughout the year, unless otherwise stated.

George Hotel
COMMENDED
6 St George's Place, Tadcaster Road, York YO2 2DR
☎ (01904) 625056
Small family-run hotel in a quiet cul-de-sac near the racecourse and convenient for the city centre. Good car parking facilities.
Bedrooms: 5 double, 2 triple, 3 family rooms
Bathrooms: 10 en-suite

Bed & breakfast per night:	£min	£max
Single	20.00	30.00
Double	35.00	50.00

Evening meal 1900 (last orders 2100)
Parking for 9
Cards accepted: Access, Visa, Diners, Amex

Gleneagles Lodge Guest House
APPROVED
27 Nunthorpe Avenue, York YO2 1PF
☎ (01904) 637000
Fax (01904) 637000
In a cul-de-sac close to the station, city centre and museums. Within easy walking distance of the racecourse.
Bedrooms: 2 double, 1 twin, 2 family rooms
Bathrooms: 2 en-suite, 2 public

Bed & breakfast per night:	£min	£max
Single	20.00	25.00
Double	35.00	42.00

Glenville Guest House
APPROVED
132 East Parade, Heworth, York YO3 7YG
☎ (01904) 425370
Warm, friendly accommodation in a quiet area 10 minutes' walk from York Minster and city centre. Special emphasis on English breakfast. En-suite available. Ample unrestricted street parking.
Bedrooms: 1 single, 1 double, 1 triple
Bathrooms: 1 en-suite, 1 public, 1 private shower

Bed & breakfast per night:	£min	£max
Single	14.00	16.00
Double	28.00	36.00

Continued ▶

YORK
Continued

Parking for 1

Granby Lodge Hotel
Listed

41-43 Scarcroft Road, York
YO2 1DA
☎ (01904) 653291
Fax (01904) 653291

Victorian family hotel offering all modern comforts and a mezzanine bar-lounge. Most rooms en-suite. Car park.
Bedrooms: 8 single, 9 double, 27 twin, 7 triple, 3 family rooms
Bathrooms: 32 en-suite, 6 public

Bed & breakfast per night:	£min	£max
Single	16.00	25.00
Double	30.00	40.00

Half board per person:	£min	£max
Daily	24.00	33.00

Evening meal 1800 (last orders 1900)
Parking for 30
Cards accepted: Access, Visa, Diners, Amex, Switch/Delta

Grange Hotel
HIGHLY COMMENDED

Clifton, York YO3 6AA
☎ (01904) 644744
Fax (01904) 612453
Classical, Regency town house hotel with all bedrooms individually decorated with antiques and English chintz. Within easy walking distance of York Minster.
Bedrooms: 3 single, 9 double, 17 twin, 1 triple
Suite available
Bathrooms: 30 en-suite

Bed & breakfast per night:	£min	£max
Single	95.00	95.00
Double	105.00	155.00

Half board per person:	£min	£max
Daily	75.50	100.50

Lunch available
Evening meal 1800 (last orders 2230)

Parking for 26
Cards accepted: Access, Visa, Diners, Amex, Switch/Delta

Grange Lodge
APPROVED

52 Bootham Crescent, Bootham, York YO3 7AH
☎ (01904) 621137
Attractive, tastefully furnished Victorian town house with a friendly atmosphere. Special emphasis is given to food, cleanliness and hospitality. Basic and en-suite rooms available. Evening meal by arrangement.
Bedrooms: 1 single, 3 double, 1 twin, 2 triple
Bathrooms: 4 en-suite, 1 public

Bed & breakfast per night:	£min	£max
Single	16.00	18.00
Double	30.00	40.00

Half board per person:	£min	£max
Daily	23.00	28.00
Weekly	150.00	190.00

Evening meal from 1800

Greenside

124 Clifton, York YO3 6BQ
☎ (01904) 623491

Owner-run guesthouse, fronting Clifton Green, ideally situated for all York's attractions. Offers many facilities and a homely atmosphere.
Bedrooms: 1 single, 3 double, 2 twin, 2 triple
Bathrooms: 3 en-suite, 2 public

Bed & breakfast per night:	£min	£max
Single	16.00	
Double	24.00	

Half board per person:	£min	£max
Daily	25.50	

Evening meal 1800 (last orders 1800)
Parking for 6

Grimston House
APPROVED

Deighton, York YO4 6HB
☎ (01904) 728328

Country house in well established gardens, 5 miles from York and close to good pub food.
Bedrooms: 1 twin, 5 triple, 1 family room
Bathrooms: 5 en-suite, 1 public

Bed & breakfast per night:	£min	£max
Single	20.00	25.00
Double	38.00	41.00

Parking for 16

Hazelmere Guest House
Listed APPROVED

65 Monkgate, York YO3 7PA
☎ (01904) 655947
Georgian cottages, tastefully linked to retain their original character. Very close to York Minster and to several restaurants. Established for over 30 years. All rooms on first floor level. Private parking.
Bedrooms: 2 single, 2 double, 2 twin, 2 triple
Bathrooms: 1 en-suite, 1 private, 2 public

Bed & breakfast per night:	£min	£max
Single	16.00	18.00
Double	32.00	40.00

Parking for 7

The Hazelwood
COMMENDED

24-25 Portland Street, Gillygate, York YO3 7EH
☎ (01904) 626548
Fax (01904) 628032
Situated in centre of York, only 400 yards from Minster, in an extremely quiet location with own car park. Elegant Victorian house. Non-smoking.
Bedrooms: 2 single, 7 double, 3 twin, 2 triple
Bathrooms: 11 en-suite, 3 public

Bed & breakfast per night:	£min	£max
Single	19.50	44.00
Double	32.00	56.00

YORKSHIRE

Parking for 12
Cards accepted: Access, Visa

Heath Holme Guest House
COMMENDED

104 Main Street, Fulford, York
YO1 4PS
☎ (01904) 629073
Secluded detached house in own grounds on outskirts of city, half a mile from A64 ring road. 1 mile city centre on bus route. River walks.
Bedrooms: 2 single, 2 double
Bathrooms: 4 en-suite

Bed & breakfast per night:	£min	£max
Single	23.00	23.00
Double	42.00	42.00

Parking for 6
Open April–November
Cards accepted: Access, Visa

Hedley House
COMMENDED

3-4 Bootham Terrace, York
YO3 7DH
☎ (01904) 637404
Family-run hotel close to the city centre. 1 ground floor bedroom. All rooms en-suite. Home cooking, special diets catered for.
Bedrooms: 2 single, 5 double, 5 twin, 2 triple, 1 family room
Bathrooms: 15 en-suite

Bed & breakfast per night:	£min	£max
Single	20.00	34.00
Double	36.00	56.00

Half board per person:	£min	£max
Daily	30.00	44.00

Lunch available
Evening meal 1830 (last orders 1900)
Parking for 13
Cards accepted: Access, Visa, Diners, Amex, Switch/Delta

Heworth Court Hotel
COMMENDED

76-78 Heworth Green, York
YO3 7TQ
☎ (01904) 425156
Fax (01904) 415290
Privately-owned, family-run hotel close to York Minster and surrounding countryside. Special short breaks. Bar, restaurant, car park, lounge. Brochure available.

Wheelchair access category 3
Bedrooms: 1 single, 18 double, 5 triple, 2 family rooms
Bathrooms: 26 en-suite

Bed & breakfast per night:	£min	£max
Single	36.00	43.00
Double	42.00	76.00

Half board per person:	£min	£max
Daily	40.00	58.95
Weekly	161.00	234.50

Lunch available
Evening meal 1830 (last orders 2130)
Parking for 26
Cards accepted: Access, Visa, Diners, Amex, Switch/Delta

Hobbits Hotel
COMMENDED

9 St Peter's Grove, York YO3 6AQ
☎ (01904) 624538 & 642926
Fax (01904) 651765
Find a friendly and comfortable welcome in this lovely old house, in a quiet cul-de-sac 10 minutes' walk from centre.
Bedrooms: 2 single, 2 double, 1 twin, 1 triple
Bathrooms: 6 en-suite

Bed & breakfast per night:	£min	£max
Single	25.00	27.00
Double	50.00	55.00

Parking for 5
Cards accepted: Access, Visa, Diners

The Hollies
Listed APPROVED

141 Fulford Road, York YO1 4HG
☎ (01904) 634279
Comfortable family-run guesthouse, close to university and golf-course and with easy access to city centre. Tea/coffee facilities, colour TV in all rooms, some en-suite. Car parking.
Bedrooms: 2 double, 2 triple, 1 family room
Bathrooms: 2 en-suite, 1 public

Bed & breakfast per night:	£min	£max
Single	16.00	25.00
Double	30.00	40.00

Parking for 5

Please check prices and other details at the time of booking.

Holly Lodge
APPROVED

206 Fulford Road, York YO1 4DD
☎ (01904) 646005
Listed Georgian building on the A19, convenient for both the north and south and within walking distance of the city centre. Close to university, golf course and Barbican centre. Quiet rooms and private car park.
Bedrooms: 3 double, 1 twin, 1 family room
Bathrooms: 5 en-suite

Bed & breakfast per night:	£min	£max
Single	20.00	30.00
Double	30.00	50.00

Parking for 5
Cards accepted: Access, Visa

Holmwood House Hotel
HIGHLY COMMENDED

112-114 Holgate Road, York
YO2 4BB
☎ (01904) 626183
Fax (01904) 670899
Two listed Victorian town houses, 5 minutes from city walls, lovingly redecorated and elegantly furnished. Offering comfort in attractive non-smoking, en-suite rooms.
Bedrooms: 10 double, 1 twin, 1 triple
Bathrooms: 12 en-suite

Bed & breakfast per night:	£min	£max
Single	40.00	55.00
Double	55.00	70.00

Parking for 9
Cards accepted: Access, Visa, Amex, Switch/Delta

Jacobean Lodge Hotel
COMMENDED

Plainville Lane, Wigginton, York
YO3 8RG
☎ (01904) 768403
Fax (01904) 768403

Converted 17th C farmhouse, 4 miles north of York. Set in picturesque gardens with ample parking. Open log fire, warm, friendly atmosphere and traditional cuisine.

Continued ▶

YORKSHIRE

YORK
Continued

Bedrooms: 2 single, 9 double, 1 twin, 2 triple
Bathrooms: 14 en-suite

Bed & breakfast per night:

	£min	£max
Single	28.00	34.00
Double	40.00	56.00

Lunch available
Evening meal 1900 (last orders 2200)
Parking for 70
Cards accepted: Access, Visa, Switch/Delta

Jarvis Abbey Park
COMMENDED
77 The Mount, York YO2 2BN
☎ (01904) 658301
Fax (01904) 621224
Jarvis/Utell International
Explore York from this centrally located yet quiet hotel. Friendly service with a full bar and English restaurant. All rooms en-suite.
Bedrooms: 5 single, 34 double, 36 twin, 9 triple, 1 family room
Bathrooms: 85 en-suite

Bed & breakfast per night:

	£min	£max
Single	47.00	77.50
Double	94.00	96.00

Half board per person:

	£min	£max
Daily	58.50	62.00

Lunch available
Evening meal 1830 (last orders 2130)
Parking for 30
Cards accepted: Access, Visa, Diners, Amex, Switch/Delta

Jorvik Hotel
APPROVED
50-52 Marygate, Bootham, York YO3 7BH
☎ (01904) 653511
Fax (01904) 627009
Well-appointed central hotel overlooking the walls of St Mary's Abbey and Museum Gardens. Close to the minster and shopping areas.
Bedrooms: 1 single, 12 double, 8 twin, 1 triple
Bathrooms: 22 en-suite

Bed & breakfast per night:

	£min	£max
Single	26.00	30.00
Double	38.00	60.00

Half board per person:

	£min	£max
Daily	27.50	40.00
Weekly	192.50	250.00

Evening meal 1830 (last orders 2100)
Parking for 8
Cards accepted: Access, Visa

Judges Lodging
HIGHLY COMMENDED
9 Lendal, York YO1 2AQ
☎ (01904) 623587 & 638733
Fax (01904) 679947
Georgian town house of exceptional historic importance, set in the centre of this ancient city. Lavishly decorated and furnished. Private parking.
Bedrooms: 2 single, 6 double, 3 twin, 2 triple
Suites available
Bathrooms: 13 en-suite

Bed & breakfast per night:

	£min	£max
Single	70.00	90.00
Double	90.00	140.00

Lunch available
Evening meal 1830 (last orders 2130)
Parking for 12
Cards accepted: Access, Visa, Diners, Amex, Switch/Delta

Keys House
Listed COMMENDED
137 Fulford Road, York YO1 4HG
☎ (01904) 658488
Comfortable Edwardian house providing spacious bedrooms with showers and WCs. Own key provided. Reductions for 3 or more nights. Walled car park.
Bedrooms: 2 double, 3 triple
Bathrooms: 5 en-suite

Bed & breakfast per night:

	£min	£max
Single	15.00	40.00
Double	30.00	55.00

Parking for 5
Cards accepted: Access, Visa

Kilima Hotel
COMMENDED
129 Holgate Road, York YO2 4DE
☎ (01904) 625787
Fax (01904) 612083
Lovingly furbished 19th C rectory with a fine restaurant serving a la carte and table d'hote. Walking distance to city centre. Private car park.
Bedrooms: 4 single, 7 double, 3 twin, 1 family room

Bathrooms: 15 en-suite

Bed & breakfast per night:

	£min	£max
Single	50.00	50.00
Double	78.00	90.00

Half board per person:

	£min	£max
Daily	57.00	63.50
Weekly	399.00	444.50

Lunch available
Evening meal 1830 (last orders 2130)
Parking for 20
Cards accepted: Access, Visa, Diners, Amex, Switch/Delta

Kismet Guest House
Listed
147 Haxby Road, York YO3 7JW
☎ (01904) 621056
18th C terraced house, 10 minutes' walk from city centre. Parking and private lock-up garage. Late keys, no petty restrictions. Heartiest of English breakfasts to satisfy any appetite.
Bedrooms: 2 single, 2 double, 1 twin, 1 triple
Bathrooms: 1 en-suite, 2 private, 1 public, 1 private shower

Bed & breakfast per night:

	£min	£max
Single	16.00	20.00
Double	30.00	36.00

Parking for 5
Open March–November

Knavesmire Manor Hotel
COMMENDED
302 Tadcaster Road, York YO2 2HE
☎ (01904) 702941
Fax (01904) 709274
Logis of Great Britain

Built in 1833, this magnificent house stands elevated, commanding uninterrupted views across the Knavesmire and parkland, site of York's famous racecourse. Tropical pool and spa.
Bedrooms: 3 single, 9 double, 5 twin, 3 triple, 1 family room
Bathrooms: 21 en-suite

Bed & breakfast per night:

	£min	£max
Single	39.50	59.00
Double	49.00	79.00

YORKSHIRE

Half board per person:	£min	£max
Daily	34.50	47.50
Weekly	210.00	260.00

Evening meal 1900 (last orders 2200)
Parking for 26
Cards accepted: Access, Visa, Diners, Amex, Switch/Delta

Linden Lodge ⋒
≝≝ COMMENDED

6 Nunthorpe Avenue, Scarcroft Road, York YO2 1PF
☎ (01904) 620107
Fax (01904) 620985
Victorian town house in a quiet cul-de-sac, 10 minutes' walk from racecourse, rail station and city centre. Easy access A64.
Bedrooms: 1 single, 6 double, 2 twin, 2 family rooms
Bathrooms: 9 en-suite, 1 public

Bed & breakfast per night:	£min	£max
Single	20.00	30.00
Double	36.00	50.00

Cards accepted: Access, Visa, Amex

The Manor at Acaster Malbis ⋒
≝≝≝ HIGHLY COMMENDED

Acaster Malbis, York YO2 1UL
☎ (01904) 706723
Fax (01904) 706723

Atmospheric manor in rural tranquillity, bordering river. Off the beaten track yet close for city, racecourse and A64. Private fishing in lake. En-suite rooms with full facilities. Wonderful conservatory dining room with view of lake and gardens.
Bedrooms: 5 double, 2 twin, 3 triple
Bathrooms: 10 en-suite

Bed & breakfast per night:	£min	£max
Double	47.00	60.00

Lunch available
Evening meal 1900 (last orders 2100)
Parking for 15

Midway House Hotel ⋒
≝≝≝ COMMENDED

145 Fulford Road, York YO1 4HG
☎ (01904) 659272
Fax (01904) 621799
Non-smoking, family-run hotel. Spacious en-suite bedrooms with four-poster and ground floor rooms available. Close to city centre and university. Private parking.
Bedrooms: 7 double, 3 twin, 2 triple
Bathrooms: 11 en-suite, 1 private, 1 public

Bed & breakfast per night:	£min	£max
Single	20.00	40.00
Double	36.00	50.00

Evening meal 1900 (last orders 1900)
Parking for 14
Cards accepted: Access, Visa, Diners, Amex

Monkbar Hotel
≝≝≝≝ COMMENDED

St Maurice's Road, York YO3 7JA
☎ (01904) 638086
Fax (01904) 629195
Ⓒ Consort/The Independents

A short walk from York Minster and all tourist attractions. Attractive bedrooms, four-poster room, jacuzzi.
Bedrooms: 23 double, 23 twin, 2 triple
Bathrooms: 48 en-suite

Bed & breakfast per night:	£min	£max
Single	56.00	72.00
Double	112.00	144.00

Half board per person:	£min	£max
Daily	69.00	110.00
Weekly	364.00	483.00

Lunch available
Evening meal 1800 (last orders 2130)
Parking for 70
Cards accepted: Access, Visa, Diners, Amex, Switch/Delta

Map references apply to the colour maps at the back of this guide.

Monkgate Lodge ⋒
≝≝

51 Monkgate, York YO3 7PB
☎ (01904) 631501
Listed Georgian city-centre house. 300 yards from York Minster and close to all amenities. En-suite rooms with colour TV and tea/coffee trays. Non-smokers welcome. Private parking.
Bedrooms: 1 double, 1 triple
Bathrooms: 2 en-suite

Bed & breakfast per night:	£min	£max
Double	45.00	50.00

Open February–December

Moorgarth Guest House ⋒
≝≝ APPROVED

158 Fulford Road, York YO1 4DA
☎ (01904) 636768
Victorian town house with a warm, friendly atmosphere. Close to all tourist attractions and 10 minutes' walk from the city centre.
Bedrooms: 2 single, 2 double, 2 triple, 1 family room
Bathrooms: 4 en-suite, 1 public

Bed & breakfast per night:	£min	£max
Single	19.00	
Double	32.00	

Parking for 5
Open March–December
Cards accepted: Access, Visa

Moorland House ⋒
≝≝

1A Moorland Road, Fulford Road, York YO1 4HF
☎ (01904) 629354
Purpose-built guesthouse with car park, close to city centre, golf club and university. Pleasant and quiet ground floor rooms en-suite with colour TV and hot drink facilities.
Bedrooms: 2 double, 1 twin, 1 triple
Bathrooms: 4 en-suite

Bed & breakfast per night:	£min	£max
Single	24.00	38.00
Double	34.00	50.00

Parking for 4
Cards accepted: Access, Visa, Switch/Delta

Establishments should be open throughout the year, unless otherwise stated.

213

YORKSHIRE

YORK
Continued

Mount Royale Hotel
HIGHLY COMMENDED
The Mount, York YO2 2DA
☎ (01904) 628856
Fax (01904) 611171

Privately owned, tastefully restored William IV building with individually furnished bedrooms. Restaurant overlooks fine English gardens. Heated outdoor swimming pool for use in summer.
Bedrooms: 2 single, 11 double, 10 twin
Suites available
Bathrooms: 23 en-suite

Bed & breakfast per night:
	£min	£max
Single	75.00	100.00
Double	85.00	140.00

Lunch available
Evening meal 1900 (last orders 2200)
Parking for 30
Cards accepted: Access, Visa, Diners, Amex, Switch/Delta

Newington Hotel
COMMENDED
147-157 Mount Vale, York YO2 2DJ
☎ (01904) 625173 & 623090
Fax (01904) 679937
Hotel in a fine Georgian terrace, next to a large open area, within walking distance of the city centre. Large car park, indoor swimming pool, sauna.
Bedrooms: 4 single, 18 double, 11 twin, 7 triple
Bathrooms: 40 en-suite

Bed & breakfast per night:
	£min	£max
Single	38.00	40.00
Double	56.00	60.00

Half board per person:
	£min	£max
Daily	38.00	41.00
Weekly	254.00	254.00

Lunch available
Evening meal 1800 (last orders 2115)
Parking for 32
Cards accepted: Access, Visa, Diners, Amex, Switch/Delta

Papillon Hotel
Listed
43 Gillygate, York YO3 7EA
☎ (01904) 636505
Small, friendly city centre guesthouse with personal attention at all times. 300 yards from York Minster. En-suite available. No smoking, please. Car parking. Phone for details.
Bedrooms: 2 single, 1 double, 2 twin, 3 triple
Bathrooms: 3 en-suite, 2 public

Bed & breakfast per night:
	£min	£max
Single	20.00	25.00
Double	35.00	50.00

Parking for 7

Park View Guest House
Listed COMMENDED
34 Grosvenor Terrace, Bootham, York YO3 7AG
☎ (01904) 620437
Family-run Victorian house with views of York Minster, close to city centre off the A19. Reductions for children sharing.
Bedrooms: 1 single, 3 double, 2 triple, 1 family room
Bathrooms: 3 en-suite, 1 public

Bed & breakfast per night:
	£min	£max
Single	16.00	20.00
Double	30.00	42.00

Priory Hotel
COMMENDED
126-128 Fulford Road, York YO1 4BE
☎ (01904) 625280
Fax (01904) 625280
Family hotel in a residential area with adjacent riverside walk to the city centre.
Bedrooms: 1 single, 9 double, 3 twin, 2 triple, 3 family rooms
Bathrooms: 18 en-suite

Bed & breakfast per night:
	£min	£max
Single	30.00	
Double	45.00	50.00

Half board per person:
	£min	£max
Daily	35.00	

Evening meal 1830 (last orders 2130)
Parking for 24
Cards accepted: Access, Visa, Diners, Amex, Switch/Delta

Riverside Walk Hotel
APPROVED
9 Earlsborough Terrace, Marygate, York YO3 7BQ
☎ (01904) 620769 & 646249

Family-run hotel, a 450-yard riverside walk from the city centre. 5 minutes' walk from the railway station, bus station, Minster and shops. Quiet location. Private car park. Bargain breaks until 1 July, 3 nights' dinner, bed and breakfast.
Bedrooms: 2 single, 6 double, 2 triple
Bathrooms: 10 en-suite

Bed & breakfast per night:
	£min	£max
Single	20.00	26.00
Double	35.00	52.00

Evening meal 1800 (last orders 1900)
Parking for 14
Cards accepted: Access, Visa

Romley Guest House
APPROVED
2 Millfield Road, Scarcroft Road, York YO2 1NQ
☎ (01904) 652822
Comfortable, friendly, family-run guesthouse offering a licensed bar and a variety of other facilities. 10 minutes from city centre.
Bedrooms: 3 single, 1 double, 1 twin, 2 triple
Bathrooms: 1 public, 2 private showers

Bed & breakfast per night:
	£min	£max
Single	13.00	18.00
Double	26.00	36.00

Rosedale Guest House
COMMENDED
Wetherby Road, Rufforth, York YO2 3QB
☎ (01904) 738297
Family-run guesthouse with a homely atmosphere and all facilities, in a delightful, unspoilt village 4 miles west of York on the B1224. Private parking available.
Bedrooms: 1 single, 4 double, 1 twin
Bathrooms: 1 en-suite, 2 public, 2 private showers

YORKSHIRE

Bed & breakfast per night:	£min	£max
Single	16.00	18.00
Double	36.00	38.00

Parking for 5

🐶⌂☐♿♥🆗🛁🛎📺🏧🅿✈🚌OAP※SP†

Royal York Hotel ⓜ

👑👑👑👑 HIGHLY COMMENDED

Station Road, York YO2 2AA
☎ (01904) 653681
Fax (01904) 623503
Ⓖ Principal/Utell International

Set in 3 acres of private grounds, this refurbished, magnificent Victorian hotel is in the centre of historic York. Major attractions within a short walking distance. Prices shown are based on minimum 2-night stay.
Bedrooms: 29 single, 71 double, 70 twin, 7 triple
Suites available
Bathrooms: 177 en-suite

Bed & breakfast per night:	£min	£max
Single	58.00	71.00
Double	86.00	112.00

Half board per person:	£min	£max
Daily	55.00	68.00

Lunch available
Evening meal 1900 (last orders 2145)
Parking for 120
Cards accepted: Access, Visa, Diners, Amex, Switch/Delta

🐶✆⌂☐♥🆗🛁🛎📺🎬🏧🅿✈🍴🍽❋❄SP🎯†

St Pauls ⓜ

👑👑 COMMENDED

120 Holgate Road, York YO2 4BB
☎ (01904) 611514

Close to York's many attractions, this small, family-run hotel has a warm atmosphere and serves a hearty breakfast. Come as a guest and leave as a friend.
Bedrooms: 1 double, 1 twin, 1 triple, 2 family rooms
Bathrooms: 5 en-suite

Bed & breakfast per night:	£min	£max
Single	20.00	
Double		36.00

Evening meal 1800 (last orders 2100)
Parking for 12

🐶⌂☐♥🆗🛁🛎📺🏧🅿✈🚌

Savages Hotel ⓜ

👑👑👑 COMMENDED

15 St Peter's Grove, Clifton, York YO3 6AQ
☎ (01904) 610818
Fax (01904) 627729
Victorian hotel in quiet tree-lined street close to city centre and all attractions. Comfortable, well equipped bedrooms (some ground floor), traditional restaurant serving fine food.
Wheelchair access category 3♿
Bedrooms: 3 single, 9 double, 5 twin, 1 triple, 2 family rooms
Bathrooms: 20 en-suite

Bed & breakfast per night:	£min	£max
Single	25.00	36.00
Double	50.00	64.00

Half board per person:	£min	£max
Daily	28.00	45.00

Lunch available
Evening meal 1800 (last orders 2100)
Parking for 14
Cards accepted: Access, Visa, Diners, Amex

🐶⌂☐♥🆗🛁🛎📺🏧🅿30✈OAP❄SP🎯†

Swallow Hotel ⓜ

👑👑👑👑 HIGHLY COMMENDED

Tadcaster Road, York YO2 2QQ
☎ (01904) 701000
Fax (01904) 702308
Ⓖ Swallow
Set on the edge of York racecourse on the Knavesmire. A traditional hotel with extensive leisure facilities, attractive bedrooms and a restaurant overlooking the hotel grounds. Short break packages available.
Wheelchair access category 1♿
Bedrooms: 7 single, 45 double, 46 twin, 10 triple, 5 family rooms
Suite available
Bathrooms: 113 en-suite

Bed & breakfast per night:	£min	£max
Single	80.00	100.00
Double	90.00	120.00

Half board per person:	£min	£max
Daily	98.95	118.95

Lunch available
Evening meal 1900 (last orders 2200)
Parking for 200
Cards accepted: Access, Visa, Diners, Amex, Switch/Delta

🐶♿⌂☐♥🆗🛁🛎📺🎬🏧🅿180✈🍴🍽❋❄SP†

Tower Guest House ⓜ

👑👑 COMMENDED

2 Feversham Crescent, Wigginton Road, York YO3 7HQ
☎ (01904) 655571 & 635924
Comfortable and spacious 19th C guesthouse with friendly, informative hosts. Strolling distance from York Minster and city centre attractions.
Bedrooms: 2 double, 1 twin, 2 triple
Bathrooms: 5 en-suite

Bed & breakfast per night:	£min	£max
Single	18.00	25.00
Double	35.00	40.00

Parking for 5
Cards accepted: Access, Visa

🐶⌂☐♥🆗🛁🛎📺🏧🅿✈OAP SP†

Warrens Guest House ⓜ

👑👑 COMMENDED

30 Scarcroft Road, York YO2 1NF
☎ (01904) 643139
Centrally situated guesthouse. All rooms en-suite with colour TV and tea/coffee-making facilities. Full English breakfast. Four-poster beds available, also some ground-floor bedrooms. Car park.
Bedrooms: 1 single, 1 double, 2 twin, 1 triple, 1 family room
Bathrooms: 5 en-suite, 1 private

Bed & breakfast per night:	£min	£max
Single	25.00	30.00
Double	35.00	42.00

Parking for 8
Open February–November

🐶♿⌂☐♥🆗🛁🛎📺🏧✈🚌SP

Winston House ⓜ

👑👑

4 Nunthorpe Drive, Bishopthorpe Road, York YO2 1DY
☎ (01904) 653171
Close to racecourse and 10 minutes' walk to city centre, railway station. Character en-suite room with all facilities. Private car park.
Bedrooms: 1 double
Bathrooms: 1 en-suite

Continued ▶

YORKSHIRE

YORK
Continued

Bed & breakfast per night:

	£min	£max
Double	30.00	34.00

Parking for 6

York Pavilion Hotel

HIGHLY COMMENDED

45 Main Street, Fulford, York
YO1 4PJ
☎ (01904) 622099
Fax (01904) 626939
CR Best Western

Charming Georgian country house near city centre. Excellent restaurant, individually designed en-suite bedrooms, car parking, all within mature, walled grounds.

Bedrooms: 22 double, 10 twin, 2 family rooms
Bathrooms: 34 en-suite

Bed & breakfast per night:

	£min	£max
Single	60.00	70.00
Double	104.00	124.00

Half board per person:

	£min	£max
Daily	60.00	75.00
Weekly	396.00	435.60

Lunch available
Evening meal 1830 (last orders 2130)
Parking for 45
Cards accepted: Access, Visa, Diners, Amex, Switch/Delta

USE YOUR *i*'s

There are more than 550 Tourist Information Centres throughout England offering friendly help with accommodation and holiday ideas as well as suggestions of places to visit and things to do. You'll find the address of your nearest Tourist Information Centre in your local Phone Book.

HEART OF ENGLAND

The heart of England is a pot pourri of rural charm and urban vitality. From the spa town of Cheltenham to the busy streets of Birmingham, from the remote grandeur of the Western Marches to the gentle beauty of tiny Cotswold villages, the area will appeal to culture buffs and country lovers alike.

Visit Shakespeare country and Stratford with its world-famous theatre. Discover the craftsmanship of the Potteries and explore the rich industrial heritage of the Black Country. Or simply escape to the Staffordshire peaks, the Malvern Hills, or the gently meandering byways of the Severn Valley.

FOR MORE INFORMATION CONTACT:
Heart of England Tourist Board
Lark Hill Road, Worcester WR5 2EZ
Tel: (01905) 763436 or 763439
Fax: (01905) 763450

Where to Go in the Heart of England -
see pages 218-221
Where to Stay in the Heart of England -
see pages 222-285

HEART OF ENGLAND

Where to Go and What to See

You will find hundreds of interesting places to visit during your stay in the Heart of England, just some of which are listed in these pages. The number against each name will help you locate it on the map (page 221). Contact any Tourist Information Centre in the region for more ideas on days out in the Heart of England.

1 Spode
Spode Works, Church Street,
Stoke-on-Trent,
Staffordshire ST4 1BX
Tel: (01782) 744220
Visitors are shown the various processes in the making of Bone China. Samples can be bought at the Spode Shop.

2 Wedgwood Visitor Centre
Barlaston, Stoke-on-Trent,
Staffordshire ST12 9ES
Tel: (01782) 204141
Located in the Wedgwood Factory which lies within a 500 acre country estate. See potters and decorators at work. Museum and shop.

3 Alton Towers Theme Park
Alton, Staffordshire ST10 4DB
Tel: (0990) 204060
Theme Park with over 125 rides and attractions including Nemesis, Haunted House, Runaway Mine Train, Congo River Rapids, Log Flume, Thunderlooper and Toyland tours.

4 Shugborough Estate
Shugborough, Milford, Stafford,
Staffordshire ST17 0XB
Tel: (01889) 881388
18thC mansion house with fine collection of furniture. Gardens and park contain beautiful neo-classical monuments.

5 The Shrewsbury Quest
193 Abbey Foregate,
Shrewsbury,
Shropshire SY2 6AH
Tel: (01743) 243324
12thC Shrewsbury historical site. Visitors are invited to solve three mysteries, creating manuscripts and playing medieval garden games.

6 Ironbridge Gorge Museum
Ironbridge, Telford,
Shropshire TF8 7AW
Tel: (01952) 433522
Worlds first cast iron bridge, Museum of the River Visitor Centre, Tar Tunnel, Jackfield Tile Museum, Coalport China Museum, Rosehill House, Blists Hill Museum and Museum of Iron.

7 Walsall Arboretum
Lichfield Street,
Walsall, West Midlands
Tel: (01922) 653141
Picturesque Victorian park with over 79 acres of gardens, lakes and parkland, just 5 minutes walk from Walsall town centre. The arboretum is home to the Walsall illuminations.

8 Black Country Museum
Tipton Road, Dudley,
West Midlands DY1 4SQ
Tel: (0121) 557 9643
Midlands open air museum with shops, chapel, canal trip into limestone cavern houses, underground mining display and electric tramway.

9 Birmingham Botanical Gardens and Glasshouses
Westbourne Road,
Edgbaston, Birmingham,

West Midlands B15 3TR
Tel: (0121) 454 1860
Fifteen acres of ornamental gardens and glasshouses. Tropical plants of botanical interest. Aviaries with exotic birds and children's play area.

10 National Sea Life Centre
The Water's Edge, Brindleyplace,
Birmingham B1 2HL
Tel: (0121) 633 4700
Over 55 fascinating displays. The opportunity to come face-to-face with literally 100's of fascinating sea creatures from sharks to shrimps.

11 Cadbury World
Linden Road, Bournville,
Birmingham,
West Midlands B30 2LD
Tel: (0121) 451 4180
Story of Chocolate from Aztec times to present day includes chocolate-making demonstration and children's fantasy factory.

12 National Motorcycle Museum
Coventry Road, Bickenhill,
Solihull, West Midlands B92 0EJ
Tel: (01675) 443311
Museum with a collection of 650 British machines from 1898-1993, housed in a new high architectural standard building.

13 Museum of British Road Transport
St Agnes Lane,
Hales Street, Coventry,
West Midlands CV1 1NN
Tel: (01203) 832425
Museum with a collection of over 400 cars, commercial vehicles, cycles and motorcycles from 1818 to present day.

14 Rugby School Museum
10 Little Church Street,
Rugby, Warwickshire CV21 3AW
Tel: (01788) 574117
Tells the story of the School, scene of Tom Brown's Schooldays, and contains early memorabilia of the game of rugby invented on the School Close.

15 Severn Valley Railway
The Railway Station, Bewdley,
Worcestershire DY12 1BG
Tel: (01299) 403816
Preserved standard gauge steam railway running 16 miles between Kidderminster, Bewdley and Bridgnorth. Collection of locomotives and passenger coaches.

16 Warwick Castle
Warwick,
Warwickshire CV34 4QU
Tel: (01926) 406500
Set in 60 acres of grounds with state rooms, armoury, dungeon, torture chamber, clock tower. Exhibits include a Royal Weekend Party 1898, a preparation for battle scene and Kingmaker Feasts.

17 Ragley Hall
Alcester,
Warwickshire B49 5NJ
Tel: (01789) 762090
17thC Palladian House, home of the Earl and Countess of Yarmouth, restored with French furnishing. Also 3D maze, woodland walk and lakeside picnic area.

18 Heritage Motor Centre
Banbury Road,
Gaydon,
Warwick,
Warwickshire CV35 0BJ
Tel: (01926) 641188
Purpose-built transport museum containing collection of historic British cars. 63 acre site including 4 wheel drive circuit, playground, picnic area and nature reserve.

19 Elgar's Birthplace Museum
Crown East Lane,
Lower Broadheath,
Worcester,
Worcestershire WR2 6RH
Tel: (01905) 333224
The cottage in which Edward Elgar was born, now houses a museum of photographs, musical scores, letters and records.

20 Shakespeare's Birthplace
Henley Street,
Stratford-upon-Avon
Warwickshire CV37 6QW
Tel: (01789) 204016
Evoking the busy market town into which he was born, the exhibition covers Shakespeare's home background, schooling, marriage and theatre career in London.

21 Worcester Cathedral
10A College Green
Worcester, WR1 2LH
Tel: (01905) 611002
Norman crypt and chapter house. King John's Tomb. Prince Arthur's Chantry, medieval cloisters and buildings.

22 Malvern Hills Children's Zoo
Solitaire, Danemoor Cross,
Welland, Malvern,
Worcestershire WR13 6NJ
Tel: (01684) 310016
Tropical animals, pets corner and creepy-crawly house. Visitors can handle the animals, reptiles and see snake demonstrations daily.

23 The New Mappa Mundi & Chained Library Museum
Hereford Cathedral,
5 The Cloister, Hereford,
Herefordshire HR1 2NG
Tel: (01432) 359880
The New Library of Hereford Cathedral is open to visitors. See also the unique Mappa Mundi, the largest and most complete map in the world, drawn in 1289.

24 The National Birds of Prey Centre
Newent, Gloucestershire GL18 1JJ
Tel: (01531) 820286
Large collection of birds of prey. Flying demonstrations daily, weather permitting, with eagles, falcons, hawks, owls and vultures. Also breeding aviaries.

25 Three Choirs Vineyards
Baldwins Farm, Newent,
Gloucestershire GL18 1LS
Tel: (01531) 890555
Home of internationally awarded Three Choirs wine. Visitors are welcome to look round the vineyards and taste the wines at no charge.

26 National Waterways Museum
Llanthony Warehouse,
Gloucester Docks,
Gloucester GL1 2EH
Tel: (01452) 318054
Three floors of dockside warehouse with lively displays telling the story of Britain's canals. Outside craft area with demonstrations. Cafe and shop.

27 Soldiers of Gloucestershire Museum
Custom House,
Gloucester Docks,
Gloucester GL1 2HE
Tel: (01452) 522682
Listed Victorian building in historic docks. The story of Gloucestershire's foot and horse soldiers in the last 300 years.

FIND OUT MORE

Further information about holidays and attractions in the Heart of England is available from: **Heart of England Tourist Board,**
Lark Hill Road,
Worcester WR5 2EZ.
Tel: (01905) 763436 (24 hours)

These publications are available free from the Heart of England Tourist Board:

■ **Bed & Breakfast Touring Map**
■ **Great Escapes - short breaks and leisure holidays for all seasons**
■ **Events list**

Also available are:
Places to Visit in the Heart of England - a comprehensive guide to over 750 varied attractions and things to see, also great ideas for where to go in winter, (over £40 in discount vouchers included). £3.99
■ **Cotswolds Map** £2.95
■ **Cotswold/Wyndean Map** £3.25
■ **Shropshire/Staffordshire Map** £3.25
Please add 60p postage for up to 3 items, plus 25p for each additional 3 items.

WHERE TO STAY (HEART OF ENGLAND)

Accommodation entries in this region are listed in alphabetical order of place name, and then in alphabetical order of establishment.

Map references refer to the colour location maps at the back of this guide. The first number indicates the map to use; the letter and number which follow refer to the grid reference on the map.

At-a-glance symbols at the end of each accommodation entry give useful information about services and facilities. A key to symbols can be found inside the back cover flap. Keep this open for easy reference.

ALCESTER
Warwickshire
Map ref 2B1

Town has Roman origins and many old buildings around the High Street. It is close to Ragley Hall, the 18th C Palladian mansion with its magnificent baroque Great Hall.

Icknield House
54 Birmingham Road, Alcester B49 5EG
☎ Alcester (Reservations) (01789) 763287
Fax (01789) 763287
Comfortable, well-furnished Victorian house of character, on the Birmingham road, a few hundred yards off A435. Close to Warwick and the Cotswolds and 10 minutes from Stratford-upon-Avon. Excellent touring centre.
Bedrooms: 2 single, 2 double, 1 twin, 1 triple
Bathrooms: 3 en-suite, 1 public, 1 private shower

Bed & breakfast
per night: £min £max
Single 19.00 25.00
Double 36.00 38.00

Half board per
person: £min £max
Daily 26.00 32.00

Evening meal 1830 (last orders 1930)
Parking for 8

Kings Court Hotel
COMMENDED
Kings Coughton, Stratford-upon-Avon B49 5QQ
☎ (01789) 763111
Fax (01789) 400242

Delightful bedrooms set around main part of the hotel, which is a listed Tudor farmhouse. Excellent home-cooked bar and restaurant meals. Close to Stratford-upon-Avon and the Cotswolds.
Bedrooms: 6 single, 18 double, 18 twin
Bathrooms: 42 en-suite

Bed & breakfast
per night: £min £max
Single 31.00
Double 52.00

Lunch available
Evening meal 1900 (last orders 2200)
Parking for 100
Cards accepted: Access, Visa, Amex, Switch/Delta

Throckmorton Arms Hotel
COMMENDED
Coughton, Alcester B49 5HX
☎ (01789) 762879
Fax (01789) 762654
Small family-owned and managed country hotel of quality. Friendly atmosphere, log fires, air conditioning. Bar meals and a la carte restaurant.

Ideally located for Stratford-upon-Avon and Cotswolds. On A435 between Studley and Alcester. Exit junction 3, M42.
Bedrooms: 5 double, 5 twin
Bathrooms: 10 en-suite

Bed & breakfast
per night: £min £max
Single 25.00 45.00
Double 40.00 60.00

Lunch available
Evening meal 1800 (last orders 2145)
Parking for 70
Cards accepted: Access, Visa, Diners, Amex, Switch/Delta

ALTON
Staffordshire
Map ref 4B2

Alton Castle, an impressive 19th C building, dominates the village which is set in spectacular scenery. Nearby is Alton Towers, a romantic 19th C ruin with innumerable tourist attractions within one of England's largest theme parks in its 800 acres of magnificent gardens.

Bulls Head Inn
APPROVED
High Street, Alton ST10 4AQ
☎ Oakamoor (01538) 702307
Fax (01538) 702065
In the village of Alton close to Alton Towers, an 18th C inn with real ale and home cooking.
Bedrooms: 3 double, 1 twin, 2 family rooms

HEART OF ENGLAND

Bathrooms: 6 en-suite, 1 public

Bed & breakfast per night:	£min	£max
Single	25.00	40.00
Double	45.00	55.00

Lunch available
Evening meal 1900 (last orders 2200)
Parking for 10
Cards accepted: Access, Visa, Switch/Delta

Fernlea Guest House

Cedar Hill, Alton, Stoke-on-Trent ST10 4BH
☎ (01538) 702327
Stone country guesthouse in the heart of village. Homely, friendly atmosphere guaranteed. Families most welcome. Walking distance to pub/restaurants.
Bedrooms: 1 double, 1 triple, 1 family room
Bathrooms: 3 en-suite

Bed & breakfast per night:	£min	£max
Single	20.00	25.00
Double	30.00	35.00

Parking for 3
Open February–November

BARTON UNDER NEEDWOOD

Staffordshire
Map ref 4B3

Fairfield Guest House M
HIGHLY COMMENDED

55 Main Street, Barton under Needwood, Burton upon Trent DE13 8AB
☎ Burton on Trent (01283) 716396
Fax (01827) 61594
Spacious, early-Victorian residence, recently carefully restored, with modern facilities but retaining many original features.
Bedrooms: 2 double, 1 twin
Bathrooms: 3 en-suite

Bed & breakfast per night:	£min	£max
Single	30.00	35.00
Double	40.00	45.00

Parking for 3
Cards accepted: Access, Visa

A key to symbols can be found inside the back cover flap.

BERKSWELL

West Midlands
Map ref 4B3

Pretty village with an unusual set of 5-holed stocks on the green. It has some fine houses, cottages, a 16th C inn and a windmill open to the public Sunday afternoons, May to end September. The Norman church is one of the finest in the area, with many interesting features.

Nailcote Hall Hotel and Restaurant M
HIGHLY COMMENDED

Nailcote Lane, Berkswell, Coventry CV7 7DE
☎ Coventry (01203) 466174
Fax (01203) 470720

Historic country house hotel and restaurant. Ideally located for Heart of England visitors. Situated on the B4101 Knowle to Coventry road.
Bedrooms: 25 double, 13 twin
Bathrooms: 38 en-suite

Bed & breakfast per night:	£min	£max
Single	110.00	110.00
Double	120.00	120.00

Half board per person:	£min	£max
Daily	80.00	80.00

Lunch available
Evening meal 1900 (last orders 2130)
Parking for 130
Cards accepted: Access, Visa, Diners, Amex, Switch/Delta

WELCOME HOST

This is a nationally recognised customer care programme which aims to promote the highest standards of service and a warm welcome. Establishments who are taking part in this initiative are indicated by the symbol.

BIBURY

Gloucestershire
Map ref 2B1

Village on the River Coln with stone houses and the famous 17th C Arlington Row, former weavers' cottages. Arlington Mill is now a folk museum. Trout farm and Bansley House Gardens nearby are open to the public.

The Swan Hotel M
DE LUXE

Bibury, Cirencester GL7 5NW
☎ Cirencester (01285) 740695
Fax (01285) 740473
Grand Heritage
De luxe family-run hotel, with riverside gardens, cosy parlours, noted restaurant, sumptuous bedrooms, some with four-posters, all with extravagant bathrooms. Centrally located for touring the Cotswolds, Stratford, Oxford and Bath.
Bedrooms: 1 single, 12 double, 4 twin, 1 family room
Bathrooms: 18 en-suite

Bed & breakfast per night:	£min	£max
Single	86.00	115.00
Double	115.00	210.00

Half board per person:	£min	£max
Daily	77.50	120.00

Lunch available
Evening meal 1930 (last orders 2130)
Parking for 20
Cards accepted: Access, Visa, Amex, Switch/Delta

The M symbol after an establishment name indicates that it is a Regional Tourist Board member.

Information on accommodation listed in this guide has been supplied by the proprietors. As changes may occur you are advised to check details at the time of booking.

HEART OF ENGLAND

BIRMINGHAM
West Midlands
Map ref 4B3

Britain's second city, whose attractions include Centenary Square and the ICC with Symphony Hall, the NEC, the City Art Gallery, Barber Institute of Fine Arts, 17th C Aston Hall, science and railway museums, Jewellery Quarter, Cadbury World, 2 cathedrals and Botanical Gardens.
Tourist Information Centre ☎ (0121) 693 6300 or 780 4321

Asquith House Hotel & Restaurant
COMMENDED
19 Portland Road, Edgbaston, Birmingham B16 9UN
☎ (0121) 454 5282 & 454 6699
Fax (0121) 456 4668
Listed building (1854) of architectural interest, converted into an exclusive licensed hotel and restaurant. Well suited for mini-conferences and business meetings. Weddings a speciality.
Bedrooms: 2 single, 2 double, 5 twin, 1 triple
Bathrooms: 10 en-suite
Bed & breakfast

per night:	£min	£max
Single	55.00	65.60
Double	71.50	76.45

Lunch available
Evening meal 1930 (last orders 2130)
Parking for 10
Cards accepted: Access, Visa, Amex

Atholl Lodge
16 Elmdon Road, Acocks Green, Birmingham B27 6LH
☎ (0121) 707 4417
Fax (0121) 707 4417
Friendly guesthouse in a quiet location on the south side of Birmingham. The National Exhibition Centre, airport and town centre are all within easy reach.
Bedrooms: 4 single, 1 double, 4 twin, 1 triple
Bathrooms: 2 en-suite, 3 public
Bed & breakfast

per night:	£min	£max
Single	16.00	22.00
Double	32.00	44.00

Half board per

person:	£min	£max
Daily	24.00	
Weekly	147.00	

Lunch available
Evening meal 1800 (last orders 2100)
Parking for 10

Bearwood Court Hotel
360-366 Bearwood Road, Bearwood, Warley B66 4ET
☎ (0121) 429 9731
Fax (0121) 429 6175
Family-run establishment with personal service, convenient for Birmingham city centre and West Bromwich. 2 miles to junction 1 of M5.
Bedrooms: 10 single, 6 double, 5 twin, 3 triple
Bathrooms: 16 en-suite, 1 public, 8 private showers
Bed & breakfast

per night:	£min	£max
Single	28.00	35.00
Double	42.00	48.00

Half board per

person:	£min	£max
Daily	38.50	45.50
Weekly	269.00	318.00

Lunch available
Evening meal 1900 (last orders 2100)
Parking for 26
Cards accepted: Access, Visa, Switch/Delta

Brentwood Hotel
APPROVED
127 Portland Road, Edgbaston, Birmingham B16 9QX
☎ (0121) 454 4079 & 454 5507
Comfortable, friendly hotel close to city centre. Rooms attractively furnished with colour TV, central heating and tea/coffee facilities. Pretty restaurant and Victorian bar, free car parking.
Bedrooms: 6 single, 3 double, 3 twin, 1 triple, 2 family rooms
Bathrooms: 3 en-suite, 3 public
Bed & breakfast

per night:	£min	£max
Single	25.00	30.00
Double	40.00	45.00

Half board per

person:	£min	£max
Daily	33.00	38.00

Lunch available
Evening meal 1900 (last orders 2030)
Parking for 15
Cards accepted: Access, Visa, Amex

Bridge House Hotel
49 Sherbourne Road, Acocks Green, Birmingham B27 6DX
☎ Bookings (0121) 706 5900
Fax (0121) 624 5900
Comfortably appointed private hotel with a range of facilities including pleasant dining room with a la carte menu, 2 licensed residential bars, TV lounge, patio and garden. Large secure car park. New executive rooms available.
Bedrooms: 15 single, 13 double, 13 twin, 1 triple
Bathrooms: 42 en-suite, 1 public
Bed & breakfast

per night:	£min	£max
Single	37.60	47.00
Double	47.00	52.87

Evening meal 1900 (last orders 2100)
Parking for 70
Cards accepted: Access, Visa, Diners, Amex, Switch/Delta

Celtic Court Hotel & Conferencecentre
Golden Hillock Road, Sparkbrook, Birmingham B11 2PN
☎ (0121) 604 8111
Fax (0121) 604 8004
Modern hotel in busy suburb of Birmingham. Within 10 minutes' drive of NEC, NAC, ICC, National Indoor Arena, airport, stations and city centre attractions.
Bedrooms: 1 single, 14 double, 21 twin, 5 family rooms
Bathrooms: 41 en-suite
Bed & breakfast

per night:	£min	£max
Single	60.00	70.00
Double	70.00	80.00

Half board per

person:	£min	£max
Daily	47.50	72.50
Weekly	332.50	507.50

Lunch available
Evening meal 1900 (last orders 2145)
Parking for 170
Cards accepted: Access, Visa, Amex, Switch/Delta

Chamberlain Hotel
Listed COMMENDED
Alcester Street, Birmingham B12 0PJ
☎ (0121) 606 9000
Fax (0121) 606 9001

HEART OF ENGLAND

Restored and refurbished Grade II listed Victorian building of character, 1 mile from city centre. Extensive conference and banqueting facilities.
Bedrooms: 69 single, 118 double, 63 twin
Bathrooms: 250 en-suite

Bed & breakfast per night:	£min	£max
Single		35.00
Double		40.00

Half board per person:	£min	£max
Daily	29.00	43.00
Weekly	203.00	301.00

Lunch available
Evening meal 1800 (last orders 2200)
Parking for 180
Cards accepted: Access, Visa, Diners, Amex, Switch/Delta

Elmdon Guest House
COMMENDED

2369 Coventry Road, Sheldon, Birmingham B26 3PN
☎ (0121) 742 1626 & 688 1720
Fax (0121) 742 1626
Family-run guesthouse with en-suite facilities. TV in all rooms, including Sky. On main A45 close to the National Exhibition Centre, airport, railway and city centre.
Bedrooms: 2 single, 4 twin, 1 triple
Bathrooms: 5 en-suite, 1 public

Bed & breakfast per night:	£min	£max
Single	20.00	26.00
Double	36.00	45.00

Half board per person:	£min	£max
Daily	30.50	36.50
Weekly	213.50	255.50

Lunch available
Evening meal 1830 (last orders 1930)
Parking for 7
Cards accepted: Access, Visa

Greenway House Hotel

978 Warwick Road, Acocks Green, Birmingham B27 6QG
☎ (0121) 706 1361
Fax (0121) 706 1361
Small, comfortable, privately-run hotel, close to the city centre, airport and National Exhibition Centre. Special weekend tariffs from £15.
Bedrooms: 8 single, 3 double, 2 twin, 1 triple
Bathrooms: 7 en-suite, 2 public, 1 private shower

Bed & breakfast per night:	£min	£max
Single	21.00	27.00
Double	30.00	36.00

Half board per person:	£min	£max
Daily	27.00	33.00
Weekly	175.00	210.00

Lunch available
Evening meal 1830 (last orders 1930)
Parking for 18

Heath Lodge Hotel

Coleshill Road, Marston Green, Birmingham B37 7HT
☎ (0121) 779 2218
Fax (0121) 779 2218

Licensed family-run hotel, quietly situated and less than 2 miles from the National Exhibition Centre and Birmingham Airport. Courtesy car to airport.
Bedrooms: 9 single, 3 double, 5 twin, 1 family room
Bathrooms: 13 en-suite, 1 public, 1 private shower

Bed & breakfast per night:	£min	£max
Single	28.50	39.50
Double	39.50	52.00

Evening meal 1830 (last orders 2030)
Parking for 24
Cards accepted: Access, Visa, Diners, Amex

Homelea
COMMENDED

2399 Coventry Road, Sheldon, Birmingham B26 3PN
☎ (0121) 742 0017
Fax (0121) 688 1879
Friendly guesthouse, close to NEC, airport and many local amenities. Comfortable rooms all with TV. Full English breakfast included.
Bedrooms: 1 single, 1 double, 1 twin
Bathrooms: 2 en-suite, 1 private

Bed & breakfast per night:	£min	£max
Single	19.00	29.00
Double	38.00	38.00

Jonathans' Hotel and Restaurant
HIGHLY COMMENDED

16-24 Wolverhampton Road, Oldbury, Warley B68 0LH
☎ (0121) 429 3757
Fax (0121) 434 3107

A restaurant and hotel offering fine, traditional English cooking, and high quality Victorian hospitality. Exciting environment with intriguing rooms, indoor Victorian street, galleries and glasshouses.
Bedrooms: 8 single, 13 double, 2 twin, 9 triple
Bathrooms: 32 en-suite

Bed & breakfast per night:	£min	£max
Single	69.00	79.00
Double	80.00	120.00

Lunch available
Evening meal 1900 (last orders 2230)
Parking for 72
Cards accepted: Access, Visa, Diners, Amex, Switch/Delta

Kensington Guest House Hotel
COMMENDED

785 Pershore Road, Selly Park, Birmingham B29 7LR
☎ (0121) 472 7086 & 414 1874
Fax (0121) 472 5520
Family atmosphere. Full central heating, evening meals, discount for long stay, ground floor rooms. Four-poster bed in bridal suite. Close to all amenities.
Bedrooms: 3 single, 13 double, 5 twin, 3 triple, 6 family rooms
Bathrooms: 19 en-suite, 4 private, 6 public, 7 private showers

Bed & breakfast per night:	£min	£max
Single	25.00	35.00
Double	35.00	40.00

Continued ▶

Please check prices and other details at the time of booking.

HEART OF ENGLAND

BIRMINGHAM
Continued

Half board per person:

	£min	£max
Daily	32.50	42.95
Weekly	227.50	300.00

Evening meal 1800 (last orders 2000)
Parking for 34
Cards accepted: Access, Visa, Diners, Amex, Switch/Delta

Lyndhurst Hotel
APPROVED

135 Kingsbury Road, Erdington, Birmingham B24 8QT
☎ (0121) 373 5695
Fax (0121) 373 5695
Within half a mile of M6 (junction 6) and within easy reach of the city and National Exhibition Centre. Comfortable bedrooms, spacious restaurant. Personal service in a quiet friendly atmosphere.
Bedrooms: 10 single, 2 double, 2 twin
Bathrooms: 13 en-suite, 1 private

Bed & breakfast per night:

	£min	£max
Single	25.00	39.50
Double	39.50	52.50

Half board per person:

	£min	£max
Daily	37.00	51.50

Evening meal 1800 (last orders 2000)
Parking for 12
Cards accepted: Access, Visa, Diners, Amex

Pineway Guest House
Listed APPROVED

5 Elmdon Road, Acocks Green, Birmingham B27 6LJ
☎ (0121) 708 2177
Victorian residence in quiet tree-lined cul-de-sac. Close to Birmingham city centre, airport and National Exhibition Centre. Clean and friendly.
Bedrooms: 3 single, 2 double, 1 twin, 1 triple
Bathrooms: 2 public

Bed & breakfast per night:

	£min	£max
Single	18.00	20.00
Double	34.00	36.00

Half board per person:

	£min	£max
Daily	27.00	30.00

Evening meal 1700 (last orders 1900)
Parking for 6

Rollason Wood Hotel

130 Wood End Road, Erdington, Birmingham B24 8BJ
☎ (0121) 373 1230
Fax (0121) 382 2578
Friendly, family-run hotel, 1 mile from M6, exit 6. Convenient for city centre, NEC and convention centre. A la carte restaurant and bar.
Bedrooms: 19 single, 3 double, 8 twin, 5 triple
Bathrooms: 11 en-suite, 5 public, 6 private showers

Bed & breakfast per night:

	£min	£max
Single	17.85	36.25
Double	30.00	52.00

Evening meal 1800 (last orders 2100)
Parking for 43
Cards accepted: Access, Visa, Diners, Amex

Sheriden House Hotel
COMMENDED

82 Handsworth Wood Road, Handsworth Wood, Birmingham B20 2PL
☎ (0121) 523 5960 & 554 2185
Fax (0121) 551 4761
Private hotel 3.5 miles from Birmingham city centre, ICC and National Indoor Arena. 20 minutes from NEC, 5 minutes from M5 and M6. Car park.
Bedrooms: 2 single, 3 double, 5 twin, 1 triple
Bathrooms: 9 en-suite, 1 public, 1 private shower

Bed & breakfast per night:

	£min	£max
Single	22.00	39.00
Double	32.00	54.00

Half board per person:

	£min	£max
Daily	35.00	52.00
Weekly	203.00	364.00

Lunch available
Evening meal 1830 (last orders 2100)
Parking for 30
Cards accepted: Access, Visa, Amex, Switch/Delta

Strathallan Thistle Hotel
COMMENDED

Hagley Road, Edgbaston, Birmingham B16 9RY
☎ (0121) 455 9777
Fax (0121) 454 9432
Utell International
Recently refurbished modern hotel with a brasserie, close to the city centre.
Bedrooms: 117 single, 16 double, 28 twin, 5 triple
Suites available
Bathrooms: 166 en-suite

Bed & breakfast per night:

	£min	£max
Single	97.00	109.00
Double	117.50	125.50

Lunch available
Evening meal 1830 (last orders 2200)
Parking for 200
Cards accepted: Access, Visa, Diners, Amex

Swallow Hotel
DE LUXE

Hagley Road, Five Ways, Birmingham B16 8SJ
☎ (0121) 452 1144
Fax (0121) 456 3442
Swallow
Luxurious hotel with air-conditioning, award-winning food, an Egyptian-themed leisure club and excellent service. Short break packages available.
Bedrooms: 14 single, 44 double, 40 twin
Suites available
Bathrooms: 98 en-suite

Bed & breakfast per night:

	£min	£max
Single	110.00	150.00
Double	120.00	160.00

Half board per person:

	£min	£max
Daily	135.00	175.00

Lunch available
Evening meal 1800 (last orders 2230)
Parking for 70
Cards accepted: Access, Visa, Diners, Amex, Switch/Delta

Wentworth Hotel
APPROVED

103 Wentworth Road, Harborne, Birmingham B17 9SU
☎ (0121) 427 2839 & 427 6818
Fax (0121) 427 2839
Family-run hotel, all bedrooms en-suite with tea and coffee facilities. Victorian

HEART OF ENGLAND

building with bar and restaurant in Victorian style. Sky TV.
Bedrooms: 6 single, 2 double, 3 twin, 1 triple
Bathrooms: 12 en-suite

Bed & breakfast per night:	£min	£max
Single	25.00	30.00
Double	40.00	45.00

Half board per person:	£min	£max
Daily	35.00	40.00

Evening meal 1800 (last orders 1930)
Parking for 10
Cards accepted: Access, Visa, Amex, Switch/Delta

Westbourne Lodge Hotel
COMMENDED

27-29 Fountain Road, Edgbaston, Birmingham B17 8NJ
☎ (0121) 429 1003
Fax (0121) 429 7436
The Independents
Family-run hotel, all rooms en-suite. Good food. Ideal for city, National Exhibition Centre, International Convention Centre, National Indoor Arena and airport. Free parking.
Bedrooms: 11 single, 2 double, 3 twin, 2 triple
Bathrooms: 17 en-suite, 1 private

Bed & breakfast per night:	£min	£max
Single	35.00	45.00
Double	45.00	55.00

Half board per person:	£min	£max
Daily	45.00	59.00
Weekly	300.00	395.00

Lunch available
Evening meal 1900 (last orders 2100)
Parking for 14
Cards accepted: Access, Visa, Amex, Switch/Delta

The Westley Hotel
HIGHLY COMMENDED

Westley Road, Acocks Green, Birmingham B27 7UJ
☎ (0121) 706 4312
Fax (0121) 706 2824
Best Western
Close to National Exhibition Centre and International Convention Centre. Two restaurants, theme bar and banqueting. Convenient for Stratford-upon-Avon and Warwick. 3 miles junction 5 of M42.
Bedrooms: 8 single, 7 double, 20 twin, 1 triple

Suite available
Bathrooms: 36 en-suite

Bed & breakfast per night:	£min	£max
Single	37.50	75.00
Double	37.50	90.00

Lunch available
Evening meal 1900 (last orders 2200)
Parking for 200
Cards accepted: Access, Visa, Diners, Amex, Switch/Delta

Westmead Hotel
COMMENDED

Redditch Road, Hopwood, Alvechurch, Birmingham B48 7AL
☎ (0121) 445 1202
Fax (0121) 445 6163
Whitbread
Hotel located off junction 2 of the M42. Within easy reach of Birmingham, Redditch, the National Exhibition Centre and Birmingham International Airport.
Bedrooms: 16 double, 40 twin, 2 family rooms
Bathrooms: 58 en-suite

Bed & breakfast per night:	£min	£max
Single	82.50	87.50
Double	90.00	96.00

Lunch available
Evening meal 1900 (last orders 2200)
Parking for 155
Cards accepted: Access, Visa, Diners, Amex, Switch/Delta

Woodville House
Listed APPROVED

39 Portland Road, Edgbaston, Birmingham B16 9HN
☎ (0121) 454 0274
Fax (0121) 421 4340
High standard accommodation, 1 mile from city centre. Full English breakfast. All rooms have colour TV and tea/coffee making facilities. En-suite bedrooms available.
Bedrooms: 4 single, 2 double, 2 twin, 1 triple
Bathrooms: 2 en-suite, 4 public

Bed & breakfast per night:	£min	£max
Single		15.00
Double	30.00	32.00

Parking for 12

BIRMINGHAM AIRPORT
West Midlands

See under Berkswell, Birmingham, Coleshill, Coventry, Hampton in Arden, Meriden, Solihull

BISHOP'S CASTLE
Shropshire
Map ref 4A3

A 12th C Planned Town with a castle site at the top of the hill and a church at the bottom of the main street. Many interesting buildings with original timber frames hidden behind present day houses. On the Welsh border close to the Clun Forest in quiet, unspoilt countryside.

The Boars Head Hotel
COMMENDED

Church Street, Bishop's Castle SY9 5AE
☎ Bishop's Castle (01588) 638521 & Mobile 0374 201272
Fax (01588) 630126
Wayfarer
Old world inn, with en-suite accommodation in original stables. Comfortable dining area serves wide choice of bar meals. A la carte restaurant also available.
Bedrooms: 1 double, 2 twin, 1 family room
Bathrooms: 4 en-suite

Bed & breakfast per night:	£min	£max
Single	33.00	38.00
Double	50.00	56.00

Lunch available
Evening meal 1830 (last orders 2130)
Parking for 20
Cards accepted: Access, Visa, Diners, Amex, Switch/Delta

WELCOME HOST

This is a nationally recognised customer care programme which aims to promote the highest standards of service and a warm welcome. Establishments who are taking part in this initiative are indicated by the symbol.

HEART OF ENGLAND

BLAKENEY

Gloucestershire
Map ref 2B1

Village in wooded hills near the Forest of Dean and the Severn Estuary. It is close to Lydney where the Dean Forest Railway has full size railway engines, a museum and steam days.

Viney Hill Country Guesthouse

COMMENDED

Blakeney GL15 4LT
☎ Dean (01594) 516000
Fax (01594) 516018

Detached period farmhouse south-west of Gloucester, set in delightful gardens of approximately half an acre. Lovely rural setting with extensive views of surrounding countryside.
Bedrooms: 4 double, 2 twin
Bathrooms: 6 en-suite

Bed & breakfast per night:	£min	£max
Single	32.00	
Double	44.00	

Half board per person:	£min	£max
Daily	36.00	

Evening meal 1900 (last orders 1700)
Parking for 7
Cards accepted: Access, Visa, Switch/Delta

BLEDINGTON

Gloucestershire
Map ref 2B1

Village close to the Oxfordshire border, with a pleasant green and a beautiful church.

Kings Head Inn & Restaurant

COMMENDED

The Green, Bledington, Oxford OX7 6HD
☎ Kingham (01608) 658365
Fax (01608) 658902

15th C inn located in the heart of the Cotswolds, facing the village green. Authentic lounge bars, notable restaurant. Delightful en-suite rooms.
Bedrooms: 10 double, 2 twin
Bathrooms: 12 en-suite

Bed & breakfast per night:	£min	£max
Single	40.00	45.00
Double	60.00	75.00

Lunch available
Evening meal 1900 (last orders 2200)
Parking for 60
Cards accepted: Access, Visa, Switch/Delta

BOURTON-ON-THE-WATER

Gloucestershire
Map ref 2B1

The River Windrush flows through this famous Cotswold village which has a green, and cottages and houses of Cotswold stone. Its many attractions include a model village, Birdland, a Motor Museum and the Cotswold Perfumery.

Bourton Lodge Hotel

APPROVED

Whiteshoots Hill, Bourton-on-the-Water, Cheltenham GL54 2LE
☎ (01451) 820387
Fax (01451) 821635
Logis of Great Britain

Family-run hotel with friendly atmosphere and traditional home cooking. Panoramic views of surrounding countryside from most bedrooms. Bourton-on-the-Water close by. Within easy driving distance of Cirencester, Cheltenham and Stratford.
Bedrooms: 7 double, 1 twin, 1 triple, 1 family room
Bathrooms: 10 en-suite

Bed & breakfast per night:	£min	£max
Double	65.00	65.00

Half board per person:	£min	£max
Daily	48.00	48.00

Lunch available
Evening meal 1900 (last orders 2130)
Parking for 30
Cards accepted: Access, Visa, Amex, Switch/Delta

Broadlands Guest House

COMMENDED

Clapton Row, Bourton-on-the-Water, Cheltenham GL54 2DN
☎ Cotswold (01451) 822002

Tastefully furnished to a high standard, offering a friendly home-from-home atmosphere. In quiet street a few minutes' level walk from beautiful village centre. Discount for weekly bookings and for minimum 3-night winter break specials.
Bedrooms: 6 double, 2 twin, 3 family rooms
Bathrooms: 11 en-suite

Bed & breakfast per night:	£min	£max
Single	25.00	30.00
Double	39.99	39.99

Half board per person:	£min	£max
Daily	31.95	31.95
Weekly	209.59	209.59

Evening meal 1800 (last orders 1900)
Parking for 11

Dial House

HIGHLY COMMENDED

The Chestnuts, High Street, Bourton-on-the-Water, Cheltenham GL54 2AN
☎ Cotswold (01451) 822244
Fax (01451) 810126

17th C hotel in 1.5 acres of beautiful walled garden, peacefully situated in village centre. Log fires, four-posters, noted a la carte restaurant. Special winter offers.
Bedrooms: 1 single, 6 double, 3 twin
Bathrooms: 9 en-suite, 1 private

Bed & breakfast per night:	£min	£max
Single	30.00	44.00
Double	60.00	105.00

Half board per person:	£min	£max
Daily	53.50	68.50
Weekly	315.00	400.00

Lunch available
Evening meal 1900 (last orders 2100)
Parking for 18
Cards accepted: Access, Visa, Amex, Switch/Delta

Old Manse Hotel

COMMENDED

Victoria Street, Bourton-on-the-Water, Cheltenham GL54 2BX
☎ Cotswold (01451) 820082
Fax (01451) 810381

Listed 18th C village centre hotel fronting the River Windrush. A la carte,

HEART OF ENGLAND

table d'hote and vegetarian menus, real ales, four-poster with whirlpool spa, log fire. Special break and winter rates available.
Bedrooms: 9 double, 3 twin
Bathrooms: 12 en-suite

Bed & breakfast

per night:	£min	£max
Single	39.50	74.50
Double	59.00	119.00

Half board per

person:	£min	£max
Daily	45.25	75.25

Lunch available
Evening meal 1830 (last orders 2130)
Parking for 12
Cards accepted: Access, Visa, Diners, Amex, Switch/Delta

Old New Inn

COMMENDED

Bourton-on-the-Water, Cheltenham GL54 2AF
☎ Cotswold (01451) 820467
Fax (01451) 810236

Built in 1712 and run by the same family for over 60 years. Traditional cooking and service. Log fires in winter. Large gardens. Ideal centre for touring.
Bedrooms: 5 single, 9 double, 5 twin
Bathrooms: 11 en-suite, 4 public

Bed & breakfast

per night:	£min	£max
Single	29.00	36.00
Double	58.00	72.00

Half board per

person:	£min	£max
Daily	46.00	52.00

Lunch available
Evening meal 1930 (last orders 2030)
Parking for 32
Cards accepted: Access, Visa

National gradings and classifications were correct at the time of going to press but are subject to change. Please check at the time of booking.

BRIDGNORTH

Shropshire
Map ref 4A3

Red sandstone riverside town in 2 parts - High and Low - linked by a cliff railway. Much of interest including a ruined Norman keep, half-timbered 16th C houses, Midland Motor Museum and Severn Valley Railway.
Tourist Information Centre ☎ (01746) 763358

The Croft Hotel

APPROVED

St. Mary's Street, Bridgnorth WV16 4DW
☎ (01746) 762416 & 767155
Listed building with a wealth of oak beams, in an old street. Family-run and an ideal centre for exploring the delightful Shropshire countryside.
Bedrooms: 3 single, 4 double, 1 twin, 4 triple
Bathrooms: 10 en-suite, 1 public

Bed & breakfast

per night:	£min	£max
Single	23.50	40.00
Double	40.00	50.00

Half board per

person:	£min	£max
Daily	35.00	50.00

Lunch available
Evening meal 1800 (last orders 2030)
Cards accepted: Access, Visa, Amex

Mill Hotel

HIGHLY COMMENDED

Alveley, Bridgnorth WV15 6HL
☎ Quatt (01746) 780437
Fax (01746) 780850
Beautiful hotel in a delightful, tranquil setting. En-suite bedrooms overlook the mill pool and landscaped gardens. Superb waterside restaurant.
Bedrooms: 2 single, 13 double, 6 twin
Suite available
Bathrooms: 21 en-suite

Bed & breakfast

per night:	£min	£max
Single	48.00	85.00
Double	60.00	85.00

Half board per

person:	£min	£max
Daily	70.50	107.50
Weekly	493.50	752.50

Lunch available
Evening meal 1900 (last orders 2215)
Parking for 200

Cards accepted: Access, Visa, Diners, Amex, Switch/Delta

Old Vicarage Hotel

DE LUXE

Worfield, Bridgnorth WV15 5JZ
☎ Worfield (01746) 716497
Fax (01746) 716552
Logis of Great Britain

Country house hotel in a quiet peaceful location, ideal for business or pleasure, close to Ironbridge Gorge and Severn Valley Railway. Half-board prices are based on minimum 2-night stay.
Wheelchair access category 2
Bedrooms: 8 double, 5 twin, 1 triple
Suite available
Bathrooms: 14 en-suite

Bed & breakfast

per night:	£min	£max
Single	68.50	89.50
Double	97.00	135.00

Half board per

person:	£min	£max
Daily	69.50	82.50

Lunch available
Evening meal 1930 (last orders 2130)
Parking for 30
Cards accepted: Access, Visa, Diners, Amex

Severn Arms Hotel

COMMENDED

Underhill Street, Bridgnorth WV16 4BB
☎ (01746) 764616
Listed private hotel overlooking the River Severn, within walking distance of Severn Valley Railway and close to the famous Ironbridge Gorge museums.
Bedrooms: 2 single, 2 double, 3 twin, 2 triple, 1 family room
Bathrooms: 6 en-suite, 2 public

Bed & breakfast

per night:	£min	£max
Single	23.50	34.50
Double	39.00	46.00

Evening meal 1830 (last orders 1900)

Continued ▶

HEART OF ENGLAND

BRIDGNORTH
Continued

Open January–November
Cards accepted: Access, Visa, Amex, Switch/Delta

BROADWAY
Hereford and Worcester
Map ref 2B1

Beautiful Cotswold village called the "Show village of England", with 16th C stone houses and cottages. Near the village is Broadway Tower with magnificent views over 12 counties and a country park with nature trails and adventure playground.

Barn House Bed & Breakfast
HIGHLY COMMENDED

Barn House, 152 High Street, Broadway, Worcestershire WR12 7AJ
☎ (01386) 858633
Fax (01386) 853593

Substantial listed 17th C house in 16 acres of scenic grounds. Superb facilities include a magnificent barn room and swimming pool.
Bedrooms: 3 double, 1 twin
Bathrooms: 3 en-suite, 1 private, 2 public

Bed & breakfast per night:	£min	£max
Single	25.00	50.00
Double	45.00	70.00

Parking for 42

Broadway Hotel

The Green, Broadway, Worcestershire WR12 7AA
☎ Evesham (01386) 852401
Fax (01386) 853879

Grade II listed 16th C family-run hotel in the heart of picturesque village. Combines old world charm with the comforts and amenities of a modern hotel. Half board price based on minimum 2-night stay.
Bedrooms: 2 single, 10 double, 6 twin
Bathrooms: 18 en-suite

Bed & breakfast per night:	£min	£max
Single	45.00	55.00
Double	70.00	85.00

Half board per person:	£min	£max
Daily	45.00	51.00
Weekly	270.00	320.00

Lunch available
Evening meal 1900 (last orders 2100)
Parking for 24
Cards accepted: Access, Visa, Diners, Amex, Switch/Delta

Collin House Hotel & Restaurant
COMMENDED

Collin Lane, Broadway, Worcestershire WR12 7PB
☎ (01386) 858354 & 852544
16th C, secluded Cotswold hotel with traditional atmosphere and charm. Four-poster bedrooms, inglenook fireplaces. Fine views, extensive gardens. Noted for food.
Bedrooms: 1 single, 3 double, 3 twin
Bathrooms: 6 en-suite, 1 private shower

Bed & breakfast per night:	£min	£max
Single	45.00	65.00
Double	87.00	97.00

Half board per person:	£min	£max
Weekly	350.00	385.00

Lunch available
Evening meal 1900 (last orders 2100)
Parking for 30
Cards accepted: Access, Visa

Eastbank

Station Drive, Broadway, Worcestershire WR12 7DF
☎ (01386) 852659
Quiet location, half a mile from village. All rooms fully en-suite (bath/shower), with colour TV and beverage facilities. Homely atmosphere. Free brochure.
Bedrooms: 2 double, 2 twin, 2 triple
Bathrooms: 6 en-suite

Bed & breakfast per night:	£min	£max
Single	15.00	
Double	32.00	50.00

Evening meal 1900 (last orders 1000)
Parking for 6

Leasow House
HIGHLY COMMENDED

Laverton Meadow, Broadway, Worcestershire WR12 7NA
☎ Stanton (01386) 584526
Fax (01386) 584596
17th C Cotswold-stone farmhouse tranquilly set in open countryside close to Broadway village.
Bedrooms: 3 double, 2 twin, 2 triple
Bathrooms: 7 en-suite

Bed & breakfast per night:	£min	£max
Double	52.00	60.00

Parking for 14
Cards accepted: Access, Visa, Amex

The Lygon Arms
HIGHLY COMMENDED

Broadway, Worcestershire WR12 7DU
☎ (01386) 852255
Fax (01386) 858611
Utell International
16th C coaching inn set in the heart of the Cotswolds, with all the comforts of the 20th C. Well situated for touring the Cotswolds and Shakespeare country.
Bedrooms: 2 single, 48 double, 9 twin, 6 triple
Bathrooms: 65 en-suite

Bed & breakfast per night:	£min	£max
Single	117.00	147.00
Double	177.50	188.50

Half board per person:	£min	£max
Daily	118.00	

Lunch available
Evening meal 1930 (last orders 2115)
Parking for 153
Cards accepted: Access, Visa, Diners, Amex, Switch/Delta

Map references apply to the colour maps at the back of this guide.

HEART OF ENGLAND

The Old Rectory
⌂⌂⌂ DE LUXE
Church Street, Willersey, Broadway,
Worcestershire WR12 7PN
☎ (01386) 853729 & Mobile 0378 356447
Fax (01386) 858061

Award-winning guesthouse. A combination of the standards of a good hotel with the warmth of a private home - the ultimate in B & B, in exceptionally quiet surroundings.
Bedrooms: 5 double, 1 twin, 2 triple
Bathrooms: 6 en-suite, 2 private

Bed & breakfast per night:	£min	£max
Single	35.00	75.00
Double	60.00	95.00

Parking for 10
Cards accepted: Access, Visa, Switch/Delta

Olive Branch Guest House
⌂⌂
78 High Street, Broadway,
Worcestershire WR12 7AJ
☎ (01386) 853440
Fax (01386) 853440

16th C house with modern amenities close to centre of village. Traditional English breakfast served. Reduced rates for 3 nights or more.
Bedrooms: 2 single, 3 double, 2 twin, 1 triple
Bathrooms: 6 en-suite, 1 private, 1 public

Bed & breakfast per night:	£min	£max
Single	19.00	19.50
Double	40.00	56.00

Evening meal 1900 (last orders 2000)
Parking for 8
Cards accepted: Amex

Pathlow House
Listed COMMENDED
82 High Street, Broadway,
Worcestershire WR12 7AJ
☎ (01386) 853444
Comfortable period house, central for village amenities.
Bedrooms: 4 double, 1 twin, 1 family room
Bathrooms: 5 en-suite, 1 private

Bed & breakfast per night:	£min	£max
Double	40.00	45.00

Parking for 6

Southwold Guest House
⌂⌂ COMMENDED
Station Road, Broadway,
Worcestershire WR12 7DE
☎ (01386) 853681 & Mobile (0589) 950833
Warm welcome, friendly service, good cooking at this large Edwardian house, only 4 minutes' walk from village centre. Reductions for 2 or more nights; bargain winter breaks.
Bedrooms: 1 single, 5 double, 2 twin
Bathrooms: 5 en-suite, 2 public

Bed & breakfast per night:	£min	£max
Single	15.00	17.00
Double	30.00	40.00

Parking for 8
Cards accepted: Access, Visa, Amex, Switch/Delta

White Acres Guesthouse
⌂⌂ HIGHLY COMMENDED
Station Road, Broadway,
Worcestershire WR12 7DE
☎ (01386) 852320
Spacious Victorian house with en-suite bedrooms, 3 with four-poster beds. Off-road parking. 4 minutes' walk from village centre. Reductions for 2 or more nights. Bargain winter breaks.
Bedrooms: 5 double, 1 twin
Bathrooms: 6 en-suite

Bed & breakfast per night:	£min	£max
Double	38.00	42.00

Parking for 8
Open March–October

Half board prices are given per person, but in some cases these may be based on double/twin occupancy.

Windrush House
⌂⌂⌂ COMMENDED
Station Road, Broadway,
Worcestershire WR12 7DE
☎ (01386) 853577
Edwardian guesthouse on the A44, 300 yards from the village centre, offering personal service. Evening meals by arrangement. 10 per cent reduction in tariff after 2 nights. A no-smoking establishment.
Bedrooms: 4 double, 1 twin
Bathrooms: 5 en-suite

Bed & breakfast per night:	£min	£max
Single	18.00	25.00
Double	36.00	44.00

Half board per person:	£min	£max
Daily	30.00	34.00
Weekly	200.00	220.00

Parking for 5

BROMSGROVE
Hereford and Worcester
Map ref 4B3

This market town near the Lickey Hills has an interesting museum and craft centre and 14th C church with fine tombs and a Carillon tower. The Avoncroft Museum of Buildings is nearby where many old buildings have been re-assembled, having been saved from destruction.
Tourist Information Centre ☎ (01527) 831809

Bromsgrove Country Hotel
⌂⌂⌂
249 Worcester Road, Stoke Heath, Bromsgrove, Worcestershire B61 7JA
☎ (01527) 835522
Fax (01527) 871257
A quiet, elegant, Victorian residence with modern amenities, suitable for business or pleasure. Close to the M6/M42/M5 junctions and historic countryside. A pleasant stay ensured under the personal supervision of the proprietors.
Bedrooms: 1 single, 4 double, 2 twin, 3 triple
Bathrooms: 9 en-suite, 1 private, 1 public

Bed & breakfast per night:	£min	£max
Single	35.00	45.00
Double	39.00	49.00

Evening meal 1930 (last orders 1400)
Parking for 20
Cards accepted: Access, Visa

HEART OF ENGLAND

BROMSGROVE
Continued

Pine Lodge Hotel
HIGHLY COMMENDED

Kidderminster Road, Bromsgrove,
Worcestershire B61 9AB
☎ (01527) 576600
Fax (01527) 878981

With convenient access to the motorway network, in beautiful countryside. This Spanish design hotel has 2 restaurants, lounge bar, 12 conference and banqueting suites and leisure club. Close to NEC, Birmingham, Cadbury World and Warwick Castle.
Bedrooms: 15 single, 70 double, 12 twin, 17 triple
Suites available
Bathrooms: 114 en-suite

Bed & breakfast
per night:	£min	£max
Single	29.95	90.00
Double	59.90	100.00

Half board per
person:	£min	£max
Daily	43.50	65.00

Lunch available
Evening meal 1900 (last orders 2200)
Parking for 250
Cards accepted: Access, Visa, Diners, Amex, Switch/Delta

BURTON UPON TRENT
Staffordshire
Map ref 4B3

An important brewing town with the Bass Museum of Brewing, where the Bass shire horses are stabled. There are 3 bridges with views over the river and some interesting public buildings including the 18th C St Modwen's Church.
Tourist Information Centre ☎ (01283) 516609 or 508589

The Queens Hotel
COMMENDED

Bridge Street, Burton upon Trent
DE14 1SY
☎ Burton upon Trent (01283) 564993
Fax (01283) 517556
A hotel within Burton's oldest licensed house. A choice of restaurants, bars and extensive conference and meeting facilities.
Bedrooms: 10 single, 14 double, 3 twin
Suites available
Bathrooms: 27 en-suite

Bed & breakfast
per night	£min	£max
Single	29.50	79.50
Double	45.00	89.50

Half board per
person:	£min	£max
Daily	32.50	89.50
Weekly	270.00	590.00

Lunch available
Evening meal 1900 (last orders 2230)
Parking for 52
Cards accepted: Access, Visa, Amex, Switch/Delta

Riverside Hotel
COMMENDED

Riverside Drive, Branston, Burton upon Trent DE14 3EP
☎ Burton-on-Trent (01283) 511234
Fax (01283) 511441
Character hotel with restaurant offering a wide choice of food, in peaceful surroundings with own river frontage.
Bedrooms: 16 single, 6 double
Bathrooms: 22 en-suite

Bed & breakfast
per night:	£min	£max
Single	28.00	58.00
Double	56.00	68.00

Half board per
person:	£min	£max
Daily	44.95	74.95
Weekly	338.65	434.65

Lunch available
Evening meal 1900 (last orders 2200)
Parking for 110
Cards accepted: Access, Visa, Amex, Switch/Delta

The symbol **CR** and a group name following an hotel address indicates that bookings can be made through a central reservations office. These offices are listed in the information pages at the back of this guide.

CHELTENHAM
Gloucestershire
Map ref 2B1

Cheltenham was developed as a spa town in the 18th C and has some beautiful Regency architecture, in particular the Pittville Pump Room. It holds international music and literature festivals and is also famous for its race meetings and cricket.
Tourist Information Centre ☎ (01242) 522878

Abbots Lee
HIGHLY COMMENDED

Priory Walk, Cheltenham
GL52 6DU
☎ (01242) 515255
Fax (01242) 515255
The house itself is modern, but we hope we have made it inviting outside and in, with an attractive approach.
Bedrooms: 1 double, 2 twin
Bathrooms: 3 en-suite

Bed & breakfast
per night:	£min	£max
Single	25.00	28.00
Double	40.00	45.00

Parking for 5

Beaumont House Hotel
HIGHLY COMMENDED

Shurdington Road, Cheltenham
GL53 0JE
☎ (01242) 245986
Fax (01242) 520044
Ideally situated where Cheltenham meets the Cotswolds, close to town centre or hill walks. Relaxation, comfort and service are our hallmarks. Private parking, garden.
Bedrooms: 2 single, 6 double, 5 twin, 1 triple, 1 family room
Bathrooms: 15 en-suite

Bed & breakfast
per night:	£min	£max
Single	37.00	37.00
Double	45.00	58.00

Half board per
person:	£min	£max
Daily	39.00	44.00
Weekly	241.00	261.00

Evening meal 1900 (last orders 2000)
Parking for 20
Cards accepted: Access, Visa, Amex

Please check prices and other details at the time of booking.

HEART OF ENGLAND

Beechworth Lawn Hotel

HIGHLY COMMENDED

133 Hales Road, Cheltenham
GL52 6ST
☎ (01242) 522583
Fax (01242) 522583
Carefully modernised and well-appointed, detached Victorian hotel, set in conifer and shrub gardens. Convenient for shopping centre and all amenities.
Bedrooms: 2 single, 2 double, 3 twin, 2 triple
Bathrooms: 5 en-suite, 1 public

Bed & breakfast

per night:	£min	£max
Single	24.50	32.00
Double	42.00	50.00

Half board per

person:	£min	£max
Daily	36.50	44.00

Evening meal 1800 (last orders 1900)
Parking for 12

Carlton Hotel

COMMENDED

Parabola Road, Cheltenham
GL50 3AQ
☎ (01242) 514453
Fax (01242) 226487
In quiet, first class position, 250 yards from famous Promenade and award-winning parks. Emphasis on traditional friendly service. Tasteful bedrooms offer today's guest all modern comforts. Excellent restaurant and bar facilities. Half board prices below apply at weekends only.
Bedrooms: 15 single, 15 double, 44 twin
Bathrooms: 74 en-suite

Bed & breakfast

per night:	£min	£max
Single	40.00	62.50
Double	65.00	83.50

Half board per

person:	£min	£max
Daily	39.50	41.50

Lunch available
Evening meal 1900 (last orders 2130)
Parking for 85
Cards accepted: Access, Visa, Diners, Amex, Switch/Delta

Charlton Kings Hotel

HIGHLY COMMENDED

London Road, Charlton Kings, Cheltenham GL52 6UU
☎ (01242) 231061
Fax (01242) 241900
Logis of Great Britain

2.5 miles from town centre in an area of outstanding beauty. Friendly staff, interesting menus and quality accommodation.
Bedrooms: 2 single, 8 double, 2 twin, 1 triple, 1 family room
Suite available
Bathrooms: 14 en-suite

Bed & breakfast

per night:	£min	£max
Single	44.50	54.50
Double	60.00	92.00

Half board per

person:	£min	£max
Weekly	294.00	308.00

Lunch available
Evening meal 1900 (last orders 2045)
Parking for 26
Cards accepted: Access, Visa, Amex, Switch/Delta

The Frogmill

COMMENDED

Shipton Oliffe, Andoversford, Cheltenham GL54 4HT
☎ (01242) 820547
Fax (01242) 820237

Magnificent building set in 5 acres by the River Coln. Turning ornamental waterwheel in the garden. 4 miles from Cheltenham, 9 miles from Gloucester.
Bedrooms: 6 double, 6 twin, 4 family rooms
Bathrooms: 16 en-suite

Bed & breakfast

per night:	£min	£max
Single	35.00	42.00
Double	58.00	77.00

Half board per

person:	£min	£max
Daily	38.00	48.00
Weekly	231.00	301.00

Lunch available
Evening meal 1830 (last orders 2145)

Parking for 200
Cards accepted: Access, Visa, Diners, Amex

George Hotel

COMMENDED

41-49 St Georges Road, Cheltenham
GL50 3DZ
☎ (01242) 235751
Fax (01242) 224359
Regency building, centrally situated. Close to promenade and Montpellier shops.
Bedrooms: 8 single, 21 double, 10 twin
Bathrooms: 39 en-suite

Bed & breakfast

per night:	£min	£max
Single	42.00	54.00
Double	54.00	64.00

Half board per

person:	£min	£max
Daily	36.00	44.00
Weekly	263.00	290.00

Lunch available
Evening meal 1900 (last orders 2115)
Parking for 28
Cards accepted: Access, Visa, Diners, Amex, Switch/Delta

Hallery House Hotel & Restaurant

48 Shurdington Road, Cheltenham
GL53 0JE
☎ (01242) 578450
Fax (01242) 529730
Logis of Great Britain
Beautiful Grade II listed house, offering a warm and friendly atmosphere. Varied food. Colour and satellite TV all rooms. Close to town centre.
Bedrooms: 6 single, 5 double, 4 twin, 1 family room
Bathrooms: 10 en-suite, 2 public

Bed & breakfast

per night:	£min	£max
Single	25.00	45.00
Double	35.00	75.00

Half board per

person:	£min	£max
Daily	35.00	60.00

Lunch available
Evening meal 1900 (last orders 2200)
Parking for 20

Continued ▶

HEART OF ENGLAND

CHELTENHAM
Continued

Cards accepted: Access, Visa, Diners, Amex

Hamilton House
COMMENDED

65 Bath Road, Cheltenham
GL53 7LH
☎ (01242) 527772

Extremely central terraced town house within easy walking distance of all Cheltenham's facilities.
Bedrooms: 2 single, 1 double, 1 twin, 2 triple
Bathrooms: 3 en-suite, 1 public

Bed & breakfast per night:	£min	£max
Single	18.00	25.00
Double	36.00	40.00

Hanover House
COMMENDED

65 St Georges Road, Cheltenham
GL50 3DU
☎ (01242) 529867
Fax (01242) 222779

Well-appointed and spacious accommodation in elegant, listed Victorian Cotswold-stone house. Close to theatre, town hall, gardens and shopping centre.
Bedrooms: 1 single, 3 double, 1 twin, 1 triple
Bathrooms: 3 en-suite, 1 public

Bed & breakfast per night:	£min	£max
Single	22.00	36.00
Double	48.00	54.50

Half board per person:	£min	£max
Daily	38.00	

Evening meal 1830 (last orders 0900)
Parking for 4
Cards accepted: Amex

Hollington House Hotel
COMMENDED

115 Hales Road, Cheltenham
GL52 6ST
☎ (01242) 256652
Fax (01242) 570280
The Independents

Easy to find, 700 yards from London road/A40. Plenty of free on-site parking. Victorian house, spacious en-suite bedrooms, a la carte menus, licensed bar. Standards maintained by resident proprietors. Special interest tours arranged in our own mini-bus. Nous parlons francais. Chakap bahasa sidikit. Wir sprechen Deutsch.
Bedrooms: 2 single, 2 double, 1 twin, 1 triple, 3 family rooms
Bathrooms: 8 en-suite, 1 private

Bed & breakfast per night:	£min	£max
Single	30.00	40.00
Double	40.00	60.00

Half board per person:	£min	£max
Daily	33.00	43.00

Evening meal 1900 (last orders 1900)
Parking for 14
Cards accepted: Access, Visa, Amex, Switch/Delta

Ivy Dene Guest House
COMMENDED

145 Hewlett Road, Cheltenham
GL52 6TS
☎ (01242) 521726 & 521776

Ideal base for exploring the Cotswolds. A charming corner house in its own grounds, situated in a residential area within walking distance of the town.
Bedrooms: 3 single, 1 twin, 4 triple, 1 family room
Bathrooms: 5 en-suite, 2 public

Bed & breakfast per night:	£min	£max
Single	18.00	25.00
Double	40.00	45.00

Parking for 6

Lawn House
COMMENDED

11 London Road, Cheltenham
GL52 6EX
☎ (01242) 578486
Fax (01242) 578486

Elegant Grade II listed house. Good parking and close to town centre. Friendly atmosphere, family-run. TVs, beverage trays, good food, comfortable rooms. A non-smoking establishment.
Bedrooms: 2 single, 3 double, 2 twin, 1 triple
Bathrooms: 3 en-suite, 2 public

Bed & breakfast per night:	£min	£max
Single	22.50	29.00
Double	39.00	49.00

Half board per person:	£min	£max
Daily	31.50	58.00
Weekly	200.00	350.00

Evening meal 1730 (last orders 1900)
Parking for 10
Cards accepted: Access, Visa, Switch/Delta

Micklinton Hotel

12 Montpellier Dr, Cheltenham
GL50 1TX
☎ (01242) 520000
Fax (01242) 260408

5 minutes' walk to theatres and town centre. Easy access to roads and motorway and ideal for touring the Cotswolds.
Bedrooms: 3 single, 2 double, 3 twin
Bathrooms: 5 en-suite, 1 public

Bed & breakfast per night:	£min	£max
Single	18.00	22.00
Double	34.00	40.00

Evening meal 1830 (last orders 2000)
Parking for 6
Cards accepted: Access, Visa, Diners

Milton House
HIGHLY COMMENDED

12 Royal Parade, Bayshill Road,
Cheltenham GL50 3AY
☎ (01242) 582601 & Cheltenham 573631
Fax (01242) 222326

Beautiful Regency listed building with freshly-decorated spacious bedrooms, set among tree-lined avenues, only 4 minutes' stroll from the Promenade.
Bedrooms: 2 single, 2 double, 2 twin, 2 triple
Bathrooms: 8 en-suite

Map references apply to the colour maps at the back of this guide.

HEART OF ENGLAND

Bed & breakfast

per night:	£min	£max
Single	38.50	45.00
Double	52.00	68.00

Evening meal from 2130
Parking for 5
Cards accepted: Access, Visa, Amex, Switch/Delta

Moorend Park Hotel
COMMENDED

11 Moorend Park Road, Cheltenham GL53 0LA
☎ (01242) 224441
Fax (01242) 572413

Elegant Victorian house, renovated and refurbished in 1996. Ample private parking. Fine Swiss orientated cuisine. Close to town centre and M5.
Bedrooms: 1 single, 2 double, 3 twin, 2 triple, 1 family room
Bathrooms: 9 en-suite

Bed & breakfast

per night:	£min	£max
Single	31.00	42.00
Double	43.50	55.00

Half board per

person:	£min	£max
Daily	37.00	57.00

Lunch available
Evening meal 1900 (last orders 2030)
Parking for 25
Cards accepted: Access, Visa, Amex

Old Stables
Listed

239A London Road, Charlton Kings, Cheltenham GL52 6YE
☎ (01242) 583660

Former coach house with separate B & B accommodation, 2 miles east of Cheltenham town centre on A40. Easy car access and parking.
Bedrooms: 1 twin, 1 triple
Bathrooms: 1 public

Bed & breakfast

per night:	£min	£max
Single	16.00	17.00
Double	20.00	30.00

Parking for 3

COLOUR MAPS

Colour maps at the back of this guide pinpoint all places in which you will find accommodation listed.

Hotel On The Park
DE LUXE

Evesham Road, Cheltenham GL52 2AH
☎ (01242) 518898
Fax (01242) 511526

Overlooking Pittville Park, this exclusive Regency town house hotel offers excellent standards of accommodation with individually designed rooms and the best of modern British cooking.
Bedrooms: 8 double, 4 twin
Suite available
Bathrooms: 12 en-suite

Bed & breakfast

per night:	£min	£max
Single	82.75	
Double	106.00	166.00

Half board per

person:	£min	£max
Daily	65.78	102.00

Lunch available
Evening meal 1900 (last orders 2130)
Parking for 10
Cards accepted: Access, Visa, Diners, Amex

4 Pittville Crescent
COMMENDED

Cheltenham GL52 2QZ
☎ (01242) 575567
Lovely Regency house with large airy rooms, beautifully situated overlooking charming parkland. 5 minutes from town centre.
Bedrooms: 1 single, 2 twin
Bathrooms: 1 public

Bed & breakfast

per night:	£min	£max
Single	17.50	20.00
Double	35.00	40.00

Parking for 20

The Prestbury House Hotel and Restaurant
COMMENDED

The Burgage, Prestbury, Cheltenham GL52 3DN
☎ (01242) 529533
Fax (01242) 227076

300-year-old Georgian country manor house set in 4 acres of secluded grounds beneath Cleeve Hill. Only 1 mile from Cheltenham centre.

Wheelchair access category 3
Bedrooms: 1 single, 6 double, 9 twin, 1 triple
Bathrooms: 17 en-suite

Bed & breakfast

per night:	£min	£max
Single	65.00	75.00
Double	80.00	90.00

Half board per

person:	£min	£max
Daily	89.00	99.00

Lunch available
Evening meal 1900 (last orders 2100)
Parking for 50
Cards accepted: Access, Visa, Diners, Amex, Switch/Delta

Regency House Hotel
HIGHLY COMMENDED

50 Clarence Square, Cheltenham GL50 4JR
☎ (01242) 582718
Fax (01242) 262697

Restored Regency house in a quiet Georgian square. Near Pittville Park but only minutes' walk from all town centre amenities.
Bedrooms: 5 double, 3 triple
Bathrooms: 8 en-suite

Bed & breakfast

per night:	£min	£max
Single	32.50	40.00
Double	44.00	54.00

Half board per

person:	£min	£max
Daily	34.95	38.95
Weekly	244.65	272.65

Evening meal 1800 (last orders 1930)
Parking for 5
Cards accepted: Access, Visa, Amex

St James Hotel

Ambrose Street, Cheltenham GL50 3LH
☎ (01242) 522860
Pub/hotel, 5 minutes from town centre, opposite St Gregory's Church.
Bedrooms: 1 double, 3 twin, 4 triple
Bathrooms: 2 public

Continued ▶

HEART OF ENGLAND

CHELTENHAM
Continued

Bed & breakfast
per night:	£min	£max
Single	15.00	20.00
Double	30.00	40.00

Lunch available
Evening meal 1900 (last orders 2100)
Cards accepted: Access, Visa

St. Michaels
COMMENDED

4 Montpellier Drive, Cheltenham GL50 1TX
☎ (01242) 513587
Elegant Edwardian guesthouse offering delightful accommodation in a friendly informal atmosphere. Quiet location five minutes' walk from town hall, Promenade, restaurants and theatres. Parking.
Bedrooms: 2 double, 1 twin, 2 triple
Bathrooms: 4 en-suite, 1 public

Bed & breakfast
per night:	£min	£max
Single	23.00	30.00
Double	35.00	44.00

Parking for 3
Cards accepted: Access, Visa

White House Hotel
COMMENDED

Gloucester Road, Staverton, Cheltenham GL51 0ST
☎ Churchdown (01452) 713226
Fax (01452) 857590
Peacefully located hotel, just a few minutes' drive from Cheltenham or Gloucester city centre. Ideal base for the Cotswolds.
Bedrooms: 1 single, 6 double, 37 twin, 3 triple, 2 family rooms
Suites available
Bathrooms: 49 en-suite

Bed & breakfast
per night:	£min	£max
Single		75.00
Double		100.00

Lunch available
Evening meal 1900 (last orders 2130)
Parking for 150
Cards accepted: Access, Visa, Diners, Amex, Switch/Delta

CHIPPING CAMPDEN
Gloucestershire
Map ref 2B1

Outstanding Cotswold wool town with many old stone gabled houses, a splendid church and 17th C almshouses. Nearby are Kiftsgate Court Gardens and Hidcote Manor Gardens (National Trust).

Cotswold House Hotel and Restaurant
HIGHLY COMMENDED

The Square, Chipping Campden GL55 6AN
☎ Evesham (01386) 840330
Fax (01386) 840310
Comfort, elegance, good food and friendly, personal service are all to be found at this delightful and historic country town house hotel.
Bedrooms: 3 single, 7 double, 5 twin
Bathrooms: 15 en-suite

Bed & breakfast
per night:	£min	£max
Single	70.00	80.00
Double	100.00	160.00

Half board per
person:	£min	£max
Daily	60.00	89.00
Weekly	420.00	620.00

Evening meal 1915 (last orders 2130)
Parking for 15
Cards accepted: Access, Visa, Diners, Amex, Switch/Delta

Malt House
HIGHLY COMMENDED

Broad Campden, Chipping Campden GL55 6UU
☎ Evesham (01386) 840295
Fax (01386) 841334
Listed 16th C Cotswold home set in 7.5 acres of secluded gardens. Bedrooms individually decorated, four-poster room available. Public rooms furnished with English antiques and with log fires. Noted restaurant serving a table d'hote evening menu.
Bedrooms: 4 double, 3 twin, 1 triple
Bathrooms: 8 en-suite

Bed & breakfast
per night:	£min	£max
Single	49.50	69.50
Double	82.50	97.50

Half board per
person:	£min	£max
Daily	72.50	87.50

Evening meal from 1930
Parking for 10

Cards accepted: Access, Visa, Switch/Delta

Three Ways House
COMMENDED

Chapel Lane, Mickleton, Chipping Campden GL55 6SB
☎ Evesham (01386) 438429
Fax (01386) 438118
Logis of Great Britain
Cotswold village hotel close to Chipping Campden, Broadway and Stratford-upon-Avon. Comfortable bedrooms, cosy bar, good food and friendly service.
Bedrooms: 3 single, 14 double, 19 twin, 3 triple, 2 family rooms
Bathrooms: 41 en-suite

Bed & breakfast
per night:	£min	£max
Single		50.00
Double		80.00

Half board per
person:	£min	£max
Daily		54.00
Weekly		343.00

Lunch available
Evening meal 1900 (last orders 2130)
Parking for 40
Cards accepted: Access, Visa, Diners, Amex, Switch/Delta

CHURCH STRETTON
Shropshire
Map ref 4A3

Church Stretton lies under the eastern slope of the Longmynd surrounded by hills. It is ideal for walkers, with marvellous views, golf and gliding. Wenlock Edge is not far away.

Belvedere Guest House
COMMENDED

Burway Road, Church Stretton SY6 6DP
☎ Church Stretton (01694) 722232
Fax (01694) 722232
Quiet detached house set in its own grounds, convenient for Church Stretton town centre and Longmynd Hills. Adequate parking.
Bedrooms: 3 single, 3 double, 2 twin, 3 triple, 1 family room
Bathrooms: 6 en-suite, 4 public

Bed & breakfast
per night:	£min	£max
Single	22.00	27.00
Double	44.00	48.00

HEART OF ENGLAND

Half board per person:	£min	£max
Daily	31.50	36.50
Weekly	198.45	230.00

Evening meal 1900 (last orders 1800)
Parking for 8
Cards accepted: Access, Visa, Switch/Delta

Denehurst Hotel & Leisure Centre ⚜

COMMENDED

Shrewsbury Road, Church Stretton SY6 6EU
☎ Church Stretton (01694) 722699
Fax (01694) 724110

In the heart of beautiful Shropshire, with a comfortable, friendly family atmosphere and recently built leisure complex. Suitable for all the family.
Bedrooms: 1 single, 7 double, 3 twin, 5 triple
Bathrooms: 16 en-suite, 1 public

Bed & breakfast per night:	£min	£max
Single	35.00	40.00
Double	50.00	55.00

Half board per person:	£min	£max
Daily	47.50	52.50
Weekly	220.00	225.00

Lunch available
Evening meal 1900 (last orders 2030)
Parking for 70
Cards accepted: Access, Visa

CIRENCESTER
Gloucestershire
Map ref 2B1

"Capital of the Cotswolds", Cirencester was Britain's second most important Roman town with many finds housed in the Corinium Museum. It has a very fine Perpendicular church and old houses around the market place.
Tourist Information Centre ☎ *(01285) 654180*

Chesil Rocks

Listed COMMENDED

Baunton Lane, Stratton, Cirencester GL7 2LL
☎ (01285) 655031

Please mention this guide when making your booking.

Pleasant and friendly home in a quiet lane, with easy access to town and country walks. Cheltenham, Gloucester and Swindon within easy reach.
Bedrooms: 2 single, 1 twin
Bathrooms: 1 public

Bed & breakfast per night:	£min	£max
Single	15.00	15.00
Double	30.00	30.00

Parking for 3

Crown of Crucis ⚜

COMMENDED

Ampney Crucis, Cirencester GL7 5RS
☎ (01285) 851806
Fax (01285) 851735

Privately owned Cotswold hotel, 2.5 miles east of Cirencester on A417. 16th C building, noted for good food and elegant bedrooms.
Bedrooms: 9 double, 16 twin
Bathrooms: 25 en-suite

Bed & breakfast per night:	£min	£max
Single	36.00	54.00
Double	54.00	76.00

Lunch available
Evening meal 1800 (last orders 2200)
Parking for 80
Cards accepted: Access, Visa, Diners, Amex, Switch/Delta

Eliot Arms Hotel Free House ⚜

COMMENDED

Clarks Hay, South Cerney, Cirencester GL7 5UA
☎ (01285) 860215
Fax (01285) 861121

Dating from the 16th C, a comfortable Cotswold freehouse hotel, 2.5 miles from Cirencester, just off the A419. Reputation for fine food and hospitality. Riverside gardens.
Bedrooms: 1 single, 5 double, 4 twin, 2 triple

Suites available
Bathrooms: 12 en-suite

Bed & breakfast per night:	£min	£max
Single	35.00	38.00
Double	49.50	55.00

Lunch available
Evening meal 1830 (last orders 2200)
Parking for 30
Cards accepted: Access, Visa, Amex, Switch/Delta

Wimborne House ⚜

COMMENDED

91 Victoria Road, Cirencester GL7 1ES
☎ (01285) 653890

Victorian Cotswold-stone house, with a warm and friendly atmosphere and spacious rooms. Four-poster room. Non-smokers only, please.
Bedrooms: 4 double, 1 twin
Bathrooms: 5 en-suite

Bed & breakfast per night:	£min	£max
Single	20.00	28.00
Double	30.00	40.00

Half board per person:	£min	£max
Daily	21.50	26.50
Weekly	145.50	180.50

Evening meal 1830 (last orders 1730)
Parking for 6

For ideas on places to visit refer to the introduction at the beginning of this section.

ACCESSIBILITY

Look for the ♿♿ symbols which indicate accessibility for wheelchair users. These are described in detail at the front of this guide.

HEART OF ENGLAND

CLEARWELL

Gloucestershire
Map ref 2A1

Attractive village in the Forest of Dean, noted for its castle, built in 1735 and one of the oldest Georgian Gothic houses in England. The old mines in Clearwell Caves are open to the public.

Wyndham Arms ♠
♛♛♛♛ HIGHLY COMMENDED

Clearwell, Coleford GL16 8JT
☎ Dean (01594) 833666
Fax (01594) 836450
Logis of Great Britain

Stay free on Sundays in this historic hotel. Under the competent management of the Stanford family since 1973.
Bedrooms: 2 single, 4 double, 9 twin, 2 triple
Bathrooms: 17 en-suite
Bed & breakfast
per night:

	£min	£max
Single	52.50	52.50
Double	61.00	65.00

Half board per person:

	£min	£max
Daily	47.50	50.00
Weekly	280.00	280.00

Lunch available
Evening meal 1900 (last orders 2130)
Parking for 52
Cards accepted: Access, Visa, Diners, Amex, Switch/Delta

CLEOBURY MORTIMER

Shropshire
Map ref 4A2

Village with attractive timbered and Georgian houses and a church with a wooden spire. It is close to the Clee Hills with marvellous views.

The Redfern Hotel ♠
♛♛♛♛ COMMENDED

Cleobury Mortimer, Kidderminster, Worcestershire DY14 8AA
☎ Cleobury Mortimer (01299) 270395
Fax (01299) 271011
Minotel/Logis of Great Britain

18th C stone-built hotel in ancient market town, bordering 6,000-acre Forest of Wyre. Conservation area. Four-poster bed and room with whirlpool bathroom available.
Bedrooms: 5 double, 5 twin, 1 triple
Bathrooms: 10 en-suite, 1 private
Bed & breakfast
per night:

	£min	£max
Single	48.00	52.00
Double	70.00	85.00

Half board per person:

	£min	£max
Daily	46.00	65.00
Weekly	260.00	330.00

Lunch available
Evening meal 1930 (last orders 2200)
Parking for 20
Cards accepted: Access, Visa, Diners, Amex, Switch/Delta

CODSALL

Staffordshire
Map ref 4B3

Expanding residential village a few miles from Wolverhampton.

Moors Farm and Country Restaurant
♛♛♛

Chillington Lane, Codsall, Wolverhampton WV8 1QF
☎ (01902) 842330
Fax (01902) 847878
100-acre mixed farm. 200-year-old farmhouse, 1 mile from pretty village. All home produce used. Many local walks and places of interest.
Bedrooms: 3 double, 1 twin, 1 family room
Bathrooms: 3 en-suite, 2 public
Bed & breakfast
per night:

	£min	£max
Single	25.00	32.00
Double	40.00	52.00

Half board per person:

	£min	£max
Daily	30.00	42.00
Weekly	200.00	280.00

Evening meal 1830 (last orders 1900)
Parking for 20

COLEFORD

Gloucestershire
Map ref 2A1

Small town in the Forest of Dean with the ancient iron mines at Clearwell Caves nearby, where mining equipment and geological samples are displayed. There are several forest trails in the area.
Tourist Information Centre ☎ (01594) 812388

Forest House Hotel ♠
♛♛

Cinder Hill, Coleford GL16 8HQ
☎ Dean (01594) 832424
18th C listed former home of industrial steel pioneers. Spacious, comfortable rooms, imaginative cuisine. Close to town centre. Ideal touring/outdoor pursuits base.
Bedrooms: 2 single, 3 double, 2 twin
Bathrooms: 2 en-suite, 2 public
Bed & breakfast
per night:

	£min	£max
Single	16.00	25.00
Double	32.00	40.00

Half board per person:

	£min	£max
Daily	25.75	34.75

Evening meal 1900 (last orders 1900)
Parking for 10

Information on accommodation listed in this guide has been supplied by the proprietors. As changes may occur you are advised to check details at the time of booking.

WELCOME HOST

This is a nationally recognised customer care programme which aims to promote the highest standards of service and a warm welcome. Establishments who are taking part in this initiative are indicated by the ✿ symbol.

The National Grading and Classification Scheme is explained in full at the back of this guide.

HEART OF ENGLAND

COLESHILL
Warwickshire
Map ref 4B3

Close to Birmingham's many attractions including the 17th C Aston Hall with its plasterwork and furnishings, the Railway Museum and Sarehole Mill, an 18th C water-powered mill restored to working order.

Coleshill Hotel
COMMENDED
152 High Street, Coleshill, Birmingham B46 3BG
☎ (01675) 465527
Fax (01675) 464013
The Independents
In traditional coaching inn style with restaurant, lounge bar and function/conference facilities. 5 minutes' drive from the National Exhibition Centre.
Bedrooms: 2 single, 11 double, 10 twin
Bathrooms: 23 en-suite

Bed & breakfast per night:	£min	£max
Single	65.00	67.50
Double	75.00	77.50

Half board per person:	£min	£max
Daily	72.50	80.00

Lunch available
Evening meal 1900 (last orders 2200)
Parking for 48
Cards accepted: Access, Visa, Diners, Amex, Switch/Delta

COTSWOLDS
*See under Bibury, Bledington, Bourton-on-the-Water, Broadway, Cheltenham, Chipping Campden, Cirencester, Fairford, Gloucester, Guiting Power, Lechlade, Long Compton, Lower Slaughter, Minchinhampton, Moreton-in-Marsh, Nailsworth, Northleach, Nympsfield, Painswick, Slimbridge, Stonehouse, Stow-on-the-Wold, Stroud, Tetbury, Tewkesbury, Wotton-under-Edge
See also Cotswolds in South of England region*

COLOUR MAPS
Colour maps at the back of this guide pinpoint all places in which you will find accommodation listed.

COVENTRY
West Midlands
Map ref 4B3

Modern city with a long history. It has many places of interest including the post-war and ruined medieval cathedrals, art gallery and museums, some 16th C almshouses, St Mary's Guildhall, Lunt Roman fort and the Belgrade Theatre.
Tourist Information Centre ☎ (01203) 832303 or 832304

Acorn Lodge Private Guest House
COMMENDED
Pond Farm, Upper Eastern Green Lane, Coventry CV5 7DP
☎ (01203) 465182
300-year-old beamed farmhouse of character in secluded position. Ideally situated for touring Stratford and Warwick and 20 miles from National Exhibition Centre and Birmingham Airport. Friendly, informal atmosphere. Paddocks and ponies.
Bedrooms: 2 single, 1 double, 2 twin
Bathrooms: 1 en-suite, 2 public

Bed & breakfast per night:	£min	£max
Single	16.00	16.00
Double	32.00	35.00

Parking for 6

Ashleigh House
17 Park Road, Coventry CV1 2LH
☎ (01203) 223804
Recently renovated guesthouse only 100 yards from the railway station. All city amenities within 5 minutes' walk.
Bedrooms: 3 single, 3 double, 2 twin, 2 triple
Bathrooms: 8 en-suite, 1 public

Bed & breakfast per night:	£min	£max
Single	18.00	25.00
Double	28.00	36.00

Half board per person:	£min	£max
Daily	23.50	30.50

Evening meal 1700 (last orders 1900)
Parking for 12

Establishments should be open throughout the year, unless otherwise stated.

Courtyard Coventry Knight Hotel
A45 London Road, Ryton-on-Dunsmore, Coventry CV8 3DY
☎ (01203) 301585
Fax (01203) 301610
Whitbread
Comfortable, modern hotel with friendly atmosphere, on the A45 just a couple of miles from Coventry. Good touring base for the Midlands and Shakespeare country. NAC/NEC and Birmingham Airport 15 miles.
Bedrooms: 1 single, 8 double, 32 twin, 2 triple
Suites available
Bathrooms: 43 en-suite

Bed & breakfast per night:	£min	£max
Single	80.00	130.00
Double	80.00	130.00

Half board per person:	£min	£max
Daily	95.00	150.00

Lunch available
Evening meal 1900 (last orders 2200)
Parking for 150
Cards accepted: Access, Visa, Diners, Amex

Falcon Hotel
13-19 Manor Road, Coventry CV1 2LH
☎ (01203) 258615
Fax (01203) 520680
Close to Coventry railway station, ideal for the travelling businessman. Ten minutes from NEC, M6 motorway and Birmingham International Airport. Large free car park. Shops, social and cultural activities readily at hand.
Bedrooms: 6 single, 2 double, 3 twin, 3 triple, 1 family room
Bathrooms: 15 en-suite

Bed & breakfast per night:	£min	£max
Single	35.00	45.00
Double	50.00	65.00

Half board per person:	£min	£max
Daily	32.00	50.00

Lunch available
Evening meal 1900 (last orders 2145)
Parking for 50
Cards accepted: Access, Visa, Diners, Amex

HEART OF ENGLAND

COVENTRY
Continued

Merrick Lodge Hotel
COMMENDED
80-82 St. Nicholas Street, Coventry
CV1 4BP
☎ (01203) 553940
Fax (01203) 550112

Former manor house, 5 minutes' walk from city centre. Table d'hote and a la carte restaurant, 3 bars. Comfortable, well-equipped, en-suite bedrooms. Superb base for visiting the area. Private functions and conferences also catered for.
Bedrooms: 5 single, 7 double, 9 twin, 5 triple
Bathrooms: 19 en-suite, 7 private

Bed & breakfast per night:
	£min	£max
Single	30.00	45.00
Double	40.00	65.00

Half board per person:
	£min	£max
Daily	27.50	60.00
Weekly	192.50	420.00

Lunch available
Evening meal 1830 (last orders 2300)
Parking for 60
Cards accepted: Access, Visa, Amex, Switch/Delta

Mount Guest House
Listed APPROVED
9 Coundon Road, Coventry
CV1 4AR
☎ (01203) 225998 & Mobile (0589) 008120
Fax (01203) 225998
Family guesthouse within walking distance of city and cathedral. Easy reach of National Exhibition Centre and Royal Showground. Snacks available.
Bedrooms: 2 single, 5 twin, 2 triple
Bathrooms: 2 public

Bed & breakfast per night:
	£min	£max
Single	14.00	14.00
Double	28.00	28.00

Northanger House
APPROVED
35 Westminster Road, Coventry
CV1 3GB
☎ (01203) 226780
Friendly home 5 minutes from the city centre. Close to railway and bus stations, and convenient for all amenities.
Bedrooms: 2 single, 3 twin, 3 triple, 1 family room
Bathrooms: 3 public

Bed & breakfast per night:
	£min	£max
Single	16.00	17.00
Double	28.00	30.00

Half board per person:
	£min	£max
Daily	19.50	20.50
Weekly	125.00	140.00

Evening meal from 1900
Cards accepted: Visa

Novotel Coventry
COMMENDED
M6, Junction 3, Wilsons Lane, Longford, Coventry CV6 6HL
☎ (01203) 365000
Fax (01203) 362422
Novotel
Coventry and the Novotel, a venue for business, holiday weekends or as a relaxing stop-over between journeys.
Bedrooms: 98 triple
Bathrooms: 98 en-suite

Bed & breakfast per night:
	£min	£max
Single	50.00	58.00
Double	52.00	63.50

Half board per person:
	£min	£max
Daily	70.00	83.00

Lunch available
Evening meal 1800 (last orders 2359)
Parking for 120
Cards accepted: Access, Visa, Diners, Amex, Switch/Delta

Windmill Village Hotel, Golf and Leisure Club
COMMENDED
Birmingham Road, Allesley, Coventry CV5 9AL
☎ (01203) 404040
Fax (01203) 407016
Mix of lodge and hotel accommodation. Own excellent leisure centre, 18-hole golf-course, fishing lakes, bowling green and tennis court.
Bedrooms: 11 single, 42 double, 32 twin, 7 family rooms
Suites available
Bathrooms: 92 en-suite

Bed & breakfast per night:
	£min	£max
Single	49.50	99.00
Double	59.50	115.00

Lunch available
Evening meal 1900 (last orders 2200)
Parking for 250
Cards accepted: Access, Visa, Diners, Amex, Switch/Delta

DROITWICH
Hereford and Worcester
Map ref 2B1

Old town with natural brine springs, now incorporated into the Brine Baths Health Centre, developed as a spa at the beginning of the 19th C. Of particular interest is the Church of the Sacred Heart with splendid mosaics. Fine parks and a Heritage Centre.
Tourist Information Centre ☎ (01905) 774312

Richmond Guest House
Listed
3 Ombersley St. West, Droitwich, Worcestershire WR9 8HZ
☎ Worcester (01905) 775722
Fax (01905) 794500
Victorian-built guesthouse in the town centre, 5 minutes from railway station and bus route. English breakfast. 30 minutes from National Exhibition Centre via M5/M42.
Bedrooms: 8 single, 1 twin, 4 triple, 2 family rooms
Bathrooms: 3 public

Bed & breakfast per night:
	£min	£max
Single	16.00	18.00
Double	28.00	30.00

Parking for 12

St. Andrews House Hotel
COMMENDED
Worcester Road, Droitwich, Worcestershire WR9 8AL
☎ Worcester (01905) 779677
Fax (01905) 779752
Country house hotel built in 1820 in the centre of Droitwich (a former spa town) yet surrounded by its own grounds. Fully modernised.
Bedrooms: 10 single, 8 double, 10 twin, 3 family rooms
Bathrooms: 28 en-suite, 3 private

HEART OF ENGLAND

Bed & breakfast per night:	£min	£max
Single	49.50	55.50
Double	72.00	79.00

Lunch available
Evening meal 1900 (last orders 2100)
Parking for 120
Cards accepted: Access, Visa, Diners, Amex

ECKINGTON

Hereford and Worcester
Map ref 2B1

Large and expanding village in a fruit growing and market gardening area beside the Avon, which is crossed here by a 15th C bridge.
Half-timbered houses are much in evidence.

The Bell Inn
COMMENDED

Church Street, Eckington, Pershore, Worcestershire WR10 3AN
☎ Evesham (01386) 750205 & 751073
Fax (01386) 750205
In the centre of Eckington village, offering comfortable, pleasant surroundings. Within easy reach of Worcester, Evesham and Cheltenham.
Bedrooms: 2 double, 1 twin, 1 triple
Bathrooms: 4 private

Bed & breakfast per night:	£min	£max
Single	27.50	50.00
Double	50.00	60.00

Half board per person:	£min	£max
Daily	35.00	60.00
Weekly	210.00	350.00

Lunch available
Evening meal 1800 (last orders 2130)
Parking for 14
Cards accepted: Access, Visa, Switch/Delta

Please check prices and other details at the time of booking.

A key to symbols can be found inside the back cover flap.

ELLESMERE

Shropshire
Map ref 4A2

Small market town with old streets and houses and situated close to 9 lakes. The largest, the Mere, has many waterfowl and recreational facilities and some of the other meres have sailing and fishing.

The Ellesmere Hotel

High Street, Ellesmere SY12 0ES
☎ (01691) 622055
Fax (01691) 622055
17th C coaching inn with stunningly redesigned interior and en-suite bedrooms. Restaurant, lounge and bar serving wholesome, hearty food. Quality wines, spirits and cask conditioned ales.
Bedrooms: 3 single, 7 double, 2 twin
Bathrooms: 12 en-suite

Bed & breakfast per night:	£min	£max
Single	25.00	30.00
Double	43.00	

Half board per person:	£min	£max
Daily	35.00	

Lunch available
Evening meal 1700 (last orders 2130)
Parking for 20
Cards accepted: Access, Visa

Greenbanks (Bed and Breakfast)
HIGHLY COMMENDED

Coptiviney, Ellesmere SY12 0ND
☎ (01691) 623420
Fax (01691) 623420
Comfortable Victorian country house set in extensive grounds. Peacefully situated in the tranquillity of this totally rural area, yet well placed for centres of Shrewsbury, Oswestry, Wrexham and Chester.
Bedrooms: 2 twin
Bathrooms: 1 en-suite, 1 private, 1 public

Bed & breakfast per night:	£min	£max
Single	27.00	30.00
Double	54.00	60.00

Half board per person:	£min	£max
Daily	44.00	47.00
Weekly	308.00	329.00

Parking for 4
Cards accepted: Visa

EVESHAM

Hereford and Worcester
Map ref 2B1

Market town in the centre of a fruit-growing area. There are pleasant walks along the River Avon and many old houses and inns. A fine 16th C bell tower stands between 2 churches near the medieval Almonry Museum.
Tourist Information Centre ☎ *(01386) 446944*

Evesham Hotel
HIGHLY COMMENDED

Cooper's Lane, Off Waterside, Evesham, Worcestershire WR11 6DA
☎ (01386) 765566 & Freephone 0800 716969
Fax (01386) 765443
Family-run Tudor mansion in 2.5-acre garden, offering unusual food and wine and all modern facilities. Ideal touring centre. Indoor pool designed for fun. Overnight half-board prices are for a minimum 2-night stay.
Bedrooms: 6 single, 22 double, 11 twin, 1 triple
Bathrooms: 40 en-suite

Bed & breakfast per night:	£min	£max
Single	57.00	65.00
Double	74.00	88.00

Half board per person:	£min	£max
Daily	47.00	61.00
Weekly	335.00	372.00

Lunch available
Evening meal 1900 (last orders 2130)
Parking for 45
Cards accepted: Access, Visa, Diners, Amex, Switch/Delta

The Mill at Harvington
HIGHLY COMMENDED

Anchor Lane, Harvington, Evesham, Worcestershire WR11 5NR
☎ (01386) 870688
Fax (01386) 870688

Peaceful, owner-run, riverside hotel tastefully converted from beautiful
Continued ▶

HEART OF ENGLAND

EVESHAM
Continued

house and mill. In acres of gardens, quarter of a mile from Evesham to Stratford road.
Bedrooms: 12 double, 3 twin
Bathrooms: 15 en-suite

Bed & breakfast per night:	£min	£max
Single	54.00	58.00
Double	85.00	89.00

Lunch available
Evening meal 1900 (last orders 2045)
Parking for 25
Cards accepted: Access, Visa, Diners, Amex, Switch/Delta

Northwick Arms Hotel
COMMENDED

Waterside, Evesham, Worcestershire WR11 6BT
☎ (01386) 40322
Fax (01386) 41070

Once a coaching inn, this traditional hotel overlooks the River Avon and is close to the centre of Evesham. En-suite bedrooms, a restaurant and two bars.
Wheelchair access category 2
Bedrooms: 8 single, 11 double, 7 twin, 4 triple
Bathrooms: 30 en-suite

Bed & breakfast per night:	£min	£max
Single	32.00	52.00
Double	48.00	80.00

Half board per person:	£min	£max
Daily	42.00	66.00
Weekly	252.00	330.00

Lunch available
Evening meal 1900 (last orders 2130)
Parking for 100
Cards accepted: Access, Visa, Diners, Amex, Switch/Delta

Park View Hotel

Waterside, Evesham, Worcestershire WR11 6BS
☎ (01386) 442639

Family-run hotel offering comfortable accommodation in a friendly atmosphere. Riverside situation, close to town centre. Ideal base for touring the Cotswolds and Shakespeare country.
Bedrooms: 10 single, 4 double, 10 twin, 1 triple, 1 family room
Bathrooms: 7 public

Bed & breakfast per night:	£min	£max
Single	20.50	24.00
Double	34.00	41.00

Evening meal 1800 (last orders 1900)
Parking for 50
Cards accepted: Access, Visa, Diners, Amex

The Waterside Hotel
HIGHLY COMMENDED

56 Waterside, Evesham, Worcestershire WR11 6JZ
☎ (01386) 442420
Fax (01386) 446272

Warm and friendly owner-run hotel, in exceptional position overlooking river and parks. Designer interior, themed restaurant, extensive menu with affordable wines.
Bedrooms: 2 single, 8 double, 4 twin, 1 triple
Bathrooms: 15 en-suite, 1 public

Bed & breakfast per night:	£min	£max
Single	40.60	54.60
Double	52.00	75.00

Half board per person:	£min	£max
Daily	38.00	66.00
Weekly	255.00

Lunch available
Evening meal 1830 (last orders 2130)
Parking for 30
Cards accepted: Access, Visa, Amex

FAIRFORD
Gloucestershire
Map ref 2B1

Small town with a 15th C wool church famous for its complete 15th C stained glass windows, interesting carvings and original wall paintings. It is an excellent touring centre and the Cotswolds Wildlife Park is nearby.

Bull Hotel
COMMENDED

Market Place, Fairford GL7 4AA
☎ Cirencester (01285) 712535 & 712217
Fax (01285) 713782

15th C family-run Cotswold hotel with a la carte restaurant. Rooms with private facilities, TV, Teasmade, telephone. Private fishing.
Bedrooms: 2 single, 13 double, 5 twin
Bathrooms: 15 en-suite, 2 private, 2 public, 1 private shower

Bed & breakfast per night:	£min	£max
Single	29.50	49.50
Double	39.50	67.50

Half board per person:	£min	£max
Daily	39.50	59.50
Weekly	210.00	350.00

Lunch available
Evening meal 1800 (last orders 2115)
Parking for 20
Cards accepted: Access, Visa, Diners, Amex, Switch/Delta

FOREST OF DEAN
See under Blakeney, Clearwell, Coleford, Newent

GLOUCESTER
Gloucestershire
Map ref 2B1

A Roman city and inland port, its cathedral is one of the most beautiful in Britain. Gloucester's many attractions include museums and the restored warehouses in the Victorian docks containing the National Waterways Museum, Robert Opie Packaging Collection and other attractions.
Tourist Information Centre ☎ (01452) 421188

Brookthorpe Lodge
COMMENDED

Stroud Road, Brookthorpe, Gloucester GL4 0UQ
☎ (01452) 812645

Three-storey Georgian house on the

The ♠ symbol after an establishment name indicates that it is a Regional Tourist Board member.

HEART OF ENGLAND

outskirts of Gloucester, set in lovely countryside at the foot of the Cotswold Escarpment.
Bedrooms: 2 single, 2 double, 3 twin, 2 family rooms
Bathrooms: 6 en-suite, 3 private, 2 public

Bed & breakfast per night:	£min	£max
Single	20.00	27.50
Double	42.00	50.00

Half board per person:	£min	£max
Daily	31.00	36.00
Weekly	215.00	250.00

Lunch available
Evening meal 1800 (last orders 2000)
Parking for 15

Cheltenham/Gloucester Moat House

HIGHLY COMMENDED

Shurdington Road, Brockworth, Gloucester GL3 4PB
☎ (01452) 519988
Fax (01452) 519977
Queens Moat/Utell International
New hotel with leisure facilities, set in extensive landscaped grounds. Directly accessible from M5, junction 11a. Rates shown below apply Friday-Sunday only. From Monday-Thursday, rate is £80 for room only.
Bedrooms: 55 double, 41 twin
Suites available
Bathrooms: 96 en-suite

Bed & breakfast per night:	£min	£max
Single	41.00	50.00
Double	82.00	115.00

Half board per person:	£min	£max
Daily	53.00	65.00

Lunch available
Evening meal 1900 (last orders 2200)
Parking for 212
Cards accepted: Access, Visa, Diners, Amex, Switch/Delta

Georgian Guest House

Listed

85 Bristol Road, Gloucester GL1 5SN
☎ (01452) 413186
On the main Bristol Road, 10 minutes' walk from Gloucester city centre.
Bedrooms: 2 single, 3 double, 3 twin, 1 triple
Bathrooms: 2 en-suite, 1 public, 2 private showers

Bed & breakfast per night:	£min	£max
Single	14.50	16.00
Double	29.00	32.00

Parking for 3

Hatherley Manor Hotel

COMMENDED

Down Hatherley Lane, Gloucester GL2 9QA
☎ (01452) 730217
Fax (01452) 731032
Lyric
Beautiful hotel in 37 acres, with notable restaurant. Mini-breaks available. Ideal base for visiting Cotswolds and Cheltenham.
Bedrooms: 8 single, 43 double, 5 twin
Bathrooms: 56 en-suite

Bed & breakfast per night:	£min	£max
Single	50.00	80.00
Double	60.00	95.00

Half board per person:	£min	£max
Daily	46.00	70.00

Lunch available
Evening meal 1900 (last orders 2130)
Parking for 250
Cards accepted: Access, Visa, Diners, Amex, Switch/Delta

Jarvis Gloucester Hotel and Country Club

COMMENDED

Matson Lane, Robinswood Hill, Gloucester GL4 6EA
☎ (01452) 525653
Fax (01452) 307212
Jarvis/Utell International
Hotel and country club specialising in golf, skiing and leisure activities, within the boundaries of the Roman city of Gloucester. Convenient for touring the Cotswolds and the Wye Valley.
Bedrooms: 9 single, 34 double, 57 twin, 7 triple
Suites available
Bathrooms: 107 en-suite, 8 public

Bed & breakfast per night:	£min	£max
Single	55.00	97.00
Double	75.00	116.00

Half board per person:	£min	£max
Daily	49.50	65.00

Lunch available
Evening meal 1930 (last orders 2200)
Parking for 400

Cards accepted: Access, Visa, Diners, Amex

Notley House and Coach House

COMMENDED

93 Hucclecote Road, Hucclecote, Gloucester GL3 3TR
☎ (01452) 611584
Fax (01452) 371229
Affordable quality accommodation. Ideal for historic Gloucester and the Cotswolds. Tastefully furnished en-suite rooms, suites with four-poster bed.
Bedrooms: 1 single, 2 double, 2 twin, 1 triple, 1 family room
Bathrooms: 5 en-suite, 2 private showers

Bed & breakfast per night:	£min	£max
Single	23.50	41.00
Double	38.00	59.00

Half board per person:	£min	£max
Daily	30.00	50.00
Weekly	185.00	315.00

Evening meal 1900 (last orders 2000)
Parking for 8
Cards accepted: Access, Visa

Pembury Guest House

COMMENDED

9 Pembury Road, St. Barnabas, Gloucester GL4 9UE
☎ (01452) 521856
Fax (01452) 303418
Licensed family-run detached house, close to ski-slope and golfing facilities. Ideal base for Cotswolds, Gloucester Docks and cathedral.
Bedrooms: 1 single, 4 double, 3 twin, 2 triple
Bathrooms: 5 en-suite, 1 public, 2 private showers

Bed & breakfast per night:	£min	£max
Single	16.00	26.00
Double	30.00	38.00

Evening meal 1900 (last orders 1930)
Parking for 10
Cards accepted: Access, Visa

> Map references apply to the colour maps at the back of this guide.

HEART OF ENGLAND

GLOUCESTER
Continued

Rotherfield House Hotel
COMMENDED
5 Horton Road, Gloucester
GL1 3PX
☎ (01452) 410500
Fax (01452) 381922
Elegant Victorian detached property in quiet side road location, 1 mile from city centre and minutes from M5. Family business. Choice of freshly-cooked dishes.
Bedrooms: 8 single, 2 double, 1 twin, 2 public
Bathrooms: 6 en-suite, 2 private, 2 public

Bed & breakfast
per night:	£min	£max
Single	21.00	32.00
Double	44.00	44.00

Half board
per person:	£min	£max
Daily	30.50	41.50
Weekly	202.00	275.00

Evening meal 1845 (last orders 1915)
Parking for 9
Cards accepted: Access, Visa, Diners, Amex

Severn Bank
COMMENDED
Minsterworth, Gloucester GL2 8JH
☎ (01452) 750357
Fax (01452) 750357
Fine riverside country house in 6 acres of grounds, 4 miles west of Gloucester. Viewpoint for Severn Bore Tidal Wave. Ideal for touring Forest of Dean and the Cotswolds.
Bedrooms: 1 single, 2 double, 3 triple
Bathrooms: 4 en-suite, 1 public

Bed & breakfast
per night:	£min	£max
Single	18.00	20.00
Double	36.00	40.00

Parking for 6

GOODRICH
Hereford and Worcester
Map ref 2A1

Village standing above the River Wye with the magnificent ruins of a red sandstone castle high above it, now in the care of English Heritage.

The Inn on the Wye
COMMENDED
Kerne Bridge, Goodrich, Ross-on-Wye, Herefordshire
HR9 5QT
☎ Symonds Yat (01600) 890872
Fax (01600) 890594
Tastefully refurbished old coaching inn on bank of River Wye. Good food and accommodation, regular entertainment, interesting architecture. Good walking country.
Bedrooms: 10 double
Bathrooms: 10 en-suite

Bed & breakfast
per night:	£min	£max
Single	39.00	43.00
Double	43.50	43.50

Half board
per person:	£min	£max
Daily	49.00	60.00
Weekly	300.00	400.00

Lunch available
Evening meal 1900 (last orders 2200)
Parking for 65
Cards accepted: Access, Visa, Diners, Amex, Switch/Delta

GREAT WITLEY
Hereford and Worcester
Map ref 2B1

Village in the Abberley Hills beside the shell of the once sumptuous palace of Witley Court, home of the Earl of Dudley.

Hundred House Hotel
COMMENDED
Great Witley, Worcester WR6 6HS
☎ Great Witley (01299) 896888
Fax (01299) 896588
Family-owned country hotel, on A443 Worcester to Tenbury road 8 miles from M5 junction 5. Close to golf-courses and places of historic interest.
Bedrooms: 2 single, 14 double, 9 twin, 2 triple
Bathrooms: 27 en-suite

Bed & breakfast
per night:	£min	£max
Single	40.00	43.00

Half board
per person:	£min	£max
Daily	55.00	60.00

Lunch available
Evening meal 1900 (last orders 2145)
Parking for 120
Cards accepted: Access, Visa, Amex

GUITING POWER
Gloucestershire
Map ref 2B1

Unspoilt village with stone cottages and a green. The Cotswold Farm Park, with a collection of rare breeds, an adventure playground and farm trail, is nearby.

Guiting Guesthouse
HIGHLY COMMENDED
Post Office Lane, Guiting Power, Cheltenham GL54 5TZ
☎ Guiting Power (01451) 850470
Fax (01451) 850034

Cotswold-stone farmhouse with inglenooks and four-posters. In centre of delightful village, convenient for Stratford-upon-Avon, Cheltenham, Oxford, Stow, etc.
Bedrooms: 3 double
Bathrooms: 2 en-suite, 1 private

Bed & breakfast
per night:	£min	£max
Single	28.00	
Double	45.00	

Half board
per person:	£min	£max
Daily	37.00	

Evening meal 1845 (last orders 1845)
Parking for 4

Information on accommodation listed in this guide has been supplied by the proprietors. As changes may occur you are advised to check details at the time of booking.

The symbols in each entry give information about services and facilities. A 'key' to these symbols appears at the back of this guide.

HEART OF ENGLAND

HAMPTON IN ARDEN
West Midlands
Map ref 4B3

Midway between Birmingham and Coventry and with the National Exhibition Centre on the doorstep.

The Hollies ⋀
COMMENDED

Kenilworth Road, Hampton in Arden, Solihull B92 0LW
☎ Hampton-in-Arden (01675) 442941 & 442681
Fax (01675) 442941

Home-from-home comfort, 2.5 miles from NEC and Birmingham International Airport. Sky TV, ample parking.
Bedrooms: 1 single, 4 double, 2 twin, 1 triple
Bathrooms: 6 en-suite, 1 public

Bed & breakfast per night:

	£min	£max
Single	20.00	25.00
Double	36.00	40.00

Parking for 10

HEREFORD
Hereford and Worcester
Map ref 2A1

Agricultural county town, its cathedral containing much Norman work and a large chained library. Among the city's varied attractions are several museums including the Cider Museum and the Old House.
Tourist Information Centre ☎ (01432) 268430

Belmont Lodge and Golf Course ⋀
COMMENDED

Belmont, Hereford HR2 9SA
☎ (01432) 352666
Fax (01432) 358090
Comfortable hotel situated off the A465, 2 miles south of Hereford city centre. Overlooking the River Wye and Herefordshire countryside, offering beautiful views.
Bedrooms: 26 twin, 4 triple
Bathrooms: 30 en-suite, 2 public

Bed & breakfast per night:

	£min	£max
Single	35.00	48.00
Double	50.00	65.00

Half board per person:

	£min	£max
Daily	45.00	60.00

Lunch available
Evening meal 1900 (last orders 2130)
Parking for 120
Cards accepted: Access, Visa, Diners, Amex

Castle Pool Hotel ⋀
COMMENDED

Castle Street, Hereford HR1 2NR
☎ (01432) 356321
Fax (01432) 356321
Ⓡ Logis of Great Britain
The hotel garden is part of the old castle moat. Located minutes from the cathedral, river and sports facilities.
Bedrooms: 8 single, 8 double, 8 twin, 2 triple
Bathrooms: 26 en-suite

Bed & breakfast per night:

	£min	£max
Single	40.00	50.00
Double	55.00	

Half board per person:

	£min	£max
Daily	51.00	
Weekly	332.50	350.00

Lunch available
Evening meal 1930 (last orders 2130)
Parking for 14
Cards accepted: Access, Visa, Diners, Amex

Cedar Guest House ⋀

123 Whitecross Road, Whitecross, Hereford HR4 0LS
☎ (01432) 267235
Situated on touring route, approximately 1 mile from Hereford, this Georgian family guesthouse has private parking.
Bedrooms: 1 twin, 3 triple
Bathrooms: 1 public, 2 private showers

Bed & breakfast per night:

	£min	£max
Single	20.00	22.00
Double	34.00	36.00

Parking for 10

Felton House ⋀
HIGHLY COMMENDED

Felton, Hereford HR1 3PH
☎ (01432) 820366
The tranquil charm of a Victorian/Edwardian stone rectory. Four-poster and brass beds. Wide breakfast choice. Modern comforts and warm welcome. Tiny hamlet 8 miles Hereford, Leominster, Bromyard, off A417.
Bedrooms: 1 single, 2 double, 1 twin
Bathrooms: 2 en-suite, 1 private, 1 public

Bed & breakfast per night:

	£min	£max
Single	18.50	21.00
Double	37.50	42.00

Parking for 6

Merton Hotel ⋀
APPROVED

Commercial Road, Hereford HR1 2BD
☎ (01432) 265925 & Mobile 0860 550288
Fax (01432) 354983
Georgian origin, this charming town house hotel has been modernised to provide comfortable, well-appointed accommodation with elegant "Governor's" restaurant.
Bedrooms: 8 single, 5 double, 3 twin, 1 triple
Bathrooms: 17 en-suite

Bed & breakfast per night:

	£min	£max
Single	45.00	50.00
Double	50.00	70.00

Half board per person:

	£min	£max
Daily	60.00	70.00
Weekly	400.00	500.00

Lunch available
Evening meal 1830 (last orders 2130)
Parking for 6
Cards accepted: Access, Visa, Diners, Amex, Switch/Delta

National gradings and classifications were correct at the time of going to press but are subject to change. Please check at the time of booking.

HEART OF ENGLAND

HEREFORD
Continued

The New Priory Hotel
APPROVED

Stretton Sugwas, Hereford
HR4 7AR
☎ (01432) 760264
Fax (01432) 760264

Really friendly family hotel set in pleasant peaceful surroundings, 2 miles from the centre of Hereford. Good home-cooked food, lots of historical interest. En-suite four-poster rooms.
Bedrooms: 2 single, 5 double, 1 twin
Bathrooms: 6 en-suite, 1 public

Bed & breakfast per night:

	£min	£max
Single	25.00	35.00
Double	45.00	75.00

Half board per person:

	£min	£max
Daily	35.00	45.00
Weekly	200.00	300.00

Lunch available
Evening meal 1900 (last orders 2145)
Parking for 60
Cards accepted: Access, Visa

Pilgrim Hotel
COMMENDED

Ross Road, Hereford HR2 8HJ
☎ Golden Valley (01981) 540742
Fax (01981) 540620
CR The Independents

Country house hotel combining modern facilities with old world charm. Popular with country lovers and golfers. Set in 4 acres of grounds, south of Hereford.
Bedrooms: 1 single, 9 double, 8 twin, 2 triple
Bathrooms: 20 en-suite

Bed & breakfast per night:

	£min	£max
Single	39.50	49.50
Double	78.00	119.00

Half board per person:

	£min	£max
Daily	44.50	49.50
Weekly	273.00	297.50

Lunch available
Evening meal 1900 (last orders 2200)
Parking for 40

Cards accepted: Access, Visa, Diners, Amex

The Somerville
COMMENDED

12 Bodenham Road, Hereford
HR1 2TS
☎ (01432) 273991

Quiet, licensed guesthouse convenient for city centre and station. Well-appointed bedrooms and views. No lunches. Children welcome. Ample parking.
Bedrooms: 4 single, 3 double, 2 twin, 1 triple
Bathrooms: 6 en-suite, 3 public

Bed & breakfast per night:

	£min	£max
Single	18.00	25.00
Double	30.00	40.00

Half board per person:

	£min	£max
Daily	28.50	30.50
Weekly	189.00	200.00

Evening meal 1830 (last orders 1900)
Parking for 10
Cards accepted: Access, Visa, Amex, Switch/Delta

Tenby Guest House
Listed

8 St. Nicholas Street, Hereford
HR4 0BG
☎ (01432) 274783

A guesthouse in the centre of Hereford close to the cathedral, offering very comfortable accommodation, friendly service and good cooking.
Bedrooms: 1 double, 3 twin, 2 triple
Bathrooms: 2 public

Bed & breakfast per night:

	£min	£max
Single	18.00	20.00
Double	30.00	32.00

Three Counties Hotel
COMMENDED

Belmont Road, Hereford HR2 7BP
☎ (01432) 299955
Fax (01432) 275114

Excellently appointed hotel set in 3.5 acres. Emphasis on traditional, friendly service. Tasteful bedrooms, restaurant and bar offer today's guest all modern comforts. Ideal base for touring Wye Valley. Town centre 1 mile. Half board prices below apply at weekends only.
Bedrooms: 17 double, 43 twin
Bathrooms: 60 en-suite

Bed & breakfast per night:

	£min	£max
Single	40.00	59.50
Double	65.00	78.50

Half board per person:

	£min	£max
Daily	35.00	36.50

Lunch available
Evening meal 1900 (last orders 2130)
Parking for 250
Cards accepted: Access, Visa, Diners, Amex

HOCKLEY HEATH
West Midlands
Map ref 4B3

Village near the National Trust property of Packwood House, with its well-known yew garden, and Kenilworth.

Nuthurst Grange Country House Hotel & Restaurant
HIGHLY COMMENDED

Nuthurst Grange Lane, Hockley Heath, Warwickshire B94 5NL
☎ Lapworth (0156478) 3972
Fax (0156478) 3919

Located close to motorway network in rural setting of 7.5 acres. Relaxed country house atmosphere with acclaimed restaurant. Bedrooms en-suite with whirlpool baths. Single price is for sole occupancy of double room.
Bedrooms: 10 double, 5 twin
Bathrooms: 15 en-suite

Bed & breakfast per night:

	£min	£max
Single	95.00	
Double	115.00	140.00

Lunch available
Evening meal 1900 (last orders 2130)
Parking for 86
Cards accepted: Access, Visa, Diners, Amex, Switch/Delta

The map references refer to the colour maps towards the end of the guide. The first figure is the map number; the letter and figure which follow indicate the grid reference on the map.

HEART OF ENGLAND

IRONBRIDGE
Shropshire
Map ref 4A3

Small town on the Severn where the Industrial Revolution began. It has the world's first iron bridge built in 1779. The Ironbridge Gorge Museum, of exceptional interest, comprises a rebuilt turn-of-the-century town and sites spread over 6 square miles.
Tourist Information Centre ☎ (01952) 432166

Broseley Guest House ♠
♛♛ COMMENDED
The Square, Broseley TF12 5EW
☎ Telford (01952) 882043
Well-appointed spacious accommodation in the centre of Broseley, 1 mile from Ironbridge and convenient for Telford business centres.
Bedrooms: 2 single, 2 double, 1 twin, 1 triple
Bathrooms: 6 en-suite
Bed & breakfast
per night: £min £max
Single 26.00 30.00
Double 42.00 46.00
Evening meal (last orders 1800)
Cards accepted: Access, Visa

Hundred House Hotel Restaurant and Inn ♠
♛♛♛ HIGHLY COMMENDED
Bridgnorth Rd., A442, Norton, Shifnal, Telford TF11 9EE
☎ Telford (01952) 730353
Fax (01952) 730355
Ⓒ Logis of Great Britain
Homely, family-run hotel, with atmospheric historic bars, interesting bar food and intimate restaurant. Antique patchwork themed bedrooms with all facilities. Beautiful, relaxing cottage gardens.
Bedrooms: 2 single, 2 double, 1 twin, 5 triple
Bathrooms: 10 en-suite
Bed & breakfast
per night: £min £max
Single 59.00 65.00
Double 79.00 90.00
Half board per
person: £min £max
Daily 55.00 62.50
Weekly 346.00 394.00
Lunch available
Evening meal 1800 (last orders 2200)

Parking for 30
Cards accepted: Access, Visa, Amex, Switch/Delta

Madeley Court Hotel ♠
♛♛♛♛ HIGHLY COMMENDED
Castlefields Way, Madeley, Telford TF7 5DW
☎ Telford (01952) 680068
Fax (01952) 684275
Ⓒ Lyric
Country house style hotel converted from 16th C manor house in the heart of the Ironbridge Gorge. Telford and motorway network 5 minutes' drive.
Bedrooms: 7 single, 31 double, 8 twin, 1 triple
Bathrooms: 47 en-suite
Bed & breakfast
per night: £min £max
Single 50.00 110.00
Double 78.00 130.00
Half board per
person: £min £max
Daily 65.00 130.00
Lunch available
Evening meal 1900 (last orders 2145)
Parking for 200
Cards accepted: Access, Visa, Diners, Amex, Switch/Delta

Severn Lodge ♠
♛♛♛ DE LUXE
New Road, Ironbridge, Telford TF8 7AS
☎ Telford (01952) 432148
Fax (01952) 432148
Georgian house set in a lovely garden and situated a few yards from the famous iron bridge and River Severn.
Bedrooms: 2 double, 1 twin
Bathrooms: 2 en-suite, 1 private
Bed & breakfast
per night: £min £max
Single 38.00 38.00
Double 48.00 48.00
Parking for 22

ACCESSIBILITY
Look for the symbols which indicate accessibility for wheelchair users. These are described in detail at the front of this guide.

Valley Hotel ♠
♛♛♛ COMMENDED
Ironbridge, Telford TF8 7DW
☎ (01952) 432247
Fax (01952) 432308
Ⓒ Consort/The Independents

Georgian listed building situated in World Heritage Site of Ironbridge. Riverside location with large car park. All Ironbridge Gorge Museum sites are within walking distance of the hotel.
Bedrooms: 9 single, 23 double, 2 twin
Bathrooms: 34 en-suite
Bed & breakfast
per night: £min £max
Single 49.00 62.00
Double 62.00 72.00
Lunch available
Evening meal 1900 (last orders 2200)
Parking for 100
Cards accepted: Access, Visa, Amex

KENILWORTH
Warwickshire
Map ref 4B3

The main feature of the town is the ruined 12th C castle. It has many royal associations but was damaged by Cromwell. A good base for visiting Coventry, Leamington Spa and Warwick.
Tourist Information Centre ☎ (01926) 852595 or 850708

Abbey Guest House ♠
♛♛ COMMENDED
41 Station Road, Kenilworth CV8 1JD
☎ (01926) 512707
Fax (01926) 859148
Cosy Victorian house, 10 minutes from National Agricultural Centre, 15 minutes from NEC. Ideally placed for Warwick, Stratford-upon-Avon, Coventry and the Cotswolds.
Bedrooms: 1 single, 2 double, 3 twin, 1 triple
Bathrooms: 3 en-suite, 1 public
Bed & breakfast
per night: £min £max
Single 21.00 25.00
Double 36.00 42.00
Parking for 2

HEART OF ENGLAND

KENILWORTH
Continued

Castle Laurels Hotel
COMMENDED
22 Castle Road, Kenilworth
CV8 1NG
☎ (01926) 856179
Fax (01926) 854954
Victorian house in conservation area beside Kenilworth Castle and Abbey Fields. Convenient for Warwick, Leamington Spa, Coventry, National Exhibition Centre and National Agricultural Centre. Non-smokers only, please.
Bedrooms: 3 single, 5 double, 3 twin, 1 triple
Bathrooms: 12 en-suite
Bed & breakfast
per night:	£min	£max
Single	31.00	38.00
Double	49.50	55.00

Evening meal 1800 (last orders 1930)
Parking for 14
Cards accepted: Access, Visa

The Cottage Inn
APPROVED
36 Stoneleigh Road, Kenilworth
CV8 2GD
☎ (01926) 853900
Traditional English pub located centrally for Warwick, Leamington, Stratford-upon-Avon, Coventry, Birmingham Airport, the National Exhibition Centre and the Royal Agricultural Showground at Stoneleigh. Home-made bar meals and snacks.
Bedrooms: 1 single, 3 double, 2 twin
Bathrooms: 6 en-suite
Bed & breakfast
per night:	£min	£max
Single	20.00	29.00
Double	30.00	40.00

Lunch available
Evening meal 1800 (last orders 1000)
Parking for 12
Cards accepted: Access, Visa, Switch/Delta

COLOUR MAPS
Colour maps at the back of this guide pinpoint all places in which you will find accommodation listed.

Enderley Guest House
APPROVED
20 Queens Road, Kenilworth
CV8 1JQ
☎ (01926) 855388 & 850450
Family-run guesthouse, quietly situated near town centre and convenient for Warwick, Stratford-upon-Avon, Stoneleigh, Warwick University and National Exhibition Centre.
Bedrooms: 2 double, 1 twin, 1 triple
Bathrooms: 4 en-suite
Bed & breakfast
per night:	£min	£max
Single	24.00	29.00
Double	37.00	42.00

Parking for 2

Ferndale Guest House
COMMENDED
45 Priory Road, Kenilworth
CV8 1LL
☎ (01926) 853214
Fax (01926) 858336
Delightfully modernised Victorian house. Attractive en-suite bedrooms with colour TV, tea/coffee facilities. Ideal for NEC, NAC and Warwick University. Private parking.
Bedrooms: 1 single, 1 double, 3 twin, 2 triple
Bathrooms: 7 en-suite
Bed & breakfast
per night:	£min	£max
Single	21.00	23.00
Double	36.00	36.00

Parking for 8

Hollyhurst Guest House
COMMENDED
47 Priory Road, Kenilworth
CV8 1LL
☎ (01926) 853882
High standard family-run guesthouse in quiet location close to town centre. Easy access to National Exhibition Centre, Royal Showground and tourist areas of Stratford-upon-Avon, Warwick and Coventry.
Bedrooms: 1 single, 1 double, 3 twin, 2 triple
Bathrooms: 3 en-suite, 2 public
Bed & breakfast
per night:	£min	£max
Single	20.00	26.00
Double	40.00	46.00

Half board per
person:	£min	£max
Daily	28.00	35.00
Weekly	175.00	200.00

Parking for 9

Victoria Lodge Hotel
HIGHLY COMMENDED
180 Warwick Road, Kenilworth
CV8 1HU
☎ (01926) 512020
Fax (01926) 858703
Prestigious small hotel with a warming ambience. Beautiful bedrooms, with individual appeal and character, are complemented by traditional hospitality. Non-smoking.
Bedrooms: 1 single, 5 double, 1 twin
Bathrooms: 7 en-suite
Bed & breakfast
per night:	£min	£max
Single	34.00	40.00
Double	45.00	55.00

Lunch available
Evening meal 1700 (last orders 1930)
Parking for 10
Cards accepted: Access, Visa, Amex, Switch/Delta

KIDDERMINSTER
Hereford and Worcester
Map ref 4B3

The town is the centre for carpet manufacturing. It has a medieval church with good monuments and a statue of Sir Rowland Hill, a native of the town and founder of the penny post. West Midlands Safari Park is nearby. Severn Valley Railway station.

Cedars Hotel
COMMENDED
Mason Road, Kidderminster, Worcestershire DY11 6AG
☎ (01562) 515595
Fax (01562) 751103
Minotel
Charming conversion of a Georgian building close to the River Severn, Severn Valley Railway and Worcestershire countryside. 15 minutes from M5.
Bedrooms: 2 single, 7 double, 7 twin, 4 triple, 2 family rooms
Bathrooms: 22 en-suite
Bed & breakfast
per night:	£min	£max
Single	31.25	53.00
Double	43.30	65.00

Evening meal 1900 (last orders 2030)
Parking for 23
Cards accepted: Access, Visa, Diners, Amex

HEART OF ENGLAND

Gainsborough House Hotel

COMMENDED

Bewdley Hill, Kidderminster, Worcestershire DY11 6BS
☎ (01562) 820041
Fax (01562) 66179
Lyric
Traditional hotel close to River Severn. The Severn Valley Railway, West Midlands Safari Park and Worcestershire countryside are all close at hand. 15 minutes from M5.
Bedrooms: 1 single, 12 double, 24 twin, 5 triple
Bathrooms: 42 en-suite

Bed & breakfast per night:	£min	£max
Single	30.00	70.00
Double	40.00	80.00

Half board per person:	£min	£max
Daily	40.00	60.00

Lunch available
Evening meal 1900 (last orders 2200)
Parking for 127
Cards accepted: Access, Visa, Diners, Amex, Switch/Delta

The Granary Hotel and Restaurant

COMMENDED

Shenstone, Kidderminster, Worcestershire DY10 4BS
☎ (01562) 777535
Fax (01562) 777722
The Independents
Family-owned restaurant and hotel renowned for food and good service. Close to Severn Valley Railway and safari park. Rural location.
Wheelchair access category 3
Bedrooms: 5 double, 13 twin
Bathrooms: 18 en-suite

Bed & breakfast per night:	£min	£max
Single	42.50	45.00
Double	45.00	50.00

Half board per person:	£min	£max
Daily	59.50	
Weekly	402.50	

Lunch available
Evening meal 1900 (last orders 2115)
Parking for 95
Cards accepted: Access, Visa, Diners, Amex, Switch/Delta

KINGSBURY

Warwickshire
Map ref 4B3

There are 420 acres of lakes at nearby Kingsbury Water Park with sailing, fishing, guided walks, a nature reserve and visitor centre. Drayton Manor with its amusement park and zoo is nearby.

Lea Marston Hotel and Leisure Complex

HIGHLY COMMENDED

Haunch Lane, Lea Marston B76 0BY
☎ Curdworth (01675) 470468
Fax (01675) 470871
Consort

Beautiful hotel set in 20 acres of landscaped grounds near junction 9 of M42. Convenient for National Exhibition Centre, The Belfry and Birmingham Airport. Extensive conference and meeting facilities with hire equipment. Golf and other leisure facilities on site.
Wheelchair access category 3
Bedrooms: 2 single, 28 double, 19 twin
Suites available
Bathrooms: 49 en-suite

Bed & breakfast per night:	£min	£max
Single	70.00	92.00
Double	80.00	102.00

Half board per person:	£min	£max
Daily	86.00	108.00
Weekly	602.00	756.00

Lunch available
Evening meal 1900 (last orders 2200)
Parking for 160
Cards accepted: Access, Visa, Amex, Switch/Delta

The M symbol after an establishment name indicates that it is a Regional Tourist Board member.

KINGTON

Hereford and Worcester
Map ref 2A1

Market town on the Welsh border, with Offa's Dyke close by. The Hergest Croft Gardens are well-known for their beautiful displays of azaleas and rhododendrons during May and June.

Burton Hotel

APPROVED

Mill Street, Kington, Herefordshire HR5 3BQ
☎ (01544) 230323
Fax (01544) 230323
Attractively modernised, authentic coaching inn, in centre of small market town near Welsh border and Offa's Dyke footpath.
Bedrooms: 1 single, 5 double, 3 twin, 6 triple
Bathrooms: 15 en-suite

Bed & breakfast per night:	£min	£max
Single	40.00	
Double	55.00	

Half board per person:	£min	£max
Daily	55.00	
Weekly	315.00	

Lunch available
Evening meal 1930 (last orders 2130)
Parking for 45
Cards accepted: Access, Visa, Diners, Amex

LEAMINGTON SPA

Warwickshire
Map ref 4B3

18th C spa town with many fine Georgian and Regency houses. Tea can be taken in the 19th C Pump Room. The attractive Jephson Gardens are laid out alongside the river and there is a museum and art gallery.
Tourist Information Centre ☎ (01926) 311470

Adams Hotel

COMMENDED

22 Avenue Road, Leamington Spa CV31 3PQ
☎ Leamington Spa (01926) 450742
Fax (01926) 313110
Privately owned 17th C listed hotel,
Continued ▶

HEART OF ENGLAND

LEAMINGTON SPA
Continued

with modern bedrooms, standing back from the road in a typical Regency setting.
Bedrooms: 4 single, 4 double, 3 twin
Bathrooms: 11 en-suite

Bed & breakfast per night:	£min	£max
Single	39.50	56.00
Double	52.50	64.50

Half board per person:	£min	£max
Daily	45.00	62.95

Evening meal 1800 (last orders 2000)
Parking for 10
Cards accepted: Access, Visa, Diners, Amex

Beech Lodge Hotel
28 Warwick New Road, Leamington Spa CV32 5JJ
☎ Leamington Spa (01926) 422227
Elegant Regency building with spacious lounge, dining room and residents' bar. All bedrooms with colour TV, radio, telephone and tea/coffee-making facilities.
Bedrooms: 7 single, 6 double, 1 twin
Bathrooms: 12 en-suite, 1 public

Bed & breakfast per night:	£min	£max
Single	30.00	42.00
Double	45.00	60.00

Half board per person:	£min	£max
Daily	38.00	58.00
Weekly	245.00	340.00

Lunch available
Evening meal 1900 (last orders 2000)
Parking for 14
Cards accepted: Access, Visa, Diners, Amex

Bungalow Farm
COMMENDED
Windmill Hill, Cubbington, Leamington Spa CV32 7LW
☎ Leamington Spa (01926) 423316
Fax (01926) 887357
Attractive and spacious detached private residence, offering comfortable and attractive bed and breakfast accommodation. Some rooms en-suite. All rooms have colour TV, radio/alarm clock and tea/coffee-making facilities.
Bedrooms: 1 double, 1 twin
Bathrooms: 1 en-suite, 1 public

Bed & breakfast per night:	£min	£max
Single	15.00	20.00
Double	30.00	40.00

Parking for 10

Charnwood Guest House
APPROVED
47 Avenue Road, Leamington Spa CV31 3PF
☎ Leamington Spa (01926) 831074
Attractive Victorian house near railway station and town centre. All rooms have colour TV and tea/coffee.
Bedrooms: 1 single, 2 double, 2 twin, 1 triple
Bathrooms: 2 en-suite, 2 public, 1 private shower

Bed & breakfast per night:	£min	£max
Single	17.00	27.00
Double	32.00	37.00

Half board per person:	£min	£max
Daily	27.00	37.00
Weekly	189.00	259.00

Evening meal 1800 (last orders 1200)
Parking for 5
Cards accepted: Access, Visa

Eaton Court Hotel
COMMENDED
1-7 St Marks Road, Leamington Spa CV32 6DL
☎ Leamington Spa (01926) 885848
Fax (01926) 885848
Privately owned and run hotel with spacious en-suite rooms and comfortable facilities including function rooms and licensed restaurant.
Bedrooms: 10 single, 12 double, 10 twin, 2 triple, 2 family rooms
Bathrooms: 36 en-suite

Bed & breakfast per night:	£min	£max
Single	30.00	55.00
Double	50.00	75.00

Half board per person:	£min	£max
Daily	44.50	69.50

Lunch available
Evening meal 1900 (last orders 2130)
Parking for 36
Cards accepted: Access, Visa, Diners, Amex

Falstaff Hotel
16-20 Warwick New Road, Leamington Spa CV32 5JQ
☎ Leamington Spa (01926) 312044
Fax (01926) 450574

Elegant Regency hotel offering every modern convenience to the business traveller. Ideally located in the Heart of England.
Bedrooms: 28 single, 13 double, 22 twin
Bathrooms: 63 en-suite

Bed & breakfast per night:	£min	£max
Single	30.00	59.50
Double	40.00	69.50

Half board per person:	£min	£max
Daily	33.00	43.00

Lunch available
Evening meal 1900 (last orders 2115)
Parking for 80
Cards accepted: Access, Visa, Diners, Amex, Switch/Delta

Flowerdale House Hotel
58 Warwick New Road, Leamington Spa CV32 6AA
☎ Leamington Spa (01926) 426002
Fax (01926) 883699
Tastefully modernised Victorian house with conservatory, overlooking a small garden. All bedrooms with private facilities and colour TV. Reduced rates for more than 1 night.
Bedrooms: 1 single, 2 double, 3 twin
Bathrooms: 5 en-suite, 1 private

Bed & breakfast per night:	£min	£max
Single	22.00	27.00
Double	36.00	44.00

Evening meal 1900 (last orders 2100)
Parking for 6
Cards accepted: Access, Visa

All accommodation in this guide has been graded, or is awaiting a grading, by a trained Tourist Board inspector.

HEART OF ENGLAND

Hedley Villa Guest House
Listed APPROVED
31 Russell Terrace, Leamington Spa
CV31 1EZ
☎ Leamington Spa (01926) 424504
Homely guesthouse close to town centre. Convenient for National Exhibition Centre, National Agricultural Centre, Stratford, Coventry, Kenilworth, M40 and Warwick.
Bedrooms: 3 single, 1 twin, 2 triple, 1 family room
Bathrooms: 1 en-suite, 2 public

Bed & breakfast per night:	£min	£max
Single	16.00	25.00
Double	32.00	50.00

Half board per person:	£min	£max
Daily	23.00	32.00
Weekly	161.00	224.00

Evening meal 1400 (last orders 2100)

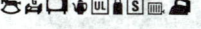

Milverton House Hotel
COMMENDED
1 Milverton Terrace, Leamington Spa
CV32 5BE
☎ Leamington Spa (01926) 428335
Graceful, modernised, 145-year-old building, licensed and centrally heated, within walking distance of the town centre. Home-cooked food.
Bedrooms: 2 single, 3 double, 4 twin, 1 triple
Bathrooms: 6 en-suite, 2 public, 1 private shower

Bed & breakfast per night:	£min	£max
Single	18.00	
Double	32.00	

Half board per person:	£min	£max
Daily	24.00	
Weekly	160.00	

Evening meal 1900 (last orders 1900)
Parking for 6
Cards accepted: Access, Visa

Victoria Park Hotel
COMMENDED
12 Adelaide Road, Leamington Spa
CV31 3PW
☎ Leamington Spa (01926) 424195
Fax (01926) 421521
Victorian house close to bus and railway stations and town centre. Park, pump room, gardens, bowls, tennis and river all three minutes' walk away.
Bedrooms: 11 single, 3 double, 1 twin, 1 triple
Bathrooms: 14 en-suite, 1 public

Bed & breakfast per night:	£min	£max
Single	28.00	33.00
Double	40.00	46.00

Half board per person:	£min	£max
Daily	40.50	45.50
Weekly	283.50	318.50

Lunch available
Evening meal 1830 (last orders 1920)
Parking for 12
Cards accepted: Access, Visa, Diners, Amex

LECHLADE
Gloucestershire
Map ref 2B1

Attractive village on the River Thames and a popular spot for boating. It has a number of fine Georgian houses and a 15th C church. Nearby is Kelmscott Manor, with its William Morris furnishings, and 18th C Buscot House (National Trust).

Cambrai Lodge
Listed COMMENDED
Oak Street, Lechlade GL7 3AY
☎ (01367) 253173 & Mobile 0860 150467
Friendly, family-run guesthouse, recently modernised, close to River Thames. Ideal base for touring the Cotswolds. Garden and ample parking.
Bedrooms: 2 single, 1 double, 1 twin
Bathrooms: 2 en-suite, 1 public

Bed & breakfast per night:	£min	£max
Single	20.00	25.00
Double	32.00	38.00

Parking for 13

New Inn Hotel
Market Square, Lechlade-on-Thames, Lechlade GL7 3AB
☎ Faringdon (01367) 252296
Fax (01367) 252315
Situated in a tranquil riverside setting, offering a comfortable blend of traditional hospitality and all modern advantages. Private parking.
Bedrooms: 2 single, 6 double, 2 twin
Bathrooms: 10 en-suite

Bed & breakfast per night:	£min	£max
Single	35.00	49.00
Double	40.00	70.00

Half board per person:	£min	£max
Daily	35.00	45.00
Weekly	210.00	249.00

Lunch available
Evening meal 1900 (last orders 2200)
Parking for 40
Cards accepted: Access, Visa, Diners, Amex, Switch/Delta

LEDBURY
Hereford and Worcester
Map ref 2B1

Town with cobbled streets and many black and white timbered houses, including the 17th C market house and old inns. Nearby is Eastnor Castle with an interesting collection of tapestries and armour. Tourist Information Centre ☎ (01531) 636147

Feathers Hotel
COMMENDED
High Street, Ledbury, Herefordshire HR8 1DS
☎ (01531) 635266
Fax (01531) 632001
Logis of Great Britain
Traditional Elizabethan coaching inn, situated in the centre of a small market town nestling under the Malvern Hills.
Bedrooms: 4 double, 4 twin, 3 triple
Bathrooms: 11 en-suite

Bed & breakfast per night:	£min	£max
Double	69.00	95.00

Lunch available
Evening meal 1830 (last orders 2130)
Parking for 20
Cards accepted: Access, Visa, Diners, Amex, Switch/Delta

TOWN INDEX

This can be found at the back of the guide. If you know where you want to stay, the index will give you the page number listing all accommodation in your chosen town, city or village.

251

HEART OF ENGLAND

LEEK
Staffordshire
Map ref 4B2

Old silk and textile town, with some interesting buildings and a number of inns dating from the 17th C. Its art gallery has displays of embroidery. Brindley Mill, designed by James Brindley, has been restored as a museum.
Tourist Information Centre ☎ (01538) 381000

Three Horseshoes Inn & Restaurant ♠
♛♛ COMMENDED

Buxton Road, Blackshaw Moor, Leek ST13 8TW
☎ (01538) 300296
Fax (01538) 300320
Ⓖ Logis of Great Britain

Log fire, slate floor, oak and pine beams, good food and wines. Cottage-style rooms. Convenient for Peak District National Park and Alton Towers.
Bedrooms: 4 double, 2 twin
Bathrooms: 6 en-suite
Bed & breakfast
per night: £min   £max
Single   40.00   46.00
Double   46.00   58.00

Lunch available
Evening meal 1900 (last orders 2100)
Parking for 100
Cards accepted: Access, Visa, Amex, Switch/Delta

WELCOME HOST
This is a nationally recognised customer care programme which aims to promote the highest standards of service and a warm welcome. Establishments who are taking part in this initiative are indicated by the ✿ symbol.

LEINTWARDINE
Hereford and Worcester
Map ref 4A3

Attractive border village where the Rivers Teme and Clun meet. It has some black and white cottages, old inns and an impressive church. It is near Hopton Castle and the beautiful scenery around Clun.

Lower House ♠
♛♛♛ HIGHLY COMMENDED

Adforton, Leintwardine, Craven Arms, Shropshire SY7 0NF
☎ Wigmore (01568) 770223
Fax (01568) 770592

House dates from early 17th C. Set in peaceful, unspoilt countryside. Excellent walking in surrounding hills. Home cooking using local produce. A no-smoking establishment.
Bedrooms: 2 double, 2 twin
Bathrooms: 3 en-suite, 1 private
Bed & breakfast
per night: £min   £max
Single   24.00   26.00
Double   48.00   52.00

Half board per person: £min   £max
Daily   41.00   43.00
Weekly   270.00 270.00

Evening meal 1900 (last orders 1930)
Parking for 10

Half board prices are given per person, but in some cases these may be based on double/twin occupancy.

Information on accommodation listed in this guide has been supplied by the proprietors. As changes may occur you are advised to check details at the time of booking.

LEOMINSTER
Hereford and Worcester
Map ref 2A1

The town owed its prosperity to wool and has many interesting buildings, notably the timber-framed Grange Court, a former town hall. The impressive Norman priory church has 3 naves and a ducking stool. Berrington Hall (National Trust) is nearby.
Tourist Information Centre ☎ (01568) 616460

Lower Bache ♠
♛♛♛ HIGHLY COMMENDED

Kimbolton, Leominster, Herefordshire HR6 0ER
☎ Leysters (01568) 750304

Award-winning 17th C Herefordshire house, set in 14 acres of private nature reserve. Three suites, each with bedroom, bath/shower room and private sitting room. Renowned cuisine. Illustrated brochure.
Bedrooms: 2 double, 1 twin
Bathrooms: 3 en-suite
Bed & breakfast
per night: £min   £max
Single   29.50
Double   49.00

Half board per person: £min   £max
Daily   33.00   42.00
Weekly   231.00 273.00

Lunch available
Evening meal 1950 (last orders 1230)
Parking for 5

Royal Oak Hotel ♠
♛♛♛

South Street, Leominster, Herefordshire HR6 8JA
☎ (01568) 612610
Fax (01568) 612710
Ⓖ Minotel
Grade II listed Georgian coaching house dating from 1723, with log fires in winter, real ales and an emphasis on good food and wines at reasonable prices.
Bedrooms: 2 single, 9 double, 5 twin, 2 triple
Bathrooms: 18 en-suite

HEART OF ENGLAND

Bed & breakfast per night:	£min	£max
Single	33.50	37.50
Double	45.00	55.00
Half board per person:	£min	£max
Daily	32.75	37.75
Weekly	206.33	237.83

Lunch available
Evening meal 1830 (last orders 2130)
Parking for 25
Cards accepted: Access, Visa, Diners, Amex

⇔♤🚗🛏🍴♿🛁S⚲♆TV🎱
1225 DAP ♠ SP 🎯 T

Talbot Hotel ⋀

◉◉◉ APPROVED

West Street, Leominster,
Herefordshire HR6 8EP
☎ (01568) 616347
Fax (01568) 614880
Ⓡ Best Western

15th C coaching inn with oak beams and log fire, now offering 20th C facilities. Ideal location for touring Mid-Wales, Shropshire and Herefordshire.
Bedrooms: 2 single, 8 double, 7 twin, 2 triple, 1 family room
Bathrooms: 20 en-suite

Bed & breakfast per night:	£min	£max
Single	35.00	45.00
Double	50.00	72.00

Lunch available
Evening meal 1900 (last orders 2130)
Parking for 25
Cards accepted: Access, Visa, Diners, Amex

⇔📞🛏🍴♿S⚲♆TV🎱◉🏊
↑150 U ⌂ ♠ SP 🎯 T

LICHFIELD

Staffordshire
Map ref 4B3

Lichfield is Dr Samuel Johnson's birthplace and commemorates him with a museum and statue. The 13th C cathedral has 3 spires and the west front is full of statues. Among the attractive town buildings is the Heritage Centre. The Regimental Museum is in Whittington Barracks.
Tourist Information Centre ☎ (01543) 252109

Coppers End ⋀

◉◉ COMMENDED

Walsall Road, Muckley Corner,
Lichfield WS14 0BG
☎ (01543) 372910
Fax (01543) 372910

Detached guesthouse of character and charm in its own grounds. Rural location with easy access to M6, Birmingham, Lichfield and M1. Residential licence. Telephone for half-board rates.
Bedrooms: 1 single, 2 double, 2 twin
Bathrooms: 1 en-suite, 1 public

Bed & breakfast per night:	£min	£max
Single	22.00	30.00
Double	35.00	42.00

Evening meal 1900 (last orders 2030)
Parking for 10
Cards accepted: Access, Visa, Diners, Amex, Switch/Delta

⇔♤🚗🛏🍴♿S⚲♆TV🎱◉🏊
🌼 🎯 SP 🎯

Little Barrow Hotel ⋀

◉◉◉

Beacon Street, Lichfield WS13 7AR
☎ (01543) 414500
Fax (01543) 415734

Popular hotel just a short distance from the centre of town and close to the cathedral. Bedrooms are well designed and the restaurant enjoys a good reputation.
Bedrooms: 2 single, 6 double, 16 twin
Bathrooms: 24 en-suite

Bed & breakfast per night:	£min	£max
Single	45.00	55.00
Double	55.00	65.00
Half board per person:	£min	£max
Daily	60.00	70.00
Weekly	400.00	470.00

Lunch available
Evening meal 1900 (last orders 2130)
Parking for 70
Cards accepted: Access, Visa, Diners, Amex, Switch/Delta

⇔📞🛏🍴♿🛁S⚲♆TV🎱◉🏊
↑100 ✈ SP

COLOUR MAPS

Colour maps at the back of this guide pinpoint all places in which you will find accommodation listed.

Oakleigh House Hotel ⋀

◉◉◉ COMMENDED

25 St. Chad's Road, Lichfield
WS13 7LZ
☎ (01543) 262688 & 255573
Fax (01543) 418556

Country house hotel standing in its own grounds, alongside a small lake, just behind Lichfield Cathedral.
Bedrooms: 4 single, 2 double, 4 twin
Bathrooms: 8 en-suite, 1 public

Bed & breakfast per night:	£min	£max
Single	35.00	45.00
Double	55.00	70.00
Half board per person:	£min	£max
Daily	42.00	60.00
Weekly	255.00	385.00

Lunch available
Evening meal 1900 (last orders 2100)
Parking for 20
Cards accepted: Access, Visa

⇔♤📞🛏🍴♿🍷🛁S⚲♆
TV🎱↑20 🌼 SP

The Swan

◉◉◉ COMMENDED

Bird Street, Lichfield WS13 6PT
☎ (01543) 414777
Fax (01543) 411321

Classic 18th C coaching inn in the heart of historic Lichfield. Within easy walking distance of Lichfield Cathedral.
Bedrooms: 2 single, 4 double, 13 twin
Bathrooms: 19 en-suite

Bed & breakfast per night:	£min	£max
Single	35.00	45.00
Double	47.00	59.50
Half board per person:	£min	£max
Daily		50.00

Lunch available
Evening meal 1900 (last orders 2145)
Parking for 56
Cards accepted: Access, Visa, Diners, Amex, Switch/Delta

⇔📞🛏🍴♿🍷🛁◉🏊↑120
🌼 SP 🎯

HEART OF ENGLAND

LONG COMPTON
Warwickshire
Map ref 2B1

Village with a restored church displaying Norman doorways and a thatched room above the lych gate. Several interesting old houses exist in the area.

The Red Lion Hotel
COMMENDED

Main Street, Long Compton, Shipston-on-Stour CV36 5JS
☎ Shipston-on-Stour (01608) 684221
Fax (01608) 684221
Friendly inn dating from 1748. Centrally located for places of interest in Stratford, Warwick and Cotswold areas.
Bedrooms: 1 single, 2 double, 1 twin, 1 triple
Bathrooms: 5 en-suite

Bed & breakfast per night:	£min	£max
Single	29.50	35.00
Double	45.00	55.00

Lunch available
Evening meal 1800 (last orders 2130)
Parking for 60
Cards accepted: Access, Visa, Switch/Delta

LOWER SLAUGHTER
Gloucestershire
Map ref 2B1

Pretty Cotswold village of stone cottages with a river running through the main street.

Washbourne Court Hotel
HIGHLY COMMENDED

Lower Slaughter, Cheltenham GL54 2HS
☎ Cotswold (01451) 822143
Fax (01451) 821045

Beautiful, tranquil 16th C hotel on the River Eye, just off the Fosseway, set in 4 acres of lovely grounds bordered by the river. Riverside terrace and restaurant, cottage suites in grounds. All-weather tennis court. New Coach House rooms with large jacuzzi tubs.

Bedrooms: 12 double, 3 twin, 6 triple
Suites available
Bathrooms: 21 en-suite

Bed & breakfast per night:	£min	£max
Single	85.00	85.00
Double	95.00	185.00

Half board per person:	£min	£max
Daily	62.50	112.50
Weekly	400.00	500.00

Lunch available
Evening meal 1930 (last orders 2115)
Parking for 69
Cards accepted: Access, Visa, Diners, Amex, Switch/Delta

LUDLOW
Shropshire
Map ref 4A3

Outstandingly interesting border town with a magnificent castle high above the River Teme, 2 half-timbered old inns and an impressive 15th C church. The Reader's House, with its 3-storey Jacobean porch, should also be seen.
Tourist Information Centre ☎ (01584) 875053

Cecil Guest House
COMMENDED

Sheet Road, Ludlow SY8 1LR
☎ (01584) 872442
Fax (01584) 872442
Attractive guesthouse 15 minutes' walk from town centre and station. Good fresh food and comfortable accommodation.
Bedrooms: 3 single, 1 double, 5 twin, 1 triple
Bathrooms: 3 en-suite, 2 public

Bed & breakfast per night:	£min	£max
Single	18.50	30.00
Double	37.00	50.00

Evening meal 1900 (last orders 0900)
Parking for 11
Cards accepted: Access, Visa

Charlton Arms Hotel
COMMENDED

Ludford Bridge, Ludlow SY8 1PJ
☎ (01584) 872813
Riverside location, adjacent to an ancient pack bridge and the Whitcliff Centre for anglers, canoeists and tourists, famous for its woods, walks and wildlife.

Bedrooms: 5 double, 1 twin
Bathrooms: 6 en-suite

Bed & breakfast per night:	£min	£max
Single	30.00
Double	40.00

Lunch available
Evening meal 1900 (last orders 2130)
Parking for 20
Cards accepted: Access, Visa, Switch/Delta

Cliffe Hotel
COMMENDED

Dinham, Ludlow SY8 2JE
☎ (01584) 872063
Hotel in its own garden conveniently placed on the edge of town, near the castle, river and forest.
Bedrooms: 1 single, 4 double, 4 twin
Bathrooms: 9 en-suite

Bed & breakfast per night:	£min	£max
Single	30.00	35.00
Double	52.00	58.00

Lunch available
Evening meal 1900 (last orders 2030)
Parking for 50
Cards accepted: Access, Visa, Amex

Dinham Hall Hotel & Restaurant
COMMENDED

Dinham, By The Castle, Ludlow SY8 1EJ
☎ (01584) 876464
Fax (01584) 876019
Best Western
Splendid Georgian residence situated opposite Ludlow Castle and with open views of the countryside from all rooms. Restaurant noted for cuisine.
Bedrooms: 2 single, 6 double, 4 twin
Bathrooms: 12 en-suite, 2 public

Bed & breakfast per night:	£min	£max
Single	62.00	72.00
Double	89.00	120.00

Half board per person:	£min	£max
Daily	63.00	78.00
Weekly	420.00	511.00

Lunch available
Evening meal 1900 (last orders 2150)
Parking for 16
Cards accepted: Access, Visa, Diners, Amex, Switch/Delta

HEART OF ENGLAND

Dinham Weir Hotel and Restaurant

APPROVED

Dinham Bridge, Ludlow SY8 1EH
☎ (01584) 874431
Logis of Great Britain

Beautifully situated on the banks of the River Teme. All bedrooms with riverside views. Intimate candlelit restaurant.
Bedrooms: 4 double, 2 twin
Bathrooms: 6 en-suite

Bed & breakfast per night:	£min	£max
Single	30.00	55.00
Double	65.00	80.00

Half board per person:	£min	£max
Daily	45.00	62.50
Weekly	252.00	350.00

Lunch available
Evening meal 1900 (last orders 2030)
Parking for 8
Cards accepted: Access, Visa, Diners, Amex

The Feathers at Ludlow

HIGHLY COMMENDED

Bull Ring, Ludlow SY8 1AA
☎ (01584) 875261
Fax (01584) 876030

Historic inn with Jacobean interior and exterior, sited within the medieval walls of Ludlow, historic capital of the English/Welsh Marches.
Wheelchair access category 3
Bedrooms: 11 single, 15 double, 11 twin, 2 triple
Suites available
Bathrooms: 39 en-suite

Bed & breakfast per night:	£min	£max
Single	65.00	80.00
Double	88.00	140.00

Half board per person:	£min	£max
Daily	64.00	95.00
Weekly	448.00	630.00

Lunch available
Evening meal 1900 (last orders 2100)
Parking for 32
Cards accepted: Access, Visa, Diners, Amex, Switch/Delta

The Moor Hall

HIGHLY COMMENDED

Cleedownton, Ludlow SY8 3EG
☎ Stoke St Millborough (01584) 823209 & 823333
Fax (01584) 823387

Built c1789, the Moor Hall is set in 5 acres of mature grounds with pools, amid unspoilt countryside, yet close to historic Ludlow. Relaxed, informal atmosphere. Fishing.
Bedrooms: 2 double, 1 twin
Bathrooms: 3 en-suite

Bed & breakfast per night:	£min	£max
Single	25.00	35.00
Double	45.00	60.00

Half board per person:	£min	£max
Daily	37.50	45.00
Weekly	235.00	285.00

Evening meal 1900 (last orders 2000)
Parking for 12

Number Twenty Eight

HIGHLY COMMENDED

28 Lower Broad Street, Ludlow SY8 1PQ
☎ (01584) 876996
Fax (01584) 876996

Listed town house of charm and character. Centrally situated. Emphasis on warm hospitality and quiet, relaxed atmosphere with good food and wines.
Bedrooms: 2 double, 1 twin, 1 triple
Bathrooms: 4 en-suite, 1 public

Bed & breakfast per night:	£min	£max
Single	27.50	50.00
Double	40.00	60.00

Half board per person:	£min	£max
Daily	37.50	47.50
Weekly	250.00	300.00

Evening meal 1930 (last orders 2030)
Cards accepted: Access, Visa, Amex

MADELEY

Shropshire
Map ref 4A2

Woodlands

COMMENDED

Park Lane, Madeley, Telford TF7 5HJ
☎ Telford (01952) 580693
Modern detached bungalow, both rooms en-suite. TV, car parking. Centrally located for museums, bridge and Telford centre.
Bedrooms: 1 double, 1 twin
Bathrooms: 2 en-suite

Bed & breakfast per night:	£min	£max
Single	20.00	25.00
Double	32.00	36.00

Parking for 6

MALVERN

Hereford and Worcester
Map ref 2B1

Spa town in Victorian times, its water is today bottled and sold worldwide. 6 resorts, set on the slopes of the Hills, form part of Malvern. Great Malvern Priory has splendid 15th C windows. It is an excellent walking centre.
Tourist Information Centre ☎ (01684) 892289

Bredon House Hotel

COMMENDED

34 Worcester Road, Malvern, Worcestershire WR14 4AA
☎ (01684) 566990
Fax (01684) 575323
Quiet, relaxed and friendly family-run hotel with spectacular views. 100 yards from town centre, Winter Gardens and theatre. Wonderful walks. Car park, pets welcome.
Bedrooms: 2 single, 3 double, 2 twin, 2 triple
Bathrooms: 9 en-suite

Continued ▶

Please check prices and other details at the time of booking.

HEART OF ENGLAND

MALVERN
Continued

Bed & breakfast per night: £min / £max
Single — 30.00 / 40.00
Double — 45.00 / 60.00
Parking for 10
Cards accepted: Access, Visa, Amex

Colwall Park Hotel
Walwyn Road, Colwall, Malvern, Worcestershire WR13 6QG
☎ Colwall (01684) 540206 & 541033
Fax (01684) 540847
Family hotel, personally run. Situated on the western side of the Malvern Hills. Quiet garden. Ideal for walking, touring and exploring.
Bedrooms: 3 single, 9 double, 7 twin, 2 triple, 2 family rooms
Suites available
Bathrooms: 23 en-suite

Bed & breakfast per night: £min / £max
Single — 49.50 / 65.00
Double — 75.00 / 90.00

Half board per person: £min / £max
Daily — 59.50 / 75.00
Weekly — 346.50 / 416.50

Lunch available
Evening meal 1930 (last orders 2100)
Parking for 40
Cards accepted: Access, Visa, Diners, Amex, Switch/Delta

For ideas on places to visit refer to the introduction at the beginning of this section.

The Cottage in the Wood Hotel
HIGHLY COMMENDED
Holywell Road, Malvern Wells, Malvern, Worcestershire WR14 4LG
☎ (01684) 575859
Fax (01684) 560662
Consort

Set high on the Malvern Hills with 30-mile views to the Cotswolds. All en-suite. Family owned and run. Exceptional food. Daily half board price based on minimum 2-night stay. Weekly is 7 nights for price of 6. Breaks available all week, all year.
Bedrooms: 16 double, 4 twin
Bathrooms: 20 en-suite

Bed & breakfast per night: £min / £max
Single — 68.00 / 74.00
Double — 89.00 / 135.00

Half board per person: £min / £max
Daily — 50.00 / 64.00
Weekly — 300.00 / 384.00

Lunch available
Evening meal 1900 (last orders 2100)
Parking for 40
Cards accepted: Access, Visa, Amex, Switch/Delta

Foley Arms Hotel & Restaurant
Worcester Road, Malvern, Worcestershire WR14 4QS
☎ (01684) 573797
Fax (01684) 569665
Best Western
Regency coaching inn with the comfort and atmosphere of a country house hotel. Ideal for touring the Cotswolds and Wales. Panoramic views and lovely walks.
Bedrooms: 6 single, 16 double, 5 twin, 1 triple
Bathrooms: 28 en-suite

Bed & breakfast per night: £min / £max
Single — 65.00 / 82.00
Double — 83.00 / 105.00

Half board per person: £min / £max
Daily — 56.00 / 61.00

Lunch available
Evening meal 1900 (last orders 2100)
Parking for 50
Cards accepted: Access, Visa, Diners, Amex, Switch/Delta

See display advertisement on this page

Great Malvern Hotel
COMMENDED
Graham Road, Malvern, Worcestershire WR14 2HN
☎ (01684) 563411
Fax (01684) 560514
Grade II listed hotel with all amenities, in the centre of Malvern close to the Winter Gardens. Run by the proprietors.
Bedrooms: 1 single, 8 double, 3 twin, 2 triple
Bathrooms: 13 en-suite, 1 private

Bed & breakfast per night: £min / £max
Single — 40.00 / 45.00
Double — 60.00 / 70.00

Lunch available
Evening meal 1800 (last orders 2100)
Parking for 9
Cards accepted: Access, Visa, Diners, Amex

The Foley Arms Hotel
in
The Malvern Hills.
Traditional coaching inn with the style and ambience of a Country House Hotel.
Merit awards for hospitality and restaurant.
Real Ale tavern.
Special offers available.

AA ★★★ RAC Merit award

Tel: 01684 573397

HEART OF ENGLAND

Harcourt Cottage ▲
👑👑👑 COMMENDED

252 West Malvern Road, West Malvern, Malvern, Worcestershire WR14 4DQ
☎ (01684) 574561
Nestling on the west side of the Malvern Hills, well placed for walking holidays or as a base for touring. English and French cuisine.
Bedrooms: 2 double, 1 twin
Bathrooms: 3 en-suite

Bed & breakfast per night:
	£min	£max
Double	38.00	40.00

Half board per person:
	£min	£max
Daily	28.00	29.00
Weekly	180.00	185.00

Evening meal 1845 (last orders 1800)
Parking for 3

Holdfast Cottage Hotel ▲
👑👑👑 HIGHLY COMMENDED

Marlbank Road, Little Malvern, Malvern, Worcestershire WR13 6NA
☎ Hanley Swan (01684) 310288
Fax (01684) 311117
ⓒ Logis of Great Britain

Small oak-beamed country house set in 2 acres of gardens at the foot of the Malvern Hills. Pretty bedrooms, log fires, wonderful views.
Bedrooms: 1 single, 5 double, 2 twin
Bathrooms: 8 en-suite, 1 public

Bed & breakfast per night:
	£min	£max
Single	42.00	44.00
Double	74.00	82.00

Half board per person:
	£min	£max
Daily	54.00	56.00
Weekly	324.00	336.00

Evening meal 1900 (last orders 2100)
Parking for 20
Cards accepted: Access, Visa

Map references apply to the colour maps at the back of this guide.

Malvern Hills Hotel ▲
👑👑👑 COMMENDED

British Camp, Wynd's Point, Malvern, Worcestershire WR13 6DW
☎ Colwall (01684) 540237 & 540690
Fax (01684) 540327
Enchanting hotel sitting atop the Malvern Hills. Magnificent views, prettily decorated en-suite rooms, oak panelled lounge, friendly and efficient staff.
Bedrooms: 2 single, 6 double, 6 twin, 2 triple
Bathrooms: 16 en-suite

Bed & breakfast per night:
	£min	£max
Single	30.00	35.00
Double	60.00	65.00

Half board per person:
	£min	£max
Daily	40.00	45.00
Weekly	250.00	300.00

Lunch available
Evening meal 1900 (last orders 2130)
Parking for 30
Cards accepted: Access, Visa

Mount Pleasant Hotel ▲
👑👑👑 COMMENDED

Belle Vue Terrace, Malvern, Worcestershire WR14 4PZ
☎ (01684) 561837
Fax (01684) 569968
ⓒ Logis of Great Britain/The Independents

Georgian building with Orangery, in 1.5 acres of garden with beautiful views. Close to theatre and shops and with direct access to Malvern Hills.
Bedrooms: 3 single, 7 double, 5 twin
Bathrooms: 14 en-suite, 1 private, 1 public

Bed & breakfast per night:
	£min	£max
Single	39.50	52.50
Double	60.00	77.50

Half board per person:
	£min	£max
Daily	39.50	47.50
Weekly	235.00	295.00

Lunch available
Evening meal 1900 (last orders 2130)

Parking for 20
Cards accepted: Access, Visa, Diners, Amex

Pembridge Hotel ▲
👑 HIGHLY COMMENDED

114 Graham Road, Malvern, Worcestershire WR14 2HX
☎ (01684) 574813
Fax (01684) 574815
Small, friendly, detached hotel, close to town centre and Malvern Hills. Ample car parking. Fresh meats and local vegetables prepared daily by chef/proprietor.
Bedrooms: 4 double, 4 twin
Bathrooms: 8 en-suite, 1 public

Bed & breakfast per night:
	£min	£max
Single	36.00	39.00
Double	55.00	62.00

Lunch available
Evening meal 1900 (last orders 2000)
Parking for 10
Cards accepted: Access, Visa, Switch/Delta

Rock House ▲
👑 COMMENDED

144 West Malvern Road, Malvern, Worcestershire WR14 4NJ
☎ (01684) 574536
Early Victorian house with wonderful views, on Malvern Hills. Ideal for rambling and touring. Comfortable bedrooms, excellent cuisine, licensed. Special midweek prices. Self-catering coach house also available.
Bedrooms: 5 double, 3 twin, 2 triple
Bathrooms: 1 private, 2 public, 2 private showers

Bed & breakfast per night:
	£min	£max
Single	22.00	26.00
Double	38.00	40.00

Half board per person:
	£min	£max
Daily	30.00	32.00
Weekly	200.00	205.00

Evening meal 1830 (last orders 1700)
Parking for 10

Establishments should be open throughout the year, unless otherwise stated.

HEART OF ENGLAND

MALVERN
Continued

Sidney House
COMMENDED

40 Worcester Road, Malvern,
Worcestershire WR14 4AA
☎ (01684) 574994 & 563265
Small, attractive Georgian hotel with personal and friendly service. Magnificent views over the Worcestershire countryside. Close to town centre and hills. Stay for 7 nights' bed and breakfast - pay for 6. Winter weekend breaks - stay for 3 pay for 2. Prices below are from 1 March.
Bedrooms: 1 single, 4 double, 2 twin, 1 triple
Bathrooms: 5 private, 1 public

Bed & breakfast per night:	£min	£max
Single	19.50	40.00
Double	39.00	59.00

Parking for 10
Cards accepted: Access, Visa, Amex

MARKET DRAYTON
Shropshire
Map ref 4A2

Old market town with black and white buildings and 17th C houses, also acclaimed for its gingerbread. Hodnet Hall is in the vicinity with its beautiful landscaped gardens covering 60 acres.
Tourist Information Centre ☎ (01630) 652139

The Bear Hotel
COMMENDED

Hodnet, Market Drayton TF9 3NH
☎ Market Drayton (01630) 685214 & 685788
Fax (01630) 685787
Privately owned 16th C inn, with the character of a bygone age but 20th C comforts, and a warm and friendly atmosphere. Oak-beamed, open fires.
Bedrooms: 1 single, 3 double, 2 twin
Bathrooms: 6 en-suite

Bed & breakfast per night:	£min	£max
Single	30.00	32.50
Double	50.00	55.00

Half board per person:	£min	£max
Daily	38.00	50.00

Lunch available
Evening meal 1900 (last orders 2145)
Parking for 100

Cards accepted: Access, Visa, Amex, Switch/Delta

Rosehill Manor Hotel & Restaurant
COMMENDED

Tern Hill, Market Drayton TF9 2JF
☎ Tern Hill (01630) 638572
Country house hotel in 1.5 acres, easy to find as adjacent to main A41. Log fires in winter, large, relaxing garden.
Bedrooms: 1 single, 5 double, 1 triple
Bathrooms: 7 en-suite, 2 public

Bed & breakfast per night:	£min	£max
Single	39.00	
Double	60.00	

Half board per person:	£min	£max
Daily	47.50	

Lunch available
Evening meal 1900 (last orders 2130)
Parking for 20
Cards accepted: Access, Visa

MAYFIELD
Staffordshire
Map ref 4B2

Village on the border between Staffordshire and Derbyshire marked by the River Dove which is crossed by the Hanging Bridge. Alton Towers and Dovedale are nearby.

Lichfield Guest House
HIGHLY COMMENDED

Bridge View, Mayfield, Ashbourne, Derbyshire DE6 2HN
☎ Ashbourne (01335) 344422
Fax (01335) 344422
Georgian house set in 2 acres of landscaped gardens. Magnificent views over River Dove and valleys. Convenient for Alton Towers, Chatsworth and the Peaks. Non-smoking.
Bedrooms: 1 single, 1 double, 1 twin, 1 family room
Bathrooms: 2 en-suite, 1 public

Bed & breakfast per night:	£min	£max
Single	20.00	20.00
Double	38.00	42.00

Parking for 10

MERIDEN
West Midlands
Map ref 4B3

Village halfway between Coventry and Birmingham. Said to be the centre of England, marked by a cross on the green.

Meriden Hotel
APPROVED

Main Road, Meriden, Solihull, Coventry CV7 7NH
☎ (01676) 522005
Fax (01676) 523744

Family-run hotel near National Exhibition Centre and Birmingham Airport. Convenient for Coventry, Birmingham, Solihull and surrounding districts.
Bedrooms: 6 single, 4 double, 5 twin
Bathrooms: 12 en-suite, 3 private

Bed & breakfast per night:	£min	£max
Single	32.50	45.00
Double	50.00	70.00

Lunch available
Evening meal 1800 (last orders 2200)
Parking for 15
Cards accepted: Access, Visa, Diners, Amex, Switch/Delta

Information on accommodation listed in this guide has been supplied by the proprietors. As changes may occur you are advised to check details at the time of booking.

The symbols in each entry give information about services and facilities. A 'key' to these symbols appears at the back of this guide.

HEART OF ENGLAND

MINCHINHAMPTON

Gloucestershire
Map ref 2B1

Stone-built town, with many 17th/18th C buildings, owing its existence to the wool and cloth trades. A 17th C pillared market house may be found in the town square, near which is the Norman and 14th C church.

The Ragged Cot Inn
COMMENDED

Hyde, Chalford, Stroud GL6 8PE
☎ Stroud (01453) 884643 & 731333
Fax (01453) 731166
Half a mile from Gatcombe Park and adjacent to 600 acres of National Trust commonland. Cheltenham 15 miles, Bath 20 miles, Stroud 5 miles and Cirencester 8 miles.
Bedrooms: 3 double, 7 twin
Bathrooms: 10 en-suite

Bed & breakfast
per night:	£min	£max
Single		35.00
Double	50.00	70.00

Lunch available
Evening meal 1900 (last orders 2130)
Parking for 55
Cards accepted: Access, Visa, Amex

MORETON-IN-MARSH

Gloucestershire
Map ref 2B1

Attractive town of Cotswold stone with 17th C houses, an ideal base for touring the Cotswolds. Some of the local attractions include Batsford Park Arboretum, the Jacobean Chastleton House and Sezincote Garden.

Blue Cedar House

Stow Road, Moreton-in-Marsh
GL56 0DW
☎ (01608) 650299
Attractive detached residence set in half-acre garden in the Cotswolds, with pleasantly decorated, well-equipped accommodation and garden room. Close to village centre.
Bedrooms: 1 single, 1 double, 1 twin, 1 family room
Bathrooms: 2 en-suite, 2 public

Bed & breakfast
per night:	£min	£max
Single	19.00	28.00
Double	34.00	44.00

Half board per person:
	£min	£max
Daily	25.00	30.00

Evening meal 1800 (last orders 1800)
Parking for 7
Open February–November

Manor House Hotel
COMMENDED

High Street, Moreton-in-Marsh
GL56 0LJ
☎ (01608) 650501
Fax (01608) 651481
16th C privately-owned manor house with original features. Some four-poster beds, indoor pool, sauna and jacuzzi. Walled garden.
Bedrooms: 4 single, 23 double, 12 twin
Bathrooms: 39 en-suite

Bed & breakfast
per night:	£min	£max
Single	55.00	85.00
Double	85.00	135.00

Half board per person:
	£min	£max
Daily	45.00	70.00
Weekly	290.00	377.50

Lunch available
Evening meal 1900 (last orders 2130)
Parking for 30
Cards accepted: Access, Visa, Diners, Amex, Switch/Delta

Moreton House
APPROVED

Moreton-in-Marsh GL56 0LQ
☎ (01608) 650747
Fax (01608) 652747
Family-run guesthouse providing full English breakfast and optional evening meal. Tea shop, open 6 days a week, lounge bar with restaurant. Ideal for touring the Cotswolds. Children and dogs welcome.
Bedrooms: 3 single, 7 double, 2 twin
Bathrooms: 5 en-suite, 2 public

Bed & breakfast
per night:	£min	£max
Single	22.00	22.00
Double	42.00	60.00

Lunch available
Evening meal 1800 (last orders 2030)
Parking for 5
Cards accepted: Access, Visa

The White Hart Royal
COMMENDED

High Street, Moreton-in-Marsh
GL56 0BA
☎ (01608) 650731
Fax (01608) 650880
Pleasant old inn of Cotswold stone in the High Street. Once a peaceful refuge for King Charles I, now a peaceful setting for our guests.
Bedrooms: 2 single, 11 double, 5 twin, 2 triple
Suite available
Bathrooms: 20 en-suite, 1 public

Bed & breakfast
per night:	£min	£max
Single	40.00	55.00
Double	65.00	80.00

Half board per person:
	£min	£max
Daily	44.00	48.00
Weekly	284.00	294.00

Lunch available
Evening meal 1830 (last orders 2100)
Parking for 10
Cards accepted: Access, Visa, Diners, Amex, Switch/Delta

MUCH WENLOCK

Shropshire
Map ref 4A3

Small town close to Wenlock Edge in beautiful scenery and full of interest. In particular there are the remains of an 11th C priory with fine carving and the black and white 16th C Guildhall.

Gaskell Arms Hotel

Much Wenlock TF13 6HF
☎ Telford (01952) 727212
Fax (01952) 727736
17th C coaching inn built of stone and brick, with beamed ceilings, log fires. Family-run freehouse. Situated on outskirts of small medieval town and Wenlock Edge, close to Ironbridge.
Bedrooms: 7 double, 3 twin, 1 family room
Bathrooms: 6 en-suite, 2 public

Bed & breakfast
per night:	£min	£max
Single	29.00	39.00
Double	46.00	60.00

Half board per person:
	£min	£max
Daily	35.00	53.00
Weekly	240.00	356.00

Continued ▶

HEART OF ENGLAND

MUCH WENLOCK
Continued

Lunch available
Evening meal 1900 (last orders 2200)
Parking for 31
Cards accepted: Access, Visa, Amex, Switch/Delta

Raven Hotel & Restaurant
HIGHLY COMMENDED

Barrow Street, Much Wenlock TF13 6EN
☎ Much Wenlock (01952) 727251
Fax (01952) 728416
Ⓒ Logis of Great Britain

A fine coaching inn which has provided hospitality since 1700. Beautifully appointed accommodation, making this an ideal base for discovering Shropshire.
Bedrooms: 1 single, 11 double, 3 twin
Suite available
Bathrooms: 15 en-suite

Bed & breakfast per night:	£min	£max
Single	48.00	55.00
Double	85.00	120.00

Half board per person:	£min	£max
Daily	70.00	

Lunch available
Evening meal 1900 (last orders 2130)
Parking for 30
Cards accepted: Access, Visa, Diners, Amex, Switch/Delta

The symbol Ⓒ and a group name following an hotel address indicates that bookings can be made through a central reservations office. These offices are listed in the information pages at the back of this guide.

NAILSWORTH
Gloucestershire
Map ref 2B1

Ancient wool town with several elegant Jacobean and Georgian houses, surrounded by wooded hillsides with fine views.

Egypt Mill
COMMENDED

Nailsworth, Stroud GL6 0AE
☎ Stroud (01453) 833449
Fax (01453) 836098
Charming 16th C Cotswold mill and miller's house with extensive bars and restaurant. Conference facilities and water gardens. Major Cotswold walkway commences from private car park. 5 golf-courses nearby.
Bedrooms: 13 double, 5 twin
Bathrooms: 18 en-suite

Bed & breakfast per night:	£min	£max
Single	37.50	42.50
Double	65.00	75.00

Half board per person:	£min	£max
Daily	42.50	50.00
Weekly	280.00	350.00

Lunch available
Evening meal 1830 (last orders 2145)
Parking for 120
Cards accepted: Access, Visa, Diners, Amex, Switch/Delta

NEWENT
Gloucestershire
Map ref 2B1

Small town with the largest collection of birds of prey in Europe at the Falconry Centre. Flying demonstrations daily. Glass workshop where visitors can watch glass being blown. There is a "seconds" shop. North of the village is the Three Choirs Vineyards.
Tourist Information Centre ☎ (01531) 822145

Old Court Hotel
APPROVED

Church Street, Newent GL18 1AB
☎ (01531) 820522

Magnificent manor house in 1 acre of walled gardens. Friendly, relaxed atmosphere in elegant surroundings. Good cuisine. Four-poster available.
Bedrooms: 3 double, 1 twin, 1 triple
Bathrooms: 4 en-suite, 1 private

Bed & breakfast per night:	£min	£max
Single	21.50	37.50
Double	37.00	65.00

Half board per person:	£min	£max
Daily	35.25	51.25
Weekly	225.25	293.50

Evening meal 1930 (last orders 2030)
Parking for 21
Cards accepted: Access, Visa, Amex, Switch/Delta

NEWPORT
Shropshire
Map ref 4A3

Small market town on the Shropshire Union Canal has a wide High Street and a church with some interesting monuments. Newport is close to Aqualate Mere which is the largest lake in Staffordshire.

Norwood House Hotel and Restaurant

Pave Lane, Newport TF10 9LQ
☎ (01952) 825896
Hotel of character just off the A41 Whitchurch to Wolverhampton road, close to Lilleshall National Sports Centre.
Bedrooms: 1 single, 3 double, 2 twin
Bathrooms: 6 en-suite

Bed & breakfast per night:	£min	£max
Single		30.00
Double		39.00

Lunch available
Evening meal 1900 (last orders 2200)
Parking for 26
Cards accepted: Access, Visa, Amex

The Old Parsonage
HIGHLY COMMENDED

High Offley, Woodseaves, Staffordshire ST20 0NE
☎ Woodseaves (01785) 284446
Fax (01785) 284446
Ⓒ Logis of Great Britain
The Old Parsonage, off the A519 Eccleshall to Newport road, offers en-suite bedrooms and a dining room

with views to the Welsh Hills. 15 minutes junction 14 of M6.
Bedrooms: 4 double
Bathrooms: 4 private
Bed & breakfast

per night:	£min	£max
Single	45.00	49.50
Double	45.00	54.00

Half board per
person:	£min	£max
Daily	45.00	49.50

Lunch available
Evening meal 1930 (last orders 2200)
Parking for 13
Cards accepted: Access, Visa, Diners, Amex, Switch/Delta

NORTHLEACH

Gloucestershire
Map ref 2B1

Village famous for its beautiful 15th C wool church with its lovely porch and interesting interior. There are also some fine houses including a 17th C wool merchant's house containing Keith Harding's World of Mechanical Music. The Cotswold Countryside Collection is in the former prison.

Northfield Bed & Breakfast
COMMENDED
Cirencester Road (A429), Northleach, Cheltenham GL54 3JL
☎ Cotswold (01451) 860427
Detached family house in the country with large gardens and home-grown produce. Excellent centre for visiting the Cotswolds and close to local services.
Bedrooms: 1 double, 2 family rooms
Bathrooms: 3 en-suite
Bed & breakfast

per night:	£min	£max
Single		20.00
Double	38.00	44.00

Half board per
person:	£min	£max
Daily	29.00	36.00

Evening meal 1800 (last orders 1900)
Parking for 10

The National Grading and Classification Scheme is explained in full at the back of this guide.

NUNEATON

Warwickshire
Map ref 4B3

Busy town with an art gallery and museum which has a permanent exhibition of the work of George Eliot. The library also has an interesting collection of material. Arbury Hall, a fine example of Gothic architecture, is nearby.
Tourist Information Centre ☎ (01203) 384027

La Tavola Calda
APPROVED
70 Midland Road, Abbey Green, Nuneaton CV11 5DY
☎ Coventry (01203) 383195 & Mobile 0850 279908
Fax (01203) 381816
Family-run Italian restaurant and hotel.
Bedrooms: 1 single, 5 twin, 2 triple
Bathrooms: 8 en-suite
Bed & breakfast

per night:	£min	£max
Single	18.00	20.00
Double	32.00	32.00

Evening meal 1900 (last orders 2200)
Parking for 30
Cards accepted: Access, Visa, Diners, Amex

NYMPSFIELD

Gloucestershire
Map ref 2B1

Pretty village high up in the Cotswolds, with a simple mid-Victorian church and a prehistoric long barrow nearby.

Rose and Crown Inn
COMMENDED
Nympsfield, Stonehouse GL10 3TU
☎ Dursley (01453) 860240
Fax (01453) 860240
Logis of Great Britain
300-year-old inn, in quiet Cotswold village, close to Cotswold Way. Easy access to M4/M5.
Bedrooms: 1 double, 3 triple
Bathrooms: 3 en-suite, 1 private
Bed & breakfast

per night:	£min	£max
Single	27.50	29.50
Double	50.00	54.00

Half board per
person:	£min	£max
Daily	35.00	49.00
Weekly	245.00	343.00

Lunch available
Evening meal 1830 (last orders 2130)

HEART OF ENGLAND

Parking for 30
Cards accepted: Access, Visa, Diners, Amex, Switch/Delta

OAKAMOOR

Staffordshire
Map ref 4B2

Small village below a steep hill amid the glorious scenery of the Churnet Valley. Its industrial links have now gone, as the site of the factory which made 20,000 miles of copper wire for the first Atlantic cable has been transformed into an attractive picnic site on the riverside.

Beehive Guest House
Listed COMMENDED
Churnet View Road, Oakamoor, Stoke-on-Trent ST10 3AE
☎ (01538) 702420
Family-run guesthouse, overlooking river and parkland, in the beautiful Churnet Valley. Within walking distance of Alton Towers.
Bedrooms: 2 double, 1 twin, 2 family rooms
Bathrooms: 3 en-suite, 2 public
Bed & breakfast

per night:	£min	£max
Single	25.00	25.00
Double	30.00	36.00

Parking for 8

OMBERSLEY

Hereford and Worcester
Map ref 2B1

A particularly fine village full of black and white houses including the 17th C Dower House and some old inns. The church contains the original box pews.

The Crown and Sandys Arms
COMMENDED
Ombersley, Droitwich, Worcestershire WR9 0EW
☎ Worcester (01905) 620252
Fax (01905) 620769
Freehouse with comfortable bedrooms, draught beers and open fires. Home-cooked meals available lunchtimes and evenings, 7 days a week.

Continued ▶

261

HEART OF ENGLAND

OMBERSLEY
Continued

Bedrooms: 1 single, 3 double, 1 twin, 1 triple, 1 family room
Bathrooms: 6 en-suite, 1 public

Bed & breakfast
per night	£min	£max
Single	25.00	30.00
Double	45.00	48.00

Lunch available
Evening meal 1800 (last orders 2145)
Parking for 100
Cards accepted: Access, Visa, Amex, Switch/Delta

⌑30 ☆ ✱ ♨

ONNELEY
Staffordshire
Map ref 4A2

Village on the line between Shropshire and Staffordshire counties, within easy reach of Bridgemere Garden World.

The Wheatsheaf Inn at Onneley
COMMENDED

Bar Hill Road, Onneley, Madeley CW3 9QF
☎ Stoke-on-Trent (01782) 751581
Fax (01782) 751499
18th C country inn with bars, Spanish restaurant, conference and function facilities. On A525, 7 miles from Newcastle-under-Lyme. Close to Potteries, Keele University and M6. Convenient for Alton Towers and Chester.
Bedrooms: 4 double, 1 twin
Bathrooms: 5 en-suite

Bed & breakfast
per night:	£min	£max
Single	45.00	45.00
Double	50.00	60.00

Half board per
person:	£min	£max
Daily	57.00	
Weekly	309.00	

Lunch available
Evening meal 1800 (last orders 2130)
Parking for 150
Cards accepted: Access, Visa, Diners, Amex

⌑100 ☆ ✱

You are advised to confirm your booking in writing.

OSWESTRY
Shropshire
Map ref 4A3

Town close to the Welsh border, the scene of many battles. To the north are the remains of a large Iron Age hill fort. An excellent centre for exploring Shropshire and Offa's Dyke.
Tourist Information Centre ☎ (01691) 662488 or 662753

Bear Hotel
COMMENDED

Salop Road, Oswestry SY11 2NR
☎ (01691) 652093
Fax (01691) 679996
Family-run hotel in the town centre, offering a warm welcome. Good home cooking in Bear's Paw Restaurant. Weekends: 1 night full price, 2nd night half price.
Bedrooms: 3 single, 4 double, 2 twin, 1 family room
Bathrooms: 5 en-suite, 1 public

Bed & breakfast
per night:	£min	£max
Single	23.00	42.00
Double	40.00	50.00

Lunch available
Evening meal 1900 (last orders 2130)
Parking for 25
Cards accepted: Access, Visa, Amex, Switch/Delta

Pen-y-Dyffryn Country Hotel
HIGHLY COMMENDED

Rhyd-y-Croesau, Oswestry SY10 7DT
☎ (01691) 653700
Fax (01691) 656526
Peaceful, stone-built Georgian former rectory in 5 acres of grounds in Shropshire/Welsh border hills. Fully licensed, extensive a la carte menu. Quiet and relaxed atmosphere. Shrewsbury and Chester 30 minutes.
Bedrooms: 1 single, 2 double, 3 twin, 1 triple
Bathrooms: 7 en-suite

Bed & breakfast
per night:	£min	£max
Single	42.00	47.00
Double	60.00	68.00

Half board per
person:	£min	£max
Daily	42.00	47.00
Weekly	270.00	300.00

Evening meal 1900 (last orders 2100)
Parking for 38

Cards accepted: Access, Visa, Amex, Switch/Delta
⌑35 ☆

Sebastian's Restaurant and Hotel
Listed HIGHLY COMMENDED

45 Willow Street, Oswestry SY11 1AQ
☎ (01691) 655444
Fax (01691) 653452
16th C small hotel with beautifully decorated and furnished en-suite bedrooms. Award-winning restaurant with table d'hote and a la carte menus, featuring the finest French cuisine. Original oak beams and panelling. Chef/patron, Mark Sebastian Fisher.
Bedrooms: 2 double, 1 twin
Bathrooms: 3 en-suite

Bed & breakfast
per night:	£min	£max
Single	28.00	
Double	35.00	

Half board per
person:	£min	£max
Daily	33.50	44.00

Lunch available
Evening meal 1830 (last orders 2200)
Parking for 3
Cards accepted: Access, Visa, Diners, Amex, Switch/Delta

⌑15 ✱

The Wynnstay
HIGHLY COMMENDED

Church Street, Oswestry SY11 2SZ
☎ (01691) 655261
Fax (01691) 670606

Attractive Georgian country house hotel, 30 minutes from Chester and Shrewsbury. Indoor swimming pool with health and beauty suite.
Bedrooms: 5 single, 9 double, 11 twin, 2 triple
Bathrooms: 27 en-suite

Bed & breakfast
per night:	£min	£max
Single	58.90	91.45
Double	67.85	117.90

Lunch available
Evening meal 1900 (last orders 2130)
Parking for 90

HEART OF ENGLAND

Cards accepted: Access, Visa, Diners, Amex, Switch/Delta

PAINSWICK
Gloucestershire
Map ref 2B1

Picturesque wool town with inns and houses dating from the 14th C. Painswick Rococo Garden is open to visitors from January to November, and the house is a Palladian mansion. The churchyard is famous for its yew trees.

Thorne
COMMENDED

Friday Street, Painswick, Stroud GL6 6QJ
☎ (01452) 812476

Thorne is one of the oldest houses in Painswick, a perfect example of Cotswold secular architecture. Part has market hall pillars "in situ". Outside used for filming "Poldark" television film. Situated on Cotswold Way Walk. Guide service available by Blue Badge Guide.

Bedrooms: 2 twin
Bathrooms: 1 en-suite, 1 private

Bed & breakfast per night:	£min	£max
Single	20.00	24.00
Double	40.00	50.00

Open February–November

PENKRIDGE
Staffordshire
Map ref 4B3

Small town south of Stafford in the wide valley of the Penk has a stately church with many monuments to the Littleton family.

Hatherton Country Hotel & Leisure Centre
COMMENDED

Pinfold Lane, Penkridge, Stafford ST19 5QP
☎ (01785) 712459
Fax (01785) 715532
CR Lyric

Listed building set in its own extensive grounds. Leisure facilities include indoor pool, squash, sauna and gym. Walking distance to picturesque Penkridge village. Leisure breaks.

Bedrooms: 13 double, 32 twin, 2 triple
Suite available
Bathrooms: 47 en-suite

Bed & breakfast per night:	£min	£max
Single	40.00	70.00
Double	50.00	85.00

Half board per person:	£min	£max
Daily	35.00	65.00

Lunch available
Evening meal 1900 (last orders 2130)
Parking for 150
Cards accepted: Access, Visa, Diners, Amex

ROSS-ON-WYE
Hereford and Worcester
Map ref 2A1

Attractive market town with a 17th C market hall, set above the River Wye. There are lovely views over the surrounding countryside from the Prospect and the town is close to Goodrich Castle and the Welsh border.
Tourist Information Centre ☎ (01989) 562768

The Arches Country House
COMMENDED

Walford Road, Ross-on-Wye, Herefordshire HR9 5PT
☎ (01989) 563348

Small, family-run hotel, set in half an acre of lawned garden, 10 minutes' walk from town centre. Warm, friendly atmosphere. All rooms furnished to a high standard with views of the garden. Victorian-style conservatory to relax in.

Bedrooms: 1 single, 4 double, 1 twin, 1 triple
Bathrooms: 4 en-suite, 2 public

Bed & breakfast per night:	£min	£max
Single	19.00	25.00
Double	36.00	44.00

Half board per person:	£min	£max
Daily	29.00	33.00
Weekly	113.00	147.00

Evening meal from 1900
Parking for 10

Bridge House Hotel
COMMENDED

Wilton, Ross-on-Wye, Herefordshire HR9 6AA
☎ (01989) 562655

Riverside hotel with panoramic views from the gardens and pride in its comfort and cuisine. All rooms en-suite. Break terms available.

Bedrooms: 5 double, 3 twin, 1 triple
Bathrooms: 8 en-suite, 1 public

Bed & breakfast per night:	£min	£max
Single	32.50	34.00
Double	50.00	54.00

Half board per person:	£min	£max
Daily	33.00	40.00
Weekly	220.00	230.00

Evening meal 1800 (last orders 2030)
Parking for 12
Cards accepted: Access, Visa, Switch/Delta

Kings Head Hotel
COMMENDED

8 High Street, Ross-on-Wye, Herefordshire HR9 5HL
☎ (01989) 763174
Fax (01989) 769578

Family-owned and managed offering en-suite accommodation, good food and a safe haven for the traveller.

Bedrooms: 10 double, 4 twin, 7 triple, 2 family rooms
Bathrooms: 23 en-suite

Bed & breakfast per night:	£min	£max
Single	40.00	48.00
Double	65.00	65.00

Half board per person:	£min	£max
Daily	45.00	50.00

Lunch available
Evening meal 1900 (last orders 2100)
Parking for 25
Cards accepted: Access, Visa, Switch/Delta

Lumleys

Kerne Bridge, Bishopswood, Ross-on-Wye, Herefordshire HR9 5QT
☎ Monmouth (01600) 890040

Lumleys only offers the best. Treat yourself to an experience.

Bedrooms: 2 double, 1 twin
Bathrooms: 3 en-suite

Bed & breakfast per night:	£min	£max
Single	25.00	26.50
Double	40.00	45.00

Half board per person:	£min	£max
Daily	30.00	32.50
Weekly	190.00	200.00

Continued ▶

HEART OF ENGLAND

ROSS-ON-WYE
Continued

Evening meal 1830 (last orders 2000)
Parking for 10
Open January, March–December

Orles Barn Hotel & Restaurant
COMMENDED
Wilton, Ross-on-Wye,
Herefordshire HR9 6AE
☎ (01989) 562155
Fax (01989) 768470
Set in large gardens with outdoor heated pool. English and Spanish cuisine by chef/proprietor using fresh local produce.
Bedrooms: 1 single, 5 double, 1 twin, 2 triple
Bathrooms: 8 en-suite, 1 private

Bed & breakfast per night:	£min	£max
Single	35.00	45.00
Double	45.00	60.00

Half board per person:	£min	£max
Daily	40.00	60.00
Weekly	225.00	275.00

Lunch available
Evening meal 1900 (last orders 2130)
Parking for 20
Cards accepted: Access, Visa, Diners, Amex, Switch/Delta

Pencraig Court Hotel
COMMENDED
Pencraig, Ross-on-Wye,
Herefordshire HR9 6HR
☎ (01989) 770306 & 770416
Fax (01989) 770040

Georgian country house hotel, privately owned, providing both English and French cooking. Elegant restaurant and extensive wine cellars. Large attractive garden with glorious views overlooking River Wye. Special breaks available.
Bedrooms: 1 single, 4 double, 4 twin, 2 triple
Bathrooms: 11 en-suite

Bed & breakfast per night:	£min	£max
Single	39.50	45.00
Double	50.00	70.00

Half board per person:	£min	£max
Daily	40.50	60.50
Weekly	245.00	350.00

Lunch available
Evening meal 1900 (last orders 2100)
Parking for 20
Cards accepted: Access, Visa, Switch/Delta

Pengethley Manor
COMMENDED
Ross-on-Wye, Herefordshire
HR9 6LL
☎ Harewood End (01989) 730211
Fax (01989) 730238
Best Western
Elegant Georgian country house in superb gardens with magnificent views over Herefordshire countryside. Extensive wine list. Restaurant specialises in fresh local produce.
Bedrooms: 2 single, 11 double, 10 twin, 1 triple
Suites available
Bathrooms: 24 en-suite

Bed & breakfast per night:	£min	£max
Single	70.00	110.00
Double	100.00	160.00

Half board per person:	£min	£max
Daily	67.50	95.00
Weekly	402.50	570.00

Lunch available
Evening meal 1900 (last orders 2130)
Parking for 70
Cards accepted: Access, Visa, Diners, Amex, Switch/Delta

Sunnymount Hotel
COMMENDED
Ryefield Road, Ross-on-Wye,
Herefordshire HR9 5LU
☎ (01989) 563880
Warm, comfortable hotel in quiet location on edge of town, offering French and English cooking with home-grown and local produce freshly cooked for each meal. Special breaks always available.
Bedrooms: 3 single, 3 double, 3 twin
Bathrooms: 7 en-suite, 1 public

Bed & breakfast per night:	£min	£max
Single	27.00	30.00
Double	47.00	51.00

Half board per person:	£min	£max
Daily	38.50	40.50
Weekly	225.00	268.00

Evening meal 1900 (last orders 1730)
Parking for 7
Cards accepted: Access, Visa, Amex

Wilton Court Hotel
Wilton Lane, Wilton, Ross-on-Wye,
Herefordshire HR9 6AQ
☎ (01989) 562569
Fax (01989) 768460
16th C hotel on the banks of the Wye, set in own delightful gardens. Restaurant and bar meals available.
Bedrooms: 2 single, 6 double, 1 twin, 1 triple
Bathrooms: 10 en-suite

Bed & breakfast per night:	£min	£max
Single	38.00	45.00
Double	43.00	70.00

Half board per person:	£min	£max
Daily	34.00	40.00
Weekly	238.00	260.00

Lunch available
Evening meal 1900 (last orders 2100)
Parking for 25
Cards accepted: Access, Visa, Amex, Switch/Delta

RUGBY
Warwickshire
Map ref 4C3

Town famous for its public school which gave its name to Rugby Union football and which featured in "Tom Brown's Schooldays".
Tourist Information Centre ☎ *(01788) 535348*

White Lion Inn
Listed APPROVED
Coventry Road, Pailton, Rugby
CV23 0QD
☎ (01788) 832359
Fax (01788) 832359
17th C coaching inn, recently refurbished but maintaining all old world features. Close to Rugby, Coventry and Stratford. Within 2 miles of motorways.
Bedrooms: 9 twin
Bathrooms: 3 en-suite, 2 public

HEART OF ENGLAND

Bed & breakfast per night:	£min	£max
Single	18.50	25.00
Double	32.00	45.00

Lunch available
Evening meal 1830 (last orders 2200)
Parking for 60
Cards accepted: Access, Visa

SEVERN STOKE

Hereford and Worcester
Map ref 2B1

Village to the south of Worcester with a picturesque group of houses surrounding the church and magnificent views across the Severn to the Malvern Hills.

The Old School House Hotel

HIGHLY COMMENDED

Severn Stoke, Worcester WR8 9JA
☎ Worcester (01905) 371268
Fax (01905) 371591
The Independents

A warm welcome awaits at this 17th C farmhouse/Victorian school near Worcester. Popular restaurant, gardens, outdoor pool. Wonderful views of the Malverns. Easy car parking. Winter discounts available.
Bedrooms: 2 single, 8 double, 2 twin, 1 family room
Bathrooms: 13 en-suite

Bed & breakfast per night:	£min	£max
Single	37.50	50.00
Double	55.00	80.00

Half board per person:	£min	£max
Daily	45.00	65.00
Weekly	250.00	355.00

Lunch available
Evening meal 1900 (last orders 2130)
Parking for 100
Cards accepted: Access, Visa, Diners, Switch/Delta

National gradings and classifications were correct at the time of going to press but are subject to change. Please check at the time of booking.

SHREWSBURY

Shropshire
Map ref 4A3

Beautiful historic town on the River Severn retaining many fine old timber-framed houses. Its attractions include Rowley's Museum with Roman finds, remains of a castle, Clive House Museum, St Chad's 18th C round church, rowing on the river and the Shrewsbury Flower Show in August.
Tourist Information Centre ☎ (01743) 350761.

Abbot's Mead Hotel

COMMENDED

9-10 St. Julian Friars, Shrewsbury SY1 1XL
☎ (01743) 235281
Fax (01743) 369133

Georgian town house between town centre and the River Severn. All bedrooms have private facilities, colour TV, tea/coffee makers, direct dial telephone. Car parking.
Bedrooms: 10 double, 4 twin
Bathrooms: 14 en-suite, 1 public

Bed & breakfast per night:	£min	£max
Single	30.00	35.90
Double	48.00	49.90

Half board per person:	£min	£max
Daily	35.00	36.50

Evening meal 1900 (last orders 2130)
Parking for 10
Cards accepted: Access, Visa, Amex, Switch/Delta

Cromwells Hotel & Wine Bar

Listed

11 Dogpole, Shrewsbury SY1 1EN
☎ (01743) 361440

15th C coaching inn in Shrewsbury town centre, offering comfortable, well-maintained character bedrooms. Cosy restaurant, with excellent local reputation, and lively wine bar.
Bedrooms: 2 single, 2 double, 1 twin, 2 triple
Bathrooms: 2 public

Bed & breakfast per night:	£min	£max
Single	23.00	28.00
Double	37.00	40.00

Lunch available
Evening meal 1900 (last orders 2200)
Cards accepted: Access, Visa, Amex, Switch/Delta

Golden Cross Hotel

Princess Street, Shrewsbury SY1 1LP
☎ (01743) 362507

15th C town centre inn, offering a friendly welcome, real ale, bar snacks and a lunch menu.
Bedrooms: 2 single, 2 double, 1 twin
Bathrooms: 1 public

Bed & breakfast per night:	£min	£max
Single	18.50	
Double	35.00	

Lunch available

Hawkstone Park Hotel, Golf, Historic Park & Follies

HIGHLY COMMENDED

Weston-under-Redcastle, Shrewsbury SY4 5UY
☎ Lee Brockhurst (01939) 200611 & 200204
Fax (01939) 200311

Fine example of a country house hotel, built in 1752, set in over 400 acres of Grade I listed landscape with panoramic views over the golf courses and beyond to the forgotten masterpiece - an Historic Park and Follies with dramatic scenery, high cliffs and grotto caves. 10 miles north of Shrewsbury off A49.
Bedrooms: 6 single, 28 double, 29 twin, 2 triple
Suites available
Bathrooms: 65 en-suite, 8 public

Bed & breakfast per night:	£min	£max
Single	50.00	79.50
Double	50.00	79.50

Half board per person:	£min	£max
Daily	66.50	95.50

Lunch available
Evening meal 1930 (last orders 2145)
Parking for 300
Cards accepted: Access, Visa, Diners, Amex, Switch/Delta

The map references refer to the colour maps towards the end of the guide. The first figure is the map number; the letter and figure which follow indicate the grid reference on the map.

HEART OF ENGLAND

SHREWSBURY
Continued

Lion and Pheasant Hotel
COMMENDED
49-50 Wyle Cop, Shrewsbury
SY1 1XJ
☎ (01743) 236288
Fax (01743) 244475
Consort
Ancient inn of character with many exposed beams and original fireplaces. Bars and restaurant open to non-residents.
Bedrooms: 5 single, 6 double, 8 twin, 1 family room
Bathrooms: 17 en-suite, 3 private, 2 public

Bed & breakfast per night:

	£min	£max
Single	28.50	45.00
Double	57.00	60.00

Half board per person:

	£min	£max
Daily	39.00	57.00

Lunch available
Evening meal 1900 (last orders 2130)
Parking for 20
Cards accepted: Access, Visa, Diners, Amex, Switch/Delta

Mytton and Mermaid Hotel
COMMENDED
Atcham, Shrewsbury SY5 6QG
☎ (01743) 761220
Fax (01743) 761292
Grade II listed manor house on the banks of the River Severn. Two miles from Shrewsbury and 7 miles from Telford.
Bedrooms: 2 single, 11 double, 4 twin, 1 family room
Bathrooms: 18 en-suite

Bed & breakfast per night:

	£min	£max
Single	29.95	50.00
Double	39.95	60.00

Half board per person:

	£min	£max
Daily	42.90	62.95
Weekly	300.00	450.00

Lunch available
Evening meal 1800 (last orders 2200)
Parking for 100
Cards accepted: Access, Visa, Diners, Amex, Switch/Delta

Sandford House Hotel
HIGHLY COMMENDED
St. Julian Friars, Shrewsbury
SY1 1XL
☎ (01743) 343829
Fax (01743) 343829
Family-run Grade II listed town house, close to the river, with pleasant walks and access to good fishing. Easy parking and within a few minutes of the town centre.
Bedrooms: 2 single, 4 double, 3 twin, 2 triple
Bathrooms: 9 en-suite, 1 public, 1 private shower

Bed & breakfast per night:

	£min	£max
Single	25.00	
Double	50.00	

Parking for 3
Cards accepted: Access, Visa, Switch/Delta

Shelton Hall Hotel
HIGHLY COMMENDED
Shelton, Shrewsbury SY3 8BH
☎ (01743) 343982
Fax (01743) 241515
Quiet, family-run hotel set in 4 acres of beautiful gardens, amidst lovely Shropshire countryside.
Bedrooms: 5 double, 2 twin, 1 triple, 1 family room
Suite available
Bathrooms: 9 en-suite

Bed & breakfast per night:

	£min	£max
Single	47.00	47.00
Double	64.00	64.00

Half board per person:

	£min	£max
Daily	39.00	49.50
Weekly		380.00

Lunch available
Evening meal 1900 (last orders 2100)
Parking for 60
Cards accepted: Access, Visa, Amex, Switch/Delta

The Stiperstones Guest House
COMMENDED
18 Coton Crescent, Coton Hill, Shrewsbury SY1 2NZ
☎ (01743) 246720 & 350303
Fax (01743) 350303
Always a warm welcome. Tastefully furnished, quality accommodation. Very comfortable and clean. Extensive facilities, off-road parking. Close to town centre and river. Special rates.
Bedrooms: 1 single, 3 double, 1 twin, 1 triple
Bathrooms: 3 public

Bed & breakfast per night:

	£min	£max
Single	18.00	20.00
Double	34.00	35.00

Half board per person:

	£min	£max
Daily	28.00	30.00
Weekly	182.00	196.00

Evening meal 1900 (last orders 1200)
Parking for 8

Sydney House Hotel
Coton Crescent, Coton Hill, Shrewsbury SY1 2LJ
☎ (01743) 354681 & Freephone 0500 130243
Fax (01743) 354681
Logis of Great Britain
Edwardian town house with period features, 10 minutes' walk from town centre and railway station. Most rooms en-suite. All with direct dial telephone, colour TV, hot drink facilities and hairdryer.
Bedrooms: 2 single, 2 double, 2 twin, 1 family room
Bathrooms: 4 en-suite, 2 public

Bed & breakfast per night:

	£min	£max
Single	35.00	47.00
Double	46.00	64.00

Half board per person:

	£min	£max
Daily	33.00	62.00
Weekly	182.00	314.00

Evening meal 1930 (last orders 2100)
Parking for 7
Cards accepted: Access, Visa, Amex

The ⋀ symbol after an establishment name indicates that it is a Regional Tourist Board member.

ACCESSIBILITY

Look for the symbols which indicate accessibility for wheelchair users. These are described in detail at the front of this guide.

HEART OF ENGLAND

SLIMBRIDGE
Gloucestershire
Map ref 2B1

The Wildfowl and Wetlands Trust Centre was founded by Sir Peter Scott and has the world's largest collection of wildfowl. Of special interest are the wild swans and the geese which wander around the grounds.

Tudor Arms Lodge
COMMENDED

Shepherds Patch, Slimbridge, Gloucester GL2 7BP
☎ Dursley (01453) 890245
Fax (01453) 890103
Newly-built lodge adjoining an 18th C freehouse, alongside Gloucester and Sharpness Canal. Renowned Slimbridge Wildfowl and Wetlands Trust Centre only 800 yards away.
Bedrooms: 4 double, 5 twin, 2 triple, 1 family room
Bathrooms: 12 en-suite

Bed & breakfast per night:	£min	£max
Single	29.50	32.50
Double	39.50	42.50

Half board per person:	£min	£max
Daily	28.60	38.40
Weekly	180.00	235.00

Lunch available
Evening meal 1900 (last orders 2200)
Parking for 70
Cards accepted: Access, Visa, Amex

SOLIHULL
West Midlands
Map ref 4B3

On the outskirts of Birmingham. Some Tudor houses and a 13th C church remain amongst the new public buildings and shopping centre. The 16th C Malvern Hall is now a school and the 15th C Chester House at Knowle is now a library.
Tourist Information Centre ☎ (0121) 704 6130 or 704 6134

Cedarwood House

347 Lyndon Road, Solihull B92 7QT
☎ (0121) 743 5844
Private guesthouse, all bedrooms elegantly furnished, en-suite facilities. Within 2 miles of the National Exhibition Centre, airport, station and Solihull centre.
Bedrooms: 4 single, 1 twin
Bathrooms: 5 en-suite

Bed & breakfast per night:	£min	£max
Single	30.00	45.00
Double	35.00	55.00

Parking for 6

The Edwardian Guest House
HIGHLY COMMENDED

7 St Bernards Road, Olton, Solihull B92 7AU
☎ (0121) 706 2138
Edwardian guesthouse of character. A warm welcome, good food. Excellent accommodation and delightful garden. 1.25 miles Solihull, 10 minutes NEC, airport and railway, 5 minutes junction 5 of M42. No smoking, please.
Bedrooms: 2 twin
Bathrooms: 2 en-suite

Bed & breakfast per night:	£min	£max
Single	25.00	35.00
Double	50.00	60.00

Parking for 7

Ivy House Guest House
COMMENDED

Warwick Road, Heronfield, Knowle, Solihull B93 0EB
☎ Knowle (01564) 770247
Fax (01564) 778063

Set in 6 acres of its own land overlooking fields. Approximately 5 miles from the NEC and airport, 20 minutes from the ICC.
Bedrooms: 4 single, 2 double, 3 twin, 1 triple
Bathrooms: 10 en-suite

Bed & breakfast per night:	£min	£max
Single	25.00	28.00
Double	40.00	46.00

Parking for 20

Regency Hotel

Stratford Road, Shirley, Solihull B90 4EB
☎ (0121) 745 6119
Fax (0121) 733 3801
Consort
Regency-style building, in its own grounds, close to NEC and city centre, with easy access from M42. Leisure centre with indoor pool.
Bedrooms: 17 single, 46 double, 41 twin, 8 triple
Suites available
Bathrooms: 112 en-suite

Bed & breakfast per night:	£min	£max
Single	55.00	102.00
Double	63.00	110.00

Lunch available
Evening meal 1900 (last orders 2145)
Parking for 275
Cards accepted: Access, Visa, Diners, Amex, Switch/Delta

St. John's Swallow Hotel
HIGHLY COMMENDED

651 Warwick Road, Solihull B91 1AT
☎ (0121) 711 3000
Fax (0121) 705 6629
Swallow
Newly refurbished hotel with leisure facilities, close to Solihull town centre. A good touring base for Stratford, Warwick and Coventry. Short break packages available.
Bedrooms: 14 single, 58 double, 100 twin, 5 family rooms
Suites available
Bathrooms: 177 en-suite

Bed & breakfast per night:	£min	£max
Single	55.00	105.00
Double	63.00	115.00

Half board per person:	£min	£max
Daily	74.95	124.95

Lunch available
Evening meal 1900 (last orders 2145)
Parking for 380
Cards accepted: Access, Visa, Diners, Amex

All accommodation in this guide has been graded, or is awaiting a grading, by a trained Tourist Board inspector.

Please check prices and other details at the time of booking.

HEART OF ENGLAND

SOLIHULL
Continued

Solihull Moat House
Homer Road, Solihull B91 3QD
☎ (0121) 623 9988
Fax (0121) 711 2696
Queens Moat/Utell International
Modern hotel, tastefully furnished in traditional English style, set in mature grounds featuring a lake and fountain. Special children's hours in health club.
Bedrooms: 47 double, 65 twin, 3 triple
Suites available
Bathrooms: 115 en-suite

Bed & breakfast per night:	£min	£max
Single	65.00	130.00
Double	75.00	140.00

Half board per person:	£min	£max
Daily	98.00	
Weekly	490.00	

Lunch available
Evening meal 1900 (last orders 2230)
Parking for 161
Cards accepted: Access, Visa, Diners, Amex, Switch/Delta

STAFFORD
Staffordshire
Map ref 4B3

The town has a long history and some half-timbered buildings still remain, notably the 16th C High House. There are several museums in the town and Shugborough Hall and the famous angler Izaak Walton's cottage, now a museum, are nearby.
Tourist Information Centre ☎ (01785) 240204

Aviemore Hotel
APPROVED
4A Lloyd Street, Stafford ST16 3AS
☎ (01785) 211986
Fax (01785) 226143
Friendly, family-run hotel close to town centre and M6 junction 14.
Bedrooms: 6 single, 1 double, 2 twin, 3 triple
Bathrooms: 5 en-suite, 3 public, 2 private showers

Bed & breakfast per night:	£min	£max
Single	15.00	30.00
Double	30.00	50.00

Lunch available
Evening meal 1800 (last orders 2130)

Parking for 15
Cards accepted: Access, Visa, Diners, Amex, Switch/Delta

Wyndale Guest House
199 Corporation Street, Stafford ST16 3LQ
☎ (01785) 223069
Family-run business en-route to showground. From town centre take A518 for Uttoxeter, first set of lights turn left by multi-storey flats. Guesthouse is on opposite side.
Bedrooms: 3 single, 2 double, 2 twin, 1 family room
Bathrooms: 5 en-suite, 2 public

Bed & breakfast per night:	£min	£max
Single	18.00	30.00
Double	35.00	45.00

Evening meal 1800 (last orders 1930)
Parking for 12

STAPENHILL
Staffordshire
Map ref 4B3

Village across the River Trent from Burton and bordering Derbyshire, within easy reach of the Bass Museum and Snowdome.

Redhill Hotel
66 Stanton Road, Stapenhill, Burton upon Trent DE15 9RS
☎ Burton-upon-Trent (01283) 564629 & 565078
Fax (01283) 564629
Licensed family-run hotel, well situated on main road on outskirts of town. Full a la carte restaurant, bar snacks, Saturday night and Sunday lunch carvery. Garden, large car park.
Bedrooms: 7 single, 5 double, 7 twin
Bathrooms: 7 en-suite, 4 private, 2 public

Bed & breakfast per night:	£min	£max
Single	25.00	35.00
Double	38.00	50.00

Half board per person:	£min	£max
Daily	37.00	47.00
Weekly	250.00	300.00

Map references apply to the colour maps at the back of this guide.

Lunch available
Evening meal 1800 (last orders 2200)
Parking for 32
Cards accepted: Access, Visa

STOKE-ON-TRENT
Staffordshire
Map ref 4B2

Famous for its pottery. Factories of several famous makers, including Josiah Wedgwood, can be visited. The City Museum has one of the finest pottery and porcelain collections in the world.
Tourist Information Centre ☎ (01782) 284600

Flower Pot Hotel
Listed
44-46 Snow Hill, Shelton, Stoke-on-Trent ST1 4LY
☎ (01782) 207204
Homely hotel with easy access to M6. Central for pottery firms and within easy reach of Alton Towers. Half a mile from rail and bus stations.
Bedrooms: 3 single, 4 double, 1 twin, 4 triple
Bathrooms: 1 en-suite, 1 private, 3 public

Bed & breakfast per night:	£min	£max
Single	15.00	19.00
Double	26.00	40.00

Haydon House Hotel
Haydon Street, Basford, Stoke-on-Trent ST4 6JD
☎ (01782) 711311
Fax (01782) 717470
Country house in the city. Fine food and service. Executive accommodation, including suites. A landmark in Staffordshire.
Bedrooms: 7 single, 7 double, 7 twin, 2 triple
Bathrooms: 23 en-suite

Bed & breakfast per night:	£min	£max
Single	38.00	57.50
Double	55.00	67.50

Half board per person:	£min	£max
Daily	54.00	73.50

Lunch available
Evening meal 1900 (last orders 2145)

HEART OF ENGLAND

Parking for 50
Cards accepted: Access, Visa, Diners, Amex, Switch/Delta
⛔🅿️🍴📞📺♿🅟ⓘⓢ🎱♨️🛏️🅿️
🏠100▶︎🐕🅢🅟🇹

The Old Dairy House ⓜ
👑👑 HIGHLY COMMENDED
Trentham Park, Stoke-on-Trent
ST4 8AE
☎ (01782) 641209
Fax (01782) 712904
Privately owned and family run former dairy, set in 2 acres of secluded wooded grounds with the benefit of a tennis court. Ample parking.
Bedrooms: 2 double
Bathrooms: 2 en-suite

Bed & breakfast per night:	£min	£max
Single	30.00	35.00
Double	40.00	45.00

Half board per person:	£min	£max
Daily	35.00	40.00
Weekly	50.00	60.00

Evening meal 1830 (last orders 1800)
Parking for 10
⛔🅿️🍴📞📺♿🇺🇱ⓘⓢ🎱♨️📺🛏️
🅿️16🔑🐕❊🚗🅟

Plough Motel
👑👑 COMMENDED
Campbell Road, Stoke-on-Trent
ST4 4EN
☎ (01782) 414685
Fax (01782) 414669

Family-run hotel situated for easy access to the Potteries and motorway. Restaurant and bar facilities. Ideal starting point for Alton Towers and the Staffordshire Moorlands.
Bedrooms: 3 single, 5 double, 12 twin
Bathrooms: 20 en-suite

Bed & breakfast per night:	£min	£max
Single	37.00	39.50
Double	45.00	47.50

Half board per person:	£min	£max
Daily	33.00	49.50

Lunch available
Evening meal 1900 (last orders 2200)

Parking for 50
Cards accepted: Access, Visa, Amex, Switch/Delta
⛔🅿️🍴📞📺♿🅟ⓘⓢ🎱✂️♨️🛏️🅿️
🏠125🎾🐕🔍🅢🅟🇹

STONE
Staffordshire
Map ref 4B2

Town on the River Trent with the remains of a 12th C Augustinian priory. It is surrounded by pleasant countryside. Trentham Gardens with 500 acres of parklands and recreational facilities is within easy reach.

Stone House Hotel
👑👑👑👑 HIGHLY COMMENDED
Stone ST15 0BQ
☎ (01785) 815531
Fax (01785) 814764
Ⓖ Whitbread
Elegant building, set in its own delightful grounds, offers extensive leisure facilities, including tennis courts and swimming pool.
Bedrooms: 9 single, 29 double, 8 twin, 1 triple
Bathrooms: 47 en-suite

Bed & breakfast per night:	£min	£max
Single	65.00	75.00
Double	72.00	82.00

Half board per person:	£min	£max
Daily	79.00	89.00

Lunch available
Evening meal 1900 (last orders 2200)
Parking for 150
Cards accepted: Access, Visa, Diners, Amex
⛔🅿️🍴📞📺♿🅟ⓘⓢ🎱✂️♨️📺
🌀🛏️🅿️🏠180🎾🐕☂️🔑▶︎❊🚗🅳🅐🅟
🅢🅟🇹

STONEHOUSE
Gloucestershire
Map ref 2B1

Village in the Stroud Valley with an Elizabethan Court, later restored and altered by Lutyens.

The Grey Cottage
👑👑👑 HIGHLY COMMENDED
Bath Road, Leonard Stanley, Stonehouse GL10 3LU
☎ Stroud (01453) 822515
Fax (01453) 822515
1807 Cotswold cottage featuring tessellated tiling, stonework and open log fires. Charming garden with distinctive Wellingtonia. Imaginative cooking and presentation.

Bedrooms: 1 single, 1 double, 1 twin
Bathrooms: 1 en-suite, 2 private, 1 public

Bed & breakfast per night:	£min	£max
Single	25.00	29.00
Double	46.00	49.00

Half board per person:	£min	£max
Daily	39.00	45.50

Evening meal from 1800
Parking for 7
⛔7🅿️🍴📞♿🇺🇱ⓘⓢ🎱✂️♨️📺🛏️
🅿️❊🍴🚗🅢🅟🏠

STOW-ON-THE-WOLD
Gloucestershire
Map ref 2B1

Attractive Cotswold wool town with a large market-place and some fine houses, especially the old grammar school. There is an interesting church dating from Norman times. Stow-on-the-Wold is surrounded by lovely countryside and Cotswold villages.
Tourist Information Centre ☎ (01451) 831082

Auld Stocks Hotel ⓜ
👑👑👑
The Square, Stow-on-the-Wold, Cheltenham GL54 1AF
☎ Cotswold (01451) 830666
Fax (01451) 870014

17th C Grade II listed hotel facing quiet village green on which the original penal stocks still stand. Refurbished to combine modern comforts with original charm and character. Friendly and caring staff make this an ideal base for exploring the Cotswolds.
Bedrooms: 1 single, 14 double, 2 twin, 1 triple
Bathrooms: 18 en-suite

Bed & breakfast per night:	£min	£max
Single		35.00
Double		70.00

Half board per person:	£min	£max
Daily	47.50	49.50
Weekly	237.50	346.50

Continued ▶

HEART OF ENGLAND

STOW-ON-THE-WOLD
Continued

Lunch available
Evening meal 1900 (last orders 2130)
Parking for 14
Cards accepted: Access, Visa, Switch/Delta

Corsham Field Farmhouse
APPROVED

Bledington Road, Stow-on-the-Wold, Cheltenham GL54 1JH
☎ Cotswold (01451) 831750
100-acre mixed farm. Homely farmhouse with breathtaking views. Ideally situated for exploring the Cotswolds. En-suite and standard rooms. TVs, guest lounge, tea/coffee facilities. Good pub food 5 minutes' walk away.
Bedrooms: 1 double, 1 twin, 2 triple, 3 family rooms
Bathrooms: 5 en-suite, 1 public

Bed & breakfast
per night:	£min	£max
Single	15.00	25.00
Double	27.00	38.00

Parking for 10

Fosse Manor Hotel
HIGHLY COMMENDED

Stow-on-the-Wold, Cheltenham GL54 1JX
☎ Cotswold (01451) 830354
Fax (01451) 832486
Consort
Rurally located Cotswold manor house in beautiful gardens. Tastefully decorated throughout. Elegant restaurant serving traditional and continental cuisine. Central to all Cotswold attractions.
Bedrooms: 3 single, 8 double, 3 twin, 3 triple
Suite available
Bathrooms: 17 en-suite

Bed & breakfast
per night:	£min	£max
Single	53.00	66.00
Double	80.00	150.00

Half board per
person:	£min	£max
Daily	53.00	88.00
Weekly	334.00	610.00

Lunch available
Evening meal 1900 (last orders 2130)
Parking for 55

Cards accepted: Access, Visa, Diners, Amex, Switch/Delta

Grapevine Hotel
HIGHLY COMMENDED

Sheep Street, Stow-on-the-Wold, Cheltenham GL54 1AU
☎ Cotswold (01451) 830344
Fax (01451) 832278
Best Western

Exceptional small hotel in antique centre of Cotswolds. Accent on food and hospitality. Lovely furnishings complement the romantic, vine-clad conservatory restaurant. Overnight half board minimum price based on 2-night stay.
Bedrooms: 1 single, 10 double, 10 twin, 1 triple, 1 family room
Bathrooms: 22 en-suite, 1 private

Bed & breakfast
per night:	£min	£max
Single	60.00	100.00
Double	120.00	160.00

Half board per
person:	£min	£max
Daily	55.00	116.00
Weekly	350.00	610.00

Lunch available
Evening meal 1900 (last orders 2130)
Parking for 23
Cards accepted: Access, Visa, Diners, Amex, Switch/Delta

Old Farmhouse Hotel
COMMENDED

Lower Swell, Stow-on-the-Wold, Cheltenham GL54 1LF
☎ Cotswold (01451) 830232 & Freephone 0500 657842
Fax (01451) 870962

Sympathetically converted 16th C Cotswold-stone farmhouse in a quiet hamlet, 1 mile west of Stow-on-the-Wold. Offers warm and unpretentious hospitality.

Bedrooms: 9 double, 4 twin, 1 family room
Suite available
Bathrooms: 14 en-suite, 1 public

Bed & breakfast
per night:	£min	£max
Single	21.50	58.00
Double	43.00	97.00

Half board per
person:	£min	£max
Daily	35.00	65.00
Weekly	245.00	455.00

Lunch available
Evening meal 1900 (last orders 2100)
Parking for 25
Cards accepted: Access, Visa, Switch/Delta

Stow Lodge Hotel
HIGHLY COMMENDED

The Square, Stow-on-the-Wold, Cheltenham GL54 1AB
☎ Cotswold (01451) 830485
Fax (01451) 831671

Family-run, Grade II listed manor house in pretty gardens overlooking market square. Open fires in bar and lounge, en-suite comfortably furnished bedrooms, candlelit restaurant with interesting wine list, private car park.
Bedrooms: 1 single, 9 double, 8 twin, 3 triple
Bathrooms: 21 en-suite

Bed & breakfast
per night:	£min	£max
Single	40.00	70.00
Double	58.00	90.00

Evening meal 1900 (last orders 2100)
Parking for 30
Open February–December
Cards accepted: Access, Visa, Diners, Amex, Switch/Delta

Information on accommodation listed in this guide has been supplied by the proprietors. As changes may occur you are advised to check details at the time of booking.

HEART OF ENGLAND

Unicorn Hotel
COMMENDED

Sheep Street, Stow-on-the-Wold,
Cheltenham GL54 1HQ
☎ Cotswold (01451) 830257
Fax (01451) 831090
Forte

17th C coaching inn, well placed for touring the Cotswolds. Business services available.
Bedrooms: 2 single, 14 double, 4 twin
Bathrooms: 20 en-suite

Bed & breakfast per night:	£min	£max
Single	54.00	64.00
Double	108.00	128.00

Half board per person:	£min	£max
Daily	59.00	74.00
Weekly	413.00	518.00

Lunch available
Evening meal 1900 (last orders 2130)
Parking for 50
Cards accepted: Access, Visa, Diners, Amex, Switch/Delta

Wyck Hill House
DE LUXE

Burford Road (A424),
Stow-on-the-Wold, Cheltenham
GL54 1HY
☎ Cotswold (01451) 831936
Fax (01451) 832243
Lyric

Country manor house hotel, set in 100 acres of its own grounds, in the heart of the Cotswolds. 2 miles south of Stow-on-the-Wold on the A424 Stow/Burford road. Splendid restaurant which affords the finest views of the Windrush Valley.

Bedrooms: 1 single, 14 double, 15 twin
Suites available
Bathrooms: 30 en-suite

Bed & breakfast per night:	£min	£max
Single	80.00	180.00
Double	105.00	180.00

Half board per person:	£min	£max
Daily	82.50	112.50

Lunch available
Evening meal 1930 (last orders 2130)
Parking for 100
Cards accepted: Access, Visa, Diners, Amex, Switch/Delta

STRATFORD-UPON-AVON

Warwickshire
Map ref 2B1

Famous as Shakespeare's home town, Stratford's many attractions include his birthplace, New Place where he died, the Royal Shakespeare Theatre and Gallery, "The World of Shakespeare" 30 minute theatre and Hall's Croft (his daughter's house).
Tourist Information Centre ☎ (01789) 293127

Aberfoyle Guest House
Listed COMMENDED

3 Evesham Place,
Stratford-upon-Avon CV37 6HT
☎ Stratford-on-Avon (01789) 295703

Charming bijou Edwardian residence with spacious bedrooms, near town centre. English breakfast. Garage. Non-smokers only, please.
Bedrooms: 1 double, 1 triple
Bathrooms: 2 en-suite

Bed & breakfast per night:	£min	£max
Double	38.00	42.00

Continued ▶

Oxstalls Farm Stud
For Farmhouse Bed & Breakfast

Warwick Road
Stratford on Avon
Warwickshire. CV37 4NR
[01789] 205277

English Tourist Board COMMENDED

The Barn
Built 1840 & a Listed Building

* Also the Old Cowshed has now been renovated into delightful ensuite bedrooms

* Five minutes from the Royal Shakespeare Theatre.
* One mile from town centre Shakespeare properties
* Thoroughbred Stud Farm, overlooking beautiful Welcombe Hills
* Adjacent to 18 hole Golf Course
* All rooms are pleasantly furnished many with ensuite facilities and TV, Tea & Coffee making etc.
* Four poster en suite available
* Convenient for touring the Cotswolds
* Twenty minutes from the N.E.C. Birmingham.
* Additional en suite rooms in the Cow Shed & Stables Complex
* Self Catering Accommodation available
* Easy access from Junction 15 M40.

Prices
From £15.00 per person
to
£25.00 per person

Main House

Oxstalls Farm is situated on the A439. Stratford Road to Warwick. 1 mile from Stratford on Avon

HEART OF ENGLAND

STRATFORD-UPON-AVON
Continued

Parking for 2

Ambleside Guest House
APPROVED

41 Grove Road,
Stratford-upon-Avon CV37 6PB
☎ (01789) 297239 &
Stratford-upon-Avon 295670
Fax (01789) 295670
Picturesque guesthouse, offering a warm welcome to all. Overlooking Firs Park and close to town centre. Delightfully furnished rooms. Private parking.
Bedrooms: 2 single, 2 double, 1 twin, 2 triple
Bathrooms: 3 en-suite, 1 public

Bed & breakfast
per night: £min £max
Single 16.00 24.00
Double 32.00 48.00

Parking for 21
Cards accepted: Access, Visa

The Arden Thistle Hotel
HIGHLY COMMENDED

44 Waterside, Stratford-upon-Avon CV37 6BA
☎ Stratford-on-Avon (01789) 294949
Fax (01789) 415874
Utell International
The ideal location for business or pleasure in the heart of Stratford. Opposite the Royal Shakespeare and Swan Theatres. Bards Restaurant offers traditional English fare, dinner and pre-theatre meals.
Bedrooms: 8 single, 19 double, 34 twin, 2 triple
Bathrooms: 63 en-suite

Bed & breakfast
per night: £min £max
Single 49.00 86.95
Double 98.00 127.90

Lunch available
Evening meal 1745 (last orders 2130)
Parking for 60
Cards accepted: Access, Visa, Diners, Amex

Brett House
COMMENDED

8 Broad Walk, Stratford-upon-Avon CV37 6HS
☎ (01789) 266374
Mature house with spacious rooms,

within easy walking distance of the theatre and town centre. Ample parking.
Bedrooms: 1 single, 1 double, 2 triple
Bathrooms: 2 en-suite, 1 public

Bed & breakfast
per night: £min £max
Single 17.00 18.00
Double 38.00 40.00

Parking for 4

Charlecote Pheasant Country Hotel
COMMENDED

Charlecote CV35 9EW
☎ (01789) 279954
Fax (01789) 470222
Queens Moat/Utell International

19th C farmhouse converted into a comfortable hotel, opposite Charlecote Park. Set in beautiful Warwickshire countryside, 4 miles from Stratford-upon-Avon and Warwick.
Bedrooms: 5 single, 16 double, 6 twin, 40 triple
Suites available
Bathrooms: 67 en-suite

Bed & breakfast
per night: £min £max
Single 70.00 150.00
Double 100.00 150.00

Lunch available
Evening meal 1900 (last orders 2200)
Parking for 130
Cards accepted: Access, Visa, Diners, Amex

The Coach House Hotel
COMMENDED

16/17 Warwick Road, Stratford-upon-Avon CV37 6YW
☎ Stratford-on-Avon (01789) 204109 & 299468
Fax (01789) 415916
Logis of Great Britain
Family-run hotel within 6 minutes' walk of town centre. Adjacent to sports centre and golf-courses. Vaulted Cellar Restaurant.
Bedrooms: 3 single, 8 double, 6 twin, 2 triple, 1 family room
Bathrooms: 20 en-suite, 1 public

Bed & breakfast
per night: £min £max
Single 28.00 57.00
Double 48.00 92.00

Half board per
person: £min £max
Daily 40.00 87.00
Weekly 280.00 374.50

Lunch available
Evening meal 1730 (last orders 2200)
Parking for 32
Cards accepted: Access, Visa, Diners, Amex, Switch/Delta

Courtland Hotel
APPROVED

12 Guild Street,
Stratford-upon-Avon CV37 6RE
☎ Stratford-on-Avon (01789) 292401
Fax (01789) 292401
Personal attention in elegant Georgian house. Town centre situation at rear of Shakespeare's birthplace and 3-4 minutes from theatre. Home-made preserves, antique furniture.
Bedrooms: 1 single, 3 double, 1 twin, 2 family rooms
Bathrooms: 3 en-suite, 2 public

Bed & breakfast
per night: £min £max
Single 20.00 38.00
Double 35.00 50.00

Parking for 3
Cards accepted: Access, Visa, Amex

Craig Cleeve House

67-69 Shipston Road,
Stratford-upon-Avon CV37 7LW
☎ Stratford-on-Avon (01789) 296573
Fax (01789) 299452
Licensed family hotel close to the town centre and theatre, offering friendly service and value for money in comfortable surroundings.
Bedrooms: 2 single, 7 double, 5 twin, 1 family room
Bathrooms: 9 en-suite, 2 public

Bed & breakfast
per night: £min £max
Single 19.50 45.00
Double 39.00 52.00

For further information on accommodation establishments use the coupons at the back of this guide.

HEART OF ENGLAND

Parking for 15
Cards accepted: Access, Visa, Diners, Amex, Switch/Delta

Dukes Hotel
COMMENDED

Payton Street, Stratford-upon-Avon CV37 6UA
☎ Stratford upon Avon (01789) 269300 & 297921
Fax (01789) 414700
Logis of Great Britain

A quiet garden setting, alongside the Stratford canal and within 2 minutes' walk of the town centre and Shakespeare's birthplace. Large private car park.
Bedrooms: 4 single, 10 double, 8 twin
Suites available
Bathrooms: 22 en-suite

Bed & breakfast per night:	£min	£max
Single	47.50	52.50
Double	67.50	115.00

Lunch available
Evening meal 1800 (last orders 2130)
Parking for 30
Cards accepted: Access, Visa, Diners, Amex, Switch/Delta

Dylan Guesthouse
Listed APPROVED

10 Evesham Place, Stratford-upon-Avon CV37 6HT
☎ (01789) 204819
Located in the town, 5 minutes' walk from shops and the Royal Shakespeare Theatre. We are a no-smoking establishment.
Bedrooms: 1 single, 2 double, 1 twin, 1 triple
Bathrooms: 5 en-suite

Bed & breakfast per night:	£min	£max
Single	20.00	23.00
Double	38.00	42.00

Parking for 3

Please check prices and other details at the time of booking.

Eastnor House Hotel
COMMENDED

Shipston Road, Stratford-upon-Avon CV37 7LN
☎ (01789) 268115
Fax (01789) 266516
Comfortable Victorian private hotel, oak panelled and tastefully furnished. Spacious bedrooms with private bathrooms. Centrally located by River Avon, theatre 350 metres.
Bedrooms: 3 double, 2 twin, 2 triple, 2 family rooms
Bathrooms: 9 en-suite

Bed & breakfast per night:	£min	£max
Single	21.00	38.00
Double	42.00	60.00

Parking for 9
Cards accepted: Access, Visa, Amex

Falcon Hotel
COMMENDED

Chapel Street, Stratford-upon-Avon CV37 6HA
☎ Stratford-on-Avon (01789) 279953
Fax (01789) 414260
Queens Moat/Utell International
A magnificently preserved 16th C timbered inn, with a skilfully blended modern extension, large enclosed garden and ample car parking, situated in the heart of Stratford.
Bedrooms: 5 single, 23 double, 31 twin, 13 triple, 1 family room
Bathrooms: 73 en-suite

Bed & breakfast per night:	£min	£max
Single	60.00	99.00
Double	70.00	145.00

Half board per person:	£min	£max
Daily	52.00	75.00
Weekly	315.00	441.00

Lunch available
Evening meal 1800 (last orders 2100)
Parking for 124
Cards accepted: Access, Visa, Diners, Amex, Switch/Delta

Green Haven

217 Evesham Road, Stratford-upon-Avon CV37 9AS
☎ (01789) 297874
Within walking distance of theatre and town centre amenities. Off-street parking. Homely atmosphere, TV in most rooms.
Bedrooms: 3 double, 2 twin
Bathrooms: 2 en-suite, 1 public

Bed & breakfast per night:	£min	£max
Single		20.00
Double	32.00	36.00

Parking for 5
Open February–November

Grosvenor House Hotel
COMMENDED

Warwick Road, Stratford-upon-Avon CV37 6YT
☎ Stratford-on-Avon (01789) 269213
Fax (01789) 266087
Independently-owned Georgian hotel, 5 minutes' walk from town centre, theatres, Shakespeare's birthplace and River Avon. Unique restaurant decor, private car park.
Wheelchair access category 3
Bedrooms: 3 single, 35 double, 14 twin, 7 triple, 1 family room
Suite available
Bathrooms: 60 en-suite

Bed & breakfast per night:	£min	£max
Single	72.00	
Double	95.00	

Half board per person:	£min	£max
Daily	61.45	
Weekly	312.00	

Lunch available
Evening meal 1800 (last orders 2130)
Parking for 50
Cards accepted: Access, Visa, Diners, Amex, Switch/Delta

Hampton Lodge Guest House
APPROVED

38 Shipston Road, Stratford-upon-Avon CV37 7LP
☎ Stratford upon Avon (01789) 299374
Fax (01789) 299374
Refurbished guesthouse. All en-suite rooms with usual facilities. 5 minutes' walk town centre and RSC Theatre. Friendly reception. Private parking.
Bedrooms: 1 single, 2 double, 1 twin, 2 triple
Bathrooms: 6 en-suite

Bed & breakfast per night:	£min	£max
Single	22.00	28.00
Double	32.00	45.00

Evening meal 1800 (last orders 1930)

Continued ▶

HEART OF ENGLAND

STRATFORD-UPON-AVON
Continued

Parking for 8
Cards accepted: Access, Visa, Amex, Switch/Delta

Hardwick House
COMMENDED
1 Avenue Road,
Stratford-upon-Avon CV37 6UY
☎ Stratford-on-Avon (01789) 204307
Fax (01789) 296760

Family-run Victorian guesthouse in a quiet area, a short walk to town, theatre, Shakespearean properties. Non-smoking bedrooms. Large car park.
Bedrooms: 2 single, 7 double, 2 twin, 2 triple, 1 family room
Bathrooms: 13 en-suite, 1 private, 1 public

Bed & breakfast
per night: £min   £max
Single   26.00   32.00
Double   48.00   56.00

Parking for 12
Cards accepted: Access, Visa, Amex, Switch/Delta

Melita Private Hotel
COMMENDED
37 Shipston Road,
Stratford-upon-Avon CV37 7LN
☎ Stratford-on-Avon (01789) 292432
Fax (01789) 204867

Appointed to a high and comfortable standard, managed by caring proprietors offering a warm, friendly atmosphere. Close to town centre and an ideal base for Cotswolds and National Exhibition Centre. Lounge bar and beautiful award-winning garden.
Bedrooms: 3 single, 4 double, 3 twin, 1 triple, 1 family room
Bathrooms: 10 en-suite, 2 private

Bed & breakfast
per night: £min   £max
Single   30.00   49.00
Double   50.00   70.00

Parking for 12
Cards accepted: Access, Visa, Amex

Moonraker House
COMMENDED
40 Alcester Road,
Stratford-upon-Avon CV37 9DB
☎ Stratford-on-Avon (01789) 299346 & 267115
Fax (01789) 295504
Minotel

Family-run, near town centre. Beautifully co-ordinated decor throughout. Some rooms with four-poster beds and garden terrace available for non-smokers.
Bedrooms: 16 double, 2 twin, 4 triple
Bathrooms: 22 en-suite

Bed & breakfast
per night: £min   £max
Single   35.00   50.00
Double   43.00   65.00

Parking for 24
Cards accepted: Access, Visa

Moss Cottage
COMMENDED
61 Evesham Road,
Stratford-upon-Avon CV37 9BA
☎ (01789) 294770

Pauline and Jim Rush welcome you to their charming detached cottage. Walking distance theatre/town. Spacious en-suite accommodation. Hospitality tray, TV. Parking.
Bedrooms: 2 double
Bathrooms: 2 en-suite

Bed & breakfast
per night: £min   £max
Single   25.00   30.00
Double   34.00   42.00

Parking for 3

The Myrtles Bed and Breakfast
Listed COMMENDED
6 Rother Street,
Stratford-upon-Avon CV37 6LU
☎ (01789) 295511
Victorian 3-storey building in town centre. En-suite bedrooms, breakfast room and patio garden.
Bedrooms: 2 double, 1 twin
Bathrooms: 3 en-suite

Bed & breakfast
per night: £min   £max
Single   25.00   35.00
Double   40.00   45.00

Cards accepted: Access, Visa

Nando's
18-19 Evesham Place,
Stratford-upon-Avon CV37 6HT
☎ Stratford-on-Avon (01789) 204907
Fax (01789) 204907
A warm welcome awaits from Pat and Peter. Convenient for theatre, town centre and Shakespeare properties. Full English breakfast.
Bedrooms: 4 single, 7 double, 5 twin, 4 triple
Bathrooms: 13 en-suite, 2 public

Bed & breakfast
per night: £min   £max
Single   18.00   30.00
Double   28.00   44.00

Half board per
person: £min   £max
Daily   21.00   27.00

Evening meal from 1800
Parking for 8
Cards accepted: Access, Visa, Diners, Amex

Newlands
COMMENDED
7 Broad Walk, Stratford-upon-Avon CV37 6HS
☎ (01789) 298449
Fax (01789) 298449
Park your car at Sue Boston's home and take a short walk to the Royal Shakespeare Theatre, town centre and Shakespeare properties.
Bedrooms: 1 single, 1 double, 2 triple
Bathrooms: 3 en-suite, 1 public

Bed & breakfast
per night: £min   £max
Single   19.00   21.00
Double   40.00   44.00

Parking for 2
Cards accepted: Access, Visa, Switch/Delta

All accommodation in this guide has been graded, or is awaiting a grading, by a trained Tourist Board inspector.

HEART OF ENGLAND

Payton Hotel
HIGHLY COMMENDED
6 John Street, Stratford-upon-Avon CV37 6UB
☎ Stratford-on-Avon (01789) 266442
Fax (01789) 266442
Listed Georgian house close to the town centre but in a quiet area. 3 minutes' walking distance from the theatre, Shakespeare Centre and shops. Friendly, personal service.
Bedrooms: 3 double, 2 twin
Bathrooms: 4 en-suite, 1 private shower

Bed & breakfast per night:	£min	£max
Single	38.00	40.00
Double	56.00	58.00

Parking for 3
Cards accepted: Access, Visa, Amex

Peartree Cottage
HIGHLY COMMENDED
7 Church Road, Wilmcote, Stratford-upon-Avon CV37 9UX
☎ (01789) 205889
Fax (01789) 262862
Elizabethan house, furnished with antiques, set in beautiful garden overlooking Mary Arden's house. Pub and restaurant within walking distance.
Bedrooms: 4 double, 2 twin, 1 triple
Bathrooms: 7 en-suite

Bed & breakfast per night:	£min	£max
Single	30.00	30.00
Double	45.00	45.00

Parking for 8

Ravenhurst
2 Broad Walk, Stratford-upon-Avon CV37 6HS
☎ Stratford-on-Avon (01789) 292515

Quietly situated, a few minutes' walk from the town centre and places of historic interest. Comfortable home, with substantial breakfast provided. Four-poster en-suite available.
Bedrooms: 4 double, 1 twin
Bathrooms: 5 en-suite

Bed & breakfast per night:	£min	£max
Double	38.00	50.00

Parking for 4
Cards accepted: Access, Visa, Diners, Amex

Sequoia House
COMMENDED
51-53 Shipston Road, Stratford-upon-Avon CV37 7LN
☎ Stratford-on-Avon (01789) 268852 & 294940
Fax (01789) 414559
Beautifully-appointed private hotel with large car park and delightful garden walk to the theatre, riverside gardens and Shakespeare properties. Fully air-conditioned dining room.
Bedrooms: 2 single, 10 double, 12 twin
Bathrooms: 8 en-suite, 12 private, 3 public

Bed & breakfast per night:	£min	£max
Single	29.00	49.00
Double	39.00	76.00

Lunch available
Parking for 33
Cards accepted: Access, Visa, Diners, Amex, Switch/Delta

The Shakespeare
HIGHLY COMMENDED
Chapel Street, Stratford-upon-Avon CV37 6ER
☎ Stratford-on-Avon (01789) 294771
Fax (01789) 415411
Forte

Dating from the 16th C, this is one of Stratford's most famous timbered buildings. Overnight half-board prices are for a minimum 2-night stay.
Bedrooms: 12 single, 21 double, 30 twin
Bathrooms: 63 en-suite

Bed & breakfast per night:	£min	£max
Single	95.00	110.00
Double	110.00	140.00

Half board per person:	£min	£max
Daily	80.00	87.50
Weekly	480.00	525.00

Lunch available
Evening meal 1800 (last orders 2130)
Parking for 45
Cards accepted: Access, Visa, Diners, Amex, Switch/Delta

The Stag at Redhill
COMMENDED
Alcester Road, Stratford-upon-Avon B49 6NQ
☎ (01789) 764634
Fax (01789) 764431

16th C coaching inn in 4 acres of grounds, 2 miles from Stratford-upon-Avon. Noted a la carte restaurant plus bar meals. En-suite bedrooms with all amenities. Open views.
Bedrooms: 4 single, 5 double, 3 twin
Bathrooms: 12 en-suite

Bed & breakfast per night:	£min	£max
Single	39.50	39.50
Double	58.00	68.00

Lunch available
Evening meal 1900 (last orders 2130)
Parking for 92
Cards accepted: Access, Visa, Diners, Amex

Stratford Court Hotel
HIGHLY COMMENDED
20 Avenue Road, Stratford-upon-Avon CV37 6UX
☎ (01789) 297799
Fax (01789) 262449

Continued ▶

> Half board prices are given per person, but in some cases these may be based on double/twin occupancy.

HEART OF ENGLAND

STRATFORD-UPON-AVON
Continued

Quietly situated Edwardian house, furnished with antiques and set in beautiful gardens with car park. Enjoy the relaxed atmosphere yet only 10 minutes' walk from the town and theatres.
Bedrooms: 4 single, 5 double, 2 twin, 2 triple
Bathrooms: 13 en-suite

Bed & breakfast

per night:	£min	£max
Single	45.00	55.00
Double	75.00	140.00

Half board per

person:	£min	£max
Daily	60.00	85.00
Weekly	400.00	560.00

Lunch available
Evening meal 1800 (last orders 2030)
Parking for 32
Cards accepted: Access, Visa

Stratford Moat House
COMMENDED
Bridgefoot, Stratford-upon-Avon CV37 6YR
☎ Stratford-on-Avon (01789) 279988
Fax (01789) 298589
Queens Moat/Utell International
Modern hotel standing in its own gardens by the River Avon. Close to the town centre and Royal Shakespeare Theatre.
Bedrooms: 66 double, 173 twin, 5 triple, 3 family rooms
Suites available
Bathrooms: 247 en-suite

Bed & breakfast

per night:	£min	£max
Single	70.00	104.50
Double	100.00	145.00

Half board per

person:	£min	£max
Daily	60.00	119.00

Lunch available
Evening meal 1800 (last orders 2200)
Parking for 350
Cards accepted: Access, Visa, Diners, Amex, Switch/Delta

Map references apply to the colour maps at the back of this guide.

Twelfth Night
COMMENDED
Evesham Place, Stratford-upon-Avon CV37 6HT
☎ (01789) 414595
Elegant Victorian villa once owned for almost a quarter of a century by the governors of the Royal Shakespeare Company. Delightfully refurbished for the connoisseur. Non-smokers only, please.
Bedrooms: 6 double
Bathrooms: 6 en-suite

Bed & breakfast

per night:	£min	£max
Double	46.00	58.00

Parking for 7
Cards accepted: Access, Visa

Victoria Spa Lodge
HIGHLY COMMENDED
Bishopton Lane, Stratford-upon-Avon CV37 9QY
☎ (01789) 267985
Fax (01789) 204728

Elegant 19th C English home in country setting, overlooking canal 1.5 miles from town centre. Your hosts are Paul and D'reen Tozer.
Bedrooms: 3 double, 1 twin, 3 family rooms
Bathrooms: 7 en-suite, 1 public

Bed & breakfast

per night:	£min	£max
Single	35.00	40.00
Double	45.00	50.00

Parking for 12
Cards accepted: Access, Visa

WELCOME HOST
This is a nationally recognised customer care programme which aims to promote the highest standards of service and a warm welcome. Establishments who are taking part in this initiative are indicated by the ❀ symbol.

STRETTON
Staffordshire
Map ref 4B3

On the outskirts of Burton upon Trent, beside the Trent and Mersey Canal and River Dove, alongside the Roman road - Ryknild Street.

Dovecliff Hall
HIGHLY COMMENDED
Dovecliff Road, Stretton, Burton upon Trent DE13 0DJ
☎ Burton-upon-Trent (01283) 531818
Fax (01283) 516546
Magnificent Georgian house, with breathtaking views, overlooking the River Dove and set in 7 acres of landscaped gardens in open countryside. Half a mile from A38.
Bedrooms: 1 single, 5 double, 1 twin
Bathrooms: 7 en-suite

Bed & breakfast

per night:	£min	£max
Single	55.00	85.00
Double	95.00	105.00

Lunch available
Evening meal 1900 (last orders 2130)
Parking for 40
Cards accepted: Access, Visa, Diners, Amex, Switch/Delta

STROUD
Gloucestershire
Map ref 2B1

This old town, surrounded by attractive hilly country, has been producing broadcloth for centuries and the local museum has an interesting display on the subject. Many of the mills have been converted into craft centres and for other uses.
Tourist Information Centre ☎ (01453) 765768

Ashleigh House
COMMENDED
Bussage, Stroud GL6 8AZ
☎ Brimscombe (01453) 883944
Fax (01453) 886931
Ideal Cotswold touring centre in beautiful village setting, providing cleanliness and comfort. All rooms en-suite.
Bedrooms: 3 double, 3 twin, 3 triple
Bathrooms: 9 en-suite

HEART OF ENGLAND

Bed & breakfast per night:	£min	£max
Single	25.00	30.00
Double	40.00	50.00

Half board per person:	£min	£max
Daily	33.50	43.50
Weekly	234.50	269.50

Evening meal 1830 (last orders 1900)
Parking for 10

Bell Hotel & Restaurant ⚜
COMMENDED
Wallbridge, Stroud GL5 3JA
☎ (01453) 763556
Fax (01453) 758611
Friendly, family-run hotel. All rooms with TV, tea/coffee facilities and telephone. Bridal suite. A la carte restaurant. Garden and bar on canal.
Bedrooms: 1 single, 7 double, 3 twin, 1 triple
Bathrooms: 10 en-suite, 1 public

Bed & breakfast per night:	£min	£max
Single	30.00	60.00
Double	40.00	80.00

Half board per person:	£min	£max
Daily	39.50	69.50

Lunch available
Evening meal 1900 (last orders 2130)
Parking for 25
Cards accepted: Access, Visa, Diners

Downfield Hotel ⚜
134 Cainscross Road, Stroud GL5 4HN
☎ (01453) 764496
Fax (01453) 753150

Imposing hotel in quiet location. Home cooking. 1 mile from town centre, 5 miles from M5 motorway, junction 13, on main A419 road.
Bedrooms: 4 single, 9 double, 7 twin, 1 triple
Bathrooms: 11 en-suite, 3 public

Bed & breakfast per night:	£min	£max
Single	20.00	29.00
Double	33.00	39.00

Half board per person:	£min	£max
Daily	28.00	35.00
Weekly	196.00	245.00

Evening meal 1830 (last orders 2000)
Parking for 23
Cards accepted: Access, Visa, Diners, Amex, Switch/Delta

The Imperial ⚜
COMMENDED
Station Road, Stroud GL5 3AP
☎ (01453) 764077
Fax (01453) 751314
Ⓖ The Independents
Covered in ivy and over 150 years old, the hotel was originally a coaching and railway inn. Recently refurbished to a high standard.
Bedrooms: 2 single, 9 double, 12 twin, 2 triple
Bathrooms: 25 en-suite

Bed & breakfast per night:	£min	£max
Single	20.00	39.95
Double	40.00	49.50

Half board per person:	£min	£max
Daily	24.75	26.75
Weekly	173.25	187.25

Lunch available
Evening meal 1800 (last orders 2200)
Parking for 20
Cards accepted: Access, Visa, Amex, Switch/Delta

Stonehouse Court Hotel ⚜
HIGHLY COMMENDED
Stonehouse GL10 3RA
☎ Stonehouse (01453) 825155
Fax (01453) 824611

Set in 6 acres of secluded gardens, yet easily accessible being just 1.5 miles from the M5, junction 13. Manor house, dating from 1601, with individually decorated bedrooms. Open fires in winter.
Bedrooms: 4 single, 26 double, 6 twin
Suites available
Bathrooms: 36 en-suite

Bed & breakfast per night:	£min	£max
Single	60.00	70.00
Double	90.00	98.00

Half board per person:	£min	£max
Daily	65.00	73.00

Lunch available
Evening meal 1900 (last orders 2145)
Parking for 204
Cards accepted: Access, Visa, Amex, Switch/Delta

SYMONDS YAT EAST
Hereford and Worcester
Map ref 2A1

Well-known beauty spot where the River Wye loops back on itself in a narrow gorge. It is close to the ruins of Goodrich Castle, the Forest of Dean and the Welsh border.

Royal Hotel ⚜
APPROVED
Symonds Yat East, Ross-on-Wye, Herefordshire HR9 6JL
☎ Symonds Yat (01600) 890238
Fax (01600) 890238
Quiet country house in Alpine-type setting, next to the River Wye. Ideal touring location. Only 6 miles from Ross-on-Wye and Monmouth.
Bedrooms: 1 single, 15 double, 4 twin
Bathrooms: 20 en-suite, 1 public

Bed & breakfast per night:	£min	£max
Single	28.00	45.00
Double	56.00	65.00

Half board per person:	£min	£max
Daily	45.50	62.50
Weekly	250.00	300.00

Lunch available
Evening meal 1900 (last orders 2100)
Parking for 90
Cards accepted: Access, Visa, Amex

National gradings and classifications were correct at the time of going to press but are subject to change. Please check at the time of booking.

HEART OF ENGLAND

SYMONDS YAT WEST
Hereford and Worcester
Map ref 2A1

Jubilee Maze and Exhibition was created here in 1977 to commemorate Queen Elizabeth II's Jubilee, and there are other attractions beside the river. The area of Symonds Yat is a world-renowned beauty spot.

Riversdale Lodge Hotel

Symonds Yat West, Ross-on-Wye, Herefordshire HR9 6BL
☎ Symonds Yat (01600) 890445
Fax (01600) 890445
High standard accommodation, set in 2 acres on the banks of the River Wye. Spectacular views of the rapids and gorge. Traditional food.
Bedrooms: 3 double, 1 twin, 1 family room
Bathrooms: 5 en-suite, 1 public

Bed & breakfast per night:	£min	£max
Single	24.00	29.00
Double	48.00	50.00

Half board per person:	£min	£max
Daily	35.00	40.00
Weekly	240.00	250.00

Lunch available
Evening meal 1900 (last orders 1300)
Parking for 11

Woodlea Hotel
COMMENDED

Symonds Yat West, Ross-on-Wye, Herefordshire HR9 6BL
☎ Symonds Yat (01600) 890206
Fax (01600) 890206
Family-run Victorian country house hotel in a quiet position amid glorious scenery. Imaginative home cooking and friendly service.
Bedrooms: 1 single, 5 double, 1 twin, 1 triple, 1 family room
Bathrooms: 6 en-suite, 2 public

Bed & breakfast per night:	£min	£max
Single	24.00	40.00
Double	48.00	60.00

Half board per person:	£min	£max
Daily	34.50	40.50
Weekly	210.00	255.00

Evening meal 1900 (last orders 1830)
Parking for 9
Cards accepted: Access, Visa

TAMWORTH
Staffordshire
Map ref 4B3

Town with a Norman castle which has a Tudor banqueting hall, and a museum with coins minted at Tamworth in Saxon times when it was an important royal town. The church has a magnificent tower.
Tourist Information Centre ☎ *(01827) 59134*

Drayton Court Hotel

65 Coleshill Street, Fazeley, Tamworth B78 3RG
☎ (01827) 285805
Fax (01827) 284842
One mile from Tamworth and Ski Dome, walking distance of Drayton Manor Park, 3 miles Belfry International Golf Centre, 15 minutes by road to NEC and Birmingham International airport.
Bedrooms: 5 single, 2 double, 4 twin, 1 triple, 3 family rooms
Bathrooms: 13 en-suite, 1 public

Bed & breakfast per night:	£min	£max
Single	40.00	50.00
Double	45.00	55.00

Evening meal 1800 (last orders 2015)
Parking for 16
Cards accepted: Access, Visa

The Plough and Harrow Inn

Atherstone Street, Fazeley, Tamworth B78 3RF
☎ Fazeley (01827) 289596
360 years old. Originally a coaching inn, retaining original ship beam timbers in all rooms and coach house with stables outside. Large gardens and car parking.
Bedrooms: 1 single, 2 double, 3 twin, 1 triple, 1 family room
Bathrooms: 8 en-suite

Bed & breakfast per night:	£min	£max
Single		30.00
Double		50.00

Lunch available
Evening meal 1830 (last orders 2030)
Parking for 50
Cards accepted: Access, Visa, Switch/Delta

TELFORD
Shropshire
Map ref 4A3

New Town named after Thomas Telford, the famous engineer who designed many of the country's canals, bridges and viaducts. It is close to Ironbridge with its monuments and museums to the Industrial Revolution, including restored 18th C buildings.
Tourist Information Centre ☎ *(01952) 291370*

Arleston Inn Hotel
COMMENDED

Arleston Lane, Wellington, Telford TF1 2LA
☎ (01952) 501881
Fax (01952) 506429
Tudor-style building with many exposed beamed ceilings. M54, 5 minutes from junction 6. A la carte and bar menus.
Bedrooms: 2 single, 4 double, 1 twin
Bathrooms: 7 en-suite

Bed & breakfast per night:	£min	£max
Single	31.00	38.00
Double	41.00	48.00

Lunch available
Evening meal 1900 (last orders 2200)
Parking for 40
Cards accepted: Access, Visa

Falcon Hotel
APPROVED

Holyhead Road, Wellington, Telford TF1 2DD
☎ (01952) 255011

Small, family-run 18th C coaching hotel, 10 miles from Shrewsbury, 4 miles from Ironbridge, 18 miles from M6 at the end of M54 (exit 7).
Bedrooms: 2 single, 4 double, 4 twin, 1 family room
Bathrooms: 7 en-suite, 2 public

Bed & breakfast per night:	£min	£max
Single	25.00	36.00
Double	33.00	45.00

HEART OF ENGLAND

Lunch available
Evening meal 1900 (last orders 2100)
Parking for 30
Cards accepted: Access, Visa

Hadley Park House Hotel
HIGHLY COMMENDED
Hadley Park, Telford TF1 4UL
☎ (01952) 677269
Fax (01952) 676938
Enjoy the lavish comforts of this 200-year-old manor house, set in 3 acres of gardens. Friendly welcome and exceptional cuisine.
Bedrooms: 2 single, 5 double, 2 twin
Bathrooms: 9 en-suite

Bed & breakfast per night:	£min	£max
Single	65.00	75.00
Double	85.00	95.00

Lunch available
Evening meal 1900 (last orders 2200)
Parking for 50
Cards accepted: Access, Visa, Diners, Amex, Switch/Delta

The Oaks Hotel & Restaurant
COMMENDED
Redhill, St Georges, Telford TF2 9NZ
☎ (01952) 620126
Fax (01952) 620257
Family-owned hotel, 2.5 miles from Telford town centre. Restaurant, public bar. En-suite bedrooms with telephone, colour TV, tea/coffee facilities.
Bedrooms: 6 single, 3 double, 3 twin
Bathrooms: 12 en-suite

Bed & breakfast per night:	£min	£max
Single	42.00	
Double	52.00	

Half board per person:	£min	£max
Daily	50.00	

Lunch available
Evening meal 1900 (last orders 2130)
Parking for 40
Cards accepted: Access, Visa, Diners, Amex

Park House Hotel
COMMENDED
Park Street, Shifnal TF11 9BA
☎ (01952) 460128
Fax (01952) 461708
Ⓡ Utell International
Magnificent character hotel converted from 2 17th C country houses. Located just a few minutes' drive from exit 4 of the M54. 40 minutes from Birmingham. Leisure facilities.
Bedrooms: 5 single, 30 double, 19 twin
Bathrooms: 54 en-suite

Bed & breakfast per night:	£min	£max
Single	40.00	92.50
Double	80.00	110.50

Half board per person:	£min	£max
Daily	50.00	112.45

Lunch available
Evening meal 1900 (last orders 2130)
Parking for 180
Cards accepted: Access, Visa, Diners, Amex, Switch/Delta

Stone House
Shifnal Road, Priorslee, Telford TF2 9NN
☎ (01952) 290119
Comfortable guesthouse, convenient for M54, station, town centre, Ironbridge and university. Personal attention assured. Good home cooking.
Bedrooms: 2 double, 3 twin
Bathrooms: 5 en-suite

Bed & breakfast per night:	£min	£max
Single	22.00	24.00
Double	36.00	38.00

Half board per person:	£min	£max
Daily		34.00

Evening meal 1800 (last orders 1930)
Parking for 4

TETBURY
Gloucestershire
Map ref 2B2

Small market town with 18th C houses and an attractive 17th C Town Hall. It is a good touring centre with many places of interest nearby including Badminton House and Westonbirt Arboretum.

Calcot Manor
HIGHLY COMMENDED
Beverston, Tetbury GL8 8YJ
☎ (01666) 890391
Fax (01666) 890500
17th C manor house quietly situated in south Cotswolds, with relaxing atmosphere amidst elegant surroundings. Daily half board prices based on minimum two-night stay.
Bedrooms: 9 double, 7 twin, 4 family rooms
Suites available
Bathrooms: 20 en-suite

Bed & breakfast per night:	£min	£max
Single	75.00	100.00
Double	97.00	135.00

Half board per person:	£min	£max
Daily	65.00	82.50
Weekly	364.00	441.00

Lunch available
Evening meal 1930 (last orders 2130)
Parking for 103
Cards accepted: Access, Visa, Diners, Amex

Tavern House
DE LUXE
Willesley, Tetbury GL8 8QU
☎ (01666) 880444
Fax (01666) 880254

Grade II listed Cotswold stone house (formerly a staging post) on the A433 Bath road, 1 mile from Westonbirt Arboretum and 4 miles from Tetbury.
Bedrooms: 3 double, 1 twin
Bathrooms: 4 en-suite

Bed & breakfast per night:	£min	£max
Single	42.50	47.50
Double	57.00	67.00

Parking for 4
Cards accepted: Access, Visa

For ideas on places to visit refer to the introduction at the beginning of this section.

The National Grading and Classification Scheme is explained in full at the back of this guide.

HEART OF ENGLAND

TEWKESBURY
Gloucestershire
Map ref 2B1

Tewkesbury's outstanding possession is its magnificent church, built as an abbey, with a great Norman tower and beautiful 14th C interior. The town stands at the confluence of the Severn and Avon and has many medieval houses, inns and several museums.
Tourist Information Centre ☎ (01684) 295027

Jessop House Hotel
COMMENDED
65 Church Street, Tewkesbury GL20 5RZ
☎ (01684) 292017
Fax (01684) 273076
Logis of Great Britain/Minotel
Georgian house facing the abbey and medieval cottages, peacefully overlooking Tewkesbury's "Ham".
Bedrooms: 3 double, 4 twin, 1 triple
Bathrooms: 8 en-suite
Bed & breakfast
per night:	£min	£max
Single	55.00	55.00
Double	75.00	75.00

Evening meal 1900 (last orders 2030)
Parking for 6
Cards accepted: Access, Visa, Amex

Puckrup Hall Hotel & Golf Club
HIGHLY COMMENDED
Puckrup, Tewkesbury GL20 6EL
☎ (01684) 296200
Fax (01684) 850788

Elegant former Regency manor house in over 140 acres of parkland, close to the M50/M5 intersection.
Bedrooms: 10 single, 55 double, 19 twin
Suites available
Bathrooms: 84 en-suite
Bed & breakfast
per night:	£min	£max
Single		91.00
Double		105.00

Half board per
person:	£min	£max
Daily		85.00

Lunch available
Evening meal 1900 (last orders 2130)
Parking for 200
Cards accepted: Access, Visa, Diners, Amex, Switch/Delta

Tewkesbury Park Hotel Country Club Resort
HIGHLY COMMENDED
Lincoln Green Lane, Tewkesbury GL20 7DN
☎ (01684) 295405
Fax (01684) 292386
Whitbread

Set between the Cotswold and Malvern Hills overlooking the historic town of Tewkesbury with its famous abbey. Extensive leisure facilities and 18-hole golf-course. Prices are for room only; half-board price is for a minimum 2-night stay.
Bedrooms: 10 double, 58 twin, 4 triple, 6 family rooms
Bathrooms: 78 en-suite, 8 public
Bed & breakfast
per night:	£min	£max
Single	79.00	79.00
Double	79.00	79.00

Half board per
person:	£min	£max
Daily	52.00	62.00

Lunch available
Evening meal 1900 (last orders 2145)
Parking for 250
Cards accepted: Access, Visa, Diners, Amex

TOWN INDEX

This can be found at the back of the guide. If you know where you want to stay, the index will give you the page number listing all accommodation in your chosen town, city or village.

TUTBURY
Staffordshire
Map ref 4B3

Small town on the River Dove with an attractive High Street, old houses and the remains of a castle where Mary Queen of Scots was imprisoned.

Ye Olde Dog & Partridge Hotel
COMMENDED
High Street, Tutbury, Burton upon Trent DE13 9LS
☎ Burton upon Trent (01283) 813030
Fax (01283) 813178

Coaching inn with wealth of beams and history. Carvery with grand piano played in the evenings. Beautiful gardens.
Bedrooms: 5 single, 7 double, 4 twin, 1 triple
Bathrooms: 17 en-suite
Bed & breakfast
per night:	£min	£max
Single	55.00	62.50
Double	72.50	78.00

Lunch available
Evening meal 1800 (last orders 2145)
Parking for 100
Cards accepted: Access, Visa, Amex, Switch/Delta

ULLINGSWICK
Hereford and Worcester
Map ref 2A1

Village close to Hereford with its many attractions including the cathedral and the Cider Museum.

The Steppes
HIGHLY COMMENDED
Ullingswick, Hereford HR1 3JG
☎ Hereford (01432) 820424
Fax (01432) 820042
Logis of Great Britain
17th C listed building with oak beams, log fires and inglenook fireplaces. Cordon Bleu cuisine. Intimate atmosphere. En-suite accommodation in restored barns.

HEART OF ENGLAND

Bedrooms: 4 double, 2 twin
Bathrooms: 6 en-suite

Bed & breakfast

per night:	£min	£max
Single	40.00	50.00
Double	70.00	80.00

Half board per

person:	£min	£max
Daily	55.00	60.00
Weekly	350.00	365.00

Evening meal 1930 (last orders 2030)
Parking for 8
Open February–December
Cards accepted: Access, Visa, Amex, Switch/Delta

UTTOXETER
Staffordshire
Map ref 4B2

Small market town, famous for its racecourse. There are half-timbered buildings around the Market Square.

Bank House Hotel
COMMENDED
Church Street, Uttoxeter ST14 8AG
☎ (01889) 566922
Fax (01889) 567565

Listed Georgian town house, tastefully converted, with restaurant, lounge bar and conference facilities.
Bedrooms: 4 single, 8 double, 3 triple
Suites available
Bathrooms: 15 en-suite

Bed & breakfast

per night:	£min	£max
Single	54.50	
Double	65.00	

Half board per

person:	£min	£max
Daily	44.95	

Lunch available
Evening meal 1830 (last orders 2130)
Parking for 16
Cards accepted: Access, Visa, Diners, Amex, Switch/Delta

WALSALL
West Midlands
Map ref 4B3

Industrial town with a magnificent collection of pictures and antiquities in its museum and art gallery, Walsall Leather Museum and Jerome K Jerome birthplace. It has a fine arboretum with lakes and walks and illuminations each September.

Beverley Hotel

58 Lichfield Road, (A461), Walsall WS4 2DJ
☎ (01922) 22999 & 614967
Fax (01922) 724187
Hotel close to motorway network, with special facilities and rates for group bookings. Convenient for National Exhibition Centre.
Bedrooms: 7 single, 8 double, 16 twin, 2 triple
Bathrooms: 33 en-suite

Bed & breakfast

per night:	£min	£max
Single	35.00	60.00
Double	45.00	75.00

Lunch available
Evening meal 1800 (last orders 2130)
Parking for 66
Cards accepted: Access, Visa, Amex, Switch/Delta

The Fairlawns at Aldridge

Little Aston Road, Aldridge, Walsall WS9 0NU
☎ Aldridge (01922) 55122
Fax (01922) 743210
Best Western
Modern hotel in its own grounds, in a quiet, rural location, 20 minutes from Birmingham and 30 minutes from the National Exhibition Centre. Award winning restaurant specialising in fresh fish.
Bedrooms: 3 single, 21 double, 5 twin, 6 triple
Suites available
Bathrooms: 35 en-suite

Bed & breakfast

per night:	£min	£max
Single	45.00	92.50
Double	57.50	99.50

Lunch available
Evening meal 1900 (last orders 2200)
Parking for 82
Cards accepted: Access, Visa, Diners, Amex, Switch/Delta

WARWICK
Warwickshire
Map ref 2B1

Castle rising above the River Avon and 15th C Beauchamp Chapel attached to St Mary's Church, medieval Lord Leycester's Hospital almshouses and several museums. Nearby is Ashorne Hall Nickelodeon and the new National Heritage museum at Gaydon.
Tourist Information Centre ☎ *(01926) 492212*

The Croft
COMMENDED
Haseley Knob, Warwick CV35 7NL
☎ Haseley Knob (01926) 484447
Fax (01926) 484447
Friendly family atmosphere in picturesque rural setting. In Haseley Knob village off the A4177 between Balsall Common and Warwick, convenient for NEC, National Agricultural Centre, Stratford and Coventry. 15 minutes from Birmingham Airport.
Bedrooms: 1 single, 1 double, 1 twin, 2 triple
Bathrooms: 5 en-suite, 2 public

Bed & breakfast

per night:	£min	£max
Single	20.00	30.00
Double	39.00	42.00

Evening meal 1800 (last orders 1900)
Parking for 10
Cards accepted: Access, Visa, Switch/Delta

Crown Hotel

Coventry Road, Warwick CV34 4NT
☎ (01926) 492087
Fax (01926) 410638
Small, family-run coaching inn, 400 years old. Home produced cooking on premises. Two minutes' walk from Warwick Castle.
Bedrooms: 2 single, 6 double, 4 twin, 2 triple
Bathrooms: 14 en-suite

Bed & breakfast

per night:	£min	£max
Single	30.00	40.00
Double	35.00	50.00

Half board per

person:	£min	£max
Daily	40.00	50.00
Weekly	385.00	490.00

Continued ▶

281

HEART OF ENGLAND

WARWICK
Continued

Lunch available
Evening meal 1900 (last orders 2200)
Parking for 12
Cards accepted: Access, Visa, Amex, Switch/Delta

The Glebe at Barford
HIGHLY COMMENDED
Church Street, Barford, Warwick CV35 8BS
☎ Barford (01926) 624218
Fax (01926) 624625
Country village location, 1 mile junction 15 of M40, 7 miles Stratford-upon-Avon. Four-poster beds, traditional cuisine, fine wines, leisure club. All en-suite facilities.
Bedrooms: 5 single, 23 double, 10 twin, 3 triple
Suites available
Bathrooms: 41 en-suite

Bed & breakfast
per night:	£min	£max
Single	60.00	90.00
Double	70.00	110.00

Half board per
person:	£min	£max
Daily	60.00	60.00
Weekly	280.00	280.00

Lunch available
Evening meal 1930 (last orders 2200)
Parking for 67
Cards accepted: Access, Visa, Diners, Amex, Switch/Delta

Honiley Court Hotel
COMMENDED
Honiley, Warwick CV8 1NP
☎ Haseley Knob (01926) 484234
Fax (01926) 484474
Whitbread
Period-style hotel built around an original 16th C inn. Tastefully furnished and with every modern comfort.
Bedrooms: 1 single, 11 double, 50 twin
Bathrooms: 62 en-suite

Bed & breakfast
per night:	£min	£max
Single	30.00	74.50
Double	60.00	82.00

Half board per
person:	£min	£max
Daily	42.00	89.50
Weekly	280.00	626.00

Lunch available
Evening meal 1900 (last orders 2130)
Parking for 110
Cards accepted: Access, Visa, Diners, Amex, Switch/Delta

Lord Leycester Hotel
APPROVED
17 Jury Street, Warwick CV34 4EJ
☎ (01926) 491481
Fax (01926) 491561
Comfortable Georgian hotel. Elegant wood panelled bar and restaurant. Short walk to castle, easy drive to Stratford, Leamington Spa, National Exhibition Centre.
Bedrooms: 13 single, 25 double, 7 twin, 6 triple
Bathrooms: 51 en-suite

Bed & breakfast
per night:	£min	£max
Single	30.00	49.50
Double	50.00	89.50

Lunch available
Evening meal 1900 (last orders 2100)
Parking for 50
Cards accepted: Access, Visa, Diners, Amex, Switch/Delta

Northleigh House
HIGHLY COMMENDED
Five Ways Road, Hatton, Warwick CV35 7HZ
☎ (01926) 484203 & Mobile 0374 101894
Fax (01926) 484006

Comfortable, peaceful country house where the elegant rooms are individually designed and have en-suite bathroom, fridge, kettle and remote-control TV.
Bedrooms: 1 single, 5 double, 1 twin
Bathrooms: 7 en-suite

Bed & breakfast
per night:	£min	£max
Single	30.00	38.00
Double	38.00	55.00

Parking for 8
Open February–November
Cards accepted: Access, Visa

The Old Fourpenny Shop Hotel
HIGHLY COMMENDED
27-29 Crompton Street, Warwick CV34 6HJ
☎ (01926) 491360
Fax (01926) 411892
Recently refurbished, offering real ale, real food and friendly hospitality. Situated in a quiet side street, close to town centre.
Bedrooms: 2 single, 5 double, 3 twin, 1 triple
Bathrooms: 11 en-suite

Bed & breakfast
per night:	£min	£max
Single	32.50	35.00
Double	59.50	65.00

Half board per
person:	£min	£max
Daily	42.50	45.00

Lunch available
Evening meal 1900 (last orders 2130)
Parking for 13
Cards accepted: Access, Visa, Diners, Amex, Switch/Delta

Old Rectory
COMMENDED
Vicarage Lane, Sherbourne, Warwick CV35 8AB
☎ Barford (01926) 624562
Fax (01926) 624995

Georgian country house with beams and inglenooks, furnished with antiques. All bedrooms en-suite, many with brass beds, all with direct-dial telephone and colour TV. Spa bath available. A la carte restaurant, bar, hearty breakfast. Half a mile from M40, junction 15.
Bedrooms: 2 single, 6 double, 3 twin, 2 triple, 1 family room
Bathrooms: 12 en-suite, 2 private

Bed & breakfast
per night:	£min	£max
Single	33.00	45.00
Double	48.00	65.00

Evening meal 1900 (last orders 2030)
Parking for 16
Cards accepted: Access, Visa, Switch/Delta

HEART OF ENGLAND

Park Cottage
HIGHLY COMMENDED

113 West Street, Warwick
CV34 6AH
☎ (01926) 410319
Fax (01926) 410319

Early 16th C Tudor building, near entrance to Warwick Castle. Beautifully restored and retaining all original features.
Bedrooms: 2 double, 1 twin, 2 triple
Bathrooms: 5 en-suite

Bed & breakfast per night:	£min	£max
Single	38.00	45.00
Double	50.00	60.00

Parking for 8
Cards accepted: Access, Visa, Switch/Delta

Shrewley House
HIGHLY COMMENDED

Hockley Road, Shrewley, Warwick
CV35 7AT
☎ Claverdon (0192684) 2549
Fax (0192684) 2216

Listed 17th C farmhouse and home set amidst beautiful 1.5 acre gardens. King-sized four-poster bedrooms, all en-suite, with many thoughtful extras. Four miles from Warwick.
Bedrooms: 3 double
Bathrooms: 3 en-suite

Bed & breakfast per night:	£min	£max
Single	35.00	42.00
Double	52.00	72.00

Evening meal (last orders 1930)
Parking for 17
Cards accepted: Access, Visa

Wheatsheaf Hotel
Listed

54 West Street, Warwick
CV34 6AN
☎ (01926) 492817
Fax (01926) 492817

Former coaching house still retaining its old charm, with brass and copper gleaming from the walls and stone hearth. Adjacent Warwick Castle.
Bedrooms: 1 double, 2 twin, 2 triple, 3 family rooms
Bathrooms: 2 public, 1 private shower

Bed & breakfast per night:	£min	£max
Single	30.00	35.00
Double	40.00	45.00

Lunch available
Evening meal 1800 (last orders 2200)
Parking for 10
Cards accepted: Access, Visa, Diners, Amex, Switch/Delta

WEM
Shropshire
Map ref 4A3

Small town connected with Judge Jeffreys who lived in Lowe Hall. Well known for its ales.

Soulton Hall
COMMENDED

Wem, Shrewsbury SY4 5RS
☎ (01939) 232786
Fax (01939) 234097

Super home cooking and en-suite rooms at this Tudor manor house ensure a relaxing holiday. Moated Domesday site in grounds, private riverside and woodland walks.
Bedrooms: 3 double, 1 twin, 1 triple
Bathrooms: 4 en-suite, 1 private

Bed & breakfast per night:	£min	£max
Single	31.50	38.00
Double	49.00	63.00

Half board per person:	£min	£max
Daily	41.50	48.50
Weekly	315.00	306.50

Evening meal 1900 (last orders 2030)
Parking for 23
Cards accepted: Access, Visa, Diners

ACCESSIBILITY

Look for the symbols which indicate accessibility for wheelchair users. These are described in detail at the front of this guide.

WEOBLEY
Hereford and Worcester
Map ref 2A1

One of the most beautiful Herefordshire villages, full of framed houses, at the heart of the Black and White Trail. It is dominated by the church which has a fine spire.

Ye Olde Salutation Inn
HIGHLY COMMENDED

Market Pitch, Weobley, Hereford
HR4 8SJ
☎ (01544) 318443
Fax (01544) 318216

Traditional black and white country inn overlooking the main Broad Street. Quality home-cooked bar meals and a la carte menu. Inglenook fireplace. Homely atmosphere.
Bedrooms: 2 single, 1 double, 1 twin
Bathrooms: 4 en-suite, 1 public

Bed & breakfast per night:	£min	£max
Single	35.00	
Double	60.00	65.00

Lunch available
Evening meal 1900 (last orders 2130)
Parking for 20
Cards accepted: Access, Visa, Diners, Amex, Switch/Delta

The symbol after an establishment name indicates that it is a Regional Tourist Board member.

Information on accommodation listed in this guide has been supplied by the proprietors. As changes may occur you are advised to check details at the time of booking.

HEART OF ENGLAND

WETTON
Staffordshire
Map ref 4B2

High-lying village with many old limestone buildings and some of Staffordshire's most glorious countryside around it. Near here one of the country's most spectacular sights, Thor's Cave, gapes from a limestone precipice in the Manifold Valley.

Croft Cottage
COMMENDED

Wetton, Ashbourne, Derbyshire DE6 2AF
☎ Alstonfield (01335) 310402
18th C cottage set in three-quarters of an acre of land surrounded by working farms. Close to Dove/Manifold Valleys. Ideal for walking.
Bedrooms: 2 double, 1 twin
Bathrooms: 2 en-suite, 1 public

Bed & breakfast per night:	£min	£max
Single	15.00	18.00
Double	30.00	36.00

Half board per person:	£min	£max
Daily	28.00	30.00
Weekly	176.40	189.00

Lunch available
Evening meal 1700 (last orders 1900)
Parking for 6

WISHAW
Warwickshire
Map ref 4B3

The Belfry
Wishaw B76 9PR
☎ Curdworth (01675) 470301
Fax (01675) 470178
More than just a golfer's paradise. Famous for 1985, 1989 and 1993 Ryder Cup matches, set in 500 acres with 2 golf courses, Brabazon and Derby, and a third under construction (the PGA National Course). Floodlit 17-bay driving range. Conference rooms, superb leisure centre nightclub in grounds.
Bedrooms: 4 single, 133 double, 118 twin, 12 family rooms
Suites available
Bathrooms: 267 en-suite

Bed & breakfast per night:	£min	£max
Single	130.00	160.00
Double	160.00	190.00

Half board per person:	£min	£max
Daily		85.00

Lunch available
Evening meal 1830 (last orders 2230)
Parking for 1500
Cards accepted: Access, Visa, Diners, Amex

WOLVERHAMPTON
West Midlands
Map ref 4B3

Modern industrial town with a long history, a fine parish church and an excellent art gallery. There are several places of interest in the vicinity including Moseley Old Hall and Wightwick Manor with its William Morris influence.
Tourist Information Centre ☎ (01902) 312051

Ely House
COMMENDED

53 Tettenhall Road, Wolverhampton WV3 9NB
☎ (01902) 311311
Fax (01902) 21098
Minotel/The Independents
Fine imposing Georgian building, fully restored, in a good central position adjacent to motorway network. Ideal base for touring the West Midlands.
Bedrooms: 6 single, 6 double, 7 twin
Bathrooms: 19 en-suite

Bed & breakfast per night:	£min	£max
Single	42.00	48.00
Double	52.00	68.00

Lunch available
Evening meal 1900 (last orders 2100)
Parking for 16
Cards accepted: Access, Visa, Diners, Amex, Switch/Delta

Featherstone Farm
Listed COMMENDED

New Road, Featherstone, Wolverhampton WV10 7NW
☎ (01902) 725371 & Mobile 0836 315258
Fax (01902) 731741
17th C farmhouse with listed barn/stables completely refurbished. Open fires. Near M6 and M54, and close to Weston Hall. Restaurant offering Indian cuisine.
Bedrooms: 5 double, 4 twin
Suites available
Bathrooms: 9 en-suite, 1 public

Bed & breakfast per night:	£min	£max
Single	30.00	45.00
Double	45.00	85.00

Half board per person:	£min	£max
Daily	45.00	65.00
Weekly	295.00	400.00

Lunch available
Evening meal 1800 (last orders 2100)
Parking for 62
Cards accepted: Access, Visa, Switch/Delta

Patshull Park Hotel Golf and Country Club
COMMENDED

Patshull Park, Pattingham, Wolverhampton WV6 7HR
☎ Pattingham (01902) 700100
Fax (01902) 700874
Modern, attractive country hotel set in picturesque estate with own golf-course and fishing lakes. Health and fitness complex includes sauna, indoor pool and solarium. 6 miles from junction 3 of M54.
Bedrooms: 7 double, 38 twin, 4 triple
Suite available
Bathrooms: 49 en-suite, 4 public

Bed & breakfast per night:	£min	£max
Single	59.00	69.00
Double	59.00	69.00

Lunch available
Evening meal 1930 (last orders 2130)
Parking for 200
Cards accepted: Access, Visa, Diners, Amex, Switch/Delta

Establishments should be open throughout the year, unless otherwise stated.

The symbols in each entry give information about services and facilities. A 'key' to these symbols appears at the back of this guide.

HEART OF ENGLAND

WORCESTER
Hereford and Worcester
Map ref 2B1

Lovely riverside city dominated by its Norman and Early English cathedral, King John's burial place. Many old buildings including the 15th C Commandery and the 18th C Guildhall. There are several museums and the Royal Worcester porcelain factory.
Tourist Information Centre ☎ (01905) 726311 or 723471

Abbott Accommodation Bed and Breakfast
Listed
85 Bromyard Road, Worcester WR2 5BZ
☎ (01905) 425271
Fax (01905) 427225
Quiet and homely guesthouse on the west side of St John's, 10 minutes from the cathedral, cricket ground and racecourse. 2 miles to Elgar's birthplace.
Bedrooms: 1 single, 2 double, 1 twin, 2 triple
Bathrooms: 6 en-suite, 1 public

Bed & breakfast per night:	£min	£max
Single	20.00	
Double	40.00	

Half board per person:	£min	£max
Daily	30.00	
Weekly	210.00	

Evening meal (last orders 2200)
Parking for 9

Bank House Hotel, Golf & Country Club
COMMENDED
Hereford Road, Bransford, Worcester WR6 5JD
☎ Bransford (01886) 833551
Fax (01886) 832461
Sympathetically converted country house hotel and golf course set in 123 acres of countryside 3 miles from Worcester. On A4103 Worcester to Hereford road, close to many local attractions.
Bedrooms: 11 single, 32 double, 23 twin
Suites available
Bathrooms: 66 en-suite

Bed & breakfast per night:	£min	£max
Single	57.50	57.50
Double	75.00	75.00

Half board per person:	£min	£max
Daily	65.00	65.00
Weekly	399.00	399.00

Lunch available
Evening meal 1900 (last orders 2145)
Parking for 300
Cards accepted: Access, Visa, Diners, Amex, Switch/Delta

Fownes Hotel
COMMENDED
City Walls Road, Worcester WR1 2AP
☎ (01905) 613151
Fax (01905) 23742
Located in the city centre near the cathedral, river and Commandery. Also close to shopping centre, cricket ground and racecourse.
Bedrooms: 13 single, 16 double, 29 twin, 3 triple
Suites available
Bathrooms: 61 en-suite

Bed & breakfast per night:	£min	£max
Single	38.00	82.50
Double	76.00	100.00

Half board per person:	£min	£max
Daily	39.00	100.00

Lunch available
Evening meal 1930 (last orders 2200)
Parking for 94
Cards accepted: Access, Visa, Diners, Amex, Switch/Delta

Loch Ryan Hotel
119 Sidbury, Worcester WR5 2DH
☎ (01905) 351143
Fax (01905) 351143
Historic hotel, once home of Bishop Gore, close to cathedral, Royal Worcester Porcelain factory and Commandery. Attractive terraced garden. Imaginative food. Holders of Heartbeat and Worcester City clean food awards.
Bedrooms: 1 single, 3 double, 5 twin, 1 family room
Bathrooms: 10 en-suite

Bed & breakfast per night:	£min	£max
Single	40.00	45.00
Double	55.00	65.00

Half board per person:	£min	£max
Daily	43.50	

Evening meal 1800 (last orders 1900)
Parking for 10
Cards accepted: Access, Visa, Diners, Amex

The Maximillian Hotel
Shrub Hill Road, Shrub Hill, Worcester WR4 9EF
☎ (01905) 23867 & 21694
Fax (01905) 724935
Homely atmosphere in newly refurbished family-run hotel at the edge of city centre. Easy access to Shrub Hill station and M5, junction 7.
Bedrooms: 8 single, 5 double, 4 twin
Bathrooms: 13 en-suite, 4 private, 1 public

Bed & breakfast per night:	£min	£max
Single	34.65	38.50
Double	45.90	51.00

Lunch available
Evening meal 1900 (last orders 2330)
Parking for 15
Cards accepted: Access, Visa, Diners, Amex

Park House Hotel
COMMENDED
12 Droitwich Road, Worcester WR3 7LJ
☎ (01905) 21816 & 612029
Fax (01905) 612178
Family-run Victorian guesthouse, near city centre, racecourse and cricket. Close junction 6 of M5. Friendly, informal atmosphere, refurbished with Laura Ashley designs.
Bedrooms: 2 single, 2 double, 2 twin, 1 triple
Bathrooms: 5 en-suite, 1 public

Bed & breakfast per night:	£min	£max
Single	24.00	30.00
Double	34.00	42.00

Lunch available
Evening meal 1830 (last orders 1930)
Parking for 10
Cards accepted: Access, Visa

> A key to symbols can be found inside the back cover flap.

HEART OF ENGLAND

WORCESTER
Continued

Wyatt Guest House
♛

40 Barbourne Road, Worcester
WR1 1HU
☎ (01905) 26311
Small, family-run guesthouse close to city centre, parks, river and racecourse. Situated on A38, half a mile north of city centre.
Bedrooms: 2 single, 3 double, 1 twin, 1 triple, 1 family room
Bathrooms: 4 en-suite, 1 public, 1 private shower

Bed & breakfast per night:	£min	£max
Single	18.00	20.00
Double	32.00	34.00

Cards accepted: Access, Visa

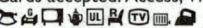

WOTTON-UNDER-EDGE
Gloucestershire
Map ref 2B2

Small town in the southern Cotswolds. Berkeley Castle is within easy reach.

Burrows Court Hotel
♛♛♛

Nibley Green, North Nibley, Dursley
GL11 6AZ
☎ Dursley (01453) 546230
18th C country house hotel in idyllic setting. Peaceful, quiet and relaxing. All en-suite, exposed beams, home-cooked food, acre of gardens.
Bedrooms: 1 single, 7 double, 2 twin
Bathrooms: 10 en-suite

Bed & breakfast per night:	£min	£max
Single	27.50	31.50
Double	40.00	48.00

Half board per person:	£min	£max
Daily	39.50	43.50
Weekly	172.00	240.00

Evening meal 1900 (last orders 2030)
Parking for 20
Open February–November
Cards accepted: Access, Visa, Amex

WYE VALLEY
See under Goodrich, Hereford, Ross-on-Wye, Symonds Yat East, Symonds Yat West

---

AT-A-GLANCE SYMBOLS

Symbols at the end of each accommodation entry give useful information about services and facilities. A key to symbols can be found inside the back cover flap.

Keep this open for easy reference.

MIDDLE ENGLAND

Middle England can be enjoyed on foot, by car - and in some places, by canal boat.

From the heights of the High Peaks to the tranquil shire countryside, this region is as rich in history as it is in colour and contrast.

The English Civil War began in Middle England; the tapestry of history is closely woven - with historic houses, heritage centres and museums bearing witness.

Don't miss Lincoln or the Lace-making city of Nottingham, elegant Buxton spa or Skegness by the sea! And then there's Sherwood Forest, haunt of the legendary Robin Hood...

FOR MORE INFORMATION CONTACT:
East Anglia Tourist Board *(Lincolnshire)*
Toppesfield Hall, Hadleigh, Suffolk IP7 5DN
Tel: (01473) 822922 **Fax:** (01473) 823063

Heart of England Tourist Board *(Derbyshire, Nottinghamshire, Leicestershire, Northamptonshire)*
Lark Hill Road, Worcester WR5 2EZ
Tel: (01905) 763436 or 763439
Fax: (01905) 763450

Where to Go in Middle England -
see pages 288-291

Where to Stay in Middle England -
see pages 292-320

MIDDLE ENGLAND
Where to Go and What to See

You will find hundreds of interesting places to visit during your stay in Middle England, just some of which are listed in these pages. The number against each name will help you locate it on the map (page 291). Contact any Tourist Information Centre in the region for more ideas on days out in Middle England.

1 Gainsborough Old Hall
Parnell Street, Gainsborough,
Lincolnshire DN21 2NB
Tel: (01427) 612669
Late medieval timber-framed manor house built c1460, with fine medieval kitchen. Displays on the building and its restoration.

2 World Of Robin Hood
Haughton, Retford,
Nottinghamshire DN22 8DZ
Tel: (01623) 860210
A hands-on medieval experience including The Crusaders, Medieval Market Place, Sherwood Forest, Castle Dungeons Armoury and the Great Hall.

3 Chatsworth House and Garden
Bakewell, Derbyshire DE45 1PP
Tel: (01246) 582204
Built 1687-1707. Collection of fine pictures, books, drawings, furniture. Garden laid out by Capability Brown with fountains and cascade. Farmyard and adventure playground.

4 Lincoln Cathedral
Lincoln LN2 1PZ
Tel: (01522) 544544
Medieval Gothic cathedral of outstanding historical and architectural merit.

5 Museum of Lincolnshire Life
Burton Road,
Lincoln LN1 3LY
Tel: (01522) 528448
The region's largest social history museum. Agricultural, industrial and social history of Lincolnshire from a teapot to a World War I tank. Victorian room setting.

6 The Heights of Abraham
Matlock Bath,
Matlock,
Derbyshire DE4 3PD
Tel: (01629) 582365
Cable car ride across Derwent Valley gives access to Alpine Centre with refreshments, superb views, woodland, prospect tower and two show caves.

7 The National Tramway Museum
Crich, Matlock,
Derbyshire DE4 5DP
Tel: (01773) 852565
Collection of 50 trams from Britain and overseas built 1873-1957. Tram rides on one-mile route, period street scene, depots, power station, workshops, exhibitions.

8 Midland Railway Centre
Butterley Station, Ripley,
Derby DE5 3QZ
Tel: (01773) 747674
Over 25 locomotives and 80 items of historic rolling stock of Midland and LMS origin. Steam-hauled passenger service, museum site. Country and farm parks.

9 American Adventure
Pit Lane, Ilkeston,
Derbyshire DE7 5SX
Tel: (01773) 531521
American theme park with more than 100 rides including Nightmare Niagara Log Flume, Rocky

Mountain, Rapids Ride, The Missile, Motion Master Simulator Cinema and many other attractions.

10 Southwell Minster
Bishop's Drive,
Southwell,
Nottinghamshire NG25 0JP
Tel: (01636) 812649
Building begun c1108. Saxon tympanum, Norman nave and crossing, early English choir. Outstanding foliage carving in Chapter House. Archbishop's Palace ruins.

11 The Galleries of Justice
Shire Hall,
High Pavement,
Nottingham NG1 1HN
Tel: (0115) 952 0555
Condemned! is the visitor attraction at the Galleries of Justice which offers a major crime and punishment experience. Based in and around former 19thC courthouse.

12 Newstead Abbey
Linby, Nottingham NG15 8GE
Tel: (01623) 793557
800-year-old remains of priory church, converted into country house in 16thC. Home of Lord Byron with possessions and manuscripts. Parkland, lake, gardens.

13 Nottingham Industrial Museum
Courtyard Buildings,
Wollaton Park,
Nottingham NG8 2AE
Tel: (0115) 928 4602
18thC stables presenting history of Nottingham's industries: printing, pharmacy, hosiery and lace. Victorian beam engine, horse gin, transport.

14 Belvoir Castle
Belvoir, Lincolnshire NG32 1PD
Tel: (01476) 870262
The present castle is fourth to be built on this site and dates from 1816. Art treasures including works by Poussin, Rubens, Holbein and Reynolds. Museum of Queen's Royal Lancers.

15 Belton House, Park & Gardens
Belton, Grantham,
Lincolnshire NG32 2LS
Tel: (01476) 66116
The crowning achievement of Restoration country house architecture, built in 1685-88 for Sir John Brownlow. Alterations by James Wyatt in 1777.

16 Sudbury Hall
Sudbury, Derbyshire DE6 5HT
Tel: (01283) 585305
Grand 17thC house. Plasterwork ceilings, ceiling paintings, carved staircase and overmantel. Museum of Childhood in old servants' wing.

17 Great Central Railway
Great Central Station,
Great Central Road,
Loughborough,
Leicestershire LE11 1RW
Tel: (01509) 230726
Preserved main line steam railway operating over 8.5 miles from Loughborough to Leicester North.

18 Ye Olde Pork Pie Shoppe
Dickinson & Morris Ltd,
10 Nottingham Street,
Melton Mowbray,
Leicestershire LE13 1NW
Pork pie shop and bakery in 17C building. History of shop and Melton Mowbray Pork Pie industry. Demonstrations of traditional craft of hand raising pork pies.

19 Spalding Tropical Forest
Glenside North,
Pinchbeck,
Spalding,
Lincolnshire PE11 3SD
Tel: (01775) 710882
One half-acre glass house enclosing a tropical environment. Four zones including tropical rain forest, Japanese and Australian tropical plants and Mediterranean temperate zone.

20 Oakham Castle
Market Place, Oakham,
Leicestershire
Tel: (01572) 723654
Splendid 12thC Great Hall of fortified manor house. Unique horseshoe forfeits left by peers of the realm.

21 Newarke Houses Museum
The Newarke, Leicester LE2 7BY
Tel: (0116) 247 3222
Local history and crafts from 1485. Toys and games, clocks, mechanical instruments. 19thC street scene, early 20thC shop. Feature on 19thC giant Daniel Lambert.

22 Twycross Zoo
Twycross, Near Atherstone,
Warwickshire CV9 3PX
Tel: (01827) 880250
Gorillas, orangutans, chimpanzees, modern gibbon complex, elephants, lions, cheetahs, giraffes, reptile house. Pets corner. Rides.

23 Rockingham Castle
Rockingham,
Leicestershire LE16 8TH
Tel: (01536) 770240
Elizabethan house within walls of Norman castle. Fine pictures. Extensive views and gardens with roses and ancient yew hedge.

24 Lamport Hall
Lamport,
Northampton NN6 9HD
Tel: (01604) 686272
17th/18thC house, home of Isham family, mainly John Webb and Francis Smith. Beautiful high room (1655) fine library (1732). Garden home to the 1st Gnome in England.

25 Holdenby House and Gardens
Holdenby,
Northampton NN6 8DJ
Tel: (01604) 770074
Remains of Elizabethan palace and gardens. Fragrant border, falconry centre, armoury, 17thC homestead, tea room and shop.

26 National Dragonfly Museum
Ashton Mill, Ashton,
Northampton PE8 5LB
Tel: (01832) 272427
Discover the wonder and plight of dragonflies. See also the Victorian diesel hydro-electric generating pumping hall and craft exhibitions. Gift shop.

27 Sulgrave Manor
Sulgrave, Near Banbury,
Oxfordshire OX17 2SD
Tel: (01295) 760205
Small manor house of Shakespeare's time, with furniture of period. Fine kitchen. Early English home of ancestors of George Washington.

FIND OUT MORE
Further information about holidays and attractions in Middle England is available from either:
East Anglia Tourist Board,
Toppesfield Hall,
Hadleigh,
Suffolk IP7 5DN.
Tel: (01473) 822922
or **Heart of England Tourist Board**,
Lark Hill Road,
Worcester WR5 2EZ
Tel: (01905) 763436 or 763439

These publications are available free from the East Anglia Tourist Board:
- **Great Escapes** - short breaks
- **Touring Map**

These publications are available free from the Heart of England Tourist Board:
- **Places to Visit** (chargeable)
- **Peak District and Derbyshire Guide**
- **Rutland, Rockingham Forest and Stamford Guide**

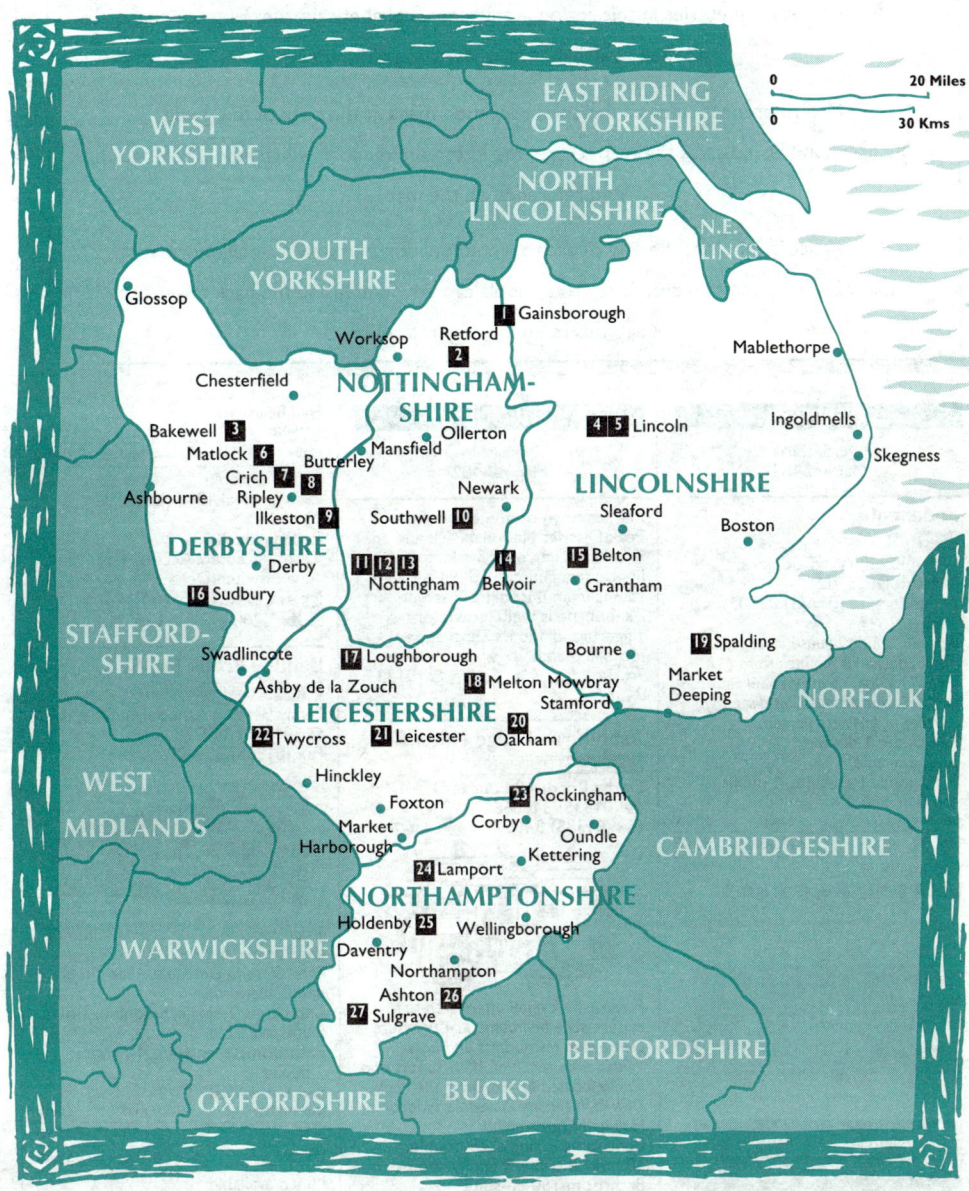

MIDDLE ENGLAND

WHERE TO STAY (MIDDLE ENGLAND)

Accommodation entries in this region are listed in alphabetical order of place name, and then in alphabetical order of establishment.

Map references refer to the colour location maps at the back of this guide. The first number indicates the map to use; the letter and number which follow refer to the grid reference on the map.

At-a-glance symbols at the end of each accommodation entry give useful information about services and facilities. A key to symbols can be found inside the back cover flap. Keep this open for easy reference.

ALFRETON
Derbyshire
Map ref 4B2

Bodencote
Lynam Road, Wingfield Park, Alfreton DE55 7LS
☎ Ambergate (01773) 853071 & 0860 477699

Victorian country house in peaceful surroundings, 10 minutes from M1. "Peak Practice" country. Excellent base for tourist attractions. Suit discerning traveller or business person.
Bedrooms: 1 double
Suite available
Bathrooms: 1 en-suite, 1 public

Bed & breakfast
per night:	£min	£max
Double	36.00	50.00

Parking for 4

A key to symbols can be found inside the back cover flap.

Information on accommodation listed in this guide has been supplied by the proprietors. As changes may occur you are advised to check details at the time of booking.

ASHBOURNE
Derbyshire
Map ref 4B2

Market town on the edge of the Peak District National Park and an excellent centre for walking. Its impressive church with 212-ft spire stands in an unspoilt old street. Ashbourne is well-known for gingerbread and its Shrovetide football match.
Tourist Information Centre ☎ (01335) 343666

Ashbourne Lodge Hotel
COMMENDED
Derby Road, Ashbourne DE6 1XH
☎ (01335) 346666
Fax (01335) 346549

Purpose-built hotel offering en-suite cottage-style bedrooms, luxury leisure centre, two restaurants and bars. Within easy reach of Alton Towers and ideally located for exploring the Peak District, including Dovedale, Haddon Hall and Chatsworth.
Bedrooms: 2 single, 25 double, 10 twin, 8 triple, 5 family rooms
Bathrooms: 50 en-suite

Bed & breakfast
per night:	£min	£max
Single	49.00	70.00
Double	76.00	89.00

Half board per
person:	£min	£max
Daily	64.00	85.00

Lunch available
Evening meal 1900 (last orders 2200)
Parking for 200
Cards accepted: Access, Visa, Diners, Amex, Switch/Delta

Bentley Brook Inn
COMMENDED
Fenny Bentley, Ashbourne DE6 1LF
☎ (01335) 350278
Fax (01335) 350422

Traditional family-run country inn with large garden in Peak District National Park. Close to Dovedale, Alton Towers and Chatsworth.
Bedrooms: 1 single, 5 double, 3 twin
Suites available
Bathrooms: 6 en-suite, 1 private, 2 public

Bed & breakfast
per night:	£min	£max
Single	32.50	37.50
Double	47.50	57.50

Lunch available
Evening meal 1900 (last orders 2130)
Parking for 60
Cards accepted: Access, Visa, Diners, Amex, Switch/Delta

MIDDLE ENGLAND

Callow Hall Country House Hotel & Restaurant ⋒

👑👑👑 HIGHLY COMMENDED

Mappleton, Ashbourne DE6 2AA
☎ (01335) 343403 & 342412
Fax (01335) 343624

Half a mile from the centre of Ashbourne and set in an elevated position in unspoilt countryside, surrounded by its own woodland and overlooking the valleys of the Bentley Brook and the River Dove.
Bedrooms: 10 double, 6 twin
Suite available
Bathrooms: 16 en-suite

Bed & breakfast per night:	£min	£max
Single	65.00	85.00
Double	95.00	120.00

Half board per person:	£min	£max
Daily	78.00	90.00
Weekly	464.00	516.00

Evening meal 1900 (last orders 2130)
Parking for 50
Cards accepted: Access, Visa, Diners, Amex

🛌♿🏠📞📺🚭💰💲🍽🛏♿
🚭🛁40 🅿🚶🐾🐕🎿🅿️🚬🏊

The Green Man Royal Hotel ⋒

St John Street, Ashbourne DE6 1GH
☎ (01335) 345783
Fax (01335) 346613

16th C town centre coaching inn, totally refurbished yet retaining its old character and charm. Situated at the gateway to the Peak District.
Bedrooms: 4 single, 5 double
Bathrooms: 9 en-suite

Bed & breakfast per night:	£min	£max
Single	34.50	39.50
Double	39.50	59.50

Half board per person:	£min	£max
Daily	41.50	46.50
Weekly	260.50	300.00

Lunch available
Evening meal 1800 (last orders 2030)
Parking for 44
Cards accepted: Access, Visa, Amex

🛌📞🏠📞♿💲📺💰🛁350 🅿
🚭 DAP 🚬🏊🚬

ASHBY-DE-LA-ZOUCH

Leicestershire
Map ref 4B3

Lovely market town with late 15th C church, impressive ruined 15th C castle, an interesting small museum and a wide, sloping main street with Georgian buildings. Twycross Zoo is nearby.
Tourist Information Centre ☎ (01530) 411767

Smisby Manor

👑👑👑 COMMENDED

Annwell Lane, Ashby-de-la-Zouch LE65 2TA
☎ (01530) 415881
Fax (01530) 411914

16th C manor house overlooking Ivanhoe tournament fields. Large lawned gardens. Close to Calke Abbey, Staunton Harold, and convenient for Alton Towers and Donington Park.
Bedrooms: 1 double, 2 twin
Bathrooms: 3 en-suite

Bed & breakfast per night:	£min	£max
Single	30.00	35.00
Double		50.00

Lunch available
Evening meal 1800 (last orders 2130)
Parking for 30
Cards accepted: Access, Visa

🛌🏠📞♿💲💰🛁30 🅿♻
🚭🍽🚬🏊

BAKEWELL

Derbyshire
Map ref 4B2

Pleasant market town, famous for its pudding. It is set in beautiful countryside on the River Wye and is an excellent centre for exploring the Derbyshire Dales, the Peak District National Park, Chatsworth and Haddon Hall.
Tourist Information Centre ☎ (01629) 813227

The Ashford Hotel and Restaurant ⋒

👑👑 COMMENDED

Church Street, Ashford in the Water, Bakewell DE4 1QB
☎ (01629) 812725
Fax (01629) 814749

Traditional, friendly country hotel where you will receive personal attention throughout your stay. There are open fires and a wealth of oak beams. An ideal location to relax.
Bedrooms: 1 single, 5 double, 1 twin
Bathrooms: 7 private

Bed & breakfast per night:	£min	£max
Single	45.00	50.00
Double	70.00	90.00

Half board per person:	£min	£max
Daily	50.00	60.00
Weekly	297.50	332.50

Lunch available
Evening meal 1900 (last orders 2130)
Parking for 45
Cards accepted: Access, Visa, Diners, Amex, Switch/Delta

🛌🐾🏠📞💲📺💰💲🛁🍽🚭🛏
🌸🚬🏊 SP 🚬

Castle Cliffe Private Hotel ⋒

👑👑 COMMENDED

Monsal Head, Bakewell DE45 1NL
☎ Great Longstone (01629) 640258
A Victorian stone house overlooking beautiful Monsal Dale. Noted for its friendly atmosphere, good food and exceptional views.
Bedrooms: 3 double, 4 twin, 2 family rooms
Bathrooms: 6 en-suite, 2 public, 3 private showers

Bed & breakfast per night:	£min	£max
Single	27.00	37.00
Double	46.00	54.00

Half board per person:	£min	£max
Daily	39.00	49.00
Weekly	225.00	260.00

Evening meal 1900 (last orders 1700)
Parking for 15
Cards accepted: Access, Visa

🛌♿💲💰🛁📺💲🛁15 🅿♻
🍽🚬🏊 SP ⓒ

The Croft Country House Hotel ⋒

👑👑👑 HIGHLY COMMENDED

Great Longstone, Bakewell DE45 1TF
☎ Great Longstone (01629) 640278
Family-run hotel, centrally located. Freshly prepared food, an imaginative wine list and personal service will help make your stay a memorable one.
Wheelchair access category 3⚛
Bedrooms: 1 single, 6 double, 2 twin
Bathrooms: 9 en-suite

Continued ▶

MIDDLE ENGLAND

BAKEWELL
Continued

Bed & breakfast per night:	£min	£max
Single	60.00	60.00
Double	97.50	97.50

Half board per person:	£min	£max
Daily	70.25	70.25
Weekly	382.50	382.50

Evening meal 1930 (last orders 1900)
Parking for 30
Open February–December
Cards accepted: Access, Visa

East Lodge Country House Hotel and Restaurant
HIGHLY COMMENDED
Rowsley, Matlock DE4 2EF
☎ Matlock (01629) 734474
Fax (01629) 733949
Logis of Great Britain
Tastefully furnished country house hotel and restaurant, set in 10 acres of grounds close to Chatsworth, Haddon Hall and the market town of Bakewell.
Bedrooms: 3 single, 6 double, 6 twin
Bathrooms: 15 en-suite

Bed & breakfast per night:	£min	£max
Single	60.00	60.00
Double	78.00	94.00

Half board per person:	£min	£max
Daily	57.00	65.00

Lunch available
Evening meal 1915 (last orders 2030)
Parking for 30
Cards accepted: Access, Visa, Amex, Switch/Delta

WELCOME HOST
This is a nationally recognised customer care programme which aims to promote the highest standards of service and a warm welcome. Establishments who are taking part in this initiative are indicated by the symbol.

BASLOW
Derbyshire
Map ref 4B2

Small village on the River Derwent with a stone-built toll-house and a packhorse bridge. Chatsworth, home of the Duke of Devonshire, is nearby.

Wheatsheaf Hotel
COMMENDED
Netherend, Baslow, Bakewell DE4 1SR
☎ Chesterfield (01246) 582240
Traditional stone-built inn in the heart of the Peak District. Oak beams, home-cooked food and an open fire in winter. Convenient for visitors to Chatsworth House.
Bedrooms: 2 double, 3 twin
Bathrooms: 3 en-suite, 2 private, 1 public

Bed & breakfast per night:	£min	£max
Single	25.00	30.00
Double	35.00	40.00

Half board per person:	£min	£max
Daily	29.50	42.00
Weekly	206.50	294.00

Lunch available
Evening meal 1800 (last orders 2130)
Parking for 100

BEESTON
Nottinghamshire
Map ref 4C2

Within easy reach of Nottingham's city centre, with its castle, museums, shopping and entertainments, and close to the university.

The Grove Guest House
8 Grove Street, Beeston, Nottingham NG9 1JL
☎ Nottingham (0115) 9259854
Small, friendly Victorian guesthouse, close to GPT, Plessey, Boots, university and tennis centre. Four miles from M1 junction 25, 6 miles East Midlands International Airport.
Bedrooms: 4 single, 1 twin
Bathrooms: 2 public

Bed & breakfast per night:	£min	£max
Single	14.00	18.00
Double	24.00	32.00

Parking for 5

BLYTH
Nottinghamshire
Map ref 4C2

Village on the old Great North Road. A busy staging post in Georgian times with many examples of Georgian Gothic architecture. The remains of a Norman Benedictine priory survive as the parish church.

The Charnwood Hotel
HIGHLY COMMENDED
Sheffield Road, Blyth, Worksop S81 8HF
☎ Worksop (01909) 591610
Fax (01909) 591429
Best Western
On the A634 Sheffield road between the villages of Blyth and Oldcotes. Stands in 3 acres of landscaped gardens with a natural wildlife pond.
Bedrooms: 2 single, 12 double, 6 twin
Bathrooms: 20 en-suite

Bed & breakfast per night:	£min	£max
Single	35.00	55.00
Double	50.00	70.00

Lunch available
Evening meal 1900 (last orders 2145)
Parking for 75
Cards accepted: Access, Visa, Diners, Amex, Switch/Delta

BUXTON
Derbyshire
Map ref 4B2

The highest market town in England and one of the oldest spas, with an elegant Crescent, Poole's Cavern, Opera House and attractive Pavilion Gardens. An excellent centre for exploring the Peak District.
Tourist Information Centre ☎ (01298) 25106

Buxton View
COMMENDED
74 Corbar Road, Buxton SK17 6RJ
☎ (01298) 79222
Guesthouse built from local stone, offering a friendly and relaxed atmosphere. In a quiet area with a commanding view over the town and surrounding hills, yet only a few minutes' walk from the town's amenities.
Bedrooms: 1 single, 2 double, 1 twin, 1 triple
Bathrooms: 4 en-suite, 1 private

MIDDLE ENGLAND

[Unnamed entry]

Bed & breakfast per night:	£min	£max
Single	18.00	20.00
Double	36.00	36.00

Half board per person:	£min	£max
Daily	28.00	28.00
Weekly	183.00	183.00

Evening meal 1900 (last orders 2000)
Parking for 7
Open January–November

Devonshire Lodge Guesthouse

2 Manchester Road, Buxton SK17 6SB
☎ (01298) 71487
Family-run guesthouse with all modern facilities and a homely atmosphere. Three minutes from Opera House, Pavilion Gardens and shopping centre.
Bedrooms: 2 double, 1 twin
Bathrooms: 1 en-suite, 1 public

Bed & breakfast per night:	£min	£max
Single	16.00	20.00
Double	28.00	32.00

Parking for 6

Fairhaven

Listed APPROVED

1 Dale Terrace, Buxton SK17 6LU
☎ (01298) 24481
Centrally placed with ample roadside parking, offering English home cooking in a warm and friendly atmosphere.
Bedrooms: 1 single, 1 double, 1 twin, 2 triple, 1 family room
Bathrooms: 1 public

Bed & breakfast per night:	£min	£max
Single	17.00	19.00
Double	30.00	32.00

Half board per person:	£min	£max
Daily	22.50	24.50
Weekly	150.50	157.50

Evening meal 1800 (last orders 1600)
Cards accepted: Access, Visa, Amex

Grosvenor House Hotel

COMMENDED

1 Broad Walk, Buxton SK17 6JE
☎ (01298) 72439
Fax (01298) 72439
Privately-run, Victorian residence enjoying splendid views of Pavilion Gardens/theatre. Homely and peaceful atmosphere. Bedrooms non-smoking.

Home-cooked traditional English food. Comfort and hospitality assured.
Bedrooms: 5 double, 1 twin, 2 triple
Bathrooms: 8 en-suite

Bed & breakfast per night:	£min	£max
Single	42.50	47.50
Double	50.00	70.00

Half board per person:	£min	£max
Daily	39.00	49.00
Weekly	238.00	280.00

Lunch available
Evening meal 1845 (last orders 1845)
Parking for 6
Cards accepted: Access, Visa

Hawthorn Farm Guesthouse

COMMENDED

Fairfield Road, Buxton SK17 7ED
☎ (01298) 23230
A 400-year-old former farmhouse which has been in the family for 10 generations. Full English breakfast.
Bedrooms: 4 single, 2 double, 2 twin, 4 triple
Bathrooms: 5 en-suite, 2 public

Bed & breakfast per night:	£min	£max
Single	20.00	21.00
Double	40.00	46.00

Parking for 15
Open April–October

Lakenham Guesthouse

COMMENDED

11 Burlington Road, Buxton SK17 9AL
☎ (01298) 79209
Elegant Victorian house in own grounds overlooking Pavilion Gardens. Furnished in Victorian manner and offering personal service in a friendly, relaxed atmosphere.
Bedrooms: 3 double, 3 triple
Bathrooms: 5 en-suite, 1 private

Bed & breakfast per night:	£min	£max
Double	40.00	50.00

Half board per person:	£min	£max
Daily	30.00	37.00

Evening meal from 1800
Parking for 10

Netherdale Guesthouse

16 Green Lane, Buxton SK17 9DP
☎ (01298) 23896
Guesthouse in a quiet, central residential area offering mostly en-suite facilities and ground floor accommodation.
Bedrooms: 2 single, 6 double, 2 twin Suites available
Bathrooms: 5 en-suite, 1 public, 1 private shower

Bed & breakfast per night:	£min	£max
Single	21.00	30.00
Double	40.00	50.00

Half board per person:	£min	£max
Daily	33.00	37.00
Weekly	225.00	240.00

Evening meal 1800 (last orders 1800)
Parking for 14

Old Hall Hotel

COMMENDED

The Square, Buxton SK17 6BD
☎ (01298) 22841
Fax (01298) 72437
This historic hotel, reputed to be the oldest in England, offers a warm and friendly service. Ideally located opposite Pavilion Gardens (with 23 acres parkland and spa water swimming pool) and Edwardian Theatre, we serve pre and post theatre dinner in our restaurant and wine bar. A visit is recommended.
Bedrooms: 8 single, 17 double, 8 twin, 4 triple
Bathrooms: 34 en-suite, 2 public, 3 private showers

Bed & breakfast per night:	£min	£max
Single	47.50	47.50
Double	75.00	80.00

Half board per person:	£min	£max
Daily	50.00	63.50
Weekly	300.00	325.00

Lunch available
Evening meal 1800 (last orders 2300)
Cards accepted: Access, Visa, Diners, Amex, Switch/Delta

Please check prices and other details at the time of booking.

Map references apply to the colour maps at the back of this guide.

MIDDLE ENGLAND

BUXTON
Continued

Portland Hotel and Park Restaurant
COMMENDED

32 St. John's Road, Buxton SK17 6XQ
☎ (01298) 71493 & 22462
Fax (01298) 27464
Ⓡ Logis of Great Britain

Situated just 100 yards from Buxton's famous Opera House, the hotel and its noted restaurant make the perfect base for touring the Peak District.
Bedrooms: 6 single, 11 double, 7 twin, 1 triple
Bathrooms: 25 en-suite

Bed & breakfast per night:	£min	£max
Single	48.00	52.00
Double	58.00	62.00

Half board per person:	£min	£max
Daily	46.00	49.00
Weekly	276.00	294.00

Lunch available
Evening meal 1845 (last orders 2130)
Parking for 17
Cards accepted: Access, Visa, Diners, Amex, Switch/Delta

Staden Grange Country House
HIGHLY COMMENDED

Staden Lane, Staden, Buxton SK17 9RZ
☎ (01298) 24965
Fax (01298) 72167
Ⓡ Minotel

250-acre dairy farm. A spacious residence 1.5 miles from Buxton, in a magnificent scenic area. It has been carefully extended and enjoys uninterrupted views over open farmland.
Bedrooms: 9 double, 5 twin
Bathrooms: 13 en-suite, 1 public, 1 private shower

Bed & breakfast per night:	£min	£max
Single	35.50	39.50
Double	50.00	85.00

Half board per person:	£min	£max
Daily	41.50	54.00

Lunch available
Evening meal 1830 (last orders 2000)
Parking for 30

Cards accepted: Access, Visa, Diners, Amex

Westminster Hotel

21 Broad Walk, Buxton SK17 6JR
☎ (01298) 23929 & 0802 375933
Fax (01298) 71121

Private, family hotel overlooking Pavilion Gardens and close to the town, shops and Opera House. Personal service and a varied menu. Ideal base for exploring the Peak District.
Bedrooms: 6 double, 6 twin
Bathrooms: 12 en-suite

Bed & breakfast per night:	£min	£max
Single	26.00	
Double	42.00	44.00

Half board per person:	£min	£max
Daily	29.00	33.00
Weekly	200.00	235.00

Evening meal 1830 (last orders 1500)
Parking for 14
Open February–November
Cards accepted: Access, Visa, Amex, Switch/Delta

CASTLE ASHBY
Northamptonshire
Map ref 2C1

Castle Ashby is a fine Elizabethan mansion open for special events, product launches and conferences and set in landscaped grounds which are open to the public in summer. The church has many monuments to the Compton family.

The Falcon
COMMENDED

Castle Ashby, Northampton NN7 1LF
☎ Northampton (01604) 696200
Fax (01604) 696673
Ⓡ Best Western

Proprietor-managed country cottage hotel. Ideal touring centre for Oxford, Cambridge, Stratford, Warwick and National Exhibition Centre. Good restaurant and bar open daily. Sky TV in all rooms.
Bedrooms: 4 single, 10 double, 2 twin
Bathrooms: 16 en-suite, 1 public

Bed & breakfast per night:	£min	£max
Single	52.50	65.00
Double	62.50	75.00

Half board per person:	£min	£max
Daily	69.50	81.50

Lunch available
Evening meal 1930 (last orders 2130)
Parking for 60
Cards accepted: Access, Visa, Amex, Switch/Delta

CASTLE DONINGTON
Leicestershire
Map ref 4C3

A Norman castle once stood here. The world's largest collection of single-seater racing cars is displayed at Donington Park alongside the racing circuit, and an Aeropark Visitor Centre can be seen at nearby East Midlands International Airport.

Delven Hotel
APPROVED

12 Delven Lane, Castle Donington, Derby DE7 2LJ
☎ Derby (01332) 810153 & 850507

Small, family-run hotel, 1 mile from Donington race track and 2 miles from East Midlands International Airport.
Bedrooms: 2 double, 4 twin, 1 triple
Bathrooms: 3 public, 2 private showers

Bed & breakfast per night:	£min	£max
Single	17.00	23.00
Double	36.00	40.00

Parking for 5
Cards accepted: Access, Visa

Donington Manor Hotel

High Street, Castle Donington, Derby DE74 2PP
☎ Derby (01332) 810253
Fax (01332) 850330
Ⓡ The Independents

This 18th C coaching inn with modern bedroom extensions has French and English menus, is 2 miles from junction 24 of the M1 and is close to Donington Park motor circuit and East Midlands International Airport.
Bedrooms: 10 single, 12 double, 7 twin, 3 family rooms
Bathrooms: 32 en-suite

Bed & breakfast per night:	£min	£max
Single	58.00	70.00
Double	65.00	80.00

MIDDLE ENGLAND

Half board per person:	£min	£max
Daily	70.00	82.00
Weekly	400.00	500.00

Lunch available
Evening meal 1900 (last orders 2130)
Parking for 60
Cards accepted: Access, Visa, Diners, Amex, Switch/Delta

Four Poster Guesthouse

73 Clapgun Street, Castle Donington, Derby DE7 2LF
☎ Derby (01332) 810335 & 812418
Fax (01332) 812418
Some four-poster beds are available in this old-world accommodation in a quiet location opposite the church.
Bedrooms: 3 single, 3 double, 2 twin, 3 family rooms
Bathrooms: 7 en-suite, 2 public

Bed & breakfast per night:	£min	£max
Single	15.00	25.00
Double	30.00	50.00

Parking for 12

Little Chimneys Guesthouse

COMMENDED

19 The Green, Diseworth, Castle Donington, Derby DE7 2QN
☎ Derby (01332) 812458
Modern building in the pleasant village of Diseworth close to the M1, East Midlands International Airport and Donington race track.
Bedrooms: 4 twin, 1 triple
Bathrooms: 5 private

Bed & breakfast per night:	£min	£max
Single	24.50	
Double	35.50	

Evening meal 1700 (last orders 2000)
Parking for 7
Cards accepted: Access, Visa

Park Farmhouse Hotel

COMMENDED

Melbourne Road, Isley Walton, Castle Donington, Derby DE74 2RN
☎ Derby (01332) 862409
Fax (01332) 862364
Logis of Great Britain
Half-timbered 17th C farmhouse, in its own grounds. Spacious rooms, farmhouse suppers. Located at competitors' entrance to Donington Park.

Wheelchair access category 2
Bedrooms: 2 single, 3 double, 3 twin, 2 triple, 1 family room
Bathrooms: 10 en-suite, 1 private

Bed & breakfast per night:	£min	£max
Single	42.00	46.00
Double	56.00	66.00

Evening meal 1800 (last orders 2030)
Parking for 15
Cards accepted: Access, Visa, Diners, Amex

CASTLETON

Derbyshire
Map ref 4B2

Large village in a spectacular Peak District setting with ruined Peveril Castle and 4 great show caverns, where the Blue John stone and lead were mined. One cavern offers a mile-long underground boat journey.

Ye Olde Nags Head

HIGHLY COMMENDED

Castleton, Sheffield S30 2WH
☎ Hope Valley (01433) 620248
Fax (01433) 621604
Old world hotel in the beautiful countryside of the Peak District National Park, near the famous caverns and ancient Peveril Castle.
Bedrooms: 6 double, 2 twin
Bathrooms: 8 en-suite

Bed & breakfast per night:	£min	£max
Single	49.50	67.50
Double	69.50	99.50

Half board per person:	£min	£max
Daily	74.45	92.45
Weekly	521.15	647.15

Lunch available
Evening meal 1900 (last orders 2200)
Parking for 16
Cards accepted: Access, Visa, Diners, Amex, Switch/Delta

National gradings and classifications were correct at the time of going to press but are subject to change. Please check at the time of booking.

CHESTERFIELD

Derbyshire
Map ref 4B2

Famous for the twisted spire of its parish church, Chesterfield has some fine modern buildings and excellent shopping facilities, including a large, traditional open-air market. Hardwick Hall and Bolsover Castle are nearby.
Tourist Information Centre ☎ (01246) 207777 or 207778

Abbeydale Hotel

COMMENDED

Cross Street, Chesterfield S40 4TD
☎ (01246) 277849
Fax (01246) 558223
Minotel/Logis of Great Britain
Resident proprietors. Quiet location within walking distance of town centre, close to Peak District and Chatsworth. Short breaks available.
Wheelchair access category 3
Bedrooms: 5 single, 2 double, 3 twin, 1 triple
Bathrooms: 9 en-suite, 1 public

Bed & breakfast per night:	£min	£max
Single	26.00	44.00
Double	58.00	58.00

Half board per person:	£min	£max
Daily	36.00	54.00

Lunch available
Evening meal 1830 (last orders 2000)
Parking for 12
Cards accepted: Access, Visa, Diners, Amex

Abigails

COMMENDED

62 Brockwell Lane, Chesterfield S40 4EE
☎ (01246) 279391
Relax taking breakfast in the conservatory overlooking Chesterfield and surrounding moorlands. Garden with pond and waterfall, private car park.
Bedrooms: 2 single, 3 double, 2 twin
Bathrooms: 7 en-suite

Bed & breakfast per night:	£min	£max
Single	19.50	22.00
Double	38.00	38.00

Half board per person:	£min	£max
Daily	29.00	31.50
Weekly	189.35	205.10

Continued ▶

MIDDLE ENGLAND

CHESTERFIELD
Continued

Evening meal from 1830
Parking for 7

Twin Oaks Motel
M1 Junction 29, Palterton Turn Off,
Church Lane, Palterton, Chesterfield
S44 6UZ
☎ (01246) 855455
Fax (01246) 851708
Adjacent to the M1 junction 29. Fully licensed bar, restaurant and conference facilities.
Bedrooms: 13 single, 5 double, 3 twin, 2 triple
Bathrooms: 3 private, 3 public

Bed & breakfast per night:
	£min	£max
Single	30.00	34.95
Double	36.00	45.90

Half board per person:
	£min	£max
Daily	40.45	58.05
Weekly	268.30	391.60

Lunch available
Evening meal 1900 (last orders 2200)
Parking for 160
Cards accepted: Access, Visa, Amex, Switch/Delta

The Van Dyk Hotel
COMMENDED
Worksop Road, Clowne,
Chesterfield S43 4TD
☎ (01246) 810219
Fax (01246) 819566
Elegant country house hotel in beautiful countryside, with 2 bars, a restaurant, banqueting and conference facilities. Approximately 1 mile from M1 junction 30.
Bedrooms: 8 single, 1 double, 5 twin, 2 triple
Bathrooms: 16 en-suite

Bed & breakfast per night:
	£min	£max
Single	27.50	45.00
Double	50.00	55.00

Half board per person:
	£min	£max
Daily	37.50	69.00
Weekly	350.00	450.00

Lunch available
Evening meal 1900 (last orders 2130)
Parking for 100
Cards accepted: Access, Visa, Amex

COALVILLE
Leicestershire
Map ref 4B3

North-west Leicestershire town, home of Snibston Discovery Park and close to Twycross Zoo and Charnwood Forest area.
Tourist Information Centre ☎ (01530) 813608

Bardon Hall
COMMENDED
Beveridge Lane, Bardon Hill,
Coalville, Leicester LE6 2TB
☎ (01530) 813644
Fax (01530) 815425
The Independents
Originally a country house, now transformed into a delightful pub and hotel with an informal atmosphere. On the A50, near junction 22 of M1. Prices below are for room only.
Bedrooms: 5 single, 26 double, 4 twin
Bathrooms: 35 en-suite

Bed & breakfast per night:
	£min	£max
Single	28.50	39.50
Double	28.50	39.50

Lunch available
Evening meal 1900 (last orders 2200)
Parking for 250
Cards accepted: Access, Visa, Amex, Switch/Delta

Hermitage Park Hotel
COMMENDED
Whitwick Road, Coalville, Leicester
LE67 3FA
☎ (01530) 814814
Fax (01530) 814202
Purpose-built hotel with a health centre, bars and a restaurant contained in a 150 feet long glazed atrium.
Bedrooms: 21 double, 4 twin
Suite available
Bathrooms: 25 en-suite

Bed & breakfast per night:
	£min	£max
Single	35.00	59.50
Double	39.50	64.50

Lunch available
Evening meal 1900 (last orders 2230)
Parking for 48
Cards accepted: Access, Visa, Amex, Switch/Delta

CRESSBROOK
Derbyshire
Map ref 4B2

Delightful dale with stone hall and pleasant houses, steep wooded slopes and superb views.

Cressbrook Hall
COMMENDED
Cressbrook, Buxton SK17 8SY
☎ Tideswell (01298) 871289 & Free Phone 0500 121248
Fax (01298) 871845

Accommodation with a difference. Enjoy this magnificent family home built in 1835, set in 23 acres, with spectacular views around the compass. Wheelchair access category 3
Bedrooms: 1 double, 1 twin, 1 family room
Bathrooms: 3 en-suite

Bed & breakfast per night:
	£min	£max
Single	28.50	45.00
Double	57.00	65.00

Evening meal from 1830
Parking for 10
Cards accepted: Access, Visa

DERBY
Derbyshire
Map ref 4B2

Modern industrial city but with ancient origins. There is a wide range of attractions including several museums (notably Royal Crown Derby), a theatre, a concert hall, and the cathedral with fine ironwork and Bess of Hardwick's tomb.
Tourist Information Centre ☎ (01332) 255802

European Inn
COMMENDED
Midland Road, Derby DE1 2SL
☎ (01332) 292000
Fax (01332) 293940

For ideas on places to visit refer to the introduction at the beginning of this section.

MIDDLE ENGLAND

Stylish, modern hotel with en-suite bedrooms. Full English buffet-style breakfast, restaurant on site. Near Derby rail station and 10 minutes off M1.
Bedrooms: 66 double, 22 twin
Bathrooms: 88 en-suite
Bed & breakfast

per night:	£min	£max
Single		46.75
Double		52.30

Parking for 90
Cards accepted: Access, Visa, Diners, Amex, Switch/Delta

International Hotel & Restaurant
COMMENDED
Burton Road (A5250), Derby DE23 6AD
☎ (01332) 369321
Fax (01332) 294430
Situated close to the city centre, this privately owned hotel makes an excellent base from which to explore the Peak District Park. Good quality restaurant offers an extensive selection of fare.
Bedrooms: 12 single, 40 double, 6 twin, 4 triple
Bathrooms: 62 en-suite
Bed & breakfast

per night:	£min	£max
Single	35.00	50.00
Double	45.00	60.00

Half board per

person:	£min	£max
Daily	35.00	65.00

Lunch available
Evening meal 1900 (last orders 2215)
Parking for 120
Cards accepted: Access, Visa, Diners, Amex, Switch/Delta

Hotel Ristorante 'La Gondola'
COMMENDED
220 Osmaston Road, Derby DE23 8JX
☎ (01332) 332895
Fax (01332) 384512
Privately owned hotel with bar, restaurant and private car park. Close to the city centre and all amenities.
Bedrooms: 11 double, 2 twin, 6 triple, 1 family room

Bathrooms: 20 en-suite
Bed & breakfast

per night:	£min	£max
Single	40.00	
Double	45.00	55.00

Half board per

person:	£min	£max
Daily	52.50	65.00
Weekly	325.00	400.00

Lunch available
Evening meal 1900 (last orders 2200)
Parking for 70
Cards accepted: Access, Visa, Diners, Amex, Switch/Delta

DOVEDALE
Derbyshire
Map ref 4B2

Very popular beauty spot best seen from the footpath bordering the River Dove. It runs in a narrow valley between high wooded banks with rocky outcrops and caves.

Izaak Walton Hotel
COMMENDED
Dovedale, Ashbourne DE6 2AY
☎ Ashbourne (01335) 350555
Fax (01335) 350539
Country hotel in open countryside, overlooking Dovedale. Walking, fishing, gardens and outstanding views surround the establishment.
Bedrooms: 3 single, 17 double, 12 twin
Bathrooms: 32 en-suite
Bed & breakfast

per night:	£min	£max
Single	80.00	
Double	100.00	120.00

Half board per

person:	£min	£max
Daily	101.50	

Lunch available
Evening meal 1930 (last orders 2130)
Parking for 100
Cards accepted: Access, Visa, Diners, Amex, Switch/Delta

ACCESSIBILITY
Look for the symbols which indicate accessibility for wheelchair users. These are described in detail at the front of this guide.

EDALE
Derbyshire
Map ref 4B2

Deep, 1,250 ft valley, a mecca for walkers. The Pennine Way starts here, also the easiest way on to Kinder via Jacobs Ladder. Most of the buildings and walls are traditionally made of stone in this picturesque village.

Stonecroft
COMMENDED
Grindsbrook, Edale, Sheffield S30 2ZA
☎ Hope Valley (01433) 670262 & 0378 517656
Licensed country house accommodation with magnificent views at start of Pennine Way. Gourmet home-cooked meals - vegetarians and vegans welcomed. Drying facilities. Non-smoking.
Bedrooms: 1 double, 1 twin
Bathrooms: 1 en-suite, 1 private, 2 public
Bed & breakfast

per night:	£min	£max
Single	28.00	31.00
Double	46.00	52.00

Half board per

person:	£min	£max
Daily	38.00	41.00
Weekly	228.00	246.00

Lunch available
Evening meal from 1930
Parking for 5
Cards accepted: Access, Visa

FINEDON
Northamptonshire
Map ref 3A2

Large ironstone village with interesting Victorian houses and cottages and an ironstone 14th C church. The inn claims to be the oldest in England.

Tudor Gate Hotel
COMMENDED
35 High Street, Finedon, Wellingborough NN9 5JN
☎ Wellingborough (01933) 680408
Fax (01933) 680745
Converted from a 16th C farmhouse, with 3 four-poster beds. Close to new A1/M1 link. 30 antique businesses within walking distance and a wide range of leisure activities locally.

Continued ▶

MIDDLE ENGLAND

FINEDON
Continued

Bedrooms: 4 single, 20 double, 3 twin
Bathrooms: 27 en-suite

Bed & breakfast per night	£min	£max
Single	40.00	75.00
Double	50.00	85.00

Lunch available
Evening meal 1900 (last orders 2145)
Parking for 40
Cards accepted: Access, Visa, Diners, Amex, Switch/Delta

FROGGATT
Derbyshire
Map ref 4B2

Small village above which to the east is Froggatt Edge where many well-known climbers have gained experience.

Chequers Inn
HIGHLY COMMENDED

Froggatt, Calver, Sheffield S30 1ZB
☎ Hope Valley (01433) 630231
Fax (01433) 631072
In the heart of the Peak District National Park, 3 miles from Chatsworth, 6 miles from Bakewell. Traditional ales, log fire and always a warm welcome.
Bedrooms: 4 double, 2 twin
Bathrooms: 6 en-suite

Bed & breakfast per night	£min	£max
Single	42.00	51.00
Double	53.00	64.00

Lunch available
Evening meal 1900 (last orders 2130)
Parking for 60
Cards accepted: Access, Visa, Switch/Delta

The map references refer to the colour maps towards the end of the guide. The first figure is the map number; the letter and figure which follow indicate the grid reference on the map.

GAINSBOROUGH
Lincolnshire
Map ref 4C2

Britain's most inland port has strong connections with the Pilgrim Fathers. Gainsborough Old Hall, where they worshipped, boasts a 15th C manor house with complete kitchens.

White Hart Hotel
APPROVED

Lord Street, Gainsborough DN21 2DD
☎ (01427) 612018
Family-run, town centre pub/hotel. Cosy restaurant, bar snacks plus fast food bar/diner. Function room for seminars, weddings, etc. Secure undercover car parking.
Bedrooms: 3 single, 2 double, 7 twin, 2 family rooms
Bathrooms: 14 en-suite

Bed & breakfast per night	£min	£max
Single	27.50	35.00
Double	37.50	48.00

Half board per person	£min	£max
Daily	35.50	48.00

Lunch available
Evening meal 1900 (last orders 2100)
Parking for 24
Cards accepted: Access, Visa, Diners, Switch/Delta

GLOSSOP
Derbyshire
Map ref 4B2

Town in dramatic moorland surroundings with views over the High Peak. The settlement can be traced back to Roman times but expanded during the Industrial Revolution.
Tourist Information Centre ☎ (01457) 855920

Avondale
Listed HIGHLY COMMENDED

28 Woodhead Road, Glossop SK13 9RH
☎ (01457) 853132
Traditional stone house overlooking old Glossop and the Peak District. Comfortable accommodation, good cuisine and superb walks all around.
Bedrooms: 1 double, 1 twin
Bathrooms: 1 public

Bed & breakfast per night	£min	£max
Single	15.00	17.50
Double	30.00	35.00

Parking for 8

Wind in the Willows Hotel
HIGHLY COMMENDED

Derbyshire Level, off Sheffield Road, (A57), Glossop SK13 9PT
☎ (01457) 868001
Fax (01457) 853354
Friendly but professional country house hotel with antiques and open fires, offering home cooking, peace and relaxation. Views over the magnificent Peak District National Park. Adjacent to golf-course in excellent walking country and handy for Manchester.
Bedrooms: 9 double, 3 twin
Suite available
Bathrooms: 12 en-suite

Bed & breakfast per night	£min	£max
Single	57.00	75.00
Double	67.00	95.00

Evening meal 1930 (last orders 1600)
Parking for 20
Cards accepted: Access, Visa, Diners, Amex

GRANTHAM
Lincolnshire
Map ref 3A1

On the old Great North Road (A1), Grantham's splendid parish church has a fine spire and chained library. Sir Isaac Newton was educated here and his statue stands in front of the museum which includes displays on Newton and other famous local people.
Tourist Information Centre ☎ (01476) 566444

Grantham Lodge Hotel
COMMENDED

Toll Bar Road, Marston, Grantham NG32 2HT
☎ Loveden (01400) 250909
Fax (01400) 250130
Lodge-style hotel including a restaurant, bar and conference centre, north of Grantham. Newly refurbished, with courtyard gardens, new restaurant and lounge.
Bedrooms: 23 double, 4 twin, 1 family room
Suite available
Bathrooms: 28 en-suite

MIDDLE ENGLAND

Swallow Hotel
HIGHLY COMMENDED

Swingbridge Road, Grantham
NG31 7XT
☎ (01476) 593000
Fax (01476) 592592
Swallow

This courtyard-style hotel is situated just off the A1 and makes a great centre for touring Lincolnshire, Nottinghamshire and Leicestershire. Short break packages available.
Bedrooms: 61 double, 29 twin
Bathrooms: 90 en-suite

Bed & breakfast per night:	£min	£max
Single	55.00	95.00
Double	68.00	105.00

Half board per person:	£min	£max
Daily	72.95	112.95

Lunch available
Evening meal 1900 (last orders 2200)
Parking for 150
Cards accepted: Access, Visa, Diners, Amex, Switch/Delta

GRINDLEFORD
Derbyshire
Map ref 4B2

Good centre for walking, at the eastern end of the Hope Valley. Longshaw Estate is nearby with 1500 acres of moorland and woodland.

Maynard Arms Hotel
HIGHLY COMMENDED

Main Road, Grindleford, Sheffield S30 1HP
☎ Hope Valley (01433) 630321
Fax (01433) 630445

An established hotel with a relaxed, friendly atmosphere and extensive facilities. Picturesque gardens with lovely views of Hope Valley and Peak Park. Excellent walking country.
Bedrooms: 1 single, 8 double, 2 twin
Suite available
Bathrooms: 11 en-suite

Bed & breakfast per night:	£min	£max
Single	49.00	55.00
Double	65.00	85.00

Lunch available
Evening meal 1900 (last orders 2130)
Parking for 80
Cards accepted: Access, Visa, Amex

Kings Hotel
COMMENDED

North Parade, Grantham
NG31 8AU
☎ (01476) 590800
Fax (01476) 590800
Logis of Great Britain

Privately owned hotel serving Grantham and the East Midlands, with a tradition of good hospitality and great value since 1974.
Wheelchair access category 3
Bedrooms: 1 single, 7 double, 13 twin
Bathrooms: 21 en-suite

Bed & breakfast per night:	£min	£max
Single	35.00	50.00
Double	45.00	65.00

Lunch available
Evening meal 1900 (last orders 2200)
Parking for 50
Cards accepted: Access, Visa, Diners, Amex, Switch/Delta

Lanchester Guesthouse

84 Harrowby Road, Grantham
NG31 9DS
☎ (01476) 574169

Well established and run professionally to high standards but retaining its warm and friendly atmosphere. All rooms can be let as singles. Light suppers can be served until 9pm.
Bedrooms: 1 double, 2 twin
Bathrooms: 1 en-suite, 1 public

Bed & breakfast per night:	£min	£max
Single	18.00	25.00
Double	30.00	35.00

Evening meal 1800 (last orders 1200)
Parking for 3

HARRINGWORTH
Northamptonshire
Map ref 3A1

Village with a medieval cross, a 12th C church, an inn and old manor house. The 82 arches of the 19th C Welland railway viaduct dominate the valley, which forms the Northamptonshire/Leicestershire border.

White Swan
COMMENDED

Seaton Road, Harringworth, Corby NN17 3AF
☎ Morcott (01572) 747543
Fax (01572) 747323
Logis of Great Britain

15th C coaching inn offering en-suite accommodation, in a delightful village, close to many historic sites. Home-cooked food and real ales.
Bedrooms: 1 single, 4 double, 1 twin
Bathrooms: 6 en-suite

Bed & breakfast per night:	£min	£max
Single	38.50	
Double	52.00	

Lunch available
Evening meal 1900 (last orders 2200)
Parking for 18
Cards accepted: Access, Visa, Amex, Switch/Delta

HATHERSAGE
Derbyshire
Map ref 4B2

Hillside village in the Peak District, dominated by the church with many good brasses and monuments to the Eyre family which provide a link with Charlotte Bronte. Little John, friend of Robin Hood, is said to be buried here.

George Hotel
COMMENDED

Main Road, Hathersage, Sheffield S30 1BB
☎ Hope Valley (01433) 650436
Fax (01433) 650099
Stagecoach

Very comfortable 16th C coaching inn with cosy en-suite bedrooms. Open fires, homely atmosphere. Set in the beautiful Peak District.
Bedrooms: 11 double, 5 twin, 2 triple
Bathrooms: 18 en-suite

Continued ▶

Bed & breakfast per night:

	£min	£max
Single	35.00	45.00
Double	45.00	55.00

Half board per person:

	£min	£max
Daily	34.00	39.00
Weekly	225.00	265.00

Lunch available
Evening meal 1830 (last orders 2130)
Parking for 60
Cards accepted: Access, Visa, Amex, Switch/Delta

MIDDLE ENGLAND

HATHERSAGE
Continued

Bed & breakfast per night:

	£min	£max
Single	59.50	59.50
Double	75.00	75.00

Half board per person:

	£min	£max
Daily	51.00	73.00

Lunch available
Evening meal 1900 (last orders 2130)
Parking for 40
Cards accepted: Access, Visa, Diners, Amex, Switch/Delta

HINCKLEY
Leicestershire
Map ref 4B3

The town has an excellent leisure centre. Bosworth Battlefield, with its Visitor Centre and Battle Trail, is 5 miles away.
Tourist Information Centre ☎ (01455) 635106

Ambion Court
COMMENDED

The Green, Dadlington, Nuneaton, Warwickshire CV13 6JB
☎ (01455) 212292
Fax (01455) 213141
Charming, modernised farmhouse hotel overlooking tranquil village green. En-suite bedrooms, restaurant. Convenient for Leicester, Coventry, Warwick and NEC.
Bedrooms: 5 double, 1 twin, 1 triple
Bathrooms: 7 en-suite

Bed & breakfast per night:

	£min	£max
Single	35.00	45.00
Double	50.00	60.00

Half board per person:

	£min	£max
Daily	50.00	60.00

Evening meal 1900 (last orders 2030)
Parking for 8
Cards accepted: Access, Visa, Amex

Hinckley Island Hotel
COMMENDED

A5, Watling Street, Hinckley LE10 3JA
☎ (01455) 631122
Fax (01455) 634536
This refreshingly different hotel combines a convenient location with its

rural surroundings and a comprehensive range of leisure facilities.
Bedrooms: 209 double, 59 twin, 2 triple
Suite available
Bathrooms: 270 en-suite

Bed & breakfast per night:

	£min	£max
Single	49.00	85.00
Double	73.00	115.00

Half board per person:

	£min	£max
Daily	49.50	115.00

Lunch available
Evening meal 1900 (last orders 2200)
Parking for 500
Cards accepted: Access, Visa, Diners, Amex, Switch/Delta

HOPE
Derbyshire
Map ref 4B2

Village in the Hope Valley which is an excellent base for walking in the Peak District and for fishing and shooting. There is a well-dressing ceremony each June and its August sheep dog trials are well-known. Castleton Caves are nearby.

Moorgate
APPROVED

Edale Road, Hope, Sheffield S30 2RF
☎ Hope Valley (01433) 621219
Recently refurbished country guesthouse in the heart of the Peak District. En-suite facilities available. Boot and drying room. Packed lunches. Ideal for walking and touring.
Bedrooms: 9 single, 3 double, 15 twin
Bathrooms: 11 en-suite, 8 public

Bed & breakfast per night:

	£min	£max
Single	18.00	25.50
Double	36.00	51.00

Half board per person:

	£min	£max
Daily	27.00	34.50
Weekly	189.00	241.00

Lunch available
Evening meal from 1900
Parking for 30
Cards accepted: Access, Visa

HORNCASTLE
Lincolnshire
Map ref 4D2

Pleasant market town near the Lincolnshire Wolds, which was once a walled Roman settlement. It was the scene of a decisive Civil War battle, relics of which can be seen in the church. Tennyson's bride lived here.

Admiral Rodney Hotel
COMMENDED

North Street, Horncastle LN9 5DX
☎ Louth (01507) 523131
Fax (01507) 523104
Located in pleasant market town just off main Lincoln to Skegness road - ideal touring base. Large car park, en-suite bedrooms, fine restaurant.
Bedrooms: 19 double, 9 twin, 1 triple, 2 family rooms
Bathrooms: 31 en-suite

Bed & breakfast per night:

	£min	£max
Single	38.00	45.00
Double	50.00	62.00

Half board per person:

	£min	£max
Daily	32.50	52.00

Lunch available
Evening meal 1900 (last orders 2130)
Parking for 70
Cards accepted: Access, Visa, Diners, Amex, Switch/Delta

HORSLEY
Derbyshire
Map ref 4B2

Small village 5 miles north of Derby, in pretty countryside with many well-used footpaths.

Horsley Lodge
COMMENDED

Smalley Mill Road, Horsley DE21 5BL
☎ Derby (01332) 780838
Fax (01332) 781118
Magnificent stone country house, 5 miles from Derby. Easy access to M1. 18 hole golf-course (free golf) and private fishing.
Bedrooms: 2 twin, 2 triple
Bathrooms: 4 en-suite

Bed & breakfast per night:

	£min	£max
Single	45.00	45.00
Double	60.00	60.00

MIDDLE ENGLAND

Lunch available
Evening meal 1800 (last orders 2200)
Parking for 200
Cards accepted: Access, Visa, Switch/Delta

KEGWORTH

Leicestershire
Map ref 4C3

Village on the River Soar close to East Midlands International Airport and Donington Park racing circuit. It has a 14th C church with a fine nave and chantry roof. The nearby churches of Staunton Harold, Melbourne and Breedon-on-the-Hill are of exceptional interest.

The Kegworth Hotel

Packington Hill, Kegworth, Derby DE74 2DF
☎ Loughborough (01509) 673367 & 672427
Fax (01509) 674664
Modern privately owned hotel half a mile from junction 24 of M1, close to Donington race track and East Midlands International Airport. Central for Nottingham, Derby and Leicester. Excellent leisure facilities.
Bedrooms: 10 single, 28 double, 11 twin, 3 triple
Bathrooms: 52 en-suite, 2 public

Bed & breakfast per night:	£min	£max
Single	57.50	72.50
Double	65.00	80.00

Half board per person:	£min	£max
Daily	69.00	84.00
Weekly	483.00	588.00

Lunch available
Evening meal 1830 (last orders 2130)
Parking for 150
Cards accepted: Access, Visa, Amex, Switch/Delta

COLOUR MAPS

Colour maps at the back of this guide pinpoint all places in which you will find accommodation listed.

KETTERING

Northamptonshire
Map ref 3A2

Ancient industrial town based on shoe-making. Wicksteed Park to the south has many children's amusements. The splendid 17th C ducal mansion of Boughton House is to the north.
Tourist Information Centre ☎ (01536) 410266 or 534212

Pennels Guesthouse

Listed COMMENDED

175 Beatrice Road, Kettering NN16 9QR
☎ (01536) 81940 & Mobile 0850 946794
Fax (01536) 410798
Family-run guesthouse where you are assured of a warm welcome. Offering quality accommodation with a private lawned garden, in a quiet area.
Bedrooms: 3 single, 1 double, 3 twin
Bathrooms: 4 en-suite, 3 private, 2 public

Bed & breakfast per night:	£min	£max
Single	17.00	19.50
Double	32.00	39.00

Half board per person:	£min	£max
Daily	26.50	29.00
Weekly	185.50	269.50

Lunch available
Evening meal 1800 (last orders 1700)
Parking for 4
Cards accepted: Access, Visa

KNIPTON

Leicestershire
Map ref 4C2

Leicestershire Wolds village close to Belvoir Castle, where medieval jousting tournaments and other special events add to the attractions in summer.

Red House Inn

APPROVED

Knipton, Grantham, Lincolnshire NG32 1RH
☎ Grantham (01476) 870352
Fax (01476) 870429
In the beautiful Vale of Belvoir, within 1 mile of the castle, this listed building was a hunting lodge for approximately 200 years.
Bedrooms: 2 single, 2 double, 4 twin
Bathrooms: 3 en-suite, 1 public

Bed & breakfast per night:	£min	£max
Single	21.50	34.50
Double	32.50	48.00

Half board per person:	£min	£max
Daily	33.50	43.50
Weekly	186.50	243.50

Lunch available
Evening meal 1900 (last orders 2130)
Parking for 60
Cards accepted: Access, Visa, Switch/Delta

LANGAR

Nottinghamshire
Map ref 4C2

Small village standing on a small escarpment. Has a fine, Early English style church and a strong village atmosphere.

Langar Hall

COMMENDED

Langar, Nottingham NG13 9HG
☎ Harby (01949) 860559
Fax (01949) 861045
Charming small hotel in peaceful rural setting, 12 miles south-east of Nottingham. Central for touring or as a stop-off for travellers between north and south.
Bedrooms: 1 single, 9 double, 1 twin
Bathrooms: 11 private

Bed & breakfast per night:	£min	£max
Single	60.00	85.00
Double	85.00	135.00

Lunch available
Evening meal 1900 (last orders 2130)
Parking for 20
Cards accepted: Access, Visa, Diners, Amex

The symbol CR and a group name following an hotel address indicates that bookings can be made through a central reservations office. These offices are listed in the information pages at the back of this guide.

LEADENHAM

Lincolnshire
Map ref 3A1

Village on the Lincoln Edge, noted for its fine church spire.

George Hotel

High Street, Leadenham, Lincoln LN5 0PN
☎ Loveden (01400) 272251
Fax (01400) 272091

17th C coaching inn where the owners take pride in the international menu and their collection of over 500 whiskies from all over the world.
Bedrooms: 2 single, 2 double, 2 twin
Bathrooms: 2 en-suite, 1 private, 2 public

Bed & breakfast per night:	£min	£max
Single	18.00	25.00
Double	25.00	35.00

Lunch available
Evening meal 1900 (last orders 2145)
Parking for 150
Cards accepted: Access, Visa, Diners, Amex, Switch/Delta

LEICESTER

Leicestershire
Map ref 4C3

Modern industrial city with a wide variety of attractions including Roman remains, ancient churches, Georgian houses and a Victorian clock tower. Excellent shopping precincts, arcades and market, museums, theatres, concert hall and sports and leisure centres.
Tourist Information Centre ☎ (0116) 265 0555

Beaumaris Guesthouse

18 Westcotes Drive, Leicester LE3 0QN
☎ (0116) 254 0261

Friendly, family-run guesthouse, away from heavy traffic, yet on a bus route to town and within 15 minutes' walking distance of it.
Bedrooms: 2 single, 1 double, 2 twin, 1 triple
Bathrooms: 1 private, 3 public

Bed & breakfast per night:	£min	£max
Single	17.00	20.00
Double	25.00	30.00

Burlington Hotel

COMMENDED

Elmfield Avenue, Stoneygate, Leicester LE2 1RB
☎ (0116) 270 5112
Fax (0116) 270 4207

A friendly welcome awaits you at this family-run hotel. Situated in a quiet residential area close to the city centre.
Bedrooms: 9 single, 4 double, 2 twin, 1 triple
Bathrooms: 11 en-suite, 1 public, 4 private showers

Bed & breakfast per night:	£min	£max
Single	29.00	38.00
Double	41.00	46.00

Half board per person:	£min	£max
Daily	39.00	48.00
Weekly	273.00	336.00

Evening meal 1900 (last orders 2030)
Parking for 18
Cards accepted: Access, Visa, Amex

Chase Hotel and Leisure Complex

The Racecourse, Oadby, Leicester LE2 3QH
☎ (0116) 270 3920
Fax (0116) 270 0008

Purpose-built, privately owned hotel and leisure complex on the south side of Leicester within 5 minutes of the M1 and the M69. Overlooks a racecourse and golf club.
Bedrooms: 6 twin, 4 triple
Bathrooms: 10 en-suite

Bed & breakfast per night:	£min	£max
Single	25.00	39.50
Double	40.00	58.00

Lunch available
Evening meal 1700 (last orders 2000)
Parking for 250
Cards accepted: Access, Visa

Glenfield Lodge Hotel

APPROVED

4 Glenfield Road, Leicester LE3 6AP
☎ (0116) 262 7554

Small, friendly hotel with an interesting ornamental courtyard, home-cooked food and cosy, relaxed surroundings. Close to city centre.
Bedrooms: 6 single, 3 double, 4 twin, 2 triple
Bathrooms: 3 public

Bed & breakfast per night:	£min	£max
Single	15.50	15.50
Double	27.00	27.00

Half board per person:	£min	£max
Daily	25.50	25.50

Evening meal 1730 (last orders 1830)
Parking for 3

The Red Cow

COMMENDED

Hinckley Road, Leicester Forest East, Leicester LE3 3PG
☎ (0116) 238 7878
Fax (0116) 238 6539
The Independents

Charming thatched pub on the A47, 4 miles from Leicester city centre and close to the interchange of M1 and M69. Reduced rates for Friday, Saturday and Sunday night stays.
Wheelchair access category 2
Bedrooms: 27 double, 4 twin
Bathrooms: 31 en-suite

Bed & breakfast per night:	£min	£max
Single	42.00	
Double	49.40	

Lunch available
Evening meal 1800 (last orders 2200)
Parking for 120
Cards accepted: Access, Visa, Amex, Switch/Delta

Regency Hotel

COMMENDED

360 London Road, Leicester LE2 2PL
☎ (0116) 270 9634
Fax (0116) 270 1375

A most elegant Victorian town house hotel, close to city centre. Formerly a convent with many interesting historical features. Individually designed bedrooms, 2 restaurants and a relaxed, friendly atmosphere.
Bedrooms: 15 single, 15 double, 2 triple
Bathrooms: 32 en-suite

Bed & breakfast per night:	£min	£max
Single	30.00	45.00
Double	40.00	55.00

MIDDLE ENGLAND

Half board per person:	£min	£max
Daily	32.75	57.75

Lunch available
Evening meal 1800 (last orders 2200)
Parking for 50
Cards accepted: Access, Visa, Amex, Switch/Delta

Hotel Saint James
COMMENDED
Abbey Street, Leicester LE1 3TE
☎ (0116) 251 0666
Fax (0116) 251 5183
In the heart of Leicester with superb panoramic views of the city. Close to Shires shopping centre. Free undercover parking.
Bedrooms: 41 single, 11 double, 21 twin
Bathrooms: 73 en-suite

Bed & breakfast per night:	£min	£max
Single	49.50	54.00
Double	57.00	62.00

Half board per person:	£min	£max
Daily	41.00	45.00

Lunch available
Evening meal 1900 (last orders 2130)
Parking for 250
Cards accepted: Access, Visa, Diners, Amex, Switch/Delta

Spindle Lodge Hotel
COMMENDED
2 West Walk, Leicester LE1 7NA
☎ (0116) 233 8801
Fax (0116) 233 8804

Victorian house with friendly atmosphere, within easy walking distance of city centre, university, station, civic and entertainment centres.
Bedrooms: 5 single, 3 double, 3 twin, 2 triple
Bathrooms: 7 en-suite, 3 public

Bed & breakfast per night:	£min	£max
Single	28.50	39.50
Double	51.00	63.50

Evening meal 1830 (last orders 1800)

Parking for 7
Cards accepted: Access, Visa, Switch/Delta

Stanfre' House Hotel
265 London Road, Leicester LE2 3BE
☎ (0116) 270 4294
Family-run hotel on the A6, 1 mile from the city centre and close to the university, racecourse, De Montfort Hall and railway station.
Bedrooms: 3 single, 1 double, 5 twin, 1 triple
Bathrooms: 2 public

Bed & breakfast per night:	£min	£max
Single	20.00	20.00
Double	32.00	32.00

Parking for 6

Waltham House
APPROVED
500 Narborough Road, Leicester LE3 2FU
☎ (0116) 289 1129
Victorian detached house. Close M1/M69 junction and approximately 2 miles from city centre. Very large rooms. Warm, friendly welcome assured.
Bedrooms: 2 single, 1 double, 1 twin
Bathrooms: 1 public

Bed & breakfast per night:	£min	£max
Single	19.00	22.00
Double	35.00	36.00

Parking for 4

LINCOLN
Lincolnshire
Map ref 4C2

Ancient city dominated by the magnificent 11th C cathedral with its triple towers. A Roman gateway is still used and there are medieval houses lining narrow, cobbled streets. Other attractions include the Norman castle, several museums and the Usher Gallery.
Tourist Information Centre ☎ (01522) 529828

Castle Hotel
COMMENDED
Westgate, Lincoln LN1 3AS
☎ (01522) 538801
Fax (01522) 575457

Privately owned traditional English hotel offering hospitality at its best. Listed building in Lincoln's historic heart. Impressive castle and cathedral views. Ample free parking. A unique welcome, and one we're confident you'll wish to experience again. Half-board prices are for a minimum 2-night stay.
Bedrooms: 4 single, 9 double, 5 twin, 1 triple
Bathrooms: 19 en-suite

Bed & breakfast per night:	£min	£max
Single	50.00	50.00
Double	65.00	70.00

Half board per person:	£min	£max
Daily	41.00	43.50
Weekly	287.00	304.50

Lunch available
Evening meal 1900 (last orders 2130)
Parking for 20
Cards accepted: Access, Visa, Switch/Delta

Damon's Motel
HIGHLY COMMENDED
997 Doddington Road, Lincoln LN6 3SE
☎ (01522) 500422
Fax (01522) 689719
Purpose-built, 2 storey motel on the Lincoln ring road. Adjacent restaurant, indoor pool, gym, solarium. Satellite TV.
Wheelchair access category 3
Bedrooms: 24 double, 18 twin, 5 triple
Bathrooms: 47 en-suite

Bed & breakfast per night:	£min	£max
Single	37.50	41.50
Double	39.50	45.00

Lunch available
Evening meal 1500 (last orders 2200)
Parking for 47
Cards accepted: Access, Visa, Diners, Amex, Switch/Delta

Please check prices and other details at the time of booking.

MIDDLE ENGLAND

LINCOLN
Continued

Grand Hotel
👑👑👑 COMMENDED
St. Mary's Street, Lincoln LN5 7EP
☎ (01522) 524211
Fax (01522) 537661
CR The Independents
Family-owned hotel, in the centre of the beautiful historic city of Lincoln. Breakaway weekends all year.
Bedrooms: 19 single, 15 double, 13 twin, 1 triple
Bathrooms: 48 en-suite

Bed & breakfast per night:	£min	£max
Single	46.00	56.00
Double	56.00	66.00

Half board per person:	£min	£max
Daily	35.00	40.00

Lunch available
Evening meal 1900 (last orders 2100)
Parking for 30
Cards accepted: Access, Visa, Diners, Amex, Switch/Delta

Hillcrest Hotel
👑👑👑 COMMENDED
15 Lindum Terrace, Lincoln LN2 5RT
☎ (01522) 510182
Fax (01522) 510182
CR Logis of Great Britain
Victorian rectory overlooking gardens and park. Peaceful location, 5 minutes' walk to cathedral and city. Short breaks available all year for a minimum 2-night stay.
Bedrooms: 6 single, 6 double, 1 twin, 4 triple
Bathrooms: 17 en-suite

Bed & breakfast per night:	£min	£max
Single	39.00	47.00
Double	62.50	65.00

Half board per person:	£min	£max
Daily	41.00	41.00

Lunch available
Evening meal 1915 (last orders 2045)
Parking for 7
Cards accepted: Access, Visa, Amex, Switch/Delta

Hollies Hotel
👑👑 COMMENDED
65 Carholme Road, Lincoln LN1 1RT
☎ (01522) 522419
Fax (01522) 522419
Privately-owned Victorian residence of considerable charm and character. A short and picturesque walk to the town, tourist areas and Brayford Marina.
Bedrooms: 2 single, 4 double, 2 twin, 1 triple, 1 family room
Bathrooms: 6 en-suite, 1 private, 2 public

Bed & breakfast per night:	£min	£max
Single	28.00	46.00
Double	46.00	66.00

Lunch available
Evening meal 1900 (last orders 2100)
Parking for 8
Cards accepted: Access, Visa, Amex

Newport Guesthouse
👑
26-28 Newport, Lincoln LN1 3DF
☎ (01522) 528590 & 0831 773622
Fax (01522) 542868
Part of a Victorian terrace, only 4 minutes' walk from cathedral and castle.
Bedrooms: 1 single, 1 double, 4 twin, 1 family room
Bathrooms: 2 public

Bed & breakfast per night:	£min	£max
Single		16.00
Double		32.00

Parking for 6

Tennyson Hotel
👑👑 COMMENDED
7 South Park Avenue, Lincoln LN5 8EN
☎ (01522) 521624
Fax (01522) 521624
Hotel with a comfortable atmosphere, overlooking the South Park, 1 mile from the city centre. Personally supervised. Leisure breaks available.
Bedrooms: 2 single, 3 double, 1 twin, 2 triple
Bathrooms: 8 en-suite

Bed & breakfast per night:	£min	£max
Single	26.00	26.00
Double	35.00	38.00

Evening meal 1830 (last orders 1945)

Parking for 8
Cards accepted: Access, Visa, Diners, Amex

Washingborough Hall Country House Hotel
👑👑👑 COMMENDED
Church Hill, Washingborough, Lincoln LN4 1BE
☎ (01522) 790340
Fax (01522) 792936
CR Minotel/The Independents
Stone-built, former manor house in grounds of 3 acres, in a pleasant village 2.5 miles from the historic cathedral city of Lincoln.
Bedrooms: 6 double, 6 twin
Bathrooms: 12 en-suite, 1 public

Bed & breakfast per night:	£min	£max
Single	53.50	64.00
Double	74.00	86.50

Half board per person:	£min	£max
Weekly	280.00	320.00

Evening meal 1900 (last orders 2030)
Parking for 50
Cards accepted: Access, Visa, Diners, Amex

LOUGHBOROUGH
Leicestershire
Map ref 4C3

Industrial town famous for its bell foundry and 47-bell Carillon Tower. The Great Central Railway operates steam railway rides of over 8 miles through the attractive scenery of Charnwood Forest.
Tourist Information Centre ☎ *(01509) 218113*

Demontfort Hotel
👑👑👑 COMMENDED
88 Leicester Road, Loughborough LE11 2AQ
☎ (01509) 216061
Fax (01509) 233667
Recently refurbished, friendly family-run hotel under new ownership. Close to town centre, Main Line Steam Trust, university and beautiful Leicestershire countryside.
Bedrooms: 2 single, 1 double, 5 twin, 1 triple
Bathrooms: 6 en-suite, 3 private, 1 public

MIDDLE ENGLAND

Bed & breakfast per night:	£min	£max
Single	20.00	28.00
Double	30.00	40.00

Half board per person:	£min	£max
Daily	25.50	43.50

Evening meal 1830 (last orders 2030)
Cards accepted: Access, Visa, Amex

East Midlands Hotel

Nottingham Road, Loughborough
LE11 1ET
☎ (01509) 233056
Fax (01509) 268465
Opposite Loughborough station, this hotel offers a restaurant, leisure club, 2 bars and a friendly atmosphere.
Bedrooms: 18 double, 33 twin, 2 triple
Bathrooms: 53 en-suite

Bed & breakfast per night:	£min	£max
Single	40.00	47.50
Double	59.50	64.50

Half board per person:	£min	£max
Daily	52.50	60.00

Lunch available
Evening meal 1900 (last orders 2200)
Parking for 55
Cards accepted: Access, Visa, Diners, Amex, Switch/Delta

Forest Rise Hotel

COMMENDED
55 Forest Road, Loughborough
LE11 3NW
☎ (01509) 215928
Fax (01509) 210506
Friendly personal service. Excellent order throughout. Easy access to M1 motorway, university and town centre. Car parking facilities at rear.
Bedrooms: 8 single, 10 double, 1 twin, 3 triple
Bathrooms: 18 en-suite, 4 private showers

Bed & breakfast per night:	£min	£max
Single	32.00	43.00
Double	51.00	59.50

Evening meal 1900 (last orders 2100)
Parking for 25
Cards accepted: Access, Visa, Switch/Delta

Garendon Lodge Guesthouse

COMMENDED
136 Leicester Road, Loughborough
LE11 2AQ
☎ (01509) 211120 & (0585) 582449
Spacious Victorian guesthouse, completely refurbished. In quiet surroundings but within 5 minutes of the town centre and nearby Charnwood Forest.
Bedrooms: 2 single, 3 double
Bathrooms: 5 en-suite

Bed & breakfast per night:	£min	£max
Single	22.00	25.00
Double	35.00	38.00

Half board per person:	£min	£max
Daily	28.00	32.00

Lunch available
Evening meal 1800 (last orders 2000)
Parking for 6
Cards accepted: Amex

Garendon Park Hotel

COMMENDED
92 Leicester Road, Loughborough
LE11 2AQ
☎ (01509) 236557
Fax (01509) 265559
Victorian building retaining many original features. Friendly personal service and comfortable atmosphere. Close to town centre, Steam Trust and university.
Bedrooms: 2 single, 2 double, 2 twin, 1 triple, 2 family rooms
Bathrooms: 6 en-suite, 2 private, 2 public

Bed & breakfast per night:	£min	£max
Single	23.00	30.00
Double	35.00	45.00

Evening meal 1830 (last orders 2030)
Cards accepted: Access, Visa, Amex, Switch/Delta

The Highbury Guesthouse

COMMENDED
146 Leicester Road, Loughborough
LE11 0BJ
☎ (01509) 230545

Guesthouse on the A6 road from Loughborough to Leicester. Within 5 minutes' walking distance of the town centre. Convenient for steam railway, junction 23 of M1, university, airport and Donington Park.
Bedrooms: 4 single, 4 double, 3 triple
Bathrooms: 7 en-suite, 1 private, 1 public, 3 private showers

Bed & breakfast per night:	£min	£max
Single	19.00	23.50
Double	30.00	36.00

Half board per person:	£min	£max
Daily	24.00	28.50
Weekly	140.00	155.00

Evening meal 1800 (last orders 2000)
Parking for 12

Jarvis Kings Head Hotel

COMMENDED
High Street, Loughborough
LE11 2QL
☎ (01509) 233222
Fax (01509) 262911
Jarvis/Utell International

Georgian-style hotel located midway between Leeds and London, only 3 miles off M1. Many interesting places to visit in the nearby English shires.
Bedrooms: 20 single, 34 double, 26 twin
Bathrooms: 78 en-suite, 4 public

Bed & breakfast per night:	£min	£max
Single	37.50	77.50
Double	75.00	96.00

Half board per person:	£min	£max
Daily	47.50	87.50

Lunch available
Evening meal 1900 (last orders 2130)
Parking for 80
Cards accepted: Access, Visa, Diners, Amex, Switch/Delta

Please mention this guide when making your booking.

MIDDLE ENGLAND

LOUGHBOROUGH
Continued

Peachnook
Listed

154 Ashby Road, Loughborough
LE11 3AG
☎ (01509) 264390
Small, friendly guesthouse built around 1890. Near all amenities. TV and tea-making facilities in all rooms. Ironing facilities.
Bedrooms: 1 twin, 2 triple
Bathrooms: 2 en-suite, 1 public
Bed & breakfast

per night:	£min	£max
Single	12.00	25.00
Double	28.00	35.00

MACKWORTH
Derbyshire
Map ref 4B2

An old Roman road lies between Mackworth and Markeaton. Built on the side is All Saints Church with a rare tower.

The Mackworth Hotel
COMMENDED

Ashbourne Road, Mackworth, Derby
DE22 4LY
☎ Kirk Langley (01332) 824324
Fax (01332) 824692

Independent hotel with ample car parking, in a rural setting. Recently refurbished restaurant and bedrooms. Within easy reach of city centre, Peak District and Alton Towers.
Bedrooms: 4 single, 5 double, 2 twin, 2 triple, 1 family room
Bathrooms: 14 en-suite
Bed & breakfast

per night:	£min	£max
Single	44.50	47.50
Double	59.00	69.50

Half board per

person:	£min	£max
Daily	52.45	64.50
Weekly	367.15	451.30

Lunch available
Evening meal 1800 (last orders 2145)
Parking for 80

Cards accepted: Access, Visa, Amex, Switch/Delta

MANSFIELD
Nottinghamshire
Map ref 4C2

Ancient town, now an industrial and shopping centre, with a popular market, in the heart of Robin Hood country. There is an impressive 19th C railway viaduct, 2 interesting churches, an 18th C Moot Hall and a museum and art gallery.

Pine Lodge Hotel
COMMENDED

281-283 Nottingham Road,
Mansfield NG18 4SE
☎ (01623) 22308
Fax (01623) 656819
Friendly and informal. Good food, good value, excellent service.
Bedrooms: 5 single, 5 double, 7 twin, 2 triple
Bathrooms: 19 en-suite
Bed & breakfast

per night:	£min	£max
Single	25.00	49.95
Double	40.00	59.95

Half board per

person:	£min	£max
Daily	33.00	63.00
Weekly	281.00	

Lunch available
Evening meal 1900 (last orders 2100)
Parking for 35
Cards accepted: Access, Visa, Diners, Amex, Switch/Delta

MARKET HARBOROUGH
Leicestershire
Map ref 4C3

There have been markets here since the early 13th C, and the town was also an important coaching centre, with several ancient hostelries. The early 17th C grammar school was once the butter market.
Tourist Information Centre ☎ (01858) 468106

The George at Great Oxendon
COMMENDED

Great Oxendon, Market Harborough LE16 8NA
☎ (01858) 465205
Fax (01858) 465105
Bedroom accommodation and restaurant with bars and conservatory, all with views of the garden. Ex-QE2 chef/proprietor.
Bedrooms: 2 double, 1 twin
Bathrooms: 3 en-suite
Bed & breakfast

per night:	£min	£max
Single	49.50	53.00
Double	59.50	

Lunch available
Evening meal 1900 (last orders 2200)
Parking for 36
Cards accepted: Access, Visa, Amex

MARSTON
Lincolnshire
Map ref 3A1

Thorold Arms
Listed COMMENDED

Main Street, Marston, Grantham
NG32 2HH
☎ Honington (01400) 250899 & 0831 340018
Fax (01400) 251030
Typical inn, circa 1830, in middle of village on the Viking Way. Traditional cask ales plus guest ales. Home-cooked food.
Bedrooms: 1 double, 1 family room
Bathrooms: 2 en-suite
Bed & breakfast

per night:	£min	£max
Single	20.00	25.00
Double	40.00	50.00

Half board per

person:	£min	£max
Daily	27.50	35.00
Weekly	140.00	175.00

Lunch available
Evening meal 1900 (last orders 2200)
Parking for 14
Cards accepted: Visa, Amex

WELCOME HOST

This is a nationally recognised customer care programme which aims to promote the highest standards of service and a warm welcome. Establishments who are taking part in this initiative are indicated by the symbol.

MIDDLE ENGLAND

MATLOCK
Derbyshire
Map ref 4B2

The town lies beside the narrow valley of the River Derwent surrounded by steep wooded hills. Good centre for exploring Derbyshire's best scenery.

Derwent House
Knowleston Place, Matlock
DE4 3BU
☎ (01629) 584681
Charming 17th/18th C house situated close to park and the River Derwent. Well-known for full English and vegetarian cooked breakfasts.
Bedrooms: 2 single, 1 double, 1 triple
Bathrooms: 1 en-suite, 1 public
Bed & breakfast

per night:	£min	£max
Single	17.00	17.00
Double	34.00	40.00

Lane End House
HIGHLY COMMENDED
Green Lane, Tansley, Matlock
DE4 5FJ
☎ (01629) 583981
Fax (01629) 583981
Georgian farmhouse, c.1730. Non-smoking. Every comfort, super healthy food and good wine cellar. Idyllically situated with spectacular views to Riber Castle. Close to Chatsworth, Haddon, Hardwick.
Bedrooms: 3 double, 1 twin
Bathrooms: 2 en-suite, 2 private
Bed & breakfast

per night:	£min	£max
Single	30.00	35.00
Double	44.00	55.00

Half board per

person:	£min	£max
Daily	36.95	42.45
Weekly	238.00	277.00

Evening meal 1930 (last orders 1900)
Parking for 8
Cards accepted: Access, Visa

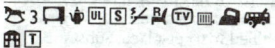

The symbol after an establishment name indicates that it is a Regional Tourist Board member.

The Red House Hotel
HIGHLY COMMENDED
Old Road, Darley Dale, Matlock
DE4 2ER
☎ (01629) 734854
Fax (01629) 734854

Attractive country house situated on the edge of the beautiful Peak District National Park. Delightful gardens and panoramic views.
Bedrooms: 1 single, 5 double, 2 twin, 1 triple
Bathrooms: 9 en-suite
Bed & breakfast

per night:	£min	£max
Single	50.00	55.00
Double	75.00	85.00

Half board per

person:	£min	£max
Daily	66.00	68.00
Weekly	300.00	462.00

Lunch available
Evening meal 1930 (last orders 2100)
Parking for 20
Cards accepted: Access, Visa, Diners, Amex, Switch/Delta

Riber Hall
HIGHLY COMMENDED
Matlock DE4 5JU
☎ (01629) 582795
Fax (01629) 580475
Enjoy pure tranquillity in the intimate atmosphere of this historic Derbyshire country house. Noted in all major hotel and restaurant guides.
Bedrooms: 11 double
Bathrooms: 11 en-suite
Bed & breakfast

per night:	£min	£max
Single	85.00	
Double	105.00	150.00

Half board per

person:	£min	£max
Daily	110.00	

Lunch available
Evening meal 1900 (last orders 2130)
Parking for 50
Cards accepted: Access, Visa, Diners, Amex, Switch/Delta

Robertswood
COMMENDED
Farley Hill, Matlock DE4 3LL
☎ (01629) 55642
Fax (01629) 55642
Spacious Victorian residence on the edge of Matlock, with panoramic views. Near Chatsworth. All bedrooms en-suite. Friendly, warm welcome.
Bedrooms: 4 double, 3 twin
Bathrooms: 7 en-suite
Bed & breakfast

per night:	£min	£max
Single	35.00	35.00
Double	40.00	50.00

Half board per

person:	£min	£max
Daily	45.00	45.00
Weekly	210.00	245.00

Evening meal 1830 (last orders 1900)
Parking for 12
Cards accepted: Access, Visa, Switch/Delta

Winstaff Guesthouse
APPROVED
Derwent Avenue, (Off Old English Road), Matlock DE4 3LX
☎ (01629) 582593
In a pleasant, quiet cul-de-sac, with a garden backing on to the River Derwent and the park, central for many tourist attractions. Private forecourt parking. Colour TV in all rooms.
Bedrooms: 2 single, 3 double, 1 twin, 1 family room
Bathrooms: 3 en-suite, 1 public
Bed & breakfast

per night:	£min	£max
Single	18.00	20.50
Double	36.00	41.00

Parking for 6

Establishments should be open throughout the year, unless otherwise stated.

All accommodation in this guide has been graded, or is awaiting a grading, by a trained Tourist Board inspector.

MIDDLE ENGLAND

MATLOCK BATH

Derbyshire
Map ref 4B2

19th C spa town with many attractions including several caverns to visit, a lead mining museum and a family fun park. There are marvellous views over the surrounding countryside from the Heights of Abraham, to which a cable car gives easy access.
Tourist Information Centre ☎ *(01629) 55082*

Hodgkinsons Hotel

COMMENDED

150 South Parade, Matlock Bath, Matlock DE4 3NR
☎ Matlock (01629) 582170
Fax (01629) 584891
Georgian hotel, beautifully restored, with original features. Open fires, antique shop and hairdressing salon. Terraced garden with lovely views.
Bedrooms: 1 single, 6 double
Bathrooms: 7 en-suite

Bed & breakfast per night:	£min	£max
Single	30.00	35.00
Double	50.00	90.00

Half board per person:	£min	£max
Daily	44.50	84.50
Weekly	260.00	380.00

Evening meal 1930 (last orders 2100)
Parking for 6
Cards accepted: Access, Visa, Amex, Switch/Delta

Temple Hotel

COMMENDED

Temple Walk, Matlock Bath, Matlock DE4 3PG
☎ Matlock (01629) 583911
Fax (01629) 580851

The hotel nestles comfortably amid "Little Switzerland" scenery of picturesque Matlock Bath, overlooking the Vale of the River Derwent from a steep, wooded hillside. All bedrooms en-suite with colour TV.
Bedrooms: 1 single, 10 double, 3 twin
Bathrooms: 14 en-suite

Bed & breakfast per night:	£min	£max
Single	39.00	44.00
Double	61.00	66.00

Half board per person:	£min	£max
Daily	51.00	56.00

Lunch available
Evening meal 1800 (last orders 2100)
Parking for 45
Cards accepted: Access, Visa, Diners, Amex

MELTON MOWBRAY

Leicestershire
Map ref 4C3

Close to the attractive Vale of Belvoir and famous for its pork pies and Stilton cheese which are the subjects of special displays in the museum. It has a beautiful church with a tower 100 ft high.
Tourist Information Centre ☎ *(01664) 480992*

Quorn Lodge Hotel

COMMENDED

46 Asfordby Road, Melton Mowbray LE13 0HR
☎ (01664) 66660 & 62590
Fax (01664) 480660
Originally a hunting lodge. Short walk from busy market town. Family owned and run. Restaurant overlooking garden serving a la carte and table d'hote meals. Large car park.
Bedrooms: 6 single, 8 double, 5 twin, 1 triple
Bathrooms: 20 en-suite

Bed & breakfast per night:	£min	£max
Single	37.50	47.50
Double	50.00	65.00

Half board per person:	£min	£max
Daily	48.00	58.00

Lunch available
Evening meal 1900 (last orders 2100)
Parking for 33
Cards accepted: Access, Visa, Diners, Switch/Delta

Sysonby Knoll Hotel

COMMENDED

Asfordby Road, Melton Mowbray LE13 0HP
☎ (01664) 63563
Fax (01664) 410364
Logis of Great Britain
Family owned and run hotel, in its own grounds, offering a cosy bar and restaurant serving table d'hote and a la carte meals. Bar snacks available lunchtime and evening. Overlooks gardens and River Eye. Private car park.
Bedrooms: 6 single, 10 double, 6 twin, 2 triple
Bathrooms: 24 en-suite

Bed & breakfast per night:	£min	£max
Single	35.00	52.00
Double	49.00	60.00

Lunch available
Evening meal 1900 (last orders 2100)
Parking for 30
Cards accepted: Access, Visa, Diners, Amex, Switch/Delta

NEWARK

Nottinghamshire
Map ref 4C2

The town has many fine old houses and ancient inns near the large, cobbled market-place. Substantial ruins of the 12th C castle, where King John died, dominate the riverside walk and there are several interesting museums. Sherwood Forest is nearby.
Tourist Information Centre ☎ *(01636) 78962*

The Grange Hotel

COMMENDED

73 London Road, Newark NG24 1RZ
☎ (01636) 703399
Fax (01636) 702328
Family-run hotel with en-suite rooms, candlelit restaurant and excellent food. Spacious bar with good selection of wines and malt whiskies. Car park.
Bedrooms: 2 single, 9 double, 3 twin, 1 triple
Bathrooms: 15 en-suite

Bed & breakfast per night:	£min	£max
Single	42.50	55.00
Double	59.50	69.50

Half board per person:	£min	£max
Daily	55.00	62.00

Lunch available
Evening meal 1900 (last orders 2100)
Parking for 18
Cards accepted: Access, Visa, Amex, Switch/Delta

MIDDLE ENGLAND

South Parade Hotel

117 Balderton Gate, Newark
NG24 1RY
☎ (01636) 703008
Fax (01636) 605593
Ⓒ The Independents
Family-run Georgian listed hotel in quiet location, 5 minutes' walk from market place. Good home-cooked food, warm and friendly bar and restaurant. Car park.
Bedrooms: 5 single, 5 double, 2 twin, 2 triple
Bathrooms: 12 en-suite, 2 private, 3 public

Bed & breakfast per night:

	£min	£max
Single	36.00	42.00
Double	45.00	64.00

Half board per person:

	£min	£max
Daily	40.00	50.45

Lunch available
Evening meal 1900 (last orders 2045)
Parking for 12
Cards accepted: Access, Visa, Amex, Switch/Delta

Willow Tree Inn
COMMENDED

Front Street, Barnby-in-the-Willows, Newark NG24 2SA
☎ Fenton Claypole (01286) 626613
Fax (01636) 626060
17th C village inn, conveniently placed for historic Lincoln, Grantham, Newark and Sherwood. Known locally for good food and ales. Off the A17 and A1.
Bedrooms: 1 double, 3 triple
Bathrooms: 4 en-suite

Bed & breakfast per night:

	£min	£max
Single	28.50	28.50
Double	37.50	37.50

Half board per person:

	£min	£max
Daily	38.00	38.00
Weekly	250.00	250.00

Lunch available
Evening meal 1900 (last orders 2130)
Parking for 50
Cards accepted: Access, Visa, Amex

A key to symbols can be found inside the back cover flap.

NORTHAMPTON

Northamptonshire
Map ref 2C1

A bustling town and a shoe manufacturing centre, with excellent shopping facilities, several museums and parks, a theatre and a concert hall. Several old churches include 1 of only 4 round churches in Britain.
Tourist Information Centre ☎ (01604) 22677

Aarandale Regent Hotel and Guesthouse

6-8 Royal Terrace, Barrack Road (A508), Northampton NN1 3RF
☎ (01604) 31096
Fax (01604) 21035
Small and cosy, family-run hotel/guesthouse within easy walking distance of town centre, bus and train stations.
Bedrooms: 4 single, 6 double, 6 twin, 4 triple
Bathrooms: 5 public

Bed & breakfast per night:

	£min	£max
Single	24.00	28.00
Double	39.00	43.00

Half board per person:

	£min	£max
Daily	29.00	33.00
Weekly	190.00	219.00

Evening meal 1930 (last orders 2130)
Parking for 14
Cards accepted: Access, Visa, Diners, Amex

Broomhill Country House Hotel and Restaurant
COMMENDED

Holdenby Road, Spratton, Northampton NN6 8LD
☎ (01604) 845959
Fax (01604) 845834
Converted Victorian country house with some splendid views. As a welcomed guest you will be offered relaxed, old fashioned hospitality, while chef will tempt you with his interesting and varied menus. 6 miles north of Northampton, 6 miles from A14.
Bedrooms: 2 single, 4 double, 7 twin
Bathrooms: 13 en-suite

Bed & breakfast per night:

	£min	£max
Single	60.00	60.00
Double	70.00	75.00

Half board per person:

	£min	£max
Daily		78.75

Lunch available
Evening meal 1900 (last orders 2145)
Parking for 100
Cards accepted: Access, Visa, Diners, Amex

Courtyard by Marriott Northampton

Bedford Road, Northampton NN4 7YF
☎ (01604) 22777
Fax (01604) 35454
Ⓒ Whitbread/Utell International
A business and leisure hotel, 5 minutes' drive from both the town centre and the M1, junction 15.
Bedrooms: 48 single, 20 twin, 36 triple
Suites available
Bathrooms: 104 en-suite

Bed & breakfast per night:

	£min	£max
Single	70.00	95.00
Double	78.25	105.00

Half board per person:

	£min	£max
Daily	85.00	110.00

Lunch available
Evening meal 1830 (last orders 2215)
Parking for 160
Cards accepted: Access, Visa, Diners, Amex, Switch/Delta

Courtyard Daventry
HIGHLY COMMENDED

High Street, Flore, Northampton NN7 4LP
☎ Weedon (01327) 349022
Fax (01327) 349017
Ⓒ Whitbread
Modern hotel in a rural setting to the west of Northampton, only 1 mile from junction 16 of the M1.
Wheelchair access category 3
Bedrooms: 2 single, 26 double, 25 twin
Bathrooms: 53 en-suite

Bed & breakfast per night:

	£min	£max
Single	24.00	75.50
Double	48.00	84.00

Half board per person:

	£min	£max
Daily	36.00	91.50
Weekly	252.00	407.00

Continued ▶

MIDDLE ENGLAND

NORTHAMPTON
Continued

Lunch available
Evening meal 1900 (last orders 2130)
Parking for 170
Cards accepted: Access, Visa, Diners, Amex, Switch/Delta

Grand Hotel
COMMENDED

Gold Street, Northampton
NN1 1RE
☎ (01604) 250511
Fax (01604) 234534
Centrally located in a busy market town with many splendid tourist attractions to see in the area. Easy access to London and the south and Birmingham and the north.
Bedrooms: 12 single, 23 double, 18 twin, 2 triple
Bathrooms: 55 en-suite

Bed & breakfast per night:

	£min	£max
Single	40.00	70.00
Double	80.00	150.00

Half board per person:

	£min	£max
Daily	50.00	80.00

Lunch available
Evening meal 1830 (last orders 2130)
Parking for 66
Cards accepted: Access, Visa, Diners, Amex

Hollington Guesthouse
Listed

22 Abington Grove, Northampton
NN1 4QW
☎ (01604) 32584
Comfortable guesthouse, close to town centre with easy access to M1. TV and tea-making facilities in all rooms.
Bedrooms: 2 single, 2 double, 1 twin, 2 triple
Bathrooms: 2 public

Bed & breakfast per night:

	£min	£max
Single	16.00	18.00
Double	30.00	34.00

Parking for 6
Cards accepted: Access, Visa, Switch/Delta

Lime Trees Hotel
COMMENDED

8 Langham Place, Barrack Road, Northampton NN2 6AA
☎ (01604) 32188
Fax (01604) 233012
The Independents

Beautifully restored, owner-managed hotel with restaurant, set in a Georgian terrace, with easy access to the motorway. Car park.
Bedrooms: 10 single, 10 double, 2 twin, 3 triple
Bathrooms: 23 en-suite, 2 public

Bed & breakfast per night:

	£min	£max
Single	37.50	49.50
Double	52.00	65.00

Half board per person:

	£min	£max
Daily	49.50	68.00

Lunch available
Evening meal 1900 (last orders 2100)
Parking for 24
Cards accepted: Access, Visa, Diners, Amex, Switch/Delta

Poplars Hotel
Listed

Cross Street, Moulton, Northampton NN3 7RZ
☎ (01604) 643983
Fax (01604) 790233
Personal attention is given at this small country hotel in the heart of Northamptonshire. Within easy reach of many tourist attractions.
Bedrooms: 11 single, 8 double, 1 twin
Bathrooms: 16 en-suite, 2 public

Bed & breakfast per night:

	£min	£max
Single	20.00	37.50
Double	39.50	49.50

Half board per person:

	£min	£max
Daily	30.00	47.50

Evening meal 1830 (last orders 1830)
Parking for 21
Cards accepted: Access, Visa, Amex

Swallow Hotel
HIGHLY COMMENDED

Eagle Drive, Northampton
NN4 7HW
☎ (01604) 768700
Fax (01604) 769011
Swallow
Modern hotel with a leisure club and choice of two restaurants, overlooking a lake and golf-course. 3 miles from junction 15 M1. Short break packages available.
Bedrooms: 82 double, 38 twin
Suites available
Bathrooms: 120 en-suite

Bed & breakfast per night:

	£min	£max
Single	60.00	99.00
Double	65.00	110.00

Half board per person:

	£min	£max
Daily	78.75	117.75

Lunch available
Evening meal 1900 (last orders 2230)
Parking for 166
Cards accepted: Access, Visa, Diners, Amex

NOTTINGHAM
Nottinghamshire
Map ref 4C2

Attractive modern city with a rich history. Outside its castle, now a museum, is Robin Hood's statue. Attractions include "The Tales of Robin Hood"; the Lace Hall; Wollaton Hall; museums and excellent facilities for shopping, sports and entertainment.
Tourist Information Centre ☎ (0115) 947 0661

Clifton Hotel
APPROVED

126 Nottingham Road, Long Eaton, Nottingham NG10 2BZ
☎ Long Eaton (0115) 973 4277
Friendly, family-run hotel close to M1, exit 25. 10 minutes from Donington Racecourse, East Midlands International Airport, Derby and Nottingham.
Bedrooms: 5 single, 2 double, 1 twin, 2 triple
Bathrooms: 2 en-suite, 2 public

Bed & breakfast per night:

	£min	£max
Single	18.00	25.00
Double	26.00	32.00

Half board per person:

	£min	£max
Daily	24.75	31.75

MIDDLE ENGLAND

Evening meal 1830 (last orders 1730)
Parking for 25

Europa Hotel
APPROVED
20-22 Derby Road, Long Eaton, Nottingham NG10 1LW
☎ Long Eaton (0115) 972 8481
Fax (0115) 946 0229
On the A6005 midway between Nottingham and Derby, 1.5 miles from M1 junction 25 and the A52, and 6 miles from East Midlands International Airport.
Bedrooms: 4 single, 3 double, 6 twin, 2 triple
Bathrooms: 13 en-suite, 1 private, 1 private shower

Bed & breakfast per night:	£min	£max
Single	27.00	34.00
Double	36.00	40.00

Half board per person:	£min	£max
Daily		40.00

Lunch available
Evening meal 1830 (last orders 2030)
Parking for 20
Cards accepted: Access, Visa, Diners, Amex, Switch/Delta

Fairhaven Private Hotel
19 Meadow Road, Beeston Rylands, Nottingham NG9 1JP
☎ (0115) 922 7509
Family-run private hotel close to the university and rail station, midway between the M1 and Nottingham city centre.
Bedrooms: 5 single, 4 double, 2 twin, 1 triple
Suites available
Bathrooms: 7 en-suite, 3 public

Bed & breakfast per night:	£min	£max
Single	20.00	30.00
Double	30.00	40.00

Evening meal 1800 (last orders 1400)
Parking for 12

Grantham Hotel
COMMENDED
24-26 Radcliffe Road, West Bridgford, Nottingham NG2 5FW
☎ (0115) 981 1373
Fax (0115) 981 8567
Family-run licensed hotel offering modern accommodation in a comfortable atmosphere. Convenient for the centre of Nottingham, Trent Bridge and the National Water Sports Centre.
Bedrooms: 13 single, 2 double, 4 twin, 2 triple, 1 family room
Bathrooms: 13 en-suite, 3 public

Bed & breakfast per night:	£min	£max
Single	19.95	27.00
Double	36.00	39.00

Half board per person:	£min	£max
Daily	26.00	34.00
Weekly	158.00	198.00

Evening meal 1800 (last orders 1900)
Parking for 20
Cards accepted: Access, Visa, Amex, Switch/Delta

Greenwood Lodge
HIGHLY COMMENDED
Third Avenue, Sherwood Rise, Nottingham NG7 6JH
☎ (0115) 962 1206
Fax (0115) 962 1206

Warm and welcoming Victorian house, 1 mile from city centre. All rooms en-suite with tea/coffee facilities, trouser press, TV and telephone.
Bedrooms: 1 single, 3 double, 1 twin
Bathrooms: 5 en-suite

Bed & breakfast per night:	£min	£max
Single	29.00	40.00
Double	42.00	50.00

Half board per person:	£min	£max
Daily	39.00	50.00
Weekly	271.00	350.00

Lunch available
Evening meal 1800 (last orders 2000)
Parking for 5
Cards accepted: Access, Visa

The Nottingham Gateway Hotel
HIGHLY COMMENDED
Nuthall Road, Nottingham NG8 6AZ
☎ (0115) 979 4949
Fax (0115) 979 4744

Privately owned hotel with impressive glass architectural features. Ground floor entrance, free and easy car parking, carvery and Thai restaurant providing comfort and personal service. Convenient for numerous places of interest including Tales of Robin Hood and the Lace Hall.
Wheelchair access category 3
Bedrooms: 69 double, 31 twin, 8 triple
Bathrooms: 108 en-suite

Bed & breakfast per night:	£min	£max
Single	25.00	64.50
Double	50.00	80.00

Half board per person:	£min	£max
Daily	35.00	74.50
Weekly	245.00	365.00

Lunch available
Evening meal 1830 (last orders 2230)
Parking for 250
Cards accepted: Access, Visa, Diners, Amex, Switch/Delta

Oakmont House
COMMENDED
51 Shearing Hill, Gedling, Nottingham NG4 3GY
☎ (0115) 961 6534
Charming Victorian house, with full central heating. All rooms private facilities. Guests' lounge, satellite TV. Freshly cooked evening dinner and full English breakfast. Car-parking. Non-smokers only, please.
Bedrooms: 1 single, 2 double, 1 twin
Bathrooms: 2 en-suite, 2 private

Bed & breakfast per night:	£min	£max
Single	25.00	32.00
Double	39.50	45.00

Half board per person:	£min	£max
Daily	35.00	45.00
Weekly	230.00	299.00

Lunch available
Evening meal 1800 (last orders 1930)
Parking for 6
Cards accepted: Access, Visa

MIDDLE ENGLAND

NOTTINGHAM
Continued

St. Andrews Private Hotel

310 Queens Road, Beeston,
Nottingham NG9 1JA
☎ (0115) 925 4902
Fax (0115) 925 4902
Friendly, family-run guesthouse with easy access to Nottingham city centre, the university, M1 and East Midlands International Airport. Nottingham Tennis Centre nearby. Convenient for Sherwood Forest and Derbyshire.
Bedrooms: 4 single, 2 double, 3 twin, 1 triple
Bathrooms: 3 en-suite, 3 public

Bed & breakfast per night:
	£min	£max
Single	20.00	30.00
Double	30.00	40.00

Half board per person:
	£min	£max
Daily	27.00	38.00
Weekly	189.00	266.00

Evening meal 1745 (last orders 1900)
Parking for 6

Swans Hotel and Restaurant
COMMENDED

84-90 Radcliffe Road, West Bridgford, Nottingham NG2 5HH
☎ (0115) 981 4042
Fax (0115) 945 5745
Minotel

An elegant hotel, where your stay will be relaxing in an atmosphere that gratifies the most discerning guest. Ideally placed for all Nottingham's major sporting facilities.
Bedrooms: 6 single, 19 double, 3 twin, 2 triple, 1 family room
Suite available
Bathrooms: 31 en-suite

Bed & breakfast per night:
	£min	£max
Single	32.50	45.00
Double	45.00	55.00

Lunch available
Evening meal 1900 (last orders 2200)
Parking for 30

Cards accepted: Access, Visa, Diners, Amex, Switch/Delta

OAKHAM
Leicestershire
Map ref 4C3

Pleasant former county town of Rutland. Fine 12th C Great Hall, part of its castle, with a historic collection of horseshoes. An octagonal Butter Cross stands in the market-place and Rutland County Museum, Rutland Farm Park and Rutland Water are of interest.
Tourist Information Centre ☎ (01572) 724329

Boultons Country House Hotel
COMMENDED

4 Catmos Street, Oakham LE15 6HW
☎ (01572) 722844
Fax (01572) 724473
Consort
In the county of Rutland. Unspoilt surroundings with many attractions, including Rutland Water. Country house ambience, pub circa 1604 and intimate restaurant.
Bedrooms: 7 single, 12 double, 6 twin
Bathrooms: 25 en-suite

Bed & breakfast per night:
	£min	£max
Single		60.00
Double		75.00

Half board per person:
	£min	£max
Daily		78.50
Weekly		471.00

Lunch available
Evening meal 1900 (last orders 2200)
Parking for 15
Cards accepted: Access, Visa, Diners, Amex, Switch/Delta

TOWN INDEX

This can be found at the back of the guide. If you know where you want to stay, the index will give you the page number listing all accommodation in your chosen town, city or village.

OLLERTON
Nottinghamshire
Map ref 4C2

A good base for exploring the Dukeries which include the 3800 acres of Clumber Park with its famous avenue of limes. Sherwood Forest is nearby.
Tourist Information Centre ☎ (01623) 824545

Hop Pole Hotel
COMMENDED

Ollerton, Newark NG22 9AD
☎ Mansfield (01623) 822573 & 822305

Former coaching inn with carvery restaurant situated in the picturesque village of Ollerton and ideally located for touring Robin Hood country.
Bedrooms: 2 single, 4 double, 4 twin, 1 triple
Bathrooms: 8 en-suite, 3 private, 1 public

Bed & breakfast per night:
	£min	£max
Single		32.00
Double		45.00

Lunch available
Evening meal 1800 (last orders 2200)
Parking for 30
Cards accepted: Access, Visa, Amex, Switch/Delta

OUNDLE
Northamptonshire
Map ref 3A1

Historic town situated on the River Nene with narrow alleys and courtyards and many stone buildings, including a fine church and historic inns.
Tourist Information Centre ☎ (01832) 274333

Talbot Hotel
COMMENDED

New Street, Oundle, Peterborough PE8 4EA
☎ (01832) 273621
Fax (01832) 274545
Forte
An inn of great charm and character,

built in 1626 from the ruins of nearby Fotheringhay Castle.
Bedrooms: 6 single, 24 double, 9 twin
Bathrooms: 39 en-suite

Bed & breakfast

per night:	£min	£max
Single	75.00	79.00
Double	79.00	97.00

Lunch available
Evening meal 1900 (last orders 2130)
Parking for 50
Cards accepted: Access, Visa, Diners, Amex, Switch/Delta

PEAK DISTRICT

See under Ashbourne, Bakewell, Baslow, Buxton, Castleton, Cressbrook, Dovedale, Edale, Froggatt, Glossop, Grindleford, Hathersage, Hope

QUORN

Leicestershire
Map ref 4C3

The Great Central Railway, a preserved steam railway, runs through attractively wooded countryside at the edge of this village.

Quorn Grange Hotel and Restaurant

COMMENDED

Quorn Grange, 88 Wood Lane, Quorn, Loughborough LE12 8DB
☎ Loughborough (01509) 412167
Fax (01509) 415621
Old country house on the edge of Bradgate Park, set in its own gardens.
Bedrooms: 10 double, 6 twin
Bathrooms: 16 en-suite

Bed & breakfast

per night:	£min	£max
Single	72.00	
Double	88.00	

Lunch available
Evening meal 1900 (last orders 2200)
Parking for 100
Cards accepted: Access, Visa, Diners, Amex, Switch/Delta

COLOUR MAPS

Colour maps at the back of this guide pinpoint all places in which you will find accommodation listed.

REDMILE

Leicestershire
Map ref 4C2

Vale of Belvoir village, overlooked by the hilltop castle.

Peacock Farm Guesthouse and Country Restaurant

Redmile, Nottingham NG13 0GQ
☎ (01949) 842475
Fax (01949) 43127
Logis of Great Britain
Nicky, Peter and Marjorie Need welcome you to their old farmhouse in the delightful Vale of Belvoir, close to the castle. A small licensed restaurant is attached, and there is a small covered pool, play room and gardens.
Bedrooms: 1 single, 2 double, 2 twin, 3 triple, 2 family rooms
Bathrooms: 9 en-suite, 2 public

Bed & breakfast

per night:	£min	£max
Single		32.00
Double		45.00

Half board per

person:	£min	£max
Daily	36.00	46.00
Weekly	227.00	286.00

Lunch available
Evening meal 1900 (last orders 2100)
Parking for 40
Cards accepted: Access, Visa, Diners, Amex, Switch/Delta

RETFORD

Nottinghamshire
Map ref 4C2

Market town on the River Idle with a pleasant market square and Georgian houses. The surrounding villages were the homes and meeting places of the early Pilgrim Fathers.
Tourist Information Centre ☎ (01777) 860780

The Old Plough

DE LUXE

Top Street, North Wheatley, Retford DN22 9DB
☎ Gainsborough (01427) 880916
Listed Georgian dwelling offering de luxe accommodation and home-cooked food in a small village between Retford and Gainsborough.
Bedrooms: 2 double, 1 twin
Bathrooms: 1 en-suite, 2 private

MIDDLE ENGLAND

Bed & breakfast

per night:	£min	£max
Single	27.50	27.50
Double	55.00	55.00

Half board per

person:	£min	£max
Daily	41.00	41.00
Weekly	287.00	287.00

Evening meal 2000 (last orders 2000)
Parking for 4

RIPLEY

Derbyshire
Map ref 4B2

Busy market town, with leisure centre.
Tourist Information Centre ☎ (01773) 841488 or 841486

Hammersmith House Hotel

Butterley Lane, Hammersmith, Ripley, Derby DE5 3RA
☎ (01773) 742574 & 745462
Fax (01773) 740266
Privately-owned hotel near A38 and M1, with a quiet, relaxed, friendly atmosphere. All rooms en-suite with colour TV and telephone.
Bedrooms: 1 single, 5 double, 1 twin, 2 triple, 3 family rooms
Bathrooms: 12 en-suite, 1 public

Bed & breakfast

per night:	£min	£max
Single	34.50	37.50
Double	40.00	43.00

Half board per

person:	£min	£max
Daily	43.45	46.45
Weekly	304.15	325.15

Evening meal 1930 (last orders 2000)
Parking for 75
Cards accepted: Access, Visa

The map references refer to the colour maps towards the end of the guide. The first figure is the map number; the letter and figure which follow indicate the grid reference on the map.

MIDDLE ENGLAND

RISLEY
Derbyshire
Map ref 4C2

Risley Hall
♛♛♛ HIGHLY COMMENDED
Derby Road, Risley, Draycott
DE72 3SS
☎ Nottingham (0115) 9399000
Fax (0115) 9397766

Risley Hall dates from the 16th C to the 20th C. A beautiful country house in an outstanding setting with period gardens. Sixteen bedrooms, leisure facilities, banqueting and conferences for up to 150 people.
Bedrooms: 16 double
Suite available
Bathrooms: 16 en-suite
Bed & breakfast
per night: £min £max
Single 50.00 80.00
Double 60.00 95.00
Half board per
person: £min £max
Daily 65.00 95.00
Weekly 472.50 693.00
Lunch available
Evening meal 1830 (last orders 2130)
Cards accepted: Access, Visa, Amex, Switch/Delta
⛔👁🗝🏧♿👜🍴🍽📺⭕🛏💶⚿
🛁🛎150 🐕🔍�️🏊🏇🎾🎯 SP

SHERWOOD FOREST
See under Mansfield, Newark, Retford, Worksop

SKEGNESS
Lincolnshire
Map ref 4D2

Famous seaside resort with 6 miles of sandy beaches and bracing air. Attractions include swimming pools, bowling greens, gardens, Natureland Marine Zoo, golf-courses and a wide range of entertainment at the Embassy Centre. Nearby is Gibraltar Point Nature Reserve.
Tourist Information Centre ☎ (01754) 764821

Grosvenor House Hotel
♛♛♛ COMMENDED
North Parade, Skegness PE25 2TE
☎ (01754) 763376

The hotel is midway along the seafront, near the bathing pool, bowling greens, Sun Castle and the Embassy Conference Centre.
Bedrooms: 9 single, 9 double, 3 twin, 11 triple, 1 family room
Bathrooms: 23 en-suite, 4 public
Bed & breakfast
per night: £min £max
Single 23.20 28.80
Double 46.40 57.60
Half board per
person: £min £max
Daily 32.00 38.10
Weekly 197.75 233.80
Lunch available
Evening meal 1830 (last orders 1915)
Parking for 6
Open April–October
Cards accepted: Access, Visa, Diners, Amex
⛔👁🗝🏧♿🍴📺⭕🛏💶⚿🛁🎯✈ SP T

Saxby Hotel
♛♛♛ COMMENDED
12 Saxby Avenue, Skegness
PE25 3LG
☎ (01754) 763905
Fax (01754) 763905
Family-run hotel on a corner in a quiet residential area of Skegness. 300 yards from seafront and close to all amenities.
Wheelchair access category 3♿
Bedrooms: 1 single, 10 double, 2 twin, 2 triple
Bathrooms: 11 en-suite, 2 public
Bed & breakfast
per night: £min £max
Single 23.00 24.00
Double 46.00 48.00
Half board per
person: £min £max
Daily 30.00 31.00
Weekly 154.00 161.00
Lunch available
Evening meal 1800 (last orders 1900)
Parking for 8
Cards accepted: Access, Visa, Diners, Amex
⛔👁🗝🏧🍴📺💶🛁✈ SP T ⭕

Seacroft Hotel
♛♛♛ APPROVED
South Parade, Skegness PE25 3EH
☎ (01754) 762301
Fax (01754) 761037
Spacious, very friendly family-run hotel, overlooking sea and close to town centre. Two bars, ballroom entertainment most nights. Ideal for all ages - children to senior citizens.
Bedrooms: 12 single, 14 double, 21 twin, 6 triple, 1 family room

Bathrooms: 47 en-suite, 3 public
Bed & breakfast
per night: £min £max
Single 23.00 27.00
Double 46.00 54.00
Half board per
person: £min £max
Daily 30.00 35.00
Weekly 157.50 210.00
Lunch available
Evening meal 1830 (last orders 2000)
Parking for 100
Open March–December
Cards accepted: Access, Visa
⛔👁🗝🏧♿🍴📺⭕🛏💶⚿🛁
🛎100 🔍🏊🎯 DAP SP ✈

SLEAFORD
Lincolnshire
Map ref 3A1

Market town whose parish church has one of the oldest stone spires in England and particularly fine tracery round the windows.
Tourist Information Centre ☎ (01529) 414294

The Lincolnshire Oak Hotel
♛♛♛ COMMENDED
East Road, Sleaford NG34 7EH
☎ (01529) 413807
Fax (01529) 413710
Situated on the edge of a market town, this comfortable hotel offers an ideal central base for exploring Lincolnshire. Excellent food and wines.
Bedrooms: 5 single, 7 double, 2 twin
Bathrooms: 14 en-suite
Bed & breakfast
per night: £min £max
Single 42.00 47.00
Double 55.00 65.00
Half board per
person: £min £max
Daily 39.00 63.00
Weekly 273.00 441.00
Lunch available
Evening meal 1900 (last orders 2100)
Parking for 60
Cards accepted: Access, Visa, Amex, Switch/Delta
⛔👁🗝🏧♿🍴📺💶🛁
🛎140 🏇✈ SP ✈

All accommodation in this guide has been graded, or is awaiting a grading, by a trained Tourist Board inspector.

MIDDLE ENGLAND

SOUTH NORMANTON
Derbyshire
Map ref 4C2

Village near the Nottinghamshire border and close to Hardwick Hall, Newstead Abbey and the National Tramway Museum at Crich.

Swallow Hotel
HIGHLY COMMENDED

Carter Lane East, Junction 28 M1, South Normanton DE55 2EH
☎ Ripley (01773) 812000
Fax (01773) 580032
Swallow
Modern hotel at junction 28 of M1 motorway. Ideal for Peak District, Chatsworth House, Sherwood Forest, Alton Towers (discounted tickets available). Leisure facilities. Short break packages available.
Wheelchair access category 3
Bedrooms: 54 single, 66 double, 41 twin
Bathrooms: 161 en-suite

Bed & breakfast
per night:	£min	£max
Single	70.00	100.00
Double	80.00	115.00

Half board per
person:	£min	£max
Daily	84.95	119.95

Lunch available
Evening meal 1900 (last orders 2200)
Parking for 280
Cards accepted: Access, Visa, Diners, Amex

SPALDING
Lincolnshire
Map ref 3A1

Fenland town famous for its bulbfields. A spectacular Flower Parade takes place at the beginning of May each year and the tulips at Springfields show gardens are followed by displays of roses and bedding plants in summer. Interesting local museum.
Tourist Information Centre ☎ (01775) 725468 or 761161

Cley Hall Hotel
COMMENDED

22 High Street, Spalding PE11 1TX
☎ (01775) 725157
Fax (01775) 710785
Georgian manor house by the River Welland, 500 metres from town centre, with unique candlelit cellar restaurant. Own car park.

Bedrooms: 6 single, 3 double, 2 twin
Bathrooms: 11 en-suite

Bed & breakfast
per night:	£min	£max
Single	30.00	48.00
Double	45.00	52.00

Half board per
person:	£min	£max
Daily	40.00	55.00

Lunch available
Evening meal 1900 (last orders 2130)
Parking for 20
Cards accepted: Access, Visa, Diners, Amex, Switch/Delta

The Red Lion Hotel

Market Place, Spalding PE11 1SU
☎ (01775) 722869
Fax (01775) 710074
Sympathetically refurbished 18th C town centre hotel offering en-suite accommodation. Real food, real ales and value for money.
Bedrooms: 1 single, 7 double, 7 twin
Bathrooms: 15 en-suite

Bed & breakfast
per night:	£min	£max
Single	35.00	45.00
Double	45.00	55.00

Lunch available
Evening meal 1900 (last orders 2100)
Cards accepted: Access, Visa, Diners, Amex, Switch/Delta

STAMFORD
Lincolnshire
Map ref 3A1

Exceptionally beautiful and historic town with many houses of architectural interest, several notable churches and other public buildings all in the local stone. Burghley House, built by William Cecil, is a magnificent Tudor mansion on the edge of the town.
Tourist Information Centre ☎ (01780) 55611

Abbey House & Coach House
COMMENDED

West End Road, Maxey, Peterborough PE6 9EJ
☎ Market Deeping (01778) 344642
Grade II listed former rectory dating in part from 1190 AD located in quiet, predominantly stone, village east of Stamford. Attractive gardens. Ideal for touring the Eastern Shires.

Bedrooms: 1 single, 4 double, 3 twin, 1 triple
Bathrooms: 7 en-suite, 1 private, 1 public

Bed & breakfast
per night:	£min	£max
Single	22.00	33.00
Double	36.00	39.00

Parking for 12

Dolphin Guesthouse
APPROVED

12 East Street, Stamford PE9 1QD
☎ (01780) 55494 & 57515 changing to 755494 & 757515
Fax (01780) 57515 changing to 757515
En-suite accommodation next to the Dolphin Inn, renowned for its cask ales, friendliness and food. Off-road secure car parking and only 100 yards from the town centre.
Bedrooms: 4 double, 3 twin, 1 triple, 1 family room
Suites available
Bathrooms: 7 en-suite, 1 public

Bed & breakfast
per night:	£min	£max
Single	18.00	25.00
Double	40.00	50.00

Lunch available
Evening meal 1800 (last orders 2130)
Parking for 5
Cards accepted: Access, Visa, Switch/Delta

Garden House Hotel
COMMENDED

St Martins, Stamford PE9 2LP
☎ (01780) 63359 changing to 763359
Fax (01780) 63339 changing to 763359
Minotel

Charming 18th C town house converted to a hotel, where guests are treated as such by their hosts. Features a conservatory full of floral extravaganza and a meandering garden of 1 acre.
Wheelchair access category 3
Bedrooms: 2 single, 9 double, 8 twin, 1 triple

Continued ▶

MIDDLE ENGLAND

STAMFORD
Continued

Bathrooms: 20 en-suite
Bed & breakfast
per night:	£min	£max
Single	45.00	65.00
Double	65.00	85.00

Half board per
person:	£min	£max
Daily	40.00	50.00

Lunch available
Evening meal 1900 (last orders 2130)
Parking for 25
Cards accepted: Access, Visa, Amex, Switch/Delta

George of Stamford
HIGHLY COMMENDED

71 St. Martins, Stamford PE9 2LB
☎ (01780) 55171 changing to 755171
Fax (01780) 57070 changing to 757070

Full of antique furniture, oak panelling and log fires, this historic coaching inn is one of England's most famous resting places. Ever popular restaurant and more informal garden lounge. Privately owned.
Bedrooms: 12 single, 24 double, 11 twin
Suite available
Bathrooms: 47 en-suite
Bed & breakfast
per night:	£min	£max
Single	72.00	85.00
Double	95.00	160.00

Lunch available
Evening meal 1800 (last orders 2230)
Parking for 120
Cards accepted: Access, Visa, Diners, Amex, Switch/Delta

The Priory
HIGHLY COMMENDED

Church Road, Ketton, Stamford PE9 3RD
☎ (01780) 720215
Fax (01780) 721881

Listed 16th C country house in peaceful setting. Award-winning bed and breakfast. En-suite rooms with every comfort overlook splendid gardens. Resident chef. Choice of menus. Brochure available.
Bedrooms: 2 double, 1 twin
Bathrooms: 3 en-suite
Bed & breakfast
per night:	£min	£max
Single	50.00	55.00
Double	65.00	80.00

Half board per
person:	£min	£max
Daily	50.00	57.50
Weekly	315.00	360.00

Lunch available
Evening meal 1900 (last orders 2000)
Parking for 10
Cards accepted: Access, Visa

TIMBERLAND
Lincolnshire
Map ref 4D2

Village close to Tattershall with its imposing 15th C castle keep, now in the care of the National Trust.

Penny Farthing Inn
APPROVED

Station Road, Timberland, Lincoln LN4 3SA
☎ Martin (01526) 378359
Fax (01526) 378359

Relaxed, family-run, beamed inn with a comfortable atmosphere, in a rural village off the A153 at Billinghay along the B1189.
Bedrooms: 2 double, 4 twin
Bathrooms: 2 public
Bed & breakfast
per night:	£min	£max
Single	25.00	25.00
Double	44.00	44.00

Lunch available
Evening meal 1930 (last orders 2200)
Parking for 35
Cards accepted: Access, Visa, Diners, Amex, Switch/Delta

The map references refer to the colour maps towards the end of the guide. The first figure is the map number; the letter and figure which follow indicate the grid reference on the map.

UPPINGHAM
Leicestershire
Map ref 4C3

Quiet market town dominated by its famous public school which was founded in 1584. It has many stone houses and is surrounded by attractive countryside.

Garden Hotel
COMMENDED

High Street West, Uppingham, Rutland LE15 9QD
☎ (01572) 822352
Fax (01572) 821156

Historic homely hotel with secluded walled garden. Restaurant open daily for all meals, specialising in traditional home-made British cuisine. Interesting, sensibly-priced wine list.
Bedrooms: 4 single, 4 double, 1 twin, 1 triple
Bathrooms: 10 en-suite
Bed & breakfast
per night:	£min	£max
Single	45.00	55.00
Double	65.00	75.00

Half board per
person:	£min	£max
Daily	45.00	55.00

Lunch available
Evening meal 1930 (last orders 2100)
Cards accepted: Access, Visa, Diners, Amex, Switch/Delta

Lake Isle Hotel
HIGHLY COMMENDED

16 High Street East, Uppingham, Oakham LE15 9PZ
☎ (01572) 822951
Fax (01572) 822955

This 18th C hotel absorbs more than a little of Uppingham's charm. The personal touch will make your stay extra special with weekly changing menus and a list of over 300 wines.
Bedrooms: 1 single, 9 double, 2 twin
Suites available
Bathrooms: 12 en-suite
Bed & breakfast
per night:	£min	£max
Single	43.00	49.00
Double	60.00	69.00

Half board per
person:	£min	£max
Daily	49.00	49.00

Lunch available
Evening meal 1930 (last orders 2130)

MIDDLE ENGLAND

Parking for 7
Cards accepted: Access, Visa, Diners, Amex

Old Rectory Guest House
COMMENDED
New Road, Belton in Rutland, Oakham LE15 9LE
☎ Belton in Rutland (01572) 717279
Fax (01572) 717343

Large Victorian country house and annexe overlooking Eye Brook valley and rolling Rutland countryside. Cottage-style en-suite rooms, quiet friendly atmosphere. 10 minutes' Rutland Water. Midway between Leicester and Peterborough.
Bedrooms: 1 single, 1 double, 2 twin, 1 triple
Bathrooms: 4 en-suite, 1 private, 2 public

Bed & breakfast per night:

	£min	£max
Single	28.00	
Double	36.00	40.00

Lunch available
Evening meal 1800 (last orders 1900)
Parking for 10
Cards accepted: Access, Visa

Rutland House
COMMENDED
61 High Street East, Uppingham LE15 9PY
☎ (01572) 822497
Fax (01572) 822497
Family-run B & B. All rooms en-suite. Close to Rutland Water. Full English or continental breakfast. Well-placed for exploring Rutland's villages and countryside.
Bedrooms: 2 single, 1 double, 1 twin, 1 triple
Bathrooms: 5 en-suite

Bed & breakfast per night:

	£min	£max
Single	29.00	29.00
Double	39.00	39.00

Parking for 3
Cards accepted: Access, Visa

WEEDON
Northamptonshire
Map ref 2C1

Old village steeped in history, with thatched cottages and several antique shops.

Globe Hotel
COMMENDED
High Street, Weedon, Northampton NN7 4QD
☎ (01327) 340336
Fax (01327) 349058
19th C countryside inn. Old world atmosphere and freehouse hospitality with good English cooking, available all day. Meeting rooms. Close to M1, Stratford and many tourist spots. Send for information pack.
Bedrooms: 4 single, 6 double, 5 twin, 3 triple
Bathrooms: 18 en-suite

Bed & breakfast per night:

	£min	£max
Single	29.50	42.50
Double	42.50	50.00

Lunch available
Evening meal (last orders 2200)
Parking for 40
Cards accepted: Access, Visa, Diners, Amex

WELLINGBOROUGH
Northamptonshire
Map ref 3A2

Manufacturing town, mentioned in the Domesday Book, with some old buildings and inns, in one of which Cromwell stayed on his way to Naseby. It has attractive gardens in the centre of the town and 2 interesting churches.
Tourist Information Centre ☎ (01933) 228101

High View Hotel
156 Midland Road, Wellingborough NN8 1NG
☎ (01933) 278733
Fax (01933) 225948
Large, detached, modernised building with pleasant gardens. In quiet tree-lined area near town centre, trading estates and railway station.
Bedrooms: 6 single, 5 double, 6 twin
Bathrooms: 14 en-suite, 1 public

Bed & breakfast per night:

	£min	£max
Single	15.00	44.00
Double	30.00	51.00

Lunch available
Evening meal 1830 (last orders 2030)
Parking for 10
Cards accepted: Access, Visa, Diners, Amex

Oak House Private Hotel
APPROVED
8-11 Broad Green, Wellingborough NN8 4LE
☎ (01933) 271133
Fax (01933) 271133
The Independents
Small, homely hotel with a comfortable atmosphere, on the edge of the town centre. Double-glazed. Enclosed car park.
Bedrooms: 5 single, 5 double, 6 twin
Bathrooms: 15 en-suite, 1 private shower

Bed & breakfast per night:

	£min	£max
Single	28.00	32.50
Double	38.00	42.00

Evening meal 1815 (last orders 1200)
Parking for 9
Cards accepted: Access, Visa, Diners, Amex

WOODHALL SPA
Lincolnshire
Map ref 4D2

Attractive town which was formerly a spa. It has excellent sporting facilities with a championship golf-course and is surrounded by pine woods.

Claremont Guesthouse
9-11 Witham Road, Woodhall Spa LN10 6RW
☎ (01526) 352000
Homely B&B in unspoilt Victorian guesthouse within easy reach of the town's sporting and leisure facilities. All rooms have TV and tea/coffee making facilities. Off-street car parking, garden for use of guests.
Bedrooms: 2 single, 1 twin, 5 triple, 1 family room
Bathrooms: 1 private, 2 public

Bed & breakfast per night:

	£min	£max
Single	15.00	20.00
Double	30.00	35.00

Continued ▶

MIDDLE ENGLAND

WOODHALL SPA
Continued

Evening meal from 1800
Parking for 6

Eagle Lodge Hotel
COMMENDED

The Broadway, Woodhall Spa
LN10 6ST
☎ (01526) 353231
Fax (01526) 352797
Mock-Tudor country house hotel, built in the 1800s and recently modernised. Close to numerous golf-courses and a short drive to Lincoln, Boston and the East Coast.
Bedrooms: 5 single, 7 double, 9 twin, 1 triple, 1 family room
Bathrooms: 22 en-suite, 1 private

Bed & breakfast

per night:	£min	£max
Single	25.00	39.50
Double	44.00	60.00

Half board per

person:	£min	£max
Daily	31.00	49.50

Lunch available
Evening meal 1900 (last orders 2130)
Parking for 28
Cards accepted: Access, Visa, Diners, Amex, Switch/Delta

Petwood House Hotel
HIGHLY COMMENDED

Stixwould Road, Woodhall Spa
LN10 6QF
☎ (01526) 352411
Fax (01526) 353473

Country house with superb restaurant, set in 30 acres. Putting green, croquet, golf practice area and snooker room. Former officers' mess of the famous Dambusters Squadron.
Wheelchair access category 3
Bedrooms: 4 single, 29 double, 13 twin
Suites available
Bathrooms: 46 en-suite

Bed & breakfast

per night:	£min	£max
Single	60.00	
Double	85.00	

Half board per

person:	£min	£max
Daily		54.00

Lunch available
Evening meal 1900 (last orders 2100)
Parking for 70
Cards accepted: Access, Visa, Diners, Amex

Pitchaway Guesthouse

The Broadway, Woodhall Spa
LN10 6SQ
☎ (01526) 352969
A warm welcome, home cooking and personal service await you at this family-run guesthouse. Close to the golf links, recreation park and wooded walks.
Bedrooms: 2 single, 1 double, 2 twin, 1 triple, 1 family room
Bathrooms: 2 en-suite, 2 public

Bed & breakfast

per night:	£min	£max
Single	16.00	18.00
Double	32.00	36.00

Half board per

person:	£min	£max
Daily	22.00	25.00

Lunch available
Evening meal 1930 (last orders 0900)
Parking for 8

WORKSOP
Nottinghamshire
Map ref 4C2

Market town close to the Dukeries, where a number of Ducal families had their estates, some of which, like Clumber Park, may be visited. The upper room of the 14th C gatehouse of the priory housed the country's first elementary school in 1628.
Tourist Information Centre ☎ (01909) 501148

Clumber Park Hotel
HIGHLY COMMENDED

Clumber Park, Sherwood Forest, Worksop S80 3PA
☎ Mansfield (01623) 835333
Fax (01623) 835525
Whitbread
Newly refurbished hotel offering traditional comfort and character. Adjacent to Clumber Park, close to Sherwood Forest and Rufford Abbey. Easily accessible from A1 via A614 towards Nottingham.
Bedrooms: 2 single, 22 double, 22 twin, 2 triple
Bathrooms: 48 en-suite

Bed & breakfast

per night:	£min	£max
Single	26.00	70.00
Double	52.00	78.00

Half board per

person:	£min	£max
Daily	38.00	85.00

Lunch available
Evening meal 1900 (last orders 2200)
Parking for 204
Cards accepted: Access, Visa, Diners, Amex, Switch/Delta

Sherwood Guesthouse
COMMENDED

57 Carlton Road, Worksop S80 1PP
☎ (01909) 474209 & 478214
In Robin Hood country, near M1 and A1 and close to station and town centre. Comfortable rooms with TV and tea/coffee facilities.
Bedrooms: 1 single, 5 twin, 1 triple
Bathrooms: 2 en-suite, 2 public

Bed & breakfast

per night:	£min	£max
Single	18.00	22.00
Double	36.00	40.00

WELCOME HOST

This is a nationally recognised customer care programme which aims to promote the highest standards of service and a warm welcome. Establishments who are taking part in this initiative are indicated by the symbol.

EAST ANGLIA

East Anglia is the ideal 'get away from it all' destination. Here you can play golf, go fishing, follow the region's nature trails or discover the pastoral beauty of Constable country.

Pretty Hertfordshire villages await you, along with the sleepy charms of the Broads, England's newest National Park.

The untamed coastline boasts a number of much-loved seaside resorts like Great Yarmouth, Clacton and Southend-on-Sea while inland, Aldeburgh hosts a famous music festival.

Discover markets, vineyards and the gourmet delights of Cromer crab, Suffolk ham and Colchester oysters, as memorable as the surroundings in which you'll savour them.

FOR MORE INFORMATION CONTACT:
East Anglia Tourist Board
Toppesfield Hall, Hadleigh, Suffolk IP7 5DN
Tel: (01473) 822922 **Fax:** (01473) 823063

Where to Go in East Anglia - see pages 322-325
Where to Stay in East Anglia - see pages 326-368

EAST ANGLIA

Where to Go and What to See

You will find hundreds of interesting places to visit during your stay in East Anglia, just some of which are listed in these pages. The number against each name will help you locate it on the map (page 325). Contact any Tourist Information Centre in the region for more ideas on days out in East Anglia.

1 Wells Walsingham Railway
Stiffkey Road,
Wells-next-the-Sea,
Norfolk NR23 1QB
Tel: (01328) 856506
Four miles of railway. The longest 10¼ railway in the World. New locomotive Norfolk Hero now in service, largest of its kind ever built.

2 Thursford Collection
Thursford Green,
Thursford, Fakenham,
Norfolk NR21 0AS
Tel: (01328) 878477
Live musical shows, nine mechanical organs and Wurlitzer show starring Robert Wolfe.

3 Penthorpe Waterfowl Park
Pensthorpe, Fakenham,
Norfolk NR21 0LN
Tel: (01328) 851465
Large waterfowl and wildfowl collection. Information centre, conservation shop, adventure play area, walks and nature trails. Licensed restaurant.

4 Norfolk Lavender
Caley Mill, Heacham,
King's Lynn, Norfolk PE31 7JE
Tel: (01485) 570384
Lavender is distilled from the flowers and the oil made in to a wide range of gifts. Slide show when distillery not working.

5 Sandringham
Sandringham, King's Lynn,
Norfolk PE35 6EN
Tel: (01553) 772675
Country retreat of HM The Queen. Delightful house and 60-acres of grounds and lakes. Museum of vehicles and royal memorabilia.

6 Banham Zoo
The Grove, Banham,
Norwich, Norfolk NR16 2HE
Tel: (01953) 887771
See some of the world's rare and endangered species.

**7 Sainsbury Centre
for Visual Arts**
University of East Anglia,
Norwich, Norfolk NR4 7TJ
Tel: (01603) 456060
The Robert and Lisa Sainsbury Collection of modern and non modern art is wide-ranging and of international importance. Housed in a building purpose designed by N Foster.

8 Sea Life Centre
Marine Parade, Great Yarmouth,
Norfolk NR30 3AH
Tel: (01493) 330631
Walk under a tropical reef. Shark tank, Ray fish and British sharks, plus 25 themed displays depicting British marine life and local settings.

**9 Somerleyton Hall
and Gardens**
Somerleyton, Lowestoft,
Suffolk NR32 5QQ
Tel: (01502) 730224
Anglo-Italian-style building with state rooms, maze. Garden with azaleas and rhododendrons. Miniature railway, shop, light luncheons and teas.

10 East Anglia Transport Museum
Chapel Road, Carlton Colville,
Lowestoft, Suffolk NR33 8BL
Tel: (01502) 518459
A working museum with one of the widest ranges of street transport vehicles on display - and in action!

11 Pleasurewood Hills
Corton, Lowestoft,
Suffolk NR32 5DZ
Tel: (01502) 508200
Log flume, chair lift, cine 180, two railways, pirate ship, fort, Aladdin's cave, parrot and sealion shows, roller coasters, waveswinger, Eye in the Sky, Star Ride Enterprise.

12 Otter Trust
Earsham, Bungay,
Suffolk NR35 2AF
Tel: (01986) 893470
A breeding and conservation headquarters with the largest collection of otters in the world. Also lakes with collection of waterfowl and deer.

13 Bressingham Steam Museum and Gardens
Bressingham, Diss,
Norfolk IP22 2AB
Tel: (01379) 687386
Steam rides through five miles of woodland, garden and nursery.

Mainline locomotives and over 50 steam engines. Alan Bloom's Dell Garden.

14 Sacrewell Farm and Country Centre
Sacrewell, Thornhaugh,
Peterborough,
Cambridgeshire PE8 6HJ
Tel: (01780) 782222
500-acre farm, with working watermill, farmhouse gardens, shrubberies, nature and general interest trails, 18C buildings, displays of farm, rural and domestic bygones.

15 Ely Cathedral
Chapter House,
The College, Ely,
Cambridgeshire CB7 4DN
Tel: (01353) 667735
One of England's finest cathedrals. Fine out buildings. Guided tours and tours of Octagon and West Tower. Brass rubbing and stained glass museum.

16 Pakenham Water Mill
Mill Road,
Grimestone End, Pakenham,
Bury St Edmunds,
Suffolk IP3 2NB
Tel: (01787) 247179
18C working water mill on Domesday site, with oil engine and other subsidiary machinery.

17 Framlingham Castle
Framlingham, Woodbridge,
Suffolk IP13 9BP
Tel: (01728) 724189
12C curtain walls with 13 towers and Tudor brick chimneys. Built by Bigod family, Earls of Norfolk. Wall walk. 17C almshouses. Home of Mary Tudor in 1553.

18 Imperial War Museum
Duxford Airfield, Duxford,
Cambridgeshire CB2 4QR
Tel: (01223) 835000
Over 120 aircraft on display, tanks, vehicles, guns. Ride simulator, adventure playground, shops and restaurant.

19 National Horseracing Museum
99 High Street, Newmarket,
Suffolk CB8 8JL
Tel: (01638) 667333
Five permanent galleries telling the story of horseracing. Opened by the Queen in 1983. British sporting art. Temporary Exhibition Gallery.

20 Ickworth House, Park and Gardens
Ickworth, Bury St Edmunds,
Suffolk IP29 5QE
Tel: (01284) 735270
Extraordinary oval house with flanking wings begun in 1795. Fine paintings and beautiful collection of Georgian silver. Italian garden and park designed by Capability Brown.

21 Helmingham Hall Gardens
Helmingham,
Suffolk IP14 6EF
Tel: (01473) 890363
Moated and walled garden with many rare roses and possibly the best kitchen garden in Britain. Also highland cattle and safari rides in park to view red and fallow deer.

22 Shuttleworth Collection
Old Warden Aerodrome,
Biggleswade,
Bedfordshire SG18 9ER
Tel: (01767) 627288
Unique historic collection of aircraft from 1909 Bleriot to 1942 Spitfire in flying condition. Cars dating from 1898 Panhard.

23 Audley End House and Park
Saffron Walden,
Essex CB11 4JF
Tel: (01799) 522842
Palatial Jacobean house remodelled in the 18-19C. Magnificent Great Hall. Rooms and furniture by Robert Adam. Park by Capability Brown.

24 Woburn Abbey
Woburn,
Milton Keynes,
Bedfordshire MK43 0TP
Tel: (01525) 290666
18C Palladian mansion altered by Henry Holland, the Prince Regent's architect. Contains a collection of English silver, French and English furniture and an important art collection.

25 Mountfitchet Castle
Stansted Mountfitchet,
Essex CM24 8SP
Tel: (01279) 813237
Reconstructed Norman motte-and-bailey castle and village of Domesday period. Grand Hall, church, prison, seige tower and weapons.

26 Colchester Castle
Colchester,
Essex CO1 1TJ
Tel: (01206) 282931
Norman Keep on foundations of Roman Temple, archaeological material includes much on Roman Colchester.

27 Whipsnade Wild Animal Park
Zoological Society of London,
Dunstable,
Bedfordshire LU6 2LF
Tel: (01582) 872171
Over 2,500 animals set in 600 acres of beautiful parkland. Great Whipsnade Railway. Free animal demonstrations.

28 Hatfield House
Hatfield Park, Hatfield,
Hertfordshire AL9 5NQ
Tel: (01707) 262823
Jacobean house built in 1611 and Old Palace built in 1497. Contains famous paintings, fine furniture and possessions of Queen Elizabeth I. Extensive park and gardens.

29 The Gardens of the Rose
The Royal National Rose Society,
Chiswell Green,
St Albans,
Hertfordshire AL2 3NR
Tel: (01727) 850461
The Royal National Rose Society's Garden, 20 acres of showground and trial grounds for new varieties of rose. 30,000 roses of all types with 1,700 different varieties.

FIND OUT MORE

Further information about holidays and attractions in East Anglia is available from:
East Anglia Tourist Board,
Toppesfield Hall,
Hadleigh,
Suffolk IP7 5DN.
Tel: (01473) 822922

These publications are available from the East Anglia Tourist Board (post free):
- **Great Escapes** - short breaks
- **Touring Map** - bed & breakfast and camping
- **Freedom Holiday Parks in Eastern England**

Also available are (prices include postage and packaging):
- **East Anglia Guide** £4.50
- **Gardens to Visit in East Anglia** £1.99

WHERE TO STAY (EAST ANGLIA)

Accommodation entries in this region are listed in alphabetical order of place name, and then in alphabetical order of establishment.

Map references refer to the colour location maps at the back of this guide. The first number indicates the map to use; the letter and number which follow refer to the grid reference on the map.

At-a-glance symbols at the end of each accommodation entry give useful information about services and facilities. A key to symbols can be found inside the back cover flap. Keep this open for easy reference.

ALDEBURGH

Suffolk
Map ref 3C2

A prosperous port in the 16th C, now famous for the Aldeburgh Music Festival held annually in June. The 16th C Moot Hall, now a museum, is a timber-framed building once used as an open market.

Uplands Hotel
COMMENDED

Victoria Road, Aldeburgh IP15 5DX
☎ (01728) 452420
Fax (01728) 454872
Comfortable family-run hotel with en-suite rooms. Restaurant using local produce overlooks award-winning gardens.
Bedrooms: 4 single, 5 double, 9 twin, 2 triple
Bathrooms: 17 en-suite, 3 private, 1 public

Bed & breakfast per night:

	£min	£max
Single	35.00	47.00
Double	63.00	65.00

Half board per person:

	£min	£max
Daily	45.00	
Weekly	290.00	

Evening meal 1900 (last orders 2030)
Parking for 20
Cards accepted: Access, Visa, Diners, Amex

White Lion Hotel

Market Cross Place, Aldeburgh
IP15 5BJ
☎ (01728) 452720
Fax (01728) 452986
Best Western
Imposing hotel standing directly on the seafront of totally unspoilt fishing town of great charm, famous for classical music concerts.
Bedrooms: 2 single, 21 double, 14 twin, 1 triple
Bathrooms: 38 en-suite

Bed & breakfast per night:

	£min	£max
Single	55.00	62.50
Double	70.00	100.00

Half board per person:

	£min	£max
Daily	52.50	70.00
Weekly	357.50	550.00

Lunch available
Evening meal 1900 (last orders 2100)
Parking for 15
Cards accepted: Access, Visa, Diners, Amex, Switch/Delta

Please check prices and other details at the time of booking.

A key to symbols can be found inside the back cover flap.

ATTLEBOROUGH

Norfolk
Map ref 3B1

Market town, mostly destroyed in 1559 by fire, now a cider-making centre. Church with fine Norman tower.

Sherbourne Country House Hotel
HIGHLY COMMENDED

Norwich Road, Attleborough
NR17 2JX
☎ (01953) 454363
Fax (01953) 453509

18th C country house in mature grounds. Recently refurbished to a high standard. Four-poster and spa baths. Noted restaurant and attractive bar.
Bedrooms: 2 single, 4 double, 2 twin
Bathrooms: 5 en-suite, 1 public, 1 private shower

Bed & breakfast per night:

	£min	£max
Single	29.00	55.00
Double	55.00	70.00

Half board per person:

	£min	£max
Daily	44.00	70.00

EAST ANGLIA

Lunch available
Evening meal 1930 (last orders 2100)
Parking for 30
Cards accepted: Access, Visa, Diners

AYLSHAM
Norfolk
Map ref 3B1

Small town on the River Bure with an attractive market place and interesting church. Nearby is Blickling Hall (National Trust). Also the terminal of the Bure Valley narrow gauge steam railway which runs on 9 miles of the old Great Eastern trackbed, between Wroxham and Aylsham.

The Aylsham Motel
COMMENDED

Norwich Road, Aylsham, Norwich NR11 6JH
☎ (01263) 734851
Fax (01263) 734851

Family-run motel. Relaxed and friendly atmosphere in peaceful surroundings. All rooms en-suite. Close to North Norfolk coast and Broads. Bar and a la carte meals available.
Bedrooms: 3 double, 10 twin, 2 triple
Bathrooms: 15 en-suite

Bed & breakfast per night:	£min	£max
Single	29.00	35.00
Double	39.00	50.00

Half board per person:	£min	£max
Weekly	156.00	180.00

Lunch available
Evening meal 1900 (last orders 2130)
Parking for 100
Cards accepted: Access, Visa, Amex, Switch/Delta

The Old Pump House
HIGHLY COMMENDED

Holman Road, Aylsham, Norwich NR11 6BY
☎ (01263) 733789

Creature comforts, steps everywhere, home cooking. Rambling 1750s house beside the thatched pump, a minute

from church and marketplace. Pine shuttered breakfast room overlooks peaceful garden. Non-smoking.
Bedrooms: 3 double, 2 twin
Bathrooms: 3 en-suite, 2 public

Bed & breakfast per night	£min	£max
Single	18.00	25.00
Double	36.00	42.00

Half board per person:	£min	£max
Daily	28.00	35.00
Weekly	148.00	165.00

Evening meal from 1800
Parking for 7

BACTON-ON-SEA
Norfolk
Map ref 3C1

Seacroft Private Hotel
APPROVED

Beach Road, Bacton-on-Sea, Norwich NR12 0HS
☎ Walcott (01692) 650302

Large Victorian house close to shops and beach. Home cooking and personal supervision. Off B1159, via Seacroft caravan park.
Bedrooms: 1 single, 3 double, 3 twin, 1 triple, 1 family room
Bathrooms: 5 en-suite, 3 public

Bed & breakfast per night:	£min	£max
Single	16.50	24.50
Double	33.00	49.00

Half board per person:	£min	£max
Daily	27.50	35.50
Weekly	173.00	223.00

Evening meal 1800 (last orders 2000)
Parking for 15
Open February–December
Cards accepted: Access, Visa

BARNHAM BROOM
Norfolk
Map ref 3B1

Barnham Broom Hotel, Golf, Conference & Leisure Centre
COMMENDED

Honingham Road, Barnham Broom, Norwich NR9 4DD
☎ (01603) 759393
Fax (01603) 758524
Best Western

In 250 acres of beautiful countryside, with a relaxed and friendly atmosphere.

Excellent sports facilities, 2 18-hole golf-courses. Large conference complex, indoor heated pool.
Bedrooms: 1 single, 7 double, 36 twin, 1 triple, 7 family rooms
Bathrooms: 52 en-suite

Bed & breakfast per night:	£min	£max
Single	62.00	65.00
Double	85.00	90.00

Half board per person:	£min	£max
Daily	78.00	81.00

Lunch available
Evening meal 1900 (last orders 2130)
Parking for 200
Cards accepted: Access, Visa, Diners, Amex, Switch/Delta

BASILDON
Essex
Map ref 3B3

One of the New Towns planned after World War II. It overlooks the estuary of the River Thames and is set in undulating countryside. The main feature is the town square with a traffic-free pedestrian concourse.

The Chichester Hotel
COMMENDED

Old London Road, Wickford SS11 8UE
☎ Wickford (01268) 560555
Fax (01268) 560580
The Independents

Picturesque family-run hotel with restaurant, dinner-dance restaurant and functions complex. Surrounded by farmland in the Basildon, Chelmsford, Southend triangle.
Bedrooms: 17 single, 10 double, 8 twin
Bathrooms: 35 en-suite

Bed & breakfast per night:	£min	£max
Single	52.00	60.00
Double	68.80	

Lunch available
Evening meal 1900 (last orders 2130)
Parking for 41
Cards accepted: Access, Visa, Diners, Amex

327

EAST ANGLIA

BATTLESBRIDGE
Essex
Map ref 3B3

The Cottages Guest House
Listed
The Cottages, Beeches Road, Battlesbridge, Wickford SS11 8TJ
☎ Southend (01702) 232105
Rural cottage, close to Southend, Chelmsford and Basildon. Good views. Half a mile from Battlesbridge Antique Centre. Extensive parking. Bridal room, licensed bar.
Bedrooms: 1 single, 1 double, 2 twin, 1 triple
Bathrooms: 1 public

Bed & breakfast per night:	£min	£max
Single	20.00	25.00
Double	35.00	45.00

Half board per person:	£min	£max
Daily	25.00	30.00
Weekly	150.00	180.00

Evening meal 1800 (last orders 2030)
Parking for 14

BECCLES
Suffolk
Map ref 3C1

Fire destroyed the town in the 16th C and it was rebuilt in Georgian red brick. The River Waveney, on which the town stands, is popular with boating enthusiasts and has an annual regatta. Home of Beccles and District Museum and the William Clowes Printing Museum.

Colville Arms Motel
APPROVED
Lowestoft Road, Worlingham, Beccles NR34 7EF
☎ (01502) 712571
Fax (01502) 712571
Quiet village location, all rooms en-suite, bar, restaurant, large car park. Half hour to Norwich, Lowestoft, Yarmouth and Broads. Blue Flag beaches.
Bedrooms: 2 double, 2 twin, 1 triple
Bathrooms: 5 en-suite

Bed & breakfast per night:	£min	£max
Single	24.50	28.00
Double	32.00	38.00

Half board per person:	£min	£max
Daily	30.50	34.00
Weekly	200.00	220.00

Lunch available
Evening meal 1900 (last orders 2200)
Parking for 40
Cards accepted: Access, Visa

BEDFORD
Bedfordshire
Map ref 2D1

Busy county town with interesting buildings and churches near the River Ouse which has pleasant riverside walks. Many associations with John Bunyan including Bunyan Meeting House, museum and statue. The Bedford Museum and Cecil Higgins Art Gallery are of interest.
Tourist Information Centre ☎ (01234) 215226

Barns Hotel & Restaurant
Cardington Road, Bedford MK44 3SA
☎ (01234) 270044
Fax (01234) 273102
Whitbread
Built around an 18th C tithe barn and a 17th C manor, on the banks of the River Great Ouse. Still retains the character of the original beamed and timbered buildings.
Bedrooms: 22 double, 27 twin
Bathrooms: 49 private

Bed & breakfast per night:	£min	£max
Single	76.50	78.50
Double	76.50	78.50

Half board per person:	£min	£max
Daily	92.00	94.00

Lunch available
Evening meal 1900 (last orders 2200)
Parking for 120
Cards accepted: Access, Visa, Diners, Amex

Bedford Oak House
33 Shakespeare Road, Bedford MK40 2DX
☎ (01234) 266972
Fax (01234) 266972

Comfortable motor hotel bed and breakfast accommodation in a large mock-Tudor house, close to the railway station and town centre. En-suite facilities and large car park.
Bedrooms: 1 single, 10 double, 3 twin, 1 triple
Bathrooms: 10 en-suite, 2 public, 1 private shower

Bed & breakfast per night:	£min	£max
Single	21.00	33.00
Double	30.00	40.00

Evening meal (last orders 1900)
Parking for 15
Cards accepted: Access, Visa, Diners, Amex

No 1 Ravensden Grange
COMMENDED
Sunderland Hill, Ravensden, Bedford MK44 2SH
☎ (01234) 771771
Well-appointed accommodation in spacious Georgian manor house overlooking lawns with great cedar trees. Cooking, comfort, hospitality all first class.
Bedrooms: 1 single, 1 double, 1 twin
Bathrooms: 2 private, 2 public

Bed & breakfast per night:	£min	£max
Single	18.00	20.00
Double	36.00	

Half board per person:	£min	£max
Daily	28.00	35.00

Lunch available
Evening meal 1830 (last orders 1200)
Parking for 10

BIGGLESWADE
Bedfordshire
Map ref 2D1

Busy centre for market gardening set on the River Ivel spanned by a 14th C bridge. Some interesting old buildings in the market-place. Nearby are the Shuttleworth collection of historic aeroplanes and Jordan's Mill.

Stratton House Hotel
COMMENDED
London Road, Biggleswade SG18 8EO
☎ (01767) 312442 & 314540
Fax (01767) 600416
The Independents

EAST ANGLIA

Completely refurbished, privately owned hotel in centre of town. Character building with en-suite rooms, grill/restaurant, attractive bar. Half a mile off A1 and 45 minutes from London. Lots of local attractions.
Bedrooms: 9 single, 9 double, 8 twin, 4 triple, 1 family room
Bathrooms: 31 en-suite

Bed & breakfast per night:	£min	£max
Single	36.00	41.00
Half board per person:	£min	£max
Daily	30.00	50.00

Lunch available
Evening meal 1800 (last orders 2200)
Parking for 40
Cards accepted: Access, Visa, Diners, Amex, Switch/Delta

BISHOP'S STORTFORD

Hertfordshire
Map ref 2D1

Fine old town on the River Stort with many interesting buildings, particularly Victorian, and an imposing parish church. The vicarage where Cecil Rhodes was born is now a museum.
Tourist Information Centre ☎ (01279) 655831

The Cottage
HIGHLY COMMENDED

71 Birchanger Lane, Birchanger, Bishop's Stortford CM23 5QA
☎ (01279) 812349
Fax (01279) 812349
17th C listed house with panelled rooms and wood stove. Conservatory dining room overlooks large, mature garden. Quiet village setting yet near M11 junction 8 and Stansted Airport.
Bedrooms: 3 single, 6 double, 6 twin
Bathrooms: 11 en-suite, 2 private, 1 public

Bed & breakfast per night:	£min	£max
Single	30.00	40.00
Double	50.00	50.00

Evening meal from 1900
Parking for 14
Cards accepted: Access, Visa

BLAKENEY

Norfolk
Map ref 3B1

Picturesque village on the north coast of Norfolk and a former port and fishing village. 15th C Guildhall. Marshy creeks extend towards Blakeney Point (National Trust) and are a paradise for naturalists, with trips to the reserve and to see the seals from Blakeney Quay.

Blakeney Hotel
COMMENDED

Quayside, Blakeney, Holt NR25 7NE
☎ Cley (01263) 740797
Fax (01263) 740795
The Independents
Traditional, privately-owned, friendly hotel overlooking National Trust harbour. Relax, sail, walk, play golf or bird-watch. Half board prices based on minimum 2 nights' stay.
Bedrooms: 9 single, 24 double, 26 twin
Bathrooms: 59 en-suite

Bed & breakfast per night:	£min	£max
Single	52.00	87.00
Double	104.00	174.00
Half board per person:	£min	£max
Daily	57.00	98.00
Weekly	364.00	609.00

Lunch available
Evening meal 1900 (last orders 2130)
Parking for 75
Cards accepted: Access, Visa, Diners, Amex, Switch/Delta

Flintstones Guest House
Listed COMMENDED

Wiveton, Holt NR25 7TL
☎ Cley (01263) 740337
Attractive licensed guesthouse in picturesque rural surroundings near village green. 1 mile from Cley and Blakeney with good sailing and bird-watching. All rooms with private facilities. Non-smokers only, please.
Bedrooms: 1 single, 1 double, 3 triple
Bathrooms: 3 en-suite, 2 private

Bed & breakfast per night:	£min	£max
Single	20.00	22.00
Double		37.00
Half board per person:	£min	£max
Daily		29.50
Weekly		192.50

Evening meal 1900 (last orders 1700)
Parking for 5

White Horse Hotel
COMMENDED

4 High Street, Blakeney, Holt NR25 7AL
☎ Cley (01263) 740574
Old Norfolk inn near picturesque harbour, offering traditional food and real beer. Restaurant closed Sunday/Monday evenings. Bar food 7 days a week. Local fish and game used. Service not included in prices shown.
Bedrooms: 2 single, 4 double, 1 twin, 2 triple
Bathrooms: 9 en-suite

Bed & breakfast per night:	£min	£max
Single	30.00	
Double	60.00	70.00

Lunch available
Evening meal 1900 (last orders 2130)
Parking for 15
Cards accepted: Access, Visa, Amex, Switch/Delta

BRAINTREE

Essex
Map ref 3B2

The Heritage Centre in the Town Hall describes Braintree's former international importance in wool, silk and engineering. St Michael's parish church includes some Roman bricks. Braintree market was first chartered in 1199.
Tourist Information Centre ☎ (01376) 550066

The White Hart Hotel
COMMENDED

Bocking End, Braintree CM7 9AB
☎ (01376) 321401
Fax (01376) 552628
Stagecoach
Warm and cosily furnished, town centre hotel, created around an original 16th C coaching inn. Excellent base for visiting East Anglia.

Continued ▶

COLOUR MAPS

Colour maps at the back of this guide pinpoint all places in which you will find accommodation listed.

329

EAST ANGLIA

BRAINTREE
Continued

Bedrooms: 3 single, 14 double, 6 twin, 8 triple
Bathrooms: 31 en-suite

Bed & breakfast
per night:	£min	£max
Single	36.00	59.50
Double	52.00	71.00

Half board per
person:	£min	£max
Daily	38.00	73.00

Lunch available
Evening meal 1800 (last orders 2200)
Parking for 51
Cards accepted: Access, Visa, Diners, Amex

BRENTWOOD
Essex
Map ref 2D2

The town grew up in the late 12th C and then developed as a staging post, being strategically placed close to the London to Chelmsford road. Deer roam by the lakes in the 428-acre park at South Weald, part of Brentwood's attractive Green Belt.
Tourist Information Centre ☎ *(01277) 200300*

Marygreen Manor Hotel
HIGHLY COMMENDED
London Road, Brentwood
CM14 4NR
☎ (01277) 225252
Fax (01277) 262809

Original Tudor building dating back to 1512. Hunting lodge visited by Catherine of Aragon. Old world garden. B&B prices below are per room.
Bedrooms: 16 double, 17 twin
Bathrooms: 33 en-suite

Bed & breakfast
per night:	£min	£max
Single	107.00	116.00
Double	119.50	128.50

Lunch available
Evening meal 1915 (last orders 2215)

Parking for 100
Cards accepted: Access, Visa, Diners, Amex, Switch/Delta

BUCKDEN
Cambridgeshire
Map ref 3A2

Pretty village with several attractive brick houses. Once a posting station and dominated by the remains of the 15th C palace of the Bishops of Lincoln. The local church is noted for its spire and carvings. Nearby is Grafham Water, a reservoir with extensive picnic areas.

Lion Hotel
HIGHLY COMMENDED
High Street, Buckden, St Neots, Huntingdon PE18 9XA
☎ Huntingdon (01480) 810313
Fax (01480) 811070

15th C coaching inn with lovely open fires, oak-panelled restaurant and comfortable bedrooms, all en-suite. Close to A1. Minimum half-board price applies to weekend breaks.
Bedrooms: 2 single, 6 double, 3 twin, 4 triple
Bathrooms: 15 en-suite, 1 public

Bed & breakfast
per night:	£min	£max
Single	59.50	61.50
Double	75.00	78.00

Half board per
person:	£min	£max
Daily	42.00	78.50

Lunch available
Evening meal 1900 (last orders 2115)
Parking for 25
Cards accepted: Access, Visa, Diners, Amex, Switch/Delta

BUNGAY
Suffolk
Map ref 3C1

Market town and yachting centre on the River Waveney with the remains of a great 12th C castle. In the market-place stands the Butter Cross, rebuilt in 1689 after being largely destroyed by fire. Nearby at Earsham is the Otter Trust.

Dove Restaurant
APPROVED
Wortwell, Harleston, Norfolk
IP20 0EN
☎ Homersfield (01986) 788315

A former railway hotel, now an established international restaurant offering accommodation. Norfolk/Suffolk border. Good centre for the Waveney Valley and coast.
Bedrooms: 1 double, 1 twin, 1 triple
Bathrooms: 1 en-suite, 1 public

Bed & breakfast
per night:	£min	£max
Single	16.50	16.50
Double	32.00	32.00

Half board per
person:	£min	£max
Daily	22.75	22.75
Weekly	136.50	136.50

Lunch available
Evening meal 1900 (last orders 2130)
Parking for 16
Cards accepted: Access, Visa

BURY ST EDMUNDS
Suffolk
Map ref 3B2

Ancient market and cathedral town which takes its name from the martyred Saxon King, St Edmund. Bury St Edmunds has many fine buildings including the Athenaeum and Moyses Hall, reputed to be the oldest Norman house in the county.
Tourist Information Centre ☎ *(01284) 764667*

Angel Hotel
HIGHLY COMMENDED
Angel Hill, Bury St Edmunds
IP33 1LT
☎ (01284) 753926
Fax (01284) 750092

Attractive Georgian hotel with individually decorated bedrooms. Four-posters and suites available. Ballroom and conference rooms. Bar food and noted restaurant.
Bedrooms: 15 single, 15 double, 12 twin
Bathrooms: 42 en-suite

Bed & breakfast
per night:	£min	£max
Single	37.00	70.00
Double	70.00	130.00

Half board per
person:	£min	£max
Daily	57.00	90.00

EAST ANGLIA

Lunch available
Evening meal 1900 (last orders 2200)
Parking for 58
Cards accepted: Access, Visa, Diners, Amex, Switch/Delta

Butterfly Hotel
COMMENDED

A14 Bury East Exit, Moreton Hall, Bury St Edmunds IP32 7BW
☎ (01284) 760884
Fax (01284) 755476
Modern building with rustic style and decor, around open central courtyard. Special weekend rates available.
Bedrooms: 32 single, 19 double, 14 twin
Bathrooms: 65 en-suite
Bed & breakfast

per night:	£min	£max
Single	59.95	61.95
Double	64.90	68.90

Lunch available
Evening meal 1800 (last orders 2200)
Parking for 70
Cards accepted: Access, Visa, Diners, Amex, Switch/Delta

The Grange Hotel
COMMENDED

Barton Road, Thurston, Bury St Edmunds IP31 3PQ
☎ Pakenham (01359) 231260
Fax (01359) 231260

Family-owned country house hotel with chef/proprietor, 4 miles from Bury St Edmunds.
Bedrooms: 2 single, 8 double, 2 twin, 1 triple
Suites available
Bathrooms: 12 en-suite
Bed & breakfast

per night:	£min	£max
Single	35.00	45.00
Double	50.00	65.00

Lunch available
Evening meal 1900 (last orders 2130)
Parking for 80
Cards accepted: Access, Visa

Hamling House Hotel
COMMENDED

Bull Road, Pakenham, Bury St Edmunds IP31 2LW
☎ Pakenham (01359) 230934
Fax (01359) 232298
Possibly west Suffolk's most revisited small hotel. Alpine tranquillity in picturesque conservation village minutes from historic Bury St Edmunds. Superb facilities and memorable dining. Short breaks available.
Bedrooms: 4 double, 2 twin
Bathrooms: 6 en-suite
Bed & breakfast

per night:	£min	£max
Single	48.00	48.00
Double	68.00	68.00

Half board per

person:	£min	£max
Daily	46.00	52.50
Weekly	322.00	367.50

Lunch available
Evening meal 1900 (last orders 2030)
Parking for 10
Cards accepted: Access, Visa, Diners, Amex, Switch/Delta

CAMBRIDGE
Cambridgeshire
Map ref 2D1

A most important and beautiful city on the River Cam with 31 colleges forming one of the oldest universities in the world. Numerous museums, good shopping centre, restaurants, theatres, cinema and fine bookshops.
Tourist Information Centre ☎ (01223) 322640

Acorn Guest House
COMMENDED

154 Chesterton Road, Cambridge CB4 1DA
☎ (01223) 353888
Fax (01223) 350527
Small guesthouse less than 1 mile from city centre. Most rooms en-suite, ground floor rooms available. Choice of breakfasts. Parking.
Bedrooms: 2 double, 1 twin, 1 triple, 1 family room
Suites available
Bathrooms: 5 en-suite, 1 public
Bed & breakfast

per night:	£min	£max
Single	20.00	42.00
Double	32.00	50.00

Half board per

person:	£min	£max
Daily	30.00	50.00

Parking for 7
Cards accepted: Access, Visa

L'Aquila Guest House

12 Rock Road, Off Cherry Hinton Road, Cambridge CB1 4UF
☎ (01223) 245432 & 564432
Comfortable family-run guesthouse. Convenient for the station and hospital and about 20 minutes' walk from the city centre.
Bedrooms: 2 double, 1 twin, 1 triple
Bathrooms: 1 en-suite, 1 private, 1 public, 1 private shower
Bed & breakfast

per night:	£min	£max
Single	25.00	28.00
Double	35.00	38.00

Parking for 2
Cards accepted: Access, Visa

Arbury Lodge Guest House
Listed COMMENDED

82 Arbury Road, Cambridge CB4 2JE
☎ (01223) 364319 & 566988
Fax (01223) 566988
Comfortable family-run guesthouse, about 20 minutes' walk to city centre and colleges. Easy access from A14. Large car park and garden.
Bedrooms: 2 single, 1 double, 2 twin
Bathrooms: 2 en-suite, 4 public
Bed & breakfast

per night:	£min	£max
Single	20.00	24.00
Double	35.00	44.00

Parking for 8

Arundel House Hotel
COMMENDED

Chesterton Road, Cambridge CB4 3AN
☎ (01223) 367701
Fax (01223) 367721
Elegant, privately-owned 19th C terraced hotel. Beautiful location overlooking River Cam and open parkland, near city centre and colleges. Reputation for some of the best food in the area.
Bedrooms: 42 single, 33 double, 24 twin, 5 triple, 1 family room
Bathrooms: 99 en-suite, 8 public
Bed & breakfast

per night:	£min	£max
Single	39.50	59.00
Double	55.50	89.00

Continued ▶

EAST ANGLIA

CAMBRIDGE
Continued

Half board per person:
	£min	£max
Daily	49.50	74.95

Lunch available
Evening meal 1830 (last orders 2130)
Parking for 70
Cards accepted: Access, Visa, Diners, Amex, Switch/Delta

Ashtrees Guest House
Listed COMMENDED

128 Perne Road, Cambridge
CB1 3RR
☎ (01223) 411233
Comfort and an enjoyable stay are the priorities. Individually decorated rooms to a high standard. Home cooking. Garden and car park.
Bedrooms: 2 single, 3 double, 1 twin, 1 triple
Bathrooms: 1 en-suite, 1 public

Bed & breakfast per night:
	£min	£max
Single	19.00	29.00
Double	36.00	40.00

Half board per person:
	£min	£max
Daily	26.00	37.00

Evening meal 1830 (last orders 1830)
Parking for 6
Cards accepted: Access, Visa

Assisi Guest House
APPROVED

193 Cherry Hinton Road, Cambridge CB1 4BX
☎ (01223) 246648 & 211466
Fax (01223) 412900

Warm, welcoming, family-run guesthouse, ideally situated for the city, colleges and Addenbrookes Hospital. All modern facilities. Large car park.
Bedrooms: 4 single, 5 double, 7 twin, 1 triple, 1 family room
Bathrooms: 18 en-suite

Bed & breakfast per night:
	£min	£max
Single	27.00	30.00
Double	37.00	40.00

Parking for 15
Cards accepted: Access, Visa, Amex

Avimore Guest House

310 Cherry Hinton Road, Cambridge CB1 4AU
☎ (01223) 410956
Fax (01223) 576957
Family-run guesthouse on the ring road, 1.75 miles from city centre and close to Addenbrookes Hospital.
Bedrooms: 2 single, 1 double, 1 twin, 2 family rooms
Bathrooms: 2 private, 2 public

Bed & breakfast per night:
	£min	£max
Single	20.00	28.00
Double	36.00	42.00

Parking for 5
Cards accepted: Access, Visa, Diners

Bridge Hotel (Motel)

Clayhythe, Waterbeach, Cambridge CB5 9NZ
☎ (01223) 860252
Fax (01223) 440448

Picturesque 17th C riverside hotel with motel rooms, between A45 and A10 (B1047), 4 miles from Cambridge. Fishing, walking, boating.
Bedrooms: 7 single, 16 double, 5 twin
Suites available
Bathrooms: 28 en-suite

Bed & breakfast per night:
	£min	£max
Single	30.00	45.00
Double	45.00	56.00

Lunch available
Evening meal 1830 (last orders 2130)
Parking for 50
Cards accepted: Access, Visa, Amex, Switch/Delta

Brooklands Guest House
COMMENDED

95 Cherry Hinton Road, Cambridge CB1 4BS
☎ (01223) 242035
Fax (01223) 242035
Friendly guesthouse, well decorated. All rooms en-suite and with telephone. Satellite TV, jacuzzi, sauna, four-poster bed.
Bedrooms: 3 double, 2 twin
Bathrooms: 5 en-suite

Bed & breakfast per night:
	£min	£max
Single	28.00	30.00
Double	40.00	46.00

Evening meal 1830 (last orders 1900)
Parking for 5
Cards accepted: Access, Visa, Diners, Amex, Switch/Delta

Cam Guest House
Listed

17 Elizabeth Way, Cambridge CB4 1DD
☎ (01223) 354512
Guesthouse close to the River Cam, within 15 minutes' walking distance of the city centre and 5 minutes from Grafton shopping centre.
Bedrooms: 3 single, 3 double, 2 triple
Bathrooms: 1 en-suite, 3 public

Bed & breakfast per night:
	£min	£max
Single	22.00	25.00
Double	35.00	48.00

Parking for 6

Centennial Hotel
COMMENDED

63-71 Hills Road, Cambridge CB2 1PG
☎ (01223) 314652
Fax (01223) 315443
Modernised family-run hotel opposite the botanical gardens. Central, near entertainment and colleges. Fully licensed bar and restaurant. Parking.
Bedrooms: 7 single, 21 double, 10 twin, 1 triple
Bathrooms: 39 en-suite

Bed & breakfast per night:
	£min	£max
Single	55.00	63.00
Double	69.00	77.00

Half board per person:
	£min	£max
Daily	68.50	76.50

Lunch available
Evening meal 1830 (last orders 2130)
Parking for 32
Cards accepted: Access, Visa, Diners, Amex

EAST ANGLIA

Cristinas
👑👑👑

47 St. Andrews Road, Cambridge
CB4 1DL
☎ (01223) 365855 & 327700
Fax (01223) 365855
Small family-run business in quiet location, a short walk from city centre and colleges.
Bedrooms: 5 double, 3 twin, 1 triple
Bathrooms: 7 en-suite, 1 public

Bed & breakfast
per night:	£min	£max
Single	26.00	38.00
Double	39.00	47.00

Parking for 8

The Crown and Punchbowl Inn 🅜
👑👑👑 COMMENDED

Horningsea, Cambridge CB5 9JG
☎ (01223) 860643
Fax (01223) 441814

Country hotel formed from 17th C inn and adjoining Georgian house. Serves fine and imaginative food in the English tradition. Off A14, 4 miles from city centre.
Bedrooms: 3 double, 2 twin
Bathrooms: 5 en-suite

Bed & breakfast
per night:	£min	£max
Single	39.50	42.50
Double	55.00	62.50

Half board per
person:	£min	£max
Daily	52.25	61.25
Weekly	365.75	428.75

Lunch available
Evening meal 1930 (last orders 2130)
Parking for 20
Cards accepted: Access, Visa

Dresden Villa Guest House 🅜
👑👑👑 APPROVED

34 Cherry Hinton Road, Cambridge
CB1 4AA
☎ (01223) 247539
Fax (01223) 410640
Family-run guesthouse offering friendly service. All rooms en-suite, tea/coffee, satellite TV. Easy access to city colleges, hospital.

Bedrooms: 4 single, 3 double, 2 twin, 2 triple
Bathrooms: 11 en-suite, 1 public

Bed & breakfast
per night:	£min	£max
Single	25.00	26.00
Double	40.00	42.00

Half board per
person:	£min	£max
Daily	35.00	36.00

Lunch available
Evening meal 1900 (last orders 2000)
Parking for 8

Duxford Lodge Hotel 🅜
👑👑👑 HIGHLY COMMENDED

Ickleton Road, Duxford, Cambridge
CB2 4RU
☎ (01223) 836444
Fax (01223) 832271

Comfortable country house hotel in beautiful grounds. 10 minutes south of Cambridge, off the M11 and very close to Duxford Air Museum.
Bedrooms: 2 single, 12 double, 1 twin
Bathrooms: 15 en-suite

Bed & breakfast
per night:	£min	£max
Single	37.00	47.00
Double	70.00	70.00

Lunch available
Evening meal 1900 (last orders 2130)
Parking for 34
Cards accepted: Access, Visa, Diners, Amex, Switch/Delta

Fairways Guest House
👑👑

141-143 Cherry Hinton Road,
Cambridge CB1 4BX
☎ (01223) 246063
Fax (01223) 212093
Charming Victorian house. Family and en-suite rooms available. Direct dial telephone, clock/radio in all rooms. Close to Addenbrookes Hospital, station and golf-course and 1 mile from city centre. English/continental breakfast, bar/lounge.
Bedrooms: 4 single, 4 double, 4 twin, 1 triple, 2 family rooms
Bathrooms: 8 en-suite, 2 public

Bed & breakfast
per night:	£min	£max
Single	20.00	29.00
Double	35.00	44.00

Parking for 20
Cards accepted: Access, Visa, Switch/Delta

Gonville Hotel 🅜
👑👑👑👑 COMMENDED

Gonville Place, Cambridge CB1 1LY
☎ (01223) 366611
Fax (01223) 315470
Ⓒ Best Western
Occupies one of the most favoured positions in Cambridge, overlooking Parkers Piece and close to most of the colleges.
Bedrooms: 24 single, 19 double, 21 twin, 1 triple
Bathrooms: 65 en-suite

Bed & breakfast
per night:	£min	£max
Single	77.00	
Double	96.00	

Half board per
person:	£min	£max
Daily	54.00	

Lunch available
Evening meal 1900 (last orders 2045)
Parking for 80
Cards accepted: Access, Visa, Diners, Amex, Switch/Delta

Hamden Guest House
Listed

89 High Street, Cherry Hinton,
Cambridge CB1 4LU
☎ (01223) 413263
High standard bed and breakfast accommodation. Comfortable rooms with private facilities, most with garden view. Full English or continental breakfast. Frequent bus service to city centre; close to Addenbrookes Hospital, shops, pubs and restaurants. Easy access to M11 and A14.
Bedrooms: 1 single, 1 double, 1 twin, 1 triple, 1 family room
Bathrooms: 5 private

Bed & breakfast
per night:	£min	£max
Single	25.00	30.00
Double	38.00	40.00

Parking for 7

EAST ANGLIA

CAMBRIDGE
Continued

Hamilton Hotel
⬥⬥⬥
156 Chesterton Road, Cambridge
CB4 1DA
☎ (01223) 365664
Fax (01223) 314866
Family-run private hotel about 1 mile from city centre. TVs, telephones, en-suites, tea and coffee-making facilities. Bar, meals, car park.
Bedrooms: 5 single, 5 double, 5 twin, 3 triple
Bathrooms: 15 en-suite, 1 public

Bed & breakfast per night:	£min	£max
Single	20.00	30.00
Double	40.00	55.00

Half board per person:	£min	£max
Daily	30.00	40.00

Evening meal 1830 (last orders 2030)
Parking for 18
Cards accepted: Access, Visa, Diners, Amex, Switch/Delta

Helen Hotel
⬥⬥⬥ APPROVED
167-169 Hills Road, Cambridge
CB2 2RJ
☎ (01223) 246465
Fax (01223) 214406
Comfortable family hotel. Beautiful Italian garden and good Italian food.
Bedrooms: 12 single, 8 double, 5 twin, 3 triple
Bathrooms: 28 en-suite

Bed & breakfast per night:	£min	£max
Single	36.00	47.50
Double	55.00	60.00

Evening meal 1900 (last orders 2000)
Parking for 20
Open January–November
Cards accepted: Access, Visa

Lensfield Hotel ⋒
⬥⬥⬥
53 Lensfield Road, Cambridge
CB2 1EN
☎ (01223) 355017
Fax (01223) 312022
Family-run hotel in central location for all parts of the city's splendour - the "Bridges and Backs", Botanical Gardens, colleges, entertainment and shopping.
Bedrooms: 8 single, 11 double, 10 twin, 4 triple
Bathrooms: 29 en-suite, 4 public

Bed & breakfast per night:	£min	£max
Single	35.00	45.00
Double	55.00	60.00

Half board per person:	£min	£max
Daily	42.00	50.00
Weekly	280.00	350.00

Evening meal 1830 (last orders 2100)
Parking for 11
Cards accepted: Access, Visa, Diners, Amex, Switch/Delta

Mowbray Lodge Guest House
⬥⬥⬥ COMMENDED
5 Mowbray Road, Cambridge
CB1 4SR
☎ (01223) 240089
Fax (01223) 240089

Comfort and a warm welcome with high standards of decoration are the priorities at Mowbray Lodge. All rooms en-suite. Car parking.
Bedrooms: 1 single, 2 double, 1 twin, 1 family room
Bathrooms: 5 en-suite

Bed & breakfast per night:	£min	£max
Single	28.00	30.00
Double	40.00	46.00

Evening meal 1800 (last orders 1900)
Parking for 7
Cards accepted: Access, Visa, Switch/Delta

Six Steps Guest House ⋒
Listed
93 Tenison Road, Cambridge
CB1 2DJ
☎ (01223) 353968 & 313802
Within 4 minutes' walking distance of the railway station, and half a mile from the city centre.
Bedrooms: 7 single, 3 double, 2 twin, 3 triple
Bathrooms: 11 en-suite, 4 private showers

You are advised to confirm your booking in writing.

Sorrento Hotel ⋒
⬥⬥⬥
190-196 Cherry Hinton Road, Cambridge CB1 4AN
☎ (01223) 243533
Fax (01223) 213463
Small family hotel in a quiet residential area. Close to town centre, with personal service and English/French/Italian cooking. All rooms en-suite. Bridal suite with jacuzzi and sauna.
Bedrooms: 9 single, 9 double, 1 twin, 3 triple
Bathrooms: 22 en-suite, 1 public

Bed & breakfast per night:	£min	£max
Single	40.50	55.00
Double	60.00	100.00

Half board per person:	£min	£max
Daily	52.00	67.00
Weekly	364.00	469.00

Evening meal 1830 (last orders 2030)
Parking for 25
Cards accepted: Access, Visa, Diners, Amex, Switch/Delta

Southampton House
Listed
7 Elizabeth Way, Cambridge
CB4 1DE
☎ (01223) 357780
Fax (01223) 314297
Victorian property with friendly atmosphere, only 8 minutes' walk along riverside to city centre, colleges and new shopping mall.
Bedrooms: 1 single, 1 double, 2 triple, 1 family room
Bathrooms: 5 en-suite

Bed & breakfast per night:	£min	£max
Single	22.00	30.00
Double	35.00	44.00

Parking for 8

The ⋒ symbol after an establishment name indicates that it is a Regional Tourist Board member.

EAST ANGLIA

CAWSTON
Norfolk
Map ref 3B1

Village with one of the finest churches in the country. St Agnes, built in the Perpendicular style, was much patronised by Michael de la Pole, Earl of Suffolk (1414), and has a magnificent hammer-beam roof and numerous carved angels.

Grey Gables Country House Hotel & Restaurant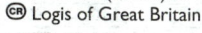

Norwich Road, Cawston, Norwich NR10 4EY
☎ Norwich (01603) 871259
Ⓖ Logis of Great Britain

Former rectory in pleasant, rural setting, 10 miles from Norwich, coast and Broads. Wine cellar, emphasis on food. Comfortably furnished with many antiques.
Bedrooms: 2 single, 5 double, 1 twin
Bathrooms: 6 en-suite, 1 public
Bed & breakfast

per night:	£min	£max
Single	20.00	40.00
Double	40.00	60.00

Half board per

person:	£min	£max
Daily	35.00	46.00
Weekly	235.00	246.00

Lunch available
Evening meal 1900 (last orders 2100)
Parking for 15
Cards accepted: Access, Visa

CHATTERIS
Cambridgeshire
Map ref 3A2

Cross Keys Inn Hotel
COMMENDED
12-16 Market Hill, Chatteris PE16 6BA
☎ March (01354) 693036 & 692644
Fax (01354) 693036

Please mention this guide when making your booking.

Elizabethan coaching inn built around 1540, Grade II listed. A la carte menu and bar meals. Friendly atmosphere, oak-beamed lounge with log fires. Ideally placed in the heart of the Fens.
Bedrooms: 2 double, 4 twin, 1 triple
Bathrooms: 5 en-suite, 1 public
Bed & breakfast

per night:	£min	£max
Single	21.00	32.50
Double	32.50	55.00

Lunch available
Evening meal 1900 (last orders 2200)
Parking for 10
Cards accepted: Access, Visa, Diners, Amex, Switch/Delta

CHEDISTON
Suffolk
Map ref 3C2

Saskiavill

Chediston, Halesworth IP19 OAR
☎ Halesworth (01986) 873067
Travelling west from Halesworth on the B1123, turn right after 2 miles at the signpost for Chediston Green. After crossing the hump-backed bridge over the stream, Saskiavill is the fourth property on the left.
Bedrooms: 1 double, 1 twin, 1 triple
Bathrooms: 3 en-suite, 2 public
Bed & breakfast

per night:	£min	£max
Single	18.00	20.00
Double	36.00	40.00

Half board per

person:	£min	£max
Daily	22.00	24.00
Weekly	135.00	148.00

Evening meal from 1830
Parking for 8
Open January–October

COLOUR MAPS

Colour maps at the back of this guide pinpoint all places in which you will find accommodation listed.

CHELMSFORD
Essex
Map ref 3B3

The county town of Essex, originally a Roman settlement, Caesaromagus, thought to have been destroyed by Boudicca. Growth of the town's industry can be traced in the excellent museum in Oaklands Park. 15th C parish church has been Chelmsford Cathedral since 1914.
Tourist Information Centre ☎ (01245) 283400

Beechcroft Private Hotel
COMMENDED
211 New London Road, Chelmsford CM2 0AJ
☎ (01245) 352462 & 250861
Fax (01245) 347833
Central hotel offering clean and comfortable accommodation with friendly service. Under family ownership and management. Within walking distance of town centre.
Bedrooms: 12 single, 3 double, 3 twin, 1 triple, 1 family room
Bathrooms: 9 en-suite, 4 public
Bed & breakfast

per night:	£min	£max
Single	25.50	37.70
Double	42.00	51.85

Parking for 15
Cards accepted: Access, Visa

Boswell House Hotel
COMMENDED
118 Springfield Road, Chelmsford CM2 6LF
☎ (01245) 287587
Fax (01245) 287587
Victorian town house in central location, offering high-standard accommodation in friendly and informal surroundings. Family atmosphere with home cooking.
Bedrooms: 5 single, 6 double, 2 triple
Bathrooms: 13 en-suite
Bed & breakfast

per night:	£min	£max
Single	42.00	
Double	60.00	

Half board per

person:	£min	£max
Daily	52.00	

Lunch available
Evening meal 1900 (last orders 2030)
Parking for 15
Cards accepted: Access, Visa, Diners, Amex

EAST ANGLIA

CHELMSFORD
Continued

The Chelmer Hotel
Listed

2-4 Hamlet Road, Chelmsford
CM2 0EU
☎ (01245) 353360 & 261751
Fax (0181) 574 3912
Friendly and homely atmosphere. Close to all amenities and priding itself as the most economic hotel in Chelmsford.
Bedrooms: 1 single, 1 double, 2 twin, 2 triple
Bathrooms: 2 public

Bed & breakfast per night	£min	£max
Single	19.00	21.50
Double	34.00	36.00

Parking for 2

County Hotel
COMMENDED

Rainsford Road, Chelmsford
CM1 2QA
☎ (01245) 491911
Fax (01245) 492762
Privately owned hotel, 10 minutes' walk from town centre. Families welcome - free cots, extra beds. Popular restaurant offering £18 - £20 three-course meal.
Bedrooms: 18 single, 7 double, 11 twin
Suite available
Bathrooms: 36 en-suite

Bed & breakfast per night	£min	£max
Single	28.00	64.00
Double	56.00	74.00

Lunch available
Evening meal 1830 (last orders 2100)
Parking for 120
Cards accepted: Access, Visa, Diners, Amex, Switch/Delta

Miami Hotel
APPROVED

Princes Road, Chelmsford CM2 9AJ
☎ (01245) 264848 & 269603
Fax (01245) 259860
The Independents
Family-run hotel, 1 mile from town centre. All rooms are twin/double size (let as singles when required).
Bedrooms: 28 single, 17 double, 10 twin
Bathrooms: 55 en-suite

Bed & breakfast per night	£min	£max
Single	55.50	60.50
Double	67.00	72.00

Half board per person	£min	£max
Daily	67.50	72.50

Lunch available
Evening meal 1830 (last orders 2130)
Parking for 80
Cards accepted: Access, Visa, Diners, Amex, Switch/Delta

Pontlands Park Country Hotel and Restaurant
HIGHLY COMMENDED

West Hanningfield Road, Great Baddow, Chelmsford CM2 8HR
☎ (01245) 476444
Fax (01245) 478393
Victorian mansion, now a leading country hotel and restaurant. Health and leisure centre, sauna, solarium, jacuzzi, indoor and outdoor swimming pool, garden coffee shop.
Bedrooms: 2 single, 14 double, 1 twin
Bathrooms: 17 en-suite

Bed & breakfast per night	£min	£max
Single	89.00	99.00
Double	115.00	125.00

Half board per person	£min	£max
Daily	123.00	133.00
Weekly	861.00	931.00

Lunch available
Evening meal 1900 (last orders 2200)
Parking for 100
Cards accepted: Access, Visa, Diners, Amex, Switch/Delta

Tanunda Hotel

217-219 New London Road, Chelmsford CM2 0AJ
☎ (01245) 354295
Fax (01245) 345503
Well-positioned commercial hotel with homely atmosphere. Snacks available.
Bedrooms: 8 single, 6 double, 6 twin
Bathrooms: 11 private, 3 public

Bed & breakfast per night	£min	£max
Single	29.00	40.00
Double	42.50	52.50

Parking for 20
Cards accepted: Access, Visa, Diners, Amex, Switch/Delta

Telford Lodge

102 Arbour Lane, Chelmsford
CM1 5RN
☎ (01245) 350011
Fax (01245) 265323
Comfortable accommodation and friendly staff, within a mile of town centre and railway station and with good access to A12/M25.
Bedrooms: 34 single, 10 twin
Suites available
Bathrooms: 3 en-suite, 14 public

Bed & breakfast per night	£min	£max
Single	21.95	41.75
Double	34.40	50.50

Half board per person	£min	£max
Daily	41.10	60.90
Weekly	287.70	426.30

Lunch available
Evening meal 1800 (last orders 1900)
Parking for 75
Cards accepted: Access, Visa

CHESHUNT

Hertfordshire
Map ref 2D1

Cheshunt Marriott Hotel
COMMENDED

Halfhide Lane, Turnford, Broxbourne
EN10 6NG
☎ Hoddesdon (01992) 451245
Fax (01992) 440120
Utell International
Only minutes' drive from the M25 motorway, the Cheshunt Marriott offers an ideal base for exploring London and the South East. Prices are per room.
Wheelchair access category 1
Bedrooms: 103 double, 39 twin
Suites available
Bathrooms: 142 en-suite

Bed & breakfast per night	£min	£max
Single	78.00	98.00
Double	78.00	98.00

Lunch available
Evening meal 1830 (last orders 2200)
Parking for 200
Cards accepted: Access, Visa, Diners, Amex, Switch/Delta

Map references apply to the colour maps at the back of this guide.

EAST ANGLIA

CLACTON-ON-SEA

Essex
Map ref 3B3

Developed in the 1870s into a popular holiday resort with pier, pavilion, funfair, theatres and traditional amusements. The Martello Towers on the seafront were built like many others in the early 19th C to defend Britain against Napoleon.
Tourist Information Centre ☎ (01255) 423400

Sandrock Hotel ♠
♛♛♛ COMMENDED
1 Penfold Road, Marine Parade West, Clacton-on-Sea CO15 1JN
☎ (01255) 428215
Private licensed hotel in central location, 50 metres from seafront. High-standard accommodation in friendly and informal surroundings. Freshly cooked meals. Free car park. Hygiene award.
Bedrooms: 5 double, 2 twin, 1 triple
Bathrooms: 8 en-suite

Bed & breakfast
per night:	£min	£max
Single		24.50
Double		48.00

Half board per
person:	£min	£max
Daily		34.50
Weekly		205.00

Lunch available
Evening meal 1830 (last orders 1900)
Parking for 6
Cards accepted: Access, Visa, Amex

CLARE

Suffolk
Map ref 3B2

Attractive village with many of the houses displaying pargetting work and the site of a castle first mentioned in 1090. Clare Country Park occupies the site of the castle bailey and old railway station. Ancient House Museum in the 15th C priest's house contains local bygones.

Bell Hotel
♛♛♛ APPROVED
Market Hill, Clare, Sudbury CO10 8NN
☎ (01787) 277741
Fax (01787) 278474

16th C posting house with beamed restaurant and wine bar. Within easy reach of ports. 60 miles from London.
Bedrooms: 1 single, 12 double, 4 twin, 2 triple
Bathrooms: 19 en-suite, 1 public

Bed & breakfast
per night:	£min	£max
Single	30.00	55.00
Double	40.00	80.00

Lunch available
Evening meal 1900 (last orders 2130)
Parking for 16
Cards accepted: Access, Visa, Amex, Switch/Delta

Cobwebs
Listed
26 Nethergate Street, Clare, Sudbury CO10 8NP
☎ Sudbury (01787) 277539
Beamed Grade II listed family house near town centre on A1092. Excellent base for touring. Set in delightful walled garden.
Bedrooms: 1 single, 2 twin
Bathrooms: 1 en-suite, 1 public

Bed & breakfast
per night:	£min	£max
Single	20.00	25.00
Double	40.00	45.00

CLEY NEXT THE SEA

Norfolk
Map ref 3B1

Due to land reclamation the village has not been "next the sea" since the 17th C. Behind the old quay the main street winds between flint-built houses. The marshes between Cley and Salthouse are bird reserves. Cley Windmill is a 160-year-old tower mill converted into a guesthouse.

Cley Windmill ♠
♛♛ APPROVED
Cley next the Sea, Holt NR25 7NN
☎ Cley (01263) 740209 & 741324
Fax (01263) 740209

Unusual, dramatic building which enjoys superb views over Cley marshes. Wonderfully comfortable and relaxed atmosphere within.
Bedrooms: 5 double, 3 twin
Bathrooms: 6 en-suite, 2 public

Bed & breakfast
per night:	£min	£max
Single	32.00	
Double		64.00

Half board per
person:	£min	£max
Daily	42.00	46.50
Weekly	266.00	297.50

Evening meal 1930 (last orders 1930)
Parking for 12
Cards accepted: Access, Visa, Switch/Delta

CODICOTE

Hertfordshire
Map ref 2D1

The Bell Inn & Motel ♠
♛♛♛ COMMENDED
High Street, Codicote SG4 8XD
☎ Stevenage (01438) 820278
Fax (01438) 821671

Recently refurbished traditional inn and restaurant with en-suite motel rooms. Beautiful village setting, with gardens. Very close to A1(M), M25 and M1. Family-run and very welcoming.
Bedrooms: 9 double, 16 twin
Bathrooms: 25 en-suite

Bed & breakfast
per night:	£min	£max
Single	35.50	49.50
Double	45.00	55.50

Half board per
person:	£min	£max
Daily	51.50	61.50
Weekly	370.00	399.50

Lunch available
Evening meal 1900 (last orders 2200)
Parking for 60

Continued ▶

EAST ANGLIA

CODICOTE
Continued

Cards accepted: Access, Visa, Diners, Amex, Switch/Delta

COGGESHALL
Essex
Map ref 3B2

The National Trust property "Paycocke's" is at Coggeshall. It is a 16th century half-timbered merchant's house featuring a richly-carved interior.

The White Hart Hotel
HIGHLY COMMENDED

Market End, Coggeshall, Colchester CO6 1NH
☎ Braintree (01376) 561654
Fax (01376) 561789

Tudor inn dating from 1432, built on a Roman road and signed off the A120 and A12, 7 miles west of Colchester.
Bedrooms: 4 single, 12 double, 2 twin
Bathrooms: 18 en-suite

Bed & breakfast per night:
	£min	£max
Single	49.20	66.50
Double	77.60	97.00

Half board per person:
	£min	£max
Daily	64.15	81.35

Lunch available
Evening meal 1900 (last orders 2200)
Parking for 41
Cards accepted: Access, Visa, Amex, Switch/Delta

All accommodation in this guide has been graded, or is awaiting a grading, by a trained Tourist Board inspector.

Information on accommodation listed in this guide has been supplied by the proprietors. As changes may occur you are advised to check details at the time of booking.

COLCHESTER
Essex
Map ref 3B2

Britain's oldest recorded town standing on the River Colne and famous for its oysters. Numerous historic buildings, ancient remains and museums. Plenty of parks and gardens, extensive shopping centre, theatre and zoo.
Tourist Information Centre ☎ (01206) 282920

Butterfly Hotel

A12-A120 Ardleigh Junction, Old Ipswich Road, Colchester CO7 7QY
☎ (01206) 230900
Fax (01206) 231095

Purpose-built hotel in traditional style. Modern coaching inn by the water's edge on the outskirts of Colchester at the junction of A12 and A120.
Bedrooms: 22 single, 12 double, 12 twin, 4 family rooms
Suites available
Bathrooms: 50 en-suite

Bed & breakfast per night:
	£min	£max
Single	59.95	61.95
Double	64.90	68.90

Lunch available
Evening meal 1800 (last orders 2200)
Parking for 75
Cards accepted: Access, Visa, Diners, Amex, Switch/Delta

George Hotel
HIGHLY COMMENDED

116 High Street, Colchester CO1 1TD
☎ (01206) 578494
Fax (01206) 761732
Best Western

Now privately-owned, this completely refurbished famous coaching inn features original wattle and daub walls. Food available all day.
Bedrooms: 5 single, 22 double, 14 twin, 3 triple, 1 family room
Bathrooms: 45 en-suite

Bed & breakfast per night:
	£min	£max
Single	39.00	62.50
Double	50.00	80.00

Lunch available
Evening meal 1900 (last orders 2200)
Parking for 50
Cards accepted: Access, Visa, Diners, Amex, Switch/Delta

The Globe Hotel
Listed APPROVED

71 North Station Road, Colchester CO1 1RQ
☎ (01206) 573881
Fax (01206) 797265

Victorian pub/hotel, now fully restored. All rooms en-suite, car park, restaurant. Close to A12, mainline station and all local amenities.
Bedrooms: 3 single, 3 double, 2 twin, 2 triple, 2 family rooms
Bathrooms: 12 en-suite

Bed & breakfast per night:
	£min	£max
Single	30.00	30.00
Double	50.00	60.00

Lunch available
Evening meal 1800 (last orders 2000)
Parking for 20
Cards accepted: Access, Visa, Diners, Amex

Kingsford Park Hotel
COMMENDED

Layer Road, Colchester CO2 OHS
☎ (01206) 734301
Fax (01206) 734512

Privately-owned 18th C manor house in 18 acres, offering good cuisine and a warm friendly atmosphere. Only 2 miles from town centre.
Bedrooms: 2 single, 3 double, 3 twin, 1 triple
Suite available
Bathrooms: 9 en-suite

Bed & breakfast per night:
	£min	£max
Single	55.00	85.00
Double	65.00	95.00

Lunch available
Evening meal 1900 (last orders 2130)
Parking for 100
Cards accepted: Access, Visa, Diners, Amex

EAST ANGLIA

Rose & Crown
✤✤✤ COMMENDED
East Street, Colchester CO1 2TZ
☎ (01206) 866677
Fax (01206) 866616
Ⓡ Logis of Great Britain

The oldest inn in the oldest recorded town in England. Early 15th C inn with charming en-suite bedrooms, log fire bar and noted restaurant. On Ipswich road 2 miles off A12 and half a mile from town centre.
Bedrooms: 1 single, 23 double, 2 twin, 4 triple
Bathrooms: 30 en-suite

Bed & breakfast per night:	£min	£max
Single	49.00	58.00
Double	49.00	58.00

Half board per person:	£min	£max
Daily	36.00	40.00

Lunch available
Evening meal 1900 (last orders 2200)
Parking for 60
Cards accepted: Access, Visa, Diners, Amex, Switch/Delta
🐕♿🏠💺🛏⚑S⅟♨TV📺
🔥🛢T120⛳❄✴DAP♺SP🏠T

The Salisbury
Listed APPROVED
112 Butt Road, Colchester CO3 3DL
☎ (01206) 572338
Fax (01206) 797265
Family-run hotel near town centre. Fully licensed restaurant/bar, private meeting facilities, pool, darts. Specialises in small, informal dinner parties.
Bedrooms: 3 single, 2 double, 2 twin, 1 triple
Bathrooms: 6 en-suite

Bed & breakfast per night:	£min	£max
Single	30.00	35.00
Double	50.00	60.00

Lunch available
Evening meal 1930 (last orders 2100)
Parking for 40
Cards accepted: Access, Visa, Amex
🐕🏠💺⚑S⅟♨TV📺🔥🛢T🌲❄✴⚡
✴DAP SP

Scheregate Hotel
 APPROVED
36 Osborne Street, via St John's Street, Colchester CO2 7DB
☎ (01206) 573034
Interesting 15th C building, centrally situated, providing accommodation at moderate prices.
Bedrooms: 12 single, 4 double, 7 twin, 1 triple, 1 family room
Bathrooms: 5 en-suite, 6 public

Bed & breakfast per night:	£min	£max
Single	18.00	30.00
Double	33.00	45.00

Parking for 28
Cards accepted: Access, Visa
🐕♿🏠💺⚑S♨📺🔥🛢❄✴T

Silver Springs Restaurant and Motel
✤✤✤
Tenpenny Hill, Thorrington, Colchester CO7 8JG
☎ (01206) 250366
Fax (01206) 250700
Ⓡ Wayfarer
A country motel set in acres of landscaped grounds with separate timbered restaurant, bar and conference facilities. On B1027, between Colchester and Clacton-on-Sea.
Bedrooms: 6 double, 6 twin, 7 triple, 2 family rooms
Suite available
Bathrooms: 21 en-suite

Bed & breakfast per night:	£min	£max
Single	29.95	34.95
Double	39.95	49.95

Lunch available
Evening meal 1830 (last orders 2100)
Parking for 50
Cards accepted: Access, Visa, Diners, Amex, Switch/Delta
🐕♿🏠💺⚑S⅟♨TV📺🔥🛢T60❄
✴♺SP T

Wivenhoe House Hotel and Conference Centre
✤✤✤ COMMENDED
Wivenhoe Park, Colchester CO4 3SQ
☎ (01206) 863666
Fax (01206) 868532

Georgian mansion in 200 acres of parkland on the outskirts of Colchester.

Bedrooms: 8 single, 10 double, 29 twin
Bathrooms: 47 en-suite

Bed & breakfast per night:	£min	£max
Single	54.30	65.80
Double	62.60	74.10

Lunch available
Evening meal 1900 (last orders 2045)
Parking for 80
Cards accepted: Access, Visa, Diners, Amex, Switch/Delta
🐕♿🏠💺⚑S⅟♨TV📺
🔥🛢T80⛳❄✴♺SP🏠T

COLTISHALL
Norfolk
Map ref 3C1

On the River Bure, with an RAF station nearby. The village is attractive with many pleasant 18th C brick houses and a thatched church.

The Norfolk Mead Hotel
✤✤✤
The Mead, Coltishall, Norwich NR12 7DN
☎ Norwich (01603) 737531
Fax (01603) 737521
Beautiful Georgian country house set in 12 secluded acres of parkland and gardens with river frontage. Boating, birdlife, fishing, outdoor swimming pool and restaurant.
Bedrooms: 5 double, 3 twin, 2 triple
Bathrooms: 10 en-suite

Bed & breakfast per night:	£min	£max
Single	49.00	75.00
Double	65.00	95.00

Half board per person:	£min	£max
Weekly	294.00	390.00

Evening meal 1900 (last orders 2100)
Parking for 50
Cards accepted: Access, Visa, Diners, Amex
🐕3🏠💺⚑S⅟♨🔥
🛢T30🏊⛳❄✴⚡♺SP🏠T

The symbols in each entry give information about services and facilities. A 'key' to these symbols appears at the back of this guide.

EAST ANGLIA

CROMER
Norfolk
Map ref 3C1

Once a small fishing village and now famous for its fishing boats that still work off the beach and offer freshly caught crabs. Excellent bathing on sandy beaches fringed by cliffs. The town boasts a fine pier, theatre, museum and a lifeboat station.
Tourist Information Centre ☎ (01263) 512497

Cliftonville Hotel
COMMENDED

Seafront, Runton Road, Cromer NR27 9AS
☎ (01263) 512543
Fax (01263) 515700
Beautifully restored Edwardian hotel on the seafront. En-suite bedrooms all with sea view. All-day coffee shop/bar, Boltons Seafood Bistro and fine a la carte restaurant.
Wheelchair access category 3
Bedrooms: 7 single, 11 double, 9 twin, 2 triple, 1 family room
Bathrooms: 30 en-suite, 1 public

Bed & breakfast per night:	£min	£max
Single	30.00	55.00
Double	60.00	110.00

Half board per person:	£min	£max
Daily	40.00	67.00
Weekly	210.00	400.00

Lunch available
Evening meal 1800 (last orders 2200)
Parking for 20
Cards accepted: Access, Visa, Amex, Switch/Delta

The Grove Guest House
COMMENDED

95 Overstrand Road, Cromer NR27 0DJ
☎ (01263) 512412
Fax (01263) 513416
Georgian holiday home in 3 acres, with beautiful walks through fields and woods to the cliffs and beach. We also have self-catering cottages in a range of converted barns which are very popular.
Bedrooms: 1 single, 3 double, 3 twin, 2 family rooms
Bathrooms: 8 en-suite, 1 public, 1 private shower

Bed & breakfast per night:	£min	£max
Single	22.50	22.50
Double	45.00	45.00

Half board per person:	£min	£max
Daily	30.00	30.00
Weekly	195.00	195.00

Evening meal 1830 (last orders 1830)
Parking for 15
Open April–September

Hotel De Paris

High Street, Cromer NR27 9HG
☎ (01263) 513141
Fax (01263) 515217
Large hotel of historic and architectural interest, overlooking pier and close to shops.
Bedrooms: 10 single, 14 double, 27 twin, 5 triple
Bathrooms: 56 en-suite, 1 public

Bed & breakfast per night:	£min	£max
Single	25.00	35.00
Double	44.00	64.00

Half board per person:	£min	£max
Daily	31.00	44.00
Weekly	150.00	231.00

Lunch available
Evening meal 1800 (last orders 1900)
Parking for 12
Open March–December
Cards accepted: Access, Visa

DEREHAM
Norfolk
Map ref 3B1

East Dereham is famous for its associations with the poet William Cowper and also Bishop Bonner, chaplain to Cardinal Wolsey. His home is now a museum. Around the charming market-place are many notable buildings.

Lynn Hill Guest House
APPROVED

Lynn Hill, Yaxham Road, Dereham NR19 1HA
☎ East Dereham (01362) 696142
Modern establishment on approach road to East Dereham, 400 yards from the town centre, 300 yards from the by-pass exit.
Bedrooms: 1 single, 1 double, 5 twin, 1 triple
Bathrooms: 3 private, 2 public

Bed & breakfast per night:	£min	£max
Single	16.00	20.00
Double	30.00	36.00

Half board per person:	£min	£max
Daily	20.00	24.00

Evening meal 1800 (last orders 2000)
Parking for 8

DISS
Norfolk
Map ref 3B2

Old market town built around 3 sides of the Mere, a placid water of 6 acres. Although modernised, some interesting Tudor, Georgian and Victorian buildings around the market-place remain. St Mary's church has a fine knapped flint chancel.
Tourist Information Centre ☎ (01379) 650523

Malt House
DE LUXE

Denmark Hill, Palgrave, Diss IP22 1AE
☎ (01379) 642107
Fax (01379) 640315
17th C malt house, beautifully renovated and with all modern amenities. Candlelit dinners in elegant dining room, after-dinner coffee in beamed lounge. 1 acre of landscaped garden with walled kitchen garden. 10 minutes' walk Diss, 2 miles Bressingham Gardens.
Bedrooms: 2 double, 1 twin
Bathrooms: 3 en-suite

Bed & breakfast per night:	£min	£max
Single	30.00	30.00
Double	60.00	60.00

Half board per person:	£min	£max
Daily	50.00	50.00
Weekly	329.00	

Evening meal 1900 (last orders 2000)
Parking for 6
Cards accepted: Access, Visa, Diners

The Park Hotel
APPROVED

29 Denmark Street, Diss IP22 3LE
☎ (01379) 642244
Fax (01379) 644218
Minotel/The Independents
Modern hotel near town centre, with fine restaurant and bar. All rooms en-suite with colour TV, telephone, hospitality tray. Ideal location for touring East Anglia.

EAST ANGLIA

Bedrooms: 1 single, 10 double,
6 twin
Bathrooms: 17 en-suite

Bed & breakfast
per night:	£min	£max
Single	30.00	55.00
Double	45.00	65.00

Half board per
person:	£min	£max
Daily	40.00	

Lunch available
Evening meal 1900 (last orders 2200)
Parking for 72
Cards accepted: Access, Visa, Diners, Amex, Switch/Delta

🛏🚗📞📺🛋♿§🗡🅿🚭
🍴400 ⌛✓✻🐕 OAP 🐕 SP

DOWNHAM MARKET

Norfolk
Map ref 3B1

Market town above the surrounding Fens on the River Ouse. Oxburgh Hall (National Trust) is 8 miles east, a magnificent 15th C moated dwelling owned by one family, the Bedingfields, for almost 500 years.

Castle Hotel M
🏵🏵 COMMENDED

High Street, Downham Market
PE38 9HF
☎ (01366) 384311
Fax (01366) 384311

17th C coaching inn in centre of town. Restaurant, bar, lounge, conference rooms and function room (max. 80 persons). Four poster room with jacuzzi. Vegetarian menu in restaurant.
Bedrooms: 6 double, 6 twin
Bathrooms: 9 en-suite, 1 public

Bed & breakfast
per night:	£min	£max
Single	32.00	36.00
Double	39.00	49.00

Half board per
person:	£min	£max
Daily	35.00	44.00
Weekly	245.00	308.00

Lunch available
Evening meal 1900 (last orders 2130)
Parking for 30
Cards accepted: Access, Visa, Amex
🛏🚗📞📺🛋♿§🗡🅿
🍴T

Half board prices are given per person, but in some cases these may be based on double/twin occupancy.

DUNSTABLE

Bedfordshire
Map ref 2D1

Modern town with remains of a 12th C Augustinian priory in the parish church. The Dunstable Downs are famous for gliding and in the parkland of Whipsnade Zoo on the edge of the Downs many animals roam freely.
Tourist Information Centre ☎ (01582) 471012

Old Palace Lodge Hotel
🏵🏵🏵 COMMENDED

Church Street, Dunstable LU5 4RT
☎ (01582) 662201
Fax (01582) 696422

Parts of the hotel are believed to date back to the lodge at the Norman palace of Dunstable circa 1100 AD. Hotel lies on edge of Chilterns, 6 miles from Luton Airport.
Bedrooms: 5 single, 37 double, 8 twin
Bathrooms: 50 en-suite

Bed & breakfast
per night:	£min	£max
Single	51.50	92.25
Double	68.00	111.00

Lunch available
Evening meal 1900 (last orders 2145)
Parking for 70
Cards accepted: Access, Visa, Diners, Amex, Switch/Delta

🛏🚗📞📺🛋♿§🗡🅿🚭
🍴🏊T46 SP 🐕

EARLS COLNE

Essex
Map ref 3B2

Riverside Inn Motel
🏵

42 Lower Holt Street A604, Earls Colne, Colchester CO6 2PH
☎ Bures (01787) 223487

Converted farm buildings in village, on A604 at Earls Colne by the bridge over River Colne. All en-suite.
Wheelchair access category 3♿
Bedrooms: 2 double, 7 twin, 2 family rooms
Bathrooms: 11 en-suite

Bed & breakfast
per night:	£min	£max
Single	30.50	32.50
Double	40.00	44.00

Lunch available
Evening meal 1930 (last orders 2200)
Parking for 40
Cards accepted: Access, Visa
🛏🚗📞📺🛋♿§🗡🅿 SP

ELSTREE

Hertfordshire
Map ref 2D2

Edgwarebury Hotel
🏵🏵🏵 HIGHLY COMMENDED

Barnet Lane, Elstree, Borehamwood WD6 3RE
☎ (0181) 953 8227
Fax (0181) 207 3668
CR Whitbread

Large country house hotel set in 10 acres of landscaped gardens.
Bedrooms: 18 single, 17 double, 12 twin
Bathrooms: 47 en-suite

Bed & breakfast
per night:	£min	£max
Single	89.00	165.00
Double	89.00	165.00

Lunch available
Evening meal 1900 (last orders 2200)
Parking for 120
Cards accepted: Access, Visa, Diners, Amex, Switch/Delta
🛏🚗📞📺🛋♿§🗡🅿🚭
🍴80 ✻🐕 SP 🐕 T

ELY

Cambridgeshire
Map ref 3A2

Until the 17th C, when the Fens were drained, Ely was an island. The cathedral, completed in 1189, dominates the surrounding area. One particular feature is the central octagonal tower with a fan-vaulted timber roof and wooden lantern.
Tourist Information Centre ☎ (01353) 662062

Lamb Hotel M
🏵🏵🏵 COMMENDED

2 Lynn Road, Ely CB7 4EJ
☎ (01353) 663574
Fax (01353) 662023
CR Consort

In the shadows of Ely Cathedral, this fully modernised former coaching inn has been used by travellers since the 14th C.

Continued ▶

EAST ANGLIA

ELY
Continued

Bedrooms: 7 single, 5 double,
13 twin, 6 triple, 1 family room
Bathrooms: 32 en-suite

Bed & breakfast per night:	£min	£max
Single	57.00	57.00
Double	80.00	80.00

Lunch available
Evening meal 1900 (last orders 2130)
Parking for 19
Cards accepted: Access, Visa, Diners, Amex, Switch/Delta

Nyton Hotel

7 Barton Road, Ely CB7 4HZ
☎ (01353) 662459
Fax (01353) 666619
In a quiet, residential area overlooking Fenland countryside and adjoining golf-course. Close to city centre and cathedral.
Bedrooms: 2 single, 4 double, 2 twin, 2 family rooms
Bathrooms: 10 en-suite

Bed & breakfast per night:	£min	£max
Single	38.00	
Double	60.00	

Half board per person:	£min	£max
Daily	45.00	
Weekly	280.00	

Lunch available
Evening meal 1900 (last orders 2030)
Parking for 25
Cards accepted: Access, Visa, Diners, Amex

ERPINGHAM
Norfolk
Map ref 3B1

The Ark Restaurant with Rooms
Listed HIGHLY COMMENDED

The Street, Erpingham, Norwich NR11 7QB
☎ Cromer (01263) 761535
Original "2 up 2 down" cottage grown to 17 rooms over 200 years. Delightful rural setting.
Bedrooms: 2 double, 1 triple
Bathrooms: 3 private

Bed & breakfast per night:	£min	£max
Single	25.00	35.00
Double	50.00	65.00

Half board per person:	£min	£max
Daily	60.00	75.00
Weekly	105.00	125.00

Evening meal 1900 (last orders 2130)
Parking for 16

Saracens Head Inn
COMMENDED

Wolterton, Erpingham, Norwich NR11 7LX
☎ Cromer (01263) 768909
Unusual country inn with comfortable en-suite rooms, delightful garden and log fires in winter. Renowned for cuisine.
Bedrooms: 3 double, 1 twin
Bathrooms: 4 en-suite

Bed & breakfast per night:	£min	£max
Single	35.00	40.00
Double	40.00	50.00

Lunch available
Evening meal 1830 (last orders 2200)
Parking for 30
Cards accepted: Access, Visa, Amex

EYE
Suffolk
Map ref 3B2

"Eye" means island and this town was once surrounded by marsh. The fine church of SS Peter and Paul has a tower over 100 ft high and a carving of the Archangel Gabriel can be seen on the 16th C Guildhall.

The Cornwallis Arms
COMMENDED

Brome, Eye IP23 8AJ
☎ (01379) 870326
Fax (01379) 870051
Family-run country house hotel with medieval origins set in beautiful spacious grounds with water garden. Well appointed bedrooms with four-poster beds. Characterful bar and elegant restaurant.
Bedrooms: 10 double, 1 twin
Bathrooms: 11 en-suite

Bed & breakfast per night:	£min	£max
Single	59.50	65.00
Double	74.00	89.00

Lunch available
Evening meal 1900 (last orders 2130)
Parking for 150
Cards accepted: Access, Visa, Diners, Amex

FELIXSTOWE
Suffolk
Map ref 3C2

Seaside resort that developed at the end of the 19th C. Lying in a gently curving bay with a 2-mile-long beach and backed by a wide promenade of lawns and floral gardens. Ferry links to the continent.
Tourist Information Centre ☎ (01394) 276770

Brook Hotel
COMMENDED

Orwell Road, Felixstowe IP11 7PF
☎ (01394) 278441
Fax (01394) 670422

Close to town centre, leisure complex and seaside. All rooms en-suite.
Bedrooms: 2 single, 17 double, 5 twin, 1 family room
Suite available
Bathrooms: 24 en-suite, 1 private

Bed & breakfast per night:	£min	£max
Single	48.00	
Double	60.00	

Half board per person:	£min	£max
Daily	55.00	
Weekly	350.00	

Lunch available
Evening meal 1900 (last orders 2130)
Parking for 15
Cards accepted: Access, Visa, Diners, Amex

Dolphin Hotel

41 Beach Station Road, Felixstowe IP11 8EY
☎ (01394) 282261
Private hotel, 5 minutes from beach and 10 minutes from town centre.
Bedrooms: 3 single, 4 double, 2 twin
Bathrooms: 2 en-suite, 2 public, 1 private shower

EAST ANGLIA

Bed & breakfast
per night:	£min	£max
Single	18.00	24.00
Double	28.00	36.00

Lunch available
Evening meal 1900 (last orders 2130)
Parking for 24
Cards accepted: Access, Visa, Amex

Fludyer Arms Hotel
APPROVED

Undercliff Rd. East, Felixstowe
IP11 7LU
☎ (01394) 283179
Fax (01394) 670754
Closest hotel to the sea in Felixstowe. Two fully licensed bars and family room overlooking the sea. All rooms have superb sea views. Colour TV. Specialises in home-cooked food, with children's and vegetarian menus available.
Bedrooms: 3 single, 4 double, 1 twin
Bathrooms: 6 en-suite, 1 public

Bed & breakfast
per night:	£min	£max
Single	18.00	26.00
Double	32.00	40.00

Lunch available
Evening meal 1900 (last orders 2100)
Parking for 14
Cards accepted: Access, Visa, Amex

Orwell Hotel
COMMENDED

Hamilton Road, Felixstowe
IP11 7DX
☎ (01394) 285511
Fax (01394) 670687
Elegant, late-Victorian hotel dating back to 1898.
Bedrooms: 7 single, 12 double, 34 twin, 5 triple
Bathrooms: 58 en-suite

Bed & breakfast
per night:	£min	£max
Single		50.00
Double		60.00

Half board per
person:	£min	£max
Daily		60.00

Lunch available
Evening meal 1900 (last orders 2145)
Parking for 215
Cards accepted: Access, Visa, Diners, Amex, Switch/Delta

FRESSINGFIELD
Suffolk
Map ref 3C2

Chippenhall Hall
HIGHLY COMMENDED

Fressingfield, Eye IP21 5TD
☎ Diss (01379) 586733 & 588180
Fax (01379) 586272
Listed Tudor manor, film location, heavily beamed and with inglenook fireplaces, in 7 secluded acres. Fine food and wines. 1 mile south of Fressingfield on B1116.
Bedrooms: 5 double
Bathrooms: 5 en-suite

Bed & breakfast
per night:	£min	£max
Single	49.00	58.00
Double	57.00	65.00

Half board per
person:	£min	£max
Daily	52.00	56.00
Weekly	348.00	377.00

Lunch available
Evening meal 1930 (last orders 1600)
Parking for 12
Cards accepted: Access, Visa

FRINTON-ON-SEA
Essex
Map ref 3C2

Sedate town that developed as a resort at the end of the 19th C and still retains an air of Victorian gentility. Fine sandy beaches, good fishing and golf.

The Rock Hotel
COMMENDED

The Esplanade, Frinton-on-Sea
CO13 9EQ
☎ (01255) 677194 & Freefone 0500 506045
Fax (01255) 675173
Facing the sea, overlooking Frinton's greensward. Table d'hote, a la carte menu and a varied wine list. 9 and 18-hole golf courses nearby.
Bedrooms: 3 double, 1 twin, 2 triple
Bathrooms: 5 en-suite, 1 private, 2 public

Bed & breakfast
per night:	£min	£max
Single	49.50	59.50
Double	74.75	81.75

Half board per
person:	£min	£max
Daily	107.75	114.75

Lunch available
Evening meal 1800 (last orders 2200)
Parking for 17
Open February–December
Cards accepted: Access, Visa, Diners, Amex

GARBOLDISHAM
Norfolk
Map ref 3B2

Ingleneuk Lodge
COMMENDED

Hopton Road, Garboldisham, Diss
IP22 2RQ
☎ (01953) 681541
Fax (01953) 681633

Modern single-level home, family-run. South-facing patio, riverside walk. Very friendly atmosphere. On B1111, 1 mile south of village.
Wheelchair access category 2
Bedrooms: 2 single, 3 double, 2 twin
Bathrooms: 6 en-suite, 1 private, 1 public

Bed & breakfast
per night:	£min	£max
Single	23.00	33.00
Double	37.50	51.00

Half board per
person:	£min	£max
Daily	33.25	40.00
Weekly	199.00	306.00

Evening meal 1830 (last orders 1300)
Parking for 20
Cards accepted: Access, Visa, Amex, Switch/Delta

WELCOME HOST

This is a nationally recognised customer care programme which aims to promote the highest standards of service and a warm welcome. Establishments who are taking part in this initiative are indicated by the symbol.

EAST ANGLIA

GREAT YARMOUTH
Norfolk
Map ref 3C1

One of Britain's major seaside resorts with 5 miles of seafront and every possible amenity including an award winning leisure complex offering a huge variety of all-weather facilities. Busy harbour and fishing centre.

The Corner House Hotel
❦❦❦ COMMENDED

Albert Square, Great Yarmouth NR30 3JH
☎ (01493) 842773
Bay-fronted Victorian house adjacent to seafront, enjoying a high reputation for good cooking and personal, courteous service.
Bedrooms: 5 double, 2 twin, 1 triple
Bathrooms: 8 en-suite, 2 public

Bed & breakfast
per night:	£min	£max
Single	18.00	24.00
Double	36.00	48.00

Half board per
person:	£min	£max
Daily	26.00	32.00
Weekly	159.00	199.00

Evening meal 1715 (last orders 1715)
Parking for 8
Open March–September
⌂☎🅲♿♻🆂🅿📺🅰🛁🅿
🅾🅰🅿 🆂🅿 ♿

Furzedown Private Hotel
❦❦❦ COMMENDED

19-20 North Drive, Great Yarmouth NR30 4EW
☎ (01493) 844138
Fax (01493) 844138

You are advised to confirm your booking in writing.

Hotel overlooking the sea and 5 minutes' walk from town centre. Centrally heated throughout. Established over 30 years.
Bedrooms: 2 single, 9 double, 6 twin, 6 triple
Bathrooms: 21 en-suite, 2 private

Bed & breakfast
per night:	£min	£max
Single	22.50	31.50
Double	45.00	51.00

Half board per
person:	£min	£max
Daily	28.50	39.50
Weekly	150.00	220.00

Lunch available
Evening meal 1800 (last orders 1900)
Parking for 25
Cards accepted: Access, Visa, Switch/Delta
⌂☎🅲♿🆂🅿📺🅾🛁🅿100
▶✳🅾🅰🅿 🆂🅿
🅰🅳 See display advertisement on this page

Horse & Groom Motel ♠
❦❦❦ COMMENDED

Rollesby, Great Yarmouth NR29 5ER
☎ (01493) 740624
Fax (01493) 740022

Recently built motel on A149 in Norfolk Broads area. All rooms en-suite with satellite TV and tea/coffee facilities. Prices are per room.

Wheelchair access category 2♿
Bedrooms: 14 double, 3 twin, 3 family rooms
Bathrooms: 20 en-suite

Bed & breakfast
per night:	£min	£max
Single	37.90	43.00
Double	39.90	47.90

Half board per
person:	£min	£max
Daily	39.95	49.95
Weekly	208.00	236.00

Lunch available
Evening meal 1800 (last orders 2115)
Parking for 50
Cards accepted: Access, Visa, Switch/Delta
⌂☎🅲♿🆂🅿📺🅰🛁🅿30❖
🅾🅰🅿 🆂🅿

New Beach Hotel ♠
❦❦❦ COMMENDED

Marine Parade, Great Yarmouth NR30 2EJ
☎ (01493) 332300
Fax (01493) 331880
Centrally situated in a lively location opposite the pier and close to most shops and attractions.
Bedrooms: 4 single, 26 double, 42 twin, 3 triple
Bathrooms: 75 en-suite

Bed & breakfast
per night:	£min	£max
Single	22.00	28.00
Double	38.00	50.00

Half board per
person:	£min	£max
Daily	31.00	37.00
Weekly	140.00	190.00

Lunch available
Evening meal 1800 (last orders 1900)
Open March–December
Cards accepted: Access, Visa
⌂☎🅲♿🆂🅿🅾⛓🛁🅿✖
🆂🅿

The Garrod family have welcomed you for over 30 years
THE FURZEDOWN HOTEL

Open all year round and occupying the finest position on the sea front, overlooking Venetian Waterways and the sea.
We are famous for the quality of our food which is served in our spacious dining room. All rooms have TV and tea making facilities, and all rooms have private bath, toilet and shower. Children welcome, with reduced rates. Business and Contract personnel welcome. Private car park at rear of hotel.

19/20 NORTH DRIVE, GREAT YARMOUTH, NORFOLK NR30 4EW TEL/FAX: 01493 844138

ETB 3 CROWN COMMENDED

EAST ANGLIA

Regency Dolphin Hotel
COMMENDED

Albert Square, Great Yarmouth
NR30 3JH
☎ (01493) 855070
Fax (01493) 853798

Friendly, relaxing hotel with many amenities. Suites, presidential suite, jacuzzis, heated swimming pool in summer, health club. Short breaks available. Pets welcome by arrangement. Weekend rate £45.00 per person per night.
Bedrooms: 6 single, 33 double, 6 twin, 4 triple
Bathrooms: 49 en-suite

Bed & breakfast
per night:	£min	£max
Single	55.00	60.00
Double	75.00	85.00

Half board per
person:	£min	£max
Daily	45.00	68.00
Weekly	275.00	

Lunch available
Evening meal 1830 (last orders 2200)
Parking for 24
Cards accepted: Access, Visa, Diners, Amex, Switch/Delta

Spindrift Private Hotel
APPROVED

36 Wellesley Road, Great Yarmouth
NR30 1EU
☎ (01493) 858674
Fax (01493) 858674

Attractively situated small private hotel, close to all amenities and with Beach Coach Station and car park at rear. Front bedrooms overlook gardens and sea.
Bedrooms: 2 single, 2 double, 1 twin, 1 triple, 1 family room
Bathrooms: 5 private, 1 public

Bed & breakfast
per night:	£min	£max
Single	16.00	26.00
Double	28.00	40.00

Cards accepted: Access, Visa, Amex

Taunton House Hotel
Listed COMMENDED

9 Nelson Road South, Great Yarmouth NR30 3JL
☎ (01493) 850043

Conveniently situated for Pleasure Beach, Marina Centre, Wellington Pier and all major attractions. High standard of food from our varied menu choice.
Bedrooms: 1 single, 5 double, 1 twin, 1 triple

Bathrooms: 8 private

Bed & breakfast
per night:	£min	£max
Single	16.00	22.00
Double	32.00	44.00

Half board per
person:	£min	£max
Daily	21.00	26.00
Weekly	120.00	160.00

Evening meal from 1730
Open February–September, December

Trotwood Private Hotel
COMMENDED

2 North Drive, Great Yarmouth
NR30 1ED
☎ (01493) 843971

Opposite bowling greens on seafront, giving unrivalled sea views. Close to Britannia Pier and all amenities. Bedrooms en-suite, licensed bar, own car park.
Bedrooms: 8 double, 1 twin
Bathrooms: 8 en-suite, 1 public, 1 private shower

Bed & breakfast
per night:	£min	£max
Single	21.00	30.00
Double	38.00	53.00

Parking for 11

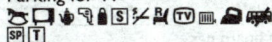

HARLESTON
Norfolk
Map ref 3C2

Attractive small town on the River Waveney with 2 market-places and a museum. Candler's House is an outstanding example of an early Georgian town house. At Starston, 1 mile away, is a restored wind-pump.

Swan Hotel
APPROVED

The Thoroughfare, Harleston
IP20 9AS
☎ (01379) 852221
Fax (01379) 854817

Situated in the centre of town, an old coaching inn with a carvery restaurant.
Bedrooms: 4 double, 6 twin
Bathrooms: 10 en-suite

Bed & breakfast
per night:	£min	£max
Single	30.00	30.00
Double	42.00	42.00

Lunch available
Evening meal 1900 (last orders 2130)
Parking for 40
Cards accepted: Access, Visa, Diners

HARPENDEN
Hertfordshire
Map ref 2D1

Delightful country town with many scenic walks through surrounding woods and fields. Harpenden train station provides a fast service into London.

Glen Eagle Hotel
COMMENDED

Luton Road, Harpenden AL5 2PX
☎ (01582) 760271
Fax (01582) 460819

Just off M1, junction 9 or 10, this pleasant country-town hotel offers comfortable facilities for businessmen and tourists. Prices shown are for room only.
Bedrooms: 10 single, 31 double, 10 twin
Bathrooms: 51 en-suite

Bed & breakfast
per night:	£min	£max
Single	73.50	83.50
Double	73.50	83.50

Lunch available
Evening meal 1900 (last orders 2200)
Parking for 100
Cards accepted: Access, Visa, Diners, Amex

Milton Hotel

25 Milton Road, Harpenden
AL5 5LA
☎ (01582) 762914

Family-run, comfortable hotel in residential area close to mainline station, junctions 9/10 of M1 and convenient for M25. Large car park.

Continued ▶

HARPENDEN
Continued

Bedrooms: 3 single, 2 double, 1 twin, 1 family room
Bathrooms: 3 en-suite, 2 public
Bed & breakfast
per night: £min £max
Single 22.00
Double 35.00 38.00

Evening meal 1900 (last orders 2100)
Parking for 9

HATFIELD
Hertfordshire
Map ref 2D1

The old town is dominated by the great Jacobean Hatfield House, built for Robert Cecil and still in the Cecil family. It has many interesting exhibits and extensive gardens open to the public.

Comet Hotel
COMMENDED

301 St Albans Road West, Hatfield AL10 9RH
☎ (01707) 265411
Fax (01707) 264019
Jarvis/Utell International
A hotel in the style of the 1930s, combining traditional comfort and service with modern design. Ideally located for London and Hertfordshire countryside.
Bedrooms: 14 single, 26 double, 15 twin
Bathrooms: 55 en-suite
Bed & breakfast
per night: £min £max
Single 46.00 85.00
Double 60.00 105.00

Half board per
person: £min £max
Daily 39.50 99.50
Weekly 276.50 696.50

Lunch available
Evening meal 1900 (last orders 2145)
Parking for 150
Cards accepted: Access, Visa, Diners, Amex, Switch/Delta

The National Grading and Classification Scheme is explained in full at the back of this guide.

HEMEL HEMPSTEAD
Hertfordshire
Map ref 2D1

Pleasant market town greatly expanded since the 1950s but with older origins. The High Street has pretty cottages and 18th C houses and the Norman parish church has a fine 14th C timber spire. The Grand Union Canal runs nearby.
Tourist Information Centre ☎ *(01442) 234222*

The Bobsleigh Inn
COMMENDED

Hempstead Road, Bovingdon, Hemel Hempstead HP3 0DS
☎ (01442) 833276 & 832000
Fax (01442) 832471
Privately owned country hotel/restaurant with reputation for good food and service. Easy access M1 and M25. 30 minutes from Luton and London Heathrow airports.
Wheelchair access category 3
Bedrooms: 5 single, 27 double, 5 twin, 5 triple, 1 family room
Bathrooms: 43 en-suite
Bed & breakfast
per night: £min £max
Single 35.00 75.00
Double 50.00 90.00

Half board per
person: £min £max
Daily 48.95 93.95
Weekly 450.00 600.00

Lunch available
Evening meal 1900 (last orders 2130)
Parking for 63
Cards accepted: Access, Visa, Diners, Amex, Switch/Delta

HERTFORD
Hertfordshire
Map ref 2D1

Old county town with attractive cottages and houses and fine public buildings. The remains of the ancient castle, childhood home of Elizabeth I, now form the council offices and the grounds are open to the public.
Tourist Information Centre ☎ *(01992) 584322*

Hall House
DE LUXE

Broad Oak End, Off Bramfield Road, Hertford SG14 2JA
☎ (01992) 582807
Tranquil, 15th C country house, rebuilt

---

in woodland setting on the edge of Hertford town. Non-smokers only, please.
Bedrooms: 3 double
Bathrooms: 2 en-suite, 1 private, 1 public
Bed & breakfast
per night: £min £max
Single 48.00 48.00
Double 65.00 65.00

Half board per
person: £min £max
Daily 52.50 68.00
Weekly 367.50 476.00

Evening meal from 1900
Parking for 6
Cards accepted: Access, Visa

HEVINGHAM
Norfolk
Map ref 3B1

Marsham Arms Inn
COMMENDED

Holt Road, Hevingham, Norwich NR10 5NP
☎ (01603) 754268
Fax (01603) 754839
Set in peaceful Norfolk countryside within reach of Norwich, the Broads and the coast. Comfortable and spacious accommodation, good food and a fine selection of ales.
Bedrooms: 3 double, 5 twin
Suites available
Bathrooms: 8 en-suite
Bed & breakfast
per night: £min £max
Single 40.00 45.00
Double 45.00 55.00

Lunch available
Evening meal 1800 (last orders 2200)
Parking for 100
Cards accepted: Access, Visa, Amex, Switch/Delta

HILLINGTON
Norfolk
Map ref 3B1

Ffolkes Arms Hotel
COMMENDED

Lynn Road, Hillington, King's Lynn PE31 6BJ
☎ (01485) 600210
Fax (01485) 601196
2 miles from Sandringham, family-run hotel with en-suite facilities on A148. Landscaped gardens in rural setting. Bar meals, carvery, restaurant.

EAST ANGLIA

Bedrooms: 6 single, 6 double, 6 twin, 2 triple
Bathrooms: 20 en-suite

Bed & breakfast
per night:	£min	£max
Single	29.00	29.00
Double	45.00	45.00

Half board per person:
	£min	£max
Daily	34.75	39.50
Weekly	197.75	276.50

Lunch available
Evening meal 1730 (last orders 2200)
Parking for 200
Cards accepted: Access, Visa, Amex, Switch/Delta

HITCHIN

Hertfordshire
Map ref 2D1

Once a flourishing wool town. Full of interest, with many fine old buildings around the market square. These include the 17th C almshouses, old inns and the Victorian Corn Exchange.

Redcoats Farmhouse Hotel ♠
COMMENDED

Redcoats Green, Hitchin SG4 7JR
☎ Stevenage (01438) 729500
Fax (01438) 723212
Ⓡ The Independents/Logis of Great Britain
15th C farmhouse in open countryside offering secluded comfort and fresh food. Luton Airport is 20 minutes away.
Bedrooms: 1 single, 10 double, 2 twin, 1 triple
Bathrooms: 11 en-suite, 1 private, 1 public

Bed & breakfast
per night:	£min	£max
Single	40.00	75.00
Double	50.00	95.00

Half board per person:
	£min	£max
Daily	65.00	100.00

Lunch available
Evening meal 1900 (last orders 2100)
Parking for 40
Cards accepted: Access, Visa, Diners, Amex, Switch/Delta

Please check prices and other details at the time of booking.

HORNING

Norfolk
Map ref 3C1

Riverside village and well-known Broadland centre. Occasional glimpses of the river can be caught between picturesque thatched cottages.

Petersfield House Hotel ♠
COMMENDED

Lower Street, Horning, Norwich NR12 8PF
☎ (01692) 630741
Fax (01692) 630745
Set slightly back from the banks of the River Bure, the hotel occupies one of the choicest positions on the Broads. Weekend breaks available.
Bedrooms: 3 single, 9 double, 5 twin, 1 triple
Bathrooms: 18 en-suite

Bed & breakfast
per night:	£min	£max
Single	58.00	63.00
Double	72.00	82.00

Half board per person:
	£min	£max
Daily	48.00	53.00
Weekly	226.00	371.00

Lunch available
Evening meal 1930 (last orders 2130)
Parking for 25
Cards accepted: Access, Visa, Diners, Amex

HUNSTANTON

Norfolk
Map ref 3B1

Seaside resort which faces the Wash. The shingle and sand beach is backed by striped cliffs and many unusual fossils can be found here. The town is predominantly Victorian. The Oasis family leisure centre has indoor and outdoor pools.
Tourist Information Centre ☎ (01485) 532610

The Linksway Country House Hotel
COMMENDED

Golf Course Road, Old Hunstanton, Hunstanton PE36 6JE
☎ (01485) 532209 & Mobile 0860 330178
Fax (01485) 532209
In quiet location overlooking Hunstanton Golf Course. Close to Beach and RSPB bird sanctuaries.

Bedrooms: 2 single, 2 double, 8 twin, 2 family rooms
Bathrooms: 13 en-suite, 1 private, 1 public

Bed & breakfast
per night:	£min	£max
Single	25.00	35.00
Double	50.00	65.00

Half board per person:
	£min	£max
Daily	38.00	48.00
Weekly	250.00	290.00

Evening meal 1900 (last orders 2100)
Parking for 15
Open March–December
Cards accepted: Access, Visa

HUNTINGDON

Cambridgeshire
Map ref 3A2

Attractive, interesting town which abounds in associations with the Cromwell family. The town is connected to Godmanchester by a beautiful 14th C bridge over the River Great Ouse.
Tourist Information Centre ☎ (01480) 388588

Old Bridge Hotel ♠

1 High Street, Huntingdon PE18 6TQ
☎ (01480) 452681
Fax (01480) 411017
Beautifully decorated Georgian town hotel by the River Ouse. Oak-panelled dining room and terrace brasserie with award-winning wine list, real ales and log fires. Privately owned.
Bedrooms: 7 single, 16 double, 3 twin
Bathrooms: 26 en-suite

Bed & breakfast
per night:	£min	£max
Single	69.50	85.00
Double	89.50	120.00

Half board per person:
	£min	£max
Daily	67.50	77.50

Lunch available
Evening meal 1830 (last orders 2200)
Parking for 70
Cards accepted: Access, Visa, Diners, Amex, Switch/Delta

EAST ANGLIA

HUNTINGDON
Continued

Prince of Wales
COMMENDED

Potton Road, Hilton, Huntingdon
PE18 9NG
☎ (01480) 830257
Fax (01480) 830257

Traditional village inn renowned for its traditional ales and good value food. Convenient for St Ives, Huntingdon, St Neots and Cambridge. On B1040, south-east of Huntingdon.
Bedrooms: 2 single, 1 double, 1 twin
Bathrooms: 4 en-suite

Bed & breakfast per night:

	£min	£max
Single	20.00	35.00
Double	40.00	50.00

Lunch available
Evening meal 1900 (last orders 2115)
Parking for 9
Cards accepted: Access, Visa, Amex, Switch/Delta

INGATESTONE
Essex
Map ref 3B3

The Heybridge Hotel
HIGHLY COMMENDED

Roman Road, Ingatestone CM4 9AB
☎ (01277) 355355
Fax (01277) 353288

Extensive conference and banqueting facilities with high quality accommodation. Restaurant offers international cuisine in a characteristic setting.
Wheelchair access category 3
Bedrooms: 14 double, 8 twin
Bathrooms: 22 en-suite

Bed & breakfast per night:

	£min	£max
Single	65.50	78.50
Double	72.00	98.50

Half board per person:

	£min	£max
Daily	82.75	120.50

Lunch available
Evening meal 1830 (last orders 2230)
Parking for 221
Cards accepted: Access, Visa, Diners, Amex

IPSWICH
Suffolk
Map ref 3B2

Interesting county town and major port on the River Orwell. Birthplace of Cardinal Wolsey. Christchurch Mansion, set in a fine park, contains a good collection of furniture and pictures, with works by Gainsborough, Constable and Munnings.
Tourist Information Centre ☎ (01473) 258070

Anglesea Hotel
APPROVED

10 Oban Street, Ipswich IP1 3PH
☎ (01473) 255630 & 0850 052764
Fax (01473) 255630
Victorian house, tastefully refurbished as a small hotel, in quiet conservation area. Within easy walking distance of town centre. Meals always available at a time to suit guests.
Bedrooms: 1 single, 1 double, 2 twin, 2 triple, 1 family room
Bathrooms: 7 en-suite

Bed & breakfast per night:

	£min	£max
Single	32.00	39.00
Double	42.00	49.00

Evening meal 1830 (last orders 2100)
Parking for 9
Cards accepted: Access, Visa, Diners, Amex

Belstead Brook Manor Hotel
HIGHLY COMMENDED

Belstead Brook Park, Belstead Road, Ipswich IP2 9HB
☎ (01473) 684241
Fax (01473) 681249
Best Western
Built in the 16th C, today's hotel is set in 9 acres of parkland and combines fine modern bedrooms and new leisure centre, with the charm of the Tudor award-winning restaurant.
Bedrooms: 16 single, 44 double, 16 twin

Suites available
Bathrooms: 76 en-suite

Bed & breakfast per night:

	£min	£max
Single	66.95	90.95
Double	75.90	132.90

Half board per person:

	£min	£max
Daily	54.50	143.45
Weekly	542.80	774.80

Lunch available
Evening meal 1900 (last orders 2130)
Parking for 120
Cards accepted: Access, Visa, Diners, Amex, Switch/Delta

Courtyard Ipswich
HIGHLY COMMENDED

The Havens, Ransomes Europark, Ipswich IP3 9SJ
☎ (01473) 272244
Fax (01473) 272484
Whitbread
Situated on outskirts of Ipswich, 4 miles from centre. Easy access to A14, ample free parking. Modern hotel offering traditional hospitality and good cuisine. Weekend breaks from £24 per person B&B.
Wheelchair access category 3
Bedrooms: 36 double, 24 twin
Bathrooms: 60 en-suite

Bed & breakfast per night:

	£min	£max
Single	24.00	70.50
Double	48.00	76.00

Half board per person:

	£min	£max
Daily	36.00	86.00

Lunch available
Evening meal 1900 (last orders 2200)
Parking for 148
Cards accepted: Access, Visa, Diners, Amex, Switch/Delta

Lochiel Guest House
Listed

216 Felixstowe Road, Ipswich IP3 9AE
☎ (01473) 727775
Fax (01473) 723201
Family-run establishment open all year. Near town centre and Suffolk Show Ground. En-suite rooms available. Car park.

Please mention this guide when making your booking.

EAST ANGLIA

Bedrooms: 3 single, 1 double, 2 twin, 1 triple
Bathrooms: 2 en-suite, 1 public, 1 private shower
Bed & breakfast

per night:	£min	£max
Single	15.00	17.00
Double	28.00	34.00

Half board per

person:	£min	£max
Daily	21.00	21.00

Evening meal 1700 (last orders 1930)
Parking for 6
Cards accepted: Access, Visa

The Marlborough at Ipswich
COMMENDED
Henley Road, Ipswich IP1 3SP
☎ (01473) 257677
Fax (01473) 226927
Best Western

Quietly situated hotel opposite Christchurch Park and Mansion. Victorian restaurant overlooking floodlit gardens. All rooms, including a suite and several with balconies, are individually decorated.
Bedrooms: 6 single, 11 double, 5 twin
Suite available
Bathrooms: 22 en-suite
Bed & breakfast

per night:	£min	£max
Single	75.00	
Double	85.00	

Lunch available
Evening meal 1930 (last orders 2130)
Parking for 60
Cards accepted: Access, Visa, Diners, Amex, Switch/Delta

Mount Pleasant
HIGHLY COMMENDED
103 Anglesea Road, Ipswich IP1 3PJ
☎ (01473) 251601
Fax (01473) 252198

Elegant Victorian house in residential road, just 10 minutes' walk from town centre. Spacious, attractive bedrooms, all with comfortable private bathrooms.
Bedrooms: 1 single, 2 double, 1 twin
Bathrooms: 3 en-suite, 1 private
Bed & breakfast

per night:	£min	£max
Single	25.00	28.00
Double		44.00

Parking for 4
Cards accepted: Diners

Novotel Ipswich
COMMENDED
Greyfriars Road, Ipswich IP1 1UP
☎ (01473) 232400
Fax (01473) 232414
Novotel
Town centre situation, access from A12/A14. 2 minutes from mainline station. All bedrooms have king-size bed and couch, radio, TV. Conference facilities, restaurant, bar. Special weekend breaks.
Wheelchair access category 3
Bedrooms: 100 double
Bathrooms: 100 en-suite
Bed & breakfast

per night:	£min	£max
Single	66.00	70.00
Double	74.00	78.00

Half board per

person:	£min	£max
Daily	72.00	75.00
Weekly	483.00	504.00

Lunch available
Evening meal 1800 (last orders midnight)
Parking for 50
Cards accepted: Access, Visa, Diners, Amex, Switch/Delta

Queenscliffe House Hotel
Queenscliffe Road, Ipswich IP2 9AS
☎ (01473) 690293
Elegant Victorian house close to station and town centre, in quiet wooded area, not on main road. 5 minutes to A12 and A45.
Bedrooms: 5 single, 1 double, 2 twin, 2 triple
Bathrooms: 8 en-suite, 3 public, 1 private shower
Bed & breakfast

per night:	£min	£max
Single	35.00	40.00
Double	42.00	49.00

Half board per

person:	£min	£max
Daily	45.00	49.00
Weekly	283.50	308.70

Evening meal 1900 (last orders 2000)
Parking for 12
Cards accepted: Access, Visa, Switch/Delta

KING'S LYNN
Norfolk
Map ref 3B1

A busy town with many outstanding buildings. The Guildhall and Town Hall are both built of flint in a striking chequer design. Behind the Guildhall in the Old Gaol House the sounds and smells of prison life 2 centuries ago are recreated.
Tourist Information Centre ☎ (01553) 763044

The Beeches Guest House
APPROVED
2 Guanock Terrace, King's Lynn PE30 5QT
☎ (01553) 766577
Fax (01553) 776664
Detached Victorian house, all rooms with TV, tea/coffee facilities and telephone. Most rooms en-suite. Full English breakfast and 3-course evening meal with coffee.
Bedrooms: 1 single, 2 double, 3 twin, 3 triple
Bathrooms: 4 en-suite, 2 private, 1 public
Bed & breakfast

per night:	£min	£max
Single	22.00	30.00
Double	35.00	44.00

Half board per

person:	£min	£max
Daily	21.50	38.00
Weekly	150.00	266.00

Evening meal 1830 (last orders 1930)
Parking for 3
Cards accepted: Access, Visa

National gradings and classifications were correct at the time of going to press but are subject to change. Please check at the time of booking.

EAST ANGLIA

KING'S LYNN
Continued

Butterfly Hotel
A10-A47 Roundabout, Hardwick Narrows, King's Lynn PE30 4NB
☎ (01553) 771707
Fax (01553) 768027
Modern building with rustic style and decor, set around an open central courtyard. Special weekend rates available.
Bedrooms: 23 single, 16 double, 11 twin
Bathrooms: 50 en-suite

Bed & breakfast

per night:	£min	£max
Single	59.95	61.95
Double	64.90	68.90

Lunch available
Evening meal 1800 (last orders 2200)
Parking for 70
Cards accepted: Access, Visa, Diners, Amex, Switch/Delta

The Duke's Head
COMMENDED
Tuesday Market Place, King's Lynn PE30 1JS
☎ (01553) 774996
Fax (01553) 763556
One of the finest classical buildings in the town. Overlooking the delightful market square, it holds a prime position from which to enjoy this interesting town. Half-board prices below are based on minimum 2-night stay.
Bedrooms: 18 single, 37 double, 14 twin, 2 triple
Bathrooms: 71 en-suite

Bed & breakfast

per night:	£min	£max
Single	65.95	68.50
Double	81.90	87.00

Half board per person:

	£min	£max
Daily	42.00	52.00
Weekly	273.00	325.00

Lunch available
Evening meal 1900 (last orders 2200)
Parking for 40
Cards accepted: Access, Visa, Diners, Amex, Switch/Delta

Fairlight Lodge
HIGHLY COMMENDED
79 Goodwins Road, King's Lynn PE30 5PE
☎ (01553) 762234
Fax (01553) 770280
Lovely owner-run Victorian house with friendly atmosphere and well appointed rooms. Ground floor en-suite rooms available. Private parking. Closed Christmas.
Bedrooms: 2 single, 1 double, 3 twin, 1 triple
Bathrooms: 4 private, 2 public

Bed & breakfast

per night:	£min	£max
Single	16.00	25.00
Double	32.00	38.00

Parking for 6

Havana Guest House
COMMENDED
117 Gaywood Road, King's Lynn PE30 2PU
☎ (01553) 772331
Comfortable bedrooms with colour co-ordinated soft furnishings. Some rooms non-smoking. Ground floor en-suites. Ample private parking. 10 minutes' walk to town centre.
Bedrooms: 1 single, 2 double, 3 twin, 1 family room
Bathrooms: 3 en-suite, 1 public, 1 private shower

Bed & breakfast

per night:	£min	£max
Single	16.00	25.00
Double	30.00	38.00

Parking for 8

Knights Hill Hotel
COMMENDED
Knights Hill Village, South Wootton, King's Lynn PE30 3HQ
☎ (01553) 675566
Fax (01553) 675568
Best Western
Sympathetically restored farm complex offering a choice of accommodation styles, 2 restaurants, a country pub and an extensive health club. Special breaks available.
Bedrooms: 5 single, 35 double, 12 twin
Bathrooms: 52 en-suite

Bed & breakfast

per night:	£min	£max
Single	41.50	77.00
Double	83.00	104.00

Half board per person:

	£min	£max
Daily	57.00	94.00

Lunch available
Evening meal 1900 (last orders 2200)
Parking for 350
Cards accepted: Access, Visa, Diners, Amex, Switch/Delta

Maranatha Guest House
APPROVED
115 Gaywood Road, Gaywood, King's Lynn PE30 2PU
☎ (01553) 774596
Large carrstone and brick residence with gardens front and rear, 10 minutes' walk from town centre, Lynnsport and Queen Elizabeth Hospital. Direct road to Sandringham and the coast.
Bedrooms: 2 single, 2 double, 3 twin
Bathrooms: 2 en-suite, 1 private, 1 public

Bed & breakfast

per night:	£min	£max
Single	17.00	20.00
Double	28.00	32.00

Half board per person:

	£min	£max
Daily	22.00	
Weekly	154.00	

Lunch available
Evening meal 1800 (last orders 1800)
Parking for 9

Russet House Hotel
COMMENDED
53 Goodwins Road, Vancouver Avenue, King's Lynn PE30 5PE
☎ (01553) 773098
Fax (01553) 773098
Lovely old house with pretty en-suite rooms. Four-poster available. Bar, dining room, gardens, ample parking. Good food.
Bedrooms: 3 single, 5 double, 4 twin
Bathrooms: 12 en-suite

Bed & breakfast

per night:	£min	£max
Single	35.00	46.00
Double	48.00	68.00

Half board per person:

	£min	£max
Daily	35.00	46.00

Evening meal 1900 (last orders 2000)
Parking for 14
Cards accepted: Access, Visa, Diners, Amex, Switch/Delta

EAST ANGLIA

The Tudor Rose Hotel

COMMENDED

St. Nicholas Street, Off Tuesday Market Place, King's Lynn PE30 1LR
☎ (01553) 762824
Fax (01553) 764894
The Independents

Built around 1500 by a local merchant and extended in 1640, the hotel offers comfortable accommodation, traditional British cooking and a choice of 4 real ales in 2 bars.
Bedrooms: 4 single, 6 double, 3 twin
Bathrooms: 11 en-suite, 2 private

Bed & breakfast
per night:	£min	£max
Single	30.00	38.50
Double	50.00	50.00

Lunch available
Evening meal 1900 (last orders 2100)
Cards accepted: Access, Visa, Diners, Amex, Switch/Delta

LAVENHAM
Suffolk
Map ref 3B2

A former prosperous wool town of timber-framed buildings with the cathedral-like church and its tall tower. The market-place is 13th C and the Guildhall now houses a museum.

Angel Hotel

HIGHLY COMMENDED

Market Place, Lavenham, Sudbury CO10 9QZ
☎ Sudbury (01787) 247388
Fax (01787) 248344
Logis of Great Britain

Family-run 15th C inn overlooking famous Guildhall. Freshly cooked local food, menu changing daily.
Bedrooms: 6 double, 1 twin, 1 triple
Bathrooms: 7 en-suite, 1 private

Bed & breakfast
per night:	£min	£max
Single	37.50	47.50
Double	50.00	60.00

Half board per
person:	£min	£max
Daily	40.00	50.00

Lunch available
Evening meal 1845 (last orders 2115)

Parking for 5
Cards accepted: Access, Visa, Amex, Switch/Delta

The Great House Restaurant and Hotel

Market Place, Lavenham, Sudbury CO10 9QZ
☎ Sudbury (01787) 247431
Fax (01787) 248007

Famous and historic 15th C house with covered outside courtyard, quietly and ideally located, full of warmth and oak furniture for a relaxing stay. Menu changing daily.
Bedrooms: 1 double, 1 twin, 1 triple, 1 family room
Bathrooms: 4 en-suite

Bed & breakfast
per night:	£min	£max
Single	49.50	60.00
Double	55.00	78.00

Half board per
person:	£min	£max
Daily		44.45

Lunch available
Evening meal 1900 (last orders 2130)
Parking for 10
Open February–December
Cards accepted: Access, Visa

LEISTON
Suffolk
Map ref 3C2

Busy industrial town near the coast. The abbey sited here in 1363 was for hundreds of years used as a farm until it was restored in 1918.

White Horse Hotel

Station Road, Leiston IP16 4HD
☎ (01728) 830694
Fax (01728) 833105

18th C Georgian hotel with a relaxed and informal atmosphere, only 2 miles from the sea, in the heart of bird-watching country.
Bedrooms: 3 single, 6 double, 4 twin
Bathrooms: 11 en-suite, 2 public

Bed & breakfast
per night:	£min	£max
Single	25.00	33.50
Double	45.00	52.00

Lunch available
Evening meal 1930 (last orders 2200)

Parking for 16
Cards accepted: Access, Visa, Diners, Amex

LENWADE
Norfolk
Map ref 3B1

Lenwade House Hotel

Fakenham Road, Lenwade, Great Witchingham, Norwich NR9 5QP
☎ Norwich (01603) 872288
Fax (01603) 872355

Tudor-style, country house hotel in 18 acres of private gardens, lakes and woodland. Extensive leisure facilities. Norwich 15 minutes.
Bedrooms: 2 single, 21 double, 11 twin, 1 triple
Bathrooms: 35 en-suite

Bed & breakfast
per night:	£min	£max
Single	45.00	49.50
Double	65.00	69.50

Half board per
person:	£min	£max
Daily	42.50	45.00

Lunch available
Evening meal 1900 (last orders 2130)
Parking for 50
Cards accepted: Access, Visa, Diners, Amex

LONG MELFORD
Suffolk
Map ref 3B2

One of Suffolk's loveliest villages, remarkable for the length of its main street. Holy Trinity Church is considered to be the finest village church in England. The National Trust own the Elizabethan Melford Hall and nearby Kentwell Hall is also open to the public.

The Crown Hotel

COMMENDED

Hall Street, Long Melford, Sudbury CO10 9JL
☎ Sudbury (01787) 377666
Fax (01787) 379045

17th C family-run hotel offering comfortable, well-equipped en-suite bedrooms. Excellent food and a wide

Continued ▶

EAST ANGLIA

LONG MELFORD
Continued

range of traditional ales are served in a relaxed and friendly atmosphere. Special long stay and weekend rates available.
Bedrooms: 2 single, 7 double, 2 twin, 1 family room
Bathrooms: 12 en-suite

Bed & breakfast per night:

	£min	£max
Single	30.00	30.00
Double	50.00	55.00

Half board per person:

	£min	£max
Daily	40.00	45.00

Lunch available
Evening meal 1900 (last orders 2100)
Parking for 6
Cards accepted: Access, Visa

LOWESTOFT
Suffolk
Map ref 3C1

Seaside town with wide sandy beaches. Important fishing port with picturesque fishing quarter. Home of the famous Lowestoft porcelain and birthplace of Benjamin Britten. East Point Pavilion's exhibition describes the Lowestoft story.
Tourist Information Centre ☎ (01502) 523000 or 523157

Fairways Guest House
COMMENDED

398 London Rd. South, Lowestoft NR33 0BQ
☎ (01502) 572659
Spacious, well furnished and comfortable, with good food and a friendly atmosphere. Central position for town, sea and country.
Bedrooms: 2 single, 1 twin, 2 triple, 2 family rooms
Bathrooms: 3 en-suite, 1 private, 2 public

Bed & breakfast per night:

	£min	£max
Single	17.00	22.00
Double	32.00	36.00

Half board per person:

	£min	£max
Daily	25.50	30.50
Weekly	150.00	185.00

Evening meal 1800 (last orders 1850)
Parking for 4
Cards accepted: Access, Visa, Diners

Longshore Guest House
Listed COMMENDED

7 Wellington Esplanade, Lowestoft NR33 0QQ
☎ (01502) 565037
Fax (01502) 582032
Family-run guesthouse in south Lowestoft, 5 minutes from town centre and close to Oulton Broad. Friendly atmosphere, most rooms with sea views. Dogs welcome.
Bedrooms: 2 single, 2 double, 1 twin, 1 triple
Bathrooms: 4 en-suite, 2 private

Bed & breakfast per night:

	£min	£max
Single	18.00	20.00
Double	40.00	42.00

Parking for 5
Cards accepted: Access, Visa, Switch/Delta

MALDON
Essex
Map ref 3B3

The Blackwater Estuary has made Maldon a natural base for yachtsmen. Boat-building is also an important industry. Numerous buildings of interest. The 13th C church of All Saints has the only triangular church tower in Britain. Also a museum and maritime centre.
Tourist Information Centre ☎ (01621) 856503

Five Lakes Hotel, Golf and Country Club
HIGHLY COMMENDED

Colchester Road, Tolleshunt Knights, Maldon CM9 8HX
☎ (01621) 868888
Fax (01621) 869696
Set in 320 acres, Five Lakes offers unparalleled sporting, health and leisure activities including two 18-hole golf courses, indoor/outdoor tennis and health spa complemented by high quality accommodation, bars and two restaurants.
Bedrooms: 2 single, 69 double, 43 twin
Suites available
Bathrooms: 114 en-suite, 25 public

Bed & breakfast per night:

	£min	£max
Single	67.00	93.00
Double	95.00	121.00

Half board per person:

	£min	£max
Daily	61.00	109.50
Weekly	365.00	560.00

Lunch available
Evening meal 1800 (last orders 2200)
Parking for 520
Cards accepted: Access, Visa, Diners, Amex, Switch/Delta

MARCH
Cambridgeshire
Map ref 3A1

This is the heart of a railway system linking the Fens to surrounding counties. St Wendreda's Church makes the town famous, for the roof is of double hammer-beam construction with a host of carved angels spreading their wings.

Olde Griffin Hotel

High Street, March PE15 9ES
☎ (01354) 52517
Fax (01354) 50086
Family-owned coaching inn/hotel in historic town centre. Offering traditional comfort, food and service. Ideal location to explore East Anglia.
Bedrooms: 4 single, 7 double, 7 twin, 1 triple, 1 family room
Bathrooms: 20 en-suite, 1 public

Bed & breakfast per night:

	£min	£max
Single	38.50	45.00
Double	55.00	65.00

Half board per person:

	£min	£max
Daily	49.00	49.00
Weekly	310.00	310.00

Lunch available
Evening meal 1900 (last orders 2130)
Parking for 100
Cards accepted: Access, Visa, Amex

WELCOME HOST

This is a nationally recognised customer care programme which aims to promote the highest standards of service and a warm welcome. Establishments who are taking part in this initiative are indicated by the ❀ symbol.

EAST ANGLIA

MILDENHALL
Suffolk
Map ref 3B2

Town that has grown considerably in size in the last 20 years but still manages to retain a pleasant small country town centre. Mildenhall and District Museum deals with local history, particularly RAF Mildenhall and the Mildenhall Treasure.

Riverside Hotel
Mill Street, Mildenhall, Bury St Edmunds IP28 7DP
☎ (01638) 717274
Best Western
Grade II Regency-style manor house in picturesque riverside setting. Recently refurbished to a high standard. Bridge weekends, Christmas breaks.
Bedrooms: 2 single, 8 double, 6 twin, 3 triple
Bathrooms: 17 en-suite, 2 private

Bed & breakfast

per night:	£min	£max
Single	53.00	63.00
Double	82.00	84.00

Lunch available
Evening meal 1830 (last orders 2100)
Parking for 50
Cards accepted: Access, Visa, Diners, Amex

Smoke House
Beck Row, Mildenhall, Bury St Edmunds IP28 8DH
☎ (01638) 713223
Fax (01638) 712202
Consort
Listed Tudor/Georgian manor house with inglenook fireplaces and comfortable, well-equipped rooms. 2 bars, licensed restaurant, barbecue in season. Conference centre.
Wheelchair access category 3
Bedrooms: 4 double, 84 twin, 16 triple
Bathrooms: 104 en-suite

Bed & breakfast

per night:	£min	£max
Single		72.00
Double		85.00

Half board per

person:	£min	£max
Daily		86.00

Lunch available
Evening meal 1700 (last orders 2200)
Parking for 200

Cards accepted: Access, Visa, Diners, Amex, Switch/Delta

MUNDESLEY
Norfolk
Map ref 3C1

Small seaside resort with a superb sandy beach and excellent bathing. Nearby is a smock-mill still with cap and sails.

Overcliff Lodge
COMMENDED
46 Cromer Road, Mundesley, Norwich NR11 8DB
☎ (01263) 720016
Fax (01263) 720016
Popular licensed family-run guesthouse offering high quality cooking and relaxed atmosphere. Ideal for touring Broadland and North Norfolk. Non-smoking establishment.
Bedrooms: 2 single, 3 double, 2 twin
Bathrooms: 4 en-suite, 1 public

Bed & breakfast

per night:	£min	£max
Single	15.50	25.00
Double	31.00	38.00

Half board per

person:	£min	£max
Daily	26.00	36.50
Weekly	168.00	196.00

Evening meal 1900 (last orders 1900)
Parking for 17

NEATISHEAD
Norfolk
Map ref 3C1

Regency Guest House
COMMENDED
The Street, Neatishead, Norwich NR12 8AD
☎ Horning (01692) 630233
Peaceful Broads village. Ideal nature rambles, wildlife, bird-watching. 6 miles coast/10 miles Norwich. Accent on personal service. Renowned for generous English breakfasts. Laura Ashley rooms with tea-making facilities, TV. Wild duck speciality in village pub/restaurant a few yards' walk.
Bedrooms: 2 double, 1 twin
Bathrooms: 2 en-suite, 1 private, 1 public

Bed & breakfast

per night:	£min	£max
Single		20.00
Double		39.00

Parking for 8
Cards accepted: Diners

NEEDHAM MARKET
Suffolk
Map ref 3B2

Interesting town on the Ipswich to Bury St Edmunds road containing Georgian houses in the High Street, the Friends' Meeting House, the 17th C timber-framed grammar school and the "Bull Inn" with carved corner-post.

The Annex
Listed COMMENDED
17 High Street, Needham Market, Ipswich IP6 8AL
☎ (01449) 720687
Fax (01449) 722230
Close to all local amenities and recreational facilities. Family suites available if required. Payphone for guests' use. Private car park.
Bedrooms: 2 single, 1 double, 1 twin
Bathrooms: 2 public

Bed & breakfast

per night:	£min	£max
Single	20.00	25.00
Double	30.00	35.00

Parking for 4

NEWMARKET
Suffolk
Map ref 3B2

Centre of the English horse-racing world and the headquarters of the Jockey Club and National Stud. Racecourse and horse sales. The National Horse Racing Museum traces the history and development of the Sport of Kings.
Tourist Information Centre ☎ (01638) 667200

Bedford Lodge Hotel, Conference and Leisure
Bury Road, Newmarket CB8 7BX
☎ (01638) 663175
Fax (01638) 667391
Best Western
Combination of a beautiful Georgian hunting lodge and an exciting, sympathetically designed, modern hotel and conference complex with extensive leisure facilities. Set in pleasant, secluded gardens, close to town centre and racecourse. Half board price based on minimum 2-night stay.

Continued ▶

353

EAST ANGLIA

NEWMARKET
Continued

Bedrooms: 43 double, 13 twin
Suites available
Bathrooms: 56 en-suite

Bed & breakfast per night

	£min	£max
Single	72.00	79.20
Double	92.50	101.75

Half board per person

	£min	£max
Daily	57.50	65.00

Lunch available
Evening meal 1900 (last orders 2130)
Parking for 90
Cards accepted: Access, Visa, Diners, Amex, Switch/Delta

Heath Court Hotel
COMMENDED
Moulton Road, Newmarket
CB8 8DY
☎ (01638) 667171
Fax (01638) 666533
Hotel of high standards in a quiet central position. Ideal location for touring, horseracing and local countryside.
Wheelchair access category 3
Bedrooms: 16 single, 13 double, 10 twin, 2 triple
Suites available
Bathrooms: 41 en-suite

Bed & breakfast per night

	£min	£max
Single	65.00	75.00
Double	80.00	95.00

Lunch available
Evening meal 1900 (last orders 2145)
Parking for 70
Cards accepted: Access, Visa, Diners, Amex, Switch/Delta

Swynford Paddocks Hotel
HIGHLY COMMENDED
Six Mile Bottom, Newmarket
CB8 0UE
☎ Six Mile Bottom (01638) 570234
Fax (01638) 570283
Country house hotel standing in extensive grounds. 6 miles from Newmarket and 8 miles from Cambridge.
Bedrooms: 3 single, 9 double, 3 twin
Bathrooms: 15 en-suite

Bed & breakfast per night

	£min	£max
Single	80.00	95.00
Double	117.00	138.00

Half board per person

	£min	£max
Daily	70.00	80.00

Lunch available
Evening meal 1900 (last orders 2130)
Parking for 120
Cards accepted: Access, Visa, Diners, Amex, Switch/Delta

NORFOLK BROADS

See under Aylsham, Beccles, Bungay, Cawston, Coltishall, Great Yarmouth, Hevingham, Horning, Lowestoft, Neatishead, North Walsham, Norwich, Oulton Broad, Stalham, Wroxham

NORTH WALSHAM
Norfolk
Map ref 3C1

Weekly market has been held here for 700 years. 1 mile south of town is a cross commemorating the Peasants' Revolt of 1381. Nelson attended the local Paston Grammar School, founded in 1606 and still flourishing.

Elderton Lodge Hotel and Restaurant
COMMENDED
Gunton Park, North Walsham
NR11 8TZ
☎ Cromer (01263) 833547
Fax (01263) 834673

Secluded Georgian shooting lodge with historical royal connections, set in 6 acres with spectacular views across the Deer Park. Elegant rooms, quality food.
Bedrooms: 1 single, 6 double, 2 twin
Suites available
Bathrooms: 9 en-suite

Bed & breakfast per night

	£min	£max
Single	42.00	50.00
Double	64.00	85.00

Half board per person

	£min	£max
Daily	44.50	59.50

Lunch available
Evening meal 1900 (last orders 2100)
Parking for 100
Cards accepted: Access, Visa, Diners, Amex, Switch/Delta

NORWICH
Norfolk
Map ref 3C1

Beautiful cathedral city and county town on the River Wensum with many fine museums and medieval churches. Norman castle, Guildhall and interesting medieval streets. Good shopping centre and market.
Tourist Information Centre ☎ (01603) 666071

Annesley House Hotel
HIGHLY COMMENDED
6 Newmarket Road, Norwich
NR2 2LA
☎ (01603) 624553
Fax (01603) 621577
Consort

Three listed Georgian buildings, restored and refurbished to a high standard. Set in landscaped grounds in a conservation area, yet just a stroll to the city centre.
Bedrooms: 8 single, 15 double, 2 twin
Bathrooms: 25 en-suite

Bed & breakfast per night

	£min	£max
Single	50.00	70.00
Double	65.00	80.00

Evening meal 1900 (last orders 2100)
Parking for 24
Cards accepted: Access, Visa, Diners, Amex, Switch/Delta

Becklands
COMMENDED
105 Holt Road, Horsford, Norwich
NR10 3AB
☎ (01603) 898582 & 898020
Quietly located modern house overlooking open countryside. 5 miles north of Norwich. Central for the Broads and coastal areas.
Bedrooms: 4 single, 3 double, 2 twin
Bathrooms: 7 en-suite, 3 public

The M symbol after an establishment name indicates that it is a Regional Tourist Board member.

EAST ANGLIA

Bed & breakfast

per night:	£min	£max
Single	18.00	20.00
Double	36.00	38.00

Parking for 30
Cards accepted: Access, Visa, Diners

Beeches Hotel & Victorian Gardens

HIGHLY COMMENDED

4-6 Earlham Road, Norwich
NR2 3DB
☎ (01603) 621167
Fax (01603) 620151
CR The Independents

Welcoming hotel, with unique and tranquil English Heritage wooded gardens. Tastefully restored to offer high standards of comfort in a relaxed, informal atmosphere. An oasis in the heart of historic Norwich.
Wheelchair access category 2
Bedrooms: 6 single, 14 double, 4 twin, 2 triple
Bathrooms: 26 en-suite

Bed & breakfast

per night:	£min	£max
Single	46.00	55.00
Double	59.00	75.00

Half board per

person:	£min	£max
Daily	56.00	65.00
Weekly		255.00

Evening meal 1830 (last orders 2030)
Parking for 24
Cards accepted: Access, Visa, Diners, Amex, Switch/Delta

Catton Old Hall

HIGHLY COMMENDED

Lodge Lane, Old Catton, Norwich
NR6 7HG
☎ (01603) 419239
Fax (01603) 400239
17th C family home offering quality accommodation for business or pleasure. Oak-beamed rooms, four-poster bed, jacuzzi bath, inglenook fireplace. Candlelit dinners.
Bedrooms: 2 double, 2 twin
Bathrooms: 4 en-suite

Bed & breakfast

per night:	£min	£max
Single	27.50	48.00
Double	55.00	95.00

Lunch available
Evening meal 1800 (last orders 2000)
Parking for 20
Cards accepted: Access, Visa, Diners, Amex

Conifers Hotel

162 Dereham Road, Norwich
NR2 3AH
☎ (01603) 628737
Friendly hotel, close to city centre, university, sports village and showground. All rooms have colour TV, tea/coffee, hairdryers.
Bedrooms: 4 single, 1 double, 3 twin
Bathrooms: 1 en-suite, 3 public

Bed & breakfast

per night:	£min	£max
Single	18.00	19.00
Double	36.00	38.00

Parking for 4

The Corner House

APPROVED

62 Earlham Road, Norwich
NR2 3DF
☎ (01603) 627928
Large Victorian house with friendly atmosphere, 10 minutes from city centre. TV, coffee/tea facilities in all bedrooms, residents' lounge area. Car parking.
Bedrooms: 3 double
Bathrooms: 2 en-suite, 1 private

Bed & breakfast

per night:	£min	£max
Single	20.00	25.00
Double	32.00	35.00

Parking for 4

Crofters Hotel

2 Earlham Road, Norwich NR2 3DA
☎ (01603) 613287
Fax (01603) 766654

Tastefully restored Victorian house set in beautiful landscaped gardens.

Comfortable accommodation at affordable rates in central Norwich. Private car park.
Bedrooms: 1 single, 6 double, 5 twin, 1 triple
Bathrooms: 13 en-suite

Bed & breakfast

per night:	£min	£max
Single	39.50	49.00
Double	54.50	64.50

Half board per

person:	£min	£max
Daily	49.00	59.00

Lunch available
Evening meal 1800 (last orders 2100)
Parking for 20
Cards accepted: Access, Visa, Switch/Delta

Earlham Guest House

COMMENDED

147 Earlham Road, Norwich
NR2 3RG
☎ (01603) 454169
Fax (01603) 54169
Susan and Derek Wright extend a warm welcome to their elegant Victorian guesthouse situated between city centre and UEA. Vegetarian foods if preferred. Mostly non-smoking.
Bedrooms: 2 single, 3 double, 2 twin
Bathrooms: 2 en-suite, 2 public

Bed & breakfast

per night:	£min	£max
Single	19.00	24.00
Double	36.00	42.00

Cards accepted: Access, Visa, Switch/Delta

Edmar Lodge

COMMENDED

64 Earlham Road, Norwich
NR2 3DF
☎ (01603) 615599
Quality, family-run accommodation with en-suite rooms. All rooms have satellite TV, tea and coffee facilities and hairdryer. Close to city and university with car parks. Hearty breakfasts.
Bedrooms: 1 single, 1 double, 1 twin, 1 triple
Bathrooms: 3 en-suite, 1 public

Bed & breakfast

per night:	£min	£max
Single	18.00	25.00
Double	30.00	36.00

Parking for 6

EAST ANGLIA

NORWICH
Continued

Elm Farm Chalet Hotel
COMMENDED
St Faiths NR10 3HH
☎ (01603) 898366
Fax (01603) 897129
Situated in quiet pretty village 4 miles north of Norwich. Ideal base for touring Norfolk and Suffolk. En-suite chalet bedrooms. Restaurant in farmhouse. Licensed.
Wheelchair access category 3
Bedrooms: 4 single, 7 double, 6 twin, 1 family room
Bathrooms: 15 en-suite, 3 private

Bed & breakfast per night:	£min	£max
Single	32.00	37.00
Double	50.50	56.00

Half board per person:	£min	£max
Daily	43.00	48.00
Weekly	253.75	336.00

Lunch available
Evening meal 1830 (last orders 1930)
Parking for 20
Cards accepted: Access, Visa, Amex

Forte Posthouse Norwich
COMMENDED
Ipswich Road, Norwich NR4 6EP
☎ (01603) 456431
Fax (01603) 506400
Forte
Recently refurbished hotel, with a health club, on the southern side of the city. Convenient for both town and country.
Bedrooms: 89 double, 21 twin, 6 triple
Bathrooms: 116 en-suite

Bed & breakfast per night:	£min	£max
Single	42.00	78.95
Double	64.00	88.90

Half board per person:	£min	£max
Daily	38.00	46.00
Weekly	245.00	294.00

Lunch available
Evening meal 1830 (last orders 2230)
Parking for 200
Cards accepted: Access, Visa, Diners, Amex, Switch/Delta

The Georgian House Hotel
APPROVED
32-34 Unthank Road, Norwich NR2 2RB
☎ (01603) 615655
Fax (01603) 765689
Minotel/The Independents

Comfortable we may be, expensive we are not. Two tastefully furnished linked Victorian houses, set in beautiful gardens, form the heart of this popular hotel. Ample parking, intimate bar and relaxed restaurant.
Bedrooms: 10 single, 10 double, 5 twin, 2 triple
Bathrooms: 27 en-suite

Bed & breakfast per night:	£min	£max
Single	34.00	39.50
Double	48.00	62.00

Half board per person:	£min	£max
Daily	41.00	50.00
Weekly	246.00	300.00

Lunch available
Evening meal 1830 (last orders 2030)
Parking for 30
Cards accepted: Access, Visa, Diners, Amex, Switch/Delta

Marlborough House Hotel
22 Stracey Road, Norwich NR1 1EZ
☎ (01603) 628005
Fax (01603) 628005
Long established family hotel, close to city centre, Castle Mall, museum, cathedral and Elm Hill. 3 minutes from railway station. Full central heating. All double, twin and family rooms are en-suite. Tea and coffee-making facilities, licensed bar, car park.
Bedrooms: 4 single, 3 double, 2 twin, 2 triple
Bathrooms: 7 en-suite, 1 public

Bed & breakfast per night:	£min	£max
Single	18.00	32.00
Double	38.00	50.00

Half board per person:	£min	£max
Daily	24.00	38.00
Weekly	160.00	260.00

Lunch available
Evening meal 1730 (last orders 1900)
Parking for 10

Hotel Nelson
HIGHLY COMMENDED
Prince of Wales Road, Norwich NR1 1DX
☎ (01603) 760260
Fax (01603) 620008
Modern, purpose-built hotel on the riverside close to railway station and city centre. Easy access to the Broads and coast. Leisure club with indoor swimming pool.
Bedrooms: 27 single, 52 double, 38 twin
Bathrooms: 117 en-suite

Bed & breakfast per night:	£min	£max
Single	77.50	99.50

Half board per person:	£min	£max
Daily	52.00	59.00

Lunch available
Evening meal 1845 (last orders 2145)
Parking for 180
Cards accepted: Access, Visa, Diners, Amex

Hotel Norwich
COMMENDED
121-131 Boundary Road, Norwich NR3 2BA
☎ (01603) 787260
Fax (01603) 400466
Best Western
Modern hotel conveniently located on the ring road, with easy access to the city centre, countryside, coastlines and Norfolk Broads. Leisure centre with indoor pool.
Wheelchair access category 2
Bedrooms: 19 single, 43 double, 30 twin, 15 triple
Suites available
Bathrooms: 107 en-suite

Bed & breakfast per night:	£min	£max
Single	64.50	99.50
Double	74.50	

Half board per person:	£min	£max
Daily	46.00	48.00
Weekly	276.00	288.00

Lunch available
Evening meal 1900 (last orders 2200)
Parking for 221

EAST ANGLIA

Cards accepted: Access, Visa, Diners, Amex

⛳🏊‍♂️🍽️📞💻♿🍴🚭🎱⛔️
🛏️🏊300🚗⭐️🎾🐟🐠DAP⛔️SP⛔️T

Norwich Sport Village and Hotel in Broadland

👑👑👑 COMMENDED

Drayton High Road, Hellesdon, Norwich NR6 5DU
☎ (01603) 789469
Fax (01603) 406845

Situated on outer Norwich Ring Road on the A1067. Providing sports facilities, including tennis, squash, badminton, snooker, health centre, sauna and £4.5m Aquapark. Three bars and three restaurants. Many facilities free to residents. Half board rates available on request.
Bedrooms: 11 double, 42 twin, 2 family rooms
Bathrooms: 55 en-suite

Bed & breakfast per night:	£min	£max
Single	52.00	64.00
Double	62.00	79.00

Lunch available
Evening meal 1830 (last orders 2130)
Parking for 1200
Cards accepted: Access, Visa, Diners, Amex

🏊‍♂️🍽️📞💻♿🍴🚭🎱📺⛔️
🛏️🏊160🚗⭐️🎾🐟🐠DAP⛔️SP⛔️T

Old Rectory

👑👑

North Walsham Road, Crostwick, Norwich NR12 7BG
☎ (01603) 738513
Fax (01603) 738712

Old Victorian rectory with bedroom extension, set amidst 2.5 acres of mature trees. Well placed for the Broads and 5 miles from Norwich. Homely accommodation.
Wheelchair access category 3♿
Bedrooms: 5 double, 6 twin, 2 family rooms
Bathrooms: 13 en-suite

Bed & breakfast per night:	£min	£max
Single	32.00	34.00
Double	45.00	47.00

Half board per person:	£min	£max
Daily	31.00	32.00
Weekly	217.00	231.00

Evening meal 1830 (last orders 1930)
Parking for 45
Cards accepted: Access, Visa

🏊‍♂️🍽️📞💻♿🍴🚭🎱📺⛔️
🚗🐟♿🌸⛔️

Spixworth Motel

👑👑 COMMENDED

145 Crostwick Lane, Spixworth, Norwich NR10 3NG
☎ (01603) 898288
Fax (01603) 897617

Motel and licensed restaurant, family owned and run, in village location just 2 miles north of Norwich off the B1150. Large car park, frequent buses. Modern en-suite, mostly ground floor, bedrooms with satellite TV (including Sky Sports) and tea/coffee maker.
Bedrooms: 3 single, 11 double, 5 twin, 3 triple
Bathrooms: 22 en-suite

Bed & breakfast per night:	£min	£max
Single	27.50	35.00
Double	40.00	45.00

Half board per person:	£min	£max
Daily	27.50	30.00
Weekly	165.00	180.00

Evening meal 1830 (last orders 2100)
Parking for 40
Cards accepted: Access, Visa, Diners, Amex

🏊10🏊‍♂️🍽️📞💻♿🍴🚭🎱📺⛔️
🛏️🏊25🚗⭐️🌸🐟SP⛔️T

Sprowston Manor Hotel

👑👑👑👑👑 HIGHLY COMMENDED

Sprowston Park, Wroxham Road, Norwich NR7 8RP
☎ (01603) 410871
Fax (01603) 423911
Ⓒ Best Western

Adjacent to 18-hole golf-course, this Victorian manor house has been extended to provide modern bedrooms and La Fontana Health Spa, with large indoor swimming pool and full range of spa facilities.
Bedrooms: 47 double, 45 twin
Bathrooms: 92 en-suite

Bed & breakfast per night:	£min	£max
Single	96.95	
Double	112.90	

Half board per person:	£min	£max
Daily	119.45	
Weekly	716.66	

Lunch available
Evening meal 1900 (last orders 2200)
Parking for 120

Cards accepted: Access, Visa, Diners, Amex, Switch/Delta

🏊‍♂️🍽️📞💻♿🍴🚭🎱⛔️
🛏️🏊🏊100🚗⭐️🎾🐟🐠⛔️
SP⛔️T

Wedgewood House

👑👑 APPROVED

42 St. Stephens Road, Norwich NR1 3RE
☎ (01603) 625730
Fax (01603) 615035

Family-run hotel, close to coach station and within walking distance of shops and places of interest. Parking.
Bedrooms: 2 single, 4 double, 2 twin, 2 triple, 1 family room
Bathrooms: 8 en-suite, 1 public

Bed & breakfast per night:	£min	£max
Single	20.00	24.00
Double	38.00	44.00

Parking for 7
Cards accepted: Access, Visa, Amex

🏊‍♂️♿💻🍴🚭🎱🐟DAP SP

OULTON BROAD

Suffolk
Map ref 3C1

Oulton Broad is the most southerly of the Broads and the centre of a very busy boating industry.

Parkhill Hotel

👑👑👑

Parkhill, Oulton, Lowestoft NR32 5DQ
☎ Lowestoft (01502) 730322
Fax (01502) 731695

Peaceful wooded grounds with gardens and lawns. The hotel offers a friendly and homely atmosphere. Minimum B&B prices below are for weekends.
Bedrooms: 7 single, 8 double, 3 twin
Suites available
Bathrooms: 17 en-suite

Bed & breakfast per night:	£min	£max
Single	45.00	60.00
Double	55.00	75.00

Half board per person:	£min	£max
Daily	40.00	60.00
Weekly	270.00	420.00

Lunch available
Evening meal 1900 (last orders 2130)
Parking for 154
Cards accepted: Access, Visa, Diners, Amex

🏊1🏊‍♂️🍽️📞💻♿🍴🚭🎱📺
⛔️🚗🏊100🐟🌸SP⛔️

EAST ANGLIA

PETERBOROUGH
Cambridgeshire
Map ref 3A1

Prosperous and rapidly expanding cathedral city on the edge of the Fens on the River Nene. Catherine of Aragon is buried in the cathedral. City Museum and Art Gallery. Ferry Meadows Country Park has numerous leisure facilities.
Tourist Information Centre ☎ (01733) 317336

The Bell Inn Hotel
HIGHLY COMMENDED
Great North Road, Stilton, Peterborough PE7 3RA
☎ (01733) 241066
Fax (01733) 245173

Old coaching inn, restored as a hotel including conference and banqueting facilities. Off A1, just south of Norman Cross roundabout.
Bedrooms: 2 single, 14 double, 2 twin, 1 triple
Bathrooms: 19 en-suite

Bed & breakfast per night:	£min	£max
Single	40.00	74.00
Double	55.00	94.00

Lunch available
Evening meal 1900 (last orders 2130)
Parking for 30
Cards accepted: Access, Visa, Switch/Delta

Butterfly Hotel
Thorpe Meadows, Off Longthorpe Parkway, Peterborough PE3 6GA
☎ (01733) 64140
Fax (01733) 65538
By the water's edge at Thorpe Meadows, this modern hotel maintains all the traditional values of design and comfort. Special weekend rates available.
Bedrooms: 33 single, 18 double, 15 twin, 4 triple
Bathrooms: 70 en-suite

Bed & breakfast per night:	£min	£max
Single	62.45	64.45
Double	67.40	71.40

Lunch available
Evening meal 1800 (last orders 2200)
Parking for 80
Cards accepted: Access, Visa, Diners, Amex, Switch/Delta

Dalwhinnie Lodge Hotel
APPROVED
31-35 Burghley Road, Peterborough PE1 2QA
☎ (01733) 65968 & Reservations (0550) 131251
Fax (01733) 890838
We believe we are the best hotel of our kind for location, comfort and value for money. High standards and a warm welcome guaranteed. 5 minutes from city centre, bus and train station. Ample parking.
Bedrooms: 3 single, 1 double, 4 twin, 2 triple
Bathrooms: 2 en-suite, 3 public, 2 private showers

Bed & breakfast per night:	£min	£max
Single	19.75	34.00
Double	32.00	41.00

Evening meal 1830 (last orders 2100)
Parking for 14
Cards accepted: Access, Visa, Diners, Amex, Switch/Delta

Hawthorn House Hotel
COMMENDED
89 Thorpe Road, Peterborough PE3 6JQ
☎ (01733) 340608
City centre licensed hotel. High standard of accommodation and service. Tastefully furnished en-suite rooms with TV and tea-making facilities.
Bedrooms: 3 single, 3 double, 2 twin
Bathrooms: 8 en-suite

Bed & breakfast per night:	£min	£max
Single	27.50	
Double	49.50	

Half board per person:	£min	£max
Daily	35.00	

Evening meal 1900 (last orders 2100)
Parking for 5
Cards accepted: Access, Visa, Amex

Orton Hall Hotel
COMMENDED
The Village, Orton Longueville, Peterborough PE2 7DN
☎ (01733) 391111
Fax (01733) 231912
Best Western
17th C manor house set in 20 acres of mature parkland. En-suite bedrooms, some with four poster beds. Huntly Restaurant or country pub for a choice of dining. Minimum half board price below based on 2-night weekend stay.
Bedrooms: 9 single, 32 double, 7 twin, 2 triple
Bathrooms: 50 en-suite

Bed & breakfast per night:	£min	£max
Single	68.00	103.00
Double	88.00	130.00

Half board per person:	£min	£max
Daily	49.50	92.90
Weekly	297.00	

Lunch available
Evening meal 1830 (last orders 2130)
Parking for 200
Cards accepted: Access, Visa, Diners, Amex, Switch/Delta

Swallow Hotel
HIGHLY COMMENDED
Peterborough Business Park, Lynch Wood, Peterborough PE2 6GB
☎ (01733) 371111 & 394442
Fax (01733) 236725
Swallow
Innovatively designed hotel 1 minute from A1/A605 junction on the edge of Nene Country Park and opposite East of England showground. In picturesque village of Alwalton. Large leisure complex. Short break packages available.
Wheelchair access category 2
Bedrooms: 125 double, 38 twin
Suites available
Bathrooms: 163 en-suite

Establishments should be open throughout the year, unless otherwise stated.

The M symbol after an establishment name indicates that it is a Regional Tourist Board member.

EAST ANGLIA

Bed & breakfast per night:	£min	£max
Single	75.00	95.00
Double	85.00	110.00

Half board per person:	£min	£max
Daily	94.75	114.75

Lunch available
Evening meal 1900 (last orders 2230)
Parking for 250
Cards accepted: Access, Visa, Diners, Amex, Switch/Delta

SAFFRON WALDEN
Essex
Map ref 2D1

Takes its name from the saffron crocus once grown around the town. The church of St Mary has superb carvings, magnificent roofs and brasses. A town maze can be seen on the common. Two miles south-west is Audley End, a magnificent Jacobean mansion owned by English Heritage.
Tourist Information Centre ☎ (01799) 510444

Queens Head Inn
COMMENDED

Littlebury, Saffron Walden
CB11 4TD
☎ (01799) 522251
Fax (01799) 513522
Logis of Great Britain
Family-run freehouse and hotel close to Audley End. All rooms en-suite. Good Pub Guide "Best Pub in Essex" 1995. Interesting and unusual menu.
Bedrooms: 2 single, 2 double, 1 twin, 1 family room
Bathrooms: 6 en-suite

Bed & breakfast per night:	£min	£max
Single	29.95	35.95
Double	49.95	59.95

Half board per person:	£min	£max
Weekly	245.00	287.00

Lunch available
Evening meal 1900 (last orders 2100)
Parking for 30
Cards accepted: Access, Visa, Diners, Switch/Delta

Map references apply to the colour maps at the back of this guide.

Saffron Hotel
COMMENDED

10-18 High Street, Saffron Walden
CB10 1AY
☎ (01799) 522676
Fax (01799) 513979
16th C hotel in market town. South of Cambridge, close to Duxford Air Museum and Stansted Airport. Noted restaurant.
Bedrooms: 3 single, 10 double, 3 twin, 1 triple
Bathrooms: 14 en-suite, 3 private

Bed & breakfast per night:	£min	£max
Single	45.00	60.00
Double	65.00	85.00

Half board per person:	£min	£max
Daily	42.50	55.50

Lunch available
Evening meal 1830 (last orders 2130)
Parking for 8
Cards accepted: Access, Visa, Diners, Amex

ST ALBANS
Hertfordshire
Map ref 2D1

As Verulamium this was one of the largest towns in Roman Britain and its remains can be seen in the museum. The Norman cathedral was built from Roman materials to commemorate Alban, the first British Christian martyr.
Tourist Information Centre ☎ (01727) 864511

The Apples Hotel
COMMENDED

133 London Road, St Albans
AL1 1TA
☎ St Albans (01727) 844111
Fax (01727) 861100
Family-run hotel in beautiful gardens within easy reach of city centre, station and major motorways. Heated swimming pool. Facilities for disabled.
Bedrooms: 1 single, 5 double, 3 twin, 1 triple
Bathrooms: 10 en-suite

Bed & breakfast per night:	£min	£max
Single	43.00	50.00
Double	50.00	59.00

Half board per person:	£min	£max
Daily	57.00	64.00

Lunch available
Evening meal 1930 (last orders 2100)
Parking for 10

Cards accepted: Access, Visa, Diners, Amex, Switch/Delta

Ardmore House
COMMENDED

54 Lemsford Road, St Albans
AL1 3PP
☎ St Albans (01727) 859313
Fax (01727) 859313
Logis of Great Britain
Large, detached Edwardian house with garden, in conservation area, close to Clarence Park and within 5 minutes of city centre and railway station. Excellent base for visitors to London.
Bedrooms: 6 single, 10 double, 4 twin, 2 triple, 4 family rooms
Bathrooms: 21 en-suite, 1 private shower

Bed & breakfast per night:	£min	£max
Single	35.00	49.50
Double	50.00	59.50

Half board per person:	£min	£max
Daily	45.00	39.75
Weekly	315.00	430.00

Evening meal 1800 (last orders 2030)
Parking for 34
Cards accepted: Access, Visa, Amex, Switch/Delta

Jarvis Aubrey Park Hotel
COMMENDED

Hemel Hempstead Road, Redbourn, St Albans AL3 7AF
☎ Redbourn (01582) 792105
Fax (01582) 792001
Jarvis/Utell International
Elegant, well-appointed, friendly hotel set in 6 acres of well-kept gardens and woodland. Only 25 miles north of London via the M1.
Bedrooms: 88 double, 31 twin
Bathrooms: 119 en-suite

Bed & breakfast per night:	£min	£max
Single	40.00	108.50
Double	70.00	127.00

Half board per person:	£min	£max
Daily	56.50	121.00

Lunch available
Evening meal 1900 (last orders 2145)
Parking for 160
Cards accepted: Access, Visa, Diners, Amex, Switch/Delta

EAST ANGLIA

ST ALBANS
Continued

Lake Hotel
COMMENDED
234 London Road, St Albans AL1 1JQ
St Albans (01727) 840904
Fax (01727) 862750
Consort
Family hotel, half a mile from the centre of the historic Roman city of Verulamium. Junction 22 of M25, junction 7 of M1, 18 minutes by train from Kings Cross. Bar, restaurant and conference suite. Large car park.
Bedrooms: 20 single, 13 double, 4 twin, 4 triple, 2 family rooms
Bathrooms: 41 en-suite

Bed & breakfast
per night:	£min	£max
Single	39.50	59.50
Double	50.00	79.50

Half board per
person:	£min	£max
Daily	53.00	73.00

Lunch available
Evening meal 1900 (last orders 2130)
Parking for 70
Cards accepted: Access, Visa, Diners, Amex, Switch/Delta

The Noke Thistle Hotel
Watford Road, St Albans AL2 3DS
St Albans (01727) 854252
Fax (01727) 841906
Utell International
Delightful country house style hotel, ideally located for Gardens of the Rose and historic houses. Close to M1, M10 and M25.
Bedrooms: 57 double, 50 twin, 4 triple
Bathrooms: 111 en-suite

Bed & breakfast
per night:	£min	£max
Single	102.00	110.00
Double	122.00	140.00

Half board per
person:	£min	£max
Daily	127.00	135.00

Lunch available
Evening meal 1900 (last orders 2200)
Parking for 150
Cards accepted: Access, Visa, Diners, Amex

ST IVES
Cambridgeshire
Map ref 3A2

Picturesque market town with a narrow 6-arched bridge spanning the River Ouse on which stands a bridge chapel. There are numerous Georgian and Victorian buildings and the Norris Museum has a good local collection.

The Dolphin Hotel
COMMENDED
Bridgefoot, London Road, St Ives, Huntingdon PE17 4EP
St Ives (01480) 466966 & 497497
Fax (01480) 495597
Modern hotel on banks of the River Great Ouse, with panoramic views across surrounding meadows. 2 minutes' walk from historic town centre and just 20 minutes' drive from centre of Cambridge and the Imperial War Museum at Duxford. Extensive restaurant menus.
Bedrooms: 2 single, 12 double, 31 twin, 2 family rooms
Bathrooms: 47 en-suite

Bed & breakfast
per night:	£min	£max
Single	65.00	70.00
Double	70.00	90.00

Half board per
person:	£min	£max
Daily		75.00

Lunch available
Evening meal 1900 (last orders 2130)
Parking for 200
Cards accepted: Access, Visa, Diners, Amex

The Golden Lion Hotel
APPROVED
Market Hill, St Ives, Huntingdon PE17 4AL
St Ives (01480) 492100
Fax (01480) 497109
16th C coaching inn of great historic interest in the town centre. Good facilities for business people and tourists, full a la carte menu. 15 minutes' drive to Cambridge. Weekend rates available.
Bedrooms: 5 single, 9 double, 3 twin, 2 triple, 1 family room
Bathrooms: 20 en-suite

Bed & breakfast
per night:	£min	£max
Single	36.00	
Double	46.00	

Lunch available
Evening meal 1900 (last orders 2200)
Parking for 4
Cards accepted: Access, Visa, Diners

The Old Ferry Boat Inn
COMMENDED
Holywell, St Ives, Huntingdon PE17 3TG
St Ives (01480) 463227
Fax (01480) 494885

Thatched riverside inn with low beamed ceilings and log fires. Extensive, interesting menu, real ales, garden. From main A14 head for St Ives, then Needingworth, then Holywell.
Bedrooms: 6 double, 1 twin
Suites available
Bathrooms: 7 en-suite

Bed & breakfast
per night:	£min	£max
Single	39.95	49.50
Double	49.50	68.00

Lunch available
Evening meal 1800 (last orders 2200)
Parking for 150
Cards accepted: Access, Visa, Switch/Delta

Slepe Hall Hotel
COMMENDED
Ramsey Road, St Ives, Huntingdon PE17 4RB
St Ives (01480) 463122
Fax (01480) 300706
Former private Victorian girls' school converted in 1966. Now a Grade II listed building, 5 minutes' walk from the River Great Ouse and historic town centre. Extensive bar and restaurant menus.
Bedrooms: 2 single, 4 double, 8 twin, 1 triple
Bathrooms: 15 en-suite

Bed & breakfast
per night:	£min	£max
Single	47.00	65.00
Double	60.00	85.00

Lunch available
Evening meal 1900 (last orders 2100)
Parking for 70

Cards accepted: Access, Visa, Diners, Amex, Switch/Delta

SANDY

Bedfordshire
Map ref 2D1

Small town on the River Ivel on the site of a Roman settlement. Sandy is mentioned in Domesday.
Tourist Information Centre ☎ (01767) 682728

Holiday Inn Garden Court (A1) Sandy

Girtford Bridge, London Road, Sandy SG19 1DH
☎ (01767) 692220
Fax (01767) 680452
This Holiday Inn combines comfort, quality and tranquillity in an ideal location.
Bedrooms: 36 double, 20 twin
Bathrooms: 56 en-suite

Bed & breakfast per night:	£min	£max
Single	39.00	51.00
Double	49.00	57.00

Half board per person:	£min	£max
Daily	51.00	75.00
Weekly	427.00	567.00

Evening meal 1845 (last orders 2145)
Parking for 150
Cards accepted: Access, Visa, Diners, Amex, Switch/Delta

SHERINGHAM

Norfolk
Map ref 3B1

Holiday resort with Victorian and Edwardian hotels and a sand and shingle beach where the fishing boats are hauled up. The North Norfolk Railway operates from Sheringham station during the summer. Other attractions include museums, theatre and Splash Fun Pool.

The Bay Leaf Guest House
COMMENDED

10 St. Peters Road, Sheringham NR26 8QY
☎ (01263) 823779
Charming Victorian licensed guesthouse, open all year. Conveniently situated in the town. Near golf-course and woodlands, adjacent to steam railway and 5 minutes from sea.
Bedrooms: 1 double, 3 twin, 2 triple
Bathrooms: 6 en-suite

Bed & breakfast per night:	£min	£max
Single	17.00	22.00
Double	34.00	44.00

Half board per person:	£min	£max
Daily	25.00	30.00
Weekly	165.00	195.00

Evening meal 1800 (last orders 1930)
Parking for 4
Cards accepted: Access, Visa

Beaumaris Hotel
COMMENDED

15 South Street, Sheringham NR26 8LL
☎ (01263) 822370
Fax (01263) 821421
Family-run hotel established in 1947. Reputation for personal service and English cuisine. Quietly located close to beach, shops and golf club.
Bedrooms: 5 single, 10 double, 7 twin
Bathrooms: 22 en-suite

Bed & breakfast per night:	£min	£max
Single	30.00	40.00
Double	50.00	80.00

Half board per person:	£min	£max
Daily	43.50	53.50
Weekly	245.00	305.00

Lunch available
Evening meal 1900 (last orders 2030)
Parking for 20
Open February–December
Cards accepted: Access, Visa, Diners, Amex, Switch/Delta

Olivedale Guest House
COMMENDED

20 Augusta Street, Sheringham NR26 8LA
☎ (01263) 825871
Charming family home, close to town centre, sea and amenities. Ideal base for exploring this beautiful area. All rooms have colour TV, radio/alarm, tea/coffee facilities.
Bedrooms: 2 double, 1 twin
Bathrooms: 1 en-suite, 1 private, 1 public

Bed & breakfast per night:	£min	£max
Single	18.00	20.00
Double	36.00	44.00

Parking for 3

SOUTHEND-ON-SEA

Essex
Map ref 3B3

On the Thames Estuary and the nearest seaside resort to London. Famous for its pier and unique pier trains. Other attractions include Peter Pan's Playground, indoor swimming pools, indoor rollerskating and ten pin bowling.
Tourist Information Centre ☎ (01702) 215120

Balmoral Hotel

32-36 Valkyrie Road, Southend-on-Sea SSO 8BU
☎ (01702) 342947
Fax (01702) 337828
Highly appealing hotel, designer furnished in 1995. En-suite rooms, excellent bar, restaurant, 24-hour service. Near station, buses, shops and sea. Secure parking.
Bedrooms: 10 single, 13 double, 6 twin
Suite available
Bathrooms: 29 en-suite

Bed & breakfast per night:	£min	£max
Single	39.00	52.00
Double	52.00	80.00

Half board per person:	£min	£max
Daily	48.00	61.00

Lunch available
Evening meal 1830 (last orders 2130)
Parking for 28
Cards accepted: Access, Visa, Amex, Switch/Delta

Camelia Hotel and Restaurant
COMMENDED

178 Eastern Esplanade, Thorpe Bay, Southend-on-Sea SS1 3AA
☎ (01702) 587917
Fax (01702) 585704
Well-appointed family-run hotel on seafront in quiet residential area. Offering good cuisine. Close to all local amenities.
Bedrooms: 6 single, 9 double, 1 triple
Bathrooms: 16 en-suite

Continued ▶

EAST ANGLIA

SOUTHEND-ON-SEA
Continued

Bed & breakfast per night:
	£min	£max
Single	42.50	55.00
Double	45.00	80.00

Half board per person:
	£min	£max
Weekly	250.00	475.00

Lunch available
Evening meal 1830 (last orders 2200)
Parking for 100
Cards accepted: Access, Visa, Amex

Tower Hotel and Restaurant

146 Alexandra Road,
Southend-on-Sea SS1 1HE
☎ (01702) 348635
Fax (01702) 433044
The Independents
Restored Victorian hotel in conservation area, 10 minutes' walk from Cliff Gardens, the sea, Cliffs Pavilion Theatre, High Street and British Rail.
Bedrooms: 16 single, 11 double, 4 twin, 2 triple
Bathrooms: 33 en-suite, 3 public

Bed & breakfast per night:
	£min	£max
Single	20.00	40.00
Double	30.00	55.00

Half board per person:
	£min	£max
Daily	20.00	55.00
Weekly	140.00	325.00

Lunch available
Evening meal 1800 (last orders 2130)
Parking for 3
Cards accepted: Access, Visa, Diners, Amex, Switch/Delta

WELCOME HOST

This is a nationally recognised customer care programme which aims to promote the highest standards of service and a warm welcome. Establishments who are taking part in this initiative are indicated by the symbol.

SOUTHWOLD
Suffolk
Map ref 3C2

Pleasant and attractive seaside town with a triangular market square and spacious greens around which stand flint, brick and colour-washed cottages. The parish church of St Edmund is one of the greatest churches in Suffolk.

Pier Avenue Hotel
COMMENDED

Station Road, Southwold IP18 6AY
☎ (01502) 722632
Fax (01502) 722632
Family-run, fully licensed hotel at the entrance to this quaint, unspoilt seaside town.
Bedrooms: 4 single, 3 double, 2 twin, 4 triple
Bathrooms: 13 en-suite

Bed & breakfast per night:
	£min	£max
Single	45.00	45.00
Double	59.00	63.00

Half board per person:
	£min	£max
Daily	44.00	48.00
Weekly	280.20	296.00

Lunch available
Evening meal 1845 (last orders 2100)
Parking for 12
Cards accepted: Access, Visa, Diners, Amex

Saxon House
COMMENDED

86 Pier Avenue, Southwold IP18 6BL
☎ (01502) 723651
Comfortable, detached guesthouse, 100 metres from beach. All rooms en-suite with clock/radio and tea/coffee facilities. Some rooms have TV. Two rooms on ground floor. Full English breakfast. Residents' car park. A non-smoking establishment.
Bedrooms: 4 double, 2 twin, 1 family room
Bathrooms: 6 en-suite, 1 private

Bed & breakfast per night:
	£min	£max
Single	25.00	30.00
Double	44.00	50.00

Parking for 6
Cards accepted: Access, Visa, Switch/Delta

Swan Hotel
COMMENDED

Market Place, Southwold IP18 6EG
☎ (01502) 722186
Fax (01502) 724800

Dating back to 17th C, originally a coaching house, kept in its traditional style. Conferences catered for.
Bedrooms: 6 single, 18 double, 19 twin, 2 triple
Suites available
Bathrooms: 42 en-suite, 3 private

Bed & breakfast per night:
	£min	£max
Single	42.00	88.00
Double	86.00	149.00

Lunch available
Evening meal 1900 (last orders 2130)
Parking for 48
Cards accepted: Access, Visa, Diners, Amex, Switch/Delta

STALHAM
Norfolk
Map ref 3C1

Lies on the edge of the Broads.

Kingfisher Hotel
COMMENDED

High Street, Stalham, Norwich NR12 9AN
☎ (01692) 581974
Fax (01692) 582544
Consort
Modern, licensed hotel with a friendly atmosphere, ideal for touring the Norfolk countryside. Children welcome. Noted for food.
Bedrooms: 3 single, 9 double, 3 twin, 2 family rooms
Bathrooms: 15 en-suite, 2 private

Bed & breakfast per night:
	£min	£max
Single	41.00	52.00
Double	50.00	69.00

Lunch available
Evening meal 1900 (last orders 2100)
Parking for 45
Cards accepted: Access, Visa

EAST ANGLIA

STOKE-BY-NAYLAND
Suffolk
Map ref 3B2

Picturesque village with a fine group of half-timbered cottages near the church of St Mary, the tower of which was one of Constable's favourite subjects. In School Street are the Guildhall and the Maltings, both 16th C timber-framed buildings.

The Angel Inn
HIGHLY COMMENDED

Polstead Street, Stoke-by-Nayland, Colchester CO6 4SA
☎ Colchester (01206) 263245
Fax (01206) 263173

Beautifully restored freehouse and restaurant in the historic village of Stoke-by-Nayland, in the heart of Constable country.

Bedrooms: 5 double, 1 twin
Bathrooms: 6 en-suite

Bed & breakfast per night:

	£min	£max
Single	45.00	45.00
Double	59.00	59.00

Lunch available
Evening meal 1830 (last orders 2100)
Parking for 25
Cards accepted: Access, Visa, Diners, Amex, Switch/Delta

STOWMARKET
Suffolk
Map ref 3B2

Small market town where routes converge. There is an open-air museum of rural life at the Museum of East Anglian Life.
Tourist Information Centre ☎ (01449) 676800

Cedars Hotel

Needham Road, Stowmarket IP14 2AJ
☎ (01449) 612668
Fax (01449) 674704
Ⓒ The Independents

Originally a 16th C farmhouse, now a family-run hotel, ideal for those wishing to tour Suffolk. Good food available in comfortable, informal atmosphere. Ample parking.

Bedrooms: 5 single, 13 double, 4 twin, 2 triple
Bathrooms: 24 en-suite

Bed & breakfast per night:

	£min	£max
Single	40.00	42.50
Double	45.00	48.00

Lunch available
Evening meal 1900 (last orders 2100)
Parking for 80
Cards accepted: Access, Visa, Diners, Amex, Switch/Delta

STRETHAM
Cambridgeshire
Map ref 3A2

The Red Lion
APPROVED

High Street, Stretham, Ely CB6 3JQ
☎ Ely (01353) 648132

Village inn dating from 1732. Recently completely refurbished and additional buildings and facilities provided. Off A10 Cambridge-Ely Road. Cambridge 12 minutes, Ely 5 minutes.

Bedrooms: 2 single, 1 double, 3 triple
Bathrooms: 6 en-suite

Bed & breakfast per night:

	£min	£max
Single	25.00	30.00
Double	35.00	40.00

Lunch available
Evening meal 1900 (last orders 2100)
Parking for 20
Cards accepted: Access, Visa, Switch/Delta

SUDBURY
Suffolk
Map ref 3B2

Former important cloth and market town on the River Stour. Birthplace of Thomas Gainsborough whose home is now an art gallery and museum. The Corn Exchange is an excellent example of early Victorian civic building.
Tourist Information Centre ☎ (01787) 881320

The Boathouse Hotel
Listed

Ballingdon Bridge, Sudbury CO10 6DA
☎ (01787) 379090

Family-owned and operated hotel set on the banks of the River Stour, offering good food and service in picturesque surroundings.

Bedrooms: 4 double, 1 triple
Bathrooms: 3 en-suite, 2 private, 1 public

Bed & breakfast per night:

	£min	£max
Single	31.00	37.00
Double	50.00	56.00

Lunch available
Evening meal 1830 (last orders 2130)
Parking for 14
Cards accepted: Access, Visa

THETFORD
Norfolk
Map ref 3B2

Small, medieval market town with numerous reminders of its long history: the ruins of the 12th C priory, Iron Age earthworks at Castle Hill and a Norman castle mound. Timber-framed Ancient House is now a museum.

The Bell
COMMENDED

King Street, Thetford IP24 2AZ
☎ (01842) 754455
Fax (01842) 755552
Ⓒ Forte

Originally a Tudor inn, with an old courtyard where the galleries have been preserved.

Bedrooms: 11 single, 19 double, 16 twin, 1 triple
Suite available
Bathrooms: 47 en-suite

Bed & breakfast per night:

	£min	£max
Single	37.00	47.00
Double	74.00	88.00

Half board per person:

	£min	£max
Daily	47.00	64.00

Lunch available
Evening meal 1900 (last orders 2130)
Parking for 65
Cards accepted: Access, Visa, Diners, Amex, Switch/Delta

ACCESSIBILITY

Look for the ♿ symbols which indicate accessibility for wheelchair users. These are described in detail at the front of this guide.

EAST ANGLIA

TITCHWELL

Norfolk
Map ref 3B1

Briarfields

⚜⚜⚜ COMMENDED

Main Street, Titchwell, King's Lynn
PE31 8BB
☎ Brancaster (01485) 210742
Fax (01485) 210933

Traditional, privately owned hotel, overlooking the Titchwell RSPB Reserve, salt marshes and beaches. Renowned for comfort and excellent menus. Ideally situated for birdwatching, beach walking, golf or visiting places of local interest. Special breaks all-year-round.
Bedrooms: 10 double, 5 twin, 2 family rooms
Bathrooms: 17 en-suite

Bed & breakfast per night:

	£min	£max
Single	33.00	35.50
Double		66.00

Half board per person:

	£min	£max
Daily		46.95
Weekly	296.00	

Lunch available
Evening meal 1845 (last orders 2100)
Parking for 40
Cards accepted: Access, Visa, Switch/Delta

TIVETSHALL ST MARY

Norfolk
Map ref 3B2

The Old Ram Coaching Inn

⚜⚜⚜ HIGHLY COMMENDED

Ipswich Road, Tivetshall St Mary, Norwich NR15 2DE
☎ Pulham Market (01379) 676794
Fax (01379) 608399
17th C coaching inn (15 miles south of Norwich) with oak beams and log fires. En-suite accommodation, extensive menu.
Bedrooms: 4 double, 1 family room
Bathrooms: 5 en-suite

Bed & breakfast per night:

	£min	£max
Single	43.00	48.00
Double	61.00	66.00

Lunch available
Evening meal 1700 (last orders 2200)
Parking for 150
Cards accepted: Access, Visa, Switch/Delta

TRING

Hertfordshire
Map ref 2C1

Pleasant town near lovely countryside and woods. Tring has a fine church with a large 14th C tower. Tring Park houses the Rothschild Zoological Collection, now part of the Natural History Museum. The Tring Reservoir's National Nature Reserve is nearby.

Stocks Hotel & Country Club

⚜⚜⚜ COMMENDED

Stocks Road, Aldbury, Tring HP23 5RX
☎ Aldbury Common (01442) 851341 & 851491
Fax (01442) 851253
A charming and friendly 18th C Georgian mansion is at the centre of this complex. Features include a spectacular 18-hole championship length golf course, golf practice facilities, stables, including bridleway and manege, jacuzzi, steam room, solarium, sauna, tennis courts and outdoor pool.
Bedrooms: 1 single, 8 double, 9 twin
Bathrooms: 15 en-suite, 3 private

Bed & breakfast per night:

	£min	£max
Single	70.00	120.00
Double	80.00	130.00

Half board per person:

	£min	£max
Daily	60.00	85.00

Lunch available
Evening meal 1900 (last orders 2130)
Parking for 200
Cards accepted: Access, Visa, Diners, Amex, Switch/Delta

COLOUR MAPS

Colour maps at the back of this guide pinpoint all places in which you will find accommodation listed.

WALTHAM ABBEY

Essex
Map ref 2D1

King Harold rebuilt the church in 1060 and it is believed he was buried here after the Battle of Hastings. Henry II founded a priory which became Waltham Abbey. Henry VIII suppressed the Abbey and it was demolished, except for the nave and great gateway.
Tourist Information Centre ☎ (01992) 652295

Swallow Hotel

⚜⚜⚜⚜ COMMENDED

Old Shire Lane, Waltham Abbey EN9 3LX
☎ Lea Valley (01992) 717170
Fax (01992) 711841
Swallow
Modern purpose-built hotel situated at junction 26 of M25. En-suite bedrooms, 2 restaurants, cocktail bar and leisure club. Short break packages available.
Bedrooms: 79 single, 31 double, 39 twin, 14 triple
Suites available
Bathrooms: 163 en-suite

Bed & breakfast per night:

	£min	£max
Single	70.00	99.00
Double	75.00	120.00

Half board per person:

	£min	£max
Daily	92.75	121.75

Lunch available
Evening meal 1800 (last orders 2300)
Parking for 240
Cards accepted: Access, Visa, Diners, Amex, Switch/Delta

WANSFORD

Cambridgeshire
Map ref 3A1

A terminus of the Nene Valley Railway with British and continental steam locomotives and rolling-stock.

Haycock Hotel

⚜⚜⚜⚜ HIGHLY COMMENDED

Wansford-in-England, Wansford, Peterborough PE8 6JA
☎ Stamford (01780) 782223
Fax (01780) 783031
17th C coaching inn with a restaurant, log fires, many fascinating rooms. Orchard room for informal eating. Five real ales and a great "village" atmosphere. Special weekend breaks.

EAST ANGLIA

Wheelchair access category 3
Bedrooms: 7 single, 32 double, 7 twin, 4 triple
Bathrooms: 50 en-suite

Bed & breakfast per night:	£min	£max
Single	75.00	110.00
Double	125.00	175.00

Lunch available
Evening meal 1900 (last orders 2230)
Parking for 300
Cards accepted: Access, Visa, Diners, Amex, Switch/Delta

WARE

Hertfordshire
Map ref 2D1

Interesting riverside town with picturesque summer-houses lining the tow-path of the River Lea. The town has many timber-framed and Georgian houses and the famous Great Bed of Ware is now in the Victoria and Albert Museum.

Marriott Hanbury Manor Hotel & Country Club

DE LUXE

Ware SG12 0SD
☎ (01920) 487722
Fax (01920) 487692
Utell International/Whitbread
Superbly located 25 miles north of London en route to Cambridge. A unique country house resort offering extensive leisure facilities, 18-hole golf course designed by Jack Nicklaus II, creche, and three restaurants including the award-winning Zodiac Restaurant.
Bedrooms: 11 single, 27 double, 43 twin, 15 triple
Bathrooms: 96 en-suite

Bed & breakfast per night:	£min	£max
Single	183.00	
Double	197.00	

Lunch available
Evening meal 1830 (last orders 2230)
Parking for 200
Cards accepted: Access, Visa, Diners, Amex

All accommodation in this guide has been graded, or is awaiting a grading, by a trained Tourist Board inspector.

WATFORD

Hertfordshire
Map ref 2D1

Large town with many industries but with some old buildings, particularly around St Mary's Church which contains some fine monuments. The grounds of Cassiobury Park, once the home of the Earls of Essex, form a public park and golf-course.

White House Hotel

COMMENDED

26-31 Upton Road, Watford WD1 2EL
☎ (01923) 237316
Fax (01923) 233109
Consort/Logis of Great Britain/The Independents
Recently refurbished town centre hotel. Full a la carte conservatory restaurant or bar meals available. Guaranteed friendly and efficient service.
Bedrooms: 10 single, 27 double, 24 twin
Bathrooms: 57 en-suite

Bed & breakfast per night:	£min	£max
Single	69.00	79.00
Double	79.00	99.00

Half board per person:	£min	£max
Daily	85.00	95.00

Lunch available
Evening meal 1830 (last orders 2145)
Parking for 45
Cards accepted: Access, Visa, Diners, Amex, Switch/Delta

WELLS-NEXT-THE-SEA

Norfolk
Map ref 3B1

Seaside resort and small port on the north coast. The Buttlands is a large tree-lined green surrounded by Georgian houses and from here narrow streets lead to the quay.

Crown Hotel

APPROVED

The Buttlands, Wells-next-the-Sea NR23 1EX
☎ Fakenham (01328) 710209
Fax (01328) 711432
Famous old coaching inn set amongst Norfolk's finest coastal scenery.
Bedrooms: 1 single, 6 double, 4 twin, 3 triple, 1 family room
Bathrooms: 11 en-suite, 1 public

Bed & breakfast per night:	£min	£max
Single	35.00	55.00
Double	58.00	68.00

Lunch available
Evening meal 1900 (last orders 2130)
Parking for 10
Cards accepted: Access, Visa, Diners, Amex

The Normans

Invaders Court, Standard Road, Wells-next-the-Sea NR23 1JW
☎ Fakenham (01328) 710657
Fax (01328) 710468
Listed Georgian house 100 yards from the quay. All rooms en-suite with colour TV and tea/coffee. Some rooms have views over saltmarshes to the sea. Dogs welcome.
Bedrooms: 5 double, 1 twin, 1 triple
Bathrooms: 7 en-suite, 1 public

Bed & breakfast per night:	£min	£max
Single	30.00	
Double	47.00	55.00

Parking for 12

Scarborough House Hotel

COMMENDED

Clubbs Lane, Wells-next-the-Sea NR23 1DP
☎ Fakenham (01328) 710309 & 711661
Licensed hotel with restaurant, log fires, four-poster beds, private parking. Perfect for bird-watchers and ramblers. Dogs welcome.
Bedrooms: 10 double, 4 twin, 1 family room
Bathrooms: 15 en-suite

Bed & breakfast per night:	£min	£max
Single	29.00	34.00
Double	48.00	68.00

Half board per person:	£min	£max
Daily	37.95	47.95
Weekly	235.00	270.00

Evening meal 1930 (last orders 2100)
Parking for 15
Cards accepted: Access, Visa, Diners, Amex, Switch/Delta

EAST ANGLIA

WHITTLESFORD

Cambridgeshire
Map ref 2D1

Red Lion Hotel

Station Road East, Whittlesford, Cambridge CB2 4NL
☎ Cambridge (01223) 832047 & 832115
Fax (01223) 837576

Traditional 13th C English inn with modern facilities. Well situated for Cambridge with excellent road and rail connections. 1 mile from Duxford Imperial War Museum.
Bedrooms: 7 single, 6 double, 1 twin, 2 triple, 2 family rooms
Bathrooms: 18 en-suite
Bed & breakfast
per night: £min £max
Single 35.00 39.00
Double 49.50 54.00

Lunch available
Evening meal 1900 (last orders 2130)
Parking for 75
Cards accepted: Access, Visa, Diners, Amex, Switch/Delta

WISBECH

Cambridgeshire
Map ref 3A1

The town is the centre of the agricultural and flower-growing industries of Fenland. Peckover House (National Trust) is an important example of domestic architecture.
Tourist Information Centre ☎ (01945) 583263

Crown Lodge Hotel
COMMENDED

Downham Road, Outwell, Wisbech PE14 8SE
☎ (01945) 773391
Fax (01945) 772668
The Independents

A warm welcome awaits you at this small hotel, which offers a relaxed, friendly atmosphere. Enjoy a meal in our bistro-style restaurant which uses only the best fresh local produce and prime select meats, poultry and fish.
Wheelchair access category 3
Bedrooms: 8 double, 2 twin
Bathrooms: 10 en-suite
Bed & breakfast
per night: £min £max
Single 38.75 40.00
Double 50.00 55.00

Half board per
person: £min £max
Daily 51.25 52.50

Lunch available
Evening meal 1830 (last orders 2230)
Parking for 100
Cards accepted: Access, Visa, Diners, Amex, Switch/Delta

WIX

Essex
Map ref 3B2

New Farm House
COMMENDED

Spinnell's Lane, Wix, Manningtree CO11 2UJ
☎ Clacton (01255) 870365
Fax (01255) 870837

Modern comfortable farmhouse in large garden, 10 minutes' drive to Harwich and convenient for Constable country. From Wix village crossroads, take Bradfield Road, turn right at top of hill; first house on left.
Bedrooms: 3 single, 1 double, 3 twin, 5 family rooms
Bathrooms: 7 en-suite, 2 public
Bed & breakfast
per night: £min £max
Single 21.50 25.00
Double 40.00 46.00

Half board per
person: £min £max
Daily 34.50 38.00
Weekly 308.35 330.40

Evening meal 1830 (last orders 1730)
Parking for 18
Cards accepted: Access, Visa, Diners, Amex

Information on accommodation listed in this guide has been supplied by the proprietors. As changes may occur you are advised to check details at the time of booking.

WOBURN

Bedfordshire
Map ref 2D1

Attractive village with thatched cottages, Victorian almshouses and an impressive inn. Woburn Abbey, an 18th C mansion set in 3000 acres of parkland, is a major tourist attraction and has a splendid art collection.

The Bell Inn
21 Bedford Street, Woburn, Milton Keynes MK17 9QD
☎ (01525) 290280
Fax (01525) 290017
Best Western

Part Georgian, part 17th C hotel. Award-winning restaurant, full table d'hote or bar food menus. Beautiful village location.
Bedrooms: 13 single, 10 double, 2 twin, 2 triple
Bathrooms: 25 en-suite, 1 public
Bed & breakfast
per night: £min £max
Single 49.00 59.00
Double 59.00 69.00

Lunch available
Evening meal 1900 (last orders 2130)
Parking for 36
Cards accepted: Access, Visa, Diners, Amex, Switch/Delta

WOODBRIDGE

Suffolk
Map ref 3C2

Once a busy seaport, the town is now a sailing centre on the River Deben. There are many buildings of architectural merit including the Bell and Angel Inns. The 18th C Tide Mill is now restored and open to the public.

Seckford Hall Hotel
HIGHLY COMMENDED

Woodbridge IP13 6NU
☎ (01394) 385678
Fax (01394) 380610
Elizabethan country house hotel with four poster beds, spa baths, indoor

EAST ANGLIA

heated swimming pool and 18-hole golf-course. Excellent cuisine in 2 restaurants.
Bedrooms: 3 single, 14 double, 10 twin, 1 triple, 4 family rooms
Suites available
Bathrooms: 32 en-suite

Bed & breakfast per night:	£min	£max
Single	79.00	110.00
Double	105.00	148.00

Lunch available
Evening meal 1915 (last orders 2130)
Parking for 102
Cards accepted: Access, Visa, Diners, Amex

Ufford Park Hotel Golf & Leisure

COMMENDED

Yarmouth Road, Ufford, Woodbridge IP12 1QW
☎ (01394) 383555
Fax (01394) 383582
Best Western

Located 2.5 miles north of Woodbridge and set in historic parkland. Extensive leisure facilities, including indoor swimming pool and 18-hole golf-course.
Bedrooms: 2 single, 5 double, 26 twin, 4 triple
Bathrooms: 37 en-suite, 4 public

Bed & breakfast per night:	£min	£max
Single	70.00	80.00
Double	80.00	90.00

Half board per person:	£min	£max
Daily	77.00	95.00
Weekly	462.00	570.00

Lunch available
Evening meal 1900 (last orders 2130)
Parking for 200
Cards accepted: Access, Visa, Diners, Amex, Switch/Delta

WORLINGTON

Suffolk
Map ref 3B2

Worlington Hall Country House Hotel

COMMENDED

The Street, Worlington, Bury St Edmunds IP28 8RX
☎ Mildenhall (01638) 712237
Fax (01638) 712631

Grade II listed former hall, dating back in parts to the 16th C. In 5 acres with frontage to the River Lark. Providing a full service and also a friendly "local".
Bedrooms: 5 double, 3 twin, 1 triple
Bathrooms: 9 en-suite

Bed & breakfast per night:	£min	£max
Single	38.00	50.00
Double	50.00	85.00

Half board per person:	£min	£max
Daily	35.00	41.00
Weekly	245.00	287.00

Lunch available
Evening meal 1900 (last orders 2145)
Parking for 150
Cards accepted: Access, Visa, Diners, Amex, Switch/Delta

WROXHAM

Norfolk
Map ref 3C1

Yachting centre on the River Bure which houses the headquarters of the Norfolk Broads Yacht Club. The church of St Mary has a famous doorway and the manor house nearby dates back to 1623.

Hotel Wroxham

COMMENDED

Wroxham, Norwich NR12 8AJ
☎ (01603) 782061
Fax (01603) 784279
Minotel

Modern, friendly hotel, privately owned, in a riverside setting next to Wroxham bridge. Busy shopping centre. In the heart of the Norfolk Broads, 8 miles from Norwich.
Bedrooms: 1 single, 7 double, 10 twin
Bathrooms: 18 en-suite

Bed & breakfast per night:	£min	£max
Single	35.00	50.00
Double	60.00	70.00

Half board per person:	£min	£max
Daily	47.95	62.95
Weekly	265.00	350.00

Lunch available
Evening meal 1900 (last orders 2130)
Parking for 60
Cards accepted: Access, Visa, Diners, Amex, Switch/Delta

WYMONDHAM

Norfolk
Map ref 3B1

Thriving historic market town of charm and architectural interest. The octagonal market cross, 12th C abbey and 15th C Green Dragon inn blend with streetscapes spanning three centuries. An excellent touring base.

Abbey Hotel

10 Church Street, Wymondham NR18 0PH
☎ (01953) 602148
Fax (01953) 606247
Best Western

Quiet location opposite 12th C abbey. Character Victorian town house with friendly, relaxed atmosphere. Proprietor-run with high rate of repeat business.
Bedrooms: 3 single, 10 double, 9 twin, 1 triple
Bathrooms: 23 en-suite

Bed & breakfast per night:	£min	£max
Single	46.50	52.50
Double	66.00	72.00

Half board per person:	£min	£max
Daily	47.50	67.00
Weekly	237.00	267.00

Lunch available
Evening meal 1900 (last orders 2130)
Parking for 4
Cards accepted: Access, Visa, Diners, Amex, Switch/Delta

The symbol CR and a group name following an hotel address indicates that bookings can be made through a central reservations office. These offices are listed in the information pages at the back of this guide.

367

EAST ANGLIA

WYMONDHAM
Continued

Wymondham Consort Hotel

COMMENDED

28 Market Street, Wymondham
NR18 0BB
☎ (01953) 606721
Fax (01953) 601361
Consort

Charming, historic town centre hotel. Proprietor-run and offering good food and accommodation. Private garden, car parking.

Bedrooms: 5 single, 6 double, 8 twin, 1 triple
Bathrooms: 20 en-suite

Bed & breakfast per night:	£min	£max
Single	40.00	50.00
Double	55.00	68.00

Half board per person:	£min	£max
Daily	55.00	65.00

Lunch available
Evening meal 1900 (last orders 2130)
Parking for 16
Cards accepted: Access, Visa, Diners, Amex, Switch/Delta

COUNTRY CODE

Always follow the Country Code ✿Enjoy the countryside and respect its life and work ✿Guard against all risk of fire ✿Fasten all gates ✿Keep your dogs under close control ✿Keep to public paths across farmland ✿Use gates and stiles to cross fences, hedges and walls ✿Leave livestock, crops and machinery alone ✿Take your litter home ✿Help to keep all water clean ✿Protect wildlife, plants and trees ✿Take special care on country roads ✿Make no unnecessary noise

WEST COUNTRY

The West Country is famous for its wildness and beauty, legends and magic... but mostly for the breathtaking variety of its scenery.

From titanic cliffs overlooking sparkling beaches to the vastness of Dartmoor and Exmoor, then on to cosy villages nestling in verdant countryside, this most compelling of regions has inspired generations of writers and artists.

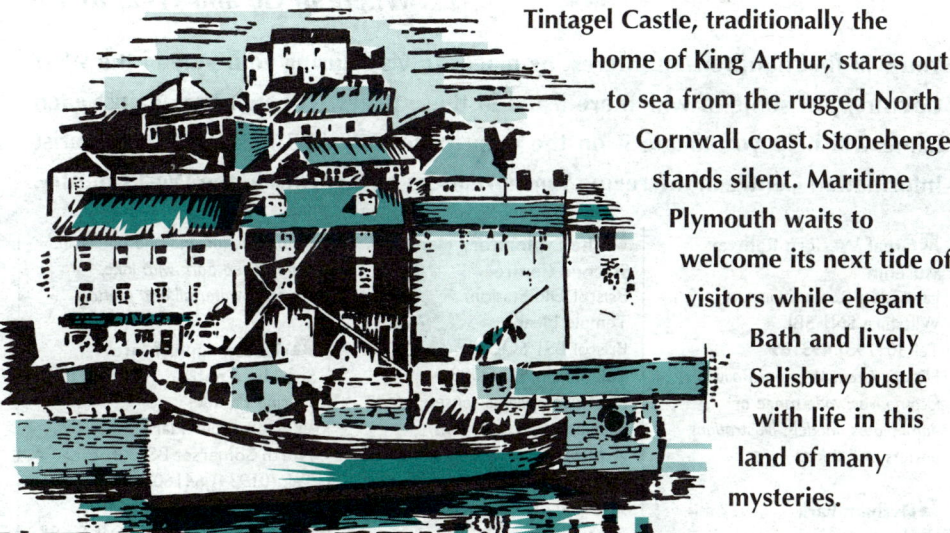

Tintagel Castle, traditionally the home of King Arthur, stares out to sea from the rugged North Cornwall coast. Stonehenge stands silent. Maritime Plymouth waits to welcome its next tide of visitors while elegant Bath and lively Salisbury bustle with life in this land of many mysteries.

FOR MORE INFORMATION CONTACT:
West Country Tourist Board
60 St Davids Hill, Exeter EX4 4SY
Tel: (01392) 425426 **Fax:** (01392) 420891

Where to Go in the West Country -
see pages 370-374
Where to Stay in the West Country -
see pages 375-471

WEST COUNTRY

Where to Go and What to See

You will find hundreds of interesting places to visit during your stay in the West Country, just some of which are listed in these pages. The number against each name will help you locate it on the map (pages 372-373). Contact any Tourist Information Centre in the region for more ideas on days out in the West Country.

1 Great Western Railway Museum
Faringdon Road, Swindon,
Wiltshire SN1 5BJ
Tel: (01793) 493189
Historic Great Western Railway locomotives, wide range of nameplates, models, illustrations, posters and tickets.

2 Dyrham Park
Dyrham,
Chippenham,
Wiltshire SN14 8ER
Tel: (0117) 937 2501
Mansion built between 1691 and 1710 for William Blathwayt. Rooms have been little changed. A herd of deer roams the 263-acre parkland.

3 Bristol Zoo Gardens
Clifton, Bristol BS8 3HA
Tel: (0117) 973 8951
Set in beautiful gardens, the zoo provides a haven for some of the world's most endangered wildlife. Plenty of activities and special events throughout the year.

4 The Exploratory Hands-on Science Centre
Bristol Old Station,
Temple Meads,
Bristol BS1 6QU
Tel: (0117) 925 2008
Exhibition of lights, lenses, lasers, bubbles, bridges, illusions, gyroscopes and much more all housed in Brunel's original engine shed and drawing office.

5 Harveys Wine Museum
12 Denmark Street,
Bristol BS1 5DQ
Tel: (0117) 927 5036
Wine museum in original 13thC cellars displaying artefacts connected with production and enjoyment of wines, especially glass, silver and corkscrews.

6 Bowood House and Gardens
Bowood Estate,
Calne, Wiltshire SN11 0LZ
Tel: (01249) 812102
18thC house by Robert Adam, collections of paintings, watercolours, Victoriana, Indiana and porcelain. Landscaped park with lake, terraces, waterfall and grottos.

7 Weston-super-Mare Sea Life Centre
Marine Parade,
Weston-super-Mare,
North Somerset BS23 1BE
Tel: (01934) 641603
All aspects of British marine life housed on Britain's first pier for 85 years.

8 Museum of Costume
Assembly Rooms, Bennett Street,
Bath BA1 2QH
Tel: (01225) 477789
Designed by John Wood the Younger in 1769. One of Bath's finest Georgian buildings. Museum of Costume housed in basement.

9 Cheddar Showcaves and Gorge
Cheddar, Somerset BS27 3QF
Tel: (01934) 742343
Beautiful caves located in Cheddar

Gorge. Gough's Cave with its cathedral-like caverns and Cox's Cave with stalagmites and stalactites. Also "The Crystal Quest" fantasy adventure.

10 Secret World
New Road Farm, East Huntspill, Highbridge, Somerset TA9 3PZ
Tel: (01278) 783250
300-year-old farm, many breeds of animals including rare breeds. Old and modern farm machinery on display. Play areas, gardens. Somerset Levels Visitor Centre.

11 Wookey Hole Caves and Papermill
Wookey Hole,
Wells,
Somerset BA5 1BB
Tel: (01749) 672243
Spectacular caves and legendary home of the Witch of Wookey. Working Victorian papermill including Fairground Memories, Old Penny Arcade, Magical Mirror Maze and Cave Diving Museum.

12 Longleat
Warminster,
Wiltshire BA12 7NW
Tel: (01985) 844400
Great Elizabethan house with lived-in atmosphere. Important libraries and Italian ceilings. Capability Brown designed parkland. Safari Park.

13 Stourhead House and Garden
Stourton, Warminster,
Wiltshire BA12 6QH
Tel: (01747) 840348
Landscaped garden laid out in 1741-80, with lakes and temples, rare trees and plants. House begun in 1721 by Colen Campbell contains fine paintings and Chippendale furniture.

14 Wilton House
Wilton, Wiltshire SP2 0BJ
Tel: (01722) 743115
Home of the Earls of Pembroke for nearly 450 years. Famous Double and Single Cube rooms. Art collection. Adventure playground. Woodland walk. Wareham Bears.

15 Salisbury and South Wiltshire Museum
The King's House, 65 The Close, Salisbury, Wiltshire SP1 2EN
Tel: (01722) 332151
Grade 1 listed building. Stonehenge collection, Salisbury Giant, Early man. History of Old Sarum, Salisbury, Romans to Saxons, ceramics, Wedgwood, pictures, costume exhibitions.

16 West Somerset Railway
The Railway Station, Minehead, Somerset TA24 5BG
Tel: (01643) 704996
Preserved steam railway operating between Minehead and Bishops Lydeard, near Taunton. Longest independent railway in Britain (20 miles).

17 Clovelly Village
Clovelly, Bideford,
Devon EX39 5SY
Tel: (01237) 431200
Unspoilt fishing village on North Devon coast with steep cobbled street and no vehicular access. Donkeys and sledges only means of transport. Visitor centre.

18 Dartington Crystal
Linden Close, Torrington,
Devon EX38 7AN
Tel: (01805) 622321
Manufacture of hand-made crystal table glassware by skilled craftsmen. Glass centre and glassware exhibition. Visitors can watch glass blowers "hand blowing" glassware.

19 Rosemoor Garden - Royal Horticultural Society's Garden
Rosemoor, Great Torrington,
Devon EX38 8PH
Tel: (01805) 624067
Garden of rare horticultural interest. Trees, shrubs, roses, alpines and arboretum. Nursery of uncommon and rare plants. 8 acres being expanded to 40 acres.

20 Haynes Motor Museum
Sparkford, Yeovil,
Somerset BA22 7LH
Tel: (01963) 440804
Motor vehicles and memorobilia covering the years from the turn of the century to the present day. Video cinema, exhibition track.

21 Montacute House
Montacute, Yeovil,
Somerset TA15 6XP
Tel: (01935) 823289
Late 16thC house built of local golden Ham stone, by Sir Edward Phelips. The Long Gallery houses a collection of Tudor and Jacobean portraits. Formal gardens and park.

22 Sherborne Castle
Sherborne, Dorset
Tel: (01935) 813182
Built by Sir Walter Raleigh in 1594 to replace the old castle. The Elizabethan Hall and Jacobean Oak Room show two of the many styles of architecture.

24 The Dinosaur Museum
Icen Way,
Dorchester,
Dorset DT1 1EW
Tel: (01305) 269880
Only museum in Britain devoted exclusively to dinosaurs. Fossils, actual-size dinosaur reconstructions, audio-visual, "hands on". Video gallery and computerised displays.

26 Weymouth Sea Life Park
Lodmoor Country Park,
Weymouth, Dorset DT4 7SX
Tel: (01305) 761070
Spectacular displays of British marine life where visitors come face to face with a wide variety of creatures. Also an exciting tropical jungle full of birds.

23 Athelhampton House and Gardens
Athelhampton, Dorset DT2 7LG
Tel: (01305) 848363
Legendary site of King Athelstan's Palace. Family home for five centuries. Fine example of 15thC architecture. Gardens with fountains, pools and waterfalls.

25 Brewers' Quay and Timewalk
Hope Square, Weymouth,
Dorset DT4 8TR
Tel: (01305) 777622
Former brewery now housing The Timewalk, depicting 600 years of Weymouth's history, also The Brewer's Tale exhibition and shopping village with restaurants.

27 Abbotsbury Swannery
New Barn Road, Abbotsbury
Weymouth, Dorset DT3 4JG
Tel: (01305) 871684
The only place in the world where over 600 swans can be visited during the nesting and hatching time (end May-end June). Audio-visual presentation. Ugly duckling trail.

28 Killerton House
Broadclyst, Exeter,
Devon EX5 3LE
Tel: (01392) 881345
18thC house built for the Acland family. Now houses a collection of costumes shown in various room settings. 15 acres of hillside garden with rare trees and shrubs.

29 Babbacombe Model Village
Hampton Avenue, Babbacombe,
Torquay, Devon TQ1 3LA
Tel: (01803) 328669
Hundreds of models and figures laid out in 4 acres of beautiful gardens to represent a model English countryside with modern town, villages and rural areas. Scale to 1/12th.

30 Woodlands Leisure Park
Blackawton, Totnes,
Devon TQ9 7DQ
Tel: (01803) 712598
A full day of variety set in 60 acres of countryside. 12 venture playzones including 500-metre toboggan run, commando course. 34000 sq ft indoor play area, toddlers' areas and animals.

31 Plymouth Dome
The Hoe, Plymouth,
Devon PL1 2NZ
Tel: (01752) 603300
Purpose-built visitor interpretation centre showing the history of Plymouth and its people from Stone Age beginnings to satellite technology. Situated on Plymouth Hoe.

32 Cotehele
St Dominick,
Saltash,
Cornwall PL12 6TA
Tel: (01579) 351346
Medieval granite house. Working watermill. Quay on River Tamar with small shipping museum. Sailing barge "Shamrock". Formal and valley gardens, pools, dovecote. Woodland walks.

33 Newquay Pearl
Southway,
Quintrell Downs,
Newquay,
Cornwall TR8 4LE
Tel: (01637) 872991
A large showroom with every range of pearl and semi-precious stone, with workshops and staff actively working. Pick your own pearl from our oyster tanks.

34 Royal Cornwall Museum
River Street,
Truro,
Cornwall TR1 2SJ
Tel: (01872) 72205
World famous mineral collection, Old Master drawings, ceramics, oil paintings by the Newlyn School and others, including John Opie and Hogarth. Geneaology library.

35 Tate Gallery St Ives
Porthmeor Beach,
St Ives,
Cornwall TR26 1TG
Tel: (01736) 796226
A major new gallery showing changing groups of work from the Tate Gallery's pre-eminent collection of St Ives painting and sculpture.

36 The Minack Theatre and Exhibition Centre
Porthcurno,
Penzance,
Cornwall
Tel: (01736) 810694
Open-air cliffside theatre with breathtaking views, presenting a 16 week season of plays and musicals. Exhibition centre telling the theatre's story.

37 Flambards Village Theme Park
Culdrose Manor,
Helston,
Cornwall TR13 0GA
Tel: (01326) 574549
Life-sized Victorian village with fully stocked shops, carriages and fashions. 'Britain in the Blitz' life-sized wartime street, historic aircraft. Exploratorium.

FIND OUT MORE
Further information about holidays and attractions in the West Country is available from:
West Country Tourist Board,
60 St Davids Hill,
Exeter EX4 4SY.
Tel: (01392) 425426
Fax: (01392) 420891

These publications are available free from the West Country Tourist Board:
- **Great Escapes in England's West Country**
- **Bed & Breakfast Touring Map**
- **West Country Inspected Holiday Homes**
- **Commended Hotels and Guesthouses**
- **Glorious Gardens of the West Country**
- **Camping and Caravan Touring Map**

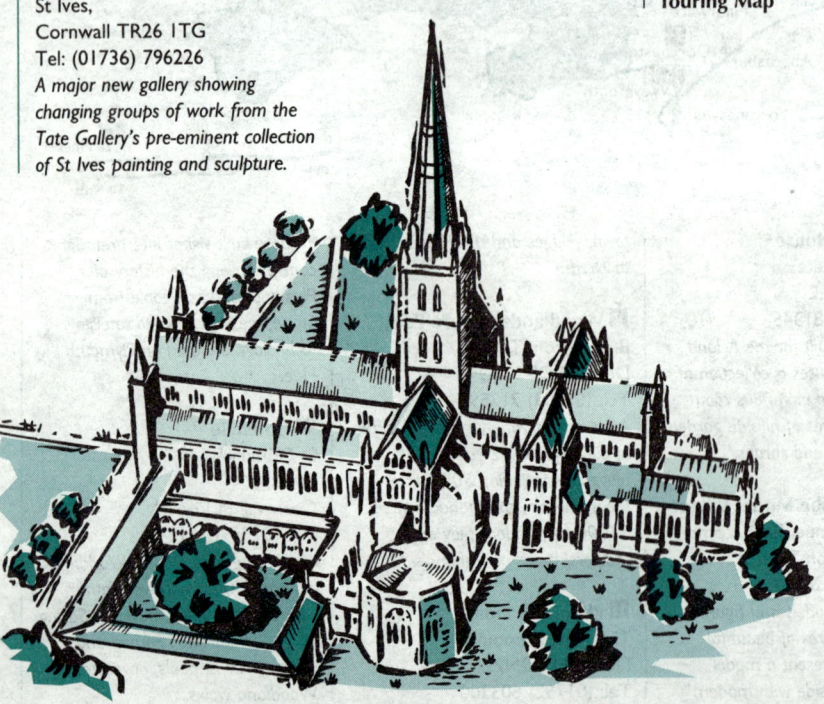

WEST COUNTRY

WHERE TO STAY (WEST COUNTRY)

Accommodation entries in this region are listed in alphabetical order of place name, and then in alphabetical order of establishment.

Map references refer to the colour location maps at the back of this guide. The first number indicates the map to use; the letter and number which follow refer to the grid reference on the map.

At-a-glance symbols at the end of each accommodation entry give useful information about services and facilities. A key to symbols can be found inside the back cover flap. Keep this open for easy reference.

ABBOTSBURY
Dorset
Map ref 2A3

Beautiful village near Chesil Beach, with a long main street of mellow stone and thatched cottages and the ruins of a Benedictine monastery. High above the village on a hill is a prominent 15th C chapel. Abbotsbury's famous swannery and sub-tropical gardens lie just outside the village.

Swan Lodge
COMMENDED

Rodden Row, Abbotsbury,
Weymouth DT3 4JL
☎ (01305) 871249
Fax (01305) 871249
Situated on the B3157 coastal road between Weymouth and Bridport. Swan Inn public house opposite, where food is served all day, is under the same ownership.
Bedrooms: 2 double, 2 twin, 1 single
Bathrooms: 4 en-suite, 1 public
Bed & breakfast per night:

	£min	£max
Single	28.00	36.00
Double	42.00	52.00

Lunch available
Evening meal 1800 (last orders 2200)
Parking for 10
Cards accepted: Access, Visa

Please mention this guide when making your booking.

ALLERFORD
Somerset
Map ref 1D1

Village with picturesque stone and thatch cottages and a packhorse bridge, set in the beautiful Vale of Porlock.

Fern Cottage
COMMENDED

Allerford, Minehead TA24 8HN
☎ Porlock (01643) 862215

Large 16th C traditional Exmoor cottage in National Trust wooded vale. Dramatic scenery and wildlife. Fine classic cooking and comprehensive wine list.
Bedrooms: 2 double, 2 triple
Bathrooms: 4 en-suite
Bed & breakfast per night:

	£min	£max
Single	28.50	28.50
Double	50.00	50.00

Half board per person:

	£min	£max
Daily	36.25	36.25
Weekly	228.40	228.40

Evening meal 1900 (last orders 1800)
Parking for 7
Cards accepted: Access, Visa, Switch/Delta

AMESBURY
Wiltshire
Map ref 2B2

Standing on the banks of the River Avon, this is the nearest town to Stonehenge on Salisbury Plain. The area is rich in prehistoric sites.
Tourist Information Centre ☎ (01980) 622833

Antrobus Arms Hotel
COMMENDED

15 Church Street, Amesbury,
Salisbury SP4 7EU
☎ (01980) 623163
Fax (01980) 622112
Ⓡ Logis of Great Britain

Traditional hotel with highly acclaimed "Fountain Restaurant". Walled Victorian garden. Near Stonehenge, A303 half a mile, Salisbury 5 miles. Well situated for visiting countryside steeped in history and rich in culture.
Bedrooms: 7 single, 7 double, 5 twin, 1 family room
Bathrooms: 14 en-suite, 2 public
Bed & breakfast per night:

	£min	£max
Single	35.00	46.00
Double	61.00	75.00

Half board per person:

	£min	£max
Daily	45.00	95.00

Continued ▶

WEST COUNTRY

AMESBURY
Continued

Lunch available
Evening meal 1900 (last orders 2130)
Parking for 60
Cards accepted: Access, Visa, Diners, Amex, Switch/Delta

Fairlawn Hotel
APPROVED

42 High Street, Amesbury, Salisbury SP4 7DJ
☎ Shrewton (01980) 622103
Family-run hotel in the middle of Salisbury Plain. Own restaurant which is open 7 days a week. Close to town centre and all amenities.
Bedrooms: 3 single, 5 double, 2 twin, 2 family rooms
Bathrooms: 9 en-suite, 3 private, 1 public

Bed & breakfast per night:

	£min	£max
Single	35.00	
Double	46.00	55.00

Half board per person:

	£min	£max
Daily	40.00	
Weekly	252.00	

Lunch available
Evening meal 1830 (last orders 2200)
Cards accepted: Access, Visa, Diners, Amex, Switch/Delta

ASHBURTON
Devon
Map ref 1C2

Formerly a thriving wool centre and important as one of Dartmoor's four stannary towns. Today's busy market town has many period buildings. Ancient tradition is maintained in the annual ale-tasting and bread-weighing ceremony. Good centre for exploring Dartmoor or the south Devon coast.

Gages Mill
COMMENDED

Buckfastleigh Road, Ashburton, Newton Abbot TQ13 7JW
☎ (01364) 652391

You are advised to confirm your booking in writing.

14th C former millhouse set in beautiful countryside on edge of Dartmoor. Comfortable accommodation, quality home cooking, large well-kept gardens.
Bedrooms: 1 single, 6 double, 1 twin
Bathrooms: 8 en-suite

Bed & breakfast per night:

	£min	£max
Single	20.00	23.00
Double	40.00	46.00

Half board per person:

	£min	£max
Daily	30.00	33.00
Weekly	196.00	206.50

Evening meal 1900 (last orders 1900)
Parking for 10
Open March–November

Holne Chase Hotel and Restaurant
HIGHLY COMMENDED

Tavistock Road, Ashburton, Newton Abbot TQ13 7NS
☎ Poundsgate (01364) 631471
Fax (01364) 631453
In one of the most romantic situations possible, Holne Chase offers that traditional hospitality which is part of Britain's heritage.
Bedrooms: 1 single, 5 double, 8 twin
Suites available
Bathrooms: 14 en-suite

Bed & breakfast per night:

	£min	£max
Single	70.00	
Double	110.00	140.00

Half board per person:

	£min	£max
Daily	87.50	100.00

Lunch available
Evening meal 1915 (last orders 2100)
Parking for 30
Cards accepted: Access, Visa, Diners, Amex, Switch/Delta

New Cott Farm
COMMENDED

Poundsgate, Newton Abbot TQ13 7PD
☎ Poundsgate (01364) 631421
Fax (01364) 631338
130-acre mixed farm. Enjoy the freedom, peace and tranquillity of moorland and valleys in the Dartmoor National Park. A warm welcome and lots of lovely home-made food to complete your stay.
Bedrooms: 2 double, 1 twin, 1 triple
Bathrooms: 4 en-suite

Bed & breakfast per night:

	£min	£max
Double	34.00	36.00

Half board per person:

	£min	£max
Daily	27.00	28.00
Weekly	175.00	

Evening meal 1830 (last orders 1700)
Parking for 4

ASHWATER
Devon
Map ref 1C2

Village 6 miles south-east of Holsworthy, with a pleasant village green dominated by its church.

Blagdon Manor Country Hotel

Ashwater EX21 5DF
☎ (01409) 211224
Fax (01409) 211634
Logis of Great Britain

17th C manor house, nestling in 8 acres with superb views of rural Devon. Central for exploring Devon and Cornwall. Country house party atmosphere, fine wine and exquisite food. Warm and cosy with open log fires.
Bedrooms: 5 double, 2 twin
Bathrooms: 7 en-suite

Bed & breakfast per night:

	£min	£max
Single	38.00	45.00
Double	76.00	90.00

Half board per person:

	£min	£max
Daily	55.00	62.00
Weekly	350.00	406.00

Evening meal 2000 (last orders 2000)
Parking for 8
Cards accepted: Access, Visa, Amex, Switch/Delta

WEST COUNTRY

AVEBURY
Wiltshire
Map ref 2B2

Set in a landscape of earthworks and megalithic standing stones, Avebury has a fine church and an Elizabethan manor. Remains from excavations may be seen in the museum. The area abounds in important prehistoric sites, among them Silbury Hill. Stonehenge stands about 20 miles due south.

New Inn
Listed APPROVED

Winterbourne Monkton, Swindon SN4 9NW
☎ (01672) 539240
Small and friendly country pub only 1 mile from Avebury. Good, central touring position.
Bedrooms: 2 double, 3 twin
Bathrooms: 5 en-suite
Bed & breakfast

per night:	£min	£max
Double	35.00	40.00

Lunch available
Evening meal 1830 (last orders 2130)
Parking for 20
Cards accepted: Access, Visa, Switch/Delta

BADMINTON
South Gloucestershire
Map ref 2B2

Small village close to Badminton House, a 17th to 18th C Palladian mansion which has been the seat of the Dukes of Beaufort for centuries. The 3-day Badminton Horse Trials are held in the Great Park every May.

Bodkin House Hotel ♠
COMMENDED

A46, Bath to Stroud Road, Badminton GL9 1AF
☎ Didmarton (01454) 238310
Fax (01454) 238422
Ⓒ Logis of Great Britain

Ideal for Bath and Cotswolds. Beautifully restored 17th C Cotswold coaching inn, providing large, well-appointed en-suite bedrooms. Renowned for its good food.

Bedrooms: 6 double, 2 twin
Bathrooms: 7 en-suite, 1 private
Bed & breakfast

per night:	£min	£max
Single	45.00	49.00
Double	55.00	70.00

Half board per

person:	£min	£max
Daily	40.00	57.00
Weekly	238.00	280.00

Lunch available
Evening meal 1900 (last orders 2130)
Parking for 30
Cards accepted: Access, Visa, Diners, Amex, Switch/Delta

BARNSTAPLE
Devon
Map ref 1C1

At the head of the Taw Estuary, once a ship-building and textile town, now an agricultural centre with attractive period buildings, a modern civic centre and leisure centre. Attractions include Queen Anne's Walk, a charming colonnaded arcade and Pannier Market.
Tourist Information Centre ☎ (01271) 388583 or 388584

Barnstaple Hotel ♠
COMMENDED

Braunton Road, Barnstaple EX31 1LE
☎ (01271) 76221
Fax (01271) 24101
The Barnstaple has undergone extensive refurbishment and now boasts a business centre and a health club with heated outdoor and indoor pools.
Bedrooms: 22 double, 32 twin, 3 triple
Suite available
Bathrooms: 57 en-suite
Bed & breakfast

per night:	£min	£max
Single	40.00	57.00
Double	55.00	77.00

Half board per

person:	£min	£max
Daily	42.50	72.00
Weekly	321.50	468.00

Lunch available
Evening meal 1900 (last orders 2130)
Parking for 200
Cards accepted: Access, Visa, Diners, Amex, Switch/Delta

Cedars Lodge Inn
COMMENDED

Bickington Road, Barnstaple EX31 2HP
☎ (01271) 71784
Fax (01271) 25733
Country house with lodges in 3 acres. All en-suite, satellite TV. Pub and restaurant. Just off North Devon link road.
Bedrooms: 10 double, 12 twin, 6 family rooms
Bathrooms: 28 en-suite
Bed & breakfast

per night:	£min	£max
Single	36.00	46.00
Double	56.00	66.00

Lunch available
Evening meal 1830 (last orders 2200)
Parking for 120
Cards accepted: Access, Visa, Amex, Switch/Delta

Downrew House Hotel ♠
COMMENDED

Bishop's Tawton, Barnstaple EX32 0DY
☎ (01271) 42497
Fax (01271) 446673
Queen Anne country house in glorious setting. English and French cuisine, own golf, heated pool, tennis. Ideal for coast and countryside.
Bedrooms: 5 double, 5 twin, 2 triple
Bathrooms: 12 en-suite, 1 public
Bed & breakfast

per night:	£min	£max
Single	39.50	48.50
Double	63.00	81.00

Half board per

person:	£min	£max
Daily	49.00	58.00
Weekly	280.00	329.00

Lunch available
Evening meal 1900 (last orders 2130)
Parking for 20
Open February–December
Cards accepted: Access, Visa, Amex

The Park Hotel ♠
COMMENDED

Taw Vale, Barnstaple EX32 8NJ
☎ (01271) 72166
Fax (01271) 23157
Overlooking parkland and River Taw, a short walk to town centre. Leisure facilities available at sister hotel, the Barnstaple Hotel.
Bedrooms: 7 single, 16 double, 19 twin

Continued ▶

WEST COUNTRY

BARNSTAPLE
Continued

Bathrooms: 42 en-suite
Bed & breakfast per night:

	£min	£max
Single	35.00	52.00
Double	50.00	72.00

Half board per person:

	£min	£max
Daily	40.00	67.00
Weekly	304.00	453.00

Lunch available
Evening meal 1900 (last orders 2130)
Parking for 90
Cards accepted: Access, Visa, Diners, Amex, Switch/Delta

Royal and Fortescue Hotel
HIGHLY COMMENDED

Boutport Street, Barnstaple EX31 1HG
☎ (01271) 42289
Fax (01271) 42289
Traditional market town hotel centrally located. Extensive refurbishments have retained the hotel's coaching inn charm while adding fine modern facilities.
Bedrooms: 4 single, 18 double, 20 twin, 5 triple
Bathrooms: 47 en-suite

Bed & breakfast per night:

	£min	£max
Single	38.00	55.00
Double	53.00	75.00

Half board per person:

	£min	£max
Daily	41.50	70.00
Weekly	314.50	454.00

Lunch available
Evening meal 1900 (last orders 2100)
Parking for 55
Cards accepted: Access, Visa, Diners, Amex, Switch/Delta

Yeo Dale Hotel
COMMENDED

Pilton Bridge, Barnstaple EX31 1PG
☎ (01271) 42954
Fax (01271) 42954
Family-run hotel located minutes from town centre and overlooking park. Ideal touring base for North Devon.
Bedrooms: 3 single, 1 double, 3 twin, 2 triple, 1 family room
Bathrooms: 6 en-suite, 2 public

Bed & breakfast per night:

	£min	£max
Single	20.00	26.00
Double	38.00	48.00

Half board per person:

	£min	£max
Daily	30.50	36.50
Weekly	213.50	255.50

Evening meal 1900 (last orders 1930)
Cards accepted: Access, Visa, Diners, Amex

BATH
Bath & North East Somerset
Map ref 2B2

Georgian spa city beside the River Avon. Important Roman site with impressive reconstructed baths, uncovered in 19th C. Bath Abbey built on site of monastery where first king of England was crowned (AD 973). Fine architecture in mellow local stone. Pump Room and museums.
Tourist Information Centre ☎ (01225) 462831

Apsley House Hotel
HIGHLY COMMENDED

141 Newbridge Hill, Bath BA1 3PT
☎ (01225) 336966
Fax (01225) 425462
Elegant William IV period house approximately 1 mile from the town centre. Beautifully furnished. Caring personal service and comfort.
Bedrooms: 5 double, 2 twin, 1 triple
Bathrooms: 8 en-suite

Bed & breakfast per night:

	£min	£max
Single	35.00	55.00
Double	55.00	85.00

Evening meal 1930 (last orders 2100)
Parking for 10
Cards accepted: Access, Visa, Amex

Ashley Villa Hotel

26 Newbridge Road, Bath BA1 3JZ
☎ (01225) 421683 & 428887
Fax (01225) 313604
Comfortably furnished licensed hotel with relaxing informal atmosphere, close to city centre. All rooms en-suite. Swimming pool. Car park.
Bedrooms: 2 single, 7 double, 2 twin, 3 triple
Bathrooms: 14 en-suite

Bed & breakfast per night:

	£min	£max
Single	45.00	49.00
Double	49.00	69.00

Evening meal 1830 (last orders 1930)
Parking for 10
Cards accepted: Access, Visa, Amex, Switch/Delta

AT-A-GLANCE SYMBOLS

Symbols at the end of each accommodation entry give useful information about services and facilities. A key to symbols can be found inside the back cover flap.

Keep this open for easy reference.

WEST COUNTRY

The Bath Spa Hotel ⋒
👑👑👑👑👑 DE LUXE
Sydney Road, Bath BA2 6JF
☎ (01225) 444424
Fax (01225) 444006
Ⓡ Utell International
Former Georgian mansion, set in 7 acres of landscaped gardens, 10 minutes' walk from the centre of Bath. Exceptional comfort is combined with attentive service and friendly informality. Rates shown below based on a minimum 2-night stay.
Bedrooms: 7 single, 45 double, 46 twin
Suites available
Bathrooms: 98 en-suite

Bed & breakfast per night:	£min	£max
Single	79.00	109.00
Double	158.00	198.00

Half board per person:	£min	£max
Daily	99.00	129.00
Weekly	554.00	722.00

Lunch available
Evening meal 1830 (last orders 2200)
Parking for 156
Cards accepted: Access, Visa, Diners, Amex, Switch/Delta

The Bath Tasburgh Hotel ⋒
👑👑 HIGHLY COMMENDED
Warminster Road, Bath BA2 6SH
☎ (01225) 425096
Fax (01225) 463842
Victorian mansion in 2 acres of beautiful, secluded gardens. Magnificent views, convenient for city centre. Individually furnished en-suite bedrooms, including four-posters. Warm hospitality. Parking.
Bedrooms: 1 single, 7 double, 2 twin, 3 triple, 3 family rooms
Bathrooms: 12 en-suite, 1 public

Bed & breakfast per night:	£min	£max
Single	39.00	56.00
Double	56.00	74.00

Parking for 15
Cards accepted: Access, Visa, Diners, Amex

Brompton House ⋒
👑👑 HIGHLY COMMENDED
Saint Johns Road, Bath BA2 6PT
☎ (01225) 420972
Fax (01225) 420505

Charming Georgian rectory in beautiful secluded gardens. 6-7 minutes' level walk to city centre. Car park. No smoking.
Bedrooms: 2 single, 9 double, 5 twin, 2 family rooms
Bathrooms: 18 en-suite

Bed & breakfast per night:	£min	£max
Single	32.00	50.00
Double	55.00	78.00

Parking for 18
Cards accepted: Access, Visa, Amex, Switch/Delta

Carfax Hotel ⋒
👑👑👑 COMMENDED
Great Pulteney Street, Bath BA2 4BS
☎ (01225) 462089
Fax (01225) 443257
In a famous Georgian street, surrounded by beautiful Bath hills. The rear of Carfax overlooks Henrietta Park. A well maintained, listed building.
Bedrooms: 13 single, 12 double, 10 twin, 3 triple
Bathrooms: 33 en-suite, 2 public

Bed & breakfast per night:	£min	£max
Single	28.00	48.50
Double	50.00	75.00

Half board per person:	£min	£max
Daily	33.00	45.50
Weekly	192.50	275.00

Evening meal 1830 (last orders 1930)
Parking for 17
Cards accepted: Access, Visa, Amex, Switch/Delta

9 Charlotte Street
Listed APPROVED
Bath BA1 2NE
☎ (01225) 424193

Grade II listed Georgian house, 3 minutes from city centre, with public car park at rear. All rooms have hot and cold water, colour TV, tea and coffee-making facilities.
Bedrooms: 2 double, 1 twin, 1 triple, 1 family room
Bathrooms: 2 public

Bed & breakfast per night:	£min	£max
Double	30.00	33.00

Chesterfield Hotel ⋒
👑👑 COMMENDED
11 Great Pulteney Street, Bath BA2 4BR
☎ (01225) 460953
Fax (01225) 448770

Centrally situated Grade I listed Georgian building. Family-run hotel with individually decorated en-suite rooms at reasonable B & B rates. Garage parking by arrangement.
Bedrooms: 4 single, 12 double, 2 twin, 2 triple
Bathrooms: 20 en-suite, 1 public

Bed & breakfast per night:	£min	£max
Single	35.00	45.00
Double	50.00	75.00

Parking for 14
Cards accepted: Access, Visa, Diners, Amex

Combe Grove Manor Hotel and Country Club ⋒
👑👑👑👑 HIGHLY COMMENDED
Brassknocker Hill, Monkton Combe, Bath BA2 7HS
☎ (01225) 834644
Fax (01225) 834961
Ⓡ Grand Heritage

Beautiful 18th C manor house and more recently built garden lodge. 2 miles from centre of Bath and with excellent sports facilities.
Bedrooms: 27 double, 11 twin, 2 triple
Suites available
Bathrooms: 40 en-suite

Continued ▶

WEST COUNTRY

BATH
Continued

Bed & breakfast per night:	£min	£max
Single	78.00	98.00
Double	98.00	265.00

Half board per person:	£min	£max
Daily	65.00	195.00
Weekly	312.00	

Lunch available
Evening meal 1900 (last orders 2130)
Parking for 200
Cards accepted: Access, Visa, Diners, Amex

Dukes Hotel
COMMENDED

Great Pulteney Street, Bath
BA2 4DN
☎ (01225) 463512
Fax (01225) 483733
Ⓖ Logis of Great Britain/The Independents

Elegantly refurbished, family-run Grade 1 Georgian town-house hotel, in city centre. Restaurant offers finest local produce and reasonably priced wines carefully selected by a Master of Wine.
Bedrooms: 4 single, 11 double, 4 twin, 4 triple
Bathrooms: 23 en-suite

Bed & breakfast per night:	£min	£max
Single	55.00	75.00
Double	65.00	95.00

Half board per person:	£min	£max
Daily	45.00	60.00

Evening meal 1845 (last orders 2030)
Cards accepted: Access, Visa, Diners, Amex, Switch/Delta

14 Dunsford Place

Bathwick Hill, Bath BA2 6HF
☎ (01225) 464134
Interesting and appealing establishment with a variety of collections from owner's travels. Easy access to the city centre. Non-smokers only, please.
Bedrooms: 1 double, 1 twin
Bathrooms: 2 private

Bed & breakfast per night:	£min	£max
Double	38.00	40.00

Open March–November

Edgar Hotel

64 Great Pulteney Street, Bath
BA2 4DN
☎ (01225) 420619
Georgian town house hotel, close to city centre and Roman Baths. Privately run. All rooms with en-suite facilities.
Bedrooms: 2 single, 9 double, 4 twin, 1 triple
Bathrooms: 16 en-suite

Bed & breakfast per night:	£min	£max
Single	25.00	35.00
Double	35.00	55.00

Cards accepted: Access, Visa

Forres Guest House

172 Newbridge Road, Lower Weston, Bath BA1 3LE
☎ (01225) 427698
Edwardian family guesthouse with helpful hosts, who are ex-teachers and love Bath. River Avon and Cotswold Way close by. Traditional and vegetarian breakfasts. Colour TV and beverages in all rooms.
Bedrooms: 3 double, 2 triple
Bathrooms: 4 en-suite, 1 private

Bed & breakfast per night:	£min	£max
Double	35.00	45.00

Parking for 5
Open April–October

Gainsborough Hotel

Weston Lane, Bath BA1 4AB
☎ (01225) 311380
Fax (01225) 447411
Ⓖ The Independents

Spacious and comfortable country house hotel in own lovely grounds near the botanical gardens, and within easy walking distance of the city. High ground, nice views, own large car park. 5-course breakfast, friendly staff, warm welcome.
Bedrooms: 2 single, 6 double, 6 twin, 1 triple, 1 family room
Bathrooms: 16 en-suite

Bed & breakfast per night:	£min	£max
Single	28.00	40.00
Double	48.00	68.00

Evening meal 1900 (last orders 2000)
Parking for 18
Cards accepted: Access, Visa, Amex

Glen View
COMMENDED

162 Newbridge Road, Bath BA1 3LE
☎ (01225) 421376
Fax (01225) 421376

Sunny, south-facing home, ideally situated for exploring Bath. Providing a high standard of traditional hospitality. Private parking, non-smoking, brochure available
Bedrooms: 1 double, 1 twin
Bathrooms: 2 en-suite

Bed & breakfast per night:	£min	£max
Single	25.00	35.00
Double	40.00	55.00

Parking for 4

Haringtons Hotel

8-10 Queen Street, Bath BA1 1HE
☎ (01225) 461728 & 445883
Fax (01225) 444804
Enjoy warm hospitality, good food and wine in charming hotel in picturesque cobbled street in the very heart of Bath.
Bedrooms: 7 double, 2 twin, 1 triple, 2 family rooms
Bathrooms: 11 en-suite, 2 public

Bed & breakfast per night:	£min	£max
Single	40.00	55.00
Double	50.00	70.00

Half board per person:	£min	£max
Daily	40.00	50.00
Weekly	280.00	350.00

WEST COUNTRY

Evening meal 1800 (last orders 2100)
Cards accepted: Access, Visa, Diners, Amex, Switch/Delta

Haute Combe Hotel
👑👑 COMMENDED
174/176 Newbridge Road, Bath BA1 3LE
☎ (01225) 420061 & 339064
Fax (01225) 420061
Fully-equipped en-suite rooms in comfortable, period surroundings. Easy access to city attractions. Special off-season rates. Telephone for brochure.
Bedrooms: 2 single, 3 double, 2 twin, 3 triple, 2 family rooms
Bathrooms: 11 en-suite, 1 private
Bed & breakfast
per night: £min £max
Single 42.00 49.00
Double 49.00 69.00
Evening meal 1900 (last orders 1800)
Parking for 12
Cards accepted: Access, Visa, Diners, Amex, Switch/Delta

Henrietta Hotel
👑👑
32 Henrietta Street, Bath BA2 6LR
☎ (01225) 447779
Fax (01225) 466916
Privately-run Georgian town house hotel, close to city centre and Roman Baths. All rooms with en-suite facilities.
Bedrooms: 7 double, 2 twin, 1 triple
Bathrooms: 10 en-suite
Bed & breakfast
per night: £min £max
Single 25.00 35.00
Double 35.00 55.00
Cards accepted: Access, Visa

Holly Lodge ♠
👑👑 DE LUXE
8 Upper Oldfield Park, Bath BA2 3JZ
☎ (01225) 424042
Fax (01225) 481138
Elegant Victorian house set in its own grounds, enjoying magnificent views of the city.
Bedrooms: 1 single, 4 double, 2 twin
Bathrooms: 7 en-suite
Bed & breakfast
per night: £min £max
Single 48.00 55.00
Double 75.00 85.00

Parking for 8
Cards accepted: Access, Visa, Diners, Amex

Kennard Hotel ♠
👑👑 COMMENDED
11 Henrietta Street, Bath BA2 6LL
☎ (01225) 310472
Fax (01225) 460054
Georgian town house hotel of charm and character in a quiet street. A few minutes' level walk to the abbey and Roman Baths.
Bedrooms: 2 single, 9 double, 1 twin, 1 family room
Bathrooms: 11 en-suite, 1 public
Bed & breakfast
per night: £min £max
Single 35.00 38.00
Double 58.00 68.00
Cards accepted: Access, Visa, Diners, Amex, Switch/Delta

Laura Place Hotel ♠
👑👑 COMMENDED
3 Laura Place, Great Pulteney Street, Bath BA2 4BH
☎ (01225) 463815
Fax (01225) 310222
18th C town house, centrally located in Georgian square. 2 minutes from Roman Baths, Pump Rooms and abbey.
Bedrooms: 5 double, 2 twin, 1 family room
Suite available
Bathrooms: 7 en-suite, 1 private
Bed & breakfast
per night: £min £max
Single 52.00
Double 66.00 86.00
Parking for 10
Open March–December
Cards accepted: Access, Visa, Amex

Leighton House ♠
139 Wells Road, Bath BA2 3AL
☎ (01225) 314769
Fax (01225) 443079

Enjoy a haven of friendliness in this elegant and spacious Victorian guesthouse with own car park, 10 minutes' walk from city centre.
Bedrooms: 3 double, 4 twin, 1 family room

Bathrooms: 8 en-suite
Bed & breakfast
per night: £min £max
Single 45.00 50.00
Double 62.00 68.00
Parking for 8
Cards accepted: Access, Visa, Switch/Delta

The Manor House
👑👑 COMMENDED
Mill Lane, Monkton Combe, Bath BA2 7HD
☎ (01225) 723128
Fax (01225) 723128

Restful, rambling 16th C manor beside mill stream in wooded valley designated as an Area of Outstanding Natural Beauty, just 2 miles south of city. Inglenook fires, Victorian conservatory, spacious bedrooms. Fine breakfasts served until noon.
Bedrooms: 2 double, 1 family room
Bathrooms: 2 en-suite, 1 private, 1 public
Bed & breakfast
per night: £min £max
Single 25.00 25.00
Double 45.00 45.00
Parking for 6

Old Malt House Hotel ♠
👑👑👑 COMMENDED
Radford, Timsbury, Bath BA3 1QF
☎ Timsbury (01761) 470106
Fax (01761) 472726
Ⓖ Minotel/Logis of Great Britain

Family-run hotel and restaurant, in lovely countryside 6 miles south-west of Bath. Tastefully converted and furnished, including antiques. Ideal for touring Bath, Wells and Mendip Hills.
Bedrooms: 1 single, 4 double, 3 twin, 2 triple
Bathrooms: 10 en-suite
Continued ▶

381

WEST COUNTRY

BATH
Continued

Bed & breakfast per night:	£min	£max
Single	32.50	39.00
Double	55.00	68.00

Half board per person:	£min	£max
Daily	49.00	55.50
Weekly	281.75	

Lunch available
Evening meal 1900 (last orders 2030)
Parking for 26
Cards accepted: Access, Visa, Diners, Amex

The Old School House
HIGHLY COMMENDED
Church Street, Bathford, Bath BA1 7RR
☎ (01225) 859593
Fax (01225) 859590

Pretty Victorian schoolhouse of Bath stone in peaceful conservation area overlooking Avon Valley. 3 miles to Bath centre. Country house ambience with antique furniture and winter log fires. Ground floor en-suite rooms. Licensed, non-smoking.
Bedrooms: 3 double, 1 twin
Bathrooms: 4 en-suite

Bed & breakfast per night:	£min	£max
Single	45.00	60.00
Double	65.00	70.00

Evening meal 1900 (last orders 2000)
Parking for 6
Cards accepted: Access, Visa

The Redcar Hotel
27-29 Henrietta Street, Bath BA2 6LR
☎ (01225) 469151
Fax (01225) 461424
Utell International

Please check prices and other details at the time of booking.

In quiet Georgian terrace a few minutes' walk from Bath city centre and with easy access to all tourist attractions.
Bedrooms: 6 single, 19 double, 6 twin
Bathrooms: 22 en-suite, 1 public, 4 private showers

Bed & breakfast per night:	£min	£max
Single	78.75	88.75
Double	97.50	107.50

Half board per person:	£min	£max
Daily	65.25	75.25
Weekly	371.00	441.00

Lunch available
Evening meal 1830 (last orders 2200)
Parking for 16
Cards accepted: Access, Visa, Diners, Amex

Rosemary House
COMMENDED
63 Wellsway, Bear Flat, Bath BA2 4RT
☎ (01225) 425667
Elegant small Edwardian house, in elevated location close to city centre on A367 Exeter road. Wide choice of traditional or vegetarian breakfasts cooked to order.
Bedrooms: 3 double, 1 twin
Bathrooms: 3 en-suite, 1 public

Bed & breakfast per night:	£min	£max
Single	22.00	36.00
Double	32.00	52.00

Half board per person:	£min	£max
Daily	25.50	48.50
Weekly	160.00	310.00

Evening meal 1930 (last orders 1700)
Open February–December

The Royal Crescent Hotel
HIGHLY COMMENDED
16 Royal Crescent, Bath BA1 2LS
☎ (01225) 739955
Fax (01225) 339401
Queens Moat/Utell International

Elegant Georgian townhouse in the heart of Bath. Individually designed bedrooms and suites. Beautiful gardens, fine cuisine.
Bedrooms: 2 single, 19 double, 11 twin, 14 triple
Suites available
Bathrooms: 46 en-suite

Bed & breakfast per night:	£min	£max
Single	98.00	105.00
Double	140.00	225.00

Lunch available
Evening meal 1900 (last orders 2130)
Parking for 52
Cards accepted: Access, Visa, Diners, Amex

Hotel Saint Clair
COMMENDED
1 Crescent Gardens, Upper Bristol Road, Bath BA1 2NA
☎ (01225) 425543 & Mobile 0378 834592
Fax (01225) 425543
Small family hotel 5 minutes' walk from city, 2 minutes from Royal Crescent. Large public car park 1 minute away. One-night stays welcome.
Bedrooms: 4 double, 2 twin, 2 triple, 1 family room
Bathrooms: 7 private, 1 public

Bed & breakfast per night:	£min	£max
Single	22.00	38.00
Double	32.00	50.00

Cards accepted: Access, Visa

Siena Hotel
HIGHLY COMMENDED
24/25 Pulteney Road, Bath BA2 4EZ
☎ (01225) 425495
Fax (01225) 469029

Fine Victorian building overlooking Bath Abbey, a few minutes' level walk from centre. Refurbished to provide spacious well-appointed en-suite rooms.
Bedrooms: 2 single, 6 double, 2 twin, 3 triple, 1 family room

WEST COUNTRY

Suite available
Bathrooms: 14 en-suite

Bed & breakfast
per night:	£min	£max
Single	42.50	57.50
Double	62.50	80.00

Half board per
person:	£min	£max
Daily	57.50	62.50

Evening meal 1900 (last orders 2030)
Parking for 14
Cards accepted: Access, Visa, Diners, Amex, Switch/Delta

Somerset House Hotel and Restaurant ⚜
HIGHLY COMMENDED
35 Bathwick Hill, Bath BA2 6LD
☎ (01225) 466451 & 463471
Fax (01225) 317188
CR Logis of Great Britain

A restaurant with rooms, this Regency house (1827) is owned and run by the Seymour family. Large garden. Good views of city. Non-smoking house. Lunch available on Sundays in winter.
Bedrooms: 1 single, 2 double, 2 twin, 5 triple
Bathrooms: 10 en-suite

Bed & breakfast
per night:	£min	£max
Single	26.00	32.00
Double	52.00	64.00

Half board per
person:	£min	£max
Daily	43.00	51.00
Weekly	275.00	282.00

Evening meal 1900 (last orders 1830)
Parking for 15
Cards accepted: Access, Visa, Amex

Villa Magdala Hotel ⚜
COMMENDED
Henrietta Road, Bath BA2 6LX
☎ (01225) 466329
Fax (01225) 483207

A key to symbols can be found inside the back cover flap.

Delightful Victorian town house hotel in a tranquil setting overlooking Henrietta Park. Only 5 minutes' level walk to Roman Baths. Parking in grounds.
Bedrooms: 2 single, 12 double, 1 twin, 2 triple
Bathrooms: 17 en-suite

Bed & breakfast
per night:	£min	£max
Single	40.00	49.00
Double	50.00	75.00

Parking for 20
Cards accepted: Access, Visa, Amex, Switch/Delta

Wellsgate
COMMENDED
131 Wells Road, Bath BA2 3AN
☎ (01225) 310688
Fax (01225) 310143

Peaceful Victorian elegance, large colourful gardens and panoramic views. Full or vegetarian breakfasts with home-made jams. Close to city centre. Private parking, non-smoking. Separate self-contained family accommodation.
Bedrooms: 2 double, 1 twin
Bathrooms: 3 en-suite

Bed & breakfast
per night:	£min	£max
Single	22.00	35.00
Double	42.00	52.00

Half board per
person:	£min	£max
Daily	30.00	45.00
Weekly	180.00	240.00

Evening meal from 1800
Parking for 9
Cards accepted: Access, Visa

Williams Guest House
Listed APPROVED
81 Wells Road, Bath BA2 3AN
☎ (01225) 312179
Long established non-smoking guesthouse, run from a Victorian town house with good views to the front. Four minutes' walk to the city, British Rail and National Express stations. Private parking available. A warm welcome awaits.
Bedrooms: 1 double, 2 triple
Bathrooms: 1 public, 1 private shower

Bed & breakfast
per night:	£min	£max
Single	20.00	25.00
Double	38.00	44.00

Parking for 5

BERRYNARBOR
Devon
Map ref 1C1

Picturesque, old-world village, winner of best-kept village awards, adjoining the lovely, wooded Sterridge Valley. On scenic route between Ilfracombe and Combe Martin.

Sandy Cove Hotel ⚜
APPROVED
Old Coast Road, Berrynarbor, Ilfracombe EX34 9SR
☎ Combe Martin (01271) 882243 & 882888
Fax (01271) 883830

In many acres of own grounds incorporating garden, cliffs, own beach and woods. Overlooks Combe Martin Bay, the beaches, sea and Exmoor. Outdoor/indoor pools, sauna, sunbed, gym equipment and whirlpool.
Bedrooms: 2 single, 16 double, 5 twin, 10 triple
Bathrooms: 33 en-suite

Bed & breakfast
per night:	£min	£max
Single	25.00	46.00
Double	50.00	92.00

Half board per
person:	£min	£max
Daily	45.00	69.00
Weekly	280.00	384.00

Lunch available
Evening meal 1900 (last orders 2130)
Parking for 70

The ⚜ symbol after an establishment name indicates that it is a Regional Tourist Board member.

WEST COUNTRY

BIDEFORD
Devon
Map ref 1C1

The home port of Sir Richard Grenville, the town with its 17th C merchants' houses flourished as a shipbuilding and cloth town. The bridge of 24 arches was built about 1460. Charles Kingsley stayed here while writing Westward Ho!
Tourist Information Centre ☎ (01237) 477676 or 421853

Durrant House Hotel
COMMENDED

Heywood Road, Northam, Bideford EX39 3QB
☎ (01237) 472361
Fax (01237) 421709
Consort

Family-managed hotel, now elegantly extended and refurbished. Outdoor swimming pool, sauna and solarium. M5 junction 27, A361 to Barnstaple, A39 to Bideford-Torridge Bridge, turn right at roundabout.
Bedrooms: 11 double, 92 twin, 12 triple
Suites available
Bathrooms: 115 en-suite

Bed & breakfast
per night: £min £max
Single 54.50 59.50
Double 85.00 89.00

Half board per
person: £min £max
Daily 45.00 49.00

Lunch available
Evening meal 1900 (last orders 2130)
Parking for 202
Cards accepted: Access, Visa, Diners, Amex, Switch/Delta

The Mount Hotel

Northdown Road, Bideford EX39 3LP
☎ (01237) 473748
Small, family-run hotel over 200 years old, with character and charm. Home cooking. Smoking in bar only. Peaceful garden. Short walk to town centre and quay. Ideal base for touring North Devon and "Tarka" country.

Bedrooms: 2 single, 3 double, 2 twin, 1 triple
Bathrooms: 7 en-suite, 1 private shower

Bed & breakfast
per night: £min £max
Single 21.00 26.00
Double 38.00 42.00

Half board per
person: £min £max
Daily 26.00 32.00
Weekly 175.00 210.00

Evening meal 1830 (last orders 1700)
Parking for 4
Cards accepted: Access, Visa

Riversford Hotel

Limers Lane, Bideford EX39 2RG
☎ (01237) 474239
Fax (01237) 421661
Peace and tranquillity, overlooking the River Torridge, delightful restaurant offering home-cooked foods (fresh fish a speciality). Individual en-suite bedrooms with character and river views. Four-poster bedrooms. Take A386 from Bideford to Northam then turn right into Limers Lane.
Bedrooms: 6 double, 7 twin, 1 family room
Bathrooms: 14 en-suite

Bed & breakfast
per night: £min £max
Single 37.00 40.00
Double 55.00 75.00

Half board per
person: £min £max
Daily 41.00 45.00
Weekly 242.00 271.00

Lunch available
Evening meal 1800 (last orders 2100)
Parking for 22
Cards accepted: Access, Visa, Diners, Amex, Switch/Delta

Royal Hotel
COMMENDED

Barnstaple Street, Bideford EX39 4AE
☎ (01237) 472005
Fax (01237) 478957
Overlooking historic Bideford Bridge and the River Torridge. Bideford's leading hotel with locally renowned restaurant and well-appointed lounges.
Bedrooms: 5 single, 10 double, 14 twin, 1 triple
Bathrooms: 30 en-suite, 3 public

Bed & breakfast
per night: £min £max
Single 35.00 52.00
Double 50.00 72.00

Half board per
person: £min £max
Daily 40.00 67.00
Weekly 304.00 453.00

Lunch available
Evening meal 1900 (last orders 2100)
Parking for 35
Cards accepted: Access, Visa, Diners, Amex, Switch/Delta

Sunset Hotel

Landcross, Bideford EX39 5JA
☎ (01237) 472962
Small, elegant country hotel in peaceful, picturesque location, specialising in home cooking. Delightful en-suite bedrooms with beverages and colour TV. Book with confidence. A non-smoking establishment.
Bedrooms: 1 double, 1 twin, 1 triple, 1 family room
Bathrooms: 4 en-suite

Bed & breakfast
per night: £min £max
Single 25.00 30.00
Double 46.00 47.50

Half board per
person: £min £max
Daily 36.00 38.00
Weekly 217.50 222.50

Evening meal 1900 (last orders 1900)
Parking for 10
Open February–November
Cards accepted: Access, Visa

Tanton's Hotel
COMMENDED

New Road, Bideford EX39 2HR
☎ (01237) 473317
Fax (01237) 473387
Overlooking the River Torridge, this Grade II listed building has been fully refurbished to maintain the hotel's 17th C character.
Bedrooms: 7 single, 16 double, 22 twin, 5 triple, 1 family room
Bathrooms: 41 en-suite, 10 private showers

Bed & breakfast
per night: £min £max
Single 30.00 37.50
Double 50.00 60.00

WEST COUNTRY

Lunch available
Evening meal 1800 (last orders 2200)
Cards accepted: Visa, Amex

Yeoldon Country House Hotel and Restaurant
HIGHLY COMMENDED
Durrant Lane, Northam, Bideford EX39 2RL
☎ (01237) 474400
Fax (01237) 476618
Logis of Great Britain

Victorian country house, now an impressive comfortable hotel. Quality English and continental cuisine and an interesting wine list. Hospitable owners, friendly and efficient staff.
Bedrooms: 6 double, 4 twin
Bathrooms: 10 en-suite
Bed & breakfast

per night:	£min	£max
Single	32.00	45.00
Double	60.00	82.00

Half board per

person:	£min	£max
Daily	46.00	60.00

Lunch available
Evening meal 1900 (last orders 2100)
Parking for 22
Cards accepted: Access, Visa, Diners, Amex, Switch/Delta

BIGBURY-ON-SEA
Devon
Map ref 1C3

Small resort on Bigbury Bay at the mouth of the River Avon. Wide sands, rugged cliffs. Burgh Island can be reached on foot at low tide.

The Henley Hotel
COMMENDED
Folly Hill, Bigbury-on-Sea, Kingsbridge TQ7 4AR
☎ Kingsbridge (01548) 810240
Fax (01548) 810020
Logis of Great Britain
Small, comfortable hotel on the edge of the sea. Spectacular views with private steps through garden down to lovely beach. A non-smoking establishment.

Bedrooms: 2 single, 4 double, 2 twin
Bathrooms: 8 en-suite
Bed & breakfast

per night:	£min	£max
Single	26.00	36.00
Double	49.00	62.00

Half board per

person:	£min	£max
Daily	40.00	47.00
Weekly	245.00	283.00

Lunch available
Evening meal 1900 (last orders 2130)
Parking for 10
Open April–October
Cards accepted: Access, Visa, Amex

BODMIN
Cornwall
Map ref 1B2

County town south-west of Bodmin Moor with a ruined priory and church dedicated to St Petroc. Nearby are Lanhydrock House and Pencarrow House.
Tourist Information Centre ☎ (01208) 76416

Mount Pleasant Moorland Hotel
HIGHLY COMMENDED
Mount Village, Bodmin PL30 4EX
☎ Cardinham (01208) 821342
Fax (01208) 821417
Small friendly hotel with bar, TV and sun lounges. Bedrooms en-suite with tea-making facilities and lovely country views. Rural location. Heated outdoor swimming pool.
Bedrooms: 1 single, 3 double, 1 twin, 2 triple
Bathrooms: 6 en-suite, 1 private
Bed & breakfast

per night:	£min	£max
Single	18.00	20.00
Double	36.00	40.00

Half board per

person:	£min	£max
Daily	26.50	28.50
Weekly	164.00	179.50

Evening meal 1900 (last orders 1700)
Parking for 10
Open April–September

Tredethy Country Hotel
Helland Bridge, Bodmin PL30 4QS
☎ St Mabyn (01208) 841262
Fax (01208) 841707
Logis of Great Britain

Gracious living with spacious rooms, log fires in winter and absolute peace and quiet in beautiful surroundings. From Bodmin take the Launceston road, then the Helland turn-off to Helland Bridge. Tredethy is up the hill over the bridge.
Bedrooms: 1 single, 7 double, 3 twin
Bathrooms: 11 en-suite
Bed & breakfast

per night:	£min	£max
Single	36.00	48.00
Double	60.00	80.00

Half board per

person:	£min	£max
Daily	42.00	56.00
Weekly	270.00	340.00

Lunch available
Evening meal 1900 (last orders 2030)
Parking for 60
Cards accepted: Access, Visa, Diners, Amex, Switch/Delta

BOSCASTLE
Cornwall
Map ref 1B2

Small, unspoilt village in Valency Valley. Active as a port until onset of railway era, its natural harbour affords rare shelter on this wild coast. Attractions include spectacular blow-hole, Celtic field strips, part-Norman church. Nearby St Juliot Church was restored by Thomas Hardy.

Tolcarne House Hotel and Restaurant
COMMENDED
Tintagel Road, Boscastle PL35 0AS
☎ (01840) 250654
Delightful late Victorian house in spacious grounds with lovely views to the dramatic Cornish coastline. All rooms en-suite. Restaurant and bar. Warm welcome.
Bedrooms: 1 single, 5 double, 2 twin
Bathrooms: 8 en-suite
Bed & breakfast

per night:	£min	£max
Single	25.00	30.00
Double	40.00	56.00

Half board per

person:	£min	£max
Daily	37.00	42.00
Weekly	195.00	270.00

Evening meal 1900 (last orders 2100)
Parking for 15

Continued ▶

385

WEST COUNTRY

BOSCASTLE
Continued

Open January–October and Christmas
Cards accepted: Access, Visa

The Wellington Hotel
COMMENDED

The Harbour, Boscastle PL35 0AQ
☎ (01840) 250202
Fax (01840) 250621
Logis of Great Britain

Historic 16th C coaching inn by Elizabethan harbour and National Trust countryside. Fine Anglo-French restaurant, specialising in regional cuisine and seafood. Freehouse with real ales, pub-grub, open fires and beams. 10 acres of private woodland walks. Pets welcome.
Bedrooms: 7 single, 11 double, 2 twin
Bathrooms: 16 en-suite, 2 public

Bed & breakfast per night:	£min	£max
Single	14.00	33.00
Double	44.00	62.00

Half board per person:	£min	£max
Daily	26.00	48.00
Weekly	171.00	305.00

Lunch available
Evening meal 1900 (last orders 2130)
Parking for 20
Cards accepted: Access, Visa, Diners, Amex, Switch/Delta

For ideas on places to visit refer to the introduction at the beginning of this section.

All accommodation in this guide has been graded, or is awaiting a grading, by a trained Tourist Board inspector.

BOVEY TRACEY
Devon
Map ref 1D2

Standing by the river just east of Dartmoor National Park, this old town has good moorland views. Its church, with a 14th C tower, holds one of Devon's finest medieval rood screens.

Edgemoor Hotel
HIGHLY COMMENDED

Haytor Road, Bovey Tracey TQ13 9LE
☎ (01626) 832466
Fax (01626) 834760
Country house hotel in peaceful wooded setting on edge of Dartmoor National Park. Good food. Elegance without pretension.
Bedrooms: 3 single, 9 double, 3 twin, 2 triple
Bathrooms: 17 en-suite

Bed & breakfast per night:	£min	£max
Single	42.50	48.50
Double	75.00	89.00

Half board per person:	£min	£max
Daily	47.50	60.00
Weekly	332.50	385.00

Lunch available
Evening meal 1930 (last orders 2100)
Parking for 50
Cards accepted: Access, Visa, Diners, Amex, Switch/Delta

BRADFORD-ON-AVON
Wiltshire
Map ref 2B2

Huddled beside the river, the buildings of this former cloth-weaving town reflect continuing prosperity from the Middle Ages. There is a tiny Anglo-Saxon church, part of a monastery. The part-14th C bridge carries a medieval chapel, later used as a gaol.
Tourist Information Centre ☎ (01225) 865797

Leigh Park Hotel
COMMENDED

Bradford-on-Avon BA15 2RA
☎ (01225) 864885
Fax (01225) 862315
Consort
Quiet and relaxing hotel set in 4 acres with a vineyard in its grounds. Personal attention from the owners. Facilities include a snooker room and croquet lawn.
Bedrooms: 5 single, 10 double, 2 twin, 5 triple
Bathrooms: 22 en-suite

Bed & breakfast per night:	£min	£max
Single	69.50	75.00
Double	76.00	90.00

Half board per person:	£min	£max
Daily	57.50	62.00
Weekly	350.00	434.00

Lunch available
Evening meal 1900 (last orders 2100)
Parking for 60
Cards accepted: Access, Visa, Diners, Amex

BRANSCOMBE
Devon
Map ref 1D2

Scattered village of unusual character. Houses of cob and thatch are sited irregularly on the steep wooded slopes of a combe, which widens towards the sea. Much of Branscombe Estate is National Trust property.

The Bulstone
COMMENDED

Higher Bulstone, Branscombe, Seaton EX12 3BL
☎ (01297) 680446
Fax (01297) 680446

Small, friendly, family-run establishment offering personal service. Catering especially for those with young children.
Bedrooms: 1 double, 1 twin, 10 family rooms
Bathrooms: 6 en-suite, 3 public

Bed & breakfast per night:	£min	£max
Double	42.00	72.00

Half board per person:	£min	£max
Daily	34.75	49.25

Evening meal 1945 (last orders 1845)
Parking for 20

WEST COUNTRY

BRATTON FLEMING
Devon
Map ref 1C1

On the western fringe of Exmoor with easy access to the magnificent beaches and coastline of North Devon.

Bracken House Country Hotel ⋔
HIGHLY COMMENDED

Bratton Fleming, Barnstaple EX31 4TG
☎ Brayford (01598) 710320

Former wealthy rectory set in 8 acres of garden, woodland, pond and paddocks on western edge of Exmoor. Extensive views.
Wheelchair access category 3
Bedrooms: 4 double, 4 twin
Bathrooms: 8 en-suite

Bed & breakfast per night:	£min	£max
Single	33.00	48.00
Double	56.00	66.00
Half board per person:	£min	£max
Daily	43.00	63.00
Weekly	259.00	294.00

Evening meal 1900 (last orders 1930)
Parking for 12
Open March–November
Cards accepted: Access, Visa

BRAUNTON
Devon
Map ref 1C1

Large village just north of the Taw Estuary and close to botanically-important dunelands, National Nature Reserve, at Braunton Burrows on Devon's north coast. Braunton Great Field shows rare example of ancient field-strip cultivation.
Tourist Information Centre ☎ (01271) 816400

Poyers Hotel ⋔
Listed APPROVED
Wrafton, Braunton, North Devon EX33 2DN
☎ (01271) 812149

16th C thatched longhouse with all en-suite accommodation. On edge of pretty village, 2 miles from coast.
Bedrooms: 2 single, 3 double, 3 twin, 1 triple
Bathrooms: 9 en-suite

Bed & breakfast per night:	£min	£max
Single	25.00	25.00
Double	44.00	44.00

Parking for 20
Cards accepted: Access, Visa, Amex

BRIDGWATER
Somerset
Map ref 1D1

Former medieval port on the River Parrett, now small industrial town with mostly 19th C or modern architecture. Georgian Castle Street leads to West Quay and site of 13th C castle razed to the ground by Cromwell. Birthplace of Cromwellian Admiral Robert Blake is now museum. Arts centre.

The Acorns ⋔
Listed
61 Taunton Road, Bridgwater TA6 3LP
☎ (01278) 445577
Large Edwardian house on the banks of the Bridgwater and Taunton Canal. Approximately 1 mile junction 24 of M5 motorway. Private car park.
Bedrooms: 2 single, 2 double, 6 twin, 2 triple, 1 family room
Bathrooms: 4 en-suite, 3 public

Bed & breakfast per night:	£min	£max
Single	15.00	17.50
Double	30.00	35.00

Parking for 12

Information on accommodation listed in this guide has been supplied by the proprietors. As changes may occur you are advised to check details at the time of booking.

Apple Tree Inn Hotel and Restaurant ⋔
COMMENDED
Keenthorne, Nether Stowey, Bridgwater TA5 1HZ
☎ Nether Stowey (01278) 733238
Fax (01278) 732693

Small family hotel easily located on the main A39, surrounded by rolling Quantock Hills. Large car park and gardens. Well known restaurant. Near Nether Stowey, some 8 miles west of Bridgwater.
Bedrooms: 2 single, 3 double, 2 twin, 2 triple, 3 family rooms
Bathrooms: 12 en-suite

Bed & breakfast per night:	£min	£max
Single	35.00	40.00
Double	40.00	50.00
Half board per person:	£min	£max
Daily	32.50	40.00
Weekly	200.00	260.00

Lunch available
Evening meal 1830 (last orders 2130)
Parking for 60
Cards accepted: Access, Visa, Amex

Friarn Court Hotel ⋔
COMMENDED
37 St Mary Street, Bridgwater TA6 3LX
☎ (01278) 452859
Fax (01278) 452988
Comfortable friendly hotel with restaurant and cosy bar, ideal base for business or pleasure. Double price is for special weekend breaks. Colour brochure.
Wheelchair access category 2
Bedrooms: 2 single, 7 double, 6 twin, 1 triple
Bathrooms: 16 en-suite

Bed & breakfast per night:	£min	£max
Single	39.90	59.90
Double	56.00	69.90

Lunch available
Evening meal 1930 (last orders 2130)
Parking for 14
Cards accepted: Access, Visa, Diners, Amex

WEST COUNTRY

BRIDGWATER
Continued

Quantock View House
APPROVED

Bridgwater Road, North Petherton, Bridgwater TA6 6PR
☎ North Petherton (01278) 663309 & Mobile 0860 137638
Fax (01278) 663309

Comfortable, family-run guesthouse in central Somerset. En-suite facilities available. Close to hills and coast. Only 200 yards from M5, junction 24.

Bedrooms: 1 double, 1 twin, 2 triple
Bathrooms: 3 en-suite, 1 private shower

Bed & breakfast
per night:	£min	£max
Single	16.00	17.50
Double	32.00	35.00

Half board per
person:	£min	£max
Daily	23.00	24.50
Weekly	140.00	150.00

Evening meal 1830 (last orders 1500)
Parking for 5
Cards accepted: Access, Visa

Walnut Tree Hotel
HIGHLY COMMENDED

North Petherton, Bridgwater TA6 6QA
☎ North Petherton (01278) 662255
Fax (01278) 663946
Best Western/The Independents

Set in the heart of Somerset. 18th C coaching inn on A38, 1 mile from M5 exit 24. A welcome stopover for businessmen and tourists.

Bedrooms: 2 single, 23 double, 8 twin
Suites available
Bathrooms: 33 en-suite

Bed & breakfast
per night:	£min	£max
Single	35.00	82.00
Double	50.00	96.00

Half board per
person:	£min	£max
Daily	49.00	

Lunch available
Evening meal 1900 (last orders 2200)
Parking for 74
Cards accepted: Access, Visa, Diners, Amex, Switch/Delta

BRIDPORT
Dorset
Map ref 2A3

Market town and chief producer of nets and ropes just inland of dramatic Dorset coast. Old, broad streets built for drying and twisting and long gardens for rope-walks. Grand arcaded Town Hall and Georgian buildings. Local history museum has Roman relics.
Tourist Information Centre ☎ (01308) 424901

Bridport Arms Hotel
APPROVED

West Bay, Bridport DT6 4EN
☎ (01308) 422994
Fax (01308) 425141

16th C thatched hotel on beach. Restaurant specialising in local sea food. 2 bars, real local ales and bar meals.

Bedrooms: 3 single, 4 double, 3 twin, 1 triple, 2 family rooms
Bathrooms: 6 en-suite, 3 public

Bed & breakfast
per night:	£min	£max
Single	21.50	29.50
Double	40.00	55.00

Half board per
person:	£min	£max
Daily	35.00	38.00
Weekly	200.00	250.00

Lunch available
Evening meal 1900 (last orders 2100)
Parking for 10
Cards accepted: Access, Visa, Switch/Delta

Britmead House
HIGHLY COMMENDED

West Bay Road, Bridport DT6 4EG
☎ (01308) 422941
Fax (01308) 422516

Elegant, spacious, tastefully decorated house. Lounge and dining room overlooking garden. West Bay Harbour/Coastal Path, 10 minutes' walk away. Renowned for hospitality, delicious meals and comfort.

Bedrooms: 4 double, 3 twin
Bathrooms: 6 en-suite, 1 private

Bed & breakfast
per night:	£min	£max
Single	25.00	35.00
Double	40.00	56.00

Half board per
person:	£min	£max
Daily	33.00	41.00
Weekly	203.00	238.00

Evening meal 1900 (last orders 1700)
Parking for 8
Cards accepted: Access, Visa, Diners, Amex

Bull Hotel
APPROVED

34 East Street, Bridport DT6 3LF
☎ (01308) 422878
Fax (01308) 422878

16th C town centre coaching inn. Bar snacks, a la carte restaurant, conferences, parties, own car park.

Bedrooms: 5 single, 8 double, 2 twin, 2 triple, 2 family rooms
Bathrooms: 12 en-suite, 3 public

Bed & breakfast
per night:	£min	£max
Single	24.50	36.00
Double	39.00	55.00

Half board per
person:	£min	£max
Daily	29.00	48.50
Weekly	180.00	297.50

Lunch available
Evening meal 1900 (last orders 2130)
Parking for 42
Cards accepted: Access, Visa, Diners, Amex

Haddon House Hotel
COMMENDED

West Bay, Bridport DT6 4EL
☎ (01308) 423626 & 425323
Fax (01308) 427348

Country house hotel, renowned for cuisine, situated yards from picturesque harbour, coast and golf course. Well situated for touring Dorset, Devon and Somerset.

Bedrooms: 2 single, 6 double, 3 twin, 2 triple
Bathrooms: 13 en-suite

WEST COUNTRY

Bed & breakfast per night:	£min	£max
Double	50.00	70.00

Lunch available
Evening meal 1900 (last orders 2100)
Parking for 44
Cards accepted: Access, Visa, Diners, Amex

Roundham House Hotel M
COMMENDED

Roundham Gardens, West Bay Road, Bridport DT6 4BD
☎ (01308) 422753
Fax (01308) 421145
CR Logis of Great Britain

Attractive stone house in elevated position, within own 1-acre gardens, giving superb country and sea views. Noted for good food (using home-grown and local produce) and wine.
Bedrooms: 1 single, 3 double, 2 twin, 2 family rooms
Bathrooms: 7 en-suite

Bed & breakfast per night:	£min	£max
Single	30.00	35.00
Double	50.00	64.00
Half board per person:	£min	£max
Daily	40.00	47.50
Weekly	270.00	350.00

Lunch available
Evening meal 1900 (last orders 2030)
Parking for 12
Open March–December
Cards accepted: Access, Visa, Amex

The symbol CR and a group name following an hotel address indicates that bookings can be made through a central reservations office. These offices are listed in the information pages at the back of this guide.

BRISTOL
Map ref 2A2

Famous for maritime links, historic harbour, Georgian terraces and Brunel's Clifton suspension bridge. Many attractions including SS Great Britain, Bristol Zoo, museums and art galleries and top name entertainments. Events include Balloon Fiesta and Regatta.
Tourist Information Centre ☎ (0117) 926 0767

Alcove Guest House
APPROVED

508/510 Fishponds Road, Bristol S16 3DT
☎ (0117) 965 3886 & 965 2436
Fax (0117) 965 3886
Clean and comfortable accommodation with personal service. Noted for its food.
Bedrooms: 1 single, 3 double, 3 twin, 1 triple, 1 family room
Bathrooms: 3 en-suite, 4 public

Bed & breakfast per night:	£min	£max
Single	25.00	28.00
Double	36.00	40.00

Parking for 9

Arches Hotel
COMMENDED

132 Cotham Brow, Cotham, Bristol BS6 6AE
☎ (0117) 9247398
Small friendly private hotel close to central stations and 100 yards from main A38. Option of traditional or vegetarian breakfast.
Bedrooms: 3 single, 4 double, 1 twin, 2 triple
Bathrooms: 2 en-suite, 2 public

Bed & breakfast per night:	£min	£max
Single	22.50	32.00
Double	39.50	45.50

Cards accepted: Access, Visa, Diners, Amex, Switch/Delta

Basca Guest House
COMMENDED

19 Broadway Road, Bishopston, Bristol BS7 8ES
☎ (0117) 9422182
Elegant Victorian home restored to high standard. Quiet residential area adjacent A38. 15 minutes' walk from centre. Friendly atmosphere. Home cooking.
Bedrooms: 2 single, 2 twin
Bathrooms: 1 public

Bed & breakfast per night:	£min	£max
Single	19.00	22.00
Double	36.00	38.00
Half board per person:	£min	£max
Daily	27.00	30.00

Evening meal 1830 (last orders 2000)
Parking for 4

Berkeley Square Hotel M
HIGHLY COMMENDED

15 Berkeley Square, Clifton, Bristol BS8 1HB
☎ (0117) 9254000
Fax (0117) 9252970
CR Utell International
Located in the tranquil Georgian square where "The House of Elliot" was filmed. Continental bar and noted restaurant offering a high standard of service.
Bedrooms: 25 single, 12 double, 6 twin
Bathrooms: 43 en-suite

Bed & breakfast per night:	£min	£max
Single	52.00	78.00
Double	72.00	106.00

Lunch available
Evening meal 1900 (last orders 2200)
Parking for 26
Cards accepted: Access, Visa, Diners, Amex, Switch/Delta

The Bowl Inn and Restaurant M
COMMENDED

16 Church Road, Lower Almondsbury, Bristol BS12 4DT
☎ Almondsbury (01454) 612757
Fax (01454) 619910
12th C building, once a priory, nestling on the edge of the Severn Vale. 3 minutes from M4/M5 interchange.
Bedrooms: 3 double, 5 twin
Bathrooms: 7 en-suite, 1 private

Bed & breakfast per night:	£min	£max
Single	25.00	56.50
Double	39.00	86.50
Half board per person:	£min	£max
Daily	41.50	68.50

Lunch available
Evening meal 1830 (last orders 2200)

Continued ▶

WEST COUNTRY

BRISTOL
Continued

Parking for 40
Cards accepted: Access, Visa, Diners, Amex, Switch/Delta

Clifton Hotel
St Paul's Road, Clifton, Bristol
BS8 1LX
☎ (0117) 9736882
Fax (0117) 9741082
Recently refurbished, this very popular hotel offers a high standard of accommodation and is home to the lively wine bar and restaurant - Racks.
Bedrooms: 27 single, 11 double, 20 twin, 2 triple
Bathrooms: 48 en-suite, 5 public, 1 private shower
Bed & breakfast

per night:	£min	£max
Single	40.00	58.00
Double	54.00	70.00

Lunch available
Evening meal 1830 (last orders 2200)
Parking for 32
Cards accepted: Access, Visa, Diners, Amex, Switch/Delta

Courtlands Hotel
COMMENDED
1 Redland Court Road, Redland, Bristol BS6 7EE
☎ (0117) 9424432
Fax (0117) 9232432

Comfortable, family-run town-house hotel. Located in a quiet residential area overlooking Redland Grove. Close to all the main attractions.
Bedrooms: 6 single, 10 double, 4 twin, 3 triple, 1 family room
Bathrooms: 24 en-suite
Bed & breakfast

per night:	£min	£max
Single	42.00	44.00
Double	52.00	54.00

Lunch available
Evening meal 1900 (last orders 2000)

Parking for 15
Cards accepted: Access, Visa

Forte Posthouse Bristol
COMMENDED
Filton Road, Hambrook, Bristol
BS16 1QX
☎ (0117) 9564242
Fax (0117) 9569735
Forte/Utell International
Set in 16 acres of quiet woodland on the outskirts of Bristol, 4 miles south-east of M4/M5 interchange. Conference and banqueting facilities. Business services available. Leisure club.
Bedrooms: 148 double, 46 twin
Suites available
Bathrooms: 194 en-suite
Bed & breakfast

per night:	£min	£max
Single	79.00	89.00

Lunch available
Evening meal 1900 (last orders 2200)
Parking for 400
Cards accepted: Access, Visa, Diners, Amex

Glenroy Hotel
COMMENDED
Victoria Square, Clifton, Bristol
BS8 4EW
☎ (0117) 9739058
Fax (0117) 9739058
Consort
Two large, detached, early Victorian houses, in one of Bristol's most attractive squares. Restaurant open Monday-Friday and for Sunday lunch. Restricted menu available on Saturday and Sunday evenings.
Bedrooms: 14 single, 14 double, 8 twin, 8 triple
Bathrooms: 44 en-suite
Bed & breakfast

per night:	£min	£max
Single	40.00	70.00
Double	48.00	80.00

Half board per

person:	£min	£max
Daily	50.00	80.00
Weekly	450.00	575.00

Evening meal 1830 (last orders 2130)
Parking for 16
Cards accepted: Access, Visa, Diners, Amex, Switch/Delta

Henbury Lodge Hotel
COMMENDED
Station Road, Henbury, Bristol
BS10 7QQ
☎ (0117) 9502615
Fax (0117) 9509532
One mile from junction 17 off M5, 15 minutes' drive from city centre. Local interest includes Blaise Castle and Blaise Hamlet. Various special diets catered for.
Bedrooms: 1 single, 12 double, 2 twin, 4 triple
Bathrooms: 19 en-suite, 1 public
Bed & breakfast

per night:	£min	£max
Single	36.00	68.00
Double	52.00	78.00

Lunch available
Evening meal 1900 (last orders 2130)
Parking for 24
Cards accepted: Access, Visa, Diners, Amex, Switch/Delta

Mayfair Hotel
5 Henleaze Road,
Westbury-on-Trym, Bristol BS9 4EX
☎ (0117) 9622008 & 9493924
Small hotel run by owners, situated close to the downs and within easy reach of both the city centre and motorway.
Bedrooms: 4 single, 2 double, 2 twin, 1 triple
Bathrooms: 3 en-suite, 2 public
Bed & breakfast

per night:	£min	£max
Single	22.00	32.00
Double	40.00	52.00

Parking for 9
Cards accepted: Access

Rodney Hotel
4 Rodney Place, Clifton, Bristol
BS8 4HY
☎ (0117) 9735422
Fax (0117) 9467095
Set in a Georgian terrace, with open fires and a delightful walled garden. Superb location in Clifton village, excellent restaurant.
Bedrooms: 14 single, 14 double, 3 twin
Bathrooms: 31 en-suite
Bed & breakfast

per night:	£min	£max
Single	42.00	56.00
Double	56.00	76.00

WEST COUNTRY

Lunch available
Evening meal 1900 (last orders 2130)
Cards accepted: Access, Visa, Diners, Amex, Switch/Delta

Rowan Lodge Hotel
APPROVED
41 Gloucester Road North, Filton Park, Bristol BS7 0SN
☎ (0117) 9312170
Fax (0117) 9753601
Small family-run hotel in residential area. On A38 with access to M4, M5 and M32 and to the city.
Bedrooms: 1 single, 1 double, 2 twin, 1 triple, 1 family room
Bathrooms: 1 en-suite, 1 private, 2 public

Bed & breakfast

per night:	£min	£max
Single	23.00	32.00
Double	36.00	42.00

Parking for 7
Cards accepted: Access, Visa

Swallow Royal Hotel
HIGHLY COMMENDED
College Green, Bristol BS1 5TA
☎ (0117) 9255100 & 9255200
Fax (0117) 9251515
Swallow
Enjoys a prime position in the centre of Bristol. Exceptionally well-appointed, with air-conditioning, award-winning food and a Roman-themed leisure club. Short break packages available.
Bedrooms: 16 single, 104 double, 108 twin, 14 triple
Suites available
Bathrooms: 242 en-suite

Bed & breakfast

per night:	£min	£max
Single	70.00	99.00
Double	95.00	125.00

Half board per

person:	£min	£max
Daily	89.00	123.00

Lunch available
Evening meal 1900 (last orders 2230)
Parking for 200
Cards accepted: Access, Visa, Diners, Amex, Switch/Delta

Thornbury House
COMMENDED
80 Chesterfield Road, St Andrews, Bristol BS6 5DR
☎ (0117) 9245654

Large Victorian house 1 mile from city centre, linked by frequent bus. Warm hospitality, en-suite rooms. 5 minutes from M32 and ideal for Cotswolds, West Country. Aromatherapy, Reflexology and Shiatsu available.
Bedrooms: 1 double, 1 twin
Bathrooms: 2 en-suite

Bed & breakfast

per night:	£min	£max
Single	22.00	25.00
Double	44.00	46.00

Parking for 2

The Town and Country Lodge
COMMENDED
A38 Bridgwater Road, Bristol BS13 8AG
☎ Long Ashton (01275) 392441
Fax (01275) 393362

Recently refurbished hotel in glorious rural surroundings halfway between city centre and Bristol Airport. Restaurant with extensive menu. Function and conference rooms.
Bedrooms: 10 single, 12 double, 10 twin, 4 triple
Suites available
Bathrooms: 36 en-suite

Bed & breakfast

per night:	£min	£max
Single	39.00	49.50
Double	54.00	64.50

Lunch available
Evening meal 1800 (last orders 2230)
Parking for 300
Cards accepted: Access, Visa, Amex, Switch/Delta

Washington Hotel
11-15 St Paul's Road, Bristol BS8 1LX
☎ (0117) 9733980
Fax (0117) 9741082
The Independents
Offering good value for money in Clifton. The hotel has its own charming breakfast room.
Bedrooms: 19 single, 10 double, 12 twin, 5 triple
Bathrooms: 35 en-suite, 5 public

Bed & breakfast

per night:	£min	£max
Single	40.00	47.00
Double	49.00	64.00

Parking for 20
Cards accepted: Access, Visa, Diners, Amex, Switch/Delta

Westbury Park Hotel
HIGHLY COMMENDED
37 Westbury Road, Bristol BS9 3AU
☎ (0117) 9620465
Fax (0117) 9628607
Friendly, family-run hotel on Durdham Downs, close to city centre and M5, junction 17.
Bedrooms: 1 single, 5 double, 2 twin
Bathrooms: 8 en-suite

Bed & breakfast

per night:	£min	£max
Single	28.00	39.00
Double	44.00	49.00

Parking for 5
Cards accepted: Access, Visa, Diners, Amex

BRIXHAM
Devon
Map ref 1D2

Famous for its trawling fleet in the 19th C, a steeply-built fishing port overlooking the harbour and fish market. A statue of William of Orange recalls his landing here before deposing James II. There is an aquarium and museum. Good cliff views and walks.
Tourist Information Centre ☎ (01803) 852861

Harbour Side Guest House
65 Berry Head Road, Brixham TQ5 9AA
☎ (01803) 858899
Overlooking the outer harbour and marina, opposite the lifeboat station and close to Breakwater Beach. Within walking distance of town.
Bedrooms: 2 single, 1 double, 1 twin, 1 triple
Bathrooms: 2 en-suite, 1 public

Bed & breakfast

per night:	£min	£max
Single	17.00	20.00
Double	30.00	36.00

WEST COUNTRY

BRIXHAM
Continued

Tor Haven Hotel
👑👑 COMMENDED
97 King Street, Brixham TQ5 9TH
☎ (01803) 882281
Small, comfortable, family hotel with superb views across Torbay. Close to the town, beach and breakwater, all within 400 yards.
Bedrooms: 2 single, 4 double, 1 twin, 1 triple, 1 family room
Bathrooms: 3 en-suite, 2 public

Bed & breakfast per night:	£min	£max
Single	17.00	19.00
Double	34.00	52.00

Parking for 5

Woodstock Guesthouse
👑👑 COMMENDED
4 Penpethy Road, Brixham TQ5 8NN
☎ (01803) 853844
Large modern detached house under personal supervision of owners, with homely atmosphere. Easy distance of harbourside.
Bedrooms: 4 double, 1 twin, 1 family room
Bathrooms: 2 public

Bed & breakfast per night:	£min	£max
Single	13.00	15.00
Double	26.00	30.00

Parking for 6

BUDE
Cornwall
Map ref 1C2

Resort on dramatic Atlantic coast. High cliffs give spectacular sea and inland views. Golf-course, cricket pitch, folly, surfing, coarse-fishing and boating. Mother-town Stratton was base of Royalist Sir Bevil Grenville.
Tourist Information Centre ☎ (01288) 354240

Atlantic House Hotel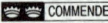
👑👑 COMMENDED
Summerleaze Crescent, Bude EX23 8HJ
☎ (01288) 352451
Superb location overlooking beach, downs and town. Renowned for good food and fine wines. Five-choice menu daily.
Bedrooms: 3 single, 9 double, 4 twin, 3 family rooms
Bathrooms: 12 en-suite, 3 public, 4 private showers

Bed & breakfast per night:	£min	£max
Single	20.00	22.50
Double	40.00	45.00

Half board per person:	£min	£max
Daily	33.00	35.50
Weekly	204.00	235.00

Lunch available
Evening meal 1830 (last orders 2000)
Parking for 10
Open March–November
Cards accepted: Access, Visa

Bude Haven Hotel
👑👑 COMMENDED
Flexbury Avenue, Bude EX23 8NS
☎ (01288) 352305
Edwardian family hotel with friendly, relaxing atmosphere in quiet area. Convenient for beach, town and golf-course. Comfort, hospitality and good food assured.
Bedrooms: 2 single, 5 double, 4 twin, 1 triple
Bathrooms: 12 en-suite

Bed & breakfast per night:	£min	£max
Single	22.00	27.00
Double	36.00	50.00

Half board per person:	£min	£max
Daily	30.00	37.00
Weekly	210.00	259.00

Evening meal 1830 (last orders 1900)
Parking for 8
Cards accepted: Access, Visa, Amex

Camelot Hotel
👑👑👑 COMMENDED
Downs View, Bude EX23 8RE
☎ (01288) 352361
Fax (01288) 355470

Comfortable family-run hotel situated close to the famous Crooklets Beach and overlooking a championship golf-course.
Bedrooms: 2 single, 6 double, 12 twin, 1 triple
Bathrooms: 21 en-suite

Bed & breakfast per night:	£min	£max
Single	22.00	26.00
Double	44.00	52.00

Half board per person:	£min	£max
Daily	33.00	39.00
Weekly	199.00	239.00

Evening meal 1900 (last orders 2030)
Parking for 21
Open February–November
Cards accepted: Access, Visa

Cliff Hotel
👑👑👑 HIGHLY COMMENDED
Crooklets Beach, Bude EX23 8NG
☎ (01288) 353110
Fax (01288) 353110

Indoor pool and spa, solarium, putting, tennis court, bowling green, 5 acres next to National Trust cliffs, 200 yards from the beach. Chef/proprietor.
Bedrooms: 2 single, 3 double, 1 twin, 9 triple
Bathrooms: 15 en-suite

Bed & breakfast per night:	£min	£max
Single	25.00	30.00
Double	50.00	60.00

Half board per person:	£min	£max
Daily	30.00	38.00
Weekly	210.00	260.00

Lunch available
Evening meal 1830 (last orders 1930)
Parking for 15
Open April–September
Cards accepted: Access, Visa, Switch/Delta

The Falcon Hotel
👑👑👑 HIGHLY COMMENDED
Breakwater Road, Bude EX23 8SD
☎ (01288) 352005
Fax (01288) 356359

WEST COUNTRY

Character hotel in lovely position overlooking the Bude Canal. Close to the beaches and shops. Self-catering apartments also available.
Bedrooms: 4 single, 14 double, 5 twin
Suites available
Bathrooms: 23 en-suite
Bed & breakfast
per night:

	£min	£max
Single	32.50	35.00
Double	65.00	70.00

Half board per person:

	£min	£max
Daily	46.00	48.50
Weekly	276.00	291.00

Lunch available
Evening meal 1900 (last orders 2100)
Parking for 40
Cards accepted: Access, Visa, Diners, Amex, Switch/Delta

Maer Lodge Hotel
APPROVED
Maer Down Road, Crooklets Beach, Bude EX23 8NG
☎ (01288) 353306
Fax (01288) 353306
Minotel/Logis of Great Britain
In own grounds in semi-rural setting overlooking the seaward end of the golf-course, near Crooklets surfing beach.
Bedrooms: 1 single, 9 double, 3 twin, 4 triple, 1 family room
Bathrooms: 18 en-suite, 2 public
Bed & breakfast
per night:

	£min	£max
Single	28.00	33.00
Double	50.00	60.00

Half board per person:

	£min	£max
Daily	33.00	41.00
Weekly	196.00	231.00

Lunch available
Evening meal 1900 (last orders 2000)
Parking for 20
Cards accepted: Access, Visa, Diners, Amex, Switch/Delta

Meva-Gwin Hotel
COMMENDED
Upton, Bude EX23 0LY
☎ (01288) 352347
Fax (01288) 352347
On Marine Drive between Bude and Widemouth Bay. Coastal and rural views from all rooms, friendly atmosphere, traditional English cooking.
Bedrooms: 2 single, 4 double, 1 twin, 2 triple, 3 family rooms

Bathrooms: 11 en-suite, 1 public
Bed & breakfast
per night:

	£min	£max
Single	20.00	22.00
Double	40.00	44.00

Half board per person:

	£min	£max
Daily	28.95	30.95
Weekly	175.00	190.00

Lunch available
Evening meal 1830 (last orders 1830)
Parking for 44
Open April–September
Cards accepted: Access, Visa

Old Rectory
HIGHLY COMMENDED
Marhamchurch, Bude EX23 0ER
☎ (01288) 361379

Offering spacious, quality en-suite accommodation, 2 minutes to Atlantic Highway (A39). Spectacular unspoilt coastline. Plentiful home cooking. No smoking.
Bedrooms: 2 double, 1 twin
Bathrooms: 3 en-suite
Bed & breakfast
per night:

	£min	£max
Single	18.00	20.00
Double	32.00	40.00

Half board per person:

	£min	£max
Daily	26.00	30.00
Weekly	182.00	210.00

Evening meal 1830 (last orders 1830)

Stratton Gardens Hotel
COMMENDED
Cot Hill, Stratton, Bude EX23 9DN
☎ (01288) 352500
Fax (01288) 352500

Charming 16th C Grade II listed hotel personally run by resident proprietors. Lovely home-cooked food. Quiet location in conservation area.
Bedrooms: 3 double, 1 twin, 1 triple
Bathrooms: 5 en-suite, 1 public

Bed & breakfast
per night:

	£min	£max
Single	20.00	25.00
Double	40.00	50.00

Half board per person:

	£min	£max
Daily	29.00	34.00
Weekly	174.00	204.00

Lunch available
Evening meal 1930 (last orders 2030)
Parking for 12
Cards accepted: Access, Visa, Switch/Delta

BURNHAM-ON-SEA
Somerset
Map ref 1D1

Small Victorian resort famous for sunsets and sandy beaches, a few minutes from junction 22 of the M5. Ideal base for touring Somerset, Cheddar and Bath. Good sporting facilities, championship golf-course.
Tourist Information Centre ☎ (01278) 787852

Queens Hotel
COMMENDED
Pier Street, Burnham-on-Sea TA8 1BT
☎ (01278) 783045
Fax (01278) 781767
Delightfully situated on the seafront. Built in 1850 and completely renovated to a high standard, offering friendly personal service. Satellite TV in all rooms.
Bedrooms: 4 single, 5 double, 4 twin, 4 triple, 1 family room
Bathrooms: 18 en-suite, 2 public
Bed & breakfast
per night:

	£min	£max
Single	30.00	40.00
Double	48.00	60.00

Half board per person:

	£min	£max
Daily	42.50	50.00

Lunch available
Evening meal 1830 (last orders 2100)
Parking for 20
Cards accepted: Access, Visa

Half board prices are given per person, but in some cases these may be based on double/twin occupancy.

WEST COUNTRY

BURRINGTON
Devon
Map ref 1C2

Charming village overlooking the River Taw, with woods all around. The church has a Norman font and a very fine carved screen.

Northcote Manor Hotel
HIGHLY COMMENDED
Burrington, Umberleigh EX37 9LZ
☎ High Bickington (01769) 560501
Fax (01769) 560770
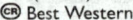 Best Western

Secluded Victorian manor, set in 18 acres of woodland, between Exmoor and Dartmoor. Excellent continental cuisine. Marriage licence. Off A377 at Portsmouth Arms (do not enter village).
Bedrooms: 10 double, 2 twin
Suite available
Bathrooms: 12 en-suite

Bed & breakfast per night:	£min	£max
Single	79.00	139.00
Double	109.00	169.00

Half board per person:	£min	£max
Daily	69.50	89.50
Weekly	486.50	626.50

Lunch available
Evening meal 1900 (last orders 2130)
Parking for 20
Open January, March–December
Cards accepted: Access, Visa, Diners, Amex, Switch/Delta

CARBIS BAY
Cornwall
Map ref 1B3

Overlooking St Ives Bay and with fine beaches.

Carbis Bay Hotel
COMMENDED
Carbis Bay, St Ives TR26 2NP
☎ Penzance (01736) 795311
Fax (01736) 797677

Perfectly situated almost on the sands of private beach. Ideal base for touring most parts of Cornwall.
Bedrooms: 3 single, 13 double, 6 twin, 4 triple, 7 family rooms
Bathrooms: 33 en-suite

Bed & breakfast per night:	£min	£max
Single	40.00	65.00
Double	50.00	90.00

Half board per person:	£min	£max
Daily	50.00	65.00
Weekly	295.00	395.00

Lunch available
Evening meal 1800 (last orders 2030)
Parking for 66
Open March–December
Cards accepted: Access, Visa, Diners, Amex, Switch/Delta

Hotel Rotorua
COMMENDED
Trencrom Lane, Carbis Bay, St Ives TR26 2TD
☎ Penzance (01736) 795419
Fax (01736) 795419
Modern private hotel in quiet wooded lane near many sporting activities and beaches.
Bedrooms: 1 single, 1 double, 1 twin, 6 triple, 4 family rooms
Bathrooms: 13 en-suite, 1 public

Bed & breakfast per night:	£min	£max
Single	18.00	26.00
Double	36.00	52.00

Half board per person:	£min	£max
Daily	25.00	33.00
Weekly	189.00	224.00

Lunch available
Evening meal 1900 (last orders 1730)
Parking for 10
Open April–October

Tregorran Hotel
APPROVED
Headland Road, Carbis Bay, St Ives TR26 2NU
☎ Penzance (01736) 795889
Mediterranean-style villa hotel in own grounds overlooking St Ives Bay, with panoramic sea views, safe beaches and tropical garden.
Bedrooms: 7 double, 2 twin, 1 triple, 6 family rooms
Bathrooms: 16 en-suite, 2 public

Bed & breakfast per night:	£min	£max
Single	18.00	35.00
Double	36.00	70.00

Half board per person:	£min	£max
Daily	27.00	44.00
Weekly	189.00	308.00

Evening meal 1830 (last orders 1900)
Parking for 25
Open April–September
Cards accepted: Access, Visa, Amex

CARLYON BAY
Cornwall
Map ref 1B3

Residential and retirement suburb near St Austell, with fine clifftop golf-course.

Carlyon Bay Hotel
HIGHLY COMMENDED
Sea Road, Carlyon Bay, St Austell PL25 3RD
☎ Par (01726) 812304
Fax (01726) 814938
High standard accommodation, complemented by extensive leisure facilites, including an 18-hole golf-course.
Bedrooms: 13 single, 16 double, 41 twin, 2 triple
Bathrooms: 72 en-suite, 1 public

Bed & breakfast per night:	£min	£max
Single	64.00	79.00
Double	122.00	182.00

Half board per person:	£min	£max
Daily	73.00	103.00
Weekly	479.50	721.00

Lunch available
Evening meal 1900 (last orders 2100)
Parking for 74
Cards accepted: Access, Visa, Diners, Amex, Switch/Delta

The National Grading and Classification Scheme is explained in full at the back of this guide.

WEST COUNTRY

CASTLE CARY
Somerset
Map ref 2B2

One of south Somerset's most attractive market towns, with a picturesque winding high street of golden stone and thatch, market-house and famous round 18th C lock-up.

George Hotel
COMMENDED
Market Place, Castle Cary BA7 7AH
☎ (01963) 350761
Fax (01963) 350035
The Independents

15th C thatched coaching inn with en-suite rooms, 2 bars and noted restaurant. Centrally located for many National Trust houses and gardens, Cheddar, Wells, Glastonbury and Bath.
Bedrooms: 4 single, 7 double, 3 twin, 1 family room
Bathrooms: 15 en-suite

Bed & breakfast per night:	£min	£max
Single	45.00	55.00
Double	70.00	85.00

Lunch available
Evening meal 1900 (last orders 2100)
Parking for 10
Cards accepted: Access, Visa, Amex, Switch/Delta

The Horse Pond Inn and Motel
COMMENDED
The Triangle, Castle Cary BA7 7BD
☎ (01963) 350318 & 351762/4
A 17th C coaching inn with its old stables converted to spacious motel units, within a few steps of the main building.
Bedrooms: 1 double, 2 twin, 3 triple
Suites available
Bathrooms: 3 en-suite, 3 private, 2 public

Bed & breakfast per night:	£min	£max
Single	32.00	35.00
Double	35.00	40.00

Half board per person:	£min	£max
Daily	43.00	46.00
Weekly	252.00	280.00

Lunch available
Evening meal 1900 (last orders 2100)
Parking for 24
Cards accepted: Access, Visa, Switch/Delta

CHAGFORD
Devon
Map ref 1C2

Handsome stone houses, some from the Middle Ages, grace this former stannary town on northern Dartmoor. It is a popular centre for walking expeditions and for tours of the antiquities on the rugged moor. There is a splendid 15th C granite church, said to be haunted by the poet Godolphin.

Easton Court Hotel
COMMENDED
Easton Cross, Chagford, Newton Abbot TQ13 8JL
☎ (01647) 433469
Fax (01647) 433469

Thatched 15th C hotel of great charm and character on the edge of Dartmoor, offering peace, comfort and good food.
Bedrooms: 6 double, 2 twin
Bathrooms: 8 en-suite

Bed & breakfast per night:	£min	£max
Single	40.00	45.00
Double	80.00	90.00

Half board per person:	£min	£max
Daily	58.00	65.00
Weekly	315.00	336.00

Evening meal 1930 (last orders 2030)
Parking for 16
Open February–December
Cards accepted: Access, Visa, Amex

Gidleigh Park
DE LUXE
Chagford TQ13 8HH
☎ (01647) 432367 & 432225
Fax (01647) 432574
Luxurious hotel and restaurant on the banks of the River Teign. Regarded by many as having the finest restaurant between Bath and Land's End.
Bedrooms: 1 double, 13 twin
Suites available
Bathrooms: 14 en-suite

Half board per person:	£min	£max
Daily	250.00	375.00

Lunch available
Evening meal 1900 (last orders 2100)
Parking for 25
Cards accepted: Access, Visa, Diners, Amex, Switch/Delta

The Mews
Listed HIGHLY COMMENDED
Meldon Hall, Chagford, Newton Abbot TQ13 8EJ
☎ (01647) 433466
Former coach house and stable block, converted in 1994, in grounds of Meldon Hall. Half a mile from centre of Chagford.
Bedrooms: 3 double
Bathrooms: 2 en-suite, 1 private

Bed & breakfast per night:	£min	£max
Single	16.50	19.00
Double	33.00	38.00

Half board per person:	£min	£max
Daily	26.50	29.00
Weekly	185.50	203.00

Lunch available
Evening meal 1800 (last orders 1930)
Parking for 3

Thornworthy House
COMMENDED
Chagford, Newton Abbot TQ13 8EY
☎ Moretonhampstead (01647) 433297
Fax (01647) 433297
Peaceful moorland setting for country lovers in search of real comfort and personal service. Stylish home cooking and fine wines.
Bedrooms: 1 single, 1 double, 1 twin
Bathrooms: 2 en-suite, 1 public

Bed & breakfast per night:	£min	£max
Single	24.00	30.00
Double	50.00	66.00

Half board per person:	£min	£max
Daily	35.00	41.00
Weekly	224.00	400.00

Continued ▶

WEST COUNTRY

CHAGFORD
Continued

Evening meal 2000 (last orders 2030)
Parking for 8

Throwleigh Manor
COMMENDED
Throwleigh, Near Chagford, Okehampton EX20 2JF
☎ Whiddon (01647) 231630
Beautiful country house set in 12 acres in lovely countryside within Dartmoor National Park. Tasteful decor and excellent breakfasts. Swimming pool, games room, private lake.
Bedrooms: 1 single, 1 double, 1 family room
Suite available
Bathrooms: 1 en-suite, 2 private

Bed & breakfast per night:	£min	£max
Single	18.00	22.00
Double	36.00	44.00

Parking for 12

CHARDSTOCK
Devon
Map ref 1D2

Tytherleigh Cot Hotel
COMMENDED
Chardstock, Axminster EX13 7BN
☎ South Chard (01460) 221170
Fax (01460) 221291
The Independents

Offers comfort and cuisine to a high standard. Four-poster beds and double jacuzzis available. Situated in an Area of Outstanding Natural Beauty.
Bedrooms: 2 single, 11 double, 5 twin, 1 triple
Bathrooms: 19 en-suite, 1 public

Bed & breakfast per night:	£min	£max
Single	55.00	
Double	98.00	

Half board per person:	£min	£max
Daily	65.00	
Weekly	357.00	

Lunch available
Evening meal 1900 (last orders 2130)
Parking for 34
Cards accepted: Access, Visa

CHARLESTOWN
Cornwall
Map Ref 1B3

Pier House Hotel
COMMENDED
Harbour Front, Charlestown, St Austell PL25 3NJ
☎ St Austell (01726) 67955
Fax (01726) 69246

Comfortable family-run hotel on the harbour front of small village. Local seafood a speciality of the a la carte restaurant.
Bedrooms: 11 single, 9 double, 1 twin, 4 triple
Bathrooms: 25 en-suite

Bed & breakfast per night:	£min	£max
Single	30.00	38.00
Double	55.00	62.00

Lunch available
Evening meal 1830 (last orders 2130)
Parking for 26
Cards accepted: Access, Visa, Switch/Delta

CHARMOUTH
Dorset
Map ref 1D2

Set back from the fossil-rich cliffs, a small coastal town where Charles II came to the Queen's Armes when seeking escape to France. Just south at low tide, the sandy beach rewards fossil-hunters; at Black Ven an ichthyosaurus (now in London's Natural History Museum) was found.

Hensleigh Hotel
HIGHLY COMMENDED
Lower Sea Lane, Charmouth, Bridport DT6 6LW
☎ (01297) 560830
Family-run hotel with a reputation for friendly service, comfort, hospitality and delicious food. Situated just 300 metres from beach.
Bedrooms: 2 single, 4 double, 4 twin, 1 triple
Bathrooms: 11 en-suite

Bed & breakfast per night:	£min	£max
Single	24.00	26.00
Double	48.00	52.00

Half board per person:	£min	£max
Daily	37.00	39.00
Weekly	234.00	250.00

Evening meal 1830 (last orders 1945)
Parking for 15
Open March–October
Cards accepted: Access, Visa, Amex

Newlands House
COMMENDED
Stonebarrow Lane, Charmouth, Bridport DT6 6RA
☎ (01297) 560212

House of character, comfortably furnished and giving an ambience of quiet relaxation, offers you excellent home-cooked food. Set in large gardens and orchard 5 minutes from the Heritage Coastal Path. No smoking except in bar lounge. About 2.5 miles east of Lyme Regis.
Bedrooms: 3 single, 4 double, 3 twin, 2 family rooms
Bathrooms: 11 en-suite, 1 public

Bed & breakfast per night:	£min	£max
Single	23.00	26.00
Double	46.00	52.00

Half board per person:	£min	£max
Daily	37.00	40.00
Weekly	235.00	251.00

Evening meal 1900 (last orders 1930)
Parking for 15
Open March–October

Establishments should be open throughout the year, unless otherwise stated.

WEST COUNTRY

CHEW STOKE
Bath & North East Somerset
Map ref 2A2

Attractive village in the Mendip Hills with an interesting Tudor rectory and the remains of a Roman villa. To the south is the Chew Valley reservoir with its extensive leisure facilities.

Orchard House
COMMENDED

Bristol Road, Chew Stoke, Bristol BS18 8UB
☎ Chew Magna (01275) 333143
Fax (01275) 333754
Comfortable accommodation in a carefully modernised Georgian house and coach house annexe. Home cooking using local produce.
Bedrooms: 1 single, 2 double, 3 twin, 1 family room
Bathrooms: 5 en-suite, 1 private, 2 public

Bed & breakfast per night:
	£min	£max
Single	17.00	22.00
Double	34.00	44.00

Half board per person:
	£min	£max
Daily	26.00	31.00

Evening meal 1830 (last orders 1000)
Parking for 9

CHIDEOCK
Dorset
Map ref 1D2

Village of sandstone thatched cottages in a valley near the dramatic Dorset coast. The church holds an interesting processional cross in mother-of-pearl and the manor house close by is associated with the Victorian Roman Catholic church. Seatown has a pebble beach and limestone cliffs.

Chideock House Hotel
APPROVED

Main Street, Chideock, Bridport DT6 6JN
☎ (01297) 489242

15th C thatched house in Chideock village. On the A35, 3 miles west of Bridport and less than 1 mile from the

sea. Oak-beamed restaurant and bar. Reputed headquarters of General Fairfax.
Bedrooms: 5 double, 3 twin, 1 triple
Bathrooms: 6 en-suite, 1 public, 3 private showers

Bed & breakfast per night:
	£min	£max
Single	30.00	30.00
Double	50.00	55.00

Half board per person:
	£min	£max
Daily	41.00	46.00
Weekly	260.00	295.00

Lunch available
Evening meal 1900 (last orders 2100)
Parking for 20
Cards accepted: Access, Visa, Switch/Delta

CHIPPENHAM
Wiltshire
Map ref 2B2

Ancient market town with modern industry. Notable early buildings include the medieval Town Hall and the gabled 15th C Yelde Hall, now a local history museum. On the outskirts Hardenhuish has a charming hilltop church by the Georgian architect John Wood of Bath.
Tourist Information Centre ☎ (01249) 657733

The Bramleys
Listed COMMENDED

73 Marshfield Road, Chippenham SN15 1JR
☎ (01249) 653770
Large Victorian listed building, close to town centre. Family-run with relaxed friendly atmosphere. All home cooking.
Bedrooms: 1 single, 3 twin, 1 triple
Bathrooms: 1 public

Bed & breakfast per night:
	£min	£max
Single	15.00	17.00
Double	30.00	32.00

Half board per person:
	£min	£max
Daily	21.00	23.00

Parking for 4

A key to symbols can be found inside the back cover flap.

CHIPPING SODBURY
South Gloucestershire
Map ref 2B2

Old market town, its buildings a mixture of Cotswold stone and mellowed brickwork. The 15th C church and the market cross are of interest. Horton Court (National Trust) stands 4 miles north-east and preserves a very rare Norman hall.

The Sodbury House Hotel
COMMENDED

Badminton Road, Old Sodbury, Bristol BS17 6LU
☎ (01454) 312847
Fax (01454) 273105
GR The Independents

Former farmhouse in extensive, well-kept grounds, offering informal but quality accommodation. Easy access M4/M5. Stepping-stone to Bath, Bristol, Cotswolds and South Wales.
Bedrooms: 6 single, 3 double, 2 twin, 2 triple
Bathrooms: 13 en-suite

Bed & breakfast per night:
	£min	£max
Single	42.50	48.00
Double	60.00	78.00

Half board per person:
	£min	£max
Daily	55.00	63.00

Evening meal 1900 (last orders 1945)
Parking for 30
Cards accepted: Access, Visa, Amex, Switch/Delta

WELCOME HOST

This is a nationally recognised customer care programme which aims to promote the highest standards of service and a warm welcome. Establishments who are taking part in this initiative are indicated by the symbol.

WEST COUNTRY

CLEVEDON

North Somerset
Map ref 1D1

Handsome Victorian resort on shingly shores of Severn Estuary. Pier, golf links with ruined folly, part-Norman clifftop church. Tennyson and Thackeray stayed at nearby Clevedon Court just to the east. Medieval with later additions, the manor overlooks terraces with rare plants.

Walton Park Hotel

1 Wellington Terrace, Clevedon
BS21 7BL
☎ (01275) 874253
Fax (01275) 343577
Consort

Country house hotel overlooking the Severn Estuary. 2 miles from M5 junction 20. Ideal base for touring the West Country.
Bedrooms: 10 single, 8 double, 22 twin
Bathrooms: 40 en-suite

Bed & breakfast
per night:	£min	£max
Single	40.00	69.95
Double	70.00	90.90

Half board
per person:	£min	£max
Daily	47.50	75.95
Weekly	315.00	315.00

Lunch available
Evening meal 1930 (last orders 2130)
Parking for 50
Cards accepted: Access, Visa, Diners, Amex, Switch/Delta

COMBE MARTIN

Devon
Map ref 1C1

On the edge of the Exmoor National Park, this seaside village is set in a long narrow valley with its natural harbour lying between towering cliffs. The main beach is a mixture of sand, rocks and pebbles and the lack of strong currents ensures safe bathing.

Channel Vista
COMMENDED

Woodlands, Combe Martin
EX34 0AT
☎ (01271) 883514

Charming, Edwardian period house, with comfortable en-suite rooms. Close to picturesque cove. Superb coastal

walks - discover beautiful Exmoor. Non smoking. Dogs welcome.
Bedrooms: 4 double, 1 twin, 1 triple, 1 family room
Bathrooms: 7 en-suite

Bed & breakfast
per night:	£min	£max
Single	20.00	25.00
Double	37.00	41.00

Half board per
person:	£min	£max
Daily	27.50	29.50
Weekly	165.00	175.00

Evening meal from 1900
Parking for 9
Open March–October and Christmas
Cards accepted: Access, Visa

Saffron House Hotel
COMMENDED

King Street, Combe Martin,
Ilfracombe EX34 0BX
☎ (01271) 883521

17th C hotel set in own grounds close to beaches and Exmoor.
Well-appointed en-suite rooms. Heated pool. Children and pets very welcome. Ideal touring centre.
Bedrooms: 5 double, 1 twin, 2 triple, 2 family rooms
Bathrooms: 8 en-suite, 1 public

Bed & breakfast
per night:	£min	£max
Single	18.00	20.00
Double	34.00	40.00

Half board per
person:	£min	£max
Daily	27.00	29.00
Weekly	154.00	179.00

Evening meal from 1830
Parking for 10
Cards accepted: Access, Visa, Switch/Delta

WELCOME HOST

This is a nationally recognised customer care programme which aims to promote the highest standards of service and a warm welcome. Establishments who are taking part in this initiative are indicated by the symbol.

CONSTANTINE

Cornwall
Map ref 1B3

Hilltop quarrying village overlooking wooded valley at the head of a creek on the Helford River. Shops, quarrymen's terraces, handsome church and chapel are all of granite. A granite-walled prehistoric cave, just north, can be explored.

Trengilly Wartha Inn
COMMENDED

Nancenoy, Constantine, Falmouth
TR11 5RP
☎ Falmouth (01326) 340332
Fax (01326) 340332
Logis of Great Britain

Inn with restaurant, serving real ales and bar meals. From Falmouth follow signs to Constantine then signs to Gweek. Close to the Helford River and convenient for beaches. Gweek is also near.
Bedrooms: 4 double, 2 twin
Bathrooms: 5 en-suite, 1 public

Bed & breakfast
per night:	£min	£max
Single	40.00	40.00
Double	56.00	60.00

Half board per
person:	£min	£max
Daily	44.50	50.00
Weekly	255.00	280.00

Lunch available
Evening meal 1830 (last orders 2130)
Parking for 80
Cards accepted: Access, Visa, Diners, Amex, Switch/Delta

COUNTISBURY

Devon
Map ref 1C1

Small village in Exmoor National Park and close to the sea. One mile south is Watersmeet (National Trust).

The Exmoor Sandpiper Inn
COMMENDED

Countisbury, Lynton EX35 6NE
☎ Brendon (01598) 741263
Fax (01598) 741358
Logis of Great Britain

Map references apply to the colour maps at the back of this guide.

WEST COUNTRY

Beamed character inn/hotel, part 13th C, amidst thousands of acres of rolling Exmoor hills. A few hundred yards from Countisbury sea cliffs and 1 mile from Lynmouth harbour.
Bedrooms: 9 double, 2 twin, 5 triple
Bathrooms: 16 en-suite
Bed & breakfast

per night:	£min	£max
Single	25.00	46.00
Double	50.00	92.00

Half board per

person:	£min	£max
Daily	45.00	69.00
Weekly	245.00	324.00

Lunch available
Evening meal 1900 (last orders 2130)
Parking for 50

CRANTOCK

Cornwall
Map ref 1B2

Pretty village of thatched cottages and seaside bungalows. Village stocks, once used against smugglers, are in the churchyard and the pub has a smugglers' hideout.

Crantock Bay Hotel ♈

⚜⚜⚜ COMMENDED
Crantock, Newquay TR8 5SE
☎ (01637) 830229
Fax (01637) 831111
Ⓒ Minotel
Long established family hotel on headland, with grounds leading directly on to beach. National Trust land nearby. Wonderful walking country.
Bedrooms: 9 single, 8 double, 15 twin, 2 family rooms
Bathrooms: 34 en-suite
Half board per

person:	£min	£max
Daily	54.00	59.00
Weekly	301.00	385.00

Lunch available
Evening meal 1900 (last orders 2030)
Parking for 36
Open March–November
Cards accepted: Access, Visa, Diners, Amex, Switch/Delta

CREDITON

Devon
Map ref 1D2

Ancient town in fertile valley, once prosperous from wool, now active in cider-making. Said to be the birthplace of St Boniface. The 13th C Chapter House, the church governors' meeting place, holds a collection of armour from the Civil War.

Coombe House Country Hotel ♈

⚜⚜⚜ COMMENDED
Coleford, Crediton EX17 5BY
☎ Copplestone (01363) 84487
Fax (01363) 84722
Georgian manor house in 5 acres of the rural heart of Devon. 20 minutes from Exeter. 2 bars, 2 restaurants, croquet, swimming, tennis.
Bedrooms: 9 double, 5 twin
Bathrooms: 14 en-suite
Bed & breakfast

per night:	£min	£max
Single	39.50	49.50
Double	64.50	79.50

Half board per

person:	£min	£max
Daily	57.00	67.00
Weekly	319.00	394.00

Lunch available
Evening meal 1900 (last orders 2130)
Parking for 90
Cards accepted: Access, Visa, Switch/Delta

CREWKERNE

Somerset
Map ref 1D2

This charming little market town on the Dorset border nestles in undulating farmland and orchards in a conservation area. Built of local sandstone with Roman and Saxon origins. The magnificent St Bartholomew's Church dates from 15th C; St Bartholomew's Fair is held in September.

Broadview Gardens ♈

⚜⚜ DE LUXE
East Crewkerne, Crewkerne TA18 7AG
☎ (01460) 73424
Fax (01460) 73424
Unusual colonial bungalow with en-suite rooms overlooking beautiful gardens. Carefully furnished with antiques. Friendly and relaxing. Quality traditional English home cooking. Truly perfect touring base, 20 minutes from coast.
Bedrooms: 1 double, 2 twin
Bathrooms: 2 en-suite, 1 private
Bed & breakfast

per night:	£min	£max
Single	25.00	35.00
Double	46.00	54.00

Half board per

person:	£min	£max
Daily	35.50	39.50
Weekly	248.50	276.50

Evening meal 1830 (last orders 1200)
Parking for 6
Cards accepted: Access, Visa

The George Hotel and Restaurant ♈

⚜⚜⚜ APPROVED
Market Square, Crewkerne TA18 7LP
☎ (01460) 73650
Fax (01460) 72974

17th C Grade II listed coaching inn, newly refurbished, situated in the market square. Ideally located for touring. Fine food, real ales. Warm welcome!
Bedrooms: 3 single, 6 double, 2 twin, 1 triple, 1 family room
Bathrooms: 10 en-suite, 2 public, 1 private shower
Bed & breakfast

per night:	£min	£max
Single	24.00	38.00
Double	48.00	70.00

Half board per

person:	£min	£max
Daily	35.00	53.00

Lunch available
Evening meal 1900 (last orders 2130)
Cards accepted: Access, Visa, Diners, Amex, Switch/Delta

The ♈ symbol after an establishment name indicates that it is a Regional Tourist Board member.

WEST COUNTRY

CROYDE

Devon
Map ref 1C1

Pretty village with thatched cottages near Croyde Bay. To the south stretch Saunton Sands and their dunelands Braunton Burrows with interesting flowers and plants, nature reserve and golf-course. Cliff walks and bird-watching at Baggy Point, west of the village.

Croyde Bay House Hotel
HIGHLY COMMENDED

Moor Lane, Croyde, Braunton EX33 1PA
☎ (01271) 890270
Small, friendly hotel beside beach, where comfort, good food and personal care are still found. Beautifully positioned sun deck and sun lounge. Peaceful garden, car parking.
Bedrooms: 3 double, 2 twin, 2 triple
Bathrooms: 7 en-suite

Half board per person:	£min	£max
Daily	42.00	53.00
Weekly	285.00	325.00

Evening meal 1915 (last orders 2000)
Parking for 7
Open March–November
Cards accepted: Access, Visa, Amex

CULLOMPTON

Devon
Map ref 1D2

Market town on former coaching routes, with pleasant tree-shaded cobbled pavements and some handsome 17th C houses. Earlier prosperity from the wool industry is reflected in the grandness of the church with its fan-vaulted aisle built by a wool-stapler in 1526.

Rullands
COMMENDED

Rull Lane, Cullompton EX15 1NQ
☎ (01884) 33356
Fax (01884) 35890
Logis of Great Britain

15th C country house amid beautiful Devon countryside. Within easy reach of all country pursuits, the M5 and the historic town of Tiverton.
Bedrooms: 1 single, 2 double, 1 triple
Bathrooms: 4 en-suite

Bed & breakfast per night:	£min	£max
Single	25.00	35.00
Double	55.00	55.00

Half board per person:	£min	£max
Daily	40.00	50.00

Evening meal 1900 (last orders 2130)
Parking for 20
Cards accepted: Access, Visa, Switch/Delta

DARTMOOR

See under Ashburton, Bovey Tracey, Chagford, Haytor, Ilsington, Lydford, Moretonhampstead, Okehampton, Poundsgate, Two Bridges, Widecombe-in-the-Moor, Yelverton

DARTMOUTH

Devon
Map ref 1D3

Ancient port at mouth of Dart. Has fine period buildings, notably town houses near Quay and Butterwalk of 1635. Harbour castle ruin. In 12th C Crusader fleets assembled here. Royal Naval College dominates from Hill. Carnival, June; Regatta, August.
Tourist Information Centre ☎ (01803) 834224

Royal Castle Hotel
HIGHLY COMMENDED

11 The Quay, Dartmouth TQ6 9PS
☎ Torbay (01803) 833033
Fax (01803) 835445

Historic 17th C quayside coaching inn, famous for traditional-style food and service. Antiques, open fires, character bars and restaurant, delightful accommodation.
Bedrooms: 4 single, 10 double, 7 twin, 4 triple
Bathrooms: 25 en-suite

Bed & breakfast per night:	£min	£max
Single	45.50	55.50
Double	80.00	120.00

Half board per person:	£min	£max
Daily	50.00	70.00
Weekly	300.00	420.00

Lunch available
Evening meal 1845 (last orders 2200)
Parking for 4
Cards accepted: Access, Visa, Switch/Delta

Townstal Farmhouse
COMMENDED

Townstal Road, Dartmouth TQ6 9HY
☎ (01803) 832300
Comfortable 16th C listed farmhouse. Varied home-cooked meals in friendly, family-run atmosphere. Within walking distance of the town and Royal Naval College.
Bedrooms: 1 single, 10 double, 1 twin, 4 triple, 1 family room
Bathrooms: 14 en-suite, 1 public

Bed & breakfast per night:	£min	£max
Single	20.00	40.00
Double	36.00	60.00

Half board per person:	£min	£max
Daily	28.00	40.00
Weekly	196.00	262.50

Evening meal from 1830
Parking for 20
Cards accepted: Visa

DAWLISH

Devon
Map ref 1D2

Small resort, developed in Regency and Victorian periods beside Dawlish Water. Town centre has ornamental riverside gardens with black swans. One of England's most scenic stretches of railway was built by Brunel alongside jagged red cliffs between the sands and the town.
Tourist Information Centre ☎ (01626) 863589

Oak Cottage
HIGHLY COMMENDED

Luscombe Hill, Dawlish EX7 0PX
☎ (01626) 863120

WEST COUNTRY

Listed Tudor revival house. Stone mullions, log fires, beautiful gardens. Woodland location close to sea and moors. Excellent candlelit dinners. Brochure available.
Bedrooms: 1 double, 1 twin
Bathrooms: 2 en-suite

Bed & breakfast per night:

	£min	£max
Double	50.00	56.00

Half board per person:

	£min	£max
Daily	37.00	42.00
Weekly	233.00	265.00

Evening meal from 1930
Parking for 3

Radfords Country Hotel
COMMENDED

Lower Dawlish Water, Dawlish
EX7 0QN
☎ (01626) 863322
Fax (01626) 888515
Highly specialised family hotel near the sea. Service, entertainment and safety standards for children of all ages.
Bedrooms: 8 triple, 29 family rooms
Bathrooms: 37 en-suite

Bed & breakfast per night:

	£min	£max
Single	25.00	30.00
Double	35.00	60.00

Half board per person:

	£min	£max
Daily	30.00	50.00
Weekly	200.00	300.00

Evening meal 1800 (last orders 1900)
Parking for 52
Open March–November and Christmas
Cards accepted: Access, Visa

All accommodation in this guide has been graded, or is awaiting a grading, by a trained Tourist Board inspector.

The symbols in each entry give information about services and facilities. A 'key' to these symbols appears at the back of this guide.

DEVIZES
Wiltshire
Map ref 2B2

Old market town standing on the Kennet and Avon Canal. Rebuilt Norman castle, good 18th C buildings. St John's church has 12th C work and Norman tower. Museum of Wiltshire's archaeology and natural history reflects wealth of prehistoric sites in the county.
Tourist Information Centre ☎ (01380) 729408

The Castle Hotel
New Park Street, Devizes
SN10 1DS
☎ (01380) 729300
Fax (01380) 729155
Well-appointed accommodation in a busy market town. A la carte restaurant and popular bar. All rooms en-suite.
Bedrooms: 5 single, 5 double, 7 twin, 1 family room
Suite available
Bathrooms: 18 en-suite

Bed & breakfast per night:

	£min	£max
Single	40.00	45.00
Double	55.00	65.00

Half board per person:

	£min	£max
Daily	50.00	55.00

Lunch available
Evening meal 1830 (last orders 2100)
Parking for 6
Cards accepted: Access, Visa, Amex

Pinecroft

Potterne Road (A360), Devizes
SN10 5DA
☎ (01380) 721433
Fax (01380) 721229
Comfortable Georgian family house with spacious rooms, exquisite garden and private parking. Only 3 minutes' walk from town centre.
Wheelchair access category 3
Bedrooms: 2 double, 2 twin, 1 family room
Suite available
Bathrooms: 4 en-suite, 1 private

Bed & breakfast per night:

	£min	£max
Single	20.00	25.00
Double	32.00	40.00

Parking for 7
Cards accepted: Access, Visa, Amex

Rathlin Guest House
COMMENDED

Wick Lane, Devizes SN10 5DP
☎ (01380) 721999
Elegant period charm, all rooms en-suite and individually furnished. Quiet location close to town centre. Tranquil gardens. Ample parking.
Bedrooms: 1 single, 1 double, 2 twin
Bathrooms: 4 en-suite

Bed & breakfast per night:

	£min	£max
Single	25.00	25.00
Double	40.00	40.00

Half board per person:

	£min	£max
Daily	30.00	35.00

Evening meal 1800 (last orders 1930)
Parking for 5
Open March–November

Spout Cottage
HIGHLY COMMENDED

Stert, Devizes SN10 3JD
☎ (01380) 724336
Delightfully situated thatched cottage in secluded valley. Idyllic peaceful retreat. Well-appointed centrally heated rooms, inglenook fireplace, beamed ceilings. Delicious, imaginative food.
Bedrooms: 1 single, 1 double, 1 twin
Bathrooms: 2 public

Bed & breakfast per night:

	£min	£max
Single	18.50	20.00
Double	33.00	36.00

Half board per person:

	£min	£max
Daily	34.00	35.50

Lunch available
Evening meal from 2000
Parking for 4

WELCOME HOST

This is a nationally recognised customer care programme which aims to promote the highest standards of service and a warm welcome. Establishments who are taking part in this initiative are indicated by the symbol.

WEST COUNTRY

DORCHESTER
Dorset
Map ref 2B3

Busy medieval county town destroyed by fires in 17th and 18th C. Cromwellian stronghold and scene of Judge Jeffreys' Bloody Assize after Monmouth Rebellion of 1685. Tolpuddle Martyrs were tried in Shire Hall. Museum has Roman and earlier exhibits and Hardy relics.
Tourist Information Centre ☎ (01305) 267992

Wessex Royale Hotel
32 High West Street, Dorchester DT1 1UP
☎ (01305) 262660
Fax (01305) 251941

Georgian town centre hotel, recently refurbished to a high standard, with extensive restaurant, bar and function facilities.
Bedrooms: 2 single, 16 double, 4 twin, 1 triple
Suite available
Bathrooms: 23 en-suite
Bed & breakfast
per night: £min   £max
Single   20.00   40.00
Double   40.00   50.00
Half board per
person: £min   £max
Daily   40.00   55.00
Weekly   199.00   299.00
Lunch available
Evening meal 1830 (last orders 2130)
Parking for 5
Cards accepted: Access, Visa, Diners, Amex, Switch/Delta

Yalbury Cottage Hotel and Restaurant
HIGHLY COMMENDED
Lower Bockhampton, Dorchester DT2 8PZ
☎ (01305) 262382
Fax (01305) 266412
Logis of Great Britain

17th C thatched hotel in beautiful countryside 2 miles east of Dorchester near Hardy's Cottage. Comfortable, oak-beamed lounge and excellent restaurant with friendly, attentive service. Well-equipped en-suite bedrooms.
Bedrooms: 6 double, 2 twin
Bathrooms: 8 en-suite
Bed & breakfast
per night: £min   £max
Single   45.00   45.00
Double   70.00   70.00
Half board per
person: £min   £max
Daily   52.00   62.00
Weekly   308.00   406.00
Evening meal 1900 (last orders 2100)
Parking for 19
Cards accepted: Access, Visa, Switch/Delta

DULVERTON
Somerset
Map ref 1D1

Set among woods and hills of south-west Exmoor, a busy riverside town with a 13th C church. The Rivers Barle and Exe are rich in salmon and trout. The information centre at the Exmoor National Park Headquarters at Dulverton is open throughout the year.

Exton House Hotel
HIGHLY COMMENDED
Exton, Dulverton TA22 9JT
☎ Winsford (01643) 851365
Fax (01643) 851213
Former rectory in a delightful rural setting on side of the Exe Valley. Turn off A396 at Bridgetown and we are half a mile on right.
Bedrooms: 1 single, 5 double, 3 twin
Bathrooms: 8 en-suite, 1 private
Bed & breakfast
per night: £min   £max
Single   29.00   35.00
Double   49.00   58.00
Half board per
person: £min   £max
Daily   37.00   43.50
Weekly   259.00   290.50
Evening meal 1930 (last orders 1400)

Parking for 10
Cards accepted: Access, Visa

DUNSTER
Somerset
Map ref 1D1

Ancient town with views of Exmoor. The hilltop castle has been continuously occupied since 1070. Medieval prosperity from cloth built 16th C octagonal Yarn Market and the church. A riverside mill, packhorse bridge and 18th C hilltop folly occupy other interesting corners in the town.

Bilbrook Lawns Hotel
COMMENDED
Bilbrook, Minehead TA24 6HE
☎ Washford (01984) 640331
Detached Georgian country house hotel set in extensive lawned gardens bordered by a stream.
Bedrooms: 4 double, 3 twin
Bathrooms: 4 en-suite, 1 public
Bed & breakfast
per night: £min   £max
Single   25.00   30.00
Double   40.00   50.00
Half board per
person: £min   £max
Daily   32.50   47.50
Weekly   175.00   210.00
Lunch available
Evening meal 1930 (last orders 1900)
Parking for 8
Open March–October and Christmas
Cards accepted: Amex

Exmoor House Hotel
HIGHLY COMMENDED
12 West Street, Dunster, Minehead TA24 6SN
☎ (01643) 821268
Fax (01643) 821268
Near Dunster Castle, Exmoor, Brendons, Quantocks and coast. Farm-fresh food (including vegetarian), interesting wines, lounges and restaurant. Home comforts. Non-smokers only, please.
Bedrooms: 4 double, 3 twin
Bathrooms: 7 en-suite, 1 public
Bed & breakfast
per night: £min   £max
Single   27.50   38.50
Double   55.00   61.00

WEST COUNTRY

Half board per person:	£min	£max
Daily	38.00	46.00
Weekly	266.00	280.00

Lunch available
Evening meal 1930 (last orders 1900)
Open February–November
Cards accepted: Access, Visa, Diners, Amex

Spears Cross Hotel

1 West Street, Dunster, Minehead
TA24 6SN
☎ (01643) 821439
Fax (01643) 821439

Pretty 15th C small hotel with old world charm but up to date facilities. In picturesque village in Exmoor National Park. No smoking. Private car parking.
Bedrooms: 1 double, 1 twin, 1 triple
Bathrooms: 3 en-suite

Bed & breakfast per night:	£min	£max
Single	21.00	33.00
Double	42.00	50.00

Half board per person:	£min	£max
Daily	33.00	37.00
Weekly	216.00	241.00

Evening meal from 1930
Parking for 4
Open February–December

Yarn Market Hotel (Exmoor)

25 High Street, Dunster, Minehead
TA24 6SF
☎ (01643) 821425
Fax (01643) 821475
Central and accessible hotel in quaint English village, an ideal location from which to explore the Exmoor National Park.
Bedrooms: 2 double, 1 twin, 1 family room
Bathrooms: 4 en-suite

Bed & breakfast per night:	£min	£max
Single	22.50	30.00
Double	45.00	60.00

Half board per person:	£min	£max
Daily	34.00	41.50
Weekly	215.50	260.50

Evening meal 1800 (last orders 2000)
Parking for 3
Cards accepted: Access, Visa, Amex, Switch/Delta

EAST PRAWLE

Devon
Map ref 1C3

The Forge on the Green

HIGHLY COMMENDED

East Prawle, Kingsbridge TQ7 2BU
☎ Kingsbridge (01548) 511210
Fax (01548) 511210

Acclaimed country cottage with picturesque views to the sea. Superbly appointed interior, en-suite bath, emperor bed, all facilities to make an extremely comfortable stay. Imaginative table d'hote evening meal £12.50.
Bedrooms: 2 double
Bathrooms: 2 en-suite

Bed & breakfast per night:	£min	£max
Single	25.00	30.00
Double	38.00	50.00

Half board per person:	£min	£max
Daily	40.00	43.00
Weekly	250.00	275.00

Evening meal 1800 (last orders 2000)

EVERSHOT

Dorset
Map ref 2A3

Set in hilly country at source of the River Frome, a small village with a sophisticated, bow-fronted High Street of raised pavements. The church has an unusual spire.

Rectory House

HIGHLY COMMENDED

Fore Street, Evershot, Dorchester DT2 0JW
☎ (01935) 83273
Fax (01935) 83273

Lovely 18th C rectory in picturesque village. Super home cooking of traditional and exotic dishes.
Bedrooms: 4 double, 2 twin
Bathrooms: 6 en-suite

Bed & breakfast per night:	£min	£max
Single	45.00	60.00
Double	70.00	80.00

Half board per person:	£min	£max
Daily	63.00	78.00
Weekly	319.00	346.00

Evening meal 1830 (last orders 1930)
Parking for 8
Open January–November
Cards accepted: Access, Visa

EXETER

Devon
Map ref 1D2

University city rebuilt after the 1940s around its cathedral. Attractions include 13th C cathedral with fine west front; notable waterfront buildings; Maritime Museum; Guildhall; Royal Albert Memorial Museum; underground passages; Northcott Theatre.
Tourist Information Centre ☎ (01392) 265700

Devon Hotel

COMMENDED

Exeter-by-Pass, Matford, Exeter EX2 8XU
☎ (01392) 59268
Fax (01392) 413142
Set in beautiful countryside, yet offering easy accessibility to the M5 and the centre of Exeter.
Bedrooms: 7 single, 15 double, 17 twin, 2 family rooms
Bathrooms: 41 en-suite

Bed & breakfast per night:	£min	£max
Single	40.00	55.00
Double	55.00	75.00

Half board per person:	£min	£max
Daily	42.50	70.00
Weekly	317.50	460.00

Lunch available
Evening meal 1900 (last orders 2100)
Parking for 200
Cards accepted: Access, Visa, Diners, Amex, Switch/Delta

WEST COUNTRY

EXETER
Continued

Ebford House Hotel ♠
♛♛♛♛ COMMENDED
Exmouth Road, Ebford, Exeter
EX3 OQH
☎ Topsham (01392) 877658
Fax (01392) 874424
Ⓡ Logis of Great Britain/The Independents
Beautiful Georgian country house surrounded by lovely gardens, fine views. Noted restaurant. Relax in our leisure area. Convenient for 8 golf courses, sea, sand and moors.
Bedrooms: 3 single, 11 double, 2 twin
Bathrooms: 16 en-suite
Bed & breakfast
per night:	£min	£max
Single	60.00	70.00
Double	80.00	90.00

Lunch available
Evening meal 1830 (last orders 2130)
Parking for 45
Cards accepted: Access, Visa, Amex, Switch/Delta

Fairwinds Hotel ♠
♛♛♛ COMMENDED
Kennford, Exeter EX6 7UD
☎ (01392) 832911
Fax (01392) 832911
Friendly little "no-smoking" hotel, offering real value for money in beautiful rural surroundings. Comfortable, well-equipped en-suite bedrooms. Excellent choice of home-made food. Perfect touring base.
Bedrooms: 2 single, 4 double, 1 twin, 1 triple
Bathrooms: 6 en-suite, 2 private showers
Bed & breakfast
per night:	£min	£max
Single	23.00	35.00
Double	45.00	48.00

Half board per
person:	£min	£max
Daily	34.00	48.00
Weekly	195.00	215.00

Evening meal 1830 (last orders 2000)
Parking for 9
Cards accepted: Access, Visa

Gipsy Hill Hotel and Restaurant ♠
♛♛♛♛ COMMENDED
Gipsy Hill Lane, Pinhoe, Exeter
EX1 3RN
☎ (01392) 465252
Fax (01392) 464302
Ⓡ Consort

Peaceful country house hotel with magnificent views. 1 mile from M5, junction 30, and 2 miles from Exeter, just off the A30. Adjacent M5 junction 29 (under construction).
Bedrooms: 9 single, 16 double, 10 twin, 2 triple, 1 family room
Bathrooms: 38 en-suite
Bed & breakfast
per night:	£min	£max
Single	40.00	67.00
Double	70.00	90.00

Half board per
person:	£min	£max
Daily	56.50	85.00

Lunch available
Evening meal 1900 (last orders 2115)
Parking for 100
Cards accepted: Access, Visa, Amex, Switch/Delta

Globe Hotel ♠
♛♛♛ COMMENDED
Fore Street, Topsham, Exeter
EX3 0HR
☎ (01392) 873471
Fax (01392) 873879

Family-run 16th C coaching inn, situated in the historic estuary town of Topsham (exit 30, M5). Exeter 4 miles.
Bedrooms: 1 single, 6 double, 7 twin, 3 triple
Bathrooms: 17 en-suite
Bed & breakfast
per night:	£min	£max
Single	35.00	40.00
Double	48.00	55.00

Lunch available
Evening meal 1900 (last orders 2130)

Parking for 14
Cards accepted: Access, Visa, Amex, Switch/Delta

The Great Western Hotel ♠
♛♛♛
Station Approach, St David's, Exeter
EX4 4NU
☎ (01392) 274039
Fax (01392) 425529
Ⓡ Minotel
Hotel has easy access to railway station. Bar, restaurant, lounge, conference room and car park.
Bedrooms: 23 single, 7 double, 9 twin, 1 triple
Bathrooms: 30 en-suite, 5 public
Bed & breakfast
per night:	£min	£max
Single	30.00	36.50
Double	48.00	52.50

Half board per
person:	£min	£max
Daily	39.00	46.50
Weekly	259.00	311.50

Lunch available
Evening meal 1900 (last orders 2130)
Parking for 25
Cards accepted: Access, Visa, Diners, Amex, Switch/Delta

Park View Hotel
♛♛ COMMENDED
8 Howell Road, Exeter EX4 4LG
☎ (01392) 271772
Fax (01392) 53047
*Charming family-run hotel, noted for peace and quiet and high standards, near city centre and stations.
Tea/coffee, colour TV and telephone in all rooms.*
Bedrooms: 3 single, 7 double, 3 twin, 2 triple
Bathrooms: 8 en-suite, 2 private, 2 public
Bed & breakfast
per night:	£min	£max
Single	20.00	28.00
Double	35.00	43.00

Parking for 6
Cards accepted: Access, Visa, Amex

Raffles Hotel
♛♛♛ COMMENDED
11 Blackall Road, Exeter EX4 4HD
☎ (01392) 270200
Restored spacious Victorian house, furnished and decorated to period. Close to city centre, university and theatres.

WEST COUNTRY

Bedrooms: 2 single, 2 double, 2 twin, 1 triple
Bathrooms: 7 en-suite

Bed & breakfast

per night:	£min	£max
Single	28.00	30.00
Double	42.00	44.00

Half board per

person:	£min	£max
Daily	33.00	40.00
Weekly	231.00	280.00

Evening meal 1900 (last orders 1200)
Parking for 4
Cards accepted: Access, Visa, Diners, Amex

St Andrews Hotel
COMMENDED
28 Alphington Road, Exeter EX2 8HN
☎ (01392) 276784
Fax (01392) 50249
Ⓒ Logis of Great Britain

A warm welcome awaits you at this long established family-run hotel. Whilst retaining the features of a large Victorian house it provides all the facilities of a modern hotel. Brochure on request. Weekend breaks available all year.

Wheelchair access category 3
Bedrooms: 4 single, 7 double, 3 twin, 2 family rooms
Bathrooms: 16 en-suite

Bed & breakfast

per night:	£min	£max
Single	39.00	
Double	49.50	

Lunch available
Evening meal 1900 (last orders 2030)
Parking for 20
Cards accepted: Access, Visa, Diners, Amex

The Southgate Exeter
HIGHLY COMMENDED
Southernhay East, Exeter EX1 1QF
☎ (01392) 412812 & 413549
Ⓒ Forte/Utell International

Situated in the heart of Exeter, this modern hotel is of Georgian design with a high standard of interior furnishings and features. Prices are for room only.

Bedrooms: 60 double, 50 twin
Suite available
Bathrooms: 110 en-suite

Bed & breakfast

per night:	£min	£max
Single	69.00	90.00
Double	69.00	90.00

Lunch available
Evening meal 1900 (last orders 2200)
Parking for 115
Cards accepted: Access, Visa, Diners, Amex

EXFORD
Somerset
Map ref 1D1

Sheltered village on the River Exe close to Exmoor. Attractive old houses, shops and inns face the village green and the Methodist chapel has 2 windows by Burne-Jones. A footpath north-eastward leads to Dunkery Beacon, Exmoor's highest point.

Exmoor House Hotel
APPROVED
Chapel Street, Exford, Minehead TA24 7PY
☎ (01643) 831304

Small family-run country hotel in the heart of Exford village, "capital" of Exmoor. Ideal for all country pursuits. Stabling can be arranged for guests' horses. Delicious home-cooked food.

Bedrooms: 1 single, 1 double, 1 twin
Suites available
Bathrooms: 2 en-suite, 1 public

Bed & breakfast

per night:	£min	£max
Single	18.00	23.50
Double	36.00	47.00

Half board per

person:	£min	£max
Daily	29.00	34.50
Weekly	185.00	245.00

Lunch available
Evening meal 1830 (last orders 1930)
Parking for 40
Cards accepted: Access, Visa

Exmoor White Horse Hotel
COMMENDED
Exford, Minehead TA24 7PY
☎ (01643) 831229
Fax (01643) 831246

Old world inn standing on the green beside the River Exe in beautiful

Exmoor village. Local blacksmith at work in village, with the rolling moors just up the road.
Bedrooms: 12 double, 3 twin, 3 triple
Bathrooms: 18 en-suite

Bed & breakfast

per night:	£min	£max
Single	25.00	46.00
Double	50.00	92.00

Half board per

person:	£min	£max
Daily	45.00	69.00
Weekly	245.00	324.00

Lunch available
Evening meal 1900 (last orders 2130)
Parking for 30

EXMOOR

See under Allerford, Combe Martin, Countisbury, Dulverton, Dunster, Exford, Heasley Mill, Lynmouth, Lynton, Porlock, Timberscombe, Wheddon Cross, Winsford

---

EXMOUTH
Devon
Map ref 1D2

Developed as a seaside resort in George III's reign, set against the woods of the Exe Estuary and red cliffs of Orcombe Point. Extensive sands, small harbour, chapel and almshouses, a model railway and A la Ronde, a 16-sided house.
Tourist Information Centre ☎ (01395) 222299

The Devoncourt Hotel
COMMENDED
Douglas Avenue, Exmouth EX8 2EX
☎ (01395) 272277
Fax (01395) 269315

The ideal family resort, commanding spectacular sea views. Full leisure
Continued ▶

COLOUR MAPS

Colour maps at the back of this guide pinpoint all places in which you will find accommodation listed.

WEST COUNTRY

EXMOUTH
Continued

complex, with 2 pools, tennis, putting, croquet and much more. Sky TV.
Located 8 miles from Exeter and M5.
Bedrooms: 6 single, 11 double, 6 twin, 17 triple, 11 family rooms
Suites available
Bathrooms: 51 en-suite

Bed & breakfast per night:	£min	£max
Single	50.00	75.00
Double	80.00	115.00

Half board per person:	£min	£max
Daily	50.00	77.50
Weekly	350.00	542.50

Lunch available
Evening meal 1900 (last orders 2130)
Parking for 54
Cards accepted: Access, Visa, Diners, Amex, Switch/Delta

FALMOUTH
Cornwall
Map ref 1B3

Busy port and fishing harbour, popular resort on the balmy Cornish Riviera. Henry VIII's Pendennis Castle faces St Mawes Castle across the broad natural harbour and yacht basin, Carrick Roads, which receives 7 rivers.
Tourist Information Centre ☎ (01326) 312300

Broadmead Hotel
COMMENDED

Kimberley Park Road, Falmouth TR11 2DD
☎ (01326) 315704 & 318036
Fax (01326) 311048
Logis of Great Britain
Small hotel, tastefully decorated and furnished, with traditional English cooking. Overlooking Kimberley Park, near the centre of Falmouth. Private car park.
Wheelchair access category 3
Bedrooms: 4 single, 4 double, 3 twin, 1 triple
Bathrooms: 11 en-suite, 1 private, 1 public

Bed & breakfast per night:	£min	£max
Single	22.00	27.00
Double	50.00	56.00

Half board per person:	£min	£max
Daily	32.50	39.75
Weekly	200.00	250.00

Lunch available
Evening meal 1900 (last orders 2000)
Parking for 8
Cards accepted: Access, Visa, Amex, Switch/Delta

Carthion Hotel
COMMENDED

Cliff Road, Falmouth TR11 4AP
☎ (01326) 313669
Fax (01326) 212828
Family hotel, situated in pleasant gardens, with a panoramic view of the sea from Pendennis Point to the Manacles.
Bedrooms: 2 single, 8 double, 4 twin, 4 triple
Bathrooms: 18 en-suite

Bed & breakfast per night:	£min	£max
Single	25.00	39.00
Double	50.00	78.00

Half board per person:	£min	£max
Daily	36.00	51.00
Weekly	252.00	357.00

Lunch available
Evening meal 1900 (last orders 2000)
Parking for 18
Cards accepted: Access, Visa, Diners, Amex

The Falmouth Hotel
HIGHLY COMMENDED

Castle Beach, Falmouth TR11 4NZ
☎ (01326) 312671
Fax (01326) 319533

Modernised Victorian building in 5 acres of prize-winning gardens, overlooking the sea. Open all year.
Bedrooms: 16 single, 12 double, 41 twin, 4 triple
Bathrooms: 73 en-suite

Bed & breakfast per night:	£min	£max
Single	35.00	60.00
Double	66.00	120.00

Half board per person:	£min	£max
Daily	48.00	75.00
Weekly	235.00	440.00

Lunch available
Evening meal 1900 (last orders 2130)
Parking for 170
Cards accepted: Access, Visa, Diners, Amex, Switch/Delta

Falmouth Beach Resort Hotel
COMMENDED

Gyllyngvase Beach, Seafront, Falmouth TR11 4NA
☎ (01326) 318084
Fax (01326) 319147
Consort

Modern hotel, right by the beach, with lifts to most floors. No steps/stairs from seafront to public rooms. Superb sea views. "All weather pleasure."
Bedrooms: 15 single, 34 double, 55 twin, 23 family rooms
Suites available
Bathrooms: 127 en-suite

Bed & breakfast per night:	£min	£max
Single	40.00	51.00
Double	64.00	86.00

Half board per person:	£min	£max
Daily	38.00	57.00
Weekly	266.00	399.00

Lunch available
Evening meal 1900 (last orders 2100)
Parking for 80
Cards accepted: Access, Visa, Diners, Amex, Switch/Delta

Green Lawns Hotel
HIGHLY COMMENDED

Western Terrace, Falmouth TR11 4QJ
☎ (01326) 312734
Fax (01326) 211427
The Independents

WEST COUNTRY

Elegant chateau-style hotel situated between the main beaches and town, with indoor leisure complex. Honeymoon and executive suites.
Bedrooms: 6 single, 17 double, 9 twin, 2 triple, 6 family rooms
Bathrooms: 40 en-suite

Bed & breakfast

per night:	£min	£max
Single	45.00	80.00
Double	74.00	106.00

Half board per

person:	£min	£max
Daily	61.00	96.00
Weekly	350.00	440.00

Lunch available
Evening meal 1845 (last orders 2200)
Parking for 60
Cards accepted: Access, Visa, Diners, Amex, Switch/Delta

Grove Hotel
APPROVED

Grove Place, Falmouth TR11 4AU
☎ (01326) 319577
Fax (01326) 319577
Harbourside Georgian hotel offering a warm welcome, good food and good value. Central to all local amenities. Public car and dinghy parks opposite.
Bedrooms: 2 single, 2 double, 3 twin, 6 triple, 2 family rooms
Bathrooms: 13 en-suite, 2 public

Bed & breakfast

per night:	£min	£max
Single	20.00	25.00
Double	40.00	47.00

Half board per

person:	£min	£max
Daily	29.00	33.50
Weekly	190.00	

Evening meal 1900 (last orders 2100)
Open January–November
Cards accepted: Access, Visa, Diners, Amex

Gyllyngdune Manor Hotel
COMMENDED

Melvill Road, Falmouth TR11 4AR
☎ (01326) 312978
Fax (01326) 211881
Old Georgian manor house situated in an acre of beautiful gardens. 10 minutes' walk from town centre, 2 minutes' walk from beach overlooking Falmouth Bay.
Bedrooms: 3 single, 13 double, 10 twin, 4 triple
Bathrooms: 30 en-suite

Bed & breakfast

per night:	£min	£max
Single	25.00	53.00
Double	50.00	106.00

Half board per

person:	£min	£max
Daily	38.00	64.00
Weekly	266.00	404.00

Lunch available
Evening meal 1900 (last orders 2100)
Parking for 20
Cards accepted: Access, Visa, Diners, Amex, Switch/Delta

Madeira Hotel
APPROVED

Sea Front, Falmouth TR11 4NY
☎ (01326) 313531
Fax (01326) 319143
Well-situated with views over Falmouth Bay. Entertainment most evenings.
Bedrooms: 6 single, 16 double, 19 twin, 8 triple
Bathrooms: 49 en-suite, 2 public

Bed & breakfast

per night:	£min	£max
Single	25.00	32.00
Double	44.00	58.00

Half board per

person:	£min	£max
Daily	31.00	38.00
Weekly	165.00	220.00

Lunch available
Evening meal 1800 (last orders 1900)
Parking for 20
Open March–November and Christmas
Cards accepted: Access, Visa

Park Grove Hotel
COMMENDED

Kimberley Park Road, Falmouth TR11 2DD
☎ (01326) 313276
Fax (01326) 211926
Family-run, long established hotel, centrally situated for harbour, beaches and town centre. Spacious restaurant serving excellent cuisine. Large car park.
Bedrooms: 3 single, 5 double, 6 twin, 5 triple
Bathrooms: 12 en-suite, 5 private, 2 public, 2 private showers

Bed & breakfast

per night:	£min	£max
Single	20.00	26.00
Double	40.00	52.00

Half board per

person:	£min	£max
Daily	27.00	33.00
Weekly	189.00	231.00

Lunch available
Evening meal 1830 (last orders 1930)
Parking for 23
Cards accepted: Access, Visa, Amex, Switch/Delta

Royal Duchy Hotel
HIGHLY COMMENDED

Cliff Road, Falmouth TR11 4NX
☎ (01326) 313042
Fax (01326) 319420
Falmouth's first and foremost hotel situated overlooking the bay. High standard accommodation with extensive leisure facilities.
Bedrooms: 4 single, 17 double, 17 twin, 4 triple, 1 family room
Suites available
Bathrooms: 43 en-suite

Bed & breakfast

per night:	£min	£max
Single	50.00	78.00
Double	96.00	190.00

Half board per

person:	£min	£max
Daily	58.00	105.00
Weekly	325.50	735.00

Lunch available
Evening meal 1900 (last orders 2100)
Parking for 56
Cards accepted: Access, Visa, Diners, Amex, Switch/Delta

Tresillian House Hotel
COMMENDED

3 Stracey Road, Falmouth TR11 4DW
☎ (01326) 312425 & 311139
Family-run hotel in a quiet area, close to safe beaches, town and harbours. Traditional English menus.
Bedrooms: 2 single, 3 double, 3 twin, 4 triple
Bathrooms: 12 en-suite

Bed & breakfast

per night:	£min	£max
Single	18.50	20.50
Double	37.00	41.00

Continued ▶

WEST COUNTRY

FALMOUTH
Continued

Half board per person:	£min	£max
Daily	26.00	29.90
Weekly	163.80	189.00

Lunch available
Evening meal 1830 (last orders 1915)
Parking for 8
Open March–October
Cards accepted: Access, Visa, Amex

Wickham Guest House
APPROVED

21 Gyllyngvase Terrace, Falmouth TR11 4DL
☎ (01326) 311140
Small guesthouse in quiet road a few minutes' walk from main beaches. Most rooms with sea views, some with colour TV and some en-suite.
Bedrooms: 2 single, 2 double, 1 twin, 1 family room
Bathrooms: 3 en-suite, 2 public

Bed & breakfast per night:	£min	£max
Single	15.00	18.00
Double	30.00	36.00

Half board per person:	£min	£max
Daily	21.50	25.00
Weekly	150.00	160.00

Evening meal 1845 (last orders 1700)
Parking for 4
Open April–October

FONTHILL GIFFORD
Wiltshire
Map ref 2B3

Village north of Tisbury. The 18th C architect, James Wyatt, built the now ruined Fonthill Abbey. Old Wardour Castle, 4 miles south.

Beckford Arms
COMMENDED

Fonthill Gifford, Tisbury, Salisbury SP3 6PX
☎ Tisbury (01747) 870385
Fax (01747) 851496
Wayfarer/Logis of Great Britain
Tastefully refurbished, stylish and comfortable 18th C inn, between Tisbury and Hindon in area of outstanding beauty. 2 miles A303. Convenient for Salisbury and Shaftesbury.

Bedrooms: 3 single, 4 double, 1 twin
Bathrooms: 5 en-suite, 3 private showers

Bed & breakfast per night:	£min	£max
Single	29.50	29.50
Double	49.50	54.50

Half board per person:	£min	£max
Daily	36.50	
Weekly	192.50	

Lunch available
Evening meal 1900 (last orders 2200)
Parking for 42
Cards accepted: Access, Visa, Amex, Switch/Delta

FOWEY
Cornwall
Map ref 1B3

Set on steep slopes at the mouth of the Fowey River, important clayport and fishing town. Ruined forts guarding the shore recall days of "Fowey Gallants" who ruled local seas. The lofty church rises above the town. Ferries to Polruan and Bodinnick; August Regatta.
Tourist Information Centre ☎ (01726) 833616

Carnethic House Hotel
COMMENDED

Lambs Barn, Fowey PL23 1HQ
☎ (01726) 833336
Fax (01726) 833336
Regency house in 1.5 acres of mature gardens. Heated pool. Home cooking with local fish a speciality. Informal atmosphere.

Bedrooms: 1 single, 4 double, 1 twin, 2 triple
Bathrooms: 6 en-suite, 1 private, 1 public, 1 private shower

Bed & breakfast per night:	£min	£max
Single	30.00	40.00
Double	46.00	62.00

Half board per person:	£min	£max
Daily	35.00	45.00
Weekly	250.00	300.00

Evening meal 1930 (last orders 2030)
Parking for 20
Open February–November
Cards accepted: Access, Visa, Diners, Amex

Cormorant Hotel
COMMENDED

Golant, Fowey PL23 1LL
☎ (01726) 833426
Fax (01726) 833426
Logis of Great Britain
Small, attractive, family-run hotel with magnificent views of the Fowey estuary. Noted for hospitality and food. Indoor heated swimming pool. Special rates for short breaks all year round.
Bedrooms: 7 double, 4 twin
Bathrooms: 11 en-suite

Bed & breakfast per night:	£min	£max
Single	42.00	52.00
Double	70.00	84.00

Half board per person:	£min	£max
Daily	58.00	60.00
Weekly	315.00	385.00

Lunch available
Evening meal 1900 (last orders 2100)
Parking for 15
Cards accepted: Access, Visa, Amex, Switch/Delta

Marina Hotel
HIGHLY COMMENDED

Esplanade, Fowey PL23 1HY
☎ (01726) 833315
Fax (01726) 832779
Privately-run, comfortably appointed Georgian hotel of character with river views and some balcony rooms. Own moorings, waterside garden and restaurant.
Bedrooms: 5 double, 5 twin
Bathrooms: 10 en-suite

Bed & breakfast per night:	£min	£max
Single	26.00	51.00
Double	52.00	88.00

Half board per person:	£min	£max
Daily	42.00	60.00
Weekly	266.00	392.00

Evening meal 1900 (last orders 2030)
Open March–December
Cards accepted: Access, Visa, Amex, Switch/Delta

Half board prices are given per person, but in some cases these may be based on double/twin occupancy.

WEST COUNTRY

FROME
Somerset
Map ref 2B2

Old market town with modern light industry, its medieval centre watered by the River Frome. Above Cheap Street with its flagstones and watercourse is the church showing work of varying periods. Interesting buildings include 18th C wool merchants' houses.
Tourist Information Centre ☎ *(01373) 467271*

Fourwinds Guest House
COMMENDED

19 Bath Road, Frome BA11 2HJ
☎ (01373) 462618
Fax (01373) 453029
Comfortable and friendly guesthouse with all the amenities of a small hotel. Half a mile north of town centre.
Wheelchair access category 3
Bedrooms: 1 single, 2 double, 2 twin, 1 family room
Bathrooms: 4 en-suite, 2 public

Bed & breakfast per night:

	£min	£max
Single	25.00	30.00
Double	40.00	45.00

Half board per person:

	£min	£max
Daily		40.00
Weekly		245.00

Evening meal 1800 (last orders 1900)
Parking for 12
Cards accepted: Access, Visa

GLASTONBURY
Somerset
Map ref 2A2

Market town associated with Joseph of Arimathea and the birth of English Christianity. Built around its 7th C abbey said to be the site of King Arthur's burial. Glastonbury Tor with its ancient tower gives panoramic views over flat country and the Mendip Hills.
Tourist Information Centre ☎ *(01458) 832954*

The Who'd A Thought It Inn
HIGHLY COMMENDED

17 Northload Street, Glastonbury BA6 9JJ
☎ (01458) 834460
Fax (01458) 831039
18th C Grade II listed traditional inn. Full of reclaimed interesting artefacts

and memorabilia. Real ales. Gourmet food always available.
Bedrooms: 1 single, 3 double, 2 twin
Bathrooms: 6 en-suite, 1 public

Bed & breakfast per night:

	£min	£max
Single	39.95	39.95
Double	55.00	55.00

Half board per person:

	£min	£max
Daily	35.50	55.00

Lunch available
Evening meal 1800 (last orders 2100)
Parking for 20
Cards accepted: Access, Visa

HARTLAND
Devon
Map ref 1C1

Hamlet on high, wild country near Hartland Point. Just west, the parish church tower makes a magnificent landmark; the light, unrestored interior holds one of Devon's finest rood screens. There are spectacular cliffs around Hartland Point and the lighthouse.

Hartland Quay Hotel

Hartland, Bideford EX39 6DU
☎ (01237) 441218
Small family-run hotel overlooking the rugged Atlantic coastline. Coastal walks. Important geological area.
Bedrooms: 2 single, 4 double, 4 twin, 3 triple, 1 family room
Bathrooms: 10 en-suite, 3 public

Bed & breakfast per night:

	£min	£max
Single	21.00	23.00
Double	42.00	46.00

Half board per person:

	£min	£max
Daily	30.00	31.00
Weekly	185.00	190.00

Lunch available
Evening meal 1900 (last orders 2100)
Parking for 100
Open February–November
Cards accepted: Access, Visa

The National Grading and Classification Scheme is explained in full at the back of this guide.

HAYLE
Cornwall
Map ref 1B3

Former mining town with modern light industry on the Hayle Estuary. Most buildings are Georgian or early Victorian, with some Regency houses along the canal.

Penellen Hotel

Riviere Towans, Hayle TR27 5AF
☎ (01736) 753777
Small family beachside hotel overlooking St Ives Bay, offering sea-bathing and glorious views. Ideal centre for touring. Restaurant, safe parking.
Bedrooms: 6 double, 2 twin, 2 family rooms
Bathrooms: 10 en-suite

Bed & breakfast per night:

	£min	£max
Single	17.00	21.00
Double	34.00	42.00

Half board per person:

	£min	£max
Daily	25.00	30.00
Weekly	158.00	212.00

Lunch available
Evening meal 1830 (last orders 2130)
Parking for 20

HAYTOR
Devon
Map ref 1C2

Rugged moorland with dramatic craggy rock formation on the eastern edge of Dartmoor National Park. Granite from local quarries was used for the British Museum, the National Gallery and London Bridge. Near Haytor Vale is a nature reserve with many species of trees and birds.

Moorland Hotel
APPROVED

Haytor, Newton Abbot TQ13 9XT
☎ (01364) 661407
Fax (01364) 661573
Set in delightful grounds below Haytor Rock. Superb views of open moorland and coast from all hotel rooms and self-catering apartments.
Bedrooms: 1 single, 11 double, 11 twin
Bathrooms: 23 en-suite

Continued ▶

WEST COUNTRY

HAYTOR
Continued

Bed & breakfast per night:	£min	£max
Single	28.00	35.00
Double	56.00	70.00

Half board per person:	£min	£max
Daily	39.50	45.00
Weekly	245.00	295.00

Lunch available
Evening meal 1900 (last orders 2100)
Parking for 50
Cards accepted: Access, Visa

HEASLEY MILL
Devon
Map Ref 1C1

Heasley House
COMMENDED

Heasley Mill, North Molton, South Molton EX36 3LE
☎ North Molton (01598) 740213
Fax (01598) 740677
A fine Georgian house, set in a Mole River valley hamlet. Uniquely tranquil, with country cooking, good wines and Exmoor hospitality.
Bedrooms: 4 double, 4 twin
Bathrooms: 5 en-suite, 2 public

Bed & breakfast per night:	£min	£max
Single	35.00	38.00
Double	51.00	64.00

Half board per person:	£min	£max
Daily	39.50	46.50
Weekly	248.00	293.00

Evening meal 1900 (last orders 2000)
Parking for 12
Open January, March–December
Cards accepted: Access, Visa, Diners

TOWN INDEX
This can be found at the back of the guide. If you know where you want to stay, the index will give you the page number listing all accommodation in your chosen town, city or village.

HELSTON
Cornwall
Map ref 1B3

Handsome town with steep, main street and narrow alleys. In medieval times it was a major port and stannary town. Most buildings date from Regency and Victorian periods. The famous May dance, the Furry, is thought to have pre- Christian origins. A museum occupies the old Butter Market.
Tourist Information Centre ☎ (01326) 565431

Gwealdues Hotel
COMMENDED

Falmouth Road, Helston TR13 8JX
☎ (01326) 572808 & 573331
Fax (01326) 561388
The Independents
Fully licensed modern hotel with en-suite rooms and central heating. Bar meals and a la carte restaurant available. Large banqueting room, satellite TV lounge.
Bedrooms: 3 single, 7 double, 2 twin, 3 triple, 2 family rooms
Bathrooms: 14 en-suite, 2 public

Bed & breakfast per night:	£min	£max
Single	30.00	45.00
Double	40.00	60.00

Lunch available
Evening meal 1930 (last orders 2100)
Parking for 60
Cards accepted: Access, Visa, Amex, Switch/Delta

HONITON
Devon
Map ref 1D2

Old coaching town in undulating farmland. Formerly famous for lace-making, it is now an antiques trade centre and market town. Small museum.
Tourist Information Centre ☎ (01404) 43716

The Belfry Country Hotel
COMMENDED

Yarcombe, Honiton EX14 9BD
☎ Upottery (01404) 861234 & 861588
Fax (01404) 861579
Minotel

Tastefully converted Victorian village school in picturesque valley with lovely views. Relaxed and friendly atmosphere, all rooms en-suite, scrumptious award-winning home cooking. No children under 12.
Bedrooms: 3 double, 2 twin, 1 triple
Bathrooms: 6 en-suite

Bed & breakfast per night:	£min	£max
Single	44.00	44.00
Double	68.00	68.00

Half board per person:	£min	£max
Daily	45.95	52.45
Weekly	308.00	308.00

Evening meal 1900 (last orders 2100)
Parking for 10
Cards accepted: Access, Visa, Amex

Home Farm Hotel
COMMENDED

Wilmington, Honiton EX14 9JR
☎ Wilmington (01404) 831278 & 831246
Fax (01404) 831411
Logis of Great Britain
Thatched 16th C farmhouse hotel in lovely countryside. Restaurant uses local produce to serve food of high standard. Bar with light meals. Log fires. 6 miles from sea.
Bedrooms: 3 single, 4 double, 2 twin, 4 triple
Suite available
Bathrooms: 13 en-suite, 1 public

Bed & breakfast per night:	£min	£max
Single		30.00
Double		56.00

Half board per person:	£min	£max
Daily		40.00

Lunch available
Evening meal 1900 (last orders 2130)
Parking for 20
Cards accepted: Access, Visa, Amex, Switch/Delta

Please mention this guide when making your booking.

WEST COUNTRY

Honiton Motel ⚜
♛♛♛ COMMENDED
Turks Head Corner, Exeter Road, Honiton EX14 8BL
☎ (01404) 43440 & 45400
Fax (01404) 47767
Comfortable, friendly licensed motel. Ideal touring base or for a one-night stay. Midway stop between Cornwall and the North.
Bedrooms: 1 single, 4 double, 8 twin, 2 triple
Bathrooms: 15 en-suite

Bed & breakfast
per night:	£min	£max
Single	30.00	32.00
Double	48.00	49.50

Half board per
person:	£min	£max
Daily	38.50	41.00

Lunch available
Evening meal 1900 (last orders 2100)
Parking for 150
Cards accepted: Access, Visa, Amex, Switch/Delta

HOPE COVE
Devon
Map ref 1C3

Sheltered by the 400-ft headland of Bolt Tail, Hope Cove lies close to a small resort with thatched cottages, Inner Hope. Between Bolt Tail and Bolt Head lie 6 miles of beautiful National Trust cliffs.

Lantern Lodge Hotel
♛♛♛ COMMENDED
Hope Cove, Kingsbridge TQ7 3HE
☎ Kingsbridge (01548) 561280
Fax (01548) 561736
Small, privately run, cliff-top hotel.
Bedrooms: 10 double, 3 twin, 1 triple
Bathrooms: 14 en-suite

Bed & breakfast
per night:	£min	£max
Single	37.51	54.45
Double	68.20	110.10

Half board per
person:	£min	£max
Daily	46.75	63.25
Weekly	308.00	408.10

Evening meal 1900 (last orders 2030)
Parking for 20
Open March–November
Cards accepted: Access, Visa, Switch/Delta

ILFRACOMBE
Devon
Map ref 1C1

Resort of Victorian grandeur set on hillside between cliffs with sandy coves. At the mouth of the harbour stands an 18th C lighthouse, built over a medieval chapel. There are fine formal gardens and a museum. Chambercombe Manor, interesting old house, nearby.
Tourist Information Centre ☎ (01271) 863001

Capstone Hotel and Restaurant ⚜
♛♛
St James Place, Ilfracombe EX34 9BJ
☎ (01271) 863540
Fax (01271) 862277
Family-run hotel with restaurant on ground floor. Close to harbour and all amenities. Local seafood a speciality.
Bedrooms: 1 single, 7 double, 1 twin, 3 family rooms
Bathrooms: 11 en-suite, 1 private

Bed & breakfast
per night:	£min	£max
Single	12.00	16.00
Double	24.00	32.00

Half board per
person:	£min	£max
Daily	24.50	28.00
Weekly	120.00	175.00

Lunch available
Evening meal 1800 (last orders 2200)
Parking for 4
Open April–October
Cards accepted: Access, Visa, Amex, Switch/Delta

Cleveland Hotel
♛♛
29 Saint James Place, Ilfracombe EX34 9BJ
☎ (01271) 867835
Fax (01271) 867835
In an excellent position on the main seafront road, close to harbour, coach station and all amenities.
Bedrooms: 4 double, 1 triple, 1 family room
Bathrooms: 6 en-suite

Bed & breakfast
per night:	£min	£max
Single	22.00	25.00
Double	28.50	33.00

Lunch available
Evening meal 1700 (last orders 1930)
Parking for 4
Cards accepted: Access, Visa

Darnley Private Hotel ⚜
♛♛♛ APPROVED
3 Belmont Road, Ilfracombe EX34 8DR
☎ Instow (01271) 863955
Elegant Victorian hotel of charm and character, quietly situated. Good home-cooked food, cosy bar, friendly personal service, ample parking, four poster.
Bedrooms: 6 double, 1 twin, 1 family room
Bathrooms: 7 en-suite, 1 private, 2 public

Bed & breakfast
per night:	£min	£max
Single	18.00	22.00
Double	36.00	44.00

Half board per
person:	£min	£max
Daily	26.00	30.00
Weekly	173.00	194.00

Evening meal 1830 (last orders 1900)
Parking for 12
Open March–December
Cards accepted: Visa, Switch/Delta

Elmfield Hotel
♛♛♛ COMMENDED
Torrs Park, Ilfracombe EX34 8AZ
☎ (01271) 863377
In quiet position close to town, with 1 acre of gardens. Adjacent to the famous Torrs Walks.
Bedrooms: 2 single, 8 double, 4 twin
Bathrooms: 14 en-suite

Bed & breakfast
per night:	£min	£max
Single	30.00	35.00
Double	60.00	66.00

Half board per
person:	£min	£max
Daily	35.00	40.00
Weekly	220.00	245.00

Lunch available
Evening meal 1900 (last orders 1930)
Parking for 15
Open March–October and Christmas
Cards accepted: Access, Visa

The ⚜ symbol after an establishment name indicates that it is a Regional Tourist Board member.

WEST COUNTRY

ILFRACOMBE
Continued

Epchris Hotel
APPROVED
Torrs Park, Ilfracombe EX34 8AZ
☎ (01271) 862751

Old stone house with a country feel, near centre of Ilfracombe and Torrs Walks. Bar, lovely terraced gardens, swimming pool.
Bedrooms: 2 single, 2 double, 1 triple, 5 family rooms
Bathrooms: 9 en-suite, 1 private, 1 public

Bed & breakfast

per night:	£min	£max
Single	19.00	21.00
Double	38.00	42.00

Half board per

person:	£min	£max
Daily	27.00	29.00
Weekly	175.00	195.00

Lunch available
Evening meal from 1830
Parking for 8
Open February–November and Christmas
Cards accepted: Access, Visa

The Ilfracombe Carlton Hotel
COMMENDED
Runnacleave Road, Ilfracombe EX34 8AR
☎ (01271) 862446 & 863711
Fax (01271) 865379
The Independents

Premier resort hotel in central location adjacent to beach and seafront. Comfortable rooms with good facilities. Buttery, dancing, 1 non-smoking lounge.
Bedrooms: 10 single, 19 double, 13 twin, 6 triple
Bathrooms: 48 en-suite, 2 public

Bed & breakfast

per night:	£min	£max
Single	25.00	27.50
Double	40.00	55.00

Half board per

person:	£min	£max
Daily	25.00	35.00
Weekly	150.00	220.00

Lunch available
Evening meal 1900 (last orders 2030)
Parking for 25
Open March–December
Cards accepted: Access, Visa, Diners, Amex

Imperial Hotel
Wilder Road, Ilfracombe EX34 9AL
☎ (01271) 862536
Fax (01271) 862571
On seafront close to all amenities. Entertainment 5 nights a week.
Bedrooms: 16 single, 34 double, 46 twin, 8 triple
Bathrooms: 104 en-suite

Bed & breakfast

per night:	£min	£max
Single	22.00	31.00
Double	38.00	56.00

Half board per

person:	£min	£max
Daily	28.00	34.00
Weekly	135.00	206.00

Lunch available
Evening meal 1800 (last orders 1930)
Parking for 12
Open March–December
Cards accepted: Access, Visa, Switch/Delta

Merlin Court Hotel
APPROVED
Torrs Park, Ilfracombe EX34 8AY
☎ (01271) 862697

Listed detached hotel, peacefully situated in own lovely terraced gardens and ideally located for exploring beautiful north Devon. Four-poster bed available. Car park.
Bedrooms: 7 double, 2 triple, 4 family rooms
Bathrooms: 12 en-suite, 1 public

Bed & breakfast

per night:	£min	£max
Single	20.00	22.00
Double	40.00	44.00

Half board per

person:	£min	£max
Daily	26.00	27.00
Weekly	169.00	180.00

Evening meal 1830 (last orders 1900)
Parking for 14
Cards accepted: Access, Visa, Amex

Sunnymeade Country House Hotel
APPROVED
Dean Cross, West Down, Ilfracombe EX34 8NT
☎ (01271) 863668

Set in over half an acre amid beautiful rolling Devon countryside. Close to beaches and Exmoor. West Down is 4 miles south of Ilfracombe.
Wheelchair access category 3
Bedrooms: 6 double, 1 twin, 1 triple, 1 family room
Bathrooms: 8 en-suite, 2 public, 1 private shower

Bed & breakfast

per night:	£min	£max
Single	20.50	24.50
Double	18.50	22.50

Half board per

person:	£min	£max
Daily	27.00	31.00
Weekly		195.00

Lunch available
Evening meal 1900 (last orders 2030)
Parking for 14
Cards accepted: Access, Visa, Diners, Switch/Delta

WELCOME HOST

This is a nationally recognised customer care programme which aims to promote the highest standards of service and a warm welcome. Establishments who are taking part in this initiative are indicated by the symbol.

WEST COUNTRY

ILLOGAN
Cornwall
Map ref 1B3

Former mining village 2 miles north-west of Redruth and close to the coast. The Victorian engineer and benefactor, Sir Richard Tangye, was born here in 1833.

Aviary Court Hotel
HIGHLY COMMENDED

Marys Well, Illogan, Redruth TR16 4QZ
☎ Portreath (01209) 842256
Fax (01209) 843744
Logis of Great Britain

Charming country house hotel set in over 2 acres of secluded gardens. Portreath 5 minutes by car or a 20 minute woodland walk.
Bedrooms: 4 double, 1 twin, 1 triple
Bathrooms: 6 en-suite

Bed & breakfast per night:	£min	£max
Single	38.00	42.00
Double	54.00	58.00

Half board per person:	£min	£max
Daily	39.50	41.50
Weekly	237.00	249.00

Evening meal 1900 (last orders 2030)
Parking for 25
Cards accepted: Access, Visa, Diners, Amex

ILSINGTON
Devon
Map ref 1D2

Village 4 miles north-east of Ashburton, and within the Dartmoor National Park. Yarner Wood National Nature Reserve to the north.

Ilsington Hotel
COMMENDED

Ilsington, Newton Abbot TQ13 9RR
☎ Haytor (01364) 661452
Fax (01364) 661307

Elegant country hotel on the edge of Dartmoor, near Exeter. Leisure facilities include indoor pool, sauna/solarium, bowls, tennis, riding. Golf nearby.

Walking, shooting, Dartmoor safaris, country life breaks. Magnificent views.
Bedrooms: 2 single, 16 double, 7 twin
Suites available
Bathrooms: 25 en-suite

Bed & breakfast per night:	£min	£max
Single		50.00
Double		80.00

Half board per person:	£min	£max
Daily		65.00
Weekly		315.00

Lunch available
Evening meal 1830 (last orders 2100)
Parking for 100
Cards accepted: Access, Visa, Diners, Amex, Switch/Delta

INSTOW
Devon
Map ref 1C1

Popular sailing centre on the Torridge Estuary, between Bideford and Barnstaple. Tapeley Park House, standing in Italian gardens, has fine 18th C plasterwork ceilings and collections of china and furniture.

The Commodore Hotel
HIGHLY COMMENDED

Marine Parade, Instow EX39 4JN
☎ (01271) 860347
Fax (01271) 861233

Family owned and managed hotel set in waterside village with sweeping estuary views. Ideally situated for golfing, walking or just relaxing. Noted for warmth of welcome, good food and hospitality.
Bedrooms: 1 single, 12 double, 7 twin
Bathrooms: 20 en-suite

Bed & breakfast per night:	£min	£max
Single	45.00	50.00
Double	80.00	90.00

Half board per person:	£min	£max
Daily	55.00	65.00
Weekly	385.00	400.00

Lunch available
Evening meal 1900 (last orders 2115)
Parking for 150
Cards accepted: Access, Visa, Diners, Amex, Switch/Delta

ISLES OF SCILLY
Map ref 1A3

Picturesque group of islands and granitic rocks south-west of Land's End. Peaceful and unspoilt, they are noted for natural beauty, romantic maritime history, silver sands, early flowers and sub-tropical gardens on Tresco. Main island is St Mary's.
Tourist Information Centre ☎ (01720) 422536

Bell Rock Hotel
COMMENDED

Church Street, St Mary's, Isles of Scilly TR21 0JS
☎ Scillonia (01720) 422575
Fax (01720) 423093

Warm welcome and friendly, informal service. All en-suite, heated indoor pool, wide choice of good food, fully licensed. In central position, 100 yards from beaches.
Bedrooms: 5 single, 11 double, 4 twin, 2 triple, 1 family room
Bathrooms: 23 en-suite

Bed & breakfast per night:	£min	£max
Single	23.50	54.00
Double	47.00	108.00

Half board per person:	£min	£max
Daily	39.50	59.00
Weekly	256.00	399.00

Lunch available
Evening meal 1830 (last orders 2000)
Cards accepted: Access, Visa

Carnwethers Country House
COMMENDED

Pelistry Bay, St Mary's, Isles of Scilly TR21 0NX
☎ Scillonia (01720) 422415
"Up-country" private hotel, family-run,
Continued ▶

WEST COUNTRY

ISLES OF SCILLY
Continued

close to quiet beaches, nature trails and coastal walks. Secluded gardens, heated pool, well-stocked bar, library and croquet lawn.
Bedrooms: 1 single, 3 double, 3 twin, 2 triple
Bathrooms: 9 en-suite
Half board per

person:	£min	£max
Daily	34.00	49.00
Weekly	230.00	335.00

Evening meal 1830 (last orders 1830)
Parking for 3
Open May–September

Harbourside Hotel
COMMENDED
The Quay, St Mary's, Isles of Scilly TR21 OHV
☎ Scillonia (01720) 422352
Fax (01720) 422352
Small hotel situated right on St Mary's Quay. Every room has private facilities and a view of the sea.
Bedrooms: 5 double, 6 twin, 1 triple
Bathrooms: 12 en-suite
Half board per

person:	£min	£max
Daily	47.50	57.50
Weekly	332.50	402.50

Evening meal 1830 (last orders 2100)
Open February–December
Cards accepted: Access, Visa

Hell Bay Hotel
HIGHLY COMMENDED
Bryher, Isles of Scilly TR23 OPR
☎ Scillonia (01720) 422947
Fax (01720) 423004
Only hotel on beautiful unspoilt island. Attractive rooms opening on to gardens. Residents' lounge overlooking Atlantic Ocean. Adjacent safe, sandy beaches. High standards of comfort and cuisine.
Bedrooms: 4 double, 3 twin, 1 triple, 2 family rooms
Suites available
Bathrooms: 10 en-suite
Half board per

person:	£min	£max
Daily	51.00	76.00

Lunch available
Evening meal 1915 (last orders 2045)

Open March–October
Cards accepted: Access, Visa, Switch/Delta

KEYNSHAM
Bath & North East Somerset
Map ref 2B2

Busy town on the River Avon between Bath and Bristol.

Grasmere Court Hotel
22-24 Bath Road, Keynsham, Bristol BS18 1SN
☎ (0117) 986 2521
Fax (0117) 986 2762
Well-appointed hotel with high standard of decor and accommodation. Private facilities. Situated on A4 between Bath and Bristol.
Bedrooms: 1 single, 10 double, 3 twin, 2 family rooms
Bathrooms: 16 en-suite
Bed & breakfast

per night:	£min	£max
Single	34.00	52.00
Double	48.00	64.00

Evening meal 1830 (last orders 1930)
Parking for 18
Cards accepted: Access, Visa, Amex, Switch/Delta

KINGSBRIDGE
Devon
Map ref 1C3

Formerly important as a port, now a market town overlooking head of beautiful, wooded estuary winding deep into rural countryside. Summer art exhibitions; Cookworthy Museum.
Tourist Information Centre ☎ (01548) 853195

Crabshell Motor Lodge
Embankment Road, Kingsbridge TQ7 1JZ
☎ (01548) 853301
Fax (01548) 856283
Logis of Great Britain

On water's edge of Salcombe Estuary.

Boat moorings. Waterside bar/restaurant with extensive seafood menu. Rooms with private balcony, colour TV, kitchenette, refrigerator.
Bedrooms: 2 double, 17 twin, 5 family rooms
Bathrooms: 24 en-suite
Bed & breakfast

per night:	£min	£max
Single	33.00	
Double	50.00	

Half board per

person:	£min	£max
Weekly	221.00	

Lunch available
Evening meal 1830 (last orders 2130)
Parking for 36
Cards accepted: Access, Visa, Diners, Amex, Switch/Delta

Kings Arms Hotel
COMMENDED
Fore Street, Kingsbridge TQ7 1AB
☎ (01548) 852071
Fax (01548) 852977
Minotel
17th C coaching inn, renowned for its hospitality, four-poster beds and historic links with this very pretty estuary town.
Bedrooms: 2 single, 8 double, 1 twin
Bathrooms: 10 en-suite, 1 private
Bed & breakfast

per night:	£min	£max
Single	35.00	35.00
Double	60.00	60.00

Half board per

person:	£min	£max
Daily	45.00	45.00
Weekly	240.00	240.00

Lunch available
Evening meal 1900 (last orders 2130)
Parking for 30
Cards accepted: Access, Visa, Switch/Delta

WELCOME HOST
This is a nationally recognised customer care programme which aims to promote the highest standards of service and a warm welcome. Establishments who are taking part in this initiative are indicated by the ✿ symbol.

WEST COUNTRY

KINGSTEIGNTON
Devon
Map ref 1D2

Large village 2 miles north of Newton Abbot and the centre of the clay industry. Ram roasting ceremony held annually on Spring Bank Holiday. National Hunt racecourse nearby.

Passage House Hotel
HIGHLY COMMENDED

Hackney Lane, Kingsteignton, Newton Abbot TQ12 3QH
☎ Newton Abbot (01626) 55515
Fax (01626) 63336

This modern hotel offers a high standard of comfort and service. Leave A380 for the A381 and follow the racecourse signs.
Bedrooms: 7 double, 31 triple, 1 family room
Bathrooms: 39 en-suite
Bed & breakfast

per night:	£min	£max
Single	59.00	69.00
Double	75.00	85.00

Lunch available
Evening meal 1900 (last orders 2130)
Parking for 200
Cards accepted: Access, Visa, Diners, Amex, Switch/Delta

LAUNCESTON
Cornwall
Map ref 1C2

Medieval "Gateway to Cornwall", county town until 1838, founded by the Normans under their hilltop castle near the original monastic settlement. This market town, overlooked by its castle ruin, has a square with Georgian houses and an elaborately-carved granite church.
Tourist Information Centre ☎ (01566) 772321 or 772333

Glencoe Villa

13 Race Hill, Launceston PL15 9BB
☎ (01566) 773012 & 775819
Large 3-storey, hilltop Victorian-type house with superb views across Tamar Valley. 4 minutes from town centre.
Bedrooms: 1 double, 1 twin, 1 triple, 1 family room
Bathrooms: 2 private, 1 public

Bed & breakfast

per night:	£min	£max
Single	14.00	25.00
Double	28.00	38.00

Parking for 10
Cards accepted: Access, Visa

LISKEARD
Cornwall
Map ref 1C2

Former stannary town with a livestock market and light industry, at the head of a valley running to the coast. Handsome Georgian and Victorian residences and a Victorian Guildhall reflect the prosperity of the mining boom. The large church has an early 20th C tower and a Norman font.

Elnor Guest House
COMMENDED

1 Russell Street, Liskeard PL14 4BP
☎ (01579) 342472
Home-from-home with friendly family atmosphere in 100-year-old town house between the station and market town.
Bedrooms: 4 single, 1 double, 2 twin, 1 triple, 1 family room
Bathrooms: 7 en-suite, 1 public
Bed & breakfast

per night:	£min	£max
Single	17.00	20.00
Double	34.00	40.00

Half board per

person:	£min	£max
Daily	29.00	32.00
Weekly	189.00	210.00

Evening meal 1800 (last orders 1800)
Parking for 6

LITTLE TORRINGTON
Devon
Map ref 1C2

Smytham Manor Holidays

Little Torrington, Torrington EX38 8PU
☎ Torrington (01805) 622110
Old manor house set in 25 acres of landscaped grounds. Close to beaches, moors, Tarka Trail and Rosemoor Gardens.
Bedrooms: 3 double, 3 twin, 1 triple
Bathrooms: 5 en-suite, 1 public
Bed & breakfast

per night:	£min	£max
Single	14.00	21.00
Double	28.00	42.00

Half board per

person:	£min	£max
Daily	20.00	31.00
Weekly	140.00	217.00

Evening meal 1900 (last orders 2100)
Parking for 20
Open March–October
Cards accepted: Access, Visa, Switch/Delta

LOOE
Cornwall
Map ref 1C2

Small resort developed around former fishing and smuggling ports occupying the deep estuary of the East and West Looe Rivers. Narrow winding streets, with old inns; museum and art gallery are housed in interesting old buildings. Shark fishing centre, boat trips; busy harbour.

Commonwood Manor Hotel
HIGHLY COMMENDED

St Martins Road, Looe PL13 1LP
☎ (01503) 262929
Fax (01503) 262632

Spacious and relaxing country house hotel. Set in 6 acre estate overlooking Looe River valley and countryside beyond, yet only 10 minutes' walk to harbour and town.
Bedrooms: 1 single, 7 double, 2 twin, 1 family room
Suite available
Bathrooms: 11 en-suite
Bed & breakfast

per night:	£min	£max
Single	29.00	37.00
Double	58.00	74.00

Half board per

person:	£min	£max
Daily	41.00	53.00
Weekly	287.00	315.00

Lunch available
Evening meal 1900 (last orders 2000)
Parking for 20
Cards accepted: Access, Visa, Amex, Switch/Delta

WEST COUNTRY

LOOE
Continued

Coombe Farm
HIGHLY COMMENDED
Widegates, Looe PL13 1QN
☎ Widegates (01503) 240223
Fax (01503) 240895

Charming country house in wonderful, tranquil setting with superb views to the sea. Warm, friendly, relaxing atmosphere. Log fires. Delicious food, candlelit dining. 3.5 miles east of Looe on B3253.
Bedrooms: 3 double, 3 twin, 2 triple, 2 family rooms
Bathrooms: 10 en-suite

Bed & breakfast
per night:	£min	£max
Single	20.00	26.00
Double	40.00	52.00

Half board per
person:	£min	£max
Daily	34.00	40.00
Weekly	224.00	266.00

Evening meal 1900 (last orders 1900)
Parking for 12
Open March–October
Cards accepted: Access, Visa, Diners, Amex, Switch/Delta

Fieldhead Hotel
HIGHLY COMMENDED
Portuan Road, Hannafore, West Looe, Looe PL13 2DR
☎ (01503) 262689
Fax (01503) 264114
Minotel/The Independents
Turn-of-the-century house set in lovely gardens in quiet area, with panoramic views of the sea and bay. Intimate candlelit restaurant.
Bedrooms: 1 single, 9 double, 3 twin, 1 triple
Bathrooms: 14 en-suite

Bed & breakfast
per night:	£min	£max
Single	35.00	37.50
Double	60.00	75.00

Half board per
person:	£min	£max
Daily	45.00	50.00
Weekly	260.00	325.00

Lunch available
Evening meal 1830 (last orders 2030)
Parking for 14
Open February–December
Cards accepted: Access, Visa, Amex, Switch/Delta

The Panorama Hotel
COMMENDED
Hannafore Road, Looe PL13 2DE
☎ (01503) 262123
Fax (01503) 265654
Family-run hotel, good food, friendly atmosphere. Magnificent setting overlooking harbour, beach and miles of beautiful coastline.
Bedrooms: 2 single, 4 double, 1 twin, 2 triple, 1 family room
Bathrooms: 10 en-suite, 1 public

Bed & breakfast
per night:	£min	£max
Single	22.50	32.50
Double	45.00	65.00

Half board per
person:	£min	£max
Daily	33.75	43.75
Weekly	202.50	262.50

Evening meal 1830 (last orders 1900)
Parking for 8
Cards accepted: Access, Visa, Diners, Amex, Switch/Delta

Rivercroft Hotel
COMMENDED
Station Road, East Looe, Looe PL13 1HL
☎ (01503) 262251

Family-run hotel overlooking beautiful Looe River, with locally renowned restaurant serving fresh seafood and local produce.
Bedrooms: 3 single, 5 double, 1 twin, 3 triple, 1 family room
Bathrooms: 10 en-suite, 2 public

Bed & breakfast
per night:	£min	£max
Single	16.00	25.00
Double	32.00	50.00

Half board per
person:	£min	£max
Daily	25.00	34.00
Weekly	160.00	220.00

Lunch available
Evening meal 1830 (last orders 2130)
Cards accepted: Access, Visa

Hotel Trevanion
COMMENDED
Hannafore Road, Looe PL13 2DE
☎ (01503) 262003 & Mobile 0860 132320
Fax (01503) 265408
Family-run hotel with panoramic views over the harbour, beach and coastline. En-suite rooms and comfortable bar.
Bedrooms: 2 single, 6 double, 1 twin, 1 triple, 2 family rooms
Bathrooms: 11 en-suite, 2 public

Bed & breakfast
per night:	£min	£max
Single	21.00	27.00
Double	38.00	50.00

Half board per
person:	£min	£max
Daily	29.50	37.50
Weekly	175.00	223.00

Evening meal 1830 (last orders 1900)
Parking for 1
Cards accepted: Access, Visa

LOSTWITHIEL
Cornwall
Map ref 1B2

Cornwall's ancient capital which gained its Royal Charter in 1189. Tin from the mines around the town was smelted and coined in the Duchy Palace. Norman Restormel Castle, with its circular keep and deep moat, overlooks the town.

Restormel Lodge Hotel
COMMENDED
19 Castle Hill, Lostwithiel PL22 0DD
☎ Bodmin (01208) 872223
Fax (01208) 873568
Consort
Set in the beautiful Fowey Valley. Warm, spacious well-equipped bedrooms. Imaginative menus of delicious food and friendly, efficient service.
Bedrooms: 2 single, 14 double, 13 twin, 3 triple
Bathrooms: 32 en-suite

Bed & breakfast
per night:	£min	£max
Single	46.00	48.00
Double	62.00	64.00

Half board per
person:	£min	£max
Daily	47.00	49.00

WEST COUNTRY

Lunch available
Evening meal 1900 (last orders 2130)
Parking for 45
Cards accepted: Access, Visa, Diners, Amex

LYDFORD
Devon
Map ref 1C2

Former important tin mining centre, a small village on edge of West Dartmoor. Remains of Norman castle where all falling foul of tinners' notorious "Lydford Law" were incarcerated. Bridge crosses River Lyd where it rushes through a mile-long gorge of boulders and trees.

Lydford House Hotel M
HIGHLY COMMENDED
Lydford, Okehampton EX20 4AU
☎ (01822) 820347
Fax (01822) 820442
Minotel

Family-run country house hotel, peacefully set in own grounds on edge of Dartmoor. Superb touring centre. Own riding stables.
Bedrooms: 3 single, 3 double, 3 twin, 2 triple, 2 family rooms
Bathrooms: 11 en-suite, 2 private

Bed & breakfast per night:	£min	£max
Single		35.00
Double		70.00

Half board per person:	£min	£max
Weekly	280.00

Lunch available
Evening meal 1900 (last orders 2030)
Parking for 30
Cards accepted: Access, Visa

Moor View House M
COMMENDED
Vale Down, Lydford, Okehampton EX20 4BB
☎ (01822) 820220

Family-run country house hotel on edge of Dartmoor, peacefully set in 2 acres of gardens. Fine food, sound wine, log fires. Walking, fishing, riding, shooting and golf. Excellent touring centre.
Bedrooms: 1 single, 2 double, 1 triple
Bathrooms: 4 en-suite

Bed & breakfast per night:	£min	£max
Single	30.00	37.50
Double	55.00	60.00

Half board per person:	£min	£max
Daily	45.00	55.00
Weekly	280.00	300.00

Evening meal 1900 (last orders 2000)
Parking for 15

LYME REGIS
Dorset
Map ref 1D2

Pretty, historic fishing town and resort set against the fossil-rich cliffs of Lyme Bay. In medieval times it was an important port and cloth centre. The Cobb, a massive stone breakwater, shelters the ancient harbour which is still lively with boats.
Tourist Information Centre ☎ (01297) 442138

Hotel Buena Vista M
COMMENDED
Pound Street, Lyme Regis DT7 3HZ
☎ (01297) 442494

Regency house with a country house atmosphere in an unrivalled position overlooking the bay. Close to the town and beaches.
Bedrooms: 4 single, 9 double, 4 twin, 1 family room
Bathrooms: 17 en-suite, 1 private

Bed & breakfast per night:	£min	£max
Single	38.00	42.00
Double	64.00	98.00

Half board per person:	£min	£max
Daily	44.00	57.00
Weekly	288.00	366.00

Evening meal 1900 (last orders 2000)
Parking for 20

Open February–November
Cards accepted: Access, Visa, Diners, Amex, Switch/Delta

The Dower House Hotel M
HIGHLY COMMENDED
Rousdon, Lyme Regis DT7 3RB
☎ Seaton (01297) 21047
Fax (01297) 24748

Originally a dower house, now a country house hotel in its own idyllic grounds. Open fires. Emphasis on good food and comfort.
Bedrooms: 1 single, 3 double, 2 twin, 3 triple
Bathrooms: 9 en-suite

Bed & breakfast per night:	£min	£max
Single	38.00	48.00
Double	60.00	80.00

Half board per person:	£min	£max
Daily	42.00	55.00
Weekly	265.00	325.00

Lunch available
Evening meal 1900 (last orders 2100)
Parking for 48
Cards accepted: Access, Visa, Diners, Amex

Kersbrook Hotel and Restaurant M
HIGHLY COMMENDED
Pound Road, Lyme Regis DT7 3HX
☎ (01297) 442596 & 442576
Fax (01297) 442596
Minotel

Thatched, 18th C listed hotel and restaurant in its own picturesque gardens, set high above Lyme Bay. For those who prefer peace and tranquillity.
Bedrooms: 2 single, 7 double, 3 twin
Bathrooms: 12 en-suite

Bed & breakfast per night:	£min	£max
Single	50.00	65.00
Double	65.00	75.00

Half board per person:	£min	£max
Daily	47.50	52.00
Weekly	300.00	340.00

Continued ▶

WEST COUNTRY

LYME REGIS
Continued

Lunch available
Evening meal 1930 (last orders 2100)
Parking for 16
Open February–November
Cards accepted: Access, Visa, Amex, Switch/Delta

Lydwell House
COMMENDED

Lyme Road, Uplyme, Lyme Regis DT7 3TJ
☎ (01297) 443522
Fax (01297) 445897
Delightful Edwardian house in attractive gardens, ideally located for coast and country walking. Short distance to Lyme Regis town centre and beaches.
Bedrooms: 1 single, 1 double, 1 twin, 2 family rooms
Bathrooms: 2 en-suite, 1 public
Bed & breakfast

per night:	£min	£max
Single	17.50	22.00
Double	33.00	38.00

Parking for 7

Swallows Eaves Hotel
HIGHLY COMMENDED

Colyford, Colyton, Devon EX13 6QJ
☎ Colyton (01297) 553184
Attractive award-winning hotel for discerning guests, in an Area of Outstanding Natural Beauty. Quality rooms and interesting food. Special breaks. Ideal centre for visiting gardens and National Trust properties.
Bedrooms: 1 single, 3 double, 4 twin
Bathrooms: 8 en-suite
Bed & breakfast

per night:	£min	£max
Single	27.00	47.00
Double	54.00	74.00

Half board per person:	£min	£max
Daily	45.00	55.00
Weekly	273.00	329.00

Lunch available
Evening meal 1900 (last orders 2000)
Parking for 10
Open February–November
Cards accepted: Access, Visa, Amex, Switch/Delta

LYNMOUTH
Devon
Map ref 1C1

Resort set beneath bracken-covered cliffs and pinewood gorges where 2 rivers meet, and cascade between boulders to the town. Lynton, set on cliffs above, can be reached by water-operated cliff railway from the Victorian esplanade. Valley of the Rocks, to the west, gives dramatic walks.

Bath Hotel
COMMENDED

Lynmouth EX35 6EL
☎ Lynton (01598) 752238
Friendly, family-run hotel by picturesque Lynmouth harbour. Ideal centre for exploring Exmoor National Park.
Bedrooms: 1 single, 10 double, 11 twin, 2 triple
Bathrooms: 24 en-suite
Bed & breakfast

per night	£min	£max
Single	27.00	37.00
Double	54.00	74.00

Half board per person:	£min	£max
Daily	35.00	45.00
Weekly	204.00	315.00

Lunch available
Evening meal 1900 (last orders 2030)
Parking for 17
Open March–October
Cards accepted: Access, Visa, Diners, Amex, Switch/Delta

Tregonwell Riverside Guesthouse
APPROVED

1 Tors Road, Lynmouth EX35 6ET
☎ Lynton (01598) 753369

Elegant Victorian riverside rock house, alongside waterfalls, cascades, dramatic scenery, enchanting harbour, in romantic old world smugglers' village. Nature lovers'/walkers' paradise.
Bedrooms: 1 single, 5 double, 1 twin
Bathrooms: 3 en-suite, 1 private, 2 public
Bed & breakfast

per night:	£min	£max
Single	16.50	20.00
Double	33.00	45.00

Half board per person:	£min	£max
Daily	30.00	35.00
Weekly	200.00	240.00

Evening meal 1800 (last orders 1815)
Parking for 9
Open February–May, July–December

LYNTON
Devon
Map ref 1C1

Hilltop resort on Exmoor coast linked to its seaside twin, Lynmouth, by a water-operated cliff railway which descends from the town hall. Spectacular surroundings of moorland cliffs with steep chasms of conifer and rocks through which rivers cascade.
Tourist Information Centre ☎ (01598) 752225

Alford House Hotel
COMMENDED

Alford Terrace, Lynton EX35 6AT
☎ (01598) 752359
Elegant Georgian hotel with spectacular views over Lynton and Exmoor coastline. Delightful en-suite rooms, some four-poster beds. Relaxing and peaceful, warm hospitality, outstanding food and fine wine. Non-smokers preferred.
Bedrooms: 1 single, 5 double, 2 twin
Bathrooms: 8 en-suite, 1 public
Bed & breakfast

per night:	£min	£max
Single	20.00	26.00
Double	40.00	56.00

Half board per person:	£min	£max
Daily	34.00	40.00
Weekly	224.00	238.00

Evening meal 1700 (last orders 1700)
Open February–October, December
Cards accepted: Access, Visa

Chough's Nest Hotel
COMMENDED

North Walk, Lynton EX35 6HJ
☎ (01598) 753315
Detached cliffside retreat with 2-acre grounds and magnificent sea views. Good food. Value for money. Within walking distance of shops.
Bedrooms: 2 single, 7 double, 1 twin, 2 triple
Bathrooms: 12 en-suite

WEST COUNTRY

Bed & breakfast per night:	£min	£max
Single	29.00	31.00
Double	58.00	62.00

Half board per person:	£min	£max
Daily	39.50	
Weekly	265.00	

Lunch available
Evening meal 1900 (last orders 1930)
Parking for 10
Open March–October
Cards accepted: Access, Visa, Amex
🛏2🗝📞♿🍽🅿️♨️🛎🧺🐕✱✈
SP 🏠 T

Ingleside Hotel ♠
◉◉◉ COMMENDED
Lynton EX35 6HW
☎ (01598) 752223
Family-run hotel with high standards in elevated position overlooking village. Ideal centre for exploring Exmoor.
Bedrooms: 4 double, 1 twin, 2 triple
Bathrooms: 7 en-suite

Bed & breakfast per night:	£min	£max
Single	27.00	29.00
Double	46.00	50.00

Half board per person:	£min	£max
Daily	36.00	38.00
Weekly	238.00	252.00

Evening meal 1900 (last orders 1800)
Parking for 10
Open March–October
Cards accepted: Access, Visa
🛏12🗝📞♿🍽🅿️♨️🛎🧺✱✈
🐕 OAP SP T

Longmead House Hotel ♠
◉◉◉ HIGHLY COMMENDED
9 Longmead, Lynton EX35 6DQ
☎ (01598) 752523

Delightful old house set in a large garden, quietly situated towards the "Valley of Rocks". Comfortable, pretty en-suite bedrooms. No smoking. A warm welcome awaits you.
Bedrooms: 1 single, 4 double, 1 twin, 1 family room
Bathrooms: 5 en-suite, 1 public

Bed & breakfast per night:	£min	£max
Single	18.00	22.00
Double	36.00	44.00

Half board per person:	£min	£max
Daily	30.00	34.00
Weekly	180.00	217.00

Evening meal 1900 (last orders 1530)
Parking for 8
Open March–October
🛏♿📞S🍽📺🛎🅿️♨️🚌SP T

Rockvale Hotel
◉◉◉ COMMENDED
Lee Road, Lynton EX35 6HW
☎ (01598) 752279 & 753343
Quiet, very sunny central location with panoramic views. Pretty en-suite rooms, bar and large level car park. Award-winning home cooking and hospitality. Non smoking.
Bedrooms: 1 single, 5 double, 1 triple, 1 family room
Bathrooms: 6 en-suite, 2 private

Bed & breakfast per night:	£min	£max
Single	20.00	22.00
Double	44.00	48.00

Half board per person:	£min	£max
Daily	33.00	37.00
Weekly	211.00	251.00

Evening meal 1900 (last orders 1600)
Parking for 10
Open March–October
Cards accepted: Access, Visa
🛏4🗝📞♿🍽🅿️♨️🛎🧺
✱✈🐕 SP

Sandrock Hotel ♠
◉◉◉ COMMENDED
Longmead, Lynton EX35 6DH
☎ (01598) 753307
Fax (01598) 752665

Relaxing Edwardian hotel with modern comforts, in delightful sunny position close to Exmoor's superb coastal scenery and beauty spots.
Bedrooms: 2 single, 4 double, 3 twin
Bathrooms: 7 en-suite, 1 public

Bed & breakfast per night:	£min	£max
Single	19.50	26.00
Double	39.00	52.00

Half board per person:	£min	£max
Daily	29.50	37.50
Weekly	205.00	240.00

Evening meal 1900 (last orders 2000)
Parking for 9
Cards accepted: Access, Visa, Amex, Switch/Delta
🛏🗝📞♿S🍽🧺🅿️♨️🐕
OAP SP T

Seawood Hotel
◉◉◉ HIGHLY COMMENDED
North Walk Drive, Lynton EX35 6HJ
☎ (01598) 752272
Family-run country house hotel nestling on wooded cliffs overlooking Lynmouth Bay and headland. Varied menu and friendly service.
Bedrooms: 1 single, 9 double, 2 twin
Bathrooms: 12 en-suite, 2 public

Bed & breakfast per night:	£min	£max
Single	27.00	29.00
Double	54.00	58.00

Half board per person:	£min	£max
Daily	37.00	39.00
Weekly	255.00	265.00

Evening meal 1900 (last orders 1930)
Parking for 10
Open April–October
🛏10🗝📞♿S🍽🧺🅿️♨️
🐕 SP 🏠 T

MALMESBURY
Wiltshire
Map ref 2B2

Overlooking the River Avon, an old town dominated by its great church, once a Benedictine abbey. The surviving Norman nave and porch are noted for fine sculptures, 12th C arches and musicians' gallery.
Tourist Information Centre ☎ (01666) 823748

Knoll House Hotel
◉◉◉ COMMENDED
Swindon Road, Malmesbury SN16 9LU
☎ (01666) 823114
Fax (01666) 823897
GR Minotel

Ideally located with easy access to M4, Bath, Cheltenham and Cotswolds. Country house with fine restaurant and outdoor heated pool.

Continued ▶

WEST COUNTRY

MALMESBURY
Continued

Bedrooms: 9 single, 10 double, 3 twin
Bathrooms: 22 en-suite

Bed & breakfast per night:	£min	£max
Single	50.00	57.30
Double	65.00	85.00

Half board per person:	£min	£max
Daily		55.00

Lunch available
Evening meal 1900 (last orders 2130)
Parking for 60
Cards accepted: Access, Visa, Amex, Switch/Delta

Mayfield House Hotel
COMMENDED

Crudwell, Malmesbury SN16 9EW
☎ (01666) 577409 & 577198
Fax (01666) 577977

Delightful country hotel with 2 acres of walled garden. Award-winning restaurant, with warm and friendly service. Close to M4, ideal for touring Cotswolds and Bath.
Bedrooms: 4 single, 8 double, 7 twin, 1 triple
Bathrooms: 20 en-suite

Bed & breakfast per night:	£min	£max
Single	40.00	42.00
Double	58.00	62.00

Half board per person:	£min	£max
Daily	37.00	45.00
Weekly	189.00	199.00

Lunch available
Evening meal 1900 (last orders 2130)
Parking for 50
Cards accepted: Access, Visa, Diners, Amex, Switch/Delta

Old Bell Hotel
HIGHLY COMMENDED

Abbey Row, Malmesbury SN16 0AG
☎ (01666) 822344
Fax (01666) 825145

Wisteria-clad frontage to England's oldest hotel. Adjacent to Norman abbey in historic town. Particularly suited to families.
Bedrooms: 4 single, 24 double, 3 twin
Suites available
Bathrooms: 31 en-suite

Bed & breakfast per night:	£min	£max
Single	60.00	85.00
Double	85.00	150.00

Lunch available
Evening meal 1930 (last orders 2130)
Parking for 30
Cards accepted: Access, Visa, Diners, Amex, Switch/Delta

MARAZION
Cornwall
Map ref 1B3

Old town sloping to Mount's Bay with views of St Michael's Mount and a causeway to the island revealed at low tide. In medieval times it catered for pilgrims. The Mount is crowned by a 15th C castle built around the former Benedictine monastery of 1044.

Chymorvah Private Hotel

Marazion TR17 0DQ
☎ Penzance (01736) 710497

Family-run hotel and tea garden overlooking St Michael's Mount and Mount's Bay. Spacious grounds with own access to beach.
Bedrooms: 1 single, 4 double, 1 twin, 1 triple, 2 family rooms
Bathrooms: 9 en-suite, 1 public

Bed & breakfast per night:	£min	£max
Single	25.00	26.50
Double	56.00	59.00

Half board per person:	£min	£max
Daily	35.00	39.50
Weekly	236.00	266.50

Lunch available
Evening meal 1830 (last orders 1830)
Parking for 9
Cards accepted: Access, Visa, Amex

For ideas on places to visit refer to the introduction at the beginning of this section.

MARLBOROUGH
Wiltshire
Map ref 2B2

Important market town, in a river valley cutting through chalk downlands. The broad main street, with colonnaded shops on one side, shows a medley of building styles, mainly from the Georgian period. Lanes wind away on either side and a church stands at each end.
Tourist Information Centre ☎ *(01672) 513989*

The Old Vicarage
HIGHLY COMMENDED

Burbage, Marlborough SN8 3AG
☎ (01672) 810495
Fax (01672) 810663

Victorian country house in 2-acre garden, offering peace, comfort and delicious food. South of Marlborough and within easy reach of Avebury, Bath, Oxford and Salisbury.
Bedrooms: 1 single, 1 double, 1 twin
Bathrooms: 3 en-suite

Bed & breakfast per night:	£min	£max
Single	30.00	40.00
Double	60.00	80.00

Parking for 10
Cards accepted: Access, Visa

MAWGAN PORTH
Cornwall
Map ref 1B2

Holiday village occupying a steep valley on the popular coastal route to Newquay. Golden sands, rugged cliffs and coves. Nearby Bedruthan Steps offers exhilarating cliff walks and views. The chapel of a Carmelite nunnery, once the home of the Arundells, may be visited.

Tredragon Hotel
COMMENDED

Mawgan Porth, Newquay TR8 4DQ
☎ St Mawgan (01637) 860213
Fax (01637) 860269
Logis of Great Britain

Grounds lead directly to sandy cove. Magnificent coastal walks/views. Relax

in our indoor pool complex. Excellent food and wine. Open all year. Ideal for short breaks.
Bedrooms: 2 single, 9 double, 5 twin, 13 family rooms
Bathrooms: 29 en-suite

Bed & breakfast per night:

	£min	£max
Single	25.00	40.00
Double	50.00	60.00

Half board per person:

	£min	£max
Daily	38.50	48.00
Weekly	269.50	336.00

Lunch available
Evening meal 1900 (last orders 2000)
Parking for 32
Cards accepted: Access, Visa, Amex, Switch/Delta

MAWNAN SMITH
Cornwall
Map ref 1B3

Budock Vean Golf and Country House Hotel

 COMMENDED

Mawnan Smith, Falmouth TR11 5LG
☎ Falmouth (01326) 250288
Fax (01326) 250892
Country house hotel set in sub-tropical grounds with own golf course. Facilities free to guests.
Bedrooms: 6 single, 16 double, 30 twin, 2 triple
Suite available
Bathrooms: 54 en-suite

Bed & breakfast per night:

	£min	£max
Single	25.00	65.00
Double	50.00	130.00

Half board per person:

	£min	£max
Daily	40.00	75.00
Weekly	245.00	480.00

Lunch available
Evening meal 1900 (last orders 2100)
Parking for 100
Open February–December
Cards accepted: Access, Visa, Diners, Switch/Delta

All accommodation in this guide has been graded, or is awaiting a grading, by a trained Tourist Board inspector.

MELKSHAM
Wiltshire
Map ref 2B2

Small industrial town standing on the banks of the River Avon. Old weavers' cottages and Regency houses are grouped around the attractive church which has traces of Norman work. The 18th C Round House, once used for dyeing fleeces, is now a craft centre.
Tourist Information Centre ☎ *(01225) 707424*

Conigre Farm Hotel

COMMENDED

Semington Road, Melksham SN12 6BZ
☎ Bath (01225) 702229
Fax (01225) 707392
Charming 17th C farmhouse and stable block tastefully converted to provide individually decorated en-suite accommodation and an informal oak-beamed restaurant.
Bedrooms: 3 single, 5 double, 1 twin
Bathrooms: 8 en-suite, 1 private, 1 public

Bed & breakfast per night:

	£min	£max
Single	40.00	45.00
Double	55.00	65.00

Half board per person:

	£min	£max
Daily	32.50	56.95
Weekly	204.75	358.00

Lunch available
Evening meal 1900 (last orders 2145)
Parking for 15
Cards accepted: Access, Visa, Switch/Delta

The Kings Arms Hotel

COMMENDED

Market Place, Melksham SN12 6EX
☎ Bath (01225) 707272
Fax (01225) 702085
Combines old world atmosphere with modern amenities and is an ideal centre for touring historic Wiltshire.
Bedrooms: 6 single, 5 double, 2 twin
Bathrooms: 10 en-suite, 2 public

Bed & breakfast per night:

	£min	£max
Single	30.00	45.00
Double	49.00	49.00

Lunch available
Evening meal 1900 (last orders 2100)

Parking for 45
Cards accepted: Access, Visa, Diners, Amex, Switch/Delta

Longhope Guest House

9 Beanacre Road, Melksham SN12 8AG
☎ (01225) 706737
Fax (01225) 706737
Situated in its own grounds on the A350 Melksham - Chippenham road. Half a mile from Melksham town centre, 10 miles from M4 junction 17.
Bedrooms: 1 single, 2 double, 1 twin, 2 triple
Bathrooms: 5 en-suite, 1 public

Bed & breakfast per night:

	£min	£max
Single		24.00
Double		35.00

Evening meal 1830 (last orders 1900)
Parking for 12

Shaw Country Hotel

COMMENDED

Bath Road, Shaw, Melksham SN12 8EF
☎ (01225) 702836 & 790321
Fax (01225) 790275

400-year-old farmhouse in own grounds, 9 miles from Bath. Licensed bar and restaurant, with table d'hote and a la carte menus.
Bedrooms: 3 single, 7 double, 3 twin
Bathrooms: 13 en-suite

Bed & breakfast per night:

	£min	£max
Single	40.00	40.00
Double	59.00	78.00

Lunch available
Evening meal 1900 (last orders 2130)
Parking for 35
Cards accepted: Access, Visa, Diners, Amex, Switch/Delta

You are advised to confirm your booking in writing.

WEST COUNTRY

MERE
Wiltshire
Map ref 2B2

Small town with a grand Perpendicular church surrounded by Georgian houses, with old inns and a 15th C chantry house. On the chalk downs overlooking the town is an Iron Age fort.
Tourist Information Centre ☎ (01747) 861211

Chetcombe House Hotel
COMMENDED

Chetcombe Road, Mere, Warminster BA12 6AZ
☎ (01747) 860219
Logis of Great Britain
Country house hotel set in 1 acre of mature gardens, close to Stourhead House and Garden. Ideal touring centre. Home-cooked local produce a speciality.
Bedrooms: 1 single, 2 double, 2 twin
Bathrooms: 5 en-suite

Bed & breakfast per night:	£min	£max
Single	29.00	33.00
Double	50.00	50.00

Half board per person:	£min	£max
Daily	38.50	46.50
Weekly	245.00	295.00

Lunch available
Evening meal 1900 (last orders 1700)
Parking for 10
Cards accepted: Access, Visa, Amex

Old Ship Hotel
APPROVED

Castle Street, Mere BA12 6JE
☎ (01747) 860258
Fax (01747) 860501
Period hotel surrounded by country gardens. Many places of interest nearby. All rooms have TV, telephone, tea and coffee makers; most have private facilities. Black and white timbered restaurant, renowned for cuisine.
Bedrooms: 4 single, 8 double, 5 twin, 4 family rooms
Bathrooms: 15 en-suite, 3 public

Bed & breakfast per night:	£min	£max
Single	32.00	
Double	53.00	

Half board per person:	£min	£max
Daily	38.00	
Weekly	214.00	

Lunch available
Evening meal 1930 (last orders 2130)
Parking for 48
Cards accepted: Access, Visa, Amex

Talbot Hotel
APPROVED

The Square, Mere BA12 6DR
☎ (01747) 860427
Fax (01747) 861210
16th C coaching inn with interesting features. Ideal for visits to Stourhead, Longleat, Stonehenge, Salisbury, Bath, Sherborne and Cheddar areas. Two-night breaks available.
Bedrooms: 1 single, 2 double, 1 twin, 3 triple
Bathrooms: 6 en-suite, 1 private

Bed & breakfast per night:	£min	£max
Single	25.00	32.50
Double	40.00	53.00

Half board per person:	£min	£max
Weekly	157.50	210.00

Lunch available
Evening meal 1830 (last orders 2130)
Parking for 20
Cards accepted: Access, Visa, Amex

MEVAGISSEY
Cornwall
Map ref 1B3

Small fishing town, a favourite with holidaymakers. Earlier prosperity came from pilchard fisheries, boat-building and smuggling. By the harbour are fish cellars, some converted, and a local history museum is housed in an old boat-building shed. Handsome Methodist chapel; shark fishing, sailing.

Mevagissey House
COMMENDED

Vicarage Hill, Mevagissey, St Austell PL26 6SZ
☎ (01726) 842427
Fax (01726) 842427
Georgian country house in woodland setting on a hillside, set in 4 acres. Sea views, elegant spacious rooms, many facilities, licensed bar.
Bedrooms: 1 double, 1 twin, 2 triple
Bathrooms: 3 en-suite, 1 private, 1 public

Bed & breakfast per night:	£min	£max
Single	20.00	25.00
Double	40.00	52.00

Parking for 12
Open March–October
Cards accepted: Access, Visa

Steep House

Portmellon Cove, Mevagissey, St Austell PL26 2PH
☎ (01726) 843732

Refreshingly clean and comfortable house with large garden and covered (summertime) pool. Superb seaside views, licensed, free off-road parking.
Bedrooms: 1 single, 5 double, 1 twin, 1 triple
Bathrooms: 2 en-suite, 1 private, 2 public

Bed & breakfast per night:	£min	£max
Single	17.00	20.00
Double	36.00	54.00

Parking for 12
Cards accepted: Access, Visa, Amex

Tremarne Hotel
COMMENDED

Polkirt, Mevagissey, St Austell PL26 6UY
☎ (01726) 842213
Fax (01726) 843420
In a quiet secluded area with views of sea and country. Within easy reach of Mevagissey harbour and Portmellon bathing beach.
Bedrooms: 2 single, 7 double, 3 twin, 1 triple, 1 family room
Bathrooms: 14 en-suite

Bed & breakfast per night:	£min	£max
Single	22.50	27.50
Double	45.00	55.00

Half board per person:	£min	£max
Daily	36.00	41.00
Weekly	250.00	275.00

Evening meal 1900 (last orders 1930)
Parking for 13

Open March–October
Cards accepted: Access, Visa, Diners, Amex, Switch/Delta

Trevalsa Court Hotel

Polstreath Hill, Mevagissey, St Austell
PL26 6TH
☎ (01726) 842468
Clifftop position with superb sea views and access to beach, in peaceful surroundings. Ideal for touring. Ample car parking. Accent on fresh food, vegetarian/special diets. Ground floor room ideal for semi-disabled persons.
Bedrooms: 2 single, 8 double, 4 twin, 1 triple
Bathrooms: 15 en-suite

Bed & breakfast per night:	£min	£max
Single	25.00	35.00
Double	50.00	70.00

Half board per person:	£min	£max
Daily	39.00	49.00
Weekly	273.00	308.70

Lunch available
Evening meal 1830 (last orders 1830)
Parking for 40
Open February–November
Cards accepted: Access, Visa

MIDSOMER NORTON
Bath & North East Somerset
Map ref 2B2

Small town in pleasant rural setting in the valley of the River Somer.

Centurion Hotel
COMMENDED

Charlton Lane, Midsomer Norton, Bath BA3 4BD
☎ Midsomer Norton (01761) 417711
Fax (01761) 418257
Ideally situated hotel, midway between Bath and Wells. Well-appointed bedrooms, golf, squash, swimming pool, indoor and outdoor bowls.
Bedrooms: 15 double, 26 twin, 2 triple
Suite available
Bathrooms: 43 en-suite

Bed & breakfast per night:	£min	£max
Single	50.00	60.00
Double	60.00	80.00

Lunch available
Evening meal 1930 (last orders 2130)
Parking for 100

Cards accepted: Access, Visa, Diners, Amex, Switch/Delta

MINEHEAD
Somerset
Map ref 1D1

Victorian resort with spreading sands developed around old fishing port on the coast below Exmoor. Former fishermen's cottages stand beside the 17th C harbour; cobbled streets climb the hill in steps to the church. Boat trips, steam railway. Hobby Horse festival 1 May.
Tourist Information Centre ☎ (01643) 702624

Channel House Hotel
HIGHLY COMMENDED

Church Path, Off Northfield Road, Minehead TA24 5QG
☎ (01643) 703229

Hotel specialising in good food and service. Beautiful gardens in peaceful location. The bedrooms will suit those who appreciate quality. Perfect for exploring Exmoor.
Bedrooms: 2 double, 5 twin, 1 triple
Bathrooms: 8 en-suite

Bed & breakfast per night:	£min	£max
Single	60.00	68.00
Double	96.00	96.00

Half board per person:	£min	£max
Daily	58.00	58.00
Weekly	329.00	346.50

Evening meal 1900 (last orders 2030)
Parking for 10
Open March–November and Christmas
Cards accepted: Access, Visa, Diners, Switch/Delta

COLOUR MAPS
Colour maps at the back of this guide pinpoint all places in which you will find accommodation listed.

Kildare Lodge
COMMENDED

Townsend Road, Minehead
TA24 5RQ
☎ (01643) 702009
Fax (01643) 706516
Family-run, Edwin Lutyens designed, Grade II listed building. Elegant a la carte restaurant; character-filled licensed bar; bar meals; well appointed en-suite accommodation, including family rooms.
Bedrooms: 1 single, 4 double, 2 twin, 2 family rooms
Suite available
Bathrooms: 9 en-suite, 1 public

Bed & breakfast per night:	£min	£max
Single	25.00	37.50
Double	44.00	68.00

Half board per person:	£min	£max
Daily	29.00	37.50
Weekly	185.00	240.00

Lunch available
Evening meal 1900 (last orders 2100)
Parking for 28
Cards accepted: Access, Visa, Diners, Amex

Mayfair Hotel and Dorchester
COMMENDED

25 The Avenue, Minehead
TA24 5AY
☎ (01643) 702719 & 702052
Victorian house hotel with lovely decor and furnishings. Family run, home cooking. On level, 3 minutes from sea and shops. Ground floor rooms.
Bedrooms: 4 single, 7 double, 5 twin, 10 triple
Bathrooms: 24 en-suite, 2 private

Bed & breakfast per night:	£min	£max
Single	24.00	25.00
Double	46.00	52.00

Half board per person:	£min	£max
Daily	33.00	35.00
Weekly	170.00	182.00

Evening meal 1830 (last orders 1900)
Parking for 21
Open March–October
Cards accepted: Access, Visa

Please check prices and other details at the time of booking.

WEST COUNTRY

MONTACUTE

Somerset
Map ref 2A3

Picturesque village named after its "steep hill" and noted for its splendid hamstone Elizabethan mansion. By the church stands the gatehouse of a Cluniac priory, built with stone from the hilltop castle. An 18th C folly now crowns the hill, where the Holy Cross of Waltham Abbey was found.

Kings Arms Inn
HIGHLY COMMENDED

Montacute TA15 6UU
☎ Martock (01935) 822513
Fax (01935) 826549
Picturesque 16th C hamstone inn situated in unspoilt Somerset village. Ideal touring location for West Country. Quality cuisine, log fires, tastefully furnished throughout.
Bedrooms: 9 double, 4 twin
Bathrooms: 13 en-suite

Bed & breakfast per night:	£min	£max
Single	49.00	56.00
Double	69.00	85.00

Half board per person:	£min	£max
Daily	69.00	76.00
Weekly		370.00

Lunch available
Evening meal 1900 (last orders 2200)
Parking for 20
Cards accepted: Access, Visa, Amex

MORETONHAMPSTEAD

Devon
Map ref 1C2

Small market town with a row of 17th C almshouses standing on the Exeter road. Surrounding moorland is scattered with ancient farmhouses, prehistoric sites.

White Hart Hotel
COMMENDED

The Square, Moretonhampstead, Newton Abbot TQ13 8NF
☎ (01647) 440406
Fax (01647) 440565
Minotel/Logis of Great Britain
Historic inn, centre of Dartmoor town. Antiques, log fires, cosy bar. Fine restaurant and bar meals. Comfortable bedrooms with courtesy trays.
Bedrooms: 1 single, 9 double, 10 twin
Bathrooms: 20 en-suite, 1 public

Bed & breakfast per night:	£min	£max
Single	40.00	45.00
Double	55.00	73.00

Lunch available
Evening meal 1800 (last orders 2030)
Parking for 12
Cards accepted: Access, Visa, Diners, Amex, Switch/Delta

MORTEHOE

Devon
Map ref 1C1

Old coastal village with small, basically Norman church. Wild cliffs, inland combes; sand and surf at Woolacombe.

Sunnycliffe Hotel
COMMENDED

Mortehoe, Woolacombe EX34 7EB
☎ Woolacombe (01271) 870597
Fax (01271) 870597
Logis of Great Britain

Small, select hotel beautifully situated above sandy cove overlooking beach. Traditional English food cooked by qualified chef/proprietor. Sorry, no children or pets.
Bedrooms: 6 double, 2 twin
Bathrooms: 8 en-suite, 2 public

Bed & breakfast per night:	£min	£max
Single	25.00	28.00
Double	50.00	56.00

Half board per person:	£min	£max
Daily	39.00	44.00
Weekly	240.00	275.00

Evening meal 1900 (last orders 1900)
Parking for 11
Open February–October

Half board prices are given per person, but in some cases these may be based on double/twin occupancy.

MOUSEHOLE

Cornwall
Map ref 1A3

Old fishing port completely rebuilt after destruction in the 16th C by Spanish raiders. Twisting lanes and granite cottages with luxuriant gardens rise steeply from the harbour; just south is a private bird sanctuary.

Carn Du Hotel

Raginnis Hill, Mousehole, Penzance TR19 6SS
☎ Penzance (01736) 731233
Elegant Victorian house in an elevated position above Mousehole. Cosy lounge, delightful cocktail bar and licensed restaurant specialising in seafood and local vegetables. Terraced gardens.
Bedrooms: 1 single, 3 double, 3 twin
Bathrooms: 6 en-suite, 1 private

Bed & breakfast per night:	£min	£max
Single	25.00	30.00
Double	50.00	60.00

Half board per person:	£min	£max
Daily	39.95	44.95
Weekly	240.00	270.00

Lunch available
Evening meal 1900 (last orders 2030)
Parking for 12
Cards accepted: Access, Visa, Amex

MULLION

Cornwall
Map ref 1B3

Small holiday village with a golf-course, set back from the coast. The church has a serpentine tower of 1500, carved roof and beautiful medieval bench-ends. Beyond Mullion Cove, with its tiny harbour, wild untouched cliffs stretch south-eastward toward Lizard Point.

Mullion Cove Hotel
COMMENDED

Mullion, Helston TR12 7EP
☎ Helston (01326) 240328
Fax (01326) 240998
Beautiful late-Victorian hotel with spectacular harbour and coastal views. Outstanding food and fine wines. Guaranteed warmth and relaxation.
Bedrooms: 9 single, 13 double, 12 twin, 4 triple
Suites available
Bathrooms: 23 en-suite, 6 public

WEST COUNTRY

Bed & breakfast per night:	£min	£max
Single	25.00	65.00
Double	40.00	110.00

Half board per person:	£min	£max
Daily	35.00	75.00
Weekly	210.00	450.00

Lunch available
Evening meal 1900 (last orders 2030)
Parking for 50
Cards accepted: Access, Visa, Switch/Delta

Polurrian Hotel, Apartments and Leisure Club

HIGHLY COMMENDED

Polurrian Cove, Mullion, Helston TR12 7EN
☎ (01326) 240421
Fax (01326) 240083
Idyllic setting for family-run hotel with own beach, surrounded by National Trust coastline. Indoor leisure club and outdoor amenities. Personal service.
Bedrooms: 1 single, 14 double, 17 twin, 6 triple
Bathrooms: 38 en-suite, 1 public

Bed & breakfast per night:	£min	£max
Single	35.00	76.00
Double	70.00	152.00

Half board per person:	£min	£max
Daily	45.00	86.00
Weekly	315.00	602.00

Lunch available
Evening meal 1900 (last orders 2145)
Parking for 60
Open February–December
Cards accepted: Access, Visa, Diners, Amex

WELCOME HOST

This is a nationally recognised customer care programme which aims to promote the highest standards of service and a warm welcome. Establishments who are taking part in this initiative are indicated by the symbol.

NEWQUAY

Cornwall
Map ref 1B2

Popular resort spread over dramatic cliffs around its old fishing port. Many beaches with abundant sands, caves and rock pools; excellent surf. Pilots' gigs are still raced from the harbour and on the headland stands the stone Huer's House from the pilchard-fishing days.
Tourist Information Centre ☎ (01637) 871345

Aloha Hotel

122/124 Henver Road, Newquay TR7 3EQ
☎ (01637) 878366
Friendly licensed hotel with en-suite rooms and home comforts. Well situated for beaches and touring Cornwall. Conservatory and garden overlooking Trencreek Valley.
Bedrooms: 2 single, 5 double, 3 triple, 3 family rooms
Bathrooms: 6 en-suite, 2 public, 4 private showers

Bed & breakfast per night:	£min	£max
Single	12.00	20.00
Double	24.00	40.00

Half board per person:	£min	£max
Daily	17.00	29.00
Weekly	100.00	160.00

Evening meal 1830 (last orders 1000)
Parking for 14
Cards accepted: Access, Visa, Diners, Amex

Arundell Hotel

COMMENDED

86/90 Mount Wise, Newquay TR7 2BS
☎ (01637) 872481
Fax (01637) 850001
Three-storey building with long, attractive road frontage. Easy access and exit. Large car park. Sea view to rear.
Bedrooms: 1 single, 17 double, 9 twin, 3 triple, 5 family rooms
Bathrooms: 35 en-suite

Bed & breakfast per night:	£min	£max
Single	15.00	27.00
Double	30.00	54.00

Half board per person:	£min	£max
Daily	19.00	31.00
Weekly	130.00	215.00

Evening meal 1800 (last orders 1830)
Parking for 37
Open February–November and Christmas
Cards accepted: Access, Visa, Diners, Amex

Carnmarth Hotel

COMMENDED

22 Headland Road, Fistral Beach, Newquay TR7 1HN
☎ (01637) 872519
Fax (01637) 878770

Faces south over golf links, Fistral Bay, the heathland and Newquay Bay to the rear. Commanding position. Full indoor bowling green 120'x 30' to Sports Council standards.
Bedrooms: 5 single, 12 double, 9 twin, 7 triple, 1 family room
Bathrooms: 34 en-suite, 1 public

Bed & breakfast per night:	£min	£max
Single	23.50	23.50
Double	47.00	47.00

Half board per person:	£min	£max
Daily	31.50	31.50
Weekly	175.00	220.50

Lunch available
Evening meal 1830 (last orders 1730)
Parking for 24
Cards accepted: Access, Visa, Amex, Switch/Delta

Corisande Manor Hotel

COMMENDED

Riverside Avenue, Pentire, Newquay TR7 1PL
☎ (01637) 872042
Unique turreted Austrian design, quietly situated and commanding an unrivalled position in 3-acre secluded grounds with private foreshore. Same proprietors since 1968.
Bedrooms: 5 single, 8 double, 3 twin, 3 triple
Bathrooms: 16 en-suite, 1 private, 4 public

Bed & breakfast per night:	£min	£max
Single	20.00	26.00
Double	40.00	52.00

Continued ▶

425

WEST COUNTRY

NEWQUAY
Continued

Half board per person:
	£min	£max
Daily	27.00	35.00
Weekly	165.00	205.00

Lunch available
Evening meal 1900 (last orders 1930)
Parking for 19
Open May–October
Cards accepted: Access, Visa

Eliot-Cavendish Hotel
Edgecumbe Avenue, Newquay TR7 2NH
☎ (01637) 878177
Fax (01637) 852053
Large family hotel situated close to beaches. Heated outdoor pool, sauna and solarium. Extensive parking.
Bedrooms: 6 single, 35 double, 24 twin, 12 triple
Bathrooms: 77 en-suite

Bed & breakfast per night:
	£min	£max
Single	22.00	28.00
Double	38.00	50.00

Half board per person:
	£min	£max
Daily	28.00	37.00
Weekly	135.00	200.00

Lunch available
Evening meal 1800 (last orders 1900)
Parking for 35
Open January, March–December
Cards accepted: Access, Visa

The Esplanade Hotel
9 Esplanade Road, Pentire, Newquay TR7 1PS
☎ (01637) 873333
Fax (01637) 851413

Modern hotel overlooking beautiful Fistral Bay. Good food, friendly service and excellent facilities for a happy, relaxing holiday.
Bedrooms: 6 single, 21 double, 10 twin, 17 triple, 20 family rooms
Bathrooms: 74 en-suite, 2 public

Bed & breakfast per night:
	£min	£max
Single	19.00	31.00
Double	38.00	62.00

Half board per person:
	£min	£max
Daily	19.00	36.00
Weekly	135.00	250.00

Lunch available
Evening meal 1900 (last orders 2030)
Parking for 32
Open February–December
Cards accepted: Access, Visa, Amex, Switch/Delta

Kilbirnie Hotel
COMMENDED
Narrowcliff, Newquay TR7 2RS
☎ (01637) 875155
Fax (01637) 850769
Superbly situated, overlooking beaches. Excellent accommodation, cuisine and service. Heated indoor and outdoor swimming pools. Lift to all floors.
Bedrooms: 7 single, 33 double, 19 twin, 6 triple, 3 family rooms
Bathrooms: 68 en-suite

Bed & breakfast per night:
	£min	£max
Single	30.00	40.00
Double	60.00	80.00

Half board per person:
	£min	£max
Daily	30.00	45.00
Weekly	370.00	420.00

Lunch available
Evening meal 1930 (last orders 2030)
Parking for 50
Cards accepted: Access, Visa, Switch/Delta

Pendeen Hotel
COMMENDED
Alexandra Road, Porth, Newquay TR7 3ND
☎ (01637) 873521
Fax (01637) 873521
Well established family-run hotel, in its own grounds, 2 miles from Newquay and close to beach. Good food served with friendly and efficient service.
Bedrooms: 1 single, 8 double, 2 twin, 2 triple, 2 family rooms
Bathrooms: 15 en-suite

Bed & breakfast per night:
	£min	£max
Single	18.50	25.00
Double	32.00	45.00

Half board per person:
	£min	£max
Daily	22.50	30.00
Weekly	135.00	195.00

Evening meal 1830 (last orders 1930)
Parking for 15
Open January–October, December
Cards accepted: Access, Visa, Amex

Philema Hotel
1 Esplanade Road, Pentire, Newquay TR7 1PY
☎ (01637) 872571
Fax (01637) 873188
Furnished to a high standard with magnificent views overlooking Fistral Beach and golf-course. Friendly informal hotel with good facilities, including indoor pool, leisure complex and apartments.
Bedrooms: 2 single, 8 double, 3 twin, 5 triple, 11 family rooms
Suites available
Bathrooms: 29 en-suite, 2 public

Bed & breakfast per night:
	£min	£max
Single	22.00	30.00
Double	44.00	60.00

Half board per person:
	£min	£max
Daily	25.00	35.00
Weekly	147.00	230.00

Evening meal 1830 (last orders 1930)
Parking for 38
Open March–October
Cards accepted: Access, Visa, Switch/Delta

Porth Enodoc Hotel
4 Esplanade Road, Pentire, Newquay TR7 1PY
☎ (01637) 872372
In its own grounds overlooking Fistral Beach, set away from the town but within walking distance of the shopping centre.
Bedrooms: 1 single, 8 double, 1 twin, 2 triple
Bathrooms: 12 en-suite

Bed & breakfast per night:
	£min	£max
Single	15.00	23.50
Double	30.00	47.00

Half board per person:
	£min	£max
Daily	21.50	31.00
Weekly	129.00	189.00

WEST COUNTRY

Evening meal 1845 (last orders 1930)
Parking for 15
Open March–October

Trebarwith Hotel
COMMENDED
Newquay TR7 1BZ
☎ (01637) 872288
Fax (01637) 875431

On the sea edge with 350 feet of private sea frontage, in a central position away from traffic noise. Same ownership since 1964.
Bedrooms: 3 single, 20 double, 12 twin, 6 family rooms
Bathrooms: 38 en-suite, 3 private

Bed & breakfast
per night:	£min	£max
Single	18.00	36.00
Double	39.00	72.00

Half board per
person:	£min	£max
Daily	21.00	42.00
Weekly	147.00	295.00

Lunch available
Evening meal 1915 (last orders 2030)
Parking for 40
Open March–October
Cards accepted: Access, Visa, Switch/Delta

Tregurrian Hotel
Watergate Bay, Newquay TR8 4AB
☎ St Mawgan (01637) 860280
Fax (01637) 860280
On coast road between Newquay and Padstow, just 100 yards from golden sandy beach in an area reputed to have some of the finest beaches and coastline in Europe.
Bedrooms: 4 single, 11 double, 4 twin, 2 triple, 6 family rooms
Suites available
Bathrooms: 22 en-suite, 2 public

Bed & breakfast
per night:	£min	£max
Single	18.00	31.00
Double	36.00	59.00

Half board per
person:	£min	£max
Daily	26.50	39.50
Weekly	158.00	230.00

Lunch available
Evening meal 1845 (last orders 1930)
Parking for 25
Open March–October
Cards accepted: Access, Visa

Trevalsa Hotel
COMMENDED
Watergate Road, Porth, Newquay TR7 3LX
☎ (01637) 873336
Fax (01637) 878843
Modern, licensed hotel above beautiful Whipsiderry beach. Panoramic views of Newquay's coastline. Golf, fishing, wind-surfing, surfing, coastal and countryside walks.
Bedrooms: 4 single, 10 double, 2 twin, 5 triple, 3 family rooms
Bathrooms: 22 en-suite, 2 public

Bed & breakfast
per night:	£min	£max
Single	16.00	24.00

Half board per
person:	£min	£max
Daily	21.00	29.50

Lunch available
Evening meal 1900 (last orders 1930)
Parking for 21
Open March–October
Cards accepted: Access, Visa, Amex, Switch/Delta

Whipsiderry Hotel
HIGHLY COMMENDED
Trevelgue Road, Porth, Newquay TR7 3LY
☎ (01637) 874777
Fax (01637) 874777
Set in own grounds overlooking Porth Beach and Newquay Bay. Noted for fine cuisine. Watch the badgers feed and play only a few feet away.
Bedrooms: 2 single, 12 double, 1 twin, 1 triple, 4 family rooms
Bathrooms: 12 en-suite, 8 private, 2 public

Bed & breakfast
per night:	£min	£max
Single	18.50	28.50
Double	37.00	57.00

Half board per
person:	£min	£max
Daily	30.00	42.00
Weekly	210.50	279.50

Evening meal 1830 (last orders 2000)
Parking for 30
Open March–October, December
Cards accepted: Access, Visa, Amex

Windsor Hotel
Mount Wise, Newquay TR7 2AY
☎ (01637) 875188
Fax (01637) 872573

A hotel for all the family, with indoor and outdoor swimming pools, jacuzzi, sauna, solarium, gym, putting, squash court. Secluded suntrap gardens.
Bedrooms: 3 single, 18 double, 8 twin, 3 triple, 12 family rooms
Bathrooms: 44 en-suite, 2 public

Half board per
person:	£min	£max
Daily	22.00	40.00
Weekly	140.00	260.00

Lunch available
Evening meal 1915 (last orders 2030)
Parking for 70
Open February–December
Cards accepted: Access, Visa, Amex, Switch/Delta

Windward Hotel
HIGHLY COMMENDED
Alexandra Road, Porth, Newquay TR7 3NB
☎ (01637) 873185
Modern hotel of fine quality with large car park and situated on coastal road to Padstow overlooking Porth Bay. 1.5 miles north of Newquay.
Bedrooms: 10 double, 1 twin, 1 triple, 2 family rooms
Bathrooms: 14 en-suite

Bed & breakfast
per night:	£min	£max
Single	22.00	27.00
Double	44.00	54.00

Half board per
person:	£min	£max
Daily	30.00	35.00
Weekly	125.00	198.00

Lunch available
Evening meal 1830 (last orders 1900)
Parking for 14
Open March–December
Cards accepted: Access, Visa, Amex, Switch/Delta

WEST COUNTRY

NEWTON ABBOT

Devon
Map ref 1D2

Lively market town at the head of the Teign Estuary. A former railway town, well placed for moorland or seaside excursions. Interesting old houses nearby include Bradley Manor, dating from the 15th C, and Forde House, visited by Charles I and William of Orange.
Tourist Information Centre ☎ *(01626) 67494*

Hazelwood Hotel
♛♛♛ COMMENDED

33a Torquay Road, Newton Abbot TQ12 2LW
☎ (01626) 66130
Fax (01626) 65021
Attractive, turn-of-the-century building in quiet residential location, 5 minutes' walk from town centre, rail and coach stations. Own garden. Licensed restaurant, residents' lounge, car park.
Bedrooms: 2 single, 3 double, 3 twin
Bathrooms: 7 en-suite, 2 public, 1 private shower
Bed & breakfast

per night:	£min	£max
Single	35.00	35.00
Double	49.00	49.00

Half board

per person:	£min	£max
Daily	44.50	47.95

Lunch available
Evening meal 1830 (last orders 1930)
Parking for 10
Cards accepted: Access, Visa, Switch/Delta

OGBOURNE ST GEORGE

Wiltshire
Map ref 2B2

The Parklands Hotel
♛♛♛ COMMENDED

High Street, Ogbourne St George, Marlborough SN8 1SL
☎ (01672) 841555
Fax (01672) 841533
Small family-run hotel and separate restaurant in rural surroundings, in village on Ridgeway path. Just off A345 between Swindon and Marlborough.
Bedrooms: 2 single, 2 double, 6 twin
Bathrooms: 10 en-suite
Bed & breakfast

per night:	£min	£max
Single	25.00	45.00
Double	50.00	60.00

Half board

per person:	£min	£max
Daily	38.50	72.00
Weekly	240.00	

Lunch available
Evening meal 1900 (last orders 2130)
Parking for 20
Cards accepted: Access, Visa, Amex

OKEHAMPTON

Devon
Map ref 1C2

Busy market town near the high tors of northern Dartmoor. The Victorian church, with William Morris windows and a 15th C tower, stands on the site of a Saxon church. A Norman castle ruin overlooks the river to the west of the town. Museum of Dartmoor Life in a restored mill.

Heathfield House
♛♛♛ COMMENDED

Klondyke Road, Okehampton EX20 1EW
☎ (01837) 54211 & Mobile 0850 881547
Fax (01837) 54211
Friendly country guesthouse specialising in the personal touch. Noted for cuisine. The ideal stopover for business or pleasure. Comfort assured. Heated pool. Non-smoking.
Bedrooms: 1 single, 1 double, 1 twin, 1 family room
Bathrooms: 3 en-suite, 1 private
Bed & breakfast

per night:	£min	£max
Single	25.00	28.00
Double	46.00	50.00

Half board

per person:	£min	£max
Daily	38.00	40.00
Weekly	245.00	260.00

Evening meal (last orders 2000)
Parking for 8
Open January–November
Cards accepted: Access, Visa

Poltimore Guest House
♛♛♛

Ramsley, South Zeal, Okehampton EX20 2PD
☎ (01837) 840209
Delightful thatched guesthouse. Comfortable en-suite bedrooms with colour TV and tea-making facilities. Licensed bar, home cooking with choice of menu. Friendly atmosphere.
Bedrooms: 2 single, 3 double, 2 twin
Bathrooms: 4 en-suite, 1 public
Bed & breakfast

per night:	£min	£max
Single	23.00	27.00
Double	46.00	50.00

Half board

per person:	£min	£max
Daily	35.50	39.50
Weekly	216.50	230.50

Lunch available
Evening meal 1900 (last orders 1700)
Parking for 15
Cards accepted: Access, Visa, Amex

OLD SODBURY

South Gloucestershire
Map ref 2B2

Cross Hands Hotel M
♛♛♛

Old Sodbury, Bristol BS17 6RJ
☎ Chipping Sodbury (01454) 313000
Fax (01454) 324409
Two miles from M4 (exit 18) towards Stroud. In 6 acres, with a garden and orchard. A la carte restaurant and large meeting rooms for over 100 delegates with private bar.
Bedrooms: 9 single, 9 double, 6 twin
Bathrooms: 20 en-suite, 2 public
Bed & breakfast

per night:	£min	£max
Single	32.50	66.45
Double	45.00	89.50

Lunch available
Evening meal 1830 (last orders 2230)
Parking for 200
Cards accepted: Access, Visa, Diners, Amex, Switch/Delta

OTTERY ST MARY

Devon
Map ref 1D2

Former wool town with modern light industry set in countryside on the River Otter. The Cromwellian commander, Fairfax, made his headquarters here briefly during the Civil War. The interesting church, dating from the 14th C, is built to cathedral plan.

Fluxton Farm Hotel M
♛♛♛

Ottery St Mary EX11 1RJ
☎ (01404) 812818
Former farmhouse in beautiful country

WEST COUNTRY

setting. Comfortable en-suite bedrooms, 2 sitting rooms, large gardens. Home-cooked food served in candlelit dining room. Log fires in season. Cat lovers' paradise.
Bedrooms: 3 single, 3 double, 4 twin, 2 triple
Bathrooms: 10 en-suite, 1 public

Bed & breakfast per night:	£min	£max
Single	23.00	25.00
Double	46.00	50.00

Half board per person:	£min	£max
Daily	30.00	34.00
Weekly	210.00	225.00

Evening meal 1850 (last orders 1800)
Parking for 20

Salston Manor Hotel
COMMENDED
Ottery St Mary, Exeter EX11 1RQ
☎ (01404) 815581
Fax (01404) 815581
Welcoming country house hotel in the heart of East Devon, with amenities for all the family. Indoor pool, squash, sauna, solarium. Ideal for business or pleasure.
Bedrooms: 3 single, 7 double, 4 twin, 12 triple, 1 family room
Bathrooms: 27 en-suite

Bed & breakfast per night:	£min	£max
Single	39.50	50.00
Double	60.00	85.00

Half board per person:	£min	£max
Daily	37.50	43.75
Weekly	250.00	300.00

Lunch available
Evening meal 1900 (last orders 2100)
Parking for 100
Cards accepted: Access, Visa, Switch/Delta

Venn Ottery Barton Country Hotel
COMMENDED
Venn Ottery, Ottery St Mary EX11 1RZ
☎ (01404) 812733

Friendly 16th C country house hotel. Beautiful location, ideal for walks and touring Dartmoor. Only 5 miles to the coast.
Bedrooms: 2 single, 5 double, 7 twin, 2 triple
Bathrooms: 11 en-suite, 3 public

Bed & breakfast per night:	£min	£max
Single	28.00	32.00
Double	52.00	60.00

Half board per person:	£min	£max
Daily	39.00	47.00
Weekly	252.00	295.00

Evening meal 1900 (last orders 1930)
Parking for 16
Cards accepted: Access, Visa

PADSTOW
Cornwall
Map ref 1B2

Old town encircling its harbour on the Camel Estuary. The 15th C church has notable bench-ends. There are fine houses on North Quay and Raleigh's Court House on South Quay. Tall cliffs and golden sands along the coast and ferry to Rock. Famous 'Obby 'Oss Festival on 1 May.
Tourist Information Centre ☎ (01841) 533449

Old Custom House Inn
COMMENDED
South Quay, Padstow PL28 8ED
☎ (01841) 532359
Fax (01841) 533372
Comfortable quayside inn in the small fishing port of Padstow. Personally run by Mrs Allen.
Bedrooms: 16 double, 2 twin, 8 triple
Bathrooms: 26 en-suite

Bed & breakfast per night:	£min	£max
Single	54.00	
Double	76.00	

Lunch available
Evening meal 1900 (last orders 2130)
Parking for 9
Cards accepted: Access, Visa, Diners, Amex, Switch/Delta

Trevone Bay Hotel
COMMENDED
Trevone Bay, Padstow PL28 8QS
☎ (01841) 520243
Fax (01841) 521195
You will find friendship, relaxation and good food in our spotless, family-run hotel. Tranquil village position overlooking beach/coastal footpath.
Bedrooms: 3 single, 3 double, 3 twin, 1 triple, 3 family rooms
Bathrooms: 13 en-suite

Bed & breakfast per night:	£min	£max
Single	24.00	29.00
Double	44.00	54.00

Half board per person:	£min	£max
Daily	29.00	35.00
Weekly	175.00	215.00

Lunch available
Evening meal 1900 (last orders 1930)
Parking for 12
Open April–October
Cards accepted: Access, Visa

Woodlands Country House Hotel
COMMENDED
Treator, Padstow PL28 8RU
☎ (01841) 532426 & 533353
Delightful country house in rural setting near beaches and golf-courses, offering picturesque walks, modern amenities and choice of cuisine.
Bedrooms: 5 double, 2 twin, 2 triple
Bathrooms: 9 en-suite

Bed & breakfast per night:	£min	£max
Single	23.00	28.00
Double	40.00	48.00

Half board per person:	£min	£max
Daily	35.00	40.00
Weekly	210.00	230.00

Evening meal 1830 (last orders 1700)
Parking for 15
Open March–October

Map references apply to the colour maps at the back of this guide.

National gradings and classifications were correct at the time of going to press but are subject to change. Please check at the time of booking.

WEST COUNTRY

PAIGNTON
Devon
Map ref 1D2

Lively seaside resort with a pretty harbour on Torbay. Bronze Age and Saxon sites are occupied by the 15th C church, which has a Norman door and font. The beautiful Chantry Chapel was built by local landowners, the Kirkhams.
Tourist Information Centre ☎ *(01803) 558383*

Cherwood Hotel
COMMENDED
26 Garfield Road, Paignton TQ4 6AX
☎ (01803) 556515
Small family-run licensed hotel offering en-suite accommodation with colour TV and tea/coffee facilities, bar lounge and separate TV lounge. Good home cooking. 100 yards to beach.
Bedrooms: 1 single, 2 double, 3 family rooms
Bathrooms: 5 en-suite, 1 public
Bed & breakfast

per night:	£min	£max
Single	13.00	16.00
Double	26.00	32.00

Half board per

person:	£min	£max
Daily	19.00	22.00
Weekly	133.00	154.00

Evening meal 1800 (last orders 1830)

Dainton Hotel and Restaurant
APPROVED
95 Dartmouth Road, Goodrington, Paignton TQ4 6NA
☎ (01803) 550067 & 525901
Fax (01803) 666339

Delightful old world Tudor-style hotel overlooking Torbay. 150 yards from beach and shops. All rooms en-suite. Previous winners of *"Torbay in Bloom"*. A warm welcome awaits you from the Richards family.
Bedrooms: 2 single, 5 double, 1 twin, 3 triple
Bathrooms: 11 en-suite, 1 public
Bed & breakfast

per night:	£min	£max
Single	26.00	
Double	52.00	

Half board per

person:	£min	£max
Weekly	230.00	

Lunch available
Evening meal 1800 (last orders 2130)
Parking for 20
Cards accepted: Access, Visa, Amex, Switch/Delta

Preston Sands Hotel
HIGHLY COMMENDED
10/12 Marine Parade, Sea Front, Paignton TQ3 2NU
☎ (01803) 558718
Fax (01803) 527345
Situated 15 yards from the water's edge. All bedrooms en-suite (some with private balcony) with radio, colour TV with satellite, tea/coffee-making facilities, direct-dial telephone, hairdryer.
Bedrooms: 2 single, 20 double, 7 twin, 3 triple
Bathrooms: 32 en-suite, 1 public
Bed & breakfast

per night:	£min	£max
Single	20.00	30.00
Double	40.00	46.00

Half board per

person:	£min	£max
Daily	28.00	36.00
Weekly	190.00	245.00

Lunch available
Evening meal 1800 (last orders 1930)
Parking for 24
Open February–November and Christmas
Cards accepted: Access, Visa, Amex, Switch/Delta

Redcliffe Hotel
COMMENDED
Marine Drive, Paignton TQ3 2NL
☎ (01803) 526397
Fax (01803) 528030
Choice location in 3 acres of grounds directly adjoining the beach. Heated outdoor swimming pool and new indoor leisure complex.
Bedrooms: 12 single, 23 double, 22 twin, 2 triple
Bathrooms: 59 en-suite, 1 public
Bed & breakfast

per night:	£min	£max
Single	38.00	56.00
Double	76.00	112.00

Half board per

person:	£min	£max
Daily	42.00	60.00
Weekly	266.00	385.00

Evening meal 1900 (last orders 2030)
Parking for 100
Cards accepted: Access, Visa, Amex, Switch/Delta

Sealawn Hotel
Sea Front, 20 Esplanade Road, Paignton TQ4 6BE
☎ (01803) 559031
On the seafront, enjoying breathtaking views across the bay. Close to all amenities. Noted for food. "Arrive as visitors - leave as friends."
Bedrooms: 7 double, 2 twin, 2 triple, 1 family room
Bathrooms: 12 en-suite
Bed & breakfast

per night:	£min	£max
Single	18.00	27.00
Double	36.00	44.00

Half board per

person:	£min	£max
Daily	24.00	33.00
Weekly	161.00	224.00

Lunch available
Evening meal 1800 (last orders 1800)
Parking for 14

South Sands Hotel
COMMENDED
12 Alta Vista Road, Paignton TQ4 6BZ
☎ (01803) 557231 & Freephone 0500 432153
Fax (01803) 529947
Family-run, wonderful fresh food. Superb, peaceful location overlooking sea, beach, park and close to harbour. Large car park. Dogs and children very welcome.
Bedrooms: 2 single, 3 double, 1 twin, 5 triple, 8 family rooms
Bathrooms: 17 en-suite, 2 private
Bed & breakfast

per night:	£min	£max
Single	20.00	28.00
Double	40.00	56.00

Half board per

person:	£min	£max
Daily	28.00	35.00
Weekly	165.00	220.00

Evening meal 1800 (last orders 1900)
Parking for 17
Open April–October and Christmas
Cards accepted: Access, Visa

WEST COUNTRY

Summerhill Hotel
👑👑👑

Braeside Road, Goodrington Sands, Paignton TQ4 6BX
☎ (01803) 558101
Fax (01803) 558101
Comfortable hotel with spacious, secluded, suntrap gardens, adjacent to sandy beaches and park. Close to harbour, leisure centre and water theme park.
Bedrooms: 2 single, 8 double, 7 twin, 5 triple, 4 family rooms
Bathrooms: 26 en-suite, 1 public

Bed & breakfast
per night:	£min	£max
Single	23.00	29.00
Double	46.00	52.00

Half board per
person:	£min	£max
Daily	29.00	33.00
Weekly	189.00	215.00

Lunch available
Evening meal 1830 (last orders 1900)
Parking for 36
Open March–November

Torbay Court Hotel
👑👑👑 COMMENDED

Stearfield Road, Paignton TQ3 2BG
☎ (01803) 663332
Fax (01803) 522680
Situated in a quiet, secluded position. A few yards' level walk to the seafront. Close to park and amenities.
Bedrooms: 11 single, 16 double, 27 twin, 3 triple, 1 family room
Bathrooms: 58 en-suite, 2 public

Bed & breakfast
per night:	£min	£max
Single	12.00	19.00

Half board per
person:	£min	£max
Daily	18.00	25.00
Weekly	106.00	146.00

Lunch available
Evening meal 1800 (last orders 1830)
Parking for 16
Open March–December

Torbay Holiday Motel
👑👑👑 COMMENDED

Totnes Road, Paignton TQ4 7PP
☎ (01803) 558226
Fax (01803) 663375
On the A385 in peaceful countryside, close to all amenities of Torbay. Ideal base for touring Devon.
Bedrooms: 2 single, 9 double, 5 twin, 2 triple
Bathrooms: 18 en-suite

Bed & breakfast
per night:	£min	£max
Single	29.50	32.50
Double	47.00	53.00

Half board per
person:	£min	£max
Daily	29.50	32.50
Weekly	206.50	227.50

Lunch available
Evening meal 1830 (last orders 2100)
Parking for 100
Cards accepted: Access, Visa, Amex

Wynncroft Hotel
👑👑👑 HIGHLY COMMENDED

2 Elmsleigh Park, Paignton TQ4 5AT
☎ (01803) 525728
Centrally situated hotel, with traditional cuisine from an a la carte menu, in the comfort of a refurbished Victorian home.
Bedrooms: 6 double, 3 twin, 2 triple
Bathrooms: 9 en-suite, 1 public, 2 private showers

Bed & breakfast
per night:	£min	£max
Single	28.00	36.00
Double	46.00	70.00

Half board per
person:	£min	£max
Daily	37.00	45.00
Weekly	222.00	270.00

Lunch available
Evening meal 1800 (last orders 1900)
Parking for 8
Open January–November
Cards accepted: Access, Visa

PENZANCE
Cornwall
Map ref 1A3

Resort and fishing port on Mount's Bay with mainly Victorian promenade and some fine Regency terraces. Former prosperity came from tin trade and pilchard fishing. Grand Georgian style church by harbour. Georgian Egyptian building at head of Chapel Street and Morrab Gardens.
Tourist Information Centre ☎ (01736) 62207

Estoril Hotel
👑👑👑 COMMENDED

46 Morrab Road, Penzance TR18 4EX
☎ (01736) 62468 & 67571
Fax (01736) 67471
Elegant Victorian house offering comfortable, comprehensive accommodation. A warm welcome and personal service in peaceful and immaculate surroundings await you.
Bedrooms: 1 single, 4 double, 3 twin, 1 triple, 1 family room
Bathrooms: 10 en-suite

Bed & breakfast
per night:	£min	£max
Single	24.00	26.00
Double	48.00	52.00

Half board per
person:	£min	£max
Daily	34.00	38.00
Weekly	238.00	252.00

Lunch available
Evening meal 1845 (last orders 1930)
Parking for 4
Open January–November
Cards accepted: Access, Visa

Keigwin Hotel
👑👑👑 APPROVED

Alexandra Road, Penzance TR18 4LZ
☎ (01736) 63930
Smoke-free, quiet, comfortable, family-run hotel, close to all amenities. Good cooking, on-street parking, colour TV. Pre-booking advised.
Bedrooms: 2 single, 4 double, 1 twin, 1 triple
Bathrooms: 4 en-suite, 1 private, 1 public

Bed & breakfast
per night:	£min	£max
Single	13.00	17.00
Double	26.00	34.00

Half board per
person:	£min	£max
Daily	24.00	28.00
Weekly	161.50	187.75

Evening meal 1800 (last orders 0900)
Cards accepted: Access, Visa

Lynwood Guest House
👑👑 APPROVED

41 Morrab Road, Penzance TR18 4EX
☎ (01736) 65871
Fax (01736) 65871
Lynwood offers a warm welcome and is situated between promenade and town centre, close to all amenities. Standard and en-suite rooms.
Bedrooms: 1 single, 2 double, 1 twin, 1 triple, 1 family room
Bathrooms: 2 en-suite, 3 public

Bed & breakfast
per night:	£min	£max
Single	11.50	16.00

Continued ▶

WEST COUNTRY

PENZANCE
Continued

Cards accepted: Access, Visa, Diners, Amex

Mount Haven Hotel and Restaurant ♠
APPROVED
Turnpike Road, Marazion, Penzance
TR17 0DQ
☎ (01736) 710249
Fax (01736) 711658
CR Minotel/Logis of Great Britain

Well-situated detached hotel in own grounds overlooking St Michael's Mount and Mount's Bay. Ideal touring centre for West Cornwall.
Bedrooms: 3 single, 7 double, 2 twin, 5 triple
Bathrooms: 17 en-suite

Bed & breakfast per night:
	£min	£max
Single	36.00	44.00
Double	56.00	83.00

Half board per person:
	£min	£max
Daily	46.50	60.00
Weekly	224.00	319.00

Lunch available
Evening meal 1900 (last orders 2100)
Parking for 30
Cards accepted: Access, Visa, Amex

Penmorvah Hotel ♠
APPROVED
Alexandra Road, Penzance
TR18 4LZ
☎ (01736) 63711
350 yards from promenade in tree-lined avenue. Easy reach of town centre and an ideal location for touring.
Bedrooms: 2 single, 1 double, 1 twin, 4 triple
Bathrooms: 8 en-suite

Bed & breakfast per night:
	£min	£max
Single	15.00	20.00
Double	30.00	40.00

Half board per person:
	£min	£max
Daily	25.00	30.00
Weekly	155.00	195.00

Evening meal 1830 (last orders 1700)
Cards accepted: Access, Visa, Amex

Sea and Horses Hotel ♠
APPROVED
Alexandra Terrace, Sea Front, Penzance TR18 4NX
☎ (01736) 61961 changing to 361961
Fax (01736) 330499
CR The Independents
In quiet terrace overlooking seafront, with uninterrupted views over Mount's Bay. Accent on cleanliness, friendliness and good food. We look forward to welcoming you.
Bedrooms: 2 single, 2 double, 3 twin, 3 triple, 1 family room
Suites available
Bathrooms: 8 en-suite, 3 private showers

Bed & breakfast per night:
	£min	£max
Single	27.00	
Double	54.00	

Half board per person:
	£min	£max
Daily	38.50	

Lunch available
Evening meal 1900 (last orders 1930)
Parking for 12
Cards accepted: Access, Visa, Diners, Amex, Switch/Delta

Tarbert Hotel ♠
COMMENDED
11 Clarence Street, Penzance
TR18 2NU
☎ (01736) 63758
Fax (01736) 331336
CR Minotel/Logis of Great Britain/The Independents
Georgian hotel, centrally located, with emphasis on quality and personal service. Restaurant featuring a la carte with fish specialities. Short breaks available.
Bedrooms: 2 single, 6 double, 4 twin
Bathrooms: 12 en-suite

Bed & breakfast per night:
	£min	£max
Single	26.00	29.50
Double	48.00	59.00

Half board per person:
	£min	£max
Daily	40.00	43.50

Evening meal 1900 (last orders 2030)
Parking for 5

Open February–December
Cards accepted: Access, Visa, Amex

Treventon Guest House
♛
Alexandra Place, Penzance
TR18 4NE
☎ (01736) 63521

Genuine Cornish granite guesthouse, 200 yards walk to promenade. Homely atmosphere. Our guest book is your guarantee.
Bedrooms: 1 single, 3 double, 2 twin, 1 triple
Bathrooms: 4 en-suite, 1 public

Bed & breakfast per night:
	£min	£max
Single	14.00	17.00
Double	28.00	34.00

Evening meal 1830 (last orders 1830)

Warwick House Hotel ♠
COMMENDED
17 Regent Terrace, Penzance
TR18 4DW
☎ (01736) 63881
Family-run hotel near the sea, station and heliport. Tastefully decorated rooms, most en-suite and with sea views. Car parking.
Bedrooms: 1 single, 3 double, 1 twin, 1 triple
Bathrooms: 4 en-suite, 1 public

Bed & breakfast per night:
	£min	£max
Single	17.00	19.00
Double	34.00	38.00

Half board per person:
	£min	£max
Daily	29.50	31.50
Weekly	206.50	220.50

Evening meal 1830 (last orders 1900)
Parking for 10
Cards accepted: Access, Visa, Switch/Delta

Woodstock Guest House
♛♛
29 Morrab Road, Penzance
TR18 4AZ
☎ (01736) 369049
Fax (01736) 369049

WEST COUNTRY

Well-appointed, centrally situated guesthouse. Helpful, friendly service. Tea-making facilities, radio and TV. Standard and en-suite rooms available.
Bedrooms: 1 single, 1 double, 2 twin, 1 triple
Bathrooms: 3 en-suite, 1 public

Bed & breakfast
per night:	£min	£max
Single	11.00	17.00
Double	22.00	37.00

Cards accepted: Access, Visa, Diners, Amex

PERRANPORTH
Cornwall
Map ref 1B2

Small seaside resort developed around a former mining village. Today's attractions include exciting surf, rocks, caves and extensive sand dunes.

Atlantic View Hotel
APPROVED

Ponsmere Road, Perranporth TR6 0BW
☎ Truro (01872) 573171
Family hotel in level position beside the beach. Welcomes children and pets. Discount for party bookings. Choice of menu. Ideal base for touring Cornwall.
Bedrooms: 3 single, 3 double, 3 twin, 4 family rooms
Bathrooms: 8 en-suite, 2 public, 1 private shower

Bed & breakfast
per night:	£min	£max
Single	15.00	25.00
Double	30.00	50.00

Half board per
person:	£min	£max
Daily	23.00	33.00
Weekly	135.00	195.00

Lunch available
Evening meal 1830 (last orders 1800)
Parking for 4
Cards accepted: Access, Visa

Chy an Kerensa Hotel
COMMENDED

Cliff Road, Perranporth TR6 0DR
☎ Truro (01872) 572470
Family-run hotel directly overlooking Perranporth beach and golf-course. Superb views from lounge, restaurant and many of the rooms.
Bedrooms: 3 single, 3 double, 2 twin, 1 triple, 1 family room
Suites available

Bathrooms: 2 en-suite, 5 private, 3 public
Bed & breakfast
per night:	£min	£max
Single	16.00	22.00
Double	32.00	44.00

Half board per
person:	£min	£max
Daily	24.00	30.00

Lunch available
Evening meal 1830 (last orders 1930)
Parking for 2
Cards accepted: Access, Visa

PIDDLETRENTHIDE
Dorset
Map ref 2B3

Old Bakehouse
COMMENDED

Piddletrenthide, Dorchester DT2 7QR
☎ (01300) 348305
Country hotel in Hardy's Wessex. All bedrooms en-suite, colour TV. Swimming pool.
Bedrooms: 1 single, 4 double, 1 twin
Bathrooms: 6 en-suite

Bed & breakfast
per night:	£min	£max
Single	24.00	27.50
Double	48.00	48.00

Parking for 8
Open February–December
Cards accepted: Access, Visa

The Poachers Inn
COMMENDED

Piddletrenthide, Dorchester DT2 7QX
☎ (01300) 348358

Inn situated in lovely Piddle Valley on B3143. En-suite rooms with colour TV, telephone, tea/coffee. Restaurant. Stay 2 nights half board October-March, get third night free.
Bedrooms: 8 double, 1 twin, 2 family rooms
Bathrooms: 11 en-suite

Bed & breakfast
per night:	£min	£max
Double	46.00	50.00

Half board per
person:	£min	£max
Daily	33.00	35.00
Weekly	230.00	245.00

Lunch available
Evening meal 1700 (last orders 2130)
Parking for 30
Cards accepted: Access, Visa

PLYMOUTH
Devon
Map ref 1C2

Devon's largest city, major port and naval base. Old houses on the Barbican and ambitious architecture in modern centre, with aquarium, museum and art gallery, the Dome - a heritage centre on the Hoe. Superb coastal views over Plymouth Sound from the hoe.
Tourist Information Centre ☎ (01752) 264849 or 266031 or 266030

Athenaeum Lodge
Listed HIGHLY COMMENDED

4 Athenaeum Street, The Hoe, Plymouth PL1 2RH
☎ (01752) 665005
Elegant Georgian Grade II listed guesthouse, close to the Hoe, historic Barbican, town centre and ferry port. Satellite TV in all rooms. Run by resident owners.
Bedrooms: 4 double, 3 twin, 3 triple
Bathrooms: 4 en-suite, 1 private, 2 public, 2 private showers

Bed & breakfast
per night:	£min	£max
Single	16.00	16.00
Double	28.00	36.00

Parking for 5
Cards accepted: Access, Visa

Berkeleys of St James
Listed

4 St James Place East, The Hoe, Plymouth PL1 3AS
☎ (01752) 221654
Elegant Victorian town house furnished to a very high standard, ideally situated for seafront, Barbican, theatre, ferry port, city centre and university. No smoking.
Bedrooms: 1 single, 1 double, 2 twin, 1 triple
Bathrooms: 1 en-suite, 1 public, 2 private showers

Bed & breakfast
per night:	£min	£max
Single	17.00	25.00
Double	30.00	36.00

Continued ▶

WEST COUNTRY

PLYMOUTH
Continued

Parking for 4
Cards accepted: Access, Visa, Diners, Switch/Delta

Forte Posthouse Plymouth
COMMENDED
Cliff Road, The Hoe, Plymouth PL1 3DL
☎ (01752) 662828
Fax (01752) 660974
Forte
Hotel of modern construction in a magnificent position overlooking the Hoe and Plymouth Sound.
Bedrooms: 15 single, 69 double, 22 twin
Bathrooms: 106 en-suite

Half board per person:
	£min	£max
Daily	46.00	60.00
Weekly	257.60	420.00

Lunch available
Evening meal 1700 (last orders 2230)
Parking for 149
Cards accepted: Access, Visa, Diners, Amex, Switch/Delta

The Grand Hotel
COMMENDED
Elliot Street, The Hoe, Plymouth PL1 2PT
☎ (01752) 661195
Fax (01752) 600653
Utell International

Victorian hotel on Plymouth Hoe. Magnificent sea views, close to city centre and historic Barbican. Leisure breaks available all year round. Live entertainment every Saturday. Balcony rooms and suites.
Bedrooms: 36 double, 36 twin, 3 triple, 2 family rooms
Suites available
Bathrooms: 77 en-suite

Bed & breakfast per night:
	£min	£max
Single	30.50	112.00
Double	45.00	132.00

Half board per person:
	£min	£max
Daily	37.50	64.30

Lunch available
Evening meal 1900 (last orders 2200)
Parking for 70
Cards accepted: Access, Visa, Diners, Amex, Switch/Delta

Grosvenor Park Hotel
COMMENDED
114-116 North Road East, Plymouth PL4 6AH
☎ (01752) 229312
Fax (01752) 252777
Popular, comfortable, recently refurbished hotel offering good food and drink and great value. Nearest hotel to the station and all city centre amenities. Look no further! Golf, bowls and diving package breaks a speciality.
Bedrooms: 8 single, 5 double, 5 twin
Bathrooms: 9 en-suite, 3 public

Bed & breakfast per night:
	£min	£max
Single	17.50	17.50
Double	30.00	35.00

Half board per person:
	£min	£max
Daily	22.50	30.00
Weekly	155.00	210.00

Lunch available
Evening meal 1900 (last orders 2000)
Parking for 6
Cards accepted: Access, Visa, Amex

Invicta Hotel
HIGHLY COMMENDED
11/12 Osborne Place, Lockyer Street, The Hoe, Plymouth PL1 2PU
☎ (01752) 664997
Fax (01752) 664994
Elegant Victorian hotel opposite Sir Francis Drake bowling green and famous Plymouth Hoe. Very close to the city centre and historic Barbican.
Bedrooms: 4 single, 6 double, 8 twin, 2 triple, 3 family rooms
Bathrooms: 19 en-suite, 1 public

Bed & breakfast per night:
	£min	£max
Single	26.00	39.00
Double	45.00	49.00

Half board per person:
	£min	£max
Daily	35.00	45.00
Weekly	250.00	280.00

Lunch available
Evening meal 1900 (last orders 2100)
Parking for 10
Cards accepted: Access, Visa, Amex

Lamplighter Hotel
103 Citadel Road, The Hoe, Plymouth PL1 2RN
☎ (01752) 663855
Fax (01752) 228139
Small friendly hotel on Plymouth Hoe, 5 minutes' walk from the city centre and seafront.
Bedrooms: 5 double, 2 twin, 1 triple, 1 family room
Bathrooms: 7 en-suite, 2 private

Bed & breakfast per night:
	£min	£max
Single	18.00	25.00
Double	28.00	35.00

Parking for 4
Cards accepted: Access, Visa

Millstones Country Hotel
436 - 438 Tavistock Road, Roborough, Plymouth PL6 7HQ
☎ (01752) 773734
Fax (01752) 769435
Elegant country hotel set in an acre of delightful lawned gardens with private parking. Located 4 miles north of the centre of Plymouth on main A386 road.
Bedrooms: 2 single, 5 double, 2 twin
Bathrooms: 9 en-suite, 1 public

Bed & breakfast per night:
	£min	£max
Single	45.00	52.00
Double	55.00	69.50

Half board per person:
	£min	£max
Daily	42.00	52.00
Weekly	294.00	364.00

Evening meal 1930 (last orders 2100)
Parking for 16
Cards accepted: Access, Visa, Diners, Amex

New Continental Hotel
COMMENDED
Millbay Road, Plymouth PL1 3LD
☎ (01752) 220782
Fax (01752) 227013

Beautifully furbished city centre hotel, within easy walking distance of the shops, Barbican and seafront and adjacent to Pavilions conference centre. Superb leisure complex.

WEST COUNTRY

Bedrooms: 22 single, 37 double, 14 twin, 2 triple, 24 family rooms
Suites available
Bathrooms: 99 en-suite

Bed & breakfast
per night:	£min	£max
Single	45.00	70.00
Double	48.00	120.00

Half board per
person:	£min	£max
Daily	34.00	55.00
Weekly	204.00	245.00

Lunch available
Evening meal 1800 (last orders 2200)
Parking for 100
Cards accepted: Access, Visa, Amex, Switch/Delta

⊃♿🏠⌂♦🍴S⚡🅿◎🍽️🏠♠🎱400🛏🎯♞🇺♻SP🛎T

Osmond Guest House 👑
👑👑👑 HIGHLY COMMENDED
42 Pier Street, Plymouth PL1 3BT
☎ (01752) 229705
Fax (01752) 269655
Elegant Edwardian house, converted to modern standards, 20 yards from seafront and within walking distance of main points of interest. Resident proprietors offer courtesy "pick-up" from stations.
Bedrooms: 1 single, 3 double, 1 twin, 1 triple
Bathrooms: 3 en-suite, 2 public, 1 private shower

Bed & breakfast
per night:	£min	£max
Single	15.00	25.00
Double	28.00	38.00

Parking for 4

⊃♿🏠⌂♦🍴📺UL S⚡🎱🍽️
🏠🚗OAP SP🛎T

Phantele Guest House 👑
👑👑 COMMENDED
176 Devonport Road, Stoke, Plymouth PL1 5RD
☎ (01752) 561506
Small family-run guesthouse about 2 miles from city centre. Convenient base for touring. Close to continental and Torpoint ferries.
Bedrooms: 2 single, 1 double, 1 twin, 2 triple
Bathrooms: 2 en-suite, 2 public

Bed & breakfast
per night:	£min	£max
Single	15.50	25.85
Double	29.00	41.80

Half board per
person:	£min	£max
Daily	21.50	33.55
Weekly	135.00	203.10

Evening meal 1830 (last orders 1700)

⊃🏠⌂♦📺S⚡🎱📺🍽️♠🚗♞T

Plymouth Hoe Moat House 👑
👑👑👑👑👑 HIGHLY COMMENDED
Armada Way, Plymouth PL1 2HJ
☎ (01752) 639988
Fax (01752) 673816
Ⓡ Queens Moat/Utell International
Situated on historic Plymouth Hoe in the heart of the city, a short walk from the shopping centre and the Barbican. Half board price based on minimum 2-night stay.
Bedrooms: 108 double, 102 twin
Suite available
Bathrooms: 210 en-suite

Bed & breakfast
per night:	£min	£max
Single	105.00	
Double	124.00	

Half board per
person:	£min	£max
Daily	47.50	

Lunch available
Evening meal 1830 (last orders 2230)
Parking for 175
Cards accepted: Access, Visa, Diners, Amex, Switch/Delta

⊃♿🏠⌂♦🍴📺UL S⚡🎱📺◎🍽️
🏠🚗♠🎱425🛏🎯♞🇺♻SP

Rosaland Hotel 👑
👑👑👑 COMMENDED
32 Houndiscombe Road, Plymouth PL4 6HQ
☎ (01752) 664749
Fax (01752) 256984
Victorian private hotel in quiet residential area, close to centre, university and railway station. Well-appointed rooms with satellite TV. Licensed bar. Warm welcome assured.
Bedrooms: 3 single, 2 double, 1 twin, 2 triple
Bathrooms: 4 en-suite, 2 public, 1 private shower

Bed & breakfast
per night:	£min	£max
Single	17.00	23.00
Double	30.00	35.00

Half board per
person:	£min	£max
Daily	25.00	31.00

Evening meal 1800 (last orders 1800)
Parking for 3
Cards accepted: Access, Visa, Diners, Amex

⊃🏠⌂♦🍴S⚡🎱📺◎🍽️♠🛏
♞OAP T

Please mention this guide when making your booking.

Squires Guest House
Listed HIGHLY COMMENDED
7 St James Place East, The Hoe, Plymouth PL1 3AS
☎ (01752) 261459
Fax (01752) 261459
Elegant Victorian establishment in a quiet secluded square on Plymouth Hoe. Converted to a high standard. Within easy walking distance of all amenities. Winner of Chairman's Cup for Excellence, awarded by Plymouth Marketing Bureau.
Bedrooms: 2 single, 4 double, 2 triple
Bathrooms: 2 private, 1 public, 1 private shower

Bed & breakfast
per night:	£min	£max
Single	16.00	18.00
Double	35.00	37.00

Parking for 4
Cards accepted: Access, Visa, Diners, Amex

⊃♿🏠⌂♦🍴S⚡📺◎🍽️🏠
♠🚗SP T

The Teviot Guest House
Listed HIGHLY COMMENDED
20 North Road East, Plymouth PL4 6AS
☎ (01752) 262656 & 251660
Early Victorian town house situated close to university, rail, bus and ferry terminals. Within a short walking distance of Plymouth Hoe and Barbican. Catering for non-smokers.
Bedrooms: 1 single, 2 double, 2 twin, 1 triple
Bathrooms: 2 en-suite, 1 public, 3 private showers

Bed & breakfast
per night:	£min	£max
Single	18.00	26.00
Double	32.00	40.00

Half board per
person:	£min	£max
Daily	28.00	36.00
Weekly	196.00	252.00

Evening meal 1830 (last orders 1600)
Parking for 2
Cards accepted: Access, Visa, Amex

⊃10📞🏠⌂♦🍴UL⚡🍽️♠🚗
T

ACCESSIBILITY
Look for the ♿ symbols which indicate accessibility for wheelchair users. These are described in detail at the front of this guide.

WEST COUNTRY

POLPERRO
Cornwall
Map ref 1C3

Picturesque fishing village clinging to steep valley slopes about its harbour. A river splashes past cottages and narrow lanes twist between. The harbour mouth, guarded by jagged rocks, is closed by heavy timbers during storms.

Brent House ⋔
Listed APPROVED

1 Brent House, Talland Hill, Polperro, Looe PL13 2RY
☎ (01503) 272495
Amazing bird's eye view of Polperro Harbour, the village and out to sea. Sun terraces, car parking. Good restaurants, pubs and shops in village, just a short walk away. Good walking area.
Bedrooms: 1 double
Bathrooms: 1 en-suite
Bed & breakfast

per night:	£min	£max
Single	18.00	20.00
Double	35.00	37.50

Claremont Hotel ⋔

The Coombes, Polperro, Looe PL13 2RG
☎ (01503) 272241
Fax (01503) 272241
Logis of Great Britain

Family-run hotel in the heart of fishing village. Splendid coastal walks and places of interest nearby. Award-winning restaurant, sun-trap patio. Off-season breaks.
Bedrooms: 1 single, 6 double, 2 twin, 1 triple
Bathrooms: 10 en-suite
Bed & breakfast

per night:	£min	£max
Single	19.00	35.00
Double	34.00	54.00

Half board per person:	£min	£max
Daily	29.00	37.00
Weekly	203.00	259.00

Lunch available
Evening meal 1900 (last orders 2000)

Parking for 16
Cards accepted: Access, Visa, Amex, Switch/Delta

Lanhael House
HIGHLY COMMENDED

Langreek Road, Polperro, Looe PL13 2PW
☎ Looe (01503) 272428
Fax (01503) 273077
17th C house set in beautiful gardens with swimming pool. Within walking distance of Polperro harbour.
Bedrooms: 4 double, 1 twin
Bathrooms: 3 private, 2 public, 1 private shower
Bed & breakfast

per night:	£min	£max
Double	38.00	42.00

Parking for 5
Open April–October

Penryn House Hotel ⋔

The Coombes, Polperro, Looe PL13 2RQ
☎ (01503) 272157
Fax (01503) 273055
Charming Victorian hotel offering comfortable en-suite accommodation and fine dining in our candlelit restaurant. Fabulous coastal walks and National Trust properties. "Murder Mystery" weekends.
Bedrooms: 9 double, 1 twin
Bathrooms: 10 en-suite, 1 public
Bed & breakfast

per night:	£min	£max
Single	23.00	38.00
Double	38.00	57.00

Half board per person:	£min	£max
Daily	33.50	39.50
Weekly	225.00	259.00

Lunch available
Evening meal 1830 (last orders 2130)
Parking for 14
Cards accepted: Access, Visa, Diners

Information on accommodation listed in this guide has been supplied by the proprietors. As changes may occur you are advised to check details at the time of booking.

POLZEATH
Cornwall
Map ref 1B2

Small resort on Padstow Bay and the widening Camel Estuary, with excellent sands and bathing. Pentire Head (National Trust), a notable viewpoint, lies to the north.

Seascape Hotel ⋔
COMMENDED

Polzeath PL27 6SX
☎ Trebetherick (01208) 863638
Catering exclusively for adults, renowned for food and a high degree of comfort with magnificent sea views. Honeymoon and Christmas specials.
Bedrooms: 1 single, 13 double, 2 twin
Bathrooms: 15 en-suite, 1 private
Bed & breakfast

per night:	£min	£max
Single	24.00	30.00
Double	48.00	60.00

Half board per person:	£min	£max
Daily	38.00	40.00
Weekly	240.00	265.00

Evening meal 1900 (last orders 1800)
Parking for 18
Open February–October, December
Cards accepted: Access, Visa

PORLOCK
Somerset
Map ref 1D1

Village set between steep Exmoor hills and the sea at the head of beautiful Porlock Vale. The narrow street shows a medley of building styles. South westward is Porlock Weir with its old houses and tiny harbour and further along the shore at Culbone is England's smallest church.

Anchor and Ship Hotel ⋔
COMMENDED

Porlock Harbour, Exmoor, Minehead TA24 8PB
☎ (01643) 862753
Fax (01643) 862843

Attractive, quiet, comfortable hotel on water's edge. Picturesque harbour amid

WEST COUNTRY

Exmoor's magnificent scenery and coastline. Wildlife everywhere, ancient villages, medieval castle, smugglers' coves.
Bedrooms: 2 single, 12 double, 4 twin, 3 triple
Bathrooms: 19 en-suite, 2 private

Bed & breakfast per night:

	£min	£max
Single	45.00	65.00
Double	70.00	100.00

Half board per person:

	£min	£max
Daily	54.75	69.75
Weekly	307.00	393.00

Lunch available
Evening meal 1900 (last orders 2115)
Parking for 30
Cards accepted: Access, Visa, Amex, Switch/Delta

The Lorna Doone Hotel

High Street, Porlock, Minehead TA24 8PS
☎ (01643) 862404
Personally run by owner and wife. Comfortable rooms, all en-suite, and a wide choice of home-cooked meals. Situated within Exmoor National Park.
Bedrooms: 2 single, 8 double, 3 twin, 2 family rooms
Bathrooms: 15 en-suite, 1 public

Bed & breakfast per night:

	£min	£max
Single	21.50	23.00
Double	38.00	50.00

Lunch available
Evening meal 1900 (last orders 2045)
Parking for 8
Cards accepted: Access, Visa

Porlock Vale House

HIGHLY COMMENDED
Porlock Weir, Minehead TA24 8NY
☎ (01643) 862338
Fax (01643) 862338
Magnificent Edwardian country house, set in 25 acres on the edge of the moor, with grounds sweeping down to the sea. En-suite accommodation.
Bedrooms: 9 double, 5 twin
Bathrooms: 13 en-suite, 1 private, 2 public

Bed & breakfast per night:

	£min	£max
Single	41.00	43.00
Double	62.00	66.00

Half board per person:

	£min	£max
Daily	48.50	50.50
Weekly	275.00	289.00

Lunch available
Evening meal 1900 (last orders 1930)
Parking for 20
Cards accepted: Access, Visa, Diners, Amex, Switch/Delta

PORT GAVERNE

Cornwall
Map ref 1B2

Small village sheltering in a narrow inlet on the dramatic north Cornish coast. In the 19th C the shingle beach was a loading site for slate from the nearby Delabole quarry.

Port Gaverne Hotel

COMMENDED
Port Gaverne, Port Isaac PL29 3SQ
☎ Bodmin (01208) 880244 & Freephone 0500 657867
Fax (01208) 880151
17th C hotel and restaurant in a tiny paradise on the North Cornwall coast. Half board daily price below based on minimum 2-day stay.
Bedrooms: 3 single, 8 double, 2 twin, 6 triple
Bathrooms: 18 en-suite, 1 private

Bed & breakfast per night:

	£min	£max
Single	46.00	49.00
Double	48.00	50.00

Half board per person:

	£min	£max
Daily	53.00	63.00
Weekly	350.00	392.00

Lunch available
Evening meal 1900 (last orders 2130)
Parking for 20
Open February–December
Cards accepted: Access, Visa, Diners, Amex, Switch/Delta

Please check prices and other details at the time of booking.

Establishments should be open throughout the year, unless otherwise stated.

PORT ISAAC

Cornwall
Map ref 1B2

Old fishing port of whitewashed cottages, twisting stairways and narrow alleys. A stream splashes down through the centre to the harbour. Nearby stands a 19th C folly, Doyden Castle, with a magnificent view of the coast.

Long Cross Hotel and Victorian Garden

APPROVED
Trelights, Port Isaac PL29 3TF
☎ Bodmin (01208) 880243

Unusual character hotel on the North Cornwall coast, with magnificent gardens open to the public. Own freehouse tavern and one of Cornwall's best tea/beer gardens.
Bedrooms: 7 double, 1 twin, 2 triple
Bathrooms: 10 en-suite

Bed & breakfast per night:

	£min	£max
Single	21.60	30.00
Double	30.00	50.00

Half board per person:

	£min	£max
Daily	27.00	37.00

Lunch available
Evening meal 1800 (last orders 2000)
Parking for 40

PORTHLEVEN

Cornwall
Map ref 1B3

Old fishing port with handsome Victorian buildings overlooking Mount's Bay. An extensive, shingly beach reaches south-east towards the Loe Bar, where the pebbles make a lake on the landward side.

Harbour Inn

COMMENDED
Commercial Road, Porthleven, Helston TR13 9JD
☎ Helston (01326) 573876
150-year-old inn on harbour edge.

Continued ▶

WEST COUNTRY

PORTHLEVEN
Continued

Restaurant open 7 days a week. Most bedrooms en-suite, many with harbour views.
Bedrooms: 1 single, 6 double, 2 twin, 1 family room
Bathrooms: 8 en-suite, 1 public, 2 private showers

Bed & breakfast
per night:	£min	£max
Single		31.00
Double		56.00

Lunch available
Evening meal 1830 (last orders 2130)
Parking for 10
Cards accepted: Access, Visa, Diners, Amex

PORTLAND
Dorset
Map ref 2B3

Joined by a narrow isthmus to the coast, a stony promontory sloping from the lofty landward side to a lighthouse on Portland Bill at its southern tip. Villages are built of the white limestone for which the "isle" is famous.

Alessandria Hotel and Italian Restaurant
APPROVED

71 Wakeham Easton, Portland, Weymouth DT5 1HW
☎ (01305) 822270 & 820108
Fax (01305) 820561

Italy on Portland. Warm and friendly Italian hospitality from chef/proprietor Giovanni. Spacious en-suite bedrooms with all facilities. Food prepared and cooked to order. Three bedrooms on ground floor.
Bedrooms: 6 single, 3 double, 3 twin, 2 triple, 1 family room
Suite available
Bathrooms: 10 en-suite, 1 private, 3 public, 1 private shower

Bed & breakfast
per night:	£min	£max
Single	26.00	46.00
Double	42.00	55.00

Half board per
person:	£min	£max
Daily	35.00	45.00
Weekly	225.00	275.00

Evening meal 1900 (last orders 2100)
Parking for 19

Cards accepted: Access, Visa, Diners, Amex, Switch/Delta

Portland Heights Hotel
COMMENDED

Yeates Corner, Portland DT5 2EN
☎ (01305) 821361
Fax (01305) 860081

Modern hotel situated on the summit of Portland. Enjoy spectacular sea views in comfortable surroundings. Excellent leisure facilities.
Bedrooms: 1 single, 20 double, 36 twin, 8 triple
Bathrooms: 65 en-suite

Bed & breakfast
per night:	£min	£max
Single	44.50	49.50
Double	54.50	59.50

Half board per
person:	£min	£max
Daily		37.50
Weekly	225.00	285.00

Lunch available
Evening meal 1900 (last orders 2130)
Parking for 250
Cards accepted: Access, Visa, Diners, Amex, Switch/Delta

PORTSCATHO
Cornwall
Map ref 1B3

Coastal village spreading along low cliffs of Gerrans Bay on the eastern side of the Roseland Peninsula. Seaside buildings show a variety of styles from late Georgian houses to small, interestingly-designed modern blocks.

Rosevine Hotel
HIGHLY COMMENDED

Porthcurnick Beach, Portscatho, Truro TR2 5EW
☎ (01872) 580230 & 580206
Fax (01872) 580230

Peaceful country house hotel with large delightful gardens and magnificent sea views over safe, sandy beach. Good food. Complimentary golf and tennis.
Bedrooms: 1 single, 4 double, 8 twin, 2 triple
Bathrooms: 15 en-suite

Bed & breakfast
per night:	£min	£max
Single	28.00	50.00
Double	56.00	100.00

Half board per
person:	£min	£max
Daily	44.00	74.00
Weekly	295.00	490.00

Lunch available
Evening meal 1915 (last orders 2030)
Parking for 40
Open March–October
Cards accepted: Access, Visa

POUNDSGATE
Devon
Map ref 1C2

Dartmoor village near the Dart Valley. River Dart Country Park is 2 miles to the south-east.

Leusdon Lodge Country House Hotel
COMMENDED

Poundsgate, Newton Abbot TQ13 7PE
☎ (01364) 631304 & 631573
Fax (01364) 631599

Family-run country house on Dartmoor. Delightful garden, splendid views. Local riding and fishing, short breaks, walking weekends.
Bedrooms: 2 double, 5 twin
Bathrooms: 7 en-suite

Bed & breakfast
per night:	£min	£max
Single		40.00
Double	60.00	88.00

Half board per
person:	£min	£max
Daily	54.00	68.00

Lunch available
Evening meal 1850
Parking for 12
Open March–December
Cards accepted: Access, Visa

Map references apply to the colour maps at the back of this guide.

WEST COUNTRY

RANGEWORTHY
South Gloucestershire
Map ref 2B2

Rangeworthy Court Hotel
COMMENDED

Church Lane, Wotton Road, Rangeworthy, Bristol BS17 5ND
☎ (01454) 228347
Fax (01454) 228945

17th C country manor house with relaxing, peaceful atmosphere and popular restaurant. Less than 20 minutes from M4, M5 and Bristol.
Bedrooms: 3 single, 7 double, 2 twin, 2 triple
Bathrooms: 14 en-suite

Bed & breakfast
per night:	£min	£max
Single	45.00	60.00
Double	60.00	80.00

Half board per
person:	£min	£max
Daily	45.00	50.00

Lunch available
Evening meal 1900 (last orders 2100)
Parking for 40
Cards accepted: Access, Visa, Diners, Amex, Switch/Delta

REDRUTH
Cornwall
Map ref 1B3

Originally west Cornwall's major mining centre, now a light-industrial town with handsome granite public buildings of the early 19th C.

Crossroads Hotel
HIGHLY COMMENDED

Scorrier, Redruth TR16 5BP
☎ St Day (01209) 820551
Fax (01209) 820392

Modern, purpose-built hotel, all private facilities. Excellent reputation for food and service. Two miles east of Redruth just off Scorrier exit of A30.
Bedrooms: 6 single, 12 double, 15 twin, 3 triple
Bathrooms: 36 en-suite

Bed & breakfast
per night:	£min	£max
Single	33.00	47.50
Double	46.00	58.00

Half board per
person:	£min	£max
Daily	33.00	58.50
Weekly	210.00	285.00

Lunch available
Evening meal 1900 (last orders 2130)

Parking for 140
Cards accepted: Access, Visa, Diners, Amex, Switch/Delta

ROCK
Cornwall
Map ref 1B2

Small resort and boating centre beside the abundant sands of the Camel Estuary. A fine golf-course stretches northward along the shore to Brea Hill, thought to be the site of a Roman settlement. Passenger ferry service from Padstow.

The Mariners Hotel
COMMENDED

The Slipway, Rock, Wadebridge PL27 6LD
☎ Trebetherick (01208) 862312
Fax (01208) 863827

Situated in a popular water sports area with panoramic views over the Camel Estuary to Padstow.
Bedrooms: 1 single, 8 double, 7 twin, 2 family rooms
Bathrooms: 18 en-suite

Bed & breakfast
per night:	£min	£max
Single	20.00	40.00
Double	30.00	70.00

Half board per
person:	£min	£max
Daily	30.00	55.00
Weekly	189.00	315.00

Lunch available
Evening meal 1900 (last orders 2130)
Parking for 29
Open April–October
Cards accepted: Access, Visa, Amex, Switch/Delta

Roskarnon House Hotel

Rock, Wadebridge PL27 6LD
☎ Trebetherick (01208) 862329
Fax (01208) 862785

Edwardian house in an acre of lawned gardens, facing south and overlooking Camel Estuary. 20 yards from the beach and 50 yards from the golf-course.
Bedrooms: 1 single, 4 double, 6 twin, 1 triple
Bathrooms: 8 en-suite, 2 private, 3 public

Bed & breakfast
per night:	£min	£max
Single	20.00	35.00
Double	45.00	65.00

Half board per
person:	£min	£max
Daily	30.00	45.00
Weekly	210.00	290.00

Lunch available
Evening meal 1900 (last orders 2000)
Parking for 16
Open March–October
Cards accepted: Amex

Silvermead
COMMENDED

Rock, Wadebridge PL27 6LB
☎ Bodmin (01208) 862425

Off main road affording superb estuary views. Sailing club and windsurfing. 150 yards from beach and adjacent to St Enodoc 36-hole golf-course. Residential licence.
Bedrooms: 2 single, 2 double, 2 twin, 2 triple
Bathrooms: 4 en-suite, 1 public

Bed & breakfast
per night:	£min	£max
Single	18.00	24.00
Double	36.00	48.00

Half board per
person:	£min	£max
Daily	28.00	34.00
Weekly	180.00	230.00

Evening meal 1800 (last orders 2000)
Parking for 13

RUAN HIGH LANES
Cornwall
Map ref 1B3

Village at the northern end of the Roseland Peninsula.

The Hundred House Hotel
HIGHLY COMMENDED

Ruan Highlanes, Truro TR2 5JR
☎ Truro (01872) 501336
Fax (01872) 501151
Minotel

Delightful 19th C house in 3-acre garden, near St Mawes. Antiques, log fires, delicious dinners. Pretty en-suite bedrooms. Ideal for walking, touring, gardens and National Trust properties.
Continued ▶

WEST COUNTRY

RUAN HIGH LANES
Continued

Bedrooms: 2 single, 4 double, 4 twin
Bathrooms: 10 en-suite

Bed & breakfast per night:	£min	£max
Single	36.00	38.50
Double	72.00	77.00

Half board per person:	£min	£max
Daily	50.00	59.00
Weekly	301.00	364.00

Evening meal 1930 (last orders 1900)
Parking for 15
Open March–October
Cards accepted: Access, Visa, Amex

ST AGNES
Cornwall
Map ref 1B3

Small town in a once-rich mining area on the north coast. Terraced cottages and granite houses slope to the church. Some old mine workings remain, but the attraction must be the magnificent coastal scenery and superb walks. St Agnes Beacon offers one of Cornwall's most extensive views.

Driftwood Spars Hotel
COMMENDED

Trevaunance Cove, St Agnes TR5 ORT
☎ St Agnes (01872) 552428 & 553323
Fax (01872) 552428

Delightful old inn with enormous beams, stone walls and log fires. Most bedrooms have wonderful sea views. Candelit restaurant. Parking.
Bedrooms: 7 double, 1 twin, 1 family room
Bathrooms: 9 en-suite

Bed & breakfast per night:	£min	£max
Single	27.00	
Double	54.00	

Lunch available
Evening meal 1900 (last orders 2300)
Parking for 100
Cards accepted: Access, Visa, Diners, Amex

Penkerris
APPROVED

Penwinnick Road, St Agnes TR5 0PA
☎ St Agnes (01872) 552262

Enchanting Edwardian residence with own grounds in unspoilt Cornish village. Beautiful rooms, log fires in winter, good home cooking. Dramatic cliff walks and beaches nearby.
Bedrooms: 1 single, 5 double, 3 twin, 3 triple
Bathrooms: 8 en-suite, 3 public

Bed & breakfast per night:	£min	£max
Single	15.00	30.00
Double	27.00	35.00

Half board per person:	£min	£max
Daily	22.50	26.00
Weekly	135.00	175.00

Lunch available
Evening meal from 1830
Parking for 9
Cards accepted: Access, Visa, Diners, Amex, Switch/Delta

ST AUSTELL
Cornwall
Map ref 1B3

Leading market town, the meeting point of old and new Cornwall. One mile from St Austell Bay with its sandy beaches, old fishing villages and attractive countryside. Ancient narrow streets, pedestrian shopping precincts. Fine church of Pentewan stone and Italianate Town Hall.

Alexandra Hotel

52-54 Alexandra Road, St Austell PL25 4QN
☎ (01726) 66111 & 74242
Fax (01726) 74242

In quietish position just 5 minutes from town centre. Within easy reach of St Austell Bay and very near bus and rail station.
Bedrooms: 5 single, 4 double, 3 twin
Bathrooms: 4 en-suite, 3 public

Bed & breakfast per night:	£min	£max
Single	24.00	29.00
Double	42.00	52.00

Half board per person:	£min	£max
Daily	33.75	38.75
Weekly	180.00	212.00

Evening meal 1830 (last orders 1700)

Parking for 16
Cards accepted: Access, Visa, Diners, Amex, Switch/Delta

Boscundle Manor
HIGHLY COMMENDED

Tregrehan, St Austell PL25 3RL
☎ St Austell (01726) 813557
Fax (01726) 814997

Lovely 18th C house in secluded grounds, furnished with many antiques and run like a private country house. 2 miles north-east of St Austell.
Bedrooms: 2 single, 3 double, 5 twin
Suites available
Bathrooms: 10 en-suite

Bed & breakfast per night:	£min	£max
Single	60.00	80.00
Double	110.00	130.00

Half board per person:	£min	£max
Daily	75.00	100.00
Weekly	455.00	560.00

Evening meal 1930 (last orders 2030)
Parking for 15
Open April–October
Cards accepted: Access, Visa, Amex

Cliff Head Hotel

Sea Road, Carlyon Bay, St Austell PL25 3RB
☎ Par (01726) 812345
Fax (01726) 815511

Family-run hotel, set in own grounds. Licensed bar, heated pool and ample parking. Central for touring Cornwall.
Bedrooms: 6 single, 17 double, 14 twin, 3 triple, 2 family rooms
Bathrooms: 42 en-suite, 3 public

Bed & breakfast per night:	£min	£max
Single	35.00	45.00
Double	65.00	75.00

Half board per person:	£min	£max
Daily	49.95	59.95
Weekly	349.65	419.65

Lunch available
Evening meal 1930 (last orders 2130)
Parking for 80

WEST COUNTRY

Cards accepted: Access, Visa, Diners, Amex, Switch/Delta

Selwood House Hotel

60 Alexandra Road, St Austell PL25 4QN
☎ St Austell (01726) 65707
Fax (01726) 68951
Detached, family-run hotel, centrally situated for holidays and business, in the beautiful St Austell Bay.
Bedrooms: 3 single, 5 double, 3 twin
Suite available
Bathrooms: 11 en-suite

Bed & breakfast per night	£min	£max
Single	31.00	31.00
Double	45.00	59.00

Half board per person	£min	£max
Daily	42.00	42.00
Weekly	250.00	250.00

Evening meal 1830 (last orders 1900)
Parking for 13
Cards accepted: Access, Visa, Diners, Amex

White Hart Hotel

COMMENDED

Church Street, St Austell PL25 4AT
☎ St Austell (01726) 72100
Fax (01726) 74705
Built in the late 16th C, became the chief coaching inn in the 17th C and is now a family-run hotel.
Bedrooms: 2 single, 13 double, 2 twin, 1 triple
Bathrooms: 18 en-suite

Bed & breakfast per night	£min	£max
Single	40.00	
Double	63.00	

Lunch available
Evening meal 1900 (last orders 2100)
Cards accepted: Access, Visa, Diners, Amex

ST IVES

Cornwall
Map ref 1B3

Old fishing port, artists' colony and holiday town with good surfing beach. Fishermen's cottages, granite fish cellars, a sandy harbour and magnificent headlands typify a charm that has survived since the 19th C pilchard boom. Tate Gallery opened in 1993.
Tourist Information Centre ☎ (01736) 796297

The Anchorage Guest House

COMMENDED

5 Bunkers Hill, St Ives TR26 1LJ
☎ Penzance (01736) 797135
18th C fisherman's cottage, 30 yards from harbour front and beaches, full of old world charm. Two minutes from Tate Gallery.
Bedrooms: 1 single, 4 double, 1 twin
Bathrooms: 4 en-suite, 1 public

Bed & breakfast per night	£min	£max
Single	16.00	20.00
Double	30.00	40.00

Cards accepted: Access, Visa, Amex

Blue Hayes Guest House

HIGHLY COMMENDED

Trelyon Avenue, St Ives TR26 2AD
☎ Penzance (01736) 797129
A country house by the sea. Quiet garden, warm and friendly atmosphere, good food.
Bedrooms: 2 single, 5 double, 2 triple
Bathrooms: 5 en-suite, 2 public

Bed & breakfast per night	£min	£max
Single	29.00	36.00
Double	56.00	74.00

Half board per person	£min	£max
Daily	42.00	50.00
Weekly	240.00	290.00

Evening meal 1830 (last orders 1830)
Parking for 9
Open March–October
Cards accepted: Access, Visa

Chy-an-Dour Hotel

COMMENDED

Trelyon Avenue, St Ives TR26 2AD
☎ Penzance (01736) 796436
Fax (01736) 795772
Former sea captain's house built of dressed granite, with superb sea views. All rooms en-suite. Chef/proprietor.
Bedrooms: 13 double, 7 twin, 1 triple, 2 family rooms
Suite available
Bathrooms: 23 en-suite

Bed & breakfast per night	£min	£max
Single	27.00	38.00
Double	54.00	76.00

Half board per person	£min	£max
Daily	41.75	52.75
Weekly	255.00	335.00

Lunch available
Evening meal 1900 (last orders 2030)
Parking for 23
Cards accepted: Access, Visa, Switch/Delta

Chy-an-Gwedhen Guest House

St Ives Road, Carbis Bay, St Ives TR26 2PN
☎ St Ives (01736) 798684
Delightful welcoming guesthouse, a haven for non-smokers. Adjacent to coastal footpath, excellent food. Tate Gallery nearby. All rooms fully en-suite.
Bedrooms: 3 double, 2 twin
Bathrooms: 5 en-suite, 1 public

Bed & breakfast per night	£min	£max
Single	20.00	20.00
Double	34.00	40.00

Half board per person	£min	£max
Daily	25.50	28.50

Parking for 9
Cards accepted: Access, Visa, Amex, Switch/Delta

Chy Harbro

COMMENDED

16 Park Avenue, St Ives TR26 2DN
☎ Penzance (01736) 794617
Superb sea views overlooking the harbour. Reputation for good food and hospitality. Some rooms en-suite and with sea views.
Bedrooms: 1 single, 3 double, 2 triple
Bathrooms: 3 en-suite, 1 public

Bed & breakfast per night	£min	£max
Single	12.50	13.50
Double	25.00	30.00

Open April–September

The symbols in each entry give information about services and facilities. A 'key' to these symbols appears at the back of this guide.

441

WEST COUNTRY

ST IVES
Continued

Dean Court Hotel
♛♛♛ COMMENDED

Trelyon Avenue, St Ives TR26 2AD
☎ Penzance (01736) 796023
Fax (01736) 796233

Former gentleman's residence set in own grounds. Enjoys panoramic views across St Ives Bay and overlooks Porthminster Beach and St Ives harbour. Good food, ample parking.
Bedrooms: 2 single, 8 double, 2 twin
Bathrooms: 12 en-suite

Bed & breakfast per night:	£min	£max
Single	30.00	36.00
Double	56.00	72.00

Half board per person:	£min	£max
Daily	36.00	42.00
Weekly	210.00	260.00

Evening meal 1830 (last orders 1800)
Parking for 12
Open March–October
Cards accepted: Access, Visa

Garrack Hotel M
♛♛♛ COMMENDED

Higher Ayr, St Ives TR26 3AA
☎ Penzance (01736) 796199
Fax (01736) 798955
Ⓖ Logis of Great Britain

Delightful family-owned hotel. Quiet location. Superb coastal views. Ample parking. Heated indoor pool and leisure centre. Fabulous bargain breaks October-March.
Bedrooms: 1 single, 8 double, 5 twin, 3 triple
Bathrooms: 17 en-suite, 1 public

Bed & breakfast per night:	£min	£max
Single	61.00	79.00
Double	84.00	158.00

Half board per person:	£min	£max
Daily	54.00	68.30
Weekly	364.00	505.00

Lunch available
Evening meal 1900 (last orders 2030)
Parking for 30
Cards accepted: Access, Visa, Diners, Amex, Switch/Delta

Longships Hotel
♛♛♛ HIGHLY COMMENDED

Talland Road, St Ives TR26 2DF
☎ Penzance (01736) 798180
Fax (01736) 798180

Overlooking St Ives Bay, minutes by foot from town centre and beaches. All rooms en-suite, most with sea view.
Bedrooms: 3 single, 9 double, 4 twin, 9 triple
Bathrooms: 25 en-suite

Bed & breakfast per night:	£min	£max
Single	18.00	26.00
Double	36.00	52.00

Half board per person:	£min	£max
Daily	22.50	29.00
Weekly	150.00	210.00

Lunch available
Evening meal 1800 (last orders 1900)
Parking for 18
Open March–October

The Nook
♛♛

Ayr, St Ives TR26 1EQ
☎ Penzance (01736) 795913

Family hotel in secluded gardens, near cliff path, beaches and harbour. Children's play area and car park. Traditional home cooking.
Bedrooms: 3 single, 5 double, 2 twin, 3 family rooms
Bathrooms: 6 en-suite, 3 public

Bed & breakfast per night:	£min	£max
Single	17.00	21.50
Double	34.00	43.00

Half board per person:	£min	£max
Daily	25.00	29.50
Weekly	160.00	205.00

Evening meal 1830 (last orders 1900)
Parking for 10
Open March–September

Pondarosa Hotel M
♛♛ COMMENDED

10 Porthminster Terrace, St Ives TR26 2DQ
☎ St Ives (01736) 795875

Charming Victorian house. Warm and friendly atmosphere, well-appointed, comfortable accommodation, convenient for town and beaches. Large private car park.
Bedrooms: 5 double, 2 triple, 2 family rooms
Bathrooms: 9 en-suite

Bed & breakfast per night:	£min	£max
Single	14.00	20.00
Double	28.00	40.00

Half board per person:	£min	£max
Daily	22.00	28.00
Weekly	154.00	189.00

Lunch available
Evening meal 1800 (last orders 1930)
Parking for 12
Cards accepted: Access, Visa, Amex

Primavera Private Hotel M
♛♛ COMMENDED

14 Draycott Terrace, St Ives TR26 2EF
☎ Penzance (01736) 795595

Small, friendly hotel overlooking Porthminster Beach, with warm, personal and efficient service. Carefully prepared food - special dietary needs catered for. Bar meals served all day.
Bedrooms: 2 single, 1 double, 1 triple, 1 family room
Bathrooms: 2 en-suite, 1 public

Bed & breakfast per night:	£min	£max
Single	14.00	18.00
Double	28.00	36.00

Lunch available
Evening meal 1830 (last orders 2100)
Open June–September

Tregenna Castle M
♛♛♛♛ APPROVED

Trelyan Avenue, St Ives TR26 2DE
☎ Penzance (01736) 795254
Fax (01736) 796066
Ⓖ Utell International

Dating back to the 18th C, this fine hotel in its own parkland commands magnificent views of St Ives Bay.
Bedrooms: 7 single, 17 double, 33 twin, 18 family rooms
Suites available
Bathrooms: 75 en-suite, 5 public

Bed & breakfast per night:	£min	£max
Single	30.00	65.00
Double	60.00	130.00

Half board per person:	£min	£max
Daily	40.00	75.00

WEST COUNTRY

Lunch available
Evening meal 1900 (last orders 2115)
Parking for 450
Cards accepted: Access, Visa, Diners, Amex, Switch/Delta

ST JUST-IN-PENWITH
Cornwall
Map ref 1A3

Coastal parish of craggy moorland scattered with engine houses and chimney stacks of disused mines. The old mining town of St Just has handsome 19th C granite buildings. North of the town are the dramatic ruined tin mines at Botallack.

Roseudian
COMMENDED

Crippas Hill, Kelynack, St. Just, Penzance TR19 7RE
☎ Penzance (01736) 788556
Comfortable modernised cottage in rural surroundings. Friendly, relaxing atmosphere. Good home cooking based on own produce. South-facing terraced gardens. Dogs by arrangement only.
Bedrooms: 2 double, 1 twin
Bathrooms: 3 en-suite
Bed & breakfast

per night:	£min	£max
Single	17.50	22.50
Double		35.00

Half board per

person:	£min	£max
Daily	27.50	32.50
Weekly	192.50	

Evening meal 1900 (last orders 1600)
Parking for 4
Open March–October

ST KEYNE
Cornwall
Map ref 1C2

The Old Rectory Country House Hotel
COMMENDED

St Keyne, Liskeard PL14 4RL
☎ Liskeard (01579) 342617

Peacefully secluded, family-run old rectory hotel in 3 acres of grounds. Modern amenities and known for its excellent food.
Bedrooms: 1 single, 5 double, 2 twin
Bathrooms: 8 en-suite, 1 public
Bed & breakfast

per night:	£min	£max
Single	25.00	35.00
Double	50.00	70.00

Half board per

person:	£min	£max
Daily	40.00	50.00
Weekly	252.00	315.00

Evening meal 1900 (last orders 2000)
Parking for 30
Cards accepted: Access, Visa

ST MELLION
Cornwall
Map ref 1C2

St Mellion Hotel, Golf and Country Club
COMMENDED

St Mellion, Saltash PL12 6SD
☎ Liskeard (01579) 351351
Fax (01579) 350116
The compass point of Devon and Cornwall. The visitor's perfect choice, with world-class golf, new leisure facilities, award-winning food and lodge/hotel accommodation.
Bedrooms: 8 double, 16 twin
Bathrooms: 24 en-suite
Bed & breakfast

per night:	£min	£max
Single	54.00	62.00
Double	58.00	71.00

Half board per

person:	£min	£max
Daily	49.00	62.00

Lunch available
Evening meal 1930 (last orders 2130)
Parking for 400
Cards accepted: Access, Visa, Diners, Amex, Switch/Delta

ST NEOT
Cornwall
Map ref 1C2

Colliford Tavern
COMMENDED

Colliford Lake, St Neot, Liskeard PL14 6PZ
☎ Cardinham (01208) 821335
Fax (01208) 821335
"An oasis on Bodmin Moor". Friendly country pub, ideally situated for exploring Cornwall. Immaculate facilities. Good home-cooked meals and fine traditional ales. Colour brochure available.
Bedrooms: 3 double, 2 twin
Bathrooms: 5 en-suite
Bed & breakfast

per night:	£min	£max
Double	29.00	50.00

Lunch available
Evening meal 1900 (last orders 2130)
Parking for 50
Open April–September
Cards accepted: Access, Visa, Amex, Switch/Delta

SALCOMBE
Devon
Map ref 1C3

Sheltered yachting resort of whitewashed houses and narrow streets in a balmy setting on the Salcombe Estuary. Palm, myrtle and other Mediterranean plants flourish. There are sandy bays and creeks for boating.
Tourist Information Centre ☎ (01548) 843927

Fern Lodge
Hope Cove, Kingsbridge TQ7 3HF
☎ Kingsbridge (01548) 561326
Small hotel, bed and breakfast, all en-suite, colour TVs. Own keys. Near beaches and coastal path. Pets welcome free of charge.
Bedrooms: 2 single, 2 double, 2 twin, 2 triple
Bathrooms: 8 en-suite
Bed & breakfast

per night:	£min	£max
Single	18.50	19.50
Double	37.00	39.00

Parking for 8
Open March–September and Christmas

Heron House Hotel
COMMENDED

Thurlestone Sands, Salcombe TQ7 3JY
☎ Kingsbridge (01548) 561308 & 561600
Fax (01548) 560180
Idyllic sea-edge location, surrounded by National Trust countryside and adjacent to bird reserve. Beautifully appointed, fine Devon cuisine/seafood.
Bedrooms: 1 single, 13 double, 2 twin, 1 family room
Bathrooms: 17 en-suite

Continued ▶

WEST COUNTRY

SALCOMBE
Continued

Bed & breakfast per night:
	£min	£max
Single	30.00	45.00
Double	60.00	120.00

Half board per person:
	£min	£max
Daily	40.00	70.00
Weekly	200.00	441.00

Evening meal 1915 (last orders 2050)
Parking for 50
Open February–December
Cards accepted: Access, Visa, Switch/Delta

Lyndhurst Hotel
COMMENDED

Bonaventure Road, Salcombe TQ8 8BG
☎ (01548) 842481
Fax (01548) 842481
Friendly hotel enjoying an atmosphere of informality. Magnificent views. Traditional menus. Resident proprietors. Non-smokers only, please. 1993/94 winners of South Hams Council tourism award for excellence, service, quality and value.
Bedrooms: 3 double, 3 twin, 1 triple, 1 family room
Bathrooms: 8 en-suite

Bed & breakfast per night:
	£min	£max
Single	22.00	27.00
Double	44.00	54.00

Half board per person:
	£min	£max
Daily	33.00	39.00
Weekly	231.00	245.00

Evening meal 1900 (last orders 1630)
Parking for 4
Open February–November

Sunnycliff Hotel
COMMENDED

Cliff Road, Salcombe TQ8 8JX
☎ (01548) 842207
Informal family hotel on water's edge. Superb sea views from all rooms. Own moorings and landing stage. English fare.
Bedrooms: 1 single, 6 double, 5 twin, 5 triple, 1 family room
Bathrooms: 11 en-suite, 3 public, 2 private showers

Bed & breakfast per night:
	£min	£max
Single	31.50	40.00
Double	63.00	80.00

Lunch available
Evening meal 1930 (last orders 2000)
Parking for 18
Cards accepted: Access, Visa, Amex, Switch/Delta

Torre View Hotel
COMMENDED

Devon Road, Salcombe TQ8 8HJ
☎ (01548) 842633
Fax (01548) 842633
Detached Victorian residence with every modern comfort, commanding extensive views of the estuary and surrounding countryside. Congenial atmosphere. No smoking, please.
Bedrooms: 6 double, 2 twin
Suites available
Bathrooms: 5 en-suite, 3 private

Bed & breakfast per night:
	£min	£max
Single	22.50	29.00
Double	45.00	52.00

Half board per person:
	£min	£max
Daily	33.00	39.00
Weekly	220.00	245.00

Evening meal 1900 (last orders 1800)
Parking for 5
Open February–October
Cards accepted: Access, Visa

SALISBURY
Wiltshire
Map ref 2B3

Beautiful city and ancient regional capital set amid water meadows. Buildings of all periods are dominated by the cathedral whose spire is the tallest in England. Built between 1220 and 1258, it is one of the purest examples of Early English architecture.
Tourist Information Centre ☎ (01722) 334956

Byways House

31 Fowlers Road, City Centre, Salisbury SP1 2QP
☎ (01722) 328364
Fax (01722) 322146
Attractive family-run Victorian house close to cathedral in quiet area of city centre. Car park. Bedrooms with private bathrooms and colour satellite TV. Traditional English and vegetarian breakfasts.
Bedrooms: 4 single, 8 double, 5 twin, 2 triple, 1 family room
Bathrooms: 17 en-suite, 1 public

Bed & breakfast per night:
	£min	£max
Single	24.00	32.50
Double	39.00	51.50

Parking for 15
Cards accepted: Access, Visa

Cranston Guest House
APPROVED

5 Wain-a-Long Road, Salisbury SP1 1LJ
☎ (01722) 336776
Large detached town house covered in Virginia Creeper. 10 minutes' walk from town centre and cathedral.
Bedrooms: 2 single, 1 double, 2 twin, 2 family rooms
Bathrooms: 5 en-suite, 1 public

Bed & breakfast per night:
	£min	£max
Single	17.00	18.00
Double	32.00	35.00

Half board per person:
	£min	£max
Daily	25.00	

Evening meal 1800 (last orders 1900)
Parking for 4

The Edwardian Lodge

59 Castle Road, Salisbury SP1 3RH
☎ (01722) 413329 & 410500
Edwardian house, home-cooked evening meals, good parking off main road, short walk city centre, cathedral, Old Sarum. Beautiful valley drive to Stonehenge.
Bedrooms: 1 single, 1 double, 3 twin, 2 family rooms
Bathrooms: 7 en-suite

Bed & breakfast per night:
	£min	£max
Single	27.50	30.00
Double	38.00	42.00

Half board per person:
	£min	£max
Daily	25.00	30.00
Weekly	160.00	195.00

Evening meal 1800 (last orders 2030)
Parking for 8

WEST COUNTRY

Glen Lyn Guest House
⬥⬥ COMMENDED

6 Bellamy Lane, Milford Hill,
Salisbury SP1 2SP
☎ (01722) 327880
Elegant Victorian house in quiet lane, 5
minutes' walk to city centre. Ample
parking. Non-smokers only, please.
Quiet, only birdsong.
Bedrooms: 1 single, 4 double, 3 twin,
1 triple
Bathrooms: 4 en-suite, 2 public

Bed & breakfast per night:	£min	£max
Single	22.00	25.00
Double	37.00	45.00

Half board per person:	£min	£max
Daily	31.00	34.00
Weekly	180.00	210.00

Evening meal (last orders 1930)
Parking for 7

The Milford Hall Hotel and Restaurant
⬥⬥⬥ HIGHLY COMMENDED

206 Castle Street, Salisbury SP1 3TE
☎ (01722) 417411
Fax (01722) 419444
This fine Georgian city centre mansion
has been sympathetically restored to
create a magnificent hotel and
restaurant that is becoming a
landmark in this historic cathedral city.
Bedrooms: 20 double, 15 twin
Bathrooms: 35 en-suite

Bed & breakfast per night:	£min	£max
Single	42.00	55.00
Double	50.00	75.00

Half board per person:	£min	£max
Daily	52.00	70.00
Weekly	350.00	500.00

Lunch available
Evening meal 1900 (last orders
2130)
Parking for 50
Cards accepted: Access, Visa, Amex,
Switch/Delta

Red Lion Hotel
⬥⬥⬥ COMMENDED

Milford Street, Salisbury SP1 2AN
☎ (01722) 323334
Fax (01722) 325756
Best Western
Originally a coaching inn, now a city
centre hotel with all modern facilities.
Ideal for business or pleasure. Daily
half-board price below based on
minimum 2-night stay.

Bedrooms: 11 single, 22 double,
19 twin, 2 family rooms
Suites available
Bathrooms: 54 en-suite

Bed & breakfast per night:	£min	£max
Single	78.50	84.00
Double	107.50	113.00

Half board per person:	£min	£max
Daily	55.00	
Weekly	330.00	

Lunch available
Evening meal 1900 (last orders
2100)
Parking for 10
Cards accepted: Access, Visa, Diners,
Amex, Switch/Delta

Victoria Lodge Guest House
⬥⬥ APPROVED

61 Castle Road, Salisbury SP1 3RH
☎ (01722) 320586
Fax (01722) 414507
Victorian lodge, a short walk from city
centre, cathedral and Old Sarum.
Home-cooked evening meals, good
parking. Stonehenge 8 miles.
Bedrooms: 3 single, 2 double,
3 triple, 5 family rooms
Bathrooms: 13 en-suite

Bed & breakfast per night:	£min	£max
Single	22.20	29.50
Double	33.30	44.00

Half board per person:	£min	£max
Daily		36.00

Lunch available
Evening meal 1800 (last orders
2100)
Parking for 13

White Hart Hotel
⬥⬥⬥ COMMENDED

St John Street, Salisbury SP1 2SD
☎ (01722) 327476
Fax (01722) 412761
Forte
The imposing pillared portico of the
White Hart is a landmark in the city.
Modern accommodation is provided in
extensions.
Bedrooms: 15 single, 28 double,
22 twin, 1 triple, 2 family rooms
Bathrooms: 68 en-suite

Bed & breakfast per night:	£min	£max
Single	92.25	95.25
Double	120.50	148.50

Half board per person:	£min	£max
Daily	55.00	65.00
Weekly	308.00	364.00

Lunch available
Evening meal 1900 (last orders
2130)
Parking for 90
Cards accepted: Access, Visa, Diners,
Amex, Switch/Delta

SALISBURY PLAIN

See under Amesbury, Salisbury,
Winterbourne Stoke

SAMPFORD PEVERELL

Devon
Map ref 1D2

Parkway House Hotel
⬥⬥ COMMENDED

Sampford Peverell, Tiverton
EX16 7BJ
☎ (01884) 820255

Friendly, family-run hotel and restaurant
set in large, attractive grounds. In a
quiet area but just 2 minutes away
from junction 27 of the M5, making it
an ideal venue for business persons,
visitors and holidaymakers when
travelling between London and
Cornwall.
Bedrooms: 4 single, 3 double, 1 twin,
2 triple
Bathrooms: 10 en-suite

Bed & breakfast per night:	£min	£max
Single	30.00	35.00
Double	40.00	45.00

Lunch available
Evening meal 1900 (last orders
2130)
Cards accepted: Access, Visa,
Switch/Delta

COLOUR MAPS

Colour maps at the back of
this guide pinpoint all places
in which you will find
accommodation listed.

445

WEST COUNTRY

SAUNTON
Devon
Map ref 1C1

Houses situated on a minor road at the end of Braunton Burrows, part of which is a nature reserve, important to botanists and ornithologists. Nearby is a fine golf-course and a 3 mile beach, Saunton Sands.

Preston House Hotel
COMMENDED

Saunton, Braunton EX33 1LG
☎ Croyde (01271) 890472
Fax (01271) 890555

Beautifully furnished Victorian country house hotel, with sea views, overlooking Saunton Sands. All rooms en-suite. Lovingly prepared country-fresh food.
Bedrooms: 2 single, 5 double, 7 twin
Bathrooms: 14 en-suite, 1 public

Bed & breakfast per night:	£min	£max
Single	35.00	70.00
Double	65.00	85.00

Half board per person:	£min	£max
Daily	50.00	60.00

Lunch available
Evening meal 1900 (last orders 2030)
Parking for 20
Open February–December
Cards accepted: Access, Visa, Switch/Delta

Saunton Sands Hotel
HIGHLY COMMENDED

Saunton, Braunton EX33 1LQ
☎ Croyde (01271) 890212
Fax (01271) 890145

Directly overlooks 5 miles of golden sands and is surrounded by unspoilt countryside. Offering a wealth of sports and leisure facilities.
Bedrooms: 17 single, 15 double, 28 twin, 32 family rooms
Suites available
Bathrooms: 92 en-suite, 5 public

Bed & breakfast per night:	£min	£max
Single	60.00	82.00
Double	116.00	236.00

Half board per person:	£min	£max
Daily	70.00	130.00
Weekly	374.50	910.00

Lunch available
Evening meal 1930 (last orders 2100)
Parking for 200

Cards accepted: Access, Visa, Diners, Amex, Switch/Delta

SEATON
Devon
Map ref 1D2

Small resort lying near the mouth of the River Axe. A mile-long beach extends to the dramatic cliffs of Beer Head. Annual art exhibition in July.
Tourist Information Centre ☎ (01297) 21660 or 21689

Beach End Guest House
HIGHLY COMMENDED

8 Trevelyan Road, Seaton EX12 2NL
☎ (01297) 23388

Enjoy unrivalled views of Seaton Bay. We offer fine food, friendly and attentive service in our lovely Edwardian guesthouse.
Bedrooms: 4 double, 1 twin
Bathrooms: 5 en-suite, 1 public

Bed & breakfast per night:	£min	£max
Double		42.00

Half board per person:	£min	£max
Daily		30.95
Weekly		206.50

Evening meal 1900 (last orders 1500)
Parking for 5
Open February–October

Beaumont
COMMENDED

Castle Hill, Seaton EX12 2QW
☎ (01297) 20832

Attractive and spacious guesthouse in select seafront position, offering en-suite comfort, personal attention and traditional home cooking.
Bedrooms: 2 double, 2 triple, 1 family room
Suites available
Bathrooms: 5 en-suite

Bed & breakfast per night:	£min	£max
Double	36.00	38.00

Half board per person:	£min	£max
Daily	29.00	30.00
Weekly	185.00	190.00

Evening meal 1900 (last orders 1700)
Parking for 6
Open January–October, December

SHALDON
Devon
Map ref 1D2

Pretty resort facing Teignmouth from the south bank of the Teign Estuary. Regency houses harmonise with others of later periods; there are old cottages and narrow lanes. On the Ness, a sandstone promontory nearby, a tunnel built in the 19th C leads to a beach revealed at low tide.

Fonthill
HIGHLY COMMENDED

Torquay Road, Shaldon, Teignmouth TQ14 0AX
☎ (01626) 872344
Fax (01626) 872344

Lovely Georgian family home in superb grounds overlooking River Teign. Very comfortable rooms in a peaceful setting. Restaurants nearby.
Bedrooms: 3 twin
Bathrooms: 2 en-suite, 1 private

Bed & breakfast per night:	£min	£max
Single	28.00	
Double	48.00	54.00

Parking for 5
Open March–November

Glenside Hotel
COMMENDED

Ringmore Road, Shaldon, Teignmouth TQ14 0EP
☎ (01626) 872448

Old world cottage-style hotel by the riverside. Licensed and family-run, with home cooking. Easy walking. Car park.
Bedrooms: 2 single, 5 double, 3 twin
Bathrooms: 7 en-suite, 1 public

Bed & breakfast per night:	£min	£max
Single	19.50	24.50
Double	38.00	49.00

Half board per person:	£min	£max
Daily	32.50	37.50
Weekly	185.00	225.00

WEST COUNTRY

Evening meal 1900 (last orders 1900)
Parking for 10
🛏4🍴♿🚭🛒✂🍽💺🅿❄🚌
SP

Ness House Hotel
👑👑👑 COMMENDED
Marine Parade, Shaldon, Teignmouth TQ14 0HP
☎ (01626) 873480
Fax (01626) 873486
Overlooking Teign Estuary. Elegant restaurant and comfortable bars. Most rooms have balconies overlooking the sea. En-suite facilities. Easy access to Torquay, Exeter and Dartmoor.
Bedrooms: 1 single, 9 double, 2 triple
Suite available
Bathrooms: 12 en-suite

Bed & breakfast
per night:	£min	£max
Single	39.00	60.00
Double	65.00	85.00

Half board per
person:	£min	£max
Daily	51.50	72.50

Lunch available
Evening meal 1900 (last orders 2215)
Parking for 20
Cards accepted: Access, Visa, Amex, Switch/Delta
🛏♿🏊🍴☎🍽♿🚭🛒✂🍽📺💺🅿❄❋🚌🅿T

SHEPTON MALLET
Somerset
Map ref 2A2

Important, stone-built market town beneath the south-west slopes of the Mendips. Thriving rural industries include glove and shoe making, dairying and cider making; the remains of a medieval "shambles" in the square date from the town's prosperity as a wool centre.

The Shrubbery Hotel M
👑👑👑 COMMENDED
Commercial Road, Shepton Mallet BA4 5BU
☎ (01749) 346671
Fax (01749) 346581
A small in-town oasis. Privately owned hotel set in delightful gardens, offering customer comfort, a quality restaurant and lounge with light eating facilities. Ideal stopping-off point for the West Country.
Bedrooms: 1 single, 6 double, 1 twin, 2 family rooms
Bathrooms: 9 en-suite, 1 private

Bed & breakfast
per night	£min	£max
Single	35.00	45.00
Double	59.50	65.00

Lunch available
Evening meal 1900 (last orders 2130)
Parking for 100
Cards accepted: Access, Visa, Diners, Switch/Delta
🛏♿🏊🍴☎🍽♿🚭🛒✂🍽💺🅿❄
T30❋🚌🅿SP

SHERBORNE
Dorset
Map ref 2B3

Dorset's "Cathedral City" of medieval streets, golden hamstone buildings and great abbey church, resting place of Saxon kings. Formidable 12th C castle ruins and Sir Walter Raleigh's splendid Tudor mansion and deer park. Street markets, leisure centre, many cultural activities.
Tourist Information Centre ☎ (01935) 815341

Britannia Inn
👑
Westbury, Sherborne DT9 3EH
☎ (01935) 813300
Originally the Lord Digby School for Girls, built in 1743, now a listed building.
Bedrooms: 1 single, 1 double, 3 twin, 2 triple
Bathrooms: 3 public

Bed & breakfast
per night:	£min	£max
Single	19.00	22.00
Double	34.00	36.00

Evening meal 1900 (last orders 2100)
Parking for 13
Cards accepted: Access, Visa
🛏♿🍴S💺🍷🚌🅿

Eastbury Hotel M
👑👑👑 COMMENDED
Long Street, Sherborne DT9 3BY
☎ (01935) 813131
Fax (01935) 817296
Gracious Georgian town house hotel with attractive walled garden, near town centre. Private car park.
Bedrooms: 6 single, 5 double, 4 twin
Bathrooms: 15 en-suite

Bed & breakfast
per night:	£min	£max
Single	45.00	60.00
Double	65.00	110.00

Half board per
person:	£min	£max
Weekly		332.50

Lunch available
Evening meal 1900 (last orders 2200)
Parking for 27
Cards accepted: Access, Visa
🛏♿🏊🍴☎🍽♿🚭🛒✂🍽💺🅿❄❋O💺🍽
T60U❋✂❄🚌SP🅿

SIDMOUTH
Devon
Map ref 1D2

Charming resort set amid lofty red cliffs where the River Sid meets the sea. The wealth of ornate Regency and Victorian villas recalls the time when this was one of the south coast's most exclusive resorts. Museum; August International Festival of Folk Arts.
Tourist Information Centre ☎ (01395) 516441

The Belmont Hotel M
👑👑👑👑 HIGHLY COMMENDED
The Esplanade, Sidmouth EX10 8RX
☎ (01395) 512555
Fax (01395) 579101
Traditionally one of Sidmouth's finest seafront hotels. Leisure facilities are available at adjacent hotel, the Victoria.
Bedrooms: 9 single, 11 double, 28 twin, 3 family rooms
Bathrooms: 51 en-suite

Bed & breakfast
per night:	£min	£max
Single	54.00	96.00
Double	94.00	192.00

Half board per
person:	£min	£max
Daily	42.00	106.00
Weekly	294.00	637.00

Lunch available
Evening meal 1900 (last orders 2100)
Parking for 45
Cards accepted: Access, Visa, Diners, Amex, Switch/Delta
🛏♿🏊🍴☎🍽♿🚭🛒✂🍽O❄
💺🅿T40▶❋🚌🅿SP🅿T

Devoran Hotel
👑👑👑 COMMENDED
Esplanade, Sidmouth EX10 8AU
☎ (01395) 513151 & Freephone 0800 317171
Fax (01395) 579929
Family-run hotel overlooking beach, very close to town centre and amenities. Relaxed, happy atmosphere, with traditional home-cooked food using local produce.
Bedrooms: 5 single, 7 double, 7 twin, 4 triple
Bathrooms: 19 en-suite, 2 public

Continued ▶

WEST COUNTRY

SIDMOUTH
Continued

Bed & breakfast per night:	£min	£max
Single	24.50	36.00
Double	49.00	68.00

Half board per person:	£min	£max
Daily	30.50	48.00
Weekly	199.00	270.00

Evening meal 1845 (last orders 1930)
Parking for 4
Open March–October
Cards accepted: Access, Visa

Kingswood Hotel
HIGHLY COMMENDED
Esplanade, Sidmouth EX10 8AX
☎ (01395) 516367
Fax (01395) 513185

Long standing family-run seafront hotel. Emphasis on good cooking using local produce. Warmth, comfort and relaxed atmosphere. Formerly Victorian spa baths.
Bedrooms: 8 single, 2 double, 9 twin, 7 triple
Bathrooms: 18 en-suite, 8 private, 1 public

Bed & breakfast per night:	£min	£max
Single	25.00	38.00
Double	50.00	76.00

Half board per person:	£min	£max
Daily	25.00	46.50
Weekly	215.00	285.00

Lunch available
Evening meal 1845 (last orders 1930)
Parking for 17
Open March–November
Cards accepted: Access, Visa, Switch/Delta

Hotel Riviera
DE LUXE
The Esplanade, Sidmouth EX10 8AY
☎ (01395) 515201
Fax (01395) 577775

Majestic Regency hotel on the Esplanade, with panoramic sea views and a splendid terrace overlooking Lyme Bay.
Bedrooms: 7 single, 6 double, 14 twin
Suites available
Bathrooms: 27 en-suite

Bed & breakfast per night:	£min	£max
Single	62.00	85.00
Double	108.00	154.00

Half board per person:	£min	£max
Daily	63.00	86.00
Weekly	441.00	539.00

Lunch available
Evening meal 1900 (last orders 2100)
Parking for 24
Cards accepted: Access, Visa, Diners, Amex

Royal York and Faulkner Hotel
COMMENDED
Esplanade, Sidmouth EX10 8AZ
☎ (01395) 513043 & 513184
Fax (01395) 577472

Charming Regency hotel on centre of Sidmouth's delightful Esplanade. Long established, family-run hotel offering all amenities and excellent leisure facilities.
Bedrooms: 22 single, 9 double, 29 twin, 8 triple
Bathrooms: 66 en-suite, 2 private, 4 public

Bed & breakfast per night:	£min	£max
Single	22.00	42.00
Double	44.00	84.00

Half board per person:	£min	£max
Daily	27.50	52.00
Weekly	197.50	315.00

Lunch available
Evening meal 1915 (last orders 2030)
Parking for 7
Open February–December
Cards accepted: Access, Visa, Switch/Delta

The Victoria Hotel
HIGHLY COMMENDED
The Esplanade, Sidmouth EX10 8RY
☎ (01395) 512651
Fax (01395) 579154

One of England's finest hotels on Sidmouth's famous Esplanade. Guests are assured of high standards of service, comfort and cuisine.
Bedrooms: 14 single, 18 double, 20 twin, 9 triple
Suites available
Bathrooms: 61 en-suite

Bed & breakfast per night:	£min	£max
Single	62.00	94.00
Double	104.00	204.00

Half board per person:	£min	£max
Daily	62.00	104.00
Weekly	308.00	679.00

Lunch available
Evening meal 1915 (last orders 2100)
Parking for 54
Cards accepted: Access, Visa, Diners, Amex, Switch/Delta

SOUTH MOLTON
Devon
Map ref 1C1

Busy market town at the mouth of the Yeo Valley near southern Exmoor. Wool, mining and coaching brought prosperity between the Middle Ages and the 19th C and the fine square with Georgian buildings, a Guildhall and Assembly Rooms reflect this former affluence.

Whitechapel Manor
HIGHLY COMMENDED
South Molton EX36 3EG
☎ (01769) 573377
Fax (01769) 573797

In the foothills of Exmoor National Park lies this Grade I listed Elizabethan manor house. All around are unspoilt woodlands, valleys, moors, rivers, gardens and National Trust properties.
Bedrooms: 1 single, 3 double, 5 twin, 1 family room
Suite available
Bathrooms: 10 en-suite

WEST COUNTRY

Bed & breakfast per night:

	£min	£max
Single	70.00	155.00
Double	110.00	170.00

Lunch available
Evening meal 1900 (last orders 2045)
Parking for 40
Cards accepted: Access, Visa, Diners, Amex, Switch/Delta

STREET
Somerset
Map ref 2A2

Busy shoe-making town set beneath the Polden Hills. A museum at the factory, which was developed with the rest of the town in the 19th C, can be visited. Just south, the National Trust has care of woodland on Ivythorn Hill which gives wide views northward.

Wessex Hotel
COMMENDED

High Street, Street BA16 0EF
☎ (01458) 443183
Fax (01458) 446589
Modern en-suite bedrooms, situated in the heart of Somerset, legendary country of King Arthur and the Knights of the Round Table. Nearby attractions include Bath, Glastonbury Abbey, Cheddar Gorge, Wookey Hole Caves and Wells Cathedral.
Bedrooms: 7 double, 43 twin
Bathrooms: 50 en-suite

Bed & breakfast per night:

	£min	£max
Single	40.00	50.00
Double	50.00	60.00

Half board per person:

	£min	£max
Daily	50.00	57.50
Weekly	240.00	350.00

Lunch available
Evening meal 1900 (last orders 2130)
Parking for 85
Cards accepted: Access, Visa, Diners, Amex, Switch/Delta

SUTTON BENGER
Wiltshire
Map ref 2B2

Bell House Hotel
APPROVED

High Street, Sutton Benger, Chippenham SN15 4RH
☎ Seagry (01249) 720401
Fax (01249) 720401
Pretty country hotel set in small quiet village. Suitable for a quiet weekend away yet near M4 and town.
Bedrooms: 3 single, 5 double, 6 twin
Bathrooms: 14 en-suite

Bed & breakfast per night:

	£min	£max
Single	32.50	66.45
Double	45.00	89.50

Lunch available
Evening meal 1830 (last orders 2230)
Parking for 35
Cards accepted: Access, Visa, Diners, Amex, Switch/Delta

SWINDON
Wiltshire
Map ref 2B2

Wiltshire's industrial and commercial centre, an important railway town in the 19th C, situated just north of the Marlborough Downs. The railway village created in the mid-19th C has been preserved. Railway museum, art gallery, theatre and leisure centre.
Tourist Information Centre ☎ (01793) 530328 or 493007

Fairview Guest House
COMMENDED

52 Swindon Road, Wootton Bassett, Swindon SN4 8EU
☎ (01793) 852283
Fax (01793) 848076
Detached guesthouse, west of Swindon, close to M4 junction 16 (1.25 miles). Ground floor rooms available.
Bedrooms: 5 single, 3 double, 2 twin, 2 triple
Bathrooms: 6 en-suite, 2 public, 1 private shower

Bed & breakfast per night:

	£min	£max
Single	19.50	35.00
Double	30.00	43.00

Evening meal 1830 (last orders 1930)
Parking for 17
Cards accepted: Access, Visa, Diners, Amex

Goddard Arms Hotel
COMMENDED

High Street, Old Town, Swindon SN1 3EW
☎ (01793) 692313
Fax (01793) 512984
Old world hotel built in 1790 and named after famous local family in the old town. Short distance from M4 motorway, Cotswolds, Avebury and Wiltshire Downs.
Bedrooms: 12 single, 16 double, 37 twin
Suite available
Bathrooms: 65 private

Bed & breakfast per night:

	£min	£max
Single	30.00	
Double	60.00	

Half board per person:

	£min	£max
Daily	39.00	
Weekly	300.00	

Continued ▶

School House Hotel and Restaurant

Hook Street,
Hook, nr Swindon, Wiltshire SN4 8EF
Telephone: 01793 851198
Fax: 01793 851025

Small but charming Country house Hotel in converted 1860 Schoolhouse, combining modern facilities and Victorian decor. Rural, on southern borders of Cotswolds yet close to M4 and Swindon.

Weekend breaks from £29.50 per person

449

WEST COUNTRY

SWINDON
Continued

Lunch available
Evening meal 1830 (last orders 2130)
Parking for 115
Cards accepted: Access, Visa, Diners, Amex, Switch/Delta

Relian Guest House

151-153 County Road, Swindon SN1 2EB
☎ (01793) 521416
Quiet house adjacent to Swindon Town Football Club and short distance from town centre. Close to bus and rail stations, and A345. Free car park at rear.
Bedrooms: 4 single, 2 double, 2 twin
Suites available
Bathrooms: 3 en-suite, 2 public, 3 private showers
Bed & breakfast

per night:	£min	£max
Single	17.00	
Double	32.00	

The School House Hotel and Restaurant

COMMENDED
Hook Street, Hook, Swindon SN4 8EF
☎ (01793) 851198
Fax (01793) 851025

Charming country house hotel in a converted 1860 school house. Combining modern facilities and Victorian decor. In rural hamlet but close to M4, Swindon and Cotswolds.
Bedrooms: 1 single, 8 double, 1 twin
Bathrooms: 10 en-suite
Bed & breakfast

per night:	£min	£max
Single	59.50	72.50
Double	69.50	79.95

Half board per

person:	£min	£max
Daily	79.95	92.50

Lunch available
Evening meal 1800 (last orders 2200)
Parking for 40

Cards accepted: Access, Visa, Diners, Amex, Switch/Delta

Ad See display advertisement on page 449

Swindon Marriott

Pipers Way, Swindon SN3 1SH
☎ (01793) 512121
Fax (01793) 513114
CR Utell International/Whitbread
Bedrooms include executive suites with king size beds, and double beds as standard in twins and singles. Indoor pool, squash and tennis courts.
Bedrooms: 110 double, 43 twin
Suites available
Bathrooms: 153 en-suite
Bed & breakfast

per night:	£min	£max
Single	85.00	115.00
Double	95.00	125.00

Half board per

person:	£min	£max
Daily	105.00	130.00

Lunch available
Evening meal 1830 (last orders 2200)
Parking for 180
Cards accepted: Access, Visa, Diners, Amex

TAUNTON
Somerset
Map ref 1D1

County town, well-known for its public schools, sheltered by gentle hill-ranges on the River Tone. Medieval prosperity from wool has continued in marketing and manufacturing and the town retains many fine period buildings.
Tourist Information Centre ☎ (01823) 336344

Falcon Hotel

COMMENDED
Henlade, Taunton TA3 5DH
☎ Henlade (01823) 442502
Fax (01823) 442670
Family-owned country house hotel in own grounds, only 1 mile east of M5 (junction 25). Informal atmosphere, comfortable and well equipped.
Bedrooms: 2 single, 3 double, 5 twin, 2 family rooms
Bathrooms: 12 en-suite
Bed & breakfast

per night:	£min	£max
Single	39.50	45.00
Double	55.00	55.00

Evening meal 1900 (last orders 2030)
Parking for 25
Cards accepted: Access, Visa, Diners, Amex

Forde House

COMMENDED
9 Upper High Street, Taunton TA1 3PX
☎ (01823) 279042
Fax (01823) 279042
Peaceful location in the centre of town, close to all amenities, including public park and golf-course. Warm welcome guaranteed.
Bedrooms: 1 single, 2 double, 2 twin
Bathrooms: 4 en-suite, 1 private
Bed & breakfast

per night:	£min	£max
Single	26.00	28.00
Double	48.00	50.00

Parking for 5

Fursdon Guest House

88-90 Greenway Road, Taunton TA2 6LE
☎ (01823) 331955
Delightful, detached Edwardian guesthouse close to town centre and railway station. En-suites available. Private car park.
Bedrooms: 5 single, 4 double, 1 twin, 1 triple, 3 family rooms
Bathrooms: 5 en-suite, 1 public, 5 private showers
Bed & breakfast

per night:	£min	£max
Single	16.00	25.00
Double	35.00	40.00

Parking for 9
Cards accepted: Access, Visa, Amex

Higher Dipford Farm

COMMENDED
Dipford, Trull, Taunton TA3 7NU
☎ (01823) 275770 & 257916
120-acre dairy farm. 14th C listed Somerset longhouse with magnificent walks and views. Antique furniture, log fires and spacious en-suite rooms. Renowned for high class cuisine using fresh dairy produce.
Bedrooms: 1 double, 1 triple, 1 family room
Bathrooms: 3 en-suite
Bed & breakfast

per night:	£min	£max
Single	27.00	32.00
Double	46.00	54.00

WEST COUNTRY

Half board per person:	£min	£max
Daily	40.00	47.00
Weekly	259.00	313.00

Lunch available
Evening meal 1900 (last orders 2130)
Parking for 6
Open January, March–December
Cards accepted: Amex

Lowdens

26 Wellington Road, Taunton TA1 4EQ
☎ (01823) 334500
Comfortable town centre hotel, close to bus station and all amenities. Private car park. Evening meals available.
Bedrooms: 1 single, 5 double, 3 twin
Bathrooms: 9 en-suite

Bed & breakfast per night:	£min	£max
Single	27.50	27.50
Double	40.00	40.00

Parking for 10
Cards accepted: Access, Visa, Amex

Meryan House Hotel

HIGHLY COMMENDED

Bishops Hull, Taunton TA1 5EG
☎ (01823) 337445
Fax (01823) 322355

Delightful 17th C period residence with beams and inglenooks, in peaceful surroundings near Taunton. Personal attention assured at all times.
Bedrooms: 2 single, 8 double, 2 twin
Bathrooms: 12 en-suite

Bed & breakfast per night:	£min	£max
Single	38.00	48.00
Double	48.00	58.00

Half board per person:	£min	£max
Daily	53.00	63.00

Evening meal 1900 (last orders 2030)
Parking for 17
Cards accepted: Access, Visa

Orchard House

HIGHLY COMMENDED

Fons George, Wilton, Taunton TA1 3JS
☎ (01823) 351783
Fax (01823) 351785

Lovely Georgian house in residential area, 5 minutes' walk from town centre and with easy access from M5. Short break reductions available. Next door is cosy 17th C "Vivary Arms" serving good food.
Bedrooms: 1 double, 5 twin
Bathrooms: 6 en-suite

Bed & breakfast per night:	£min	£max
Single	30.00	35.00
Double	50.00	55.00

Lunch available
Evening meal 1900 (last orders 2130)
Parking for 8
Cards accepted: Access, Visa, Switch/Delta

Roadchef Lodge

COMMENDED

Taunton Deane Motorway Service Area, M5 Southbound, Trull, Taunton TA1 4BA
☎ (01823) 332228 & Freephone 0800 834719
Fax (01823) 338131
RoadChef

RoadChef Lodges offer high specification rooms at affordable prices, in popular locations suited to both the business and private traveller. Prices are per room and do not include breakfast.
Bedrooms: 39 double
Bathrooms: 39 en-suite

Bed & breakfast per night:	£min	£max
Single	37.95	39.95

Parking for 500
Cards accepted: Access, Visa, Diners, Amex, Switch/Delta

A key to symbols can be found inside the back cover flap.

TEDBURN ST MARY

Devon
Map ref 1D2

Fingle Glen Family Golf Centre

APPROVED

Tedburn St Mary, Exeter EX6 6AF
☎ (01647) 61817 & 61818
Fax (01647) 61135
Family hotel with 9-hole golf centre and driving range, offering excellent teaching and practice facilities. First class function and golfing break venue.
Bedrooms: 1 single, 2 double, 2 twin, 2 family rooms
Bathrooms: 7 en-suite

Bed & breakfast per night:	£min	£max
Single	30.50	
Double	57.00	

Half board per person:	£min	£max
Daily	39.50	

Lunch available
Evening meal 1800 (last orders 2130)
Parking for 200
Cards accepted: Access, Visa, Amex, Switch/Delta

TEIGNMOUTH

Devon
Map ref 1D2

Set on the north bank of the beautiful Teign Estuary, busy fishing and shipbuilding port handling timber and locally-quarried ball-clay. A bridge crosses to the pretty village of Shaldon and there are good views of the estuary from here.
Tourist Information Centre ☎ (01626) 779769

Belvedere Hotel

COMMENDED

Barnpark Road, Teignmouth TQ14 8PJ
☎ (01626) 774561
Fax (01626) 770009
Comfortable detached family-run Victorian villa with its own garden and car park. Close to beach and town centre. Many rooms with sea views.
Bedrooms: 1 single, 6 double, 2 twin, 2 triple, 2 family rooms
Bathrooms: 12 en-suite, 1 private

Bed & breakfast per night:	£min	£max
Single	20.00	23.00
Double	40.00	45.00

Continued ▶

WEST COUNTRY

TEIGNMOUTH
Continued

Half board per person:

	£min	£max
Daily	28.00	30.00
Weekly	180.00	195.00

Lunch available
Evening meal 1830 (last orders 2000)
Parking for 10
Cards accepted: Access, Visa, Amex, Switch/Delta

The Coombe Bank Hotel
APPROVED

Landscore Road, Teignmouth
TQ14 9JL
☎ (01626) 772369
Fax (01626) 772369
Spacious, detached Victorian house, quietly situated above town centre, 10 minutes' walk from shops and beach. Well-appointed bedrooms with private facilities. Private parking.
Bedrooms: 2 single, 5 double, 3 twin
Bathrooms: 6 en-suite, 4 private

Bed & breakfast per night:

	£min	£max
Single	20.00	24.00
Double	40.00	48.00

Half board per person:

	£min	£max
Daily	29.00	36.00
Weekly	200.00	252.00

Lunch available
Evening meal 1900 (last orders 2030)
Parking for 12
Cards accepted: Access, Visa, Switch/Delta

London Hotel
APPROVED

Bank Street, Teignmouth
TQ14 8AW
☎ (01626) 776336
Fax (01626) 778457
Situated in town centre with easy access to beaches and moors. Families catered for. Leisure facilities include indoor swimming pool.
Bedrooms: 1 single, 17 double, 2 twin, 6 triple, 6 family rooms
Bathrooms: 32 en-suite

Bed & breakfast per night:

	£min	£max
Single	30.00	37.00
Double	64.00	64.00

Half board per person:

	£min	£max
Daily	32.00	40.00
Weekly	224.00	280.00

Lunch available
Evening meal 1800 (last orders 2200)
Parking for 8
Cards accepted: Access, Visa, Diners, Amex, Switch/Delta

THURLESTONE
Devon
Map ref 1C3

Small resort of thatched cottages standing above coastal cliffs near the winding estuary of Devon's River Avon. The village has a fine golf-course and a good beach.

Thurlestone Hotel
HIGHLY COMMENDED

Thurlestone, Kingsbridge TQ7 3NN
☎ Kingsbridge (01548) 560382
Fax (01548) 561069
A peaceful setting in old world village with thatched cottages. International cuisine and outstanding indoor sporting amenities.
Bedrooms: 7 single, 16 double, 32 twin, 13 triple
Bathrooms: 68 en-suite

Bed & breakfast per night:

	£min	£max
Single	35.00	80.00
Double	70.00	160.00

Half board per person:

	£min	£max
Daily	40.00	98.00
Weekly	280.00	651.00

Lunch available
Evening meal 1930 (last orders 2100)
Parking for 119
Cards accepted: Access, Visa

TIMBERSCOMBE
Somerset
Map ref 1D1

Knowle Riding Centre
APPROVED

Timberscombe, Minehead
TA24 6TZ
☎ (01643) 841342
Fax (01643) 841644
Riding holiday/activity centre with over 40 horses. Manor house accommodation. Trout lake and river fishing, croquet lawn, 4 hole golf practice area, indoor heated pool and gardens. Non-riders very welcome. Golf/fishing breaks.
Bedrooms: 2 single, 3 double, 5 twin, 7 triple, 3 family rooms
Bathrooms: 8 en-suite, 1 private, 4 public

Bed & breakfast per night:

	£min	£max
Single	20.00	25.00
Double	40.00	50.00

Half board per person:

	£min	£max
Daily	27.50	32.50
Weekly		250.00

Lunch available
Evening meal 1830 (last orders 1900)
Parking for 40

TINTAGEL
Cornwall
Map ref 1B2

Coastal village near the legendary home of King Arthur. There is a lofty headland with the ruin of a Norman castle and traces of a Celtic monastery are still visible in the turf.

Atlantic View Hotel
APPROVED

Treknow, Tintagel PL34 0EJ
☎ Camelford (01840) 770221
Victorian coastal hotel in superb clifftop position. All en-suite with four-posters and magnificent sea views. Licensed. Indoor pool. Minutes from beach.
Bedrooms: 1 single, 5 double, 1 twin, 1 triple
Bathrooms: 8 en-suite

Bed & breakfast per night:

	£min	£max
Single	19.50	24.00
Double	39.00	48.00

Half board per person:

	£min	£max
Daily	29.50	38.00
Weekly	195.00	252.00

Lunch available
Evening meal 1900 (last orders 2115)
Parking for 20
Cards accepted: Access, Visa

The Cornishman Inn
COMMENDED

Fore Street, Tintagel PL34 0DB
☎ Camelford (01840) 770238
Fax (01840) 770078
Beautiful old world inn offering en-suite

WEST COUNTRY

bedrooms with TV and tea/coffee-making facilities. Three bars, extensive menus, beautiful gardens.
Bedrooms: 4 double, 4 twin, 1 triple, 1 family room
Suites available
Bathrooms: 10 en-suite
Bed & breakfast

per night:	£min	£max
Single	20.00	
Double	39.00	

Lunch available
Evening meal 1800 (last orders 2130)
Parking for 30
Cards accepted: Access, Visa, Diners, Amex, Switch/Delta

King Arthur's Castle Hotel
APPROVED
Atlanta Road, Tintagel PL34 0DQ
☎ Camelford (01840) 770202
Fax (01840) 770978
Located in one of the most spectacular parts of Cornwall, standing on a very high and rugged coastline which commands majestic views. Overlooks the ruins of Tintagel Castle, reputedly the home of King Arthur.
Bedrooms: 12 single, 14 double, 18 twin, 6 triple
Bathrooms: 50 en-suite, 12 public
Bed & breakfast

per night:	£min	£max
Single	25.00	
Double	50.00	

Half board per

person:	£min	£max
Daily	33.50	
Weekly	231.00	

Lunch available
Evening meal 1900 (last orders 2200)
Parking for 106
Open April–October
Cards accepted: Access, Visa

Polkerr Guest House
HIGHLY COMMENDED
Tintagel PL34 0BY
☎ Camelford (01840) 770382
Period country house offering quality accommodation, central heating, TV and tea-making facilities in all rooms. Ideal for touring, bathing, golf and coastal walks.
Bedrooms: 1 single, 3 double, 2 twin, 1 family room
Bathrooms: 6 en-suite, 1 public
Bed & breakfast

per night:	£min	£max
Single	17.00	20.00
Double	34.00	40.00

Half board per

person:	£min	£max
Daily	25.00	28.00

Evening meal 1830 (last orders 1200)
Parking for 9

Port William Inn
COMMENDED
Trebarwith Strand, Tintagel PL34 0HB
☎ (01840) 770230
Fax (01840) 770936

Probably the best located inn in Cornwall, overlooking sea and beach. All rooms en-suite with TV and telephone. Extensive menu, including local seafood. Open all day, all year.
Bedrooms: 2 double, 1 twin, 1 triple, 2 family rooms
Bathrooms: 6 en-suite
Bed & breakfast

per night:	£min	£max
Single	30.00	38.50
Double	40.00	57.00

Lunch available
Evening meal 1800 (last orders 2130)
Parking for 50
Cards accepted: Access, Visa, Amex, Switch/Delta

Willapark Manor Hotel
COMMENDED
Bossiney, Tintagel PL34 0BA
☎ Camelford (01840) 770782

One of the most beautifully situated hotels in England, set in 14 acres of garden and woodland, overlooking bay. Warm welcome and good cuisine ensure a memorable holiday.
Bedrooms: 3 single, 7 double, 2 twin, 1 triple, 1 family room
Bathrooms: 14 en-suite
Bed & breakfast

per night:	£min	£max
Single	24.00	29.00
Double	48.00	58.00

Half board per

person:	£min	£max
Daily	38.00	45.00
Weekly	217.00	250.00

Lunch available
Evening meal 1900 (last orders 2000)
Parking for 20

TIVERTON
Devon
Map ref 1D2

Busy market and textile town, settled since the 9th C, at the meeting of 2 rivers. Town houses, Tudor almshouses and parts of the fine church were built by wealthy cloth merchants; a medieval castle is incorporated into a private house; Blundells School.
Tourist Information Centre ☎ *(01884) 255827*

Bridge Guest House
COMMENDED
23 Angel Hill, Tiverton EX16 6PE
☎ (01884) 252804

Attractive Victorian town house on a bank of the River Exe, with pretty riverside tea garden. Ideal for touring the heart of Devon.
Bedrooms: 4 single, 2 double, 1 twin, 2 triple
Bathrooms: 5 en-suite, 2 public
Bed & breakfast

per night:	£min	£max
Single	17.00	25.00
Double	35.00	45.00

Half board per

person:	£min	£max
Daily	27.50	32.00
Weekly	170.00	200.00

Evening meal 1830 (last orders 1930)
Parking for 7

For ideas on places to visit refer to the introduction at the beginning of this section.

WEST COUNTRY

TIVERTON
Continued

Lodge Hill Farm Guesthouse
COMMENDED
Tiverton EX16 5PA
☎ (01884) 252907
Fax (01884) 242090

Ideally situated in a peaceful rural setting in the beautiful Exe Valley. Perfect base for exploring Devon. Easily accessible on A396, 1 mile south of Tiverton.
Bedrooms: 2 single, 2 double, 2 twin, 2 family rooms
Bathrooms: 8 en-suite, 1 public

Bed & breakfast per night:	£min	£max
Single	18.00	
Double	36.00	

Half board per person:	£min	£max
Daily	28.00	
Weekly	178.00	

Lunch available
Evening meal 1730 (last orders 2000)
Parking for 10
Cards accepted: Access, Visa, Amex, Switch/Delta

TORMARTON
South Gloucestershire
Map ref 2B2

Compass Inn
COMMENDED
Tormarton, Badminton GL9 1JB
☎ Badminton (01454) 218242
Fax (01454) 218741
Best Western

Traditional Cotswold-stone inn with log fires and modern bedrooms. Hot and cold buffet and a la carte restaurant.
Bedrooms: 1 single, 9 double, 12 twin, 6 triple
Bathrooms: 28 en-suite

Bed & breakfast per night:	£min	£max
Single	59.95	75.95
Double	73.45	93.95

Half board per person:	£min	£max
Daily	49.00	59.00

Lunch available
Evening meal 1900 (last orders 2200)
Parking for 100
Cards accepted: Access, Visa, Diners, Amex, Switch/Delta

TORPOINT
Cornwall
Map ref 1C2

Town beside the part of the Tamar Estuary known as the Hamoaze, linked by car ferry to Devonport. The fine 18th C Anthony House (National Trust) is noted for its 19th C entrance portico.

Whitsand Bay Hotel
Portwrinkle, Torpoint PL11 3BU
☎ St Germans (01503) 230276
Fax (01503) 230329

Spectacularly sited elegant country mansion with sea views. Own 18-hole golf-course. Indoor heated pools and leisure complex. Self-catering units also available.
Bedrooms: 5 single, 9 double, 9 twin, 2 triple, 11 family rooms
Suites available
Bathrooms: 35 en-suite, 2 public

Bed & breakfast per night:	£min	£max
Single	21.00	31.00
Double	42.00	62.00

Half board per person:	£min	£max
Daily	36.00	46.00

Lunch available
Evening meal 1930 (last orders 2030)
Parking for 60
Open March–December
Cards accepted: Access, Visa

TORQUAY
Devon
Map ref 1D2

Devon's grandest resort, developed from a fishing village. Smart apartments and terraces rise from the seafront and Marine Drive along the headland gives views of beaches and colourful cliffs.
Tourist Information Centre ☎ (01803) 297428

Avron Hotel
70 Windsor Road, Torquay TQ1 1SZ
☎ (01803) 294182
Hotel with family atmosphere.

Everything home made, including sweets for trolley and bread rolls hot for breakfast. En-suite rooms available. Children under 3 free, special rates for OAPs, short breaks early/late season.
Bedrooms: 2 single, 9 double, 2 twin, 1 triple
Bathrooms: 8 en-suite, 2 public, 2 private showers

Bed & breakfast per night:	£min	£max
Single	13.00	22.00
Double	26.00	44.00

Half board per person:	£min	£max
Daily	18.00	25.00
Weekly	118.00	160.00

Evening meal 1830 (last orders 1630)
Parking for 7
Open May–September

Bahamas Hotel
COMMENDED
17 Avenue Road, Torquay TQ2 5LB
☎ (01803) 296005 & Freephone 0500 526022

Family hotel with emphasis on food and service. 5 minutes from the sea and English Riviera Centre. All en-suite rooms with TV.
Bedrooms: 1 single, 3 double, 4 twin, 1 triple, 2 family rooms
Bathrooms: 11 en-suite

Bed & breakfast per night:	£min	£max
Single	19.00	23.00
Double	38.00	46.00

Half board per person:	£min	£max
Daily	28.00	32.00
Weekly	185.00	210.00

Evening meal 1830 (last orders 1830)
Parking for 14
Cards accepted: Access, Visa, Diners, Amex

Barn Hayes Country Hotel
HIGHLY COMMENDED
Brim Hill, Maidencombe, Torquay TQ1 4TR
☎ (01803) 327980
Fax (01803) 327980

Warm, friendly and comfortable country house hotel in an Area of

WEST COUNTRY

Outstanding Natural Beauty overlooking countryside and sea. Relaxation is guaranteed in these lovely surroundings by personal service, good food and fine wines.
Bedrooms: 2 single, 4 double, 2 twin, 2 triple, 2 family rooms
Bathrooms: 10 en-suite, 2 private

Bed & breakfast
per night:	£min	£max
Single	25.00	28.00
Double	50.00	56.00

Half board per
person:	£min	£max
Daily	38.00	41.00
Weekly	230.00	259.00

Lunch available
Evening meal 1830 (last orders 1900)
Parking for 16
Open February–December
Cards accepted: Access, Visa

Bowden Close Hotel
APPROVED
Teignmouth Road, Maidencombe, Torquay TQ1 4TJ
☎ (01803) 328029
Fax (01803) 327331
Licensed Victorian country house hotel in tranquil setting, with panoramic sea/coastal views. Family-run, offering personal service in relaxed surroundings.
Bedrooms: 1 single, 5 double, 2 twin, 2 family rooms
Bathrooms: 10 en-suite, 1 public

Bed & breakfast
per night:	£min	£max
Single	19.00	24.00
Double	38.00	48.00

Half board per
person:	£min	£max
Daily	26.00	32.00
Weekly	154.00	196.00

Lunch available
Evening meal 1830 (last orders 1930)
Parking for 32
Cards accepted: Access, Visa, Diners, Amex

Bute Court Hotel
COMMENDED
Belgrave Road, Torquay TQ2 5HQ
☎ (01803) 213055
Fax (01803) 213429
Family-run hotel overlooking Torbay and adjoining English Riviera Centre. Large lounges and bar. 5-course choice menu.
Bedrooms: 10 single, 15 double, 13 twin, 9 triple, 1 family room

Bathrooms: 44 en-suite, 4 public

Bed & breakfast
per night:	£min	£max
Single	20.00	32.00
Double	40.00	64.00

Half board per
person:	£min	£max
Daily	25.00	37.00
Weekly	145.00	265.00

Lunch available
Evening meal 1830 (last orders 2000)
Parking for 38
Cards accepted: Access, Visa, Diners, Amex

Clevedon Hotel
COMMENDED
Meadfoot Sea Road, Torquay TQ1 2LQ
☎ (01803) 294260
Fax (01803) 299396
Elegant Victorian villa set in own peaceful grounds, 300 yards from Meadfoot Beach. Home-from-home atmosphere, delicious traditional cooking. Families welcome. All rooms with en-suite facilities. Car parking.
Bedrooms: 1 single, 6 double, 2 twin, 2 triple, 1 family room
Bathrooms: 12 en-suite, 1 public

Bed & breakfast
per night:	£min	£max
Single	19.00	29.00
Double	38.00	48.00

Half board per
person:	£min	£max
Daily	27.00	32.00
Weekly	162.00	192.00

Evening meal 1800 (last orders 1815)
Parking for 8
Cards accepted: Access, Visa

Clovelly Guest House
91 Avenue Road, Torquay TQ2 5LH
☎ (01803) 292286
Homely accommodation with friendly service. Home cooking with choice of menu. Special rates for senior citizens and children. On level main road to beach.
Bedrooms: 1 single, 2 double, 1 twin, 1 triple, 1 family room
Bathrooms: 1 en-suite, 1 public

Bed & breakfast
per night:	£min	£max
Single	12.00	14.00
Double	24.00	28.00

Half board per
person:	£min	£max
Daily	18.00	20.00
Weekly	126.00	140.00

Evening meal 1800 (last orders 1900)
Parking for 4
Cards accepted: Access, Diners

Cranmore Guest House
APPROVED
89 Avenue Road, Torquay TQ2 5LH
☎ (01803) 298488
Friendly, family-run, small hotel offering home cooking. No restrictions, close to all amenities. Level walk to seafront.
Bedrooms: 4 double, 2 twin, 2 family rooms
Bathrooms: 7 en-suite, 1 private

Bed & breakfast
per night:	£min	£max
Single	15.00	17.00
Double	28.00	34.00

Half board per
person:	£min	£max
Daily	20.50	23.50
Weekly	143.50	164.50

Lunch available
Evening meal 1800 (last orders 1830)
Parking for 4
Cards accepted: Access, Visa, Diners, Amex

Devonshire Hotel
COMMENDED
Parkhill Road, Torquay TQ1 2DY
☎ (01803) 291123
Fax (01803) 291710
Hotel is set in its own delightful gardens which are tranquil, yet sufficiently close to harbour, beaches and shops.
Bedrooms: 8 single, 14 double, 40 twin, 10 triple
Bathrooms: 72 en-suite

Bed & breakfast
per night:	£min	£max
Single	26.00	36.00
Double	52.00	72.00

Half board per
person:	£min	£max
Daily	32.00	42.00
Weekly	224.00	294.00

Evening meal 1845 (last orders 2045)
Parking for 53
Cards accepted: Access, Visa, Diners, Switch/Delta

WEST COUNTRY

TORQUAY
Continued

Fairmount House Hotel
👑👑👑 HIGHLY COMMENDED
Herbert Road, Chelston, Torquay
TQ2 6RW
☎ (01803) 605446
Fax (01803) 605446
Ⓖ Logis of Great Britain
Small hotel offering real home cooking, high quality accommodation and friendly service. Peaceful setting near Cockington village. Dogs welcome.
Bedrooms: 2 single, 4 double, 2 triple
Bathrooms: 8 en-suite, 2 public

Bed & breakfast per night:	£min	£max
Single	23.00	30.00
Double	46.00	60.00

Half board per person:	£min	£max
Daily	34.50	41.50
Weekly	221.50	270.50

Lunch available
Evening meal 1830 (last orders 1930)
Parking for 8
Open March–October
Cards accepted: Access, Visa, Amex

Frognel Hall
👑👑👑 COMMENDED
Higher Woodfield Road, Torquay
TQ1 2LD
☎ (01803) 298339
Fax (01803) 215115
Warm and friendly listed mansion, set in 2 acres of peaceful gardens with beautiful views. Close to town centre and lovely Meadfoot Beach. Intimate restaurant - holder of the Bay Award for Hygiene and Healthy Eating.
Bedrooms: 4 single, 8 double, 7 twin, 7 triple, 2 family rooms
Bathrooms: 26 en-suite, 2 private, 1 public

Bed & breakfast per night:	£min	£max
Single	20.00	30.00
Double	40.00	60.00

Half board per person:	£min	£max
Daily	25.00	38.00

Lunch available
Evening meal 1830 (last orders 2000)
Parking for 20
Cards accepted: Access, Visa, Switch/Delta

Kings Hotel
👑👑👑 HIGHLY COMMENDED
44 Bampfylde Road, Torquay
TQ2 5AY
☎ (01803) 293108
Delightful licensed Victorian hotel situated in peaceful yet convenient position minutes from Abbey Sands/Conference Centre. Perfect for a memorable holiday.
Bedrooms: 1 single, 3 double, 1 twin, 2 triple, 1 family room
Bathrooms: 8 en-suite

Bed & breakfast per night:	£min	£max
Single	20.00	25.00
Double	40.00	50.00

Half board per person:	£min	£max
Daily	24.00	33.00
Weekly	161.00	224.00

Evening meal 1800 (last orders 1830)
Parking for 5
Open March–November
Cards accepted: Access, Visa

Livermead House Hotel
👑👑👑👑 COMMENDED
Sea Front, Torquay TQ2 6QJ
☎ (01803) 294361
Fax (01803) 200758

This elegant Victorian hotel, personally supervised by the Rew family, provides the comforts and service expected of a 4 Crown commended seafront hotel.
Bedrooms: 11 single, 34 double, 15 twin, 5 triple
Bathrooms: 65 en-suite

Bed & breakfast per night:	£min	£max
Single	39.00	56.00
Double	78.00	122.00

Half board per person:	£min	£max
Daily	47.00	68.00
Weekly	280.00	427.00

Lunch available
Evening meal 1900 (last orders 2030)
Parking for 120
Cards accepted: Access, Visa, Diners, Amex

Meadfoot Bay Hotel
👑👑👑 COMMENDED
Meadford Sea Road, Torquay
TQ1 2LQ
☎ (01803) 294722
Fax (01803) 292871

Delightful hotel in own grounds with friendly family atmosphere. Peaceful location close by the sea. Delicious home cooking.
Bedrooms: 4 single, 8 double, 10 twin
Bathrooms: 22 en-suite

Bed & breakfast per night:	£min	£max
Single	23.00	30.00
Double	46.00	60.00

Half board per person:	£min	£max
Daily	28.00	36.00
Weekly	169.00	212.00

Lunch available
Evening meal 1830 (last orders 1930)
Parking for 16
Open February–December
Cards accepted: Access, Visa, Switch/Delta

Morgan House Hotel
👑👑👑 COMMENDED
Aveland Road, Babbacombe, Torquay
TQ1 3PT
☎ (01803) 328940
A friendly welcome at this family-run hotel. Ample car parking. Quiet location by Carey Park. Few minutes' level walk to Babbacombe. Choice of menu. Quality assured.
Bedrooms: 2 single, 4 double, 2 twin, 2 triple, 1 family room
Bathrooms: 11 en-suite, 1 public

Bed & breakfast per night:	£min	£max
Single	15.00	19.00
Double	30.00	38.00

Half board per person:	£min	£max
Daily	23.00	27.00
Weekly	138.00	164.00

Evening meal 1800 (last orders 1830)
Parking for 10

WEST COUNTRY

Open March–October
Cards accepted: Access, Visa, Switch/Delta

Mount Edgcombe Hotel

23 Avenue Road, Torquay TQ2 5LB
☎ (01803) 292310
Detached, family-run hotel, providing good food, bar, TV lounge. Level walk to seafront, gardens, theatre and shops.
Bedrooms: 5 double, 1 twin, 2 triple, 2 family rooms
Bathrooms: 10 en-suite

Bed & breakfast

per night:	£min	£max
Single	17.00	25.00
Double	30.00	42.00

Half board per

person:	£min	£max
Daily	23.00	33.50
Weekly	154.00	210.00

Evening meal 1830 (last orders 1930)
Parking for 12
Open March–December
Cards accepted: Access, Visa, Diners, Amex, Switch/Delta

Newton House

COMMENDED

31 Newton Road, Torre, Torquay TQ2 5DB
☎ (01803) 297520

Detached guesthouse, family-run for 12 years. Tastefully decorated, well-appointed rooms, separate tables. Cleanliness assured. Bus and walking distance to town centre amenities.
Bedrooms: 1 single, 4 double, 3 triple
Bathrooms: 7 en-suite, 1 public

Bed & breakfast

per night:	£min	£max
Double	36.00	42.00

Parking for 15

Palace Hotel

COMMENDED

Babbacombe Road, Torquay TQ1 3TG
☎ (01803) 200200
Fax (01803) 299899

Gracious former Bishop's Palace situated in 25 acres of beautiful gardens and woodland stretching to the edge of the sea.
Bedrooms: 45 single, 40 double, 36 twin, 6 triple, 14 family rooms
Suites available
Bathrooms: 141 en-suite

Bed & breakfast

per night:	£min	£max
Single	55.00	65.00
Double	110.00	130.00

Half board per

person:	£min	£max
Daily	140.00	160.00

Lunch available
Evening meal 1930 (last orders 2115)
Parking for 140
Cards accepted: Access, Visa, Diners, Amex, Switch/Delta

Princes Hotel

COMMENDED

Parkhill Road, Torquay TQ1 2DU
☎ (01803) 291803
Fax (01803) 291710
Enjoying a regal name and ancestry, the former home of the Earl of Cork and Orrery. Fine panoramic sea views over Torbay.
Bedrooms: 12 single, 12 double, 23 twin, 5 triple, 1 family room
Bathrooms: 53 en-suite, 4 public

Bed & breakfast

per night:	£min	£max
Single	26.00	36.00
Double	52.00	72.00

Half board per

person:	£min	£max
Daily	32.00	42.00
Weekly	224.00	294.00

Evening meal 1900 (last orders 2045)
Parking for 40
Open March–November and Christmas
Cards accepted: Access, Visa, Diners, Switch/Delta

You are advised to confirm your booking in writing.

Red House Hotel

COMMENDED

Rousdown Road, Chelston, Torquay TQ2 6PB
☎ (01803) 607811
Fax (01803) 200592
Small friendly hotel offering indoor/outdoor pools, spa, sauna, gym. Adjoining self-catering or serviced apartments. Convenient for seafront and other amenities.
Bedrooms: 1 single, 3 double, 1 twin, 3 triple, 2 family rooms
Bathrooms: 10 en-suite

Bed & breakfast

per night:	£min	£max
Single	23.00	40.00
Double	46.00	60.00

Half board per

person:	£min	£max
Daily	28.00	36.00
Weekly	182.00	238.00

Lunch available
Evening meal 1830 (last orders 2000)
Parking for 12
Cards accepted: Access, Visa

Hotel Regina

APPROVED

Victoria Parade, Torquay TQ1 2BE
☎ (01803) 292904
Fax (01803) 290270
Pleasant hotel adjacent to Torquay harbour, in level position and within walking distance of many of the resort's amenities.
Bedrooms: 9 single, 22 double, 33 twin, 5 triple
Bathrooms: 69 en-suite

Bed & breakfast

per night:	£min	£max
Single	22.00	31.00
Double	38.00	56.00

Half board per

person:	£min	£max
Daily	31.00	40.00
Weekly	140.00	231.00

Evening meal 1800 (last orders 1900)
Parking for 12
Open March–November and Christmas
Cards accepted: Access, Visa

Sherwood Hotel

Belgrave Road, Torquay TQ2 5HP
☎ (01803) 294534
Fax (01803) 294534
Independently owned hotel in an ideal
Continued ▶

WEST COUNTRY

TORQUAY
Continued

position, 200 yards from seafront. Close to conference/leisure centre and all amenities. Coach parties welcomed.
Bedrooms: 2 single, 41 double, 17 twin, 2 triple, 1 family room
Bathrooms: 57 en-suite, 2 public

Bed & breakfast per night:

	£min	£max
Single	22.00	31.00
Double	44.00	62.00

Half board per person:

	£min	£max
Daily	31.00	40.00
Weekly	217.00	280.00

Evening meal 1830 (last orders 1900)
Parking for 27
Cards accepted: Access, Visa, Switch/Delta

TOTNES
Devon
Map ref 1D2

Old market town steeply built near the head of the Dart Estuary. Remains of medieval gateways, a noble church, 16th C Guildhall and medley of period houses recall former wealth from cloth and shipping, continued in rural and water industries.
Tourist Information Centre ☎ (01803) 863168

Old Church House Inn
COMMENDED

Torbryan, Newton Abbot TQ12 5UR
☎ Ipplepen (01803) 812372 & 812180
Fax (01803) 812180
Minotel

13th C coaching house of immense character and old world charm with inglenook fireplaces, stone walls and oak beamed ceilings. Situated in a beautiful valley between Dartmoor and Torquay.
Bedrooms: 1 single, 6 double, 2 twin, 2 triple, 1 family room
Bathrooms: 12 en-suite

Bed & breakfast per night:

	£min	£max
Single	35.00	50.00
Double	35.00	55.00

Half board per person:

	£min	£max
Daily	30.00	40.00
Weekly	210.00	280.00

Lunch available
Evening meal 1800 (last orders 2130)
Parking for 30
Cards accepted: Access, Visa

The Old Forge at Totnes
HIGHLY COMMENDED

Seymour Place, Totnes TQ9 5AY
☎ (01803) 862174

Delightful 600-year-old stone building, with walled garden and working smithy. Cottage suite suitable for family or disabled guests. No smoking indoors. Extensive breakfast menu including traditional, vegetarian, fish and continental. Whirlpool spa, leisure lounge.
Bedrooms: 2 single, 4 double, 2 twin, 2 family rooms
Suites available
Bathrooms: 9 en-suite, 1 private, 1 public

Bed & breakfast per night:

	£min	£max
Single	35.00	55.00
Double	48.00	66.00

Parking for 10
Cards accepted: Access, Visa, Switch/Delta

Royal Seven Stars Hotel

The Plains, Totnes TQ9 5DD
☎ (01803) 862125 & 863241
Fax (01803) 867925

Old coaching inn in the centre of Totnes, near River Dart. Short drive to coast and Dartmoor. Brochures available on request. Weekend breaks available.
Bedrooms: 1 single, 12 double, 3 twin, 1 triple, 1 family room
Bathrooms: 12 en-suite, 3 public

Bed & breakfast per night:

	£min	£max
Single	40.00	54.00
Double	54.00	70.00

Half board per person:

	£min	£max
Daily	44.00	54.00
Weekly	230.00	340.00

Lunch available
Evening meal 1900 (last orders 2115)
Parking for 20
Cards accepted: Access, Visa, Diners

Sea Trout Inn
COMMENDED

Staverton, Totnes TQ9 6PA
☎ (01803) 762274
Fax (01803) 762506

Delightful beamed country inn, in attractive village by the River Dart, offering good food and friendly atmosphere. Good base for walking and touring Dartmoor and South Devon.
Bedrooms: 6 double, 3 twin, 1 triple
Bathrooms: 10 en-suite

Bed & breakfast per night:

	£min	£max
Single	39.50	42.50
Double	48.00	62.00

Half board per person:

	£min	£max
Daily	38.00	42.00
Weekly	245.00	275.00

Lunch available
Evening meal 1900 (last orders 2145)
Parking for 50
Cards accepted: Access, Visa, Amex

TREYARNON BAY
Cornwall
Map ref 1B2

Waterbeach Hotel
COMMENDED

Treyarnon Bay, Padstow PL28 8JW
☎ Padstow (01841) 520292
Fax (01841) 521102

Designed to take advantage of the sunshine and views across the Atlantic. Accommodates 30 people in comfort.
Bedrooms: 4 single, 5 double, 5 twin, 7 triple
Bathrooms: 14 en-suite, 2 public

Bed & breakfast per night:

	£min	£max
Single	27.00	38.00
Double	54.00	76.00

Half board per person:

	£min	£max
Daily	33.00	45.00
Weekly	220.00	295.00

Evening meal 1930 (last orders 2015)
Parking for 25

WEST COUNTRY

Open March–October
Cards accepted: Access, Visa, Switch/Delta

TROWBRIDGE
Wiltshire
Map ref 2B2

Wiltshire's administrative centre, a handsome market and manufacturing town with a wealth of merchants' houses and other Georgian buildings.
Tourist Information Centre ☎ (01225) 777054

Old Manor Hotel
HIGHLY COMMENDED
Trowle, Trowbridge BA14 9BL
☎ (01225) 777393
Fax (01225) 765443
Ⓖ Logis of Great Britain
Quiet hotel near Bradford-upon-Avon, set in 4 acres around 500-year-old manor farmhouse. Most rooms on ground floor. Antiques, pine, distinctive beds, en-suite all rooms. Licensed residents' restaurant. Parking.
Bedrooms: 1 single, 12 double, 1 twin
Bathrooms: 14 en-suite

Bed & breakfast per night:

	£min	£max
Single	48.50	48.50
Double	50.00	80.00

Half board per person:

	£min	£max
Daily	40.00	55.00

Evening meal 1830 (last orders 2030)
Parking for 20
Cards accepted: Access, Visa, Diners, Amex, Switch/Delta

Establishments should be open throughout the year, unless otherwise stated.

National gradings and classifications were correct at the time of going to press but are subject to change. Please check at the time of booking.

TRURO
Cornwall
Map ref 1B3

Cornwall's administrative centre and cathedral city, set at the head of Truro River on the Fal Estuary. A medieval stannary town, it handled mineral ore from west Cornwall; fine Georgian buildings recall its heyday as a society haunt in the second mining boom.
Tourist Information Centre ☎ (01872) 74555

Alverton Manor
HIGHLY COMMENDED
Tregolls Road, Truro TR1 1XQ
☎ (01872) 76633 changing to 276633
Fax (01872) 222989
Country house hotel in 6 acres of grounds, overlooking city of Truro. Award-winning restaurant. Ideal base for exploring Cornwall.
Bedrooms: 6 single, 23 double, 5 twin
Suites available
Bathrooms: 34 en-suite

Bed & breakfast per night:

	£min	£max
Single	63.00	104.00
Double	99.00	130.00

Half board per person:

	£min	£max
Daily	52.00	77.00
Weekly	328.00	486.00

Lunch available
Evening meal 1900 (last orders 2130)
Parking for 60
Cards accepted: Access, Visa, Diners, Amex, Switch/Delta

Bissick Old Mill
HIGHLY COMMENDED
Ladock, Truro TR2 4PG
☎ St Austell (01726) 882557
Fax (01726) 884057
17th C water mill sympathetically converted to provide well-appointed accommodation with exceptional standards of comfort, cuisine and hospitality. Central rural location makes ideal base for touring or business.
Bedrooms: 2 single, 2 double, 1 twin
Bathrooms: 3 en-suite, 1 public

Bed & breakfast per night:

	£min	£max
Single	27.00	35.00
Double	50.00	58.00

Half board per person:

	£min	£max
Daily	44.00	50.00
Weekly	266.00	350.00

Lunch available
Evening meal 1900 (last orders 1700)
Parking for 9
Cards accepted: Access, Visa, Switch/Delta

Carlton Hotel
APPROVED
Falmouth Road, Truro TR1 2HL
☎ (01872) 72450
Fax (01872) 223938
Established and family-run hotel with friendly atmosphere. Varied choice of menus. Sauna, spa bath and solarium available.
Bedrooms: 7 single, 13 double, 8 twin, 3 triple
Bathrooms: 31 en-suite, 1 public

Bed & breakfast per night:

	£min	£max
Single	29.00	38.50
Double	40.00	45.00

Half board per person:

	£min	£max
Daily	37.75	47.25
Weekly	219.00	256.00

Evening meal 1900 (last orders 2000)
Parking for 35
Cards accepted: Access, Visa, Diners, Amex, Switch/Delta

Cliftons
APPROVED
46 Tregolls Road, Truro TR1 1LA
☎ (01872) 74116
Charming detached Victorian house within a few minutes' walk of the town centre. Friendly family atmosphere. Ideal touring base. Private parking.
Bedrooms: 2 single, 2 twin, 1 triple
Bathrooms: 1 public, 5 private showers

Bed & breakfast per night:

	£min	£max
Single		18.00
Double		36.00

Parking for 5
Open January–November

WEST COUNTRY

TRURO
Continued

Marcorrie Hotel
APPROVED

20 Falmouth Road, Truro TR1 2HX
☎ (01872) 77374
Fax (01872) 41666

Family-run hotel 5 minutes' walk from city centre and cathedral. Ideal for business or holiday, central for visiting the country houses and gardens of Cornwall.
Bedrooms: 3 single, 3 double, 2 twin, 1 triple, 3 family rooms
Bathrooms: 9 en-suite, 1 public, 1 private shower

Bed & breakfast per night:	£min	£max
Single	21.50	32.50
Double	42.00	46.00

Half board per person:	£min	£max
Daily	30.00	41.00
Weekly	200.00	260.00

Evening meal 1900 (last orders 1600)
Parking for 16
Cards accepted: Access, Visa, Diners, Amex, Switch/Delta

The Royal Hotel
COMMENDED

Lemon Street, Truro TR1 2QB
☎ (01872) 70345
Fax (01872) 42453
The Independents

Recently refurbished and offering every comfort. Superb central location with own car park. Lively and sophisticated Manning's Restaurant open all day. Very friendly staff. Executive rooms available.
Bedrooms: 13 single, 11 double, 7 twin, 4 triple
Bathrooms: 35 en-suite

Bed & breakfast per night:	£min	£max
Single	35.00	75.00
Double	55.00	90.00

Half board per person:	£min	£max
Daily	49.95	89.95
Weekly	350.00	630.00

Lunch available
Evening meal 1700 (last orders 2200)
Parking for 40
Cards accepted: Access, Visa, Amex, Switch/Delta

Tregarthen Country Cottage Hotel
COMMENDED

Banns Road, Mount Hawke, Truro TR4 8BW
☎ Porthtowan (01209) 890399
Fax (01209) 891041

Small, tastefully furnished hotel in pleasant rural surroundings west of Truro. Lovely bedrooms with private facilities. 2 miles from the North Cornish coast.
Bedrooms: 3 double, 2 twin
Bathrooms: 5 en-suite

Bed & breakfast per night:	£min	£max
Single	25.00	27.50
Double	50.00	55.00

Half board per person:	£min	£max
Daily	35.00	42.00
Weekly	200.00	200.00

Evening meal 1900 (last orders 2000)
Parking for 12

TWO BRIDGES
Devon
Map ref 1C2

Dartmoor hamlet on the banks of the West Dart River, at the heart of the moor.

Cherrybrook Hotel
COMMENDED

Two Bridges, Yelverton PL20 6SP
☎ Tavistock (01822) 880260
Fax (01822) 880260

Old Dartmoor farmhouse in the middle of the national park, now run as a comfortable licensed hotel.
Bedrooms: 1 single, 3 double, 1 twin, 2 triple
Bathrooms: 3 en-suite, 1 private, 1 public

Bed & breakfast per night:	£min	£max
Single	26.00	27.00
Double	52.00	54.00

Half board per person:	£min	£max
Daily	40.00	42.00
Weekly	245.00	250.00

Evening meal 1930 (last orders 1915)
Parking for 10

Prince Hall Hotel
COMMENDED

Two Bridges, Yelverton PL20 6SA
☎ Princetown (01822) 890403
Fax (01822) 890676
Logis of Great Britain

Small, friendly, country house hotel set in the heart of Dartmoor. Owner/chef. Good wine list. Ideal for walking, riding and fishing.
Bedrooms: 1 single, 3 double, 3 twin, 1 triple
Bathrooms: 8 en-suite

Bed & breakfast per night:	£min	£max
Single	35.00	
Double	65.00	75.00

Half board per person:	£min	£max
Daily	50.50	55.50
Weekly	318.50	353.50

Evening meal 1900 (last orders 2030)
Parking for 15
Cards accepted: Access, Visa, Diners, Amex

Two Bridges Hotel
APPROVED

Two Bridges, Dartmoor, Princetown PL20 6SW
☎ Princetown (01822) 890581
Fax (01822) 890575
Consort

18th C riverside inn, old world atmosphere, log fires, good food, wine and own real ales. Ideal for walking, riding, fishing and golf. Heart of Dartmoor. Addictive.
Bedrooms: 1 single, 16 double, 6 twin, 2 triple
Bathrooms: 25 en-suite

WEST COUNTRY

Bed & breakfast per night:	£min	£max
Single	38.00	43.00
Double	66.00	95.00

Half board per person:	£min	£max
Daily	48.00	62.00
Weekly	288.00	375.00

Lunch available
Evening meal 1800 (last orders 2100)
Parking for 120
Cards accepted: Access, Visa, Diners, Amex, Switch/Delta

WADEBRIDGE

Cornwall
Map ref 1B2

Old market town with Cornwall's finest medieval bridge, spanning the Camel at its highest navigable point. Twice widened, the bridge is said to have been built on woolpacks sunk in the unstable sands of the river bed.

Hendra Country House
COMMENDED

St Kew Highway, Wadebridge, Bodmin PL30 3EQ
☎ St Mabyn (01208) 841343
Fax (01208) 841343

19th C manor house in quiet seclusion in rural tranquillity, 3 miles north-east of Wadebridge. Exceptional menu using home-grown produce. Warm, friendly atmosphere.
Bedrooms: 1 single, 2 double, 2 twin
Bathrooms: 4 en-suite, 1 private

Bed & breakfast per night:	£min	£max
Single	20.00	25.00
Double	40.00	50.00

Half board per person:	£min	£max
Daily	34.50	39.50
Weekly	230.00	260.00

Evening meal 1930 (last orders 1730)
Parking for 8
Open February–December
Cards accepted: Access, Visa, Amex

The National Grading and Classification Scheme is explained in full at the back of this guide.

WELLS

Somerset
Map ref 2A2

Small city set beneath the southern slopes of the Mendips. Built between 1180 and 1424, the magnificent cathedral is preserved in much of its original glory and with its ancient precincts forms one of our loveliest and most unified groups of medieval buildings.
Tourist Information Centre ☎ (01749) 672552

Ancient Gate House Hotel
20 Sadler Street, Wells BA5 2RR
☎ (01749) 672029

14th C gatehouse overlooking cathedral. Interesting hotel with Italian restaurant, friendly atmosphere. 1 mile from Wells Golf Club. Mini-break terms available for 2 days or more.
Bedrooms: 1 single, 7 double, 1 twin, 1 triple
Bathrooms: 7 en-suite, 1 public

Bed & breakfast per night:	£min	£max
Single	30.00	40.00
Double	50.00	60.00

Half board per person:	£min	£max
Daily	40.00	50.00

Lunch available
Evening meal 1900 (last orders 2200)
Cards accepted: Access, Visa, Diners, Amex, Switch/Delta

Beryl
HIGHLY COMMENDED

Beryl, Wells BA5 3JP
☎ (01749) 678738
Fax (01749) 670508

Bed and breakfast accommodation in 13 acres of parkland, 1 mile from Wells. Take the Radstock road from Wells, turn opposite the BP garage.
Bedrooms: 2 double, 4 twin
Bathrooms: 6 en-suite

Bed & breakfast per night:	£min	£max
Single	50.00	50.00
Double	65.00	75.00

Half board per person:	£min	£max
Daily	52.50	57.50

Evening meal from 2000
Parking for 14
Cards accepted: Access, Visa

Fenny Castle House
COMMENDED

Fenny Castle, Wookey, Wells BA5 1NN
☎ (01749) 672265 & Mobile (0585) 616140
Fax (01749) 676799

Riverside setting overlooking motte and bailey castle. Country house in 60 acres on boundary of Levels. Restaurant, lounge bar, delightful accommodation.
Bedrooms: 1 single, 3 double, 2 twin
Suites available
Bathrooms: 6 en-suite

Bed & breakfast per night:	£min	£max
Single	28.00	
Double	55.00	

Half board per person:	£min	£max
Daily	40.00	
Weekly	245.00	

Lunch available
Evening meal 1800 (last orders 2130)
Parking for 60
Cards accepted: Access, Visa, Amex

Home Farm

Stoppers Lane, Coxley, Wells BA5 1QS
☎ (01749) 672434

1.5 miles from Wells, in a quiet spot just off A39. Extensive views of Mendip Hills. Pleasant rooms.
Bedrooms: 1 single, 3 double, 2 twin, 1 triple
Bathrooms: 2 en-suite, 1 private, 2 public

Bed & breakfast per night:	£min	£max
Single	17.50	24.00
Double	35.00	48.00

Parking for 12

WEST COUNTRY

WELLS
Continued

Swan Hotel
HIGHLY COMMENDED
Sadler Street, Wells BA5 2RX
☎ (01749) 678877
Fax (01749) 677647
Best Western
Privately-owned 15th C hotel with views of the cathedral's west front. Restaurant, saddle bar, log fires. Four-poster beds available.
Bedrooms: 9 single, 19 double, 10 twin
Bathrooms: 38 en-suite

Bed & breakfast per night	£min	£max
Single	65.00	70.00
Double	86.00	95.00

Half board per person	£min	£max
Daily	53.00	55.00

Lunch available
Evening meal 1900 (last orders 2130)
Parking for 35
Cards accepted: Access, Visa, Diners, Amex, Switch/Delta

Tor House
HIGHLY COMMENDED
20 Tor Street, Wells BA5 2US
☎ (01749) 672322 & 672084
Fax (01749) 672322
Historic, sympathetically restored 17th C building in delightful grounds overlooking the cathedral and Bishop's Palace. Attractive, comfortable and tastefully furnished throughout. 3 minutes' walk to town centre. Ample parking.
Bedrooms: 1 single, 3 double, 1 twin, 3 family rooms
Bathrooms: 5 en-suite, 2 public

Bed & breakfast per night	£min	£max
Single	26.00	40.00
Double	38.00	54.00

Evening meal 1830 (last orders 1000)
Parking for 12
Cards accepted: Access, Visa, Switch/Delta

WEST BAY
Dorset
Map ref 2A3

Westpoint Tavern
APPROVED
The Esplanade, West Bay, Bridport DT6 4HG
☎ Bridport (01308) 423636
On seafront and promenade. All rooms en-suite with TV, coffee facilities and sea or harbour views. Fishing, golf, cliff walks in Thomas Hardy country. Daily half-board prices apply to 2-day breaks.
Bedrooms: 2 double, 3 twin
Bathrooms: 5 en-suite

Bed & breakfast per night	£min	£max
Single	23.00	25.00
Double	34.00	38.00

Half board per person	£min	£max
Daily	57.00	62.00
Weekly	137.00	179.00

Lunch available
Evening meal 1900 (last orders 2200)
Parking for 6
Cards accepted: Access, Visa, Switch/Delta

WEST BEXINGTON
Dorset
Map ref 2A3

The Manor Hotel
COMMENDED
West Bexington, Dorchester DT2 9DF
☎ Burton Bradstock (01308) 897616 & 897785
Fax (01308) 897035
Logis of Great Britain

16th C manor house, 500 yards from Chesil Beach. Panoramic views from most bedrooms. 3 real ales and character cellar bar.
Bedrooms: 1 single, 8 double, 3 twin, 1 triple
Bathrooms: 13 en-suite

Bed & breakfast per night	£min	£max
Single	47.00	51.00
Double	80.00	86.00

Half board per person	£min	£max
Daily	59.00	64.00
Weekly	335.00	375.00

Lunch available
Evening meal 1900 (last orders 2200)
Parking for 20
Cards accepted: Access, Visa, Diners, Amex

WESTBURY
Wiltshire
Map ref 2B2

Wiltshire's best-known white horse looks down on the town with its Georgian houses around the Market Place. Handsome Perpendicular church with fine carved chancel screen and stone reredos. Above the white horse are the prehistoric earthworks of Bratton Castle.
Tourist Information Centre ☎ (01373) 827158

The Cedar Hotel
COMMENDED
Warminster Road, Westbury BA13 3PR
☎ (01373) 822753
Fax (01373) 858423
Logis of Great Britain
18th C country house hotel with a friendly and relaxed atmosphere. Offering comfortable, well-appointed accommodation and good cuisine.
Bedrooms: 1 single, 12 double, 3 twin
Bathrooms: 16 en-suite

Bed & breakfast per night	£min	£max
Single	40.00	48.00
Double	48.00	58.00

Half board per person	£min	£max
Daily	52.00	60.00
Weekly	312.00	360.00

Lunch available
Evening meal 1900 (last orders 2100)
Parking for 35
Cards accepted: Access, Visa, Amex, Switch/Delta

A key to symbols can be found inside the back cover flap.

The symbol after an establishment name indicates that it is a Regional Tourist Board member.

WEST COUNTRY

WESTON-SUPER-MARE
North Somerset
Map ref 1D1

Large, friendly resort developed in the 19th C. Traditional seaside attractions include theatres and a dance hall. The museum has a Victorian seaside gallery and has Iron Age finds from a hill fort on Worlebury Hill in Weston Woods. *Tourist Information Centre ☎ (01934) 888800*

Anchor Head Hotel
APPROVED

Claremont Crescent,
Weston-super-Mare BS23 2EE
☎ (01934) 620880
Fax (01934) 621767
Situated at edge of sea between Weston's two piers, with panoramic Bristol Channel views.
Bedrooms: 5 single, 8 double,
37 twin, 2 triple
Bathrooms: 52 en-suite
Bed & breakfast

per night:	£min	£max
Single	19.00	25.00
Double	38.00	50.00

Half board per

person:	£min	£max
Daily	28.00	34.00
Weekly	140.00	190.00

Lunch available
Evening meal 1800 (last orders 1900)
Open March–December
Cards accepted: Access, Visa

Arosfa Hotel
COMMENDED

Lower Church Road,
Weston-super-Mare BS23 2AG
☎ (01934) 419523
Fax (01934) 636084
The Independents
Refurbished hotel with 3 lounges, bars, dining room and comfortable bedrooms. Situated on level ground 100 yards from the town centre and seafront.
Bedrooms: 15 single, 12 double,
15 twin, 3 triple, 2 family rooms
Bathrooms: 47 en-suite
Bed & breakfast

per night:	£min	£max
Single	40.00	45.00
Double	50.00	60.00

Half board per

person:	£min	£max
Daily	39.00	45.00
Weekly	273.00	315.00

Lunch available
Evening meal 1830 (last orders 2030)
Parking for 6
Cards accepted: Access, Visa, Diners, Amex, Switch/Delta

Baymead Hotel

19/23 Longton Grove Road,
Weston-super-Mare BS23 1LS
☎ (01934) 622951
Fax (01934) 628110
Central, level and quiet location, 500 yards from seafront. Privately owned by Cutler family since 1965. Comfortable en-suite rooms with TV, tea/coffee making. Lift to all levels.
Bedrooms: 10 single, 8 double,
12 twin, 3 triple
Bathrooms: 28 en-suite, 3 private,
2 public, 2 private showers
Bed & breakfast

per night:	£min	£max
Single	15.00	23.00
Double	35.00	40.00

Half board per

person:	£min	£max
Daily	20.00	27.00
Weekly	150.00	195.00

Evening meal 1815 (last orders 1900)
Parking for 10

Braeside Hotel
COMMENDED

2 Victoria Park, Weston-super-Mare BS23 2HZ
☎ (01934) 626642
Fax (01934) 626642
Delightful, family-run hotel, ideally situated near seafront. All rooms en-suite. Single rooms always available. Unrestricted on-street parking.
Bedrooms: 2 single, 4 double, 1 twin,
1 triple, 1 family room
Bathrooms: 9 en-suite
Bed & breakfast

per night:	£min	£max
Single	22.50	22.50
Double	45.00	45.00

Half board per

person:	£min	£max
Daily	32.00	32.00
Weekly	186.00	186.00

Lunch available
Evening meal 1830 (last orders 1800)

Commodore Hotel
HIGHLY COMMENDED

Sand Bay, Kewstoke,
Weston-super-Mare BS22 9UZ
☎ (01934) 415778
Fax (01934) 636483
Traditional hotel facilities with popular restaurant, lounge bar and buffet services. Situated in unspoilt bay close to major resort amenities.
Bedrooms: 2 single, 10 double,
3 twin, 3 family rooms
Bathrooms: 18 en-suite
Bed & breakfast

per night:	£min	£max
Single	50.00	
Double	65.00	

Half board per

person:	£min	£max
Daily	40.00	
Weekly	265.00	

Lunch available
Evening meal 1830 (last orders 2130)
Parking for 80
Cards accepted: Access, Visa, Diners, Amex

Daunceys Hotels
COMMENDED

9-14 Claremont Crescent,
Weston-super-Mare BS23 2EE
☎ (01934) 621144 & 621212
Fax (01934) 620281
Family-run hotel, directly overlooking the sea. Garden for guests' enjoyment. Lifts to all floors. Fully licensed. Open all year, special breaks available.
Bedrooms: 24 single, 20 double,
28 twin, 3 triple, 8 family rooms
Bathrooms: 73 en-suite, 5 public
Bed & breakfast

per night:	£min	£max
Single	27.50	30.00
Double	55.00	60.00

Half board per

person:	£min	£max
Daily	35.50	39.00
Weekly	223.50	245.50

Lunch available
Evening meal 1830 (last orders 1900)
Cards accepted: Access, Visa

Dorville Hotel

Madeira Road, Weston-super-Mare
BS23 2EX
☎ (01934) 621522 & 621139
Fax (01934) 645585
Fully licensed, friendly family hotel.

Continued ▶

WEST COUNTRY

WESTON-SUPER-MARE
Continued

Some four-poster rooms and penthouse. Two bars, lounge, terrace lounge. Quiet position overlooking sea. Established over 65 years.
Bedrooms: 10 single, 20 double, 8 twin, 2 triple
Bathrooms: 25 en-suite, 6 public

Bed & breakfast per night:	£min	£max
Single	22.00	29.00
Double	40.00	56.00

Half board per person:	£min	£max
Daily	25.00	32.00
Weekly	121.50	210.00

Lunch available
Evening meal 1800 (last orders 1930)
Parking for 14
Open April–November

The Grand Atlantic
COMMENDED

Beach Road, Weston-super-Mare BS23 1BA
☎ (01934) 626543
Fax (01934) 415048
Spacious hotel in a splendid position overlooking the sea and sandy beach, offering the best in service, comfort and traditional food in a friendly and relaxing atmosphere.
Bedrooms: 17 single, 32 double, 23 twin, 3 triple, 1 family room
Suite available
Bathrooms: 76 en-suite

Half board per person:	£min	£max
Daily	35.00	54.00
Weekly	245.00	330.00

Lunch available
Evening meal 1830 (last orders 2130)
Parking for 100
Cards accepted: Access, Visa, Diners, Amex, Switch/Delta

Moorlands
COMMENDED

Hutton, Weston-super-Mare, Somerset BS24 9QH
☎ Bleadon (01934) 812283
Family-run 18th C house in mature landscaped grounds. Beach 10 minutes' drive. Good centre for many places of beauty and interest. Log fires.
Wheelchair access category 3
Bedrooms: 1 single, 2 double, 2 twin, 2 family rooms

Bathrooms: 5 en-suite, 1 public

Bed & breakfast per night:	£min	£max
Single	18.00	28.00
Double	36.00	46.00

Half board per person:	£min	£max
Daily	27.50	38.00
Weekly	156.00	216.00

Evening meal 1830 (last orders 1700)
Parking for 8
Cards accepted: Access, Visa, Amex

Royal Pier Hotel

Birnbeck Road, Weston-super-Mare BS23 2EJ
☎ (01934) 626644
Fax (01934) 624169
Situated on the water's edge overlooking Weston Bay. Refurbished throughout to high standards, complementing food and service. Free parking.
Bedrooms: 7 single, 8 double, 21 twin, 4 triple
Bathrooms: 38 en-suite, 3 public

Bed & breakfast per night:	£min	£max
Single	45.00	60.00
Double	65.00	85.00

Half board per person:	£min	£max
Daily	46.00	58.00
Weekly	232.00	272.00

Lunch available
Evening meal 1900 (last orders 2115)
Parking for 70
Cards accepted: Access, Visa, Diners, Amex, Switch/Delta

Saxonia

95 Locking Road, Weston-super-Mare BS23 3EW
☎ (01934) 633856
Fax (01934) 623141
Friendly, family-run guesthouse near beach, 15 minutes from Tropicana Leisure Centre and Sea Life Centre. All rooms en-suite with shower, hairdryer, colour TV. French spoken.
Bedrooms: 2 single, 2 double, 3 twin, 2 triple, 1 family room
Bathrooms: 10 en-suite

Bed & breakfast per night:	£min	£max
Single	18.00	
Double	30.00	

Evening meal 1830 (last orders 1600)

Parking for 4
Cards accepted: Access, Visa, Diners, Amex, Switch/Delta

Tralee Hotel

Sea Front, Madeira Cove, Weston-super-Mare BS23 2BX
☎ (01934) 626707
Detached, licensed, seafront hotel with views across Weston Bay. Lift. Entertainment. Easy level walk to all main amenities.
Bedrooms: 7 single, 7 double, 9 twin, 9 triple
Bathrooms: 30 en-suite, 3 public

Bed & breakfast per night:	£min	£max
Single	20.00	23.00
Double	41.00	22.50

Half board per person:	£min	£max
Daily	26.00	132.00
Weekly	148.00	

Evening meal 1800 (last orders 1800)
Parking for 8
Open April–October

Wychwood Private Hotel
COMMENDED

148 Milton Road, Weston-super-Mare BS23 2UZ
☎ (01934) 627793
Small family hotel, all rooms en-suite. Easy access seafront, all major town attractions. Home cooking, friendly atmosphere. Heated swimming pool.
Bedrooms: 1 single, 3 double, 1 twin, 2 triple, 1 family room
Bathrooms: 8 en-suite, 1 public

Bed & breakfast per night:	£min	£max
Single	25.00	25.00
Double	36.00	42.00

Half board per person:	£min	£max
Daily	26.50	33.50
Weekly	178.50	201.00

Evening meal 1800 (last orders 1900)
Parking for 12
Cards accepted: Access, Visa

All accommodation in this guide has been graded, or is awaiting a grading, by a trained Tourist Board inspector.

WEST COUNTRY

WESTWARD HO!
Devon
Map ref 1C1

Small resort, whose name comes from the title of Charles Kingsley's famous novel, on Barnstaple Bay, close to the Taw and Torridge Estuary. There are good sands and a notable golf-course - one of the oldest in Britain.

Buckleigh Lodge
COMMENDED

135 Bay View Road, Westward Ho!, Bideford EX39 1BJ
☎ Bideford (01237) 475988
Fine late Victorian house in own grounds, with magnificent views over the bay and close to a large, safe sandy beach. Ideal touring centre.
Bedrooms: 1 single, 3 double, 2 twin
Suites available
Bathrooms: 4 en-suite, 1 public, 1 private shower

Bed & breakfast
per night:

	£min	£max
Single	18.00	
Double	36.00	

Half board per person:

	£min	£max
Daily	26.00	
Weekly	172.00	

Evening meal 1900 (last orders 1700)
Parking for 7

Culloden House Hotel
APPROVED

Fosketh Hill, Westward Ho!, Bideford EX39 1JA
☎ Bideford (01237) 479421
Carefully converted Victorian house with fabulous sea views. Family-run, good food. Ideal base for golfing, walking and family holidays.
Bedrooms: 7 twin, 2 family rooms
Suites available
Bathrooms: 7 en-suite, 1 public
Bed & breakfast
per night:

	£min	£max
Single	25.00	33.00
Double	45.00	55.00

Half board per person:

	£min	£max
Daily	35.00	39.95
Weekly	225.00	260.00

Evening meal 1900 (last orders 2030)
Parking for 12

Open February-December
Cards accepted: Access, Visa, Switch/Delta

WEYMOUTH
Dorset
Map ref 2B3

Ancient port and one of the south's earliest resorts. Curving beside a long, sandy beach, the elegant Georgian Esplanade is graced with a statue of George III and a cheerful Victorian Jubilee clock tower.
Tourist Information Centre ☎ (01305) 765221 or 785747

Bay Lodge
HIGHLY COMMENDED

27 Greenhill, Weymouth DT4 7SW
☎ (01305) 782419
Fax (01305) 782828

Panoramic seafront position with private parking. Bedrooms Laura Ashley themed, some with king size beds, jacuzzi, open log fires and balcony. Dinner menu using fresh local produce. Bargain breaks available.
Bedrooms: 1 single, 5 double, 4 twin, 2 triple
Bathrooms: 12 en-suite
Bed & breakfast
per night:

	£min	£max
Single	29.50	55.00
Double	44.00	86.00

Half board per person:

	£min	£max
Daily	30.00	70.50
Weekly	210.00	350.00

Lunch available
Evening meal 1830 (last orders 1930)
Parking for 18
Cards accepted: Access, Visa, Diners, Amex, Switch/Delta

Channel View
COMMENDED

10 Brunswick Terrace, Esplanade, Weymouth DT4 7RW
☎ (01305) 782527
Fax (01305) 782527
Elegant Georgian house with modern facilities, 10 yards from beach. Ideal for a relaxing holiday or as a touring base. Close to all amenities. Parking can be arranged.
Bedrooms: 2 single, 2 double, 2 twin, 1 family room
Bathrooms: 5 en-suite, 1 public, 1 private shower
Bed & breakfast
per night:

	£min	£max
Single	18.00	22.00
Double	36.00	44.00

Evening meal 1800 (last orders 1830)
Cards accepted: Access, Visa

Cumberland Hotel

95 Esplanade, Weymouth DT4 7BA
☎ (01305) 785644
Fax (01305) 785644
Centre of Weymouth Bay, close to all amenities, rail and bus stations. All rooms en-suite with TV, tea tray, hairdryer.
Bedrooms: 7 double, 2 twin, 3 triple
Bathrooms: 12 en-suite
Bed & breakfast
per night:

	£min	£max
Single	25.00	35.00
Double	40.00	55.00

Half board per person:

	£min	£max
Daily	29.50	35.00
Weekly	175.00	250.00

Evening meal 1800 (last orders 1830)
Parking for 2
Cards accepted: Access, Visa

Kenora Private Hotel
COMMENDED

5 Stavordale Road, Weymouth DT4 0AB
☎ (01305) 771215 & Mobile 0374 690780
Family-run hotel offering good food, comfortable accommodation, easy parking, garden and play area. 700 metres from town, harbour and sandy beach.
Bedrooms: 3 single, 7 double, 1 twin, 2 triple, 2 family rooms
Bathrooms: 13 en-suite, 1 public
Bed & breakfast
per night:

	£min	£max
Single	24.00	34.00
Double	46.00	57.00

Half board per person:

	£min	£max
Daily	39.50	177.00
Weekly	239.00	

Continued ▶

WEST COUNTRY

WEYMOUTH
Continued

Evening meal 1830 (last orders 1630)
Parking for 15
Open May–September
Cards accepted: Access, Visa, Switch/Delta

Moonfleet Manor
Fleet Road, Weymouth DT3 4ED
☎ (01305) 786948
Fax (01305) 774395
The Independents/Logis of Great Britain
Georgian manor house in 5 acres along Dorset coast. A complete resort, with indoor bowls, indoor pool, 2 tennis courts, squash, snooker, automatic skittles, children's adventure play area.
Bedrooms: 3 single, 19 double, 6 twin, 9 triple
Bathrooms: 37 en-suite

Bed & breakfast per night:	£min	£max
Single	35.00	45.00
Double	60.00	70.00

Lunch available
Evening meal 1900 (last orders 2100)
Parking for 200
Cards accepted: Access, Visa, Diners, Amex

New Salsudas Hotel
22 Lennox Street, Weymouth DT4 7HE
☎ (01305) 771903
Private hotel close to town centre in quiet position 300 yards from beach, station and gardens. Convenient for nature reserve, windsurfing and many attractions. Warm and friendly, winter or summer. JCB card also accepted.
Bedrooms: 1 double, 2 twin, 1 triple, 2 family rooms
Bathrooms: 6 en-suite, 1 public

Bed & breakfast per night:	£min	£max
Single	18.00	25.00
Double	32.00	45.00

Half board per person:	£min	£max
Daily	25.00	33.00
Weekly	135.00	175.00

Evening meal 1800 (last orders 1830)

Parking for 3
Cards accepted: Access, Visa, Switch/Delta

Rembrandt Hotel
COMMENDED
12-16 Dorchester Road, Weymouth DT4 7JU
☎ (01305) 764000
Fax (01305) 764022

Premier hotel in Weymouth, walking distance from the seafront and town centre. Hotel has leisure club with sauna, whirlpool bath, sunbeds, toning beds, large heated indoor swimming pool.
Bedrooms: 10 single, 22 double, 10 twin, 36 triple, 6 family rooms
Bathrooms: 76 en-suite, 3 public, 3 private showers

Bed & breakfast per night:	£min	£max
Single	35.00	70.00
Double	62.00	120.00

Half board per person:	£min	£max
Daily	35.00	75.00
Weekly	195.00	350.00

Lunch available
Evening meal 1830 (last orders 2115)
Parking for 80
Cards accepted: Access, Visa, Diners, Amex

Hotel Rex
COMMENDED
29 The Esplanade, Weymouth DT4 8DN
☎ (01305) 760400
Fax (01305) 760500
Georgian town house situated on the Esplanade overlooking Weymouth Bay, adjacent to the harbour and town centre, close to the Pavilion.
Bedrooms: 13 single, 6 double, 7 twin, 5 triple
Bathrooms: 31 en-suite

Bed & breakfast per night:	£min	£max
Single	40.00	48.00
Double	61.00	90.00

Half board per person: £min £max
Daily 48.50 59.00
Weekly 240.00 260.00

Lunch available
Evening meal 1800 (last orders 2200)
Parking for 8
Cards accepted: Access, Visa, Diners, Amex

Southbrook
13 Preston Road, Weymouth DT3 6PU
☎ Preston (01305) 832208
Modern house on the edge of Weymouth with views of Weymouth Bay and RSPB reserve. Close to beach. Bathing, windsurfing and country pursuits.
Bedrooms: 2 single, 5 double, 2 twin, 1 family room
Bathrooms: 4 en-suite, 2 public

Bed & breakfast per night:	£min	£max
Single	16.00	18.50
Double	30.00	46.00

Half board per person:	£min	£max
Daily	26.00	28.50
Weekly	150.00	195.00

Evening meal from 1830
Parking for 15
Cards accepted: Access, Visa, Switch/Delta

Streamside Hotel
COMMENDED
29 Preston Road, Weymouth DT3 6PX
☎ Preston (01305) 833121
Fax (01305) 832043
Logis of Great Britain
Full of old world charm in a picturesque setting, surrounded by award winning gardens. 200 yards from beach. Games room.
Bedrooms: 1 single, 7 double, 3 twin, 4 triple
Bathrooms: 9 en-suite, 3 public

Bed & breakfast per night:	£min	£max
Single	36.00	48.00
Double	54.00	72.00

Half board per person:	£min	£max
Daily	34.00	42.00
Weekly	204.00	252.00

Lunch available
Evening meal 1830 (last orders 2100)

WEST COUNTRY

Parking for 25
Cards accepted: Access, Visa, Diners, Amex

Sunningdale Hotel

52 Preston Road, Weymouth DT3 6QD
☎ Preston (01305) 832179
Fax (01305) 832179
Family hotel with a relaxed and comfortable atmosphere, set in attractive gardens with an outdoor swimming pool. 2 miles to the town centre.
Bedrooms: 1 single, 7 double, 3 twin, 3 triple, 4 family rooms
Suite available
Bathrooms: 11 en-suite, 3 public, 4 private showers

Bed & breakfast
per night:	£min	£max
Single	21.00	27.00
Double	42.00	54.00

Half board per
person:	£min	£max
Daily	28.00	35.00
Weekly	167.00	210.00

Lunch available
Evening meal 1800 (last orders 1900)
Parking for 25

Open April–October
Cards accepted: Access, Visa, Diners, Switch/Delta

WHEDDON CROSS
Somerset
Map ref 1D1

Crossroads hamlet in the heart of Exmoor National Park.

The Rest And Be Thankful Inn
HIGHLY COMMENDED

Wheddon Cross, Exmoor, Minehead TA24 7DR
☎ Timberscombe (01643) 841222
Fax (01643) 841222
Superior accommodation in the heart of Exmoor. Beautiful walking and touring base. Restaurant, fine wines, real ale, log fires in cooler months.
Bedrooms: 1 single, 3 double, 1 twin
Bathrooms: 5 en-suite, 1 public

Bed & breakfast
per night:	£min	£max
Single	26.00	26.00
Double	52.00	52.00

Half board per
person:	£min	£max
Daily	36.00	36.00
Weekly	250.00	250.00

Lunch available
Evening meal 1900 (last orders 2200)
Parking for 35
Cards accepted: Access, Visa, Amex, Switch/Delta

WIDECOMBE-IN-THE-MOOR
Devon
Map ref 1C2

Old village in pastoral country under the high tors of East Dartmoor. The "Cathedral of the Moor" stands near a tiny square, once used for archery practice, which has a 16th C Church House among other old buildings.

Sheena Tower

Widecombe-in-the-Moor, Newton Abbot TQ13 7TE
☎ (01364) 621308
Comfortable moorland guesthouse overlooking Widecombe village, offering a relaxed holiday in picturesque

Continued ▶

USE YOUR *i*'s

There are more than 550 Tourist Information Centres throughout England offering friendly help with accommodation and holiday ideas as well as suggestions of places to visit and things to do. There may well be a centre in your home town which can help you before you set out. You'll find the address of your nearest Tourist Information Centre in your local Phone Book.

467

WEST COUNTRY

WIDECOMBE-IN-THE-MOOR
Continued

surroundings. Well placed for discovering Dartmoor.
Bedrooms: 1 single, 2 double, 1 twin, 1 triple, 1 family room
Bathrooms: 2 en-suite, 2 public

Bed & breakfast per night:
	£min	£max
Single	16.00	18.00
Double	32.00	36.00

Half board per person:
	£min	£max
Daily	24.50	26.50

Evening meal 1900 (last orders 1200)
Parking for 6
Open February–October

For ideas on places to visit refer to the introduction at the beginning of this section.

Half board prices are given per person, but in some cases these may be based on double/twin occupancy.

WINSFORD
Somerset
Map ref 1D1

Small village on the River Exe in splendid walking country under Winsford Hill. On the other side of the hill is a Celtic standing stone, the Caratacus Stone, and nearby across the River Barle stretches an ancient packhorse bridge, Tarr Steps, built of great stone slabs.

Karslake House
 COMMENDED
Winsford, Minehead TA24 7JE
☎ (01643) 851242
Fax (01643) 851242

Converted 15th C malt house with beams and winding passageways leading to modern bedrooms with bathrooms. On edge of pretty Exmoor village.
Bedrooms: 4 double, 3 twin
Suites available
Bathrooms: 5 en-suite, 1 public, 2 private showers

Bed & breakfast per night:
	£min	£max
Single	26.75	43.00
Double	37.50	70.00

Half board per person:
	£min	£max
Daily	34.25	50.50
Weekly	186.35	311.50

Evening meal 1930 (last orders 2000)
Parking for 9
Open March–November

WINTERBOURNE STOKE
Wiltshire
Map ref 2B2

Scotland Lodge
COMMENDED
Winterbourne Stoke, Salisbury SP3 4TF
☎ Shrewton (01980) 620943 & Mobile 0860 272599
Fax (01980) 620943
Historic, comfortable country house with private bathrooms. Helpful service, delicious breakfasts. Ideal touring base. French and some German spoken. Self-contained unit also available for self-catering.
Bedrooms: 1 double, 1 twin, 1 triple
Bathrooms: 3 en-suite

COUNTRY CODE

Always follow the Country Code

🍀 Enjoy the countryside and respect its life and work 🍀 Guard against all risk of fire 🍀 Fasten all gates 🍀 Keep your dogs under close control 🍀 Keep to public paths across farmland 🍀 Use gates and stiles to cross fences, hedges and walls 🍀 Leave livestock, crops and machinery alone 🍀 Take your litter home 🍀 Help to keep all water clean 🍀 Protect wildlife, plants and trees 🍀 Take special care on country roads 🍀 Make no unnecessary noise

WEST COUNTRY

Bed & breakfast per night:	£min	£max
Single	25.00	35.00
Double	17.50	22.50

Parking for 5

WIVELISCOMBE
Somerset
Map ref 1D1

Small, friendly town at the foot of the Brendon Hills, leading to the wonderful wilderness of Exmoor National Park. Well served with local facilities, it is an ideal centre for walking, fishing, riding and relaxing.

Alpine House ♨
HIGHLY COMMENDED

10 West Road, Wiveliscombe, Taunton TA4 2TF
☎ (01984) 623526

Elegant Victorian house in the rolling countryside of the Brendons. Excellent base for enjoying the beauty of West Somerset, including Exmoor and the coastline. Evening meals can be arranged.
Bedrooms: 3 double, 1 twin
Bathrooms: 3 en-suite, 1 private

Bed & breakfast per night:	£min	£max
Single	26.50	27.50
Double	48.00	50.00

Cards accepted: Access, Visa, Switch/Delta

WOOKEY HOLE
Somerset
Map ref 2A2

A series of spectacular limestone caverns on the southern slopes of the Mendips, near the source of the River Axe. The river flows through elaborate formations of stalactites and stalagmites.

Glencot House ♨
HIGHLY COMMENDED

Glencot Lane, Wookey Hole, Wells BA5 1BH
☎ Wells (01749) 677160
Fax (01749) 670210
Logis of Great Britain

Establishments should be open throughout the year, unless otherwise stated.

Elegant country house in idyllic setting with river frontage. Small indoor pool, sauna, snooker and table-tennis.
Bedrooms: 2 single, 8 double, 2 twin
Bathrooms: 12 en-suite

Bed & breakfast per night:	£min	£max
Single	55.00	60.00
Double	80.00	90.00

Half board per person:	£min	£max
Daily	60.00	68.00

Lunch available
Evening meal 1830 (last orders 2030)
Parking for 21
Cards accepted: Access, Visa, Amex

WOOLACOMBE
Devon
Map ref 1C1

Between Morte Point and Baggy Point, Woolacombe and Mortehoe offer 3 miles of the finest sand and surf on this outstanding coastline. Much of the area is owned by the National Trust.

Crossways Hotel
COMMENDED

The Esplanade, Woolacombe EX34 7DJ
☎ (01271) 870395

Friendly, family-run hotel in quiet seafront position overlooking Combesgate beach and Lundy. Personal service, menu choice. Children and pets welcome.
Bedrooms: 1 single, 3 double, 2 twin, 3 family rooms
Bathrooms: 6 en-suite, 1 public, 1 private shower

Bed & breakfast per night:	£min	£max
Single	20.00	26.00
Double	40.00	52.00

Half board per person:	£min	£max
Daily	25.00	31.00
Weekly	168.00	208.00

Lunch available
Evening meal 1830 (last orders 1830)
Parking for 10
Open March–October

Woolacombe Bay Hotel ♨
HIGHLY COMMENDED

Woolacombe EX34 7BN
☎ (01271) 870388
Fax (01271) 870613

Gracious hotel in 6 acres of gardens leading to the sea. With heated pools, squash, tennis, solarium, sauna, pitch and putt, short-mat bowling. Self-catering also available.
Bedrooms: 1 single, 26 double, 11 twin, 5 triple, 22 family rooms
Bathrooms: 65 en-suite

Bed & breakfast per night:	£min	£max
Single	40.00	65.00
Double	80.00	130.00

Half board per person:	£min	£max
Daily	58.00	83.00
Weekly	325.00	465.00

Lunch available
Evening meal 1930 (last orders 2130)
Parking for 150
Open February–December
Cards accepted: Access, Visa, Diners, Amex, Switch/Delta

YELVERTON
Devon
Map ref 1C2

Village on the edge of Dartmoor, where ponies wander over the flat common. Buckland Abbey is 2 miles south-west, while Burrator Reservoir is 2 miles to the east.

Blowiscombe Barton ♨
COMMENDED

Milton Combe, Yelverton PL20 6HR
☎ (01822) 854853
Fax (01822) 854853

Modernised farmhouse surrounded by rolling farmland. Beautiful garden and heated swimming pool. Close village
Continued ▶

469

WEST COUNTRY

YELVERTON
Continued

pub and Dartmoor National Park.
Plymouth/Tavistock 8 miles.
Bedrooms: 2 double, 1 twin
Bathrooms: 3 en-suite, 1 public

Bed & breakfast per night:

	£min	£max
Single	21.00	24.00
Double	37.00	40.00

Half board per person:

	£min	£max
Daily	27.00	34.00

Evening meal 1830 (last orders 1200)
Parking for 6
Cards accepted: Access, Visa

Harrabeer Country House Hotel
COMMENDED

Harrowbeer Lane, Yelverton
PL20 6EA
☎ (01822) 853302
Delightful country house hotel, formerly a Devon longhouse, set in secluded gardens. Specialising in good food, comfort and hospitality.
Bedrooms: 1 single, 4 double, 2 twin
Bathrooms: 4 en-suite, 1 private, 1 public

Bed & breakfast per night:

	£min	£max
Single	20.00	24.00
Double	48.00	55.00

Half board per person:

	£min	£max
Daily	32.00	35.00
Weekly	210.00	250.00

Evening meal 1930 (last orders 2100)
Parking for 7
Cards accepted: Access, Visa, Amex

YEOVIL
Somerset
Map ref 2A3

Lively market town, famous for glove making, set in dairying country beside the River Yeo. Interesting parish church. Museum of South Somerset at Hendford Manor.
Tourist Information Centre ☎ (01935) 71279

Preston Hotel and Motel
APPROVED

64 Preston Road, Yeovil BA20 2DL
☎ (01935) 74400 changing to 474400
Fax (01935) 410142
The Independents
Friendly, comfortable hotel, bar and restaurant. All rooms have private bath, TV and telephone. Facilities for disabled.
Bedrooms: 1 single, 7 double, 7 triple
Suite available
Bathrooms: 15 en-suite

Bed & breakfast per night:

	£min	£max
Single	30.00	45.00
Double	40.00	55.00

Lunch available
Evening meal 1900 (last orders 2100)
Parking for 20
Cards accepted: Access, Visa, Diners, Amex

AT-A-GLANCE SYMBOLS

Symbols at the end of each accommodation entry give useful information about services and facilities. A key to symbols can be found inside the back cover flap.

Keep this open for easy reference.

USE YOUR *i*'s

There are more than 550 Tourist Information Centres throughout England offering friendly help with accommodation and holiday ideas as well as suggestions of places to visit and things to do. There may well be a centre in your home town which can help you before you set out. You'll find the address of your nearest Tourist Information Centre in your local Phone Book.

COUNTRY CODE

Always follow the Country Code ✿Enjoy the countryside and respect its life and work ✿Guard against all risk of fire ✿Fasten all gates ✿Keep your dogs under close control ✿Keep to public paths across farmland ✿Use gates and stiles to cross fences, hedges and walls ✿Leave livestock, crops and machinery alone ✿Take your litter home ✿Help to keep all water clean ✿Protect wildlife, plants and trees ✿Take special care on country roads ✿Make no unnecessary noise

ENQUIRY COUPONS

To help you obtain further information about advertisers and accommodation featured in this guide you will find enquiry coupons at the back. Send these directly to the establishments in which you are interested. Remember to complete both sides of the coupon.

COUNTRY CODE

Always follow the Country Code ⚘ Enjoy the countryside and respect its life and work ⚘ Guard against all risk of fire ⚘ Fasten all gates ⚘ Keep your dogs under close control ⚘ Keep to public paths across farmland ⚘ Use gates and stiles to cross fences, hedges and walls ⚘ Leave livestock, crops and machinery alone ⚘ Take your litter home ⚘ Help to keep all water clean ⚘ Protect wildlife, plants and trees ⚘ Take special care on country roads ⚘ Make no unnecessary noise

CHECK THE MAPS

The colour maps at the back of this guide show all the cities, towns and villages for which you will find accommodation entries.

Refer to the town index to find the page on which it is listed.

AT-A-GLANCE SYMBOLS

Symbols at the end of each accommodation entry give useful information about services and facilities. A key to symbols can be found inside the back cover flap.

Keep this open for easy reference.

SOUTH OF ENGLAND

The South of England is a region of contrast and fascination. While the New Forest and Chiltern Hills offer mile upon mile of unspoilt countryside, there is much to please those who prefer town life - not to mention smart little Thameside villages crammed with antiques shops, quaint tea shops and exclusive boutiques.

Historic Oxford, Winchester and Windsor fall within the region, as does Henley, home of the famous Regatta.

The bucolic charms of Dorset await - along with the delightful seaside resorts of Poole, Weymouth and Bournemouth. And don't overlook the pretty Isle of Wight, just a ferry ride away.

FOR MORE INFORMATION CONTACT:
Southern Tourist Board
40 Chamberlayne Road, Eastleigh,
Hampshire SO50 5JH
Tel: (01703) 620555 **Fax:** (01703) 620010

Where to Go in the South of England - see pages 474-477
Where to Stay in the South of England - see pages 478-522

SOUTH OF ENGLAND

Where to Go and What to See

You will find hundreds of interesting places to visit during your stay in the South of England, just some of which are listed in these pages. The number against each name will help you locate it on the map (page 477). Contact any Tourist Information Centre in the region for more ideas on days out in the South of England.

1 Broughton Castle
Banbury, Oxfordshire OX15 5EB
Tel: (01295) 262624
Medieval moated house built in 1300 and enlarged between 1550-1600. The home of Lord and Lady Saye and Sele and family home for 600 years. Civil War connections.

2 Blenheim Palace
Woodstock,
Oxfordshire OX20 1PX
Tel: (01993) 811091
Birthplace of Sir Winston Churchill, designed by Vanbrugh. Park designed by Capability Brown. Adventure play area, maze, butterfly house and Churchill exhibition.

3 The Oxford Story
6 Broad Street, Oxford OX1 3AJ
Tel: (01865) 728822
Heritage centre depicting eight centuries of history in sights, sounds, personalities and smells. Visitors are transported in moving desks with commentary of their choice.

4 Didcot Railway Centre
Great Western Society, Didcot, Oxfordshire OX11 7NJ
Tel: (01235) 817200
Living museum recreating the golden age of the Great Western Railway. Steam locomotives and trains, engine shed and small relics museum.

5 Bekonscot Model Village
Warwick Road, Beaconsfield, Buckinghamshire HP9 2PL
Tel: (01494) 672919
A complete model village of the 1930's, with outdoor gauge 1 model railway. Zoo, cinema, minster, cricket match and 1,400 inhabitants.

6 Beale Park
The Child-Beale Wildlife Trust
Lower Basildon,
Berkshire RG8 9NH
Tel: (01734) 845172
Established 38 years ago, the park features wildfowl, pheasants, highland cattle, rare sheep, llamas, narrow guage railway and pet corner.

7 Windsor Castle
Windsor, Berkshire SL4 1NJ
Tel: (01753) 868286
Official residence of HM The Queen and royal residence for nine centuries. State apartments, Queen Mary's Dolls' House, exhibition of The Queen's presents and carriages.

8 Legoland Windsor
Winkfield Road, Windsor, Berkshire SL4 4AY
Tel: (0990) 626375
A unique family park with hands-on activities, rides, themed playscapes and more Lego bricks than you ever dreamed possible.

9 Museum of Army Flying
Middle Wallop,
Hampshire SO20 8DY
Tel: (01980) 674421
Award-winning and unique collection of flying machines and

displays depicting the role of army flying since the late 19thC.

10 Jane Austen's House
Chawton, Hampshire GU34 1SD
Tel: (01420) 83262
17thC house where Jane Austen lived from 1809-1817, and wrote or revised her six great novels. Letters, pictures, memorabilia, garden.

11 Winchester Cathedral
5 The Close, Winchester, Hampshire SO23 9LS
Tel: (01962) 853137
Originally Norman with 16thC additions. Old Saxon site adjacent. Tombs, library and medieval wall paintings.

12 The Sir Harold Hillier Gardens and Arboretum
Jermyns Lane, Ampfield, Hampshire SO51 0QA
Tel: (01794) 368787
The largest collection of trees and shrubs of its kind in the British Isles planted within an attractive landscape of over 166 acres.

13 Marwell Zoological Park
Colden Common, Winchester, Hampshire SO21 1JH
Tel: (01962) 777407
Set in 100 acres of parkland surrounding Marwell Hall. Venue suitable for all age groups including disabled.

14 Broadlands
Romsey, Hampshire SO51 9ZD
Tel: (01794) 517888
Home of the late Lord Mountbatten. Magnificent 18thC house and contents. Superb views across River Test. Mountbatten exhibition and audio-visual presentation.

15 Paultons Park
Ower, Romsey, Hampshire SO51 6AL
Tel: (01703) 814442
A whole day out for all the family in beautiful surroundings. Over 40 different attractions including rides, museums, birds, animals and entertainment.

16 Exbury Gardens
Exbury, Southampton SO4 1AZ
Tel: (01703) 891203
Over 200 acres of woodland garden, including the Rothschild collection of rhododendrons, azaleas, camellias and magnolias.

17 Tudor House Museum
St. Michael's Square, Bugle Street, Southampton SO14 2AD
Tel: (01703) 332513
Large half-timbered Tudor house with exhibitions on Tudor, Georgian, and Victorian domestic and local history. Unique Tudor garden.

18 Royal Signals Museum
Blandford Camp, Blandford Forum, Dorset DT11 8RH
Tel: (01258) 482248
History of Army communication from Crimean War to Gulf War. Vehicles, uniforms, medals and badges on display.

19 The New Forest Owl Sanctuary
Crow Lane, Crow, Ringwood, Hampshire BH24 1EA
Tel: (01425) 476487
All the barn owls are destined to be released into the wild. The sanctuary includes an incubation room, hospital unit and 100 aviaries of various size.

20 National Motor Museum
Beaulieu, Hampshire SO42 7ZN
Tel: (01590) 612345
Motor museum with over 200 exhibits showing history of motoring from 1895. Palace House, Wheels Experience, abbey ruins with a display of monastic life.

21 HMS Victory
Portsmouth Historic Ships,
HM Naval Base,
Portsmouth PO1 3LJ
Tel: (01705) 839766
Vice Admiral Lord Nelson's flagship at Trafalgar. See his cabin, the "cockpit," where he died. Memorable tours of the sombre gun decks where men lived.

22 Osborne House
East Cowes,
Isle of Wight PO32 6JY
Tel: (01983) 200022
Queen Victoria and Prince Albert's seaside holiday home. Swiss Cottage where royal children learnt cooking and gardening. Victorian carriage service to Swiss Cottage.

23 Carisbrooke Castle
Newport,
Isle of Wight PO30 1XY
Tel: (01983) 522107
A splendid Norman castle, where Charles I was imprisoned. Governors' lodge houses the county museum, wheelhouse operated by donkeys.

24 Alice in Wonderland Maze and Family Park
Merritown Farm, Hurn,
Christchurch, Dorset BH23 6BA
Tel: (01202) 483444
Hedge maze, Mad Hatter's tea garden, Queen of Heart's croquet lawn, Cheshire Cat's adventure playground, Duchess' rose and herb garden, rare breeds farmyard and bouncy colour maze.

25 Kingston Lacy
Wimborne Minster,
Dorset BH21 4EA
Tel: (01202) 883402
17thC house designed for Sir Ralph Bankes by Sir Roger Pratt, altered by Sir Charles Barry in the 19thC. Collection of paintings. 250 acres wooded park, herd of Devon cattle.

26 Brownsea Island
Poole Harbour, Poole,
Dorset BH15 1EE
Tel: (01202) 707744
An island of 500 acres of woodland with beaches, glades and nature reserve. Site of Lord Baden Powell's first scout camp.

27 Compton Acres
Canford Cliffs Road,
Canford Cliffs, Poole,
Dorset BH13 7ES
Tel: (01202) 700778
Nine separate and distinct gardens of the world. The gardens include Italian, Japanese, sub tropical glen, rock, water and heather garden. Collection of statues.

28 Poole Pottery
The Quay, Poole,
Dorset BH15 1RF
Tel: (01202) 666200
Factory tour, self-guided commentary includes museum, cinema, factory and craft area. 'Have-a-go area', craft village, throwing, painting, plus craft demonstrations.

29 Corfe Castle
Corfe Castle, Wareham,
Dorset BH20 5EZ
Tel: (01929) 481294
Ruins of former Royal Castle sieged and "slighted" in 1646 by Parliamentary forces.

30 The Tank Museum
Bovington Camp, Wareham,
Dorset BH20 6JG
Tel: (01929) 405096
Largest and most comprehensive museum collection of armoured fighting vehicles in the world. Over 300 vehicles on show with supporting displays and video theatres.

WHERE TO STAY (SOUTH OF ENGLAND)

Accommodation entries in this region are listed in alphabetical order of place name, and then in alphabetical order of establishment.

Map references refer to the colour location maps at the back of this guide. The first number indicates the map to use; the letter and number which follow refer to the grid reference on the map.

At-a-glance symbols at the end of each accommodation entry give useful information about services and facilities. A key to symbols can be found inside the back cover flap. Keep this open for easy reference.

ABINGDON

Oxfordshire
Map ref 2C1

Attractive former county town on River Thames with many interesting buildings, including 17th C County Hall, now a museum, in the market-place and the remains of an abbey.
Tourist Information Centre ☎ (01235) 522711

The Upper Reaches
COMMENDED

Thames Street, Abingdon OX14 3JA
☎ (01235) 522311
Fax (01235) 555182
Forte
This small hotel is on an island site and the restaurant was once the cornmill for the abbey.
Bedrooms: 4 single, 15 double, 6 twin
Bathrooms: 25 en-suite

Bed & breakfast per night:	£min	£max
Single	103.00	108.00
Double	123.00	138.00

Half board per person:	£min	£max
Daily	60.00	65.00
Weekly	420.00	455.00

Lunch available
Evening meal 1900 (last orders 2130)
Parking for 90
Cards accepted: Access, Visa, Diners, Amex, Switch/Delta

ANDOVER

Hampshire
Map ref 2C2

Town that achieved importance from the wool trade and now has much modern development. A good centre for visiting places of interest.
Tourist Information Centre ☎ (01264) 324320

Amberley Hotel
APPROVED

70 Weyhill Road, Andover SP10 3NP
☎ (01264) 352224
Fax (01264) 392455
Small, comfortably furnished hotel, with attractive restaurant open to non-residents. Private meetings, luncheons and wedding receptions can be booked.
Bedrooms: 6 single, 4 double, 5 twin, 1 triple, 1 family room
Bathrooms: 9 en-suite, 2 public

Bed & breakfast per night:	£min	£max
Single	28.00	40.00
Double	44.00	52.00

Half board per person:	£min	£max
Daily	30.00

Lunch available
Evening meal 1845 (last orders 2115)
Parking for 16
Cards accepted: Access, Visa, Diners, Amex, Switch/Delta

Ashley Court Hotel
COMMENDED

Micheldever Road, Andover SP11 6LA
☎ (01264) 357344
Fax (01264) 356755
Half a mile from town centre, quietly set in nearly 3 acres of grounds. Friendly atmosphere, good restaurant, conference and air conditioned banqueting facilities.
Bedrooms: 8 single, 14 double, 13 twin
Bathrooms: 35 en-suite

Bed & breakfast per night:	£min	£max
Single	39.50	59.50
Double	45.00	85.00

Half board per person:	£min	£max
Daily	49.50	69.50
Weekly	260.00	395.00

Lunch available
Evening meal 1900 (last orders 2130)
Parking for 80
Cards accepted: Access, Visa, Amex

The symbol CR and a group name following an hotel address indicates that bookings can be made through a central reservations office. These offices are listed in the information pages at the back of this guide.

SOUTH OF ENGLAND

AYLESBURY

Buckinghamshire
Map ref 2C1

Historic county town in the Vale of Aylesbury. The cobbled market square has a Victorian clock tower and the 15th C King's Head Inn (National Trust). Interesting county museum and 13th C parish church. Twice-weekly livestock market.
Tourist Information Centre ☎ (01296) 330559

West Lodge Hotel M

COMMENDED

45 London Road, Aston Clinton, Aylesbury HP22 5HL
☎ (01296) 630331 & 630362
Fax (01296) 630151
Ⓒ The Independents
Elegant Victorian hotel offering indoor swimming and sauna facilities and hot-air balloon trips. On A41, within 50 minutes of London, Heathrow and Birmingham and close to Aylesbury.
Bedrooms: 2 single, 2 double, 2 twin
Bathrooms: 6 en-suite

Bed & breakfast per night:	£min	£max
Single	32.50	46.00
Double	45.00	55.00

Half board per person:	£min	£max
Daily	44.50	58.00
Weekly	311.50	406.00

Evening meal 1900 (last orders 2000)
Parking for 11
Cards accepted: Access, Visa, Diners, Amex

BANBURY

Oxfordshire
Map ref 2C1

Famous for its cattle market, cakes and nursery rhyme Cross. Founded in Saxon times, it has some fine houses and interesting old inns. A good centre for touring Warwickshire and the Cotswolds.
Tourist Information Centre ☎ (01295) 259855

Banbury House Hotel

COMMENDED

Oxford Road, Banbury OX16 9AH
☎ (01295) 259361
Fax (01295) 270954
Ⓒ Consort
An elegant Georgian building with all modern facilities. Ideal for touring the Cotswolds, Stratford and Oxford.
Bedrooms: 14 single, 24 double, 7 twin, 4 triple
Suites available
Bathrooms: 49 en-suite

Bed & breakfast per night:	£min	£max
Single	35.00	79.95
Double	70.00	98.90

Half board per person:	£min	£max
Daily	45.00	66.45
Weekly	315.00	465.15

Evening meal 1900 (last orders 2145)
Parking for 40
Cards accepted: Access, Visa, Diners, Amex

Prospect House Guest House M

COMMENDED

70 Oxford Road, Banbury OX16 9AN
☎ (01295) 268749 & Mobile 0831 802708
Fax (01295) 268749
Detached house with lovely grounds, in the most convenient area of town.
Bedrooms: 1 single, 6 double, 2 twin, 1 triple
Bathrooms: 7 en-suite, 3 private

Bed & breakfast per night:	£min	£max
Single	29.00	35.00
Double	39.50	45.00

Parking for 10
Cards accepted: Access, Visa, Amex

BASINGSTOKE

Hampshire
Map ref 2C2

Rapidly developing commercial and industrial centre. The town is surrounded by charming villages and places to visit.
Tourist Information Centre ☎ (01256) 817618

Cedar Court

Reading Road, Hook, Basingstoke RG27 9DB
☎ (01256) 762178
Comfortable ground floor accommodation with delightful gardens. On B3349 between the M3 and M4, 6 miles east of Basingstoke, 1 hour from London and the coast.
Bedrooms: 2 single, 3 double, 1 twin
Bathrooms: 5 en-suite, 1 public

Bed & breakfast per night:	£min	£max
Single	20.00	22.00
Double	35.00	37.00

Parking for 6
Cards accepted: Access, Visa

The Centrecourt Hotel & Tennis & Health Club M

HIGHLY COMMENDED

Centre Drive, Chineham, Basingstoke RG24 8FY
☎ (01256) 816664
Fax (01256) 816727
Hotel is complemented by a superb purpose-built tennis centre, including 5 indoor and 5 outdoor tennis courts, indoor heated pool, spa bath, steam room, sauna and gym.
Bedrooms: 24 double, 26 twin
Bathrooms: 50 en-suite

Bed & breakfast per night:	£min	£max
Single	50.00	90.00
Double	50.00	105.00

Half board per person:	£min	£max
Daily	85.00	100.00
Weekly	510.00	615.00

Lunch available
Evening meal 1900 (last orders 2130)
Parking for 123
Cards accepted: Access, Visa, Diners, Amex, Switch/Delta

Fernbank Hotel M

HIGHLY COMMENDED

4 Fairfields Road, Basingstoke RG21 3DR
☎ (01256) 21191
Fax (01256) 21191
Extremely well-appointed family-run hotel, full of character. In residential area within a short walk of town's facilities. Charming conservatory/lounge. First class breakfast.
Bedrooms: 8 single, 5 double, 2 twin, 1 triple
Bathrooms: 16 en-suite, 3 public

Bed & breakfast per night:	£min	£max
Single	39.00	52.00
Double	45.00	57.00

Parking for 18
Cards accepted: Access, Visa, Switch/Delta

SOUTH OF ENGLAND

BASINGSTOKE
Continued

The Wheatsheaf Hotel
COMMENDED
North Waltham, Basingstoke RG25 2BB
☎ (01256) 398282
Fax (01256) 398253
Stagecoach

Rural hotel, well placed for Basingstoke and the Hampshire countryside. Good food, fine wine and real ales.
Bedrooms: 4 single, 18 double, 5 twin, 1 triple
Bathrooms: 28 en-suite

Bed & breakfast per night:	£min	£max
Single	38.00	59.30
Double	52.00	71.00

Half board per person:	£min	£max
Daily	39.50	73.00

Lunch available
Evening meal 1900 (last orders 2145)
Parking for 70
Cards accepted: Access, Visa, Diners, Amex

BEACONSFIELD
Buckinghamshire
Map ref 2D2

Former coaching town with several inns still surviving. The old town has many fine houses and an interesting church. Beautiful countryside and beech woods nearby.

Highclere Farm
COMMENDED
Newbarn Lane, Seer Green, Beaconsfield HP9 2QZ
☎ Chalfont St Giles (01494) 875665 & 874505
Fax (01494) 875238

Six en-suite, twin-bedded rooms with views to horse paddock. Quiet location, close to M25, M40 and only half an hour by train to London (Marylebone).
Bedrooms: 6 twin
Bathrooms: 6 en-suite

Bed & breakfast per night:	£min	£max
Single	35.00	35.00
Double	48.00	48.00

Parking for 12
Open January, March–December
Cards accepted: Access, Visa, Switch/Delta

BICESTER
Oxfordshire
Map ref 2C1

Market town with large army depot and well-known hunting centre with hunt established in the late 18th C. The ancient parish church displays work of many periods. Nearby is the Jacobean mansion of Rousham House with gardens landscaped by William Kent.
Tourist Information Centre ☎ (01869) 369055

Littlebury Hotel
COMMENDED
Kings End, Bicester OX6 7DR
☎ (01869) 252595
Fax (01869) 253225

Family-owned and run town centre hotel in quiet location with plenty of parking, offering fine food and hospitality.
Bedrooms: 5 single, 5 double, 16 twin, 2 triple, 7 family rooms
Bathrooms: 35 en-suite

Bed & breakfast per night:	£min	£max
Single	41.50	54.50
Double	57.00	71.50

Half board per person:	£min	£max
Daily	46.00	75.00

Lunch available
Evening meal 1900 (last orders 2200)
Parking for 52
Cards accepted: Access, Visa, Diners, Amex

BLANDFORD FORUM
Dorset
Map ref 2B3

Almost completely destroyed by fire in 1731, the town was rebuilt in a handsome Georgian style. The church is large and grand and the town is the hub of a rich farming area.
Tourist Information Centre ☎ (01258) 454770

Anvil Hotel & Restaurant
COMMENDED
Salisbury Road, Pimperne, Blandford Forum DT11 8UQ
☎ Blandford (01258) 453431 & 480182
Fax (01258) 480182
The Independents

Picturesque 16th C thatched, fully licensed hotel. Separate beamed a la carte restaurant with log fire.

Mouth-watering menu with delicious desserts. Comprehensive tasty bar meals. Clay pigeon tuition.
Bedrooms: 2 single, 5 double, 2 twin, 1 triple
Bathrooms: 10 en-suite

Bed & breakfast per night:	£min	£max
Single	45.00	47.50
Double	70.00	75.00

Lunch available
Evening meal 1900 (last orders 2145)
Parking for 25
Cards accepted: Access, Visa, Diners, Amex, Switch/Delta

Crown Hotel
COMMENDED
1 West Street, Blandford Forum DT11 7AJ
☎ (01258) 456626
Fax (01258) 451084
Consort

An original Georgian coaching hotel built in 1756, overlooking watermeadows on the southern edge of town.
Bedrooms: 12 single, 7 double, 11 twin, 2 triple
Bathrooms: 32 en-suite

Bed & breakfast per night:	£min	£max
Single	50.00	60.00
Double	72.00	75.00

Lunch available
Evening meal 1915 (last orders 2115)
Parking for 255
Cards accepted: Access, Visa, Diners, Amex, Switch/Delta

BONCHURCH
Isle of Wight
Map ref 2C3

Sheltered suburb at the foot of St Boniface Down.

The Lake Hotel
COMMENDED
Shore Road, Bonchurch, Ventnor PO38 1RF
☎ Isle of Wight (01983) 852613
Fax (01983) 852613

Charming country house hotel set in 2 acres of beautiful gardens, in secluded situation 400 metres from beach. In the old world village of Bonchurch.
Bedrooms: 9 double, 4 twin, 4 triple, 3 family rooms
Bathrooms: 20 en-suite, 3 public

SOUTH OF ENGLAND

Bed & breakfast per night:	£min	£max
Single	20.00	40.00
Double	40.00	50.00

Half board per person:	£min	£max
Daily	30.00	35.00
Weekly	185.00	199.00

Evening meal 1830 (last orders 1900)
Parking for 20
Open March–October

Leconfield Hotel
COMMENDED

85 Leeson Road, Upper Bonchurch, Bonchurch, Ventnor PO38 1PU
☎ Isle of Wight (01983) 852196
Fax (01983) 852196
Small, comfortable hotel, with heated outdoor pool, superb sea views and informal, relaxing atmosphere. A la carte restaurant with extensive wine list and freehouse bar.
Bedrooms: 6 double, 2 triple, 5 family rooms
Bathrooms: 13 en-suite

Bed & breakfast per night:	£min	£max
Single	23.00	31.00
Double	46.00	62.00

Half board per person:	£min	£max
Daily	30.00	38.00
Weekly	210.00	266.00

Lunch available
Evening meal 1830 (last orders 2000)
Parking for 20

BOURNEMOUTH
Dorset
Map ref 2B3

Seaside town set among the pines with a mild climate, sandy beaches and fine coastal views. The town has wide streets with excellent shops, a pier, a pavilion, museums and conference centre.
Tourist Information Centre ☎ (01202) 451700

Babbacombe Court Hotel

28 West Hill Road, West Cliff, Bournemouth BH2 5PG
☎ (01202) 552823 & 551746
Fax (01202) 789030

Family-run hotel, with good home cooking. Close to shops, beach and Bournemouth International Centre. Ample parking.
Bedrooms: 4 single, 6 double, 2 twin, 2 triple, 1 family room
Bathrooms: 13 en-suite, 2 public

Bed & breakfast per night:	£min	£max
Single	15.00	24.00
Double	30.00	48.00

Half board per person:	£min	£max
Daily	21.00	30.00
Weekly	145.00	200.00

Evening meal 1800 (last orders 1700)
Parking for 24
Cards accepted: Access, Visa, Diners, Amex, Switch/Delta

Bella Vista Hotel

5 Studland Road, Alum Chine, Bournemouth BH4 8HZ
☎ (01202) 763591
Small family hotel, 3 minutes' walk to beach at beautiful Alum Chine, 20 minutes' walk from centre of Bournemouth. All usual amenities. A welcome awaits.
Bedrooms: 2 single, 6 double, 2 triple, 3 family rooms
Bathrooms: 6 en-suite, 4 private, 3 public

Bed & breakfast per night:	£min	£max
Single	14.00	16.00
Double	28.00	32.00

Half board per person:	£min	£max
Daily	20.00	24.00
Weekly	140.00	160.00

Evening meal 1800 (last orders 1900)
Parking for 8
Open May–September

Belvedere Hotel
HIGHLY COMMENDED

Bath Road, Bournemouth BH1 2EU
☎ (01202) 297556
Fax (01202) 294699
Centrally located with a large car park. Superb food and friendly service. Ideal for both business and holidays, offering high standards all round. Minimum B&B prices are based on group rates.
Bedrooms: 12 single, 25 double, 15 twin, 9 triple, 1 family room
Bathrooms: 62 en-suite

Bed & breakfast per night:	£min	£max
Single	20.00	46.00
Double	35.00	84.00

Half board per person:	£min	£max
Daily	32.50	38.50
Weekly	262.50	311.50

Lunch available
Evening meal 1830 (last orders 2100)
Parking for 55
Cards accepted: Access, Visa, Diners, Amex, Switch/Delta

Carisbrooke Hotel

42 Tregonwell Road, Bournemouth BH2 5NT
☎ (01202) 290432
Fax (01202) 310499
Modernised traditional family-owned hotel in excellent central location close sea and International Centre. High standards of home cooking, special diets. Ground floor rooms. Golf holidays arranged.
Bedrooms: 3 single, 6 double, 3 twin, 10 triple
Bathrooms: 19 en-suite, 2 public

Bed & breakfast per night:	£min	£max
Single	17.00	27.00
Double	32.00	55.00

Half board per person:	£min	£max
Daily	24.00	36.00
Weekly	140.00	215.00

Evening meal 1830 (last orders 1900)
Parking for 19
Cards accepted: Access, Visa, Diners, Amex

Chedworth Hotel

45 Westby Road, Boscombe, Bournemouth BH5 1HB
☎ (01202) 395848
Friendly, family hotel, minutes from safe, sandy beach and shopping centre. English cooking, non-smoking rooms, lounge bar and own car space.
Bedrooms: 1 single, 10 double, 3 twin, 3 triple
Bathrooms: 9 en-suite, 3 public

Continued ▶

SOUTH OF ENGLAND

BOURNEMOUTH
Continued

[Bournemouth header hotel]

Bed & breakfast per night:

	£min	£max
Single	18.00	23.00
Double	36.00	46.00

Half board per person:

	£min	£max
Daily	24.00	29.00
Weekly	160.00	190.00

Evening meal from 1800
Parking for 17
Cards accepted: Amex

Cherry View Hotel

66 Alumchine Road, Alum Chine, Bournemouth BH4 8DZ
☎ (01202) 760910
Family-run hotel offering good home cooking, convenient for sea and shops.
Bedrooms: 8 double, 2 twin, 1 family room
Bathrooms: 11 en-suite

Bed & breakfast per night:

	£min	£max
Single	26.00	29.00
Double	36.00	40.00

Half board per person:

	£min	£max
Daily	25.00	27.00
Weekly	160.00	180.00

Evening meal 1800 (last orders 1845)
Parking for 12
Cards accepted: Access, Visa, Diners, Amex

Cliffeside Hotel
COMMENDED

East Overcliff Drive, Bournemouth BH1 3AQ
☎ (01202) 555724
Fax (01202) 555724
On East Cliff with views to the Isle of Wight and the Purbeck Hills. Within easy reach of the town centre.
Bedrooms: 7 single, 27 double, 23 twin, 1 triple, 3 family rooms
Bathrooms: 61 en-suite

Bed & breakfast per night:

	£min	£max
Single	40.00	50.00
Double	80.00	100.00

Half board per person:

	£min	£max
Daily	46.00	55.00
Weekly	276.00	330.00

Lunch available
Evening meal 1845 (last orders 2030)
Parking for 50
Cards accepted: Access, Visa, Diners, Amex, Switch/Delta

The Cottage
COMMENDED

12 Southern Road, Southbourne, Bournemouth BH6 3SR
☎ (01202) 422764
Charming character family-run hotel. Restful location. Noted for home-prepared fresh cooking, cleanliness and tastefully furnished accommodation. Ample parking. Non-smoking.
Bedrooms: 1 single, 1 double, 2 twin, 1 triple, 2 family rooms
Bathrooms: 4 en-suite, 2 public, 1 private shower

Bed & breakfast per night:

	£min	£max
Single	17.50	19.00
Double	35.00	42.00

Half board per person:

	£min	£max
Daily	25.50	27.00
Weekly	165.00	175.00

Evening meal 1800 (last orders 1800)
Parking for 8
Open February–November

Crosbie Hall Hotel
COMMENDED

21 Florence Road, Boscombe, Bournemouth BH5 1HJ
☎ (01202) 394714
Fax (01202) 394714
Delightful character hotel offering comfort, cleanliness, fine food, friendly atmosphere and good value. Near beach, gardens, shops and transport.
Bedrooms: 3 single, 8 double, 2 twin, 4 triple
Bathrooms: 12 en-suite, 2 public

Bed & breakfast per night:

	£min	£max
Single	15.00	19.50
Double	30.00	39.00

Half board per person:

	£min	£max
Daily	21.00	27.00
Weekly	119.00	169.00

Evening meal 1800 (last orders 1800)
Parking for 10
Cards accepted: Access, Visa

Cumberland Hotel
COMMENDED

East Overcliff Drive, Bournemouth BH1 3AF
☎ (01202) 290722
Fax (01202) 311394
Family hotel on East Cliff overlooking the bay and offering a high standard of service and cuisine for all ages. Complimentary use of nearby indoor leisure facility.
Bedrooms: 12 single, 34 double, 44 twin, 12 triple
Suite available
Bathrooms: 102 en-suite

Bed & breakfast per night:

	£min	£max
Single	39.50	49.50
Double	79.00	99.00

Half board per person:

	£min	£max
Daily	46.50	56.50
Weekly	263.00	340.00

Lunch available
Evening meal 1900 (last orders 2030)
Parking for 50
Cards accepted: Access, Visa, Diners, Amex, Switch/Delta

Dene Court Hotel

19 Boscombe Spa Road, Bournemouth BH5 1AR
☎ (01202) 394874
Family-run hotel 5 minutes from sandy beach. Good home cooking served in relaxed surroundings. Come as a guest, leave as a friend.
Bedrooms: 1 single, 6 double, 5 twin, 8 triple
Bathrooms: 17 en-suite, 1 public

Bed & breakfast per night:

	£min	£max
Single	11.50	21.50
Double	23.00	43.00

Half board per person:

	£min	£max
Daily	19.00	27.00

Evening meal 1800 (last orders 1800)
Parking for 12
Cards accepted: Visa

Fircroft Hotel

Owls Road, Bournemouth BH5 1AE
☎ (01202) 309771
Fax (01202) 395644
Long-established family hotel, close to sea and comprehensive shopping. Free entry to hotel-owned sports and leisure club between 9am and 6pm.

SOUTH OF ENGLAND

Bedrooms: 6 single, 16 double, 12 twin, 16 triple
Bathrooms: 50 en-suite

Bed & breakfast per night:

	£min	£max
Single	18.00	25.00
Double	36.00	50.00

Half board per person:

	£min	£max
Daily	25.00	33.00
Weekly	160.00	217.00

Lunch available
Evening meal 1830 (last orders 2000)
Parking for 50
Cards accepted: Access, Visa, Diners, Amex, Switch/Delta

The Five Ways Hotel ⋀
👑👑 COMMENDED

23 Argyll Road, Sea Road, Boscombe, Bournemouth BH5 1EB
☎ (01202) 301509 & 304971
Fax (01202) 391107
Tastefully decorated and comfortable hotel with excellent English/continental cooking. Close to bus stops, shops and beaches. All rooms en-suite. Car park.
Bedrooms: 4 single, 5 double, 2 twin, 4 triple
Bathrooms: 15 en-suite

Bed & breakfast per night:

	£min	£max
Single	16.50	19.50
Double	33.00	39.00

Half board per person:

	£min	£max
Daily	24.00	27.00
Weekly	150.00	180.00

Lunch available
Evening meal 1800 (last orders 1830)
Parking for 10
Open February–December
Cards accepted: Access, Visa

The Garthlyn Hotel ⋀
👑👑 COMMENDED

6 Sandbourne Road, Alum Chine, Westbourne, Bournemouth BH4 8JH
☎ (01202) 761016
Hotel of character with award-winning gardens. Good quality beds. 4 minutes' walk to beaches (hut available). Car park in grounds.
Bedrooms: 1 single, 5 double, 1 twin, 1 triple, 2 family rooms
Bathrooms: 9 en-suite, 1 public

Bed & breakfast per night:

	£min	£max
Single	21.00	33.00
Double	40.00	60.00

Half board per person:

	£min	£max
Daily	28.50	41.00
Weekly	171.50	230.00

Evening meal 1800 (last orders 1900)
Parking for 9
Cards accepted: Access, Visa, Switch/Delta

Hawaiian Hotel ⋀
👑👑

4 Glen Road, Boscombe, Bournemouth BH5 1HR
☎ (01202) 393234
Immaculate, small, licensed family hotel. Short walk from beach and shops. Fresh home cooking. En-suite rooms available. Winner of "Saga Hotel of the Year" award for 6 years running.
Bedrooms: 2 single, 6 double, 1 twin, 3 triple
Bathrooms: 7 en-suite, 1 public

Bed & breakfast per night:

	£min	£max
Single	14.50	20.00
Double	28.00	40.00

Half board per person:

	£min	£max
Daily	22.00	26.00
Weekly	139.00	169.00

Evening meal from 1800
Parking for 8
Open March–October

Highclere Private Hotel
👑👑👑

15 Burnaby Road, Alum Chine, Bournemouth BH4 8JF
☎ (01202) 761350
Small family hotel with garden, playroom. Some bedrooms with sea views. Children very welcome at reduced tariff.
Bedrooms: 3 double, 1 twin, 1 triple, 4 family rooms
Bathrooms: 9 en-suite

Bed & breakfast per night:

	£min	£max
Single	19.00	23.00
Double	38.00	46.00

Half board per person:

	£min	£max
Daily	22.00	25.00
Weekly	150.00	165.00

Evening meal 1800 (last orders 1630)
Parking for 7

Open April–October
Cards accepted: Access, Visa, Diners, Amex, Switch/Delta

Holmcroft Hotel ⋀
👑👑👑 COMMENDED

Earle Road, Alum Chine, Bournemouth BH4 8JQ
☎ (01202) 761289 & 761395
Fax (01202) 761289

Subtly elegant family-run hotel, quietly situated. Enjoy a choice of menu, all fresh vegetables, within a relaxed, friendly atmosphere. No smoking.
Bedrooms: 2 single, 12 double, 3 twin, 2 family rooms
Bathrooms: 19 en-suite, 1 public

Bed & breakfast per night:

	£min	£max
Single	18.00	25.00
Double	36.00	50.00

Half board per person:

	£min	£max
Daily	28.00	35.00
Weekly	154.00	203.00

Evening meal 1800 (last orders 1745)
Parking for 12
Cards accepted: Access, Visa

Langdale Hotel ⋀
👑👑👑 COMMENDED

6 Earle Road, Alum Chine, Bournemouth BH4 8JQ
☎ (01202) 761174
Fax (01202) 761174
Quietly located in pine-clad Alum Chine, close to seafront. All rooms en-suite (bath or shower) with TV. Trouble free parking.
Bedrooms: 2 single, 5 double, 2 twin, 1 triple
Bathrooms: 10 en-suite

Bed & breakfast per night:

	£min	£max
Single	22.00	24.00
Double	42.00	48.00

Half board per person:

	£min	£max
Daily	27.00	30.00
Weekly	153.00	175.00

Evening meal 1800 (last orders 1930)

Continued ▶

SOUTH OF ENGLAND

BOURNEMOUTH
Continued

Parking for 12
Cards accepted: Access, Visa, Diners, Amex

Marsham Court Hotel
COMMENDED
Russell-Cotes Road, East Cliff, Bournemouth BH1 3AB
☎ (01202) 552111
Fax (01202) 294744
Overlooking bay in quiet central situation with sun terraces, outdoor swimming pool. Edwardian bar and summer entertainment. Free accommodation for children. Snooker. Parking.
Bedrooms: 10 single, 21 double, 44 twin, 11 triple
Suites available
Bathrooms: 86 en-suite

Bed & breakfast
per night:	£min	£max
Single	42.00	52.00
Double	64.00	84.00

Half board per
person:	£min	£max
Daily	49.00	59.00
Weekly	258.00	315.00

Lunch available
Evening meal 1900 (last orders 2100)
Parking for 100
Cards accepted: Access, Visa, Diners, Amex, Switch/Delta

The Marven Hotel
COMMENDED
5 Watkin Road, Boscombe, Bournemouth BH5 1HP
☎ (01202) 397099
Non-smoking hotel. Friendly and family-run in quiet location. Close to sandy beach, shopping centre and the amenities of Boscombe and Bournemouth.
Bedrooms: 1 single, 3 double, 2 triple, 2 family rooms
Bathrooms: 7 en-suite, 2 public

Bed & breakfast
per night:	£min	£max
Single	15.00	22.00
Double	30.00	44.00

Half board per
person:	£min	£max
Daily	21.00	29.00
Weekly	145.00	165.00

Evening meal 1800 (last orders 1830)
Parking for 8
Open April–October

Mayfield Private Hotel
46 Frances Road, Bournemouth BH1 3SA
☎ (01202) 551839
Overlooking public gardens with tennis, bowling greens, crazy-golf. Central for sea, shops and main rail/coach stations. Some rooms have shower or toilet/shower. Licensed.
Bedrooms: 1 single, 4 double, 2 twin, 1 family room
Bathrooms: 5 en-suite, 2 public, 2 private showers

Bed & breakfast
per night:	£min	£max
Single	13.00	16.00
Double	26.00	32.00

Half board per
person:	£min	£max
Daily	19.00	22.00
Weekly	110.00	130.00

Evening meal from 1800
Parking for 5
Open January–November

Norfolk Royale Hotel
HIGHLY COMMENDED
Richmond Hill, Bournemouth BH2 6EN
☎ (01202) 551521
Fax (01202) 299729

Beautifully restored Edwardian hotel, within minutes of theatres, shops, gardens and beaches, provides the perfect blend of fine food and wine with warm, friendly hospitality. Indoor pool for hotel residents.
Wheelchair access category 3
Bedrooms: 9 single, 46 double, 32 twin, 8 triple
Suites available
Bathrooms: 95 en-suite

Bed & breakfast
per night:	£min	£max
Single	75.00	170.00
Double	90.00	170.00

Half board per
person:	£min	£max
Daily	109.50	187.50
Weekly	413.00	1326.00

Lunch available
Evening meal 1900 (last orders 2300)
Parking for 88
Cards accepted: Access, Visa, Diners, Amex

Queen's Hotel
COMMENDED
Meyrick Road, East Cliff, Bournemouth BH1 3DL
☎ (01202) 554415
Fax (01202) 294810
Modern, family-run hotel near the beach, ideal for family holidays, with facilities for business conventions. Leisure club.
Bedrooms: 12 single, 43 double, 46 twin, 8 triple
Bathrooms: 109 en-suite

Half board per
person:	£min	£max
Daily	96.50	116.00

Lunch available
Evening meal 1900 (last orders 2100)
Parking for 80
Cards accepted: Access, Visa, Amex

Riviera Hotel
COMMENDED
12-16 Burnaby Road, Alum Chine, Bournemouth BH4 8JF
☎ (01202) 763653
Fax (01202) 768422
Family hotel in Alum Chine, views of the Isle of Wight. Short walk to sandy beach. Extensive leisure facilities including indoor/outdoor pools.
Bedrooms: 6 single, 22 double, 22 twin, 23 triple, 7 family rooms
Bathrooms: 80 en-suite

Half board per
person:	£min	£max
Daily	26.00	96.00

Lunch available
Evening meal 1845 (last orders 2015)
Parking for 70
Open February–December
Cards accepted: Access, Visa, Switch/Delta

SOUTH OF ENGLAND

Hotel Riviera
COMMENDED

Westcliff Gardens, Bournemouth
BH2 5HL
☎ (01202) 552845
On the West Cliff of Bournemouth overlooking the sea, with an award-winning garden which has direct access to the clifftop.
Bedrooms: 8 single, 14 double, 8 twin, 4 triple
Bathrooms: 34 en-suite
Bed & breakfast

per night:	£min	£max
Single	23.00	29.00
Double	46.00	58.00

Half board per

person:	£min	£max
Daily	30.00	36.00
Weekly	180.00	220.00

Lunch available
Evening meal 1830 (last orders 1930)
Parking for 24
Open April–October and Christmas
Cards accepted: Access, Visa

Shoreline Hotel
COMMENDED

7 Pinecliffe Avenue, Southbourne, Bournemouth BH6 3PY
☎ (01202) 429654
Small, licensed hotel providing comfortable accommodation and home cooking. Close to beach and local shops, in quiet area.
Bedrooms: 1 single, 5 double, 2 twin, 2 triple
Bathrooms: 6 en-suite, 2 public
Bed & breakfast

per night:	£min	£max
Single	13.00	20.00
Double	26.00	40.00

Half board per

person:	£min	£max
Daily	19.00	26.00
Weekly	114.00	156.00

Evening meal 1800 (last orders 1900)
Parking for 5

Suncliff Hotel ⋀
COMMENDED

East Overcliff Drive, Bournemouth BH1 3AG
☎ (01202) 291711
Fax (01202) 293788
Clifftop location overlooking bay. Short walk to sandy beach and town centre. Extensive indoor leisure facilities including pool and evening entertainment.

Bedrooms: 12 single, 29 double, 24 twin, 18 triple, 11 family rooms
Bathrooms: 94 en-suite
Half board per

person:	£min	£max
Daily	39.00	115.00

Lunch available
Evening meal 1900 (last orders 2045)
Parking for 60
Cards accepted: Access, Visa, Diners, Amex, Switch/Delta

Swallow Highcliff Hotel ⋀
HIGHLY COMMENDED

St Michael's Road, West Cliff, Bournemouth BH2 5DU
☎ (01202) 557702
Fax (01202) 292734
Swallow
Hotel with clifftop position, close to main shopping area and seafront. New £1m leisure club, free parking. Short break packages available.
Bedrooms: 13 single, 83 double, 19 twin, 35 triple, 7 family rooms
Suites available
Bathrooms: 157 en-suite
Bed & breakfast

per night:	£min	£max
Single	80.00	95.00
Double	90.00	135.00

Half board per

person:	£min	£max
Daily	100.00	115.00

Lunch available
Evening meal 1900 (last orders 2130)
Parking for 130
Cards accepted: Access, Visa, Diners, Amex, Switch/Delta

Tralee Hotel ⋀
APPROVED

West Hill Road, West Cliff, Bournemouth BH2 5EQ
☎ (01202) 556246
Fax (01202) 295229

Leisure and entertainment facilities for all the family. Clifftop position close to town centre, shops, shows and leisure centre. Children free offer year round.
Bedrooms: 4 single, 24 double, 5 twin, 38 triple, 14 family rooms
Suites available

Bathrooms: 83 en-suite
Bed & breakfast

per night:	£min	£max
Single	34.50	44.50
Double	59.50	89.50

Half board per

person:	£min	£max
Daily	34.50	49.50
Weekly	206.50	339.50

Lunch available
Evening meal 1845 (last orders 2000)
Parking for 40
Cards accepted: Access, Visa, Diners, Amex, Switch/Delta

Trouville Hotel ⋀
COMMENDED

Priory Road, West Cliff, Bournemouth BH2 5DH
☎ (01202) 552262
Fax (01202) 293324
Centrally located close to all amenities, the Trouville boasts a leisure centre and has a fine reputation for friendly service and superb food.
Bedrooms: 9 single, 27 double, 29 twin, 14 triple
Bathrooms: 79 en-suite, 1 public
Bed & breakfast

per night:	£min	£max
Single	43.50	47.00
Double	87.00	94.00

Half board per

person:	£min	£max
Daily	53.00	56.50
Weekly	318.00	339.00

Lunch available
Evening meal 1900 (last orders 2030)
Parking for 76
Cards accepted: Access, Visa, Diners, Amex, Switch/Delta

Ullswater Hotel ⋀
COMMENDED

Westcliff Gardens, Bournemouth BH2 5HW
☎ (01202) 555181
Fax (01202) 317896
On the West Cliff, a few minutes from the town centre and shops, 150 yards from the clifftop and path to beach.
Bedrooms: 9 single, 13 double, 13 twin, 7 triple
Bathrooms: 42 en-suite
Bed & breakfast

per night:	£min	£max
Single	20.00	29.00
Double	40.00	58.00

Continued ▶

SOUTH OF ENGLAND

BOURNEMOUTH
Continued

[First column hotel — continued entry]

Half board per person:	£min	£max
Daily	25.00	35.00
Weekly	140.00	220.00

Lunch available
Evening meal 1900 (last orders 2000)
Parking for 10
Cards accepted: Access, Visa, Amex

West Cliff Hall Hotel
14 Priory Road, Bournemouth BH2 5DN
☎ (01202) 299715
Fax (01202) 552669
Friendly family-run hotel, close to sea, shops and entertainments, and 200 yards from the conference centre. Generous, varied menu.
Bedrooms: 7 single, 16 double, 13 twin, 9 triple
Bathrooms: 45 en-suite, 1 public

Bed & breakfast per night:	£min	£max
Single	22.00	33.00
Double	44.00	66.00

Half board per person:	£min	£max
Daily	27.50	37.50
Weekly	165.00	220.00

Evening meal 1830 (last orders 2000)
Parking for 36
Cards accepted: Access, Visa, Diners, Amex, Switch/Delta

West Cliff Towers Hotel
COMMENDED
12 Priory Road, Bournemouth BH2 5DG
☎ (01202) 553319
Fax (01202) 553319
Hotel in an excellent position on the lovely West Cliff. All rooms with private facilities.
Bedrooms: 4 single, 11 double, 5 twin, 6 triple, 1 family room
Bathrooms: 27 en-suite

Bed & breakfast per night:	£min	£max
Single	22.00	28.00
Double	44.00	56.00

Half board per person:	£min	£max
Daily	30.00	38.00
Weekly	150.00	210.00

Evening meal 1800 (last orders 1930)
Parking for 22
Cards accepted: Access, Visa

Westleigh Hotel
COMMENDED
26 West Hill Road, West Cliff, Bournemouth BH2 5PG
☎ (01202) 296989
Fax (01202) 296989
Central location close to shops and beaches. All rooms with colour TV, tea/coffee facilities, hairdryer. Sauna, spa bath, solarium, indoor pool, lift, car park.
Bedrooms: 3 single, 14 double, 9 twin, 4 triple, 1 family room
Bathrooms: 28 en-suite, 2 public

Bed & breakfast per night:	£min	£max
Single	37.00	40.00
Double	60.00	70.00

Half board per person:	£min	£max
Daily	35.00	40.00
Weekly	245.00	280.00

Lunch available
Evening meal 1800 (last orders 1930)
Parking for 27
Cards accepted: Access, Visa, Diners, Amex

Willowdene Hotel
HIGHLY COMMENDED
43 Grand Avenue, Southbourne, Bournemouth BH6 3SY
☎ (01202) 425370
Detached Edwardian house, for those who require quality accommodation with a happy, relaxed atmosphere. 200 yards from sandy beach, with views over Poole Bay, Isle of Wight Needles and Purbeck Hills. 5 miles from New Forest. Non smoking.
Bedrooms: 3 double, 1 twin, 1 triple
Bathrooms: 4 en-suite, 1 private, 1 public

Bed & breakfast per night:	£min	£max
Single	19.00	23.00
Double	34.00	44.00

Parking for 7
Open March–October

Winterbourne Hotel
COMMENDED
Priory Road, Bournemouth BH2 5DJ
☎ (01202) 296366
Fax (01202) 780073
The Independents
Enjoying a prime position with magnificent sea views, the hotel is within 400 metres of shops, theatres, pier and beaches. Free golf tickets.
Bedrooms: 6 single, 13 double, 10 twin, 12 triple
Bathrooms: 41 en-suite

Bed & breakfast per night:	£min	£max
Single	29.00	40.00
Double	50.00	72.00

Half board per person:	£min	£max
Daily	30.00	46.00
Weekly	189.00	290.00

Lunch available
Evening meal 1830 (last orders 2030)
Parking for 34
Cards accepted: Access, Visa, Amex, Switch/Delta

Wychcote Hotel
COMMENDED
2 Somerville Road, West Cliff, Bournemouth BH2 5LH
☎ (01202) 557898
Small, well-appointed Victorian house hotel standing in its own tree-lined grounds. Quiet but near all facilities. Home cooking.
Bedrooms: 3 single, 5 double, 3 twin, 1 triple
Bathrooms: 11 en-suite, 1 private

Bed & breakfast per night:	£min	£max
Single	21.00	30.00
Double	42.00	60.00

Half board per person:	£min	£max
Daily	27.00	37.00
Weekly	144.00	225.00

Evening meal 1815 (last orders 2000)
Parking for 15
Open February–November and Christmas
Cards accepted: Access, Visa, Switch/Delta

Please check prices and other details at the time of booking.

A key to symbols can be found inside the back cover flap.

SOUTH OF ENGLAND

BRACKNELL

Berkshire
Map ref 2C2

Designated a New Town in 1949, the town has ancient origins. Set in heathlands, it is an excellent centre for golf and walking. South Hill Park, an 18th C mansion, houses an art centre.
Tourist Information Centre ☎ (01344) 868196

Coppid Beech Hotel

HIGHLY COMMENDED

John Nike Way, Bracknell RG12 8TF
☎ (01344) 303333
Fax (01344) 301200
Alpine-style hotel close to Ascot, Legoland, Windsor and Henley. Attractions include dry ski-slope, ice-skating, Brasserie at the Keller, health club and nightclub. Five minutes from junction 10 of M4. Half board prices below are for weekends only (minimum 2 nights' stay).
Wheelchair access category 1
Bedrooms: 44 single, 50 double, 111 twin
Bathrooms: 205 en-suite

Bed & breakfast per night:	£min	£max
Single	62.50	120.00
Double	72.50	195.00

Half board per person:	£min	£max
Daily	55.50	195.00

Lunch available
Evening meal 1800 (last orders 2230)
Parking for 350
Cards accepted: Access, Visa, Diners, Amex, Switch/Delta

BROCKENHURST

Hampshire
Map ref 2C3

Attractive village with thatched cottages and a ford in its main street. Well placed for visiting the New Forest.

Cloud Hotel

HIGHLY COMMENDED

Meerut Road, Brockenhurst SO42 7TD
☎ Lymington (01590) 622165
Fax (01590) 622165
Quiet country hotel in award-winning location. Panoramic views of the forest. Excellent service and cuisine. Ideal place to relax and unwind. Midweek breaks.
Bedrooms: 3 single, 8 double, 4 twin, 1 family room
Bathrooms: 16 en-suite, 1 public

Bed & breakfast per night:	£min	£max
Single	48.00	
Double	80.00	

Half board per person:	£min	£max
Daily	57.00	
Weekly	300.00	

Lunch available
Evening meal 1900 (last orders 2030)
Parking for 20
Cards accepted: Access, Visa

The Cottage Hotel

HIGHLY COMMENDED

Sway Road, Brockenhurst SO42 7SH
☎ Lymington (01590) 622296
Fax (01590) 623014
Delightfully converted cosy oak-beamed forester's cottage, noted for comfort and service. Two minutes' walk from forest and village centre.
Bedrooms: 1 single, 5 double, 1 twin
Bathrooms: 6 en-suite, 1 private shower

Bed & breakfast per night:	£min	£max
Single	30.00	60.00
Double	60.00	78.00

Evening meal 1900 (last orders 2000)
Parking for 12
Open February–November
Cards accepted: Access, Visa, Switch/Delta

New Park Manor Hotel

HIGHLY COMMENDED

Lyndhurst Road, Brockenhurst SO42 7QH
☎ Lymington (01590) 623467
Fax (01590) 622268

Prestigious and romantic country house hotel, dating from 16th C. Former royal hunting lodge of Charles II, set amidst New Forest parklands. Log fire ambience, Stag Head Restaurant, individually designed rooms. Horse riding, seasonal heated swimming pool, tennis court.
Bedrooms: 20 double, 4 twin
Bathrooms: 24 en-suite

Bed & breakfast per night:	£min	£max
Single	75.00	150.00
Double	90.00	150.00

Half board per person:	£min	£max
Daily	65.00	85.00
Weekly	455.00	595.00

Lunch available
Evening meal 1930 (last orders 2145)
Parking for 40
Cards accepted: Access, Visa, Amex

The Watersplash Hotel

COMMENDED

The Rise, Brockenhurst SO42 7ZP
☎ Lymington (01590) 622344
Fax (01590) 624047
Quiet Victorian country house hotel, set in beautiful gardens. Renowned for its family-run atmosphere, good food, service and accommodation.
Bedrooms: 3 single, 9 double, 8 twin, 3 family rooms
Bathrooms: 23 en-suite

Bed & breakfast per night:	£min	£max
Single	55.00	58.00
Double	80.00	90.00

Half board per person:	£min	£max
Daily	60.00	80.00
Weekly	290.00	340.00

Lunch available
Evening meal 1930 (last orders 2030)
Parking for 33
Cards accepted: Access, Visa, Amex

Whitley Ridge Country House Hotel

HIGHLY COMMENDED

Beaulieu Road, Brockenhurst SO42 7QL
☎ Lymington (01590) 622354
Fax (01590) 622856
Logis of Great Britain

New Forest. Beautiful Georgian country house in quiet, secluded grounds amidst the forest wildlife. Renowned for food and friendly atmosphere.

Continued ▶

SOUTH OF ENGLAND

BROCKENHURST
Continued

Bedrooms: 2 single, 8 double, 3 twin
Bathrooms: 13 en-suite

Bed & breakfast
per night:	£min	£max
Single	54.00	58.00
Double	88.00	96.00

Half board per
person:	£min	£max
Daily	58.00	63.00
Weekly	315.00	329.00

Lunch available
Evening meal 1900 (last orders 2030)
Parking for 24
Cards accepted: Access, Visa, Diners, Amex, Switch/Delta

BUCKINGHAM
Buckinghamshire
Map ref 2C1

Interesting old market town surrounded by rich farmland. It has many Georgian buildings, including the Town Hall and Old Jail and many old almshouses and inns. Stowe School nearby has magnificent 18th C landscaped gardens.
Tourist Information Centre ☎ (01280) 823020

Villiers Hotel
HIGHLY COMMENDED

3 Castle Street, Buckingham MK18 1BS
☎ (01280) 822444
Fax (01280) 822113

Individually designed bedrooms are set around an old coaching inn courtyard, incorporating English cookery restaurant, Italian bistro and Jacobean pub.

Bedrooms: 3 single, 18 double, 17 twin
Suites available
Bathrooms: 38 en-suite

Bed & breakfast
per night:	£min	£max
Single	54.00	75.00
Double	75.00	85.00

Half board per
person:	£min	£max
Daily	42.50	57.50

Lunch available
Evening meal 1900 (last orders 2230)
Parking for 36
Cards accepted: Access, Visa, Diners, Amex, Switch/Delta

BURFORD
Oxfordshire
Map ref 2B1

One of the most beautiful Cotswold wool towns with Georgian and Tudor houses, many antique shops and a picturesque High Street sloping to the River Windrush.
Tourist Information Centre ☎ (01993) 823558

The Bird in Hand
HIGHLY COMMENDED

Whiteoak Green, Hailey, Witney OX8 5XP
☎ Witney (01993) 868321 & 868811
Fax (01993) 868702
Logis of Great Britain

Recently restored inn, with attractive cottage-style bedrooms surrounding a quiet courtyard. Home-cooked food, real ales and open fires.

Bedrooms: 10 double, 4 twin, 2 family rooms
Bathrooms: 16 en-suite

Bed & breakfast
per night:	£min	£max
Single	50.00	58.00
Double	60.00	70.00

Half board per
person:	£min	£max
Daily	43.00	50.00

Lunch available
Evening meal 1900 (last orders 2130)
Parking for 100
Cards accepted: Access, Visa, Switch/Delta

Elm House Hotel
HIGHLY COMMENDED

Meadow Lane, Fulbrook, Burford OX18 4BW
☎ (01993) 823611
Fax (01993) 823937

Cotswold-stone manor-style house with attractive walled gardens. Homely, welcoming atmosphere, fine home-cooked food served in comfortable surroundings. Centrally located for exploring Cotswolds and Oxfordshire.

Bedrooms: 4 double, 3 twin
Bathrooms: 6 en-suite, 1 private

Bed & breakfast
per night:	£min	£max
Single	36.00	60.00
Double	45.00	75.00

Half board per
person:	£min	£max
Daily	40.50	55.50
Weekly	283.50	388.50

Evening meal 1900 (last orders 2030)
Parking for 10
Cards accepted: Access, Visa

Golden Pheasant Hotel
COMMENDED

High Street, Burford, Oxford OX18 4QA
☎ (01993) 823223 & 823417
Fax (01993) 822621
Logis of Great Britain

Beautifully restored 15th C inn. An informal and friendly atmosphere, large open fireplaces and antique furniture. Notable restaurant. Individually styled rooms.

Bedrooms: 8 double, 4 twin
Bathrooms: 11 en-suite, 1 private

Bed & breakfast
per night:	£min	£max
Single	45.00	60.00
Double	65.00	105.00

Lunch available
Evening meal 1900 (last orders 2130)
Parking for 10
Cards accepted: Access, Visa, Amex

Romany Inn
APPROVED

Bridge Street, Bampton, Oxford OX18 2HA
☎ Bampton Castle (01993) 850237

17th C listed Georgian building, recently refurbished, at nearby Bampton. Lounge bar, separate restaurant, chef/proprietor. Noted in pub and beer guides. Brochure available.

Bedrooms: 3 double, 2 twin, 3 triple
Bathrooms: 8 en-suite

Bed & breakfast
per night:	£min	£max
Single	21.00	25.00
Double	30.00	35.00

Half board per
person:	£min	£max
Daily	30.00	35.00
Weekly	180.00	210.00

Lunch available
Evening meal 1830 (last orders 2200)
Parking for 6
Cards accepted: Access, Visa

SOUTH OF ENGLAND

CHALE
Isle of Wight
Map ref 2C3

Village overlooking Chale Bay and near Blackgang Chine which has a children's maze, a water garden and a museum displaying many objects from shipwrecks.

Clarendon Hotel & Wight Mouse Inn

HIGHLY COMMENDED

Nr Blackgang, Chale, Ventnor
PO38 2HA
☎ Isle of Wight (01983) 730431
Fax (01983) 730431

17th C coaching hotel overlooking Freshwater Bay and the Needles. Children most welcome. 6 real ales, 365 whiskies and live entertainment nightly, all year round. Well-appointed bedrooms, good food, service and hospitality.
Bedrooms: 1 single, 3 double, 9 family rooms
Suites available
Bathrooms: 10 en-suite, 2 public

Bed & breakfast

per night:	£min	£max
Single	20.00	35.00
Double	40.00	70.00

Half board per

person:	£min	£max
Daily	35.00	50.00
Weekly	200.00	275.00

Lunch available
Evening meal 1900 (last orders 2200)
Parking for 200
Cards accepted: Access, Visa, Switch/Delta

TOWN INDEX

This can be found at the back of the guide. If you know where you want to stay, the index will give you the page number listing all accommodation in your chosen town, city or village.

CHALFONT ST GILES
Buckinghamshire
Map ref 2D2

Pretty, old village in wooded Chiltern Hills yet only 20 miles from London and a good base for visiting the city. Excellent base for Windsor, Henley, the Thames Valley, Oxford and the Cotswolds.

The White Hart Inn

COMMENDED

Three Households, Chalfont St Giles HP8 4LP
☎ High Wycombe (01494) 872441
100-year-old village pub with non-smoking restaurant, large gardens and parking. Accommodation in detached stable conversion.
Bedrooms: 1 double, 3 twin
Bathrooms: 4 en-suite

Bed & breakfast

per night:	£min	£max
Single	40.00	44.00
Double	54.00	59.00

Half board per

person:	£min	£max
Daily	50.00	54.00
Weekly	340.00	368.00

Lunch available
Evening meal 1800 (last orders 2130)
Parking for 36
Cards accepted: Access, Visa, Switch/Delta

CHENIES
Buckinghamshire
Map ref 2D1

Picturesque village built by the Russell family with attractive estate houses around a green. Chenies Manor is open to visitors in the summer.

The Bedford Arms Hotel

Chenies, Rickmansworth, Hertfordshire WD3 6EQ
☎ Watford (01923) 283301
Fax (01923) 284825
A delightful Elizabethan-style country hotel in a small historic village. Classic French cooking.
Bedrooms: 3 single, 7 double
Bathrooms: 10 en-suite

Bed & breakfast

per night:	£min	£max
Single	47.00	130.00
Double	94.00	135.00

Lunch available
Evening meal 1930 (last orders 2200)
Parking for 80

Cards accepted: Access, Visa, Diners, Amex

CHIPPING NORTON
Oxfordshire
Map ref 2C1

Old market town set high in the Cotswolds and an ideal touring centre. The wide market-place contains many 16th C and 17th C stone houses and the Town Hall and Tudor Guildhall.
Tourist Information Centre ☎ (01608) 644379

Southcombe Lodge Guest House

Southcombe, Chipping Norton OX7 5QH
☎ (01608) 643068
Well-decorated pebbledash guesthouse set in 3.5 acres, at the junction of the A44/A3400, close to Chipping Norton.
Bedrooms: 3 double, 2 twin, 1 triple
Bathrooms: 2 en-suite, 2 public

Bed & breakfast

per night:	£min	£max
Single	21.00	27.00
Double	38.00	44.00

Lunch available
Evening meal 1900 (last orders 1800)
Parking for 10

CHOLDERTON
Hampshire
Map ref 2B2

Parkhouse Motel

COMMENDED

Cholderton, Salisbury, Wiltshire SP4 0EG
☎ (01980) 629256
Fax (01980) 629256
17th C former coaching inn built of brick and flint with slate roof. 5 miles east of Stonehenge, 10 miles north of Salisbury and 9 miles west of Andover.
Bedrooms: 6 single, 18 double, 6 twin, 3 triple
Suites available
Bathrooms: 23 en-suite, 10 private

Bed & breakfast

per night:	£min	£max
Single	22.00	34.00
Double	30.00	44.00

Continued ▶

SOUTH OF ENGLAND

CHOLDERTON
Continued

Half board per person:

	£min	£max
Daily	27.00	40.00
Weekly	189.00	280.00

Evening meal 1900 (last orders 2030)
Parking for 30
Cards accepted: Access, Visa

CHRISTCHURCH
Dorset
Map ref 2B3

Tranquil town lying between the Avon and Stour just before they converge and flow into Christchurch Harbour. A fine 11th C church and the remains of a Norman castle and house can be seen.
Tourist Information Centre ☎ (01202) 471780

Avonmouth Hotel
COMMENDED

95 Mudeford, Christchurch
BH23 3NT
☎ Bournemouth (01202) 483434
Fax (01202) 479004
Forte
The hotel is set on the eastern edge of Christchurch Harbour with an excellent view over the estuary.
Bedrooms: 26 double, 11 twin, 3 triple
Bathrooms: 40 en-suite

Bed & breakfast per night:

	£min	£max
Single	75.00	80.00
Double	110.00	120.00

Half board per person:

	£min	£max
Daily	47.00	74.00
Weekly	260.00	425.00

Lunch available
Evening meal 1900 (last orders 2045)
Parking for 70
Cards accepted: Access, Visa, Diners, Amex

The ⋀ symbol after an establishment name indicates that it is a Regional Tourist Board member.

CHURCHILL
Oxfordshire
Map ref 2B1

The Forge House
HIGHLY COMMENDED

Churchill, Chipping Norton
OX7 6NJ
☎ Chipping Norton (01608) 658173
Fax (01608) 658173
The ultimate B&B. Relax and be spoilt in Old Forge House. Four-poster beds, all bedrooms en-suite (one with jacuzzi), colour TV, tea/coffee facilities and central heating. Ideal for touring, walking or just lazing. Central for the Cotswolds, Blenheim Palace, Warwick Castle, Stratford-upon-Avon and Oxford.
Bedrooms: 3 double, 1 twin
Bathrooms: 4 en-suite

Bed & breakfast per night:

	£min	£max
Single	35.00	60.00
Double	50.00	65.00

Parking for 6

CLANFIELD
Oxfordshire
Map ref 2B1

Pretty brookside village. Nearby lies the moated Friars Court, on the site of which once stood a building of the Knights Hospitallers.

Plough Hotel & Restaurant
HIGHLY COMMENDED

Clanfield, Oxford OX18 2RB
☎ (01367) 810222
Fax (01367) 810596
Elizabethan manor, dating from 1560, in the heart of the Cotswolds.
Bedrooms: 6 double
Bathrooms: 6 en-suite

Bed & breakfast per night:

	£min	£max
Single	65.00	75.00
Double	90.00	105.00

Half board per person:

	£min	£max
Daily	65.00	75.00

Lunch available
Evening meal 1900 (last orders 2100)
Parking for 40
Cards accepted: Access, Visa, Diners, Amex, Switch/Delta

COLWELL BAY
Isle of Wight
Map ref 2C3

2-mile curving stretch of sand.

Ontario Private Hotel

Colwell Common Road, Colwell Bay, Freshwater PO39 0DD
☎ Freshwater (01983) 753237
Four minutes from seaside award beach, offering accommodation of a high standard with licensed bar, choice of menu. Children and pets welcome.
Bedrooms: 1 single, 2 double, 1 twin, 2 triple, 1 family room
Bathrooms: 3 en-suite, 2 public, 1 private shower

Bed & breakfast per night:

	£min	£max
Single	20.00	24.00
Double	40.00	48.00

Half board per person:

	£min	£max
Daily	28.00	32.00
Weekly	182.00	206.00

Evening meal 1830 (last orders 1900)
Parking for 9

CORFE CASTLE
Dorset
Map ref 2B3

One of the most spectacular ruined castles in Britain. Norman in origin, the castle was a Royalist stronghold during the Civil War and held out until 1645. The village had a considerable marble-carving industry in the Middle Ages.

Bankes Hotel

East Street, Corfe Castle, Wareham
BH20 5ED
☎ Wareham (01929) 480206
Fax (01929) 480186
16th C hotel with restaurant and bar food facilities, just 80 yards from the entrance to Corfe Castle.
Bedrooms: 1 single, 9 double
Bathrooms: 5 en-suite, 2 public, 2 private showers

Bed & breakfast per night:

	£min	£max
Single	25.00	45.00
Double	45.00	65.00

Half board per person:

	£min	£max
Daily	35.00	55.00

Lunch available
Evening meal 1800 (last orders 2130)

SOUTH OF ENGLAND

Parking for 10
Cards accepted: Access, Visa, Diners, Amex, Switch/Delta

Mortons House Hotel
HIGHLY COMMENDED

East Street, Corfe Castle, Wareham BH20 5EE
☎ Wareham (01929) 480988
Fax (01929) 480820

Attractive Elizabethan manor house with castle views. Walled gardens, coastal and country pursuits. Suites and four-poster bed. Licensed gourmet restaurant.
Bedrooms: 13 double, 3 twin, 1 family room
Suite available
Bathrooms: 17 en-suite

Bed & breakfast per night:	£min	£max
Single	60.00	70.00
Double	80.00	96.00

Half board per person:	£min	£max
Daily	60.00	68.00
Weekly	320.00	375.00

Lunch available
Evening meal 1900 (last orders 2030)
Parking for 35
Cards accepted: Access, Visa, Diners, Amex, Switch/Delta

COTSWOLDS

See under Burford, Chipping Norton, Churchill, Clanfield, Deddington, Witney, Woodstock
See also Cotswolds in Heart of England region

CRANBORNE
Dorset
Map ref 2B3

Village with an interesting Jacobean manor house. Lies south-east of Cranborne Chase, formerly a forest and hunting preserve.

The Fleur de Lys

5 Wimborne Street, Cranborne, Wimborne Minster BH21 5PP
☎ (01725) 517282
Fax (01725) 517631

Charming old-world coaching inn, close to the New Forest. Cosy atmosphere, friendly hospitality. Restaurant, bar, en-suite accommodation.
Bedrooms: 1 single, 4 double, 3 twin
Bathrooms: 7 en-suite, 1 private shower

Bed & breakfast per night:	£min	£max
Single	20.00	38.00
Double	38.00	55.00

Half board per person:	£min	£max
Daily	38.00	50.00
Weekly	190.00	300.00

Lunch available
Evening meal 1900 (last orders 2145)
Parking for 35
Cards accepted: Access, Visa, Amex, Switch/Delta

DEDDINGTON
Oxfordshire
Map ref 2C1

On the edge of the Cotswolds and settled since the Stone Age, this is the only village in England to have been granted a full Coat of Arms, displayed on the 16th C Town Hall in the picturesque market square. Many places of interest include the Church of St Peter and St Paul.

The Deddington Arms
COMMENDED

Horsefair, Deddington, Banbury OX15 0SH
☎ (01869) 338364
Fax (01869) 337010

16th C coaching inn, tastefully refurbishd to provide air-conditioned restaurant and en-suite bedrooms whilst retaining the village inn atmosphere. Ideal base for Banbury, Oxford, Stratford, Warwick, Blenheim Palace and the Cotswolds.
Bedrooms: 2 double, 3 twin, 1 triple, 1 family room
Bathrooms: 7 en-suite

Bed & breakfast per night:	£min	£max
Single	49.50	75.00
Double	59.50	75.00

Lunch available
Evening meal 1830 (last orders 2130)
Parking for 24
Cards accepted: Access, Visa, Switch/Delta

Holcombe Hotel & Restaurant
COMMENDED

High Street, Deddington, Banbury OX15 0SL
☎ (01869) 338274
Fax (01869) 337167
Best Western/The Independents

Delightful 17th C award-winning family-run hotel in lovely village on A4260 Banbury to Oxford road, M40 exit 10. Ideal for visiting the Cotswolds, Stratford, Warwick and Blenheim-Woodstock.
Bedrooms: 2 single, 8 double, 6 twin, 1 triple
Bathrooms: 17 en-suite

Bed & breakfast per night:	£min	£max
Single	56.00	69.00
Double	78.00	95.00

Half board per person:	£min	£max
Daily	48.00	56.00
Weekly	290.00	330.00

Lunch available
Evening meal 1900 (last orders 2200)
Parking for 60
Cards accepted: Access, Visa, Amex, Switch/Delta

EMSWORTH
Hampshire
Map ref 2C3

Old port, now a yachting centre, set between 2 small creeks on Chichester Harbour. Yachtbuilding is the chief industry. There are some good Georgian buildings and 2 tide-mills.

The Brookfield Hotel
HIGHLY COMMENDED

Havant Road, Emsworth PO10 7LF
☎ (01243) 373363
Fax (01243) 376342

Privately owned and run country house hotel, near the old fishing village of Emsworth and close to Chichester and its festival theatre. Bargain break rates at weekends.
Bedrooms: 5 single, 23 double, 12 twin
Suite available

Continued ▶

SOUTH OF ENGLAND

EMSWORTH
Continued

Bathrooms: 40 en-suite
Bed & breakfast

per night:	£min	£max
Single	54.00	
Double	79.50	

Half board per

person:	£min	£max
Daily	68.00	

Lunch available
Evening meal 1900 (last orders 2130)
Parking for 80
Cards accepted: Access, Visa, Diners, Amex, Switch/Delta

Jingles Hotel
COMMENDED

77 Horndean Road, Emsworth
PO10 7PU
☎ (01243) 373755
Fax (01243) 373755
Fully modernised and comfortably furnished Victorian house located between the South Downs and Chichester harbour.
Bedrooms: 5 single, 5 double, 3 twin
Bathrooms: 6 en-suite, 2 private, 2 public
Bed & breakfast

per night:	£min	£max
Single	24.00	31.00
Double	40.00	52.00

Lunch available
Evening meal 1900 (last orders 2000)
Parking for 14
Cards accepted: Access, Visa

FAREHAM
Hampshire
Map ref 2C3

Lies on a quiet backwater of Portsmouth Harbour. The High Street is lined with fine Georgian buildings.
Tourist Information Centre ☎ (01329) 221342 or 824896

Avenue House Hotel
COMMENDED

22 The Avenue, Fareham PO14 1NS
☎ (01329) 232175
Fax (01329) 232196
Logis of Great Britain
Comfortable, small hotel, with charm and character, set in mature gardens. 5 minutes' walk to town centre, railway station and restaurants.

Wheelchair access category 3
Bedrooms: 3 single, 8 double, 3 twin, 3 triple
Bathrooms: 17 en-suite
Bed & breakfast

per night:	£min	£max
Single	39.50	44.50
Double	46.00	55.00

Parking for 17
Cards accepted: Access, Visa, Diners, Amex

Maylings Manor Hotel

11A Highlands Road, Fareham
PO16 7XJ
☎ (01329) 286451
Fax (01329) 822584
Picturesque Georgian manor house set in 2.5 acres of landscaped gardens. Close to M27, with easy access to Portsmouth, Southampton and Winchester.
Bedrooms: 1 single, 10 double, 8 twin, 1 triple
Bathrooms: 20 en-suite, 1 public
Bed & breakfast

per night:	£min	£max
Single	32.50	45.00
Double	35.00	50.00

Half board per

person:	£min	£max
Daily	42.50	55.00

Lunch available
Evening meal 1900 (last orders 2130)
Parking for 89
Cards accepted: Access, Visa, Diners, Amex

The Roundabout Hotel
APPROVED

Wallington Shore Road, Fareham
PO16 8SB
☎ (01329) 822542
Fax (01329) 234533
Charming 19th C hotel with modern bedrooms. Fully licensed restaurant and lounge bar. Easy access to south coast towns via M27.
Bedrooms: 5 single, 5 double, 3 twin, 2 triple, 2 family rooms
Bathrooms: 13 en-suite, 1 public
Bed & breakfast

per night:	£min	£max
Single	39.50	43.00
Double	43.00	48.50

Half board per

person:	£min	£max
Daily	45.00	
Weekly	225.00	

Lunch available
Evening meal 1800 (last orders 2200)
Parking for 42
Cards accepted: Access, Visa, Diners, Amex, Switch/Delta

FARINGDON
Oxfordshire
Map ref 2B2

Ancient stone-built market town in the Vale of the White Horse. The 17th C market hall stands on pillars and the 13th C church has some fine monuments. A great monastic tithe barn is nearby at Great Coxwell.

Faringdon Hotel

Market Place, Faringdon SN7 7HL
☎ (01367) 240536
Fax (01367) 243250
All en-suite rooms, equipped with remote-control colour TV, direct-dial telephone, tea/coffee-making facilities, hairdryer. Open fire, lounge bar and restaurant.
Bedrooms: 3 single, 13 double, 1 twin, 3 triple
Bathrooms: 20 en-suite
Bed & breakfast

per night:	£min	£max
Single	42.00	46.50
Double	50.00	56.50

Lunch available
Evening meal 1900 (last orders 2100)
Parking for 5
Cards accepted: Access, Visa, Diners, Amex

Sudbury House Hotel
HIGHLY COMMENDED

56 London Street, Faringdon
SN7 8AA
☎ (01367) 241272
Fax (01367) 242346
Peacefully situated midway between Oxford and Swindon, within an easy drive of the Cotswolds, Blenheim Palace and Warwick Castle. Special weekend rates.
Bedrooms: 39 double, 10 twin
Bathrooms: 49 en-suite
Bed & breakfast

per night:	£min	£max
Single	55.00	70.00
Double	60.00	85.00

Half board per

person:	£min	£max
Daily	45.00	

SOUTH OF ENGLAND

Lunch available
Evening meal 1900 (last orders 2115)
Parking for 85
Cards accepted: Access, Visa, Diners, Amex, Switch/Delta

FERNDOWN
Dorset
Map ref 2B3

Sharing the attractions of Bournemouth, of which it is now a part, and well placed for exploring the New Forest.

Coach House Inn

579 Wimborne Road East, Ferndown BH22 9NW
☎ Bournemouth (01202) 861222
Fax (01202) 894130
Consort
Set in beautiful wooded surroundings, close to the New Forest and 6 miles from Bournemouth with its golden beaches. Half board price based on a minimum 2 night stay.
Bedrooms: 16 double, 20 twin, 3 triple, 4 family rooms
Bathrooms: 43 en-suite

Bed & breakfast
per night:	£min	£max
Single	45.50	48.50
Double	51.00	55.00

Half board per
person:	£min	£max
Daily	37.50	49.00
Weekly	225.00	228.00

Lunch available
Evening meal 1900 (last orders 2130)
Parking for 118
Cards accepted: Access, Visa, Diners, Amex, Switch/Delta

FLEET
Hampshire
Map ref 2C2

Tourist Information Centre ☎ (01252) 811151

Lismoyne Hotel

Church Road, Fleet, Aldershot GU13 8NA
☎ (01252) 628555
Fax (01252) 811761

Attractive privately owned country hotel set in 2.25 acres of wooded seclusion. A la carte and table d'hote menus. Ideal for countryside.
Bedrooms: 20 single, 16 double, 6 twin
Bathrooms: 42 en-suite

Bed & breakfast
per night:	£min	£max
Single	25.00	65.00
Double	49.00	85.00

Half board per
person:	£min	£max
Daily	39.00	85.00
Weekly	273.00	595.00

Lunch available
Evening meal 1930 (last orders 2130)
Parking for 90
Cards accepted: Access, Visa, Diners, Amex, Switch/Delta

FORDINGBRIDGE
Hampshire
Map ref 2B3

On the north-west edge of the New Forest. A medieval bridge crosses the Avon at this point and gave the town its name. A good centre for walking, exploring and fishing.

Lion's Court Restaurant & Hotel

COMMENDED
29-31 The High Street, Fordingbridge SP6 1AS
☎ (01425) 652006
Fax (01425) 657946
Logis of Great Britain

Intimate 17th C hotel on edge of New Forest. A la carte restaurant, gardens extending to River Avon. Fishing, private parking.
Bedrooms: 2 single, 4 double, 1 twin
Bathrooms: 7 en-suite

Bed & breakfast
per night:	£min	£max
Single	25.00	40.00
Double	50.00	80.00

Half board per
person:	£min	£max
Daily	37.50	52.50
Weekly	262.50	367.50

Lunch available
Evening meal 1900 (last orders 2130)
Parking for 10
Cards accepted: Access, Visa, Switch/Delta

FRESHWATER
Isle of Wight
Map ref 2C3

This part of the island is associated with Tennyson, who lived in the village for 30 years. A monument on Tennyson's Down commemorates the poet.

Farringford Hotel

COMMENDED
Bedbury Lane, Freshwater PO40 9PE
☎ Isle of Wight (01983) 752500 & 752700
Fax (01983) 756515
Set in 33-acre grounds, offering traditional hotel service and also self-catering suites, the best of both worlds. 9-hole golf-course, swimming and tennis.
Bedrooms: 3 single, 2 double, 7 twin, 7 triple
Bathrooms: 19 en-suite

Bed & breakfast
per night:	£min	£max
Single	25.00	45.00
Double	50.00	90.00

Half board per
person:	£min	£max
Daily	38.00	58.00
Weekly	228.00	348.00

Lunch available
Evening meal 1930 (last orders 2130)
Parking for 152
Cards accepted: Access, Visa, Diners, Amex, Switch/Delta

Royal Standard Hotel

APPROVED
School Green Road, Freshwater PO40 9AJ
☎ Isle of Wight (01983) 753227
Small, family-run hotel, serving comprehensive bar meals. Freehouse with 2 bars, restaurant, function room.
Bedrooms: 4 single, 3 double, 1 twin, 2 triple, 1 family room

Continued ▶

SOUTH OF ENGLAND

FRESHWATER
Continued

Bathrooms: 9 en-suite, 2 private showers

Bed & breakfast per night:

	£min	£max
Single	20.00	25.00
Double	40.00	50.00

Lunch available
Evening meal 1800 (last orders 2200)
Parking for 5

GORING
Oxfordshire
Map ref 2C2

Riverside town on the Oxfordshire/Berkshire border, linked by an attractive bridge to Streatley with views to the Goring Gap.

Miller of Mansfield

High Street, Goring, Reading, Berkshire RG8 9AW
☎ (01491) 872829
Fax (01491) 874200

Ivy-covered inn with Tudor style exterior. Interior has original beams, open fires and comfortable bedrooms.
Bedrooms: 2 single, 5 double, 3 twin
Bathrooms: 6 en-suite, 2 public

Bed & breakfast per night:

	£min	£max
Single	29.50	41.00
Double	45.00	57.00

Lunch available
Evening meal 1900 (last orders 2200)
Parking for 10
Cards accepted: Access, Visa, Switch/Delta

WELCOME HOST

This is a nationally recognised customer care programme which aims to promote the highest standards of service and a warm welcome. Establishments who are taking part in this initiative are indicated by the symbol.

HAVANT
Hampshire
Map ref 2C3

Once a market town famous for making parchment. Nearby at Leigh Park extensive early 19th C landscape gardens and parklands are open to the public. Right in the centre of the town stands the interesting 13th C church of St Faith.
Tourist Information Centre ☎ (01705) 480024

The Old Mill Guest House
COMMENDED

Mill Lane, Bedhampton, Havant PO9 3JH
☎ Portsmouth (01705) 454948
Fax (01705) 499677

Georgian house in large grounds by a lake abundant in wildlife. Modernised, comfortable retreat. John Keats rested here.
Bedrooms: 1 double, 4 triple
Bathrooms: 4 en-suite, 1 private

Bed & breakfast per night:

	£min	£max
Single	24.00	28.00
Double	38.00	45.00

Parking for 10

HAYING ISLAND
Hampshire
Map ref 2C3

Small island of historic interest, surrounded by natural harbours and with fine sandy beaches, linked to the mainland by an attractive bridge under which boats sail. Birthplace of windsurfing and home to many international sailing events.

Cockle Warren Cottage Hotel
HIGHLY COMMENDED

36 Seafront, Hayling Island PO11 9HL
☎ (01705) 464961
Fax (01705) 464838
Logis of Great Britain

Lovely seaside farmhouse-style hotel with large garden and heated swimming pool. French and English country cooking, home-made bread, four-poster and Victorian beds, log fires in winter.
Bedrooms: 4 double, 1 triple
Bathrooms: 5 en-suite

Bed & breakfast per night:

	£min	£max
Single	45.00	65.00
Double	54.00	88.00

Evening meal 2000 (last orders 1600)
Parking for 11
Cards accepted: Access, Visa, Amex

Forte Posthouse Havant
COMMENDED

Northney Road, Hayling Island PO11 0NQ
☎ Portsmouth (01705) 465011
Fax (01705) 466468
Forte

Modern hotel on the north side of Hayling Island, overlooking Langstone Harbour.
Bedrooms: 32 double, 54 twin, 6 family rooms
Bathrooms: 92 en-suite

Bed & breakfast per night:

	£min	£max
Single	40.00	58.00
Double	60.00	76.00

Half board per person:

	£min	£max
Daily	43.00	50.00
Weekly	245.00	350.00

Lunch available
Evening meal 1845 (last orders 2230)
Parking for 200
Cards accepted: Access, Visa, Diners, Amex, Switch/Delta

Newtown House Hotel
APPROVED

Manor Road, Hayling Island PO11 0QR
☎ Portsmouth (01705) 466131
Fax (01705) 461366

18th C converted farmhouse, set in own grounds a quarter of a mile from seafront. Indoor leisure complex with heated pool, gym, steamroom, jacuzzi and sauna. Tennis.

SOUTH OF ENGLAND

Bedrooms: 9 single, 9 double, 4 twin, 3 triple
Bathrooms: 25 en-suite, 1 public

Bed & breakfast per night:	£min	£max
Single	35.00	
Double	55.00	

Half board per person:	£min	£max
Daily	48.00	
Weekly	290.00	

Lunch available
Evening meal 1900 (last orders 2130)
Parking for 45
Cards accepted: Access, Visa, Diners, Amex, Switch/Delta

HIGH WYCOMBE

Buckinghamshire
Map ref 2C2

Famous for furniture-making, historic examples of which feature in the museum. The 18th C Guildhall and the octagonal market house were designed by the Adam brothers. West Wycombe Park and Hughenden Manor (National Trust) are nearby.
Tourist Information Centre ☎ *(01494) 421892*

The Alexandra Hotel
COMMENDED

Queen Alexandra Road, High Wycombe HP11 2JX
☎ (01494) 463494
Fax (01494) 463560
Town centre hotel with tastefully furnished bedrooms and an emphasis on quality. Conference facilities. Easy access to major motorways and tourist towns such as Windsor and Oxford.
Bedrooms: 11 single, 15 double, 2 twin
Bathrooms: 28 en-suite

Bed & breakfast per night:	£min	£max
Single	44.95	72.90
Double	49.90	79.80

Half board per person:	£min	£max
Daily	50.95	84.90

Evening meal 1900 (last orders 2030)
Parking for 30
Cards accepted: Access, Visa, Amex, Switch/Delta

Clifton Lodge Hotel
COMMENDED

210 West Wycombe Road, High Wycombe HP12 3AR
☎ (01494) 440095 & 529062
Fax (01494) 536322
Situated on the A40 approximately 1 mile from the M40 Oxford to London motorway. Ideal for touring Thames Valley and Oxford.
Bedrooms: 10 single, 13 double, 7 twin, 2 family rooms
Bathrooms: 15 en-suite, 4 private, 4 public, 2 private showers

Bed & breakfast per night:	£min	£max
Single	30.00	65.00
Double	40.00	70.00

Half board per person:	£min	£max
Daily	30.00	75.00

Lunch available
Evening meal 1900 (last orders 2100)
Parking for 30
Cards accepted: Access, Visa, Diners, Amex

HIGHCLIFFE

Dorset
Map ref 2B3

Seaside district of Christchurch some 3 miles to the east. Highcliffe Castle is of interest.

Beverly Glen Guest House
COMMENDED

1 Stuart Road, Highcliffe, Christchurch BH23 5JS
☎ (01425) 273811
On A337, close to clean beach and shops. Christchurch Priory, river fishing, New Forest and Bournemouth a short drive away. Home cooking.
Bedrooms: 1 single, 3 double, 2 twin
Bathrooms: 5 en-suite, 1 private, 1 public

Bed & breakfast per night:	£min	£max
Single	18.00	23.00
Double	36.00	44.00

Half board per person:	£min	£max
Daily	27.50	30.00
Weekly	196.00	210.00

Evening meal 1800 (last orders 1900)
Parking for 7
Cards accepted: Access, Visa, Switch/Delta

HORTON CUM STUDLEY

Oxfordshire
Map ref 2C1

Village with attractive timbered and thatched cottages, on the edge of Ot Moor. The Oxfordshire Way footpath passes close to the village.

King's Arms Hotel
COMMENDED

The Old Green, Horton cum Studley, Oxford OX33 1AY
☎ Stanton-St-John (01865) 351235
Fax (01865) 351721
Charming Cotswold-stone country hotel in village location with golf course nearby. Ideal base for visiting Oxford, Blenheim Palace and the Cotswolds.
Bedrooms: 2 single, 5 double, 2 twin, 1 triple
Bathrooms: 10 en-suite

Bed & breakfast per night:	£min	£max
Single	25.00	35.00
Double	45.00	60.00

Half board per person:	£min	£max
Daily	32.50	48.00
Weekly	227.50	266.00

Lunch available
Evening meal 1900 (last orders 2100)
Parking for 30
Cards accepted: Access, Visa, Amex, Switch/Delta

HUNGERFORD

Berkshire
Map ref 2C2

Attractive town on the Avon Canal and the River Kennet, famous for its fishing. It has a wide High Street and many antique shops. Nearby is the Tudor manor of Littlecote with its large Roman mosaic.

The Bear at Hungerford
COMMENDED

Charnham Street, Hungerford RG17 0EL
☎ (01488) 682512
Fax (01488) 684357
Jarvis/Utell International
13th C coaching inn, traditionally furnished, with timber beams and open fires. 3 miles from junction 14 of the M4, ideally situated for the Cotswolds, Berkshire Downs and Newbury races. A Jarvis Hotel.

Continued ▶

SOUTH OF ENGLAND

HUNGERFORD
Continued

Bedrooms: 3 single, 29 double, 9 twin
Bathrooms: 41 en-suite

Bed & breakfast per night:
	£min	£max
Single	36.00	77.25
Double	70.00	93.75

Half board per person:
	£min	£max
Daily	39.50	93.25
Weekly	250.00	455.00

Lunch available
Evening meal 1900 (last orders 2130)
Parking for 60
Cards accepted: Access, Visa, Diners, Amex, Switch/Delta

ISLE OF WIGHT

See under Bonchurch, Chale, Colwell Bay, Freshwater, Sandown, Shanklin, Totland Bay, Ventnor

KNOWL HILL

Berkshire
Map ref 2C2

Bird In Hand
COMMENDED

Bath Road, Knowl Hill, Reading RG10 9UP
☎ (01628) 822781 & 826622
Fax (01628) 826748
Extended 14th C coaching inn, between London and Oxford. Close to Henley, Maidenhead and Windsor. 25 minutes to Heathrow.
Bedrooms: 1 single, 4 double, 10 twin
Bathrooms: 15 en-suite

Bed & breakfast per night:
	£min	£max
Single	55.00	75.00
Double	60.00	95.00

Half board per person:
	£min	£max
Daily	75.00	75.00
Weekly	500.00	500.00

Lunch available
Evening meal 1900 (last orders 2200)
Parking for 80
Cards accepted: Access, Visa, Diners, Amex, Switch/Delta

LIPHOOK

Hampshire
Map ref 2C3

Large village astride the A3 and close to the West Sussex border.

Old Thorns Golf Course, Hotel & Restaurants
COMMENDED

Longmoor Road, Griggs Green, Liphook GU30 7PE
☎ (01428) 724555
Fax (01428) 725322
Consort

Old Thorns is set in 400 acres of Hampshire parkland with an 18-hole golf course, hotel, Japanese and European restaurants and leisure complex. 1 hour's drive from London, Heathrow and Gatwick airports.
Bedrooms: 3 double, 28 twin, 1 triple
Bathrooms: 32 en-suite, 5 public

Bed & breakfast per night:
	£min	£max
Single	79.50	
Double	99.50	145.00

Half board per person:
	£min	£max
Daily	58.00	63.00

Lunch available
Evening meal 1930 (last orders 2130)
Parking for 200
Cards accepted: Access, Visa, Diners, Amex, Switch/Delta

LYMINGTON

Hampshire
Map ref 2C3

Small, pleasant town with bright cottages and attractive Georgian houses, lying on the edge of the New Forest with a ferry service to the Isle of Wight. A sheltered harbour makes it a busy yachting centre.

Our Bench
COMMENDED

9 Lodge Road, Pennington, Lymington SO41 8HH
☎ (01590) 673141
Fax (01590) 673141

All en-suite bedrooms, separate TV lounge, indoor heated pool, jacuzzi and sauna. Non-smokers only, please. Sorry, no children. Large quiet garden.
Bedrooms: 2 double, 1 twin
Bathrooms: 3 en-suite

Bed & breakfast per night:
	£min	£max
Single	20.00	26.00
Double	38.00	48.00

Half board per person:
	£min	£max
Daily	25.50	30.50
Weekly	175.00	210.00

Evening meal 1800 (last orders 2000)
Parking for 5

LYNDHURST

Hampshire
Map ref 2C3

The "capital" of the New Forest, surrounded by attractive woodland scenery and delightful villages. The town is dominated by the Victorian Gothic-style church where the original Alice in Wonderland is buried.
Tourist Information Centre ☎ (01703) 282269

Burwood Lodge

Romsey Road, Lyndhurst SO43 7AA
☎ Southampton (01703) 282445
Lovely house in half-acre garden, near the village centre. All rooms with en-suite shower, WC and washbasin. Parking in grounds.
Bedrooms: 1 single, 4 double, 1 triple, 1 family room
Bathrooms: 6 en-suite, 1 private

Bed & breakfast per night:
	£min	£max
Single	20.00	25.00
Double	40.00	50.00

Parking for 8

Knightwood Lodge
HIGHLY COMMENDED

Southampton Road, Lyndhurst SO43 7BU
☎ Southampton (01703) 282502
Fax (01703) 283730
Minotel/The Independents

Map references apply to the colour maps at the back of this guide.

SOUTH OF ENGLAND

On the edge of Lyndhurst overlooking the New Forest. Facilities include an indoor health centre with spa, sauna, swimming pool and steam room. Cosy bar. Parking.
Bedrooms: 3 single, 9 double, 1 twin, 2 triple
Bathrooms: 15 en-suite, 1 public

Bed & breakfast
per night:	£min	£max
Single	30.00	40.00
Double	60.00	80.00

Half board per person:
	£min	£max
Daily	42.00	56.00

Lunch available
Evening meal 1830 (last orders 2000)
Parking for 15
Cards accepted: Access, Visa, Diners, Amex

The Penny Farthing Hotel
COMMENDED
Romsey Road, Lyndhurst SO43 7AA
☎ Southampton (01703) 284422
Fax (01703) 284488
Perfectly situated, friendly small hotel, 1 minute's walk from village centre, shops, restaurants, 2 minutes from open forest. Tastefully furnished rooms ensure a comfortable stay.
Bedrooms: 3 single, 5 double, 1 twin, 1 triple
Bathrooms: 10 en-suite

Bed & breakfast
per night:	£min	£max
Single	25.00	35.00
Double	45.00	70.00

Parking for 15
Cards accepted: Access, Visa
See display advertisement on this page

MAIDENHEAD
Berkshire
Map ref 2C2

Attractive town on the River Thames which is crossed by an elegant 18th C bridge and by Brunel's well-known railway bridge. It is a popular place for boating with delightful riverside walks. The Courage Shire Horse Centre is nearby.
Tourist Information Centre ☎ *(01628) 781110*

Clifton Guest House
21 Crauford Rise, Maidenhead SL6 7LR
☎ (01628) 23572
Fax (01628) 23572
Fully-licensed, family-run hotel near town centre. Convenient for Heathrow, Windsor Castle and the M4, M40 and M25 motorways.
Bedrooms: 3 single, 5 double, 2 twin, 2 triple
Bathrooms: 9 en-suite, 3 public

Bed & breakfast
per night:	£min	£max
Single	28.00	
Double	45.00	

Half board per person:
	£min	£max
Daily	38.00	

Evening meal 1800 (last orders 2130)
Parking for 10
Cards accepted: Access, Visa, Amex, Switch/Delta

Elva Lodge Hotel
APPROVED
Castle Hill, Maidenhead SL6 4AD
☎ (01628) 22948 & 34883
Fax (01628) 38855
Family-run hotel in central Maidenhead. Friendly atmosphere and personal attention. Ideal for Heathrow, Windsor, Henley and Ascot. M4 5 minutes, M40 and M25 10 minutes.
Bedrooms: 10 single, 10 double, 4 twin, 2 triple, 1 family room
Bathrooms: 14 en-suite, 6 public, 6 private showers

Bed & breakfast
per night:	£min	£max
Single	35.00	67.00
Double	50.00	80.00

Half board per person:
	£min	£max
Daily	49.00	82.00
Weekly	308.70	516.60

Lunch available
Evening meal 1830 (last orders 2130)
Parking for 31
Cards accepted: Access, Visa, Diners, Amex, Switch/Delta

Monkey Island Hotel
HIGHLY COMMENDED
Bray, Maidenhead SL6 2EE
☎ (01628) 23400
Fax (01628) 784732

Unique, romantic and historic with elegance and charm. Monkey Island boasts award-winning cuisine and en-suite bedrooms and suites. Within easy reach of Royal Windsor, Eton and London.

Continued ▶

The Penny Farthing Hotel

This cheerful private hotel offers rooms with en-suite, colour TV and tea/coffee facilities. We also provide a licenced bar, a resident's lounge with satellite TV, a large car park and a lock-up bicycle store. Lyndhurst is home to the New Forest Tourist Information Centre, and offers a charming variety of shops, restaurants and bistros all within a moments walk. The Penny Farthing is centrally situated and provides an excellent location from which you can explore some of England's most beautiful countryside.

Romsey Rd, Lyndhurst, Hampshire SO43 7AA
Tel: 01703 284422 Fax: 01703 284488

SOUTH OF ENGLAND

MAIDENHEAD
Continued

Bedrooms: 1 single, 8 double,
13 twin, 3 triple
Suites available
Bathrooms: 25 en-suite

Bed & breakfast per night	£min	£max
Single	85.00	105.00
Double	120.00	140.00

Half board per person:	£min	£max
Daily	80.00	95.00
Weekly	560.00	665.00

Lunch available
Evening meal 1930 (last orders 2145)
Parking for 100
Cards accepted: Access, Visa, Diners, Amex

Moor Farm
HIGHLY COMMENDED

Ascot Road, Holyport, Maidenhead SL6 2HY
☎ (01628) 33761
Fax (01628) 33761
100-acre mixed farm. 700-year-old medieval manor in picturesque Holyport village. 4 miles from Windsor.
Bedrooms: 1 double, 2 twin
Bathrooms: 3 en-suite

Bed & breakfast per night	£min	£max
Double	39.00	49.00

Parking for 4

MARLOW
Buckinghamshire
Map ref 2C2

Attractive Georgian town on the River Thames, famous for its 19th C suspension bridge. The High Street contains many old houses and there are connections with writers including Shelley and T S Eliot.

The Country House
HIGHLY COMMENDED

Bisham Road, Marlow SL7 1RP
☎ (01628) 890606
Fax (01628) 890983
Edwardian house in lovely garden. 200 yards' level walk from Marlow Bridge and the High Street.
Bedrooms: 4 single, 4 double, 1 twin, 1 triple
Bathrooms: 10 en-suite

Bed & breakfast per night	£min	£max
Single	66.00	
Double	82.00	

Parking for 10
Cards accepted: Access, Visa, Amex

Holly Tree House
HIGHLY COMMENDED

Burford Close, Marlow Bottom, Marlow SL7 3NF
☎ (01628) 891110 & Mobile 0370 275437
Fax (01628) 481278
Detached house set in large gardens with fine views over the valley. Quiet yet convenient location. Large car park. All rooms fully en-suite. Outdoor heated swimming pool.
Bedrooms: 1 single, 4 double
Bathrooms: 5 en-suite

Bed & breakfast per night	£min	£max
Single	57.50	
Double	64.50	69.50

Parking for 10
Cards accepted: Access, Visa, Amex

The White House

194 Little Marlow Road, Marlow SL7 1HX
☎ (01628) 485765
Victorian house of character, convenient for M4 and M40. Evening meal on request.
Bedrooms: 1 single, 2 twin
Bathrooms: 2 en-suite, 1 private

Bed & breakfast per night	£min	£max
Single	27.00	35.00
Double	40.50	45.00

Parking for 2
Cards accepted: Access, Visa

MILFORD-ON-SEA
Hampshire
Map ref 2C3

Victorian seaside resort with shingle beach and good bathing, set in pleasant countryside and looking out over the Isle of Wight. Nearby is Hurst Castle, built by Henry VIII.

Compton Hotel

59 Keyhaven Road, Milford-on-Sea, Lymington SO41 0QX
☎ Lymington (01590) 643112
Small, private hotel with en-suite rooms and TV. Outdoor heated swimming pool. English and vegetarian cooking. Licensed.
Bedrooms: 3 double, 1 twin, 1 triple
Bathrooms: 4 en-suite, 1 public

Bed & breakfast per night	£min	£max
Single	22.00	25.00
Double	38.00	40.00

Half board per person:	£min	£max
Daily	29.00	30.00
Weekly	180.00	210.00

Evening meal from 1830
Parking for 7

MILTON COMMON
Oxfordshire
Map ref 2C1

Belfry Hotel
HIGHLY COMMENDED

Milton Common, Thame OX9 2JW
☎ Great Milton (01844) 279381
Fax (01844) 279624
Tudor-style country hotel, privately owned. Well-placed for touring. Indoor leisure complex with swimming pool, sauna, solarium, mini-gym.
Bedrooms: 11 single, 34 double, 30 twin
Suites available
Bathrooms: 75 en-suite

Bed & breakfast per night	£min	£max
Single	75.00	90.00
Double	95.00	120.00

Lunch available
Evening meal 1930 (last orders 2130)
Parking for 200
Cards accepted: Access, Visa, Diners, Amex, Switch/Delta

For ideas on places to visit refer to the introduction at the beginning of this section.

Information on accommodation listed in this guide has been supplied by the proprietors. As changes may occur you are advised to check details at the time of booking.

SOUTH OF ENGLAND

MILTON KEYNES

Buckinghamshire
Map ref 2C1

Designated a New Town in 1967, Milton Keynes offers a wide range of housing and is abundantly planted with trees. It has excellent shopping facilities and 3 centres for leisure and sporting activities. The Open University is based here.
Tourist Information Centre ☎ *(01908) 232525 or 231742*

The Different Drummer Hotel

COMMENDED

94 High Street, Stony Stratford, Milton Keynes MK11 1AH
☎ (01908) 564733
Fax (01908) 260646
Historic oak-beamed coaching inn, circa 1470, tastefully restored and modernised throughout and incorporating a high class Italian and English restaurant.
Bedrooms: 5 single, 5 double, 2 twin
Bathrooms: 12 en-suite

Bed & breakfast
per night:	£min	£max
Single	50.00	65.00
Double	50.00	75.00

Half board per
person:	£min	£max
Daily	70.00	80.00
Weekly	350.00	400.00

Lunch available
Evening meal 1900 (last orders 2200)
Cards accepted: Access, Visa, Diners, Amex, Switch/Delta

Kingfishers

Listed COMMENDED

9 Rylstone Close, Heelands, Milton Keynes MK13 7QT
☎ (01908) 310231
Fax (01908) 310231
Large private home set in quarter of an acre of grounds, close to Milton Keynes city centre, bus and railway stations.
Bedrooms: 1 single, 1 double, 1 triple
Bathrooms: 2 en-suite, 1 private

Bed & breakfast
per night:	£min	£max
Single	18.00	25.00
Double	32.00	37.00

Half board per
person:	£min	£max
Daily	25.00	35.00
Weekly	175.00	195.00

Evening meal 1800 (last orders 2000)
Parking for 6

The Old Bakery Hotel

HIGHLY COMMENDED

Main Street, Cosgrove, Milton Keynes MK19 7JL
☎ (01908) 263103 & 262255
Fax (01908) 263620

17th C former village bakery in the main street of idyllic village, 2 miles from Milton Keynes.
Bedrooms: 3 single, 2 double, 2 twin, 1 triple
Bathrooms: 8 en-suite

Bed & breakfast
per night:	£min	£max
Single	35.00	48.50
Double	45.00	62.50

Half board per
person:	£min	£max
Daily	47.50	68.00
Weekly	332.50	476.00

Evening meal 1900 (last orders 2100)
Parking for 10
Cards accepted: Access, Visa, Amex, Switch/Delta

Swan Revived Hotel

HIGHLY COMMENDED

High Street, Newport Pagnell, Milton Keynes MK16 8AR
☎ (01908) 610565
Fax (01908) 210995
The Independents
Independently owned famous coaching inn, where guests can enjoy every modern comfort. Convenient for thriving new city of Milton Keynes, Woburn, Towcester, Silverstone.
Bedrooms: 17 single, 19 double, 4 twin, 2 triple
Suites available
Bathrooms: 42 en-suite

Bed & breakfast
per night:	£min	£max
Single	39.50	62.50
Double	55.00	70.00

Half board per
person:	£min	£max
Daily	40.00	75.00

Lunch available
Evening meal 1915 (last orders 2200)
Parking for 18
Cards accepted: Access, Visa, Diners, Amex, Switch/Delta

NETLEY ABBEY

Hampshire
Map ref 2C3

Romantic ruin, set in green lawns against a background of trees on the east bank of Southampton Water. The abbey was built in the 13th C by Cistercian monks from Beaulieu.

La Casa Blanca

COMMENDED

48 Victoria Road, Netley Abbey, Southampton SO31 5DQ
☎ Southampton (01703) 453718
Fax (01703) 453718
Small, pleasantly situated licensed hotel. Friendly welcome, well-equipped en-suite bedrooms and home cooking.
Bedrooms: 4 single, 1 double, 1 twin, 2 triple, 1 family room
Bathrooms: 9 en-suite, 1 public

Bed & breakfast
per night:	£min	£max
Single	26.00	26.00
Double	46.00	46.00

Half board per
person:	£min	£max
Daily	25.00	35.00
Weekly	175.00	200.00

Lunch available
Evening meal 1830 (last orders 2100)
Parking for 8
Cards accepted: Access, Visa

NEW FOREST

See under Brockenhurst, Fordingbridge, Lymington, Lyndhurst, Milford-on-Sea, New Milton, Ringwood, Sway

---

Establishments should be open throughout the year, unless otherwise stated.

All accommodation in this guide has been graded, or is awaiting a grading, by a trained Tourist Board inspector.

SOUTH OF ENGLAND

NEW MILTON

Hampshire
Map ref 2B3

New Forest residential town on the mainline railway.

Chewton Glen Hotel, Health & Country Club
DE LUXE

Christchurch Road, New Milton
BH25 6QS
☎ Highcliffe (01425) 275341
Fax (01425) 272310

House of Georgian origin with unobtrusive additions and high standard of interior decoration. Set in 70 acres of parkland.
Bedrooms: 53 double
Suites available
Bathrooms: 53 en-suite
Bed & breakfast

per night:	£min	£max
Single	209.50	409.50
Double	224.00	424.00

Half board per

person:	£min	£max
Daily	152.50	240.00
Weekly	938.00	1477.00

Lunch available
Evening meal 1930 (last orders 2130)
Parking for 125
Cards accepted: Access, Visa, Diners, Amex, Switch/Delta

NEWBURY

Berkshire
Map ref 2C2

Ancient town surrounded by the Downs and on the Kennet and Avon Canal. It has many buildings of interest, including the 17th C Cloth Hall, which is now a museum. The famous racecourse is nearby.
Tourist Information Centre ☎ (01635) 30267

Foley Lodge Hotel
COMMENDED

Stockcross, Newbury RG20 8JU
☎ (01635) 528770
Fax (01635) 528398
Elegant country house hotel in tranquil setting. Indoor pool, golf, croquet. Award-winning restaurant plus brasserie. Central location for touring southern England.
Bedrooms: 12 single, 42 double, 14 twin
Suites available
Bathrooms: 68 en-suite
Bed & breakfast

per night:	£min	£max
Single	55.00	95.00
Double	80.00	110.00

Lunch available
Evening meal 1900 (last orders 2130)
Parking for 140
Cards accepted: Access, Visa, Diners, Amex, Switch/Delta

Regency Park Hotel
HIGHLY COMMENDED

Bowling Green Road, Thatcham, Newbury RG18 3RP
☎ (01635) 871555
Fax (01635) 871571
Standing in 5 acres of Berkshire countryside, 7 minutes from junction 13 of M4. Renowned restaurant and bar. Ideal weekend retreat. Weekend breaks from £54 per person per night.
Bedrooms: 19 single, 15 double, 14 twin, 1 triple
Suite available
Bathrooms: 49 en-suite
Bed & breakfast

per night:	£min	£max
Single	94.50	102.00
Double	113.00	124.00

Half board per

person:	£min	£max
Daily	113.50	121.50

Lunch available
Evening meal 1830 (last orders 2230)
Parking for 125
Cards accepted: Access, Visa, Diners, Amex, Switch/Delta

The symbol CR and a group name following an hotel address indicates that bookings can be made through a central reservations office. These offices are listed in the information pages at the back of this guide.

OXFORD

Oxfordshire
Map ref 2C1

Beautiful university town with many ancient colleges, some dating from the 13th C, and numerous buildings of historic and architectural interest. The Ashmolean Museum has outstanding collections. Lovely gardens and meadows with punting on the Cherwell.
Tourist Information Centre ☎ (01865) 726871

Acorn Guest House
Listed

260 Iffley Road, Oxford OX4 1SE
☎ (01865) 247998
Victorian house situated midway between the city centre and the ring-road. Convenient for all local amenities and more distant attractions.
Bedrooms: 2 single, 1 twin, 3 triple
Bathrooms: 2 public
Bed & breakfast

per night:	£min	£max
Single	20.00	26.00
Double	34.00	40.00

Parking for 5
Cards accepted: Access, Visa, Diners

The Athena Guest House
Listed

253-255 Cowley Road, Oxford OX4 1XQ
☎ (01865) 243124
Fax (01865) 791007
Large, comfortable Victorian guesthouse with colour TV and tea/coffee in all rooms. Close to shops and restaurants. Easy transport to station and city centre. Ideal for small or large groups.
Bedrooms: 3 single, 3 double, 3 twin, 3 triple, 1 family room
Bathrooms: 2 en-suite, 1 private, 3 public, 3 private showers
Bed & breakfast

per night:	£min	£max
Single	20.00	22.00
Double	38.00	42.00

Parking for 7

The Balkan Lodge

315 Iffley Road, Oxford OX4 4AG
☎ (01865) 244524
Delightful small hotel, recently refurbished. En-suite rooms with colour TV, hairdryer, tea/coffee facilities. Good standard of accommodation. Car park at rear.
Bedrooms: 1 single, 4 double, 3 twin
Bathrooms: 8 en-suite, 1 public

SOUTH OF ENGLAND

Bed & breakfast per night:	£min	£max
Single	35.00	40.00
Double	45.00	55.00

Parking for 8
Cards accepted: Access, Visa

Bravalla Guest House
Listed

242 Iffley Road, Oxford OX4 1SE
☎ (01865) 241326 & 250511
Fax (01865) 790096
A small family-run guesthouse within half a mile of Magdalen College with its famous deer park. 1 mile from city centre.
Bedrooms: 2 double, 2 twin, 1 triple, 1 family room
Bathrooms: 5 en-suite, 2 public, 1 private shower

Bed & breakfast per night:	£min	£max
Single	25.00	35.00
Double	36.00	45.00

Parking for 4
Cards accepted: Access, Visa, Diners

Brown's Guest House
Listed

281 Iffley Road, Oxford OX4 4AQ
☎ (01865) 246822
Fax (01865) 246822
Family guesthouse off the centre of Oxford. Clean, comfortable accommodation, some rooms en-suite.
Bedrooms: 2 single, 2 double, 3 triple, 2 family rooms
Bathrooms: 2 en-suite, 3 public

Bed & breakfast per night:	£min	£max
Single	22.00	25.00
Double	36.00	50.00

Parking for 3
Cards accepted: Access, Visa, Diners

The Coach & Horses

Stadhampton Road, Chislehampton, Oxford OX44 7UX
☎ Stadhampton (01865) 890255
Fax (01865) 891995
Picturesque 16th C listed coaching inn with beamed restaurant. Rooms with views of the countryside surround a landscaped and cobbled courtyard. One room has been thoughtfully designed for disabled guests. South-east of Oxford.
Bedrooms: 6 double, 2 twin, 1 triple
Bathrooms: 9 en-suite

Bed & breakfast per night:	£min	£max
Single	45.00	45.00
Double	50.00	55.00

Lunch available
Evening meal 1900 (last orders 2200)
Parking for 40
Cards accepted: Access, Visa, Diners, Amex

College Guest House

103-105 Woodstock Road, Oxford OX2 6HL
☎ (01865) 552579
Fax (01865) 311244
Early Victorian residence, north of the city in residential area. Within walking distance of colleges, restaurants and shops. Children welcome.
Bedrooms: 4 single, 4 double, 4 twin
Bathrooms: 2 en-suite, 2 private, 2 public

Bed & breakfast per night:	£min	£max
Single	20.00	30.00
Double	35.00	50.00

Half board per person:	£min	£max
Daily	20.00	30.00

Parking for 10
Cards accepted: Access, Visa, Amex, Switch/Delta

Combermere House
Listed

11 Polstead Road, Oxford OX2 6TW
☎ (01865) 556971
Fax (01865) 556971
Family-run Victorian house in quiet tree-lined road in residential north Oxford, 1 mile from city centre and colleges.
Bedrooms: 4 single, 1 double, 3 triple, 1 family room
Bathrooms: 9 en-suite

Bed & breakfast per night:	£min	£max
Single	23.00	35.00
Double	38.00	55.00

Parking for 3
Cards accepted: Access, Visa, Diners, Amex

Please check prices and other details at the time of booking.

Conifer Lodge

159 Eynsham Road, Botley, Oxford OX2 9NE
☎ (01865) 862280
House on the outskirts of Oxford city, overlooking farmland and offering a warm, friendly welcome.
Bedrooms: 1 single, 1 double, 1 twin, 1 triple
Bathrooms: 4 en-suite

Bed & breakfast per night:	£min	£max
Single	20.00	25.00
Double	40.00	46.00

Parking for 8

Cotswold House
HIGHLY COMMENDED

363 Banbury Road, Oxford OX2 7PL
☎ (01865) 310558
Fax (01865) 310558
Well-situated elegant property offering a high standard of furnishings and facilities in each of its rooms.
Bedrooms: 2 single, 2 double, 1 twin, 2 triple
Bathrooms: 7 en-suite

Bed & breakfast per night:	£min	£max
Single	37.00	39.00
Double	54.00	57.00

Parking for 7

Cotswold Lodge Hotel
COMMENDED

66A Banbury Road, Oxford OX2 6JP
☎ (01865) 512121
Fax (01865) 512490
The Independents
Splendid Victorian building set well back from the main road, in quiet conservation area half a mile from city centre. Interior tastefully modernised.
Bedrooms: 17 single, 13 double, 18 twin, 2 triple
Bathrooms: 50 en-suite

Bed & breakfast per night:	£min	£max
Single	65.00	85.00
Double	90.00	105.00

Half board per person:	£min	£max
Daily	82.50	102.50

Lunch available
Evening meal 1830 (last orders 2230)
Parking for 60
Cards accepted: Access, Visa, Diners, Amex

501

SOUTH OF ENGLAND

OXFORD
Continued

Falcon Private Hotel
COMMENDED
88-90 Abingdon Road, Oxford
OX1 4PX
☎ (01865) 722995
Fax (01865) 246642
Victorian building with modern facilities, overlooking Queens College playing fields. 10 minutes' walk to colleges and city centre.
Bedrooms: 2 single, 3 double, 2 twin, 2 triple, 2 family rooms
Bathrooms: 11 en-suite, 1 public
Bed & breakfast
per night:	£min	£max
Single		29.00
Double		49.00

Evening meal 1800 (last orders 1830)
Parking for 8
Cards accepted: Access, Visa, Amex, Switch/Delta

Isis Guest House
Listed APPROVED
45-53 Iffley Road, Oxford OX4 1ED
☎ (01865) 248894 & 242466
Fax (01865) 243492
Modernised, Victorian, city centre guesthouse within walking distance of colleges and shops. Easy access to ring road.
Bedrooms: 12 single, 6 double, 17 twin, 2 triple
Bathrooms: 14 private, 10 public
Bed & breakfast
per night	£min	£max
Single	20.00	25.00
Double	40.00	44.00

Parking for 18
Open June–September
Cards accepted: Access, Visa

Lakeside Guest House
118 Abingdon Road, Oxford
OX1 4PZ
☎ (01865) 244725
Fax (01865) 244725
Victorian house adjacent to river, overlooking meadows and park. Within walking distance of city centre and colleges. Warm and friendly atmosphere.
Bedrooms: 2 double, 1 twin, 1 triple, 2 family rooms
Bathrooms: 3 en-suite, 2 public

Bed & breakfast
per night	£min	£max
Single	30.00	40.00
Double	40.00	50.00

Parking for 4

Marlborough House Hotel
Listed HIGHLY COMMENDED
321 Woodstock Road, Oxford
OX2 7NY
☎ (01865) 311321
Fax (01865) 515329

1.5 miles from Oxford city centre. All rooms en-suite with telephone, TV, fridge, desk, armchair, tea/coffee facilities. Continental breakfast. Parking.
Bedrooms: 2 single, 4 double, 4 twin, 2 triple
Bathrooms: 12 en-suite, 1 public
Bed & breakfast
per night	£min	£max
Single	58.00	58.00
Double	68.00	68.00

Parking for 6
Cards accepted: Access, Visa, Amex, Switch/Delta

Milka's Guest House
COMMENDED
379 Iffley Road, Oxford OX4 4DP
☎ (01865) 778458
Fax (01865) 776477
Pleasant semi-detached house on main road, 1 mile from city centre.
Bedrooms: 2 double, 1 twin
Bathrooms: 1 en-suite, 1 public
Bed & breakfast
per night	£min	£max
Single	25.00	35.00
Double	45.00	55.00

Parking for 3

Mount Pleasant
APPROVED
76 London Road, Headington, Oxford OX3 9AJ
☎ (01865) 62749 changing to 762749
Fax (01865) 62749 changing to 762749
Small, family-run hotel offering full facilities. On the A40 and convenient for Oxford shopping, hospitals, colleges, visiting the Chilterns and the Cotswolds.
Bedrooms: 2 double, 5 twin, 1 triple
Bathrooms: 8 en-suite
Bed & breakfast
per night	£min	£max
Single	37.50	45.00
Double	48.00	65.00

Half board per
person:	£min	£max
Daily	52.50	60.00

Lunch available
Evening meal 1800 (last orders 2130)
Parking for 6
Cards accepted: Access, Visa, Diners, Amex

Newton House
82-84 Abingdon Road, Oxford
OX1 4PL
☎ (01865) 240561 & Mobile (0585) 485656
Fax (01865) 244647
Centrally located, Victorian townhouse with comfortable homely accommodation, warm welcome and friendly atmosphere. Special diets catered for on request.
Bedrooms: 7 double, 4 twin, 2 family rooms
Bathrooms: 5 private, 3 public
Bed & breakfast
per night	£min	£max
Single	22.00	38.00
Double	34.00	48.00

Parking for 8
Cards accepted: Access, Visa, Amex, Switch/Delta

The Old Black Horse Hotel
COMMENDED
102 St Clements, Oxford OX4 1AR
☎ (01865) 244691
Fax (01865) 242771
Former coaching inn with private car park, close to Magdalen Bridge, colleges, riverside walks and city centre. Easy access M40 north and south.
Bedrooms: 1 single, 4 double, 3 twin, 2 triple
Bathrooms: 10 en-suite, 1 public
Bed & breakfast
per night	£min	£max
Single	50.00	65.00
Double	75.00	85.00

Please mention this guide when making your booking.

SOUTH OF ENGLAND

Lunch available
Evening meal 1900 (last orders 2100)
Parking for 25
Cards accepted: Access, Visa, Amex

The Old Parsonage Hotel
HIGHLY COMMENDED

1 Banbury Road, Oxford OX2 6NN
☎ (01865) 310210
Fax (01865) 311262
Independently owned hotel in the centre of the city. 17th C building with an informal restaurant, open from 7am until late.
Bedrooms: 1 single, 19 double, 6 twin, 4 triple
Bathrooms: 30 en-suite
Bed & breakfast

per night:	£min	£max
Single	115.00	120.00
Double	150.00	155.00

Lunch available
Evening meal 1800 (last orders 2300)
Parking for 15
Cards accepted: Access, Visa, Diners, Amex, Switch/Delta

Pine Castle Hotel
HIGHLY COMMENDED

290 Iffley Road, Oxford OX4 4AE
☎ (01865) 241497 & 728287
Fax (01865) 727230
Characterful Edwardian guesthouse close to city centre and picturesque River Thames. A warm welcome awaits you from the resident proprietor.
Bedrooms: 5 double, 2 twin, 1 family room
Bathrooms: 8 en-suite
Bed & breakfast

per night:	£min	£max
Double	50.00	60.00

Half board per

person:	£min	£max
Daily	33.00	

Evening meal 1800 (last orders 1900)
Parking for 4
Cards accepted: Access, Visa

River Hotel

17 Botley Road, Oxford OX2 0AA
☎ (01865) 243475
Fax (01865) 724206
Dine overlooking the Thames in this riverside hotel. Residents' bar. Within walking distance of city and colleges. Ample parking. Ideal for tourists and business travellers.

Bedrooms: 8 single, 9 double, 1 twin, 3 triple, 1 family room
Bathrooms: 18 en-suite, 2 private, 2 private showers
Bed & breakfast

per night:	£min	£max
Single	39.00	57.00
Double	64.00	70.00

Half board per

person:	£min	£max
Daily	42.00	67.00

Evening meal 1830 (last orders 2000)
Parking for 25
Cards accepted: Access, Visa

Sportsview Guest House

106-110 Abingdon Road, Oxford OX1 4PX
☎ (01865) 244268
Fax (01865) 244268
Guesthouse with garden, located near the city centre. Views over tennis and cricket grounds and the River Thames.
Bedrooms: 6 single, 8 double, 5 twin, 1 triple
Bathrooms: 8 private, 4 public
Bed & breakfast

per night:	£min	£max
Single	22.00	30.00
Double	34.00	48.00

Parking for 8
Cards accepted: Access, Visa, Amex, Switch/Delta

Studley Priory Hotel
HIGHLY COMMENDED

Horton cum Studley, Oxford OX33 1AZ
☎ Stanton St John (01865) 351203 & 351254
Fax (01865) 351613
Thames Valley
Converted Elizabethan manor house in a rural setting north east of Oxford, with a restaurant that specialises in English cooking.
Bedrooms: 6 single, 8 double, 5 twin
Suite available
Bathrooms: 19 en-suite
Bed & breakfast

per night:	£min	£max
Single	100.00	125.00
Double	115.00	200.00

Lunch available
Evening meal 1930 (last orders 2130)
Parking for 101
Cards accepted: Access, Visa, Diners, Amex, Switch/Delta

Victoria Hotel

180 Abingdon Road, Oxford OX1 4RA
☎ (01865) 724536
Fax (01865) 794909
En-suite rooms with direct-dial telephone, colour TV, radio, hairdryer, tea/coffee facilities. Walking distance to city centre. Competitive prices. Car park at rear.
Bedrooms: 7 single, 8 double, 1 twin, 1 triple, 1 family room
Bathrooms: 18 en-suite, 2 public
Bed & breakfast

per night:	£min	£max
Single	37.50	55.50
Double	58.50	72.50

Lunch available
Evening meal 1900 (last orders 2100)
Parking for 20
Cards accepted: Access, Visa

Walton Guest House
Listed

169 Walton Street, Oxford OX1 2HD
☎ (01865) 552137
In city centre, with bus and rail stations and university area within walking distance. Colour TV and tea/coffee facilities in all rooms.
Bedrooms: 1 single, 2 double, 3 twin, 1 triple
Bathrooms: 2 public
Bed & breakfast

per night:	£min	£max
Single	20.00	22.00
Double	38.00	40.00

Westwood Country Hotel
COMMENDED

Hinksey Hill Top, Oxford OX1 5BG
☎ (01865) 735408
Fax (01865) 736536
Minotel/Logis of Great Britain

In 4 acres of woodland and wildlife gardens, opened by David Bellamy. Winner of award for facilities for disabled people. High standard of cuisine. Oxford city centre 3.5 miles.
Wheelchair access category 1
Bedrooms: 7 single, 8 double, 4 twin, 1 triple

Continued ▶

SOUTH OF ENGLAND

OXFORD
Continued

Bathrooms: 20 en-suite, 1 public

Bed & breakfast per night:	£min	£max
Single	55.00	65.00
Double	80.00	90.00

Half board per person:	£min	£max
Daily	56.00	
Weekly	266.00	

Lunch available
Evening meal 1900 (last orders 2030)
Parking for 50
Cards accepted: Access, Visa, Diners, Amex, Switch/Delta

Willow Reaches Private Hotel

APPROVED

1 Wytham Street, Oxford OX1 4SU
☎ (01865) 721545
Fax (01865) 251139
Comfortable, small hotel in a quiet location, 20 minutes' walk from the city centre. English and Indian cuisine with pre-bookings.
Bedrooms: 4 single, 2 double, 2 twin, 1 triple
Bathrooms: 9 en-suite, 1 public

Bed & breakfast per night:	£min	£max
Single	33.00	36.00
Double	45.00	49.00

Half board per person:	£min	£max
Daily	40.00	51.00
Weekly	280.00	300.00

Evening meal 1900 (last orders 2100)
Parking for 9
Cards accepted: Access, Visa, Diners, Amex

WELCOME HOST

This is a nationally recognised customer care programme which aims to promote the highest standards of service and a warm welcome. Establishments who are taking part in this initiative are indicated by the symbol.

PANGBOURNE

Berkshire
Map ref 2C2

A pretty stretch of river where the Pang joins the Thames with views of the lock, weir and toll bridge. Once the home of Kenneth Grahame, author of "Wind in the Willows".

The Copper Inn Hotel & Restaurant

HIGHLY COMMENDED

Church Road, Pangbourne, Reading RG8 7AR
☎ Reading (0118) 9842244
Fax (0118) 9845542
Thames Valley

Elegantly restored Georgian coaching inn with a restaurant overlooking secluded gardens. Good base for exploring the beautiful Thames Valley and all its attractions. Special weekend rates.
Bedrooms: 2 single, 14 double, 5 twin, 1 triple
Bathrooms: 22 en-suite

Bed & breakfast per night:	£min	£max
Single	85.00	90.00
Double	105.00	115.00

Half board per person:	£min	£max
Daily	100.00	105.00

Lunch available
Evening meal 1900 (last orders 2200)
Parking for 20
Cards accepted: Access, Visa, Diners, Amex, Switch/Delta

A key to symbols can be found inside the back cover flap.

Half board prices are given per person, but in some cases these may be based on double/twin occupancy.

POOLE

Dorset
Map ref 2B3

Tremendous natural harbour makes Poole a superb boating centre. The harbour area is crowded with historic buildings including the 15th C Town Cellars housing a maritime museum.
Tourist Information Centre ☎ *(01202) 673322*

The Golden Sovereigns Hotel

97 Alumhurst Road, Alum Chine, Bournemouth BH4 8HR
☎ Bournemouth (01202) 762088
Attractively decorated Victorian character hotel. Quiet, convenient location; beach 4 minutes' walk. Comfortable rooms, traditional home-cooking. Early booking special discounts.
Bedrooms: 1 single, 2 double, 1 twin, 2 triple, 2 family rooms
Bathrooms: 5 en-suite, 1 private, 2 public

Bed & breakfast per night:	£min	£max
Single	15.00	30.00
Double	30.00	50.00

Half board per person:	£min	£max
Daily	22.50	32.50
Weekly	140.00	200.00

Lunch available
Evening meal 1800 (last orders 1600)
Parking for 9
Cards accepted: Access, Visa

Harmony Hotel

APPROVED

19 St Peter's Road, Parkstone, Poole BH14 0NZ
☎ Parkstone (01202) 747510
Fax (01202) 747510
Friendly service in peaceful, residential area close to all local amenities. Ideally placed as a touring centre.
Bedrooms: 4 double, 4 twin, 3 triple
Bathrooms: 8 en-suite, 1 public, 1 private shower

Bed & breakfast per night:	£min	£max
Single	21.00	27.00
Double	36.00	44.00

Half board per person:	£min	£max
Daily	27.00	38.00
Weekly	150.00	220.00

Lunch available
Evening meal 1900 (last orders 1945)
Parking for 14
Cards accepted: Access, Visa

Heathwood Guest House
COMMENDED

266 Wimborne Road, Oakdale, Poole BH15 3EF
☎ (01202) 679176 & 679746
Fax (01202) 679176
Family-run, friendly atmosphere, satellite channels and TV in all rooms. Large breakfasts and evening meals. Close to Tower Park and Poole.
Bedrooms: 2 single, 3 double, 1 twin, 2 family rooms
Bathrooms: 8 en-suite, 1 public

Bed & breakfast per night:	£min	£max
Single	22.00	22.00
Double	36.00	40.00

Half board per person:	£min	£max
Daily	25.00	29.00

Parking for 10
Cards accepted: Access, Visa

Little Haven Guest House
Listed COMMENDED

126 Sandbanks Road, Parkstone, Poole BH14 8DA
☎ Bournemouth (01202) 746944
Comfortable, homely accommodation, near all amenities. Tea/coffee, colour TV and hot and cold in all rooms, TV lounge, parking. Non-smokers only, please.
Bedrooms: 1 double, 2 twin, 1 triple
Bathrooms: 2 public

Bed & breakfast per night:	£min	£max
Single	14.00	25.00
Double	28.00	38.00

Parking for 6

The Rosemount Hotel
COMMENDED

167 Bournemouth Road, Lower Parkstone, Poole BH14 9HT
☎ Bournemouth (01202) 732138
Small, family-run hotel on main road between Poole and Bournemouth, offering varied food, cleanliness and friendly service. Colour TV in all rooms, some en-suite.
Bedrooms: 1 single, 3 double, 2 twin, 1 triple
Bathrooms: 2 en-suite, 2 public, 1 private shower

Bed & breakfast per night:	£min	£max
Single	16.00	18.00
Double	32.00	34.00

Parking for 6
Cards accepted: Access, Visa

PORTSMOUTH & SOUTHSEA
Hampshire
Map ref 2C3

The first dock was built in 1194. HMS Victory, Nelson's flagship, is here and Charles Dickens' former home is open to the public. Neighbouring Southsea has a promenade with magnificent views of Spithead.
Tourist Information Centre ☎ *(01705) 838635 or 826722*

April House
APPROVED

7 Malvern Road, Southsea, Hampshire PO5 2LZ
☎ Portsmouth (01705) 814824 & Mobile (0585) 931720
Clean, comfortable guesthouse, close to Rock Gardens, Pyramid centre, beach and all facilities. All rooms have colour TV and electric kettle.
Bedrooms: 2 single, 3 double, 2 triple, 2 family rooms
Bathrooms: 2 public, 1 private shower

Bed & breakfast per night:	£min	£max
Single	13.00	15.00
Double	26.00	30.00

Parking for 4

Beaufort Hotel
HIGHLY COMMENDED

71 Festing Road, Southsea, Portsmouth, Hampshire PO4 0NQ
☎ Portsmouth (01705) 823707 & Freephone Reservations (0808) 919237
Fax (01705) 870270
Logis of Great Britain
Hotel with en-suite bedrooms standing in its own grounds, 1 minute's walk from seafront. Car park.
Bedrooms: 3 single, 11 double, 2 twin, 2 triple, 1 family room
Bathrooms: 19 en-suite

Bed & breakfast per night:	£min	£max
Single	32.00	48.00
Double	46.00	68.00

Half board per person:	£min	£max
Daily	30.00	38.00
Weekly	185.00	260.00

Lunch available
Evening meal 1830 (last orders 2030)
Parking for 10
Cards accepted: Access, Visa, Amex, Switch/Delta

Bembell Court Hotel

69 Festing Road, Southsea, Portsmouth, Hampshire PO4 0NQ
☎ Portsmouth (01705) 735915 & 750497
Friendly, family-run, licensed hotel, ideally situated in Southsea's prime holiday area, with an excellent selection of shops, pubs and restaurants nearby.
Bedrooms: 2 single, 4 double, 4 twin, 3 triple, 1 family room
Bathrooms: 8 en-suite, 3 public

Bed & breakfast per night:	£min	£max
Single	25.00	34.00
Double	39.00	45.00

Half board per person:	£min	£max
Daily	35.00	44.00
Weekly	210.00	295.00

Evening meal 1800 (last orders 1900)
Parking for 12
Cards accepted: Access, Visa, Diners, Amex, Switch/Delta

The Dolphins Hotel & Snobbs Cocktail Bar & Restaurant

10-11 Western Parade, Southsea, Hampshire PO5 3JF
☎ Portsmouth (01705) 823823 & 820833
Fax (01705) 820833
On the seafront, overlooking the common. Attractive bar and restaurant. Near Mary Rose, HMS Victory, HMS Warrior, ferry terminals, shopping centres, museums, sport and entertainment.
Bedrooms: 10 single, 6 double, 13 twin, 4 triple
Bathrooms: 20 en-suite, 2 private, 5 public

Bed & breakfast per night:	£min	£max
Single	22.00	33.00
Double	36.00	45.00

Continued ▶

SOUTH OF ENGLAND

PORTSMOUTH & SOUTHSEA
Continued

The Elms Guest House

48 Victoria Road South, Southsea, Hampshire PO5 2BT
☎ Portsmouth (01705) 823924
Fax (01705) 823917
Small, family-run guesthouse, close to ferry port and local attractions. Family rooms available.
Bedrooms: 1 single, 4 triple, 1 family room
Bathrooms: 2 en-suite, 1 public

Bed & breakfast per night:	£min	£max
Single	18.00	21.00
Double	36.00	42.00

Parking for 2

Half board per person:
	£min	£max
Weekly	200.00	250.00

Evening meal 1930 (last orders 2145)
Cards accepted: Access, Visa, Diners, Amex

Forte Posthouse Portsmouth
COMMENDED

Pembroke Road, Portsmouth, Hampshire PO1 2TA
☎ Portsmouth (01705) 827651
Fax (01705) 756715
Forte
Completely refurbished to include full leisure facilities. In a central position overlooking the seafront at Southsea. Business services available.
Bedrooms: 79 double, 75 twin, 9 family rooms
Bathrooms: 163 en-suite

Bed & breakfast per night:	£min	£max
Single	67.95	77.95
Double	76.20	86.30

Half board per person:	£min	£max
Daily	46.00	54.00

Lunch available
Evening meal 1730 (last orders 2230)
Parking for 70
Cards accepted: Access, Visa, Diners, Amex, Switch/Delta

Ocean Hotel & Apartments

8-10 St Helens Parade, Southsea, Hampshire PO4 0RW
☎ Portsmouth (01705) 734233
Fax (01705) 297046
Imposing building in foremost seafront position between South Parade Pier and Canoe Lake with magnificent sea views. Choice of hotel rooms, suites, or self-contained apartments. Car park.
Bedrooms: 1 single, 4 double, 4 triple, 7 family rooms
Suites available
Bathrooms: 15 en-suite, 4 public

Bed & breakfast per night:	£min	£max
Single	20.00	35.00
Double	35.00	50.00

Half board per person:	£min	£max
Daily	30.00	45.00
Weekly	210.00	320.00

Evening meal 1830 (last orders 2130)
Parking for 37
Cards accepted: Access, Visa

Sally Port Inn
COMMENDED

57-58 High Street, Portsmouth, Hampshire PO1 2LU
☎ Portsmouth (01705) 821860
Fax (01705) 821293

16th C timber-framed inn, with a charming atmosphere of bygone days. Situated opposite the cathedral in the heart of the "old" city. Nearby are museums, promenades and historic ships.
Bedrooms: 4 single, 3 double, 2 twin, 1 triple
Bathrooms: 2 public, 7 private showers

Bed & breakfast per night:	£min	£max
Single	32.00	39.00
Double	49.00	59.00

Lunch available
Evening meal 1900 (last orders 2200)
Cards accepted: Access, Visa, Diners, Amex, Switch/Delta

The Sandringham Hotel
COMMENDED

Osborne Road/Clarence Parade, Southsea, Hampshire PO5 3LR
☎ Portsmouth (01705) 826969 & 822914
Fax (01705) 822330
Seafront hotel with sea views from most bedrooms. Recently refurbished to the highest standards. 100-seat restaurant, function/conference room, large ballroom. Free car park opposite. Two minutes' walk to Southsea shopping centre.
Bedrooms: 7 single, 14 double, 10 twin, 7 triple, 4 family rooms
Bathrooms: 42 en-suite, 2 public

Bed & breakfast per night:	£min	£max
Single	34.00	
Double	48.00	

Half board per person:	£min	£max
Daily	34.00	
Weekly	195.00	

Lunch available
Evening meal 1900 (last orders 2130)
Parking for 5
Cards accepted: Access, Visa, Diners, Amex

Solent Hotel

14-17 South Parade, Southsea, Hampshire PO5 2JB
☎ Portsmouth (01705) 875566
Fax (01705) 872023
Recently refurbished hotel occupying a prime position on the seafront, with magnificent views of the Solent and Isle of Wight. Lift to all floors. Restaurant and games rooms.
Bedrooms: 9 single, 21 double, 9 twin, 6 triple, 4 family rooms
Bathrooms: 48 en-suite, 4 public, 1 private shower

Bed & breakfast per night:	£min	£max
Single	33.50	45.00
Double	45.00	65.00

Half board per person:	£min	£max
Daily	45.00	56.50
Weekly	207.50	265.00

Lunch available
Evening meal 1900 (last orders 2100)
Parking for 6
Cards accepted: Access, Visa, Diners, Amex

SOUTH OF ENGLAND

Westfield Hall Hotel
HIGHLY COMMENDED

65 Festing Road, Southsea,
Hampshire PO4 0NQ
☎ Portsmouth (01705) 826971
Fax (01705) 870200
Logis of Great Britain
Small, exclusive hotel in own grounds, with large car park, 3 minutes from Southsea's seafront, promenade and canoe lake.
Bedrooms: 2 single, 7 double, 4 twin, 4 triple, 3 family rooms
Bathrooms: 20 en-suite

Bed & breakfast per night:	£min	£max
Single	38.00	40.00
Double	48.00	60.00

Half board per person:	£min	£max
Daily	48.00	50.00
Weekly	228.00	248.00

Evening meal 1830 (last orders 2030)
Parking for 18
Cards accepted: Access, Visa, Diners, Amex, Switch/Delta

READING
Berkshire
Map ref 2C2

Busy, modern county town with large shopping centre and many leisure and recreation facilities. There are several interesting museums and the Duke of Wellington's Stratfield Saye is nearby.
Tourist Information Centre ☎ *(0118) 956 6226*

Abbey House Private Hotel
COMMENDED

118 Connaught Road, Reading RG30 2UF
☎ (0118) 959 0549
Fax (0118) 956 9299
Minotel
Hotel run by the proprietors and situated close to the town centre.
Bedrooms: 6 single, 5 double, 9 twin
Bathrooms: 17 en-suite, 2 public, 1 private shower

Bed & breakfast per night:	£min	£max
Single	29.00	47.50
Double	44.00	62.50

Evening meal 1900 (last orders 2030)
Parking for 14
Cards accepted: Access, Visa, Diners, Amex

Crescent Hotel

35 Coley Avenue, Reading RG1 6LL
☎ (0118) 950 7980
Friendly, licensed hotel in the centre of Reading, close to all amenities. TV and tea-making facilities in all rooms. Large car park.
Bedrooms: 5 single, 4 double, 7 twin
Bathrooms: 5 public, 2 private showers

Bed & breakfast per night:	£min	£max
Single	20.00	25.00
Double	38.00	45.00

Evening meal 1800 (last orders 2100)
Parking for 16
Cards accepted: Access, Visa, Amex

Dittisham Guest House
Listed COMMENDED

63 Tilehurst Road, Reading RG3 2JL
☎ (0118) 956 9483 & Mobile (0589) 605193
Renovated Edwardian property with garden, in a quiet but central location. Good value and quality. On bus routes for centre of town.
Bedrooms: 4 single, 1 twin
Bathrooms: 3 en-suite, 1 public

Bed & breakfast per night:	£min	£max
Single	21.00	28.50
Double	33.50	45.00

Parking for 7
Cards accepted: Access, Visa

The Great House at Sonning
COMMENDED

Thames Street, Sonning-on-Thames, Reading RG4 6UT
☎ (0118) 969 2277
Fax (0118) 944 1296
Thames Valley

Riverside hotel, dating from 16th C, in 4-acre estate. Moorings Restaurant and Hideaway Bistro. Riverside terrace dining in summer. Beautiful, traditional bedrooms.
Bedrooms: 3 single, 24 double, 9 twin, 2 triple
Bathrooms: 38 en-suite

Bed & breakfast per night:	£min	£max
Single	49.50	99.50
Double	79.50	129.50

Half board per person:	£min	£max
Daily	64.50	114.50
Weekly	651.50	651.50

Lunch available
Evening meal 1900 (last orders 2215)
Parking for 100
Cards accepted: Access, Visa, Diners, Amex, Switch/Delta

Kirtons Hotel & Country Club
HIGHLY COMMENDED

Pingewood, Reading RG30 3UN
☎ (0118) 950 0885
Fax (0118) 939 1996

Unrivalled combination of spacious lakeside bedrooms with private balconies, choice of restaurants and extensive leisure facilities, including water-skiing, tennis and squash. Call for details.
Bedrooms: 57 double, 24 twin
Suites available
Bathrooms: 81 en-suite

Bed & breakfast per night:	£min	£max
Single	42.50	90.00
Double	85.00	130.00

Half board per person:	£min	£max
Daily	55.00	110.00

Lunch available
Evening meal 1900 (last orders 2130)
Parking for 250
Cards accepted: Access, Visa, Diners, Amex, Switch/Delta

SOUTH OF ENGLAND

READING
Continued

Rainbow Corner Hotel
COMMENDED

132-138 Caversham Road, Reading
RG1 8AY
☎ (0118) 958 8140
Fax (0118) 958 6500
Victorian hotel. All rooms fully en-suite, bar and restaurant. 15 minutes from station, town centre and River Thames. Car parking facilities at rear.
Bedrooms: 6 single, 12 double, 3 twin, 1 triple
Bathrooms: 22 en-suite

Bed & breakfast
per night:	£min	£max
Single	38.00	59.95
Double	46.00	70.90

Half board per
person:	£min	£max
Daily	50.00	80.00
Weekly	350.00	560.00

Lunch available
Evening meal 1900 (last orders 2130)
Parking for 21
Cards accepted: Access, Visa, Diners, Amex, Switch/Delta

The Ship Hotel
COMMENDED

4-8 Duke Street, Reading RG1 4RY
☎ (0118) 958 3455
Fax (0118) 950 4450
Best Western
Town centre location, with easy access to M4, A4, M40. Few minutes' walk from rail station. Own free parking.
Bedrooms: 10 single, 16 double, 4 twin, 1 triple
Suite available
Bathrooms: 31 en-suite

Bed & breakfast
per night:	£min	£max
Single	35.00	81.95
Double	50.00	91.95

Half board per
person:	£min	£max
Daily	50.00	96.95

Lunch available
Evening meal 1900 (last orders 2130)
Parking for 30
Cards accepted: Access, Visa, Diners, Amex, Switch/Delta

Upcross Hotel
COMMENDED

68 Berkeley Avenue, Reading
RG1 6HY
☎ (0118) 959 0796
Fax (0118) 957 6517
Privately-owned country house hotel of character and warmth, featured on BBC TV. Reputed to have one of the best restaurants in Berkshire. Large garden, ample parking. Town centre/railway station 10 minutes. Easy access M4, junctions 11 and 12.
Bedrooms: 7 single, 6 double, 6 twin, 1 triple
Bathrooms: 20 en-suite

Bed & breakfast
per night:	£min	£max
Single	53.00	55.00
Double	59.00	65.00

Half board per
person:	£min	£max
Daily	60.00	65.00

Lunch available
Evening meal 1900 (last orders 2200)
Parking for 40
Cards accepted: Access, Visa, Diners, Amex, Switch/Delta

RINGWOOD
Hampshire
Map ref 2B3

Market town by the River Avon comprising old cottages, many of them thatched. Although just outside the New Forest, there is heath and woodland nearby and it is a good centre for horse-riding and walking.

Moortown Lodge Hotel & Restaurant
HIGHLY COMMENDED

244 Christchurch Road, Ringwood
BH24 3AS
☎ (01425) 471404
Fax (01425) 476052
Logis of Great Britain
Charming Georgian hotel which originally formed part of the Gladstone family estate. Chef/proprietor. Freshly-cooked food. At edge of New Forest, 1 mile from town centre on B3347.
Bedrooms: 1 single, 3 double, 2 twin
Bathrooms: 5 en-suite, 1 private, 1 public

Bed & breakfast
per night:	£min	£max
Single	35.00	42.00
Double	50.00	75.00

Half board per
person:	£min	£max
Daily	52.00	59.00
Weekly	294.00	364.00

Evening meal 1900 (last orders 2030)
Parking for 7
Cards accepted: Access, Visa, Amex

The Struan Hotel
HIGHLY COMMENDED

Horton Road, Ashley Heath, Ringwood BH24 2EG
☎ (01425) 473553
Fax (01425) 480529
Country inn with a la carte restaurant, on the edge of the New Forest not far from the historic market town of Ringwood. Convenient for Bournemouth.
Bedrooms: 2 single, 6 double, 2 twin
Bathrooms: 10 en-suite

Bed & breakfast
per night:	£min	£max
Single	40.00	50.00
Double	50.00	70.00

Half board per
person:	£min	£max
Daily	50.00	60.00
Weekly	230.00	275.00

Lunch available
Evening meal 1900 (last orders 2200)
Parking for 75
Cards accepted: Access, Visa, Diners, Amex, Switch/Delta

ROMSEY
Hampshire
Map ref 2C3

Town grew up around the important abbey and lies on the banks of the River Test, famous for trout and salmon. Broadlands House, home of the late Lord Mountbatten, is open to the public.
Tourist Information Centre ☎ (01794) 512987

Country Accommodation
COMMENDED

The Old Post Office, New Road, Michelmersh, Romsey SO51 0NL
☎ (01794) 368739 & Mobile 0374 734478

Map references apply to the colour maps at the back of this guide.

SOUTH OF ENGLAND

Character rooms in ground floor independent annexe. Quiet village, 3 miles from Romsey. All en-suite, tea/coffee, TV. Good local pubs and restaurants.
Bedrooms: 2 double, 1 twin
Bathrooms: 3 en-suite

Bed & breakfast per night:	£min	£max
Single	25.00	25.00
Double	40.00	40.00

Parking for 10
Cards accepted: Access, Visa

Highfield House
HIGHLY COMMENDED

Newtown Road, Awbridge, Romsey SO51 0GG
☎ (01794) 340727
Fax (01794) 341450

In unspoilt rural village, overlooking golf-course. Delightful setting and charming gardens. Home cooking a speciality. Close to Mottisfont Abbey National Trust and Hillier Arboretum.
Bedrooms: 1 double, 2 twin
Bathrooms: 3 en-suite, 1 public

Bed & breakfast per night:	£min	£max
Double	40.00	45.00

Evening meal from 1900
Parking for 10

Kintail
COMMENDED

Salisbury Road, Shootash, Romsey SO51 6GA
☎ (01794) 513849
Modern bungalow in rural surrounds on edge of New Forest. Within easy distance of Winchester, Salisbury, Stonehenge, Hilliers Arboretum and M27.
Bedrooms: 1 double, 1 twin
Bathrooms: 1 en-suite, 1 private

Bed & breakfast per night:	£min	£max
Double	32.00	34.00

Parking for 6
Open February–November

Potters Heron Hotel
HIGHLY COMMENDED

Ampfield, Romsey SO51 9ZF
☎ Southampton (01703) 266611
Fax (01703) 251359
Whitbread
Thatched building in rural surroundings. Recently completely refurbished. Well placed for Winchester, New Forest and Test Valley.
Bedrooms: 31 double, 23 twin
Bathrooms: 54 en-suite

Bed & breakfast per night:	£min	£max
Single	34.00	82.50
Double	50.00	90.00

Half board per person:	£min	£max
Daily	40.00	100.00
Weekly	280.00	700.00

Lunch available
Evening meal 1900 (last orders 2200)
Parking for 200
Cards accepted: Access, Visa, Diners, Amex

Wessex Guest House
Listed

5 Palmerston Street, Romsey SO51 8GF
☎ (01794) 512038
200 yards from Broadlands Park, home of the late Lord Mountbatten, which is open to the public.
Bedrooms: 1 single, 4 double, 1 twin, 1 triple, 1 family room
Bathrooms: 3 public

Bed & breakfast per night:	£min	£max
Single	18.00	20.00
Double	36.00	40.00

Cards accepted: Amex

The White Horse
COMMENDED

Market Place, Romsey SO51 8ZJ
☎ (01794) 512431
Fax (01794) 517485
Forte
Attractive hotel with traces of Elizabethan work behind its Georgian facade.
Bedrooms: 9 single, 11 double, 6 twin, 7 triple
Bathrooms: 33 en-suite

Bed & breakfast per night:	£min	£max
Single	65.00	74.00
Double	85.00	103.00

Half board per person:	£min	£max
Daily	49.00	63.00

Lunch available
Evening meal 1900 (last orders 2100)
Parking for 60
Cards accepted: Access, Visa, Diners, Amex, Switch/Delta

SANDOWN
Isle of Wight
Map ref 2C3

The 6-mile sweep of Sandown Bay is one of the island's finest stretches, with excellent sands. The pier has a pavilion and sun terrace; the esplanade has amusements, bars, eating-places and gardens.
Tourist Information Centre ☎ (01983) 403886

The Hazelwood Hotel
Listed APPROVED

19 Carter Street, Sandown PO36 8BL
☎ Isle of Wight (01983) 402536
Small, friendly, family-run, licensed hotel, close to beach, with car parking and reduced rates for children.
Bedrooms: 2 double, 2 twin, 2 triple, 1 family room
Bathrooms: 2 public

Bed & breakfast per night:	£min	£max
Single	14.00	15.00
Double	28.00	30.00

Half board per person:	£min	£max
Daily	18.00	20.00
Weekly	110.00	130.00

Evening meal 1800 (last orders 2030)
Parking for 10

Inglewood Guest House
COMMENDED

15 Avenue Road, Sandown PO36 8BN
☎ Isle of Wight (01983) 403485
Family-run, well-situated guesthouse. Close to sea and amenities, including pitch and putt, tennis and sports centre.
Bedrooms: 1 single, 2 double, 1 twin, 1 triple, 3 family rooms

Continued ▶

SOUTH OF ENGLAND

SANDOWN
Continued

Bathrooms: 3 en-suite, 3 public

Bed & breakfast
per night:	£min	£max
Single	13.00	15.00
Double	26.00	30.00

Half board per person:
	£min	£max
Daily	15.00	17.00
Weekly	104.00	119.00

Evening meal from 1800
Open April–September

Woodlynch Hall Hotel
COMMENDED

Broadway, Sandown PO36 9BB
☎ Isle of Wight (01983) 403733
Ideally situated family-run hotel offering good cuisine and all-round value for money. Heated swimming pool, live entertainment, parking.
Bedrooms: 6 single, 6 double, 6 twin, 1 triple, 6 family rooms
Bathrooms: 25 en-suite, 1 public

Bed & breakfast
per night:	£min	£max
Single	18.00	27.00
Double	36.00	54.00

Half board per person:
	£min	£max
Daily	20.00	30.00
Weekly	129.00	194.00

Evening meal 1800 (last orders 1800)
Parking for 18
Open April–October
Cards accepted: Visa

SAUNDERTON
Buckinghamshire
Map ref 2C1

Small village close to the Ridgeway long distance footpath. The site of a Roman villa is near the church.

The Rose & Crown Inn
COMMENDED

Wycombe Road, Saunderton, Princes Risborough HP27 9NP
☎ Princes Risborough (01844) 345299
Fax (01844) 343140
© Logis of Great Britain
Family-run, Georgian-style country inn set in Chiltern Hills. Log fires. 1 mile from the village of Saunderton, half a mile from Ridgeway Path.

Bedrooms: 6 single, 10 double, 1 twin
Bathrooms: 14 en-suite, 1 public

Bed & breakfast
per night:	£min	£max
Single	41.95	66.25
Double	72.40	76.65

Lunch available
Evening meal 1900 (last orders 2130)
Parking for 40
Cards accepted: Access, Visa, Diners, Amex

SHANKLIN
Isle of Wight
Map ref 2C3

Set on a cliff with gentle slopes leading down to the beach, esplanade and marine gardens. The picturesque, old thatched village nestles at the end of the wooded chine.
Tourist Information Centre ☎ (01983) 862942

Alverstone Manor Hotel
HIGHLY COMMENDED

32 Luccombe Road, Shanklin PO37 6RR
☎ Isle of Wight (01983) 862586

Charming country house hotel overlooking Sandown/Shanklin Bay. Within easy reach of Old Village, town and beach. 2 acres of gardens with heated swimming pool, lawn tennis court and putting green.
Bedrooms: 1 single, 3 double, 1 twin, 7 triple
Bathrooms: 10 en-suite, 3 public

Bed & breakfast
per night:	£min	£max
Single	24.00	30.00
Double	48.00	60.00

Half board per person:
	£min	£max
Daily	33.00	39.00
Weekly	231.00	273.00

Lunch available
Evening meal 1830 (last orders 1930)
Parking for 15
Open March–October
Cards accepted: Access, Visa

Atholl Court Guest House
Listed COMMENDED

1 Atherley Road, Shanklin PO37 7AT
☎ Isle of Wight (01983) 862414 & Mobile (0589) 731227
Victorian guesthouse with relaxing atmosphere. All rooms have toilet and washbasin, full en-suite available. Good home cooking, residential licence. Sorry, no children or pets.
Bedrooms: 3 single, 4 double, 2 twin
Bathrooms: 4 en-suite, 1 public

Bed & breakfast
per night:	£min	£max
Single	14.00	18.00
Double	28.00	36.00

Half board per person:
	£min	£max
Daily	19.00	23.00
Weekly	120.00	142.50

Evening meal 1800 (last orders 1800)
Parking for 6
Open March–October

Chine Court Hotel
HIGHLY COMMENDED

Popham Road, Shanklin PO37 6RG
☎ Isle of Wight (01983) 862732
Fax (01983) 862732
Elegant, lavishly decorated Victorian residence situated in large grounds and enjoying magnificent sea views from its elevated clifftop position.
Bedrooms: 3 single, 8 double, 6 twin, 5 triple, 4 family rooms
Bathrooms: 25 en-suite, 1 public

Bed & breakfast
per night:	£min	£max
Single	22.50	31.50
Double	45.00	63.00

Half board per person:
	£min	£max
Daily	31.00	41.00
Weekly	199.00	260.00

Evening meal 1830 (last orders 1915)
Parking for 24
Open April–October

Cliff Hall Hotel
COMMENDED

Crescent Road, Shanklin PO37 6DH
☎ Isle of Wight (01983) 862828

SOUTH OF ENGLAND

Spacious hotel, with beautiful sea views, heated swimming pool, showers, sun patio and garden. All day refreshments service, games room and ample parking. In central but quiet position, overlooking sea.
Bedrooms: 4 single, 7 double, 5 twin, 12 triple
Bathrooms: 28 en-suite, 3 public

Bed & breakfast
per night:	£min	£max
Single	19.00	25.00
Double	38.00	50.00

Half board per
person:	£min	£max
Daily	29.12	35.27
Weekly	203.86	246.75

Evening meal 1845 (last orders 1915)
Parking for 30
Open April–October and Christmas
Cards accepted: Access, Visa

Culham Lodge Hotel ⚜
COMMENDED
31 Landguard Manor Road, Shanklin PO37 7HZ
☎ Isle of Wight (01983) 862880
Fax (01983) 862880
Charming hotel in beautiful tree-lined road. Heated swimming pool, conservatory, home cooking and personal service. TV in all rooms with Sky movies and sport.
Bedrooms: 1 single, 6 double, 4 twin
Bathrooms: 9 en-suite, 2 private, 2 public

Bed & breakfast
per night:	£min	£max
Single	17.00	21.00
Double	34.00	42.00

Half board per
person:	£min	£max
Daily	22.00	26.00
Weekly	144.00	180.00

Evening meal 1800 (last orders 1600)
Parking for 8
Cards accepted: Access, Visa

The Edgecliffe Hotel ⚜
COMMENDED
7 Clarence Gardens, Shanklin PO37 6HA
☎ Isle of Wight (01983) 866199
Fax (01983) 866199
Home-cooked food, comfortable, well-equipped rooms and a refreshingly smoke-free atmosphere. Vegetarian meals available. Non-smokers only, please.
Bedrooms: 1 single, 4 double, 2 twin, 3 triple

Bathrooms: 6 en-suite, 1 public
Bed & breakfast
per night:	£min	£max
Single	15.00	24.50
Double	30.00	49.00

Half board per
person:	£min	£max
Daily	22.00	31.00
Weekly	140.00	195.00

Evening meal from 1830
Parking for 3
Cards accepted: Access, Visa, Diners, Amex, Switch/Delta

Kings Lodge Hotel ⚜
COMMENDED
Acacia House, 20 Queens Road, Shanklin PO37 6AW
☎ Isle of Wight (01983) 862990
Fax (01983) 868685
Licensed, 150 year old character hotel and restaurant. All bedrooms have telephone, colour TV, tea/coffee making facilities, hairdryer, mostly en-suite rooms. Car park.
Bedrooms: 7 double, 4 twin, 1 family room
Suites available
Bathrooms: 11 en-suite, 1 private, 1 public

Bed & breakfast
per night:	£min	£max
Single	16.00	25.00
Double	32.00	50.00

Half board per
person:	£min	£max
Daily	22.00	32.00
Weekly	140.00	204.00

Lunch available
Evening meal 1900 (last orders 2100)
Parking for 12
Cards accepted: Access, Visa, Diners, Amex, Switch/Delta

Osborne House Hotel ⚜
HIGHLY COMMENDED
Esplanade, Shanklin PO37 6BN
☎ Isle of Wight (01983) 862501
Fax (01983) 862501
Tastefully modernised Victorian residence, 25 yards from the sea, where bookings are accepted on a daily basis. Dining room is non-smoking.
Bedrooms: 1 single, 9 double, 2 twin
Bathrooms: 12 en-suite, 2 public

Bed & breakfast
per night:	£min	£max
Single	25.00	
Double	50.00	

Half board per
person:	£min	£max
Daily	38.75	43.75

Evening meal 1900 (last orders 2000)
Open January–October
Cards accepted: Access, Visa

West Coombe Hotel
COMMENDED
Westhill Road, Shanklin PO37 6PT
☎ Isle of Wight (01983) 866323 & Freephone 0500 131258
Fax (01983) 866323
Hotel standing in half an acre of secluded garden, minutes from Old Village, noted for good food and friendly service. Specialising in quiet, relaxing holidays. Sorry, no children.
Bedrooms: 3 single, 5 double, 4 twin, 5 family rooms
Bathrooms: 17 private

Bed & breakfast
per night:	£min	£max
Single	18.50	25.50
Double	37.00	51.00

Half board per
person:	£min	£max
Daily	27.50	36.00
Weekly	175.00	220.00

Evening meal 1815 (last orders 1900)
Parking for 18
Open March–November
Cards accepted: Access, Visa, Amex

SLOUGH
Berkshire
Map ref 2D2

A busy town with a large trading estate, Slough is an excellent centre for recreation with many open spaces. The ancient village of Upton, now part of Slough, has an interesting Norman church and Cliveden House is nearby.

Quality Hotel ⚜
COMMENDED
London Road, Heathrow, Slough SL3 8QB
☎ (01753) 684001
Fax (01753) 685767
Close to Heathrow Airport. Not far from Windsor, Legoland and Ascot, with easy access to central London.
Bedrooms: 33 double, 68 twin, 11 triple
Bathrooms: 112 en-suite

Continued ▶

SOUTH OF ENGLAND

SLOUGH
Continued

Bed & breakfast per night:	£min	£max
Single	86.00	
Double	95.00	105.00

Half board per person:	£min	£max
Daily	106.50	126.00

Lunch available
Evening meal 1830 (last orders 2200)
Parking for 115
Cards accepted: Access, Visa, Diners, Amex, Switch/Delta

SOUTHAMPTON
Hampshire
Map ref 2C3

One of Britain's leading seaports with a long history, now a major container port. In the 18th C it became a fashionable resort with the assembly rooms and theatre. The old Guildhall and the Wool House are now museums. Sections of the medieval wall can still be seen.
Tourist Information Centre ☎ *(01703) 221106*

Acorn Lodge Guest House
Listed
75 Morris Road, Polygon, Southampton SO12 2BQ
☎ (01703) 224837
Friendly, owner-managed guesthouse, recently refurbished. 3 minutes from city centre and train station. Convenient for hospitals, airport, docks and M27. Car parking facilities. Sky TV.
Bedrooms: 1 single, 3 twin, 2 family rooms
Bathrooms: 2 en-suite, 1 public

Bed & breakfast per night:	£min	£max
Single	16.00	19.00
Double	32.00	38.00

Evening meal from 1800
Parking for 7

Addenro House Hotel
Listed
40-42 Howard Road, Shirley, Southampton SO15 5BD
☎ (01703) 227144
Family-run small hotel, offering friendly, reliable service at a reasonable cost.
Bedrooms: 7 single, 2 double, 4 twin, 5 triple
Bathrooms: 9 en-suite, 5 public

Bed & breakfast per night:	£min	£max
Single	15.00	15.00
Double	30.00	30.00

Parking for 18

Banister House Hotel
COMMENDED
Banister Road, Southampton SO15 2JJ
☎ (01703) 221279
Fax (01703) 221279
Friendly welcome in this family-run hotel which is central and in a residential area. Off A33 (The Avenue) into Southampton.
Bedrooms: 13 single, 4 double, 3 twin, 2 triple, 1 family room
Bathrooms: 13 en-suite, 4 public, 3 private showers

Bed & breakfast per night:	£min	£max
Single	22.50	26.50
Double	31.50	35.00

Half board per person:	£min	£max
Daily	22.50	26.50

Evening meal 1800 (last orders 1945)
Parking for 14
Cards accepted: Access, Visa, Amex

Botley Park Hotel, Golf & Country Club
HIGHLY COMMENDED
Winchester Road, Boorley Green, Botley, Southampton SO3 2UA
☎ Botley (01489) 780888
Fax (01489) 789242
Utell International
Purpose-designed to cater for the evolving leisure and business demands of the 1990s. Few minutes' drive from M27, 60 minutes from London, 50 minutes to Heathrow. Golf, sauna, solaria, gymnasium, jacuzzi, indoor heated pool, tennis and squash courts.
Wheelchair access category 1
Bedrooms: 44 double, 56 twin
Bathrooms: 100 private

Bed & breakfast per night:	£min	£max
Single	90.00	
Double	105.00	

Lunch available
Evening meal 1900 (last orders 2145)
Parking for 250
Cards accepted: Access, Visa, Diners, Amex, Switch/Delta

Hunters Lodge Hotel
COMMENDED
25 Landguard Road, Shirley, Southampton SO15 5DL
☎ (01703) 227919
Fax (01703) 230913
Friendly, family hotel, aiming to give a good service to all guests, 2 minutes' walk from central Southampton and close to the general hospital and university.
Bedrooms: 5 single, 6 double, 3 twin, 1 triple
Bathrooms: 9 en-suite, 2 public, 3 private showers

Bed & breakfast per night:	£min	£max
Single	23.50	28.50
Double	38.00	50.00

Half board per person:	£min	£max
Daily	33.00	38.00
Weekly	165.00	190.00

Evening meal 1830 (last orders 1830)
Parking for 21
Cards accepted: Access, Visa, Amex, Switch/Delta

The Lodge
No 1 Winn Road, The Avenue, Southampton SO12 1EH
☎ (01703) 557537
The Independents
Friendly owner-managed hotel in quiet surroundings close to city centre and university, convenient for airport.
Bedrooms: 9 single, 2 double, 2 twin, 1 triple
Bathrooms: 8 en-suite, 2 public

Bed & breakfast per night:	£min	£max
Single	22.50	32.50
Double	39.50	44.50

Half board per person:	£min	£max
Daily	26.50	38.00

Lunch available
Evening meal 1900 (last orders 2100)
Parking for 10
Cards accepted: Access, Visa, Amex

Madison House
137 Hill Lane, Southampton SO15 5AF
☎ (01703) 333374
Fax (01703) 322264
Elegant Victorian house in tree conservation area three-quarters of a mile from centre. Ideal for touring the

SOUTH OF ENGLAND

south or relishing Southampton's medieval history. Friendly family atmosphere.
Bedrooms: 2 single, 3 double, 3 twin, 1 triple
Bathrooms: 3 en-suite, 2 public

Bed & breakfast per night:	£min	£max
Single	15.00	22.00
Double	30.00	42.00

Parking for 6
Cards accepted: Access, Visa

Novotel Southampton
COMMENDED
1 West Quay Road, Southampton SO15 1RA
☎ (01703) 330550
Fax (01703) 222158
Novotel
Modern city centre hotel, 5 minutes' walk from railway station. Easy access from M3, M27 and docks. Conference and banqueting facilities for 500. Indoor leisure centre with heated indoor swimming pool, sauna, exercise area.
Bedrooms: 121 double
Bathrooms: 121 en-suite

Bed & breakfast per night:	£min	£max
Single	65.00	67.50
Double	80.00	85.00

Half board per person:	£min	£max
Daily	80.00	85.00

Lunch available
Evening meal 1800 (last orders 2359)
Parking for 300
Cards accepted: Access, Visa, Diners, Amex, Switch/Delta

Roadchef Lodge Rownhams
COMMENDED
Motorway Service Area, M27 Southbound, Rownhams, Southampton SO51 8AW
☎ (01703) 734180
Fax (01703) 739517
RoadChef
RoadChef Lodges offer high specification rooms at affordable prices, in popular locations suited to both the business and private traveller. Prices are per room and do not include breakfast.
Bedrooms: 23 double, 15 twin, 1 family room
Bathrooms: 39 en-suite

Bed & breakfast per night:	£min	£max
Single	37.95	39.95

Parking for 65
Cards accepted: Access, Visa, Diners, Amex, Switch/Delta

De Vere Grand Harbour
DE LUXE
West Quay Road, Southampton SO15 1AG
☎ (01703) 633033
Fax (01703) 633066
Newly built, finished in exquisite granite and natural timber. Set in its own beautiful grounds which include delightful water features.
Bedrooms: 98 double, 34 twin, 20 triple, 20 family rooms
Suites available
Bathrooms: 172 en-suite

Bed & breakfast per night:	£min	£max
Single	115.00	125.00
Double	125.00	145.00

Half board per person:	£min	£max
Daily	75.00	

Lunch available
Evening meal 1900 (last orders 2145)
Parking for 190
Cards accepted: Access, Visa, Diners, Amex, Switch/Delta

SOUTHSEA
Hampshire

See under Portsmouth & Southsea

STEEPLE ASTON
Oxfordshire
Map ref 2C1

Oxfordshire village whose church has one of the finest examples of church embroidery in the world. Nearby is the Jacobean Rousham House which stands in William Kent's only surviving landscaped garden.

Westfield Farm Motel
COMMENDED
Fenway, Steeple Aston, Bicester OX6 3SS
☎ (01869) 340591
Fax (01869) 347594
Logis of Great Britain
Converted stable block with comfortable en-suite bedroom units. Combined lounge, dining room and bar. TV all rooms. Good touring centre.

Fringe of Cotswolds, off A4260, 9 miles from Banbury and 5 miles from Woodstock.
Bedrooms: 1 single, 3 double, 3 twin
Suite available
Bathrooms: 7 en-suite

Bed & breakfast per night:	£min	£max
Single	34.00	38.00
Double	50.00	65.00

Half board per person:	£min	£max
Daily	39.50	47.00

Evening meal 1900 (last orders 2030)
Parking for 24
Cards accepted: Access, Visa, Amex, Switch/Delta

STOCKBRIDGE
Hampshire
Map ref 2C2

Set in the Test Valley which has some of the best fishing in England. The wide main street has houses of all styles.

Carbery Guest House
COMMENDED
Salisbury Hill, Stockbridge SO20 6EZ
☎ Andover (01264) 810771
Fax (01264) 811022

Fine old Georgian house in an acre of landscaped gardens and lawns, overlooking the River Test. Games and swimming facilities, riding and fishing can be arranged. Ideal for touring the south coast and the New Forest.
Bedrooms: 4 single, 3 double, 2 twin, 1 triple, 1 family room
Bathrooms: 8 en-suite, 1 public

Bed & breakfast per night:	£min	£max
Single	24.00	31.00
Double	46.00	50.00

Half board per person:	£min	£max
Daily	36.00	43.00
Weekly	248.00	297.00

Evening meal 1900 (last orders 1800)
Parking for 12

SOUTH OF ENGLAND

STONOR

Oxfordshire
Map ref 2C2

The fine manor house of Stonor Park has been a family home for over 800 years and its private chapel has been a centre of catholicism since Tudor times. The park is one of the most beautiful in southern England.

The Stonor Arms
HIGHLY COMMENDED

Stonor, Henley-on-Thames RG9 6HE
☎ Turville Heath (01491) 638345 & 638866
Fax (01491) 638863
Situated in the Stonor Valley, 4 miles from Henley-on-Thames on the B480 and 4 miles from M40 junction 6. A charming English country house hotel and award-winning restaurant.
Bedrooms: 5 double, 5 twin
Suite available
Bathrooms: 10 en-suite
Bed & breakfast

per night:	£min	£max
Single	85.00	
Double	95.00	

Lunch available
Evening meal 1900 (last orders 2130)
Parking for 35
Cards accepted: Access, Visa, Amex, Switch/Delta

STRATFIELD TURGIS

Hampshire
Map ref 2C2

The Wellington Arms
HIGHLY COMMENDED

Stratfield Turgis, Hook RG27 0AS
☎ Basingstoke (01256) 882214
Fax (01256) 882934
Logis of Great Britain
Traditional coaching inn on the Duke of Wellington's estate. Situated midway between Basingstoke and Reading on the main A33. Motorway access is from junction 6 of M3, junction 11 of M4.
Bedrooms: 7 single, 19 double, 5 twin, 2 family rooms
Bathrooms: 33 en-suite
Bed & breakfast

per night:	£min	£max
Single	45.00	80.00
Double	55.00	90.00

Lunch available
Evening meal 1900 (last orders 2200)

Parking for 75
Cards accepted: Access, Visa, Diners, Amex, Switch/Delta

STREATLEY

Berkshire
Map ref 2C2

Pretty village on the River Thames, linked to Goring by an attractive bridge. It has Georgian houses and cottages and beautiful views over the countryside and the Goring Gap.

The Swan Diplomat
HIGHLY COMMENDED

Streatley on Thames, Streatley, Reading RG8 9HR
☎ Goring-on-Thames (01491) 873737
Fax (01491) 872554
Beautifully situated on the banks of the River Thames, within one hour's drive of Oxford, Windsor, London and London Heathrow Airport. Price shown below is per person for 2-night weekend break.
Bedrooms: 9 single, 27 double, 10 twin
Suite available
Bathrooms: 46 en-suite
Half board per

person:	£min	£max
Daily	72.50	

Lunch available
Evening meal 1930 (last orders 2130)
Parking for 145
Cards accepted: Access, Visa, Diners, Amex, Switch/Delta

STUDLAND

Dorset
Map ref 2B3

On a beautiful stretch of coast and good for walking, with a National Nature Reserve to the north. The Norman church is the finest in the country, with superb rounded arches and vaulting. Brownsea Island, where the first scout camp was held, lies in Poole Harbour.

Knoll House Hotel
COMMENDED

Studland, Swanage BH19 3AH
☎ (01929) 450450 & 450251
Fax (01929) 450423

Independent country hotel in National Trust reserve. Access to 3-mile beach from 100-acre grounds. Many facilities. Weekly rates below are for full board.
Bedrooms: 29 single, 20 twin, 30 triple
Bathrooms: 57 en-suite, 10 public
Half board per

person:	£min	£max
Daily	62.00	95.00
Weekly	434.00	665.00

Lunch available
Evening meal 1930 (last orders 2015)
Parking for 100
Open April–October
Cards accepted: Access, Visa, Switch/Delta

The Manor House Hotel
COMMENDED

Beach Road, Studland, Swanage BH19 3AU
☎ (01929) 450288
Fax (01929) 450288

18th C manor house in secluded gardens overlooking the sea and safe, sandy beaches. Oak-panelled bar and dining room, with conservatory. Two hard tennis courts.
Bedrooms: 6 double, 6 twin, 6 triple
Suites available
Bathrooms: 18 en-suite, 1 public
Bed & breakfast

per night:	£min	£max
Single	33.50	50.00
Double	67.00	101.00

Half board per

person:	£min	£max
Daily	55.00	68.00
Weekly	278.50	380.00

Lunch available
Evening meal 1900 (last orders 2030)
Parking for 65
Open February–December
Cards accepted: Access, Visa, Amex

SOUTH OF ENGLAND

STURMINSTER NEWTON

Dorset
Map ref 2B3

Every Monday this small town holds a livestock market. One of the bridges over the River Stour is a fine medieval example and bears a plaque declaring that anyone "injuring" it will be deported.

Plumber Manor
HIGHLY COMMENDED

Sturminster Newton DT10 2AF
☎ (01258) 472507
Fax (01258) 473170

Run as a restaurant with bedrooms and supervised by the family. Set in the middle of Hardy's Dorset and surrounded by the home farm.
Bedrooms: 10 double, 6 twin
Bathrooms: 15 en-suite, 1 private

Bed & breakfast
per night:	£min	£max
Single	65.00	85.00
Double	90.00	120.00

Evening meal 1930 (last orders 2130)
Parking for 25
Open January, March–December
Cards accepted: Access, Visa, Diners, Amex, Switch/Delta

The symbols in each entry give information about services and facilities. A 'key' to these symbols appears at the back of this guide.

National gradings and classifications were correct at the time of going to press but are subject to change. Please check at the time of booking.

Swan Inn
COMMENDED

Market Place, Sturminster Newton DT10 1AR
☎ Blandford (01258) 472208
Old coaching inn, located in the heart of Thomas Hardy's Blackmore Vale. All rooms en-suite with remote-control TV. Extensive a la carte menu plus bar meals.
Bedrooms: 1 single, 3 double, 1 twin
Bathrooms: 5 en-suite

Bed & breakfast
per night:	£min	£max
Single	39.00	42.00
Double	52.50	55.00

Half board per
person:	£min	£max
Daily	37.50	40.00

Lunch available
Evening meal 1830 (last orders 2100)
Parking for 20
Cards accepted: Access, Visa, Diners, Amex

SWANAGE

Dorset
Map ref 2B3

Began life as an Anglo-Saxon port, then a quarrying centre of Purbeck marble. Now the safe, sandy beach set in a sweeping bay and flanked by downs is good walking country, making it an ideal resort.
Tourist Information Centre ☎ (01929) 422885

Glenlee Hotel

6 Cauldon Avenue, Swanage BH19 1PQ
☎ (01929) 425794
Delightful position overlooking beach gardens, bowling green and tennis courts. 150 yards to beach. All rooms en-suite, with colour TV and hot drinks facilities.
Bedrooms: 4 double, 2 twin, 1 triple
Bathrooms: 7 en-suite

Bed & breakfast
per night:	£min	£max
Double	36.00	48.00

Half board per
person:	£min	£max
Daily	25.00	31.00
Weekly	162.00	208.00

Evening meal 1830 (last orders 1700)
Parking for 8
Open March–October
Cards accepted: Access, Visa

The Pines Hotel
COMMENDED

Burlington Road, Swanage BH19 1LT
☎ (01929) 425211
Fax (01929) 422075
Family-run hotel set amid the Purbeck countryside at quiet end of Swanage Bay. Own access to beach.
Wheelchair access category 3
Bedrooms: 4 single, 10 double, 11 twin, 24 triple
Bathrooms: 47 en-suite, 1 public

Bed & breakfast
per night:	£min	£max
Single	35.00	45.00
Double	70.00	90.00

Half board per
person:	£min	£max
Daily	45.00	60.50
Weekly	330.00	400.00

Lunch available
Evening meal 1930 (last orders 2100)
Parking for 60
Cards accepted: Access, Visa

Purbeck House Hotel
HIGHLY COMMENDED

91 High Street, Swanage BH19 2LZ
☎ (01929) 422872
Fax (01929) 421194
Family-run hotel, set in 2 acres of gardens, 300 yards from beach. Off-street parking. Fully licensed.
Bedrooms: 2 single, 9 double, 2 twin, 1 triple, 4 family rooms
Bathrooms: 18 en-suite

Bed & breakfast
per night:	£min	£max
Single	30.00	40.00
Double	60.00	80.00

Half board per
person:	£min	£max
Daily	44.00	53.00
Weekly	265.00	325.00

Lunch available
Evening meal 1830 (last orders 2130)
Parking for 23
Cards accepted: Access, Visa, Diners, Amex, Switch/Delta

COLOUR MAPS

Colour maps at the back of this guide pinpoint all places in which you will find accommodation listed.

SOUTH OF ENGLAND

SWAY
Hampshire
Map ref 2C3

Small village on the south-western edge of the New Forest. It is noted for its 220-ft tower, Peterson's Folly, built in the 1870s by a retired Indian judge to demonstrate the value of concrete as a building material.

The Nurse's Cottage
HIGHLY COMMENDED

Station Road, Sway, Lymington SO41 6BA
☎ Lymington (01590) 683402
Fax (01590) 683402
Popular award-winning guesthouse, offering good value half-board packages, including Wine and Dine, Romance!, etc. Extensive menu and wine list.
Bedrooms: 1 single, 1 double, 1 twin
Bathrooms: 3 en-suite, 1 public

Half board per person:	£min	£max
Daily	42.50	47.50
Weekly	245.00	280.00

Lunch available
Evening meal 1830 (last orders 1930)
Parking for 4
Cards accepted: Access, Visa, Amex, Switch/Delta

String of Horses
HIGHLY COMMENDED

Mead End Road, Sway, Lymington SO41 6EH
☎ Lymington (01590) 682631
Fax (01590) 682631
Unique, secluded hotel set in 4 acres in the New Forest. Individually designed bedrooms with fantasy bathrooms. Intimate candlelit restaurant.
Bedrooms: 7 double
Bathrooms: 7 en-suite

Bed & breakfast per night:	£min	£max
Single	50.00	55.00
Double	70.00	95.00

Half board per person:	£min	£max
Daily	53.95	68.95
Weekly	339.00	425.00

Lunch available
Evening meal 1900 (last orders 2030)
Parking for 24
Cards accepted: Access, Visa, Diners, Amex, Switch/Delta

White Rose Hotel
COMMENDED

Village Centre, Sway, Lymington SO41 6BA
☎ Lymington (01590) 682754
Family-run country house hotel with 5 acres of grounds, in quiet, unspoilt village on edge of New Forest.
Bedrooms: 7 double, 3 twin, 1 triple, 1 family room
Bathrooms: 11 en-suite, 2 public

Bed & breakfast per night:	£min	£max
Single	39.00	45.00
Double	58.00	70.00

Half board per person:	£min	£max
Daily	39.00	55.00
Weekly	210.00	350.00

Lunch available
Evening meal 1900 (last orders 2100)
Parking for 50
Cards accepted: Access, Visa, Amex

THAME
Oxfordshire
Map ref 2C1

Historic market town on the River Thame. The wide, unspoilt High Street has many styles of architecture with medieval timber-framed cottages, Georgian houses and some famous inns.
Tourist Information Centre ☎ (01844) 212834

The Spread Eagle Hotel
HIGHLY COMMENDED

Cornmarket, Thame OX9 2BW
☎ (01844) 213661
Fax (01844) 261380
Thames Valley/Best Western
Converted 17th C coaching inn, in centre of small country market town. Fothergills Restaurant features a choice of menus. Banqueting and conference facilities. Good base for touring the Thames Valley.
Bedrooms: 5 single, 22 double, 5 twin, 1 triple
Suites available
Bathrooms: 33 en-suite

Bed & breakfast per night:	£min	£max
Single	89.75	99.95
Double	107.90	123.95

Half board per person:	£min	£max
Daily	111.95	121.95
Weekly	625.00	685.00

Lunch available
Evening meal 1900 (last orders 2200)

Parking for 80
Cards accepted: Access, Visa, Diners, Amex

TOTLAND BAY
Isle of Wight
Map ref 2C3

On the Freshwater Peninsula. It is possible to walk from here around to Alum Bay.

Country Garden Hotel
COMMENDED

Church Hill, Totland Bay PO39 1QE
☎ Isle of Wight (01983) 754521
Fax (01983) 754521
Country house hotel set in lovely gardens overlooking the Solent and Totland Bay. Restaurant, modern facilities and personal supervision by the proprietors.
Bedrooms: 2 single, 9 double, 5 twin
Suite available
Bathrooms: 16 en-suite

Bed & breakfast per night:	£min	£max
Single	36.00	44.00
Double	72.00	88.00

Half board per person:	£min	£max
Daily	44.00	52.00
Weekly	285.00	320.00

Lunch available
Evening meal 1900 (last orders 2100)
Parking for 30
Open February–December
Cards accepted: Access, Visa

VENTNOR
Isle of Wight
Map ref 2C3

Town lies at the bottom of an 800-ft hill and has a reputation as a winter holiday and health resort due to its mild climate. There is a pier, small esplanade and Winter Gardens.

Burlington Hotel
HIGHLY COMMENDED

Bellevue Road, Ventnor PO38 1DB
☎ Isle of Wight (01983) 852113
Fax (01983) 852113
Friendly family-run hotel with heated swimming pool, commanding wonderful sea views. Central, yet affords peace and quiet.
Bedrooms: 4 single, 5 double, 9 twin, 5 triple
Bathrooms: 23 en-suite, 1 public

SOUTH OF ENGLAND

Bed & breakfast per night:	£min	£max
Single	25.50	31.50
Double	51.00	63.00

Half board per person:	£min	£max
Daily	33.50	39.50
Weekly	234.00	276.00

Evening meal 1900 (last orders 2030)
Parking for 20
Open March–October
Cards accepted: Access, Visa

🛏3♨🍴🅿📞🛋♿🈁🅿♨🈁
📺🏧🚗♣✲🔪🅶🅿🆂🅿

WANTAGE
Oxfordshire
Map ref 2C2

Market town in the Vale of the White Horse where King Alfred was born. His statue stands in the town square.
Tourist Information Centre ☎ (01235) 760176

The Bear Hotel ▲
♔♔♔ APPROVED

Market Place, Wantage OX12 8AB
☎ (01235) 766366
Fax (01235) 768826
Character 16th C coaching inn. Ideal for touring the Vale of White Horse. Traditional good food and emphasis on customer service.
Bedrooms: 9 single, 14 double, 10 twin, 3 triple
Bathrooms: 36 en-suite

Bed & breakfast per night:	£min	£max
Single	25.00	60.00
Double	50.00	70.00

Lunch available
Evening meal 1900 (last orders 2130)
Cards accepted: Access, Visa, Diners, Amex, Switch/Delta

🛏🍴📞🛋♿🈁🅿🆂🅿⛳🗻📺🏧🚗
🈁70✂🆂🅿🍴🅃

Establishments should be open throughout the year, unless otherwise stated.

The National Grading and Classification Scheme is explained in full at the back of this guide.

WAREHAM
Dorset
Map ref 2B3

This site has been occupied since pre-Roman times and has a turbulent history. In 1762 fire destroyed much of the town, so the buildings now are mostly Georgian.
Tourist Information Centre ☎ (01929) 552740

Springfield Country Hotel & Leisure Club ▲
♔♔♔♔ COMMENDED

Grange Road, Wareham BH20 5AL
☎ (01929) 552177
Fax (01929) 551862
Country hotel set in 6 acres of secluded landscaped gardens. Splendid new sports and leisure facilities. En-suite bedrooms.
Bedrooms: 4 single, 22 double, 13 twin, 7 triple, 2 family rooms
Bathrooms: 48 en-suite

Bed & breakfast per night:	£min	£max
Single		63.00
Double		100.00

Half board per person:	£min	£max
Daily		81.00
Weekly		406.00

Lunch available
Evening meal 1900 (last orders 2130)
Parking for 150
Cards accepted: Access, Visa, Amex

🛏♨🍴📞🛋♿🈁🅂🅿📺◉
⛳🏧🚗200🈁♣✲🗻🔪🅿
✲🚂✂🆂🅿

WEST LULWORTH
Dorset
Map ref 2B3

Well-known for Lulworth Cove, the almost landlocked circular bay of chalk and limestone cliffs.

Cromwell House Hotel ▲
♔♔♔ COMMENDED

Lulworth Cove, West Lulworth, Wareham BH20 5RJ
☎ (01929) 400253 & 400332
Fax (01929) 400566

Family hotel on the Dorset Heritage Coast footpath. Outstanding sea views

over Lulworth Cove. Secluded garden. Good walking country. Swimming pool (May-October).
Bedrooms: 1 single, 7 double, 5 twin, 1 triple
Bathrooms: 14 en-suite

Bed & breakfast per night:	£min	£max
Single	25.50	36.50
Double	51.00	61.00

Half board per person:	£min	£max
Daily	36.50	41.50
Weekly	220.00	250.00

Evening meal 1900 (last orders 2030)
Parking for 15
Cards accepted: Access, Visa, Amex, Switch/Delta

🛏♨🍴📞🛋♿🈁🅂🅿📺🏧🚗
🍴🅿✲🆂🅿

Lulworth Cove Hotel ▲
♔♔

Main Road, West Lulworth, Wareham BH20 5RQ
☎ (01929) 400333
Fax (01929) 400534
One hundred yards from the cove on the Dorset Coastal Path. Some sea-view balcony rooms. Wide variety of restaurant and bar meals.
Bedrooms: 1 single, 12 double, 1 triple, 1 family room
Bathrooms: 10 en-suite, 1 public, 4 private showers

Bed & breakfast per night:	£min	£max
Single	18.50	23.50
Double	37.00	47.00

Half board per person:	£min	£max
Daily	28.50	33.50
Weekly	179.55	211.05

Lunch available
Evening meal 1900 (last orders 2150)
Cards accepted: Access, Visa, Amex

🛏🍴📞🛋♿🈁🅂🅿📺🏧🚗♣✲
🆂🅿🅃

Shirley Hotel ▲
♔♔♔ HIGHLY COMMENDED

West Lulworth, Wareham BH20 5RL
☎ (01929) 400358
Fax (01929) 400358

In the country by the sea. Small, Continued ▶

517

SOUTH OF ENGLAND

WEST LULWORTH
Continued

friendly hotel close to Lulworth Cove. Good food and relaxed atmosphere. Indoor heated pool and jacuzzi.
Bedrooms: 3 single, 8 double, 4 twin, 1 triple, 2 family rooms
Bathrooms: 18 en-suite, 1 public

Bed & breakfast per night:	£min	£max
Single	29.00	31.00
Double	58.00	62.00

Half board per person:	£min	£max
Daily	41.00	44.00
Weekly	257.75	275.75

Evening meal 1830 (last orders 1930)
Parking for 22
Open February–November and Christmas
Cards accepted: Access, Visa, Diners, Amex, Switch/Delta

WIMBORNE MINSTER
Dorset
Map ref 2B3

Market town centred on the twin-towered Minster Church of St Cuthberga which gave the town the second part of its name. Good touring base for the surrounding countryside, depicted in the writings of Thomas Hardy.
Tourist Information Centre ☎ (01202) 886116

Beechleas Hotel
HIGHLY COMMENDED

17 Poole Road, Wimborne Minster BH21 1QA
☎ Bournemouth (01202) 841684
Fax (01202) 849344
Georgian building, beautifully restored, with large double bedrooms, lounge, dining room, conservatory, attractive garden, own car park. Recognised for hospitality, service and food.
Bedrooms: 1 single, 6 double, 2 twin
Bathrooms: 9 en-suite

Bed & breakfast per night:	£min	£max
Single	60.00	80.00
Double	75.00	95.00

Evening meal 1900 (last orders 2100)
Parking for 9
Cards accepted: Access, Visa, Amex

Northill House
COMMENDED

Horton, Wimborne Minster BH21 7HL
☎ Witchampton (01258) 840407

Mid-Victorian former farmhouse, modernised to provide comfortable bedrooms, all en-suite. Log fires and cooking using fresh produce. Ideal touring centre.
Wheelchair access category 1
Bedrooms: 5 double, 3 twin, 1 triple
Bathrooms: 9 en-suite

Bed & breakfast per night:	£min	£max
Single	39.00	39.00
Double	69.00	69.00

Half board per person:	£min	£max
Daily	48.50	48.50
Weekly	305.55	305.55

Evening meal 1930 (last orders 1830)
Parking for 12
Open February–December
Cards accepted: Access, Visa, Amex

WINCHESTER
Hampshire
Map ref 2C3

King Alfred the Great made Winchester the capital of Saxon England. A magnificent Norman cathedral, with one of the longest naves in Europe, dominates the city.
Tourist Information Centre ☎ (01962) 840500 or 848180

Cathedral View
COMMENDED

9A Magdalen Hill, Winchester SO23 0HJ
☎ (01962) 863802
Guesthouse with views across historic city and cathedral. 5 minutes' walk from city centre. En-suite facilities, TV, parking.
Bedrooms: 3 double, 1 twin, 1 family room
Bathrooms: 3 en-suite, 2 private

Bed & breakfast per night:	£min	£max
Single	30.00	35.00
Double	40.00	45.00

Parking for 4

Harestock Lodge Hotel
COMMENDED

Harestock Road, Winchester SO22 6NX
☎ (01962) 881870 & 880038
Fax (01962) 886959
Privately-run country house hotel set in secluded gardens on the edge of historic Winchester. Offering a warm welcome and good food with menus to suit all tastes.
Bedrooms: 4 single, 8 double, 4 twin, 2 triple
Bathrooms: 14 en-suite, 1 public, 4 private showers

Bed & breakfast per night:	£min	£max
Single	35.00	45.00
Double	45.00	58.00

Lunch available
Evening meal 1830 (last orders 2245)
Parking for 26
Cards accepted: Access, Visa, Amex

Stratton House

Stratton Road, St Giles Hill, Winchester SO23 0JQ
☎ (01962) 863919 & 864529
Fax (01962) 842095
Lovely old Victorian house with an acre of grounds, in an elevated position on St Giles Hill.
Bedrooms: 1 single, 3 double, 2 twin, 1 triple
Bathrooms: 6 en-suite, 1 private

Bed & breakfast per night:	£min	£max
Single	22.00	30.00
Double	44.00	50.00

Half board per person:	£min	£max
Daily	29.00	37.00
Weekly	199.00	249.00

Evening meal 1800 (last orders 1600)
Parking for 8
Cards accepted: Access, Visa, Switch/Delta

The symbols in each entry give information about services and facilities. A 'key' to these symbols appears at the back of this guide.

SOUTH OF ENGLAND

WINDSOR
Berkshire
Map ref 2D2

Town dominated by the spectacular castle, home of the Royal Family for over 900 years. Parts are open to the public. There are many attractions including the Great Park, Eton and trips on the river.
Tourist Information Centre ☎ *(01753) 852010*

Beaumont Lodge
COMMENDED

1 Beaumont Road, Windsor SL4 1HY
☎ (01753) 863436 & Mobile 0374 841273
Fax (01753) 863436
Very close to town centre. All rooms have colour TV, clock radio alarm, tea/coffee facilities and trouser press. Double has spa bath.
Bedrooms: 1 double, 2 twin
Bathrooms: 3 en-suite

Bed & breakfast per night:	£min	£max
Single	38.00	40.00
Double	46.00	50.00

Clarence Hotel
Listed APPROVED

9 Clarence Road, Windsor SL4 5AE
☎ (01753) 864436
Fax (01753) 857060
Comfortable hotel with licensed bar and steam room, near town centre, castle and Eton. All rooms en-suite, TV, hairdryer, radio and tea-maker. Convenient for Heathrow Airport.
Bedrooms: 4 single, 4 double, 7 twin, 4 triple, 2 family rooms
Bathrooms: 21 en-suite, 1 public

Bed & breakfast per night:	£min	£max
Single	35.00	40.00
Double	39.00	52.00

Parking for 4
Cards accepted: Access, Visa, Diners, Amex, Switch/Delta

Fairlight Lodge Royal Windsor Hotel
COMMENDED

41 Frances Road, Windsor SL4 3AQ
☎ (01753) 861207
Fax (01753) 865963
Comfortable Victorian property, once the mayoral residence, quietly situated, but close to River Thames, castle and town centre. Fully licensed bar and restaurant.
Bedrooms: 2 single, 5 double, 2 twin, 1 family room
Bathrooms: 10 en-suite

Bed & breakfast per night	£min	£max
Single	47.00	52.00
Double	62.00	75.00

Half board per person:	£min	£max
Daily	39.50	46.00
Weekly	249.00	289.00

Evening meal 1900 (last orders 2130)
Parking for 10
Cards accepted: Access, Visa, Amex

The Manor Hotel
COMMENDED

The Village Green, Datchet, Slough SL3 9EA
☎ Slough (01753) 543442
Fax (01753) 545292
Tudor period hotel overlooking village green, within easy reach of Windsor and Heathrow. Renowned cuisine in Alexander's restaurant. Traditional ales in bar.
Bedrooms: 7 single, 14 double, 10 twin
Bathrooms: 31 en-suite

Bed & breakfast per night:	£min	£max
Single	25.00	72.50
Double	50.00	92.50

Lunch available
Evening meal 1900 (last orders 2145)
Parking for 15
Cards accepted: Access, Visa, Diners, Amex, Switch/Delta

Melrose House
COMMENDED

53 Frances Road, Windsor SL4 3AQ
☎ (01753) 865328
Fax (01753) 865328
Elegant Victorian detached residence, in the heart of Windsor. Five minutes' walk from the castle.
Bedrooms: 1 single, 2 double, 1 twin, 1 triple, 1 family room
Bathrooms: 6 en-suite

Bed & breakfast per night	£min	£max
Single	35.00	40.00
Double	45.00	50.00

Half board per person:	£min	£max
Daily	43.50	48.50

Parking for 9
Cards accepted: Access, Visa, Switch/Delta

Oscar Hotel

65 Vansittart Road, Windsor SL4 5DB
☎ (01753) 830613
Fax (01753) 833744
Fully licensed bar, all rooms en-suite with direct-dial telephone, colour TV, tea/coffee facilities. Own car park.
Bedrooms: 3 single, 4 double, 2 twin, 1 triple, 2 family rooms
Bathrooms: 12 en-suite

Bed & breakfast per night:	£min	£max
Single	35.00	45.00
Double	45.00	60.00

Half board per person:	£min	£max
Daily	42.00	52.00

Evening meal 1800 (last orders 1930)
Parking for 10
Cards accepted: Access, Visa, Diners, Amex, Switch/Delta

Sir Christopher Wren's House, Hotel & Business Centre
COMMENDED

Thames Street, Windsor SL4 1PX
☎ (01753) 861354
Fax (01753) 860172
Thames Valley

Situated beneath Windsor Castle and on the banks of the River Thames. Historic house, built by Sir Christopher Wren in 1676, with restaurant bar and terraced garden.
Bedrooms: 7 single, 21 double, 10 twin, 1 triple
Suite available
Bathrooms: 39 en-suite

Bed & breakfast per night:	£min	£max
Single	49.50	
Double	79.00	

Half board per person:	£min	£max
Daily	59.50	

Continued ▶

SOUTH OF ENGLAND

WINDSOR
Continued

Lunch available
Evening meal 1900 (last orders 2215)
Parking for 20
Cards accepted: Access, Visa, Diners, Amex, Switch/Delta

Stirrups Country House Hotel
HIGHLY COMMENDED

Maidens Green, Bracknell RG42 6LD
☎ Winkfield Row (01344) 882284
Fax (01344) 882300
Best Western
Privately owned hotel in Berkshire, situated between Windsor, Ascot and Bracknell and only 3 miles from the Windsor Legoland park.
Bedrooms: 1 single, 18 double, 4 twin, 1 triple
Bathrooms: 24 en-suite
Bed & breakfast

per night:	£min	£max
Single	50.00	90.00
Double	65.00	110.00

Half board per

person:	£min	£max
Daily	55.00	65.00
Weekly	385.00	455.00

Lunch available
Evening meal 1900 (last orders 2200)
Parking for 100
Cards accepted: Access, Visa, Diners, Amex, Switch/Delta

Suffolk Lodge
4 Bolton Avenue, Windsor SL4 3JB
☎ (01753) 864186
Fax (01753) 862640
Elegant Victorian detached house in tree-lined avenue. Private parking, indoor heated swimming pool. Close to castle, river and town.
Bedrooms: 1 double, 1 twin, 1 triple
Bathrooms: 3 en-suite
Bed & breakfast

per night:	£min	£max
Single	27.00	42.00
Double	48.00	52.00

Parking for 4
Cards accepted: Access, Visa, Switch/Delta

WITNEY
Oxfordshire
Map ref 2C1

Town famous for its blanket-making and mentioned in the Domesday Book. The market-place contains the Butter Cross, a medieval meeting place, and there is a green with merchants' houses.
Tourist Information Centre ☎ *(01993) 775802*

Crofters Guest House
HIGHLY COMMENDED

29 Oxford Hill, Witney OX8 6JU
☎ (01993) 778165
Fax (01993) 778165
Within 10 minutes' walk of Witney, providing a comfortable and homely atmosphere. Convenient for Oxford, Stratford-upon-Avon, Blenheim Palace and Cotswolds. "Arrive as a guest, leave as a friend".
Bedrooms: 1 double, 1 twin, 3 triple
Bathrooms: 2 en-suite, 1 public
Bed & breakfast

per night:	£min	£max
Single	25.00	32.00
Double	34.00	44.00

Parking for 6

Greystones Lodge Hotel
HIGHLY COMMENDED

34 Tower Hill, Witney OX8 5ES
☎ (01993) 771898
Fax (01993) 771898
Quiet, comfortable private hotel set in three-quarters of an acre of pleasant garden. Conveniently located for visiting Oxford and the Cotswolds.
Bedrooms: 4 single, 4 double, 2 twin, 1 triple
Bathrooms: 6 en-suite, 1 public, 5 private showers
Bed & breakfast

per night:	£min	£max
Single	27.00	32.00
Double	42.00	48.00

Half board per

person:	£min	£max
Daily	35.50	42.50

Evening meal 1900 (last orders 2100)
Parking for 20
Cards accepted: Access, Visa, Diners, Amex, Switch/Delta

Hawthorn House
COMMENDED

79 Burford Road, Witney OX8 5DR
☎ (01993) 772768
Modernised Victorian house with large, comfortable rooms, all en-suite. Short drive to Oxford, Blenheim Palace and the Cotswolds. Off-street parking.
Bedrooms: 1 double, 2 twin
Bathrooms: 3 en-suite, 1 public
Bed & breakfast

per night:	£min	£max
Single	20.00	25.00
Double	40.00	45.00

Parking for 4
Cards accepted: Access, Visa, Amex

ENQUIRY COUPONS

To help you obtain further information about advertisers and accommodation featured in this guide you will find enquiry coupons at the back. Send these directly to the establishments in which you are interested. Remember to complete both sides of the coupon.

SOUTH OF ENGLAND

WOBURN SANDS
Buckinghamshire
Map ref 2C1

The Old Stables
Listed COMMENDED

Woodleys Farm, Bow Brickhill Road, Woburn Sands MK17 8DE
☎ Milton Keynes (01908) 281340 & Mobile 0378 313906
Fax (01908) 584812

28-acre horses farm. Formerly a granary and stables, part of the Woburn Park Farm Estate, c 1900.

Bedrooms: 2 single, 3 double, 1 twin
Bathrooms: 5 en-suite, 1 private

Bed & breakfast
per night: £min   £max
Single   29.50   29.50
Double   39.50   39.50

Parking for 6

WOKINGHAM
Berkshire
Map ref 2C2

Pleasant town which grew up around the silk trade and has some half-timbered and Georgian houses.
Tourist Information Centre ☎ *(01734) 774722*

Cantley House Hotel
COMMENDED

Milton Road, Wokingham RG11 5QG
☎ (01734) 789912
Fax (01734) 774294

Victorian country house hotel of great charm and character, set in quiet parkland just outside Wokingham. En-suite rooms, splendid restaurant and bistro. Only 5 minutes from M4, junction 10.

Bedrooms: 15 single, 12 double, 2 twin
Suite available

Bathrooms: 29 en-suite

Bed & breakfast
per night: £min   £max
Single   45.00   82.50
Double   60.00   87.50

Lunch available
Evening meal 1900 (last orders 2200)
Parking for 70
Cards accepted: Access, Visa, Diners, Amex, Switch/Delta

WOODSTOCK
Oxfordshire
Map ref 2C1

Small country town clustered around the park gates of Blenheim Palace, the superb 18th C home of the Duke of Marlborough. The town has well-known inns and an interesting museum. Sir Winston Churchill was born and buried nearby.
Tourist Information Centre ☎ *(01993) 811038*

Gorselands Farmhouse Auberge

Boddington Lane, Long Hanborough, Witney OX8 6PU
☎ Freeland (01993) 881895
Fax (01993) 882799

Stone country farmhouse with exposed beams, snooker room, conservatory. Convenient for Blenheim Palace, Oxford and Cotswold villages. Evening meals available. Licensed for wine and beer. Grass tennis court.

Bedrooms: 1 single, 2 double, 1 twin, 2 family rooms
Suite available
Bathrooms: 6 en-suite

Bed & breakfast
per night: £min   £max
Single   21.00   29.00
Double   35.00   42.00

Half board per
person: £min   £max
Daily   27.45   38.95
Weekly   179.00 250.00

Evening meal 1900 (last orders 2100)
Parking for 7
Cards accepted: Access, Visa, Amex

USE YOUR *i*'s

There are more than 550 Tourist Information Centres throughout England offering friendly help with accommodation and holiday ideas as well as suggestions of places to visit and things to do. You'll find the address of your nearest Tourist Information Centre in your local Phone Book.

COUNTRY CODE

Always follow the Country Code
🌿 Enjoy the countryside and respect its life and work 🌿 Guard against all risk of fire 🌿 Fasten all gates 🌿 Keep your dogs under close control 🌿 Keep to public paths across farmland 🌿 Use gates and stiles to cross fences, hedges and walls 🌿 Leave livestock, crops and machinery alone 🌿 Take your litter home 🌿 Help to keep all water clean 🌿 Protect wildlife, plants and trees 🌿 Take special care on country roads 🌿 Make no unnecessary noise

CHECK THE MAPS

The colour maps at the back of this guide show all the cities, towns and villages for which you will find accommodation entries.

Refer to the town index to find the page on which it is listed.

AT-A-GLANCE SYMBOLS

Symbols at the end of each accommodation entry give useful information about services and facilities. A key to symbols can be found inside the back cover flap.

Keep this open for easy reference.

SOUTH EAST ENGLAND

South East England conjures up images of cricket on the village green, traditional village pubs and Sussex cream teas with lashings of home-made jam!

The beauty is, the fantasy is reality. South East England truly is unspoilt.

Visit Kent, the Garden of England, with its oasthouses, abundant vineyards, fruitful orchards and pretty weatherboard cottages.

Wander across the glorious South Downs, the heathland of Surrey, or head for Dover's white cliffs or the buzz of Regency Brighton.

Explore the medieval Cinque Ports and the region's churches, castles, manor houses and gardens. It's all here. As it has been for centuries.

FOR MORE INFORMATION CONTACT:
South East England Tourist Board,
The Old Brew House, Warwick Park,
Tunbridge Wells, Kent TN2 5TU
Tel: (01892) 540766 **Fax:** (01892) 511008

Where to Go in South East England -
see pages 524-527
Where to Stay in South East England -
see pages 528-565

SOUTH EAST ENGLAND
Where to Go and What to See

You will find hundreds of interesting places to visit during your stay in South East England, just some of which are listed in these pages. The number against each name will help you locate it on the map (page 527). Contact any Tourist Information Centre in the region for more ideas on days out in South East England.

1 Royal Engineers Museum
Prince Arthur Road,
Gillingham,
Kent ME4 4UG
Tel: (01634) 406397
The characters, lives and work of Britain's soldier-engineers 1066-1945. Medals, uniforms, scientific and technical equipement. Collection of ethnography and decorative arts.

2 The Historic Dockyard
Chatham, Kent ME4 4TE
Tel: (01634) 812551
Historic 18thC 80 acre dockyard. Museum with seven major attractions including the award-winning 'Wooden Walls' gallery, sail and colour loft, working ropery.

3 Brogdale Horticultural Trust
Brogdale Farm,
Brogdale Road,
Faversham, Kent ME13 8XZ
Tel: (01795) 535286
National Fruit Collection with 4,000 varieties of fruit in 30 acres of orchards: apples, pears, cherries, plums, currants, quinces, medlars and other fruits.

4 Belmont
Belmont Park,
Throwley,
Kent ME13 0HH
Tel: (01795) 890202
Late 18thC country mansion designed by Samuel Wyatt, seat of the Harris family since 1801. Harris clock collection, mementos of connections with India. Gardens and pinetum.

5 Leeds Castle
Leeds, Maidstone,
Kent ME17 1PL
Tel: (01622) 765400
Castle on two islands in lake dating from 12thC. Furniture, tapestries, art treasures. Dog Collar Museum. Gardens, parkland, duckery, aviaries, maze, grotto, small vineyard, greenhouses.

6 The Royal Horticultural Society's Garden
Wisley, Surrey GU23 6QB
Tel: (01483) 224234
World famous RHS garden covering 250 acres of vegetable, fruit and ornamental gardening. Trial grounds, glasshouses, rock garden, ponds. Rose, model and specialist gardens.

7 Guildford Boat House River Trips
Millbrook, Guildford,
Surrey GU1 3XJ
Tel: (01483) 504494
Regular trips from Guildford to St. Catherine's Lock and Farncombe along River Wey. Also 'Alfred Leroy' cruising restaurant. Rowing boats and canoes.

8 Guildford Cathedral
Stag Hill, Guildford,
Surrey GU2 5UP
Tel: (01483) 565287
New Anglican cathedral, foundation

stone laid 1936 and consecrated 1961. Notable glass engravings, embroidered kneelers. Modern furnishings. Brass Rubbing Centre.

9 Loseley House and Park Farm
Loseley Park,
Guildford,
Surrey GU3 1HS
Tel: (01483) 304440
Elizabethan mansion with decorated ceilings, unusual chalk fireplace, period furniture and paintings. Parkland and farm with famous Jersey cows, rare breeds and trailer tours.

10 Denbies Wine Estate
London Road, Dorking,
Surrey RH5 6AA
Tel: (01306) 876616
England's largest wine estate, 250 acres in beautiful countryside. Winery and visitor centre featuring 3-D time-lapse film of vine growing. Viewing and picture galleries.

11 Birdworld and Underwaterworld
Holt Pound, Farnham,
Surrey GU10 4LD
Tel: (01420) 22140
20 acres of garden and parkland with ostriches, flamingos, hornbills, parrots, emus, pelicans etc. Penguin island, tropical and marine fish. Plant area, seashore walk.

12 Hever Castle and Gardens
Hever, Edenbridge,
Kent TN8 7NG
Tel: (01732) 865224
Moated castle, family home of Anne Boleyn. Restored by Astor family. Fine interior, furniture, paintings and panelling. Gardens, lake, topiary, maze, minature model houses exhibition.

13 Headcorn Flower Centre and Vineyard
Grigg Lane, Headcorn,
Ashford, Kent TN27 9LX
Tel: (01622) 890250
Walk around 6 acres of vines. Reservoir with wildlife. Weekend and group tours visit flowerhouses with chrysanthemums and orchid lilies flowering all year.

14 Dover Castle and Hellfire Corner
Dover, Kent CT16 1HU
Tel: (01304) 201628
One of the most powerful medieval fortresses in Western Europe. St Mary-in-Castro Saxon church. Roman lighthouse, Hellfire Corner, 'All The Queen's Men' exhibition.

15 Groombridge Place Gardens
Groombridge,
Royal Tunbridge Wells,
Kent TN3 9QG
Tel: (01892) 863999
Grade I listed 17thC restored walled gardens. Drunken topiary garden, oriental and sculpture gardens, ancient and mystical woodland with spring-fed pools.

16 Bedgebury National Pinetum
Goudhurst, Kent TN17 2SL
Tel: (01580) 211044
The Forestry Commission's superb collection of specimen conifers in 150 acres with lake and streams. Plus many rhododendrons and azaleas.

17 Leonardslee Gardens
Lower Beeding,
West Sussex RH13 6PP
Tel: (01403) 891212
Rhododendrons and azaleas in a peaceful 240-acre valley garden with seven beautiful lakes. Rock garden, Bonsai exhibition and wallabies.

18 The Bluebell Railway
Sheffield Park,
East Sussex TN22 3QL
Tel: (01825) 722370
9 miles of vintage steam and train railway from Sheffield Park to Horsted Keynes and extension to Kingscote. Largest collection of engines in the south. Victorian stations and museum.

19 Brickwall House and Gardens
Northiam,
East Sussex TN31 6NL
Tel: (01797) 223329
Formal gardens with terracotta entrance gates, 18thC bowling alley, sunken topiary garden, yew hedges, chess garden, arboretum. Jacobean house with 17thC plaster ceilings.

20 Great Dixter House and Gardens
Northiam,
East Sussex TN31 6PH
Tel: (01797) 253107
Fine example of 15thC manor house with antique furniture and needlework. Unique great hall restored by Lutyens who also designed garden – topiary, meadow garden, flower beds.

21 Buckleys Yesterday's World
89-90 High Street, Battle,
East Sussex TN33 0AQ
Tel: (01424) 775378
Over 100,000 exhibits in a Wealden hall house recall shopping and domestic life from 1850 to 1950 with smells and commentaries. Railway station, play village, garden.

22 A Smugglers Adventure At St. Clements Caves
West Hill, Hastings,
East Sussex TN34 3HY
Tel: (01424) 422964
An extensive exhibition of 18thC smuggling, housed in 2000 sq m of caves. Exhibition, museum, video theatre, extensive Adventure Walk incorporating dramatic special effects.

23 Brighton Sea Life Centre
Marine Parade,
Brighton,
East Sussex BN2 1TB
Tel: (01273) 604234
Discover the thrilling world beneath the waves as the Brighton Sea Life Centre takes you on an unforgettable voyage of discovery.

24 Foredown Tower Countryside Centre
Foredown Road, Portslade,
East Sussex BN41 2EW
Tel: (01273) 422540
Water tower housing a camera obscura, an unusual viewing device used by artists and astronomers since the 17thC. Popular entertainment in Victorian times.

25 Charleston Farmhouse
Firle, Lewes, East Sussex BN8 6LL
Tel: (01323) 811265
A 17-18thC farmhouse, home of Vanessa and Clive Bell and Duncan Grant. House and contents decorated by the artists. Restored garden room. Traditional flint-walled garden.

26 Amberley Museum
Houghton Bridge, Amberley,
Arundel, West Sussex BN18 9LT
Tel: (01798) 831370
Open-air industrial history centre in chalk quarry. Working craftsmen, narrow gauge railway, early buses, working machines and many other exhibits. Nature trail and visitor centre.

27 The Wildfowl and Wetlands Centre
Mill Road, Arundel,
West Sussex BN18 9PB
Tel: (01903) 883355
Reserve in 60 acres of watermeadows. Tame swans, ducks, geese and many wild birds. Film theatre and visitor centre with gallery.

28 Weald and Downland Open Air Museum
Singleton,
West Sussex PO18 0EU
Tel: (01243) 811348
Open-air museum of rescued historic buildings from South East England reconstructed on downland. 35 buildings include medieval farmstead and watermill.

29 Pallant House
9 North Pallant, Chichester,
West Sussex PO19 1TJ
Tel: (01243) 774557
Queen Anne townhouse with important works by British and European masters of the 20thC. Antiques include the world's greatest collection of Bow porcelain.

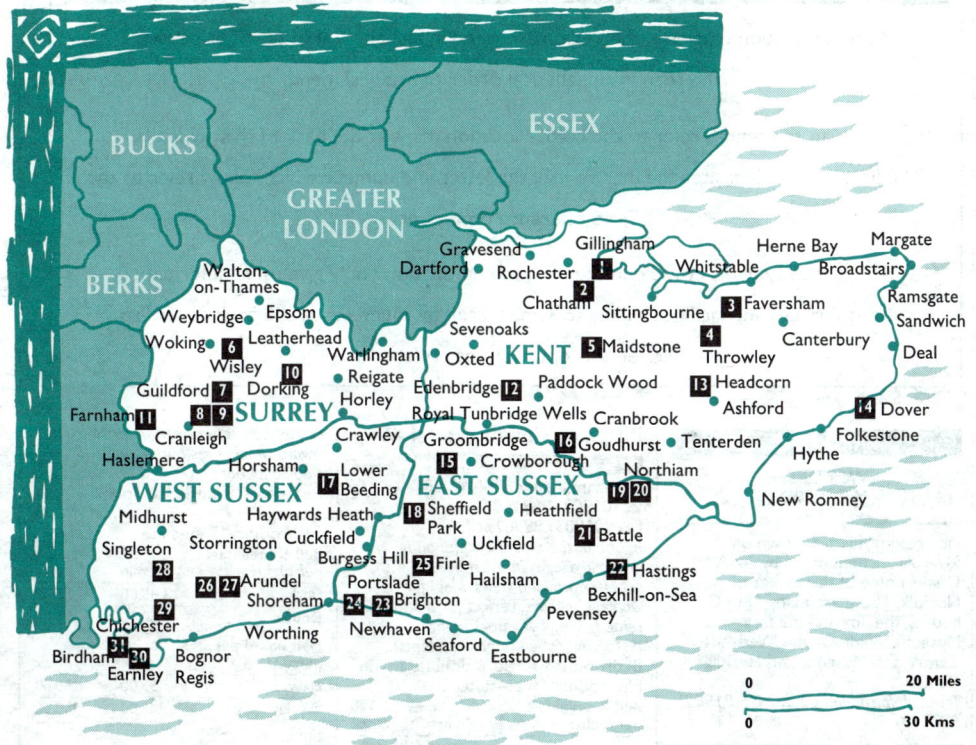

30 Earnley Butterflies and Gardens

133 Almodington Lane, Earnley,
West Sussex PO20 7JR
Tel: (01243) 512637
Ornamental butterfly house, covered theme gardens from around the world, exotic bird garden, children's play area, small animal farm and pottery.

31 Sussex Falconry Centre

Locksacre Aquatic Nursery,
Wophams Lane, Birdham,
West Sussex PO20 7BS
Tel: (01243) 512472
Aviaries containing birds of prey including hawks, falcons and owls. Flying displays of birds throughout the day, weather permitting.

FIND OUT MORE

Further information about holidays and attractions in South East England is available from:

South East England Tourist Board,
The Old Brew House,
Warwick Park,
Tunbridge Wells,
Kent TN2 5TU.
Tel: (01892) 540766

These publications are available free from the South East England Tourist Board:
- **Great Escapes**
- **Accommodation Guide**
- **Events South East**
- **Bed and Breakfast Touring Map**

■ **Outstanding Churches and Cathedrals**

Also available is (price includes postage and packaging):
- **South East England Leisure Map** £4
- **Hundreds of Place to Visit in the South East** £2.80
- **Villages to Visit** £2.50

527

WHERE TO STAY (SOUTH EAST ENGLAND)

Accommodation entries in this region are listed in alphabetical order of place name, and then in alphabetical order of establishment.

Map references refer to the colour location maps at the back of this guide. The first number indicates the map to use; the letter and number which follow refer to the grid reference on the map.

At-a-glance symbols at the end of each accommodation entry give useful information about services and facilities. A key to symbols can be found inside the back cover flap. Keep this open for easy reference.

ARUNDEL
West Sussex
Map ref 2D3

Picturesque, historic town on the River Arun, dominated by Arundel Castle, home of the Dukes of Norfolk. There are many 18th C houses, the Toy and Military Museum, Wildfowl and Wetlands Centre and Museum and Heritage Centre.
Tourist Information Centre ☎ (01903) 882268

Bridge House
COMMENDED
18 Queen Street, Arundel BN18 9JG
☎ (01903) 882779 & Freephone 0500 323224
Fax (01903) 883600
Family-run guesthouse, in centre of town, with views of castle, river, and Downs. Ideal centre for exploring beautiful Sussex, ancestral homes, Roman ruins and for visiting Fontwell and Goodwood racecourses.
Bedrooms: 2 single, 8 double, 2 twin, 4 triple, 3 family rooms
Bathrooms: 13 en-suite, 2 public
Bed & breakfast
per night: £min   £max
Single   22.00   28.00
Double   32.00   42.00
Lunch available
Evening meal 1800 (last orders 1930)
Parking for 10
Cards accepted: Access, Visa, Switch/Delta

Burpham Country Hotel
HIGHLY COMMENDED
Burpham, Arundel BN18 9RJ
☎ (01903) 882160
Fax (01903) 884627
In one of the most peaceful and unspoilt villages in West Sussex, with superb downland views. Ideal for walking holidays. Perfect for a stress remedy break. Award-winning restaurant (open to non-residents).
Bedrooms: 1 single, 6 double, 3 twin
Bathrooms: 10 en-suite
Bed & breakfast
per night: £min   £max
Single   35.00
Double   72.00   79.00
Half board per
person: £min   £max
Daily   53.50   58.00
Weekly   339.50 367.50
Evening meal 1915 (last orders 2045)
Parking for 12
Cards accepted: Access, Visa, Amex

Swan Hotel
HIGHLY COMMENDED
27-29 High Street, Arundel BN18 9AG
☎ (01903) 882314
Fax (01903) 883759

Elegant Grade II listed building situated in the heart of historic Arundel.

Completely refurbished in 1994. Award-winning restaurant with traditional bar.
Bedrooms: 3 single, 10 double, 2 twin
Bathrooms: 15 en-suite
Bed & breakfast
per night: £min   £max
Single   45.00   55.00
Double   50.00   70.00
Half board per
person: £min   £max
Daily   35.00   50.00
Weekly   245.00 350.00
Lunch available
Evening meal 1830 (last orders 2200)
Parking for 20
Cards accepted: Access, Visa, Diners, Amex, Switch/Delta

ASHFORD
Kent
Map ref 3B4

Once a market centre for the farmers of the Weald of Kent and Romney Marsh. The town centre has a number of Tudor and Georgian houses.
Tourist Information Centre ☎ (01233) 629165

Croft Hotel
COMMENDED
Canterbury Road, Kennington, Ashford TN25 4DU
☎ (01233) 622140
Fax (01233) 622140
Ⓡ The Independents

SOUTH EAST ENGLAND

Country house in 2 acres of gardens. Channel Tunnel 10 miles, Canterbury 12 miles, Dover 22 miles. Ideal for business people and tourists alike.
Bedrooms: 6 single, 8 double, 9 twin, 4 triple, 1 family room
Bathrooms: 28 en-suite
Bed & breakfast

per night:	£min	£max
Single	37.50	43.50
Double	47.50	57.50

Evening meal 1830 (last orders 2000)
Parking for 32
Cards accepted: Access, Visa, Amex

Warren Cottage

APPROVED

136 The Street, Willesborough, Ashford TN24 0NB
☎ (01233) 621905 & 632929
Fax (01233) 623400

300-year-old guesthouse with oak beams, open fireplaces and a cosy atmosphere. On old coaching route with easy access to M20 and a short drive from many places of interest.
Email: 101666.571@compuserve.com.
Bedrooms: 2 single, 2 double
Bathrooms: 4 en-suite, 1 public
Bed & breakfast

per night:	£min	£max
Single	25.00	29.90
Double	42.00	59.80

Half board per

person:	£min	£max
Daily	35.00	39.90
Weekly	245.00	275.00

Lunch available
Evening meal 1830 (last orders 2130)
Parking for 13
Cards accepted: Access, Visa, Switch/Delta

BENENDEN
Kent
Map ref 3B4

Set on a high ridge, with a big tree-lined village green where cricket is played on summer weekends. Tile-hung cottages and a white weatherboarded post office mingle with 19th C houses and a sandstone church.

Crit Hall

Listed DE LUXE

Cranbrook Road, Benenden, Cranbrook TN17 4EU
☎ Cranbrook (01580) 240609
Fax (01580) 241743
Elegant Georgian country house, near Sissinghurst, with panoramic views. Imaginative dinners. Licensed. Many National Trust properties and gardens nearby.
Bedrooms: 1 double, 2 twin
Bathrooms: 1 en-suite, 2 private
Bed & breakfast

per night:	£min	£max
Single	33.00	38.00
Double	50.00	52.00

Half board per

person:	£min	£max
Daily	43.50	56.50
Weekly	273.00	335.50

Evening meal from 1930
Parking for 6
Cards accepted: Access, Visa, Switch/Delta

BEXHILL-ON-SEA
East Sussex
Map ref 3B4

Popular resort with beach of shingle and firm sand at low tide. The De la Warr Pavilion has good entertainment facilities.
Tourist Information Centre ☎ (01424) 212023 or 732208

Bedford Lodge Hotel

COMMENDED

Cantelupe Road, Bexhill-on-Sea TN40 1PR
☎ (01424) 730097
Comfortable, family-run, Victorian building in quiet residential area close to promenade and town. Appetising home cooking. Easy parking.
Bedrooms: 2 single, 2 double, 2 twin
Bathrooms: 3 en-suite, 3 public
Bed & breakfast

per night:	£min	£max
Single	20.00	25.00
Double	39.00	50.00

Half board per

person:	£min	£max
Daily	25.00	34.00
Weekly	158.00	210.00

Lunch available
Evening meal 1800 (last orders 1900)
Parking for 1
Cards accepted: Access, Visa, Switch/Delta

BIRLING GAP
East Sussex
Map ref 2D3

Birling Gap Hotel

APPROVED

Birling Gap, Seven Sisters Cliffs, East Dean, Eastbourne BN20 0AB
☎ Eastbourne (01323) 423197
Fax (01323) 423030
Logis of Great Britain

Magnificent Seven Sisters clifftop position, with views of country, sea, beach. Superb downland and beach walks. Old world "Thatched Bar" and "Oak Room Restaurant". Coffee shop and games room, function and conference suite. Off A259 coast road at East Dean, 1.5 miles west of Beachy Head.
Bedrooms: 1 single, 2 double, 3 twin, 3 triple
Bathrooms: 9 en-suite, 1 public
Bed & breakfast

per night:	£min	£max
Single	20.00	50.00
Double	30.00	60.00

Half board per

person:	£min	£max
Daily	29.00	38.00
Weekly	183.00	245.00

Lunch available
Evening meal 1830 (last orders 2115)
Parking for 100
Cards accepted: Access, Visa, Diners, Amex, Switch/Delta

Please mention this guide when making your booking.

SOUTH EAST ENGLAND

BOGNOR REGIS
West Sussex
Map ref 2D3

5 miles of firm, flat sand have made the town a popular family resort. Well supplied with gardens, children's activities in Hotham Park and the Bognor Regis Centre for entertainment.
Tourist Information Centre ☎ (01243) 823140

Beachcroft Hotel
COMMENDED

Clyde Road, Felpham, Bognor Regis PO22 7AH
☎ (01243) 827142
Fax (01243) 827142
Family-run hotel in south-facing beachside village location. Garden, indoor heated pool, car park. All rooms en-suite with TV, telephone, tea and coffee. Comprehensive restaurant and bar facilities.
Bedrooms: 11 single, 6 double, 16 twin, 1 triple, 4 family rooms
Bathrooms: 38 en-suite
Bed & breakfast per night:	£min	£max
Single	25.50	30.00
Double	43.00	57.75

Half board per person:	£min	£max
Daily	31.75	49.00
Weekly	187.50	300.00

Evening meal 1900 (last orders 2100)
Parking for 40
Cards accepted: Access, Visa, Amex

Camelot Hotel & Restaurant
COMMENDED

3 Flansham Lane, Felpham, Bognor Regis PO22 6AA
☎ Middleton-on-Sea (01243) 585875
Fax (01243) 587500
Whilst away from home do what King Arthur did: think of Camelot. Situated on A259 Littlehampton-Bognor main road in the village of Felpham, West Sussex.
Bedrooms: 1 single, 7 double, 1 twin
Bathrooms: 9 en-suite

Bed & breakfast per night:	£min	£max
Single	32.50	40.00
Double	48.50	52.50

Half board per person:	£min	£max
Daily	37.50	52.50
Weekly	236.25	297.50

Lunch available
Evening meal 1910 (last orders 2145)
Parking for 25
Cards accepted: Access, Visa, Diners, Amex, Switch/Delta

Jubilee Guest House
Listed COMMENDED

5 Gloucester Road, Bognor Regis PO21 1NU
☎ (01243) 863016
Just 45 yards from sea. Ideal base for sightseeing. Local places of interest include Arundel, Chichester and Goodwood.
Bedrooms: 2 single, 1 double, 1 triple, 1 family room
Bathrooms: 1 private, 1 public, 2 private showers

Bed & breakfast per night:	£min	£max
Single	16.00	18.00
Double	30.00	34.00

Parking for 4
Open April–October

BRIGHTON & HOVE
East Sussex
Map ref 2D3

Brighton's attractions include the Royal Pavilion, Volks Electric Railway, Sea Life Centre and Marina Village, Conference Centre and "The Lanes" and several theatres. Neighbouring Hove is a resort in its own right.
Tourist Information Centre ☎ (01273) 323755; for Hove (01273) 746100 or 778087

Aegean Hotel
APPROVED

5 New Steine, Brighton, East Sussex BN2 1PB
☎ Brighton (01273) 686547
Family-run hotel where you can be sure of a warm welcome and satisfaction for your long or short stay.
Bedrooms: 4 single, 1 double, 1 twin, 4 triple
Bathrooms: 7 en-suite, 1 public, 1 private shower

Bed & breakfast per night:	£min	£max
Single	18.00	28.00
Double	36.00	52.00

Half board per person:	£min	£max
Daily	29.00	39.00
Weekly	190.00	260.00

Evening meal 1830 (last orders 1930)
Cards accepted: Access, Visa, Diners, Amex

Ainsley House Hotel
COMMENDED

28 New Steine, Brighton, East Sussex BN2 1PD
☎ Brighton (01273) 605310
Fax (01273) 688604
Elegant listed Regency town house overlooking a garden square and the sea. 10 minutes from conference centre, shops and theatres.
Bedrooms: 3 single, 3 double, 1 twin, 3 triple
Bathrooms: 8 en-suite, 1 public

Bed & breakfast per night:	£min	£max
Single	24.00	30.00
Double	48.00	60.00

Cards accepted: Access, Visa, Diners, Amex

Allendale Hotel
COMMENDED

3 New Steine, Brighton, East Sussex BN2 1PB
☎ Brighton (01273) 675436
Fax (01273) 602603
Regency hotel, offering every facility for a comfortable, enjoyable and stress-free stay. Privately run, overlooking garden square and sea.
Bedrooms: 5 single, 3 double, 1 twin, 2 triple, 1 family room
Bathrooms: 9 en-suite, 2 public, 1 private shower

Bed & breakfast per night:	£min	£max
Single	25.00	35.00
Double	48.00	70.00

Half board per person:	£min	£max
Daily	40.00	40.00

Evening meal 1800 (last orders 2000)
Cards accepted: Access, Visa, Amex

Ambassador Hotel

22 New Steine, Marine Parade, Brighton, East Sussex BN2 1PD
☎ Brighton (01273) 676869
Fax (01273) 689988
Family-run, licensed hotel overlooking sea, near conference centres. Colour TV, telephone, radio, tea/coffee facilities.
Bedrooms: 3 single, 4 double, 3 triple
Bathrooms: 10 en-suite

SOUTH EAST ENGLAND

Bed & breakfast
per night:	£min	£max
Single	28.00	35.00
Double	40.00	60.00

Cards accepted: Access, Visa, Diners, Amex

Arlanda Hotel

HIGHLY COMMENDED

20 New Steine, Brighton, East Sussex BN2 1PD
☎ Brighton (01273) 699300
Fax (01273) 600930
Enjoy good food and company in a licensed, family-run hotel. Our warm rooms have full en-suite facilities. The hotel is in a quiet 200-year-old Regency square, yet close to Brighton's attractions.
Bedrooms: 4 single, 4 double, 1 twin, 3 triple
Bathrooms: 12 en-suite
Bed & breakfast
per night:	£min	£max
Single	22.00	36.00
Double	46.00	80.00

Lunch available
Evening meal 1800 (last orders 2000)

Cards accepted: Access, Visa, Diners, Amex

Ascott House Hotel

HIGHLY COMMENDED

21 New Steine, Marine Parade, Brighton, East Sussex BN2 1PD
☎ Brighton (01273) 688085
Fax (01273) 623733
Well established, popular hotel with sea views close to all amenities. Reputation for comfort, cleanliness and delicious breakfasts.
Bedrooms: 4 single, 6 triple, 2 family rooms
Bathrooms: 10 en-suite, 1 public, 1 private shower
Bed & breakfast
per night:	£min	£max
Single	20.00	40.00
Double	40.00	80.00

Evening meal 1830 (last orders 1930)
Cards accepted: Access, Visa, Diners, Amex

'Brighton' Marina House Hotel

8 Charlotte Street, Marine Parade, Brighton, East Sussex BN2 1AG
☎ Brighton (01273) 605349 & Freephone 0500 099989
Fax (01273) 605349

Cosy, elegantly furnished, well-equipped, clean, comfortable, caring, family-run. Near sea, central for Palace Pier, Royal Pavilion, conference and exhibition halls, the famous Lanes, tourist attractions. Flexible breakfast, check-in/out times. Offering all facilities. Free street parking. Best in price range.
Bedrooms: 3 single, 2 double, 2 twin, 3 triple
Bathrooms: 7 en-suite, 1 public
Bed & breakfast
per night:	£min	£max
Single	15.00	39.00
Double	35.00	59.00

Continued ▶

THE TWENTY ONE

HOTEL DESCRIPTION
This highly acclaimed hotel is the charm of Brighton.
We are only a few steps from the beach and walking distance from all the major attractions.

ROOM DESCRIPTION
The delightful rooms are en-suite and fully equipped for business and leisure.

In Our collection there are some classic rooms. These include:
The twin **GOLDEN** room is unique in the hotel world as it contains two single four poster beds. An ideal setting for friends and couples alike.

The double **VICTORIAN** room is exquisitely furnished with antique pieces and includes a most attractive brass double bed.

The four poster **PATIO SUITE** boasts a large double vanity-unit washroom with its own separate WC, and a cosy conservatory which, in turn, leads onto a charming ivy-clad court-yard.

21 CHARLOTTE STREET
BRIGHTON BN2 1AG

TEL:(44) 01273 686450 / 681517
FAX:(44) 01273 695560
E-MAIL:the21@pavilion.co.uk

BREAKFAST MENU
In the Bon Appetite Room, we are committed to creating the ultimate breakfast experience. Dive into an eight section menu, catering for Vegans, Low calorie intake, a continental section and, of course the full English.

SPECIAL BREAKS
1) Stay any 2 nights and claim a **10%** discount off our normal tariff.
2) Stay any 4 nights and claim a **20%** discount off our normal tariff.
3) Stay any 7 nights and claim a **30%** discount off our normal tariff.

ROOM TARIFF		
	•	*
DOUBLE	£35.00	£65.00
TWIN/ FAMILY	£42.00	£60.00
SUITE	£60.00	£86.00

• 7 day stay price with **30%** discount
* Normal Tariff

SOUTH EAST ENGLAND

BRIGHTON & HOVE
Continued

Half board per person:
	£min	£max
Daily	25.00	49.00
Weekly	160.00	304.00

Lunch available
Evening meal 1830 (last orders 1700)
Cards accepted: Access, Visa, Diners, Amex

Brighton Oak Hotel
COMMENDED

West Street, Brighton, East Sussex BN1 2RQ
☎ Brighton (01273) 220033
Fax (01273) 778000
Elegant new city centre hotel, designed in 1930s art deco style, close to the seafront, adjoining the conference centre and the famous Lanes.
Wheelchair access category 3
Bedrooms: 2 single, 56 double, 80 twin
Bathrooms: 138 en-suite

Bed & breakfast per night:
	£min	£max
Single	55.50	97.50
Double	73.00	120.00

Half board per person:
	£min	£max
Daily	47.00	74.25
Weekly	282.00	445.50

Lunch available
Evening meal 1830 (last orders 2200)
Cards accepted: Access, Visa, Diners, Amex, Switch/Delta

The Brighton Twenty One Hotel

21 Charlotte Street, Marine Parade, Brighton, East Sussex BN2 1AG
☎ Brighton (01273) 686450
Fax (01273) 695560

Early Victorian town house with elegantly furnished bedrooms. Exquisite Victorian room features a grand brass bed. Discounts: 10% 2 nights, 20% 4 nights, 30% 7 nights.

Bedrooms: 4 double, 2 twin
Suite available
Bathrooms: 6 en-suite, 1 public

Bed & breakfast per night:
	£min	£max
Single	25.00	50.00
Double	35.00	80.00

Half board per person:
	£min	£max
Daily	35.00	45.00
Weekly	171.00	220.00

Evening meal 1830 (last orders 2000)
Cards accepted: Access, Visa, Diners, Amex

Ad See display advertisement on page 531

Cavalaire House
COMMENDED

34 Upper Rock Gardens, Brighton, East Sussex BN2 1QF
☎ Brighton (01273) 696899
Fax (01273) 600504
Victorian townhouse, close to sea and town centre. Resident proprietors offer comfortably furnished rooms with or without private facilities. Book 7 nights and get 1 night free.
Bedrooms: 1 single, 3 double, 3 twin, 2 triple
Bathrooms: 1 en-suite, 2 private, 1 public, 3 private showers

Bed & breakfast per night:
	£min	£max
Single	18.00	19.00
Double	42.00	48.00

Cards accepted: Access, Visa, Amex

Chatsworth Hotel

9 Salisbury Road, Hove, East Sussex BN3 3AB
☎ Brighton (01273) 737360
Long established, well-appointed, comfortable hotel in quiet position close to sea and county cricket ground. Accent on food.
Bedrooms: 4 single, 1 double, 2 twin, 1 triple
Bathrooms: 1 en-suite, 3 public

Bed & breakfast per night:
	£min	£max
Single	20.00	24.00
Double	40.00	50.00

Half board per person:
	£min	£max
Daily	26.00	28.00
Weekly	130.00	140.00

Lunch available
Evening meal 1830 (last orders 1900)
Cards accepted: Access, Visa, Switch/Delta

Cosmopolitan Hotel

31 New Steine, Marine Parade, Brighton, East Sussex BN2 1PD
☎ Brighton (01273) 682461
Fax (01273) 622311
In a commanding position in seafront square, overlooking the beach and Palace Pier. Central for shopping, entertainments and conference centres.
Bedrooms: 12 single, 11 double, 3 twin, 10 triple, 2 family rooms
Bathrooms: 32 en-suite, 4 private, 3 public, 2 private showers

Bed & breakfast per night:
	£min	£max
Single	20.00	30.00
Double	38.00	55.00

Cards accepted: Access, Visa, Diners, Amex

Diana House
Listed APPROVED

25 St Georges Terrace, Brighton, East Sussex BN2 1JJ
☎ Brighton (01273) 605797
Large, friendly guesthouse close to sea, town and conference centre. All rooms have TV, hospitality tray, clock/radio, shaver point. Some rooms en-suite. 24-hour access.
Bedrooms: 4 double, 2 twin, 2 triple, 1 family room
Bathrooms: 3 private, 1 public, 5 private showers

Bed & breakfast per night:
	£min	£max
Single	16.00	19.00
Double	32.00	38.00

Evening meal 1800 (last orders 2000)
Cards accepted: Access, Visa

Fyfield House
COMMENDED

26 New Steine, Brighton, East Sussex BN2 1PD
☎ Brighton (01273) 602770
Fax (01273) 602770
Established over 25 years. Excellent home-from-home hotel, close to all attractions in and out of town. Peter and Anna ensure a nice stay.
Bedrooms: 4 single, 5 double
Bathrooms: 5 en-suite, 1 public

SOUTH EAST ENGLAND

Bed & breakfast per night:	£min	£max
Single	16.00	28.00
Double	32.00	56.00

Half board per person:	£min	£max
Daily	26.00	40.00

Evening meal 1800 (last orders 1900)
Cards accepted: Access, Visa, Diners, Amex, Switch/Delta

Kempton House Hotel

COMMENDED

33-34 Marine Parade, Brighton, East Sussex BN2 1TR
☎ Brighton (01273) 570248
Fax (01273) 570248
Seafront hotel overlooking beach and Palace Pier. Central to all amenities. En-suite sea view rooms. Licensed bar and sea-facing patio garden.
Bedrooms: 7 double, 2 twin, 3 triple
Bathrooms: 12 en-suite

Bed & breakfast per night:	£min	£max
Single	29.00	39.00
Double	40.00	59.00

Evening meal from 1800
Cards accepted: Access, Visa, Amex, Switch/Delta

Kimberley Hotel

APPROVED

17 Atlingworth Street, Brighton, East Sussex BN2 1PL
☎ Brighton (01273) 603504
Fax (01273) 603504
Family-run hotel, 2 minutes from seafront and central for amusements, shopping, marina and conference centre. Licensed residents' bar.
Bedrooms: 3 single, 3 double, 5 twin, 2 triple, 2 family rooms
Bathrooms: 4 en-suite, 1 public, 11 private showers

Bed & breakfast per night:	£min	£max
Single	18.00	22.00
Double	35.00	42.00

Cards accepted: Access, Visa, Diners, Amex, Switch/Delta

Leona House

74 Middle Street, Brighton, East Sussex BN1 1AL
☎ Brighton (01273) 327309
Privately run guesthouse close to sea, conference centre and all amenities.

Bedrooms: 2 single, 3 double, 2 twin, 1 triple
Bathrooms: 3 en-suite, 1 public

Bed & breakfast per night:	£min	£max
Single	17.00	19.00
Double	26.00	38.00

Cards accepted: Access, Visa, Amex

Melford Hall Hotel

APPROVED

41 Marine Parade, Brighton, East Sussex BN2 1PE
☎ Brighton (01273) 681435
Fax (01273) 624186
Listed building, well positioned on seafront and within easy walking distance of all the entertainment that Brighton has to offer. Many rooms with sea views.
Bedrooms: 4 single, 16 double, 4 twin, 1 triple
Bathrooms: 23 en-suite, 1 public, 2 private showers

Bed & breakfast per night:	£min	£max
Single	30.00	34.00
Double	46.00	54.00

Parking for 12
Cards accepted: Access, Visa, Diners, Amex

Old Ship Hotel

COMMENDED

King's Road, Brighton, East Sussex BN1 1NR
☎ Brighton (01273) 329001
Fax (01273) 820718
Best Western
Refurbished old world character hotel on Brighton's seafront. Noted restaurant. Sea view and executive rooms available.
Bedrooms: 11 single, 88 double, 53 twin
Bathrooms: 152 en-suite

Bed & breakfast per night:	£min	£max
Single	50.00	80.00
Double	80.00	125.00

Half board per person:	£min	£max
Daily	80.00	108.00
Weekly	280.00	630.00

Lunch available
Evening meal 1930 (last orders 2130)
Parking for 70
Cards accepted: Access, Visa, Diners, Amex

Ryford Hotel

6-7 New Steine, Hove, East Sussex BN2 1PB
☎ Brighton (01273) 681576
Fax (01273) 693397
Family hotel in one of the finest positions on the seafront. Close to Palace Pier, Brighton Centre and main shopping amenities. Most bedrooms en-suite with TV and tea/coffee-making.
Bedrooms: 9 single, 9 double, 6 twin
Suites available
Bathrooms: 15 en-suite, 4 public, 6 private showers

Bed & breakfast per night:	£min	£max
Single	20.00	25.00
Double	35.00	45.00

Open March–October
Cards accepted: Diners, Amex

St. Catherines Lodge Hotel

COMMENDED

Kingsway, Hove, East Sussex BN3 2RZ
☎ Brighton (01273) 778181
Fax (01273) 774949

Well-established seafront hotel. Restaurant specialises in traditional English dishes. Four-poster honeymoon rooms. Attractive cocktail bar, games rooms, garden, and easy parking. Opposite King Alfred sports and leisure centre.
Bedrooms: 8 single, 17 double, 11 twin, 1 triple, 3 family rooms
Bathrooms: 40 en-suite, 5 public

Bed & breakfast per night:	£min	£max
Single	36.00	45.00
Double	54.00	65.00

Half board per person:	£min	£max
Daily	37.00	40.00
Weekly	190.00	240.00

Lunch available
Evening meal 1900 (last orders 2100)
Parking for 4
Cards accepted: Access, Visa, Diners, Amex

SOUTH EAST ENGLAND

BRIGHTON & HOVE
Continued

Hotel Seafield
APPROVED
23 Seafield Road, Hove, East Sussex BN3 2TP
☎ Brighton (01273) 735912
Fax (01273) 735912
Family-run hotel with home-cooked food, close to the seafront and main shopping centre. Free street parking in addition to private parking. Most rooms en-suite with shower/toilet.
Bedrooms: 1 single, 5 double, 1 twin, 2 triple, 3 family rooms
Bathrooms: 11 en-suite, 3 public

Bed & breakfast per night:
	£min	£max
Single	18.00	35.00
Double	36.00	55.00

Half board per person:
	£min	£max
Daily	35.00	50.00

Lunch available
Evening meal 1900 (last orders 1700)
Parking for 8

CAMBERLEY
Surrey
Map ref 2C2

Well-known for the Royal Staff College and the nearby Royal Military Academy, Sandhurst.

Burwood House Hotel
15 London Road, Camberley GU15 3UQ
☎ (01276) 685686
Fax (01276) 62220
Friendly, family-run hotel where Richard and Jenny Cave enjoy looking after you. Approximately 2 miles from junctions 3 and 4 of M3.
Bedrooms: 8 single, 7 double, 2 twin, 2 triple
Bathrooms: 19 en-suite

Bed & breakfast per night:
	£min	£max
Single	35.00	60.00
Double	45.00	75.00

Half board per person:
	£min	£max
Daily	47.00	72.00

Evening meal 1900 (last orders 2030)
Parking for 21
Cards accepted: Access, Visa, Diners, Amex, Switch/Delta

CANTERBURY
Kent
Map ref 3B3

Place of pilgrimage since the martyrdom of Becket in 1170 and the site of Canterbury Cathedral. Visit St Augustine's Abbey, St Martin's (the oldest church in England), Royal Museum and Art Gallery and the Canterbury Tales. Nearby is Howletts Wild Animal Park. Good shopping centre.
Tourist Information Centre ☎ (01227) 766567

Anns House
63 London Road, Canterbury CT2 8JZ
☎ (01227) 768767
Fax (01227) 768172

Comfortable Victorian guesthouse with private car park, close to city centre. Restored with love and care to accommodate the modern traveller who wants to tread the Pilgrims' Way or commute to and from the Continent.
Bedrooms: 4 single, 7 double, 3 twin, 1 triple, 3 family rooms
Bathrooms: 10 en-suite, 3 public, 5 private showers

Bed & breakfast per night:
	£min	£max
Single	20.00	30.00
Double	40.00	50.00

Parking for 10
Cards accepted: Access, Visa

Canterbury Hotel
71 New Dover Road, Canterbury CT1 3DZ
☎ (01227) 450551
Fax (01227) 780145
Elegant Victorian hotel, 10 minutes from city centre, providing high standards of personal service and comfort. Licensed French/English restaurant, bar, lift, car park.
Bedrooms: 4 single, 7 double, 13 twin, 2 triple
Bathrooms: 26 en-suite

Bed & breakfast per night:
	£min	£max
Single	40.00	45.00
Double	55.00	58.00

Half board per person:
	£min	£max
Daily	40.00	

Lunch available
Evening meal 1900 (last orders 2200)
Parking for 40
Cards accepted: Access, Visa, Diners, Amex

Cathedral Gate Hotel
36 Burgate, Canterbury CT1 2HA
☎ (01227) 464381
Fax (01227) 462800
Central position at main entrance to the cathedral. Car parking nearby. Baby listening service. Old world charm at reasonable prices. English breakfast extra.
Bedrooms: 5 single, 7 double, 7 twin, 3 triple, 2 family rooms
Bathrooms: 12 en-suite, 3 public, 2 private showers

Bed & breakfast per night:
	£min	£max
Single	21.00	47.50
Double	40.00	72.00

Evening meal 1900 (last orders 2100)
Parking for 12
Cards accepted: Access, Visa, Diners, Amex, Switch/Delta

Chaucer Lodge
HIGHLY COMMENDED
62 New Dover Road, Canterbury CT1 3DT
☎ (01227) 459141
Maria and Alistair Wilson extend a warm, friendly welcome to this comfortable family guesthouse. City 10 minutes' walk, county cricket ground 5 minutes. High standard of cleanliness and furnishings. Breakfast menu.
Bedrooms: 3 double, 2 twin, 1 triple, 1 family room
Bathrooms: 6 en-suite, 1 private

Bed & breakfast per night:
	£min	£max
Single	30.00	50.00
Double	40.00	55.00

Evening meal 1800 (last orders 2000)
Parking for 12

SOUTH EAST ENGLAND

Clare-Ellen Guest House ♠
HIGHLY COMMENDED
9 Victoria Road, Wincheap,
Canterbury CT1 3SG
☎ (01227) 760205
Fax (01227) 784482

Victorian house with large, elegant en-suite rooms, 6 minutes' walk to town centre. 5 minutes to Canterbury East train station. Car park and garage available.
Bedrooms: 1 single, 1 double, 1 twin, 1 triple, 1 family room
Bathrooms: 4 en-suite, 1 private, 1 public

Bed & breakfast per night:	£min	£max
Single	22.00	28.00
Double	42.00	48.00

Parking for 9
Cards accepted: Access, Visa, Switch/Delta

Ebury Hotel ♠
HIGHLY COMMENDED
New Dover Road, Canterbury
CT1 3DX
☎ (01227) 768433
Fax (01227) 459187
Family-run, Victorian hotel just outside city centre. Licensed restaurant, large public rooms and bedrooms. Heated indoor pool and spa. Overnight half board prices based on minimum 2-night stay.
Bedrooms: 2 single, 7 double, 4 twin, 1 triple, 1 family room
Bathrooms: 15 en-suite

Bed & breakfast per night:	£min	£max
Single	41.00	48.00
Double	60.00	66.00

Half board per person:	£min	£max
Daily	39.00	63.00
Weekly	235.00	275.00

Evening meal 1900 (last orders 2030)
Parking for 21
Cards accepted: Access, Visa, Amex, Switch/Delta

Ersham Lodge Hotel ♠
COMMENDED
12 New Dover Road, Canterbury
CT1 3AP
☎ (01227) 463174
Fax (01227) 455482
Delightfully appointed rooms, furnished with exquisite taste and elegance. Colour TV, telephone, radio, hairdryer. Well-stocked bar, bright breakfast room, pleasant patio. Close to amenities.
Bedrooms: 1 single, 5 double, 5 twin, 1 triple, 1 family room
Bathrooms: 12 en-suite, 1 private

Bed & breakfast per night:	£min	£max
Single	39.00	43.00
Double	54.00	62.00

Parking for 12
Cards accepted: Access, Visa, Amex

Falstaff Hotel ♠
HIGHLY COMMENDED
St Dunstans Street, Canterbury
CT2 8AF
☎ (01227) 462138
Fax (01227) 463525
GR Whitbread
A former coaching inn dating back to the 15th C, in the heart of the town close to Westgate Towers.
Bedrooms: 6 single, 14 double, 3 twin, 2 triple
Bathrooms: 25 en-suite

Bed & breakfast per night:	£min	£max
Single	70.00	75.00
Double	78.00	85.00

Half board per person:	£min	£max
Daily	95.00	100.00

Lunch available
Evening meal 1900 (last orders 2145)
Parking for 40
Cards accepted: Access, Visa, Diners, Amex, Switch/Delta

House of Agnes Hotel ♠
APPROVED
71 St Dunstan's Street, Canterbury
CT2 8BN
☎ (01227) 472173 & 472185
Fax (01227) 464527
Home of Agnes Wickfield from Charles Dickens' novel "David Copperfield", this friendly hotel combines the atmosphere of bygone days with modern comforts.
Bedrooms: 1 single, 4 double, 1 twin, 3 family rooms
Bathrooms: 9 en-suite

Bed & breakfast per night:	£min	£max
Single	33.95	43.45
Double	47.40	57.40

Half board per person:	£min	£max
Daily	29.50	39.50
Weekly	190.00	276.50

Lunch available
Evening meal 1830 (last orders 2130)
Parking for 31
Cards accepted: Access, Visa, Diners, Amex, Switch/Delta

London Guest House ♠
Listed COMMENDED
14 London Road, Canterbury
CT2 8LR
☎ (01227) 765860
Elegant town house near the city centre, offering a warm welcome. Home cooking.
Bedrooms: 1 single, 1 double, 2 twin, 1 family room
Bathrooms: 2 public

Bed & breakfast per night:	£min	£max
Single	18.00	25.00
Double	36.00	38.00

Cards accepted: Access, Visa

Magnolia House ♠
HIGHLY COMMENDED
36 St Dunstans Terrace, Canterbury
CT2 8AX
☎ (01227) 765121 & Mobile (0585) 595970
Fax (01227) 765121

Quiet Georgian house in attractive city street. Close to university, gardens, river and city centre. Walled garden, ideal for guests to relax in. Winner 1995 "Welcome to Kent Hospitality Award".
Bedrooms: 1 single, 4 double, 2 twin
Bathrooms: 7 en-suite

Bed & breakfast per night:	£min	£max
Single	36.00	45.00
Double	58.00	80.00

Evening meal 1800 (last orders 1900)
Parking for 4

Continued ▶

CANTERBURY
Continued

Cards accepted: Access, Visa, Amex, Switch/Delta

Oriel Lodge

HIGHLY COMMENDED

3 Queens Avenue, Canterbury
CT2 8AY
☎ (01227) 462845
Edwardian house in residential area near city centre and restaurants. Clean, well-furnished rooms, lounge, log fire. Private parking. Smoking in lounge area only.
Bedrooms: 1 single, 3 double, 1 twin, 1 triple
Bathrooms: 2 en-suite, 2 public

Bed & breakfast per night:

	£min	£max
Single	20.00	27.00
Double	36.00	57.00

Parking for 6
Cards accepted: Access, Visa

Pointers Hotel

COMMENDED

1 London Road, Canterbury
CT2 8LR
☎ (01227) 456846
Fax (01227) 831131
Logis of Great Britain

Family-run Georgian hotel close to city centre, cathedral and university. Licensed restaurant.
Bedrooms: 1 single, 6 double, 2 twin, 3 family rooms
Bathrooms: 11 en-suite, 1 private

Bed & breakfast per night:

	£min	£max
Single	38.00	40.00
Double	50.00	60.00

Half board per person:

	£min	£max
Daily	39.00	54.00
Weekly	273.00	378.00

Evening meal 1930 (last orders 2030)
Parking for 10
Cards accepted: Access, Visa, Diners, Amex, Switch/Delta

St Stephens Guest House

Listed COMMENDED

100 St Stephens Road, Canterbury
CT2 7JL
☎ (01227) 767644
Mock-Tudor house set in attractive garden within easy walking distance of city centre and cathedral. Colour TV in rooms. Car park.
Bedrooms: 3 single, 8 double, 1 twin
Bathrooms: 3 en-suite, 3 public

Bed & breakfast per night:

	£min	£max
Single	20.00	
Double	35.00	46.00

Parking for 10
Cards accepted: Access, Visa

Thanington Hotel

HIGHLY COMMENDED

140 Wincheap, Canterbury
CT1 3RY
☎ (01227) 453227
Fax (01227) 453225

Beautiful, spacious Georgian bed and breakfast hotel close to city centre. All rooms en-suite, heated indoor pool, snooker room, secure car park. 30 minutes' drive Channel ports and tunnel.
Bedrooms: 5 double, 3 twin, 2 family rooms
Bathrooms: 10 en-suite, 2 public

Bed & breakfast per night:

	£min	£max
Single	43.00	49.50
Double	60.00	68.00

Parking for 12
Cards accepted: Access, Visa, Diners, Amex

Waltham Court Hotel

COMMENDED

Kake Street, Petham, Canterbury
CT4 5SB
☎ Petham (01227) 700413
Fax (01227) 700127
Tasteful conversion of an elegant 18th C house, set in idyllic and tranquil surroundings 10 minutes from Canterbury. Extensive gardens.
Bedrooms: 1 double, 2 twin, 1 triple
Bathrooms: 4 en-suite

Bed & breakfast per night:

	£min	£max
Single	35.00	45.00
Double	50.00	65.00

Half board per person:

	£min	£max
Daily	40.00	52.00
Weekly	280.00	364.00

Evening meal 1900 (last orders 2200)
Parking for 70
Cards accepted: Access, Visa, Amex, Switch/Delta

The White House

COMMENDED

6 St Peters Lane, Canterbury
CT1 2BP
☎ (01227) 761836
Regency house situated within the city walls next to the Marlowe Theatre. Superior family-run accommodation with all rooms en-suite.
Bedrooms: 1 single, 5 double, 1 twin, 1 triple, 1 family room
Bathrooms: 9 en-suite

Bed & breakfast per night:

	£min	£max
Single	25.00	35.00
Double	40.00	50.00

Parking for 2

CHICHESTER

West Sussex
Map ref 2C3

The county town of West Sussex with a beautiful Norman cathedral. Noted for its Georgian architecture but also has modern buildings like the Festival Theatre. Surrounded by places of interest, including Fishbourne Roman Palace and Weald and Downland Open-Air Museum.
Tourist Information Centre ☎ (01243) 775888

The Dolphin and Anchor

COMMENDED

West Street, Chichester PO19 1QE
☎ (01243) 785121
Fax (01243) 533408
Forte
Opposite the cathedral, this attractive, skilfully modernised hotel is a combination of 2 ancient inns.
Bedrooms: 33 double, 14 twin, 2 triple
Bathrooms: 49 en-suite

SOUTH EAST ENGLAND

Bed & breakfast per night:	£min	£max
Single	57.00	78.00
Double	108.00	132.00

Half board per person:	£min	£max
Daily	62.00	75.00
Weekly	345.00	455.00

Lunch available
Evening meal 1900 (last orders 2100)
Parking for 7
Cards accepted: Access, Visa, Diners, Amex, Switch/Delta

Marriott Goodwood Park Hotel & Country Club

HIGHLY COMMENDED

Goodwood, Chichester PO18 0QB
☎ (01243) 775537
Whitbread

In the grounds of Goodwood House, home to the Dukes of Richmond for 300 years, the hotel has been tastefully developed and retains the original character of its 1786 forebear. Extensive leisure facilities and 18-hole golf-course.
Bedrooms: 49 double, 44 twin, 1 triple
Suite available
Bathrooms: 94 en-suite

Bed & breakfast per night:	£min	£max
Single	66.00	69.00
Double	66.00	138.00

Half board per person:	£min	£max
Daily	74.00	84.00

Lunch available
Evening meal 1900 (last orders 2130)
Parking for 250
Cards accepted: Access, Visa, Diners, Amex, Switch/Delta

CLIFTONVILLE

Kent

See under Margate

Information on accommodation listed in this guide has been supplied by the proprietors. As changes may occur you are advised to check details at the time of booking.

COBHAM

Surrey
Map ref 2D2

Village in 2 parts, Street Cobham on the A3 Portsmouth Road and Church Cobham with the restored Norman church of St Andrew and a 19th C mill.

Cedar House Hotel

Mill Road, Cobham KT11 3AN
☎ (01932) 863424
Fax (01932) 862023

15th C house with later additions, timbered dining hall and garden overlooking River Mole. Close to village. Excellent access to M25 and London.
Bedrooms: 2 single, 2 double, 2 twin
Bathrooms: 4 en-suite, 2 public

Bed & breakfast per night:	£min	£max
Single	40.00	65.00
Double	75.00	85.00

Evening meal 1900 (last orders 2130)
Parking for 15
Cards accepted: Access, Visa, Amex

COPTHORNE

Surrey
Map ref 2D2

Residential village on the Surrey/West Sussex border, near Crawley and within easy reach of Gatwick Airport.

The Copthorne Effingham Park

Copthorne, West Sussex RH10 3EU
☎ (01342) 714994
Fax (01342) 716039
Millennium & Copthorne

Versatile venue for business and pleasure, with 9-hole golf-course in grounds. All facilities for conferences, new product launches and banqueting for up to 600 people. Catering by own chefs. Leisure club, swimming pool, restaurants.
Bedrooms: 71 double, 42 twin, 9 triple
Suites available
Bathrooms: 122 en-suite

Bed & breakfast per night:	£min	£max
Single	120.00	140.00
Double	130.00	150.00

Half board per person:	£min	£max
Daily	140.00	160.00
Weekly	980.00	1120.00

Lunch available
Evening meal 1830 (last orders 2215)
Parking for 500
Cards accepted: Access, Visa, Diners, Amex, Switch/Delta

The Copthorne London Gatwick

Copthorne, West Sussex RH10 3PG
☎ (01342) 714971
Fax (01342) 717375
Millennium & Copthorne

Country house hotel, in over 100 acres of Sussex countryside, within easy reach of Gatwick Airport. Courtesy bus service. Health club on site.
Bedrooms: 136 double, 75 twin, 16 triple
Suites available
Bathrooms: 227 en-suite

Bed & breakfast per night:	£min	£max
Single	120.00	140.00
Double	130.00	150.00

Half board per person:	£min	£max
Daily	138.00	158.00
Weekly	966.00	1106.00

Lunch available
Evening meal 1900 (last orders 2130)
Parking for 400
Cards accepted: Access, Visa, Diners, Amex, Switch/Delta

CUCKFIELD

West Sussex
Map ref 2D3

The High Street is lined with Elizabethan and Georgian shops, inns and houses and was once part of the London to Brighton coach road. Nearby Nymans (National Trust) is a 30-acre garden with fine topiary work.

Hilton Park Hotel

APPROVED

Cuckfield, Haywards Heath
RH17 5EG
☎ Haywards Heath (01444) 454555
Fax (01444) 457222

Victorian country house in 3 acres of
Continued ▶

SOUTH EAST ENGLAND

CUCKFIELD
Continued

gardens, with magnificent views of South Downs from conservatory bar and bedrooms.
Bedrooms: 5 double, 1 twin, 3 triple
Bathrooms: 9 en-suite, 2 public

Bed & breakfast per night:	£min	£max
Single	55.00	
Double	75.00	

Lunch available
Evening meal 1900 (last orders 2030)
Parking for 52
Cards accepted: Access, Visa, Diners, Amex

DARTFORD
Kent
Map ref 2D2

Industrial town probably most famous for the Dartford Tunnel and now the new Queen Elizabeth II bridge across the Thames. Large Orchard Theatre has a fine variety of entertainment.
Tourist Information Centre ☎ (01322) 343243

Brands Hatch Thistle Hotel
COMMENDED
Brands Hatch, Dartford DA3 8PE
☎ (01474) 854900
Fax (01474) 853220
Utell International
Set at the entrance to the world-famous motor racing circuit, the hotel offers elegance and varied cuisine. Easy access, near M20, M25 and M26.
Bedrooms: 67 double, 63 twin, 7 triple
Suites available
Bathrooms: 137 en-suite

Bed & breakfast per night:	£min	£max
Single	88.50	
Double	111.00	

Half board per person:	£min	£max
Daily	109.50	
Weekly	706.50	

Lunch available
Evening meal 1930 (last orders 2230)
Parking for 180
Cards accepted: Access, Visa, Diners, Amex

DEAL
Kent
Map ref 3C4

Coastal town and popular holiday resort. Deal Castle was built by Henry VIII as a fort and the museum is devoted to finds excavated in the area. Also the Time-Ball Tower museum. Angling available from both beach and pier.
Tourist Information Centre ☎ (01304) 369576

Blencathra Country Hotel
Kingsdown Hill, Kingsdown, Deal CT14 8EA
☎ (01304) 373725
Peaceful situation in a private road, with commanding views of the Channel and countryside. Convenient for ferries and hoverport.
Bedrooms: 1 single, 1 double, 1 triple, 2 family rooms
Bathrooms: 4 en-suite, 2 public

Bed & breakfast per night:	£min	£max
Single	17.00	25.00
Double	34.00	40.00

Parking for 7

Hardicot Guest House
COMMENDED
Kingsdown Road, Walmer, Deal CT14 8AW
☎ (01304) 373867

Large, quiet, detached Victorian house with Channel views and secluded garden. Ideal for sea fishing, cliff walks and golfing.
Bedrooms: 1 double, 2 twin
Bathrooms: 1 en-suite, 2 private

Bed & breakfast per night:	£min	£max
Single	18.00	20.00
Double	36.00	40.00

Parking for 4

Please check prices and other details at the time of booking.

Royal Hotel
APPROVED
Beach Street, Deal CT14 6JD
☎ (01304) 375555
Fax (01304) 375555

Built about 1700, the Royal has accommodated Lord Nelson, Lady Hamilton and the Duke of Wellington. Comfortable accommodation with all modern conveniences. Fish restaurant overlooking the Channel.
Bedrooms: 5 double, 4 twin, 2 family rooms
Bathrooms: 11 en-suite

Bed & breakfast per night:	£min	£max
Single	40.00	50.00
Double	60.00	95.00

Half board per person:	£min	£max
Daily	50.00	60.00
Weekly	315.00	378.00

Lunch available
Evening meal 1800 (last orders 2200)
Parking for 3
Open February–December
Cards accepted: Access, Visa, Amex, Switch/Delta

Sutherland House Hotel
HIGHLY COMMENDED
186 London Road, Deal CT14 9PT
☎ (01304) 362853 & 381146
Fax (01304) 361268
Semi-detached Edwardian house, retaining its character and with decor of the period, in a quiet residential area on the A258 Deal – Sandwich road. Licensed restaurant. Golf nearby.
Bedrooms: 1 double, 2 twin
Bathrooms: 2 en-suite, 1 private

Bed & breakfast per night:	£min	£max
Single	35.00	37.50
Double	45.00	48.00

Lunch available
Evening meal 1900 (last orders 2200)
Parking for 7
Cards accepted: Access, Visa, Amex, Switch/Delta

SOUTH EAST ENGLAND

DORKING
Surrey
Map ref 2D2

Ancient market town and a good centre for walking, delightfully set between Box Hill and the Downs.

Fairdene Guest House
APPROVED

Moores Road, Dorking RH4 2BG
☎ (01306) 888337
Late-Victorian house in convenient location, close to town centre and Gatwick Airport. Friendly and homely atmosphere. Off-street parking.
Bedrooms: 2 double, 2 twin, 1 triple
Bathrooms: 2 public

Bed & breakfast per night:	£min	£max
Single	20.00	25.00
Double	35.00	40.00

Parking for 7

Gatton Manor Hotel, Golf And Country Club
COMMENDED

Standon Lane, Ockley, Dorking RH5 5PQ
☎ Oakwoodhill (01306) 627555
Fax (01306) 627713
18th C manor house on 200-acre estate. Championship length golf-course, hotel, a la carte restaurants, conference suites, bowls, fishing, tennis, gym and health club. Village is 6 miles south of Dorking.
Bedrooms: 2 double, 12 twin
Bathrooms: 14 en-suite

Bed & breakfast per night:	£min	£max
Single	40.00	60.00
Double	60.00	80.00

Lunch available
Evening meal 1900 (last orders 2130)
Parking for 200
Cards accepted: Access, Visa, Diners, Amex, Switch/Delta

The map references refer to the colour maps towards the end of the guide. The first figure is the map number; the letter and figure which follow indicate the grid reference on the map.

DOVER
Kent
Map ref 3C4

A Cinque Port and busiest passenger port in the world. Still a historic town and seaside resort beside the famous White Cliffs. The White Cliffs Experience attraction traces the town's history through the Roman, Saxon, Norman and Victorian periods.
Tourist Information Centre ☎ (01304) 205108

Ardmore Private Hotel
COMMENDED

18 Castle Hill Road, Dover CT16 1QW
☎ (01304) 205895
Fax (01304) 208229
Situated next door to Dover Castle. Near sports complex and ruins of Saxon church. Views of harbour and town.
Bedrooms: 2 double, 1 twin, 1 family room
Bathrooms: 3 en-suite, 1 private

Bed & breakfast per night:	£min	£max
Single	30.00	35.00
Double	35.00	45.00

Cards accepted: Access, Visa, Switch/Delta

Castle Guest House
COMMENDED

10 Castle Hill Road, Dover CT16 1QW
☎ (01304) 201656
Fax (01304) 210197
Non-smoking Grade II listed Georgian guesthouse providing good food and comfortable accommodation. Ideally located for castle, ports and town centre.
Bedrooms: 1 single, 3 double, 1 twin, 1 family room
Bathrooms: 6 en-suite

Bed & breakfast per night:	£min	£max
Single	20.00	28.00
Double	30.00	40.00

Half board per person:	£min	£max
Daily	23.00	28.00

Evening meal 1800 (last orders 2100)
Cards accepted: Access, Visa, Amex, Switch/Delta

Conifers Guest House

241 Folkestone Road, Dover CT17 9LL
☎ (01304) 205609
Family guesthouse, 5 minutes from rail station, town centre, seafront and Channel Tunnel terminus. En-suite rooms. Early breakfast available.
Bedrooms: 1 single, 2 double, 1 twin, 2 family rooms
Bathrooms: 4 en-suite, 2 public

Bed & breakfast per night:	£min	£max
Single	15.00	18.00
Double	30.00	40.00

Parking for 6

Dover Hotel
APPROVED

122-124 Folkestone Road, Dover CT17 9SP
☎ (01304) 206559 & 208109
Fax (01304) 203936
Family-run business, 200 yards from the railway station and minutes away from the docks. Bar, restaurant and pool table facilities.
Bedrooms: 2 single, 6 double, 4 twin, 3 triple, 3 family rooms
Bathrooms: 11 en-suite, 6 private, 3 public

Bed & breakfast per night:	£min	£max
Single	25.00	30.00
Double	40.00	45.00

Half board per person:	£min	£max
Daily	31.50	
Weekly	264.60	

Lunch available
Evening meal (last orders 2030)
Parking for 50
Cards accepted: Access, Visa, Diners, Amex

Gordon Guest House
APPROVED

23 Castle Street, Dover CT16 1PT
☎ (01304) 201894
Friendly welcome at this family guesthouse. Most rooms en-suite, all with private shower. Approximately 3 minutes' drive to ferries, 10/15 minutes to Channel Tunnel terminal.
Bedrooms: 2 double, 2 twin, 1 triple, 1 family room
Bathrooms: 4 en-suite, 1 public, 2 private showers

Bed & breakfast per night:	£min	£max
Single	13.00	18.00
Double	26.00	42.00

Continued ▶

539

SOUTH EAST ENGLAND

DOVER
Continued

Cards accepted: Access, Visa

Hubert House Guest House
9 Castle Hill Road, Dover
CT16 1QW
☎ (01304) 202253
Comfortable guesthouse, all en-suite rooms. Close to amenities and ferries, 10 minutes from Channel Tunnel. Overnight or longer stays.
Bedrooms: 1 single, 2 double, 1 twin, 2 triple, 2 family rooms
Bathrooms: 8 en-suite, 1 public
Bed & breakfast
per night: £min   £max
Single   26.00   30.00
Double   36.00   46.00
Parking for 7
Cards accepted: Access, Visa, Switch/Delta

Linden Guest House
COMMENDED
231 Folkestone Road, Dover
CT17 9SL
☎ (01304) 205449 & Mobile (0370) 367915
Fax (01304) 205449
Convenient for town centre and port, this clean, comfortable guesthouse provides comprehensive room facilities, secure parking and a courtesy service to/from station and ferries.
Bedrooms: 1 single, 1 double, 3 triple
Bathrooms: 1 private, 1 public, 2 private showers
Bed & breakfast
per night: £min   £max
Single   15.00   19.00
Double   30.00   40.00
Parking for 4
Cards accepted: Access, Visa, Switch/Delta

Loddington House Hotel
HIGHLY COMMENDED
14 East Cliff, (Seafront - Marine Parade), Dover CT16 1LX
☎ (01304) 201901
Fax (01304) 201907
Logis of Great Britain
Well-positioned small hotel in Georgian terrace overlooking harbour. Quality food and wine - prices on request. Yards from east ferry terminal.

Bedrooms: 1 single, 3 double, 2 twin
Bathrooms: 4 en-suite, 2 private
Bed & breakfast
per night: £min   £max
Single   28.00   35.00
Double   40.00   52.00
Evening meal 1830 (last orders 2000)
Parking for 3
Cards accepted: Access, Visa, Amex

St Martins Guest House
COMMENDED
17 Castle Hill Road, Dover
CT16 1QW
☎ (01304) 205938
Fax (01304) 208229
Situated in the lee of Dover Castle, rear of sports complex and ruins of Saxon church. Views of harbour and town.
Bedrooms: 1 single, 1 double, 1 twin, 3 family rooms
Bathrooms: 6 en-suite
Bed & breakfast
per night: £min   £max
Single   25.00   30.00
Double   32.00   40.00
Cards accepted: Access, Visa, Switch/Delta

Walletts Court Hotel and Restaurant
HIGHLY COMMENDED
West-Cliffe, St-Margarets-at-Cliffe, Dover CT15 6EW
☎ (01304) 852424
Fax (01304) 853430

Lovely 17th C manor and barns, with carved oak beams and inglenook fireplaces. Ideal for history enthusiasts. In rural setting, 3 miles from Dover Docks and Castle. Open as a full evening restaurant, Monday to Sunday.
Bedrooms: 7 double, 2 twin, 2 triple
Bathrooms: 11 en-suite
Bed & breakfast
per night: £min   £max
Single   50.00   60.00
Double   60.00   80.00
Half board per
person: £min   £max
Daily   53.00   73.00
Evening meal 1900 (last orders 2130)
Parking for 20

Cards accepted: Access, Visa, Diners, Amex, Switch/Delta

DYMCHURCH
Kent
Map ref 3B4

For centuries the headquarters of the Lords of the Level, the local government of this area. Probably best known today because of the fame of its fictional parson, the notorious Dr Syn, who has inspired a regular festival.

Waterside Guest House
COMMENDED
15 Hythe Road, Dymchurch, Romney Marsh TN29 0LN
☎ Folkestone (01303) 872255
Ideally situated for Channel Tunnel, ferry ports or touring the historic countryside of Kent, overlooking Romney, Hythe and Dymchurch railway. Sandy beaches close by. Home cooking, catering for all tastes.
Bedrooms: 1 single, 3 double, 2 twin, 1 family room
Bathrooms: 2 en-suite, 2 public, 1 private shower
Bed & breakfast
per night: £min   £max
Single   15.00   20.00
Double   28.00   37.00
Half board per
person: £min   £max
Daily   21.00   26.00
Weekly   132.00   164.00
Lunch available
Evening meal 1730 (last orders 2000)
Parking for 7

EASTBOURNE
East Sussex
Map ref 3B4

One of the finest, most elegant resorts on the south-east coast situated beside Beachy Head. Long promenade, plenty of gardens, theatres, Towner Art Gallery, "How We Lived Then" museum of shops and social history.
Tourist Information Centre ☎ (01323) 411400

Bay Lodge Hotel
COMMENDED
61-62 Royal Parade, Eastbourne
BN22 7AQ
☎ (01323) 732515
Fax (01323) 735009

SOUTH EAST ENGLAND

Small seafront hotel opposite Pavilion Gardens, close to bowling greens and marina. Large sun-lounge. All double/twin bedrooms are en-suite. Non-smokers' lounge.
Bedrooms: 3 single, 5 double, 4 twin
Bathrooms: 9 en-suite, 2 public

Bed & breakfast
per night: | £min | £max
Single | 19.00 | 25.00
Double | 38.00 | 48.00

Half board per
person: | £min | £max
Daily | 27.00 | 33.00
Weekly | 179.00 | 222.00

Evening meal 1800 (last orders 1800)
Open March–October and Christmas
Cards accepted: Access, Visa

Bella Vista
COMMENDED
30 Redoubt Road, Eastbourne
BN22 7DH
☎ (01323) 724222
Distinctive Victorian flint house with front car park. Interior maintained in good decorative order and all bedrooms have en-suite facilities.
Bedrooms: 6 double, 5 twin, 1 triple
Bathrooms: 12 en-suite, 1 public

Bed & breakfast
per night: | £min | £max
Double | 26.00 | 40.00

Half board per
person: | £min | £max
Daily | 18.00 | 26.00
Weekly | 110.00 | 150.00

Evening meal from 1800
Parking for 10
Open April–October and Christmas

Bracken Guest House
COMMENDED
3 Hampden Terrace, Latimer Road, Eastbourne BN22 7BL
☎ (01323) 725779
Friendly, comfortable family-run guesthouse, serving traditional English food. Close to seafront, town centre and entertainment.
Bedrooms: 1 single, 1 double, 2 twin, 1 triple
Bathrooms: 1 en-suite, 1 public

Bed & breakfast
per night: | £min | £max
Single | 15.00 | 19.00
Double | 30.00 | 38.00

Half board per
person: | £min | £max
Daily | 19.00 | 25.00
Weekly | 95.00 | 125.00

Evening meal from 1800

Brayscroft Private Hotel
HIGHLY COMMENDED
13 South Cliff Avenue, Eastbourne
BN20 7AH
☎ (01323) 647005

Elegant Edwardian town house in quiet Meads area. Two minutes from seafront. Ideally situated for South Downs, theatres and town.
Bedrooms: 1 single, 2 double, 2 twin
Bathrooms: 5 en-suite

Bed & breakfast
per night: | £min | £max
Single | 18.00 | 21.00
Double | 36.00 | 42.00

Half board per
person: | £min | £max
Daily | 27.00 | 30.00
Weekly | 165.00 | 170.00

Evening meal 1800 (last orders 2200)

Brownings Hotel
COMMENDED
28 Upperton Road, Eastbourne
BN21 1JS
☎ (01323) 724358
Fax (01323) 731288
All the charm and graciousness of a Victorian mansion. Centrally heated en-suite rooms with colour TV, direct-dial telephone and mini-bar.
Bedrooms: 2 single, 6 double, 2 twin
Bathrooms: 10 en-suite

Bed & breakfast
per night: | £min | £max
Single | 40.00 | 50.00
Double | 70.00 | 90.00

Half board per
person: | £min | £max
Daily | 54.00 | 64.00
Weekly | 350.00 | 380.00

Evening meal 1900 (last orders 2100)
Parking for 8

Chalk Farm Hotel
COMMENDED
Coopers Hill, Willingdon, Eastbourne BN20 9JD
☎ (01323) 503800
Fax (01323) 520331
Converted 17th C farmhouse set in 2 acres, on the edge of the Sussex Downs, only a few miles from Eastbourne.
Bedrooms: 1 single, 5 double, 1 twin, 2 triple
Bathrooms: 6 en-suite, 1 public

Bed & breakfast
per night: | £min | £max
Single | 30.00 | 37.50
Double | 43.00 | 49.50

Lunch available
Evening meal 1830 (last orders 2100)
Parking for 20
Cards accepted: Access, Visa, Diners, Amex

Chatsworth Hotel
APPROVED
Grand Parade, Eastbourne
BN21 3YR
☎ (01323) 411016
Fax (01323) 643270
Elegant Victorian detached hotel in a prominent position on seafront, very close to shops and theatres.
Bedrooms: 10 single, 12 double, 22 twin, 2 family rooms
Suites available
Bathrooms: 46 en-suite

Bed & breakfast
per night: | £min | £max
Single | 35.00 | 50.00
Double | 65.00 | 90.00

Half board per
person: | £min | £max
Daily | 45.00 | 65.00

Lunch available
Evening meal 1900 (last orders 2030)
Cards accepted: Access, Visa, Diners, Amex, Switch/Delta

Cherry Tree Hotel
COMMENDED
15 Silverdale Road, Eastbourne
BN20 7AJ
☎ (01323) 722406
Fax (01323) 648838

Continued ▶

541

SOUTH EAST ENGLAND

EASTBOURNE
Continued

Small hotel and restaurant. All bedrooms en-suite with colour TV, telephone, tea/coffee-making. A la carte, table d'hote restaurant.
Bedrooms: 2 single, 3 double, 3 twin, 2 triple
Bathrooms: 10 en-suite

Bed & breakfast per night:

	£min	£max
Single	23.00	28.00
Double	46.00	56.00

Half board per person:

	£min	£max
Daily	34.00	39.00
Weekly	205.00	235.00

Evening meal 1800 (last orders 2100)
Cards accepted: Access, Visa, Amex

Congress Hotel
APPROVED

31-41 Carlisle Road, Eastbourne
BN21 4JS
☎ (01323) 732118 & 644605
Fax (01323) 720016
Family-run hotel in peaceful location. Close to theatres and seafront.
Wheelchair access category 3
Bedrooms: 15 single, 11 double, 31 twin, 5 triple
Bathrooms: 57 en-suite, 1 public

Bed & breakfast per night:

	£min	£max
Single	29.00	36.00
Double	58.00	72.00

Half board per person:

	£min	£max
Daily	32.50	39.00
Weekly	225.00	270.00

Lunch available
Evening meal 1830 (last orders 1945)
Parking for 16
Open March–November and Christmas
Cards accepted: Access, Visa, Switch/Delta

Cumberland Hotel
COMMENDED

Grand Parade, Eastbourne
BN21 3YT
☎ (01323) 730342
Fax (01323) 646174
Beautiful hotel right on the seafront, opposite bandstand. Spacious, comfortable lounge and elegant dining room, both sea-facing. Friendly, professional service. Close to shops and theatres.
Bedrooms: 17 single, 9 double, 46 twin
Bathrooms: 72 private

Bed & breakfast per night:

	£min	£max
Single	28.00	37.00
Double	56.00	74.00

Half board per person:

	£min	£max
Daily	32.00	41.00
Weekly	224.00	287.00

Lunch available
Evening meal 1845 (last orders 2030)
Cards accepted: Access, Visa, Amex, Switch/Delta

Downland Hotel
COMMENDED

37 Lewes Road, Eastbourne
BN21 2BU
☎ (01323) 732689
Minotel
Charming small hotel in quiet yet convenient location. Warm welcome, relaxed atmosphere, personal service. Award-winning restaurant, private car park.
Bedrooms: 1 single, 9 double, 3 twin, 2 triple
Suite available
Bathrooms: 15 en-suite

Bed & breakfast per night:

	£min	£max
Single	27.50	37.50
Double	55.00	75.00

Half board per person:

	£min	£max
Daily	45.00	55.00
Weekly	195.00	245.00

Evening meal 1830 (last orders 2030)
Parking for 10
Open February–December
Cards accepted: Access, Visa, Diners, Amex

Edelweiss Private Hotel
APPROVED

10-12 Elms Avenue, Eastbourne
BN21 3DN
☎ (01323) 732071
Fax (01323) 732071
Small family-run hotel 50 yards from the pier. Comfortable bedrooms with TV and tea-making. En-suite rooms available. Guests' lounge and bar. Off-peak rates available.
Bedrooms: 2 single, 6 double, 5 twin, 1 family room
Bathrooms: 3 en-suite, 4 public

Bed & breakfast per night:

	£min	£max
Single	13.50	16.00
Double	27.00	36.00

Half board per person:

	£min	£max
Daily	18.50	23.00
Weekly	119.00	151.00

Evening meal 1800 (last orders 1500)
Cards accepted: Access, Visa

Farrar's Hotel

Wilmington Gardens, Eastbourne
BN21 4JN
☎ (01323) 723737
Fax (01323) 732902
Family-run hotel in quiet square, 200 yards from the seafront, opposite Devonshire Park and Congress Theatre. Send for brochure giving details of mini-breaks.
Bedrooms: 13 single, 7 double, 23 twin, 2 triple
Bathrooms: 45 en-suite

Bed & breakfast per night:

	£min	£max
Single	20.00	34.00
Double	40.00	64.00

Half board per person:

	£min	£max
Daily	29.00	42.00
Weekly	196.00	287.00

Lunch available
Evening meal 1845 (last orders 2030)
Parking for 26
Open February–December
Cards accepted: Access, Visa, Amex, Switch/Delta

Heatherdene Hotel
APPROVED

26-28 Elms Avenue, Eastbourne
BN21 3DN
☎ (01323) 723598
Family-run licensed hotel. Plenty of home-cooked food served in our pleasant dining room. Close to seafront and town centre.
Wheelchair access category 3
Bedrooms: 3 single, 3 double, 8 twin, 1 triple
Bathrooms: 5 en-suite, 4 public

Bed & breakfast per night:

	£min	£max
Single	16.00	20.50
Double	32.00	41.00

SOUTH EAST ENGLAND

Half board per person:	£min	£max
Daily	21.50	26.00
Weekly	138.00	171.50

Evening meal 1800 (last orders 1800)

Hydro Hotel
HIGHLY COMMENDED

Mount Road, Eastbourne BN20 7HZ
☎ (01323) 720643
Fax (01323) 641167
Elegant hotel overlooking the sea. Attractive gardens, ample parking. Good facilities. A country house by the sea.
Bedrooms: 18 single, 22 double, 41 twin, 2 triple
Bathrooms: 83 en-suite

Bed & breakfast per night:	£min	£max
Single	28.00	50.00
Double	50.00	90.00

Half board per person:	£min	£max
Daily	38.00	58.00
Weekly	245.00	378.00

Lunch available
Evening meal 1845 (last orders 2030)
Parking for 50
Cards accepted: Access, Visa, Diners, Switch/Delta

Lansdowne Hotel
COMMENDED

King Edward's Parade, Eastbourne BN21 4EE
☎ (01323) 725174
Fax (01323) 739721
Ⓒ Best Western
Privately owned and run hotel in premier seafront position, with bar, spacious lounges and elegant public areas. Theatres, shops and sporting facilities nearby. Minimum half-board prices are special off-season rates.
Bedrooms: 42 single, 18 double, 58 twin, 4 triple
Bathrooms: 122 en-suite, 2 public

Bed & breakfast per night:	£min	£max
Single	50.00	56.00
Double	78.00	96.00

Half board per person:	£min	£max
Daily	33.00	68.00
Weekly	215.00	476.00

Lunch available
Evening meal 1830 (last orders 2030)
Parking for 23

Cards accepted: Access, Visa, Diners, Amex, Switch/Delta

Princes Hotel
COMMENDED

Lascelles Terrace, Eastbourne BN21 4BL
☎ (01323) 722056
Fax (01323) 727469

Friendly family hotel, ideal centre for exploring the many historic monuments and beauty spots of Sussex.
Bedrooms: 13 single, 13 double, 16 twin, 2 triple
Bathrooms: 44 en-suite, 2 public

Bed & breakfast per night:	£min	£max
Single	27.50	40.00
Double	55.00	75.00

Half board per person:	£min	£max
Daily	40.00	50.00
Weekly	195.00	325.00

Lunch available
Evening meal 1845 (last orders 2030)
Cards accepted: Access, Visa, Diners, Amex

St Omer Hotel
COMMENDED

13 Royal Parade, Eastbourne BN22 7AR
☎ (01323) 722152
Fax (01323) 726756
Fine seafront licensed family-run hotel. Sun lounge and terrace. Colour TV and tea-making in all rooms. Home-cooked meals.
Bedrooms: 1 single, 2 double, 6 twin, 1 triple
Bathrooms: 6 en-suite, 2 public

Bed & breakfast per night:	£min	£max
Single	18.00	25.50
Double	36.00	51.00

Half board per person:	£min	£max
Daily	25.50	33.00
Weekly	162.00	209.00

Lunch available
Evening meal 1800 (last orders 1700)

Open April–September and Christmas
Cards accepted: Access, Visa, Switch/Delta

Stratford Hotel and Restaurant
APPROVED

59 Cavendish Place, Eastbourne BN21 3RL
☎ (01323) 724051 & Visitors 726391
Ideally situated near promenade, coaches and shopping centre. Licensed, centrally heated throughout. Ground floor and family rooms available. Tea-making facilities and colour TV in all rooms. Most rooms with modern en-suite.
Bedrooms: 2 single, 5 double, 4 twin, 2 triple
Bathrooms: 11 en-suite, 1 public

Bed & breakfast per night:	£min	£max
Single	18.00	20.00
Double	36.00	40.00

Half board per person:	£min	£max
Daily	25.00	28.00
Weekly	138.00	165.00

Lunch available
Evening meal 1800 (last orders 2300)
Cards accepted: Access, Visa, Diners, Amex

The Wish Tower Hotel
COMMENDED

King Edward's Parade, Eastbourne BN21 4EB
☎ (01323) 722676
Fax (01323) 721474
Ⓒ Principal/Utell International
Elegant seaside hotel within easy reach of all attractions. Most rooms have sea views. Refurbished public rooms invite total relaxation.
Bedrooms: 25 single, 12 double, 28 twin
Bathrooms: 65 en-suite

Bed & breakfast per night:	£min	£max
Single	25.00	50.00
Double	50.00	100.00

Half board per person:	£min	£max
Daily	30.00	60.00
Weekly	210.00	420.00

Lunch available
Evening meal 1830 (last orders 2045)

Continued ▶

SOUTH EAST ENGLAND

EASTBOURNE
Continued

Parking for 3
Cards accepted: Access, Visa, Diners, Amex, Switch/Delta

York House Hotel
COMMENDED

14-22 Royal Parade, Eastbourne BN22 7AP
☎ (01323) 412918
Fax (01323) 646238
Consort

Exceptional sea-views and bar lunches on the terrace of the Verandah Bar. 5-course dinner, followed by dancing in the Lancaster Room. An early dip in the heated indoor pool.
Bedrooms: 24 single, 26 double, 40 twin, 6 triple, 1 family room
Bathrooms: 97 en-suite, 5 public

Bed & breakfast per night:	£min	£max
Single	39.50	39.50
Double	70.00	70.00

Half board per person:	£min	£max
Daily	45.00	45.00
Weekly	171.50	266.00

Lunch available
Evening meal 1830 (last orders 2000)
Cards accepted: Access, Visa, Diners, Amex, Switch/Delta

EGHAM
Surrey
Map ref 2D2

In attractive and historic area beside the Thames, adjoining Runnymede and near Windsor, Thorpe Park and Savill Garden. Convenient for Heathrow Airport and good base for London, Wisley and Hampton Court.

Great Fosters
HIGHLY COMMENDED

Stroude Road, Egham TW20 9UR
☎ (01784) 433822
Fax (01784) 472455

16th C hunting lodge, now a comfortable hotel, retaining decor and atmosphere of former times. Set in 17 acres of formal grounds.
Bedrooms: 25 single, 11 double, 9 twin
Suites available
Bathrooms: 44 en-suite, 1 private

Bed & breakfast per night:	£min	£max
Single	78.00	100.00
Double	98.50	190.00

Lunch available
Evening meal 1930 (last orders 2115)
Parking for 150
Cards accepted: Access, Visa, Diners, Amex, Switch/Delta

Runnymede Hotel
HIGHLY COMMENDED

Windsor Road, Egham TW20 0AG
☎ (01784) 436171
Fax (01784) 436340

Delightfully situated overlooking the Thames at Bell-Weir Lock, a privately owned modern hotel standing in 12 acres of landscaped gardens. On A308, off the M25 junction 13. Prices below are for weekends.
Bedrooms: 80 single, 56 double, 24 twin, 11 triple
Bathrooms: 171 en-suite

Bed & breakfast per night:	£min	£max
Single	56.00	76.00
Double	112.00	132.00

Half board per person:	£min	£max
Daily	70.00	90.00

Lunch available
Evening meal 1900 (last orders 2145)
Parking for 300
Cards accepted: Access, Visa, Diners, Amex

EPSOM
Surrey
Map ref 2D2

Horse races have been held on the slopes of Epsom Downs for centuries. The racecourse is the home of the world-famous Derby. Many famous old homes are here, among them the 17th C Waterloo House.

Angleside Guest House
Listed COMMENDED

27 Ashley Road, Epsom KT18 5BD
☎ (01372) 724303

Owner-run establishment midway between Gatwick and Heathrow Airports, close to the High Street, downs and racecourse.
Bedrooms: 1 single, 3 twin, 3 triple, 1 family room
Bathrooms: 1 public, 4 private showers

Bed & breakfast per night:	£min	£max
Single	18.00	27.00
Double	32.00	36.00

Parking for 8

White House Hotel
COMMENDED

Downs Hill Road, Epsom KT18 5HW
☎ (01372) 722472
Fax (01372) 744447

Charming, spacious, traditional mansion converted into a modern hotel. Epsom town and station only minutes away with regular train services to London.
Bedrooms: 7 single, 2 double, 3 twin, 1 family room
Bathrooms: 7 en-suite, 1 public, 6 private showers

Bed & breakfast per night:	£min	£max
Single	39.50	49.50
Double	55.50	69.50

Half board per person:	£min	£max
Daily	52.00	59.70
Weekly	364.00	417.90

Lunch available
Evening meal 1800 (last orders 2300)
Parking for 15
Cards accepted: Access, Visa

All accommodation in this guide has been graded, or is awaiting a grading, by a trained Tourist Board inspector.

The symbols in each entry give information about services and facilities. A 'key' to these symbols appears at the back of this guide.

SOUTH EAST ENGLAND

FARNHAM
Surrey
Map ref 2C2

Town noted for its Georgian houses. Willmer House (now a museum) has a facade of cut and moulded brick with fine carving and panelling in the interior. The 12th C castle has been occupied by Bishops of both Winchester and Guildford.
Tourist Information Centre ☎ (01252) 715109

The Bishop's Table Hotel & Restaurant
HIGHLY COMMENDED

27 West Street, Farnham GU9 7DR
☎ (01252) 710222 & 715545
Fax (01252) 733194
Consort

An 18th C inn, once used as a training school for clergy, well situated for exploring Surrey and Hampshire.
Bedrooms: 7 single, 9 double, 2 twin
Bathrooms: 17 en-suite, 1 private

Bed & breakfast per night:
	£min	£max
Single	70.00	76.50
Double	85.00	110.00

Half board per person:
	£min	£max
Daily	88.50	95.00
Weekly	589.50	615.50

Lunch available
Evening meal 1900 (last orders 2145)
Cards accepted: Access, Visa, Diners, Amex

FOLKESTONE
Kent
Map ref 3C4

Popular resort and important cross-channel port. The town has a fine promenade, the Leas, from where orchestral concerts and other entertainments are presented. Horse-racing at Westenhanger Racecourse nearby.
Tourist Information Centre ☎ (01303) 258594

Abbey House Hotel

5-6 Westbourne Gardens, off Sandgate Road, Folkestone CT20 2JA
☎ (01303) 255514
Fax (01303) 245098

Pleasant garden square location in residential West End, close to Leas Cliff Hall and bandstand. Easy access to ferry and Channel Tunnel. Unlimited street parking.
Bedrooms: 3 single, 2 double, 5 twin, 4 family rooms
Bathrooms: 3 en-suite, 4 public

Bed & breakfast per night:
	£min	£max
Single	19.00	26.00
Double	35.00	45.00

Half board per person:
	£min	£max
Daily	29.00	36.00
Weekly	177.00	199.00

Evening meal 1830 (last orders 1930)
Cards accepted: Visa

Augusta Hotel
APPROVED

4 Augusta Gardens, Folkestone CT20 2RR
☎ (01303) 850952
Fax (01303) 240282

Small, licensed hotel in central position, close to sea and Leas and with easy access to ferries and Eurotunnel. Spacious patio with access to private gardens. An elegant Victorian building with style (but no lift).
Bedrooms: 3 single, 8 double, 1 twin
Bathrooms: 12 en-suite, 1 public

Bed & breakfast per night:
	£min	£max
Single	15.00	26.00
Double	30.00	52.00

Half board per person:
	£min	£max
Daily	22.00	30.00
Weekly	130.00	165.00

Lunch available
Evening meal 1830 (last orders 2030)
Cards accepted: Access, Visa, Diners, Amex, Switch/Delta

Clifton Hotel
COMMENDED

The Leas, Clifton Gardens, Folkestone CT20 2EB
☎ (01303) 851231
Fax (01303) 851231
Consort

Regency-style house in centre of the Leas, minutes from town centre, ferry and Channel tunnel and with views of the English Channel. Good base for Canterbury, Weald of Kent and France.
Bedrooms: 23 single, 26 double, 27 twin, 4 triple
Suite available
Bathrooms: 80 en-suite

Bed & breakfast per night:
	£min	£max
Single	55.00	69.50
Double	74.00	92.00

Half board per person:
	£min	£max
Daily	51.00	72.00
Weekly	318.50	402.50

Lunch available
Evening meal 1900 (last orders 2115)
Cards accepted: Access, Visa, Diners, Amex, Switch/Delta

Normandie Guest House
Listed APPROVED

39 Cheriton Road, Folkestone CT20 1DD
☎ (01303) 256233

Central, near all local amenities, with parking nearby. Early breakfast served. Convenient for the harbour and trips to the continent.
Bedrooms: 1 single, 1 double, 2 twin, 1 triple, 1 family room
Bathrooms: 1 public

Bed & breakfast per night:
	£min	£max
Single	14.00	16.00
Double	28.00	32.00

Sunny Lodge Guest House
APPROVED

85 Cheriton Road, Folkestone CT20 2QL
☎ (01303) 251498

Long established guesthouse noted for its high standard, surrounded by lovely garden. Walking distance town centre, railway station, seafront, 10 minutes Seacat, Channel Tunnel. M20 junction 12. Private car park.
Bedrooms: 2 single, 2 double, 2 twin, 2 family rooms
Bathrooms: 2 public

Bed & breakfast per night:
	£min	£max
Single	16.00	17.00
Double	32.00	34.00

Parking for 5

GATWICK AIRPORT
West Sussex

See under Copthorne, Horley, Redhill

Please check prices and other details at the time of booking.

SOUTH EAST ENGLAND

GILLINGHAM
Kent
Map ref 3B3

The largest Medway Town merging into its neighbour Chatham. The Royal Engineers Museum is an interesting attraction.

King Charles Hotel
APPROVED

Brompton Road, Gillingham
ME7 5QT
☎ Medway (01634) 830303
Fax (01634) 829430

Friendly, modern hotel run by family, catering for all requirements at very reasonable rates in comfortable accommodation.
Bedrooms: 1 single, 30 double, 23 twin, 21 triple, 5 family rooms
Bathrooms: 80 en-suite

Bed & breakfast per night:	£min	£max
Single	25.00	25.00
Double	30.00	30.00

Half board per person:	£min	£max
Daily	30.00	35.00

Lunch available
Evening meal 1900 (last orders 2230)
Parking for 201
Cards accepted: Access, Visa, Diners, Amex, Switch/Delta

GUILDFORD
Surrey
Map ref 2D2

Bustling town with many historic monuments, one of which is the Guildhall clock jutting out over the old High Street. The modern cathedral occupies a commanding position on Stag Hill.
Tourist Information Centre ☎ (01483) 444333

Carlton Hotel

London Road, Guildford GU1 2AF
☎ (01483) 575158 & 576539
Fax (01483) 34669
Comfortable hotel, 2 minutes' walk from high street and close to London

Road station. Most rooms en-suite, all have TV, telephone and hospitality tray.
Bedrooms: 13 single, 6 double, 6 twin, 10 triple
Bathrooms: 29 en-suite, 5 public

Bed & breakfast per night:	£min	£max
Single	26.00	36.00
Double	40.00	46.00

Evening meal 1830 (last orders 2030)
Parking for 50
Cards accepted: Access, Visa, Amex, Switch/Delta

Stream Cottage
COMMENDED

The Street, Albury, Guildford
GU5 9AG
☎ (01483) 202228 & Mobile 0860 726090
Fax (01483) 202793
Picturesque village location in beautiful countryside. Charming period beamed cottage with lounge, dining room, sauna, spa bath. Pub food locally. Courtesy transport to and from Gatwick/Heathrow.
Bedrooms: 1 double, 2 twin
Suites available
Bathrooms: 1 en-suite, 2 private

Bed & breakfast per night:	£min	£max
Single	28.00	35.00
Double	45.00	55.00

Parking for 3
Open February–December
Cards accepted: Access, Visa, Switch/Delta

HAILSHAM
East Sussex
Map ref 2D3

An important market town since Norman times and still one of the largest markets in Sussex. Two miles west, at Upper Dicker, is Michelham Priory, an Augustinian house founded in 1229.
Tourist Information Centre ☎ (01323) 844426

Olde Forge Hotel and Restaurant
COMMENDED

Magham Down, Hailsham
BN27 1PN
☎ (01323) 842893
Fax (01323) 842893
Pretty, beamed 16th C building on A271. Comfortable bedrooms, log fires and candlelit dining room. Traditional and reasonably priced menu.

Bedrooms: 2 single, 4 double, 2 twin
Bathrooms: 6 en-suite, 2 private

Bed & breakfast per night:	£min	£max
Single	38.00	40.00
Double	45.00	60.00

Evening meal 1900 (last orders 2130)
Parking for 11
Cards accepted: Access, Visa, Diners, Amex, Switch/Delta

HASLEMERE
Surrey
Map ref 2C2

Town set in hilly, wooded countryside, much of it in the keeping of the National Trust. Its attractions include the educational museum and the annual music festival.

Lythe Hill Hotel
HIGHLY COMMENDED

Petworth Road, Haslemere
GU27 3BQ
☎ (01428) 651251
Fax (01428) 644131

Hotel forms a hamlet of beautifully restored historic buildings in 14 acres of parkland in the Surrey hills. French and English restaurant, tennis, croquet. One hour from London.
Bedrooms: 4 single, 20 double, 8 twin, 8 family rooms
Suites available
Bathrooms: 40 en-suite

Bed & breakfast per night:	£min	£max
Single	84.00	135.00
Double	95.00	175.00

Half board per person:	£min	£max
Daily	111.50	161.50

Lunch available
Evening meal 1915 (last orders 2115)
Parking for 150
Cards accepted: Access, Visa, Diners, Amex, Switch/Delta

SOUTH EAST ENGLAND

HASTINGS
East Sussex
Map ref 3B4

Ancient town which became famous as the base from which William the Conqueror set out to fight the Battle of Hastings. Later became one of the Cinque Ports, now a leading resort. Castle, Hastings Embroidery inspired by the Bayeux Tapestry and Sea Life Centre.
Tourist Information Centre ☎ (01424) 781111

Beauport Park Hotel
HIGHLY COMMENDED
Battle Road, Hastings TN38 8EA
☎ (01424) 851222
Fax (01424) 852465
Best Western
Country house hotel in 33 acres of woodland and landscaped gardens. Many leisure activities, including golf, riding and swimming. Half board price based on minimum 2-night stay.
Bedrooms: 4 single, 10 double, 7 twin, 2 triple
Bathrooms: 23 en-suite

Bed & breakfast
per night:	£min	£max
Single	69.00	
Double	90.00	

Half board per
person:	£min	£max
Daily	57.00	62.00
Weekly	371.00	399.00

Lunch available
Evening meal 1900 (last orders 2130)
Parking for 64
Cards accepted: Access, Visa, Diners, Amex, Switch/Delta

Beechwood Hotel
APPROVED
59 Baldslow Road, Hastings TN34 2EY
☎ (01424) 420078
Late Victorian building with panoramic views of sea, castle and park, in quiet residential area. 1 mile from station and beach.
Bedrooms: 3 double, 1 twin, 1 triple, 2 family rooms
Bathrooms: 3 en-suite, 1 public

Bed & breakfast
per night:	£min	£max
Single	15.00	27.00
Double	28.00	45.00

Half board per
person:	£min	£max
Daily	23.00	35.00
Weekly	146.00	218.00

Lunch available
Evening meal 1800 (last orders 2200)
Parking for 6

Cinque Ports Hotel
COMMENDED
Summerfields, Bohemia Road, Hastings TN34 1ET
☎ (01424) 439222
Fax (01424) 437277
New hotel in a woodland setting yet only a few minutes' walk to the sea, shops, Old Town, sports centre and museum.
Bedrooms: 10 double, 26 twin, 4 triple
Bathrooms: 40 en-suite

Bed & breakfast
per night:	£min	£max
Single	58.00	65.00
Double	65.00	72.00

Half board per
person:	£min	£max
Daily	70.00	79.00
Weekly	400.00	550.00

Lunch available
Evening meal 1900 (last orders 2200)
Parking for 90
Cards accepted: Access, Visa, Diners, Amex, Switch/Delta

Eagle House Hotel
COMMENDED
12 Pevensey Road, St. Leonards-on-Sea, Hastings TN38 0JZ
☎ (01424) 430535 & 441273
Fax (01424) 437771
Large Victorian residence in its own grounds. Well placed for most local amenities and for visiting "1066" country.
Bedrooms: 14 double, 4 twin
Bathrooms: 18 en-suite, 2 public

Bed & breakfast
per night:	£min	£max
Single	31.60	31.60
Double	49.00	49.00

Half board per
person:	£min	£max
Daily	43.45	43.45
Weekly	282.15	282.15

Lunch available
Evening meal 1830 (last orders 2030)
Parking for 14
Cards accepted: Access, Visa, Diners, Amex

Grand Hotel
Grand Parade, St Leonards-on-Sea, Hastings TN38 0DD
☎ (01424) 428510
Fax (01424) 722387
Family-run seafront hotel, close to all amenities. Licensed, international cooking. Radio room call/baby listening in all rooms. Unrestricted parking and own parking for disabled guests. Ici on parle francais.
Wheelchair access category 3
Bedrooms: 4 single, 8 double, 4 twin, 2 triple, 2 family rooms
Bathrooms: 8 en-suite, 3 public

Bed & breakfast
per night:	£min	£max
Single	13.00	50.00
Double	26.00	100.00

Half board per
person:	£min	£max
Daily	18.00	65.00
Weekly	126.00	340.00

Lunch available
Evening meal 1800 (last orders 1900)

High Beech Hotel
COMMENDED
Battle Road, St. Leonards-on-Sea, Hastings TN37 7BS
☎ (01424) 851383
Fax (01424) 854265
Quality accommodation with all rooms en-suite. Beautifully situated between the historic towns of Hastings and Battle, 500 yards off A2100.
Bedrooms: 1 single, 14 double, 2 twin
Bathrooms: 17 en-suite

Bed & breakfast
per night:	£min	£max
Single	40.00	45.00
Double	70.00	80.00

Half board per
person:	£min	£max
Daily	56.00	61.00
Weekly	195.00	230.00

Lunch available
Evening meal 1900 (last orders 2130)
Parking for 100
Cards accepted: Access, Visa, Diners, Amex

Map references apply to the colour maps at the back of this guide.

SOUTH EAST ENGLAND

HASTINGS
Continued

Mayfair Hotel
APPROVED
9 Eversfield Place, St Leonards-on-Sea, Hastings TN37 6BY
☎ (01424) 434161
Family-owned and run hotel on the seafront. Several rooms are en-suite and face the sea. Close to town centre.
Bedrooms: 3 single, 2 double, 3 twin, 3 triple
Bathrooms: 7 en-suite, 1 public, 2 private showers

Bed & breakfast per night:
	£min	£max
Single	15.00	25.00
Double	30.00	50.00

Half board per person:
	£min	£max
Daily	21.00	32.00
Weekly	95.00	185.00

Evening meal 1800 (last orders 1900)
Cards accepted: Access, Visa

Royal Victoria Hotel
COMMENDED
Marina, St Leonards-on-Sea, Hastings TN38 OBD
☎ (01424) 445544
Fax (01424) 721995
Consort

Right on the seafront, a short distance from historic Hastings, stands this grand "oldtimer", tastefully furnished, offering comfort in its bar, lounge and sea terrace restaurant overlooking the Channel.
Bedrooms: 34 double, 11 twin, 5 triple
Bathrooms: 50 en-suite

Bed & breakfast per night:
	£min	£max
Single	33.00	65.00
Double	66.00	90.00

Half board per person:
	£min	£max
Daily	45.00	80.00

Evening meal 1900 (last orders 2130)
Parking for 6

Cards accepted: Access, Visa, Diners, Amex, Switch/Delta

Tower House
HIGHLY COMMENDED
28 Tower Road West, St Leonards-on-Sea, Hastings TN38 0RG
☎ (01424) 427217 & 423771
Fax (01424) 427217
Elegant Victorian house situated half a mile from seafront. Pleasant gardens. Separate licensed bar leading to garden patio. Freshly-cooked meals. Ample parking.
Bedrooms: 1 single, 7 double, 2 twin
Bathrooms: 10 en-suite

Bed & breakfast per night:
	£min	£max
Single	28.50	40.00
Double	45.00	55.00

Half board per person:
	£min	£max
Daily	40.00	50.00
Weekly	258.50	327.50

Evening meal 1800 (last orders 1900)
Cards accepted: Access, Visa, Diners, Amex

HORLEY
Surrey
Map ref 2D2

Town on the London to Brighton road, just north of Gatwick Airport, with an ancient parish church and 15th C inn.

Aintree & Gables Guest House
Listed
50 Bonehurst Road, Horley RH6 8QG
☎ (01293) 774553
Approximately 2 miles from Gatwick and the railway station. Long term parking. Transport to the airport available.
Bedrooms: 3 single, 7 double, 9 twin, 5 triple
Bathrooms: 9 en-suite, 4 public

Bed & breakfast per night:
	£min	£max
Single	25.00	35.00
Double	32.00	38.00

Parking for 25

Belmont House
COMMENDED
46 Massetts Road, Horley RH6 7DS
☎ (01293) 820500 & 775341
Fax (01293) 783812
Friendly family guesthouse in pleasant, quiet and green residential area, 2 minutes from shops, restaurants and railway station. 1.5 miles from Gatwick Airport.
Bedrooms: 2 double, 2 twin, 3 triple
Bathrooms: 4 en-suite, 1 public

Bed & breakfast per night:
	£min	£max
Single	26.00	35.00
Double	36.00	45.00

Parking for 22
Cards accepted: Access, Visa, Amex

Chalet Guest House
COMMENDED
77 Massetts Road, Horley RH6 7EB
☎ (01293) 821666
Fax (01293) 821619
Comfortable modern guesthouse. Convenient for Gatwick Airport, motorways, railway station, local bus, shops, pubs and restaurants.
Bedrooms: 3 single, 1 double, 1 twin, 1 triple
Bathrooms: 5 en-suite, 1 public

Bed & breakfast per night:
	£min	£max
Single	26.00	34.00
Double	44.00	44.00

Parking for 14
Cards accepted: Access, Visa

Felcourt Guest House
Listed APPROVED
79 Massetts Road, Horley RH6 7EB
☎ (01293) 782651 & 776255
Fax (01293) 782651
Friendly Victorian house, close to pubs, restaurants, shopping centre and railway station. One mile from motorway and Gatwick Airport. Long-term parking available at £10 per week.
Bedrooms: 2 single, 3 triple
Bathrooms: 3 en-suite, 1 public

Bed & breakfast per night:
	£min	£max
Single	18.00	28.00
Double	28.00	38.00

Half board per person:
	£min	£max
Daily	23.00	33.00
Weekly	161.00	231.00

Evening meal 1800 (last orders 2000)
Parking for 12

SOUTH EAST ENGLAND

Cards accepted: Access, Visa, Diners, Amex

Gainsborough Lodge
COMMENDED
39 Massetts Road, Gatwick, West Sussex RH6 7DT
☎ (01293) 783982
Fax (01293) 785365
Extended Edwardian house set in attractive garden. Five minutes' walk from Horley station and town centre. Five minutes' drive from Gatwick Airport.
Bedrooms: 3 single, 4 double, 4 twin, 4 triple, 3 family rooms
Bathrooms: 18 en-suite, 1 public
Bed & breakfast
per night:	£min	£max
Single	29.00	35.00
Double	40.00	45.00

Parking for 16
Cards accepted: Access, Visa, Diners, Amex, Switch/Delta

High Trees Gatwick Guest House
HIGHLY COMMENDED
Oldfield Road, Horley RH6 7EP
☎ (01293) 776397
Fax (01293) 785693

High Trees offers high standard accommodation, 1 mile from Gatwick. Good road and rail links to London. All rooms have TV and are en-suite.
Bedrooms: 2 single, 1 double, 2 twin, 2 family rooms
Bathrooms: 7 en-suite
Bed & breakfast
per night:	£min	£max
Single	33.00	36.00
Double	44.00	50.00

Parking for 10
Cards accepted: Access, Visa

The Lawn Guest House
HIGHLY COMMENDED
30 Massetts Road, Horley RH6 7DE
☎ (01293) 775751
Fax (01293) 821203
Classic Victorian house with mature garden, 2 minutes from Horley centre, restaurants, pubs and main rail station

to London/Brighton. 5 minutes' drive to Gatwick, long-term parking. Non-smoking.
Bedrooms: 1 double, 4 twin, 2 triple
Bathrooms: 7 en-suite
Bed & breakfast
per night:	£min	£max
Double	42.00	45.00

Parking for 10
Cards accepted: Access, Visa, Amex

Oakdene Guest House
Listed APPROVED
32 Massetts Road, Horley RH6 7DS
☎ (01293) 772047
Family-run guesthouse, 5 minutes from Gatwick Airport and 30 minutes by train from London or the coast. Long-term car parking available.
Bedrooms: 3 single, 2 triple, 1 family room
Bathrooms: 3 public
Bed & breakfast
per night:	£min	£max
Single	20.00	22.00
Double	30.00	32.00

Parking for 10
Cards accepted: Access, Visa, Amex

Stanhill Court Hotel
HIGHLY COMMENDED
Stanhill, Charlwood, Horley RH6 0EP
☎ (01293) 862166
Fax (01293) 862773

Award-winning Victorian country house hotel. 4 miles from Gatwick Airport and British Rail, but quiet. Magnificent architecture set in 35 acres of ancient woodland. Fully licensed restaurant.
Bedrooms: 12 double, 2 twin, 3 triple
Bathrooms: 17 en-suite
Bed & breakfast
per night:	£min	£max
Double		135.00

Lunch available
Evening meal 1900 (last orders 2130)
Parking for 150
Cards accepted: Access, Visa, Diners, Amex, Switch/Delta

Vulcan Lodge Guest House
HIGHLY COMMENDED
27 Massetts Road, Horley RH6 7DQ
☎ (01293) 771522
Picturesque, comfortable house featuring exposed beams, 5 minutes from Gatwick Airport. Local restaurants, shops, pubs and trains within easy walking distance.
Bedrooms: 2 single, 1 double, 1 twin
Bathrooms: 3 en-suite, 1 private, 1 public
Bed & breakfast
per night:	£min	£max
Single	25.00	31.00
Double	42.00	44.00

Parking for 8
Cards accepted: Access, Visa

Yew Tree
Listed
31 Massetts Road, Horley RH6 7DQ
☎ (01293) 785855
Fax (01293) 785855
Tudor-style house with half an acre of garden. 3 minutes by taxi from Gatwick Airport and 3 minutes' walk from town centre.
Bedrooms: 1 single, 2 double, 1 twin, 1 triple
Bathrooms: 1 public
Bed & breakfast
per night:	£min	£max
Single	15.00	20.00
Double	30.00	35.00

Parking for 10
Cards accepted: Access, Visa, Diners

HOVE
East Sussex

See under Brighton & Hove

HYTHE
Kent
Map ref 3B4

Once one of the Cinque Ports, the town today stands back from the sea. The Royal Military Canal is the scene of a summer pageant, the Romney, Hythe and Dymchurch Railway terminates here and Port Lympne Wild Animal Park, Mansion and Gardens is nearby.

Stade Court Hotel
HIGHLY COMMENDED
West Parade, Hythe CT21 6DT
☎ (01303) 268263
Fax (01303) 261803
Best Western

Continued ▶

SOUTH EAST ENGLAND

HYTHE
Continued

Seafront hotel, with well-appointed family suites. Indoor heated pool, golf, squash, sauna, solarium and so much more, 600 metres away at our sister hotel.
Bedrooms: 10 single, 11 double, 16 twin, 5 triple
Suites available
Bathrooms: 42 en-suite

Bed & breakfast
per night:	£min	£max
Single	61.50	65.00
Double	85.00	90.00

Half board per
person:	£min	£max
Daily	49.00	54.00
Weekly	330.00	350.00

Lunch available
Evening meal 1900 (last orders 2100)
Parking for 12
Cards accepted: Access, Visa, Diners, Amex, Switch/Delta

KINGSDOWN
Kent
Map ref 3C4

Quaint, tranquil, historic fishing village surrounded by castles, first-class golf courses and scenic cliff and country walks. Overlooking the Goodwin Sands towards the French coast.

Kingsdown Country Hotel & Captains Table
COMMENDED

Cliffe Road, Kingsdown, Deal CT14 8AJ
☎ Dover (01304) 373755
Fax (01304) 373755
Family-run, seaside hotel with full en-suite bedrooms, licensed restaurant, secluded car park and private rear gardens with gate to beach.
Bedrooms: 2 single, 2 double
Bathrooms: 4 en-suite

Bed & breakfast
per night:	£min	£max
Single	25.00	35.00
Double	44.00	60.00

Half board per
person:	£min	£max
Daily	32.00	45.00

Evening meal 1830 (last orders 2130)
Parking for 6
Cards accepted: Access, Visa

LEATHERHEAD
Surrey
Map ref 2D2

Old county town in the Green Belt, with the modern Thorndike Theatre.

Bookham Grange Hotel
APPROVED

Little Bookham Common, Bookham, Leatherhead KT23 3HS
☎ Bookham (01372) 452742
Fax (01372) 450080
Minotel/The Independents/Logis of Great Britain
Country house hotel in ideal location for M25, A3, Gatwick, Heathrow and central London. Good food and friendly service.
Bedrooms: 3 single, 8 double, 5 twin, 2 triple
Bathrooms: 18 en-suite

Bed & breakfast
per night:	£min	£max
Single	60.00	60.00
Double	75.00	75.00

Half board per
person:	£min	£max
Daily	50.00	75.00
Weekly	350.00	525.00

Lunch available
Evening meal 1900 (last orders 2200)
Parking for 100
Cards accepted: Access, Visa, Diners, Amex, Switch/Delta

LENHAM
Kent
Map ref 3B4

Shops, inns and houses, many displaying timber-work of the late Middle Ages, surround a square which is the centre of the village. The 14th C parish church has one of the best examples of a Kentish tower.

Lime Tree Restaurant & Hotel
COMMENDED

8-10 The Limes, Lenham, Maidstone ME17 2PQ
☎ Maidstone (01622) 859509 & 850096
Fax (01622) 850096
Situated in a picturesque Kent village near A20. Historic building. Family run, friendly atmosphere.
Bedrooms: 1 single, 3 double, 2 twin, 1 triple
Bathrooms: 7 en-suite

Bed & breakfast
per night:	£min	£max
Single	42.50	45.00
Double	56.50	75.00

Half board per
person:	£min	£max
Daily	60.00	

Lunch available
Evening meal 1900 (last orders 2200)
Cards accepted: Access, Visa, Diners, Amex, Switch/Delta

LEWES
East Sussex
Map ref 2D3

Historic county town with Norman castle. The steep High Street has mainly Georgian buildings. There is a folk museum at Anne of Cleves House and the archaeological museum is in Barbican House.
Tourist Information Centre ☎ (01273) 483448

Shelleys Hotel
HIGHLY COMMENDED

High Street, Lewes BN7 1XS
☎ (01273) 472361
Fax (01273) 483152

16th C manor house in 1 acre of garden. Convenient for the South Downs and Glyndebourne.
Bedrooms: 1 single, 9 double, 9 twin
Suite available
Bathrooms: 19 en-suite

Bed & breakfast
per night:	£min	£max
Single	45.00	105.50
Double	90.00	201.00

Half board per
person:	£min	£max
Daily	70.00	129.50

Lunch available
Evening meal 1900 (last orders 2115)
Parking for 25
Cards accepted: Access, Visa, Diners, Amex

SOUTH EAST ENGLAND

LITTLEHAMPTON
West Sussex
Map ref 2D3

Ancient port at the mouth of the River Arun, now a popular holiday resort, offering flat, sandy beaches, sailing, fishing and boat trips. The Sussex Downs are a short walk inland.

The Colbern Hotel
South Terrace, Seafront, Littlehampton BN17 5LQ
☎ (01903) 714270 & Mobile 0385 541436
Fax (01903) 730955
Friendly family-run hotel overlooking the seafront, greens and English Channel. Close to the River Arun, all leisure facilities, shops and business parks.
Bedrooms: 2 single, 4 double, 3 twin
Bathrooms: 9 en-suite, 1 public

Bed & breakfast per night:	£min	£max
Single	23.50	35.00
Double	47.00	50.00

Half board per person:	£min	£max
Daily	35.00	47.50
Weekly	180.00	210.00

Evening meal 1800 (last orders 1900)
Cards accepted: Access, Visa, Diners, Amex

MAIDSTONE
Kent
Map ref 3B3

Busy county town of Kent on the River Medway has many interesting features and is an excellent centre for excursions. Museum of Carriages, Museum and Art Gallery, Archbishop's Palace, Mote Park.
Tourist Information Centre ☎ (01622) 673581 or 602169

Grangemoor Hotel
COMMENDED
St. Michael's Road, Maidstone ME16 8BS
☎ (01622) 677623
Fax (01622) 678246
One hour from London and the Kent coast, in a quiet position on the edge of town. The hotel has rear gardens, restaurant and bar.
Bedrooms: 10 single, 15 double, 15 twin, 5 triple, 2 family rooms
Bathrooms: 47 en-suite, 3 public

Bed & breakfast per night:	£min	£max
Single	30.00	48.00
Double	45.00	56.00

Lunch available
Evening meal 1830 (last orders 2200)
Parking for 79
Cards accepted: Access, Visa

Rock House Hotel
COMMENDED
102 Tonbridge Road, Maidstone ME16 8SL
☎ (01622) 751616
Fax (01622) 756119
Family-run guesthouse 5 minutes from M20 junction 5 and close to town centre. Convenient for London, Gatwick and Channel ports. French and Spanish spoken.
Bedrooms: 3 single, 2 double, 3 twin, 3 triple
Bathrooms: 5 en-suite, 1 public, 4 private showers

Bed & breakfast per night:	£min	£max
Single	30.00	38.00
Double	38.00	46.00

Parking for 7
Cards accepted: Access, Visa, Amex

Russell Hotel
COMMENDED
136 Boxley Road, Maidstone ME14 2AH
☎ (01622) 692221
Fax (01622) 762084
Consort
Converted convent school a few minutes from Maidstone and 1.5 miles from the M20. Set in secluded grounds with ample parking.
Bedrooms: 14 single, 16 double, 7 twin, 2 triple, 2 family rooms
Bathrooms: 41 en-suite

Bed & breakfast per night:	£min	£max
Single	45.00	60.00
Double	60.00	85.00

Half board per person:	£min	£max
Daily	50.00	65.00
Weekly	300.00	360.00

Lunch available
Evening meal 1900 (last orders 2130)
Parking for 100
Cards accepted: Access, Visa, Diners, Amex, Switch/Delta

Wateringbury Hotel
COMMENDED
Tonbridge Road, Wateringbury, Maidstone ME18 5NS
☎ (01622) 812632
Fax (01622) 812720
Stagecoach
Traditional country hotel in village centre overlooking the picturesque Teston valley. Exit M20 at junction 4, follow signs for A228 West Malling then A26 Tonbridge road.
Bedrooms: 24 double, 16 twin
Bathrooms: 40 en-suite

Bed & breakfast per night:	£min	£max
Single	34.50	59.50
Double	49.00	71.00

Half board per person:	£min	£max
Daily	36.50	73.00

Lunch available
Evening meal 1900 (last orders 2200)
Parking for 90
Cards accepted: Access, Visa, Diners, Amex, Switch/Delta

Willington Court
HIGHLY COMMENDED
Willington Street, Maidstone ME15 8JW
☎ (01622) 738885
Fax (01622) 631790
Charming Grade II listed building. Antiques, four-poster bed. Friendly and relaxed atmosphere. Adjacent to Mote Park and near Leeds Castle.
Bedrooms: 2 double, 1 twin
Bathrooms: 2 en-suite, 1 private

Bed & breakfast per night:	£min	£max
Single	26.00	34.00
Double	40.00	48.00

Parking for 6
Cards accepted: Access, Visa, Diners, Amex

The symbol (CR) and a group name following an hotel address indicates that bookings can be made through a central reservations office. These offices are listed in the information pages at the back of this guide.

SOUTH EAST ENGLAND

MARGATE
Kent
Map ref 3C3

Oldest and most famous resort in Kent. Many Regency and Victorian buildings survive from the town's early days. There are 9 miles of sandy beach. "Dreamland" is a 20-acre amusement park and the Winter Gardens offers concert hall entertainment.
Tourist Information Centre ☎ (01843) 220241

Clintons
👑👑

9 Dalby Square, Cliftonville, Margate CT9 2ER
☎ Thanet (01843) 290598 & 299550
Set in illuminated garden square, this elegant hotel offers comfortable en-suite bedrooms, spacious lounge, licensed restaurant, saunas, jacuzzi, gymnasium and solarium.
Bedrooms: 5 double, 5 twin, 3 triple
Bathrooms: 13 en-suite, 4 public

Bed & breakfast
per night:	£min	£max
Double	40.00	48.00

Half board per person:
	£min	£max
Daily	27.00	30.00
Weekly	160.00	180.00

Evening meal 1800 (last orders 1930)
Parking for 4
Cards accepted: Access, Visa, Diners

Ivyside Hotel 𝐌
👑👑👑

25 Sea Road, Westgate on Sea, Margate CT8 8SB
☎ Thanet (01843) 831082
Fax (01843) 831082

Seafront hotel offering special weekend and midweek breaks with excellent reductions. Facilities for families and conferences.
Bedrooms: 11 single, 9 double, 20 twin, 35 family rooms
Bathrooms: 75 en-suite, 3 public

Bed & breakfast
per night:	£min	£max
Single	30.00	32.00
Double	50.00	56.00

Half board per person:
	£min	£max
Daily	35.00	42.00
Weekly	200.00	235.00

Lunch available
Evening meal 1830 (last orders 2030)
Parking for 25
Cards accepted: Access, Visa, Amex

The Malvern Hotel 𝐌
COMMENDED

29 Eastern Esplanade, Cliftonville, Margate CT9 2HL
☎ Thanet (01843) 290192
Overlooking the sea, promenade and lawns. Close indoor/outdoor bowls complex, Margate Winter Gardens, amenities and Channel ports. Parking (unrestricted) outside and opposite hotel. TV and tea-making facilities - most rooms en-suite with shower and toilet (no baths).
Bedrooms: 1 single, 6 double, 2 twin, 1 family room
Bathrooms: 8 en-suite, 1 public

Bed & breakfast
per night:	£min	£max
Single	20.00	30.00
Double	36.00	42.00

Cards accepted: Access, Visa, Diners, Amex

Westbrook Bay House 𝐌
COMMENDED

12 Royal Esplanade, Westbrook, Margate CT9 5DW
☎ Thanet (01843) 292700
Family-run guesthouse on the seafront. Licensed bar. Clean food award-winner. Some en-suite rooms, also some with showers.
Bedrooms: 1 single, 3 double, 2 twin, 2 triple, 2 family rooms
Bathrooms: 4 en-suite, 2 public, 2 private showers

Bed & breakfast
per night:	£min	£max
Single	15.00	16.00
Double	30.00	32.00

Half board per person:
	£min	£max
Daily	22.00	23.00
Weekly	128.00	136.00

Evening meal 1800 (last orders 1600)

Please check prices and other details at the time of booking.

MIDHURST
West Sussex
Map ref 2C3

Historic, picturesque town just north of the South Downs, with the ruins of Cowdray House, medieval castle and 15th C parish church. Polo at Cowdray Park. Excellent base for Chichester, Petworth, Glorious Goodwood and the South Downs Way.
Tourist Information Centre ☎ (01730) 817322

The Angel Hotel 𝐌
👑👑👑👑 **HIGHLY COMMENDED**

North Street, Midhurst GU29 9DN
☎ (01730) 812421
Fax (01730) 815928
Midway between Haslemere and Chichester, this 16th C inn with 2 function rooms, 85-seat restaurant and 2 bars, serving food at lunchtimes and evenings, has picturesque gardens overlooking Cowdray ruins.
Bedrooms: 2 single, 8 double, 8 twin, 3 triple
Bathrooms: 20 en-suite

Bed & breakfast
per night:	£min	£max
Single	69.00	85.00
Double	75.00	140.00

Half board per person:
	£min	£max
Daily	85.00	110.00
Weekly	550.00	650.00

Lunch available
Evening meal 1800 (last orders 2200)
Parking for 40
Cards accepted: Access, Visa, Diners, Amex, Switch/Delta

Park House Hotel 𝐌
👑👑👑👑 **HIGHLY COMMENDED**

Bepton, Midhurst GU29 0JB
☎ (0173081) 2880 & 3543
Fax (0173081) 5643
Beautifully situated country house hotel, equipped to give maximum comfort, with the atmosphere and amenities of an English country home. Outdoor pool, pitch and putt course, tennis courts, conference facilities.
Bedrooms: 1 single, 4 double, 7 twin, 1 triple
Bathrooms: 13 en-suite, 1 public

Bed & breakfast
per night:	£min	£max
Single	50.00	65.00
Double	95.00	120.00

SOUTH EAST ENGLAND

Half board per person:	£min	£max
Daily	65.00	80.00

Lunch available
Evening meal from 2000
Parking for 60
Cards accepted: Access, Visa, Amex, Switch/Delta

Southdown's Country Hotel & Restaurant

COMMENDED

Trotton, Rogate GU31 5JN
☎ Rogate (01730) 821521
Fax (01730) 821790
Best Western

Country hotel set in its own gardens with full leisure facilities. Ideal for a peaceful rest away from it all. 3 miles west of Midhurst.
Bedrooms: 9 double, 9 twin, 2 triple
Bathrooms: 20 en-suite

Bed & breakfast per night:	£min	£max
Single	60.00	80.00
Double	92.00	110.00

Half board per person:	£min	£max
Daily	72.00	100.00

Lunch available
Evening meal 1900 (last orders 2130)
Parking for 70
Cards accepted: Access, Visa, Diners, Amex

NEW ROMNEY

Kent
Map ref 3B4

Capital of Romney Marsh. Now a mile from the sea, it was one of the original Cinque Ports. Romney, Hythe and Dymchurch Railway's main station is here.

Broadacre Hotel

COMMENDED

North Street, New Romney TN28 8DR
☎ (01797) 362381
Fax (01797) 362381

Small 16th C family-run hotel offering a warm, friendly welcome and personal attention. Intimate restaurants, lounge bar, garden. Weekend breaks.
Bedrooms: 3 single, 4 double, 2 twin, 1 family room
Bathrooms: 10 en-suite

Bed & breakfast per night:	£min	£max
Single	33.00	35.00
Double	45.00	60.00

Half board per person:	£min	£max
Daily	32.50	48.00
Weekly	200.00	

Lunch available
Evening meal 1900 (last orders 2100)
Parking for 9
Cards accepted: Access, Visa

NEWHAVEN

East Sussex
Map ref 2D3

Town has the terminal of a car-ferry service to Dieppe in France.

The Brighton Motel

1 South Coast Road, Peacehaven, Newhaven BN10 8SY
☎ Brighton (01273) 583736
Fax (01273) 586499

Cliff-top motel with quiet rooms, fully licensed restaurant and freehouse bar. Disabled guests catered for.
Wheelchair access category 2
Bedrooms: 1 single, 14 double, 6 twin, 5 triple, 2 family rooms
Bathrooms: 27 en-suite

Bed & breakfast per night:	£min	£max
Single	35.00	
Double	46.00	

Lunch available
Evening meal 1900 (last orders 2130)
Parking for 60
Cards accepted: Access, Visa, Diners, Amex, Switch/Delta

OCKHAM

Surrey
Map ref 2D2

Attractive village with many Victorian buildings including pretty cottages. The Royal Horticultural Society's Garden at Wisley is nearby.

The Hautboy

HIGHLY COMMENDED

Ockham, Woking GU23 6NP
☎ Woking (01483) 225355
Fax (01483) 211176

19th C hotel built in local hand-made bricks by William, first Earl of Lovelace. All suites are individually furnished, complementing the style generated throughout the hotel.
Bedrooms: 3 double, 2 twin
Bathrooms: 5 en-suite

Bed & breakfast per night:	£min	£max
Single	78.00	88.00
Double	98.00	125.00

Half board per person:	£min	£max
Daily	91.75	110.95

Lunch available
Evening meal 1900 (last orders 2200)
Parking for 80
Cards accepted: Access, Visa, Diners, Amex, Switch/Delta

OCKLEY

Surrey
Map ref 2D2

Village by the Roman road Stane Street. In 851 King Ethelwulf defeated the Danes in battle on Ockley Green. Behind the village is Leith Hill with its outstanding views.

Kings Arms Inn

COMMENDED

Stane Street, Ockley, Dorking RH5 5TP
☎ (01306) 711224
Fax (01306) 711224

Built between 1580-1620, this freehouse is the second oldest property in the picturesque village of Ockley, between Dorking and Horsham and 34 miles from seaside town of Bognor Regis. Oak beams dominate.
Bedrooms: 6 double
Bathrooms: 5 en-suite, 1 private

Continued ▶

SOUTH EAST ENGLAND

OCKLEY
Continued

Bed & breakfast per night:	£min	£max
Single	39.50	42.50
Double	58.75	60.00

Lunch available
Evening meal 1900 (last orders 2100)
Parking for 40
Cards accepted: Access, Visa

PENSHURST
Kent
Map ref 2D2

Pretty village in a hilly wooded setting with Penshurst Place, the ancestral home of the Sidney family since 1552, standing in delightful grounds with a formal Tudor garden.

Swale Cottage
Listed HIGHLY COMMENDED

Old Swaylands Lane, Off Poundsbridge Lane, Penshurst, Tonbridge TN11 8AH
☎ (01892) 870738

Charmingly converted Grade II* listed barn overlooking medieval manor house and gardens. Idyllic and tranquil. Delightful en-suite rooms (1 four-poster). Close to Penshurst Place, Hever and Chartwell. Near A26 off B2176.
Bedrooms: 2 double, 1 twin
Bathrooms: 2 en-suite, 1 private

Bed & breakfast per night:	£min	£max
Single	36.00	40.00
Double	52.00	62.00

Parking for 7

COLOUR MAPS
Colour maps at the back of this guide pinpoint all places in which you will find accommodation listed.

PETWORTH
West Sussex
Map ref 2D3

Town dominated by Petworth House (National Trust), the great 17th C mansion, set in 2000 acres of parkland laid out by Capability Brown. The house contains wood-carvings by Grinling Gibbons.
Tourist Information Centre ☎ (01798) 343523

White Horse Inn
HIGHLY COMMENDED

The Street, Sutton, Pulborough RH20 1PS
☎ Sutton (01798) 869221
Fax (01798) 869291
Logis of Great Britain

Pretty Georgian village inn close to South Downs Way. Roman villa 1 mile. Garden, log fires. 4 miles Petworth, 5 miles Pulborough.
Bedrooms: 4 double, 2 twin
Bathrooms: 5 en-suite, 1 private shower

Bed & breakfast per night:	£min	£max
Single	48.00	48.00
Double	58.00	68.00

Half board per person:	£min	£max
Daily	43.00	62.00
Weekly	218.00	302.00

Lunch available
Evening meal 1900 (last orders 2145)
Parking for 10
Cards accepted: Access, Visa, Diners, Amex

A key to symbols can be found inside the back cover flap.

Half board prices are given per person, but in some cases these may be based on double/twin occupancy.

PULBOROUGH
West Sussex
Map ref 2D3

Here is Parham, an Elizabethan mansion with unusually tall, mullioned windows and a long gallery measuring 158 ft. The house and the surrounding park and garden can be visited. In the grounds stands the church of St Peter.

Chequers Hotel
HIGHLY COMMENDED

Church Place, Pulborough RH20 1AD
☎ (01798) 872486
Fax (01798) 872715
Minotel/Logis of Great Britain/The Independents

Queen Anne hotel in picturesque village, overlooking the South Downs. Licensed restaurant, coffee shop. Bedrooms with all facilities, some on ground floor and some with four-posters. Lovely walks in private 9 acre meadow.
Bedrooms: 1 single, 5 double, 2 twin, 3 triple
Bathrooms: 10 en-suite, 1 private

Bed & breakfast per night:	£min	£max
Single	49.50	54.50
Double	77.00	87.00

Half board per person:	£min	£max
Daily	46.00	56.00
Weekly	299.00	333.00

Lunch available
Evening meal 1930 (last orders 2045)
Parking for 16
Cards accepted: Access, Visa, Diners, Amex

RAMSGATE
Kent
Map ref 3C3

Popular holiday resort with good sandy beaches. At Pegwell Bay is replica of a Viking longship. Terminal for car-ferry service to Dunkirk and Ostend.
Tourist Information Centre ☎ (01843) 583333

Eastwood Guest House
Listed COMMENDED

28 Augusta Road, Ramsgate CT11 8JS
☎ Thanet (01843) 591505
Fax (01843) 591505

SOUTH EAST ENGLAND

Pretty Victorian villa, close to ferry port and amenities. Comfortable rooms, mostly en-suite. Lock-up garages available. Breakfast served from 6.45 am, dinner available.
Bedrooms: 1 single, 4 double, 4 twin, 6 family rooms
Bathrooms: 10 en-suite, 3 public

Bed & breakfast per night:

	£min	£max
Single	15.00	25.00
Double	30.00	35.00

Half board per person:

	£min	£max
Daily	20.00	25.00
Weekly	140.00	175.00

Evening meal 1830 (last orders 1930)
Parking for 20

Goodwin View Hotel

APPROVED

19 Wellington Cres, Ramsgate CT11 8JD
☎ Thanet (01843) 591419
Seafront licensed hotel in Grade II listed historic building overlooking harbour and beach. Bookings made for ferry-users. Terminal and town within walking distance. Ideal base for touring Kent.
Bedrooms: 4 single, 3 double, 2 twin, 2 triple, 2 family rooms
Bathrooms: 4 en-suite, 3 public

Bed & breakfast per night:

	£min	£max
Single	19.00	26.00
Double	32.00	42.00

Evening meal from 1800
Cards accepted: Access, Visa, Diners, Amex, Switch/Delta

San Clu Hotel

COMMENDED

Victoria Parade, East Cliff, Ramsgate CT11 8DT
☎ Thanet (01843) 592345
Fax (01737) 580157
Grade II listed Victorian, recently refurbished cliff top hotel overlooking sea and sands. Near cross-Channel ferry terminals and harbour. Quiet location out of town centre, but within easy reach of ample parking.
Bedrooms: 7 single, 18 double, 5 twin, 12 triple, 2 family rooms

Suites available
Bathrooms: 33 en-suite

Bed & breakfast per night:

	£min	£max
Single	40.00	70.00
Double	60.00	135.00

Half board per person:

	£min	£max
Daily	45.00	95.00
Weekly	315.00	665.00

Lunch available
Evening meal 1900 (last orders 2130)
Parking for 22
Cards accepted: Access, Visa, Diners, Amex, Switch/Delta

Shirley's Hotel

APPROVED

8 Nelson Cres, Ramsgate CT11 9JF
☎ (01843) 584198
Overlooking Ramsgate harbour and Sally Line ferry terminal. 2 minutes from town centre. All rooms have colour TV and tea-making facilities and some rooms are en-suite.
Bedrooms: 2 single, 2 double, 3 twin, 2 triple, 2 family rooms
Bathrooms: 4 en-suite, 2 public

Bed & breakfast per night:

	£min	£max
Single	15.00	18.00
Double	30.00	35.00

Spencer Court Hotel

COMMENDED

37 Spencer Square, Ramsgate CT11 9LD
☎ Thanet (01843) 594582
Grade II listed building in quiet square overlooking tennis courts, 200 yards from seafront, directly above Sally Line ferry terminal.
Bedrooms: 3 single, 3 double, 2 twin, 1 triple
Bathrooms: 4 en-suite, 2 public

Bed & breakfast per night:

	£min	£max
Single	17.00	20.00
Double	30.00	44.00

Evening meal 1830 (last orders 1000)
Cards accepted: Access, Visa, Diners

The National Grading and Classification Scheme is explained in full at the back of this guide.

REDHILL

Surrey
Map ref 2D2

Part of the borough of Reigate and now the commercial centre with good shopping facilities. Gatwick Airport is 3 miles to the south.

Ashleigh House Hotel

Listed HIGHLY COMMENDED

39 Redstone Hill, Redhill RH1 4BG
☎ (01737) 764763
Fax (01737) 780308
Friendly, family-run early Edwardian house, 500 yards from railway station, London 30 minutes, Gatwick Airport 15 minutes.
Bedrooms: 1 single, 2 double, 3 twin, 1 triple, 1 family room
Bathrooms: 6 en-suite, 1 public

Bed & breakfast per night:

	£min	£max
Single	26.00	42.00
Double	45.00	52.00

Parking for 9
Cards accepted: Access, Visa

Nutfield Priory

HIGHLY COMMENDED

Nutfield, Redhill RH1 4EN
☎ (01737) 822066
Fax (01737) 823321
Thames Valley

In 40 acres of countryside with unsurpassed views. Large ornate building of towers, elaborate carvings, stonework cloisters and stained glass windows. Extensive leisure club - free to hotel guests. Generous weekend, anytime and beauty packages available.
Bedrooms: 10 single, 33 double, 17 twin
Suites available
Bathrooms: 60 en-suite

Bed & breakfast per night:

	£min	£max
Single	110.00	125.00
Double	130.00	250.00

Lunch available
Evening meal 1900 (last orders 2200)
Parking for 170

Continued ▶

SOUTH EAST ENGLAND

REDHILL
Continued

Cards accepted: Access, Visa, Diners, Amex, Switch/Delta

ROCHESTER
Kent
Map ref 3B3

Ancient cathedral city on the River Medway. Has many places of interest connected with Charles Dickens (who lived nearby) including the fascinating Dickens Centre. Also massive castle overlooking the river and Guildhall Museum.
Tourist Information Centre ☎ (01634) 843666

Medway Manor Hotel
APPROVED

14 - 16 New Road, Rochester ME1 1BG
☎ Chatham (01634) 847985
Fax (01634) 832430
Family-run hotel with historic and scenic views, convenient for London and south east coast. Leisure facilities available.
Bedrooms: 8 single, 19 double, 9 twin, 2 triple, 4 family rooms
Bathrooms: 42 en-suite, 2 public
Bed & breakfast
per night: £min   £max
Single   35.00   75.00
Double   45.00   90.00

Half board per
person: £min   £max
Daily   40.00   95.00
Weekly   280.00   630.00

Lunch available
Evening meal 1800 (last orders 2200)
Parking for 42
Cards accepted: Access, Visa, Diners, Amex, Switch/Delta

TOWN INDEX
This can be found at the back of the guide. If you know where you want to stay, the index will give you the page number listing all accommodation in your chosen town, city or village.

ROYAL TUNBRIDGE WELLS
Kent
Map ref 2D2

This "Royal" town became famous as a spa in the 17th C and much of its charm is retained, as in the Pantiles, a shaded walk lined with elegant shops. Heritage attraction "A Day at the Wells". Rich in parks and gardens and a good centre for walks. Excellent shopping centre.
Tourist Information Centre ☎ (01892) 515675

Danehurst
HIGHLY COMMENDED

41 Lower Green Road, Rusthall, Royal Tunbridge Wells TN4 8TW
☎ Tunbridge Wells (01892) 527739
Fax (01892) 514804
Logis of Great Britain

Charming gabled house in a village setting in the heart of Kent. Our bedrooms afford excellent accommodation. Breakfast is served in our Victorian conservatory and you can enjoy a candlelit dinner in our elegant dining room. We would be delighted to welcome you to our home.
Bedrooms: 2 double, 2 twin
Bathrooms: 4 en-suite
Bed & breakfast
per night: £min   £max
Single   39.50   45.00
Double   59.50   65.00

Half board per
person: £min   £max
Daily   58.45   67.95
Weekly   409.15   475.65

Evening meal 1900 (last orders 1800)
Parking for 5
Cards accepted: Access, Visa, Amex

The Old Parsonage
DE LUXE

Church Lane, Frant, Royal Tunbridge Wells TN3 9DX
☎ Frant (01892) 750773
Fax (01892) 750773
Peacefully situated by the village church (2 pubs and restaurant nearby), this classic Georgian country house provides superior accommodation: en-suite bedrooms, antique-furnished reception rooms, spacious conservatory and

ballustraded terrace overlooking the secluded walled garden. SEETB 1995 "Bed and Breakfast of the Year" Award winner.
Bedrooms: 2 double, 1 twin
Bathrooms: 3 en-suite
Bed & breakfast
per night: £min   £max
Single   34.00   44.00
Double   54.00   64.00

Parking for 12
Cards accepted: Access, Visa

Russell Hotel

80 London Road, Royal Tunbridge Wells TN1 1DZ
☎ Tunbridge Wells (01892) 544833
Fax (01892) 515846
Logis of Great Britain

Large Victorian house facing common, only minutes from town centre. Totally refurbished to highest modern standards.
Bedrooms: 11 double, 10 twin, 3 triple
Suites available
Bathrooms: 24 en-suite
Bed & breakfast
per night: £min   £max
Single   68.00
Double   82.00

Lunch available
Evening meal 1900 (last orders 2130)
Parking for 20
Cards accepted: Access, Visa, Diners, Amex, Switch/Delta

The Spa Hotel
COMMENDED

Mount Ephraim, Royal Tunbridge Wells TN4 8XJ
☎ Tunbridge Wells (01892) 520331
Fax (01892) 510575
Best Western
Elegant mansion overlooking the historic town of Royal Tunbridge Wells. Extensive leisure facilities, fine dining. Ideal for weekend breaks.
Wheelchair access category 3
Bedrooms: 16 single, 32 double, 22 twin, 4 triple
Suites available
Bathrooms: 74 en-suite

SOUTH EAST ENGLAND

Bed & breakfast per night:

	£min	£max
Single	77.50	
Double	101.00	

Half board per person:

	£min	£max
Daily	62.00	

Lunch available
Evening meal 1930 (last orders 2130)
Parking for 150
Cards accepted: Access, Visa, Diners, Amex, Switch/Delta

RUSTINGTON
West Sussex
Map ref 2D3

Village with thatched cottages and a medieval church.

Kenmore M
HIGHLY COMMENDED

Claigmar Road, Rustington BN16 2NL
☎ (01903) 784634
Fax (01903) 784634
Secluded Edwardian house in the heart of village close to sea. Ideal for historic towns, castles, cathedrals and stately homes.
Bedrooms: 1 single, 1 double, 1 twin, 3 triple, 1 family room
Bathrooms: 7 en-suite, 1 public

Bed & breakfast per night:

	£min	£max
Single	22.50	25.00
Double	45.00	50.00

Half board per person:

	£min	£max
Daily	32.50	35.00
Weekly	215.00	230.00

Evening meal from 1830
Parking for 7
Cards accepted: Access, Visa, Amex, Switch/Delta

Mayday Hotel M
COMMENDED

12 Broadmark Lane, Rustington, Littlehampton BN16 2HH
☎ (01903) 771198 & Freephone 0500 121227
Fax (01903) 850742
In own gardens 400 yards from the beach yet ideally placed for exploring the countryside with its many attractions. Under the personal supervision of the proprietors, a warm welcome assured.
Bedrooms: 1 single, 2 double, 4 twin, 1 triple
Bathrooms: 7 en-suite, 1 public

Bed & breakfast per night:

	£min	£max
Single	28.00	30.00
Double	55.00	59.00

Half board per person:

	£min	£max
Daily	38.00	39.00
Weekly	220.50	240.00

Evening meal 1900 (last orders 1800)
Parking for 20
Cards accepted: Access, Visa

RYE
East Sussex
Map ref 3B4

Cobbled, hilly streets and fine old buildings make Rye, once a Cinque Port, a most picturesque town. Noted for its church with ancient clock, potteries and antique shops. Town Model Sound and Light Show gives a good introduction to the town.
Tourist Information Centre ☎ *(01797) 226696*

Aviemore Guest House M
APPROVED

28/30 Fishmarket Road, Rye TN31 7LP
☎ (01797) 223052
Fax (01797) 223052

Owner-run, friendly guesthouse offering a warm welcome and hearty breakfast. Overlooking "Town Salts" and the River Rother. 2 minutes from town centre.
Bedrooms: 1 single, 4 double, 3 twin
Bathrooms: 4 en-suite, 2 public

Bed & breakfast per night:

	£min	£max
Single	17.00	22.00
Double	30.00	42.00

Half board per person:

	£min	£max
Daily	23.00	28.00
Weekly	151.00	179.00

Evening meal 1800 (last orders 2200)
Cards accepted: Access, Visa, Amex

Camber Sands Lodge M

Camber Sands Leisure Park, 93 Lydd Road, Camber, Rye TN31 7RS
☎ (01797) 225555
Fax (01792) 225756
Modern, friendly hotel situated 100 yards from sandy beach. Ancient Rye a short ride away. Health club, swimming pools adjacent.
Bedrooms: 6 double, 2 twin, 1 triple
Bathrooms: 9 en-suite

Bed & breakfast per night:

	£min	£max
Single	15.00	20.00
Double	20.00	30.00

Evening meal 1900 (last orders 2100)
Parking for 14
Open March–October
Cards accepted: Access, Visa, Switch/Delta

Flackley Ash Hotel & Restaurant M
HIGHLY COMMENDED

London Road, Peasmarsh, Rye TN31 6YH
☎ Peasmarsh (01797) 230651
Fax (01797) 230510
Best Western/Logis of Great Britain
Georgian country house hotel in 5 acres. Swimming pool and leisure centre. Fresh fish, well-stocked cellar. Half board rate based on minimum 2-night stay.
Bedrooms: 21 double, 9 twin, 1 triple, 1 family room
Bathrooms: 32 en-suite

Bed & breakfast per night:

	£min	£max
Double	108.00	124.00

Half board per person:

	£min	£max
Daily	63.50	68.00
Weekly	299.00	400.00

Lunch available
Evening meal 1900 (last orders 2130)
Parking for 60
Cards accepted: Access, Visa, Diners, Amex, Switch/Delta

The M symbol after an establishment name indicates that it is a Regional Tourist Board member.

SOUTH EAST ENGLAND

RYE
Continued

Jeake's House
HIGHLY COMMENDED
Mermaid Street, Rye TN31 7ET
☎ (01797) 222828
Fax (01797) 222623

Recapture the past in this historic building, in a cobblestoned street at the heart of the old town. Honeymoon suite available.
Bedrooms: 1 single, 7 double, 1 twin, 2 triple, 1 family room
Bathrooms: 7 en-suite, 1 private, 2 public, 2 private showers

Bed & breakfast per night:
	£min	£max
Single	22.50	54.00
Double	41.00	59.00

Cards accepted: Access, Visa, Amex

Little Orchard House
HIGHLY COMMENDED
West Street, Rye TN31 7ES
☎ (01797) 223831
Georgian town house in centre of Rye. Antique furnishings and large walled garden give country house atmosphere.
Bedrooms: 2 double, 1 twin
Bathrooms: 3 en-suite

Bed & breakfast per night:
	£min	£max
Single	45.00	65.00
Double	60.00	84.00

Cards accepted: Access, Visa

The Old Vicarage Hotel
HIGHLY COMMENDED
15 East Street, Rye TN31 7JY
☎ (01797) 225131
Fax (01797) 225131
Logis of Great Britain
Family-run Queen Anne hotel and restaurant in conservation area. Spacious rooms and elegant restaurant with panoramic views over Romney Marsh.
Bedrooms: 2 double, 2 triple
Bathrooms: 4 en-suite

Bed & breakfast per night:
	£min	£max
Double	64.00	84.00

Half board per person:
	£min	£max
Daily	46.00	54.00
Weekly	276.00	324.00

Evening meal 1900 (last orders 2100)
Open February–December
Cards accepted: Access, Visa, Amex, Switch/Delta

Playden Cottage Guesthouse
HIGHLY COMMENDED
Military Road, Rye TN31 7NY
☎ (01797) 222234

Large character cottage, said to be "Grebe" from E. F. Benson's Mapp and Lucia novels. Personal service in a comfortable family home. Pretty gardens, rural aspect, peaceful.
Bedrooms: 1 double, 2 twin
Bathrooms: 3 en-suite, 1 public

Bed & breakfast per night:
	£min	£max
Single	37.50	60.00
Double	50.00	60.00

Half board per person:
	£min	£max
Daily	37.00	72.00
Weekly	241.50	273.00

Evening meal 1800 (last orders 2030)
Parking for 7
Cards accepted: Access, Visa

Rye Lodge Hotel
HIGHLY COMMENDED
Hilders Cliff, Rye TN31 7LD
☎ (01797) 223838
Fax (01797) 223585
Stunning estuary views. Close to town centre. Elegant rooms all en-suite. Candlelit dinners, delicious food and wine. Room service (breakfast in bed!). Car park. Attentive service.
Bedrooms: 1 single, 10 double, 4 twin
Bathrooms: 15 en-suite

Bed & breakfast per night:
	£min	£max
Single	47.50	65.00
Double	65.00	105.00

Half board per person:
	£min	£max
Daily	50.00	70.00
Weekly	297.50	397.50

Evening meal 1930 (last orders 2130)
Parking for 20
Cards accepted: Access, Visa, Diners, Amex, Switch/Delta

Strand House
COMMENDED
Winchelsea TN36 4JT
☎ (01797) 226276
Fax (01797) 224806

The old-world charm of one of Winchelsea's oldest houses, dating from the 15th C, with oak beams and inglenooks. Overlooking National Trust pastureland. Four-poster bedroom. Residents' licence.
Bedrooms: 8 double, 1 twin, 1 triple
Bathrooms: 8 en-suite, 1 public

Bed & breakfast per night:
	£min	£max
Single	28.00	34.00
Double	40.00	60.00

Evening meal 1800 (last orders 1900)
Parking for 12
Cards accepted: Access, Visa

Top o' The Hill at Rye
COMMENDED
Rye Hill, Rye TN31 7NH
☎ (01797) 223284
Fax (01797) 227030
Small, friendly inn offering fine traditional food and cottage-style accommodation. Central for touring Kent and Sussex, Channel ports nearby. Large car park, garden.
Bedrooms: 5 double, 2 twin, 1 triple
Bathrooms: 8 en-suite

Bed & breakfast per night:
	£min	£max
Single	25.00	26.00
Double	42.00	48.00

Lunch available
Evening meal 1900 (last orders 2100)
Parking for 32
Cards accepted: Access, Visa

SOUTH EAST ENGLAND

SANDWICH
Kent
Map ref 3C3

Delightful old market town, once a Cinque Port, now 2 miles from the sea. Many interesting old buildings including the 16th C Barbican and the Guildhall which contains the town's treasures. Several excellent golf-courses.

Bell Hotel M
👑👑👑👑 COMMENDED

The Quay, Sandwich CT13 9EF
☎ (01304) 613388
Fax (01304) 615308
17th C riverside inn extended during Victorian times, recently refurbished in traditional manner to provide individual and comfortable accommodation with quality restaurant and cellar. Own golf club, Princes, just a short drive away.
Bedrooms: 7 single, 6 double, 19 twin, 1 family room
Bathrooms: 33 private

Bed & breakfast per night:
	£min	£max
Single	70.00	110.00
Double	90.00	140.00

Half board per person:
	£min	£max
Daily	79.95	119.95

Lunch available
Evening meal 1900 (last orders 2145)
Parking for 10
Cards accepted: Access, Visa, Diners, Amex, Switch/Delta

SELSEY
West Sussex
Map ref 2C3

Almost surrounded by water, with the English Channel on two sides and an inland lake, once Pagham Harbour, and the Brook on the other two. Ideal for yachting, swimming, fishing and wildlife.

St Andrews Lodge M
👑👑👑 COMMENDED

Chichester Road, Selsey, Chichester PO20 0LX
☎ Chichester (01243) 606899
Fax (01243) 607826
Logis of Great Britain

Map references apply to the colour maps at the back of this guide.

Family-run, friendly relaxed atmosphere, licensed, en-suite bedrooms, cosy lounge, log fire. Peaceful sun trap garden. Close to natural beaches and countryside, south of Chichester.
Wheelchair access category 1
Bedrooms: 1 single, 3 double, 3 twin, 2 family rooms
Bathrooms: 9 en-suite

Bed & breakfast per night:
	£min	£max
Single	25.00	40.00
Double	40.00	55.00

Half board per person:
	£min	£max
Daily	29.50	37.50

Evening meal 1800 (last orders 1930)
Parking for 15
Cards accepted: Access, Visa, Amex, Switch/Delta

SEVENOAKS
Kent
Map ref 2D2

Set in pleasant wooded country, with a distinctive character and charm. Nearby is Knole (National Trust), home of the Sackville family and one of the largest houses in England, set in a vast deer park.
Tourist Information Centre ☎ (01732) 450305

The Bull Hotel M
👑👑👑 APPROVED

Wrotham, Sevenoaks TN15 7RF
☎ (01732) 885522 & 883092
Fax (01732) 886288
The Independents

Privately-run 14th C coaching inn, in secluded historic village 15 minutes from Sevenoaks. Just off M20 and M25/4, 30 minutes from Gatwick and London, 1 hour from Dover. Oak beams and inglenook fireplaces. Ideal for local places of interest.
Bedrooms: 1 single, 3 double, 6 twin
Bathrooms: 6 en-suite, 4 private, 1 public

Bed & breakfast per night:
	£min	£max
Single	35.00	40.00
Double	45.00	50.00

Lunch available
Evening meal 1900 (last orders 2200)
Parking for 50
Cards accepted: Access, Visa, Diners, Amex

Donnington Manor Hotel M
👑👑👑👑

London Road, Dunton Green, Sevenoaks TN13 2TD
☎ (01732) 462681
Fax (01732) 458116
Hotel with restaurant, squash and leisure facilities, in delightful countryside of the Kentish Weald, close to many places of interest.
Bedrooms: 34 double, 26 twin, 3 triple
Bathrooms: 63 en-suite, 1 public

Bed & breakfast per night:
	£min	£max
Single	50.00	75.00
Double	60.00	85.00

Half board per person:
	£min	£max
Daily	62.50	90.00
Weekly	437.50	630.00

Lunch available
Evening meal 1900 (last orders 2130)
Parking for 120
Cards accepted: Access, Visa, Diners, Amex, Switch/Delta

The Moorings Hotel M
👑👑👑 APPROVED

97 Hitchen Hatch Lane, Sevenoaks TN13 3BE
☎ (01732) 452589 & 742323
Fax (01732) 456462
Friendly family hotel offering high standard accommodation for tourists and business travellers. 30 minutes from London. Close to BR station.
Bedrooms: 5 single, 5 double, 9 twin, 2 triple
Bathrooms: 21 en-suite, 1 public

Bed & breakfast per night:
	£min	£max
Single	25.00	42.00
Double	35.00	59.00

Half board per person:
	£min	£max
Daily	35.00	52.00
Weekly	245.00	364.00

Continued ▶

SOUTH EAST ENGLAND

SEVENOAKS
Continued

Lunch available
Evening meal 1900 (last orders 2130)
Parking for 24
Cards accepted: Access, Visa, Amex, Switch/Delta

SHEPPERTON
Surrey
Map ref 2D2

Made famous by its connections with the British film industry, this town by the Thames retains an air of detachment from London, despite being only 10 miles from the centre of the capital.

Warren Lodge Hotel & Restaurant
COMMENDED

Church Square, Shepperton, Middlesex TW17 9JZ
☎ Walton-on-Thames (01932) 242972
Fax (01932) 253883

300-year-old hotel standing in a delightful, shady garden by the river, just off the main road. A mulberry tree from Hampton Court was planted here by Cardinal Wolsey.

Bedrooms: 15 single, 25 double, 5 twin, 3 triple
Bathrooms: 48 en-suite

Bed & breakfast per night:

	£min	£max
Single	35.00	76.00
Double	70.00	92.00

Half board per person:

	£min	£max
Daily	44.00	90.00

Lunch available
Evening meal 1900 (last orders 2200)
Parking for 30
Cards accepted: Access, Visa, Diners, Amex, Switch/Delta

SHIPBOURNE
Kent
Map ref 2D2

Due north of Tonbridge and halfway to Ightham, Shipbourne is sandwiched between acres of Forestry Commission conifers and the park of Fairbourne.

The Chaser Inn
COMMENDED

Stumble Hill, Shipbourne, Tonbridge TN11 9PE
☎ Plaxtol (01732) 810360
Fax (01732) 810941
Wayfarer

Recently refurbished village inn next to Shipbourne Church and set around an attractive courtyard. Imaginative bar and restaurant food served. All rooms with private facilities.

Bedrooms: 5 single, 6 double, 4 twin
Bathrooms: 15 en-suite

Bed & breakfast per night:

	£min	£max
Single	45.00	50.00
Double	60.00	65.00

Lunch available
Evening meal 1900 (last orders 2130)
Parking for 40
Cards accepted: Access, Visa, Amex, Switch/Delta

SISSINGHURST
Kent
Map ref 3B4

Kennel Holt Hotel
HIGHLY COMMENDED

Goudhurst Road, Cranbrook TN17 2PT
☎ Cranbrook (01580) 712032
Fax (01580) 715495

Elizabethan manor, 300 yards off the road. Delightful gardens. Calm and quiet. Within 30 minutes of many historic houses and gardens.

Bedrooms: 2 single, 6 double, 2 twin
Bathrooms: 10 en-suite

Bed & breakfast per night:

	£min	£max
Single	85.00	
Double	125.00	

Half board per person:

	£min	£max
Daily	105.00	
Weekly	735.00	

Lunch available
Evening meal 1930 (last orders 2100)
Parking for 35
Cards accepted: Access, Visa, Diners, Amex, Switch/Delta

SITTINGBOURNE
Kent
Map ref 3B3

The town's position and its ample supply of water make it an ideal site for the paper-making industry. Delightful villages and orchards lie round about.

The Beaumont
COMMENDED

74 London Road, Sittingbourne ME10 1NS
☎ (01795) 472536
Fax (01795) 425921

Comfortable, friendly 17th C former farmhouse, conveniently located for historic Canterbury, Rochester and Leeds Castle. Superb prize-winning breakfast menu and private car park.

Bedrooms: 3 single, 4 double, 1 twin, 1 family room
Bathrooms: 5 en-suite, 1 private, 1 public, 2 private showers

Bed & breakfast per night:

	£min	£max
Single	22.00	42.00
Double	44.00	50.00

Parking for 9
Cards accepted: Access, Visa, Switch/Delta

Hempstead House
HIGHLY COMMENDED

London Road, Bapchild, Sittingbourne ME9 9PP
☎ (01795) 428020
Logis of Great Britain

National gradings and classifications were correct at the time of going to press but are subject to change. Please check at the time of booking.

Please check prices and other details at the time of booking.

SOUTH EAST ENGLAND

Exclusive private Victorian country house hotel on main A2 between Canterbury and Sittingbourne, offering quality accommodation, fine cuisine and friendly hospitality.
Bedrooms: 5 double, 1 twin, 1 family room
Bathrooms: 7 en-suite

Bed & breakfast

per night:	£min	£max
Single	59.00	59.00
Double	69.00	69.00

Half board per

person:	£min	£max
Daily	53.00	78.50

Lunch available
Evening meal 1800 (last orders 2200)
Parking for 12
Cards accepted: Access, Visa, Diners, Amex, Switch/Delta

STEYNING
West Sussex
Map ref 2D3

An important market town and thriving port before the Norman Conquest, lying at the foot of the South Downs. Retains a picturesque charm with fascinating timber-framed and stone buildings.

The Old Tollgate Restaurant and Hotel ♠
HIGHLY COMMENDED

The Street, Bramber, Steyning
BN44 3WE
☎ (01903) 879494
Fax (01903) 813399
Best Western

Beautifully appointed hotel at the foot of South Downs, opposite Bramber Castle ruins. Extremely popular "visual a la carte" restaurant.
Bedrooms: 21 double, 10 twin
Suites available
Bathrooms: 31 en-suite

Bed & breakfast

per night:	£min	£max
Single	63.95	83.95
Double	69.90	89.90

Half board per

person:	£min	£max
Daily	49.63	101.60

Lunch available
Evening meal 1900 (last orders 2130)
Parking for 60
Cards accepted: Access, Visa, Diners, Amex, Switch/Delta

TADWORTH
Surrey
Map ref 2D2

Suburban location 3 miles south-west of Banstead.

Heathside Hotel ♠

A217-Brighton Road, Burgh Heath, Tadworth KT20 6BW
☎ Burgh Heath (01737) 353355
Fax (01737) 370857
En-suite bedrooms, restaurant, indoor pool, ladies' and gentlemen's sauna, conference facilities. Close to M25, Gatwick Airport, Epsom Downs racing, golf and central London.
Bedrooms: 18 double, 21 twin, 32 triple
Bathrooms: 71 en-suite

Bed & breakfast

per night:	£min	£max
Single	65.00	75.00
Double	75.00	85.00

Half board per

person:	£min	£max
Daily	78.00	88.00

Evening meal 1800 (last orders 2200)
Parking for 140
Cards accepted: Access, Visa, Diners, Amex

The symbol ⓒⓡ and a group name following an hotel address indicates that bookings can be made through a central reservations office. These offices are listed in the information pages at the back of this guide.

TENTERDEN
Kent
Map ref 3B4

Most attractive market town with a broad main street full of 16th C houses and shops. The tower of the 15th C parish church is the finest in Kent. Fine antiques centre.

Little Silver Country Hotel ♠
HIGHLY COMMENDED

Ashford Road, St Michaels, Tenterden TN30 6SP
☎ (01233) 850321
Fax (01233) 850647

Quality accommodation in Tudor-style country house hotel. Four-poster, brass bedded, family, disabled facilities (all en-suite). A la carte menu. Personal service in a truly delightful unique atmosphere. Landscaped gardens.
Wheelchair access category 3
Bedrooms: 5 double, 3 twin, 1 triple, 1 family room
Bathrooms: 10 en-suite

Bed & breakfast

per night:	£min	£max
Single	60.00	85.00
Double	85.00	110.00

Half board per

person:	£min	£max
Daily	64.00	110.00
Weekly	400.00	700.00

Lunch available
Evening meal 1830 (last orders 2200)
Parking for 50
Cards accepted: Access, Visa, Amex, Switch/Delta

TICEHURST
East Sussex
Map ref 3B4

Dale Hill Hotel & Golf Club ♠

Ticehurst, Wadhurst TN5 7DQ
☎ (01580) 200112
Fax (01580) 201249
Situated high on the Weald in an Area of Outstanding Natural Beauty, with its own golf course and leisure facilities.
Continued ▶

SOUTH EAST ENGLAND

TICEHURST
Continued

Bedrooms: 6 double, 20 twin
Suite available
Bathrooms: 26 en-suite

Bed & breakfast
per night:	£min	£max
Single	43.00	58.00
Double	66.00	116.00

Lunch available
Evening meal 1900 (last orders 2130)
Parking for 220
Cards accepted: Access, Visa, Amex, Switch/Delta

TUNBRIDGE WELLS
See under Royal Tunbridge Wells

UCKFIELD
East Sussex
Map ref 2D3

Once a medieval market town and centre of the iron industry, Uckfield is now a busy country town on the edge of the Ashdown Forest.

Halland Forge Hotel & Restaurant
COMMENDED

Halland, Lewes BN8 6PW
☎ Halland (01825) 840456
Fax (01825) 840773
Logis of Great Britain/The Independents

Attractive hotel with fully licensed restaurant and coffee shop. Facilities for meetings and functions. Garden and woodland walks. Ideal touring centre, 4 miles from Uckfield, 15 miles from Brighton and Eastbourne.
Bedrooms: 11 double, 7 twin, 2 triple
Bathrooms: 20 en-suite

Bed & breakfast
per night:	£min	£max
Single	44.00	56.00
Double	52.00	77.00

Half board per
person:	£min	£max
Daily	60.50	72.50
Weekly	273.00	286.50

Lunch available
Evening meal 1900 (last orders 2130)
Parking for 70
Cards accepted: Access, Visa, Diners, Amex, Switch/Delta

Hooke Hall
HIGHLY COMMENDED

250 High Street, Uckfield
TN22 1EN
☎ (01825) 761578
Fax (01825) 768025
Elegant Queen Anne town house, recently completely refurbished, with individual comfortably designed rooms equipped to a high standard. Friendly and informal atmosphere.
Bedrooms: 5 double, 4 twin
Bathrooms: 8 en-suite, 1 private

Bed & breakfast
per night:	£min	£max
Single	40.00	75.00
Double	75.00	115.00

Half board per
person:	£min	£max
Daily	60.00	80.00

Lunch available
Evening meal 1930 (last orders 2100)
Parking for 7
Cards accepted: Access, Visa, Amex

WESTERHAM
Kent
Map ref 2D2

This small country town near the Kent/Surrey border sits in the wooded slopes of the glorious North Downs. Famous as the birthplace of General Wolfe and close to Churchill's house at Chartwell (National Trust).
Tourist Information Centre ☎ (01959) 565063

Road Chef Lodge
COMMENDED

Clacket Lane Motorway Service Area, M25 Westbound, Westerham
TN16 2ER
☎ (01959) 565789
RoadChef
RoadChef Lodges offer high specification rooms at affordable prices, in popular locations suited to both the business and private traveller. Prices are per room and do not include breakfast.
Bedrooms: 35 double
Bathrooms: 35 en-suite

Bed & breakfast
per night:	£min	£max
Single	37.95	39.95

Lunch available
Cards accepted: Access, Visa, Diners, Amex, Switch/Delta

WEYBRIDGE
Surrey
Map ref 2D2

Old town on the site where, according to tradition, Julius Caesar crossed the Thames in 55BC. Now a large suburb with luxurious houses and a famous golf club.

Oatlands Park Hotel
HIGHLY COMMENDED

Oatlands Drive, Weybridge
KT13 9HB
☎ (01932) 847242
Fax (01932) 842252
Best Western/Grand Heritage
Country house hotel in its own grounds, with easy access from central London, Heathrow and M25. Special weekend rates available on request.
Bedrooms: 22 single, 48 double, 47 twin
Suites available
Bathrooms: 117 en-suite

Bed & breakfast
per night:	£min	£max
Single	47.50	110.00
Double	75.00	145.00

Half board per
person:	£min	£max
Daily	67.00	129.50

Lunch available
Evening meal 1930 (last orders 2200)
Parking for 100
Cards accepted: Access, Visa, Diners, Amex

WELCOME HOST

This is a nationally recognised customer care programme which aims to promote the highest standards of service and a warm welcome. Establishments who are taking part in this initiative are indicated by the symbol.

SOUTH EAST ENGLAND

WHITSTABLE
Kent
Map ref 3B3

Seaside resort and yachting centre on Kent's north shore. The beach is shingle and there are the usual seaside amenities and entertainments and a museum.
Tourist Information Centre ☎ (01227) 275482

Marine ♠
♛♛♛ COMMENDED

Marine Parade, Tankerton, Whitstable CT5 2BE
☎ Canterbury (01227) 272672
Fax (01227) 264721

A hotel of original character recently refurbished with every modern facility. Good food, Kentish beers, comfortable en-suite accommodation, sea-facing bedrooms.
Bedrooms: 5 double, 6 twin
Bathrooms: 11 en-suite
Bed & breakfast

per night:	£min	£max
Single	35.00	37.50
Double	49.50	52.00

Half board per

person:	£min	£max
Daily	37.50	40.00
Weekly	262.50	280.00

Lunch available
Evening meal 1900 (last orders 2100)
Parking for 20
Cards accepted: Access, Visa, Switch/Delta

For ideas on places to visit refer to the introduction at the beginning of this section.

The ♠ symbol after an establishment name indicates that it is a Regional Tourist Board member.

WOKING
Surrey
Map ref 2D2

One of the largest towns in Surrey, which developed with the coming of the railway in the 1830s. Old Woking was a market town in the 17th C and still retains several interesting buildings. Large arts and entertainment centre.

The Dutch
♛♛♛

Woodham Road, Woking
GU21 4EQ
☎ (01483) 724255
Fax (01483) 724255
Small, peaceful, private hotel, ideally situated for touring Surrey and for business visits to Woking. 27 minutes from London.
Bedrooms: 2 double, 2 twin
Bathrooms: 4 en-suite, 1 public
Bed & breakfast

per night:	£min	£max
Single	40.00	50.00
Double	54.00	64.00

Half board per

person:	£min	£max
Daily	52.00	62.00
Weekly	330.00	330.00

Evening meal 1900 (last orders 2000)
Parking for 6
Cards accepted: Access, Visa

WORTHING
West Sussex
Map ref 2D3

Largest town in West Sussex, a popular seaside resort with extensive sand and shingle beaches. Seafishing is excellent here. The museum contains finds from Cissbury Ring.
Tourist Information Centre ☎ (01903) 210022

Ardington Hotel ♠
♛♛♛♛ HIGHLY COMMENDED

Steyne Gardens, Worthing
BN11 3DZ
☎ (01903) 230451
Fax (01903) 230451
Privately-owned and managed hotel overlooking Steyne Gardens adjacent to seafront. Town centre, national bowling greens 5 minutes' walk. Conference facilities. All bedrooms have "work stations".
Bedrooms: 20 single, 17 double, 8 twin, 3 triple

Bathrooms: 48 en-suite, 1 public
Bed & breakfast

per night	£min	£max
Single	50.00	70.00
Double	65.00	90.00

Half board per

person:	£min	£max
Daily	53.00	84.00
Weekly	290.50	399.00

Lunch available
Evening meal 1900 (last orders 2030)
Parking for 20
Cards accepted: Access, Visa, Diners, Amex, Switch/Delta

Aspen House
♛♛♛ HIGHLY COMMENDED

13 Winchester Road, Worthing
BN11 4DJ
☎ (01903) 230584
Edwardian house in quiet location near town, sea and station. All bedrooms beautifully modernised and furnished. Breakfast served in elegant period dining room.
Bedrooms: 2 double, 1 twin
Bathrooms: 3 en-suite
Bed & breakfast

per night:	£min	£max
Single	20.00	30.00
Double	40.00	48.00

Parking for 4

Berkeley Hotel ♠
♛♛♛♛ COMMENDED

86-95 Marine Parade, Worthing
BN11 3QD
☎ (01903) 820000
Fax (01903) 821333
Victorian fronted hotel overlooking the sea, 2 minutes' walk from the town centre. All bedrooms recently modernised. Two lifts.
Bedrooms: 37 single, 21 double, 25 twin, 1 triple
Bathrooms: 84 en-suite
Bed & breakfast

per night:	£min	£max
Single	49.00	53.00
Double	69.00	73.00

Half board per

person:	£min	£max
Daily	39.00	65.50
Weekly		280.00

Evening meal 1830 (last orders 2030)
Parking for 35
Cards accepted: Access, Visa, Diners, Amex, Switch/Delta

SOUTH EAST ENGLAND

WORTHING
Continued

Cavendish Hotel

APPROVED

115-116 Marine Parade, Worthing
BN11 3QG
☎ (01903) 236767
Fax (01903) 823840
Minotel

Fully licensed seafront hotel with en-suite rooms. A la carte and extensive bar snack menus. Open to non-residents.
Bedrooms: 6 single, 6 double, 3 twin, 1 triple
Bathrooms: 13 en-suite, 1 public

Bed & breakfast
per night: £min   £max
Single   40.00   45.00
Double   50.00   65.00

Half board per
person: £min   £max
Daily   52.50   57.50
Weekly   280.00

Lunch available
Evening meal 1900 (last orders 2100)
Parking for 4
Cards accepted: Access, Visa, Diners, Amex

Delmar Hotel

1-2 New Parade, Worthing
BN11 2BQ
☎ (01903) 211834 & (0589) 890393
Fax (01903) 219052

Family-run licensed hotel, extensively refurbished, overlooking sea and gardens. In quiet situation, convenient for all local amenities and town.
Bedrooms: 6 single, 3 double, 2 twin, 3 triple
Bathrooms: 13 en-suite, 1 private shower

Bed & breakfast
per night: £min   £max
Single   28.50   29.50
Double   55.00   60.00

Half board per
person: £min   £max
Daily   46.00   47.00
Weekly   289.80 296.10

Evening meal 1830 (last orders 1630)
Parking for 5
Cards accepted: Access, Visa, Diners, Amex, Switch/Delta

Tudor Guest House

5 Windsor Road, Worthing
BN11 2LU
☎ (01903) 210265 & 202042

Ideally situated! 1 minute from seafront, restaurants, pubs, entertainment, etc. Very friendly atmosphere, top class service. Comfortable bedrooms with free trays tea/coffee/chocolate. 3 satellite channels in all rooms. Parking on premises. En-suite rooms available. English or continental breakfast.
Bedrooms: 5 single, 3 double, 1 twin
Bathrooms: 3 en-suite, 1 public, 1 private shower

Bed & breakfast
per night: £min   £max
Single   13.50   17.50
Double   26.00   40.00

Parking for 5

Woodlands Guest House

COMMENDED

20-22 Warwick Gardens, Worthing
BN11 1PF
☎ (01903) 233557 & 231957

Family-run guesthouse providing home-cooked food and friendly service. All bedrooms are well-appointed and comfortably furnished.
Bedrooms: 3 single, 3 double, 3 twin, 2 triple
Bathrooms: 6 en-suite, 2 public

Bed & breakfast
per night: £min   £max
Single   18.00   25.00
Double   34.00   48.00

Half board per
person: £min   £max
Daily   26.00   33.00
Weekly   165.00 220.00

Evening meal 1800 (last orders 1700)
Parking for 8
Cards accepted: Access, Visa

WYCH CROSS
East Sussex
Map ref 2D2

Ashdown Park Hotel

DE LUXE

Wych Cross, Forest Row RH18 5JR
☎ Forest Row (01342) 824988
Fax (01342) 826206

Built in the 1860s, Ashdown Park has been sympathetically restored for luxury in the 1990s. Relaxation is guaranteed, with 187 acres of landscaped grounds, lake and parkland, a superb restaurant and wine cellar, large elegant rooms and suites and impressive leisure facilities. Just off the A22.
Bedrooms: 6 single, 42 double, 47 twin
Suites available
Bathrooms: 95 en-suite

Bed & breakfast
per night: £min   £max
Single   99.00   199.00
Double   124.00 244.00

Lunch available
Evening meal 1930 (last orders 2200)
Parking for 120
Cards accepted: Access, Visa, Diners, Amex, Switch/Delta

WELCOME HOST

This is a nationally recognised customer care programme which aims to promote the highest standards of service and a warm welcome. Establishments who are taking part in this initiative are indicated by the symbol.

USE YOUR *i*'s

There are more than 550 Tourist Information Centres throughout England offering friendly help with accommodation and holiday ideas as well as suggestions of places to visit and things to do. There may well be a centre in your home town which can help you before you set out. You'll find the address of your nearest Tourist Information Centre in your local Phone Book.

ENQUIRY COUPONS

To help you obtain further information about advertisers and accommodation featured in this guide you will find enquiry coupons at the back. Send these directly to the establishments in which you are interested. Remember to complete both sides of the coupon.

AT-A-GLANCE SYMBOLS

Symbols at the end of each accommodation entry give useful information about services and facilities. A key to symbols can be found inside the back cover flap.

Keep this open for easy reference.

COUNTRY CODE

Always follow the Country Code

🍀 Enjoy the countryside and respect its life and work 🍀 Guard against all risk of fire 🍀 Fasten all gates 🍀 Keep your dogs under close control 🍀 Keep to public paths across farmland 🍀 Use gates and stiles to cross fences, hedges and walls 🍀 Leave livestock, crops and machinery alone 🍀 Take your litter home 🍀 Help to keep all water clean 🍀 Protect wildlife, plants and trees 🍀 Take special care on country roads 🍀 Make no unnecessary noise

CHECK THE MAPS

The colour maps at the back of this guide show all the cities, towns and villages for which you will find accommodation entries.

Refer to the town index to find the page on which it is listed.

USE YOUR *i*'s

There are more than 550 Tourist Information Centres throughout England offering friendly help with accommodation and holiday ideas as well as suggestions of places to visit and things to do. You'll find the address of your nearest Tourist Information Centre in your local Phone Book.

INFORMATION PAGES

National Grading and Classification Scheme   568

General Advice and Information   569

About the Guide Entries   572

Central Reservations Offices   574

Events for 1997   576

Enquiry Coupons   583

Town Index   591

Index to Advertisers   597

Mileage Chart   598

Reader Survey   599

Location Maps   601

InterCity Rail Map   615

NATIONAL GRADING AND CLASSIFICATION SCHEME

Sure Signs

The Tourist Boards in Britain operate a National Quality Grading and Classification Scheme for all types of accommodation. The purpose of the scheme is to identify and promote those establishments that the public can use with confidence. The system of facility classification and quality grading also acknowledges those that provide a wider range of facilities and services and higher quality standards. Over 30,000 places to stay are inspected under the scheme and offer the reassurance of a national grading and classification.

For 'serviced' accommodation (which includes hotels, motels, guesthouses, inns, B&B's and farmhouses) there are six classification bands, starting with LISTED and then from ONE to FIVE CROWN. For the new generation of 'lodges', offering budget accommodation along major roads and motorways, there are three classification bands, from ONE to THREE MOON.

Quite simply, the more Crowns or Moons, the wider the range of facilities and services offered.

Quality Grading

To help you find accommodation that offers even higher standards than those required for a Crown or Moon rating, there are four levels of quality grading, using the terms DE LUXE, HIGHLY COMMENDED, COMMENDED and APPROVED. Wherever you see a national grading and classification sign, you can be sure that a Tourist Board inspector has been there before you, checking the place on your behalf - and will be there again, because every place with a national rating is inspected annually.

Establishments are subject to a detailed inspection that assesses the quality standard of the facilities and services provided. The initial inspection invariably involves the Tourist Board inspector staying overnight, as a normal guest, until the bill is paid the following morning. This quality assessment includes such aspects as warmth of welcome and efficiency of service, as well as the standard of furnishing, fittings and decor. The standard of meals and their presentation is also taken into account. Everything that impinges on the experience of a guest is included in the assessment. Tourist Board inspectors receive careful training to enable them to apply the quality standards consistently and fairly. Only those facilities and services provided are assessed, and due consideration is given to the style and nature of the establishment. B&B's, farmhouses and guesthouses are not expected to operate in the style of large city centre hotels, and vice versa. This means that all types of establishment, whatever their Crown or Moon classification, can achieve a high quality grade if the facilities and services they provide, however limited in range, are to a high quality standard.

The quality grade that is awarded to an establishment is a reflection of the overall standard, taking everything into account. It is a balanced view of what is provided and, as such, cannot acknowledge individual areas of excellence. Quality grades are not intended to indicate value for money. A high quality product can be over-priced; a product of modest quality, if offered at a low price, can represent good value. The information provided by the combination of the classification and quality grade will enable you to determine for yourself what represents good value for money.

All Inspected

All establishments listed in this guide have been inspected or are awaiting inspection under the National Grading and Classification Scheme. The ratings that appear in the accommodation entries were correct at the time of going to press but are subject to change. If no rating appears in that entry it means that the inspection had not been carried out by the time of going to press. An information leaflet giving full details of the National Grading and Classification Scheme - which also covers self-catering holiday homes and caravan, chalet and camping parks - is available from any Tourist Information Centre.

INFORMATION PAGES

GENERAL ADVICE AND INFORMATION

Making a Booking

When enquiring about accommodation, make sure you check prices and other important details. You will also need to state your requirements, clearly and precisely - for example:
- **Arrival and departure dates**, with acceptable alternatives if appropriate.
- **The type of accommodation** you need; for example, room with twin beds, private bathroom.
- **The terms**, you want; for example, room only, bed and breakfast, half board, full board.
- **If you have children** with you; their ages, whether you want them to share your room or be next door, any other special requirements, such as a cot.
- **Particular requirements** you may have, such as a special diet.

Booking by letter

Misunderstandings can easily happen over the telephone, so we strongly advise you to confirm your booking in writing if there is time.

If you decide to enquire in writing in the first place, you might find it helpful to use the Accommodation Coupons on pages 583-586, which can be cut out and posted to the places of your choice.

Remember to include your name and address, and a stamped self-addressed envelope, or an international reply coupon if you are writing from outside Britain.

Please note that the English Tourist Board does not make reservations - you should write direct to the accommodation.

Deposits

If you make you reservation weeks or months in advance, you will probably be asked for a deposit. The amount will vary according to the time of year, the number of people in your party and how long you plan to stay. The deposit will then be deducted from the final bill when you leave.

Payment on Arrival

Some establishments, especially large hotels in big towns ask you to pay for you room on arrival if you have not booked it in advance. This is especially likely to happen if you arrive late and have little or no luggage.

If you are asked to pay on arrival, it is a good idea to see your room first, to make sure it meets your requirements.

Cancellations

Legal contract
When you accept accommodation that is offered to you, by telephone or in writing, you enter a legally binding contract with the proprietor.

This means that if you cancel your booking, fail to take up the accommodation or leave early, the proprietor may be entitled to compensation if he cannot re-let for all or a good part of the booked period. You will probably forfeit any deposit you have paid, and may well be asked for an additional payment.

The proprietor cannot make a claim until after the booked period, however, and during that time every effort should be made by the proprietor to re-let the accommodation.

If there is a dispute it is sensible for both sides to seek legal advice on the matter.

If you do have to change your travel plans, it is in your own interests to let the proprietors know in writing as soon as possible, to give them a chance to re-let your accommodation.

And remember, if you book by telephone and are asked for your credit card number, you should check whether the proprietor intends charging your credit card account should you later cancel your reservation. A proprietor should not be able to charge your credit card account with a cancellation unless he or she has made this clear at the time of your booking and you have agreed. However, to avoid later disputes, we suggest you check with the proprietor whether he or she intends to charge you credit card account if you cancel.

569

INFORMATION PAGES

Insurance

A travel or holiday insurance policy will safeguard you if you have to cancel or change your holiday plans. You can arrange a policy quite cheaply through your insurance company or travel agent. Some hotels also offer their own insurance schemes.

Arriving Late

If you know you will be arriving late in the evening, it is a good idea to say so when you book. If you are delayed on your way, a telephone call to say that you will be late will help prevent any problems when you arrive.

Service Charges and Tipping

These days many places levy service charges automatically. If they do, they must clearly say so in their offer of accommodation, at the time of booking. Then the service charge becomes part of the legal contract when you accept the offer of accommodation.

If a service charge is levied automatically, there is no need to tip the staff, unless they provide some exceptional service. The usual tip for meals is ten per cent of the total bill.

Telephone Charges

Hotels can set their own charges for telephone calls made through their switchboard or from direct-dial telephones in bedrooms. These charges are often much higher than telephone companies' standard charges (to defray the cost of providing the service).

Comparing costs

It is a condition of the National Grading and Classification Scheme, that hotel's unit charges are on display, by the telephones or with the room information. But in practice it is not always easy to compare these charges with standard telephone rates. Before using a hotel telephone for long-distance calls, you may decide to ask how the charges compare.

Security of Valuables

You can deposit your valuables with the proprietor or manager during your stay, and we recommend you do this as a sensible precaution. Make sure you obtain a receipt for them.

Some places do not accept articles for safe custody, and in that case it is wisest to keep your valuables with you.

Disclaimer

Some proprietors put up a notice which disclaims liability for property brought on to their premises by a guest. In fact, they can only restrict their liability to a minimum laid down by law (The Hotel Proprietors Act 1956).

Under that Act, a proprietor is liable for the value of the loss or damage to any property (except a motor car or its contents) of a guest who has engaged overnight accommodation, but if the proprietor has the prescribed notice on display as prescribed under that Act, liability is limited to £50 for one article and a total of £100 for any one guest. The notice must be prominently displayed in the reception area or main entrance. These limits do not apply to valuables you have deposited with the proprietor for safe-keeping, or to property lost through the default, neglect of wilful act of the proprietor or his staff.

Code of Conduct

All the places featured in this guide have agreed to observe the following Codes of Conduct:

1 To ensure high standards of courtesy and cleanliness, catering and service appropriate to the type of establishment.

2 To describe fairly to all visitors and prospective visitors the amenities, facilities and services provided by the establishment, whether by advertisement, brochure, word of mouth or any other means. To allow visitors to see accommodation, if requested, before booking.

3 To make clear to visitors exactly what is included in all prices quoted for accommodation, meals and refreshments, including service charges, taxes and other surcharges. Details of charges, if any, for heating or additional service of facilities should also be made clear.

4 To adhere to, and not to exceed, prices current at time of occupation for accommodation or other services.

5 To advise visitors at the time of booking, and subsequently of any change, if the accommodation offered is in an unconnected annexe, or similar, or by boarding out; and to indicate the location of such accommodation and any difference in comfort or amenities from accommodation in the main establishment.

6 To give each visitor, on request, details of payments due and a

INFORMATION PAGES

receipt if required.

7 To deal promptly and courteously with all enquiries, requests, reservations, correspondence and complaints from visitors.

8 To allow an English Tourist Board representative reasonable access to the establishment, on request, to confirm that the Code of Conduct is being observed.

Comments and Complaints

Hotels and the law
Places that offer accommodation have legal and statutory responsibilities to their customers, such as providing information about prices, providing adequate fire precautions and safeguarding valuables. Like other businesses, they must also abide by the Trades Description Acts 1968 and 1972 when they describe their accommodation and facilities.

All the places featured in this guide have declared that they do fulfil all applicable statutory obligations.

Information
The proprietors themselves supply the descriptions of their establishments and other information for the listings, and they pay to have their entries included in the guide. All the places featured in the guide have also been inspected or have applied for inspection under the National Grading and Classification Scheme.

The English Tourist Board cannot guarantee accuracy of information in this guide, and accepts no responsibility for any error or misrepresentation. All liability for loss, disappointment, negligence or other damage caused by reliance on the information contained in this guide, or in the event of bankruptcy or liquidation or cessation of trade of any company, individual or firm mentioned, is hereby excluded.

We strongly recommend that you carefully check prices and other details when you book your accommodation.

Problems
Of course, we hope you will not have cause for complaint, but problems do occur from time to time.

If you are dissatisfied with anything, make your complaint to the management immediately. Then the management can take action at once to investigate the matter and put things right. The longer you leave a complaint, the harder it is to deal with it effectively.

In certain circumstances, the English Tourist Board may look into complaints. However, the Board has no statutory control over establishments or their methods of operating. The Board cannot become involved in legal or contractual matters.

Feedback Questionnaire
We find it very helpful to receive your comments about the places featured in *Where to Stay* and your suggestions on how to improve the guide. Please send us your views using the Customer Feedback Questionnaire on pages 599-600 - we would like to hear from you.

Return it to:

Department AS,
English Tourist Board,
Thames Tower,
Black's Road,
Hammersmith,
London W6 9EL.

ENQUIRY COUPONS

To help you obtain further information about advertisers and accommodation featured in this guide you will find enquiry coupons at the back. Send these directly to the establishments in which you are interested. Remember to complete both sides of the coupon.

INFORMATION PAGES

ABOUT THE GUIDE ENTRIES

Locations

Places to stay are listed under the town, city or village where they are located. If a place is out in the countryside, you will find it listed under the nearest village or town.

Town names are listed alphabetically within each regional section of the guide, along with the name of the county they fall under, and their map reference.

Map references

These refer to the colour location maps at the back of the guide. The first figure shown is the map number, the following letter and figure indicate the grid reference on the map.

Some entries were included just before the guide went to press, so they do not appear on the maps.

Addresses

County names, which appear in the town headings, are not repeated in the entries. When you are writing, you should of course make sure you use the full address and postcode.

Telephone numbers

Telephone numbers are listed below the accommodation address for each entry. Area codes are shown in brackets, and the exchange name is also included (before the code) if it differs from that of the town under which a place is listed.

Price

The prices shown in *Where to Stay 1997* are only a general guide; they were supplied to us by proprietors in summer 1996. Remember, changes may occur after the guide goes to press, so we strongly advise you to check prices when you book your accommodation.

Prices are shown in pounds sterling and include VAT where applicable. Some places also include a service charge in their standard tariff so check this when you book.

Standardised method

There are many different ways of quoting prices for accommodation. We use a standardised method in the guide to allow you to compare prices. For example when we show:
Bed and breakfast, the prices shown are for overnight accommodation with breakfast, for single and double rooms.
The double-room price is for two people. If a double room is occupied by one person there is sometimes a reduction in price.
Halfboard, the prices shown are for room, breakfast and evening meal, per person per day and per person per week.

Some places provide only a continental breakfast in the set price, and you may have to pay extra if you want a full English breakfast.

Checking prices

According to the law, hotels with at least four bedrooms or eight beds must display their overnight accommodation charges in the reception area or entrance. In your own interests, do make sure you check prices and what they include.

Children's rates

You will find that many places charge a reduced rate for children especially if they share a room with their parents. Some places charge the full rate, however, when a child occupies a room which might otherwise have been let to an adult.

The upper age limit for reductions for children varies from one hotel to another, so check this when you book.

Seasonal packages

Prices often vary through the year, and may be significantly lower outside peak holiday weeks. Many places offer special package rates - fully inclusive weekend breaks, for example - in the autumn, winter and spring.

You can get details of bargain packages from the establishment themselves, the Regional Tourist Boards or your local Tourist Information Centre (TIC). Your local travel agent may also have information, and can help you make bookings.

INFORMATION PAGES

Bathrooms

Each accommodation entry shows you the number of private bathrooms available, the number of private showers, and the number of public bathrooms.

'Private bathroom' means a bath and/or shower with a WC en-suite with the bedroom, or a separate bathroom with a bath plus a WC solely for the occupants of that bedroom; 'private shower' means a shower en-suite but no WC.

Public bathrooms normally have a bath, sometimes with a shower attachment. If the availability of a bath is important to you, remember to check when you book.

Meals

If an establishment serves evening meals, you will find the starting time and the last order times shown in the listing; some smaller places may ask you at breakfast or at midday whether you want an evening meal.

The prices shown in each entry are for bed and breakfast or half board, but many places also offer lunch, as you will see indicated on the listing.

Opening Period

All places are open all year, except where a specific opening period is indicated.

Symbols

The at-a-glance symbols included at the end of each entry show many of the services and facilities available at each place.

You will find the key to these symbols on the back cover flap. Open out the flap and you can check the meanings of the symbols as you go.

Alcoholic Drinks

All the places listed in the guide are licensed to serve alcohol, unless the symbol ⌴ appears. The license may be restricted - to diners only, for example - so you may want to check this when you book.

Smoking

Many places provide non-smoking areas - from no-smoking bedrooms and lounges to no-smoking sections of the restaurant. Some places prefer not to accommodate smokers, and in such cases the listing information makes this clear.

Pets

Many places accept guests with pets, but we do advise you to check this when you book, and ask about any extra charges or any rules about exactly where your pet is allowed.

Some establishments do not accept dogs at all, and these places are marked with the symbol ✈.

Visitors from overseas must not bring pets of any kind into Britain, unless they are prepared for the animals to go into lengthy quarantine. Because of the continuing threat of rabies, the penalties for ignoring these regulations are extremely severe

Credit and Charge Cards

The credit and charge cards accepted by a place are listed immediately above the line of symbols at the end of each entry. The abbreviations used are:
Access - Access/Eurocard/Mastercard
Visa - Visa/Barclaycard
Diners - Diners
Amex - American Express
Switch/Delta - Direct debit cards

If you do plan to pay by card, check that the establishment will take your card before you book.

Some proprietors will charge you a higher rate if you pay by credit card rather than cash or cheque. The difference is to cover the percentage paid by the proprietor to the credit card company.

If you are planning to pay by credit card, you may want to ask whether it would, in fact, be cheaper to pay by cheque or cash. When you book by telephone, you may be asked for your credit card number as 'confirmation'. But remember, the proprietor may then charge your credit card account if you cancel your booking. See under Cancellations on page 569.

Conferences and Groups

Places which cater for conferences and meetings are marked with the symbol ⌶ (the number that follows the symbol shows the capacity). Rates are often negotiable, depending on the time of year, numbers of people involved and any special requirements you may have.

INFORMATION PAGES

CENTRAL RESERVATIONS OFFICES

Some of the accommodation establishments in this guide are members of hotel groups or consortia which maintain a central reservations office. These entries are identified with the symbol (CR), and the name of the group or consortium, appearing after the establishment's address and telephone number. Bookings or enquiries can be made direct to the establishment or to the central reservations office.

Best Western
Best Western Hotels,
Vine House, 143 London Road,
Kingston upon Thames,
Surrey KT2 6NA
Tel: (0181) 541 0033
Fax: (0181) 547 3941

Consort
Consort Hotels,
Consort House,
180-182 Fulford Road,
York YO1 4DA
Reservations: (01904) 643151
Information: (01904) 620137
Fax: (01904) 611320

Forte
Forte Hotels, Forte House,
72-80 Gatehouse Road,
Aylesbury,
Buckinghamshire HP19 3EB
Tel: 0345 40 40 40
Fax: (01296) 81391

Grand Heritage Hotels
London House,
19 Old Court Place,
London W8 4PL
Tel: (0171) 376 1777
Fax: (0171) 376 2004
0800 28 28 11 (toll free)

The Independents
The Independents Hotel
Consortium,
Beambridge, Sampford,
Arundel, Wellington,
Somerset TA21 0HB
Information line: (01823) 672100
Bookings: 0800 885544
Fax: (01823) 673100

Jarvis
Jarvis Reservations Centre,
PO Box 671,
London SW7 5JQ
Tel: (0171) 590 5406
Fax: (0171) 589 3207

Logis of Great Britain
Logis of Great Britain,
20 Church Road,
Horspath, Oxford OX9 1RU
Tel: (01865) 875888
Fax: (01865) 875777

Lyric
Lyric Hotels,
Bredbury Business Park,
Bredbury Parkway,
Stockport SK6 2TN
Tel: 0345 626633 (calls charged at local rate)
Fax: (0161) 406 8784

Millennium & Copthorne
Millennium & Copthorne Hotels,
Central Reservations,
c/o Copthorne London Gatwick,
Copthorne,
West Sussex RH10 3PG
Tel: 0645 455445 (calls charged at local rate)
Fax: (01342) 717353

Minotel
Minotel, 37 Springfield Road,
Blackpool FY1 1PZ
Tel: (01253) 292000
Fax: (01253) 291111

Novotel
Central Reservation Office,
Resinter, 1 Shortlands,
Hammersmith International
Centre, Hammersmith W6 8DR
Tel: (0181) 748 3433
Fax: (0181) 748 9116

Principal
Principal Hotels Group,
Principal House,
11 Ripon Road,
Harrogate,
North Yorkshire HG1 2JA
Tel: 0800 454454 (calls are free)
Fax: (01423) 500086

INFORMATION PAGES

Queens Moat Houses Hotels
Queens-Line UK Reservations,
Queens Court,
9-17 Eastern Road,
Romford, Essex RM1 3NG
Tel: (01708) 766677
Telex: 922781
Fax: (01708) 761033

RoadChef Lodges
Freephone: 0800 834719
Fax: (01823) 338131

Stagecoach
Hotel Management
International Ltd,
86 East Lane,
Wembley,
Middlesex HA0 3NJ
Tel: (0181) 908 3348
Fax: (0181) 904 0094

Swallow
Swallow Hotels Ltd,
PO Box 30,
Washington,
Tyne & Wear NE37 1QS
Tel: 0645 404 404 (local call)
Fax: (0191) 415 1777
E-mail: info@swallowhotels.com

Thames Valley
Thames Valley Hotels,
Northway House,
1379 High Road,
London N20 9LP
Tel: (0181) 446 6533

Utell International
Quadrant House,
The Quadrant, Sutton,
Surrey SM2 5AR
Tel: 0990 300200
Northern Ireland: 0800 660066

Wayfarer Inns
Wayfarer Inns,
16 Little London,
Chichester,
West Sussex PO19 1PA
Tel: (01243) 528733
Fax: (01243) 531331

Whitbread Hotel Company
Oakley House,
Oakley Road,
Leagrave,
Luton,
Bedfordshire LU4 9QH
For Marriott Group, contact:
Tel: (01582) 567899
Fax: (01582) 400024
For Country Club Hotel Group, contact:
Tel: (01582) 562256
Fax: (01582) 400024

CHECK THE MAPS

The colour maps at the back of this guide show all the cities, towns and villages for which you will find accommodation entries.

Refer to the town index to find the page on which it is listed.

AT-A-GLANCE SYMBOLS

Symbols at the end of each accommodation entry give useful information about services and facilities. A key to symbols can be found inside the back cover flap.

Keep this open for easy reference.

575

INFORMATION PAGES

EVENTS FOR 1997

This is a selection of the many cultural, sporting and other events that will be taking place throughout England during 1997. Dates marked with an asterisk* were provisional at the time of going to press.

January 1997

2-13 January*
43rd London International Boat Show
Earls Court Exhibition Centre,
Warwick Road, London SW5
Contact: (01784) 473377

6 January
Old Custom: Haxey Hood Game
The Village, Haxey,
North Lincolnshire
Contact: (01427) 752845

9-12 January
Autosports International
National Exhibition Centre,
Birmingham, West Midlands
Contact: (0171) 402 2555

February 1997

7-16 February
Great St Valentine's Fair
City Centre,
Leeds, West Yorkshire
Contact: (0113) 247 4293

9 February*
Chinese New Year Celebrations: Year of the Ox
Centered on Gerrard Street
and Leicester Square,
London, WC2
Contact: (0171) 734 5161

9 February-16 March
Wildlife Photographer of the Year 1995
Lancaster City Museum,
Market Square,
Lancaster, Lancashire
Contact: (01524) 841692

9-14 February*
The Wordsworth Winter School
Dove Cottage & Wordsworth Museum, Town End,
Grasmere, Cumbria
Contact: (015394) 35544

20-23 February
Harrogate Antique and Fine Art Fair
Royal Baths Assembly Rooms,
Crescent Road, Harrogate,
North Yorkshire
Contact: (01823) 323363

March 1997

6-9 March
Crufts Dog Show
National Exhibition Centre,
Birmingham, West Midlands
Contact: (0171) 4936651

7-9 March
Working Days
Abbeydale Industrial Hamlet,
Abbeydale Road South,
Sheffield, South Yorkshire
Contact: (0114) 236 7731

11-13 March
Cheltenham Gold Cup National Hunt Racing Festival
Cheltenham Racecourse,
Cheltenham, Gloucestershire
Contact: (01242) 513014

13 March-6 April
Daily Mail Ideal Home Exhibition
Earls Court Exhibition Centre,
Warwick Road,
London SW5
Contact: (01895) 677677

22 March-6 April
Easter Activities
Salford Museum & Art Gallery,
Peel Park, The Crescent,
Salford, Greater Manchester
Contact: (0161) 736 2649

28 March
Old Custom: Pace Egg Plays
Various venues in and around
Hebden Bridge,
West Yorkshire
Contact: (01422) 843831

29 March*
Oxford and Cambridge Boat Race
River Thames, London

April 1997

3-5 April
Grand National Meeting
Aintree Racecourse,
Ormskirk Road,
Aintree, Merseyside
Contact: (0151) 523 2600

INFORMATION PAGES

4 April
Birkenhead Park 150th Anniversary
Birkenhead Park, Merseyside

8 April
Old Custom: World Coal Carrying Championship
Royal Oak Public House,
Owl Lane, Ossett,
West Yorkshire

11-13 April
2nd North East Knitting and Needlecraft Exhibition
Leeds University Exhibition
& Conference Centre,
Willow Terrace Road,
Leeds, West Yorkshire
Contact: (0117) 970 1370

11-13 April
County Spring Flower Show - 100th Anniversary
The Lost Gardens of Heligan,
Heligan, Pentewan, Cornwall
Contact: (01872) 74057

13 April*
London Marathon
Greenwich Park,
London SE10
Contact: (0171) 620 4117

19-20 April
Bike Expo 97
Sheffield Arena,
Broughton Lane,
Sheffield, South Yorkshire
Contact: (01484) 605555

26-27 April
Centennial Orchid Society
The Floral Halls,
Marine Parade, Southport,
Merseyside

26-27 April
Rainbow Craft Fair
Meols Hall, Churchtown,
Southport, Merseyside
Contact: (01704) 28326

27 April
Three Peaks Race
Playing Field,
Horton-in-Ribblesdale,
North Yorkshire
Contact: (0113) 258 5586

May 1997

2-3 May
Nottinghamshire County Show
Newark and Notts Show Ground,
Winthorpe, Nottinghamshire
Contact: (01636) 610642

2-4 May
Cleethorpes Beer Festival
Winter Gardens, Kingsway,
Cleethorpes,
North East Lincolnshire
Contact: (01472) 692925

3 May
Gawthorpe Maypole Procession
High Street, Gawthorpe,
Ossett, West Yorkshire

3-5 May*
Rochester Sweeps Festival
Various venues,
Rochester, Kent
Contact: (01634) 843666

3-5 May*
Spalding Flower Parade and Springfields Country Fair
Springfields Show Gardens,
Spalding, Lincolnshire
Contact: (01775) 724543

3-25 May
Brighton International Festival
Various venues,
Brighton, East Sussex
Contact: (01273) 676926

4-5 May
Kids International
Telford Town Park,
Telford, Shropshire
Contact: (01952) 203009

8-11 May
Living Crafts Exhibition
Hatfield House, Hatfield,
Hertfordshire
Contact: (01582) 761235

10-25 May
Bournemouth International Festival
Various venues,
Bournemouth, Dorset
Contact: (01202) 297327

16-18 May
Keswick Jazz Festival
Keswick, Cumbria
Contact: (01900) 602122

17 May
Football: FA Challenge Cup Final
Wembley Stadium, London
Contact: (0171) 402 7151

20-23 May
Chelsea Flower Show
Royal Hospital Chelsea,
Royal Hospital Road,
London SW3

24-25 May
Air Fete 97
RAF Mildenhall, Suffolk

24 May-9 June
Salisbury Festival
Various venues,
Salisbury, Wiltshire
Contact: (01722) 323883

577

INFORMATION PAGES

25-26 May
Southend Air Show
Western Esplanade,
Southend-on-Sea, Essex

25-26 May*
North Shields Fishquay Festival
North Shields, Tyne and Wear
Contact: (0191) 257 5544

26 May
Northumberland County Show
Tynedale Park Rugby Ground,
Corbridge, Northumberland
Contact: (01434) 344443

26 May
Surrey County Show
Stoke Park, Guildford, Surrey
Contact: (01483) 414651

28-29 May
Corpus Christi Carpet of Flowers and Floral Festival
Cathedral of Our Lady
and St Philip Howard,
Cathedral House,
Arundel, West Sussex
Contact: (01903) 882297

28-31 May
The Royal Bath and West Show
The Royal Bath & West
Showground,
Shepton Mallet, Somerset
Contact: (01749) 822200

29-31 May*
Dickens Festival
Various venues,
Rochester, Kent
Contact: (01634) 843666

30 May-1 June
Great Garden and Countryside Festival
Holker Hall and Gardens,
Cark in Cartmel, Cumbria
Contact: (015395) 58838

June 1997

1 June*
229th Royal Academy Summer Exhibition
Royal Academy of Arts,
Burlington House, Piccadilly,
London W1
Contact: (0171) 494 5615

5-7 June
South of England Agricultural Show
South of England Showground,
Ardingly, West Sussex
Contact: (01444) 892048

8 June
Open Day
Myerscough College,
Bilsborrow, Lancashire
Contact: (01995) 640611

13-29 June
50th Aldeburgh Foundation of Music and the Arts
Snape Maltings Concert Hall,
Snape, Suffolk
Contact: (01728) 452935

14 June*
Durham Regatta
River Wear, Durham
Contact: (0191) 383 1594

14 June*
Trooping the Colour - The Queen's Birthday Parade
Horse Guards Parade,
London SW1
Contact: (0171) 414 2479

25-26 June
Royal Norfolk Show 97
The Showground, Dereham Road,
Norwich, Norfolk
Contact: (01603) 748931

28-29 June
Middlesex Show
Uxbridge Showground,
Park Road, Uxbridge, London
Contact: (01895) 252131

28-29 June
Royal Air Force Waddington Air Show
RAF Waddington, Lincolnshire
Contact: (01522) 726100

28-29 June
Vintage Vehicle Rally
Meols Hall, Churchtown,
Southport, Merseyside
Contact: (01704) 28326

30 June-3 July
The Royal Show
National Agricultural Centre,
Stoneleigh Park, Warwickshire
Contact: (01203) 696969

July 1997

1-31 July*
Hull International Festival
Various venues, Hull,
Kingston-upon-Hull
Contact: (01482) 615623

2-6 July
Henley Royal Regatta
Henley-on-Thames, Oxfordshire
Contact: (01491) 572153/4

3-20 July
The Exeter Festival
Various venues, Exeter, Devon
Contact: (01392) 265118

5-6 July
International Kite Festival
Northern Playing Fields,
Washington, Tyne and Wear
Contact: (0191) 514235

INFORMATION PAGES

6-22 July
Chichester Festivities
Various venues,
Chichester, West Sussex
Contact: (01243) 785718

8-10 July
Great Yorkshire Show
Great Yorkshire Showground,
Harrogate, North Yorkshire
Contact: (01423) 561536

9-12 July
Claremont Fete Champetre
Claremont Landscape Garden,
Portsmouth Road,
Esher, Surrey
Contact: (01372) 453401

11-13 July*
British Grand Prix 97
Silverstone,
Northamptonshire
Contact: (01327) 857271

11, 12, 13 July
Swanage Jazz Festival
Various venues,
Swanage, Dorset
Contact: (01929) 422885

11-20 July
**"Ways with Words"
Literature Festival**
Dartington Hall,
Dartington, Devon
Contact: (01803) 867311

12-13 July
Durham County Show
Clondyke Garden Centre,
Lambton Park,
Chester-Le-Street, Durham
Contact: (0191) 3885459

15-26 July
The Royal Tournament
Earls Court Exhibition Centre,
Warwick Road,
London SW5
Contact: (0171) 370 8202

19 July
Cumberland County Show
Rickerby Park,
Carlisle, Cumbria
Contact: (01228) 560364

19-20 July
Holkham Country Fair
Holkham Hall,
Wells-next-the-Sea, Norfolk
Contact: (01328) 830367

19-27 July
Whitstable Oyster Festival
Whitstable Harbour, Kent
Contact: (01227) 273570

19 July-2 August
King's Lynn Festival 97
King's Lynn Arts Centre,
King Street,
King's Lynn, Norfolk
Contact: (01553) 774725

25 July
Horse Racing: Glorious Goodwood
Goodwood Racecourse,
Goodwood, West Sussex
Contact: (01243) 774107

26-27 July
Cumbria Steam Gathering
Cark Airfield, Flookburgh,
Cumbria
Contact: (015242) 71584

26-31 July*
Teesside International Eisteddfod
Middlesbrough Festival Town
Centre,
Middlesbrough,
Tees Valley
Contact: (01642) 327088

August 1997

1-8 August
43rd Sidmouth International Festival of Folk Arts
The Arena and other Venues,
Sidmouth, Devon

2-9 August
Cowes Week
Cowes, Isle of Wight
Contact: (01983) 293303

2-17 August
International Gilbert and Sullivan Festival
Buxton Opera House,
Water Street,
Buxton, Derbyshire
Contact: (01422) 359161

6-7 August
167th Bakewell Show
The Showground, Coombs Road,
Bakewell, Derbyshire
Contact: (01629) 812736

8-10 August
Bristol International Balloon Fiesta
Ashton Court Estate,
Long Ashton, Bristol
Contact: (0117) 953 5884

8-10 August
Lowther Horse Driving Trials and Country Fair
Lowther Castle,
Lowther, Cumbria
Contact: (01931) 712378

579

INFORMATION PAGES

9-16 August*
Billingham International Folklore Festival
Queensway, Billingham,
Tees Valley
Contact: (01642) 558212

15-16 August
Shrewsbury Flower Show
Quarry Park, Shrewsbury,
Shropshire
Contact: (01743) 364051

15-17 August
International Birdwatching Fair
Egleton Reserve, Rutland Water,
Oakham, Leicestershire
Contact: (01572) 770651

15-17 August
Northampton Hot Air Balloon Festival
Northampton Racecourse,
St. George's Avenue,
Northampton, Northamptonshire
Contact: (01604) 233500

16-22 August
Whitby Folk Week
Various venues,
Whitby, North Yorkshire
Contact: (01757) 708424

20 August
Weymouth Carnival
The Seafront, Weymouth, Dorset
Contact: (01305) 772444

20-22 August
Ladies British Amateur Stroke Play Championships
Silloth-on-Solway Golf Club,
The Clubhouse, Silloth, Cumbria
Contact: (016973) 31304

21-26 August
International Beatles Festival
Various venues,
Liverpool, Merseyside
Contact: (0151) 236 9091

22-25 August
Clacton Jazz Festival
Various venues,
Clacton-on-Sea, Essex
Contact: (01255) 425501

23-30 August
Bude Jazz Festival
Various venues, Bude, Cornwall
Contact: (01684) 566956

24 August
Leicester International Air Display
Leicester Airport, Gartree Road,
Leicester, Leicestershire
Contact: (0116) 259 2360

24-25 August
Eye Show
Eye Show Ground, Dragon Hill,
Eye, Suffolk
Contact: (01379) 870224

25 August
Mathew Street Festival
Cavern Quarter,
Liverpool City Centre,
Mathew Street,
Liverpool
Contact: (0151) 236 9091

27-31 August
Great Dorset Steam Fair
South Down,
Tarrant Hinton, Dorset
Contact: (01258) 860361

28 August
Buckinghamshire County Show
Weedon Park, Weedon,
Aylesbury, Buckinghamshire
Contact: (01296) 83734

28 August
Muncaster Country Fair and Sheepdog Trials
Muncaster, Ravenglass,
Cumbria
Contact: (01229) 717608

29-31 August
Shepway Festival
The Leas, Folkestone, Kent
Contact: (01303) 852321

30 August
Hesket Newmarket Agricultural Show
Hog House Field, Hudscales,
Hesket Newmarket, Cumbria
Contact: (016974) 78663

September 1997

4 September
The Blenheim International Horse Trials
Blenheim Palace,
Woodstock, Oxfordshire
Contact: (01993) 813335

5-7 September
Swanage Folk Festival
Various venues,
Swanage, Dorset
Contact: (01929) 427490

6-7 September
Chatsworth Country Fair
Chatsworth House and Garden,
Bakewell, Derbyshire
Contact: (01328) 830367

6-7 September
Kirby Lonsdale Victorian Fair
Kirkby Lonsdale,
Cumbria
Contact: (015242) 71237

13 September
Romsey Show
Broadlands Park,
Romsey, Hampshire
Contact: (01794) 517521

INFORMATION PAGES

13-14 September
Essex Steam Rally and Craft Fair
Barleylands Farm Museum,
Billericay, Essex
Contact: (01268) 532253

13-15 September*
Stanhope Agricultural Show
Unthank Park,
Stanhope, Durham
Contact: (01833) 650879

13-21 September
Southampton International Boat Show
Western Esplanade,
Southampton, Hampshire
Contact: (01784) 473277

14-20 September
Egremont Crab Fair and Sports
Baybarrow, Egremont, Cumbria
Contact: (01946) 821554

20-21 September
Newbury and Royal County of Berkshire Show
Newbury Showground,
Chieveley, Berkshire
Contact: (01635) 247111

28 September
Urswick Rushbearing
Urswick Church, Urswick,
Ulverston, Cumbria

October 1997

1-5 October
Horse of the Year Show
Wembley Arena, Empire Way,
Wembley, London
Contact: (01203) 693088

9-19 October
Norfolk and Norwich Festival 97
Various venues,
Norwich, Norfolk
Contact: (01603) 614921

10-18 October*
Hull Fair
Walton Street Fairground, Hull,
Kingston upon Hull
Contact: (01482) 615623

10-19 October
Cheltenham Festival of Literature
Town Hall, Imperial Square,
Cheltenham, Gloucestershire
Contact: (01242) 521621

11-25 October
Canterbury Festival
Various venues,
Canterbury, Kent
Contact: (01227) 455600

12 October
World Conker Championships
The Village Green,
Ashton, Northamptonshire

16-26 October
The London Motor Show
Earls Court Exhibition Centre,
Warwick Road, London SW5

19 October
Trafalgar Day Parade - The Sea Cadet Corps
Trafalgar Square, London WC2
Contact: (0171) 928 8978

November 1997

1 November
Grand Firework Spectacular
Leeds Castle, Leeds, Kent
Contact: (01622) 765400

1 November
Firework Displays
Christchurch Park,
Ipswich, Suffolk

1 November
Bonfire and Firework Display
Meols Hall, Churchtown,
Southport, Merseyside
Contact: (01704) 28326

6 November
Bridgwater Guy Fawkes Carnival
Town Centre,
Bridgwater, Somerset
Contact: (01278) 425344

8 November
Lord Mayor's Show
City of London
Contact: (01992) 505306

20 November
Biggest Liar in the World Competition
Bridge Inn, Wasdale,
Santon Bridge, Cumbria
Contact: (01946) 67575

December 1997

18-22 December
Olympia International Showjumping Championships
Olympia, Hammersmith Road,
London W14
Contact: (0171) 370 8202

30 December*
Carlisle Races Christmas Meet
Carlisle Racecourse,
Durdar, Cumbria
Contact: (016973) 42634

31 December
Allendale Baal Festival
Market Square, Allendale,
Northumberland
Contact: (01434) 683763

INFORMATION PAGES

USE YOUR *i*'S

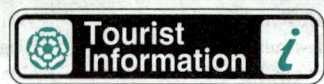

When it comes to your next England break, the first stage of your journey could be closer than you think. You've probably got a Tourist Information Centre nearby which is there to serve the local community - as well as visitors.

So make us your first stop. We'll be happy to help you, wherever you're heading.

Many Tourist Information Centres can provide you with maps and guides, helping you plan well in advance. And sometimes it's even possible for us to book your accommodation, too.

A visit to your nearest Tourist Information Centre can pay off in other ways as well. We can point you in the right direction when it comes to finding out about all the special events which are happening in the local region.

In fact, we can give you details of places to visit within easy reach... and perhaps tempt you to plan a day trip or weekend away.

Across the country, there are more than 550 Tourist Information Centres so you're never far away. You'll find the address of your nearest Tourist Information Centre in your local Phone Book.

IS IT ACCESSIBLE?

If you are a wheelchair user or someone who has difficulty walking, look for the national 'Accessible' symbol when choosing where to stay.

All the places that display a symbol have been checked by a Tourist Board inspector against standard criteria that reflect the practical needs of wheelchair users.

There are three categories of accessibility:

Category 1 Accessible to all wheelchair users including those travelling independently

Category 2 Accessible to a wheelchair user with assistance

Category 3 Accessible to a wheelchair user able to walk short distances and up at least three steps

Establishments in this guide which have a wheelchair access category are listed on pages 10 and 11.

ACCOMMODATION COUPONS

▶ **Complete this coupon and mail it direct to the establishment in which you are interested. Do not send it to the English Tourist Board. Remember to enclose a stamped addressed envelope (or international reply coupon).**

▶ **Tick as appropriate and complete the reverse side if you are interested in making a booking.**

❑ Please send me a brochure or further information, and details of prices charged.
❑ Please advise me, as soon as possible, if accommodation is available as detailed overleaf.

Name: _____ (BLOCK CAPITALS)

Address: _____

_____

_____ Postcode: _____

Telephone number: _____ Date: _____

Where to Stay 1997
Hotels & Guesthouses

English Tourist Board

▶ **Complete this coupon and mail it direct to the establishment in which you are interested. Do not send it to the English Tourist Board. Remember to enclose a stamped addressed envelope (or international reply coupon).**

▶ **Tick as appropriate and complete the reverse side if you are interested in making a booking.**

❑ Please send me a brochure or further information, and details of prices charged.
❑ Please advise me, as soon as possible, if accommodation is available as detailed overleaf.

Name: _____ (BLOCK CAPITALS)

Address: _____

_____

_____ Postcode: _____

Telephone number: _____ Date: _____

Where to Stay 1997
Hotels & Guesthouses

English Tourist Board

ACCOMMODATION COUPONS

▶ **Complete this side if you are interested in making a booking.**
▶ **Please read the information on pages 569-573 before confirming any booking.**

Please advise me if accommodation is available as detailed below.

From (date of arrival): _____ To (date of departure): _____

or alternatively from: _____ To: _____

Adults _____ Children _____ (ages _____)
Please give the number of people and ages of children

Accommodation required: _____
_____
_____

Meals required: _____

Other/special requirements: _____

▶ **Please enclose a stamped addressed envelope (or international reply coupon).**

▶ **Complete this side if you are interested in making a booking.**
▶ **Please read the information on pages 569-573 before confirming any booking.**

Please advise me if accommodation is available as detailed below.

From (date of arrival): _____ To (date of departure): _____

or alternatively from: _____ To: _____

Adults _____ Children _____ (ages _____)
Please give the number of people and ages of children

Accommodation required: _____
_____
_____

Meals required: _____

Other/special requirements: _____

▶ **Please enclose a stamped addressed envelope (or international reply coupon).**

ACCOMMODATION COUPONS

▶ *Complete this coupon and mail it direct to the establishment in which you are interested. Do not send it to the English Tourist Board. Remember to enclose a stamped addressed envelope (or international reply coupon).*

▶ *Tick as appropriate and complete the reverse side if you are interested in making a booking.*

❏ Please send me a brochure or further information, and details of prices charged.
❏ Please advise me, as soon as possible, if accommodation is available as detailed overleaf.

Name: _____ (BLOCK CAPITALS)

Address: _____

_____

_____ Postcode: _____

Telephone number: _____ Date: _____

Where to Stay 1997
Hotels & Guesthouses

English Tourist Board

▶ *Complete this coupon and mail it direct to the establishment in which you are interested. Do not send it to the English Tourist Board. Remember to enclose a stamped addressed envelope (or international reply coupon).*

▶ *Tick as appropriate and complete the reverse side if you are interested in making a booking.*

❏ Please send me a brochure or further information, and details of prices charged.
❏ Please advise me, as soon as possible, if accommodation is available as detailed overleaf.

Name: _____ (BLOCK CAPITALS)

Address: _____

_____

_____ Postcode: _____

Telephone number: _____ Date: _____

Where to Stay 1997
Hotels & Guesthouses

English Tourist Board

ACCOMMODATION COUPONS

▶ **Complete this side if you are interested in making a booking.**

▶ **Please read the information on pages 569-573 before confirming any booking.**

Please advise me if accommodation is available as detailed below.

From (date of arrival): _____ To (date of departure): _____

or alternatively from: _____ To: _____

Adults _____ Children _____ (ages _____)
Please give the number of people and ages of children

Accommodation required:
_____
_____
_____

Meals required:
_____

Other/special requirements:
_____

▶ **Please enclose a stamped addressed envelope (or international reply coupon).**

▶ **Complete this side if you are interested in making a booking.**

▶ **Please read the information on pages 569-573 before confirming any booking.**

Please advise me if accommodation is available as detailed below.

From (date of arrival): _____ To (date of departure): _____

or alternatively from: _____ To: _____

Adults _____ Children _____ (ages _____)
Please give the number of people and ages of children

Accommodation required:
_____
_____
_____

Meals required:
_____

Other/special requirements:
_____

▶ **Please enclose a stamped addressed envelope (or international reply coupon).**

ADVERTISEMENT COUPONS

▶ **Complete this coupon and mail it direct to the advertiser from whom you would like to receive further information. Do not send it to the English Tourist Board.**

To (advertiser's name): _____

Please send me a brochure or further information on the following, as advertised by you in the English Tourist Board's **Where to Stay 1997** Guide:

_____

▶ **Complete this coupon and mail it direct to the advertiser from whom you would like to receive further information. Do not send it to the English Tourist Board.**

To (advertiser's name): _____

Please send me a brochure or further information on the following, as advertised by you in the English Tourist Board's **Where to Stay 1997** Guide:

_____

▶ **Complete this coupon and mail it direct to the advertiser from whom you would like to receive further information. Do not send it to the English Tourist Board.**

To (advertiser's name): _____

Please send me a brochure or further information on the following, as advertised by you in the English Tourist Board's **Where to Stay 1997** Guide:

_____

ADVERTISEMENT COUPONS

Name: _____ (BLOCK CAPITALS)

Address: _____

_____

_____ Postcode: _____

Telephone Number: _____ Date: _____

Where to Stay 1997
Hotels & Guesthouses

English Tourist Board

Name: _____ (BLOCK CAPITALS)

Address: _____

_____

_____ Postcode: _____

Telephone Number: _____ Date: _____

Where to Stay 1997
Hotels & Guesthouses

English Tourist Board

Name: _____ (BLOCK CAPITALS)

Address: _____

_____

_____ Postcode: _____

Telephone Number: _____ Date: _____

Where to Stay 1997
Hotels & Guesthouses

English Tourist Board

ADVERTISEMENT COUPONS

▶ **Complete this coupon and mail it direct to the advertiser from whom you would like to receive further information. Do not send it to the English Tourist Board.**

To (advertiser's name): _____

Please send me a brochure or further information on the following, as advertised by you in the English Tourist Board's **Where to Stay 1997** Guide:

_____

▶ **Complete this coupon and mail it direct to the advertiser from whom you would like to receive further information. Do not send it to the English Tourist Board.**

To (advertiser's name): _____

Please send me a brochure or further information on the following, as advertised by you in the English Tourist Board's **Where to Stay 1997** Guide:

_____

▶ **Complete this coupon and mail it direct to the advertiser from whom you would like to receive further information. Do not send it to the English Tourist Board.**

To (advertiser's name): _____

Please send me a brochure or further information on the following, as advertised by you in the English Tourist Board's **Where to Stay 1997** Guide:

_____

ADVERTISEMENT COUPONS

Name: _____ (BLOCK CAPITALS)

Address: _____

_____

_____ Postcode: _____

Telephone Number: _____ Date: _____

Where to Stay 1997
Hotels & Guesthouses

English Tourist Board

Name: _____ (BLOCK CAPITALS)

Address: _____

_____

_____ Postcode: _____

Telephone Number: _____ Date: _____

Where to Stay 1997
Hotels & Guesthouses

English Tourist Board

Name: _____ (BLOCK CAPITALS)

Address: _____

_____

_____ Postcode: _____

Telephone Number: _____ Date: _____

Where to Stay 1997
Hotels & Guesthouses

English Tourist Board

TOWN INDEX

The following cities, towns and villages all have accommodation listed in this guide.
If the place where you wish to stay is not shown, the location maps (starting on page 601)
will help you to find somewhere suitable in the same area.

A — page no

Abbotsbury *Dorset*	375
Abingdon *Oxfordshire*	478
Alcester *Warwickshire*	222
Aldeburgh *Suffolk*	326
Alderley Edge *Cheshire*	130
Alfreton *Derbyshire*	292
Allerford *Somerset*	375
Alnmouth *Northumberland*	104
Alnwick *Northumberland*	104
Alston *Cumbria*	56
Alton *Staffordshire*	222
Altrincham *Greater Manchester*	130
Ambleside *Cumbria*	56
Amesbury *Wiltshire*	375
Andover *Hampshire*	478
Appleby-in-Westmorland *Cumbria*	61
Appleton-le-Moors *North Yorkshire*	162
Ardsley *South Yorkshire*	162
Arkengarthdale *North Yorkshire*	162
Arncliffe *North Yorkshire*	163
Arnside *Cumbria*	61
Arundel *West Sussex*	528
Ashbourne *Derbyshire*	292
Ashburton *Devon*	376
Ashby-de-la-Zouch *Leicestershire*	293
Ashford *Kent*	528
Ashton-under-Lyne *Greater Manchester*	131
Ashwater *Devon*	376
Askrigg *North Yorkshire*	163
Attleborough *Norfolk*	326
Austwick *North Yorkshire*	163
Avebury *Wiltshire*	377
Aylesbury *Buckinghamshire*	479
Aylsham *Norfolk*	327

B — page no

Bacton-on-Sea *Norfolk*	327
Badminton *South Gloucestershire*	377
Bakewell *Derbyshire*	293
Bamburgh *Northumberland*	105
Banbury *Oxfordshire*	479
Bardon Mill *Northumberland*	105
Barnet *Greater London*	43
Barnham Broom *Norfolk*	327
Barnstaple *Devon*	377
Barrasford *Northumberland*	106
Barrow-in-Furness *Cumbria*	62
Barton under Needwood *Staffordshire*	223
Basildon *Essex*	327
Basingstoke *Hampshire*	479
Baslow *Derbyshire*	294
Bassenthwaite *Cumbria*	62
Bassenthwaite Lake *Cumbria*	63
Bath *Bath & North East Somerset*	378
Batley *West Yorkshire*	163
Battlesbridge *Essex*	328
Beaconsfield *Buckinghamshire*	480
Beadnell *Northumberland*	106
Beccles *Suffolk*	328
Bedale *North Yorkshire*	164
Bedford *Bedfordshire*	328
Beeston *Cheshire*	131
Beeston *Nottinghamshire*	294
Belford *Northumberland*	106
Bellingham *Northumberland*	106
Benenden *Kent*	529
Berkswell *West Midlands*	223
Berrynarbor *Devon*	383
Berwick-upon-Tweed *Northumberland*	107
Beverley *East Riding of Yorkshire*	164
Bexhill-on-Sea *East Sussex*	529
Bexley *Greater London*	43
Bexleyheath *Greater London*	43
Bibury *Gloucestershire*	223
Bicester *Oxfordshire*	480
Bideford *Devon*	384
Bigbury-on-Sea *Devon*	385
Biggleswade *Bedfordshire*	328
Bingley *West Yorkshire*	164
Birkenhead *Merseyside*	131
Birling Gap *East Sussex*	529
Birmingham *West Midlands*	224
Birmingham Airport *West Midlands* (See under Berkswell, Birmingham, Coleshill, Coventry, Hampton in Arden, Meriden, Solihull)	
Bishop's Castle *Shropshire*	227
Bishop's Stortford *Hertfordshire*	329
Blackburn *Lancashire*	132
Blackpool *Lancashire*	132
Blakeney *Gloucestershire*	228
Blakeney *Norfolk*	329
Blanchland *Northumberland*	107
Blandford Forum *Dorset*	480
Bledington *Gloucestershire*	228
Blyth *Nottinghamshire*	294
Bodmin *Cornwall*	385
Bognor Regis *West Sussex*	530
Bolton *Greater Manchester*	136
Bolton Abbey *North Yorkshire*	165
Bolton-by-Bowland *Lancashire*	136
Bonchurch *Isle of Wight*	480
Boroughbridge *North Yorkshire*	165
Borrowdale *Cumbria*	63
Boscastle *Cornwall*	385
Bournemouth *Dorset*	481
Bourton-on-the-Water *Gloucestershire*	228
Bovey Tracey *Devon*	386
Bracknell *Berkshire*	487
Bradford *West Yorkshire*	166
Bradford-on-Avon *Wiltshire*	386
Braintree *Essex*	329
Braithwaite *Cumbria*	64
Brampton *Cumbria*	64
Brandesburton *East Riding of Yorkshire*	167
Branscombe *Devon*	386
Bratton Fleming *Devon*	387
Braunton *Devon*	387
Brentwood *Essex*	330
Bridgnorth *Shropshire*	229
Bridgwater *Somerset*	387
Bridlington *East Riding of Yorkshire*	167
Bridport *Dorset*	388
Brigg *North Lincolnshire*	168
Brighton & Hove *East Sussex*	530
Bristol	389
Brixham *Devon*	391
Broadway *Hereford and Worcester*	230
Brockenhurst *Hampshire*	487
Bromley *Greater London*	44
Bromsgrove *Hereford and Worcester*	231
Broughton-in-Furness *Cumbria*	65
Buckden *Cambridgeshire*	330
Buckingham *Buckinghamshire*	488
Bude *Cornwall*	392
Bungay *Suffolk*	330
Burford *Oxfordshire*	488
Burnham-on-Sea *Somerset*	393
Burnley *Lancashire*	136
Burrington *Devon*	394
Burton upon Trent *Staffordshire*	232
Burwardsley *Cheshire*	137
Bury *Greater Manchester*	137
Bury St Edmunds *Suffolk*	330
Buttermere *Cumbria*	65
Buxton *Derbyshire*	294

C — page no

Caldbeck *Cumbria*	66
Camberley *Surrey*	534
Cambridge *Cambridgeshire*	331
Canterbury *Kent*	534
Carbis Bay *Cornwall*	394
Carlisle *Cumbria*	66
Carlyon Bay *Cornwall*	394
Cartmel *Cumbria*	68
Castle Ashby *Northamptonshire*	296
Castle Cary *Somerset*	395
Castle Donington *Leicestershire*	296
Castleton *Derbyshire*	297
Catterick *North Yorkshire*	168
Cawston *Norfolk*	335

591

TOWN INDEX

Chagford *Devon*	395	
Chale *Isle of Wight*	489	
Chalfont St Giles *Buckinghamshire*	489	
Chardstock *Devon*	396	
Charlestown *Cornwall*	396	
Charmouth *Dorset*	396	
Chatteris *Cambridgeshire*	335	
Cheadle Hulme *Greater Manchester*	137	
Chediston *Suffolk*	335	
Chelmsford *Essex*	335	
Cheltenham *Gloucestershire*	232	
Chenies *Buckinghamshire*	489	
Cheshunt *Hertfordshire*	336	
Chester *Cheshire*	138	
Chesterfield *Derbyshire*	297	
Chew Stoke *Bath & North East Somerset*	397	
Chichester *West Sussex*	536	
Chideock *Dorset*	397	
Chippenham *Wiltshire*	397	
Chipping *Lancashire*	140	
Chipping Campden *Gloucestershire*	236	
Chipping Norton *Oxfordshire*	489	
Chipping Sodbury *South Gloucestershire*	397	
Cholderton *Hampshire*	489	
Chollerford *Northumberland*	107	
Chorley *Lancashire*	140	
Christchurch *Dorset*	490	
Church Stretton *Shropshire*	236	
Churchill *Oxfordshire*	490	
Cirencester *Gloucestershire*	237	
Clacton-on-Sea *Essex*	337	
Clanfield *Oxfordshire*	490	
Clapham *North Yorkshire*	168	
Clare *Suffolk*	337	
Clearwell *Gloucestershire*	238	
Cleator *Cumbria*	68	
Cleckheaton *West Yorkshire*	168	
Cleethorpes *North East Lincolnshire*	169	
Cleobury Mortimer *Shropshire*	238	
Clevedon *North Somerset*	398	
Cley next the Sea *Norfolk*	337	
Cliftonville *Kent* (See under Margate)		
Clitheroe *Lancashire*	140	
Coalville *Leicestershire*	298	
Cobham *Surrey*	537	
Cockermouth *Cumbria*	68	

Codicote *Hertfordshire*	337	
Codsall *Staffordshire*	238	
Coggeshall *Essex*	338	
Colchester *Essex*	338	
Coleford *Gloucestershire*	238	
Coleshill *Warwickshire*	239	
Coltishall *Norfolk*	339	
Colwell Bay *Isle of Wight*	490	
Combe Martin *Devon*	398	
Coniston *Cumbria*	69	
Consett *Durham*	108	
Constantine *Cornwall*	398	
Copthorne *Surrey*	537	
Corbridge *Northumberland*	108	
Corfe Castle *Dorset*	490	
Cotswolds: *Heart of England* (See under Bibury, Bledington, Bourton-on-the-Water, Broadway, Cheltenham, Chipping Campden, Cirencester, Fairford, Gloucester, Guiting Power, Lechlade, Long Compton, Lower Slaughter, Minchinhampton, Moreton-in-Marsh, Nailsworth, Northleach, Nympsfield, Painswick, Slimbridge, Stonehouse, Stow-on-the-Wold, Stroud, Tetbury, Tewkesbury, Wotton-under-Edge)		
Cotswolds: *South of England* (See under Burford, Chipping Norton, Churchill, Clanfield, Deddington, Witney, Woodstock)		
Countisbury *Devon*	398	
Coventry *West Midlands*	239	
Cranborne *Dorset*	491	
Crantock *Cornwall*	399	
Crediton *Devon*	399	
Cressbrook *Derbyshire*	298	
Crewe *Cheshire*	141	
Crewkerne *Somerset*	399	
Cromer *Norfolk*	340	
Crook *Durham*	108	
Crookham *Northumberland*	109	
Crosthwaite *Cumbria*	70	
Croyde *Devon*	400	
Croydon *Greater London*	44	
Cuckfield *West Sussex*	537	
Cullompton *Devon*	400	

D	page no
Darlington *Durham*	109
Dartford *Kent*	538
Dartmoor (See under Ashburton, Bovey Tracey, Chagford, Haytor, Ilsington, Lydford, Moretonhampstead, Okehampton, Poundsgate, Two Bridges, Widecombe-in-the-Moor, Yelverton)	
Dartmouth *Devon*	400
Darwen *Lancashire*	141
Dawlish *Devon*	400
Deal *Kent*	538
Deddington *Oxfordshire*	491
Dent *Cumbria*	70
Derby *Derbyshire*	298
Dereham *Norfolk*	340
Devizes *Wiltshire*	401
Dewsbury *West Yorkshire*	169
Diss *Norfolk*	340
Doncaster *South Yorkshire*	169
Dorchester *Dorset*	402
Dorking *Surrey*	539
Dovedale *Derbyshire*	299
Dover *Kent*	539
Downham Market *Norfolk*	341
Driffield *East Riding of Yorkshire*	170
Droitwich *Hereford and Worcester*	240
Dulverton *Somerset*	402
Dunstable *Bedfordshire*	341
Dunster *Somerset*	402
Durham *Durham*	110
Dymchurch *Kent*	540

E	page no
Eaglescliffe *Tees Valley*	112
Earls Colne *Essex*	341
Easingwold *North Yorkshire*	170
East Prawle *Devon*	403
Eastbourne *East Sussex*	540
Ebchester *Durham*	112
Eckington *Hereford and Worcester*	241
Edale *Derbyshire*	299
Egham *Surrey*	544
Egremont *Cumbria*	70
Ellerby *North Yorkshire*	170
Ellesmere *Shropshire*	241

AT-A-GLANCE SYMBOLS

Symbols at the end of each accommodation entry give useful information about services and facilities. A key to symbols can be found inside the back cover flap.

Keep this open for easy reference.

TOWN INDEX

Elstree Hertfordshire	341	
Ely Cambridgeshire	341	
Embleton Northumberland	112	
Emsworth Hampshire	491	
Endmoor Cumbria	71	
Enfield Greater London	45	
Epsom Surrey	544	
Erpingham Norfolk	342	
Eskdale Cumbria	71	
Evershot Dorset	403	
Evesham Hereford and Worcester	241	
Exeter Devon	403	
Exford Somerset	405	
Exmoor		
(See under Allerford, Combe Martin, Countisbury, Dulverton, Dunster, Exford, Heasley Mill, Lynmouth, Lynton, Porlock, Timbercombe, Wheddon Cross, Winsford)		
Exmouth Devon	405	
Eye Suffolk	342	

F — page no

Fairford Gloucestershire	242
Falmouth Cornwall	406
Fareham Hampshire	492
Faringdon Oxfordshire	492
Farnham Surrey	545
Felixstowe Suffolk	342
Ferndown Dorset	493
Filey North Yorkshire	171
Finedon Northamptonshire	299
Fir Tree Durham	113
Flamborough East Riding of Yorkshire	171
Fleet Hampshire	493
Folkestone Kent	545
Fonthill Gifford Wiltshire	408
Fordingbridge Hampshire	493
Forest-in-Teesdale Durham	114
Forest of Dean	
(See under Blakeney, Clearwell, Coleford, Newent)	
Fowey Cornwall	408
Freshwater Isle of Wight	493
Fressingfield Suffolk	343
Frinton-on-Sea Essex	343
Froggatt Derbyshire	300
Frome Somerset	409

G — page no

Gainsborough Lincolnshire	300
Garboldisham Norfolk	343
Garstang Lancashire	141
Gateshead Tyne and Wear	114
Gatwick Airport West Sussex	
(See under Copthorne, Horley, Redhill)	
Gillingham Kent	546
Glastonbury Somerset	409
Glossop Derbyshire	300
Gloucester Gloucestershire	242
Goathland North Yorkshire	171
Goodrich Hereford and Worcester	244
Goole North Lincolnshire	172
Goring Oxfordshire	494
Gosforth Cumbria	71

Grange-over-Sands Cumbria	71
Grantham Lincolnshire	300
Grasmere Cumbria	72
Grassington North Yorkshire	172
Great Langdale Cumbria	74
Great Witley Hereford and Worcester	244
Great Yarmouth Norfolk	344
Grimsby North East Lincolnshire	173
Grindleford Derbyshire	301
Guildford Surrey	546
Guiting Power Gloucestershire	244

H — page no

Hailsham East Sussex	546
Halifax West Yorkshire	173
Hampton in Arden West Midlands	245
Hamsterley Forest Durham	
(See under Crook, Fir Tree)	
Harleston Norfolk	345
Harpenden Hertfordshire	345
Harringworth Northamptonshire	301
Harrogate North Yorkshire	174
Harrow Greater London	45
Hartland Devon	409
Hartlepool Tees Valley	114
Haslemere Surrey	546
Hastings East Sussex	547
Hatfield Hertfordshire	346
Hathersage Derbyshire	301
Havant Hampshire	494
Hawes North Yorkshire	177
Hawkshead Cumbria	74
Haworth West Yorkshire	178
Hayes Greater London	46
Hayle Cornwall	409
Hayling Island Hampshire	494
Haytor Devon	409
Heasley Mill Devon	410
Heathrow Airport Greater London	
(See under Hayes, Hounslow)	
Hebden Bridge West Yorkshire	179
Helmsley North Yorkshire	179
Helston Cornwall	410
Helton Cumbria	74
Hemel Hempstead Hertfordshire	346
Hereford Hereford and Worcester	245
Hertford Hertfordshire	346
Heversham Cumbria	75
Hevingham Norfolk	346
Hexham Northumberland	115
High Wycombe Buckinghamshire	495
Highcliffe Dorset	495
Hillington Norfolk	346
Hinckley Leicestershire	302
Hitchin Hertfordshire	347
Hockley Heath West Midlands	246
Holmes Chapel Cheshire	142
Holy Island Northumberland	115
Honiton Devon	410
Hope Derbyshire	302
Hope Cove Devon	411
Horley Surrey	548
Horncastle Lincolnshire	302
Horning Norfolk	347
Horsley Derbyshire	302
Horton cum Studley Oxfordshire	495
Hounslow Greater London	46

Hove East Sussex	
(See under Brighton & Hove)	
Howden East Riding of Yorkshire	180
Hoylake Merseyside	142
Huddersfield West Yorkshire	180
Hull Kingston upon Hull	181
Hungerford Berkshire	495
Hunstanton Norfolk	347
Huntingdon Cambridgeshire	347
Hythe Kent	549

I — page no

Ilford Greater London	46
Ilfracombe Devon	411
Ilkley West Yorkshire	181
Illogan Cornwall	413
Ilsington Devon	413
Ingatestone Essex	348
Ingleton North Yorkshire	182
Instow Devon	413
Ipswich Suffolk	348
Ironbridge Shropshire	247
Isle of Wight	
(See under Bonchurch, Chale, Colwell Bay, Freshwater, Sandown, Shanklin, Totland Bay, Ventnor)	
Isles of Scilly	413

K — page no

Kegworth Leicestershire	303
Keighley West Yorkshire	183
Kendal Cumbria	75
Kenilworth Warwickshire	247
Keswick Cumbria	76
Kettering Northamptonshire	303
Keynsham Bath & North East Somerset	414
Kidderminster Hereford and Worcester	248
Kielder Forest Northumberland	
(See under Bellingham, Kielder Water)	
Kielder Water Northumberland	115
King's Lynn Norfolk	349
Kingsbridge Devon	414
Kingsbury Warwickshire	249
Kingsdown Kent	550
Kingsteignton Devon	415
Kingston upon Thames Greater London	47
Kington Hereford and Worcester	249
Kirkby Lonsdale Cumbria	81
Kirkby Stephen Cumbria	82
Kirkbymoorside North Yorkshire	183
Knaresborough North Yorkshire	183
Knipton Leicestershire	303
Knowl Hill Berkshire	496
Knutsford Cheshire	142

L — page no

Lancaster Lancashire	143
Langar Nottinghamshire	303
Langdale Cumbria	82
Langho Lancashire	143
Langley-on-Tyne Northumberland	116
Launceston Cornwall	415

TOWN INDEX

Lavenham *Suffolk*	351
Leadenham *Lincolnshire*	304
Leamington Spa *Warwickshire*	249
Leatherhead *Surrey*	550
Lechlade *Gloucestershire*	251
Ledbury *Hereford and Worcester*	251
Leeds *West Yorkshire*	184
Leeds/Bradford Airport	
(See under Bingley, Bradford, Leeds, Pool in Wharfedale)	
Leek *Staffordshire*	252
Leeming Bar *North Yorkshire*	185
Leicester *Leicestershire*	304
Leintwardine *Hereford and Worcester*	252
Leiston *Suffolk*	351
Lenham *Kent*	550
Lenwade *Norfolk*	351
Leominster *Hereford and Worcester*	252
Lewes *East Sussex*	550
Leyburn *North Yorkshire*	186
Lichfield *Staffordshire*	253
Lincoln *Lincolnshire*	305
Liphook *Hampshire*	496
Liskeard *Cornwall*	415
Little Torrington *Devon*	415
Littlehampton *West Sussex*	551
Liverpool *Merseyside*	143
Liversedge *West Yorkshire*	186
Long Compton *Warwickshire*	254
Long Melford *Suffolk*	351
Longridge *Lancashire*	144
London	25
Looe *Cornwall*	415
Lorton *Cumbria*	83
Lostwithiel *Cornwall*	416
Loughborough *Leicestershire*	306
Lower Slaughter *Gloucestershire*	254
Lowestoft *Suffolk*	352
Ludlow *Shropshire*	254
Lupton *Cumbria*	83
Lydford *Devon*	417
Lyme Regis *Dorset*	417
Lymington *Hampshire*	496
Lyndhurst *Hampshire*	496
Lynmouth *Devon*	418
Lynton *Devon*	418
Lytham St Annes *Lancashire*	145

M	page no
Macclesfield *Cheshire*	146
Mackworth *Derbyshire*	308
Madeley *Shropshire*	255
Maidenhead *Berkshire*	497
Maidstone *Kent*	551
Maldon *Essex*	352
Malham *North Yorkshire*	186
Malmesbury *Wiltshire*	419
Malton *North Yorkshire*	187
Malvern *Hereford and Worcester*	255
Manchester *Greater Manchester*	146
Manchester Airport	
(See under Alderley Edge, Altrincham, Cheadle Hulme, Knutsford, Manchester, Salford, Stockport, Urmston, Wilmslow)	
Mansfield *Nottinghamshire*	308
Marazion *Cornwall*	420
March *Cambridgeshire*	352
Margate *Kent*	552
Market Drayton *Shropshire*	258
Market Harborough *Leicestershire*	308
Marlborough *Wiltshire*	420
Marlow *Buckinghamshire*	498
Marston *Lincolnshire*	308
Matlock *Derbyshire*	309
Matlock Bath *Derbyshire*	310
Mawdesley *Lancashire*	149
Mawgan Porth *Cornwall*	420
Mawnan Smith *Cornwall*	421
Mayfield *Staffordshire*	258
Melksham *Wiltshire*	421
Melton Mowbray *Leicestershire*	310
Mere *Wiltshire*	422
Meriden *West Midlands*	258
Mevagissey *Cornwall*	422
Middleham *North Yorkshire*	187
Middlesbrough *Tees Valley*	116
Middleton-in-Teesdale *Durham*	116
Midhurst *West Sussex*	552
Midsomer Norton *Bath & North East Somerset*	423
Mildenhall *Suffolk*	353
Milford-on-Sea *Hampshire*	498
Milton Common *Oxfordshire*	498
Milton Keynes *Buckinghamshire*	499
Minchinhampton *Gloucestershire*	259
Minehead *Somerset*	423
Mobberley *Cheshire*	149
Monk Fryston *North Yorkshire*	187

Montacute *Somerset*	424
Morecambe *Lancashire*	149
Moreton-in-Marsh *Gloucestershire*	259
Moretonhampstead *Devon*	424
Morley *West Yorkshire*	188
Mortehoe *Devon*	424
Mousehole *Cornwall*	424
Much Wenlock *Shropshire*	259
Mullion *Cornwall*	424
Mundesley *Norfolk*	353
Mungrisdale *Cumbria*	83

N	page no
Nailsworth *Gloucestershire*	260
Nantwich *Cheshire*	149
Neatishead *Norfolk*	353
Needham Market *Suffolk*	353
Netley Abbey *Hampshire*	499
New Forest	
(See under Brockenhurst, Fordingbridge, Lymington, Lyndhurst, Milford-on-Sea, New Milton, Ringwood, Sway)	
New Milton *Hampshire*	500
New Romney *Kent*	553
Newark *Nottinghamshire*	310
Newbury *Berkshire*	500
Newby Bridge *Cumbria*	83
Newby Wiske *North Yorkshire*	188
Newcastle upon Tyne *Tyne and Wear*	116
Newent *Gloucestershire*	260
Newhaven *East Sussex*	553
Newmarket *Suffolk*	353
Newport *Shropshire*	260
Newquay *Cornwall*	425
Newton Abbot *Devon*	428
Newton Aycliffe *Durham*	119
Norfolk Broads	
(See under Aylsham, Beccles, Bungay, Cawston, Coltishall, Great Yarmouth, Hevingham, Horning, Lowestoft, Neatishead, North Walsham, Norwich, Oulton Broad, Stalham, Wroxham)	
North Walsham *Norfolk*	354
Northallerton *North Yorkshire*	188
Northampton *Northamptonshire*	311
Northleach *Gloucestershire*	261
Norwich *Norfolk*	354

USE YOUR *i*'s

There are more than 550 Tourist Information Centres throughout England offering friendly help with accommodation and holiday ideas as well as suggestions of places to visit and things to do. You'll find the address of your nearest Tourist Information Centre in your local Phone Book.

TOWN INDEX

Nottingham *Nottinghamshire*	312	
Nuneaton *Warwickshire*	261	
Nympsfield *Gloucestershire*	261	

O — page no

Oakamoor *Staffordshire*	261
Oakham *Leicestershire*	314
Ockham *Surrey*	553
Ockley *Surrey*	553
Ogbourne St George *Wiltshire*	428
Okehampton *Devon*	428
Old Sodbury *South Gloucestershire*	428
Ollerton *Nottinghamshire*	314
Ombersley *Hereford and Worcester*	261
Onneley *Staffordshire*	262
Orpington *Greater London*	47
Orton *Cumbria*	84
Oswestry *Shropshire*	262
Otterburn *Northumberland*	119
Ottery St Mary *Devon*	428
Oulton Broad *Suffolk*	357
Oundle *Northamptonshire*	314
Oxford *Oxfordshire*	500

P — page no

Padstow *Cornwall*	429
Paignton *Devon*	430
Painswick *Gloucestershire*	263
Pangbourne *Berkshire*	504
Pateley Bridge *North Yorkshire*	188
Peak District (See under Ashbourne, Bakewell, Baslow, Buxton, Castleton, Cressbrook, Dovedale, Edale, Froggatt, Glossop, Grindleford, Hathersage, Hope)	
Penkridge *Staffordshire*	263
Penrith *Cumbria*	84
Penshurst *Kent*	554
Penzance *Cornwall*	431
Perranporth *Cornwall*	433
Peterborough *Cambridgeshire*	358
Petworth *West Sussex*	554
Pickering *North Yorkshire*	189
Piddletrenthide *Dorset*	433
Plymouth *Devon*	433
Polperro *Cornwall*	436
Polzeath *Cornwall*	436

Pool in Wharfedale *West Yorkshire*	190
Poole *Dorset*	504
Porlock *Somerset*	436
Port Gaverne *Cornwall*	437
Port Isaac *Cornwall*	437
Porthleven *Cornwall*	437
Portland *Dorset*	438
Portscatho *Cornwall*	438
Portsmouth & Southsea *Hampshire*	505
Pott Shrigley *Cheshire*	149
Poundsgate *Devon*	438
Preston *Lancashire*	150
Pulborough *West Sussex*	554

Q — page no

Quorn *Leicestershire*	315

R — page no

Radcliffe *Greater Manchester*	150
Ramsgate *Kent*	554
Rangeworthy *South Gloucestershire*	439
Ravenscar *North Yorkshire*	190
Ravenstonedale *Cumbria*	85
Reading *Berkshire*	507
Redcar *Tees Valley*	119
Redhill *Surrey*	555
Redmile *Leicestershire*	315
Redruth *Cornwall*	439
Reeth *North Yorkshire*	190
Retford *Nottinghamshire*	315
Ribble Valley (See under Chipping, Clitheroe, Langho)	
Richmond *Greater London*	47
Richmond *North Yorkshire*	190
Ringwood *Hampshire*	508
Ripley *Derbyshire*	315
Risley *Derbyshire*	316
Rochdale *Greater Manchester*	150
Rochester *Kent*	556
Rock *Cornwall*	439
Romsey *Hampshire*	508
Rosedale Abbey *North Yorkshire*	191
Ross-on-Wye *Hereford and Worcester*	263
Rothbury *Northumberland*	119
Rotherham *South Yorkshire*	191
Rowlands Gill *Tyne and Wear*	120

Royal Tunbridge Wells *Kent*	556
Ruan High Lanes *Cornwall*	439
Rugby *Warwickshire*	264
Runcorn *Cheshire*	150
Runswick *North Yorkshire*	192
Rushyford *Durham*	120
Rustington *West Sussex*	557
Rydal *Cumbria*	85
Rye *East Sussex*	557

S — page no

Saddleworth *Greater Manchester*	151
Saffron Walden *Essex*	359
St Agnes *Cornwall*	440
St Albans *Hertfordshire*	359
St Austell *Cornwall*	440
St Helens *Merseyside*	151
St Ives *Cambridgeshire*	360
St Ives *Cornwall*	441
St Just-in-Penwith *Cornwall*	443
St Keyne *Cornwall*	443
St Mellion *Cornwall*	443
St Neot *Cornwall*	443
Salcombe *Devon*	443
Salford *Greater Manchester*	151
Salisbury *Wiltshire*	444
Salisbury Plain (See under Amesbury, Salisbury, Winterbourne Stoke)	
Samlesbury *Lancashire*	151
Sampford Peverell *Devon*	445
Sandbach *Cheshire*	151
Sandown *Isle of Wight*	509
Sandside *Cumbria*	86
Sandwich *Kent*	559
Sandy *Bedfordshire*	361
Saunderton *Buckinghamshire*	510
Saunton *Devon*	446
Sawrey *Cumbria*	86
Scarborough *North Yorkshire*	192
Scunthorpe *North Lincolnshire*	195
Seahouses *Northumberland*	120
Seaton *Devon*	446
Sedbergh *Cumbria*	86
Selby *North Yorkshire*	195
Selsey *West Sussex*	559
Settle *North Yorkshire*	195
Sevenoaks *Kent*	559
Severn Stoke *Hereford and Worcester*	265
Shaldon *Devon*	446
Shanklin *Isle of Wight*	510

COUNTRY CODE

Always follow the Country Code ❦ Enjoy the countryside and respect its life and work ❦ Guard against all risk of fire ❦ Fasten all gates ❦ Keep your dogs under close control ❦ Keep to public paths across farmland ❦ Use gates and stiles to cross fences, hedges and walls ❦ Leave livestock, crops and machinery alone ❦ Take your litter home ❦ Help to keep all water clean ❦ Protect wildlife, plants and trees ❦ Take special care on country roads ❦ Make no unnecessary noise

TOWN INDEX

Shap *Cumbria*	87
Sheffield *South Yorkshire*	196
Shelley *West Yorkshire*	197
Shepperton *Surrey*	560
Shepton Mallet *Somerset*	447
Sherborne *Dorset*	447
Sheringham *Norfolk*	361
Sherwood Forest (See under Mansfield, Newark, Retford, Worksop)	
Shipbourne *Kent*	560
Shrewsbury *Shropshire*	265
Sidmouth *Devon*	447
Sissinghurst *Kent*	560
Sittingbourne *Kent*	560
Skegness *Lincolnshire*	316
Skipton *North Yorkshire*	198
Slaley *Northumberland*	121
Sleaford *Lincolnshire*	316
Slimbridge *Gloucestershire*	267
Slough *Berkshire*	511
Solihull *West Midlands*	267
South Cave *East Riding of Yorkshire*	198
South Molton *Devon*	448
South Normanton *Derbyshire*	317
South Shields *Tyne and Wear*	121
Southampton *Hampshire*	512
Southend-on-Sea *Essex*	361
Southport *Merseyside*	152
Southsea *Hampshire* (See under Portsmouth & Southsea)	
Southwold *Suffolk*	362
Spalding *Lincolnshire*	317
Stafford *Staffordshire*	268
Stalham *Norfolk*	362
Stamford *Lincolnshire*	317
Stanley *Durham*	121
Stapenhill *Staffordshire*	268
Staveley *Cumbria*	87
Steeple Aston *Oxfordshire*	513
Steyning *West Sussex*	561
Stockbridge *Hampshire*	513
Stockport *Greater Manchester*	153
Stockton-on-Tees *Tees Valley*	122
Stoke-by-Nayland *Suffolk*	363
Stoke-on-Trent *Staffordshire*	268
Stone *Staffordshire*	269
Stonehouse *Gloucestershire*	269
Stonor *Oxfordshire*	514
Stow-on-the-Wold *Gloucestershire*	269
Stowmarket *Suffolk*	363
Stratfield Turgis *Hampshire*	514

Stratford-upon-Avon *Warwickshire*	271
Streatley *Berkshire*	514
Street *Somerset*	449
Stretham *Cambridgeshire*	363
Stretton *Staffordshire*	276
Stroud *Gloucestershire*	276
Studland *Dorset*	514
Sturminster Newton *Dorset*	515
Sudbury *Suffolk*	363
Sunderland *Tyne and Wear*	122
Sutton *Greater London*	48
Sutton Benger *Wiltshire*	449
Swanage *Dorset*	515
Sway *Hampshire*	516
Swindon *Wiltshire*	449
Symonds Yat East *Hereford and Worcester*	277
Symonds Yat West *Hereford and Worcester*	278

T — page no

Tadworth *Surrey*	561
Tamworth *Staffordshire*	278
Tarporley *Cheshire*	153
Taunton *Somerset*	450
Tedburn St Mary *Devon*	451
Teignmouth *Devon*	451
Telford *Shropshire*	278
Tenterden *Kent*	561
Tetbury *Gloucestershire*	279
Tewkesbury *Gloucestershire*	280
Thame *Oxfordshire*	516
Thetford *Norfolk*	363
Thirsk *North Yorkshire*	198
Thornthwaite *Cumbria*	87
Thornton Watlass *North Yorkshire*	199
Thurlestone *Devon*	452
Thwaite *North Yorkshire*	199
Ticehurst *East Sussex*	561
Timberland *Lincolnshire*	318
Timberscombe *Somerset*	452
Tintagel *Cornwall*	452
Titchwell *Norfolk*	364
Tiverton *Devon*	453
Tivetshall St Mary *Norfolk*	364
Tormarton *South Gloucestershire*	454
Torpoint *Cornwall*	454
Torquay *Devon*	454
Totland Bay *Isle of Wight*	516
Totnes *Devon*	458
Treyarnon Bay *Cornwall*	458

Tring *Hertfordshire*	364
Troutbeck *Cumbria*	87
Troutbeck *Cumbria*	87
Trowbridge *Wiltshire*	459
Truro *Cornwall*	459
Tunbridge Wells (See under Royal Tunbridge Wells)	
Tutbury *Staffordshire*	280
Two Bridges *Devon*	460
Tynemouth *Tyne and Wear*	123

U — page no

Uckfield *East Sussex*	562
Ullingswick *Hereford and Worcester*	280
Ullswater *Cumbria*	88
Ulverston *Cumbria*	88
Uppingham *Leicestershire*	318
Urmston *Greater Manchester*	154
Uttoxeter *Staffordshire*	281

V — page no

Ventnor *Isle of Wight*	516

W — page no

Waddington *Lancashire*	154
Wadebridge *Cornwall*	461
Wakefield *West Yorkshire*	200
Walsall *West Midlands*	281
Waltham Abbey *Essex*	364
Wansford *Cambridgeshire*	364
Wantage *Oxfordshire*	517
Ware *Hertfordshire*	365
Wareham *Dorset*	517
Warrington *Cheshire*	154
Warwick *Warwickshire*	281
Wasdale *Cumbria*	89
Watford *Hertfordshire*	365
Weedon *Northamptonshire*	319
Wellingborough *Northamptonshire*	319
Wells *Somerset*	461
Wells-next-the-Sea *Norfolk*	365
Wem *Shropshire*	283
Wembley *Greater London*	48
Weobley *Hereford and Worcester*	283
West Bay *Dorset*	462
West Bexington *Dorset*	462

CHECK THE MAPS

The colour maps at the back of this guide show all the cities, towns and villages for which you will find accommodation entries.

Refer to the town index to find the page on which it is listed.

TOWN INDEX

West Lulworth *Dorset*	517	
West Witton *North Yorkshire*	201	
Westbury *Wiltshire*	462	
Westerham *Kent*	562	
Weston-super-Mare *North Somerset*	463	
Westward Ho! *Devon*	465	
Wetherby *West Yorkshire*	201	
Wetton *Staffordshire*	284	
Weybridge *Surrey*	562	
Weymouth *Dorset*	465	
Wheddon Cross *Somerset*	467	
Whitby *North Yorkshire*	201	
Whitehaven *Cumbria*	89	
Whitley Bay *Tyne and Wear*	123	
Whitstable *Kent*	563	
Whittlesford *Cambridgeshire*	366	
Widecombe-in-the-Moor *Devon*	467	
Wigan *Greater Manchester*	154	
Willington *Cheshire*	155	
Wilmslow *Cheshire*	155	
Wimborne Minster *Dorset*	518	
Winchester *Hampshire*	518	
Windermere *Cumbria*	89	
Windsor *Berkshire*	519	
Winsford *Somerset*	468	
Winterbourne Stoke *Wiltshire*	468	
Wirral *Merseyside* (See under Birkenhead, Hoylake)		
Wisbech *Cambridgeshire*	366	
Wishaw *Warwickshire*	284	
Witherslack *Cumbria*	97	
Witney *Oxfordshire*	520	
Wiveliscombe *Somerset*	469	
Wix *Essex*	366	
Woburn *Bedfordshire*	366	
Woburn Sands *Buckinghamshire*	521	
Woking *Surrey*	563	
Wokingham *Berkshire*	521	
Wolverhampton *West Midlands*	284	
Woodbridge *Suffolk*	366	
Woodford Green *Greater London*	49	
Woodhall Spa *Lincolnshire*	319	
Woodstock *Oxfordshire*	521	
Wookey Hole *Somerset*	469	
Woolacombe *Devon*	469	
Wooler *Northumberland*	124	
Worcester *Hereford and Worcester*	285	
Workington *Cumbria*	97	
Worksop *Nottinghamshire*	320	
Worlington *Suffolk*	367	
Worthing *West Sussex*	563	
Wotton-under-Edge *Gloucestershire*	286	
Wroxham *Norfolk*	367	
Wych Cross *East Sussex*	564	
Wye Valley (See under Goodrich, Hereford, Ross-on-Wye, Symonds Yat East, Symonds Yat West)		
Wymondham *Norfolk*	367	

Y	page no
Yelverton *Devon*	469
Yeovil *Somerset*	470
York	203

INDEX TO ADVERTISERS

You can obtain further information from any display advertiser in this guide by completing an advertisement enquiry coupon. You will find these coupons on pages 587 - 590.

Abbey Court Hotel, London W2	38, IBC
Abbots Mews Hotel, York	203
Branston Hall Hotel, Branston	15
The Brighton Twenty One Hotel, Brighton & Hove	531
Campanile	IFC
The Chadwick Hotel, Lytham St Annes	145
Chase Lodge, Hampton, Kingston upon Thames	14
Country Club Hotel Group	IBC
Derwentwater Hotel, Keswick	76
Elizabeth Hotel, London SW1	29
The Foley Arms Hotel, Malvern	256
The Furzedown Hotel, Great Yarmouth	344
Helme Park Hall Country House Hotel, Fir Tree	113
Langdale Hotel and Country Club, Ambleside	57
Oxstalls Farm Stud, Stratford-upon-Avon	271
The Penny Farthing Hotel, Lyndhurst	497
Rasool Court Hotel, London SW5	15
Sass House Hotel, London W2	38, IBC
School House Hotel and Restaurant, Swindon	449
Westpoint Hotel, London W2	38, IBC
Windsor House Hotel, London SW5	33

597

MILEAGE CHART

The distances between towns on the mileage chart are given to the nearest mile, and are measured along routes based on the quickest travelling time, making maximum use of motorways or dual-carriageway roads. The chart is based upon information supplied by the Automobile Association.

CUSTOMER FEEDBACK QUESTIONNAIRE

We hope you have found this guide useful in selecting accommodation in England which suits your needs.

It is very helpful to the English Tourist Board to receive comments about establishments in *Where to Stay* and suggestions on how to improve the guide, and also on the National Grading and Classification Schemes.

We would like to hear from you. If you wish to do so, you can send us your views using this questionnaire. You need not name the establishment concerned.

Q1 Did you use the *Where to Stay* guide to find:
- Holiday accommodation ☐
- Business accommodation ☐
- Both ☐

Q2 Did you use the establishment's Quality Grading/Crown or Key Classification to help you in making your choice?
- Yes ☐
- No ☐

Q3 If you did, was it the Quality Grading (Approved, Commended, Highly Commended or De Luxe) or the number of Crowns or Keys for facilities that influenced you most?
- The Quality Grading ☐
- The number of Crowns/Keys ☐
- Both ☐

Q4 What was the Quality Grading and Crown or Key Classification of the establishment you chose?

....

Q5 Do you find the National Grades and Classifications:
- Very easy to understand ☐
- Fairly easy to understand ☐
- Difficult to understand ☐

If you find them difficult to understand, please specify why:

....
....

Q6 Was the accommodation you used:
- Hotel ☐
- Guesthouse ☐
- Farmhouse ☐
- Bed & Breakfast ☐
- Self-Catering Holiday Home ☐

Q7 Did the establishment chosen:
- Exceed your expectations ☐
- Meet your expectations ☐
- Fail to meet your expectations ☐

If it failed to meet your expectations, please specify how:

....
....

Q8 Would you say the establishment offered good value for money?
- Yes ☐
- No ☐

Q9 Was there any feature of your stay that you would particularly praise or criticise (please specify):

....
....
....

Q10 Have you bought a *Where to Stay* guide before?
Yes ☐
No ☐
If yes, how long ago:
Last year ☐
2 years ago ☐
More than 2 years ago ☐

Q11 Did you find the *Where to Stay* guide:
Very easy to use ☐
Fairly easy to use ☐
Difficult to use ☐

Q12 Are there any aspects of the *Where to Stay* guide that you would particularly praise or criticise (please specify):

....
....
....

Q13 Is there any additional information not already featured in this guide that you would find helpful (please specify):

....
....
....

Please would you give us a few details about yourself:

Q14 Are you:
Married ☐
Single ☐

Q15 Do you have dependent children?
Yes ☐
No ☐
If yes, how many ....

Q16 Into which age group do you fall?
17-24 ☐
25-34 ☐
35-44 ☐
45-54 ☐
55+ ☐

Q17 Are you an overseas visitor (i.e. from outside the UK visiting this country)?
Yes ☐
No ☐

Q18 Did you travel alone or with a party?
Alone ☐
Party of people ☐
of which .... were adults
and .... children

Q19 How long did you stay in the establishment?
.... nights

Q20 Do you plan to use the guide to book any further stays this year?
Yes ☐
No ☐
If yes, how many ....

Q21 What other sources of information did you use in selecting your accommodation (please specify):

....
....

Q22 Did you obtain your copy of *Where to Stay* from
Bookshop ☐
Tourist Information Centre ☐
Other (please specify) .... ☐

Thank you for giving us your views. Please return this questionnaire to: Department AS, English Tourist Board, Thames Tower, Black's Road, Hammersmith, London W6 9EL.

LOCATION MAPS

Every place name featured in the accommodation listings pages of this *Where to Stay* guide has a map reference to help you locate it on the maps which follow. For example, to find Colchester, Essex, which has 'Map ref 3B2', turn to Map 3 and refer to grid square B2.

All place names in the listings pages are shown in black type on the maps. This enables you to find other places in your chosen area which may have suitable accommodation - the Town Index (preceding pages) gives page numbers.

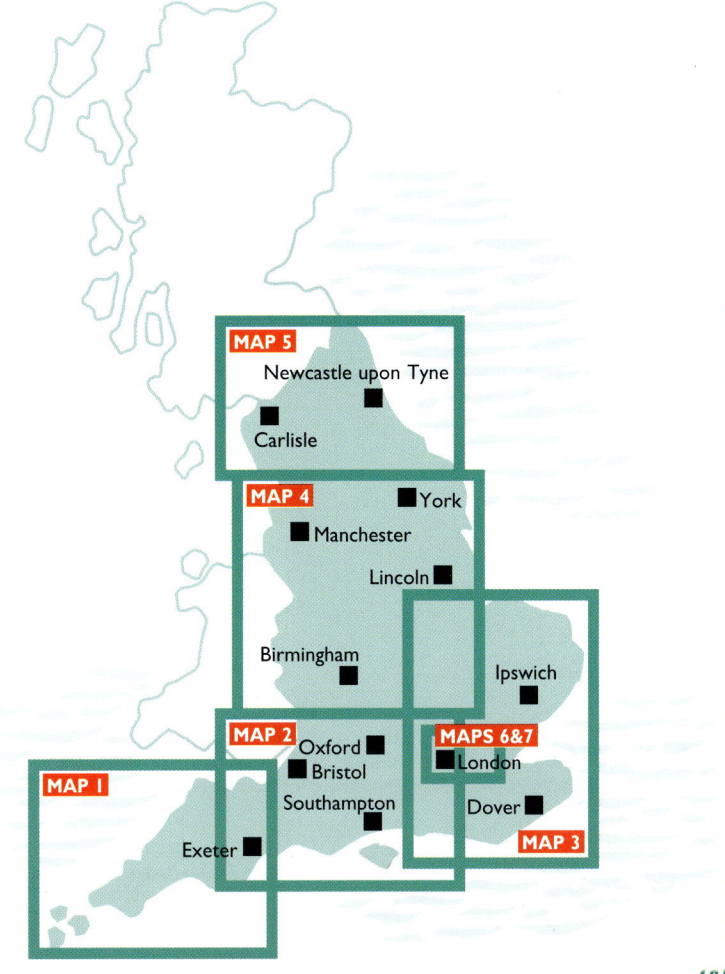

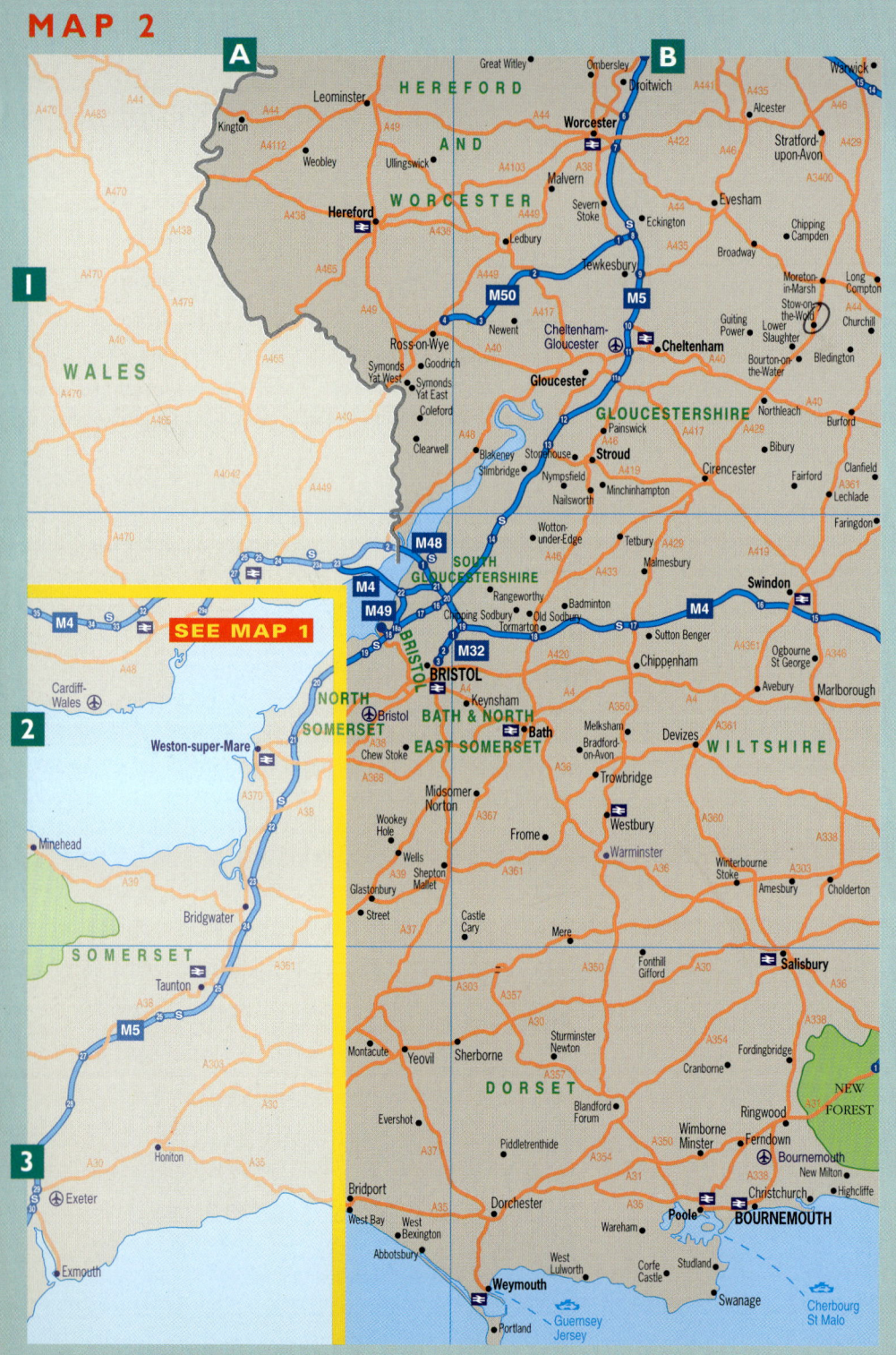

MAP 6

LONDON See also Map 7

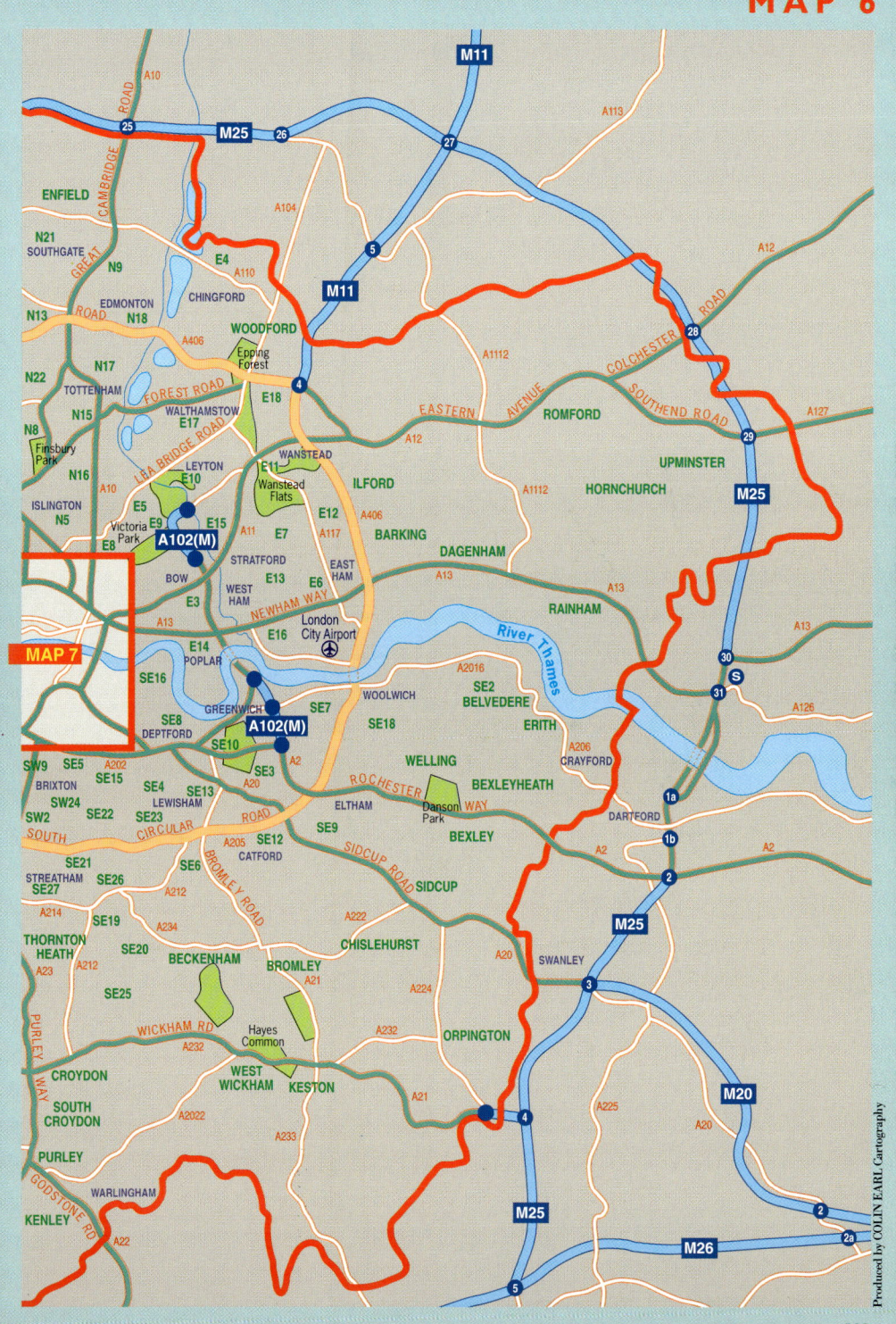

MAP 6

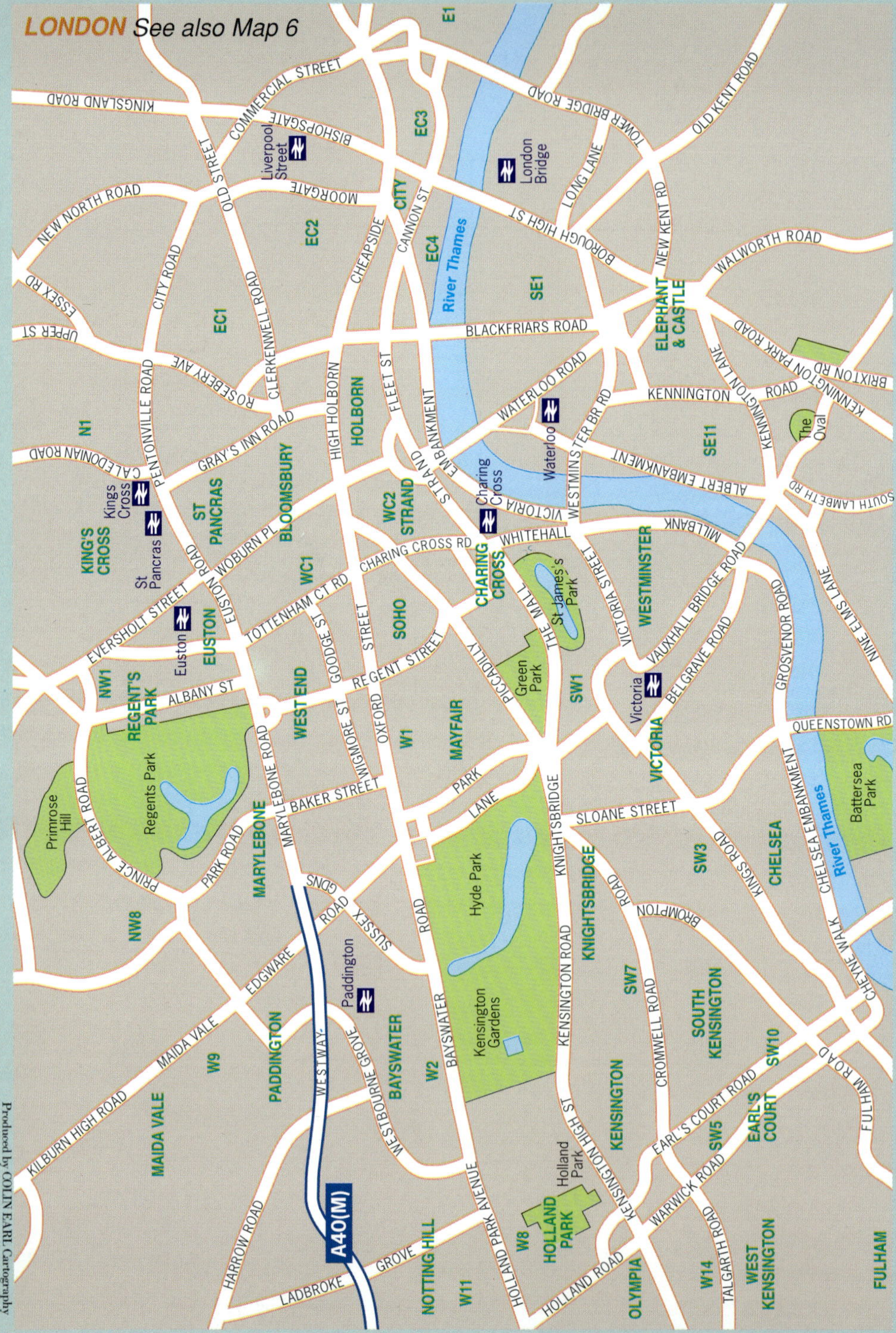

MAP 7

LONDON See also Map 6

YOUR QUICK GUIDE

Where to Stay makes it quick and easy to find a place to stay that offers the standard of quality and facilities you're looking for.

The TOWN INDEX (starting on page 591) and the LOCATION MAPS (starting on page 601) show all cities, towns and villages with accommodation listings in this guide.

1 Town Index

If the place you plan to visit is included in the town index, turn to the page number given to find accommodation available there. Also check that location on the colour maps to find other places nearby which also have accommodation listings in this guide.

Batley West Yorkshire	158
Battlesbridge Essex	317
Beadnell Northumberland	100
Bedale North Yorkshire	158
Bedford Bedfordshire	317
Belford Northumberland	100
Bellingham Northumberland	100
Belper Derbyshire	285
Belton Leicestershire	286
Berkhamsted Hertfordshire	318
Berrynarbor Devon	372
Berwick-upon-Tweed Northumberland	100
Bexhill-on-Sea East Sussex	509
Bexleyheath Greater London	43
Bibury Gloucestershire	217

2 Location Maps

If the place you want is not in the town index - or you only have a general idea of the area in which you wish to stay - use the colour location maps to find places in the area which have accommodation listings in this guide.

When you have found suitable accommodation, check its availability with the establishment and also confirm any other information in the published entry which may be important to you (price, whether bath and/or shower available, children/dogs/credit cards welcome, months open, etc).

If you are happy with everything, make your booking and, if time permits, confirm it in writing.